MAYFLOWER FAMILIES

Through

Five Generations

DESCENDANTS OF THE PILGRIMS
WHO LANDED AT
PLYMOUTH, MASS., DECEMBER 1620

VOLUME TWENTY-TWO

FAMILY OF

WILLIAM BRADFORD

Compiled by
Ann Smith Lainhart
and
Robert S. Wakefield, FASG

Published by
General Society of Mayflower Descendants
2004

Library of Congress Cataloging-in-Publication Data (revised for volume 22)

Mayflower Families Through Five Generations

Edited by L.M. Kellogg and others. Includes bibliographical references and indexes.

Contents:

1. Pilgrims (New Plymouth Colony): Genealogy.
    2. Massachusetts--Genealogy.
        I. Kellogg, Lucy Mary.
        II. General Society of Mayflower Descendants.

F63.M39   929'.2'0973   75-30145

ISBN   0-930270-34-7

DEDICATED TO

Robert S. Wakefield, FASG

1925 - 2002

History of the Five-Generations Project

The Five-Generations Project was authorized by the Board of the General Society of Mayflower Descendants in September 1959 with the goal of providing documentation from primary sources, whenever possible, for all statements, and of publishing the findings for the use of the Historian General, the State Historians, the membership, and the general public. Thus was formalized a project first conceived many years earlier, around the turn of the 19th and 20th centuries, by Herbert Folger in San Francisco and George E. Bowman in Boston.

Lewis Edwin Neff was the first chairman of the Five Generation Project. He was the driving force for this venture and recruited the first compilers. Dr. Lee D. van Antwerp was an early committee chairman in the formative years of the Project, serving from 1967 to 1975. Lucy Mary Kellogg, FASG, became chairman and gave professional advice and encouragement for a short time.

Robert Moody Sherman, FASG, served as chairman from 1976 to 1979. During his tenure the first two volumes entitled *Mayflower Families Through Five Generations* were published in "silver" hard cover: Francis Eaton, Samuel Fuller, and William White, in Volume 1 (1975); and James Chilton, Richard More, and Thomas Rogers, in Volume 2 (1978).

In 1980, Volume 3, the Descendants of George Soule, was published by the Society and the Soule Kindred in America, Inc.

Cathryn P. Lanham became the chairman of the "5Gs," as the project was familiarly called, before serving as Governor General, and she has continued preparing manuscripts for publication until recently. Under her supervision, beginning in 1986, a "pink" paperback was published under the title *Mayflower Families in Progress.* The publication of *MFIP*s has been continued under the present chairmanship and there are now many pink volumes in print.

Edith Bates Thomas, appointed director of the project in 1987, has accomplished much, beginning with the publication of Volume 4, Edward Fuller, in 1990, and continuing through the publication of Volume 22, William Bradford, in 2004, including several revised editions, and additional volumes of the John Alden family. *Mayflower Families in Progress* has expanded to include allied families — Delano, Church, Bartlett — as well as fifth-generation treatments of the Brewster family and part of the Soule family.

The Society Expresses Thanks

The Society is grateful to the many people who assisted in the research on this volume.

Lee D. van Antwerp, M.D., former CG, was the original Prime Researcher on this family and turned in an outline of the Bradford family before he died.

The Mayflower Society wishes to thank the following persons who provided research on this family: Richard Batt, Ann S. Lainhart, David A. Lambert, Charles C. Loper, Ann T. Reevers, Jean Rumsey, FASG, Peter F. Stevenson, Eugene Stratton, FASG, Edith Bates Thomas, and Neil D. Thompson, FASG. The contributions of the late Claude W. Barlow, FASG, and Ruth Wilder Sherman, FASG, are also gratefully acknowledged.

COMPUTERIZED BY Ann Smith Lainhart

EDITING, PREPARATION OF CAMERA-READY COPY,
AND INDEXING BY Jane Fletcher Fiske, FASG

PUBLICATION: Robert Allen Greene

We welcome any additions and/or corrections to this book that are supported by primary source documentation. Any such changes should be mailed to:

Five Generations Project
P. O. Box 3297
Plymouth MA 02361

vi

OFFICERS OF THE GENERAL SOCIETY

2002 – 2005

Ann Smith Lainhart

Ann Smith Lainhart is a descendant of *Mayflower* Pilgrim Richard Warren. She joined the Massachusetts Society of Mayflower Descendants in 1979, served on the Board of Assistants in the early 1980s, and then returned in 1996. Since March 1999, she has served as Historian of the Massachusetts Society.

In 1994, Ms. Lainhart became researcher of the Alden family for the Five Generations Project and is continuing that work for future volumes. In 1999 she also took on the research for the descendants of William Bradford.

She is the author, editor, or co-editor of many genealogical works, including State Census Records, Digging for Genealogical Treasure in New England Town Records; Massachusetts State Censuses of 1855 and 1865 (for 72 towns); The New North Church, Boston; Roxbury Town Records; John Haven Dexter's Memoranda of the Town of Boston; Records of the Hollis Street Church, Boston; Deaths in Boston 1700 to 1799; and Inscriptions of the Old Cemeteries of Boston. Rose Cottage Chronicles, Civil War Letters of the Bryant–Stephens Families of North Florida is a fascinating account taken from hundreds of family letters and diaries kept by Ms. Lainhart's family during the War Between the States. Ms. Lainhart's most recent work is Researcher's Guide to Boston, published in 2003.

Ms. Lainhart was born in Seattle, Washington, 6 January 1951, daughter of William Smith and Catherine Bryant (Stephens) Lainhart. After a year and a half at Macalester College, St. Paul, Minnesota, she earned an associate degree in Culinary Arts from the Culinary Institute of America. She then returned to college at Sarah Lawrence College and graduated with a BA in History. She joined the staff at the New England Historic Genealogical Society in Boston as a reference librarian in 1978. In 1981 she started working as a self-employed genealogist and worked for private clients for thirteen years.

Since 1994 Ms. Lainhart has also pursued her interest in quilting by opening *The Quilted Gallery*, with a website at *www.quiltedgallery.com*.

Robert S. Wakefield

Robert Sidney Wakefield, FASG, a descendant of both Stephen Hopkins and John Howland, was born 20 October 1925 in San Mateo, California, son of Cyril Horace and Christobel Mina (Gunn) Wakefield. He died 1 June 2002 in Redwood City, California where he had lived most of his life. Never married, he was survived by a brother, Kenneth V. Wakefield of Sonora, California, and the latter's children and grandchildren.

Bob served in the 910th Heavy Car Maintenance Ordinance Company of the United States Army in Germany during World War II and was awarded a Bronze Star. His early interests were photography and Big Band music, and he was an avid stamp collector as well as a San Francisco '49ers fan. He was employed by the Southern Pacific Transportation Company in their San Francisco office as Senior Assistant Manager of Operating Data Systems, opting for retirement after 37 years of service.

His interest in genealogy began early, and by 1965 he had begun writing corrections and notes on recent findings for the major genealogical journals. He joined the California Society of Mayflower Descendants in 1973 and soon found kindred spirits in Robert Moody Sherman, who headed the Five Generations Project from 1975 to 1979, and his wife, Ruth Ann (Wilder) Sherman. After joining the 5-Gs Committee in 1976, Bob prepared the Richard More manuscript for publication in the second volume of that series in 1978. He began work in 1977 on the Peter Brown Family, which was published in 1992. He co-authored the Edward Winslow family in Volume 5, and contributed substantially to many other Project families.

Many of his articles were published in leading genealogical journals, and in 1977 he was elected a Fellow of the American Society of Genealogists. A bibliography of his work, filling four pages, appears with his obituary in the *Mayflower Descendant*, 51 [Summer 2002], along with his Ancestor Table.

One of the most respected genealogists of his time, Bob preferred working behind the scenes, editing and advising without public recognition. Although few of his colleagues ever had the privilege of meeting him in person, his quiet presence in the field, his in-depth knowledge of Plymouth Colony, and his willing help—on which so many other Five-Generations workers often relied—are most sincerely missed.

A Note To The Reader

No five-generation genealogy is ever complete. The authors have assembled the family as correctly and as completely as circumstances have permitted. The work is based largely on carefully-researched articles in genealogical journals and family histories, verified wherever possible by research in probate and land records, town and church vital records, and other primary sources. Family tradition, in the absence of confirmatory evidence, has not been accepted as proof of a line, although it may be mentioned in order to provide possible clues for future research. Regretfully, a few lines that were accepted by the Society in its early years have been found to be based on insufficient or erroneous evidence and have thus had to be eliminated, but on the other hand, many new potential lines have been uncovered.

Paucity of records sometimes renders it virtually impossible to follow a family or an individual in a migration to a different area, and thus a whole family may disappear, or some of the children may be labeled "n.f.r.," meaning that no further record of them was found. Occasionally the author offers tentative identifications using the word "probable," indicating that the evidence is *nearly* conclusive but positive proof has not been found. The word "possible" indicates that more research is needed to prove a connection for which the evidence is merely suggestive, such as an identical name or location. While some might argue that these unproven links should not be mentioned at all, we feel that they may provide valuable clues to direct further research, resulting in the discovery of more compelling evidence.

Spelling was far from consistent, even after the Revolutionary War. To a great extent names in this book have been spelled as found in each record. This practice often provides different spellings of an individual's name at his birth, upon marriage, and in a deed or will. For example, Hayward is found as Heywood and even Howard for the same person; Marcy and Mercy are often interchangeable. Mary was often called Polly, Martha was known as Patty, and Margaret as Peggy. With variant spellings so commonplace, use of "[*sic*]" is restricted to exceptional examples. To assist the reader, most variant spellings of a surname are lumped together in the Index and cross-referenced, rather than separately alphabetized. Most given names have been standardized.

All places are assumed to be in Massachusetts unless otherwise indicated.

A reader who finds either an error or additional information regarding any family or individual in this volume down to the birth of sixth-generation children (but not beyond) is urgently requested to send such materials, with documention, to:

FIVE GENERATIONS PROJECT, P.O. BOX 3297, PLYMOUTH MA 02361

TABLE OF CONTENTS

First Generation

1. WILLIAM¹ BRADFORD, bp. Austerfield, Yorkshire, England 19 March 1589/90; d. Plymouth 9 May 1657; son of William and Alice (Hanson) Bradford.

He m. (1) Amsterdam, Holland 10 Dec. 1613 **DOROTHY MAY**, b. ca. 1597; drowned Cape Cod Harbor 7 Dec. 1620; daughter of Henry May of Wisbeach, Cambridgeshire, England. The marriage intention of William Bradford and Dorothy May in November. 1613 says he was from Austerfield, 23 years old, and that she was from Wisbeach in England, 16 years old.

He m. (2) Plymouth 14 Aug. 1623 **ALICE (CARPENTER) SOUTHWORTH**, b. prob. Wrington, Somerset, England say 1595; d. Plymouth 26 or 27 March 1670; daughter of Alexander Carpenter. She m. (1) Leyden, Holland 28 May 1613 EDWARD SOUTHWORTH with whom she had sons Constant and Thomas.

In the 1623 Division of Land William Bradford received three acres. In the 1627 Division of Cattle William Bradford, wife Alles Bradford, William Bradford Junior, and Mercy Bradford were named.

William Bradford was Governor of Plymouth Colony 1621-33, 1635, 1637, 1639-43 and 1645-56.

On 2 May 1642 at a town meeting "It is agreed upon that Mr Bradford will fynd a Bull for the Towne Cowes this summer." At meetings in 1642, 1644, and 1645, he served on committees that decided with whom "the Townes stock of cattell called the Poores Cattell" would be placed. Town meetings in 1649, 1650, and 1651 were held at Gov. Bradford's house and in 1663 a meeting was held at Mistress Bradford's.

In the town records on a list of "The Names of those that have Interest and proprieties in the Townes land att Punckateesett over against Road Iland" appear the names of Mr. William Bradford and Mistris Allice Bradford. A footnote says that a line was drawn through William's name.

"The last Will and Testament Nuncupative of Mr. William Bradford senⁱʳ: Deceased May the Ninth 1657 and exhibited to the court held att Plymouth June 3ᵈ 1657":

> Mr. William Bradford senⁱʳ: being weake in body but in prfect memory haveing Defered the forming of his Will in hopes of haveing the healp of Mr. Thomas Prence therin; feeling himselfe very weake and drawing on to the conclusion of his mortall life spake as followeth; I could hav Desired abler then

myselfe in the Deposing of that I have; how my estate is none knowes better then youerselfe, said hee to Lieftenant Southworth; I have Desposed to John and Willam alreddy their proportions of land which they are possessed of;

My Will is that what I stand Ingaged to p'forme to my Children and others may bee made good out of my estate that my Name Suffer not;

ffurther my Will is that my son Josepth bee made in some sort equall to his brethern out of my estate;

My further Will is that my Deare & loveing wife Allice Bradford shalbee the sole Exequitrix of my estate; and for her future maintainance my Will is that my Stocke in the Kennebecke Trad bee reserved for her Comfortable Subsistence as farr as it will extend and soe further in any such way as may bee Judged best for her;

I further request and appoint my welbeloved Christian ffrinds Mr Thomas Prence, Captaine Thomas Willett and Lieftenant Thomas Southworth to bee the Suppervissors for the Desposing of my estate according to the prmises Confiding much in theire faithfulnes

I comend unto youer Wisdome and Descretions some smale bookes written by my owne hand to bee Improved as you shall see meet; In speciall I comend to you a little booke with a blacke cover wherin there is a word to Plymouth, a word to Boston and a word to New England with sundry usefull verses;

These pticulars were expressed by the said Willam Bradford Govr the 9th of May 1657 in the prsence of us Thomas Cushman, Thomas Southworth, Nathaniell Morton; whoe were Deposed before the court held att Plymouth the 3d of June 1657 to the truth of the abovesaid Will that it is the last Will and Testament of the abovesaid Mr Willam Bradford senir.

William Bradford left an extensive estate which included many books.

On 22 March 1663 Mistress Bradford and Mistress Attwood are listed in the town records with lot #30.

Allis Bradford Sr. of Plymouth, widow, in her will dated 29 Dec. 1669, exhibited 7 June 1670, asked to be "Intered as neare unto my Deceased husband; Mr. Willam Bradford as Conveniently may be," and made bequests to her sister Mary Carpenter; son Constant Southworth; son Joseph Bradford; son Capt. William Bradford; honored friend Mr. Thomas Prence; grandchild Elizabeth Howland, daughter of son Thomas Southworth deceased, for the benefit of her son James Howland; and servant maid Mary Smith. Alice Bradford also left an extensive estate, including books.

Child of William and Dorothy (May) Bradford, b. Leyden Holland:

2   i JOHN[2] BRADFORD, b. ca. 1618

Children of William and Alice (Carpenter) (Southworth) Bradford, b. Plymouth:

→ 3   ii   WILLIAM BRADFORD, b. 17 June 1624(recorded in his "Table-book")

4   iii   MERCY BRADFORD, b. before May 1627

5   iv   JOSEPH BRADFORD, b. ca. 1630 (based on age at d.)

Note: *Bradford Desc* p. 1, *TAG* 46:117 and *NEHGR* 50:462-5 all say Dorothy May is daughter of John May. It seems more likely she is daughter of Henry May. See *Plymouth Colony Its History And People 1620-1691*, Eugene A. Stratton (Salt Lake City, 1986), pp. 324-6, for a discussion of this problem.

References: *MD* 2:228-234(will); 3:144-9(will Alice); 7:65(bp. England); 9:115-7(1ˢᵗ m.); 15:213(d. Alice); 18:68(d. Alice); 22:63-4(1ˢᵗ m.); 29:97-102(d. Dorothy May); 30:4(m., b. William); 39:182(Carpenter). *Plymouth Colony Recs* 8:33(d. Alice); 12:4(1623 div.), 12(1627 div.). *MQ* 27:6. *NEHGR* 97:339-364(Southworth). *Great Migration Begins* 1:207-9(Bradford), 313-4(Carpenter). *Plymouth Town Recs.* 1:8, 10, 18, 29, 31-2, 36, 58, 68.

Second Generation

2. JOHN[2] BRADFORD (*William[1]*), b. Leyden, Holland ca. 1618; d. Norwich, Conn., before 21 Sept. 1676.

He m. 1650 or earlier **MARTHA BOURNE**, b. prob. England ca. 1614; d. Norwich, Conn., between 20 Feb. 1679/80 and 1683 (Thomas Tracy's 3rd m.); daughter of Thomas and Elizabeth (_____) Bourne. She m. (2) Norwich, Conn., ca. 1679 THOMAS TRACY. The will of Thomas Bourne of Marshfield dated 2 May 1664 names daughter Bradford.

A 1650 Marshfield town record states John Phillips put his son Wm. Phillips unto John Bradford of the town of Duxborough and his now wife.

All that remains of John Bradford's estate proceedings is the statement that his will was exhibited in court, accepted, and ordered to be recorded on 21 Sept. 1676. On 20 Feb. 1679/80 Martha Tracy, executrix of the will of John Bradford, her late husband, sold 50 acres to Caleb Fobes. Martha's will has also been lost.

John and Martha Bradford left no children.

References: *MD* 16:24-5(Thomas Bourne will). *Marshfield By Richards* 1:28. *Waterman Gen* 1:610, 615-9. Plymouth Colony PR 2(2):20(Thomas Bourne). New London Co. CT Court Rec. 3:83(rec. John's will). *History Of Norwich CT*, Frances M. Caulkins, Hartford CT, 1866, p. 201(Tracy).

3. WILLIAM[2] BRADFORD (*William[1]*), b. Plymouth 17 June 1624; d. there 20 Feb. 1703/4 aged 71 [*sic*]. The Plymouth church says "dyed Major William Bradford in the 80th year of his age. He was the son of ye honourable Governour Bradford, and did for many years sustaine the place of Leivtenant Govern[r] of ye Colony of New plimouth and did almost from his Youth serve God and his Generation in both Civill & military posts. he dyed in a good old age and went to his grave in peace."

He m. (1) shortly after 23 April 1650 **ALICE RICHARDS**, bp. Pitminster, Somerset, England 7 April 1629; d. Plymouth 12 Dec. 1671 aged 44 yrs.; daughter of Thomas and Welthean (Loring) Richards. The will of Wealthian Richards, widow of Boston, drawn 3 July 1679, names Thomas, Alice, Hannah, Mercy, William Jr., John, Samuel, Melatiah, Mary, and Sarah Bradford "children of William Bradford of Plimoth Colony & my daughter Al[ice] deceased."

He m. (2) probably at Norwich, Conn., about 1674, **SARAH (____) GRISWOLD**; d. prob. Plymouth ca. 1676. She m. (1) ca. 1652 Francis Griswold with whom she had Sarah, Joseph, Mary, Hannah, Deborah, Lydia, Samuel, Margaret, and Lydia.**

He m. (3) at Plymouth about 1676, **MARY (WOOD) HOLMES**, b. Plymouth ca. 1643; d. there 6 Jan. 1714/5; daughter of John and Mary (Masterson) Wood (or Atwood). She m. (1) Plymouth 11 Dec. 1661 JOHN HOLMES with whom she had Joseph, Mary, and Isaac. The March 1675/6 division of the estate of John Wood Jr. (Mary's brother) names "Mistris Mary Holmes," therefore the marriage was after that date. The will of John Holmes of Duxbury dated 16 Dec. 1675 names wife Mary Holmes and children Joseph, Mary and Isaac.

On 23 April 1650 William Bradford deeded land to his son William upon his agreement to marry Allice, daughter of Mr. Thomas Richards of Weymouth.

On 28 11 mo. [January] 1650/1 William Bradford signed a letter with the other heirs of Thomas Richards.

At a town meeting 27 Oct. 1662 Captaine Bradford was one of those "who desire meadow on the south side of Turkey Swamp." Capt. William Bradford appears 18 May 1668 on a list of "The names of such as have voated in Towne meeting in the Towne of Plymouth." In February 1668/9 he appears on a list of "The names of those who were found to be Townsmen of Plymouth ... which Relates unto the time of the establishment of the Towne of Plymouth and the bounds therof sett by the court which was in the yeare 1640."

He served the town on several committees, as moderator of town meetings, on the town council, and laying out bounds and highways. He is called Captain from 1662 through 1675, and Major after that.

On 11 Sept. 1679 William and Mary Bradford, late wife of Mr. John Holmes late of Duxbury, conveyed land for the use of the children of John Holmes.

On 6 June 1682 Major William Bradford was chosen Deputy Governor.

On 23 April 1687 William Bradford, in consideration of the natural love he bears for his grandchild William Bradford, only son of his son William Bradford deceased, gave to his grandson one parcel of upland on which his son built his house "Given unto me from my father William Bradford Esqr." Before acknowledging the deed on 4 Sept. 1696, William added a paragraph saying that when his grandson William reached the age of 21, he "shall enjoy the lands without Interruption." On 29 Oct. 1709 John Bradford, Samuel

Bradford, Israel Bradford, Ephraim Bradford, David Bradford, and Hezekiah Bradford all of Plymouth County, gave their right in a cedar swamp to their kinsman William Bradford, son of their brother William Bradford deceased (this deed was not acknowledged until 26 March 1747).

On 18 March 1688/9 William Bradford of Plymouth gave to son-in-law [stepson] Joseph Holmes 30 acres in Plymouth.

John Richards of Boston, merchant, in his will dated 1 April, proved 10 May 1694, named, among others, the children of his late sister Alice the wife of Major William Bradford of Plymouth: Thomas Bradford of Connecticut; Mercy the wife of Mr. Steel of Hartford [Conn.]; Alice the wife of Major James Fitch of Norwich [Conn.]; Hannah the wife of Joshua Ripley of Norwich; Melatiah the wife of John Steel of Norwich; the children of William Bradford Jr. of Plymouth to receive the share of their grandfather Major William Bradford to be equally divided among them; John Bradford; Samuel Bradford; Mary the wife of William Hunt of Weymouth; Sarah the wife of Mr. Baker of Duxbury; and Elizabeth Adams the daughter of Alice the wife of the late Rev. William Adams of Dedham.

At the December 1699 term of the Court of General Sessions John Gray was presented "for reviling and rayling speeches against Major William Bradford and Mr. Ephraim Little, Minister of Plimouth."

The will of William Bradford "living in the Township of Plimouth," dated 29 June 1703, proved 10 March 1703[/4], names wife Mary Bradford; sons David, Ephraim, Hezekiah, and eldest son John who was to have "my father's manuscript viz.: a Narrative of the begining of New Plimouth"; grandson William, son of son William deceased; son Thomas to have lands in Norwich, Conn., which were the lands of my brother John Bradford; sons Samuel and Joseph, the latter to have "a portion of lands near Norwich part of which was his mother's"; son Israel; grandsons John Bradford and William Bradford sons of son John; daughters Mercy Steel, Hannah Riply, Melatiah Steel, Mary Hunt, Alce Fitch, and Sarah Baker; Hannah wife of son Samuel; sons John, Samuel and Israel were to be executors.

On 17 March 1704/5, Israel, Ephraim, David, and Hezekiah Bradford divided land given them by their father Major William Bradford. They acknowledged the deed 15 Dec. 1713.

No Plymouth Colony land or probate records were found for Mary Bradford. No Plymouth Colony land records were found for William Bradford that mentioned his wives.

Children of William and Alice (Richards) Bradford, b. Plymouth:

6   i JOHN[3] BRADFORD, b. 20 Feb. 1652/3

7	ii	WILLIAM BRADFORD, b. 11 March 1654/5
8	iii	THOMAS BRADFORD, b. ca. 1658 (based on age at d.)
→ 9	iv	ALICE BRADFORD, b. 1659
10	v	MERCY BRADFORD, bp. Boston 2 Sept. 1660
11	vi	HANNAH BRADFORD, b. 9 May 1662*
12	vii	MELATIAH BRADFORD, b. 1 Nov. 1664*
13	viii	SAMUEL BRADFORD, b. ca. 1667 (based on age at d.)
14	ix	MARY BRADFORD, b. 1668
15	x	SARAH BRADFORD, b. 1671

Child of William and Sarah (----) (Griswold) Bradford, b. Plymouth:

| 16 | xi | JOSEPH , b. 18 April 1675.* |

Children of William and Mary (Wood) (Holmes) Bradford, b. Plymouth:

17	xii	ISRAEL BRADFORD, b. ca. 1677 (based on age at d.).
18	xiii	EPHRAIM BRADFORD, b. 1685.
19	xiv	DAVID BRADFORD, b. prob. before 1687 (if he was 21 when he signed deed).
20	xv	HEZEKIAH BRADFORD, b. prob. before 1687 (if 21 when he signed deed).

*The births of Hannah, Melatiah and Joseph are from *Bradford Desc* (p.4). Hannah's, b. is also given in *Waterman Gen* (1:626). No primary record has been found to confirm these birth dates.

** David Jay Webber makes a very strong case that the second wife of William Bradford was Sarah (____) Griswold (*NEHGR* 155:245-50). The often-repeated statement that she was the "widow Wiswall" is quite unlikely.

References: *MD* 4:143-7(will); 9:65-6(m. settl.), 89-91(Richard's will); 15:212(d. Wm.); 16:238(b. John); 17:71(b. Wm.); 18:68(d. Alice); 27:129. *Waterman Gen* 1:626-30. *Plymouth Ch Recs* 1:195(d. Wm.). *PN&Q* 5:123(deed). *(Plymouth) Burial Hill* p. 8(d. Wm.). *Plymouth Colony Recs* 6:83(chosen Dep. Gov.); 8:14-16(b. 2 ch.), 33(d. Alice). *Weymouth By Chamberlain* 3:589 (Richards). *BRC* 9:77(bp. Mercy). Plymouth Colony PR 3:1:169(John Holmes); 5:188(John Wood Jr.). Plymouth Co. LR 1:70(to Joseph Holmes); 3:254(to grandson Wm.); 14:43(to ch. of John Holmes); 27:155(Israel Bradford *et al*); 41:80(uncles to grandson Wm.). Plymouth Co. PR 2:40 (Wm. Bradford). Suffolk Co. PR 1:64-5(Thomas Richards); 6:314 (Welthian Richards); #2140 13:416(John Richards). Plymouth Colony LR 3(2):104(m. agreement). *NEHGR* 144:23-8. *Plymouth VR* pp. 132(d. William), 660(b. John), 661(b. William), 663(Mary's 1st m.). *Great Migration Begins* 3:1575-9(bp. Alice). *MEHGR* 155:245-50(Sarah Griswold). *Savage* 2:317(Griswold). *Plymouth Co Ct Recs* 1:234. *Plymouth Town Recs* 1:49, 100, 108, 148.

4. MERCY² BRADFORD (*William¹*), b. Plymouth before May 1627; d. probably before 9 May 1657 (not mentioned in father's will).

She m. Plymouth 21 Dec. 1648 **BENJAMIN VERMAYES** (or **FEARMAYES**), b. ca. 1624; d. at "Ginne" (Africa?) before 28:9:1665.

Benjamin Fermaies was admitted to the Salem Church 6:1:1642.

On 1 June 1654 Benjamin Fyrmaes (being aged 30 years or thereabout) deposed in a deed.

The probate record of Capt. Benjamin Fearemayes dated 28:9:1665 says he died at "Ginne." The administration of the estate "in this country" was granted to Hester Estwick 26:4:1666.

Benjamin and Mercy Fearmayes left no known children.

References: *MD* 15:28(m.).   Suffolk Co. LR 2:27(Benj. Fyrmaes).   *Essex Co PR* 2:21(Benjamin Fearemayes). *Suffolk Deeds* 2:27(depos.). *Salem First Ch* p. 11. *Plymouth VR* p. 656(m.).

5. JOSEPH² BRADFORD (*William¹*), b. Plymouth ca. 1630; d. there 10 July 1715 in 85th yr.

He m. Hingham 25 May 1664 **JAEL HOBART**, bp. Hingham 30 Dec. 1643; d. Kingston 14 April 1730 in 87th yr.; daughter of Rev. Peter and Elizabeth (Ilbrook) Hobart of Hingham. The will of Rev. Peter Hobart of Hingham dated 16 Jan. 1678 mentions his daughter Jael Bradford, wife of Joseph Bradford of Plymouth.

Joseph Bradford first appears in the Plymouth town records when land granted to William Nelson is described as bounding on land of Joseph Bradford. He next appears 18 May 1668 as Mr. Joseph Bradford on a list of "The names of such as have voated in Towne meeting in the Towne of Plymouth." In February 1668/9 he appears on a list of "The names of those who were found to be Townsmen of Plymouth ... which Relates unto the time of the establishment of the Towne of Plymouth and the bounds therof sett by the court which was in the yeare 1640."

On 15 Oct. 1685 Joseph Bradford and Elder Cushman went with the pastor to the ordination of Mr. Thomas Mighil at the Scituate church.

Joseph Bradford of Plymouth, innholder, was granted a license to sell liquor in 1688, 1690-92, 1698-99, and 1703.

On 10 March 1703 Joseph Bradford and his wife Jael appear on a list of members of the Plymouth church.

The will of Joseph Bradford of Plymouth, planter, dated 8 Oct. 1712, with inventory taken 27 July 1715, names his wife Jael and son Elisha. The will was refused probate following testimony that it was not written according to the wishes of the decedent.

In 1716 Jael Bradford, widow of Joseph Bradford, and Elisha Bradford, son of Joseph Bradford, sold off land in four deeds, in one of which Elisha's wife Hannah participated.

The will of Jael Bradford of Kingston, widow, dated 25 March 1729, sworn 22 May 1730, names [grand]daughter Hannah Bradford, "daughter of my son Elisha"; grandsons Joseph and Nehemiah Bradford; and granddaughter Uranie Bradford.

Children of Joseph and Jael (Hobart) Bradford:

    i JOSEPH[3] BRADFORD, b. Plymouth 18 April 1665; n.f.r. (not named in father's will)

21   ii ELISHA BRADFORD, b. prob. Plymouth ca. 1669

    iii PETER BRADFORD, b. Hingham 1 March 1676/7; n.f.r. (not named in father's will)

References: *MD* 5:217-24(will); 7:23(d. Jael); 15:212(d. Joseph); 16:85(d. Joseph), 114(will Jael); 17:185(b. Jos.); 19:187(will Hobart). *VR Kingston* p. 320(d. Jael). *Waterman Gen* 1:625. *(Plymouth) Burial Hill* p. 10(d. Joseph). Suffolk Co. PR 6:293(Peter Hobart). Plymouth Co. PR 5:753(Jael Bradford). *Plymouth Colony Recs* 8:25(b. Joseph). *Plymouth Ch Recs* 1:160, 191-2(members), 256(to Scituate), 214(d. Joseph). *Hingham Hist* 2:90(bp. Jael; m., b. Peter). *Plymouth VR* pp. 133(d. Joseph), 665(b. Joseph). Plymouth Co. LR 15:78, 91; 18:77, 157(Jael & Elisha). *Plymouth Town Recs* 1:62, 102, 109.

Third Generation

6. JOHN³ BRADFORD (*William²⁻¹*), b. Plymouth 20 Feb. 1652/3; d. Kingston 8 Dec. 1736 in 84th yr. as "Major."

He m. Plymouth 6 Jan. 1674/5 **MERCY WARREN**, b. Plymouth 23 Sept. 1653; d. Kingston in March 1747 aged 93y 6m; daughter of Joseph and Priscilla (Faunce) Warren, a granddaughter of Pilgrim **Richard Warren**. The will of Joseph Warren of Plymouth dated 4 May 1689 names wife Priscilla and daughter Mercy Bradford.

John Bradford first appears in the Plymouth town records in February 1668/9 on a list of "The names of those who were found to be Townsmen of Plymouth ... which Relates unto the time of the establishment of the Towne of Plymouth and the bounds therof sett by the court which was in the yeare 1640." He served the town on various committees, running bounds, on juries, as selectman, and as deputy. On 6 May 1695 he was chosen to be Plymouth's representative at the General Court. In the town records he is called Major beginning in 1695.

In the town records on 13 April 1683 he recorded his cattle mark as "the topp of the Right Eare Cutt off; and a Slitt on the under side of the Left Eare."

In 1690 John Bradford and his wife Mercy were admitted to the Plymouth church. On 10 March 1703 they both appear on a list of members.

On 11 Sept. 1692 John Bradford was one of the men nominated as sutable to read the Psalms.

John Richards of Boston, merchant, in his will dated 1 April, proved 10 May 1694, named, among others, the children of his late sister Alice the wife of Major William Bradford of Plymouth: Thomas Bradford of Connecticut; Mercy the wife of Mr. Steel of Hartford [Conn.]; Alice the wife of Major James Fitch of Norwich [Conn.]; Hannah the wife of Joshua Ripley of Norwich; Melatiah the wife of John Steel of Norwich; the children of William Bradford Jr. of Plymouth to receive the share of their grandfather Major William Bradford to be equally divided among them; John Bradford; Samuel Bradford; Mary the wife of William Hunt of Weymouth; Sarah the wife of Mr. Baker of Duxbury; and Elizabeth Adams the daughter of Alice the wife of the late Rev. William Adams of Dedham.

On 13 Oct. 1703 John Bradford and James Warren were chosen to attend the ordination of Mr. Samuel Arnold at the Rochester church.

On 22 Dec. 1703 John Bradford of Plymouth for love and affection gave to his son John Bradford of Plymouth several pieces of land totaling over 60 acres including two acres of salt meadow that he had been given by his father Major William Bradford after his decease. On 20 June 1711 John gave to his son Samuel Bradford of Plymouth three pieces of land of more than 50 acres. On 9 Sept. 1713 his gave to his son William Bradford of Plymouth five acres of his homestead reserving to his other sons, John and Samuel, liberty to egress and regress. On 16 Feb. 1721/2 he gave to his daughter Priscilla Chipman, wife of Seth of Plymouth, several parcels "which join together where I now dwell." And on 11 Sept. 1732 he sold to his son Samuel Bradford of Plimpton 135 acres in Kingston.

On 17 Jan. 1732/3 John Bradford of Kingston, Gentleman, for love and affection gave to his five grandsons, sons of his son William deceased, James, Zadok, Samuel, Eliphalet, and William, all his homestead, 1/3 of several other pieces of land and a grist mill and fulling mill, £20 each, his carts, plows, chains, and other husbandry utensils, reserving the use and improvement to himself during his natural life and the life of his wife Mercy. He also left his gun to his grandson James and £20 to his granddaughter Hannah Bradford.

The will of John Bradford of Kingston, gentleman, dated 2 Oct. 1732, proved 21 Dec. 1736, names wife Marcy; grandson Robert Bradford, son of John Bradford deceased; son Samuel Bradford; daughter Alice Hearsy, wife of Joshua of Hingham; daughter Marcy Cushman, widow of Isaac Jr. late of Plimpton; daughter Pricilla Chipman, wife of Seth; five grandsons, James, Zadock, Samuel, Eliphalet, and William, sons of William Bradford deceased; granddaughter Hannah Bradford, daughter of William Bradford deceased; and wife and son Samuel as joint executors.

At the March 1738/9 Court of Common Pleas James Bradford of Preston, Conn., housewright, sued Mercy Bradford, widow of Kingston and Samuel Bradford, gentleman of Plympton, executors of John Bradford of Kingston, for the £20 promised him in the will of John Bradford.

At the May 1747 Court of Common Pleas John Brewster, innholder, Samuel Foster, blacksmith, and William Bradford, a minor, all of Kingston sued Seth Chipman of Kingston, cooper, for ejectment from a dwelling house and land in Kingston "it being the House which Major Bradford's son William dwelt in." The plantiffs said that on 13 May 1747 they were seised of the premises in their own right (John ¼ part, Samuel ½ part, William ¼ part) and that Seth illegally entered. The parties agreed to referees to settle the matter. The referees reported that they "Considered the Deed made by John Bradford to his Grand Children James, Zadoch, Samuel, Eliphlet, and William Bradford, Dated January 17 1732/33 on which both parties agreed before us their Title ought to be determined, are of Opinion that said Deed Created an Estate in fee to the said Grand Children, and that the Deft. has in Interest by Vertue thereof or by the Death of any of said Grand Children, and Therefore that the Pltfs. recover Possession of the premisses."

Children of John and Mercy (Warren) Bradford, b. Plymouth, bp. there 1 March 1691:

22	i	JOHN[4] BRADFORD, b. 29 Dec. 1675
23	ii	ALICE BRADFORD, b. 28 Jan. 1677
	iii	ABIGAIL BRADFORD, b. 10 Dec. 1679; prob. the one who d. Plymouth 4 May 1697*
24	iv	MERCY BRADFORD, b. 20 Dec. 1681
25	v	SAMUEL BRADFORD, b. 23 Dec. 1683
26	vi	PRISCILLA BRADFORD, b. 10 March 1686
27	vii	WILLIAM BRADFORD, b. 15 April 1688

*Bradford Desc (p.14) claims she m. Gideon Sampson but this is in error as she is called Abigail Bradford when she died.

References: MD 1:147(b. ch.); 4:14-17(J. Warren will); 7:23(d. John, Mercy); 13:205(m.); 16:63(d. Abig.); 17:192 (m.); 20:133-7(will). VR Kingston pp. 320(d. John), 321(d. Mercy). Plymouth Ch Recs 1:191-2(members), 270-1(bp. ch.), 268(admitted), 279(read Psalmes). Plymouth Co Ct Recs 6:146-7 #67; 7:79-80 #23. Plymouth VR pp. 7(b. ch.), 86(m.), 135(m.), 667(b. Mercy).   Plymouth Co. PR 1:38-9(Joseph Warren); 4:439(John Bradford). Plymouth Co. LR 5:164; 9:48; 10:231; 22:26; 27:175(John to sons); 27:175(John to grandchildren). Suffolk Co. PR #2140 13:416(John Richards). Plymouth Town Recs 1:100, 213, 236.

7. WILLIAM[3] BRADFORD (*William[2-1]*), b. Plymouth 11 March 1654/5; d. there 5 July 1687.

He m. ca. 1679 **REBECCA BARTLETT**, b. prob. Duxbury before 1664 or earlier; prob. the Rebecca Samson who d. Duxbury 14 Dec. 1741 "wife of Caleb Samson Sr."; daughter of Benjamin and Sarah (Brewster) Bartlett, a descendant of Pilgrims **William Brewster** and **Richard Warren**. The will of Benjamin Bartlett of Duxborough dated 21 Aug. 1691 names daughter Rebecca Bradford and her daughters Alice and Sarah by William Bradford. She m. (2) between 21 Aug. 1691 and 30 Aug. 1697 ROBERT STANFORD with whom she had Robert and perhaps others. She m. (3) Duxbury 30 Jan. 1728/9 CALEB SAMSON Sr., a son of Pilgrim **Henry Samson**.

William Bradford Jr. became a freeman on 27 May 1681

On 23 April 1687 William Bradford, "in consideration of the natural love he bears for his grandchild William Bradford, only son of his son William Bradford deceased," gave to his grandson one parcel of upland on which his son had built his house "Given unto me from my father William Bradford Esqr." Before acknowledging the deed on 4 Sept. 1696, William added a paragraph saying that when his grandson William reached the age of 21, he "shall enjoy the lands without Interruption." This deed clearly says that his son William is deceased, though the Plymouth records list his death on 5 July 1687, ten weeks later (the original Plymouth records were checked and the death record is very plain and falls chronologically on the page between a death on 2 July 1687 and another on 7 Jan. 1687[/8]). The purpose of this deed was to make sure that William's widow and children could continue to live in the house.

On 7 July 1687 a report on the inquest into the death of William Bradford was presented to the Plymouth County Court of General Session and Common Pleas. The committee reported "that he being Driving of his Cart and his Cartt overturned upon him and gave him a violent blow upon his head and back which blow we Judge was the Cause of his Death."

On 11 July 1687 the inventory of the estate of William Bradford late of Plymouth was taken. On 23 July 1687 administration of the estate of William Bradford, late of Plymouth, was granted to John Bradford.

John Richards of Boston, merchant, in his will dated 1 April, proved 10 May 1694, named, among others, the children of his late sister Alice the wife of Major William Bradford of Plymouth: Thomas Bradford of Connecticut; Mercy the wife of Mr. Steel of Hartford, [Conn.]; Alice the wife of Major James Fitch of Norwich, [Conn.]; Hannah the wife of Joshua Ripley of Norwich; Melatiah the wife of John Steel of Norwich; the children of William Bradford Jr. of Plymouth to receive the share of their grandfather Major William Bradford to be equally divided among them; John Bradford; Samuel Bradford; Mary the wife of William Hunt of Weymouth; Sarah the wife of Mr. Baker of Duxbury; and Elizabeth Adams the daughter of Alice the wife of the late Rev. William Adams of Dedham.

On 18 Dec. 1700 William, Alice, and Sarah Bradford, children of William Bradford Jr. late of Plymouth deceased, chose "their uncle Mr. Joseph Bartlett and Mr. Nathaniel Warren" as guardians.

On 29 Oct. 1709 John Bradford, Samuel Bradford, Israel Bradford, Ephraim Bradford, David Bradford, and Hezekiah Bradford all of Plymouth Co. gave their right in a cedar swamp to their kinsman William Bradford, son of their brother William Bradford deceased (this deed was not acknowledged until 26 March 1747).

Children of William and Rebecca (Bartlett) Bradford, b. Plymouth:

28   i ALICE[4] BRADFORD, b. 28 Jan. 1680*

29   ii WILLIAM BRADFORD, b. before 18 Dec. 1686

30   iii SARAH BRADFORD, b. ca. 1686 (based on age at d.)

* Date is from *Bradford Desc* (p.8). No primary record has been found.

References: *VR Duxbury* pp. 302(her 3rd m.), 414(d. Rebecca). *MD* 6:44-9(Bartlett will); 11:80(3rd m.); 15:213(d. Wm.); 16:115-6 (gdn.). *Waterman Gen* 1:627. NGSQ 71:84-9. *Gen Advertiser* 1:18(Wm. Bradford estate). *Plymouth VR* p. 134(d. William). *MF* 18:1:48-9. Plymouth Co. PR 1:6(William Bradford), 113-5(Benj. Bartlett), 328(gdn.). *Plymouth Co Ct Recs* 1:190(inquest). Suffolk Co. PR #2140 13:416(John Richards). *Plymouth Town Recs* 1:174.

8.   THOMAS[3] BRADFORD (*William[2-1]*), b. Plymouth ca. 1658; d. Windham, Conn., 1 Oct. 1731 aged 73 (g.s.).

He m. (1) ca. 1681 **ANNE RAYMOND**, b. New London, Conn., 12 May 1664; d. before 8 May 1705 (will of her aunt Mary Raymond); daughter of Joshua and Elizabeth (Smith) Raymond. The will of Josiah Raymond of Block Island, R.I., dated 21 July 1704, proved 1 June 1711, names his daughter Ann.

He m. (2) **KATHERINE _____**, b. ca. 1659; d. Lyme, Conn., 6 Nov. 1733, "widow" aged 74.

On 10 June 1690 John Bradford of Plymouth sold to brother Thomas Bradford the land aunt Martha, formerly the widow of uncle John Bradford, late of Norwich, left him in her will.

John Richards of Boston, merchant, made his will 1 April, proved 10 May 1694, naming, among others, the children of his late sister Alice the wife of Major William Bradford of Plymouth: Thomas Bradford of Connecticut; Mercy the wife of Mr. Steel of Hartford [Conn.]; Alice the wife of Major James Fitch of Norwich [Conn.]; Hannah the wife of Joshua Ripley of Norwich; Melatiah the wife of John Steel of Norwich; the children of William Bradford Jr. of Plymouth to receive the share of their grandfather Major William Bradford to be equally divided among them; John Bradford; Samuel Bradford; Mary the wife of William Hunt of Weymouth; Sarah the wife of Mr. Baker of Duxbury; and Elizabeth Adams the daughter of Alice the wife of the late Rev. William Adams of Dedham.

On 12 Oct. 1713 Thomas Bradford and Joshua Bradford of Lyme sold land in New London.

The will of Mary Raymond of New London dated 8 May 1705, mentions the children of "cosen" [niece] Ann Bradford deceased; only James is named.

Thomas Bradford was lieutenant of the militia company at Nahantick Quarter, Lyme, Conn., in May 1709.

In a court case concerning Lt. Thomas Bradford of Lyme, Nathaniel Havens of Lyme deposed on 23 June 1713 that "Edward Dewolfe was married to Mr. Bradford's daughter some time last winter."

On 2 April 1735 James Bradford of Canterbury sold the right of the heirs of his father, Thomas Bradford, deceased, in the third part of the fourth division to Ebenezer Darrow and John Champlin of Lyme. This deed apparently was not sufficient to pass the title of all the heirs, so on 30 May 1735 a second deed was made by James Bradford of Canterbury, Hezekiah Newcomb and his wife Jerusha of Lebanon, and Joseph Hebard Jr. and his wife Ann of Windham to Champlin and Darrow.

No Windham, Conn., probate or land records were found for Thomas Bradford.*

Children of Thomas and Anne (Raymond) Bradford, b. Norwich, Conn.:

31   i   JOSHUA⁴ BRADFORD, b. 23 Nov. 1682

32   ii JAMES BRADFORD, b. 24 March 1689

33   iii ANN BRADFORD, b. ca. 1690-1692

34   iv JERUSHA BRADFORD, bp. New London, Conn., 28 May 1693

          v   WILLIAM BRADFORD, bp. 1695; prob. d.y.

* [1986 letter from Kendall P. Hayward: Starting in 1710 he "went astray" and by 1713 had mortgaged his Lyme property. I doubt if he is the one who married Katherine ---- for as early as 1710 he was enamored of the wife of Henry Merrow, a sailing master, who shipped goods along the coast. By 1713 Henry Merrow apparently discovered that about 100 pounds of his goods were missing, and then brought suit against Thomas Bradford. Henry Merrow also accused Bradford of alienating the affections of his wife Miriam. When the case was to come to trial, Bradford had disappeared.]

References: *Norwich CT VR* 1:27(b. Joshua). *Lyme CT VR* p. 219(d. Kath.). *Bradford Desc* p. 8. *Waterman Gen* 1:628. Hale Cem Coll:Windham p. 231(d. Thomas). New London Co. Court recs. Nov. 1713. New London CT VR 1:14(b. Anne). Norwich CT LR 2A:201(Thomas Bradford). *TAG* 11:12-4(1ˢᵗ wife proof; Thomas g.s.); 24:63(d. Katherine). Lyme CT LR 5:332(James Bradford); 9:26(James Bradford *et al.*). New London CT PR #4299(Josiah Raymond); 1:299(Mary Raymond). New London CT Church Rec 1:3(bp. Jerusha). New London CT LR 6:313(Thomas & Joshua). Suffolk Co. PR #2140 13:416(John Richards).

9. ALICE³ BRADFORD (*William²⁻¹*), b. Plymouth ca. 1659; d. Canterbury, Conn., 15 March 1745/6 in 84th yr. [*sic*].

She m. (1) Dedham 29:1:1680 Rev. **WILLIAM ADAMS**, b. Ipswich 27 May 1650; d. Dedham 17:6:1685; son of William Adams. He m. (1) Dedham 15 Oct. 1674 Mary Manning with whom he had Mary who d.y.; Eliphalet; and William, who d.y. William Adams was a graduate of Harvard College in 1671 and was ordained second minister of Dedham 3 Dec. 1673.

She m. (2) Norwich, Conn., 8 May 1687 Major **JAMES FITCH**, b. Saybrook, Conn., 2 Aug. 1649; d. Canterbury, Conn., 10 Nov. 1727; son of James and Abigail (Whitfield) Fitch. He m. (1) Norwich, Conn., Jan. 1676/7 ELIZABETH MASON with whom he had James, James, Jedediah, and Samuel.

James Fitch served in King Philip's War and was an Assistant in 1681.

John Richards of Boston, merchant, made his will 1 April, proved 10 May 1694, naming, among others, the children of his late sister Alice the wife of Major William Bradford of Plymouth: Thomas Bradford of Connecticut; Mercy the wife of Mr. Steel of Hartford [Conn.]; Alice the wife of Major James Fitch of Norwich [Conn.]; Hannah the wife of Joshua Ripley of Norwich; Melatiah the wife of John Steel of Norwich; the children of William Bradford Jr. of Plymouth to receive the share of their grandfather Major William Bradford to be equally divided among them; John Bradford; Samuel Bradford; Mary the wife of William Hunt of Weymouth; Sarah the wife of Mr. Baker of Duxbury; and Elizabeth Adams the daughter of Alice the wife of the late Rev. William Adams of Dedham.

On 10 April 1696 Elizabeth Adams, aged 16, daughter of William Adams of Dedham, clerk, deceased, chose Thomas Hunt of Boston, blacksmith, as guardian.

On 7 April 1710 James Fitch of Canterbury, Esq., sold land in Little Compton which he had bought in 1703.

On 9 March 1712 James Fitch of Canterbury gave his son Ebenezer Fitch of Canterbury 3 pieces of land; Ebenezer was of Windsor when he sold this land on 29 Jan. 1712/3. On 4 Aug. 1714 James gave Ebenezer more land. On 4 Feb. 1719 James gave his son Daniel Fitch of Canterbury 350 acres. On 8 May 1722 James sold to son Theophilus Fitch land in Canterbury. On 29 June 1722 James gave his son Jabez Fitch of Canterbury 100 acres. And on 28 March 1723 James sold his son-in-law John Dyar all land in Canterbury not otherwise disposed of.

On 22 Sept. 1718 William Whiting and John Fitch both of Hartford Co. for £500 secured for the use of the family of Major James Fitch and Alice his wife during their natural lives by Daniel Fitch and Theophilus Fitch both of

Canterbury give Daniel and Theophilus 250 acres being part of Major Fitch's farm.

On 13 May 1731 Daniel Fitch; Jno Dyer and Abigail his wife; Henry Cleaveland and Lucy his wife; Theophelus Fitch & Jabez Fitch, all of Canterbury; Daniel Bissel and Jerusha his wife of Winsor; Jno Fitch and Alice his wife; and James Fitch, Elijah Fitch, Eliezer Fitch, Medinah Fitch, and Ebenezer Fitch, all of Ashford, minor children of Ebenezer Fitch late of Winsor, petitioned the court over lands conveyed to Ebenezer Fitch 24 May 1723 by a grant which had been lost.

No Windham, Conn., probate records were found for James Fitch.

Children of William and Alice (Bradford) Adams, b. Dedham:

35	i	ELIZABETH ADAMS[4], b. 23 Feb. 1681
36	ii	ALICE ADAMS, b. 3 April 1682
	iii	WILLIAM ADAMS, b. 17 Dec. 1683; d. 1699
37	iv	ABIELL (or ABIGAIL) ADAMS, b. 15 Dec. 1685

Children of James and Alice (Bradford) (Adams) Fitch:

38	v	ABIGAIL FITCH, b. Norwich, Conn., 22 Feb. 1687/8
39	vi	EBENEZER FITCH, b. Norwich, Conn., 10 Jan. 1689/90
40	vii	DANIEL FITCH, b. Norwich, Conn., Feb. 1692/3
41	viii	JERUSHA FITCH, b. Canterbury, Conn., ca. 1696
42	ix	LUCY FITCH, b. Canterbury, Conn., ca. 1698
43	x	THEOPHILUS FITCH, b. ca. 1701
44	xi	JABEZ FITCH, b. Canterbury, Conn., 30 Jan. 1702; bp. Preston, Conn., 7 June 1702

NOTE: *Waterman Gen* 1:650 also lists sons John, b. 1695 and William, b. 1701. They are not in Barbour. *Windsor, Conn., By Stiles* 2:62 gives them John, William and Bridget. See *TAG* 46:36-46 for a rebuttal of these children. (Eldest daughter Elizabeth gave Dr. Ezra Stiles an account of her brothers and sisters naming all those listed above except William who had died young. She did <u>not</u> mention John, William or Bridget.)

References: *Dedham VR* 1:1(b. Adams ch.); 2:1(d. Wm.); 3:1(1st m.; his 1st m.). *Dedham Ch* p. 278(ministers). *Harvard Grads* 2:380. *Waterman Gen* 1:649-1. *NEHGR* 70:344(d. James). *TAG* 46:36-46. Canterbury CT LR 2:25, 63, 93; 3:91, 210, 218, 239(James Fitch); 3:83(Wm. Whiting & John Fitch). Connecticut Archives: Towns & Lands 6:89a-89b(petition). Canterbury CT VR 1:148(d. Alice). Norwich CT VR 1:6(both J. Fitch m., b. 3 ch.). Preston CT VR 7:23(bp. Jabez). Suffolk Co. PR #1456(Wm. Adams); 11:153 (gdn.); #2140 13:416(John Richards). *Saybrook Colony VR* p. 28(b. James). *Fitch Gen* pp. 10-13. Bristol Co. LR 6:247(Little Compton land).

10.   MERCY³ BRADFORD (*William²⁻¹*), bp. Boston 2 Sept. 1660; d. Hartford, Conn., before 5 April 1720.

She m. Hartford, Conn., 16 Sept. 1680 **SAMUEL STEELE**, b. Farmington, Conn., 15 March 1652; d. Hartford before 2 Jan. 1709/10; son of John and Mary (Warner) Steele.

John Richards of Boston, merchant, made his will 1 April, proved 10 May 1694, naming, among others, the children of his late sister Alice the wife of Major William Bradford of Plymouth: Thomas Bradford of Connecticut; Mercy the wife of Mr. Steel of Hartford [Conn.]; Alice the wife of Major James Fitch of Norwich [Conn.]; Hannah the wife of Joshua Ripley of Norwich; Melatiah the wife of John Steel of Norwich; the children of William Bradford Jr. of Plymouth to receive the share of their grandfather Major William Bradford to be equally divided among them; John Bradford; Samuel Bradford; Mary the wife of William Hunt of Weymouth; Sarah the wife of Mr. Baker of Duxbury; and Elizabeth Adams the daughter of Alice the wife of the late Rev. William Adams of Dedham.

Samuel Steel and his wife Mary were received into full communion in the Second Hartford church on 2 June 1695.

On 21 Feb. 1709/10, administration of the estate of Samuel Steele Sr. of Hartford was granted to Thomas and William Steele, sons of the deceased

On 1 Oct. 1711 widow Mary Steele of Hartford was named guardian of her sons Eliphalet aged 11 and Daniel aged 14½. Distribution of the estate on 28 Feb. 1711/2 was among widow Marcy Steele, eldest son Thomas, and William, Daniel, Eliphalet, and Abiall Steele.

On 5 April 1720 Thomas Steel was appointed administrator of the estate of Mercy Steel. The April 1724 agreement to division of the estate of their mother Mercy Steele was made by Thomas Steele, Daniel Steele, Eliphalet Steele and John Webster in right of wife Abiell.

On 10 April 1749 Daniel, Eliphalet, Samuel, Nathaniel, and John Steele of Hartford; John Webster and wife Abiah of Farmington; William Steele of New Hartford, and Daniel and Jerusha Mills of Simsbury sold to Phinias Lewis of Farmington a tract in Farmington laid out in the right of Samuel Steele, deceased. On the same date the grantors sold to Ebenezer Buck 41 acres in Southington laid out in the right of Samuel Steele deceased

On 21 Sept. 1756 Daniel, Elphialet, Samuel, Nathaniel, and John Steel of Hartford, Thomas Hosmer and wife Susannah of Hartford, Stephen Hopkins and wife Abiel of Waterbury, and William and James Steel of New Hartford sold to Silas Spencer a lot held in common with the heirs of Samuel Hubbard.

(Samuel, Nathaniel, John, Susanna, William and James were children of son Thomas who was deceased).

Children of Samuel and Mercy (Bradford) Steele, b. Hartford, Conn., and bp. in the Second Church:

45   i   THOMAS STEELE[4], b. 9 Sept. 1681, bp. 11 Sept. 1681

        ii   ELIZABETH STEELE, bp. 25 Feb. 1682/3; d. before 5 Feb. 1711/2 (not in distribution)

       iii   SAMUEL STEELE (twin), b. and bp. 15 Feb. 1684/5; d. before 2 Jan. 1709/10, when Thomas & William Steele were appointed administrators of the estate of their brother Samuel Steele Jr. of Hartford, blacksmith, deceased

       iv   JERUSHA STEELE (twin), b. and bp. 15 Feb. 1684/5; d. before 5 Feb. 1711/2 (not in distribution)

        v   WILLIAM STEELE, b. 20 Feb. 1687/8, bp. 25 Feb. 1687/8; d. Hartford, Conn., before 2 Feb. 1712/3 when Thomas Steele was appointed administrator on the estate of his brother William late of Hartford

46   vi   ABIEL STEELE (daughter), b. 8 Oct. 1693 [gap in baptisms 1689 to 1694]

47   vii   DANIEL STEELE, b. 3 April 1697, bp. 4 April 1697

48   viii   ELIPHALET STEELE, b. 23 June 1700, bp. 24 June 1700

References: *Savage* 4:181. *Manwaring* 2:307(Samuel Steele Sr. & Jr. PR). *Waterman Gen* 1:629. *Bradford Desc* p. 9. *Hartford By Barbour* p. 578. Farmington CT LR 2:330(b. Samuel); 7:466, 486(Daniel Steele *et al.*). Hartford CT PR #5196(Mercy Steele); #5209(William Steele); 8:38(Samuel Steele Jr.); 8:39(gdn); 8:55(div. of est. of Samuel Steele). Hartford CT LR 9:406(Daniel Steele *et al.*). Hartford CT VR FFS:46(b. ch.), FFS:52(m.). Suffolk Co. PR #2140 13:416(John Richards). *Hartford CT Second Ch* pp. 293(full com.), 302(bp. Thomas), 303(bp. Elizabeth, Samuel, Jerusha), 305(bp. William), 307(bp. Daniel), 309(bp. Eliphalet).

11. HANNAH[3] BRADFORD (*William[2-1]*), b. Plymouth 9 May 1662; d. Windham, Conn., 28 May 1738 in 76th yr.

She m. Plymouth 28 Nov. 1682 **JOSHUA RIPLEY**, b. Hingham 9 Nov. 1658; d. Windham, Conn., 18 May 1739 in 81st yr.; son of John and Elizabeth (Hobart) Ripley. The will of John Ripley of Hingham dated 31 Jan. 1683, proved 27 March 1684, names his son Joshua.

John Richards of Boston, merchant, made his will 1 April, proved 10 May 1694, naming, among others, the children of his late sister Alice the wife of Major William Bradford of Plymouth: Thomas Bradford of Connecticut; Mercy the wife of Mr. Steel of Hartford [Conn.]; Alice the wife of Major James

Fitch of Norwich [Conn.]; Hannah the wife of Joshua Ripley of Norwich; Melatiah the wife of John Steel of Norwich; the children of William Bradford Jr. of Plymouth to receive the share of their grandfather Major William Bradford to be equally divided among them; John Bradford; Samuel Bradford; Mary the wife of William Hunt of Weymouth; Sarah the wife of Mr. Baker of Duxbury; and Elizabeth Adams the daughter of Alice the wife of the late Rev. William Adams of Dedham.

On 21 Feb. 1712/3 Joshua Ripley of Windham gave his son Joshua Ripley of Windham 40 acres. On 2 June 1729 Joshua sold his son Joshua Jr. another 174 acres and on the same day Joshua Jr. sold his father one-third part of a dam, land, iron ore, iron works and "Cole" house, and two forges. On 24 Feb. 1721/2 Joshua gave land in Windham to son David Ripley of Windham. On 20 July 1738 Joshua gave to his son Hezekiah more than 150 acres and his home lot except for part reserved for his daughter Jerusha.

The will of Joshua Ripley of Windham, yeoman, dated 6 Jan. 1738/9, proved 27 June 1739, names sons Joshua, Hezekiah, and David; grandchildren Ann Bingham, Abigail Manning, and Samuel Manning; daughters Alice Egerton, Hannah Webb, Leah Cook, and Rachel Tracy; Faith Bingham deceased; Margaret Seabury; Irena Manning deceased; and daughters Jerusha Ripley and Ann Wheat; son Hezekiah to be executor.

Children of Joshua and Hannah (Bradford) Ripley:

49	i	ALICE RIPLEY[4], b. Hingham 17 or 18 Sept. 1683
50	ii	HANNAH RIPLEY, b. Hingham 2 March 1684/5
51	iii	FAITH RIPLEY, b. Hingham 20 Sept. 1686
52	iv	JOSHUA RIPLEY, b. Hingham 13 May 1688
53	v	MARGARET RIPLEY, b. Norwich, Conn., 4 Nov. 1690
54	vi	RACHEL RIPLEY (twin), b. Windham, Conn., 17 April 1693
55	vii	LEAH RIPLEY (twin), b. Windham, Conn., 17 April 1693
56	viii	HEZEKIAH RIPLEY, b. Windham, Conn., 10 June 1695
57	ix	DAVID RIPLEY, b. Windham, Conn., 20 May 1697
58	x	IRENA RIPLEY, b. Windham, Conn., 28 Aug. 1700
59	xi	JERUSHA RIPLEY (twin), b. Windham, Conn., 1 Nov. 1704
60	xii	ANN RIPLEY (twin), b. Windham, Conn., 1 Nov. 1704

References: *MD* 28:97-104(g.s.; fam. acct.). *Ripley Gen* pp. 11-13. *Hingham Hist* 3:132-3(b. 4 ch.). Windham CT VR A:16-7(m.; b. ch.); 1:188(d. Hannah, Joshua). Windham CT PR 2:204-5, 212-3(Joshua Ripley). *NEHGR* 121:211(m.). Hale Cem Coll:Windham p. 281(d.

Hannah). Windham CT LR D:336; F:377; G:60-1, 544(Joshua Ripley). Suffolk Co. PR 6:459(John Ripley); #2140, 13:406(John Richards). Bible with GS #58617.

12.   MELATIAH³ BRADFORD (*William²⁻¹*), b. Plymouth 1 Nov. 1664; d. after 24 April 1739.

She m. (1) ca. 1689 **JOHN STEELE**, b. Hartford, Conn., ca. 1660; d. there 6 March 1697/8 (inv.); son of James and Bethia (Bishop) Steele.

She m. (2) prob. Killingworth, Conn., after 23 June 1702 **SAMUEL STEVENS**, b. Guilford, Conn., 1 March 1656; d. Killingworth, Conn., before 7 July 1712 (inv.); son of William and Mary (Meiggs) Stevens. He m. (1) ELIZABETH _____ with whom he had Temperance, John, Samuel, Tameson, and Mary.

John Richards of Boston, merchant, in his will dated 1 April, proved 10 May 1694, named, among others, the children of his late sister Alice the wife of Major William Bradford of Plymouth: Thomas Bradford of Connecticut; Mercy the wife of Mr. Steel of Hartford [Conn.]; Alice the wife of Major James Fitch of Norwich [Conn.]; Hannah the wife of Joshua Ripley of Norwich; Melatiah the wife of John Steel of Norwich; the children of William Bradford Jr. of Plymouth to receive the share of their grandfather Major William Bradford to be equally divided among them; John Bradford; Samuel Bradford; Mary the wife of William Hunt of Weymouth; Sarah the wife of Mr. Baker of Duxbury; and Elizabeth Adams the daughter of Alice the wife of the late Rev. William Adams of Dedham.

On 23 June 1702 James Steele Jr., father of the deceased, was appointed guardian to Bethia, John, and Ebenezer, minor children of John Steele of Hartford, deceased. In August 1712 Melatiah Stevens and "son-in-law" [stepson] John Stevens gave their bond as administrators of the estate of Samuel Stevens late of Killingworth deceased. A list of the children with their ages is included in the probate records, giving Elizabeth as 9 years old and William as 6.

On 15 Dec. 1715 Samuel Shepherd of Hartford, in right of his wife Bethia, who was the daughter of John Steele Sr., petitioned for distribution of the estate of John Steele Jr., son of John Sr., who died in his minority. At that time the court requested the appearance of Melatiah Stevens of Killingworth, widow, and Ebenezer Steele, minor son of John Sr.

On 7 Feb. 1715/6 Ebenezer Steele, a minor about 19 years of age, son of John Steele, chose Thomas Steele as his guardian.

On 4 Aug. 1722 Temperance Denton of Jamaica, N.Y., sold to Samuel Willcocks of Killingworth her right in five acres of meadow now in possession of her mother-in-law Malletiah Steevens, widow.

On 3 March 1724/5 Samuel Steevens, John Hubbard and his wife Elizabeth, and Samuel Willcocks Jr. and his wife Mary sold to their brother John Steevens their right in a lot of land which had been part of the estate of their father Samuel Steevens.

Melatiah Stevens received several grants of land in Killingworth, the latest 7 Dec. 1737 which she sold to "my son-in-law" [i.e., stepson] Samuel Steevens 24 April 1739.

Children John and Melatiah (Bradford) Steele:

61		i	BETHIA STEELE[4], b. ca. 1690
		ii	JOHN STEELE, b. ca. 1692; d. between 23 June 1702 and 15 Dec. 1715
62		iii	EBENEZER STEELE, b. Killingworth, Conn., 13 Aug. 1695

Children of Samuel and Melatiah (Bradford) (Steele) Stevens:

| 63 | | iv | ELIZABETH STEVENS, b. Guilford, Conn., ca. 1703 (based on age at d.) |
| 64 | | v | WILLIAM STEVENS, b. Killingworth, Conn., 2 Feb. 1705/6* |

* CSL Barbour Index says 1715/6 but this must be an error for 1705/6, as his father was dead by 10 June 1712 (adm.), and the age given in the probate calculates to 1705/6.

References: *NEHGR* 129:18-22(Stevens). *TAG* 36:186-90(Steele). *Manwaring* 1:587(PR for John Steele). *Bradford Desc* pp. 4, 9, 10. *Stevens Desc* pp. 38-9, 194-5. Guilford CT VR A 60(b. S. Stevens). Killingworth CT VR 2:160(b. Wm.). Hartford CT PR #5188(John Steele). Killingworth CT LR 3: 124(Temperance Denton);174(Samuel Steevens et.al.), 6:270(Melatiah Stevens). New London CT PR 1:619(Samuel Stevens), 642(bond); 653(inv.). Suffolk Co. PR #2140, 13:416(John Richards).

13. SAMUEL[3] BRADFORD (*William[2-1]*), b. Plymouth ca. 1667; d. Duxbury 11 April 1714 aged 46.

He m. Plymouth 31 July 1689 **HANNAH ROGERS**, b. Duxbury 16 Nov. 1668; d. Hingham Sept. 1754; daughter of John and Elizabeth (Pabodie) Rogers, a descendant of Pilgrims **John Alden** and **Thomas Rogers**.

On 17 May 1686 Samuel Bradford recorded his mark for cattle, horse, and swine in the Plymouth town records as "A Cropp of the neare eare." At town meetings on 13 March 1692/3, 2 March 1695/6, and 8 March 1696/7, he was chosen one of the surveyors of highways.

John Richards of Boston, merchant, in his will dated 1 April, proved 10 May 1694, named, among others, the children of his late sister Alice the wife of Major William Bradford of Plymouth: Thomas Bradford of Connecticut; Mercy the wife of Mr. Steel of Hartford [Conn.]; Alice the wife of Major James Fitch of Norwich [Conn.]; Hannah the wife of Joshua Ripley of Norwich; Melatiah the wife of John Steel of Norwich; the children of William Bradford Jr. of Plymouth to receive the share of their grandfather Major William Bradford to be equally divided among them; John Bradford; Samuel Bradford; Mary the wife of William Hunt of Weymouth; Sarah the wife of Mr. Baker of Duxbury; and Elizabeth Adams the daughter of Alice the wife of the late Rev. William Adams of Dedham.

On 8 April 1696 Samuel Bradford of Plimoth and wife Hannah deeded land in Little Compton to John Rogers, because of land given them "by our Hond Father John Rogers of Bristol."

On 15 Jan. 1700 Samuel Bradford of Duxbury sold land in Middleborough to Nathaniel Thomas of Marshfield.

On 4 July 1703 Hannah, wife of Samuel Bradford, having removed to Duxboro, was dismissed from the Plymouth Church to the Duxbury Church.

The will of Samuel Bradford of Duxbury dated 26 Jan. 1713/4, proved 16 June 1714, names eldest son Gershom, son Perez, father William Bradford deceased, and youngest son Gamaliel under 21; daughter Hannah Gilbert wife of Nathaniel of Taunton; daughters Elizabeth, Jerusha, and Welthea Bradford all under 21; wife Hannah; and negro servant William; executors wife Hannah and son Gershom Bradford.

On 27 Nov. 1731 Nathaniel Gilbert of Taunton, yeoman, sold to his mother Hannah Bradford late of Duxbury, now of Taunton, two acres where his father Thomas Gilbert did dwell as well as one-quarter of a dwelling house.

The will of Hannah Bradford of Duxbury, widow, dated 16 April 1734, codicil 1 June 1747, sworn to at Hingham 5 Nov. 1754, names sons Gershom, Peres, and Gamaliel Bradford, and daughters "Hannah Gilburd, Elizabeth Whiton, Jerusha Gay and Welthean Lane"; son [-in-law] Peter Lane executor.

On 8 April 1747 Gershom Bradford of Kingston, Gentleman, sold 100 acres, part of the homestead given him by his father's will together with his dwelling house and other buildings; Gershom's wife Priscilla released her dower rights.

On 25 Nov. 1754 Gershom Bradford of Bristol, R.I., Gentleman, sold to Peter Lane of Hingham, executor of the will of his mother Hannah Bradford, 20 acres out of 100 give to Gershom by his father Samuel Bradford and sold by Gershom to his grandfather John Rogers, Esq., and given by John Rogers to Gershom's mother. On the same day Gershom for and in consideration of 16 acres out of the estate of his mother, traded with Peter Lane 10 acres to be subject to a division by Hannah's daughters.

Children of Samuel and Hannah (Rogers) Bradford, b. Plymouth except last two b. perhaps Duxbury:

65   i   HANNAH⁴ BRADFORD, b. 14 Feb. 1689(/90), bp. 1692

66   ii   GERSHOM BRADFORD, b. 21 Dec. 1691, bp. 1692

67   iii PEREZ BRADFORD, b. 28 Dec. 1694

68   iv   ELIZABETH BRADFORD, b. 15 Dec. 1696

69   v   JERUSHA BRADFORD, b. 10 March 1699

70   vi   WELTHEA BRADFORD, b. 15 May 1702

71   vii GAMALIEL BRADFORD, b. 18 May 1704

References: *VR Duxbury* pp. 136(b. Hannah), 353(d. Samuel). *MD* 2:18(b. ch.); 9:160(d. Samuel), 172(b. Hannah); 13:205(m.); 16:116-9(Samuel's will); 20:21-2(1696 deed). *MF* 19:45-6. *Plymouth Ch Recs* 1:197(dismissal), 274(bp. Hannah, Gershom). Suffolk Co. PR #12505(Hannah Bradford); #2140, 13:416(John Richards). Hingham VR 2:15(d. Hannah). Plymouth Co. PR 3:301(Samuel Bradford). *Plymouth VR* pp. 14(b. ch.), 86(m.). Plymouth Co. LR 4:140(Samuel Bradford); 38:194; 46:166(Gershom Bradford). Bristol Co. LR 20:76(Nathaniel Gilbert). *Plymouth Town Recs* 1:211, 223, 241, 247.

14. MARY³ BRADFORD (*William²⁻¹*), b. prob. Plymouth 1668; d. Chilmark 7 May 1720.

She m. ca. 1687 **WILLIAM HUNT**, b. Weymouth 1655; d. Chilmark 2 Jan. 1727 aged abt. 73; son of Ephraim and Ebbet (Brimsmead) Hunt. He m. (2) prob. Chilmark HANNAH (SKIFF) MAYHEW. On 3 Nov. 1729 Hannah Mayhew and William Hunt of Chilmark divided land they had bought from the heirs of Nathan Skiff.

John Richards of Boston, merchant, made his will 1 April, proved 10 May 1694, naming, among others, the children of his late sister Alice the wife of Major William Bradford of Plymouth: Thomas Bradford of Connecticut; Mercy the wife of Mr. Steel of Hartford [Conn.]; Alice the wife of Major James Fitch of Norwich [Conn.]; Hannah the wife of Joshua Ripley of Norwich; Melatiah the wife of John Steel of Norwich; the children of William Bradford Jr. of Plymouth to receive the share of their grandfather Major William Bradford to be equally divided among them; John Bradford; Samuel Bradford; Mary the wife of William Hunt of Weymouth; Sarah the wife of Mr. Baker of

Duxbury; and Elizabeth Adams the daughter of Alice the wife of the late Rev. William Adams of Dedham.

The will of William Hunt of Chilmark, yeoman, dated 13 March 1721/2, presented 5 April 1727, names son William; and granddaughters Mary Knowles, Rebecca Knowles, and Malatiah Knowles.

Children of William and Mary (Bradford) Hunt, b. Weymouth:

72   i MARY HUNT[4], b. 18 Feb. 1687/8

73   ii WILLIAM HUNT, b. 17 May 1693

References: *VR Chilmark* p. 88(d. William). *VR Weymouth* 1:150(b. Mary), 154(b. William; son William). *Martha's Vineyard By Banks* 3:212-3. *Weymouth By Chamberlain* 3:313-4. *Mayflower Source Recs* p. 108(d. Mary). Dukes Co. PR 2:19-20(William Hunt). Dukes Co. LR 5:66(Hannah Mayhew & William Hunt). Suffolk Co. PR #2140, 13:416(John Richards).

15. SARAH[3] BRADFORD (*William[2-1]*), b. prob. Plymouth 1671; d. Marshfield between 18 Oct. 1705 and 29 Sept. 1712.

She m. ca. 1687 **KENELM BAKER**, b. Marshfield 23 March 1657/8; d. there between 29 Sept. 1712 and 30 March 1713; son of Samuel and Eleanor (Winslow) Baker.

John Richards of Boston, merchant, made his will 1 April, proved 10 May 1694, naming, among others, the children of his late sister Alice the wife of Major William Bradford of Plymouth: Thomas Bradford of Connecticut; Mercy the wife of Mr. Steel of Hartford [Conn.]; Alice the wife of Major James Fitch of Norwich [Conn.]; Hannah the wife of Joshua Ripley of Norwich; Melatiah the wife of John Steel of Norwich; the children of William Bradford Jr. of Plymouth to receive the share of their grandfather Major William Bradford to be equally divided among them; John Bradford; Samuel Bradford; Mary the wife of William Hunt of Weymouth; Sarah the wife of Mr. Baker of Duxbury; and Elizabeth Adams the daughter of Alice the wife of the late Rev. William Adams of Dedham.

On 5 Jan. 1700 Kenelm Baker of Marshfield sold one-half of a 100-acre lot given him by his grandfather Mr Kenelm Winslow of Marshfield.

The will of Kenelm Baker of Marshfield dated 29 Sept. 1712, proved 6 April 1713, names sons Kenelm, Samuel, William, and Edward, the last two under 21; daughter Sarah wife of John Sherman; daughters Alice, Eleanor, Abigail, Bethiah, and Keziah, (no surnames) the last two under 18; executors uncle Capt. Nathaniel Winslow of Marshfield, brother Major John Bradford of

Plymouth, and kinsman Mr. Isaac Winslow of Marshfield. The inventory was dated 30 March 1713.

On 8 March 1713/4 guardians were appointed or chosen by Abigail, William, Kenelm, Bethiah, Edward, Keziah, and Samuel.

Children of Kenelm and Sarah (Bradford) Baker, b. Marshfield:

74	i	SARAH BAKER[4], b. 28 Oct. 1688
75	ii	ALICE BAKER, b. 3 Nov. 1690
76	iii	ELEANOR BAKER, b. 31 March 1692
77	iv	ABIGAIL BAKER, b. 23 Dec. 1693
78	v	KENELM BAKER, b. 3 Nov. 1695
79	vi	BETHIAH BAKER, b. 12 May 1699
80	vii	KEZIAH BAKER, b. 15 Aug. 1701
81	viii	SAMUEL BAKER, b. 5 Feb. 1702/3
82	ix	WILLIAM BAKER (twin), b. 18 Oct. 1705
83	x	EDWARD BAKER (twin), b. 18 Oct. 1705

References: *MD* 2:7(b. Kenelm); 5:234(b. first 4 ch.), 235(b. Kenelm); 6:20(b. next 3 ch.), 21(b. twins); 11:121(ch. rec.); 24:27-30(will); 31:117(bp. Ed., Wm.). *Marshfield VR* pp. 4(b. Kenelm), 20(b. 3 ch.), 21(b. Abigail), 26(b. rest ch.). Plymouth Co. PR 3:236(Kenelm Baker), 279(gdn.). Plymouth Co. LR 7:274(Kenelm Baker). Lebanon CT LR 1:231(Kenelm buys), 275(Kenelm sells). Suffolk Co. PR #2140, 13:416(John Richards).

16. JOSEPH[3] BRADFORD (*William[2-1]*), b. Plymouth 18 April 1675; d. New London, Conn., 17 Jan. 1747 in 73rd yr.

He m. (1) Lebanon, Conn., 5 Oct. 1698 **ANNA FITCH**, b. Norwich, Conn., 6 April 1675; d. Lebanon, Conn., 7 Oct. 1715; daughter of James and Priscilla (Mason) Fitch of Norwich.

He m. (2) int. New London, Conn., 25 Feb. 1715/6 **MARY (SHERWOOD) FITCH**, b. 1674; d. Montville, Conn., 16 Sept. 1752; daughter of Matthew and Mary (Fitch) Sherwood. She m. (1) Preston, Conn., 4 March 1698 DANIEL FITCH with whom she had Adonijah, James, Lemuel, Mary, and Daniel. The will of Matthew Sherwood dated 14 April 1713 names daughter Mary Fitch. The will of Mary Sherwood of Stratfield dated 9 July 1726 names daughter Mary Bradford.

Joseph is called Ensign when he bought land on 30 March 1703 and Lieutenant when he sold land on 28 July 1704 in Lebanon.

On 1 March 1714/5 Joseph Bradford of Lebanon sold 52 acres in Norwich and Windham to Jonathan Lad.

On 8 Jan. 1741/2 Joseph Bradford of New London sold to John Bradford of New London 20 acres.

The will of Joseph Bradford of New London, Conn., dated 14 Sept. 1731, proved 10 March 1746/7, names wife Mary Bradford; sons Joseph and John; eldest daughter Ann Demick; daughters Priscilla Hide, Sarah Turthill, Hannah Buele, Elizabeth Bradford, Alithea Bradford, and Irene Bradford, to have the farm at Stafford. An acquittance from Joseph Bradford's heirs dated 18 June 1747, was signed by Samuel and Priscilla Hide, David and Alitha Hide, Jonathan and Irene Janes, and Andrew and Elizabeth Lisk, all of Lebanon; Israel and Sarah Lothrop of Norwich; and Timothy and Hannah Buele of Hebron.

On 23 June 1748 James Harris and Robert Denison of New London, William Whiting of Norwich, Timothy Buel and his wife Hannah of Hebron, Andrew Lisk and his wife Elizabeth, David Hide and his wife Alethea, and Jonathan Janes and his wife Irenia all of Lebanon sold 30 acres in New London to Ezekiel Fox.

Children of Joseph and Anna (Fitch) Bradford, 1st, b. New London CT, rest, b. Lebanon, Conn.:

84	i	ANN[4] BRADFORD, b. 26 July 1699
85	ii	JOSEPH BRADFORD (twin), b. 9 April 1702
86	iii	PRISCILLA BRADFORD (twin), b. 9 April 1702
	iv	ALTHEA BRADFORD (twin), b. 6 April 1704; d. April 1704
	v	IRENE BRADFORD (twin), b. 6 April 1704; d. 16 Aug. 1704
87	vi	SARAH BRADFORD, b. 21 Sept. 1706
88	vii	HANNAH BRADFORD, b. 24 May 1709
89	viii	ELIZABETH BRADFORD, b. 21 Oct. 1712
90	ix	ALTHEA BRADFORD (twin), b. 19 Sept. 1715
91	x	IRENA BRADFORD (twin), b. 19 Sept. 1715

Child of Joseph and Mary (Sherwood) (Fitch) Bradford, b. Lebanon, Conn.:

92	xi	JOHN BRADFORD, b. 20 May 1717

References: New London CT PR #666(Joseph Bradford). *Waterman Gen* 1:629-30(d. Irene), 652. *Fitch Fam* 2:20-1. *Torrey's Marriages* p. 269(m. Dan Fitch). *Fairfield CT Fams* 1:551-2. Norwich CT VR 1:39(b. Anna). New London CT VR 1:49(b. John). Lebanon CT VR 1:20(m., b. 10 ch.). *MD* 40:56(will). Norwich CT LR 2B:801(Joseph Bradford). Hale Cem Coll:Montville p. 71(d. Joseph). Fairfield CT PR #5772(Matthew Sherwood); #5764(Mary Sherwood). *Hempstead Diary* p. 54(int. 2nd m.). New London CT LR 15:45(Joseph Bradford); 15:118(James Harris *et al.*).

17. ISRAEL³ BRADFORD (*William²⁻¹*), b. Plymouth ca. 1677; d. Kingston 26 March 1760 in 83ʳᵈ yr.

He m. Plymouth 27 Nov. 1701 **SARAH BARTLETT**, b. probably Duxbury ca. 1681; d. Kingston 3 April 1761 in 80th yr.; daughter of Benjamin and Ruth (Pabodie) Bartlett, a descendant of Pilgrims **John Alden, William Brewster,** and **Richard Warren**. The will of Benjamin Bartlett of Duxboro dated 10 Dec. 1717 names among others wife Ruth and daughter Sarah Bradford.

On 2 March 1723/4 at a town meeting Israel Bradford was chosen constable.

On 15, 24, and 25 March 1724/5, 27 March 1725, and 8 Dec. 1742 Israel Bradford and wife Sarah and the other children of Benjamin Bartlett sold off land from Benjamin's estate or agreed to divide Benjamin's land.

At the December 1731 term of the Plymouth County Court of General Sessions, Ephraim Bradford, Hezekiah Bradford, and Israel Bradford, "the Heirs of David Bradford," all of whom "are Severally Proprietors in certain Tracts of Land lying" in Kingston, petitioned that a cartway from the county road to their lands be laid out.

On 5 Aug. 1748, recorded 2 May 1760, Israel Bradford of Kingston for love gave to oldest son Benjamin and youngest son Elisha his home and farm in Kingston. No other Plymouth County land records to children were found.

No Plymouth County probate records were found for Israel or Sarah Bradford.

Children of Israel and Sarah (Bartlett) Bradford, b. Plymouth:

	i	RUTH⁴ BRADFORD, b. 11 Dec. 1702; d. Feb. 1702/3
93	ii	BATHSHEBA BRADFORD, b. 8 Nov. 1703
94	iii	BENJAMIN BRADFORD, b. 17 Oct. 1705
95	iv	ABNER BRADFORD, b. 25 Dec. 1707
96	v	JOSHUA BRADFORD, b. 23 June 1710
97	vi	ICHABOD BRADFORD, b. 22 Sept. 1713
98	vii	ELISHA BRADFORD, b. 26 March 1718

References: *MD* 7:23(d. Israel, Sarah); 13:167-8(b. ch.), 207 (m.); 18:177-183(Bartlett will, div.), 242-4(Bartlett data). *VR Kingston* pp. 320(d. Israel), 322(d. Ruth). Plymouth Co. LR 18:225(Israel Bradford); 46:75(Israel Bradford). Plymouth Co. PR 4:40(Benj. Bartlett). *Plymouth VR* pp. 72(b. ch.; d. Ruth), 87(m.). *Plymouth Co Ct Recs* 2:125. *Plymouth Town Recs* 2:224.

18. EPHRAIM³ BRADFORD (*William²⁻¹*), b. Plymouth 1685; d. Kingston between 20 Feb. 1743/4 (deed) and 6 Oct. 1746.

He m. Plymouth 13 Feb. 1709/10* **ELIZABETH BREWSTER**, b. Duxbury ca. 1690; d. Kingston 5 Dec. 1741 in 51ˢᵗ yr., "wife of Ephraim Bradford"; daughter of Wrestling and Mary (_____) Brewster, a descendant of Pilgrim **William Brewster**. A deed of Elizabeth Brewster of Duxbury and others who were sons-in-law and daughters of Wrestling Brewster, dated 3 Oct. 1707, was acknowledged by Ephraim Bradford and his wife Elizabeth on 15 Jan. 1713.

On 15 May 1702 at a Plymouth town meeting Ephraim Bradford was granted 30 acres on the north side of Blackwater. On 6 Sept. 1708, 13 Dec. 1711, 15 May 1713, and 11 Sept. 1718 he was chosen a juror. On 21 March 1710/11 he was chosen surveyor of highways, on 18 March 1716/7 fence viewer, and on 18 March 1722/3 constable.

On 22 Dec. 1730 Ephraim Bradford of Kingston having sold to his brother David two acres of land, and David dying before Ephraim gave him a deed, Ephraim confirmed this sale to David's heirs.

At the December 1731 term of the Court of General Sessions, Ephraim Bradford, Hezekiah Bradford, and Israel Bradford, "the Heirs of David Bradford," all of whom "are Severally Proprietors in certain Tracts of Land lying" in Kingston, petitioned that a cartway from the county road to their lands be laid out.

On 20 Feb. 1743/4 Ephraim Bradford and Israel Bradford divided a tract of cedar swamp with members of the Churchill and Bonney families.

The will of Ephraim Bradford of Kingston, yeoman, dated 16 Dec. 1741, presented 6 Oct. 1746, mentions "my three sons" and "my daughters" but does not name them. On 3 Feb. 1747 Wrestling Brewster was appointed guardian of the three sons of Ephraim Bradford late of Kingston deceased: Ezekiel, Simeon, and Wait Bradford. Named in the executor's account are Ruth Chandler, wife of Nathan; Anna Chandler, wife of Ebenezer; Abigail Holmes, wife of Peleg; and Elizabeth and Lucy Bradford.

Children of Ephraim and Elizabeth (Brewster) Bradford, first 10 b. Plymouth, rest b. probably Kingston:

> i   DEBORAH⁴ BRADFORD, b. 21 June 1712; d. Kingston 10 June 1732 ae 19y 11m 20d; unm.
>
> ii [SON] BRADFORD, b. and d. June 1714
>
> iii ANNA BRADFORD, b. 25 July 1715
>
> iv [DAUGHTER] BRADFORD, b. Oct. 1716; d. 1716

99

100	v	ELIZABETH BRADFORD, b. 3 Nov. 1717
	vi	EPHRAIM BRADFORD, b. 1 Jan. 1718/9; d. before 16 Dec. 1741 (father's will)
101	vii	ABIGAIL BRADFORD, b. 28 Feb. 1719/20
102	viii	LUSANNA (or LUCY) BRADFORD, b. 3 May 1721
	ix	ELIJAH BRADFORD, b. 23 Jan. 1722/3; d. before 16 Dec. 1741 (father's will)
	x	[SON] BRADFORD, b. ca. 28 March 1723/4 [sic]; d. before 16 Dec. 1741 (father's will)
103	xi	RUTH BRADFORD, b. ca. 1725 (based on age at d.)
104	xii	EZEKIEL BRADFORD, b. 14 March 1728
105	xiii	SIMEON BRADFORD, b. 28 Aug. 1729
106	xiv	WAIT BRADFORD, b. ca. 1730

* Plymouth VR says Ephraim m. on that date Elizabeth Bartlett.

NOTE: No record was found for a daughter Deborah, b. 20 June 1732, d. 10 June 1752 as rec. in *Bradford Desc* (p.12). Note similarity to the dates of the first child, except 20 years later.

References: *MD* 7:22-3(deaths); 13:32(b. 1st 10 ch.); 14:36 (m.); 20:112-6(Brewster deed); 21:189-91(will). *VR Kingston* pp. 30(b. Simeon), 319(d. Elizabeth). Plymouth Co. LR 10 (2):244(Elizabeth Brewster); 26:53(Ephraim Bradford); 36:204(Ephraim & Israel Bradford). Plymouth Co. PR 10:343; 13:75(Ephraim Bradford); 10:523; 11:76, 77(gdns.). *Plymouth VR* pp. 58(b. 1st 4 ch.), 59(b. next 6 ch.), 89(m.). *Plymouth Co Ct Recs* 2:125. *Plymouth Town Recs* 1:299; 2:21, 51, 80,94, 176, 191, 221.

19. DAVID³ BRADFORD (*William²⁻¹*), b. prob. Plymouth before 1687; d. Kingston 16 March 1729/30.

He m. Plymouth 23 Feb. 1713/4 **ELIZABETH PHINNEY**, bp. Bristol 27 Oct. 1695; living Braintree 9 Oct. 1746; daughter of Jonathan and Joanna (Kinnicut) Phinney. The will of Jonathan Phinney of Swanzey dated 27 Aug. 1724 names wife Johannah and daughter Elizabeth Bradford. An account in the estate of Joanna Phinney of Swanzey, widow, allowed 17 Nov. 1741, states that daughter Elizabeth Ludden had received her portion. She m. (2) int. Kingston 10 Aug. 1733 BENJAMIN LUDDEN of Braintree.

On 18 March 1717/8 David Bradford of Plymouth sold to Wrestling Brewster of Plymouth all his houselot on the north side of his house.

At a Plymouth town meeting 9 May 1720, David Bradford was chosen as a juror.

On 1 April 1730 Mrs. Elizabeth Bradford of Kingston was appointed administratrix of the estate of her husband David Bradford late of Kingston deceased and in Sept. 1733 Samuel Foster of Kingston was appointed guardian to Nathaniel and Jonathan, both over 14, and Nathan, Lemuel, and Lydia, all under 14, children of David Bradford late of Kingston deceased.

On 22 Dec 1730 Ephraim Bradford of Kingston having sold his brother David two acres of land, and David dying before Ephraim gave him a deed, Ephraim confirmed this sale to David's heirs.

On 13 April 1742, acknowledged 26 April 1742, Elkanah Cushman of Plymouth, mariner, and wife Lydia sold their rights in land of David Bradford of Kingston deceased and of Jonathan Bradford of Plymouth deceased. On 9 Oct. 1746 Benjamin Ludden of Braintree and wife Elizabeth, who was widow of David Bradford late of Kingston, sold their rights to land of her late husband and of deceased [sons] Jonathan and Lemuel Bradford.

No Suffolk County probate or later land records were found for Benjamin or Elizabeth Ludden.

Children of David and Elizabeth (Phinney) Bradford, first four, b. Plymouth, last, b. Kingston:

107	i	NATHANIEL⁴ BRADFORD, b. 10 Dec. 1715
	ii	JONATHAN BRADFORD, b. 13 Nov. 1717; d. between 28 Sept. 1733 and 13 April 1742
108	iii	LYDIA BRADFORD, b. 23 Dec. 1719
109	iv	NATHAN BRADFORD, b. 3 April 1722
	v	LEMUEL BRADFORD, b. 1 March 1726/7; d. before 9 Oct. 1746

References: *MD* 12:85(b. 4 ch.); 14:37(m.); 23:165-8(Phinney est.), 181-5(est.; gdn.; deeds). *VR Kingston* pp. 28(b. Lemuel), 319(d. David). *Waterman Gen* 1:630. *Finney-Phinney* pp. 2-3. Bristol Co. PR 6:137(Jonathan Phinney); 10:103(Joanna Phinney). Plymouth Co. PR 5:664; 6:395-7(David Bradford). *Plymouth VR* pp. 51(b. 1ˢᵗ 4 ch.), 90(m.). *TAG* 68:250(bp. Elizabeth). Plymouth Co. LR 16:64(David Bradford); 35:24(Elkanah Cushman); 38:122 (Benjamin Ludden). *Plymouth Town Recs* 2:203.

20. HEZEKIAH³ BRADFORD (*William²⁻¹*), b. prob. Plymouth before 1687; d. after 23 April 1761 (deed).

He m. Plymouth 21 May 1714 **MARY CHANDLER**, b. Duxbury; d. aft. 23 April 1761 (deed); daughter of Joseph & Mercy (_____) Chandler. The will of Joseph Chandler of Duxboro dated 21 April 1721 names wife Mercy, daughter Mary Bradford and others.

On 16 May 1716 Hezekiah Bradford of Plymouth, yeoman, sold to Wrestling Brewster, land that was part of the farm of "Olde Maiger Bradford." On 30 Jan. 1718/9 Hezekiah sold to Wrestling another 10 acres of his farm.

At the Dec. 1731 term of the Plymouth County Court of General Sessions, Ephraim Bradford, Hezekiah Bradford, and Israel Bradford, "the Heirs of David Bradford," all of whom "are Severally Proprietors in certain Tracts of Land lying" in Kingston, petitioned that a cartway from the county road to their lands be laid out.

On 10 April 1761, acknowledged 23 April 1761, Hezekiah Bradford, yeoman, and Mary Bradford, his wife, of Kingston, sold to Jonathan Chandler of Duxbury land in Duxbury that Mr. Joseph Chandler, late of Duxbury, had given to his three daughters Esther, Mary and Sarah Chandler.

On 8 March 1781 Mary Bradford of Duxbury, weaver, sold to Elijah Chandler her interest in the farm that her father Hezekiah Bradford had owned.

No Plymouth County probate records were found for Hezekiah Bradford.

Child of Hezekiah and Mary (Chandler) Bradford:

    i MARY[4] BRADFORD, b. 26 Oct. 1717 (based on age at d.); d. Duxbury 24 Oct. 1803 ae 86 wanting 2 days. The will of Mary Bradford of Duxbury, singlewoman, dated 21 Dec. 1792, proved 18 Nov. 1803, leaves everything to her cousin Joseph Chandler, son of Nathan Chandler of Duxbury by his second wife, and in default to Joseph's brother Ira Chandler.

References: *Small Desc* 2:1053-5, 1059-60(Chandler will). *MD* 14:37(m.), 66(Chandlers); 27:131-3(deed). *VR Duxbury* p. 353(d. daughter Mary). Plymouth Co. PR 4:309(Joseph Chandler); 38:461(Mary Bradford). Plymouth Co. LR 12:111; 16:65; 52:74(Hezekiah Bradford); 64:223(Mary Bradford). *Plymouth VR* p. 90(m.). *Plymouth Co Ct Recs* 2:125.

21. ELISHA[3] BRADFORD (*Joseph[2], William[1]*), b. prob. Plymouth ca. 1669; d. Kingston 16 June 1747.

He m. (1) before 28 Jan. 1702/3 (deed) **HANNAH COLE**, b. Plymouth; d. there 15 Aug. 1718; daughter of James and Mary (Tilson) Cole. On 25 Jan. 1706/7 and 8 March 1707/8 Elisha Bradford and wife Hannah of Plymouth and others sold all their rights to land of their father James Cole of Plymouth deceased. Apparently Hannah and Elisha had no children.

He m. (2) Plymouth 7 Sept. 1719 **BATHSHEBA BROCK** (or **LEBROCKE**), b. Scituate 21 May 1703; living 17 Nov. 1758 (deed); daughter of Francis and Sarah (Hobart) Brock. The will of Israel Hobart of Scituate dated 14 July 1729 names his granddaughter Bathsheba Bradford, daughter of his daughter Sarah Brock deceased. She m. (2) int. Kingston 21 March 1752 JOSHUA OLDHAM of Scituate.

In an undated deposition made about June 1698 Elisha Bradford stated that he was aged 29 years or thereabout, thus born about 1669.

Elisha Bradford served the town of Plymouth in various capacities; he was chosen a juror 9 Feb. 1701/2, surveyor of highways 16 March 1701/2, constable 1 March 1702/3, grand juror 26 Feb. 1704/5, juror 2 Sept. 1706, tithingman 22 March 1708, juror 9 May 1709, tithingman 17 March 1711/2 and 1 March 1716, and grand juror 22 Feb. 1719/20. On 14 May 1711 he was one of several people granted permission by the town to build a gallery over the stairs in the meeting house.

On 1 Aug. 1729 Elisha Bradford and his family were warned from the town of Roxbury. On 23 Sept. 1729 Elisha Bradford of Roxborough in Suffolk County, yeoman, sold to Thomas Croade of Kingston, Gentleman, 25 acres adjoyning Elisha's farm in Kingston.

On 14 Oct. 1734 Elisha Bradford and his family, who arrived in town on or about 27 Aug., were warned out of Kingston. In the Common Pleas records he is called of Kingston "Now Resident in Roxbury" in March 1729/30, of Newtown "alias of Plymouth" in March 1730/1, and of Kingston "Alias of Hingham" in December 1734.

On 24 Oct. 1744 Elisha Bradford of Kingston, husbandman, sold to Nehemiah Bradford of Kingston, seafaringman, 100 acres in Kingston.

On 6 Oct. 1747 Bathsheba Bradford of Kingston, widow of Elisha, sold to Phebe Cook of Kingston, widow of John, all dower rights in land John had bought of Elisha, and on 4 June 1748 she sold to Thomas Torrey all rights to land in Kingston which Elisha owned during their marriage and had sold to Isaac Thomas on 18 March 1728/9. It was not until 26 June 1750 that Samuel Foster of Kingston was appointed administrator of the estate of Elisha Bradford late of Kingston deceased intestate.

Widow Barsheba Bradford from Kingston was warned from Plympton 28 Sept. 1750.

On 25 May 1758, ack. 17 Nov. 1758, Joshua Oldham of Scituate sold half his homestead and half his dwelling house to Israel Turner. Bathsheba acknowledged the deed 17 Nov. 1758.

No Plymouth County probate records were found for Joshua or Bathsheba Oldham.

Children of Elisha and Bathsheba (Brock) Bradford, by second wife, first five b. Plymouth, rest b. Kingston:

110   i   HANNAH[4] BRADFORD, b. 10 April 1720

        ii JOSEPH BRADFORD, b. 7 Dec. 1721; bp. Kingston in July 1722; d. 4 Sept. 1743*

      iii SYLVANUS BRADFORD, b. 6 July 1723; d. 12 July 1723

      iv NEHEMIAH BRADFORD, b. 27 July 1724; living 24 Oct. 1744 when his father sold him land

111   v LAURANNA (or URANIE) BRADFORD, b. 27 March 1726

      vi MARY BRADFORD, b. 1 Aug. 1727; d. 21 Aug. 1727*

     vii ELISHA BRADFORD, b. 6 Oct. 1729, bp. 2nd Ch Roxbury 21 Dec. 1729; d. March 1753*

    viii LOIS BRADFORD, b. 30 Jan. 1730/1, bp. 2nd Ch Roxbury 17 Jan. 1730/1; d. 10 Oct. 1752* †

112   ix DEBORAH BRADFORD, b. 18 Nov. 1732

113   x ALICE BRADFORD, b. 3 Nov. 1734

114   xi AZENATH BRADFORD, b. 15 Sept. 1736

115   xii CARPENTER BRADFORD, b. 7 Feb. 1738/9

    xiii ABIGAIL BRADFORD, b. 20 June 1741; d. 17 Dec. 1760*

    xiv CHLOE BRADFORD, bp. Kingston 6 April 1743; d. 21 Feb. 1747/8*

    xv CONTENT BRADFORD, b. 21 May 1745; d. 22 May 1745

* The deaths of Joseph, Mary, Elisha, Lois, Abigail, and Chloe are from the Bowman file.

† *Bradford Desc* says Lois may have m. and lived on Long Island and Abigail m. an English officer and resided in Halifax, Nova Scotia. Neither is likely.

References: *MD* 8:256(James Cole deed); 13:112(b. 1st 2 ch.); 14:38(2nd m.); 18:127(Brock), 142(int.); 27:41. *VR Kingston* pp. 26(bp. Chloe, Content), 27(bp. Joseph), 258(int. Bathsheba's 2nd m.). *VR Scituate* 1:50(b. Bathsheba). *Plymouth Ch Recs* 1:219(d. Hannah). *NEHGR* 1:275-6 (b. ch.; d. Content, Silvanus); 111:242 (Bible rec.). Plymouth Co. PR 6:111(Israel Hobart); 11:446 (Elisha Bradford). *Roxbury TR* p. 449(warning). Plymouth Co. LR 6:137; 21:95(Elisha Bradford *et al.*); 7:119; 9:211; 27:17; 37:19(Elisha Bradford); 39:64, 153(Bathsheba Bradford); 41:85(Joshua Oldham). *PN&Q* 2:136(depos.). *Plymouth Co Ct Recs* 2:125; 269(warning); 5:322 #107, 375 #122, 511 #1. *MQ* 31:4:22(Bible rec.). *Plymouth VR* pp. 64(b. 1st 5 ch.; d. Sylvanus). *Plymouth Town Recs* 1:294, 296, 308, 328; 2:7, 16, 26, 46, 62, 128, 201.

Fourth Generation

22. JOHN[4] BRADFORD (*John[3]*, *William[2-1]*), b. Plymouth 29 Dec. 1675; d. Plymouth (recorded Kingston) 27 March 1724 aged 48y 2m 27d.

He m. Plymouth 27 Nov. 1701 **REBECCA BARTLETT**, b. Duxbury; living 2 March 1749/50 (ack. deed); daughter of Benjamin and Ruth (Pabodie) Bartlett, a descendant of Pilgrims **John Alden**, **William Brewster** and **Richard Warren**. The division of the real estate of Benjamin Bartlett late of Duxbury deceased among his children, on 27 March 1724, includes Rebecca Bradford, widow of John deceased She also participated in deeds on 15, 24, and 25 March 1724/5 and 8 Dec. 1742 selling off or dividing the land of Benjamin Bartlett.

On 22 Dec. 1703 John Bradford of Plymouth gave his son John Bradford of Plymouth several pieces of land including 8 acres of upland where son John's now stands and 2 acres of salt meadow that "my father Maj[r] William Bradford hath given unto me after his decease."

John Bradford Jr. first appears in the Plymouth town records on 20 March 1710 when he was chosen as a surveyor of highways; on 15 March 1713/4 and 21 Feb. 1714, an inspector of lumber and timber; on 23 March 1719, a field driver; on 20 July 1719, a juror; on 1 March 1721/2, a selectman; and on 18 March 1722/3, an assesor. On 2 March 1723/4, Jacob Mitchell was chosen a selectman since John Bradford was deceased.

The will of John Bradford Jr. of Plymouth, undated, names his wife Rebecca and children Robert and Rebecca. On 28 April 1724 witnesses swore they had seen John sign the will the "later end of March last."

On 28 Dec. 1742, ack. 2 March 1749/50, Rebecca Bradford, widow of John Bradford, and others sold land in Duxborough to John Samson of Duxbury.

No Plymouth Co. PR for Rebecca Bradford.

Children of John and Rebecca (Bartlett) Bradford, b. Plymouth:

116   i   ROBERT[5] BRADFORD, b. 18 Oct. 1706
117   ii REBECCA BRADFORD, b. 14 Dec. 1710

References: *MD* 7:23(d. John); 12:13(b. ch.); 13:207(m.); 16:119-120(will); 18:179-81(Bartlett div.). *Waterman Gen* 1:626. *VR Kingston* p. 320(d. John). Plymouth Co. LR 5:164(John Bradford); 18:225(Bartlett div.); 19:7, 72; 22:154; 41:13(Bartlett heirs); 41:13(Rebecca Bradford). Plymouth Co. PR 4:439(John Bradford). *Plymouth VR* pp. 50(b. ch.), 87(m.). *Plymouth Town Recs* 2:34, 94, 103, 195, 196, 205, 214, 221, 225.

23. ALICE[4] BRADFORD (*John[3], William[2-1]*), b. Plymouth 28 Jan. 1677; d. Hingham 14 July 1746 aged 69 yrs.

She m. (1) Plymouth 26 Aug. 1708 **EDWARD MITCHELL**, b. Duxbury ca. 1647; d. Bridgewater 15 March 1716/7 (stated in inv.); son of Experience and prob. Mary (_____) Mitchell. He m. (1) Bridgewater MARY HAYWARD "and lived with her 40 years without children."

She m. (2) int. Hingham 20 Nov. 1718 **JOSHUA HERSEY**, b. Hingham 29 March 1678/9; d. there 30 Sept. 1740 aged 63; son of William and Rebecca (Chubbuck) Hersey. He m. (1) Hingham 19 Jan. 1703/4 SARAH HAWKE with whom he had Joshua, Jonathan, Noah, and Elijah. The will of William Hearsy Sr. of Hingham dated 5 July 1689, proved 27 Jan. 1691/2, names his son Joshua Hearsy.

The will of Edward Mitchell of Bridgewater, gentleman, dated 4 Feb. 1716/7, names son Edward and daughters Mary and Alice. The inventory was dated 9 April 1717.

The will of Joshua Hersey of Hingham, yeoman, dated 5 Aug. 1740, proved 24 Dec. 1740, names wife Alice; eldest son Joshua; grandsons Thomas and Ebed, sons of son Jonathan deceased; sons Noah and Elijah; daughter Sarah Loring; grandson Joshua Hearsey; and daughter-in-law Lydia Hearsey "my son's widow."

The will of Alice Hersey of Hingham, widow, dated 23 June 1746, proved 5 Aug. 1746, acquits son Edward Mitchell of paying her a yearly amount given her by her husband Edward Mitchell; names children of daughter Mary Hearsey deceased: Abel, Joshua, Bradford, Benjamin, and Mercy Hearsey; daughters Alice Hearsey and Sarah Loring; and divides among all her children land given her by her father John Bradford deceased

Children of Edward and Alice (Bradford) Mitchell, b. Bridgewater:

118   i   MARY MITCHELL[5], b. 19 July 1709
119   ii   ALICE MITCHELL, b. 23 Dec. 1714
120   iii   EDWARD MITCHELL, b. 7 Feb. 1715/6

Child of Joshua and Alice (Bradford) (Mitchell) Hersey, b. Hingham:

121   iv   SARAH HERSEY, b. 4 July 1719

Note: *Bradford Desc* pp. 14, 47 gives Alice a fifth child Alice Hersey, b. 3 Nov. 1720 who m. Hingham 26 July 1739 Solomon Loring and had 12 children. She is not named in her mother's will. The Alice Hersey in the will would be ii Alice Mitchell who m. Noah Hersey.

References: *MD* 14:36(1st m.), 184(b. Mitchell ch.); 20:140 (Mitchell will). *VR Bridgewater* 1:225(b. 3 Mitchell ch.). *Hingham Hist* 2:300-1(Hersey data). Suffolk Co. PR 8:67(William Hearsy); 35:141(Joshua Hersey); 39:135(Alice Hersey). *TAG* 59:28-31(Mitchell). Plymouth Co. PR 4:17, 19(Edward Mitchell). *Plymouth VR* p. 89(m.).

24. MERCY⁴ BRADFORD (*John³, William²⁻¹*), b. Plymouth 20 Dec. 1681; d. Plympton 27 June 1738 in 57th yr.

She m. (1) Plymouth 12 Oct. 1708 **JONATHAN FREEMAN**, b. Harwich 11 Nov. 1678; d. there 27 April 1714; son of Thomas and Rebecca (Sparrow) Freeman, a descendant of Pilgrim **William Brewster**.

She m. (2) Harwich 10 Oct. 1717 **ISAAC CUSHMAN**, b. Plymouth 15 Nov. 1676; d. Plympton 18 Sept. 1727 in 51st yr.; son of Isaac and Rebecca (Rickard) Cushman, a descendant of Pilgrim **Isaac Allerton**. He m. (1) Plymouth 28 Jan. 1701/2 SARAH GIBBS, a descendant of Pilgrim **Richard Warren**, with whom he had Phebe, Alice, Rebecca, Sarah, Nathaniel, and a daughter who died young.

On 7 April 1715 Mercy Freeman, widow, was appointed administratrix of the estate of her husband Jonathan Freeman late of Harwich deceased. On 27 May 1718 Mercy Cushman, wife of Isaac, and late widow of Jonathan Freeman of Harwich was allowed household goods for the support her children.

On 6 Nov. 1727 Mercy Cushman, widow, was appointed administratrix of the estate of Isaac Cushman. The estate was divided among the widow; only son Nathaniel Cushman; daughters Abigail Cushman, Priscilla Cushman, Fear Cushman, and Phebe Spooner who was wife of Nathaniel Spooner of Dartmouth deceased.

On 2 June 1740 Ichabod Freeman of Plympton was appointed to administer the estate of his mother Mercy Cushman in place of Samuel Bradford, deceased, executor. On 17 April 1741 he filed his account and on the same day there was a division of her dower land held from Isaac Cushman Jr. among Zebedee Chandler as assignee of Fear Sturtevant, wife of Nehemiah Sturtevant of Plymouth and Phebe wife of Barnabas Hatch of Tolland, Conn., "the two daughters of Isaac and Mercy Cushman"*; Priscilla, wife of Israel Holmes of Plympton, and Abigail Cushman.

On 7 June Israel Holmes of Plimton, cordwainer, and his wife Priscilla sold land from the estate of their father Isaac Cushman of Plimton deceased.

On 21 March 1747 Nehemiah Sturtevant of Plimton and his wife Fear sold land she had received from the estate of her father Isaac Cushman deceased.

Children of Jonathan and Mercy (Bradford) Freeman, b. Harwich:

122   i   JONATHAN FREEMAN[5], b. 26 March 1709/10

123   ii   MERCY FREEMAN, b. 24 April 1711

124   iii   BRADFORD FREEMAN, b. 15 Aug. 1713

125   iv   ICHABOD FREEMAN, b. 2 Aug. 1714

Children of Isaac and Mercy (Bradford) (Freeman) Cushman, b. Plympton:

126   v   FEAR CUSHMAN, b. 10 July 1718

127   vi   PRISCILLA CUSHMAN, b. 12 Dec. 1719

        vii   ISAAC CUSHMAN, b. 29 Sept. 1721; d. Plympton 18 Oct. 1721 ae 19d

128   viii   ABIGAIL CUSHMAN, b. 31 Dec. 1722

* Phebe was actually a daughter of Isaac Cushman's first wife Sarah Gibbs.

References: *MD* 2:226(Cushman ch.); 3:93(ch. by 2nd m.), 116 (Cushman ch.), 174(b. Jonathan); 5:86(b. ch. by 1st m.); 7:197(2nd m.); 8:93(b. Jonathan); 10:111-2; 13:20 (est. Jonathan), 207(m. Gibbs); 14:36(1st m.). *VR Plympton* pp. 82(b. Abigail), 84(b. Fear, Isaac), 86(b. Priscilla), 87(his 1st m.), 470(d. Isaac, son Isaac), 471(d. Mercy). *Waterman Gen* 1:38, 82. *TAG* 36:194. Barnstable Co. PR 3:204, 488(Jonathan Freeman). Plymouth Co. PR #5881; 5:317, 378, 380, 400-1(gdns. Cushman ch.); 7:20(Isaac Cushman); 8:215, 299(Mercy Cushman). Plymouth Co. LR 36:36(Israel Holmes); 40:190(Nehemiah Sturtevant); 119:222 (Jonathan Freeman). *Harwich VR* pp. 1(b. Jonathan), 10(b. ch.), 27(2nd m.). *Small Desc* 2:749-751. *Plymouth VR* pp. 11(b. Ichabod), 89(m.). *MF* 17:40-1

25. SAMUEL⁴ BRADFORD (*John³, William²⁻¹*), b. Plymouth 23 Dec. 1683; d. Plympton 26 March 1740 in 56th yr.

He m. Plympton 21 Oct. 1714 **SARAH GRAY**, b. Tiverton 25 April 1697; d. Chilmark 16 Oct. 1770 in 74th yr.; daughter of Edward and Mary (Smith) Gray. She m. (2) Plympton 7 Sept. 1749 WILLIAM HUNT (see #73). The will of Edward Gray of Tiverton dated 10 Dec. 1722 names daughter Sarah wife of Samuel Bradford.

On 20 June 1711 John Bradford of Plymouth gave to his son Samuel Bradford of Plymouth three pieces of land in Plymouth.

At the June 1723 term of the Plymouth Court of General Sessions "Caleb Indian Servant of Mr. Samuel Bradford of Plimton" appeared to answer for "running away from his said Master Sometime in March last and Stealing Several things viz: A Porringer, Some Meat, and a Mare from his said Master ... And also for his Stealing Several things from John Finney of Plimton." Caleb was fined but he was unable to pay the fine so the court bound him as a servant for two years "after the Expiration of the present term that the said

Bradford has in said Caleb by Indenture" to Samuel Bradford, who paid hid fine and fees.

At the September 1730 term of the Court of General Sessions, Nathaniel Harden of Pembroke, husbandman, was presented for "Assaulting and abuseing Mr. Samuel Bradford of Plympton ... Gent, on Saturday the fifteenth Day of August last in the Evening at Kingston ... in the Kings High way." The court convicted Nathaniel and ordered him to pay a fine. At the March 1730/1 term of the Court of Common Pleas Samuel Bradford of Plympton, Gentleman, sued Nathaniel Harden of Bridgewater, laborer, for assault with a "Large Club or Cudgel." Nathaniel pleaded not guilty, "But afterwards the Parties Came into Court and Declared they had agreed."

At the March 1736/7 term of the Court of Common Pleas Samuel Bradford of Plympton, Gentleman, sued Nathaniel Thomas Esq. of Plymouth "Otherwise ... of Marshfield" and others also known as "Nathaniel Thomas and Company, Partners" for failure to pay rent. On 25 Jan.1720/1 the parties agreed mutually to build a furnace on Samuel's land. Samuel granted his partners the right to use the land as needed, and promised to maintain the water level in an adjacent dam so that they might "Keep their Furnace Blowing." In return Nathaniel and Company were to pay a yearly rent, but Samuel says he performed his obligations but the defendants "did not pay any of the said Sums." The court found in Samuel's favor.

On 12 Dec. 1737 Samuel Bradford of Plymton, Gentleman, Robert Bradford of Kingston, yeoman, and George Partridge of Duxbury guardian of James Bradford, Samuel Bradford, Zadock Bradford, Eliphalet Bradford, and William Bradford grandsons of the Honorable John Bradford late of Plymouth, Esq., sold 1/9 part of land located near Muscongus in Lincoln County, Maine. This deed was acknowledged in Boston on 27 Dec. 1737 but not recorded in Lincoln County until 25 Aug. 1763.

At the Sept. 1738 term of the Court of General Sessions, Samuel Bradford of Plympton, Gentleman, was presented for committing "an assault on the body of Polycarpus Loreing of said Plymton, Physician ... and him with a Large Stick One blow did Strike and him ... thereby Greviously Wounded, bruized and him Evilly Entreated." The court ordered Samuel to pay a fine.

Samuel Bradford was a member of the Massachusetts House of Representatives.

The will of Samuel Bradford of Plympton, gentleman, dated 26 Jan. 1729/30, proved 20 May 1740, names his wife Sarah; sons John, Gideon, and William; and daughters Mary Bradford and Sarah Bradford. On 14 May 1745 the estate was redistributed; children Abigail and Phebe having been born since the will was drawn and Samuel born posthumously, they were granted shares.

On 15 Jan. 1742/3 Sarah Bradford of Plympton was named guardian of Samuel, William, Phebe, and Abigail Bradford her children. On 2 July 1751 Mrs. Sarah Hunt swore to her account as guardian for her son William Bradford. On 19 Dec. 1754 she filed her account as guardian of Abigail Bradford, "now Stetson." On 3 Aug. 1757 Samuel Bradford, over 14, requested that his brother William Bradford of Bristol, R.I., be appointed his guardian.

Sarah Bradford of Plimton, widow, received a judgement against Joshua Bradford of Kingston, cooper, and on 11 Oct. 1744 part of Joshua's house and land was set off to Sarah to satisfy the judgement. On 24 March 1748 Sarah sold her part of the house and land to Benjamin Bartlett of Duxbury, cooper.

At the September 1748 term of the Court of Common Pleas, Sarah Bradford of Plympton, widow and executrix of the estate of Samuel Bradford, sued John Faunce of Kingson, yeoman, for ejectment from four acres of salt meadow and sedge in Kingston which Gershom Bradford had sold to Sameul Bradford on 21 Aug. 1731. The court found in Sarah's favor.

Children of Samuel and Sarah (Gray) Bradford, b. Plympton:

129	i	JOHN[5] BRADFORD, b. 8 April 1717
130	ii	GIDEON BRADFORD, b. 27 Oct. 1718
	iii	WILLIAM BRADFORD, b. 16 Dec. 1720; d. Plympton 15 Feb. 1724/5
131	iv	MARY BRADFORD, b. 16 Oct. 1722
132	v	SARAH BRADFORD, b. 4 April 1725
133	vi	WILLIAM BRADFORD, b. 4 Nov. 1728
	vii	MERCY BRADFORD, b. 12 April 1731; d. Plympton 1 June 1731
134	viii	ABIGAIL BRADFORD, b. 12 June 1732
135	ix	PHEBE BRADFORD, b. 30 March 1735
136	x	SAMUEL BRADFORD, b. 13 April 1740

References: *MD* 2:235(d. Wm.); 3:94(b. 1st 6 ch.); 8:154(ds.); 23:14-23(will); 28:105-8(g.s. *et al.*). *VR Chilmark* p. 88(d. Sarah). *VR Plympton* pp. 30-9(b. ch.), 336(her 2nd m.), 448(d. Mercy), 450(d. Samuel, William). *RIVR* Tiverton 4:7:83(b. Sarah). Plymouth Co. PR 8:199; 9:447; 12:388-90(Samuel Bradford); 9:34-6; 14:10, 427(gdns.). *PN&Q* 3:104-6(b. ch.; Bible rec.). *Torrey's Marriages* p. 319(Mary Smith). *Boston News Obits* 2:120(d. Sam.). Plymouth Co. LR 9:48(John Bradford); 37:62(judgement); 40:62(Sarah Bradford). Lincoln Co. ME LR 3:140(Samuel Bradford). *Plymouth Co Ct Recs* 2:41(servant Caleb), 111(Nathaniel Harden), 192(Samuel B Bradford); 7:115 #22(Sarah Bradford).

26. PRISCILLA⁴ BRADFORD (*John³, William²⁻¹*), b. Plymouth 10 March 1686; living 23 March 1732/3 (when she ack. deed).

She m. Kingston 17 Sept. 1721 **SETH CHIPMAN**, b. Barnstable 24 Feb. 1697; d. after 10 May 1764 (when his son Seth was called Jr. in a deed); son of Samuel and Sarah (Cobb) Chipman, a descendant of Pilgrim **John Howland.**

At a Plymouth town meeting on 1 March 1720/1 Seth Chipman was chosen one of the cullers of lumber, and he was chosen a juror on 31 Aug. 1724.

On 16 Feb. 1721/2 John Bradford of Plymouth gave to his daughter Priscilla Chipman, wife of Seth of Plymouth, several parcels of land. On 7 April 1727 Seth Chipman of Kingston, cooper, sold land given to him by Major John Bradford; Priscilla also signed the deed.

On 21 March 1732/3, ack. 23 March 1732/3 by both, Seth Chipman of Kingston and his wife Priscilla, sold a lot in Kingston to Nicholas Sever.

On 3 May 1733 the Plymouth church met and a letter from the church in Kingston

> ... was read Desireing the Presence of this Chh by yᵉ Elders and one Messenger to set in Council on the case of Seth Chipman whom they had suspend[ed] from special ordinances   the Church made Choice of Brother Stephen Churchil to attend with the Elders   the Council met there on May 15 – and adjourned to June the 20 and then gave in a Result Justifying the Chh and exhorting said Chipman to a Penitent Humiliation.

At the March 1737/8 term of the Court of Common Pleas, Seth Chipman of Kingston, cooper or yeoman, sued Joseph Ryder of Plymouth (Boatman or coaster) for refusing to render accounts.   Seth had leases from George Partridge for

> the Landing Place in Kingston ... with all the Priveledge of the Warehouse, and all the New and Old Wharfe for the Space of Two Years ... the Deft. being Master of a Vessell or Sloop which Usually passed and Repassed to and from said Landing Place to Plymouth aforesaid and other Places, and Took divers Laiding of from said Premises, as Boards, Shingles, Joyce, Coopers Stuff, and other Merchandize and Promised to deliver the Plant. an acompt of them and pay the Wharfage of all he Took ... Yet he Refuses to Render the Plant. any account.

At the May 1747 Court of Common Pleas John Brewster, innholder, Samuel Foster, blacksmith, and William Bradford, a minor, all of Kingston sued Seth Chipman of Kingston, cooper, for ejectment from a dwelling house and land in Kingston "it being the House which Major Bradford's son William dwelt in." The plantiffs said that on 13 May 1747 they were seised of the premises in their own right (John ¼ part, Samuel ½ part, William ¼ part) and that Seth had illegally entered. The parties agreed to referees to settle the matter. The referees reported that they

> Considered the Deed made by John Bradford to his Grand Children James, Zadoch, Samuel, Eliphlet, and William Bradford, Dated January 17 1732/33 on which both parties agreed before us their Title ought to be determined, are of Opinion that said Deed Created an Estate in fee to the said Grand Children, and that the Deft. has in Interest by Vertue thereof or by the Death of any of said Grand Children, and Therefore that the Pltfs. recover Possession of the premises.

On 29 Sept. 1747 Seth Chipman of Kingston, cooper, executor of the estate of his brother Jacob Chipman, sold part of Jacob's land to Charles Sturtevant.

No Plymouth County probates were found for Seth or Priscilla Chipman. There are no later Plymouth County land records for Seth Chipman.

Children of Seth and Priscilla (Bradford) Chipman, first two b. Plymouth, last two b. Kingston:

	i	[CHILD] CHIPMAN[5], b. 11 Aug. 1723; d. Plymouth 31 Oct. 1723
137	ii	SETH CHIPMAN, b. 31 Oct. 1724
138	iii	MERCY CHIPMAN, b. 19 Nov. 1725
139	iv	BENJAMIN CHIPMAN, b. 23 May 1729

References: *MD* 4:121(b. Seth); 13:167(b. ch. Seth); 18:143(int.). *VR Kingston* pp. 39(b. Benjamin), 40(b. other ch.), 191(m.). *Barnstable Fams* 1:163. *Chipman Gen* 1970 pp. 10-11. *Bradford Desc* p. 15(d. Seth). Plymouth Co. LR 22:26(John Bradford); 22:27; 27:220; 39:45(Seth Chipman); 65:172(Seth Chipman, Jr.). *Plymouth VR* p. 71(b. son Seth). *Plymouth Co Ct Recs* 6:81 #46(Seth Chipman); 7:79-80 #23(John Brewster *et al.*). *Plymouth Ch Recs* 1:289(Seth Chipman). *Plymouth Town Recs* 2:206, 229.

27. WILLIAM[4] BRADFORD (*John[3], William[2-1]*), b. Plymouth 15 Aug. 1688; d. Kingston 8 May 1728 in 41st yr.

He m. Plymouth 9 Dec. 1714 **HANNAH FOSTER**, b. Plymouth 25 July 1694; d. Duxbury 17 Dec. 1778 aged 84y 4m; daughter of John and Hannah (Stetson) Foster. The will of John Foster of Plymouth dated 9 Jan. 1739/40 names daughter Hannah and grandson Eliphalet Bradford. She m. (2) Boston 19 Nov. 1729 JAMES STUBBS of Boston. She m. (3) Kingston 20 July 1734 GEORGE PARTRIDGE with whom she had a son George.

On 6 Dec. 1711 William Bradford Jr. of Plymouth sold to his brother-in-law William Barnes his share in a cedar swamp.

On 9 Sept. 1713 John Bradford of Plymouth gave to his son William five acres of his homestead reserving to his other sons, John and Samuel, the liberty to egress and regress.

At a Plymouth town meeting 17 March 1718, William Bradford Jr. was chosen as a "precints of Agawame"; on 28 March 1720, surveyor of lumber and timber and hog constable; on 18 March 1722/3, surveyor of highways; and on 29 March 1724/5, tithingman.

On 22 June 1728 Mrs. Hannah Bradford was appointed administratrix of the estate of her husband William Bradford Jr. of Kingston.

On 17 March 1736 George Partridge was chosen guardian by James, Zadock, and Eliphalet Bradford, and also guardian of William Bradford, under 14, sons of William Bradford of Kingston deceased.

On 12 Dec. 1737 Samuel Bradford of Plymton, Gentleman, Robert Bradford of Kingston, yeoman, and George Partridge of Duxbury guardian of James Bradford, Samuel Bradford, Zadock Bradford, Eliphalet Bradford, and William Bradford grandsons of the Honorable John Bradford late of Plymouth, Esq., sold 1/9 part of land located near Muscongus in Lincoln County, Maine. This deed was acknowledged in Boston on 27 Dec. 1737 but not recorded in Lincoln County until 25 Aug. 1763.

At the May 1747 Court of Common Pleas John Brewster, innholder, Samuel Foster, blacksmith, and William Bradford, a minor, all of Kingston sued Seth Chipman of Kingston, cooper, for ejectment from a dwelling house and land in Kingston "it being the House which Major Bradford's son William dwelt in." The plantiffs said that on 13 May 1747 they were seised of the premises in their own right (John ¼ part, Samuel ½ part, William ¼ part) and that Seth had illegally entered. The parties agreed to referees to settle the matter. The referees reported that they

> Considered the Deed made by John Bradford to his Grand Children James, Zadoch, Samuel, Eliphlet, and William Bradford, Dated January 17 1732/33 on which both parties agreed before us their Title ought to be determined, are of Opinion that said Deed Created an Estate in fee to the said Grand Children, and that the Deft. has in Interest by Vertue thereof or by the Death of any of said Grand Children, and Therefore that the Pltfs. recover Possession of the premisses.

On 15 March 1749/50 Willard Spaulding of Killingly, Conn., husbandman, and his wife Hannah sold to John Brewster of Kingston land in Kingston that belonged "to our honoured father William Bradford."

On 23 Jan. 1755 the estate was divided between Hannah Partredge, the widow; eldest son James; heirs of son Samuel Bradford deceased; heirs of son

Zadock Bradford deceased; son Eliphalet; heirs of son William Bradford deceased; and daughter Hannah (no surname).

The division of the dower estate of Hannah Bradford dated 6 June 1785 names son James; heirs of son William; heirs of son Zadock; heirs of son Samuel; son Eliphalet; heirs of daughter Hannah Spaulding.

Children of William and Hannah (Foster) Bradford, first four b. Plymouth:

140   i   JAMES[5] BRADFORD, b. 2 July 1717

      ii   ZADOCK BRADFORD, b. 30 July 1719; d. Kingston 23 Jan. 1745; unm. On 12 March 1745 Samuel Foster, gentleman, of Kingston was appointed administrator of the estate of Zadock Bradford, late of Kingston deceased. The will of Zadock Bradford now residing Newport, R.I., shipcarpenter, dated 28 Feb. 1744, sworn 2 Sept. 1745, gives his estate to friend Mercy Power, spinster of Newport, who was to be executor.

      iii   SAMUEL BRADFORD, b. 4 April 1721; d. Marshfield 4 Feb. 1735 ae 15

141   iv   ELIPHALET BRADFORD, b. 20 Jan. 1722/3

142   v   HANNAH BRADFORD, b. Kingston 29 May 1724

      vi   WILLIAM BRADFORD, b. Kingston 25 Jan. 1726/7; d. Plainfield, Conn., 10 Dec. 1753. The will of William Bradford of Plainfield, Conn., dated 29 Nov. 1753, names sister Hannah and Abigail Haskell, brother James Bradford executor. Inv. dated 9 April 1754.

Note: No evidence was found for a son Spaulding as stated in *Bradford Desc.*

References: *MD* 2:20(b. Hannah); 7:23(d. Wm.); 9:161(d. Hannah); 12:56(d. Sam.), 224(b. 4 ch.); 14:37(m.); 23:155-161(Wm. est.); 24:24-6(John Foster will). *VR Duxbury* p. 397(d. Hannah). *VR Kingston* pp. 27(b. Hannah), 30(b. William), 286(int. her 2nd m.), 260(her 3rd m.). *Marshfield VR* p. 399(d. Samuel). *Waterman Gen* 1:627. Plymouth Co. PR 5:403, 601; 14:90(William Bradford); 6:22(gdn.); 8:466 (John Foster); 10:85(Zadock Bradford); 29:293(Hannah Bradford). Newport RI TC 9:94(Zadock Bradford). Plainfield CT PR #240(Wm. Bradford); 2:374(Wm. Bradford, the son). *Plymouth VR* pp. 15(b. Hannah), 56(b. 1st 4 ch.), 90(m.). *BRC* 28:167(her 2nd m.). Plymouth Co. LR 9:430(William Bradford); 10:231(John Bradford); 41:58(Willard Spaulding). Lincoln Co. LR ME 3:140(Samuel Bradford). *Plymouth Co Ct Recs* 7:79-80 #23(John Brewster *et al.*). *Plymouth Town Recs* 2:189, 202, 205, 221, 232.

28. ALICE[4] BRADFORD (*William[3-2-1]*), b. prob. Plymouth 28 Jan. 1680; d. aft. 2 Aug. 1773; apparently the Else Barnes aged 75 [*sic*] who d. Plymouth 22 Aug. 1775.

She m. Plymouth 20 Nov. 1704 **WILLIAM BARNES**, b. Plymouth 14 Feb. 1670; d. there 31 March 1751 in 81st yr.; son of Jonathan and Elizabeth (Hedge) Barnes.

William Barnes served the town of Plymouth in various capacities; on 16 Dec. 1706, 21 Feb. 1708/9, 8 Sept. 1712, and 9 Aug. 1736 he was chosen as a juror and on 23 March 1719 and 2 March 1723/4 as a field driver. On 21 March 1710/1 he bought 13½ acres from the town. He recorded his cattle mark on 31 Dec. 1744 as "a half penny on the underside of the Left Ear."

At a town meeting 13 Dec. 1711 it was voted "That aney of the Inhabitants of the Town who shall betwixt this and the next town meeting subscribe their names To the Instrument shall have liberty to plant oysters in aney such place or places within sd bay as they shall Judg most likely for the groath and Increase of oysters." William Barns signed this document.

On 6 Dec. 1711 William Bradford Jr. of Plymouth sold his brother-in-law William Barnes his share in a cedar swamp.

On 1 April 1735 John Barnes and William Barnes, yeomen, and Jonathan Barnes, gentleman, all of Plymouth sold to George Bryant land purchased by their late father Jonathan Barnes.

On 3 June 1742 William Barnes, yeoman, and wife Alice, of Plymouth sold to Robert Stanford of Duxborough their interest in land previously owned by "their grandfather" Benjamin Bartlett, deceased.

The will of William Barnes of Plymouth, written 23 Jan. 1749, proved 6 May 1751, names wife Else [or Alice]; daughter Mercy Hedge (to have land at Hebron, Conn., owned with heirs of his brother John Barnes and others); sons Lemuel and Benjamin Barnes executors. A 22 Nov. 1775 warrant to divide the estate mentions equal division to the heirs of Lemuel Barnes and Benjamin Barnes, sons of William Barnes.

On 23 March 1773 the following relatives and friends of Alice Barnes of Plymouth, widow of William Barnes, petitioned that she was *non compos mentis*: Benjamin Churchill, Benjamin Barnes, Seth Harlow, Ebenezer Samson, Isaac Harlow, Elisha Corbin, Experience Corbin, Samuel Battles, Alice Battles, Bradford Barnes, and Josiah Barnes. On 31 July 1773 it was stated that Alice was about 93 years old and retained her intellectual faculties, and on 2 Aug. 1773 it was ruled that she was of sound mind.

Children of William and Alice (Bradford) Barnes, b. Plymouth:

    i WILLIAM BARNES[5], b. 5 Jan. 1706; drowned 16 April 1730

143   ii LEMUEL BARNES, b. 16 Feb. 1707

144   iii MERCY BARNES, b. 19 Dec. 1708

iv BENJAMIN BARNES, b. 11 Dec. 1711; d.y.
145 v BENJAMIN BARNES, b. 20 Dec. 1717

References: *MD* 5:53(b. ch.; d. Wm.); 14:35(m.). *(Plymouth) Burial Hill* p. 29(d. William). Plymouth Co. PR 12:197(Wm. Barnes); 21:276(Alice Barnes); 25:203(warrant). *Savage* 1:121(b. Wm.). *Bradford Desc* pp. 15-6(d. Alice). *Plymouth Ch Recs* 1:404(d. Else). Plymouth Co. LR 9:430(William Bradford); 29:170(John Barnes *et al.*); 35:48(Wm. Barnes). *Plymouth VR* pp. 38(b. ch.; d. son Wm.), 89(m.). *Plymouth Town Recs* 2:7, 22, 54-5, 84-5, 165, 195, 226

29. WILLIAM[4] BRADFORD (*William[3-2-1]*), b. prob. Plymouth before 18 Dec. 1686; d. Kingston 9 March 1729/30.

He m. Plymouth 18 Nov. 1712 **ELIZABETH FINNEY**, b. Plymouth 8 Feb. 1690; d. there between 31 Dec. 1772 and 15 July 1778; daughter of Josiah and Elizabeth (Warren) Finney, a descendant of Pilgrim **Richard Warren**. The will of Josiah Finney of Plymouth, yeoman, dated 2 Jan. 1723 names daughter Elizabeth Bradford.

On 23 April 1687 William Bradford in consideration of the natural love he bore for his grandchild William Bradford, only son of his son William Bradford deceased, gives to his grandson one parcel of upland on which his son had built his house "Given unto me from my father William Bradford Esq[r]." Before acknowledging the deed on 4 Sept. 1696, William added a paragraph saying that when his grandson William reached the age of 21, he "shall enjoy the lands without Interruption." On 29 Oct. 1709 John Bradford, Samuel Bradford, Israel Bradford, Ephraim Bradford, David Bradford, and Hezekiah Bradford all of Plymouth County gave their right in a cedar swamp to their kinsman William Bradford, son of their brother William Bradford deceased. This deed was not acknowledged until 26 March 1747.

On 1 April 1730 Elizabeth Bradford of Kingston, widow, was appointed administratrix of the estate of her husband William Bradford late of Kingston deceased. Division of the estate of William Bradford, son of William Bradford, late of Kingston was made 15 Dec. 1737 with dower set off to widow Elizabeth Bradford and the rest divided into six parts with John Brewster and Thomas Adams receiving two shares in the right of Charles Bradford and single shares going to Sarah, Jerusha, Josiah, and Marcy Bradford.

On 11 March 1730/1 Josiah Finney was appointed guardian of Charles Bradford, over 14. On 29 Nov. 1736 George Partridge of Duxborough was appointed guardian of Sarah and Jerusha Bradford, over 14, and of Mercy and Josiah, under 14. On 21 May 1741 Gershom Bradford was appointed guardian of Josiah.

On 27 Dec. 1739 Zephaniah Holmes of Plymouth, cordwainer, and his wife Sarah sold to John Adams land in Kingston from the estate of her father William Bradford.

On 14 Nov. 1743 Edward Sparrow of Plymouth, mariner, and his wife Jerusha sold to Thomas Adams land received from her father William Bradford.

On 17 April 1745 Josiah Bradford of Plymouth, cordwainer, sold to Thomas Adams of Kingston, mariner, four acres from the division of William Bradford's estate. On 24 April 1747 Elizabeth Bradford, widow of William, sold to Thomas Adams her part of an old dwelling house where her husband dwelt; Thomas owned the other two-thirds of the house. On 25 Oct. 1749 Samuel Harlow of Plymouth, mariner, and his wife Mercy, sold Thomas Adams the 4th lot in the First Division, being four acres from the estate of William Bradford. On 16 Aug. 1759 Elizabeth Bradford, widow, and Josiah Bradford, cordwainer, both of Middleborough sold to Thomas Adams land and garden set off to Elizabeth as her dower, now in the actual improvement of Thomas.

On 21 Dec. 1772, acknowledged 31 Dec. 1772, Elizabeth Bradford of Plymouth, widow, sold land to son Josiah Bradford which "was quit claimed to me and my two sisters by our Brothers Josiah Finney and John Finney."

On 15 July 1778 Sarah Holmes, widow of Plymouth, was appointed administratrix on the estate of Elizabeth Bradford late of Plymouth, widow.

On 21 Aug. 1779 Sarah Holmes, widow and administratrix of the estate of Elizabeth Bradford, being allowed to sell land to pay debts, sold Elizabeth's part of a dwelling house to William Bradford of Plymouth, cordwainer.

Children of William and Elizabeth (Phinney) Bradford, first five b. Plymouth, rest b. Kingston:

      i ELIZABETH[5] BRADFORD, b. 10 Jan. 1714/5; d. there 21 Jan. 1714/5

      ii CHARLES BRADFORD, b. 4 Jan. 1715/6; d. aft. 6 Feb. 1738/9. On 18 July 1738, ack. 6 Feb. 1738, Charles Bradford of Kingston, seafaring man, sold to Thomas Adams land which was part of the estate of his father William Bradford.

146   iii SARAH BRADFORD, b. 15 Dec. 1718

147   iv JERUSHA BRADFORD, b. 20 Dec. 1722

148   v JOSIAH BRADFORD, b. 29 March (poss. 1724)

      vi WILLIAM BRADFORD, b. 9 May 1726; d. Kingston 16 or 23 July 1726 ae 9w

149   vii MERCY BRADFORD, b. 15 Jan. 1728/9

      viii ELIZABETH BRADFORD, b. 15 Sept. 1730; d. Kingston 10 Oct. 1730

References: *MD* 1:208(b. Eliz.); 7:23(d. ch.; Wm.); 12:87(b. 4 ch.; d. Eliz.); 14:37(m.); 20:97-9(Phinney will); 24:154-164(est. Wm.); 25:25-29(deed; est. Eliz.). Plymouth Co. PR 5:219(Josiah Finney); 5:839; 7:249; 8:342(gdn.); 7:437, 440(Wm. Bradford); 23:186(Elizabeth Bradford). *VR Kingston* pp. 26(b. Elizabeth), 28(b. Mercy), 30(b. William), 319 (d. Elizabeth), 322(d. Wm.; son Wm.). Plymouth Co. LR 32:138 (Charles Bradford); 33:74(Zephaniah Holmes); 36:77(Edward Sparrow); 37:146(Josiah Bradford); 38:194(Elizabeth Bradford; **40:128(Samuel Harlow)**; 45:245; 57:44(Elizabeth Bradford); 60:19(Sarah Holmes). *Plymouth VR* pp. 10(b. Elizabeth), 53(b. 1st 4 ch.; d. dau. Eliz.), 90(m.). *MF* 18:1:174-5.

30. SARAH[4] BRADFORD (*William[3-2-1]*), b. prob. Plymouth ca. 1686; d. there 11 April 1718 aged about 32.

She m. Plymouth ca. 1708 **JONATHAN BARNES**, b. Plymouth 1684; d. before 27 Dec. 1736; son of Jonathan and Elizabeth (Hedge) Barnes. He m. (2) int. Plymouth 25 Aug. 1722 Mercy (Ellis) Doten.

At a town meeting on 9 May 1709 Jonathan Barnes Jr. was granted a house lot. On 1 March 1723/4 he was chosen as a hog reeve, on 20 March 1731/2 as a juror, on 4 March 1710/1 as a leather sealer, and on 31 March 1735 as a tythingman.

On 13 Dec. 1709 Jonathan and Sarah Barnes of Plymouth sold to William Barnes their half interest in the land inherited by Sarah Barnes and her sister Alice from their grandfather Benjamin Bartlett.

At a town meeting 13 Dec. 1711 it was voted "That aney of the Inhabitants of the Town who shall betwixt this and the next town meeting subscribe their names To the Instrument shall have liberty to plant oysters in aney such place or places within sd bay as they shall Judg most likely for the groath and Increase of oysters." Jonathan Barns Jr. signed this document.

At the Dec. 1720 term of the Court of Common Pleas, Samuel Clarke of Plymouth, weaver, sued Jonathan Barnes of Plymouth, whale fisherman, "for a ninth Part of what a Certain Whale Boat whereof the said Clarke was part owner cleared in 2 Voyages at North Carolina."

At the Sept. 1729 term of the Court of Common Pleas, James Warren of Plymouth, Gentleman, sued Jonathan Barnes of Plymouth, whale fisherman, claiming that James was due a share after "Deft. Shipped the Plant.'s [Plaintiff's] Indian man Servant Named Sion Hood to Go with him on a whale voyage to North Carolina (he Being Stearman of a Boat Crew) assumeing to pay or allow the Plant. for his said Servant a whole Share According to Custome … the Effects of said voyage being Disposed of and the accompts of the whole voyage being made up," but James said that Jonathan had not paid him.

On 27 Dec. 1736 Thomas Doane of Chatham, mariner, was appointed administrator on the estate of his father-in-law Jonathan Barnes late of Plymouth, seafaring man, deceased, but on 10 March 1740 Stephen Churchill Jr., cooper of Plymouth, and Joseph Smith, seafaring man of Plymouth, petitioned that a new administrator be appointed for the estate of their father-in-law Jonathan Barnes of Plymouth because Thomas was "almost always at sea and has now gone to Holland."

On 21 Jan. 1772 Ebenezer Phinney of Barnstable and his wife Rebecca sold land that fell to them from their father Jonathan Barnes.

Children of Jonathan and Sarah (Bradford) Barnes, b. Plymouth:

150	i	SARAH BARNES[5], b. 9 Oct. 1709
151	ii	REBECCA BARNES, b. 14 March 1711
152	iii	LYDIA BARNES, b. 30 Jan. 1714/5
153	iv	HANNAH BARNES, b. ca. 1717 (based on age at d.)

References: *MD* 7:176(b. ch.); 17:254(deed); 18:144(2nd m. int.). *(Plymouth) Burial Hill* p. 11(d. Sarah). Plymouth Co. PR 7:248: 8:283-5; 9:171(Jonathan Barnes). Plymouth Co. LR 7:333(Jonathan Barnes); 56:175(Ebenezer Phinney). *Plymouth VR* pp. 42(b. 1st 3 ch.), 178(int. his 2nd m.). *Plymouth Co Ct Recs* 5:119 #15(Samuel Clarke), 293 #21(James Warren). *Plymouth Town Recs* 2:28, 54-5, 256, 278, 293, 305

31. JOSHUA[4] BRADFORD (*Thomas[3], William[2-1]*), b. Norwich, Conn., 23 Nov. 1682; d. before 31 May 1735 (did not sign deed disposing of his father's land).

He m. int. Norwich, Conn., 17 Feb. 1711/12, **MARY BROOKS**, b. Woburn 15 Sept. 1693; d. before 29 May 1727 (not in father's will); daughter of Henry and Mary (Graves) Brooks. The will of Henry Brooke of New London dated 29 May 1727 is very detailed and does not mention this daughter Mary. It does mention his minor daughter Mary by his second wife.

Joshua's father Thomas Bradford owned 1/3 of a farm in New London and on 12 Oct. 1713 Thomas Bradford and Joshua Bradford of Lyme, Conn., sold their part of this farm.

No Connecticut probate or land records have been found for Joshua Bradford.

No known children.

Note: The two marriages and eight children attributed to purported son Sylvannus in *Bradford Desc* p. 57 belong to Sylvanus BRAMHALL. The daughter Elizabeth who later becomes Hannah in *Bradford Desc* surely does not belong to this family as she did not sign the deed disposing of her grandfather's land. *Bradford Desc* gives Joshua a second wife Katherine. She is clearly the wife of his father Thomas Bradford as she was born ca. 1659.

References: *VR Woburn* p. 28(b. Mary). *Bradford Desc* p. 16. *NEHGR* 58:128(int.). New London CT LR 6:313(Thomas Bradford).

32. JAMES⁴ BRADFORD (*Thomas³, William²⁻¹*), b. Norwich, Conn., 24 March 1689; d. Canterbury, Conn., 26 March 1762 aged 73y.

He m. (1) ca. 1711 **EDITH ADAMS**, b. Chelmsford 25 June 1688; d. before 7 Dec. 1724; daughter of Peletiah and Ruth (_____) Adams.

He m. (2) Canterbury, Conn., 7 Dec. 1724 **SUSANNA ADAMS**, b. Charlestown 13 March 1692/3; d. Canterbury, Conn., 17 March 1752; daughter of Samuel and Mary (Meeker) Adams. On 24 Oct. 1727, 28 Oct. 1729, and 6 Feb. 1745/6 James and Susannah Bradford of Canterbury sold land set out to Susannah in the distribution of the estate of her father Samuel Adams.

He m. (3) Scotland, Conn., 9 Nov. 1752 **LEAH (RIPLEY) COOK**, b. Windham, Conn., 17 April 1693; d. there 28 April 1775 [g.s. Leah Cook, wife of Samuel Cook, last wife of James Bradford, d. 28 April 1766 aged 82y]; daughter of Joshua and Hannah (Bradford) Ripley, a descendant of Pilgrim **William Bradford** (see #55).

On 12 July 1713 James Bradford and his wife owned the covenant in the Canterbury Church and Edith Bradford was admitted on 4 Dec. 1715.

On 2 April 1735 James Bradford of Canterbury sold lot 3 in the 4th division of Lyme allowed to the heirs of Thomas Bradford deceased.

On 27 March 1746 James Bradford of Canterbury gave to his son William Bradford of Canterbury 150 acres.

On 31 March 1762 Thomas and William Bradford gave their bond as administrators on the estate of James Bradford late of Canterbury deceased. Distribution of the estate 14 June 1762 names widow Leah Bradford; oldest daughter Jerusha Pellet wife of Jonathan; 2nd daughter Sarah Adams wife of Lt. Joseph; 3rd daughter Anna Cleaveland wife of Mr. Elezer; youngest daughter Mary Woodard wife of Mr. John; eldest son Thomas, and 2nd son William Bradford.

On 26 April 1762 Leah Bradford, widow of James, sold her right in James' real estate to Thomas Bradford, William Bradford, Jonathan and Jerusha Pellet, Joseph and Sarah Adams, Elezer and Anna Cleveland, and Joseph and Mary Woodard all of Canterbury. In 1762 (ack. 8 May 1762) the heirs of James Bradford sold their right in land in Canterbury.

On 24 Nov. 1762 Paul Davenport and Joseph and Mary Woodard all of Canterbury sold to Asa Aspanwell of Canterbury land that had been distributed to Mrs. Susannah Bradford, the mother of Mary Woodard, and to Mrs. Abigail Davenport, the mother of Paul Davenport, out of the estate of Mrs. Margaret Adams late of Canterbury.

See #55 for will of Leah (Ripley) (Cook) Bradford.

Children of James and Edith (Adams) Bradford, b. Canterbury, Conn.:

154   i   THOMAS[5] BRADFORD, b. 14 Nov. 1712; bp. 12 July 1713
        ii   JOHN BRADFORD, b. 30 Jan. 1714/5; bp. 27 Feb. 1715; d. 1714/5
155   iii JERUSHA BRADFORD, b. 27 June 1716; bp. 1 July 1716
156   iv   WILLIAM BRADFORD, b. 1 July 1718; bp. 10 Aug. 1718
157   v   SARAH BRADFORD, b. 27 Aug. 1720; bp. 2 Oct. 1720

Children of James and Susanna (Adams) Bradford, b. Canterbury, Conn.:

158   vi   ANN BRADFORD, bp. 10 July 1726
159   vii MARY BRADFORD, bp. June 1729
        viii JAMES BRADFORD, bp. 4 Feb. 1733; d.y.

References: Canterbury 1st Ch pp. 4(Edith adm.), 38(m.), 45(James, Susanna adm.), 49(bp. Thomas), 50(bp. John), 51 (bp. Jerusha), 53(bp. Wm.), 54(bp. John), 55(bp. Jerusha), 57(bp. William), 59(bp. Sarah), 60(bp. Ann), 68(bp. Mary), 73(bp. James), 99(2nd m.). *Bradford Desc* pp. 16-7. Plainfield CT PR #229(James Bradford). *CT Marr* 2:122(2nd m.); 3:45(3rd m.). *Charlestown VR* 1:156(b. Susanna). Canterbury CT VR 1:74(b. 5 ch.), 96(d. James, Susannah). Windham CT VR A:16(b. Leah). *VR Chelmsford* p. 10(b. Edith). Canterbury CT LR 4:6, 70; 5:209; 6:100(James Bradford); 7:55(Leah Bradford), 107(Paul Davenport), 228(heirs of James). Hale Cem. Coll.:Canterbury p. 34(James Bradford); Windham p. 281(Leah Cook). Lyme CT LR 5:332(James Bradford).

33. ANN[4] BRADFORD (*Thomas[3], William[2-1]*) d. before 31 May 1735 (not in deed).

She m. (1) **PETER STRICKLAND,** bp. New London, Conn., 11 Aug. 1676; d. before 27 Feb. 1718/9 (before 23 June 1713 if Ann m. Edward Dewolfe); son of Peter and Elizabeth (Comstock) Strickland. The will of Peter Strickland of New London dated 27 Feb. 1718/9 mentions deceased son Peter and a granddaughter Anne, Peter's daughter.

She almost surely m. (2) before 23 June 1713 **EDWARD DEWOLFE,** b. Lyme, Conn., in March 1685/6; son of Stephen Dewolfe and an unknown wife. (see court case mentioned under #8.) On the inventory of Stephen

DeWolfe's estate dated 24 Oct. 1702 are listed his children including "Also his sone Edwarde that he had by his first wife is 16 year old Last march."

On 7 April 1718/9 [sic] Ann, only daughter of Peter Strickland Jr. of New London, deceased chose her [great-] uncle Samuel Comstock to be her guardian.

No Connecticut probate records or Lyme land records have been found for Edward Dewolfe, nor any Connecticut probate records for Peter Strickland Jr.

    Child of Peter and Ann (Bradford) Strickland, b. prob. New London, Conn.:

160   i   ANN STRICKLAND[5], b. ca. 1704; bp. 21 May 1710

References: New London CT PR #1752(Stephen DeWolfe); #5201(Peter Strickland). First Church of Christ in New London CT pp. 61(bp. Peter), 86(bp. Ann). *Lyme CT VR* p. 230(b. Edward).

34. JERUSHA[4] BRADFORD (*Thomas[3]*, *William[2-1]*), b. Norwich, Conn., 26 Nov. 1692; d. Lebanon, Conn., 4 Nov. 1739 in her 47th yr.

She m. Norwich, Conn., 14 Nov. 1716 **HEZEKIAH NEWCOMB**, b. Edgartown ca. 1693; d. Lebanon, Conn., 15 Aug. 1772 in 79th yr. (g.s.); son of Simon and Deborah (_____) Newcomb. He m. (2) HANNAH _____, with whom he had no children.

On 25 Dec. 1742 Hezekiah Newcomb of Lebanon, yeoman, deeded land in Falltown to son Silas Newcomb of Falltown [later called Bernardson]. On the same date he deeded other land to his son Peter Newcomb of Falltown.

On 15 June 1770 Hezekiah Newcomb of Lebanon deeded land in Falltown, Franklin County, to grandson Hezekiah Newcomb.

The will of Hezekiah Newcomb of Lebanon dated 30 Aug. 1770, proved 1 Sept. 1772, names wife Hannah; sons Silas, Peter, and James; grandson Joseph Newcomb, son of son Thomas deceased; Samuel and Dan Smith, sons of daughter Anne deceased; and daughters Jerusha, Elizabeth, and Jemima (without surnames). In the 20 April 1773 distribution of the estate, 17 acres with the dwelling house, were set off to son James.

On 8 Nov. 1774 James Newcomb of Lebanon sold to Paul Newcomb a barn standing on his father's farm that had been given to James by his father Hezekiah Newcomb's will. On 22 Sept. 1782 James sold to Timothy Larrabee of Lebanon 200 acres in several pieces that were from his father Hezekiah.

On 2 Nov. 1779 Calvin Newcomb of Lebanon sold to Jesse Newcomb of Lebanon land set out to him from the estate of his father that had come from his grandfather Hezekiah Newcomb. Jesse then sold this land to John Newcomb of Lebanon on 7 Feb. 1782.

Children of Hezekiah and Jerusha (Bradford) Newcomb, b. Lebanon, Conn.:

161   i   SILAS NEWCOMB⁵, b. 2 Sept. 1717
162   ii   PETER NEWCOMB, b. 28 Nov. 1718
163   iii ANNE NEWCOMB, b. 4 April 1720
       iv   HEZEKIAH NEWCOMB, b. 27 Dec. 1722; d.y.
164   v   THOMAS NEWCOMB, b. 3 Sept. 1724
165   vi   JERUSHA NEWCOMB, b. 24 March 1726
166   vii ELIZABETH NEWCOMB, b. 19 Dec. 1727
       viii SAMUEL NEWCOMB, b. 2 Sept. 1729; d. Lebanon 9 Sept. 1748; no issue
167   ix   JEMIMA NEWCOMB, b. 14 Dec. 1730
168   x   JAMES NEWCOMB, b. 7 Feb. 1732/3

References: Lebanon CT VR 1:223(m.; b. ch.; d. Jerusha). *Bradford Desc* p. 17. *Newcomb Gen* pp. 37-45. Hampshire Co. LR P:167; T:20; 10:255(Hezekiah Newcomb). Windham CT PR 8:284, 397, 532(Hezekiah Newcomb). Lebanon CT LR 13:121; 14:141(James Newcomb). Hale Cem. Coll.: Lebanon(Jerusha Newcomb).

35. ELIZABETH ADAMS⁴ (*Alice³ Bradford, William²⁻¹*), b. Dedham 23 Feb. 1680/1; d. New Haven, Conn., 21 Dec. 1766 aged 86.

She m. (1) Windham, Conn., 14 Sept. 1696 Rev. **SAMUEL WHITING**, bp. Hartford, Conn., 24 April 1670; d. Enfield, Conn., 27 Sept. 1725 in 56th yr.; son of John and Sybil (Collins) Whiting. Samuel Whiting is included in the 13 Sept. 1692 distribution of John Whiting's estate. On 3 March [year blank] John's widow Phoebe petitioned for funds from the court saying that "neither is there any allowance to me for twentie pound Expended on Samuell Whiting since his fathers death for his board & Education at mr Fiches of Norwich."

She m. (2) Windham, Conn., 22 Dec. 1737 Rev. **SAMUEL NILES**, b. New Shoreham [Block Island], R.I., 1 May 1674; d. Braintree 1 May 1762 in 85th yr.; son of Nathaniel and Sarah (Sand) Niles. He m. (1) Milton 29 May 1701 ELIZABETH THATCHER with whom he had Samuel, Elizabeth, Mary, and Nathaniel. He m. (2) Newport, R.I., 22 Nov. 1716 ANN CODDINGTON with whom he had Elisha and Susanna.

On 27 Sept. 1725 the estate of Rev. Samuel Whiting of Windham was divided to widow Elizabeth Whiting; sons John, Eliphalet, Elisha, Samuel, Joseph, and Nathan; and daughters Ann Fitch, Elizabeth Gouger, Sibill

Backus, and Mary Whiting. The account mentions William Whiting eldest son; Mr. Joseph Fitch husband of eldest daughter; John Backus husband of 3rd daughter Sibil; William Gager husband of 2nd daughter Elizabeth *et al.* On 16 Sept. 1726 £90 were set out to the widow "Intended for the answering the Charge of bringing up the Children...three were under five years of age at the Death of their parent."

Samuel Niles graduated from Harvard in 1699.

On 15 May 1741 Thomas Clapp of New Haven, Clerk, sold Stephen White of Windham, Clerk, 36 acres reserving to Mrs. Elizabeth Niles of "Brantry," late the relict of Rev. Mr. Samuel Whiting of Windham, the use and improvement of part of the house.

The will of Samuel Niles of Braintree, clerk, dated 29 April 1762, sworn 21 May 1762, names sons Samuel and Elisha; wife Elizabeth; grandchildren Ebenezer and Elisha, children of "daughter Thayer deceased"; daughter Elizabeth Hayward (mentions her grandfather Rev. Mr. Thatcher – her mother's father); daughter Mary Wales; grandchild Elizabeth Thayer; and children of grandchild Ann Thayer.

On 16 March Nathan Whiting of New Haven was appointed adminIstrator of the estate of Elizabeth Niles late of New Haven. An addition to the inventory dated 29 Feb. 1768 mentions a legacy left to her by Rev. Samuel Niles.

Children of Samuel and Elizabeth (Adams) Whiting, b. Windham, Conn.:

169	i	ANNE WHITING[5], b. 2 Jan. 1698
	ii	SAMUEL WHITING, b. 20 Feb. 1700; d. 1718 at sea ae 18; unm.
170	iii	ELIZABETH WHITING, b. 11 Feb. 1702
171	iv	WILLIAM WHITING, b. 22 Jan. 1704
	v	JOSEPH WHITING, b. 17 Feb. 1705; d. 1 March 1722; unm.
172	vi	JOHN WHITING, b. 20 Feb. 1705/6
173	vii	SYBIL WHITING, b. 6 May 1708
	viii	MARTHA WHITING, b. 12 March 1710; d. 29 June 1719
174	ix	MARY WHITING, b. 24 Nov. 1712
	x	ELIPHALET WHITING, b. 8 April 1715; d. 9 Aug. 1736
	xi	ELISHA WHITING, b. 17 Jan. 1717; living 27 Sept. 1725 (dist.)
175	xii	SAMUEL WHITING, b. 15 March 1720
	xiii	JOSEPH WHITING living 27 Sept. 1725 (dist.)
176	xiv	NATHAN WHITING, b. 4 May 1724

References: *Bradford Desc* p. 18. *Waterman Gen* 1:628. *Boston News Obits* 3:177(Niles), 550(Whiting). *CT Settlers By Goodwin* p. 333. *TAG* 46:43. *Harvard Grads* 4:485-491(Samuel Niles). *Hartford By Barbour* p. 677. *NEHGR* 85:149. *New Haven Fams* pp. 1971-3. *RIVR* New Shoreham 4:4:31(b. Samuel). *RIVR* Newport 4:2:51(Sam's 2nd m.). Windham CT VR A:25(m.); 1:54(d. Sam.), 166-7 (b.ch.). Suffolk Co. PR 60:371(Samuel Niles). Windham CT PR #4145(Samuel Whiting). New Haven CT PR #7588(Elizabeth Niles). *Enfield CT Hist* 3:2394(d. Samuel). *Braintree Recs* p. 864(d. Samuel Niles). Hale Cem. Coll.: New Haven p. 389(Elizabeth Niles); Enfield p. 59(Samuel Whiting). Hartford CT PR #5950(John Whiting). Windham CT LR H:89(Thomas Clapp).

36. ALICE ADAMS[4] (*Alice*[3] *Bradford, William*[2-1]), b. Dedham 3 April 1682; d. Enfield, Conn., 19 Feb. 1734/5 aged 52.

She m. Enfield, Conn., 7 Jan. 1700/1 Rev. **NATHANIEL COLLINS**, b. Middletown, Conn., 13 June 1677; d. Glastonbury, Conn., 31 Dec. 1756 aged 79; son of Nathaniel and Mary (Whiting) Collins. He m. (2) before 22 June 1737 RACHEL SMITH. On the inventory of the estate of Nathaniel Collins taken in 1684/5 is a listing of his children including Nathaniel aged about 7 years. On 5 May 1712 Nathaniel and his siblings signed an agreement to distribute their mother's estate.

Nathaniel Collins graduated from Harvard in 1697. He was the first Pastor of the Church of Christ in Enfield, Conn., 1699 to 1724. The church and Nathaniel had several years of conflict over his salary until he resigned in 1724. He then served the town as moderator, town clerk, and representative to the General Court of Massachusetts.

He moved to Glastonbury where his second wife had land. On 14 April 1738 Nathaniel Collins of Glastonbury sold to his son John Collins of Enfield three acres.

On 29 April 1734 Samuel Smith sold Rachel Smith land in Glastonbury. On 13 Jan. 1756 Nathaniel and Rachel Collins of Glastonbury sold land that Rachel had from her brother Samuel Smith. On 16 Nov. 1761 Rachel Collins of Glastonbury sold some land off her homelot.

On 21 Feb. 1763 Ephraim Terry of Enfield, Conn., sold to Elijah Terry of Enfield, Conn., a houselot formerly owned by the Rev. Nathaniel Collins deceased

No Connecticut probate records have been found for Nathaniel Collins.

Children of Nathaniel and Alice (Adams) Collins, b. Enfield, Conn.:

    i MARY COLLINS[5], b. 15 Nov. 1701; d. 17 Feb. 1701/2

177   ii ANN COLLINS, b. 20 Dec. 1702

178   iii JOHN COLLINS, b. 7 Jan. 1704/5

	iv	ALICE COLLINS, b. 19 Feb. 1706/7; d. there 25 Aug. 1709
179	v	NATHANIEL COLLINS, b. 17 Aug. 1709
180	vi	WILLIAM COLLINS, b. 24 June 1711
181	vii	EDWARD COLLINS, b. 26 Nov. 1713
182	viii	ALICE COLLINS, b. 14 March 1716

References: Hale Cem Coll:Enfield p. 59(bur. Nathaniel & Alice). *Enfield CT Hist* 2:1591(b., d. Mary; b. Ann), 1592(b. John), 1593 (b. Alice), 1595(b. Nathaniel), 1596(b. William), 1598(b. Edward), 1612(b. Alice), 1766(m.); 3:2327(d. Alice), 2328 (d. Nath.), 2511 (first pastor). *Bradford Desc* p. 18. *Waterman Gen* 1:628. *Harvard Grads* 4:345-9. Middletown CT LR 1:13(b. Nath.). Enfield CT VR 1:12, 14, 16, 18, 21, 27, 58, 66(b. ch.), 119(d. Alice); 1-A:91(m.). *Boston News Obits* 2:234(d. Alice). *NEHGR* 61:281-3. Enfield Proprietor's Recs. 1:163(Nathaniel Collins). Glastonbury CT LR 4:197(Samuel Smith); 6:25(Nathaniel Collins); 6:102(Rachel Collins). Hartford CT PR #1341(Nathaniel Collins). Enfield CT LR 3:409(Ephraim Terry).

37. ABIEL ADAMS[4] (*Alice*[3] *Bradford, William*[2-1]), b. Dedham 15 Dec. 1685; d. Mansfield, Conn., 30 July 1758 aged 72 years.

She m. (1) int. Falmouth 3 Sept. 1707 Rev. **JOSEPH METCALF**, b. Dedham 11 April 1682; d. Falmouth 24 May 1723 aged 41 years; son of Jonathan and Hannah (Kenric) Metcalf.

She m. (2) Rev. **ISAAC CHAUNCEY**, b. Stratford, Conn., 5 Oct. 1670; d. Hadley 2 May 1745 aged 74; son of Israel and Mary (Nichols) Chauncey. He m. (1) ca. 1697 SARAH BLACKLEACH with whom he had Israel, Josiah, Richard, Charles, Abigail, Catherine, and Jerusha. The will of Israel Chauncey of Stratford dated 20 Jan. 1697/8, proved 22 July 1703, names his son Isaac, who signed a receipt for his portion on 29 Dec. 1703.

Joseph Metcalf graduated from Harvard in 1703.

On 18 June 1723 Capt. Hope Lathrop of Falmouth and Left. John Metcalf of Dedham were appointed administrators of the estate of Rev. Joseph Metcalf late of Falmouth deceased. On 26 May 1725 Abiel Metcalf widow of Joseph Metcalf, clerk (or minister), petitioned to sell real estate, said Joseph having left seven minor children mostly very young and some months after his death another child was born.

Isaac Chauncey graduated from Harvard in 1693.

On 20 Sept. 1736 Isaac Chauncey of Hadley, clerk, and wife Abial, deeded land in Hadley to son Richard Chauncey.

On 9 Sept. 1738 Isaac Chauncey of Hadley, clerk, with wife Abiel, deeded all his real and other property to son Josiah on condition he let Abiel live in the family home during widowhood and he make payments to brothers Richard and Charles and to sisters Abigail, Catherine, and Jerusha.

No probate records were found for Isaac Chauncey.

Children of Joseph and Abiel (Adams) Metcalf, b. Falmouth:

	i	ABIGAIL METCALF[5], b. 13 June 1708; d.y.
	ii	ABIJAH METCALF (twin), b. 15 Nov. 1709; d.y.
183	iii	ABIEL METCALF (twin), b. 15 Nov. 1709
184	iv	ALICE METCALF (twin), b. 2 May 1712
185	v	HANNAH METCALF (twin), b. 2 May 1712
186	vi	MARY METCALF, b. 17 Dec. 1715
187	vii	ELIZABETH METCALF, b. 6 March 1716/7
188	viii	DELIGHT METCALF, b. 1 May 1719
189	ix	SARAH METCALF, b. 10 Feb. 1720/1
	x	SYBIL METCALF, b. 10 Nov. 1722; d. Falmouth 26 Dec. 1722
190	xi	AZUBA METCALF, b. 1723

Note: *VR Falmouth* does not include, b. of Abijah or Azuba.

References: *Bradford Desc* p. 18. *Harvard Grads* 4:160-2(Chauncey); 5:220-3(Metcalf; b. ch. Azuba). Barnstable Co. PR 4:118, 279(Joseph Metcalf). *VR Falmouth* pp. 89(b. first 9 ch.), 191(int.), 248(d. Joseph, Sybil). *TAG* 46:44. Stratford CT LR 1:54(b. Isaac). Hampshire Co. LR L:120; O:416(Isaac Chauncey). *Mansfield CT Records* p. 310(d. Abiel). *VR Dedham* 1:227(b. Joseph). Hale Cem Coll:Mansfield p. 95(Abiel Chauncey). Fairfield CT PR #1607(Israel Chauncey).

38. ABIGAIL FITCH[4] (*Alice[3] Bradford, William[2-1]*), b. Norwich, Conn., 22 Feb. 1687/8; d. Canterbury, Conn., 19 May 1759 aged 71.

She m. Canterbury, Conn., 22 Oct. 1713 **JOHN DYAR**, b. Weymouth 9 April 1692; d. Canterbury, Conn., 25 Feb. 1779 aged 86; son of Joseph and Hannah (Baxter) Dyer. He m. (2) Canterbury, Conn., 4 Oct. 1759 JOANE (CHRISTOPHERS) LEFFINGWELL.

On 12 Jan. 1721/2 James Fitch of Canterbury sold to John Dyer 12 acres and on 28 March 1723 he sold to his son-in-law John Dyer all his land in Canterbury not otherwise disposed of.

On 4 May 1743 John Dyar of Canterbury gave to his eldest son Elijah Dyar part of his home farm and 25 acres. On 10 May 1743 John sold to his son James Dyar land with a dwelling house and barn. On 24 May 1749 John sold to his son John 35 acres. On 23 March 1752 John sold to his son James another 55 acres. On 25 Sept. 1759 John gave to Elijah another three pieces of land, and on 1 Oct. 1759 he gave his son Joseph 100 acres with a dwelling house.

The will of John Dyar of Canterbury dated 8 April 1773, proved 2 March 1779, mentions a covenant made with wife Joanna which is in the keeping of Thomas Leffingwell; his negro woman Gene; son-in-law Benjamin Throo [*sic*] to have negro man Shem; daughters Sibel Throop, Abigal Cobb, and Sarah Hares; and sons John, Joseph, Elija, and James. In a codocil dated 18 March 1773 he gave to his wife his youngest negro child Rose.

Children of John and Abigail (Fitch) Dyar, b. Canterbury, Conn.:

191	i	SYBIL DYAR[5], b. 26 Oct. 1714
192	ii	ELIJAH DYAR, b. 10 Sept. 1716
193	iii	ABIGAIL DYAR, b. 10 April 1718
194	iv	JAMES DYAR, b. 16 Feb. 1719/20
→195	v	JOHN DYAR, b. 13 May 1722
196	vi	JOSEPH DYAR, b. 5 Feb. 1723/4
197	vii	SARAH DYAR, b. 14 Nov. 1727
	viii	EBENEZER DYAR, b. 19 June 1729; graduated from Yale in 1750. On 5 May 1758 Col. John Dyar was appointed adm. of the estate of Major Ebenezer Dyar who was taken captive and since deceased. The inventory was dated 23 April 1759.

References: *Bradford Desc* p. 19. *CT Marr* 2:120. *Dyar Gen* p. 7. Canterbury 1st Ch pp. 51(bp. Elijah), 52(bp. Abigail), 54(bp. James), 56(bp. John), 62(bp. Sarah), 63(bp. Eben.), 95(m.). *TAG* 46:44. Plainfield PR #732(Ebenezer Dyar); #735(John Dyar). *VR Weymouth* 1:96(b. John, under Diar). Canterbury CT VR 1:120(m.), 122(b. ch.), 131(d. Abigail). *Fitch Gen* pp. 35-7. Canterbury CT LR 3:183, 239(James Fitch); 5:158, 164, 375; 6:5; 7:61, 240(John Dyar). Hale Cem Coll:Canterbury pp. 23(Abigail Dyer), 24(John Dyer).

39. EBENEZER FITCH[4] (*Alice[3] Bradford, William[2-1]*), b. Norwich, Conn., 10 Jan. 1689/90; d. Windsor, Conn., 20 Nov. 1724 aged 40.

He m. Canterbury, Conn., 18 Sept. 1712 **BRIDGET BROWN**, b. Chelmsford 7 July 1685; d. Wallingford, Conn., 22 Nov. 1756; daughter of Eleazer and Dinah (Spaulding) Brown. She m. (2) before 25 Dec. 1729 Capt. John Perry of Ashford, Conn., with whom she had Bridget. She m. (3) before 1748 Samuel Hall of Wallingford, Conn.

Ebenezer Fitch served in the Annapolis expedition in 1710 and was Deputy for Windsor, Conn., in the General Assembly 1718 - 1723.

James Fitch of Canterbury gave or sold land to his son Ebenezer three times: 90 acres (part of Maj[r] Fitches Farm) 13 April 1711, 3 pieces 9 March 1912, and 650 acres 4 Aug. 1714. On 29 Jan. 1712/3 Ebenezer Fitch of Windsor returned the land from the first deed to his father and sold the three pieces in the second deed to John Fitch of Windham and William Whiting of Hartford.

The inventory of the estate of Ebenezer Fitch of Windsor was dated 29 Dec. 1724. On 18 Dec. 1724 administration was granted to Bridget Fitch, widow, and Samuel Strong. On 25 Dec. 1729 Mr. John Perrie, husband to Bridget Perrie, formerly Bridget Fitch, requested additional time to render the account. On 5 Sept. 1730 Alice Fitch chose her uncle Deliverance Brown as guardian. On 18 May 1731 Daniel Bissell of Windsor was appointed guardian to James Fitch, 15 yrs. of age, and John Fitch Jr. of Windham was appointed guardian to Elijah 13 yrs., Eleazer 11 yrs., Medinah 9 yrs., and Ebenezer 6 yrs. On 29 May 1746 Bridget Perry of Ashford, widow and administratrix of Ebenezer Fitch, paid the heirs in full viz.: John and Alice Fitch, James Fitch, Elijah Fitch, Eleazer Fitch, Medinah Fitch, and Ebenezer Fitch.

On 25 April 1726 Atherton Mather of Suffield, Mass. (now Conn.) sold Mrs. Briggit Fitch of Windsor and her present heirs (Alice, James, Elijah, Eleazer, Medinah, and Ebenezer) his right in 4½ acres with a dwelling house and other buildings in Windsor.

In a deed acknowledged 2 May 1741 James Fitch of Durham, Conn., sold Elijah Fitch of Ashford, Conn., his right in land in Windsor that Ebenezer Fitch died seized of. On 29 June 1741 Eleazer Fitch of Windham sold Elijah Fitch of Ashford, his one-seventh share of their father's land in Windsor.

The will of John Perry of Ashford dated 29 Sept. 1743, sworn 17 Feb. 1745/6, names wife Bridget; children John, Thomas, Sarah, Esther, Dorothy, Hepzibah, and Bridget.

On 14 Aug. 1741 sons Eleazer, James, and Elijah Fitch and son-in-law John Fitch quitclaimed their rights to their father's land in Canterbury to their uncle Jabez Fitch.

Children of Ebenezer and Bridget (Brown) Fitch, b. Windsor, Conn.:

198	i	ALICE FITCH[5], b. 30 June 1713
199	ii	JAMES FITCH, b. 24 July 1715
200	iii	ELIJAH FITCH, b. 23 Feb. 1717/8
201	iv	ELEAZER FITCH, b. 18 May 1720
202	v	MEDINA FITCH, b. 20 Nov. 1722
203	vi	EBENEZER FITCH, b. 10 March 1724/5

Note: Stiles mentions a David, b. 20 Nov. 1715 who is not found in Barbour Index and has been deleted.

References: *TAG* 46:44. *Bradford Desc* p. 19. *Torrey's Marriages* p. 105. *Windsor CT By Stiles* 2:263. *Manwaring* 2:505-8(Ebenezer Fitch). Canterbury CT VR 1:138(m.). Windsor CT VR 2:32-34(b. ch.), 234(d. Eben.). *CT Marr* 2:120. *VR Chelmsford* p. 32(b. Bridget). Wallingford CT LR 13:54(d. Bridget). Windham CT PR 3:276, 279; 4:44(John Perry). Canterbury CT LR 2:12, 25, 93(James Fitch); 2:62-3(Ebenezer Fitch); 4:323(quitclaim). *Fitch Gen* pp. 37-39. Windsor CT LR 5:192(Atherton Mather); 7:205(James Fitch and Eleazer Fitch). Hale Cem Coll:Windsor p. 79(Ebenezer Fitch).

40. DANIEL FITCH[4] (Alice[3] Bradford, William[2-1]), b. Norwich, Conn., Feb. 1692/3; d. Canterbury, Conn., 3 Aug. 1752.

He m. (1) Killingly, Conn., 5 March 1718/9 **ANNA COOK**, prob. the one b. Canterbury 1695; d. there 27 July 1735; daughter of Stephen Cook.

He m. (2) before 9 Nov. 1744 **ABIGAIL _____**[*].

On 31 Oct. 1715 James Fitch of Canterbury sold to Daniel Fitch of Canterbury 20 acres and on 4 Feb. 1719 James gave 350 acres to his son Daniel.

On 9 Nov. 1744 Daniel and Abigail Fitch of Pomfret sold 10 acres in Preston deeded to her by Joshua Whitney to James Fitch of Pomfret.

No Connecticut probate records were found for Daniel Fitch. No Norwich, Killingly, or Canterbury, Conn., land records were found for Daniel Fitch to his children.

Children of Daniel and Anna (Cook) Fitch, b. Canterbury, Conn.:

204	i	WILLIAM FITCH[5], bp. 17 July 1720
	ii	JAMES FITCH, b. 27 May 1722
205	iii	EBENEZER FITCH, b. 14 July 1724
	iv	JOHN FITCH, b. 30 Sept. 1726; lost at sea 22 April 1754; unm.
	v	DANIEL FITCH, b. 6 Jan. 1728/9; d. 8 March 1739/40
206	vi	THEOPHILUS FITCH, b. 14 July 1731

[*] Poss. Abigail Tyler, b. Andover 4 Jan. 1687; d. Preston, Conn., 13 March 1771 in 84th yr.; daughter of Hopestill and Mary (Lovett) Tyler. The will of Hopestill Tyler of Preston, written 15 May 1733, proved 12 Feb. 1733/4, names his daughter Abigail Tyler. She signed a receipt for her portion on 8 Sept. 1734 (New London PR #5431).

References: *TAG* 46:45. *Bradford Desc* p. 19. Canterbury CT VR 1:138(m.; b. John), 140(b. ch.), 147(d. Daniel, Anna, son Dan.). *Killingly Ch Rec* p. 10(m.). Preston CT LR 5:403(Daniel Fitch). *Fitch Gen* pp. 39-40. Canterbury CT LR 2:166; 3:91(James Fitch).

41. JERUSHA FITCH[4] (*Alice³ Bradford, William²⁻¹*), b. Canterbury, Conn., ca. 1696; d. Windsor, Conn., 19 Feb. 1780.

She m. Canterbury, Conn., 18 March 1717/8 **DANIEL BISSELL**, b. Windsor, Conn., 31 Oct. 1694; d. there 11 Nov. 1770 in 76th yr.; son of Daniel and Margaret (Dewey) Bissell. On 13 Dec. 1714 and 15 Jan. 1730/1 Daniel Bissell of Windsor deeded to his son Daniel 72 acres and then three pieces of land, one being where his house stood. The will of Daniel Bissell of Windsor dated 25 Nov. 1738, proved 4 Jan. 1738/9, names his son Daniel.

On 19 Nov. 1719 Daniel Fitch of Canterbury sold to Daniel Bissell of Windsor and Henry Cleveland of Canterbury 600 acres in Canterbury.

On 16 Dec. 1755 Daniel Bissell deeded half a lot in Windsor to his son Ebenezer Fitch Bissell.

Daniel Bissell of Windsor sold to his daughter Jerusha the wife of John Palmer Jr. of Windsor 33 acres. On 4 April 1774 John Palmer Jr. and his wife Jerusha sold Daniel Bissell and Eb: Fitch Bissell of Windsor 33 acres "Our Honᵈ Father Daniel Bissell late of Windsor Decᵈ Gave to the said Jerusha Palmer Wife of said John Palmer Junʳ said Thirty Three Acres Lyes in Common and undivided with the Heirs of Said Deceased."

The will of Daniel Bissell of Windsor dated 31 Oct. 1765, sworn 29 Nov. 1770, names wife Jerusha; sons Jabish, Daniel, and Fitch; and daughters Jerusha, Margirt, and Lousy (without surnames).

On 20 March 1786 Ebenezer Fitch Bissell of Windsor sold to Daniel Bissell of Windsor and Jerusha Skinner of East Windsor, Conn., his right in two pieces of land from the estate of his father Daniel Bissell. On 29 Sept. 1786 Margaret Loomis of Windsor sold to Daniel Bissell of Windsor her right in two lots; the first was from her father Daniel Bissell's estate and the second was undivided with Daniel Bissell, Ebenezer Fitch Bissell, and Jerusha Skinner all heirs of their sister Lucy Bissell late of Windsor. On 24 Jan. 1787 Jerusha Skinner late of East Windsor now of Elington, Conn., sold to Daniel Bissell of Windsor her right in seven acres that had been part of her father's estate.

Children of Daniel and Jerusha (Fitch) Bissell, b. Windsor, Conn.:

207	i	JABEZ BISSELL[5], b. 16 Feb. 1718
208	ii	JERUSHA BISSELL, b. 11 April 1721
209	iii	MARGARET BISSELL, b. 24 May 1723
210	iv	DANIEL BISSELL, b. 2 Feb. 1724
211	v	EBENEZER FITCH BISSELL, b. 1736
	vi	LUCY BISSELL (named in will); living 29 Nov. 1770; d. by 29 Sept. 1786

References: *TAG* 26:92; 46:45. *Windsor CT By Stiles* 2:80. *Bradford Desc* pp. 19-20. *CT Marr* 2:121. Windsor CT VR 2:13-4(b. ch.), 129(m.). Canterbury CT VR 2:7(b. Daniel). Hartford CT PR #570(Daniel Bissell); #571(Dan. Bissell).   Windsor CT LR 4:31; 6:64(Daniel Bissell to his son); 11:152(Dan. Bissell); 15:326(Daniel Bissell), 236(John Palmer); 17:47(Ebenezer F. Bissell), 59(Margaret Loomis); 19:57(Jerusha Skinner). *Fitch Gen* p. 43.   Hale Cem Coll:Windsor p. 40(Daniel Bissell).   Canterbury CT LR 3:71(Daniel Fitch).

42.   LUCY FITCH[4] (*Alice*[3] *Bradford, William*[2-1]), b. Canterbury, Conn., ca. 1698; living 8 Nov. 1770.

She m. (1) Canterbury, Conn., 19 March 1719 **HENRY CLEVELAND**, b. Chelmsford 22 Feb. 1699; d. Mansfield, Conn., between 18 Dec. 1769 and 8 Oct. 1770; son of Josiah and Mary (Bates) Cleveland. On 23 March 1720 Henry Cleveland of Canterbury, fourth son of Josiah Cleveland, signed a receipt for his share of his father's estate. On 26 July 1721 Henry Cleveland and others sold Josiah Cleveland a house and land now in the possession of their mother Mary Cleveland distributed to her from the estate of their father Josiah Cleveland.

She m. (2) after 8 Nov. 1770 _____ _____ (see *TAG* 46:37).

On 19 Nov. 1719 Daniel Fitch of Canterbury sold to Daniel Bissell of Windsor and Henry Cleveland of Canterbury 600 acres in Canterbury.

On 20 March 1742/3 Henry Cleveland of Mansfield sold to his son Nehemiah Cleveland of Mansfield 20 acres in Canterbury.

Henry Cleveland served during the French and Indian Wars from 1745-8 including the expedition against Louisbourg in May 1746.

Henry and Lucy Cleveland were admitted to the First Church of Mansfield, Conn., 19 April 1747.

On 20 March 1742/3 Henry Cleveland of Mansfield sold to his son Nehemiah Cleveland of Mansfield 20 acres in Canterbury. On 2 Feb. 1748/9 Henry sold a large tract of land to son Nehemiah. On 21 Dec. 1749 he sold land to son William. And on 29 April 1761 he sold land in Mansfield to son Jabez.

On 11 Dec. 1750 William Cleveland of Mansfield sold to his father Henry Cleveland his right in six acres.

On 24 Jan. 1755 Nehemiah Cleveland sold to his father Henry Cleveland 20 acres being part of the farm they bought from Prince Storrs; Henry sold these 20 acres on 28 May 1763. On 15 Jan. 1759 Henry and Nehemiah sold 20 acres of the farm on which Nehemiah lived to John Slapp.

On 10 April 1760 Henry Cleveland sold to his son Jabez several lots of land, the farm on which Henry lived. On 29 April 1761 Henry sold more land in Mansfield to his son Jabez. On 10 Oct. 1764 Jabez sold half of a home lot with a house to his father Henry.

On 18 Dec. 1769, acknowledged the same day, Henry Cleveland sold part of a lot and his dwelling house to John Salter.

On 8 Oct. 1770 widow Lucy Cleveland was appointed to administer the estate of Lt. Henry Cleveland of Mansfield. The inventory was dated 8 Nov. 1770.

Children of Henry and Lucy (Fitch) Cleveland, b. Canterbury, Conn.:

212	i	WILLIAM CLEVELAND[5], b. 7 July 1719
213	ii	NEHEMIAH CLEVELAND, b. 30 July 1721
214	iii	LUCY CLEVELAND, b. 2 March 1724/5
	iv	JABEZ CLEVELAND, b. 13 Nov. 1736; d. 13 Nov. 1736
215	v	JABEZ CLEVELAND, b. 4 Nov. 1737

References: *TAG* 46:37. Canterbury CT VR 1:103-5, 117(b. ch.). *CT Marr* 2:121. Windham CT PR #904(Henry Cleveland). Mansfield First Ch. Recs. A:40-41. Mansfield CT LR 5:150, 198(Henry Cleveland), 282(William Cleveland); 6:408, 180; 7:41, 55, 473(Henry Cleveland), 264(Jabez Cleveland). *Fitch Gen* pp.42-3. *VR Chelmsford* p. 46(b. Henry). Canterbury CT LR 3:71(Daniel Fitch); 3:136(Henry Cleveland *et al.*); 5:164(Henry Cleveland). New London CT PR #1290(Josiah Cleveland).

43. THEOPHILUS FITCH[4] (*Alice[3] Bradford, William[2-1]*), b. ca. 1701; d. Canterbury, Conn., 20 July 1751.

He m. (1) Canterbury, Conn., 15 Dec. 1731 **MARY HUNTINGTON**, b. Windham, Conn., 4 Aug. 1707; d. Canterbury, Conn., 12 March 1732/3 aged 25; daughter of Joseph and Rebeccah (Adgate) Huntington.

He m. (2) Stonington, Conn., 2 Oct. 1734 **GRACE (PRENTICE) GRANT**, b. Newton 26 Jan. 1704; daughter of Samuel and Esther (Hammond) Prentice. She m. (1) Stonington, Conn., 30 Nov. 1721 JOSIAH GRANT with whom she had Rebecca, John, Lucy, and Sarah. The will of Samuel Prentice of Stonington dated 22 April 1728, proved 11 June 1728, names his daughter Grace (without surname). On 12 July 1739 Grace Fitch signed a receipt for her portion of her father's estate.

On 4 June 1723 Daniel and Theophilus Fitch of Canterbury agreed to divide their shares of "Major Fitches Farm."

On 19 April 1750 Daniel Fitch of Canterbury and Theophilos Fitch of Stonington, yeoman, sold to Samuel Adams 10 acres in Canterbury.

On 17 Oct. 1752 Samuel Fitch, minor son of Mr. Theophilus Fitch deceased, chose Lt. Elijah Duar (Dyer) of Canterbury to be his guardian. No other probate record was found for Theophilus Fitch.

Children of Theophilus and Grace (Prentice) (Grant) Fitch, b. Stonington, Conn.:

216   i   SAMUEL FITCH[5], b. 17 June 1735

217   ii THEOPHILUS FITCH, b. 8 May 1737

        iii PHINEAS FITCH, b. 12 April 1739; d. 19 April 1739

        iv JAMES FITCH, b. 5 Nov. 1740

        v DANIEL FITCH, b. 30 Jan. 1742/3; d. 22 May 1743

218   vi MARY FITCH, b. 22 April 1744

        vii SARAH FITCH, b. 12 March 1748

Note: The fact that there are no guardianship records for the younger children suggests that they may have died before their father.

References: *TAG* 46:36-45. Plainfield CT PR 1:157(Theophilus Fitch.). *Torrey's Marriages* p. 405(Huntington). Canterbury CT VR 1:138(1st m.; d.). Windham CT VR A:10(b. Mary). Stonington CT VR 3:45(2nd m.; b. ch.; d. Daniel). *Stonington CT Hist* p. 401. *NEHGR* 70:344(Mary's g.s.; her parents). *VR Newton* p. 159(b. Grace). Canterbury CT LR 3:234; 5:376(Daniel & Theo. Fitch). *Fitch Gen* pp. 40-2. New London CT PR #4230(Samuel Prentice).

44. JABEZ FITCH[4] (*Alice[3] Bradford, William[2-1]*), b. Canterbury, Conn., 30 Jan. 1702/3; d. there 3/31 Jan. 1784 aged 80.

He m. (1) Canterbury, Conn., 29 May 1722 **LYDIA GALE**, b. Watertown 9 July 1699; d. Canterbury, Conn., 20/22 Aug. 1753 aged 52; daughter of Abraham and Sarah (Fiske) Gale.

He m. (2) Canterbury, 14 Jan. 1754, **ELIZABETH (SPAULDING) DARBE/DARBY**, b. Chelmsford 15 Aug 1698; daughter of Edward and Mary (Adams) Spaulding; widow of William Darby. Elizabeth m. (1) Canterbury 9 June 1718 WILLIAM DARBY and with him had Elizabeth, Mary, John, Martha, William, Jedediah, Ruth, and Blanchard.

He m. (3) in 1782 **REBECCA (ENSWORTH or AINSWORTH) KING**.

On 29 June 1722 James Fitch of Canterbury gave to his son Jabez of Canterbury 100 acres.

Jabez and Lydiah Fitch owned the covenant at the Canterbury church on 23 June 1723 and Lydia, wife of Jabez, was admitted to the church on 11 April 1731.

Jabez Fitch was a Deputy for Canterbury to the General Assembly almost every year from 1734 to 1775.

On 4 Feb. 1754 Jabez Fitch of Canterbury sold to his son Jabez Jr. all his farm "I now live on" and on 4 April 1758 they partitioned the farm; Lucy Fitch and Asahel Fitch witnessed this second deed.

In an undated deed (ack. 27 March 1765) Jabez Fitch and Elizabeth Fitch, formerly the widow of William Darbee formerly of Pomfret and now the wife of Jabez, sold Jabez Fitch Jr. half of a dwelling house where Jabez Jr. now lived and 10 acres.

On 17 Nov. 1773 Jabez mortgaged 27 acres to son Perez Fitch of Stamford. On 10 May 1774 Jabez sold 17 acres to Jabez Jr. reserving the right to cut wood and rails.

The will of Jabez Fitch of Canterbury, Conn., dated 10 Dec. 1783, proved 10 Feb. 1784, names sons Jabez and Asahel; daughters Jerusha, Lydia, and Lucy; heirs of son Perez Fitch, late of Stamford; and heirs of daughter Alice, deceased, the late wife of Rev. James Cogswell.

Children of Jabez and Lydia (Gale) Fitch, by 1st wife; all but Jabez, b. prob. Canterbury, Conn.:

219	i	JERUSHA FITCH[5], b. 30 Jan. 1723
220	ii	ALICE FITCH, b. 8 Jan. 1724/5
221	iii	PEREZ FITCH, b. 5 Dec. 1726
222	iv	JABEZ FITCH, b. Norwich, Conn., 23 May 1729
223	v	LYDIA FITCH, bp. Canterbury, Conn., 27 Jan. 1734
224	vi	LUCY FITCH, b. 24 June 1736; bp. Canterbury, Conn., 27 June 1736
225	vii	ASHAEL FITCH, bp. 27 Aug. 1738
	viii	ABIGAIL FITCH, bp. 19 April 1741; d. 1 May 1749

References: *TAG* 46:45-6. *Bradford Desc* p. 20. Canterbury CT VR 1:138(2nd m.), 140(b. 1st 3 ch.; Lucy), 147 (d. Lydia, Abigail). *CT Marr* 2:122(1st m.). Norwich CT VR 1:106(b. Jabez). Plainfield CT PR 8:48, 49, 180(Jabez Fitch). *Canterbury 1st Ch* pp. 43(Lydia adm.), 68(bp. Lydia), 71(bp. Lucy), 96(1st m. Elizabeth), 103(Jabez & Lydia owned cov.). *Watertown By Bond* p. 227 (Gale). *Watertown Recs* 2:15(b. Lydia). *Fitch Gen* pp. 43-5(3rd m.). Canterbury CT LR 3:218(James Fitch); 6:118, 297; 7:200; 9:56, 194(Jabez Fitch). Hale Cem Coll:Canterbury p. 30(Jabez & Lydia). *The Spaulding Memorial*, Charles Warren Spalding (Chicago 1897), p. 69. *VR Chelmsford* p. 152(b. Elizabeth).

45.   THOMAS STEELE[4] (*Mercy*[3] *Bradford, William*[2-1]), b. Hartford, Conn., 9 Sept. 1681, bp. Second Ch. 11 Sept. 1681; d. W. Hartford, Conn., June 1739 aged 57 or 2 Jan. 1739 aged 57.

He m. Hartford, Conn., 10 May 1709 **SUSANNA WEBSTER**, b. Hartford 25 April 1686, bp. Second Church 26 April 1686; d. W. Hartford, Conn., 27 Nov. 1757; daughter of Jonathan and Dorcas (Hopkins) Webster. The will of Jonathan Webster of Hartford dated 7 April 1732, proved 5 Aug. 1735, names his daughter Susanah Steel. She m. (2d) _____ MERRELS.

Thomas Steele "and wife" were admitted to the West Hartford Church 18 Oct. 1719.

On 25 Dec. 1739 Thomas Steele of Hartford gave to his son William Steele of New Hartford 33 acres in New Hartford.

The will of Thomas Steele of Hartford, Conn., dated 20 Sept. 1737, proved Feb. 1739/40, names wife Susanna; sons Samuel, John, William, Nathaniel, and James Steele; daughter Jerusha Steele, alias Mills; and daughter Susannah Steele, alias Hosmer.

On 21 March 1745 and 10 April 1749 Thomas Steele's children (Samuel, Nathaniel, and John Steele of Hartford, William Steele of New Hartford, and Daniel and Jerusha Mills of Simsbury) with other heirs of Samuel Steele sold two tracts of land laid out in the right of Samuel Steele in Farmington. On 21 Sept. 1756 Thomas' children (Samuel, Nathaniel, and John Steele of Hartford, Thomas and Susannah Hosmer of Hartford, and William and James Steele of New Hartford) with other heirs of Samuel Steele sold a lot in Hartford held in common with the heirs of Samuel Hubbard.

Susannah Steel, widow of Thomas Steel late of Hartford, in her will dated 8 March 1750/1, proved 11 Oct. 1757, named her five sons Samuel, William, James, Nathaniel, and John and her two daughters Jerusha wife of Daniel Mills and Susannah wife of Thomas Hosmer. The inventory taken on 4 Oct. 1757 calls her Susannah Steel alias Merrels.

Children of Thomas and Susanna (Webster) Steele, first four, b. Hartford, Conn., first three bp. Second Church:

226   i   JERUSHA STEELE[5], b. 1 July 1710, bp. 2 July 1710
227   ii SAMUEL STEELE, b. 11 March 1712, bp. 16 March 1712
228   iii WILLIAM STEELE, b. 10 Dec. 1713, bp. 13 Dec. 1713
229   iv SUSANNA STEELE, b. 15 Dec. 1715
         v   THOMAS STEELE, bp. W. Hartford, Conn., 1 Dec. 1717 (not in father's will)
230   vi JAMES STEELE, b. W. Hartford, Conn., 22 Dec. 1719

231 vii NATHANIEL STEELE, b. W. Hartford, Conn., 11 March (or 3 Nov.) 1721

232 viii JOHN STEELE, bp. W. Hartford, Conn., 17 Nov. 1723

References: *Hartford By Barbour* pp. 579-80, 647. W. Hartford 1st Ch. Recs. 1:26(bp. Thomas), 29(bp. John). *Hartford CT Second Ch.* pp. 302(bp. Thomas), 319(bp. Jerusha), 320(bp. Samuel), 321(bp. William). *Bradford Desc* p. 21. *Manwaring* 3:344-5(Thomas Steele will). Hartford CT PR #5205(Susannah Steel); #5208(Thomas Steele); #5769(Jonathan Webster). Hartford CT VR D:19(b. wife Susanna), 29(m.); FFS:60(b. Jerusha, Samuel, William). Hale Cem Coll:West Hartford p. 6(Thomas Steele). Farmington CT LR 7:466, 486(Samuel Steele's heirs). Hartford CT LR 9:406(Samuel Steele's heirs).

46. ABIEL STEELE⁴ (*Mercy³ Bradford, William²⁻¹*), b. Hartford, Conn., 8 Oct. 1693; living 18 March 1769.

She m. (1) Hartford, Conn., 25 Dec. 1712 **JOHN WEBSTER**, bp. Hartford, Conn., Second Church 26 Dec. 1680; d. Hartford between 30 June 1752 and 1 Sept. 1753; son of John and Sarah (Myatt) Webster. The 7 Aug. 1728 distribution of the estate of John Webster of Hartford included his son John.

She m. (2) Waterbury, Conn., 25 May 1756 **STEPHEN HOPKINS**, b. Waterbury, Conn., 19 Nov. 1689; d. there 4/11 Jan. 1769 aged 80; son of John and Hannah (Strong) Hopkins. He m. (1) Waterbury, Conn., 20 Aug. 1718 SUSANNA PECK with whom he had John, Stephen, Anna, Susanna, Mary, Joseph, Jesse, Mary, Lois, and David. The will of John Hopkins of Waterbury dated 15 Feb. 1731, proved 17 Nov. 1732, names his son Stephen and Stephen was included in the 28 May 1734 distribution of the estate.

On 24 Nov. 1717 Abiel, wife of John Webster, was admitted in full communion with the West Hartford Church.

On 6 Aug. 1728 John Webster and Abiel his wife of Hartford sold 14 acres to Daniel Steel of Hartford.

On 14 March 1728/9 John Webster of Farmington bought 124 acres from James Pike.

On 13 Dec. 1742 John Webster of Southington in Farmington for love and affection gave to his second son Aaron Webster of Southington in Farmington 80 acres.

On 10 April 1749 John Webster and his wife Abiah of Farmington, along with other heirs of her father Samuel Steele, sold two pieces of land in Farmington laid out in the right of Samuel Steele.

On 13 June 1752 John Webster of Southington gave to his son John Webster of Southington four acres.

The will of John Webster dated 30 June 1752 names wife Abial; sons Osee, Elisha, Aaron, and John; and daughters Jerusha, Mary, Sarah, Ann, Susannah, and Abigail. The inventory was taken 1 Sept. 1753.

On 21 Sept. 1756 Stephen Hopkins and his wife Abiel of Waterbury, along with other heirs of her father Samuel Steele, sold a lot in Hartford held in common with the heirs of Samuel Hubbard.

On 7 Sept. 1757 Stephen and Abial Hopkins of Waterbury gave to "their son" Aaron Webster whatever interest they might have in Farmington land derived from her father Samuel Steele or her uncle Benoni Steele.

The will of Stephen Hopkins dated 7 July 1767, proved 16 Feb. 1769, names wife Abiah; sons John, Stephen, and Joseph; daughters Anna Royce and Lois Johnson. An 18 March 1769 distribution of the land among the heirs shows that the widow was still alive then.

Children of John and Abiel (Steele) Webster, first nine b. Hartford, Conn.:

233	i	ELISHA WEBSTER[5], b. 12 Nov. 1713, bp. 2nd Ch. 15 Nov. 1713
234	ii	JERUSHA WEBSTER, b. 8 Jan. 1714/5, bp. W. Hartford Sept. 1714
235	iii	AARON WEBSTER, b. 24 Feb. 1716/7, bp. W. Hartford March 1717
	iv	ABIEL WEBSTER, b. 31 July 1718, bp. W. Hartford 3 Aug. 1718; d. before 30 June 1752 (not in father's will)
236	v	MARY WEBSTER, b. 23 July 1720, bp. W. Hartford 24 July 1720
237	vi	SARAH WEBSTER, b. 17 April 1722, bp. W. Hartford 22 April 1722
238	vii	ANN WEBSTER, b. 18 April 1724, bp. W. Hartford 19 April 1724
239	viii	SUSANNAH WEBSTER, b. 8 July 1726, bp. W. Hartford 10 July 1726
240	ix	JOHN WEBSTER, b. 4 Sept. 1728
241	x	ABIGAIL WEBSTER, b. Farmington, Conn., 23 Sept. 1731
242	xi	OSEE WEBSTER, bp. 7 April 1734
	xii	ROBERT WEBSTER, b. Farmington, Conn., 8 April 1736; d. before 30 June 1752 (not in father's will)

References: *CT Hist Coll* 14:618. *Bradford Desc* p. 21(some dates wrong). *Hartford CT Second Ch*, pp. 301(bp. John Webster), 321(bp. Elisha). *Webster Fam*, W. H. Webster 1915, pp. 46-7. *Hopkins Gen* pp. 17-19, 32-5. *Hartford By Barbour* pp. 314, 649-50. Hartford CT VR D:29(1st m.); FFS:63(b. ch.). Waterbury CT VR 1:10 (b. Hopkins ch.; 2nd m.; d. Stephen), 85(b. Stephen; his 1st m.). Farmington CT LR 4:528(John Webster); 6:7(b. Robert), 427(John Webster); 7:466, 486(Samuel Steele's heirs); 8:408(John Webster); 12:450(Stephen Hopkins). Woodbury CT PR #2126(John Hopkins); #2128(Stephen Hopkins). Hartford CT PR #5766, 17:1-2(John Webster). Hartford CT LR 5:99(John Webster); 9:406(Samuel Steele's heirs). Hale Cem Coll:Waterbury p. 776(Stephen Hopkins).

47. DANIEL STEELE[4] (*Mercy*[3] *Bradford, William*[2-1]), b. Hartford, Conn., 3 April 1697, bp. Second Church 4 April 1697; d. West Hartford, Conn., 13 March 1788 aged 92.

He m. Hartford, Conn., 20 June 1725 **MARY HOPKINS**, b. Hartford, Conn., 30 Jan. 1702/3, bp. First Ch. 30 Jan. 1703/4; d. there 9 Aug. 1796 aged 94 (*Hartford, Conn., Second Ch* p. 382: Widow Mary Steele d. 18 Aug. 1796, aged 94y); daughter of Ebenezer and Mary (Butler) Hopkins. Mary Hopkins was included in the 4 April 1721 distribution of the estate of Ebenezer Hopkins of Hartford.

On 20 Feb. 1725[/6] Mary, wife to Daniel Steele, was received into full communion with the Hartford Second Church.

On 10 April 1749 Daniel Steele of Hartford, along with other heirs of his father Samuel Steele, sold two pieces of land in Farmington laid out in the right of Samuel Steele. On 21 Sept. 1756 Daniel Steele of Hartford, along with other heirs of his father Samuel Steele, sold a lot in Hartford held in common with the heirs of Samuel Hubbard.

The will of Daniel Steel of Hartford, Conn., dated 7 July 1785, proved 1 April 1788, names wife Mary; sons Timothy, Lemuel, and Thomas; and daughters Mary Goodwin wife of Capt. Ozias, Wealthy Sheldon late wife of Asher, and Submit Burr wife of William. Final distribution of the estate on 14 March 1811 set off land to Lemuel, Thomas, and heirs of Roswell Steele.

Children of Daniel and Mary (Hopkins) Steele, b. Hartford, Conn.:

	i	DANIEL STEELE[5], bp. Second Ch. 19 June 1726; n.f.r.
243	ii	MARY STEELE, bp. Second Ch. 2 Feb. 1728/9
244	iii	WELTHIA STEELE, bp. Second Ch. 14 Feb. 1730/1
245	iv	TIMOTHY STEELE, bp. 19 June 1736
246	v	ROSWELL STEELE, bp. 4 Feb. 1738/9
247	vi	THOMAS STEELE, b. 1740
248	vii	LEMUEL STEELE, b. ca. 1742
249	viii	SUBMIT STEELE, b. 1746?

Refernces: *NEHGR* 12:334. Hartford First Ch. Recs. *Hartford CT Second Ch.* pp. 296(Mary received), 297(bp. Welthia), 307(bp. Daniel), 327(bp. son Daniel), 328(bp. Mary). Hartford Center Ch. Recs. *Steele Fam* pp. 11, 14. *Bradford Desc* p. 21. *Boston News Obits* 3:409(d. Daniel). Hartford CT PR #2856(Ebenezer Hopkins); #5173(Daniel Steele). *Hartford By Barbour* p. 581. Hartford CT VR FFS:42(b. wife Mary). Farmington CT LR 7:466, 486(Samuel Steele's heirs). Hartford CT LR 9:406(Samuel Steele's heirs).

48. ELIPHALET STEELE⁴ (*Mercy³ Bradford, William²⁻¹*), b. Hartford, Conn., 23 June 1700, bp. Second Church 24 June 1700; d. Hartford in July 1773 aged 73.

He m. Hartford, Conn., 4 Oct. 1722 **KATHARINE MARSHFIELD**, b. Springfield 2 Feb. 1701/2; d. West Hartford, Conn., 7 June 1788 aged 87; daughter of Josiah and Rachel (Gilbert) Marshfield.

On 31 Dec. 1724 Eliphalet Steel of Hartford sold to Daniel Steel of Hartford one-half of a dwelling house, barn, and houselot which was their father Samuel Steel's; Katherine also signed the deed.

On 5 Feb. 1727 Katharine Steele, wife of Eliphalet, was admitted to full communion with the West Hartford Church. Eliphalet was admitted on 27 Jan. 1734.

On 10 April 1749 Eliphalet Steele of Hartford, along with other heirs of his father Samuel Steele, sold two pieces of land in Farmington laid out in the right of Samuel Steele. On 21 Sept. 1756 Elphialet Steele of Hartford, along with other heirs of his father Samuel Steele, sold a lot in Hartford held in common with the heirs of Samuel Hubbard.

On 8 Nov. 1752 Eliphalet Steele gave seven acres in Hartford to his son Josiah. No other Hartford deeds have been found from Eliphalet to any of his children.

The will of Eliphalet Steele of Hartford, Conn., dated 16 July 1773, proved 13 Dec. 1773, left all to wife Catherine Steele. Catherine and eldest son Josiah were named executors.

No Connecticut probate records were found for Katherine Steele.

Children of Eliphalet and Katharine (Marshfield) Steele, b. Hartford, Conn.:

	i	ELIPHALET STEELE⁵, b. 1723; d.y.
250	ii	JOSIAH STEELE, bp. Hartford, Conn., 2nd Ch. 16 Feb. 1723/4
	iii	KATHERINE STEELE, bp. 27 Jan. 1726; d.y.
251	iv	MERCY STEELE, bp. W. Hartford, Conn., 8 Oct. 1727
252	v	THEOPHILUS STEELE, bp. W. Hartford, Conn., 31 May 1730
	vi	ELIPHAZ STEELE, bp. W. Hartford, Conn., 10 Dec. 1732; d.y.
253	vii	ELIJAH STEELE, bp. W. Hartford, Conn., 20 April 1735
254	viii	RACHEL STEELE, bp. W. Hartford, Conn., 4 Sept. 1737
255	ix	KATHERINE STEELE, bp. W. Hartford, Conn., 27 Jan. 1740
256	x	ELIPHALET STEELE, bp. W. Hartford, Conn., 27 June 1742
	xi	JERUSHA STEELE, bp. W. Hartford, Conn., 6 April 1746; living 25 Sept. 1763

Note: No proof was found for a daughter Ruth, b. 1740 as included in *Bradford Desc.*

References: Hartford CT VR. *Steele Fam* pp. 11, 14-5. *Bradford Desc* p. 22. *Hartford CT Second Ch.* pp. 309(bp. Eliphalet), 326(bp. Josiah). W. Hartford CT Ch. Recs. 1:31(bp. Mercy), 33(bp. Theophilus), 35(bp. Eliphaz), 37(bp. Rachel), 38(bp. Katherine), 40(bp. Eliphalet), 43(bp. Jerusha), 57(bp. Elijah). Hartford CT PR #5178(Eliphalet Steele). Hartford CT LR 5:97; 8:498(Eliphalet Steele); 9:406(Samuel Steele's heirs). *Hartford By Barbour* p. 581. Farmington CT LR 7:466, 486(Samuel Steele's heirs).

49. ALICE RIPLEY[4] (*Hannah*[3] *Bradford, William*[2-1]), b. Hingham 18 Sept. 1683; d. Norwich, Conn., 18 Dec. 1768 aged 86.

She m. Norwich, Conn., 18 April 1703 **SAMUEL EDGERTON**, b. Norwich, Conn., May 1670; d. there 7 June 1748 in 81st yr.; son of Richard and Mary (Sylvester) Edgerton.

Samuel Edgerton gave or sold land to his sons over many years; to his son Samuel: 13 acres on 19 May 1727, 70 acres 11 Nov. 1730, 2 acres 7 May 1742, and a final piece of land on 17 April 1745. To his son Peter: 30 acres of his farm 13 Jan. 1728/9 and 21 acres on 11 Nov. 1730. To his son William: 70 acres 11 Nov. 1730, 3 acres 25 Jan. 1736/7, another piece of land 9 Jan. 1737/8, and 3 acres 27 May 1742. To his son Joshua: land 11 Nov. 1730, 5 acres 6 April 1736, 4 acres 13 July 1742, and one acre 14 April 1743. To his son Elijah: 17 acres 9 Sept. 1740, 50 acres 27 May 1742, and 36 acres and 20 acres 15 March 1743/4. To his son David: 50 acres 27 May 1742. On 15 March 1743/4 Elijah Edgerton agreed to pay yearly rents in exchange for the land, orchards, and buildings where Samuel Edgerton and his wife Alice now live; the rent was "one Indian Kernel of Corn, or Corn of wheat."

On 21 June 1748 Samuel Edgerton, administrator, and Joshua Edgerton, both of Norwich, posted bond to administer the estate of Samuel Edgerton of Norwich. On 25 July 1748 the following gave receipts to Samuel Edgerton for their share of the estate of Samuel Edgerton: Daniel and Mary Fuller; Peter, Joshua, David, William, Alice, and Elijah Edgerton; and widow Alice Edgerton.

On 9 Aug. 1774 Samuel Edgerton of Norwich sold to his son John Edgerton of Norwich two pieces of land "Reserving Liberty to and for Such of the Heirs of Mr Samuel Edgerton late of said Norwich Deceased that Necessarily shall have occasion to pass and Repass ... as it is Expressed in the Deeds of Conveyance of the said Samuel Deceased to his Children."

Children of Samuel and Alice (Ripley) Edgerton, b. Norwich, Conn.:

257   i SAMUEL EDGERTON[5], b. 15 March 1704

258   ii   PETER EDGERTON, b. 14 Jan. 1705/6

259   iii   JOSHUA EDGERTON, b. 26 Feb. 1707/8

260   iv   WILLIAM EDGERTON (twin), b. 25 April 1710

           v   JOHN EDGERTON (twin), b. 25 April 1710; d. 13 July 1730 in 21st yr.; unm.

261   vi   MARY EDGERTON, b. 17 May 1713

262   vii   ELIJAH EDGERTON, b. 1 Dec. 1715

263   viii DAVID EDGERTON, b. 28 Aug. 1718

           ix   ALICE EDGERTON, b. 25 Dec. 1721; living 25 July 1748

           x   DANIEL EDGERTON, b. 10 July 1725; d. 31 Aug. 1726

References: *Norwich CT VR* 1:34(b. Samuel), 60(m.; b. ch.; d. Samuel, Daniel). *Bradford Desc* p. 22. New London CT PR #1884(Sam. Edgerton). Hale Cem Coll:Franklin p. 44 (g.s. Alice, Samuel, John). Norwich CT LR 5:61; 6:9, 219, 221, 224, 249; 7:245, 365; 8:131, 310, 401, 404, 501, 503, 505; 9:345, 543, 546(Samuel to his sons); 9:544(Elijah Edgerton); 21:411(Samuel Edgerton).

50.   HANNAH RIPLEY[4] (*Hannah*[3] *Bradford, William*[2-1]), b. Hingham 2 March 1685; d. Windham, Conn., 19 March 1751.

She m. Windham, Conn., 8 Oct. 1711 **SAMUEL WEBB**, b. Braintree 14 May 1690; d. Rockingham, Vt., 6 March 1779 aged 89 yrs.; son of Samuel and Mary (Adams) Webb. He m. (2) Windham, Conn., 14 May 1752 ELIZABETH (DURKEE) FISK.

On 8 April 1713 Samuel Webb of Windham gave to his son Samuel 100 acres. On 17 Aug. 1716 and 2 Jan. 1719/20 he sold to his son Samuel more land. On 24 Sept. 1736 he gave to his son Samuel one half of his farm and in 1747 (ack. 1 April 1748) he gave Lemuel the other half.

On 1 April 1743 Samuel [Jr.] gave land in Windham to son Ebenezer Webb, and on 15 July 1743 to son Joshua Webb. On 26 Feb. 1749/50 Samuel sold to Joshua Webb 10 acres lying in partnership between them.

On 21 Dec. 1753 Edward and James Houghton of Union [Conn.] sold a lease for 987 years on six acres in Union including a grist mill to Samuel Webb of Windham. On 27 June 1758 Samuel Webb of Union sold the rest of the lease to Joshua Webb of Union.

No Vermont probate records were found for Samuel Webb.

Children of Samuel and Hannah (Ripley) Webb, b. Windham, Conn.:

           i   EBENEZER WEBB[5], b. 26 April 1712; d. 8 June 1713 ae 1y 12d

264   ii   HANNAH WEBB, b. 29 June 1715

265   iii EBENEZER WEBB, b. 12 Jan. 1718/9

266   iv   JOSHUA WEBB, b. 2 Feb. 1721/2

References: *Bradford Desc* p. 22. *Braintree Recs* p. 666(b. Sam.). Windham CT VR 1:7(m.; b. ch.; d. Hannah). Rockingham VT Cemetery at the Old Rockingham Meeting House(d. Samuel). Windham CT LR D:304; E:155, 407(to Samuel); G:395; I:189(to Lemuel); H:191(to Ebenezer); H:266; I:408(to Joshua). Union CT LR 2:91(Edward & James Houghton); 2:146(Samuel Webb). Hale Cem Coll:Windham p. 283(Ebenezer Webb).

51. FAITH RIPLEY[4] (*Hannah*[3] *Bradford, William*[2-1]), b. Hingham 20 Sept. 1686; d. Windham, Conn., 11 Feb. 1720/1.

She m. Windham, Conn., 5 Jan. 1708/9 **SAMUEL BINGHAM**, b. Windham, Conn., 28 March 1685; d. there 1 March 1760 aged 74; son of Thomas and Mary (Rudd) Bingham. He m. (2) Windham, Conn., 23 Nov. 1721 ELIZABETH MANNING with whom he had Samuel, Thomas, Jonathan, Deborah, Mary, and Abigail.

The will of Samuel Bingham of Windham dated 12 Feb. 1751/2, sworn 13 March 1760, names wife Elizabeth; sons Abishai, Lemuel, Samuel, Thomas, and Jonathan; and daughters Jerusha Robinson, Ann Fullsom, Deborah Bingham, Mary Bingham, and Abigail Bingham.

Children of Samuel and Faith (Ripley) Bingham, b. Windham, Conn.:

267   i   JERUSHA BINGHAM[5], b. 2 Feb. 1708

268   ii   ABISHA BINGHAM, b. 29 Jan. 1709/10

269   iii LEMUEL BINGHAM, b. 20 Sept. 1713

270   iv   ANNE BINGHAM, b. Nov. 1716

       v   MARAH BINGHAM, b. 10 Feb. 1720/1; d. Windham 22 Feb. 1720/1

References: Windham CT VR 1:3(m.; b. ch.; d. Faith, Marah; 2nd m.), 8(b. Sam.), 142(d. Sam.). *Bingham Fam* (1972) 1:170, 227-8. *Bradford Desc* pp. 22-3. Windham CT PR #394(Sam. Bingham). Norwich CT VR 1:8(b. Samuel).

52. JOSHUA RIPLEY[4] (*Hannah*[3] *Bradford, William*[2-1]), b. Hingham 13 May 1688; d. Windham, Conn., 18 Nov. 1773 (in Bible) or 1774 in 86th yr.

He m. Windham, Conn., 3 Dec. 1712 **MARY BACKUS**, b. Windham, Conn., 8 Nov. 1692; d. there 19 Oct. 1770 in 78th yr.; daughter of John and Mary (Bingham) Backus. On 11 Aug. 1752 Joshua and Mary Ripley signed a receipt from the estate of John Backus late of Windham.

On 21 Feb. 1712/3 Joshua Ripley of Windham gave to his son Joshua
Ripley Jr. of Windham two tracts in Windham. On 2 June 1729 Joshua sold
his son Joshua Jr. three additional tracts of land. On the same day Joshua Jr.
sold his father Joshua one-third part of a dam and land, iron ore, iron works,
"Cole house," and two forges.

On 24 May 1731 Joshua Ripley Jr. of Windham sold to Hezekiah Ripley
and Thomas Dyer of Windham the dwelling house in which Joshua dwelt with
all utensels, iron, brass, puter, household stuff both beds and beding, chests,
trunks, "Chars" and tables, all white ware, one yearling Colt, a red one, and a
black one with a white face.

On 21 Feb. 1744/5 Samuel Hebard sold to Phinehas Ripley land in Windham but Phineas died before a deed was made up. Therefore, on 1 March
1747/8, Hebard conveyed the tract to the heirs of Phinehas Ripley: Nathaniel,
Joshua Jr., Ebenezer, William, and John Jr. Ripley; Mary, wife of Joshua Abbe;
and Hannah Ripley, all of Windham; and Elizabeth, wife of John Alden of
Lebanon.

On 19 July 1749 Joshua Ripley Jr. sold to Nathaniel Ripley his right in
land now in the improvement of his father Joshua "on which he dwells" that
his late brother Phineas in his will bequeathed to his father during his life. On
7 July 1750 Ebenezer Ripley also sold his right to this land to Nathaniel.

In Nov. 1751 Joshua Ripley and wife Mary; Joshua Abbe and wife Mary;
Nathaniel Ripley and Ebenezer Ripley of Windham; and John Alden and wife
Elizabeth of Lebanon quitclaimed to Joshua Ripley Jr. of Windham their rights
to land conveyed to Mary Ripley for life and then to her daughter Hannah
Ripley, now deceased

No Windham, Conn., probate records were found for Joshua Ripley.

Children of Joshua and Mary (Backus) Ripley, b. Windham, Conn.:

271   i   MARY RIPLEY[5], b. 18 Nov. 1714

       ii PHINEAS RIPLEY, b. 25 Nov. 1716; d. Windham, Conn., 4 Aug. 1746
           ae 29; unm. The will of Phinehas Ripley of Windham dated 4 Aug.
           1746, proved 19 Aug. 1746, names father and mother, Joshua and Mary
           Ripley; siblings Mary, Hannah, Nathaniel, Elizabeth, Joshua, Ebenezer,
           William, and John.

       iii HANNAH RIPLEY, b. 12 Jan. 1718/9; d. Windham, Conn., 8 Nov. 1750
           ae 1y [*sic*]; unm. No probate record found.

272   iv NATHANIEL RIPLEY, b. 30 June 1721

273   v   ELIZABETH RIPLEY, b. 4 Nov. 1724

274   vi   JOSHUA RIPLEY, b. 30 Oct. 1726
275   vii EBENEZER RIPLEY, b. 27 June 1729
276   viii WILLIAM RIPLEY, b. 12 Feb. 1733/4
277   ix   JOHN RIPLEY, b. 31 March 1738

References: *MD* 28:101-2(m.; b. ch.; deaths). Windham CT VR 1:39(b. ch.; m.), 55(4 deaths); A:2(b. Mary). Windham CT LR D:336(to son Joshua); G:143, 60(Joshua Ripley), 61(Joshua Ripley Jr.); I:247(Samuel Hebard); I:295(Joshua Ripley Jr.); I:444(Ebenezer Ripley); K:128(quitclaim). Windham CT PR #152(John Backus); 3:287(Phinehas Ripley). Hale Cem Coll:Windham pp. 278(Joshua & Mary), 281(Phineas & Hannah). Bible with GS #58617.

53. MARGARET RIPLEY[4] (*Hannah[3] Bradford, William[2-1]*), b. Norwich, Conn., 4 Nov. 1690; d. Lebanon, Conn., 3 May 1774 aged 83.

She m. **BENJAMIN SEABURY**, b. Duxbury 24 Sept. 1689; d. Lebanon, Conn., 9 April 1787 aged 97; son of Samuel and Abigail (Allen) Seabury.

On 3 Jan. 1758 Benjamin Seabury deeded 100 acres in Lebanon to his son Samuel Seabury, and on the same date he deeded 100 acres there to his son Elisha. On 10 April 1773 he deeded 16 acres in Lebanon to his grandson Benjamin Seabury. In 1781 (date not shown) he deeded a tract of land to daughter Abigail.

No Connecticut probate records were found for Benjamin Seabury.

Children of Benjamin and Margaret (Ripley) Seabury, b. prob. Lebanon, Conn.:

        i   ABIGAIL SEABURY[5], b. ca. 1715; d. Lebanon, Conn., 11 or 12 June
             1802 ae 87; unm.
278   ii   SAMUEL SEABURY, b. ca. 1718
279   iii ELISHA SEABURY, b. ca. 1721
280   iv   SARAH SEABURY, bp. Lebanon, Conn., 29 Dec. 1723

References: *VR Duxbury* p. 148(b. Benj.). *Bradford Desc* p. 23. *Torrey's Marriages* p. 658. Records of the First Church of Lebanon CT 4:37(bp. Sarah); 5:159(d. Benj.), 166(d. Abigail). Hale Cem Coll:Lebanon p. 69(Abigail, Margaret, Benjamin). Windham CT PR 14:382(Samuel Seabury). Lebanon CT LR 9:342(to Sam.), 343(to Elisha), 12:227(to grandson); 13:185(to Abigail). *NEHGR* 74:69(g.s.).

54. RACHEL RIPLEY[4] (*Hannah³ Bradford, William²⁻¹*), b. Windham, Conn., 17 April 1693; d. there 4 April 1782.

She m. Norwich, Conn., 21 June 1714 **WINSLOW TRACY**, b. Norwich, Conn., 9 Feb. 1688/9; d. there 22 Jan. 1768 in 79th yr.; son of John and Mary (Winslow) Tracy. The will of John Tracy of Norwich dated 15 July 1702, proved 29 Oct. 1702, names his son Winslow and says "I desire that Winslow maybe put out a whill into some good place unto some trade & alsoe to have him better perfected in reading & writing."

Winslow Tracy of Norwich gave or sold land to his sons; to his son Josiah: 20 acres 22 Dec. 1744, 39 acres 14 May 1752, 1 acre 8 April 1751, and 22 acres 21 Nov. 1752. To his son Eliphalet: 20 acres 22 Dec. 1744, 4 acres 28 Feb. 1752, 23 acres 14 May 1752, and 23 acres 21 Nov. 1752. To his son Solomon: 20 acres 26 July 1749 and 15 acres 21 Nov. 1752. And to his son Samuel: 3 acres 11 Dec. 1752.

The will of Winslow Tracy of Norwich "of great age" dated 26 Nov. 1767, sworn 2 Feb. 1768, names wife Rachel and sons Eliphalet, Samuel, Nehemiah, Perez, Josiah, and Solomon.

Children of Winslow and Rachel (Ripley) Tracy, b. Norwich, Conn.:

	i	JOSHUA TRACY[5], b. 19 June 1715; d. 13 Dec. 1715
281	ii	PEREZ TRACY, b. 13 Nov. 1716
282	iii	JOSIAH TRACY, b. 10 May 1718
283	iv	ELIPHALET TRACY, b. 14 Nov. 1720
284	v	NEHEMIAH TRACY, b. 18 March 1722
	vi	SAMUEL TRACY, b. 5 Dec. 1724; d. 1774; unm.
285	vii	SOLOMON TRACY, b. 23 May 1728

References: Norwich CT VR 1:8(b. Winslow), 25(m.; b. ch.). *Bradford Desc* p. 23. Norwich CT PR #10856(Winslow Tracy). Hale Cem Coll:Franklin p. 63(d. Winslow). Norwich CT LR 9:317-8; 10:330; 12:16, 22, 34-5, 137, 353-5(Winslow to his sons). New London CT PR #5348(John Tracy).

55. LEAH RIPLEY[4] (*Hannah³ Bradford, William²⁻¹*), b. Windham, Conn., 17 April 1693; d. there 28 April 1775.

She m. (1) Windham 14 March 1716 **SAMUEL COOK**, b. Newton 3 Dec. 1690; d. Windham, Conn., 27 Aug. 1745; son of Stephen and Rebecca (Flagg) Cook.

She m. (2) Scotland, Conn., 9 Nov. 1752 **JAMES BRADFORD**, b. Norwich, Conn., 24 March 1689; d. Canterbury, Conn., 26 March 1762; son of

Thomas and Anna (Raymond) Bradford, a descendant of Pilgrim **William Bradford** (see #32). He m. (1) ca. 1711 EDITH ADAMS with whom he had Thomas, John, Jerusha, William, & Sarah. He m. (2) Canterbury, Conn., 7 Dec. 1724 SUSANNA ADAMS with whom he had Ann, Mary, and James.

The will of Samuel Cook of Windham dated 17 Aug. 1741, proved 11 Sept. 1745, names wife Leah; eldest daughter Rebeckah; daughters Jerusha, Welthean, and Mary; sons Samuel and Phineas; and wife's brother Hezekiah Ripley.

On 13 Sept. 1748 Samuel Cook, son of Samuel Cook, chose Mrs. Leah Cook to be his guardian. Phineas Cook chose Leah Cook his guardian 5 Feb. 1750/1.

On 26 June 1755 Samuel Cook of Windham sold to Joseph Allen of Windham part of a farm partly in Windham and partly in Canterbury that his father Samuel Cook willed to "me and my brother Phineas Cook," excepting the widow Leah's thirds.

On 8 Oct. 1757 James Bradford and his wife Leah for love and affection gave to Phineas Cook of Newtown, Mass., son of Samuel Cook late of Windham and of Leah, their right in the lands of Samuel Cook partly in Windham and partly in Canterbury.

The will of Leah Bradford of Windham dated 9 Sept. 1772, sworn 8 May 1775, mentions daughters of eldest daughter; granddaughter Jerusha Wheat; daughter Welthy Pardy; daughter Mary Manning; Samuel, Sibble and Leah children of son Samuel Cook deceased; and son Phineas Cook.

Children of Samuel and Leah (Ripley) Cook, b. Windham, Conn.:

	i	PHINEAS COOK[5], b. 6 Dec. 1716; d. Windham, Conn., 22 Jan. 1728/9
286	ii	REBECCA COOK, b. 26 Nov. 1718
287	iii	JERUSHA COOK, b. 20 Feb. 1721/2
	iv	MARY COOK, b. 31 Aug. 1723; d.y.
288	v	WELTHEAN COOK, b. 20 Aug. 1724
289	vi	MARY COOK, b. 25 July 1729
	vii	DANIEL COOK, b. 25 Aug. 1732; d. before 17 Aug. 1741 (not in will)
290	viii	SAMUEL COOK, b. 8 Oct. 1734
291	ix	PHINEAS COOK, b. 7 June 1736

References: *VR Newton* p. 43(b. Sam.). *Bradford Desc* pp. 23-4. Windham CT VR 1:38(m.; b. 4 ch.), 105(b. 3 ch.). Canterbury CT VR 1:96(d. James). Windham CT PR 3:231 (Samuel Cook); Special 2:195, 274(gdns.). Windham CT LR L:306(Samuel Cook); M:85(James Bradford).

56. HEZEKIAH RIPLEY[4] (*Hannah*[3] *Bradford, William*[2-1]), b. Windham, Conn., 10 June 1695; d. there 7 Feb. 1779 aged 83 yrs.

He m. (1) Windham, Conn., 16 Oct. 1740 **MIRIAM FITCH**, b. Windham, Conn., 17 Oct. 1699; d. there 19 Dec. 1744; daughter of John and Elizabeth (Waterman) Fitch. The will of John Fitch of Windham, Conn., dated 19 June 1741 names wife Elizabeth and daughter Miriam (without surname).

He m. (2) Windham, Conn., 25 Nov. 1746 **MARY SKINNER**, b. and bp. Hartford, Conn., 28 May 1704; d. Windham, Conn., 17 Nov. 1787 in 84th yr.; daughter of John and Rachel (Pratt) Skinner. The will of John Skinner of Hartford, written 19 Sept. 1741, proved 16 Jan. 1743/4, names daughter Mary Skinner, and Mary is mentioned also in the codicil written 6 Feb. 1742/3.

On 24 May 1731 Joshua Ripley Jr. of Windham sold to Hezekiah Ripley and Thomas Dyer of Windham the dwelling house Joshua was dwelling in with all utensels, iron, brass, puter, household stuff both beds and beding, chests, trunks, "Chars" and tables, all white ware, one yearling Colt, a red one, and a black one with a white face.

On 20 July 1738 Joshua Ripley of Windham gave his son Hezekiah Ripley of Windham his homelot with 21 acres with housing and buildings except what is reserved for his daughter Jerusha and 6 other parcels of land.

No Windham, Conn., probate records were found for Hezekiah Ripley.

Child of Hezekiah and second wife Mary (Skinner) Ripley, b. Windham, Conn.:

292   ﹣   i HEZEKIAH RIPLEY[5], b. 25 Sept. 1748

References: *Bradford Desc* p. 24. Windham CT VR 1:205(b. Miriam), 256(d. Miriam), 262(2nd m.; b. ch.; d. Hezekiah, Mary). *Waterman Gen* 1:50, 629. Windham CT PR 3:11-3(John Fitch). Hale Cem Coll:Windham p. 284(g.s. Hezekiah, Mary). *NEHGR* 71:204(d. Hezekiah). *Hartford CT First Ch* 1:180, 248. Hartford CT PR #4894(John Skinner). *Skinner Kinsmen* pp. 19-24(b. Mary). Windham CT LR G:143, 544(Joshua Ripley).

57. DAVID RIPLEY[4] (*Hannah*[3] *Bradford, William*[2-1]), b. Windham, Conn., 20 May 1697; d. there 16 Feb. 1781 aged 83.

He m. Windham, Conn., 21 March 1720 **LYDIA CARY**, b. Bristol 12 Feb. 1705/6; d. Windham, Conn., 7 April 1784 aged 78; daughter of Eleazer and Lydia (Throope) Cary. The will of Eleazer Cary of Windham dated 6 March 1752, proved 17 Aug. 1754, names his daughter Lydia Ripley.

On 5 Oct. 1754 David Ripley, Lydia Ripley and the other heirs of Deacon Eleazer Cary quitclaimed their rights to two tracts in Windham, Conn.

On 10 June 1757 David Ripley of Windham gave 40 acres in Windham to son William Ripley. On 11 May 1760 he gave to son William 50 more acres. On 7 May 1762 William sold to David Ripley 40 acres, "part of the land which my father gave me and part of the house in which he now dwells."

On 5 Jan. 1779 David Ripley sold 60 acres in Windham to son Gamaliel Ripley of Windham.

On 25 Oct. 1779 David Ripley of Windham sold to Job, a negro man, of Canterbury, one mulato girl named Silvia for the term of her natural life.

The will of David Ripley of Windham dated 8 Jan. 1779, recorded 17 March 1781, names wife Lydia; sons Gamaliel, David, William, and Hezekiah; daughters Faith, Lydia, Anne, Irene, and Hannah; and grandson Elisha Lord, son of deceased daughter Alathea.

Children of David and Lydia (Cary) Ripley, b. Windham, Conn.:

293	i	FAITH RIPLEY[5], b. 1 May 1722
294	ii	LYDIA RIPLEY, b. 20 Feb. 1723/4
295	iii	ANN RIPLEY, b. 24 Aug. 1726
296	iv	IRENE RIPLEY, b. 11 Feb. 1728/9
297	v	DAVID RIPLEY, b. 7 Feb. 1730/1
298	vi	WILLIAM RIPLEY, b. 12 July 1734
	vii	GAMALIEL RIPLEY, b. 19 April 1736; d. 30 May 1737
299	viii	ALETHEA RIPLEY, b. 24 April 1738
300	ix	GAMALIEL RIPLEY, b. 20 Oct. 1740
301	x	HEZEKIAH RIPLEY, b. 3 Feb. 1743
	xi	BRADFORD RIPLEY, b. 26 Feb. 1744; d. at sea 1775; unm.? No probate, cemetery or church record of his death
302	xii	HANNAH RIPLEY, b. 27 Feb. 1750

References: *Bradford Desc* p. 24. *RIVR* Bristol 6:1:68(b. Lydia). Windham CT VR A:16(m.); 1:61(b. 7 ch.), 66(d. Gamaliel), 149(b. 3 ch.), 248(b. last 2 ch.; d. David). Windham CT PR #669(Eleazer Cary); 10:377(David Ripley). Hale Cem Coll:Windham p. 17(d. David, Lydia). Windham CT LR L:287(to son William); L:318(heirs of Eleazer Cary); M:208 (William Ripley); N:74(to son William Ripley); Q:293(to son Gamaliel); P:556(Silvia to Job).

58. IRENA RIPLEY[4] (*Hannah[3] Bradford, William[2-1]*), b. Windham, Conn., 28 Aug. 1700; d. there 20 Jan. 1726/7.

She m. Windham, Conn., 20 April 1719 **SAMUEL MANNING**, b. Billerica 14 Jan. 1690/1; d. Windham, Conn., 3 June 1727; son of Samuel and

Deborah (Spaulding) Manning. The will of Samuel Manning of Windham dated 2 March 1750, proved 3 March 1755, names his two grandchildren Josiah and Hezekiah Manning the two eldest sons of his son Samuel Manning deceased to whom he left his whole farm. Josiah was to pay legacies to his sisters Abigail Welch and Sarah Tracy; and Hezekaih was to pay legacies to his brothers Samuel and David. Receipts were signed by Eliphalet and Sarah Tracy and John and Abigail Welch.

On 6 March 1749/50 Samuel Manning of Windham for love and affection gave to Hezekiah Manning and Josiah Manning of Windham all his farm "on which he now lives."

The inventory of the estate of Samuel Manning of Windham was dated 14 June 1728. A distribution dated 14 Jan. 1727/8, approved 3 July 1729, names Abigail, Sarah, Josiah, Hezekiah, Samuel, and David Manning. On 3 July 1729 Samuel Manning of Windham filed bond as guardian of Josiah, son of Samuel Manning, deceased.

Children of Samuel and Irena (Ripley) Manning, b. Windham, Conn.:

303	i	JOSIAH MANNING[5], b. 18 March 1720
304	ii	HEZEKIAH MANNING, b. 8 Aug. 1721
305	iii	ABIGAIL MANNING, b. 25 Nov. 1722
306	iv	SARAH MANNING, b. 22 Feb. 1723/4
307	v	SAMUEL MANNING, b. 22 Oct. 1725
308	vi	DAVID MANNING, b. 14 Jan. 1726/7

References: *Bradford Desc* pp. 24-5. *VR Billerica* p. 131(b. Sam.). Windham CT VR 1:3(m.; b. Josiah, Hezekiah, Abigail, Samuel), 77(b. Sarah, David; d. Irena, Samuel). Windham CT PR #2626(Samuel Manning); 1:194, 307, 309(Samuel Manning). Windham CT LR I:402(Samuel Manning).

59. JERUSHA RIPLEY[4] (*Hannah³ Bradford, William²⁻¹*), b. Windham, Conn., 1 Nov. 1704; d. there 8 Nov. 1792 in 88th yr.

She m. Windham, Conn., 9 Sept. 1744 **EDWARD BROWN**, d. Windham, Conn., 28 July 1791.

She is apparently the Jerusha Ripley who sued Elias Frink on 4 May 1731 because she was pregnant. In 1732 Elias Frink had to pay the town of Windham, Conn., for the child's maintenance.

On 29 April 1771 Edward Brown of Windham sold Hubbard Brown of Windham one-quarter of an acre with a dwelling house. On 23 May 1771 Hubbard sold the land and house back to Edward.

The will of Edward Brown of Windham dated 3 June 1785, sworn 19 Aug. 1791, names wife Jerusha; son Hubbard Brown "if he become a free inhabitant or citizen of the United States"; otherwise his share to friends Hezekiah Manning Esq., Major John Ripley, and Mr. Hezekiah Ripley.

Child (surname unknown), b. Windham, Conn.:

    i [CHILD] RIPLEY / FRINK[6], b. 1731

Child of Edward and Jerusha (Ripley) Brown, b. Windham, Conn.:

    ii HUBBARD BROWN[6], b. 11 Dec. 1745; living 3 June 1785

References: Windham CT VR A:253(m.; deaths; b. Hubbard).   Windham CT PR #521(Edward Brown). Windham Co. CT Court Rec. Vol. 2(bastard child). Windham CT LR O:212(Edward Brown); P:19(Hubbard Brown).

60.   ANNA RIPLEY[4] (*Hannah[3] Bradford, William[2-1]*), b. Windham, Conn., 1 Nov. 1704; d. before 17 Feb. 1747 (2nd m.).

She m. probably at Windham, Conn., ca. 1730 **SOLOMON WHEAT**, d. before 24 Oct. 1797; son of Samuel and Lydia (_____) Wheat. He m. (2) Windham, Conn., 17 Feb. 1747 MARGARET GREEN with whom he had Elizabeth and Solomon.

Solomon and Anna's six children were baptized at six different churches, an indication of the family's frequent moves.

On 4 April 1745 Solomon Wheat of Windham sold to his brother Benjamin Wheat of Norwich a 100-acre lot.

On 10 March 1753 Solomon Wheat of Mendon, physician, bought a homelot with buildings in Uxbridge. On 13 March 1754 Dr. Solomon Wheat of Uxbridge sold land in Mendon. On 4 Aug. 1755 Solomon Wheat of Uxbridge sold 50 acres in Windham, Conn. On 8 Jan. 1759 Solomon Wheat of Uxbridge sold the home place where he was living with 60 acres and another piece of land in Uxbridge; [second] wife Margaret also signed the deed.

On 24 Aug. 1767 Solomon Wheat of Needham, physician, purchased 10 acres and a house in Westford from Eleazer Taylor. He sold this land on 6 Feb. 1771 to Isaac Underwood.

Solomon Wheat was last taxed in Westford on 11 Nov. 1774.

On 24 Oct. 1797 Solomon Wheat of Chatham, Middlesex Co., Conn., clerk, sold to Daniel Goodhue of Westford "4 acres with an old dwelling house which my honoured father Solomon Wheat lately owned."

No probate records were found for Solomon Wheat in Suffolk, Middlesex, or Worcester counties.

Children of Solomon and Anna (Ripley) Wheat:

309   i   SARAH WHEAT[5], bp. Windham, Conn., 3 Oct. 1731

       ii SOLOMON WHEAT, bp. Canterbury, Conn., 19 Dec. 1731; d.y.

310   iii MARY WHEAT, bp. Old Lyme, Conn., 1 July 1733

311   iv ANNA WHEAT, b. Windham, Conn., 8 July 1736; bp. Scotland, Conn., 11 July 1736 as "Janna"

312   v   HANNAH WHEAT, b. Windham, Conn., 16 July 1738; bp. Hampton, Conn., 3 Sept. 1738

313   vi JEMIMA WHEAT, bp. Ashford, Conn., 28 July 1740

References: Windham CT VR 1:21(b. Anna, Hannah, Eliz.). *CT Marr* 4:171(2nd m.). Windham Ch Rec p. 18(bp. Sarah). *Bradford Desc* p. 25. Middlesex Co. LR 71:249(from Eleazer Taylor), 250 (Solomon Wheat); 126:444(Solomon Wheat). Westford Tax Lists 1:414. *Wheat Genealogy*, Silas C. Wheat, Brooklyn NY, 1903, pp. 59-61. Windham CT LR H:388; L:316(Solomon Wheat). Worcester Co. LR 34:270-1; 42:365(Solomon Wheat).

61. BETHIA STEELE[4] (*Melatiah[3] Bradford, William[2-1]*), b. Hartford, Conn., ca. 1690; d. by 1731.

She m. Hartford, Conn., 17 May 1709 **SAMUEL SHEPERD**, b. Hartford, Conn., 2 Feb. 1682/3; d. there 5 June 1750; son of John and Hannah (Peck) Sheperd. He m. (2) by 1731 and probably by 1721 EUNICE BUTLER with whom he probably had Bethiah, Hannah, Sarah, Samuel, Stephen, William, and Amos. The will of John Shepherd of Hartford dated 1 Aug. 1728, proved 6 April 1736, names his son Samuel and grandson John "the eldest son of my son Samuel."

On 20 July 1712 Samuel Shepard was admitted to full communion with the Hartford Second Church. His wife Bethiah was admitted on 20 July 1712.

On 2 March 1735/6 Samuel Shepherd signed a receipt for his wife's share of the estate of her father Joseph Butler.

On 16 May 1735 Ebenezer Steel, John Shepard 2d, and James Shepard, all of Hartford quitclaimed to Jonathan Steel their interests in the estate of James Steel. (This deed suggests that John and James were the only living descendants of Bethia.)

On 5 Nov. 1740 Samuel Shepherd of Hartford gave to his son James Shepherd of Hartford three acres reserving to Samuel two acres for his use during his life and if his wife Eunice should survive him, James shall pay her one-third of the yearly value. On 17 Dec. 1745 Samuel sold James one-half of a lot lying undivided with the heirs of John Shepherd.

The inventory of the estate of Samuel Shepherd of Hartford dated 31 July 1750, says he died 5 June 1750; on the front of the inventory is written, "Samuel Sheperd of Hartford son of John Sheperd, of the same town, and grandson of Sargeant John Shepard." The 13 Dec. 1740 distribution of the estate mentions the widow; son Samuel; eldest son John; sons James, William, and Amos Sheperd; and daughters Hannah and Sarah Shepherd.

Children of Samuel and Bethia (Steele) Sheperd, b. Hartford, Conn.:

314   i   JOHN SHEPERD[5], b. 28 April 1710, bp. Second Ch. 30 April 1710
315   ii JAMES SHEPERD, b. 27 April 1714, bp. Second Ch. 2 May 1714
       iii BETHIA SHEPERD, bp. First Ch. 23 Oct. 1720; not in distrib. of father's estate

Note: *Bradford Desc* gives Bethiah nine children. This is apparently in error as Jacobus (*Hale-House* p. 259) says Eunice was prob. the mother of seven of them. Apparently there is a document showing she was married to Samuel Sheperd in 1731 and Jacobus says prob. by 1721. The question is: which wife was the mother of Bethia?

References: *Bradford Desc* p. 25. *Hale House* p. 259. *Hartford By Barbour* pp. 523-4. Hartford CT VR D:32(m.); FFS:47(b. Samuel); FFS:60(b. John, James). *Manwaring* 3:642 (Samuel's est.). Hartford CT LR 5:675(Ebenezer Steel *et al.*); 8:53, 66(Samuel Shepherd). Hartford CT PR 12:349(Joseph Butler); #4850(John Shepherd; #4857(Samuel Shepherd). *Hartford CT Second Ch* (bp. John & James).

62. EBENEZER STEELE[4] (*Melatiah[3] Bradford, William[2-1]*), b. Killingworth, Conn., 13 Aug. 1695; d. Hartford, Conn., between 26 Dec. 1745 and 3 March 1746/7.

He m. ca. 1717 **SUSANNAH MERRILL**, b. Hartford, Conn., 18 Aug. 1700; living 3 March 1746/7; daughter of Daniel and Susanna (Pratt) Merrill. The will of Daniel Merrells of Hartford dated 26 Dec. 1745 names daughter Susanna Steele and her children viz.: John, Mary, Daniel, Susannah, Hulda, Meletiah, Bradford, and Elisha.

The will of Ebenezer Steele of Hartford dated 26 June 1745, proved 3 March 1746/7, names wife Susanna; sons John, Daniel, Bradford, and Elisha; and daughters Mary, Susannah, Huldah, and Malatiah (without surnames).

Children of Ebenezer and Susannah (Merrill) Steele, b. prob. Hartford, Conn.:

316   i   JOHN STEELE[5], bp. 22 Feb. 1718/9

317   ii   MARY STEELE, bp. 1 Jan. 1721

318   iii SUSANNA STEELE, bp. 30 June 1728

        iv   DANIEL STEELE living 26 Dec. 1745 (grandfather's will)

319   v   HULDAH STEELE, bp. 8 March 1729/30

        vi   MELETIAH STEELE, bp. 19 March 1731/2; d. Hartford, Conn., 22
             April 1760 ae 28; unm.

320   vii BRADFORD STEELE, bp. 22 Sept. 1734

321   viii ELISHA STEELE, b. ca. 1737

References: *Bradford Desc* p. 25.   *Hartford By Barbour* p. 580.   *Manwaring* 3:595-6(Daniel
Merrill), 655(Ebenezer Steele).   Hartford CT PR #5176(Ebenezer Steel).   Hartford CT
VR FFS:44(b. Susannah).   *Hartford CT Second Ch* pp. 324(bp. John, Mary), 328(bp.
Susanna), 329(bp. Huldah).   West Hartford CT Ch. Rec. 1:57(bp. Bradford).

63. ELIZABETH STEVENS[4] (*Melatiah*[3] *Bradford, William*[2-1]), b. Guilford,
Conn., ca. 1703; d. New Haven, Conn., 25 Aug. 1744 aged 42.

She m. Killingworth, Conn., 30 Aug. 1724 **JOHN HUBBARD**, b.
Jamaica, Long Island, N.Y., 30 Nov. 1703; d. New Haven, Conn., 30 Oct.
1773 aged 70; son of John and Mable (Russel) Hubbard. He m. (2) New
Haven, Conn., 13 Sept. 1745 MARY (DICKERMAN) TODD. He m. (3) New
Haven, Conn., 10 Nov. 1761 MARY (_____) STEVENS.

On 3 March 1724/5 Samuel Steevens, John and Elizabeth Hubbard, and
Samuel and Mary Willcocks Jr. all of Killingworth sold to their brother John
Steevens their right in the 132nd lot in the 8th division laid out in the right of
their father Samuel Steevens.

On 5 Feb. 1759 John Hubbard of New Haven sold to his son Daniel
Hubbard of New Haven half of a house and one and a half acres.

On 3 April 1765 John Hubbard of New Haven sold to his son Leverett
Hubbard of New Haven 19½ acres.

The inventory of the estate of John Hubbard Esq. of New Haven, Conn.,
was taken 30 April 1774.

On 4 Jan. 1791 John Hubbard of Hamden, Conn., and Isaac Hubbard of
Wallingford, Conn., sold to their uncle Col. Leveret Hubbard of New Haven
several pieces of land which were the estate of their grandfather Col. John
Hubbard late of New Haven.

Children of John and Elizabeth (Stevens) Hubbard, b. New Haven, Conn.,
except Leverrett:

322   i   LEVERRETT HUBBARD[5], b. Killingworth, Conn., 21 July 1725

323   ii JOHN HUBBARD, b. 24 Jan. 1727/8

324   iii DANIEL HUBBARD, b. 24 Dec. 1729

325   iv ELIZABETH HUBBARD, b. 3 July 1731

        v WILLIAM HUBBARD, b. 20 March 1732/3; d. 14 Nov. 1736 ae 4

326   vi WILLIAM ABDIEL HUBBARD, b. 15 Dec. 1736

        vii NATHANIEL HUBBARD, bp. 12 Nov. 1738; d. Havana, Cuba 30 Sept. 1762 ae 23

327   viii AMELIA HUBBARD, bp. 24 Oct. 1742

References: *New Haven Fams* 4:864-5. Killingworth CT VR 2:188 (b. Leverett), 193(1st m.). New Haven CT VR 1:357(b. John, Daniel), 368(b. Eliz.), 380(b. Wm.), 545(2nd m.), 594(b. Wm. Abdiel); 2:160(3rd m.). New Haven CT PR #5511(John Hubbard). *Bradford Desc* p. 105(d. Nath.). *Boston News Obits* 2:548 (d. John), 549(d. Nath.). Hale Cem Coll:New Haven p. 403(Elizabeth Hubbard). New Haven CT LR 22:67(John Hubbard); 27:131(John Hubbard); 44:192(John & Isaac Hubbard). Killingworth CT LR 3:174(Samuel Steevens).

64. WILLIAM STEVENS[4] (*Melatiah*[3] *Bradford, William*[2-1]), b. Killingworth, Conn., 2 Feb. 1705/6; d. before 3 Sept. 1751 (inv.).

He m. Killingworth, Conn., 26 Aug. 1734 **RUHAMAH EARL**, who apparently d. before 1751.

On 29 Nov. 1737 William Steevens of Killingworth sold to his brother Samuel Steevens of Killingworth four acres.

On 29 Aug. 1751 Samuel Steevens 2nd of Killingworth, Conn., was appointed administrator of the estate of William Steevens of Killingworth. The division of 21 Nov. 1753 names Ruhamah, William, Christopher, John, Leverett, and Moses Steevens.

Children of William and Ruhamah (Earl) Stevens, b. Killingworth, Conn.:

        i RUHAMAH[5] STEVENS, b. 20 April 1735; living 15 Jan. 1754 (receipt)

328   ii WILLIAM STEVENS, b. 1 Sept. 1736

329   iii CHRISTOPHER STEVENS, b. 13 Sept. 1738

        iv JOHN STEVENS, b. 4 Aug. 1740. On 2 June 1770 he was a resident of Guadeloupe in the West Indies when his brother Leverett leased his land to Theophilus Morgan.

330   v LEVERETT STEVENS, b. 19 Sept. 1742

        vi MOSES STEVENS, b. 30 Aug. 1747; d. before 9 March 1762 (deed)

References: *NEHGR* 129:18-20. Killingworth CT VR 2:160(b. ch.), 191(m.). Guilford CT PR 4:716; 5:118, 337; 6:71(William Steevens). *Steevens Desc* pp. 130, 196-7. Killingworth CT VR 6:122(William Steevens).

65. HANNAH⁴ BRADFORD (*Samuel³, William²⁻¹*), b. Plymouth 14 Feb. 1689/90; d. Berkley 28 Jan. 1772 in 82nd yr.

She m. Duxbury 16 June 1709 **NATHANIEL GILBERT**, b. Taunton 19 July 1683; d. Berkley 17 Aug. 1765 in 83rd yr.; son of Thomas and Hannah (Blake) Gilbert.

On 27 March 1705 Thomas Gilbert of Taunton deeded to son Nathaniel Gilbert of Taunton a tract of land in Taunton. On 22 March 1720/1 he gave another four parcels of land to his son Nathaniel.

On 27 Nov. 1731 Nathaniel Gilbert of Taunton, yeoman, sold to his mother Hannah Bradford, widow, late of Duxbury now of Taunton, two acres with one-fourth of a house where his father Thomas Gilbert late of Taunton dwelled.

On 17 Sept. 1736 Nathaniel Gilbert of Berkley, gentleman, deeded to son Thomas Gilbert of Berkley, husbandman, the westerly part of his homestead lying part in Taunton and part in Berkley; wife Hannah also signed. Thomas Gilbert (with wife Mary signing) deeded it back to his father 25 Dec. 1740. On 28 Feb. 1745 Nathaniel gave to his son Thomas 100 acres of his farm; wife Hannah also signed. On 1 Dec. 1749 Nathaniel gave to his son Thomas 150 acres of his farm with the dwelling house where Nathaniel was living, together with a parcel that was granted to his father Thomas Gilbert deceased. On the same day Thomas sold to his father Nathaniel 88 acres. And finally on 15 April 1763 Nathaniel of Berkley gave to his son Thomas of Freetown 20 acres with a dwelling house.

On 26 Nov. 1746 Nathaniel Gilbert of Berkley, Gentleman, deeded four acres in Taunton to daughter Hannah Smith of Taunton, widow of Ebenezer Smith.

On 28 Feb. 1745/6 Nathaniel Gilbert deeded land and a house in Taunton to son Nathaniel Gilbert.

On 30 July 1752 Nathaniel Gilbert deeded 134 acres in Norton to son Samuel Gilbert of Berkley.

The will of Nathaniel Gilbert of Berkley, gentleman, advanced to old age, dated 2 June 1757, proved 11 Sept. 1765, names wife Hannah; eldest son Thomas; father Mr. Thomas Gilbert; grandson Nathaniel Gilbert, son of son Nathaniel late of Taunton deceased; grandson George Gilbert; son Samuel Gilbert to have my mansion house in Berkley; children of late daughter

Hannah Smith wife of Ebenezer deceased: Lemuel, John, Ebenezer, and Mary Smith; Sibel wife of Doget [sic] my granddaughter; Hannah and Abigail, daughters of my daughter Hannah; daughter Mary Godfrey of Norton; and daughter Welthia Hathaway wife of Ebenezer Jr.; sons Thomas and Samuel to be administrators. He mentions "land in Taunton where I have buried two of my daughters."

On 13 July 1759 Nathaniel Gilbert of Berkley, Gentleman, and wife Hannah deeded to children James Godfrey of Norton and wife Mary one-quarter of a house and lot in Boston given to Hannah by her mother Hannah Bradford. On 30 Dec. 1760 James and Mary Godfrey sold this property to Martin Gay of Boston.

On 13 July 1759 Nathaniel Gilbert and wife Hannah deeded to children Ebenezer Hathaway of Freetown and wife Welthean one-quarter of a tract of land in Kingston devised to Hannah by her mother Hannah Bradford.

Children of Nathanial and Hannah (Bradford) Gilbert, b. prob. Taunton:

331   i   HANNAH GILBERT[5], b. 5 Feb. 1711/12

332   ii THOMAS GILBERT, b. 25 Nov. 1714

333   iii MARY GILBERT, b. 21 May 1717

334   iv NATHANIEL GILBERT, b. 1719

335   v   SAMUEL GILBERT, b. ca. 1723 (based on age at d.)

336   vi WELTHIA GILBERT, b. ca. 1725

         vii ABIGAIL GILBERT, b. ca. 1727; d. 17 Sept. 1747 in 20th yr.

References: *MD* 11:23(m.); 21:117-120(will). *VR Duxbury* p. 258(m.). *VR Taunton* 1:176(b. Nath.); 3:87(d. Hannah, Abigail), 88(d. Nathaniel). *MF* 19:149-50. George G. Gilbert *et al.*, *Gilberts of NE* pp. 84-7(b. dates of 1st 4 ch.). Suffolk Co. LR 95:196(Nath. Gilbert), 198(James Godfrey). Plymouth Co. LR 50:29(Nath. Gilbert). Bristol Co. LR 5:46, 48(Thomas Gilbert); 13:554(Thomas Gilbert); 20:76; 25:148; 36:512; 37:130(Nath. Gilbert); 30:241(Thomas Gilbert); 36:403, 530; 37:130(Nathaniel Gilbert), 211(Thomas Gilbert); 41:312(Nathaniel Gilbert); 47:69 (Nathaniel Gilbert).

66. GERSHOM[4] BRADFORD (*Samuel[3], William[2-1]*), b. Plymouth 21 Dec. 1691; d. Bristol, R.I., 4 April 1757 aged 66.

He m. Plymouth 23 Oct. 1716 **PRISCILLA WISWALL**, b. Duxbury 25 July 1690; d. Bristol, R.I., 12 Sept. 1780 in 90th yr.; daughter of Ichabod and Priscilla (Pabodie) Wiswall, a descendant of Pilgrim **John Alden**.

At a town meeting on 7 March 1714/5 Girsham Bradford was chosen as a surveyor of highways and on 28 March 1720 as a fence viewer.

Court records show he was living in Plymouth as late as March 1722/3, but in Kingston by December 1729.

On 30 June 1747 Gershom Bradford of Kingston, Gentleman, sold John Faunce of Kingston, yeoman, several pieces of land with "liberty to Cart from said swamp as was given me from my Honoured Father Samuel Bradford deceased"; Priscilla also signed the deed. On 28 Sept. 1749 Gershom Bradford of Bristol deeded land to son Daniel Bradford of Bristol.

On 25 Nov. 1754 Gershom Bradford of Bristol, Gentleman, sold to Peter Lane of Hingham, executor of the will of his mother Hannah Bradford, 20 acres out of 100 acres given Gershom by his father Samuel Bradford and then sold by Gershom to his grandfather John Rogers who gave it to Hannah. On the same day Gershom in exchange for 16 acres from Hannah's estate sold to Peter Lane 10 acres to be subjected to a division among Hannah's daughters.

On 2 May 1757 Daniel Bradford was appointed administrator of the estate of his father Capt. Gershom Bradford late of Bristol deceased.

Plymouth County land records show that a meadow in Plympton, once owned by Samuel Bradford and then belonging to heirs of Gershom Bradford of Bristol, R.I., Gentleman, deceased, was divided into eight parts with four of his children selling their shares: Alexander Bradford of Stonington, Conn., Gentleman, sold his share 4 Nov. 1763; Solomon Bradford of Bristol, R.I., laborer, sold his share to Joseph Nash 2 July 1762; Daniel Bradford of Bristol Esq. sold his to Joseph Nash 25 May 1769; and Joseph Nash of Providence, R.I., and wife Hopestill sold half a lot (4 shares) of land that was their father's Capt. Gershom Bradford of Bristol on 9 June 1763.

On 23 Sept. 1791 William Bowes Bradford and Joseph Nash Bradford sold to John Faunce of Kingston the 1/8 share of the Jones River Meadow that had in turn belonged to Samuel Bradford, Gershom Bradford, and their deceased father Job Bradford of Boston.

Children of Gershom and Priscilla (Wiswall) Bradford, b. Plymouth and Kingston:

337   i   PRISCILLA[5] BRADFORD, b. 31 Jan. 1717/8 (g.s.)

338   ii DANIEL BRADFORD, b. ca. 1721 (based on age at d.)

339   iii NOAH BRADFORD

340   iv JOB BRADFORD, b. ca. 1725

341   v ALEXANDER BRADFORD, b. 26 Oct. 1726

342   vi SOLOMON BRADFORD, b. ca. 1728 (based on age at d.)

343   vii HOPESTILL BRADFORD

344   viii JEREMIAH BRADFORD

Note: Proof is needed for Priscilla, Noah and Jeremiah. No proof has been found for purported children Rachel and Eliphalet. Eliphalet is apparently the son of #27 William Bradford.

References: *RIVR* Bristol 6:1:119(d. yr. & ae wrong). *MF* 19:150-1. *MD* 14:38(m.); 19:1(Wiswall data). *Plymouth Co Ct Recs* 5:151, 302. *NEHGR* 101:296-307; 110:44-50. Bristol RI PR 1:243, 247(Gershom Bradford). Plymouth Co. LR 39:21; 46:166(Gershom Bradford); 48:166(Solomon & Daniel Bradford, Jos. Nash); 49:34(Alex. Bradford; Solomon & Daniel Bradford & Jos. Nash); 72:185(William Bowes Bradford *et al.*). Bristol RI LE 1:176(to David Bradford). *Plymouth VR* p. 91(m.). Island Cemetery, Newport RI(g.s. daughter Priscilla). *MF* 16:1:216-20. *Plymouth Town Recs* 2:102, 202 *et al.*

67. PEREZ⁴ BRADFORD (*Samuel³, William²⁻¹*), b. Plymouth 28 Dec. 1694; d. Attleboro 19 June 1746 in 52nd yr.

He m. Dedham 14 April 1720 **ABIGAIL BELCHER**, b. Dedham 22 Aug. 1695; d. Attleboro 15 Nov. 1746 in 52nd yr.; daughter of Joseph and Abigail (Thompson) Belcher. On 9 Jan. 1726 Perez Bradford, Gentleman, and his wife Abigail, with other heirs of Joseph Belcher sold Eleazer Dorby their right in a house and wharf that had come from an inheritance from Joseph Belcher's grandfather John Gill.

On 4 April 1720 Perez Bradford of Duxbury, yeoman, sold to Ephraim Bradford of Plymouth, yeoman, 45 acres of a 60-acre lot laid out to Samuel Bradford deceased and had been given by Samuel at his decease to Perez.

Perez Bradford graduated from Harvard in 1713 and received an M.A. in 1716. On 30 Oct. 1737 Perez Bradford was dismissed from the Milton Church and recommended to Rev. Turner's church in Rehoboth.

On 24 Nov. 1737 Perez Bradford of Swanzey sold to his brother Gamaliel Bradford of Duxbury land in Kingston.

The will of Perez Bradford of Attleboro Esq., dated 12 June 1746, proved 5 Aug. 1746, names wife Abigail; eldest son Perez under 21; sons Joel, George, John and Joseph; daughter Abigail Lee wife of Samuel Lee Jr.; and daughters Hannah, Elizabeth, and Mary Bradford. Wife Abigail was to be executrix.

On 24 Dec. 1746 Samuel Lee Jr. of Swansea, shipwright, and Hannah Bradford of Attleborough, spinster, were appointed administrators of the estate of their father Peres Bradford of Attleborough as widow Abigail Bradford was now deceased.

On 24 Dec. 1746 Gershom Bradford of Kingston was appointed guardian of Joel (a minor over 14). On 3 March 1746 Samuel Lee was appointed guardian of Perez (a minor over 14). On 7 June 1748 Gershom Bradford was appointed guardian of John and Joseph (both under 14). On 17 June 1748 Gershom Bradford of Bristol, R.I., was appointed guardian of George.

On 24 Oct. 1749 Jabez Gay and his wife Hannah of Attleboro, Mary Gould of Cumberland, R.I., Elizabeth Bradford, Perez Bradford, Joel Bradford, George Bradford, John Bradford, and Joseph Bradford all of Attleboro sold to Samuel Lee Jr. of Swanzey 11 acres in Swanzey "being the homestead on which Samuel Lee dwells with dwelling house and orchards from the estate of Perez Bradford deceased."

On 21 March 1750 Samuel Lee and his wife Abigail of Swanzey, Jabez Gay and his wife Hannah, Samuel Sweetland and his wife Elizabeth, Mary Gould widow, and Perez Bradford all of Attleboro, heirs of Perez Bradford, Esq., sold three pieces of land in Attleboro.

On 7 Aug. 1753 Samuel Lee and Hannah Gay, administrators of the estate of Perez Bradford, Esq. of Attleboro rendered an account. It included legacies to Hannah Gay and Elizabeth Sweetland. On 6 Oct. 1761 a second account was rendered which included payments to Samuel Lee ("my own part"), Jabez Gay, Samuel Sweetland, John Bradford, John Bradford for Joel Bradford, George Bradford, Joseph Bradford, and Mary Searle.

On 27 Feb. 1760 Jabez Gay and his wife Hannah of Attleboro and Samuel Sweetland and his wife Elizabeth of Marblehead sold 2/8 of the land their brother Joel Bradford died seized of to Noah Wood. John Bradford of Albany, N.Y., and Samuel Lea Jr. of Swanzey and his wife Abigail sold another 2/8 of Joel's land.

Children of Perez and Abigail (Belcher) Bradford, first b. Dedham, rest b. Swansea or bp. Milton:

345   i   ABIGAIL[5] BRADFORD, b. 15 May 1721

346   ii   MARY BRADFORD, b. ca. 1723 (based on age at d.)

347   iii   HANNAH BRADFORD, b. prob. Milton ca. 1724 (based on age at d.)

348   iv   ELIZABETH BRADFORD, b. prob. Milton ca. 1728

349   v   PEREZ BRADFORD, bp. Milton 5 Jan. 1728/9

      vi JOEL BRADFORD, bp. Milton 20 Sept. 1730; d. 1757 in Army unm.
On 23 Jan. 1758 John Bradford of Albany, N.Y., was appointed adm. of the est. of Joel Bradford of Attleboro, deceased

350   vii GEORGE BRADFORD, bp. Milton 22 Oct. 1732

351   viii JOHN BRADFORD, b. Swansea 25 Jan. 1734/5

352   ix JOSEPH BRADFORD, b. Swansea 13 June 1737

References: *Swansea VR* p. 93(b. John, Joseph). *Dedham VR* 1:26(b. wife Abigail); 3:19(m.). *Bradford Desc* p. 26. Bristol Co. PR 11:168-70, 229-30; 17:602-3(Perez Bradford); 11:230, 232-3, 475-7(gdns.); 15:528-9(Joel Bradford). *VR Attleboro* p. 640(deaths). *MF* 19:151-2. *Boston News Obits* 2:120(d. Perez). *Harvard Grads* 6:5-8. *RIVR* 14:257(d. Mary). *NEHGR* 23:261(bp. Perez, Joel), 446(bp. George); 24:47(dismissal to Rehoboth). Plymouth Co. LR 27:156; 31:171(Perez Bradford). Bristol Co. LR 41:278(Samuel Lee); 44:517-8(Joel's heirs); 48:368(Jabez Gay *et al.*). Suffolk Co. LR 40:297(heirs of Joseph Belcher).

68. ELIZABETH⁴ BRADFORD (*Samuel³, William²⁻¹*), b. Plymouth 15 Dec. 1696; d. Norwich or Stonington, Conn., 10 May 1777.

She m. (1) Hartford, Conn., 10 Jan. 1716/7 **CHARLES WHITING** (or **WHITON**), b. Hartford, Conn., 5 July 1692; d. New London, Conn., 7 March 1738; son of William and Mary (Allyn) Whiting.

She "of New London" m. (2) Stonington, Conn., 13 March 1739 **JOHN NOYES**, b. Stonington, Conn., 13 June 1685; d. there 17 Sept. 1751; son of James and Dorothy (Stanton) Noyes. He m. (1) Stonington, Conn., 16 March 1714/5 MARY GALLUP with whom he had William, John, Joseph, James, Mary, Sarah, Anna, and Joseph. The will of James Noyes of Stonington dated 12 Nov. 1716, proved 29 Jan. 1719/20, names his son John.

The first seven children were baptized at the Second Church of Hartford, Conn.

On 22 March 1730/1 Charles Whiting of Hartford quitclaimed his share of a tract in Hartford to John Whiting. On 29 March 1736 Charles Whiting and William Whiting quitclaimed land in Hartford to Daniel and Wolterton Morrell.

On 11 Dec. 1738 Elizabeth Whiting petitioned the court to appoint Joseph Bradford Jr. administrator of the estate of Charles Whiting late of New London deceased.

Proof that Elizabeth (Bradford) Whiting married a second husband named Noyes is found in a Plymouth County deed dated 9 Oct. 1780 in which the heirs of Elizabeth Noyes deceased sold land in Kingston that had been given to her and [her sisters] Jerusha Gay, Hannah Gilbert, and Wealthea Lane by their grandmother Hannah Bradford late of Hingham deceased These heirs were: Mary Gardner of Hingham; Gamaliel Whiting of Great Barrington; Sibel Noyes of Groton, Conn.; (heirs of John Whiting) James Houghton and wife Philena, Elizabeth Leffingwell, Mary Whiting, and James Woolf Whiting of Norwich; William B. Whiting of New Canaan, Albany County, N.Y.; Elizabeth Goodrich of Hebron, Conn; Honor Belding of Wethersfield, Conn., administratrix of Charles Whiting late of Norwich deceased; Ebenezer Whiting; and Dorothy Noyes of Norwich.

A Suffolk County probate record includes receipts dated 1787, where most of the above heirs of Elizabeth Noyes received payment for sale of land in that county given them under Hannah's will. Distribution was delayed until Martin Gay, a staunch Loyalist who left Boston for Nova Scotia in 1776, returned for a visit in 1787.

The will of John Noyes of Stonington dated 5 Aug. 1748, codicil dated Sept. 1751, sworn 30 Sept. 1751, names wife Elizabeth; sons William, John, James, and Joseph Noyes; daughters Mary Noyes, Sarah Stanton, Ann Noyes, and Dorothy Noyes. The daughters are named in the codicil.

Children of Charles and Elizabeth (Bradford) Whiting, first 7 b. Hartford, Conn.:

353	i	MARY WHITING[5], bp. 2 March 1717
354	ii	JOHN WHITING, b. 3 Aug. 1719
355	iii	SYBIL WHITING, bp. 29 July 1722
356	iv	CHARLES WHITING (twin), b. 1725; bp. 8 Aug. 1725
357	v	ELIZABETH WHITING (twin), b. 1725; bp. 8 Aug. 1725
358	vi	GAMALIEL WHITING, bp. 24 Sept. 1727
359	vii	WILLIAM BRADFORD WHITING, bp. 11 April 1731
? poss.	viii	BERNICE WHITING, b. 1733; d.y. (according to *MF* 2:262)
360	ix	EBENEZER WHITING, b. New London, Conn., 18 May 1735

Child of John and Elizabeth (Bradford) (Whiting) Noyes, b. Stonington, Conn.:

	x	DOROTHY NOYES, b. 24 March 1740; living unm. in 1790 when she was listed in the census of New London, Conn. No PR.

References: *Hartford By Barbour* pp. 677-9. *Stonington CT Hist* p. 489. *Montville CT Hist* pp. 715-6(d. Eliz.). Hartford CT VR D:19(b. Charles). Stonington CT VR 2:31(b. of 8 Noyes ch. by Mary); 3:97(2nd m.; d. John). New London CT PR #3839(James Noyes); #3841(John Noyes); #5691(Charles Whiting). Suffolk Co. PR #12505(Hannah Bradford). Plymouth Co. LR 60:112(Mary Gardner *et al.*). *MF* 19:152-4. *Hartford CT Second Ch* pp. 297(bp. ch.), 325(bp. John). Hartford CT LR 5:311(Charles Whiting); 6:59(Charles & William Whiting).

69. JERUSHA⁴ BRADFORD (*Samuel³*, *William²⁻¹*), b. Plymouth 10 March 1699; d. Hingham 19 Aug. 1783 aged 85 yrs.

She m. Duxbury 13 Nov. 1719, Rev. **EBENEZER GAY**, b. Dedham 15 Aug. 1696; d. Hingham 8 March 1787 in 91ˢᵗ yr.; son of Nathaniel and Lydia (Lusher) Gay.

Ebenezer Gay graduated from Harvard in 1714. He was minister of the Church of Christ in Hingham nearly 69 years, and has been called "father of American Unitarianism."

On 30 Sept. 1760 Ebenezer Gay and wife Jerusha sold to son Martin Gay of Boston her one-fourth interest in a Union St. property that had been devised to her by her mother Hannah Bradford.

On 21 March 1765 Ebenezer Gay of Hingham, clerk, and his wife Jerusha sold to John Adams land in Kingston formerly owned by Samuel Bradford.

The will of Ebenezer Gay of Hingham, clerk, dated 23 Oct. 1783, proved 1 May 1787, divides his estate among his four children: Martin Gay, Jotham Gay, Abigail Gay, and Jerusha Gay, with a bequest to granddaughter Christiana Jones. Bartholomew and Christiana Jones signed a receipt for their share at Wells [Maine?] 2 July 1789.

On 3 May 1790 Martin Gay, Esq., of Westmoreland, New Brunswick (now residing in Boston) sold to Jotham Gay of Hingham, Esq., his interest in one fourth part of the real estate given by Ebenezer Gay in his will equally to his four children, Martin, Jotham, Abigail, and Jerusha.

Children of Ebenezer and Jerusha (Bradford) Gay, b. Hingham:

    i   SAMUEL GAY⁵, b. 15 Jan. 1720/1; bur. St. Lukes, Chelsea, England, 21 March 1745/6

    ii ABIGAIL GAY, b. 8 Sept. 1722; d. Hingham 8 Feb. 1728/9 ae 6y 6m.

361   iii CALVIN GAY, b. 14 Sept. 1724.

362   iv MARTIN GAY, b. 29 Dec. 1726.

    v ABIGAIL GAY, b. 20 Aug. 1729; d. Hingham 7 April 1804 in 75th yr.; unm.

    vi CELIA GAY, b. 13 Aug. 1731; d. 18 Feb. 1749.

    vii JOTHAM GAY, b. 11 April 1733; d. Hingham 16 Oct. 1802 in 70th yr.; prob. unm. Jotham Gay of Hingham Esq., in his will dated 6 June 1801, proved 25 Oct. 1802, left all real estate to his niece Frances Gay, reserving the use of real estate to his sisters Abigail Gay and Jerusha Howard during their lives. On 8 Nov. 1802 Fanny Gay of Hingham, singlewoman, posted bond as administratrix.

363   viii JERUSHA GAY, b. 17 March 1734/5

ix   EBENEZER GAY, b. 3 March 1736/7; d. Hingham 3 July 1738 in 17th yr.

x   PERSIS GAY, b. 2 Nov. 1739; d. 24 March 1752

xi   JOANNA GAY, b. 23 Nov. 1741; d. Hingham 23 July 1772 ae 31; unm.

References: *MD* 11:239(m.). *VR Cohasset* p. 199(d. ch. Abigail, Eben.). *VR Duxbury* p. 257(m.). Suffolk Co. PR #18890 86:246-7(Eben. Gay); #21776; 100; 495, 516(Jotham Gay). *Boston News Obits* 2:418-9. *Hingham Hist* 2:264-5. *NEHGR* 33:45-56(John Gay); 84:359. *Harvard Grads* 6:59-66(Ebenezer Gay); 10:496(Samuel). Plymouth Co. LR 49:237(Ebenezer Gay). Suffolk Co. LR 95:198(Ebenezer Gay); 180:14(Martin Gay). Rev. Ebenezer Gay's records(b., bp., d. ch.). *Dedham VR* 1:148(b. Ebenezer).

70. WELTHEA⁴ BRADFORD (*Samuel³, William²⁻¹*), b. Plymouth 15 May 1702; d. Hingham 2 June 1755 aged 53.

She m. Swansea 10 Aug. 1721 **PETER LANE**, b. Hingham 25 May 1697; d. there 17 March 1764 aged 67; son of Ebenezer and Hannah (Hersey) Lane. On 1 Jan. 1722 Ebenezer Lane of Hingham sold his son Peter Lane of Hingham 10 shares of land. The will of Ebenezer Lane of Hingham dated 8 Jan. 1722/3, proved 27 Dec. 1726, names his son Peter.

On 13 May 1760 Peter Lane, yeoman, George Lane, Gentleman, Samuel Johnson, mariner, and wife Hannah, Syble Lane and Sarah Lane, both singlewomen, all of Hingham; Ebenezer Wisweall and Irania his wife, Daniel Johnson and Lucie his wife, all of Worcester; all children and heirs of Welthian Lane deceased, late wife of Peter Lane, sold to Martin Gay of Boston their share of land in Boston, formerly part of the estate of John Rogers Esq. of Swansea deceased, which was set off to his eldest daughter Hannah Bradford and by her will given to her four daughters, of whom said Welthian was one. On 19 May 1760 the same grantors sold their right in 20 acres sold by Gershom Bradford and 1/4 part of 10 acres bought of Gershom.

On 20 May 1760 Peter Lane of Hingham, yeoman, sold to George Lane of Hingham, gentleman, a tract near his dwelling house with a house occupied by George.

On 27 March 1764 Ebenezer Wiswall, glazier, and wife Irana; Daniel Johnson, yeoman, of Worcester; John Holbrook and wife Sibyl; and Sarah Lane, spinster, of Hingham quitclaimed to Samuel Johnson of Hingham their interests in land in Scituate formerly owned by Peter Lane, deceased.

On 25 Jan. 1765 John J. Holbrook Jr. was appointed administrator of the estate of Peter Lane of Hingham.

Children of Peter and Wealtha (Bradford) Lane, b. Hingham:

364   i   HANNAH LANE⁵, b. 27 May 1724

365   ii IRENE LANE, b. 6 Jan. 1725/6

       iii LUCY LANE, b. 6 June 1728; d. 9 Feb. 1733/4 ae 5

366   iv GEORGE LANE, bp. 6 June 1731

367   v LUCY LANE, bp. 16 March 1734/5

       vi [Child] LANE stillborn 22 May 1739

368   vii SYBIL LANE, bp. 26 July 1741

369 viii SARAH LANE, bp. 6 Oct. 1745

References: Suffolk Co. LR 37:221(Ebenezer Lane); 94:143(Peter Lane); 95:197(Peter Lane *et al.*). *Hingham Hist* 2:414-5. *MF* 19:155-6. Suffolk Co. PR 64:20; 65:591(Peter Lane). *Swansea VR* p. 199(m.). Rev. Gay's records (bp. ch.). Plymouth Co. LR 46:166; 57:3(Ebenezer Wiswall *et al.*).

71. GAMALIEL⁴ BRADFORD (*Samuel³, William²⁻¹*), b. perhaps Duxbury 18 May 1704; d. there 24 April 1778 aged 73y 11m 6d.

He m. Duxbury 30 Aug. 1728 **ABIGAIL BARTLETT**, b. Duxbury 18 March 1704*; d. there 30 Aug. 1776 aged 73y 3m 26d; daughter of Benjamin and Ruth (Pabodie) Bartlett, a descendant of Pilgrims **John Alden** and **Richard Warren**.

On 25 April 1729 Gamaliel Bradford of Duxbury, husbandman, and his wife Abigail, sold to Josiah Thomas their right in the farm whereon "our father Benjamin Bartlett" dwelt. On 8 Dec. 1742 they, with other Bartlett heirs, sold 41 acres in Duxbury.

In the French and Indian Wars Gamaliel Bradford was a Colonel in September 1756 with service to Crown Point. He was also a Colonel in January 1759 with service to Fort William Henry. In February 1759 and 1760 he was a Captain with service to Canada and Nova Scotia. In 1761 and 1762 he was a Major in Col. Jonathan Hoar's regiment.

The will of Gamaliel Bradford of Duxbury Esq. dated 4 April 1778, proved 6 July 1778, mentions his grandchildren, children of his eldest son Samuel Bradford deceased; sons Gamaliel, Seth, Peabody, Peter, and Andrew; land in township of Winslow, Cumberland Co. [now Maine]; and three daughters Abigail Wadsworth, Hannah Stanford, and Ruth Sampson; executors named were Seth and Peter Bradford.

On 1 July 1782 Gamaliel Bradford, Esq., Seth Bradford, Gentleman, Peabody Bradford, yeoman, Peter Bradford, yeoman, all of Duxbury, Andrew Bradford of Pembrook, Gentleman, and Samuel Bradford of Duxbury, yeoman, as legal representative of his father Samuel Bradford deceased, agreed to divide 90 acres in Winslow, Maine, given to them by their father and grandfather Gamaliel Bradford.

Children of Gamaliel and Abigail (Bartlett) Bradford, b. Duxbury:

370	i	ABIGAIL[5] BRADFORD, b. 24 Sept. 1728
371	ii	SAMUEL BRADFORD, b. 2 Jan. 1729/30
372	iii	GAMALIEL BRADFORD, b. 2 Sept. 1731
373	iv	SETH BRADFORD, b. 14 Sept. 1733
374	v	PEABODY BRADFORD, b. 8 March 1734/5
	vi	DEBORAH BRADFORD, b. 17 Aug. 1738; d. 1 Aug. 1739
375	vii	HANNAH BRADFORD, b. 30 July 1740
376	viii	RUTH BRADFORD, b. 5 July 1743
377	ix	PETER BRADFORD (twin), b. 2 June 1745
378	x	ANDREW BRADFORD (twin), b. 2 June 1745

* The birth of Abigail is from *Bradford Desc* p. 28. Original source has not been found.

References: *VR Duxbury* pp. 29-32(b. ch.), 222(m.), 352(d. Gamaliel, Abigail, Deborah). Plymouth Co. PR 25:17(Gam. Bradford). *MD* 9:160(d. Gam., Abigail); 11:149(b. ch.; d. Deborah). *MF* 19:156. Plymouth Co. LR 34:31(Gamaliel Bradford); 41:13(Bartlett heirs). Kennebec Co. ME LR 5:206(Gamaliel Bradford *et al.*). *Mass Officers French & Indian Wars* #703-711.

72. MARY HUNT[4] (*Mary[3] Bradford, William[2-1]*), b. Weymouth 18 Feb. 1687/8; d. Windham, Conn., 10 June 1716.

She m. Chilmark Feb. 1706/7 **NATHANIEL KNOWLES**, b. Eastham 15 May 1686; d. between 1 June 1732 (when he was mentioned in his father's will) and 6 June 1737 (when called deceased in codicil to father's will); son of Samuel and Mercy (Freeman) Knowles. He m. (2) Windham, Conn., 25 April 1717 ELIZABETH BACON with whom he had Ruth, Nathaniel, Mercy, Freeman, Elizabeth, and Samuel. The will of Samuel Knowles of Eastham, yeoman, dated 1 June 1732, codicil dated 6 June 1737, left son Nathaniel 20 shillings and mentions his son's wife Elizabeth and his granddaughter Rebecca Knowles. In the codicil Elizabeth's share was to go to the children of his son Nathaniel "now deceased."

On 12 Jan. 1709/10 Samuel Knowles of Eastham, yeoman, deeded to son Nathaniel Knowles of Eastham, but now of Chilmark, Dukes Co., yeoman, 160 acres in Windham.

On 8 Aug. 1722 Joseph Foot of Branford sold to Nathaniel Knowles of Windham, husbandman, a house and 3 acres in Branford. On 16 Sept. 1726 Nathaniel Knowles of Branford sold the tract where he dwelled to John Bird of Branford.

On 1 Feb. 1724/5 Samuel Knowles of Eastham, but now of Chilmark, Dukes Co., gave to Nathaniel Knowles of Branford, New Haven Co., a tract in Windham.

Mercy Knowles of Eastham in her will dated 5 Sept. 1739, proved 17 April 1745, left 20 shillings each to the children of her son Nathaniel deceased except for Rebecca "who has had Something given to her by my Deced Husband her Grandfather."

No Connecticut, or Barnstable County probate records were found for Nathaniel Knowles.

Children of Nathaniel and Mary (Hunt) Knowles, recorded Windham, Conn.:

379　　i　REBECCA KNOWLES[5], b. Martha's Vineyard 30 Jan. 1710/1
380　　ii　MARY KNOWLES, b. Sept. 1713
　　　iii　MALITHIAH KNOWLES, b. 4 Jan. 1715; living 13 March 1721/2 (grandfather's will); n.f.r.

References: *VR Chilmark* p. 58(m.). *MD* 6:205(b. Nathaniel). Windham CT VR 1:32(b. ch.; d. Mary). Barnstable Co. PR 5:295(Samuel Knowles); 8:87(Mercy Knowles). Windham CT LR E:21; F:118 (Samuel Knowles). Branford CT LR 4:462(Joseph Foot); 4:705(Nathaniel Knowles). *NEHGR* 79:383-4.

73. WILLIAM HUNT[4] (*Mary[3] Bradford, William[2-1]*), b. Weymouth 17 May 1693; d. before 19 July 1769 in 94th yr. [*sic*].

He m. (1) Chilmark 2 June 1718 **JANE TILTON**, b. Chilmark 2 Aug. 1697; d. there 19 Oct. 1732 in 56th yr. [*sic*]; daughter of William and Abiah (Mayhew) Tilton.

He m. (2) Plympton 7 Sept. 1749 **SARAH (GRAY) BRADFORD**, b. Tiverton 25 April 1697; d. Chilmark 16 Oct. 1770 in 74th yr.; daughter of Edward and Mary (Smith) Gray. She m. (1) Plympton 21 Oct. 1714 **Samuel Bradford** (#25).

The will of William Hunt of Chillmark, gentleman, dated 19 March 1760, proved 19 July 1769, names wife Sarah; son Samuel Hunt; grandson Beriah

Nickerson, son of daughter Jane Nickerson, deceased; grandchildren Jane Nickerson and Nathll Nickerson, children of Jane; daughter Mary Hunt; daughter Sarah Hatch; and daughter Hannah Hunt.

On 29 Aug. 1769 Mary Hunt and Hannah Hunt seamstresses, Timothy Hatch and his wife Sarah, Robert Thomson and his wife Jean all of Chilmark, and Samuel Hunt of Liverpool, Nova Scotia, sold to Samuel Bradford of Chilmark the dwelling house in which Timothy Hatch "now lives" reserving the use and improvement of it during the natural life of Sarah Hunt, widow, of Chilmark.

On 9 Jan. 1771 Samuel Bradford of Chillmark was appointed administrator of the estate of Sarah Hunt of Chillmark, widow.

On 1, 12, 16, and 20 Nov. 1771 Samuel Hunt of Liverpool, executor of the will of William Hunt of Chilmark, sold off portions of William's estate to pay debts.

Children of William and Jane (Tilton) Hunt, all with first wife, b. Chilmark:

	i	ABIA HUNT[5], bp. Martha's Vineyard 5 July 1719; n.f.r. (not in father's will)
	ii	MARY HUNT, b. 1721; d. 8 March 1789; unm.
381	iii	JANE HUNT, bp. Martha's Vineyard 18 Aug. 1723
	iv	HANNAH HUNT, bp. 10 July 1726; living 29 Aug. 1769; unm.*
383	v	SARAH HUNT, bp. 10 July 1726
384	vi	SAMUEL HUNT, b. 1727

* Hannah did not marry Elisha Sylvester in 1746/7 as stated in *Bradford Desc* p. 118.

References: *MD* 28:105-8(Sarah's g.s., will *et al.*). *Bradford Desc* p. 29. *VR Plympton* pp. 265(Sarah's 1st m.), 336(2nd m.). *Martha's Vineyard By Banks* 3:213, 471. *VR Chilmark* pp. 32(b. Jane), 88(d. Jane, Sarah). *Mayflower Source Recs* pp. 98(1st m.), 108(bp. Abia), 109(bp. Jane), 111(bp. Hannah, Sarah). Dukes Co. PR 6:14(Wm. Hunt), 38(Sarah Hunt). *Torrey's Marriages* p. 319(Mary Smith). *RIVR* Tiverton 4:7:83(b. Sarah). Dukes Co. LR 9:674(Mary Hunt et.al.); 9:805; 10:3, 30, 328(Samuel Hunt).

74. SARAH BAKER[4] (*Sarah³ Bradford, William²⁻¹*), b. Marshfield 28 Oct. 1688; d. Rochester after 26 July 1765 (deed).

She m. Marshfield 26 March 1712 **JOHN SHERMAN**, b. Marshfield 17 Oct. 1682; d. Rochester after 26 July 1765 (deed); son of John and Jane (Hatch) Sherman.

On 26 July 1765 John and Sarah Sherman of Rochester, for love and affection, deeded their homestead farm to sons John Sherman, William Sherman, and Samuel Sherman, all of Rochester.

No Plymouth County probate record was found for John or Sarah Sherman. There are no deeds recorded giving land to the daughters.

Children of John and Sarah (Baker) Sherman, b. Rochester:

385	i	SARAH SHERMAN[5], b. 15 Aug. 1714
386	ii	JANE SHERMAN, b. 2 Oct. 1716
387	iii	ALICE SHERMAN, b. 29 July 1719
388	iv	JOHN SHERMAN, b. 27 July 1721
389	v	ABIGAIL SHERMAN, b. ca. 1723
390	vi	BETHIAH SHERMAN, b. 26 Jan. 1724
391	vii	WILLIAM SHERMAN, b. 11 Jan. 1726
392	viii	KEZIAH SHERMAN, b. 28 Oct. 1728
393	ix	SAMUEL SHERMAN, b. 2 Jan. 1730/1

References: *Marshfield VR* pp. 13(b. John), 39(m.). *VR Rochester* 1:264-8(b. ch.). Plymouth Co. LR 50:235(John & Sarah Sherman). *Sherman Fam* pp. 36-9.

75. ALICE BAKER[4] (*Sarah[3] Bradford, William[2-1]*), b. Marshfield 3 Nov. 1690; d. there 14 June 1715.

She m. Marshfield 4 March 1713/4 **NATHAN THOMAS**, b. Marshfield 21 Nov. 1688; d. there 3 Nov. 1741 aged 53 yrs.; son of Samuel and Mercy (Ford) Thomas. He m. (2) Marshfield 2 Jan. 1716/7 ABIAH SNOW. He m. (3) Plymouth 17 June 1719 SARAH (FOSTER) BARTLETT with whom he had Sarah, Alice, Nathan, William, Nathan, Ichabod, Sarah, and Nathaniel.

In the Court of General Sessions Nathan Thomas of Marshfield, retailer, was granted a license to sell liquor from 1726 to 1728.

On 6 May 1742 Mrs. Sarah Thomas of Plymouth, widow, was granted administration of the estate of her husband Nathan Thomas, late of Marshfield, yeoman, deceased. Sarah's account of 3 Oct. 1743 includes 15 shillings for letter of guardianship for Alice Thomas.

Nathan and Alice (Baker) Thomas had no children.

References: *MD* 7:131(2nd m.); 10:49(d. Alice); 14:38(3rd m.). *Marshfield VR* pp. 16(b. Nathan), 36(m.), 40(Nathan's 2nd m.), 388(d. Alice), 411(d. Nathan). Plymouth Co. PR 8:459, 478; 9:149(Nathan Thomas). *Thomas Gen* pp. 165-6. *Plymouth VR* p. 92(Nathan's 3rd m.). *Plymouth Co CT Recs* vol. 2.

76. ELEANOR BAKER⁴ (*Sarah³ Bradford, William²⁻¹*), b. Marshfield 31 March 1692; d. there 6 May 1727 aged 37 yrs.

She m. Marshfield 17 Jan. 1716/7 **BENJAMIN PHILLIPS**, b. Marshfield 20 May 1687; d. there May 1750 in 63rd yr.; son of Benjamin and Sarah (Thomas) Phillips.   He m. (2) Marshfield 18 Jan. 1728 DESIRE SHERMAN with whom he had Desire, Ellanor, and Penelope.

On 4 June 1750 Benjamin Phillips of Boston, "warfinger," was appointed administrator of the estate of his father Benjamin Phillips, late of Marshfield, yeoman, deceased. Receipts were given 9 Feb. 1750 by John Carver, Jacob Dingley Jr., John Phillips, and Jeremiah Phillips, John Carver, Jacob Dingley, John Phillips, and Benjamin Phillips, stating they had received of Jeremiah Phillips equal portions of the real estate which they prayed would be settled on him "our brother."

Children of Benjamin and Eleanor (Baker) Phillips, b. Marshfield:

394   i   JEREMIAH PHILLIPS⁵, b. 17 Nov. 1717

395   ii BENJAMIN PHILLIPS, b. 3 Aug. 1719

      iii JOHN PHILLIPS, b. 1 Sept. 1721; bp. 22 Oct. 1727; living 9 Feb. 1750. No Plymouth Co. PR.

      iv [CHILD] PHILLIPS, b. 4 May 1727; d. ae 2 days

References: *Marshfield VR* pp. 17(b. Benjamin), 34(b. 3 ch.), 36(m.), 47(b. Penelope), 49(b. Desire), 85(d. Elinore), 90(b. Elinore), 146(2nd m.), 406(d. Elinore, Benj. & ch.). *MD* 31:67(bp. John). Plymouth Co. PR 11:400, 443; 12:220, 228(Benjamin Phillips).

77. ABIGAIL BAKER⁴ (*Sarah³ Bradford, William²⁻¹*), b. Marshfield 23 Dec. 1693; d. there 25 Sept. 1753 aged 59y 9m 28d.

She m. Marshfield 9 Feb. 1720/1 **GIDEON THOMAS**, b. Marshfield 23 Dec. 1692; d. there 14 Dec. 1766 in 74th yr.; son of Samuel and Mercy (Ford) Thomas.

The will of Gideon Thomas of Marshfield, yeoman, dated 10 May 1764, proved 26 Dec. 1766, names daughter Mercy White, wife of Benjamin; grandson Gideon Harlow; daughter Anna Damon, wife of Elijah; daughter Sarah Low, wife of Jeremiah; daughter Eleanor Ford, wife of Elijah Ford; grandson Nathaniel Otis; and grandson Gideon Thomas White.

On 17 March 1780 Elijah Dammon of Pembroke and his wife Anna, yeoman and seamster, sold to Benjamin White Jr. of Marshfield, tanner, a salt meadow given by Gideon Thomas of Marshfield to his grandson Nathan Otis [*sic* - prob. Nathaniel Olds].

Children of Gideon and Abigail (Baker) Thomas, b. Marshfield:

396   i   ABIGAIL THOMAS[5], b. 4 Dec. 1722

397   ii MERCY THOMAS, b. 27 June 1725

398   iii ANNA THOMAS, b. 7 Aug. 1726

        iv ELIZABETH THOMAS, b. 10 May 1729; d. Marshfield 3 May 1761 ae 31y 11m 23d; unm. No PR.

399   v   SARAH THOMAS (twin), b. 10 Feb. 1732/3

400   vi ELEANOR THOMAS (twin), b. 10 Feb. 1732/3

References: *Marshfield VR* pp. 48(b. Anna), 82(b. twins), 87(b. 1st 2 ch.), 143(m.), 410(deaths). Plymouth Co. PR 19:415(Gideon Thomas). *Thomas Gen* p. 166. Plymouth Co. LR 92:106(Elijah Dammon).

78.   KENELM BAKER[4] (*Sarah[3] Bradford, William[2-1]*), b. Marshfield 3 Nov. 1695; d. there 22 May 1771 in 76th yr.

He m. Duxbury 22 Jan. 1718/9 **PATIENCE DOTY**, b. Plymouth 3 July 1697; d. Marshfield 18 Feb. 1784 in 87th yr.; daughter of John and Sarah (Jones) Doty, a descendant of Pilgrims **Edward Doty** and **Richard Warren**.

At the May 1737 term of the Plymouth Court of General Sessions, Kenelm Baker of Marshfield, yeoman, was presented for assaulting Isaac Barker. Kenelm "with his hand one Blow on said Barker's face ... and ... called the said Barker a plaging Knave." Kenelm was convicted of "A Breach of the peace" and was fined.

The Court of General Sessions also shows that Kenelm Baker of Marshfield, innholder, was granted a license to sell liquor in 1751, 1753, and 1757-59.

The will of Kenelm Baker of Marshfield, yeoman, dated 13 April 1770, proved 3 June 1771, names wife Patience; sons John, Kenelm, and William; daughters Alice Little, wife of Ephraim; Sarah Little, wife of Thomas Little; Betty Turner, wife of Abner Turner; and Lucy Fisher, wife of Daniel Fisher.

In the 1771 Valuation List, Patience Baker, widow, appears in Marshfield with 2 goats or sheep and 1 swine.

No Plymouth County probate records were found for Patience Baker.

Children of Kenelm and Patience (Doty) Baker, b. Marshfield:

401   i   JOHN BAKER[5], b. 18 Oct. 1719

402	ii	ALICE BAKER, b. 26 Jan. 1722
	iii	KENELM BAKER, bp. 4 Oct. 1724; d.y.
403	iv	SARAH BAKER, b. 21 April 1726
404	v	KENELM BAKER, b. 1 July 1728
405	vi	ELIZABETH BAKER, b. 29 July 1730
406	vii	WILLIAM BAKER, b. 16 Oct. 1734
407	viii	LUCY BAKER, b. 15 May 1737

References: *MD* 1:206(b. Patience); 12:55(d. Kenelm, Patience); 31:167(bp. 1st Kenelm). *Marshfield VR* pp. 49(b. Sarah, Kenelm, Eliz.), 79(b. Wm., Lucy), 87(b. John, Alice), 398(d. Kenelm), 399(d. Patience). *VR Duxbury* p. 215(m.). Plymouth Co. PR 20:496-7(Kenelm Baker). *Boston News Obits* 2:46(d. Kenelm.). *Plymouth VR* p. 8(b. Patience). *MF* 11:1:19. *Plymouth Co Ct Recs* 2:172; Vol. 3. *1771 Valuation* p. 646.

79. BETHIAH BAKER[4] (*Sarah³ Bradford, William²⁻¹*), b. Marshfield 12 May 1699; d. Boston 13 July 1741 aged 42; buried in Granary Burial Ground.

She m. Boston 29 Dec. 1720 **JAMES SCOLLEY**, bp. Boston 19 March 1699/1700; d. there before 30 Oct. 1721 (when Bethiah was appointed administratrix); son of John and Lydia (Grover) Scolley.

The inventory of the estate of James Scollay of Boston, baker, was taken 1 Nov. 1721. The widow's account mentions "grave Bells for the Deceased and child."

On 19 July 1722 Bethia Scolley, widow, and James Scolley, shopkeeper, of Boston, administrators of the estate of James Scolley late of Boston, baker, sold a bakehouse or tenement with land. On the same day Bethia Scolley sold to James Scolley her dower rights in this land.

On 21 July 1741 William Baker of Boston was appointed to administer the estate of his sister Bethiah Scollay, late of Boston, widow.

Child of James and Bethia (Baker) Scolley, b. prob. Boston:

    i   [Child] SCOLLEY[5], d.y.; poss. the child of James bur. 24 May 1718
    ii [Child] SCOLLEY, poss. the child of James bur. 27 Aug. 1718

References: *BRC* 28:89(m.). Suffolk Co. PR #4449(James Scollay); #7631(Bethiah Scollay). *History Of The Second Church*, Chandler Robbins, Boston, 1852, p. 276(bp. James). *Boston Deaths* 2:803(d. ch.). Suffolk Co. LR 36:99(Bethia Scolley).

80. KEZIAH BAKER[4] (*Sarah[3] Bradford, William[2-1]*), b. Marshfield 15 Aug. 1701; d. Rochester 12 May 1790 in 89th yr.

She m. before 14 Jan. 1727/8, when she witnessed a deed, **NATHANIEL SPRAGUE**, b. Duxbury 10 Jan. 1701/2; d. Rochester 29 July 1739; son of Samuel and Ruth (Alden) Sprague, a descendant of Pilgrim **John Alden.**

On 14 Jan. 1727/8 Keziah Sprague witnessed a partition of lands formerly in the right of David Alden.

On 27 Aug. 1739 widow Keziah Sprague was appointed administratrix of the estate of Nathaniel Sprague. The inventory was dated 17 Sept. 1739.

On 20 Dec. 1768 Keziah Sprague of Rochester, widow, gave to son Nathaniel Sprague of Rochester, mariner, all her right to son Micah's lands.

On 4 Dec. 1788 Nathaniel Sprague of Rochester, Esq. and Micah Haskell of Rochester, taylor, and his wife Lucy, heirs of Nathaniel Sprague, divided the homestead farm of their grandfather Samuel Sprague.

At the August 1804 term of the Plymouth Court of Common Pleas, Nathaniel Clap of Rochester, Gentleman, sued Solomon Hall of Rochester, yeoman, for ejectment from "at undivided 3d part of one undivided ½ part of a certain tract of Land with its buildings ... in ... Rochester." The land descended to Nathaniel in this manner: Micah Sprague was seized of one undivided half described above, 1 Jan. 1759. He died intestate and without issue 1 Oct. 1759, leaving his mother Keziah Sprague ("who was Grandmother of" Nathaniel), Nathaniel Sprague his brother, and Lucy Sprague his sister, "his only heirs at Law." An undivided third part descended to his mother Keziah, and by her deed of 20 Dec. 1768 she granted her part to "my only and beloved son Nathaniel Sprague of Rochester, mariner," reserving to herself "the whole and sole use and improvement of all the whole mentioned premises during my natural life," with reversion to her grandson Nathaniel Clap if her son Nathaniel Sprague should die without issue. Keziah Sprague died 12 May 1791, and Nathaniel Sprague died 9 Jan. 1797 without issue. Nathaniel Clap claimed that Solomon Hall entered the premises after the death of Keziah and continued there during the lifetime of Nathaniel Sprague, but "now refuses to leave."

No Plymouth County probate records were found for Keziah Sprague.

Children of Nathaniel and Keziah (Baker) Sprague, b. Rochester:

408   i   LUCY (or LUCE) SPRAGUE[5], b. 23 Feb. 1731/2

      ii MICAH SPRAGUE, b. 31 Jan. 1735/6; d. before 10 July 1762 when Nathaniel Sprague was appointed administrator of the estate of his brother "Michael" Sprague.

409   iii NATHANIEL SPRAGUE, b. 21 May 1738

Note: *Marshfield By Richards* 2:143 and *Bradford Desc* pp. 30-1 say Keziah married _____ CLAPP. Keziah's daughter Luce married Ebenezer Clapp and this is obviously the basis for the confusion about Keziah's husband.

References: *VR Duxbury* p. 169(b. Nathaniel). *VR Rochester* 1:283(b. ch.); 2:436(deaths). Plymouth Co. LR 25:80(Keziah witness); 54:225(Keziah Sprague); 67:219(Nathaniel Sprague). Plymouth Co. PR 8:84, 127(Nathaniel Sprague). *MD* 39:179-80. *Plymouth Co CT Recs* 11:302.

81. SAMUEL BAKER⁴ (*Sarah³ Bradford, William²⁻¹*), b. Marshfield 5 Feb. 1702/3; d. Duxbury (rec. Marshfield) 4 Nov. 1793 in 91st yr.

He m. Marshfield 9 Nov. 1726 **HANNAH FORD**, b. Marshfield 18 Oct. 1705; d. there 28 April 1800 in 95th yr.; daughter of James and Hannah (Dingley) Ford, a descendant of Pilgrim **Richard Warren**.

Samuel Baker's household in Duxbury in 1790 consisted of one man, 3 boys under 16, and 3 females.

The will of Samuel Baker of Duxbury, yeoman, dated 3 Aug. 1790, proved 2 Dec. 1793, names wife Hannah; sons James, Thomas, Charles, and Elijah; and daughters Eleanor, Hannah, Bethiah, and Abigail (no surnames).

On 13 April 1796 James Baker of Marshfield, yeoman, Charles Baker of Marshfield, yeoman, Thomas Baker of Duxbury, yeoman, and Elijah Baker of Duxbury, Gentleman, equal owners of the real estate of "our father Samuel Baker late of Duxbury, yeoman," given to them by his will, agreed to divide the land.

On 20 Feb. 1799 Selah Baker Jr. and Polly Baker both of Marshfield, seamsters, sold to Charles Baker of Marshfield, yeoman, 30 acres in Duxbury, part of the farm of "our grandfather Samuel Baker in division to our father James Baker deceased and his brothers."

No Plymouth County probate records were found for Hannah Baker.

Children of Samuel and Hannah (Ford) Baker, b. Duxbury:

410   i ELEANOR BAKER⁵, b. 21 Sept. 1727

411   ii HANNAH BAKER, b. 25 Feb. 1729

412   iii BETHIAH BAKER, b. 11 May 1733

        iv SAMUEL BAKER, b. 26 Feb. 1735; d. May 1759 "drowned at Sea Eastward"; prob. unm. No PR.

413   v JAMES BAKER, b. 4 Jan. 1737

414   vi THOMAS BAKER, b. 24 Jan. 1739

415   vii CHARLES BAKER, b. 26 April 1741

416   viii ELIJAH BAKER, b. 1 July 1744

417   ix   ABIGAIL BAKER, b. 24 Sept. 1746

References: *VR Duxbury* pp. 21-2(b. ch.), 349(d. ch. Samuel). *Marshfield VR* pp. 30(b. Hannah), 145(m.), 398(d. Hannah), 399(d. Samuel). *MD* 11:238-9(b. ch.); 12:55(d. Samuel, Hannah). Plymouth Co. PR 33:498(Samuel Baker). Plymouth Co. LR 86:175(James Baker *et al.*); 88:206(Selah & Polly Baker).

82. WILLIAM BAKER⁴ (*Sarah³ Bradford, William²⁻¹*), b. Marshfield 18 Oct. 1705; d. Boston 10 Dec. 1785 in 81ˢᵗ yr.

He m. Charlestown 31 Jan. 1739 **SARAH (HURD) PERKINS**, b. Charlestown 20 Nov. 1712; d. Boston 5 May 1744 aged 32; daughter of Jacob and Elizabeth (Tufts) Hurd. She m. (1) Boston 12 Oct. 1732 ISAAC PERKINS with whom she had Houghton.

In the 1771 Valuation List, William Baker appears in Boston with one poll and one house.

In his will dated 19 April 1785, proved 20 Dec. 1785, William Baker of Boston, gentleman, named son-in-law Henry Bass as executor, and made bequests to grandchildren William, Betsy, Else, and Phillips Baker, children of son William; and children Sarah and Bethiah (surname not given). The well-known Paul Revere was one of the executors and among the bequests was a pew in Mr. Thatcher's meeting house.

Children of William and Sarah (Hurd) (Perkins) Baker, b. Boston:

418   i   WILLIAM BAKER⁵, b. 13 June 1741

419   ii   SARAH BAKER, b. 7 July 1742

420   iii BETHIAH BAKER, b. 30 March 1744

References: *Charlestown By Wyman* pp. 531, 738. *BRC* 24:242(b. Wm.), 245(b. Sarah), 252(b. Bethiah); 28:179(her 1ˢᵗ m.). *Marshfield VR* p. 352(m.). Suffolk Co. PR #18583; 84:719(Wm. Baker). *Boston News Obits* 1:14(d. Wm.). *Charlestown VR* 1:237(b. Sarah), 365(m.). *Boston Deaths* 1700-1799 1:42(d. Sarah, William). *1771 Valuation* p. 38.

83. EDWARD BAKER⁴ (*Sarah³ Bradford, William²⁻¹*), b. Marshfield 18 Oct. 1705; d. Boston 1 March 1781 aged 74 yrs.

He m. (1) at New South Church, Boston 16 Dec. 1742 **MEHETABLE BLANCHARD**, b. Boston 16 March 1718/9; d. before 23 May 1748 when Edward remarried, daughter of Caleb and Alice (Wheeler) Blanchard.

He m. (2) Boston 23 May 1748 **HANNAH (MARKS) GIBBON**, d. New London, Conn., 23 Oct. 1791 (Boston newspaper account); daughter of John and Letice/Lattia/Letitia (___) Marks. She m. (1) at Boston 11 April 1741 HENRY GIBBON with whom she had a daughter Hannah. On 19 Feb. 1745 dower was set off to Hannah Gibbon, widow of Henry, and included parts of four messuages and one and a half pews in Mr. Byles meeting house. On 2 Jan. 1746 Samuel Gibbon of Roxbury, merchant, sold to Hannah Gibbon, widow, and Jacob Sheaff, Gentleman, administrators of the estate of Henry Gibbon, his right in a messuage in Boston mortgaged by Henry to Samuel. On 6 Oct. 1752 Sands Gibbon of Boston, ropemaker, and Samuel Gibbon of Roxbury, Gentleman, sold their rights in tenements in Boston to Edward Baker and his wife Hannah "which said lands and tenements Edward … and Hannah his wife are now in possession claiming to hold the Same in right of the said Hannah as heir to her Child Hannah Gibbon had by Our said Brother [Henry] to whom the said Hannah was formerly married which child deceased since our said Brothers death." Lattia Marks of Boston, widow, wrote her will on 30 Aug. 1759, proved 24 Jan. 1765, leaving everything to her daughter Hannah Baker, wife of Edward Baker of Boston, shopkeeper, and after Hannah's death to her children.

On 18 March 1749 Edward Baker was admitted to full communion in the New South Church in Boston by dismission from the First Church of Marshfield. The seven children of Edward and Hannah Baker were baptized at the New South Church.

On 27 Oct. 1752 Edward Baker of Boston, coaster, and his wife Hannah sold to Samuel Gibbon of Roxbury, Gentleman, two tenements on Gibbon's Court.

On 24 Aug. 1759 and 8 Oct. 1761 Edward Baker of Boston (shopkeeper in first deed and mariner in second) and his wife Hannah sold a dwelling house and land on Gibbon's Court to Letitia Marks, widow.

At a Selectmen's meeting on 7 July 1769 "Information was this Day given the Selectmen, that Mr Edwd Crafts who lives near Liberty Tree, has his Wife and Daughter ill of the Small Pox, and as they do not consent to be removed, Mr Williston was directed to see that a Flag was hung out as a signal of Infection; and mr Edward Baker was appointed a Guard for said House at three Shilling & four Pence p. Day."

On 22 May 1781 widow Hannah Baker signed bond as administratrix of the estate of her late husband Edward Baker of Boston, Gentleman, deceased.

The will of Hannah Baker late of Boston dated 25 July 1786, proved 29 Nov. 1791, names son Edward; Edward's children Hannah Baker and William Baker; and daughters Mehitable, Letitia, and Anna.

On 1 April 1800 Anna Durivage, widow, Letitia Baker, and Hannah Baker, singlewomen, and William Baker, tobacconist, all of Boston, mortgaged a house and land in Gibbons Court to John Freeland of Boston, tobacconist.

On 13 Oct. 1819 Anne Durivage of Boston, widow, sold to Letitia Baker of Boston, singlewoman, one-half of land and a house on Newbury Street, her share of the estates of Hannah Baker and Mehitable Baker, both deceased.

Children of Edward and second wife Hannah (Marks) (Gibbon) Baker, b. Boston and bp. New South Church:

421   i   EDWARD BAKER⁵, b. 6 March 1748/9; bp. 12 March 1748

       ii MEHITABLE BAKER, b. 11 March 1749/50; bp. 19 March 1749; bur. Boston 27 Sept. 1793; unm. The will of Mehitable Baker of Boston, singlewoman, dated 16 Sept. 1793, proved 29 Oct. 1793, names brother Edward Baker, sisters Letitia Baker and Hannah wife of Nicholas Durviage, now residing in New London, Conn.

      iii HANNAH BAKER, bp. 12 April 1752; d.y.

      iv HANNAH BAKER, b. 9 Nov. 1753; bp. 10 Nov 1753; not in mother's will

      v SHUTE BAKER, b. 7 Nov. 1756; bp. 14 Nov. 1756; bur. Boston 18 Aug. 1775 ae 18

      vi LETITIA BAKER, b. 22 Oct. 1758; bp. 22 Oct. 1758; d. Williamsburgh, Kings Co., N.Y., 16 May 1844 ae 85; unm. The will of Letitia Baker of Boston, singlewoman, dated 17 May 1839, proved 10 June 1844, names niece Hannah Bennett wife of William Bennett of Long Island, N.Y.; grandniece Hannah, wife of John J. Bennet and daughter of William Baker of Boston; nephew Francis S. Durivage and his wife Lucy Durivage; the children of Francis Durivage: Francis Alexander, Oliver Everett, John Everett, and Robert D.; and niece Anne Letitia Aldworth, wife of Henry Aldworth of Long Island, N.Y.

422   vii ANNA BAKER, b. 16 March 1761; bp. 29 March 1761

References: BRC 24:265(b. Edward), 269(b. Mehitable), 281(b. Hannah), 288(b. Shute), 293(b. Lettita), 300(b. Anna); 28:239(2nd m.), 273(1st int.), 345(1st m.). *Boston News Obits* 1:14(d. Edward, Hannah, dau. Mehitable). Suffolk Co. PR #8121 39:54(Henry Gibbon); #13783 65:25(Lattia Marks); #17438(Edward Baker); #19843(Hannah Baker), #20219(Mehitable Baker); #34002(Letitia Baker). *Gravestone Inscriptions In The Granary Burying Ground, Boston, Mass.*, Salem, 1918, p. 29(d. Letita). *Boston Deaths* 1700-1799 1:42(d. Shute). Suffolk Co. LR 73:160(Samuel Gibbon); 81:146; 93:96; 97:2(Edward Baker); 194:118; 264:66(Anne Durivage). Boston Churchs on CD(m., bp. of children). BRC 23:22(guard).

84. ANN⁴ BRADFORD (*Joseph³, William²⁻¹*), b. Lebanon, Conn., 26 July 1699; d. Mansfield, Conn., 9 Oct. 1788 aged 91.

She m. Mansfield, Conn., 15 Aug. 1723 **TIMOTHY DIMMICK**, b. Barnstable July 1698; d. Mansfield, Conn., 27 Dec. 1785 aged 87; son of John and Elizabeth (Lumbert) Dimmick.

On 23 Jan. 1748/9 Timothy Dimmick of Mansfield gave land in Mansfield to daughter Ann Clark of Mansfield. On 29 March 1749 he gave two lots in Mansfield to son John Dimmick of Mansfield, part of the farm on which Timothy was living. On 2 July 1753 he gave land in Mansfield to son Timothy Dimmick of Coventry. On 10 July 1753 he gave more land to daughter Ann Clark of Mansfield.

On 11 June 1764 John Dimmock of late of Mansfield now of Stafford, Hartford County, sold the two lots in Mansfield to his father Timothy Dimmock.

On 14 June 1774 Timothy Dimmock of Mansfield gave 130 acres "I now live on" to son Oliver Dimmock. On 8 Feb. 1775 he gave more land to son Oliver.

On 8 Dec. 1780 Timothy Dimmock gave to Mary, Eunice, Lavina, and Diantha Dimock of Mansfield, children of deceased son Dan Dimock, land in Mansfield.

No Connecticut probate records were found for Timothy Dimmick.

Children of Timothy and Ann (Bradford) Dimmick, b. Mansfield, Conn.:

423   i ANN DIMMICK⁵, b. 23 May 1724
424   ii TIMOTHY DIMMICK, b. 8 April 1726
425   iii JOHN DIMMICK, b. 24 March 1727/8
426   iv JOHANNA DIMMICK, b. 28 Aug. 1730
        v JOSIAH DIMMICK, b. 2 March 1732/3; d.y.
        vi SIMEON DIMMICK, b. 19 Sept. 1735; d. 9 March 1737
        vii SYLVANUS DIMMICK, b. 18 June 1738; d.y.
427   viii OLIVER DIMMICK, b. 31 Dec. 1740
428   ix DAN DIMMICK, b. 13 May 1743

References: *Mansfield CT VR*, pp. 62(b. 1ˢᵗ 2 ch.), 63(b. last 7 ch.), 231(m.). *Bradford Desc* p. 31. *MD* 4:222(b. Timothy). Mansfield CT VR D62-3(b. ch.); D231(m.). *Boston News Obits* 2:309(d. Ann). Mansfield CT LR 5:115(to Ann), 133(to John), 525(to Timothy), 550(to Ann); 7:87(from John); 9:71(to Oliver), 307(to Oliver); 10:277(to grandchildren).

85. JOSEPH⁴ BRADFORD (*Joseph³, William²⁻¹*), b. Lebanon, Conn., 9 April 1702; d. Haddam, Conn., 1777 aged 77.

He m. New London, Conn., March 1730 **HENRIETTA SWIFT**, b. ca. 1701; d. Haddam, Conn., Oct. 1758 aged 57.

On 23 Sept. 1772 Joseph Bradford of Haddam gave to his son Robert Bradford of Haddam land and half his house.

On 5 Jan. 1778 William Bradford was appointed administrator of the estate of Mr. Joseph Bradford, late of Haddam, deceased. The 7 April 1778 distribution of the estate of Capt. Joseph Bradford of Haddam, names William Bradford, eldest son; Robert Bradford, Henry Bradford, Elezebeth Mayo, Ann Lyman, and Hannah Russell.

On 4 May 1781 William Bradford of Chatham and Robert Bradford of Haddam sold 70 acres in Haddam, abutting land of Hannah Russell and Henry Bradford, to Solomon Hubbard of Middletown.

Children of Joseph and Henrietta (Swift) Bradford, b. New London, Conn.:

429	i	ELIZABETH⁵ BRADFORD, b. 17 Jan. 1731.
430	ii	ANNA BRADFORD, b. 23 July 1732.
431	iii	WILLIAM BRADFORD, b. 13 April 1734.
432	iv	HENRY SWIFT BRADFORD, b. 21 Aug. 1736.
433	v	ROBERT BRADFORD, b. 21 July 1739.
434	vi	HANNAH BRADFORD, b. 10 March 1740/1.
	vii	JOSEPH BRADFORD, b. 10 Jan. 1744/5; prob. d.y. (not in div.).

Note: *Montfield, Conn., Hist* shows the fourth child as Honora Swift Bradford who m. Charles Whiting. *NEHGR* 14 calls him Honora Swift. Neither is correct.

References: New London CT VR 2:4-6(m.; b. 5 ch.), 26(b. last 2 ch.). *Bradford Desc* pp. 31-2. Middletown CT PR #494; 4:192-3, 217, 238(Joseph Bradford). First Congregational Ch. Rec. Haddam CT 5:4(d. Joseph), 34(d. Henrietta). Haddam CT LR 9:203(Joseph Bradford); 10:304(William Bradford *et al.*). Hale Cem Coll:Haddam p. 103(d. Henrietta).

86. PRISCILLA⁴ BRADFORD (*Joseph³, William²⁻¹*), b. Lebanon, Conn., 9 April 1702; d. there 14 May 1778.

She m. Lebanon, Conn., 14 Jan. 1724/5 **SAMUEL HYDE**, b. Windham, Conn., 10 Sept. 1691; d. Greenwich, Conn., 14 Feb. 1776; son of Samuel and Elizabeth (Caulkins) Hyde.

On 27 April 1741 Samuel Hide of Lebanon sold his son Samuel Hide Jr. of Lebanon his right in his whole farm, partly in Lebanon and partly in Norwich, on which his son now lives.

The will of Samuel Hide of Lebanon dated 30 Jan. 1775, proved 30 April 1776, names wife Priscilla; daughter Ann, wife of Jared Hinckley; daughter Sibel, wife of Jabez Metcalf; daughter Zeruiah, wife of Andrew Metcel; daughter Abigail; grandchildren Mary and Priscilla daughters of a deceased daughter; grandsons Gurden and David, the only sons of daughter Hannah deceased; and son Samuel.

The will of Priscilla Hyde of Lebanon dated 7 Dec. 1777, proved 22 June 1778, mentions but does not name her son Samuel's children; daughter Ann wife of Jared Hinckley; daughter Sibel wife of Jabesh Metcalf; daughter Zerviah wife of Andrew Metcalf; daughter Abigail Hyde; grandchildren Mary and Priscilla daughters of her son Dan; and grandchildren Gurdon and Daniel sons of her daughter Hannah deceased. On 23 Sept. 1778 a receipt was signed by Ann Hinckley, Jared Hinckley, Sibal Metcalf, Jabez Metcalf, Zerviah Metcalf, Andrew Metcalf, and Abigail Hyde. On 31 Oct. 1778 Jared Hinckley signed a receipt as guardian of Gurdon and Daniel sons of Hannah Moulton, and Samuel Hyde signed as guardian of Mary and Priscilla daughters of Dan Hyde.

Children of Samuel and Priscilla (Bradford) Hyde, b. Lebanon, Conn.:

435   i   SAMUEL HYDE[5], b. 24 Oct. 1725.

436   ii   ANNE HYDE, b. 22 Oct. 1727.

437   iii SYBIL HYDE (twin), b. 16 April 1731.

       iv   PRISCILLA HYDE (twin), b. 16 April 1731; d. 5 Oct. 1732.

438   v   DAN HYDE, b. 7 May 1733.

       vi   PRISCILLA HYDE, b. 4 June 1735; d. Litchfield, Conn., 4 July 1759; unm.

439   vii HANNAH HYDE, b. 19 July 1738.

440   viii ZERVIAH HYDE, b. 15 Dec. 1740.

       ix   ABIGAIL HYDE, b. 4 Nov. 1744; d. Litchfield, Conn., 20 Feb. 1830 or 20 Dec. 1830 ae 86; unm.

References: *Bradford Desc* p. 32. Windham CT VR A22(b. Sam.). Lebanon CT VR 1:146(m.; b. ch.), 151(d. Sam.). Windham CT PR #2145(Samuel Hide). Lebanon CT LR 6:179(Samuel Hide). Hale Cem Coll:Lebanon p. 62(Abigail Hyde).

87. SARAH⁴ BRADFORD (*Joseph³, William²⁻¹*), b. Lebanon, Conn., 21 Sept. 1706; living 25 Nov. 1774.

She m. (1) before 14 Sept. 1731 _____ **TUTTLE** (father's will).

She m. (2) Norwich, Conn., 9 June 1747 **ISRAEL LATHROP**, b. Norwich, Conn., 1 Feb. 1687; d. before 9 June 1774; son of Israel and Rebecca (Bliss) Lathrop. He m. (1) Norwich, Conn., 20 June 1710 MARY FELLOWS with whom he had Israel, Ephraim, Mary, Jedidiah, Catherine, Simeon, and Ezekiel. On 27 June 1733 Israel signed an agreement with the other heirs of Israel Lothrop of Norwich to divide the land and in three deeds on 19 Feb. 1733/4 Israel sold land with the other heirs of Israel Lathrop.

On 28 May 1765 Israel Lothrop of Norwich and his wife Sarah sold to John Bradford Jr. of New London 4¼ acres with a "Mantion" house.

The will of Israel Lathrop dated 22 March 1758, proved 9 June 1774, names wife Sarah; deceased son Israel's three daughters Ann, Lois, and Ednah; daughter Mary Birchard; daughter Catherine Hackly; youngest daughter Prudence; and sons Jedidiah, Simeon, and Ezekiel. On 25 Nov. 1774 the estate was divided between the widow Sarah; sons Jedediah and Simeon; four children and heirs of deceased son Ezekiel; children of deceased daughter Mary Birchard; daughter Katherine Hackley; and daughter Prudence Crocker late Prudence Lathrop.

Child of Israel and Sarah (Bradford) (Tuttle) Lathrop, b. Norwich, Conn.:

441   i   PRUDENCE LATHROP⁵, b. 16 March 1748

Note: *Bradford Desc* p. 32 gives Sarah a son John Tuttle, b. 1736. He was the son of Daniel and Sarah (Comstock) Tuttle.

References: *Lo-Lathrop Fam* pp. 47, 59, 79. Norwich CT VR 1:42(b. Israel), 77(m. to Mary Fellows; b. of their ch), 113(2ⁿᵈ m.), 152(b. Prudence). Norwich CT PR #6659; 5:94, 96(Israel Lathrop). New London CT LR 18:99(Israel Lothrop). Norwich CT LR 7:69-71(heirs of Israel Lothrop). New London CT PR #3288a(Israel Lothrop).

88. HANNAH⁴ BRADFORD (*Joseph³, WIlliam²⁻¹*), b. Lebanon, Conn., 24 May 1709; living 29 May 1749.

She m. Hebron, Conn., 20 Jan. 1730 **TIMOTHY BUELL**, b. Lebanon, Conn., 24 Oct. 1711; d. Hebron, Conn., 1794; son of William and Elizabeth (Collier) Buell. The will of William Buel of Lebanon dated 22 June 1757, proved 26 April 1763, names his son Timothy.

On 18 June 1747 Timothy and Hannah Bewell of Hebron, Conn., gave receipt for their legacy from their father's estate.

On 23 June 1748 James Harris and Robert Denison of New London, William Whiting of Norwich, Timothy and Hannah Buel of Hebron, Andrew and Elizabeth Lisk, David and Alethea Hide, and Jonathan and Ivernia Janes all of Lebanon sold to Ezekiel Fox of New London 30 acres in New London.

On 15 April 1757 Timothy Buel of Middletown, Conn., sold to John Thomson of Hebron 52 acres in New London, Conn.

No Connecticut probate records were found for Timothy Buell or land records to children. He is not in 1790 census.

Children of Timothy and Hannah (Bradford) Buell, b. Hebron, Conn.:

442	i	TIMOTHY BUELL⁵, b. 20 Nov. 1732
443	ii	ELIJAH BUELL (twin), b. 9 Nov. 1735
444	iii	HANNAH BUELL (twin), b. 9 Nov. 1735
445	iv	DEBORAH BUELL, b. 13 Sept. 1738
446	v	ICHABOD BUELL, b. 15 Feb. 1741
447	vi	OLIVER BUELL, b. 6 May 1746
448	vii	JOSEPH BUELL, b. 29 May 1749

References: Hebron CT VR 1:38(m.; b. 5 ch.), 45(b. Oliver), 54(b. Joseph). Lebanon CT VR 1:25(b. Timothy). *Bradford Desc* p. 32. *Waterman Gen* 1:629-30. *TAG* 23:190(Elizabeth Collier). New London CT LR 15:118(James Harris); 16:176(Timothy Buel). Windham CT PR #555(William Buel).

89. ELIZABETH⁴ BRADFORD (*Joseph³, William²⁻¹*), b. Lebanon, Conn., 21 Oct. 1712; d. there 27 June 1808.

She m. Lebanon, Conn., 15 June 1736 **ANDREW LISK**, b. ca. 1714; d. Lebanon, Conn., 20 Feb. 1797.

On 18 June 1747 Andrew and Elizabeth Lisk of Lebanon gave receipt for their legacy from their father's estate.

On 23 June 1748 James Harris and Robert Denison of New London, William Whiting of Norwich, Timothy and Hannah Buel of Hebron, Andrew and Elizabeth Lisk, David and Alethea Hide, and Jonathan and Ivernia Janes all of Lebanon sold to Ezekiel Fox of New London 30 acres in New London.

The will of Andrew Lisk of Lebanon dated 28 Dec. 1789, presented 1 April 1797, names wife Elizabeth; son William; daughters Ann Belden, Martha Flint, Betty Graves, Amy Palmer, and Huldah Cook.

On 30 June 1808 Ebenezer Fitch posted bond as the administrator of the estates of Elizabeth Lisk and William Lisk. Her personal property was sold at auction. No list of heirs was found.

Children of Andrew and Elizabeth (Bradford) Lisk, b. Lebanon, Conn.:

449	i	WILLIAM LISK[5], b. 17 Dec. 1738
450	ii	ANN LISK, b. 24 March 1740
451	iii	MARTHA LISK, b. 30 May 1742
	iv	ANDREW LISK, b. 4 Nov. 1744 (not in will)
452	v	BETTY LISK, b. 22 Nov. 1746
	vi	SARAH LISK, b. 7 March 1748/9 (not in will)
453	vii	AMY LISK, b. 15 Jan. 1752
454	viii	HULDAH LISK, b. 18 Aug. 1754

References: Lebanon CT VR 1:182(m.; b. ch.). Windham CT PR #2460 14:73(Andrew Lisk); #2461(William Lisk); #2462 (Elizabeth Lisk). *Waterman Gen* 1:629-30. First Church Lebanon CT Rec. 5:169(d. Eliz. & Wm.). New London CT LR 15:118(James Harris).

90. ALTHEA[4] BRADFORD (*Joseph[3], William[2-1]*), b. Lebanon, Conn., 19 Sept. 1715.

She m. ca. 1739 (based on church rec.) **DAVID HIDE**, bp. Lebanon, Conn., 22 March 1719; d. Lebanon 26 Dec. 1770; son of Samuel and Elizabeth (Caulkins) Hide.

On 24 Feb. 1739/40 David and Althea Hide confessed fornication before the First Church of Lebanon, Conn.

On 2 May 1747 David Hide of Sharon sold two tracts in Lebanon to Daniel Hide of Norwich and Caleb Hide of Lebanon. The deed mentions his "honored father" Samuel Hide.

On 18 June 1747 David and Alithea Hide gave receipt for their legacy from their father's estate.

On 23 June 1748 James Harris and Robert Denison of New London, William Whiting of Norwich, Timothy and Hannah Buel of Hebron, Andrew and Elizabeth Lisk, David and Alethea Hide, and Jonathan and Ivernia Janes all of Lebanon sold to Ezekiel Fox of New London 30 acres in New London.

On 1 Feb. 1747/8 Samuel Gillet sold 120 acres in Sharon to David Hide of Lebanon. On 14 July 1763 Captain David Hide of Sharon sold this tract and another to Daniel Griswold. On 6 Feb. 1764 he sold 2½ acres to the selectmen of the Town of Sharon.

No Connecticut probate records were found for David or Althea Hide.

Children of David and Althea (Bradford) Hide, first 5, bp. Lebanon, Conn.:

455   i   ELEANOR HIDE⁵, bp. 16 March 1739/40

      ii   DAVID HIDE, bp. 4 Jan. 1740/1; n.f.r.

456   iii   SIMEON HIDE, b. 14 or 15 Sept. 1742

     iv   ZEBULON HIDE, bp. 6 Oct. 1745; n.f.r.

457   v   AVIS HIDE, bp. 28 Feb. 1747/8

     vi   AZEL HIDE, b. prob. Sharon, Conn., ca. 1750 (based on age at d.). He d. Walton, Delaware Co., N.Y., 1828 aged 78, without surviving children; perhaps unm. The will of Azel Hide dated 29 April 1828, proved 22 Oct. 1828, names David Cole, Caleb Cole, and Richard B. Cole, children of his sister Eleanor Cole wife of Daniel Cole.

458   vii   ANN HIDE, b. prob. Sharon, Conn., ca. 1753 (based on age at d.)

459   viii   ELIZABETH HIDE, b. Sharon, Conn., 8 Sept. 1758

Note: The *Hyde Genealogy* (Reuben Walworth, Albany, N.Y., 1864), errs when it says David Hide died in 1740 with only one child. His father's will of 25 Oct. 1742 (Windham, Conn., PR 3:63) clearly shows David was alive then, as does the deed of 2 May 1747.

References: First Church, Lebanon CT Records 4:33(bp. David), 44(bp. Eleanor, David), 47(bp. Simeon), 48(bp. Zebulon), 49(bp. Avis), 86(fornication). Lebanon CT LR 7:226 (David Hyde). Sharon CT LR 2:376(Samuel Gilbert); 5:453; 6:234(David Hide). *NYGBR* 62:202(d. Azel). Delaware Co. NY PR C2:222 (Azel Hide). *Boston Evening Transcript* of 24 March 1715 (#4587). *Waterman Gen* 1:629-30. New London CT LR 15:118(James Harris).

91. IRENA⁴ BRADFORD (*Joseph³, William²⁻¹*), b. Lebanon, Conn., 19 Sept. 1715; d. after 12 Dec. 1761.

She m. Lebanon, Conn., 18 March 1735/6 **JONATHAN JANES**, b. Lebanon, Conn., 12 March 1713; d. probably after 27 Nov. 1784 (as son Jonathan was called Jr. on that date); son of William and Abigail (Loomis) Janes.

On 23 June 1748 James Harris and Robert Denison of New London, William Whiting of Norwich, Timothy and Hannah Buel of Hebron, Andrew and Elizabeth Lisk, David and Alethea Hide, and Jonathan and Ivernia Janes all of Lebanon sold Ezekiel Fox of New London 30 acres in New London.

On 13 Aug. 1764 William Janes of Woodstock, Conn., sold 88 acres in Brimfield to son Jonathan Janes of Brimfield, Hampshire County.

In the 1771 Valuation List, Jonathan Jones [*sic*] appears in Brimfield with 2 polls, 1 house, 1 iron works, 2 horses, 2 oxen, 2 cattle, 11 goats or sheep, 2 swine, 6 acres of pasture, 7 acres of tillage which produced 100 bushels of grain, 7 acres of upland which produced 4 tons of hay, and 4 acres of fresh meadow which produced 8 tons of hay.

On 25 Dec. 1773 Jonathan and Eliphalet Janes of Brimfield, yeomen, sold 15 acres in Brimfield to Solomon and Daniel Janes of Brimfield, clothiers.

On 27 Nov. 1784 Daniel Janes, clothier, and Jonathan Janes Jr., cordwainer, both of Monson sold 13 acres in Monson to Joseph and Asahel Utley of Monson.

No Hampshire County or Connecticut probate records were found for Jonathan or Irene Janes.

Children of Jonathan and Irena (Bradford) Janes, first seven b. Lebanon, Conn., last four b. Brimfield:

460	i	DAVID JANES[5], b. 23 Dec. 1736
	ii	JONATHAN JANES, b. 28 Jan. 1738/9; d. Brimfield 16 March 1752
	iii	IRENE JANES, b. 5 April 1741; d. Lebanon, Conn., 28 June 1743
461	iv	ELIPHALET JANES, b. 23 Feb. 1742/3
462	v	IRENE JANES, b. 30 July 1745
463	vi	SOLOMON JANES, b. 20 June 1748
464	vii	DANIEL JANES, b. 17 March 1751
465	viii	MARY JANES, b. 28 April 1753
466	ix	JONATHAN JANES, b. 8 Jan. 1756
	x	ABIGAIL JANES, b. 24 Jan. 1759; d. Brimfield 12 Feb. 1759
	xi	ANN JANES, b. 12 Dec. 1761; d. Brimfield 27 Oct. 1779

References: Brimfield VR pp. 80-1(b. last 4 ch.). *Bradford Desc* p. 33. *CT Marr* 2:41. Lebanon CT VR 1:160(m.; b. first 7 ch.). Hampden Co. LR 9:59(William Janes); 12:562 (Jonathan and Eliphalet); 23:159(Daniel & Jonathan Janes). New London CT LR 15:118(James Harris). *1771 Valuation* p. 416.

92. JOHN[4] BRADFORD (*Joseph[3], William[2-1]*), b. New London, Conn., 20 May 1717; d. Montville, Conn., 10 March 1787 aged 70.

He m. Montville, Conn., 15 Dec. 1736 **ESTHER SHERWOOD**, b. New London, Conn., 20 Nov. 1717; d. Montville, Conn., 10 Dec. 1799 aged 82; daughter of Samuel and Rebecca (Burr) Sherwood. The will of Samuel Sherwood dated 7 Nov. 1732, names among others (second) wife Mary and daughter Esther.

On 28 May 1765 Israel Lothrop of Norwich and his wife Sarah sold to John Bradford Jr. of New London 4 ¼ acres with a "Mantion" house.

John Bradford of New London conveyed land to his sons in a series of deeds: to Samuel 31 Aug. 1765; to Joseph 31 Aug. 1765; to John 31 Aug. 1765; to John 28 Sept. 1765; to Samuel 28 Sept. 1765; to John 2 Feb. 1770; to Perez 2 Feb. 1770; to Benjamin 2 Feb. 1770; to Perez and Benjamin 29 March 1781; to Benjamin and Perez 28 March 1785.

No Connecticut probate records were found for John Bradford.

Children of John and Esther (Sherwood) Bradford, b. Montville, Conn.:

467	i	SAMUEL[5] BRADFORD, b. 4 Jan. 1737/8
	ii	[SON] BRADFORD, d.y.
468	iii	JOHN BRADFORD, b. 7 Dec. 1739
469	iv	JOSEPH BRADFORD, b. 17 June 1742
470	v	SARAH BRADFORD, b. 27 July 1744
	vi	[SON] BRADFORD, d.y.
	vii	[SON] BRADFORD, d.y.
471	viii	PEREZ BRADFORD, b. 11 Oct. 1746
472	ix	BENJAMIN BRADFORD, b. 8 Oct. 1748
	x	ELEANOR BRADFORD d. "about a year old."
473	xi	REBECCA BRADFORD, b. Jan. 1754
474	xii	MARY BRADFORD, b. 17 Jan. 1756

References: *Bradford Desc* pp. 33-4. *CT Marr* 1:70. *Fairfield CT Fams* 1:556-7(Sherwood). New London CT VR 1:49 (b. Esther). Montville Church records 3:18(b. ch.; d. 4 ch.). New London CT LR 18:99(Israel Lothrop); 18:97-100, 106; 19:299; 20:198; 21:143, 144; 22:60; 25:96(John Bradford). Hale Cem Coll:Montville p. 65(Esther Bradford); 69(John Bradford).

93. BATHSHEBA[4] BRADFORD (*Israel[3], William[2-1]*), b. Plymouth 8 Nov. 1703; d. Kingston 23 Dec. 1773 aged 70y 1m 4d.

She m. int. Kingston 23 Dec. 1731 **THOMAS ADAMS**, b. Plymouth 5 May 1709; d. Kingston 12 Dec. 1768 aged 59y 7m; son of Francis and Mary (Buck) Adams.

On 1 Dec. 1762 Thomas Adams of Kingston, gentleman, sold to Joshua Adams of Kingston, mariner, one acre and a house near the house Thomas lived in.

On 1 May 1769 Joshua Adams of Kingston, mariner, and Perez Loring of Duxboro, yeoman, were appointed administrators of the estate of Thomas Adams late of Kingston, yeoman, deceased. On 7 Oct. 1784 Perez Loring, only surviving administrator, rendered an account.

In the 1771 Valuation List, widow Bathsheba Adams appears in Kingston with half a house, 2 cattle, 6 goats or sheep, and one acre of tillage which produced 10 bushels of grain. John Adams is listed next to her.

On 11 Dec. 1771 Joshua Adams, mariner; Gershom Cobb, joyner, and his wife Sarah; and Deborah Adams, weaver, all of Kingston, being the heirs of Thomas Adams, sold to John Adams of Kingston some cedar swamp.

No Plymouth County probate records were found for Bathsheba Adams.

Children of Thomas and Bathsheba (Bradford) Adams, b. Kingston:

475   i   SARAH ADAMS[5], b. 3 Dec. 1732
476   ii JOSHUA ADAMS, b. 21 Nov. 1735
       iii BARTLETT ADAMS, b. 19 March 1738/9; d. 27 May 1741 ae 2y 2m 9d
       iv NATHANIEL ADAMS, b. 18 Nov. 1740; apparently d. before 11 Dec. 1771 (not in deed)
       v   MARY ADAMS, b. 3 Sept. 1744; d. Kingston 17 Feb. 1764 ae 19y 4m 26d
       vi DEBORAH ADAMS, b. 17 Oct. 1747; d. Kingston 23 Feb. 1826 ae 78y; unm. The will of Deborah Adams of Kingston, singlewoman, dated 20 Jan. 1826, proved 15 March 1826, names niece Sally Bradford, widow of Nathaniel Bradford; niece Molly, widow of Seth Perkins; and Deborah A. Cushing, daughter of aforsaid Sally Bradford.

References: *VR Kingston* pp. 11-5(b. ch.), 167(int.), 311-3 (deaths). *MD* 2:227(b. Thomas). Plymouth Co. PR 20:204, 249; 28:461(Thomas Adams); 60:335-6(Deborah Adams). *Plymouth VR* p. 25(b. Thomas). Plymouth Co. LR 54:77(Thomas Adams); 56:193-4(Joshua Adams *et al.*). *1771 Valuation* p. 640.

94. BENJAMIN[4] BRADFORD (*Israel[3], William[2-1]*), b. Plymouth 17 Oct. 1705; d. Kingston 16 Oct. or Nov. 1783 aged 77.

He m. (1) int. Kingston 18 Dec. 1731 **ZERESH STETSON**, b. Plymouth 29 Nov. 1712; d. Kingston 6 April 1763 in 51st yr.; daughter of Elisha and Abigail (Brewster) Stetson, a descendant of Pilgrim **William Brewster.** The agreement of the heirs of Elisha Stetson, late of Kingston deceased, includes daughter Zeresh wife of Benja Bradford (no date is mentioned, but after 3 March 1755).

He m. (2) Kingston 7 Dec. 1763 **MERCY CHIPMAN**, b. Kingston 19 Nov. 1725; d. there 13 Feb. 1782 in 57th yr.; daughter of Seth and Priscilla (Bradford) Chipman, a descendant of Pilgrims **William Bradford** (see #138) and **John Howland.**

Two of Benjamin and Zeresh's children died in infancy, and they lost all their remaining children in July 1748; daughter Lydia, the only survivor of the family, was born the following year.

On 4 April 1761 Benjamin Bradford of Kingston, yeoman, and Elisha Bradford of Kingston, cooper, divided the homestead held in common that came to them from their father Israel Bradford. On 9 July 1778 Benjamin sold Elisha and Levi Bradford of Kingston, yeomen, sold 21 acres whereon Abner Bradford was dwelling and that had come to him from his father Israel.

In the 1771 Valuation List, Benjamin Bradford appears in Kingston with 1 poll, 1 house, 1 cattle, 12 goats or sheep, 1 swine, 5 acres pasture, 4 acres tillage which produced 40 bushels grain, and 2 acres salt marsh which produced 2 tons of hay.

Benjamin Bradford of Kingston, retailer, was granted a license to sell liquor from 1778 to 1782.

On 7 April 1784 Levi Holmes of Kingston was appointed administrator of the estate of Benjamin Bradford of Kingston, yeoman.

On 7 Dec. 1785 Levi Holmes of Kingston, yeoman, and his wife Lydia, sold to Thomas Brewer land in Kingston of which Benjamin Bradford late of Kingston died seized, with reference to the division deeds of the estate of Israel Bradford. It states that Lydia is sole heir of Benjamin Bradford. On 17 July 1790 Levi and Lydia sold Jedidiah Holmes of Kingston, Gentleman, a salt meadow that was assigned to "our father Benjamin Bradford" in the division of his father's estate between him and his brother Elisha, part of the estate that came to Lydia.

Children of Benjamin and first wife Zeresh (Stetson) Bradford, b. Kingston:

- i   THOMAS[5] BRADFORD, b. 9 Feb. 1732/3; d. 7 July 1748
- ii   MICHAEL BRADFORD, b. 16 May 1735; d. 2 Oct. 1735
- iii   PEREZ BRADFORD, b. 3 Sept. 1736; d. 12 July 1748
- iv   LYDIA BRADFORD, b. 22 June 1739; d. 16 July 1748
- v   BENJAMIN BRADFORD, b. 8 Feb. 1742; d. 19 July 1748
- vi   MARCY BRADFORD, b. 13 March 1745; d. 9 Aug. 1745
- vii   LEMUEL BRADFORD, b. 16 June 1747; d. 12 July 1748

477   viii   LYDIA BRADFORD, b. 7 June 1749

References: *VR Kingston* pp. 25-30(b. ch.), 40(b. wife Mercy), 179(int. 1st m.; 2nd m.), 319-22(deaths). *MD* 7:22-4(d..), 178(b. Zeresh); 36:147(Elisha Stetson agree.). Plymouth Co. PR 27:146(Benj. Bradford). *Plymouth VR* p. 44(b. Zeresh). Plymouth Co. LR 57:161; 59:194(Benjamin Bradford); 72:12(Levi Holmes). *Plymouth Co CT Recs* Vol. 3, 4. *1771 Valuation* p.644.

95. ABNER⁴ BRADFORD (*Israel³, William²⁻¹*), b. Plymouth 25 Dec. 1707; d. Kingston 18 June 1784 aged 77.

He m. int. Kingston 4 Nov. 1733 **SUSANNAH POTTER**, b. Swansea 15 Oct. 1715; living 1 July 1765 when she acknowledged a deed; daughter of Hopestill and Lydia (Phinney) Potter. On 14 July 1806 the heirs of Simeon Potter who held land in common in nine shares divided the estate. Levi Bradford, Mary Chapman, Lucy Sheldon, Elisha Bradford, Margaret Ripley, Lydia Orcutt, and Hannah Bates each owned one share.

At the April 1765 term of the Plymouth County Court of Common Pleas, Cornelius Samson of Kingston, trader, sued Abner Bradford of Kingston, laborer, for ejectment from "a small house-lot" in Kingston. Cornelius claimed that on 1 March 1760 Abner had conveyed the land to him by deed, to be void on payment of a sum with interest within two years, and that Abner had not paid. On 29 June 1765, acknowledged 1 July 1765 by Abner and Susannah, Abner Bradford sold a house and lot in Kingston to Cornelius Sampson.

In the 1771 Valuation List, Abner Bradford appears in Kingston with nothing.

No other useful Plymouth County land records were found for Abner Bradford, or any probate records for Abner or Susanna Bradford.

Children of Abner and Susannah (Potter) Bradford, b. Kingston:

478	i	ELIJAH⁵ BRADFORD, b. 11 April 1735
	ii	LEVI BRADFORD, b. 1 Oct. 1737; d. June 1758; unm. No PR.
	iii	ZENAS BRADFORD, b. 6 July 1739; d. July 1749
479	iv	MARY BRADFORD, b. 13 June 1742
	v	ABIGAIL BRADFORD, b. 21 Aug. 1744
	vi	ISRAEL BRADFORD, b. 17 July 1748; d. July 1749
480	vii	LYDIA BRADFORD, b. 20 Dec. 1749
481	viii	HANNAH BRADFORD, b. 28 Feb. 1751
482	ix	ELISHA BRADFORD, b. 10 May 1753
482A	x	LUCY BRADFORD, b. 10 May 1755
483	xi	PEGGY (or MARGARET) BRADFORD, b. 8 May 1757
484	xii	LEVI BRADFORD, b. 1 July 1759

References: *MD* 7:22(d. Abner). *VR Kingston* pp. 25-31(b. ch.), 179(m.), 319-22(deaths). *Swansea VR* p. 148(b. Susannah). Plymouth Co. LR 50:72(Abner Bradford). *Plymouth Co CT Recs* 8:159. *1771 Valuation* p.644.

96. JOSHUA⁴ BRADFORD (*Israel³, William²⁻¹*), b. Plymouth 23 June 1710; d. Friendship, Maine, 22 May 1758, killed by Indians.

He m. Kingston 17 Feb. 1736 **HANNAH BRADFORD**, b. Plymouth 10 April 1720; d. Friendship, Maine, 22 May 1758, killed by Indians; daughter of Elisha and Bathsheba (Brock) Bradford, a descendant of Pilgrim **William Bradford** (see #110).

Sarah Bradford of Plimton, widow, received a judgement against Joshua Bradford of Kingston, cooper, and on 11 Oct. 1744 part of Joshua's house and land was set off to Sarah to satisfy the judgement. On 24 March 1748 Sarah sold her part of the house and land to Benjamin Bartlett of Duxbury.

The *Boston News Letter* of 1 June 1758, quoting from a letter dated 22 May 1758, says "They [Indians] killed and scalped Mr. Bradford, his wife and Mr. Mills' wife and killed her children. Two of Mr. Bradford's boys they carried off prisoners, wounded one of his daughters and a boy of Mills dangerously."

No York County, Maine, or Plymouth County probate or land records were found for Joshua and Hannah Bradford.

Children of Joshua and Hannah (Bradford) Bradford, b. Kingston:

485	i	CORNELIUS⁵ BRADFORD, b. 10 Dec. 1737
486	ii	SARAH BRADFORD, b. 16 Oct. 1739
487	iii	RACHEL BRADFORD, b. 28 Jan. 1741
488	iv	MARY BRADFORD (twin), b. 16 March 1744
489	v	MELATIAH BRADFORD (twin), b. 16 March 1744
490	vi	JOSHUA BRADFORD, b. 2 April 1746
491	vii	HANNAH BRADFORD, b. 9 March 1748
492	viii	JOSEPH BRADFORD, b. 19 March 1751
493	ix	BENJAMIN BRADFORD, b. 28 May 1753
494	x	ELISHA BRADFORD, b. 15 Oct. 1755
	xi	WINSLOW BRADFORD, bp. Marshfield 30 July 1757; killed by Indians 22 May 1758

References: *MD* 13:112(b. Hannah). *MQ* 46:130(bp. Winslow). *VR Kingston* pp. 25-30(b. ch.), 180(m.). *Bradford Desc* p. 35(d.. in ME). *Boston News Obits* 2:121(d. Joshua, Hannah). *Plymouth VR* p. 64(b. Hannah). Plymouth Co. LR 37:62(judgement); 40:62(Sarah Bradford).

97. ICHABOD⁴ BRADFORD (*Israel³, William²⁻¹*), b. Plymouth 22 Sept. 1713; d. Kingston 6 April 1791 aged 77.

He m. (1) Kingston 25 Nov. 1743 **MARY JOHNSON***, d. Kingston 13 July 1761.

He m. (2) Kingston 31 May 1763 **MARY (SAMSON) COOKE**, b. Pembroke 6 Jan. 1724; living 28 Oct. 1766 (b. last ch.); daughter of Peleg and Mary (Ring) Samson, a descendant of Pilgrims **John Alden, Stephen Hopkins,** and **Myles Standish.** She m. (1) int. Kingston 26 Sept. 1741 NATHANIEL COOKE with whom she had Mary, Peleg, Nathaniel, Susannah, Isaac, Deborah, and Levi.

In the 1771 Valuation List, Ichabod Bradford appears in Kingston with two polls and one house.

Figures for Ichabod Bradford's household in Kingston in 1790 suggest that he and his wife were living by themselves.

No Plymouth County probate or useful land records were found for Ichabod Bradford.

Children of Ichabod and Mary (Johnson) Bradford, b. Kingston:

495	i	ICHABOD⁵ BRADFORD, b. 28 Aug. 1744
496	ii	ELIZABETH BRADFORD, b. 10 July 1747
497	iii	RHODA BRADFORD, b. 20 July 1751
	iv	LEMUEL BRADFORD, b. 22 Aug. 1755
498	v	ANNE BRADFORD, b. 15 April 1758

Child of Ichabod and Mary (Samson) (Cooke) Bradford, b. Kingston:

499	vi	ISRAEL BRADFORD, b. 28 Oct. 1766

* MARY is called JOHNSON in int. and GORSON in mar. rec. in *VR Kingston*.

References: *VR Kingston* pp. 25-30(b. 5 ch.), 180(both m.), 198(Mary's 1ˢᵗ m.), 320(d. Ichabod), 321(d. first wife). *VR Pembroke* p. 182(b. Mary). *VR Plympton* p. 33(b. Israel). *MF* 14:82-3. *1771 Valuation* p. 640.

98. ELISHA⁴ BRADFORD (*Israel³, William²⁻¹*), b. Plymouth 25 March 1718; d. Kingston 26 Feb. 1801 aged 83.

He m. int. Halifax 17 Jan. 1761 **MARY STURTEVANT**, b. Kingston ca. 1728; d. there May 1813 aged 85; daughter of James and Susanna (Cooke) Sturtevant, a descendant of Pilgrims **James Chilton, Francis Cooke,** and **Stephen Hopkins.** On 9 April 1771 and 7 May 1774 Elisha Bradford and his wife Mary sold land that had come to them from their father James Sturtevant.

On 11 June 1770 Elisha and Mary Bradford of Kingston and others divided land of their father James Sturtevant late of Halifax. On 3 July 1773 Elisha Bradford of Kingston, cooper, sold land of his father Israel Bradford that had been conveyed to his brother Benjamin and to him.

In the 1771 Valuation List, Elisha Bradford appears in Kingston with one poll, one house, 3 cattle, 12 goats or sheep, 1 swine, 4 acres of pasture, 4 acres of tillage which produced 40 bushels of grain, and 2 acres of salt marsh which produced 2 tons of hay.

Elisha Bradford's household in 1790 in Kingston consisted of two males 16 or older and two females.

No Plymouth County probate records were found for Elisha or Mary Bradford. There is no record that they had children.

References: *VR Kingston* pp. 319(d. Elisha), 320(d. Mary). *Halifax VR* p. 61(int.). Plymouth Co. LR 55:168; 57:162(Elisha Bradford); 58:148; 61:39(Sturtevant land). Plymouth Co. PR #19752(James Sturtevant). *MF* 15:98-9. *1771 Valuation* p. 644.

99. ANNA⁴ BRADFORD (*Ephraim³, William²⁻¹*), b. Plymouth 25 July 1715; d. after 12 June 1757.

She m. Kingston 23 Feb. 1737 **EBENEZER CHANDLER**, b. Duxbury 8 Sept. 1712; living 28 March 1787 when he acknowledged a deed; son of Joseph and Martha (Hunt) Chandler.

Ebenezer Chandler and his family were warned out of Kingston on 20 Aug. 1749.

On 24 Oct. 1786, acknowledged 28 March 1787, Ebenezer Chandler of Duxbury, miller, sold his house and land in Duxbury to Sceva Chandler of Duxbury, blacksmith.

No Plymouth County probate records were found for Ebenezer Chandler.

Children of Ebenezer and Anna (Bradford) Chandler, b. or bp. Duxbury:

500 i   LYDIA CHANDLER⁵, b. 14 March 1740/1
     ii ZILPAH CHANDLER, b. 15 Feb. 1741/2; d. Duxbury 7 May 1837 ae 95; unm. No PR
     iii SIMEON CHANDLER, b. 23 June 1744; d. Duxbury 17 April 1767 ae 22y 10m. No PR
     iv ANNA CHANDLER, b. 14 June 1746
     v   NATHANIEL CHANDLER, bp. 14 Nov. 1756; d. Duxbury 14 June 1773 ae 20y 9m

vi JUDAH CHANDLER, bp. 14 Nov. 1756; d. Duxbury 24 April 1772 ae
        21y 2m. No PR

501   vii SCEVA CHANDLER, bp. 12 June 1757

References: *VR Kingston* p. 189(m.). *VR Duxbury* pp. 39-47(b. Ebenezer; b.&bp. ch.),
360-2(d. ch.). *Small Desc* 2:1075-6. *MD* 11:150(b. Eben.); 12:121 (b. 4 ch.). Plymouth Co.
LR 66:238(Ebenezer Chandler). *Plymouth Co CT Recs* 2:179(warning).

100. ELIZABETH⁴ BRADFORD (*Ephraim³, William²⁻¹*), b. Plymouth 3
Nov. 1717; living 30 Sept. 1772 when she was named in her husband's will.

She m. Kingston 12 July 1753 **AZARIAH WHITING**, b. Plympton
9 Aug. 1711; living 30 Sept. 1772; son of John and Bethia (Crocker) Whiting, a
descendant of Pilgrim **John Howland**. He m. (1) Plympton 10 June 1736
ELIZABETH BARROWS with whom he had Phebe, Elizabeth, Bethea, and
Ruth. He m. (2) Plymouth 10 Sept. 1745 REBECCA (CHURCHILL) HOLMES
with whom he had Hannah, Thomas, Priscilla, and Ebenezer.

At the March 1730/1 term of the Plymouth County Court of General
Sessions, Joseph Cole was presented "for fiting and Striking Azariah Whiting,"
and Azariah Whiting was presented for striking Joseph Cole.

On 6 Feb. 1767, acknowledged 25 Feb. 1768, Azariah Whitton of
Plympton, yeoman, sold land to Elisha Whiton of Plympton.

In the 1771 Valuation List, Azariah Whiton appears in Plympton with
2 polls, 1 house, 1 shop, 1 oxen, 1 cattle, 17 goats or sheep, 2 swine, 6 acres
pasture, 12 acres of tillage which produced 50 bushels of grain, 3 barrels of
cider, 4 acres of upland which produced 2½ tons of hay, and 6 acres of fresh
meadow which produced 7 tons of hay.

The will of Azariah Witon of Plimpton, yeoman, dated 30 Sept. 1772,
proved 1773, names wife Elizabeth; son John (under age); son Thomas;
daughter Phebe Bradford the wife of Simeon Bradford; daughter Hannah
Donham the wife of Israel Donham; daughter Priscilla Witon; daughter
Patience Witon; and daughter Elizabeth Witon.

No Plymouth County probate records were found for Elizabeth Whiting.

Children of Azariah and Elizabeth (Bradford) Whiting, b. Plympton:

    i   JOHN WHITING⁵, b. 6 Aug. 1754; living 30 Sept. 1772 (will)

    ii   EPHRAIM WHITING (twin), b. 21 Jan. 1757 (not in will)

502   iii PATIENCE WHITING (twin), b. 21 Jan. 1757

503   iv   ELIZABETH WHITING, b. 6 Oct. 1759

References: *VR Plympton* pp. 227(b. ch.), 229(b. Azariah), 427 (his 3rd m.). *Whiton Fam* pp. 37-8. Plymouth Co. LR 56:235(Azariah Whitton). Plymouth Co. PR 21:306-7(Azariah Witon). *Plymouth Co CT Recs* 2:116.

101. ABIGAIL[4] BRADFORD (*Ephraim[3], William[2-1]*), b. Plymouth 28 Feb. 1719/20; d. Yarmouth, Nova Scotia, 13 Sept. 1790 aged 75y.

She m., int. Kingston 4 Oct. 1740, **PELEG HOLMES**, b. Plymouth 28 Sept. 1715; d. Yarmouth, Nova Scotia, before 7 Nov. 1799 (will sworn); son of John and Mercy (Ford) Holmes.

On 1 June 1762 Peleg Holmes of Kingston, yeoman, sold land to Josiah Holmes of Kingston. The deed was signed by Peleg and Abigail Holmes, and acknowledged only by Peleg 10 June 1762.

The will of Peleg Holmes of Yarmouth, husbandman, dated 12 Jan. 1795, sworn 7 Nov. 1799, names son Nathaniel; daughter Lydia Holmes; daughter Abigail, wife of Cornelius Rogers of Yarmouth; daughter Elizabeth, wife of James Winslow of New England; daughter Mary, wife of Elishama Eldredge of Yarmouth; daughter Sarah, widow of Joseph Baley; daughter Lucy, wife of Elkanah Clements of Yarmouth; and grandson Samuel Kimble. Named in a division dated 18 March 1818 are Nathaniel Holmes, widow Abigail Rogers, Lydia Holmes, Sarah Baily, Samuel Kimble, heirs of Elizabeth Winslow, deceased, heirs of Lucy Clements, deceased, and heirs of Mary Eldredge, deceased

Children of Peleg and Abigail (Bradford) Holmes, first 9 b. Kingston, last 2 b. Yarmouth, N.S.:

	i	ABIGAIL HOLMES[5], b. 4 June 1741; d. 20 June 1742
	ii	DEBORAH HOLMES, b. 3 April 1743; d. 26 Jan. 1748
504	iii	ABIGAIL HOLMES, b. 6 July 1746
	iv	PELEG HOLMES, b. 6 Jan. 1749; d. Yarmouth, N.S., 28 Dec. 1772
505	v	ELIZABETH HOLMES, b. 18 Feb. 1751
	vi	LYDIA HOLMES, b. 29 June 1753; living 18 March 1818
506	vii	NATHANIEL HOLMES, b. 21 Oct. 1755
507	viii	MARY HOLMES, b. 20 Feb. 1758
508	ix	SARAH HOLMES, b. 23 April 1760
509	x	LUCY HOLMES, b. 12 Sept. 1762
	xi	[DAUGHTER] HOLMES , b. 26 May 1767; d. 27 May 1767

References: *VR Kingston* pp. 89-97(b. ch.), 240(int.), 356-7(d. 1st 2 ch.). *MD* 7:209(b. Peleg). *Bradford Desc* p. 36. Plymouth Co. LR 47:236(Peleg Holmes). *NGSQ* 74:214-5.

Yarmouth NS VR p. 1-18(b. Lucy; b.& d. daughter; d. Peleg Jr.). Yarmouth Cemetery Records. Yarmouth Co. NS PR H-10, 27(Peleg Holmes). *Plymouth VR* p. 46(b. Peleg).

102. LUSANNA⁴ BRADFORD (*Ephraim³, William²⁻¹*), b. Plymouth 3 May 1721; d. Kingston 9 Dec. 1805.

She m. Kingston 28 April 1752 **SETH EVERSON**, d. Kingston before 13 Sept. 1768.

On 13 Sept. 1768 Seth Cushing of Plimton and Lusanna Everson of Kingston, widow, were appointed to administer the estate of Seth Everson, late of Kingston, mariner, deceased. Dower was set off to widow Lusanna Everson 1 Oct. 1787. On 19 Dec. 1787 the estate was divided to heirs of James Everson, Jr.; Seth Everson; Hannah Lincoln, wife of James; Lydia Everson; and heirs of Oliver who died in his minority.

On 10 Dec. 1781 Lydia Everson of Kingston, weaver, sold to [her brother] James Everson Jr. of Kingston her right in the estate of their father Seth Everson deceased.

On 4 March 1797 Lusanna Everson of Kingston, spinster, sold to Amos Cook of Kingston half an acre; the deed was not recorded until 8 Oct. 1822.

The 6 June 1807 division of the dower of widow Lusanna Everson, late of Kingston, deceased, in the real estate of Seth Everson late of Kingston, names heirs of eldest son James, deceased; Seth Everson; Hannah, wife of James Lincoln; and Lydia Everson.

Children of Seth and Lusanna (Bradford) Everson, b. or bp. Kingston:

510   i HANNAH EVERSON⁵, bp. 15 April 1753

511   ii JAMES EVERSON, bp. 29 Sept. 1754

        iii OLIVER EVERSON, bp. 9 Jan. 1757; d. before 1778; unm.

        iv LYDIA EVERSON, bp. 17 June 1759; d. Kingston 15 April 1813 ae 54; unm. The deathbed verbal will of Lydia Everson on 15 April 1813, proved 5 July 1813, names brother Seth and sister Lincoln.

512   v SETH EVERSON, b. 11 July 1761

Note: *Bradford Desc* lists a son Bradford who d.y. but gives no dates.

References: *VR Kingston* pp. 69-71(b.&bp. ch.), 217(m.), 345(d. Lusanna, Lydia), 346(d. Seth). *MD* 7:85(d. Lusanna). Plymouth Co. PR 17:112; 19:13; 30:196, 364, 405(Seth Everson); 42:140(Lusanna Everson); 45:32(Lydia Everson). Plymouth Co. LR 67:55(Lydia Everson); 147:75(Lusanna Everson).

103. RUTH⁴ BRADFORD (*Ephraim³, William²⁻¹*), b. Plymouth ca. 1725; d. Duxbury 26 Aug. 1767 aged 42y 6m.

She m. Kingston 3 Aug. 1749 **NATHAN CHANDLER**, b. Duxbury 28 Oct. 1726; d. there 21 Sept. 1795 in 69th yr.; son of Philip and Rebecca (Phillips) Chandler. He m. (2) Duxbury 20 Feb. 1770 ESTHER GLASS with whom he had Joseph and Ira.

The will of Nathan Chandler of Duxbury dated 26 Feb. 1795, presented 27 Oct. 1795, names wife Esther; children of eldest son who is deceased: two oldest sons Nathan and Isaac and two youngest sons Ephraim and John; daughters Ruth, Lucy, and Hannah (without surnames); and son Ira Chandler.

Children of Nathan and Ruth (Bradford) Chandler, b. or bp. Duxbury:

513   i   EPHRAIM CHANDLER⁵, b. 18 May 1750
        ii   SELAH CHANDLER, bp. 6 June 1756; d. 21 May 1773 ae 19
        iii LUCY CHANDLER, bp. 6 June 1756; living 26 Feb. 1795(will). No PR
        iv   HANNAH CHANDLER, bp. 12 June 1757; living 26 Feb. 1795 (will). No PR
        v   [DAUGHTER] CHANDLER, b. 27 Nov. 1760; d. 30 Nov. 1760
514   vi   RUTH CHANDLER, bp. 24 Oct. 1762
        vii SARAH CHANDLER, d. 23 July 1764 ae 16d
        viii DEBORAH CHANDLER, b. June 1766; d. 13 Aug. 1767 ae 1y 2m

References: *VR Duxbury* pp. 40-8(b. ch.), 49(b. Nathan), 232 (his 2nd m.), 359-62(deaths). *VR Kingston* p. 190 (m.). *MD* 11:149(b. Nathan). Plymouth Co. PR 35:324(Nathan Chandler).

104. EZEKIEL⁴ BRADFORD (*Ephraim³, William²⁻¹*), b. rec. Kingston 14 March 1728; d. Turner, Maine, 26 Sept. 1816 aged 88.

He m. Duxbury 21 July 1750 **BETTY CHANDLER**, b. Duxbury 21 Oct. 1728; d. Turner, Maine, 24 Oct. 1811 aged 83; daughter of Philip and Rebecca (Phillips) Chandler. The will of Philip Chandler of Duxbury dated 9 Oct. 1762 names wife Rebecca and daughter Betty (without surname).

On 13 July 1767 Ezekiel and Betty Bradford of Kingston sold land in Plympton to Ebenezer Soule of Plympton. On 11 Dec. 1773 Ezekiel Bradford of Kingston, yeoman, sold two acres of a cedar swamp in Kingston to Ephraim Chandler of Duxbury. On 1 May 1779 Ezekiel Bradford of Kingston, husbandman, sold his homestead in Kingston to John Adams of Kingston.

In the 1771 Valuation List, Ezekiel Bradford appears in Kingston with 2 polls, 1 house, 1 horse, 4 oxen, 2 cattle, 10 goats or sheep, 2 swine, 6 acres pasture, 8 acres of tillage which produced 50 bushels of grain, 3 barrels of cider, 1 acre of salt marsh which produced 1 ton of hay, and 3 acres of fresh meadon which produced 4 tons of hay.

On 14 May 1794 Ezekiel Bradford of Turner, yeoman, quitclaimed half a lot in Turner "I now live on" to son Chandler Bradford of Turner, yeoman. On the same day Ezekiel and Chandler Bradford of Turner, yeomen, quitclaimed a lot in Turner to Martin Bradford of Turner, yeoman.

Ezekiel Bradford served as a private during the Revolutionary War.

No Maine probate records were found for Ezekiel Bradford.

Children of Ezekiel and Betty (Chandler) Bradford, b. Kingston:

515	i	EPHRAIM[5] BRADFORD, b. 13 Dec. 1750
516	ii	DEBORAH BRADFORD, b. 18 Aug. 1752
517	iii	WILLIAM BRADFORD, b. 9 March 1754
518	iv	REBECCA BRADFORD, b. 22 Sept. 1756
519	v	JESSE BRADFORD, b. 7 March 1758
520	vi	EZEKIEL BRADFORD, b. 15 Dec. 1759
521	vii	CHANDLER BRADFORD, b. 15 Aug. 1761
522	viii	MARTIN BRADFORD, b. 17 Oct. 1763
523	ix	PHILIP BRADFORD, b. 8 June 1765
524	x	BETTY BRADFORD, b. 22 Aug. 1767

References: *VR Duxbury* pp. 48(b. Betty), 222(m.). *VR Kingston* pp. 25-30(b. ch.). *Bradford Desc* p. 37. *MD* 11:149 (b. Betty). *Small Desc* 2:1066. Turner ME VR, unpaged(d. Ezekiel, Betty). *Turner ME Hist* p. 58(ch. & their spouses). Plymouth Co. LR 53:223; 60:62; 75:169(Ezekiel Bradford). Cumberland Co. ME LR 21:230(Ezekiel Bradford), 231(Ezekiel and Chandler). *DAR Patriot Index* p. 78. *1771 Valuation* p. 640.

105. SIMEON[4] BRADFORD (*Ephraim[3], William[2-1]*), b. rec. Kingston 28 Aug. 1729; d. Springfield, Vt., 6 Oct. 1793 aged 64.

He m. Plympton 23 Jan. 1755 **PHEBE WHITON**, b. Plympton 16 March 1736/7; d. Springfield, Vt., between 11 April 1794 (div.) and 10 Dec. 1796 (deed); daughter of Azariah and Elizabeth (Barrows) Whiton. The will of Azariah Witon of Plimpton dated 30 Sept. 1772 names daughter Phebe Bradford the wife of Simeon Bradford.

On 21 Sept. 1765 Simeon Bradford of Kingston, yeoman, sold to Ezekiel Bradford of Kingston, yeoman, his right in the homestead, undivided with Ezekiel, given to them by the will of their father Ephraim Bradford.

Simeon Bradford served as a private during the Revolutionary War.

On 3 Sept. 1790 Simeon Bradford of Springfield, yeoman, sold to Asa Bradford of Springfield three acres in that town. Hosea and Joel Bradford were witnesses.

On 16 Nov. 1793 administration of the estate of Simeon Bradford, late of Springfield, was granted to Asa Bradford. On 11 April 1794 the property was divided among Phebe Bradford, widow; sons Joel, Simeon, Ephraim, Asa, and Hosea Bradford; daughters Lucy McRoberts, wife of John McRoberts; Nabby Bradford Holmes, wife of Walter Holmes; Cynthia Bradford; Deborah Bradford; and Ruth Bradford Smith, wife of Isaac Smith.

On 10 Dec. 1796 Joel Bradford and Hosea Bradford of Springfield sold to Asa Bradford of Springfield 29 acres and 9½ acres, part of their mother's thirds "being the whole of the Land sett off to us out of our late Father's Estate likewise Two Thirds of the House & Barn."

Children of Simeon and Phebe (Whiton) Bradford, first three b. Kingston, rest b. prob. Springfield, Vt.:

525	i	ASA[5] BRADFORD, b. 5 July 1758
525A	ii	SIMEON BRADFORD, b. 3 Sept. 1760
526	iii	LUCY BRADFORD, b. 2 Oct. 1762
527	iv	HOSEA BRADFORD, b. ca. 1763
528	v	ABIGAIL BRADFORD, b. 23 Jan. 1765
529	vi	RUTH BRADFORD, b. 17 Jan. 1768
	vii	DEBORAH BRADFORD living 16 Nov. 1793 (div.)
530	viii	JOEL BRADFORD, b. 25 Jan. 1773
531	ix	EPHRAIM BRADFORD, b. Vermont 1780
	x	REBECCA BRADFORD, d. prob. y.
	xi	CYNTHIA BRADFORD living 16 Nov. 1793 (div.)

Note: *Bradford Desc* lists a daughter Elizabeth, b. 23 Dec. 1774 (p.37) and also gives her a second birthdate of 23 Sept. 1767 and claims she m. 31 Jan. 1771 Melatiah Holmes (pp. 150–151). These statements are obviously incorrect.

References: *VR Kingston* pp. 25(b. Asa), 28(b. Lucy), 30(b. Simeon). *VR Plympton* pp. 229(b. Phebe), 266(m.). *Bradford Desc* p. 37. Springfield VT LR 1:77(Simeon Bradford); 2:316(Joel Bradford *et al.*). Windsor Dist. VT PR 2:121, 124(Simeon Bradford). Plymouth Co. PR 21:306-7(Azariah Whiton). *DAR Patriot Index* p. 79. Plymouth Co. LR 53:10(Simeon Bradford). Springfield VT VR cards (d. Simeon).

106. WAIT⁴ BRADFORD (*Ephraim³, William²⁻¹*), b. prob. Kingston ca. 1730; d. Turner, Maine, 24 Oct. 1801.

He m. Kingston 1 Nov. 1765 **WELTHEA BASSETT**, b. Kingston 4 July 1742; d. Turner, Maine, 25 Sept. 1815 aged 77; daughter of Moses and Lydia (Cooke) Bassett, a descendant of Pilgrims **Francis Cooke** and **Stephen Hopkins.**

On 23 Feb. 1768 Wait Bradford of Kingston, yeoman, sold his homestead farm in Kingston and Duxbury to Elijah Chandler, and Welthey Bradford also signed.

In the 1771 Valuation List, Wait Bradford appears in Kingston with one poll.

Wait Bradford served as a private during the Revolutionary War.

Wait Bradford, wife Wilthea, and their children Simeon, Sarah, and Deborah who came from Kingston were warned from Duxbury 10 Dec. 1779.

On 21 May 1782, acknowledged 28 Dec. 1782, Wait Bradford of Duxborough, yeoman, sold his dwelling house to David Holles, and wife Wealthy gave up her dower rights.

No Maine probate records were found for Wait Bradford.

Children of Wait and Welthea (Bassett) Bradford, b. prob. Kingston:

532	i	SARAH⁵ BRADFORD, b. ca. 1768; bp. Kingston 9 Oct. 1774
533	ii	SIMEON BRADFORD, b. ca. 1770; bp. Kingston 9 Oct. 1774
534	iii	DEBORAH BRADFORD, b. ca. 1777; bp. Kingston Sept. 1777
535	iv	EPHRAIM BRADFORD, b. ca. 1783; bp. Kingston 14 Aug. 1785

References: *VR Kingston* pp. 21(b. Welthea), 26-30(b. ch.), 182(m.). *Bradford Desc* p. 38. *Plymouth Co Ct Recs* 3:391(warning). Turner ME VR unpaged(d. Wait, Welthea). Plymouth Co. LR 54:68; 62:272 (Wait Bradford). *MF* 12:397-8. *DAR Patriot Index* p. 79. *1771 Valuation* p. 640

107. NATHANIEL⁴ BRADFORD (*David³, William²⁻¹*), b. Plymouth 10 Dec. 1715; d. there 27 March 1751 in 36th yr.

He m. Plymouth 24 Nov. 1746 **SARAH SPOONER**, b. Plymouth 31 Jan. 1726/7; d. Bridgewater 1 July 1782 in 59th yr.; daughter of Thomas and Sarah (Nelson) Spooner. She m. (2) Plymouth 17 Dec. 1761 BENJAMIN WILLIS with whom she had Mary, Benjamin, and Sarah.

On 16 May 1751 Sarah Bradford of Plymouth, widow, was appointed administratrix of the estate of Nathaniel Bradford of Plymouth, housewright. In a petition of 27 May 1752 in which Sarah Bradford requested permission to sell lands held in common with Nathan Bradford of Kingston and Lydia, wife of Lazarus LeBarron of Plymouth, she mentioned that she had two small children.

On 13 July 1751 Sarah Bradford of Plymouth, widow, was appointed guardian of Lemuel and Nathaniel Bradford.

On 15 Sept. 1752 Sarah Bradford of Plymouth, widow and administratrix of the estate of Nathaniel Bradford and guardian to his children, sold to Nathan Bradford her right in the homestead that was his father David Bradford's, held in common with Nathan Bradford of Kingston, cordwainer, and Lydia the wife of Lazarus LeBaron of Plymouth, physician.

On 30 Jan. 1760 Sarah Bradford, widow, appears on a list of members of the Plymouth church.

On 12 April 1792 Nathaniel Bradford of Plymouth, cordwainer, and Lemuel Bradford of Plymouth, housewright, sold meadow land.

No Plymouth County probate records were found for Sarah Bradford.

Children of Nathaniel and Sarah (Spooner) Bradford, b. Plymouth:

536	i	NATHANIEL[5] BRADFORD, b. 26 July 1748, bp. 31 July 1748
537	ii	LEMUEL BRADFORD, b. 20 Feb. 1750/1, bp. 24 Feb. 1751

References: *MD* 12:13(b. ch.); 13:33(b. Sarah); 16:87(d. Nath.); 17:5(m.). *VR Bridgewater* 2:409(her 2nd m.), 583(d. Sarah). *Spooner Desc* pp. 134-6. *(Plymouth) Burial Hill* p. 29(d. Nathaniel). Plymouth Co. PR #2583(Nathaniel Bradford); #2563(gdn.). *Plymouth VR* pp. 50(b. ch.), 60(b. Sarah), 154(m.). Plymouth Co. LR 42:11(Sarah Bradford); 72:220(Nathaniel Bradford). *Plymouth Ch Recs* 1:444(bp. Nathaniel), 447(bp. Lemuel); 2:492(her 2nd m.).

108. LYDIA[4] BRADFORD (*David[3], William[2-1]*), b. Plymouth 23 Dec. 1719; d. there 28 Oct. 1756.

She m. (1) Plymouth 31 March 1740 **ELKANAH CUSHMAN**, b. Plymouth 10 July 1706; d. between 26 April 1742 (deed under #19) and 21 Jan. 1742/3; son of Elkanah and Hester (Barnes) Cushman, a descendant of Pilgrim **Isaac Allerton**.

She m. (2) Plymouth 2 May 1743 **LAZARUS LE BARON**, b. Plymouth 26 Dec. 1698; d. there 2 Sept. 1773 aged 75; son of Francis and Mary (Wilder) LeBaron. He m. (1) Plymouth 16 May 1720 LYDIA BARTLETT with whom he had Lazarus, Joseph, Lydia, Mary, Hannah, Terress, and Bartlett.

At a town meeting on 10 March 1728/9 Lazarus LeBarron was chosen a hog reve, but he soon moved on to be one of the leading men in town. A footnote in *Plymouth Town Recs* says "Dr. LeBarron was one of the Selectmen of Plymouth from 1735 to 1756 inclusive, and from 1766 to 1769 inclusive. He presided at the Annual Meetings of the Town from 1743 to 1745, in 1747, from 1751 to 1757, in 1759, 1761, 1763 and 1764."

At the January 1741/2 term of the Plymouth County Court of General Sessions "John Coshat [also "Corhatt"], a Minor of Plymouth ... Mariner, and Scipeo, a Negro Slave belonging to Capt. John Pickard of Plymouth ... Labourer" were presented because they "at a place Called Carlile Bay in the Island of Barbadoes in the West Indies did take and Conceal on board the sloop *Molly* (Elkanah Cushman, Commander), a Certain Negro man called Charles, being Servant for life as said Charles Saith to Benjamin Bissett of the Island of Barbadoes." The court found them guilty "of Carrying Charles ... on board the Sloop *Molly* (Elkanah Cushman, Master) at Barbadoes unknown unto the said Master and him, the said Charles, concealing from the said Master on the passage from that porte till their arrival at Plymouth."

On 21 Jan. 1742 appraisers were appointed for the estate of Elkanah Cushman late of Plymouth, mariner. Inventory was taken 18 Feb. 1742. On 10 Nov. 1742 widow Lydia Cushman of Plymouth was appointed administratrix of the estate of Elkanah Cushman.

On 4 June 1743 Lazarus LeBaron, physician, and wife Lydia, both of Plymouth were appointed guardians of Elkanah Cushman, minor son of Elkanah Cushman, deceased

On 13 Oct. 1749 Scipio, negro man belonging to Deacon Torrey, married Hagar, negro woman belonging to Dr. Lazarus LeBarron. And on 2 Sept. 1756 Quosh, negro man servant to Dr. Lazarus LeBarron married Phillis, negro woman servant to Capt. Theophilus Cotton.

On 16 Dec. 1753 Doctor LeBaron was chosen with others to attend the ordination of Mr. Elijah Packard at the Second church of Plymouth. In 1759 he was on a committee to entreat Mr. Job Whitney to become pastor of the Plymouth church, then later that year to entreat Mr. Potter; neither accepted. Finally the committee met with Mr Robbins, who accepted the call. On 8 April 1770 he was chosen to attend the ordination of Mr. Ivory Hovey at the Second church. On 5 Jan. 1772 he was chosen to attend the ordination of Mr. Lemuel LeBaron at the Second Church of Christ in Rochester.

On 30 Jan. 1760 Lazarus LeBaron appears on a list of members of the Plymouth church.

In the 1771 Valuation List, Dr. Lazarus Lebaron appears in Plymouth with 1 poll, 4 houses or shops, 1 servant for life, £13:6:8 of merchandise, £266:13:4 lent at interest, 1 horse, 2 cattle, 2 swine, 25 acres of pasture, 1½ acres of tillage producing 30 bushels of grain, 6 acres salt marsh producing 5 tons of hay, and 5½ acres of upland which produced 4 tons of hay.

The will of Lazarus LeBaron of Plymouth, physician, dated 24 Sept. 1772, presented 2 June 1777, names sons Lazarus, Bartlett, Isaac, Lemuel, Frances, and William; daughters Lydia Goodwin, widow of Nathaniel; Mary Bradford, wife of "Doct Bradford of Bristol"; Hannah Goodwin, wife of Benjamin of Boston; Elizabeth Robins, wife of Ammy of Norfolk, Conn.; and Priscilla LeBaron; granddaughter Sarah Hazen, wife of Mr. Hazen, daughter to son Joseph deceased; son-in-law [stepson] Elkanah Cushman; and "four sons I had by last wife viz: Isaac, Lemuel, Francis, and William."

Child of Elkanah and Lydia (Bradford) Cushman, b. Plymouth:

538   i   ELKANAH CUSHMAN[5], b. 13 Nov. 1741.

Children of Lazarus and Lydia (Bradford) (Cushman) Le Baron, b. Plymouth:

539   ii   ISAAC LEBARON, b. 25 Jan. 1743/4, bp. 29 Jan. 1743/4
540   iii ELIZABETH LEBARON, b. 21 Dec. 1745
541   iv   LEMUEL LEBARON, b. 1 Sept. 1747, bp. 6 Sept. 1747
           v   FRANCIS LEBARON, b. 3 Sept. 1749, bp. 10 Sept. 1749; d. S. Carolina Sept. 1773; unm.? On 3 Feb. 1775, Isaac LeBaron of Plymouth, cordwainer,   was appointed administrator of the estate of Francis LeBaron late of Plymouth, goldsmith.
542   vi   WILLIAM LEBARON, b. 8 Aug. 1751, bp. 11 Aug. 1751
543   vii PRISCILLA LEBARON, b. 3 Aug. 1753, bp. 5 Aug. 1753
           viii MARGARET LEBARON, b. 5 July 1755, bp. 13 July 1755; d. 20 Nov. 1756

References: *MD* 2:78(b.&d. Lazarus), 226(b. Elkanah); 13:111-112(ch. by 1st LeBaron wife); 14:159(1st m.), 160(2nd m.); 15:159(b. son Elkanah), 161(b. LeBaron ch.; d. ch.); 16:87(d. Lydia). *(Plymouth) Burial Hill* p. 44(d. Lazarus). Plymouth Co. PR 9:46, 230, 231(Elkanah Cushman); 21:324, 610(Lazarus LeBaron); 23:40(Francis LeBaron). *NEHGR* 25:181. *Boston News Obits* 3:50(d. Lazarus). *Plymouth VR* pp. 16(b.&d. Lazarus), 24(b. Elkanah), 63-4(b. LeBaron ch. by his 1st wife), 92(1st m. Lazarus), 101(1st m.), 103(2nd m.), 123(b. son Elkanah), 125(b. LeBaron ch.), 151(m. Quosh), 156(m. Hagar). *MF* 17:137-8. *Plymouth Co CT Recs* 2:213. *Plymouth Ch Recs* 1:300, 307, 340(to ordinations), 314(entreat Whitney), 317(entreat Potter), 322(Mr. Robbins), 402(d. Lazarus), 438(bp. Isaac), 444(bp. Lemuel), 445(bp. Francis), 447(bp. William), 448(bp. Priscilla), 450(bp. Margaret). *1771 Valuation* p. 654. *Plymouth Town Recs* 3:5,

109. NATHAN⁴ BRADFORD (*David³*, *William²⁻¹*), b. Plymouth 3 April 1722; d. Kingston 14 Oct. 1787 aged 64.

He m. (1) Hingham 27 Oct. 1748 **ELIZABETH GROCE**, bp. Hingham 12 July 1730; d. Kingston 30 April 1773 aged 42y 11m 19d; daughter of Isaac and Dorothy (Cobb) Groce.

He m. (2) Kingston 19 March 1776 **SARAH STURTEVANT**, b. Kingston 28 Oct. 1732; d. there 11 Oct. 1796 aged 64; daughter of David and Sarah (Holmes) Sturtevant.

On 4 Jan. 1753 Nathan Bradford of Kingston, cordwainer, sold to Ezekiel Bradford of Kingston, husbandman, 42 acres of woodland which was formerly his father David Bradford's.

In the 1771 Valuation List, Nathan Bradford appears in Kingston with 1 poll, 1 house, £66:13:4 lent at interest, 2 oxen, 3 cattle, 25 goats or sheep, 7 acres pasture, 4 acres tillage which produced 40 bushels of grain, 2 barrels of cider, 2 acres of salt marsh which produced 3 tons of hay, and 2 acres of fresh meadow which produced 1 ton of hay.

The will of Nathan Bradford of Kingston, husbandman, dated 11 Sept. 1787, proved 5 Dec. 1787, names wife Sarah, and sons Jonathan and David. The probate record calls them the "only heirs at law of Nathan Bradford."

On 7 Jan. 1797 Jonathan Bradford of Poland, Maine, housewright, sold to his brother David Bradford of Kingston one-half of the real estate of his father Nathan Bradford; his wife Mary also signed the deed.

No Plymouth County probate records were found for Sarah Bradford.

Children of Nathan and first wife Elizabeth (Groce) Bradford, b. Kingston:

    i LYDIA⁵ BRADFORD, b. 17 Jan. 1750; d. 31 July 1751

544   ii JONATHAN BRADFORD, b. 15 May 1752

    iii ELIZABETH BRADFORD, b. 11 April 1754 (not in will)*

    iv THOMAS BRADFORD, b. 18 June 1755; d.y.

545   v DAVID BRADFORD, b. 27 March 1757

---

* *Bradford Desc* p. 155 says Elizabeth m. _____ Woodman. "Her grandmother's sister Dorothy (d. 1800 unm.) gave bequest to Betsy." As Elizabeth apparently d. before 11 Sept. 1787 (will), the purported marriage seems doubtful.

References: *VR Kingston* pp. 26-30(b. ch.), 140(b. Sarah), 181(2ⁿᵈ m.), 320-2(deaths). *Hingham Hist* 2:281(b. Eliz. & par.). Plymouth Co. PR 30:273(Nathan Bradford). Plymouth Co. LR 53:10(Nathan Bradford); 81:182(Jonathan Bradford). *1771 Valuation* p. 640.

110. HANNAH⁴ BRADFORD (*Elisha³, Joseph², William¹*), b. Plymouth 10 April 1720; d. Friendship, Maine, 22 May 1758, killed by Indians.

She m. Kingston 17 Feb. 1736 **JOSHUA BRADFORD**, b. Plymouth 23 June 1710; d. Friendship, Maine, 22 May 1758, killed by Indians; son of Israel and Sarah (Bartlett) Bradford.

See #96 for an account of this family.

References: *VR Kingston* p. 180(m.). *Bradford Desc* p. 35. *MD* 13:168(b. Joshua). *Plymouth VR* p. 72(b. Joshua).

111. LAURANA⁴ BRADFORD (*Elisha³, Joseph², William¹*), b. Plymouth 27 March 1726; living Rochester 7 May 1782 when "widow Lurany Mackfarland and her family belonging to Plympton were warned out of Rochester."

She m. Plympton 14 Nov. 1745 **ELIJAH McFARLIN**, b. probably Plympton ca. 1722; d. 29 Nov. 1777; son of Solomon and Susanna (Huit) McFarlin.

On 15 March 1760 Elijah MacFarland of Plympton, laborer, sold to Seth Cushing land that was given him in the will of the late James Churchill of Plymouth deceased. On 1 Feb. 1754 James Churchill had bequeathed his estate to several "cousins" who were nieces or nephews, with part going to "cousin Elijah McFarling," his parentage not stated.

At the September 1756 term of the Plymouth County Court of Common Pleas, Gideon Bradford of Plympton, yeoman and deputy sheriff, sued Elijah McFarland of Plympton, laborer, for failing to keep an agreement. On 25 Dec. 1752 Gideon agreed to let Elijah cut down and remove the trees for his own use from 3¼ acres and to use the land for three years for his own profit while he prepared the land "fitt for Planting, Sowing or any kind of Husbandry." Gideon now claimed that Elijah cut down and took the trees but did not prepare the land. The jury found in Gideon's favor.

At the October 1762 and January 1763 terms of the Court of General Sessions, Elijah Mcfarling was presented for being absent from public worship. At the January 1765 term, Elijah Mcfarland of Plympton, laborer, was presented for theft. On 2 Sept. 1764 "being the Lords day ... one Sheep ... belonging to Isaac Churchell of said Plimton did feloniously take, Steal and Carry away." The jury found him guilty and he was to "pay a fine of twenty four shillings ... or be whipt ten stripes on his naked body." In July 1766 he was presented for being drunk and in July 1767 "did wittingly and willingly drink strong drink to excess and was thereby made drunk."

Elijah McFarland served as a private in the Revolutionary War.

No Plymouth County probate records were found for Elijah or Lauranna McFarlin.

Children of Elijah and Laurana (Bradford) McFarlin, b. prob. Plympton:

546   i MARY McFARLIN⁵, b. 18 July 1746
547   ii ELIJAH McFARLIN, b. ca. 1751
548   iii HANNAH McFARLIN
         iv JOSEPH McFARLIN
549   v LAURANA McFARLIN, b. 18 Aug. 1755
550   vi ABIGAIL McFARLIN
        vii SABA McFARLIN d.y.
       viii DAVID McFARLIN d. in Rev. War 25 Aug. 1778; apparently unm.

Note: The children are listed in *VR Plympton* without birth dates except for the two dates shown. The VR mentions one or two children who died young.

References: *VR Plympton* pp. 136(b. Mary, Laurana), 347(m.). *Bradford Desc* pp. 39, 40. *DAR Patriot Index* p. 453(d. Elijah). *Plymouth Co Ct Recs* 3:404 (warning); 3:173, 176; 7:344(Elijah presented). Plymouth Co. PR 13:384(James Churchill). Plymouth Co. LR 46:32(Elijah MacFarland). *MSSR* 10:486(d. David).

112. DEBORAH⁴ BRADFORD (*Elisha³, Joseph², William¹*), b. Kingston 18 Nov. 1732; d. after 11 March 1811.

She m. Plympton 27 Oct. 1751 **JONATHAN SAMPSON,** b. Plympton 3 April 1729; d. before 19 Nov. 1810; son of Jonathan and Joanna (Lucas) Sampson, a descendant of Pilgrims **John Alden** and **Myles Standish**.

On 23 Feb. 1758 Jonathan Samson of Plympton, laborer, with wife Deborah sold to Joseph Parrall land that was formerly his father's which had been given to his mother by his grandfather Lucas.

Jonathan Sampson deserted his family about 1767 and lived in Maine with a common law wife named Martha.

Jonathan Sampson served in the Revolutionary War.

Deborah Sampson, the widow of Jonathan Sampson, was moved from Plympton to Fayette, Maine, by the town of Fayette 19 Nov. 1810 and was living 11 March 1811.

No Maine probate or land records were found for Jonathan Sampson.

An extensive account of this family appears in *MQ* 48:172-177.

Children of Jonathan and Deborah (Bradford) Sampson, most or all b. Plympton:

551   i   JONATHAN SAMPSON[5], b. ca. 1753

           ii ELISHA SAMPSON Was he the Elisha Sampson who enlisted in the Rev. from Duxbury and d. 1776 in NY?

           iii HANNAH SAMPSON

553   iv EPHRAIM SAMPSON

554   v   DEBORAH SAMPSON, b. 17 Dec. 1760

555   vi NEHEMIAH SAMPSON, b. 17 July 1764

556   vii SYLVIA SAMPSON, b. 1 April 1766

References: *VR Duxbury* p. 409(d. Elisha). *VR Plympton* pp. 176(b. Jonathan), 178(b. Sylvia), 383(m.). *MQ* 48:172-177. Plymouth Co. LR 46:55(Jonathan Sampson). *MSSR* 13:760-1.

113. ALICE[4] BRADFORD (*Elisha[3], Joseph[2], William[1]*), b. Kingston 3 Nov. 1734; d. Stoughton 6 July 1795 aged 60 yrs. and about 6 months.

She m. Stoughton 21 Sept. 1757 **ZEBULON WATERS**, b. Easton 3 Jan. 1734/5; d. Stoughton 29 May 1790 aged 55 yrs.; son of Samuel and Bethia (Thayer) Waters. The will of Samuel Waters of Stoughton dated 23 May 1750, proved 28 Aug. 1750, names his son Zebulon.

On 29 March 1764 Daniel Waters and Zebulon Waters of Stoughton divided land they held in common. On the same day Daniel sold Zebulon his half of this land.

In the 1771 Valuation List, Zebulon Waters appears in Stoughton with 1 poll, 1 house, 2 cattle, 1 swine, 5 acres pasture, 3 acres of tillage which produced 36 bushels of grain, 15 barrels of cider, and 12 acres of upland which produced 4 tons of hay.

Zebulon Waters served as a private during the Revolutionary War.

On 20 March 1787 Zebulon Waters of Stoughton, yeoman, sold to Asa Waters of Stoughton, farmer, 40 acres with a dwelling house and barn.

The will of Zebulon Waters of Stoughton, yeoman, dated 4 May 1790, presented 29 June 1790, names wife Alice; sons Asa, Zebulon, and Samuel; daughters Matilda Nash, Hannah Drake, Molly Waters, and Chloe Waters.

On 21 May 1816 and 10 Feb. 1817 Zebulon Waters and his wife Lucy sold land formerly of Zebulon Waters deceased.

Children of Zebulon and Alice (Bradford) Waters, b. Stoughton:

	i	NEHEMIAH WATERS⁵, b. 9 July 1758; d. before 4 May 1790 (not in will)

  557 ii ASA WATERS, b. 11 Feb. 1760

  558 iii MATILDA WATERS, b. 31 May 1761

       iv REBECCA WATERS, b. 8 Oct. 1762; d.y.

       v DANIEL WATERS, b. 5 July 1765; d. New Jersey 1781 in Rev. War

  559 vi HANNAH WATERS, b. 12 Jan. 1767

  560 vii ZEBULON WATERS, b. 23 Aug. 1768

       viii SAMUEL WATERS, b. 6 Oct. 1770; living 4 May 1790

  561 ix MOLEY (or MARY) WATERS, b. 6 April 1773

  562 x CHLOE WATERS, b. 19 Sept. 1775

References: *Stoughton VR* pp. 10(b. Asa), 22(b. Zebulon), 52 (b. Nehemiah), 79(int.), 89(b. Daniel), 94(b. Matilda), 97(b. Rebecca), 100(b. Hannah, Zebulon), 115(b. Samuel, Molly, Chloe), 177(m.). *Bradford Desc* pp. 40-1. Suffolk Co. PR 44:252(Samuel Waters); 89:455(Zebulon Waters). *MD* 44:134(b. Zebulon). *DAR Patriot Index* p. 721. Suffolk Co. LR 160:131(Zebulon Waters); 168:50-1(Daniel & Zebulon Waters). *1771 Valuation* p. 522. Norfolk Co. LR 49:170; 54:202(Zebulon Waters).

114. AZENATH⁴ BRADFORD (*Elisha³, Joseph², William¹*), b. Kingston 15 Sept. 1736; d. Stoughton 15 Nov. 1818.

She m. (1) Stoughton 22 July 1753 **NATHAN ESTEY**, b. Stoughton 26 Nov. 1727; d. Nova Scotia; son of Benjamin and Sarah (Chandler) Estey.

She m. (2) int. Stoughton 30 Oct. 1756, **DANIEL WATERS**, d. before 14 Sept. 1764 (adm.); son of Samuel and Bethia (Thayer) Waters. He m. (1) Stoughton 25 Feb. 1752 SUSANNA MORGAN. The will of Samuel Waters of Stoughton dated 23 May 1750, proved 28 Aug. 1750, names his son Daniel.

She m. (3) int. Stoughton 30 April 1765 **BENJAMIN PACKARD**, b. 1743; d. Stoughton 18 Feb. 1825 aged 81; son of Joseph and Hannah (Manley) Packard. On 10 Jan. 1788 Benjamin Packard of Stoughton and Hezekiah Drake and his wife Elizabeth of Easton sold their rights in the estate of their father Joseph Packard.

On 29 March 1764 Daniel Waters and Zebulon Waters of Stoughton divided land they held in common. On the same day Daniel sold Zebulon his half of this land.

On 14 Sept. 1764 Asenath Waters was appointed administratrix of the estate of her husband Daniel Waters of Stoughton. As Asenath Packard she rendered an account on 23 March 1770.

On 7 April 1766 Benjamin Packard, yeoman, and his wife Asenath of Stoughton, Aseneth being the widow of Daniel Waters and administratrix of his estate, sold 1¾ acres to Hezekiah Gay Jr. of Stoughton to pay estate debts. On 14 May 1770 Benjamin Packard and his wife Aseneth, admistrators of the estate of Daniel Waters late of Stoughton, sold 17 acres to Joseph Smith of Stoughton.

In the 1771 Valuation List, Benjamin Packard appears in Stoughton with 1 poll, 1 house, 1 horse, 3 cattle, 2 swine, 5 acres of pasture, 3 acres of tillage which produced 40 bushells of grain, 15 barrels of cider, 4 acres of upland which produced 2 tons of hay, and 3 acres of fresh meadow which produced 3 tons of hay.

Benjamin Packard served as a private. during the Revolutionary War.

In 1790 Benjamin Packard was head of a household in Stoughton consisting of 2 males 16 or older, one boy under 16, and 3 females.

No Suffolk County probate or land records were found for Nathan Estey, and no Suffolk or Norfolk County probate for Benjamin Packard.

Children of Daniel and Asenath (Bradford) Waters, b. Stoughton:

563   i BETHIA WATERS⁵, b. 28 Dec. 1757

         ii LUCEE WATERS, b. 20 Oct. 1759

       iii SAMUEL WATERS, b. 27 Nov. 1762

Children of Benjamin and Asenath (Bradford) (Waters) Packard, b. Stoughton:

564   iv JOHN PACKARD, b. 19 Dec. 1765

        v LOIS PACKARD, b. 31 Aug. 1767

565   vi JEDEDIAH PACKARD, b. 18 Feb. 1771

566   vii MELATIAH PACKARD, b. 31 July 1773

References: *Bradford Desc* p. 41. *Stoughton VR* pp. 18(b. Nathan), 64(m. Daniel & Susanna), 74(1ˢᵗ m. int.), 78(2ⁿᵈ m. int.), 83(b. Bethia, Lucee), 95(b. John, Lois), 96 (b. Jedediah, Melatiah), 102(b. Samuel), 132(3ʳᵈ m. int.), 176(1ˢᵗ m.). Suffolk Co. PR 44:252(Samuel Waters); 63:349, 493; 69:14(Dan. Waters). *DAR Patriot Index* p. 510. Suffolk Co. LR 128:222(Benjamin & Asenath); 168:50-1(Daniel & Zebulon Waters); 170:47(Benjamin & Asenath); 171:232(Benjamin Packard & Hezekiah Drake). *1771 Valuation* p. 522.

115. CARPENTER⁴ BRADFORD (*Elisha³, Joseph², William¹*), b. prob. Kingston 7 Feb. 1739; d. Friendship, Maine, 27 Jan. 1823.

He m. (1) Stoughton 18 June 1761 **MARY GAY**, b. Stoughton 17 Sept. 1736; d. 1815; daughter of David and Hannah (Tabor) Gay.

He m. (2) Cushing, Maine, 26 June 1815 (int. Friendship, Maine, 9 June 1815) **MARY STEELE** of Boston, b. Maine ca. 1767; living 1850 (census).

Carpenter Bradford was listed in Onslow, N.S., in the 1770 census with 1 man, 1 boy, 1 woman, 3 girls, all American.

Carpenter Bradford served as a private during the Revolutionary War.

The 1790 census listed Carpenter Bradford with a household of 2 men 16 or older and 3 females, in Meduncook (Friendship). He was listed in Meduncook in the 1798 Direct Tax of Massachusetts.

On 7 Nov. 1811 Carpenter Bradford of Friendship, Gentleman, sold to William Jameson of Friendship, Gentleman, and Enoch Wentworth of Cushing, blacksmith, 9 acres in Friendship. On 26 June 1815 Carpenter sold to William Jameson, Enoch Wentworth, and Levi Morse of Union, Maine, yeomen, 91 acres in Friendship, the northerly half of the land Carpenter lived on.

On 13 March 1837 Mary Bradford was sent to live at the home of Alexander McCobb at Friendship, and in 1850 the census showed her still with that family, aged 83, born in Maine.

No Maine probate records were found for Carpenter Bradford.

Children of Carpenter and Mary (Gay) Bradford:

	i	CHLOE⁵ BRADFORD, b. Stoughton 4 Jan. 1762; d. 4 March 1770
567	ii	AZUBAH BRADFORD, b. Truro, N.S., 21 May 1765
568	iii	HANNAH BRADFORD, b. 28 June 1767
569	iv	WILLIAM BRADFORD, b. Onslow, N.S., 15 Dec. 1770
570	v	MARY GAY BRADFORD, b. Onslow, N.S., 8 Nov. 1772
571	vi.	CHLOE BRADFORD, b. Truro, N.S., 5 Jan. 1776
	vii.	EMILY BRADFORD, b. 6 March 1781; d.y.

References: *Stoughton VR* pp. 83(b. Mary), 89(b. Chloe), 174(int.), 178(m.). *Cushing ME VR*, p. 9(m.). *Bradford Desc.* p. 41. Bernice C. Richard, *Nova Scotia 1770 Census* (1972), p. 20. *DAR Patriot Index* p. 78. *Friendship ME Recs* pp. 53 (int. 2ⁿᵈ m.), 71(sent to McCobb family). Lincoln Co. LR 91:46; 94:135 (Carpenter Bradford).

Fifth Generation

116. ROBERT⁵ BRADFORD *(John⁴⁻³, William²⁻¹)*, b. Plymouth 18 Oct. 1706; d. Kingston 9 or 12 Aug. 1782 in 76th year, or aged 77.

He m. Kingston 4 Nov. 1726 **SARAH STETSON**, b. Plymouth 26 Aug. 1708; d. Kingston 23 Feb. 1792 aged 84; daughter of Elisha and Abigail (Brewster) Stetson, a descendant of Pilgrim **William Brewster**. Order for settlement of the estate of Elisha Stetson late of Kingston deceased, dated 20 July 1756, names daughters Sarah, wife of Robert Bradford and Zerash, wife of Benjamin Bradford.

On 12 Dec. 1737 Samuel Bradford of Plympton, Gentleman, Robert Bradford of Kingston, yeoman, and George Partridge of Duxbury guardian of James Bradford, Samuel Bradford, Zadock Bradford, Eliphalet Bradford, and William Bradford grandsons of the Honorable John Bradford late of Plymouth, Esq., sold 1/9 part of land located near Muscongus in Lincoln County, Maine. This deed was acknowledged in Boston on 27 Dec. 1737 but not recorded in Lincoln County until 25 Aug. 1763.

The court records show that Robert Bradford served the town of Kingston as a selectman at least 13 years from 1744 to 1769.

In the 1771 Valuation List, Capt. Robert Bradford was listed in Kingston with 1 poll, 1 house, 1 horse, 4 oxen, 4 cattle, 8 goats or sheep, 6 acres of pasture, 6 acres of tillage which produced 60 bushels of grain, 8 barrels of cider, 2 acres of salt marsh which produced 2 tons of hay, 4 acres of upland which produced 3 tons of hay, and 5 acres of fresh meadow which produced 5 tons of hay.

On 25 July 1782 Robert Bradford of Kingston, gentleman, sold three acres to his son John Bradford of Kingston, yeoman.

The will of Robert Bradford of Kingston dated 8 Aug. 1782, proved 2 Sept. 1782, mentions but does not name his wife, names daughter Orpah (without surname), sons Stetson, Robert, and Peleg; daughter Zilpah, and the heirs of daughter Rebecca (without surnames); friend William Drew to be executor. On 13 April 1784 dower was set off to Sarah Bradford, widow of Captain Robert Bradford, late of Kingston deceased.

On 29 July 1784 William Drew of Kingston, Esq., executor of the will of Capt. Robert Bradford late of Kingston sold to Robert Bradford of Kingston, Gentleman, to pay debts owed by the estate, a cedar swamp lot in Pembroke, part of an undivided swamp (reserving for the widow the improvement of one acre) and two acres of swamp in Halifax.

On 5 Sept. 1787 Robert Bradford of Kingston, Gentleman, sold to Thankful Baty of Boston, widow, and Thomas Whiting of Concord, merchant, executors of the estate of Gideon Baty late of Boston, one half of the lot bought with his brother Stetson from William Drew; Robert's wife Keziah released her dower rights and Orpha Bradford was one of the witnesses.

In April 1789 the following heirs participated in the division of Robert's estate: Zilpha Loring, John Bradford, Stetson Bradford, Rebecca Holmes, and Orpha Bradford, all of Kingston. On 17 May 1789 Stetson Bradford of Kingston, yeoman, and Robert Bradford of Kingston, Gentleman, divided land they received from their father's estate. Robert then sold his part to Uriah Bartlett of Kingston, yeoman.

Sarah Bradford's household in Sharon in the 1790 census consisted of only 3 females. Listed next to her was Stetson Bradford, with 2 men over 16, 3 boys under 16, and 2 females.

Children of Robert and Sarah (Stetson) Bradford, b. Kingston:

    i   PELEG[6] BRADFORD, b. 9 March 1727

    ii   ZILPAH BRADFORD, b. 6 April 1728

   iii REBECCA BRADFORD, b. 31 Dec. 1730

   iv JOHN BRADFORD, b. 18 Oct. 1732

    v   ELTHEA BRADFORD, b. 13 Dec. 1734; d. 11 June 1737

   vi ORPHA BRADFORD, b. 28 Dec. 1736; d. Kingston 3 May 1830 ae 93

  vii STETSON BRADFORD, b. 17 Feb. 1738/9

 viii ROBERT BRADFORD, b. 19 Jan. 1740/1; d. Sept. 1747

   ix SARAH BRADFORD, b. 20 Feb. 1742/3; d. Sept. 1747

    x   CONSIDER BRADFORD, b. 3 Dec. 1744/5; d. Sept. 1747

   xi SARAH BRADFORD, b. 4 Feb. 1747/8 (not in will)

  xii ROBERT BRADFORD, b. 11 July 1750

References: *MD* 7:23(d. Robert); 7:178(b. Sarah); 12:13. *VR Kingston* pp. 26-31(b. ch.), 182(m.), 319-22(deaths), 321(d. Orpha, Robert, son Robert), 322(d. Sarah, dau. Sarah). *Waterman Gen* 1:626. *Bradford Desc* p. 46. Plymouth Co. PR 15:97(Elisha Stetson); 28:460-1; 29:135(Robert Bradford). *Plymouth VR* p. 44(b. Sarah). Plymouth Co. LR 67:56(Robert Bradford); 69:60(William Drew; div.), 77(Stetson Bradford, Robert Bradford); 90:20(Robert Bradford). Lincoln Co. ME LR 3:140(Samuel Bradford). *1771 Valuation* p. 644.

117. REBECCA[5] BRADFORD (*John[4-3]*, *William[2-1]*), b. Plymouth 14 Dec. 1710; d. bet. 6 Aug. 1770 (swore to inv.) and 7 Jan. 1771.

She m. int. Kingston 18 Oct. 1729 **JOHN BREWSTER**, b. probably Duxbury ca. 1697; d. Kingston bet. 20 Sept. 1769 (ack. deed) and 1 Jan. 1770, son of Wrestling and Mary (_____) Brewster, a descendant of Pilgrim **William Brewster.**

John Brewster of Kingston, innholder, was granted a license to sell liquor six times from 1739 to 1752. The court records show that he served the town of Kingston as a selectman from 1757 through 1764.

At the March 1757 term of the Plymouth County Court of Common Pleas, Samuell Foster of Kingston, gentleman, brought suit against Wrestling Brewster of Kingston, yeoman, for speaking and writing "false Scandalous and Opprobrious and Lying Words." Samuel said that on 1 Sept. 1756 Wrestling publicly said "Samuel Foster … has Stolen Hay from John Brewster (meaning John Brewster of said Kingston Inholder) in August Last."

On 5 July 1763 John Brewster of Kingston, innholder, sold to Isaac Brewster of Kingston, blacksmith, half an acre in Kingston and 1½ acres in Duxbury; John's wife Rebecca also signed the deed.

On 30 Aug. 1768 John Brewster of Kingston, yeoman, sold to Gershom Cobb of Kingston, housewright, a house lot adjoining land that was formerly set off to William Bradford's widow [see #29] now Elizabeth Bradford's thirds. John acknowledged this deed on 20 Sept. 1769.

The will of John Brewster of Kingston, innholder, dated 24 June 1766, proved 1 Jan. 1770, names wife Rebecca executrix; daughter Rebecca Samson deceased and her children Elisha and Rebecca Samson; daughter Abigail Brewster, wife of Lemuel Brewster; and daughter Sarah Brewster.

On 7 Jan. 1771 Robert Bradford was appointed administrator of the estate of John Brewster of Kingston, left incomplete by the death of widow Rebecca.

On 15 Jan. 1773 Robert Bradford of Kingston, gentleman, administrator of the estate of John Brewster, sold to John Adams of Plymouth, cloathier, one-sixth share in a woodlot from the estate of William Bradford deceased, and the second share in a cedar swamp.

Children of John and Rebecca (Bradford) Brewster, b. Kingston:

    i JOHN BREWSTER[6], b. 7 Oct. 1730; d. 23 July 1748 ae 17y 9m 16d

    ii REBECCA BREWSTER, b. 25 March 1733

    iii ABIGAIL BREWSTER, b. 17 Dec. 1736

    iv SARAH BREWSTER, b. 15 Sept. 1745; d. 25 Sept. 1747 ae 2y 14d

    v SARAH BREWSTER, bp. 28 Oct. 1750

References: *MD* 7:24(d. Sarah, son John); 12:13. *VR Kingston* pp. 31-3(b. ch.), 186(m.), 324(d. Sarah), 325(d. son John). *Waterman Gen* 1:626. *Bradford Desc* pp. 14, 46. Plymouth Co. PR 20:296, 409; 27:494(John Brewster). *Gen Advertiser* 2:29. Plymouth Co. LR 48:195; 55:77(John Brewster); 57:111(Robert Bradford). *Plymouth Co Ct Recs* 7:351(Samuel Foster).

118. MARY MITCHELL[5] (*Alice[4] Bradford, John[3], William[2-1]*), b. Bridgewater 19 July 1709; d. Hingham 4 Sept. 1745 in 37th yr.

She m. Hingham 30 Jan. 1728/9 her step-brother **JOSHUA HERSEY JR.**, b. Hingham 22 Dec. 1704; d. there 1 Nov. 1784 aged 80; son of Joshua and Sarah (Hawke) Hersey. He m. (2) Hingham 15 June 1750 MARY (FEARING) LINCOLN with whom he had Mary and Rachel. He m. (3) Boston 27 May 1762 SARAH (FOSTER) HANNERS.

On 17 April 1741 Edward Mitchell of Bridgewater, Joshua Hearsey, yeoman, and his wife Mary, and Noah Hearsey, yeoman, and his wife Alice all of Hingham sold to Nehemiah Washburn of Bridgewater, Gentleman, their right in 200 acres on the south side of the [Quatcbiquat?] River.

On 6 May 1762 Joshua Hearsey of Hingham, gentleman, sold to Abel Hearsey of Hingham, yeoman, the dwelling house Abel "now lives in lately built and joining to Joshua's dwelling house with part of the celler and half of the garden." On the same day Joshua sold to Bradford Hersey of Hingham, yeoman, five acres paid for "out of the Money of his part ... of his mother & grandmother's Estate sold to in Bridgewater to his uncle Mitchel and others."

In his will dated 26 Sept. 1776, proved 24 Nov. 1784, Joshua Hersey of Hingham, gentleman, gave to wife Sarah Hersey "the household stuff she brought me at marriage"; and named sons Abel and Joshua; daughter Mercy Lincoln; son Bradford Hersey; and daughters (of his second marriage) Mary Thaxter and Rachel Hersey deceased, who was heir to Daniel Lincoln deceased.

On 11 April 1786 Abel Hearsey and Bradford Hearsey of Hingham, tenants-in-common of the home lot which Deacon Joshua Hearsey late of Hingham died siezed of, agreed to divide the 20 acres.

On 4 June 1787 Sarah Hearsey of Hingham, widow of Joshua Hearsey, gave her son [-in-law] Samuel Newell of Newburyport her power of attorney. On 9 June Sarah Hearsey and Samuel Newell and his wife Sarah in her right sold land that had been set off to Sarah Hearsey in the division of the estate of her father Hopestill Foster.

Children of Joshua and Mary (Mitchell) Hersey, b. Hingham:

    i   ABEL HERSEY[6], b. 23 Jan. 1729/30
    ii JOSHUA HERSEY, b. 11 Feb. 1731/2

   iii MERCY HERSEY, b. 29 March 1733; d. 15 Aug. 1733

   iv EDWARD HERSEY, b. 15 Dec. 1734; d. 3 Feb. 1735/6

   v EDWARD HERSEY, b. 7 April 1736; d. 20 Aug. 1736

   vi MERCY HERSEY, b. 21 Sept. 1737

   vii EDWARD HERSEY, b. 24 Feb. 1738/9; d. 23 April 1740

   viii BRADFORD HERSEY, b. 3 April 1741; d. Hingham 7 Oct. 1796 ae 55; unm. No PR.

   ix BENJAMIN HERSEY, b. 20 Oct. 1744; d. 31 Oct. 1751

References: *MD* 14:36. *Hingham Hist* 2:302. *Bradford Desc* p. 46. Suffolk Co. PR 83:1021(Joshua Hersey). *BRC:* 30:51(3rd m.). Suffolk Co. LR 99:44-46 (Joshua Hersey); 158:85(Abel Hersey); 160:222-3(Sarah Hersey). Plymouth Co. LR 35:90 (Edward Mitchell *et al.*).

119.   ALICE MITCHELL[5] (*Alice*[4] *Bradford, John*[3], *William*[2-1]), b. Bridgewater 23 Dec. 1714; d. Hingham 20 Dec. 1779 in her 66th yr.

She m. Hingham 12 Feb. 1735/6 **NOAH HERSEY**, b. Hingham 24 Feb. 1709/10; d. there 29 June 1755 aged 45; son of Joshua and Sarah (Hawke) Hersey.

On 17 April 1741 Edward Mitchell of Bridgewater, Joshua Hearsey, yeoman, and his wife Mary, and Noah Hearsey, yeoman, and his wife Alice, all of Hingham, sold to Nehemiah Washburn of Bridgewater, Gentleman, their right in 200 acres on the south side of the [Quatcbiquat?] River.

The will of Noah Hersey of Hingham, yeoman, dated 26 June 1755, proved 21 July 1744, names wife Alice; eldest son Peleg; daughter Sarah; and sons Noah, Jacob, and Levi, all of the children under 21.

On 1 Dec. 1763 Peleg Hersey of Hingham, yeoman, sold to Jeremiah Lincoln of Hingham, gentleman, half of a dwelling house and 11 acres of land as well as his right in the other half of the house and land at the marriage or death of his mother Alis Hersey; Peleg's wife Lucy also signed the deed. The four sons of Noah Hersey divided Noah's land; this division was agreed to by Peleg on 8 March 1764, by Noah on 7 Dec. 1767, by Jacob on 13 Jan. 1772, and by Levi on 5 Aug. 1772.

On 17 March 1764 Peleg Hearsey of Hingham, yeoman, sold to Joshua Hearsey of Hingham, gentleman, 14¾ acres bounded on "land of Noah Hearsey lately set out to him upon the division of his father Noah Hearsey decd. Estate"; Peleg's wife Lucy released her dower rights.

Children of Noah and Alice (Mitchell) Hersey, b. Hingham:

  i　PELEG HERSEY[6], b. 22 Nov. 1737

 ii　SARAH HERSEY, b. 28 Aug. 1741

iii　JACOB HERSEY, b. 23 April 1744; d. 12 Jan. 1747/8

 iv　NOAH HERSEY, b. 6 Oct. 1746

  v　JACOB HERSEY, b. 6 Aug. 1748; d. Hingham 7 Aug. 1773

 vi　LEVI HERSEY, b. 23 July 1751

References: *Hingham Hist* 2:302-3. *Bradford Desc* p. 47. Suffolk Co. PR 50:356(Noah Hersey). Suffolk Co. LR 108:82; 118:176(Peleg Hersey); 121:276(division). Plymouth Co. LR 35:90(Edward Mitchell *et al.*).

120. EDWARD MITCHELL[5] (*Alice⁴ Bradford, John³, William²⁻¹*), b. Bridgewater 7 Feb. 1715/6; d. E. Bridgewater 25 Dec. 1801 aged 85y 10m.

He m. Hingham 14 Dec. 1738 **ELIZABETH CUSHING**, b. Hingham 21 May 1714; d. E. Bridgewater 9 May 1799 aged 85; daughter of Elisha and Leah (Loring) Cushing. On 8 July 1740 Edward Mitchell of Bridgewater, tanner, and his wife Elizabeth sold to Abel Cushing eight acres of land in Hingham bounded on land belonging to the heirs of Elisha Cushing deceased. In his will written 6 Oct. 1734, proved 22 Oct. 1734, Elisha Cushing of Hingham named his wife Leah, sons Elisha and John, and daughter Elizabeth.

On 17 April 1741 Edward Mitchell of Bridgewater, Joshua Hearsey, yeoman, and his wife Mary, and Noah Hearsey, yeoman, and his wife Alice, all of Hingham, sold to Nehemiah Washburn of Bridgewater, Gentleman, their right in 200 acres on the south side of the [Quatcbiquat?] River.

The court records show that Edward Mitchell served as a Bridgewater Selectman in 1756, 1766, 1767, and 1773, and as a Justice of the Peace.

On 6 June 1757 Edward Mitchell of Plymouth, Gentleman, and Alice Hearsey of Hingham, widow, sold to Seth Mitchell of Bridgewater, bricklayer, 13½ in Bridgewater being the north corner of 19 acres laid out to Ensign Edward Mitchell; Alice acknowledged this deed on 6 June 1757, but Edward did not acknowledge it until 22 Nov. 1792. On 20 Jan. 1767 Alice Hearsey of Hingham sold to Edward Mitchell Jr. of Bridgewater, yeoman, one-half of a piece of cedar swamp in Bridgewater and a piece of woodland laid out on the purchase right of Edward Mitchell deceased. On 9 June 1771 Alice sold to Edward Jr. one-eighth part of 33 acres.

Edward Mitchell gave or sold to his sons land: on 30 Sept.1765 to Edward 15 acres; on 25 Dec. 1771 to Edward 40 acres with buildings; same day to

Elisha 37½ acres; same day to Cushing 36¼ acres with buildings; same day to John 55 acres; same day to William 36¼ acres; on 9 April 1772 to Edward his right in 33 acres; on 8 April 1774 to Bradford 22 acres; and on 17 Feb. 1784 to Bela Mitchell of Charlestown, tanner, 19 acres in Bridgewater and his right in 24 acres (5 acres of which were laid out to Edward and his sisters) with half of his tanyard, half of his [bark house?], and half of his currying shop. On 8 Feb. 1787 Edward sold to Elisha 30 rods with half of the house, cellar, and well. On 11 Oct. 1800 Edward sold to Bradford seven acres and on 13 May 1801 he sold to Bradford two lots of 1¼ and 7½ acres.

In the 1771 Valuation List, Edward Mitchell was listed in Bridgewater with 3 polls, 1 house, 1 tan house, 2 horses, 4 oxen, 6 cattle, 17 goats or sheep, 3 swine, 45 acres of pasture, 12 acres of tillage which produced 146 bushels of grain, 15 barrels of cider, 25 acres of upland which produced 12 tons of hay, and 16 acres of fresh meadow which produced 14 tons of hay.

At the Dec. 1773 term of the Court of Common Pleas, Richard Perkins of Bridgewater, Surgeon, sued Edward Mitchell of Bridgewater, Gentleman, for not paying his account. Richard said that he had

> ... made the several visits, given advice council and direction and administred the several medicines, dressed the wounds and amputated the foot of one Margaret Robbins alias Peg Wampus, and had also visited and taken care of the said Margaret alias Peg, the youngest daughter of the said Margaret alias Peg both of whom were sick and wounded at the said Edwards special instance and request, all of which ... the said Edward in consideration thereof then and there promised the said Richard to pay him therefor so much money as the said Richard reasonbly deserved to have, upon demand.

Edward said that he never promised to pay, but the jury decided in Richard's favor.

In the 1790 census Edward Mitchell was listed in Bridgewater with 4 men over 16, 3 boys under 16, and no females. Listed next to him was Cushing Mitchell with 3 men over 16, 3 boys under 16, and 5 females.

The will of Edward Mitchell of Bridgewater, yeoman, dated 10 Feb. 1787, proved 15 Jan. 1802, names wife Elizabeth; daughters Bettee Keith, wife of Eleazer; Molly Keith, wife of James Jr.; Celia Harris, wife of Arthur; and Sarah Mitchell; granddaughter Alice Keith, daughter of John; and sons Edward, Cushing, Elisha, John, William, Bradford, and Bela. A codicil dated 3 March 1790 notes that Elisha is deceased and gives his share to his son Asa Mitchell.

Children of Edward and Elizabeth (Cushing) Mitchell, b. Bridgewater:

   i EDWARD MITCHELL[6], b. 1 Sept. 1739

   ii CUSHING MITCHELL, b. 8 Dec. 1740

  iii ELIZABETH MITCHELL, b. 26 April 1742

  iv ALICE MITCHELL, b. 5 April 1744 (not in will)

   v ELISHA MITCHELL, b. 28 March 1746; d. before 3 March 1790 (codicil)

  vi JOHN MITCHELL, b. 8 March 1747/8

 vii WILLIAM MITCHELL, b. 13 March 1749/50

viii BRADFORD MITCHELL, b. 17 May 1752

  ix MARY (or MOLLY) MITCHELL, b. 4 April 1754

   x CELIA MITCHELL, b. 20 Aug. 1757

  xi SARAH MITCHELL, b. 26 April 1759

 xii BELA MITCHELL, b. 30 Oct. 1761

References: *VR Bridgewater* 1:225-31(b. ch.). *VR E Bridgewater* p. 372(d. Edward, Elizabeth). *Bradford Desc* p. 47. Plymouth Co. PR 38:3(Edward Mitchell). *Hingham Hist* 2:154(b. Elizabeth; m.). Suffolk Co. LR 60:210(Edward Mitchell). Plymouth Co. LR 35:90(Edward Mitchell *et al.*); 57:119; 58:124; 62:201; 63:163; 67:52, 53; 69:5-7, 40; 89:272-3(Edward to his sons); 69:6(Alice Hearsey); 73:141(Edward & Alice to Seth). Suffolk Co. PR #6635, 30:194(Elisha Cushing). *Plymouth Co Ct Recs* 9:35(Richard Perkins). *1771 Valuation* p. 630.

121. SARAH HERSEY[5] (*Alice⁴ Bradford, John³, William²⁻¹*), b. Hingham 4 July 1719; d. there 24 Oct. 1798.

She m. Hingham 17 May 1739 **THOMAS LORING**, b. Hull 30 Aug. 1713; d. Hingham 23 Aug. 1795; son of John and Jane (Baker) Loring.

On 18 May 1769 Thomas Loring of Hingham, yeoman, sold to Jotham Loring of Hingham, hatter, 3 acres with a dwelling house and outhouses.

On 12 Sept. 1793 Thomas Loring of Hingham, hatter, sold to Thomas Loring Jr. of Hingham, gentleman, a building or store; Rachel Loring and Christiana Loring were witnesses.

The will of Thomas Loring of Hingham, hatter, dated 21 Feb. 1795, presented 8 Sept. 1795, names wife Sarah; daughters Jane Thaxter, Rachel Loring, and Christiana Loring; sons Asa, Thomas, and Jotham. A codicil dated 29 July 1795 directs that at Asa's death his share be divided among Jotham, Thomas, Rachel, and Christiana.

Children of Thomas and Sarah (Hersey) Loring, b. Hingham:

   i JOTHAM LORING[6], b. 30 April 1740

  ii ASA LORING, b. 17 March 1741/2; d. Hingham 24 June 1800; unm.

iii THOMAS LORING, b. 29 July 1744; d. 31 Dec. 1745

iv SARAH LORING, b. 20 July 1747; d. 31 Dec. 1764

v JANE LORING, b. 10 Dec. 1749; d. 5 April 1752

vi JANE LORING, b. 5 Nov. 1752

vii THOMAS LORING, b. 10 March 1755

viii RACHEL LORING, b. 17 July 1758; d. Hingham 6 Nov. 1813; unm.

ix CHRISTIANA LORING, b. 16 June 1760; Hingham 12 May 1827; unm.

References: *Loring Gen* pp. 32, 53. *Hersey Gen* p. 301. *Bradford Desc* p. 47. Suffolk Co. PR 94:122(Thomas Loring). *Hingham Hist* 3:30, 32. *VR Hull* p. 26(b. Thomas). Suffolk Co. LR 115:52; 177:218(Thomas Loring).

122. JONATHAN FREEMAN[5] (*Mercy*[4] *Bradford, John*[3], *William*[2-1]), b. Harwich 26 1709/10; d. before 13 July 1748.

He m. Plymouth 19 Dec. 1728 **SARAH RIDER**, b. Plymouth 25 Dec. 1712; perhaps the "Sarah Curtis widow" who d. Plymouth 19 Jan. 1800; daughter of John and Mary (_____) Rider. She prob. m. (2) Plymouth 31 Jan. 1750/1 EDWARD CURTIS. She apparently had no children by either marriage.

In the Court of General Sessions, Jonathan Freeman of Halifax, retailer, was granted a license to sell liquor in 1738.

The will of Jonathan Freeman of Halifax, yeoman, dated 12 Jan. 1743, proved 13 July 1748, leaves all to his wife Sarah.

References: *MD* 12:223(b. Sarah); 13:72(m.). *Plymouth VR* pp. 55(b. Sarah), 95(m.), 148(her 2nd m.). Plymouth Co. PR #8114(Jonathan Freeman). *Plymouth Co Ct Recs* 2:190.

123. MERCY FREEMAN[5] (*Mercy*[4] *Bradford, John*[3], *William*[2-1]), b. Harwich 24 April 1711; d. before 5 Jan. 1763.

She m. Plympton 12 June 1728 **THOMAS WATERMAN**, b. Plympton in Oct. 1707; d. there 22 Aug. 1789 in 82nd yr.; son of Robert and Mary (Cushman) Waterman, a descendant of Pilgrim **Isaac Allerton**. He m. (2) Plympton 5 Jan. 1763 JOANNA (PADDOCK) HARLOW. He m. (3) Kingston 1 Aug. 1765 LYDIA (FAUNCE) WASHBURN.

On 21 April 1752 Thomas Waterman of Plympton, yeoman, sold to Jonathan Waterman of Plympton two pieces of land; Thomas' wife Mercy also signed this deed. On 31 March 1758 Thomas gave his son Jonathan 50 acres. On 10 Jan. 1759 Thomas sold to Jonathan 11 acres, part of Thomas' homestead.

In the 1771 Valuation List, Thomas Waterman appears in Plympton with 1 poll, 1 house, 1 shop, 1 horse, 4 cattle, 1 swine, 7 acres of pasture, 4 acres of tillage which produced 80 bushels of grain, and 3 acres of upland which produced 4 tons of hay. Listed next to him is Thomas Waterman Jr.

On 22 April 1781 Freeman Waterman of Halifax, trader, sold to Robert Waterman of Plympton five acres in Plympton that Freeman had bought of his father Waterman and bounded on land of Jonathan Waterman late of Plympton deceased; Freeman's wife Joanna also signed this deed.

On 8 Jan. 1783 Robert Waterman of Plympton, yeoman, sold to Timothy Ripley of Plympton five acres including his right in the dower land of his mother in the estate of his father Jonathan Waterman.

The will of Thomas Waterman of Halifax dated 16 July 1784, proved 5 Oct. 1789, names sons Thomas and Freeman; the children of daughter Rebecca Heferds deceased; daughter Mercy Josling; and grandson Robert Waterman.

Children of Thomas and Mercy (Freeman) Waterman, b. Plympton:

    i JONATHAN WATERMAN[6], b. 16 Dec. 1730 (not in will)

    ii ABIGAIL WATERMAN, b. 16 May 1733 (not in will)

    iii REBECCA WATERMAN, b. 19 April 1736

    iv MARY (or MERCY) WATERMAN, b. 10 June 1739

    v THOMAS WATERMAN, b. 28 July 1742

    vi PRISCILLA WATERMAN, b. 22 April 1745; d.y.

    vii FREEMAN WATERMAN, b. 16 July 1748

References: *Waterman Gen* 1:38, 82, 84. *Bradford Desc* p. 48. Plymouth Co. PR 31:78(Thomas Waterman). *VR Plympton* pp. 220(b. ch.), 221(b. Thomas), 421(all 3 m.), 529(d. Thomas). *VR Kingston* p. 300(his 3rd m.). Plymouth Co. LR 49:140-1(Thomas Waterman); 64:206(Freeman Waterman), 207(Robert Waterman). *1771 Valuation* p. 660.

124. BRADFORD FREEMAN[5] (*Mercy[4] Bradford, John[3], William[2-1]*), b. Harwich 15 Aug. 1713; d. after 9 Nov. 1758.

He m. Kingston 4 Sept. 1734 **SARAH CHURCH**, b. Plymouth 26 Feb. 1717/8; living 17 Oct. 1758; daughter of Charles and Mary (Pope) Church, a descendant of Pilgrim **Richard Warren**.

No Plymouth County probate records were found for Bradford or Sarah Freeman, nor guardianships for the children, and the only land record was dated 17 Oct. 1758 when Bradford Freeman of Plympton sold land in

Plympton with wife Sarah giving up her dower rights. He acknowledged his signature 9 Nov. 1758.

Children of Bradford and Sarah (Church) Freeman, b. Plympton:

    i CHARLES FREEMAN[6], b. 15 Oct. 1735; d. 28 Sept. 1736

    ii HANNAH FREEMAN, b. 19 July 1737

    iii MOLLEY FREEMAN, b. 20 Oct. 1739; d. 22 Oct. 1756 in 17th yr.

    iv MERCY FREEMAN, b. 10 Oct. 1742

    v JONATHAN FREEMAN, b. 24 Oct. 1745

    vi CHARLES FREEMAN, b. 26 March 1751

    vii MARY FREEMAN, b. 18 April 1757

References: *MD* 5:56(b. Sarah), 86. *VR Plympton* pp. 102-3(b. ch.), 478(d. Charles, Molley). *Bradford Desc* p. 48. Plymouth Co. LR 46:138(Bradford Freeman). *Plymouth VR* p. 40(b. Sarah). *VR Kingston* p. 224(m.).

125.   ICHABOD FREEMAN[5] (*Mercy[4] Bradford, John[3], William[2-1]*), b. Harwich 2 Aug. 1714; d. Columbia , Conn., 12 Jan. 1782 aged 66.

He m. **ANNE** _____, b. ca. 1728; d. Columbia, Conn., 10 Feb. 1792 aged 64.

On 17 Nov. 1750 Ichabod Freeman of Lebanon, Conn., laborer, sold one acre in Halifax to John Waterman Jr.

On 9 March 1785 widow Anne Freeman and daughter Phebe Loomis "only surviving child" and her husband Nathan Loomis divided the estate of Ichabod Freeman.

Child of Ichabod and Anne (_____) Freeman:

    i PHEBE FREEMAN[6], b. ca. 1755 (based on age at d.).

References: Hale Cem Coll:Columbia p. 14(d. Ichabod, Anne, Phebe). Plymouth Co. LR 41:185(Ichabod Freeman). Windham CT PR #1471(Ichabod Freeman).

126.   FEAR CUSHMAN[5] (*Mercy[4] Bradford, John[3], William[2-1]*), b. Plympton 10 July 1718; d. Kent, Conn., 29 May 1760.

She m. Plympton 11 Dec. 1734 **NEHEMIAH STURTEVANT**, b. Plympton 18 Nov. 1710; d. Kent, Conn., 18 April 1774; son of Nehemiah and Ruth (Sampson) Sturtevant.

On 21 March 1747 Nehemiah Sturtevant of Plimton and wife Fear sold land she had received from the estate of her father Isaac Cushman deceased.

On 8 Dec. 1748 Nehemiah Sturtevant of Lebanon, Conn., and wife Fear bought land in Kent, Conn.

There are no Connecticut wills for Nehemiah or Fear Sturtevant.

Children of Nehemiah and Fear (Cushman) Sturtevant, b. Plympton (exc. Lucy); rec. Kent, Conn.:

    i   PELEG STURTEVANT[6], b. 25 Jan. 1735/6

    ii PERES STURTEVANT, b. 15 Nov. 1737

    iii REMEMBER STURTEVANT, b. 6 Oct. 1740

    iv RUTH STURTEVANT, b. 12 Sept. 1743

    v FEAR STURTEVANT, b. 6 Dec. 1745

    vi ABIAH STURTEVANT, b. 27 Nov. 1748

    vii LUCY (or LUCIA) STURTEVANT, b. Kent, Conn., 6 Oct. 1752; bp. 1752

References: *VR Plympton* pp. 201(b. Peleg, Peres), 206(b. Remember, Ruth, Fear), 206(b. Nehemiah), 405(m.). *Bradford Desc* pp. 48-9. Kent CT LR 1:6(b. Peleg, Remember, Ruth, Fear, Abiah, Lucy), 62(d. Fear, Nehemiah), 367(Nehemiah Sturtevant deed). Plymouth Co. LR 40:190(Nehemiah Sturtevant).

127. PRISCILLA CUSHMAN[5] (*Mercy[4] Bradford, John[3], William[2-1]*), b. Plympton 12 Dec. 1719; d. Kent, Conn., 30 July 1763 in 44th yr.

She m. Plympton 6 Sept. 1739 **ISRAEL HOLMES**, b. ca. 1713; d. Burlington, Vt., 29 Aug. (prob. 1807) aged 95; son of John Holmes. He m. (2) Kent, Conn., 7 May 1766, ANNA NOBLE.

On 7 June 1743 Israel Holmes of Plimton, cordwainer, and wife Priscilla sold land from the estate of their father Isaac Cushman of Plimton deceased; Israel acknowledged the deed 7 July 1743.

The will of Israel Holmes of Warren, Litchfield Co., Conn., dated 25 Aug. 1803, established 22 Dec. 1807 (inv. certified in Warren 10 Dec. 1807 stating he d. in Burlington, Vt.) names daughters Sarah Buel, Priscilla Buel, Betty Bliss, and Abigail Bentley, and sons Gershom and Peleg.

Children of Israel and Priscilla (Cushman) Holmes, first two b. Plympton, third b. Lebanon, Conn., birthplace of fourth unknown, rest b. Kent, Conn.:

    i   SARAH HOLMES[6], b. 1 May 1742

    ii PRISCILLA HOLMES, bp. 24 June 1744

    iii BETTEY HOLMES, b. 31 July 1746

    iv ABIGAIL HOLMES (named in will)

v   GERSHOM HOLMES, b. 27 Sept. 1752

vi PELEG HOLMES, b. 15 May 1755

References: *VR Plympton* pp. 120(b. Sarah, bp. Priscilla), 344(1st m.). *Bradford Desc* p. 49. Plymouth Co. LR 36:36(Israel Holmes). Litchfield CT PR(Israel Holmes). Kent CT VR 2:19(b. Gershom, Peleg; d. Priscilla, Israel; 2nd m.). Lebanon CT VR 1:148(b. Betty).

128. ABIGAIL CUSHMAN⁵ (*Mercy⁴ Bradford, John³, William²⁻¹*), b. Plympton 31 Dec. 1722; d. there 8 Feb. 1784 in her 62nd yr.

She m. Plympton 31 Dec. 1741 **GIDEON SAMPSON**, b. Plympton 24 (or 15) Oct. 1719; d. there 30 Oct. 1794 aged 75y 6d; son of George and Hannah (Soule) Sampson, a descendant of Pilgrims **George Soule** and **Myles Standish**. He m. (2) Duxbury 22 Dec. 1784 REBECCA SOULE.

The court records show that Gideon Sampson served the town of Plympton as a constable in 1764 and as a selectman in 1772, 1773, and 1777.

In the 1771 Valuation List, Gideon Samson appears in Plympton with 1 poll, 1 house, 1 shop, £1:4 lent at interest, 1 horse, 2 cattle, 2 goats or sheep, 1 swine, 10 acres of pasture, 2 acres of tillage which produced 10 bushels of grain, 4 barrels of cider, and 4 acres of upland which produced 2½ tons of hay.

Gideon Sampson's household in Plympton in the 1790 census consisted of 2 men over 16 and 2 females.

The will of Gideon Sampson of Plympton dated 28 Oct. 1794, proved 9 Dec. 1794, names wife Rebecca; kinswomen Rebecca Killey, Hannah Perkins, Elizabeth Cushman, and Abigail Cushman, daughter of Joseph Cushman of Duxborough; and relative Joseph Cushman.

Gideon and Abigail apparently had no children.

References: *VR Duxbury* p. 298(his 2nd m.). *VR Plympton* pp. 381(m.), 513(d. Abigail, Gideon). *MD* 11:117(d. Abigail), 118(d. Gideon). Plymouth Co. PR 35:193(Gideon Sampson). *1771 Valuation* p. 666.

129. JOHN⁵ BRADFORD (*Samuel⁴, John³, William²⁻¹*), b. Plympton 8 April 1717; d. there 28 Sept. 1770 aged 53y 5m 9d.

He m. Plymouth 10 Nov. 1743 **ELIZABETH HOLMES**, b. Plymouth 13 Oct. 1723; d. Plympton 30 Dec. 1806 in 85th yr.; daughter of Eleazer and Hannah (Sylvester) Holmes, a descendant of Pilgrim **Richard Warren**.

On 22 Nov. 1770 widow Elizabeth Bradford and John Bradford, yeoman, both of Plimton, were appointed administrators of the estate of Capt. John Bradford late of Plympton deceased. Division of the estate into 12 shares on

31 May 1776 gave two shares to eldest son Capt. John Bradford, and single shares to sons Perez, Oliver, and William, and daughters Elizabeth Magoun, Mary Churchel, Priscilla Rider, Hannah Waterman, Lydia Bradford, Mercy Bradford, and Sarah Bradford.

On 29 May 1778 Nathaniel Rider of Plympton and his wife Priscilla sold to John Bradford, Gentleman, one-third of a mill set off to Priscilla from the estate of her father John Bradford; this deed was not recorded until 24 April 1812.

On 24 Oct. 1783 John Bradford, Gentleman; Peres Bradford, yeoman; Oliver Bradford, yeoman; Mercy Bradford, spinster; James Magoun, yeoman, and his wife Elizabeth; Levy Bryant, Gentleman, and his wife Lydia all of Plimpton; Nathaniel Rider, yeoman, and his wife Priscilla; and Jabez Waterman, yeoman, and his wife Hannah, all of Halifax, sold 2/3 of 2/9 parts "which was Set off to our Grandmother as her Right of Dower in the Real Estate of Samuel Bradford Late of Plimpton" to Freeman Norton, mariner; Phebe Norton, spinster both of Williamsborgh; Caleb Stetson, housewright; and Isaac Lobdell Jr., yeoman, and his wife Molly all of Plimton.

Elizabeth Bradford was listed in Plympton in the 1790 census with one man over 16 and 3 females. Listed next to her were Jabez Bradford (with one man over 16, 2 boys under 16, and 5 females) and Perez Bradford (with one man over 16, one boy under 16, and 6 females).

On 2 Jan. 1807 Perez Bradford of Plympton gave bond as administrator of the estate of Elizabeth Bradford, widow, deceased. On 20 April 1807 the estate was divided among: John Bradford, heirs of Elizabeth Magoun, Lydia Bryant, heirs of William Bradford, Mary Churchill, Priscilla Rider, Marcy Sears, Oliver Bradford, Perez Bradford, Hannah Waterman, and Sarah Bosworth

On 28 May 1807 Oliver Bradford of Rochester, yeoman, sold to John Bradford Jr. of Plympton his share of the land set off to him from his mother's thirds from the estate of his father John Bradford; Oliver's wife Sarah released her dower rights. On 14 May 1807 Holmes Sears of Halifax and his wife Mary sold to John their share of the thirds.

Children of John and Elizabeth (Holmes) Bradford, b. Plympton:

    i   ELIZABETH[6] BRADFORD, b. 9 Aug. 1744
   ii   MOLLY (or MARY) BRADFORD, b. 15 May 1746
  iii   JOHN BRADFORD, b. 18 July 1748
  iv   PRISCILLA BRADFORD, b. 4 Sept. 1750
   v   PEREZ BRADFORD, b. 10 Nov. 1752

  vi HANNAH BRADFORD, b. 16 Jan. 1755

  vii LYDIA BRADFORD, b. 16 Feb. 1757

  viii OLIVER BRADFORD, b. 10 Jan. 1759

  ix MARCY BRADFORD, b. 20 Dec. 1761

  x WILLIAM BRADFORD, b. 8 June 1766

  xi SARAH BRADFORD, b. 8 Oct. 1769

References: *MD* 8:153-4(deaths); 12:12(b. Elizabeth); 14:160(m.); 17:131. *VR Plympton* pp. 31-9(b. ch.), 446(d. Elizabeth), 447(d. John). *Bradford Desc* p. 49. Plymouth Co. PR 20:409; 24:116(John Bradford); 39:97; 42:141(Elizabeth Bradford). *Plymouth VR* pp. 49(b. Elizabeth), 103(m.). Plymouth Co. LR 119:7(Nathaniel Rider), 8(Oliver Bradford, Holmes Sears).

130. GIDEON[5] BRADFORD (*Samuel[4], John[3], William[2-1]*), b. Plympton 27 Oct. 1718; d. there 18 Oct. 1793 in 75th yr.

He m. Plymouth 8 Oct. 1741 **JANE PADDOCK**, b. Yarmouth 30 Aug. 1717; d. Plympton 18 April 1795 in 78th yr.; daughter of Ichabod and Joanna (Faunce) Paddock.

On 21 April 1761 Gideon Bradford and his wife Jane and Elkanah Cushman and his wife Patience of Plympton sold to Henry Thomas of Middleborough two-eighths of one-sixth of two acres in Middleborough that had come from the will of Jane and Patience's grandfather Thomas Faunce. On 21 April 1762 Gideon Bradford of Plympton, Esq., sold to William Crombie of Plymouth, tanner, a house lot with house, corn house, out houses, and fences in Plymouth; Gideon's wife Jane also signed this deed.

Land records show that Gideon was a selectman in 1761.

In the 1771 Valuation List, Gideon Bradford appears in Plympton with 3 polls, 1 house, 1 shop, 1 saw mill, 1 iron works, 1 horse, 6 oxen, 5 cattle, 15 goats or sheep, 4 swine, 35 acres of pasture, 24 acres of tillage which produced 120 bushels of grain, 4 barrels of cider, 12 acres of upland which produced 8 tons of hay, and 16 acres of fresh meadow which produced 13 tons of hay. Listed next to him are Levi and Samuel Bradford.

Gideon Bradford Esq. was in Plympton in the 1790 census, head of a household consisting of himself and 3 females. Listed next to him were Levi Bradford (with 3 men over 16, one boy under 16, and 3 females); Samuel Bradford (with 1 man, 3 boys under 16, and 3 females); Gideon Bradford Jr. (with 1 man, 4 boys under 16, and 4 females); and Calvin Bradford (with 1 man, 2 boys under 16, and 4 females).

The will of Gideon Bradford of Plympton Esq. dated 11 May 1784, proved 11 Nov. 1793, names wife Jane; sons Levi, Joseph, Samuel, Gideon, and Calvin who were to have all his law books; and daughters Sarah Ellis, wife of Freeman, and Jane Bisbee, wife of Noah.

On 15 Jan. 1794 Gideon Bradford, Gentleman, and Calvin Bradford, yeoman, both of Plympton, divided 220 acres partly in Plympton and partly in Carver that had formerly belonged to their father Gideon Bradford Esq., deceased. On 2 July 1801 Gideon mortgaged his half to Joshua Thomas.

The will of Jane Bradford of Plympton, widow of Gideon Bradford Esq., dated 31 May 1794, sworn 4 Jan. 1796, names son Levi; dau. Jenny Bisbee, wife of Noah; and dau. Sarah Ellis, wife of Freeman.

Children of Gideon and Jane (Paddock) Bradford, b. Plympton:

   i   LEVI[6] BRADFORD, b. 16 Feb. 1742/3
   ii JOSEPH BRADFORD, b. 19 Oct. 1745
   iii SARAH BRADFORD, b. 19 May 1748
   iv SAMUEL BRADFORD, b. 20 June 1750
   v   GIDEON BRADFORD, b. 30 May 1752
   vi CALVIN BRADFORD, b. 25 July 1754
   vii JENNY (or JANE) BRADFORD, b. 12 March 1756

References: *MD* 8:153-4(deaths); 14:159(m.); 18:117. *VR Plympton* pp. 30-8(b. ch.), 263(m.), 447(d. Gideon, Jane). *Yarmouth VR* 1:40(b. Jane). *Bradford Desc* pp. 49-50. Plymouth Co. PR 33:467(Gideon Bradford); #2550(Jane Bradford). *Plymouth VR* p. 102(m.). Plymouth Co. LR 47:263; 50:82; 91:46, 77(Gideon Bradford). *1771 Valuation* p. 662.

131. MARY[5] BRADFORD (*Samuel[4], John[3], William[2-1]*), b. Plympton 16 Oct. 1722; d. Tiverton, R.I., 3 Feb. 1792 in her 70th year.

She m. Tiverton 1 Dec. 1743 **ABIEL COOKE**, b. Tiverton ca. 1719; d. there 15 July 1808; son of John and Alice (Southworth) Cooke, a descendant of Pilgrim **John Alden**. This is not a *Mayflower* Cooke line. Abiel Cooke had four illegitimate children by Mary / "Moll" Briggs.

Abiel Cooke was a Loyalist in the Revolutionary War.

Abiel Cooke of Tiverton died intestate and his daughter Sarah Cook was appointed administratrix of his estate. On 6 Feb. 1809 she was named guardian of her brothers Nathaniel and William and her sister Priscilla who were apparently unable to take care of their portions.

On 9 July 1812 the heirs of Abiel Cook signed a deed. They were David Cook and wife Alice of Plymouth, N.Y.; Gilbert Eddy and wife Nancy of

Oxford; Samuel Knight of Oxford, Chenango Co., N.Y.; Philip Knight [*worn*] of Schenectady; Samuel Swain and wife Mary of Nantucket; Sarah Cook of Tiverton, singlewoman; Sarah Cook as guardian of Nathaniel and William Cook; Abiel Cook; and Priscilla Cook.

Children of Abiel and Mary (Bradford) Cooke,* b. Little Compton, R.I.:

    i   MARY COOKE[6], b. 8 Aug. 1744

    ii JOSEPH COOKE, b. 21 Aug. 1746

    iii WILLIAM COOKE, b. ca. 1750; d. before 1818; unm.

    iv ALICE COOKE, b. 6 June 1752

    v SAMUEL COOKE, b. 4 Oct. 1754

    vi NATHANIEL COOKE, b. 28 Dec. 1756; d. Little Compton, R.I., 4 Jan. 1817

    vii SARAH COOKE, b. 2 July 1759; d. summer 1840; unm. The will of Sarah Cook, singlewoman of Little Compton dated 29 April 1837, proved 3 Aug. 1840, names kinsmen Joseph Cook, John Stanton Cook, and Isaac Sanford Cook, sons of kinsman Samuel Cook Sr.; Mary, wife of Pardon Almy and her dau. Mary Almy, and Nabby Hill and "her second daughter" all of whom were daus. or granddaus. of kinsman Samuel Cook Sr.

    viii PRISCILLA COOKE, b. 10 Dec. 1761; d. before 1809; unm.

* Note: No proof found for a son THADDEUS listed in *Bradford Desc.*

References: *RIVR* Little Compton 4:6:108(b. ch. exc. William). *Bradford Desc* p. 50. *Cooke (Thomas)* 1:158-161. Tiverton RI PR 12:2(Sarah Cook). *RIVR* Tiverton 4:7:16(m.). *NEHGR* 117:21(d. Mary). Little Compton RI LE 6:183-7(heirs).

132. SARAH[5] BRADFORD (*Samuel[4], John[3], William[2-1]*), b. Plympton 4 April 1725; living Warren 4 Nov. 1759 (last child).

She m. Plympton 25 Nov. 1742 **EPHRAIM PADDOCK**, b. Yarmouth 15 April 1721; d. Ware after 1790; son of Ichabod and Joanna (Faunce) Paddock. The will of Elder Thomas Faunce of Plymouth drawn 21 March 1745, bequeathed lands in Middleboro to his dau. Joanna, wife of Ichabod Paddock [and mother of Ephraim].

On 19 Jan. 1746/7 Ephraim Paddock "a late inhabitant of Hanover for the Space of one month resided in this town" was warned from Pembroke.

On 19 July 1756 Ephraim Paddock of Pembroke, blacksmith, sold land in Pembroke with wife Sarah releasing her dower.

On 15 Oct. 1763 Ephraim Paddock of Brookfield, blacksmith, sold land in Middleboro which Elder Thomas Faunce late of Plymouth dec. gave to Jabez Barnes, provided he had issue. This deed was acknowledged 23 Aug. 1765 before Gideon Bradford, JP.

In the 1771 Valuation List, Ephraim Paddock was listed in Ware with 1 poll, 1 house, 1 tanhouse, 1 horse, 1 cattle, 25 goats or sheep, 5 acres of tillage which produced 35 bushels of grain, and 5 acres of fresh meadow which produced 4 tons of hay.

Ephraim Paddock's household in the 1790 census of Ware consisted of one man over 16 and one female. Listed next to him was Bradford Paddock (with 1 man and 3 females).

No probate records were found for Ephraim Paddock. No land transactions for him were found in Worcester, Hampshire, or Hampden counties.

Children of Ephraim and Sarah (Bradford) Paddock, first 2 b. Pembroke [no additional children found in Pembroke, Plymouth, Plympton, Middleborough, or Hanover]:

  i   SARAH PADDOCK⁶, b. 6 Jan. 1754
  ii EPHRAIM PADDOCK, bp. 20 June 1756
  iii BRADFORD PADDOCK, b. Warren 4 Nov. 1759

References: *MD* 18:118.   *VR Pembroke* p. 158(b. Sarah, Ephraim).   *VR Plympton* p. 355(m).   *Yarmouth VR* 1:40(b. Ephraim).   *Bradford Desc* p. 50.   Plymouth Co. PR 10:101(Thomas Faunce). Plymouth Co. LR 44:4; 50:82(Ephraim Paddock).   *VR Warren* p. 52(b. Bradford). *Plymouth Co Ct Recs* 2:247(warning). *1771 Valuation* p. 406.

133. WILLIAM⁵ BRADFORD (*Samuel⁴, John³, William²⁻¹*), b. Plympton 4 Nov. 1728; d. Bristol, R.I., 6 July 1808 aged 79.

He m. Plymouth 22 March 1750/1 **MARY LE BARON**, b. Plymouth 20 March 1731/2; d. Bristol, R.I., 2 Oct. 1775; daughter of Lazarus and Lydia (Bartlett) LeBaron, a descendant of Pilgrim **Richard Warren**. The will of Lazarus LeBaron of Plymouth, physician, dated 24 Sept. 1772, names daughter Mary Bradford wife of Dr. Bradford of Bristol.

On 11 Nov. 1796 William Bradford of Bristol, physician, sold ten acres of his farm in Bristol to John Bradford of Bristol, gentleman.

William Bradford was a physician, lawyer, the last Deputy Governor of Rhode Island under the Crown, and the first Governor under the Continental Congress. He was U. S. Senator 1793–1797.

The will of William Bradford of Bristol, physician and attorney, dated 9 Oct. 1807, proved 1 Aug. 1808, names sons William, John, Henry, and LeBaron Bradford; Sarah, widow of LeBaron and their son LeBaron Bradford; daughters Mary Goodwin, widow, Hannah wife of Gustavus Baylis, and Lydia wife of Charles Collins Jr.; grandson Henry Goodwin; and niece Hannah LeBaron.

Children of William and Mary (LeBaron) Bradford, first b. Warren, R.I., next seven b. Bristol, R.I.:

    i   WILLIAM[6] BRADFORD, b. 15 Sept. 1752
   ii   LE BARON BRADFORD, b. 31 May 1754
  iii   JOHN BRADFORD, b. 9 Oct. 1758; d. 30 Oct. 1765
   iv   MARY BRADFORD, b. 2 Sept. 1760
    v   HANNAH BRADFORD, b. 22 Nov. 1762; d. 5 Sept. 1763
   vi   [SON] BRADFORD, b. 15 July 1764; d. 5 Aug. 1764
  vii   HANNAH BRADFORD, b. 14 June 1767
 viii   JOHN BRADFORD, b. 17 July 1768
   ix   ANN / NANCY BRADFORD, b. 6 Aug. 1770 (not in will)
    x   EZEKIEL HERSEY BRADFORD, b. 8 March 1772
   xi   LYDIA BRADFORD, b. 11 April 1774

References: *MD* 13:112(b. Mary); 16:167(int.), 171(m.). *RIVR* Bristol 6:1:65(b. 1st 4 ch., 2nd Hannah, John), 119(d. William, Mary, children). *PN&Q* 3:105 (Bible rec.). *Bradford Desc* p. 50-1. Plymouth PR 21:324(Lazarus LeBaron). Bristol RI PR 3:142(William Bradford). *Plymouth VR* p. 148(m.). Bristol RI LE 7:95(William Bradford).

134. ABIGAIL[5] BRADFORD (*Samuel[4], John[3], William[2-1]*), b. Plympton 12 June 1732; d. there 31 Jan. 1776 in 44th yr.

She m. int. Plymouth 7 Sept. 1754 **CALEB STETSON**, bp. Plymouth Nov. 1734; d. after 1790; son of Caleb and Deborah (Morton) Stetson.

At a Plymouth town meeting 20 March 1758, Caleb Stetson was chosen one of the hogreeves and on 18 Sept. of the same year, he was chosen a juror.

In 1762 Abigail Stetson and her son Caleb from Plymouth were warned from Plympton.

On 24 Oct. 1780 Caleb Stetson and Isaac Lobdel and wife Molly, heirs of Abigail Stetson late of Plympton, deceased, and others, quitclaimed to Gideon Bradford items given to Gideon in the will of Samuel Bradford deceased. On

24 Oct. 1783 John Bradford, Gentleman; Peres Bradford, yeoman; Oliver Bradford, yeoman; Mercy Bradford, spinster; James Magoun, yeoman, and his wife Elizabeth; Levy Bryant, Gentleman, and his wife Lydia all of Plimpton; Nathaniel Rider, yeoman, and his wife Priscilla; and Jabez Waterman, yeoman, and his wife Hannah all of Halifax sold to 2/3 of 2/9 parts "which was Set off to our Grandmother as her Right of Dower in the Real Estate of Samuel Bradford Late of Plimpton" to Freeman Norton, mariner; Phebe Norton, spinster both of Williamsborgh; Caleb Stetson, housewright; and Isaac Lobdell Jr., yeoman, and his wife Molly all of Plimton.

Caleb Stetson's household in Plympton in the 1790 census consisted of one man over 16, one boy under 16, and 5 females.

No Plymouth County probate records were found for Caleb or Abigail Stetson.

Children of Caleb and Abigail (Bradford) Stetson, first two b. Plymouth:

  i   CALEB STETSON[6], b. 12 Aug. 1755
  ii BRADFORD STETSON, b. 20 May 1757; d. 5 Sept. 1758 ae 1yr 3mo 13d
  iii MARY/MOLLY STETSON, b. 7 Sept. 1759

References: *MD* 11:163(d. Abigail); 18:216(b. 1st 2 ch.); 25:51 (int.). *VR Plympton* p. 522(d. Abigail). *Bradford Desc* p. 52(b. Mary). Plymouth Co. LR 65:75(Caleb Stetson *et al.*). *Plymouth Ch Recs* 1:435(bp. Caleb). *Plymouth VR* pp. 187(b. 1st 2 ch.), 244(int.). *(Plymouth) Burial Hill* p. 34(d. Bradford). *Plymouth Town Recs* 3:107, 109. *Plymouth Co Ct Recs* 3:107(warning).

135. PHEBE[5] BRADFORD (*Samuel[4], John[3], William[2-1]*), b. Plympton 30 March 1735; living Williamsburg 24 Oct. 1780.

She m. Plympton 10 Sept. 1753 **SHUBAL NORTON**, b. Chilmark 21 Aug. 1733; d. there 15 Feb. 1760 in 27th yr.; son of Jacob and Bethia (Mayhew) Norton.

In the 1771 Valuation List, Phebe Norton appears in Chilmark with 1 poll, 1 cattle, and 40 acres of tillage which produced 60 bushels of grain.

On 27 Oct. 1780 Freeman Norton of Williamsburg, mariner, as attorney to his mother Phebe Norton also of Williamsburg, with Caleb Stetson and Isaac Lobdel and his wife Molly, all of Plympton, being heirs of Abigail Stetson late of Plympton deceased, quitclaimed to Gideon Bradford items given to Gideon in the will of Samuel Bradford late of Plympton deceased. On 24 Oct. 1783 John Bradford, Gentleman; Peres Bradford, yeoman; Oliver Bradford, yeoman; Mercy Bradford, spinster; James Magoun, yeoman, and his wife Elizabeth; Levy Bryant, Gentleman, and his wife Lydia all of Plimpton; Nathaniel Rider, yeoman, and his wife Priscilla; and Jabez Waterman, yeoman, and his wife Hannah all of Halifax sold to 2/3 of 2/9 parts "which was Set off to our Grandmother as her Right of Dower in the Real Estate of Samuel Bradford Late of Plimpton" to Freeman Norton, mariner; Phebe Norton, spinster both of Williamsborgh; Caleb Stetson, housewright; and Isaac Lobdell Jr., yeoman, and his wife Molly all of Plimton.

Children of Shubal and Phebe (Bradford) Norton, b. Chilmark:

    i   FREEMAN NORTON[6], b. 21 Aug. 1754

    ii SARAH NORTON, b. 27 May 1756

    iii BETHIA NORTON, b. 20 Nov. 1758

References: *VR Chilmark* pp. 26(b. Bethia, Freeman), 37(b. Sarah, Shubal), 92(d. Shubal). *VR Plympton* p. 353(m. - no date). *Bradford Desc* p. 52. Plymouth Co. LR 65:75(Freeman Norton *et al.*). *1771 Valuation* p. 692.

136. SAMUEL[5] BRADFORD (*Samuel[4], John[3], William[2-1]*), b. Plympton 13 April 1740; d. Williamsburg 1 Aug. 1813.

He m. Chilmark 25 Nov. 1762 **LYDIA PEASE**, b. Chilmark in 1740; d. Williamsburg 21 Nov. 1825; daughter of John and Abigail (Burgess) Pease.

On 16 June 1766 and 20 Aug. 1774 Samuel Bradford of Chilmark sold land in Chilmark; his wife Lydia signed both deeds.

In the 1771 Valuation List, Samuel Bradford appears in Chilmark with 1 poll, 1 house, 1 horse, 2 cattle, 2 swine, and 20 acres of pasture.

Samuel Bradford's household in Williamsburg in the 1790 census consisted of four men over 16, one boy under 16, and two females.

In his will dated 3 Feb. 1801, with administrator's bond dated "last day of Feb. 1814," Samuel Bradford of Williamsburg mentioned but did not name his "loving wife"; he named son Shubel, daughter Sarah, sons Samuel, Edward Gray, and Pardon, and gave to daughter Lydia the use of a room in the house. On 27 Dec. 1813 Shubael Bradford and Edward Gray Bradford, both of Conway, Franklin Co., Ephraim Hill and wife Sarah, and Lydia Bradford, all of Williamsburg, sold to Pardon Bradford of Williamsburg, real estate of their father Samuel Bradford late of Williamsburg, deceased.

Children of Samuel and Lydia (Pease) Bradford, b. Williamsburg:

    i SARAH[6] BRADFORD, b. 22 Sept. 1763; d. 30 Oct. 1763

    ii SHUBAEL BRADFORD, b. 5 Oct. 1764

iii JOHN BRADFORD, b. 6 May 1766; d. Williamsburg 26 March 1782

iv SARAH BRADFORD, b. 15 March 1768

v   SAMUEL BRADFORD, b. 5 Sept. 1770

vi EDWARD GRAY BRADFORD, b. 22 Aug. 1772

vii [SON] BRADFORD, b. 13 March 1774; d. 3 May 1774

viii PARDON BRADFORD, b. 27 June 1775

ix LYDIA BRADFORD, b. 25 Sept. 1778; d. Williamsburg 16 March 1859; unm.

x   ABIGAIL BRADFORD, b. 28 Jan. 1782; d. Williamsburg 10 June 1790

References: *VR Chilmark* p. 43(m.). *Bradford Desc* p. 52. Hampshire Co. PR Box 19:4(Samuel Bradford). Hampshire Co. LR 37:184(Shubael Bradford *et al.*). Dukes Co. LR 9:512; 10:213(Samuel Bradford). Williamsburg VR 1:26; 2:18(b.&d. ch.); 1:129(d. Lydia). *1771 Valuation* p. 694.

137. SETH CHIPMAN[5] (*Priscilla[4] Bradford, John[3], William[2-1]*), b. Kingston 1 Nov. 1724; d. prob. at sea before 23 May 1766.

He m. Kingston 3 Dec. 1746 **SARAH RIPLEY**, b. Plympton 22 Jan. 1728; living 1779; daughter of William and Hannah (Bosworth) Ripley, a descendant of Pilgrim **John Howland**.

On 23 May 1766 Cornelius Samson of Kingston, gentleman, was appointed administrator on the estate of Seth Chipman late of Kingston, mariner.

On 15 March 1770 Sarah Chipman of Kingston, widow of Seth Chipman of Kingston, mariner, and her father William Ripley of Plimton, housewright, petitioned to sell land, she being left with two female children aged about 5 and 3 years.

On 14 Sept. 1771 William Ripley Jr. of Plimton was appointed guardian to Sarah and Mercy Chipman daughters of Seth Chipman Jr. late of Kingston, mariner, deceased, minors under 14.

In 1779 Sarah Chipman, widow, and daughter Sarah from Kingston were warned from Plympton.

Children of Seth and Sarah (Ripley) Chipman, b. Kingston:

i   SARAH CHIPMAN[6], b. 5 May 1764

ii MERCY CHIPMAN, b. 22 June 1766; d. prob. by 1779 when not in warning.

References: *VR Kingston* p. 40(b. ch.), 191(m.). *VR Plympton* p. 170(b. Sarah). *Bradford Desc* p. 53. Plymouth Co. PR 17:162; 20:552(Seth Chipman); 21:30(gdn.). *Plymouth Co Ct Recs* 3:360(warning).

138. MERCY CHIPMAN⁵ (*Priscilla⁴ Bradford, John³, William²⁻¹*), b. Kingston 19 Nov. 1725; d. there 13 Feb. 1782 in her 57th yr.

She m. Kingston 7 Dec. 1763 **BENJAMIN BRADFORD**, b. Plymouth 17 Oct. 1705; d. Kingston 16 Oct./Nov. 1783 aged 77; son of Israel and Sarah (Bartlett) Bradford, a descendant of Pilgrims **John Alden, William Bradford, William Brewster**, and **Richard Warren**. He m. (1) int. Kingston 18 Dec. 1731 ZERESH STETSON with whom he had Thomas, Michael, Perez, Lydia, Benjamin, Marcy, Lemuel, and Lydia.

No children. See Family #94 for account.

References: *MD* 13:167(b. Benjamin). *VR Kingston* pp. 179(m., int. his 1ˢᵗ m.), 319(d. Benjamin, 16 Oct. in Ch. Rec; 16 Nov. on g.s.), 322(d. Mercy). *Plymouth VR* p. 72(b. Benjamin).

139. BENJAMIN CHIPMAN⁵ (*Priscilla⁴ Bradford, John³, William²⁻¹*), b. Kingston 23 May 1729; d. Poland, Maine, in May 1787.

He m. Kingston 9 May 1751 **HANNAH WADSWORTH**, b. Duxbury 6 Dec. 1732; d. Poland, Maine, 26 Dec. 1822; daughter of Ichabod and Margaret (Marshall) Wadsworth.

The General Sessions court records show that Benjamin Chipman served as a deputy sheriff in 1752 and 1777.

In the 1771 Valuation List, Benjamin Chipman appears in Kingston with 2 polls and 1 house.

On 30 Sept. 1774 Benjamin Chipman of Kingston, cooper, sold land in Kingston with buildings, with Hannah Chipman also signing.

On 16 May 1777 Barnabas Winslow of New Gloucester [Maine] sold 30 acres there to Benjamin Chipman of New Gloucester, cooper.

On 22 April 1797 Hannah Chipman, widow of Benjamin Chipman, William Chipman, Daniel Chipman, Benjamin Chipman, John T. Merrill and his wife Hannah, William and Margaret (Peggy in acknowledgement) Alden, all of Poland [Maine] conveyed half of lot #58 in the second division laid out to the late Benjamin Chipman to Josiah Little of Newbury. On 23 Feb. 1801 Josiah Little sold Isaac Currier and Thomas Brown of Newbury 105 acres with buildings in Poland; Josiah's wife Sarah also signed this deed.

The Cumberland County, Maine, probate records for this period do not survive.

At the August 1817 term of the court of Common Pleas, Judah Alden, Esq., Reuben Delano, yeoman, and his wife Luna, and Luther Peterson, yeoman, and his wife Priscilla, all of Duxbury; Thomas Browne of Portland [Maine], merchant; Benjamin Chipman of Poland [Maine], yeoman; William Alden of Poland and Margaret his wife; Joshua Berry of Poland, yeoman, and his wife Hannah; Daniel Chipman of Raymond [Maine], yeoman; Lydia Chipman of Westbrook [Maine], seamstress; and William Chipman of Hebron [Maine], yeoman, brought suit against the Duxbury South River Manufacturing Company. The plaintiffs claimed that 10 acres of meadow and pasture land in Duxbury on both sides of the South River had been flooded for two years by the defendant's dam across the South River and that they operated a Grist Mill and a Cotton Factory on the dam. The flowage had caused the "utter ruin of the herbage thereof and entire destruction of an excellent Spring of cold water." The court ordered that the plantiffs be paid $24.00 for past damage and $12.00 annually.

Children of Benjamin and Hannah (Wadsworth) Chipman, b. Kingston:

    i BENJAMIN CHIPMAN[6], b. 24 Jan. 1752

    ii MARGARET CHIPMAN, b. 16 June 1756

    iii SARAH CHIPMAN, b. 3 Dec. 1759

    iv PRISCILLA CHIPMAN, b. 25 July 1761

    v LYDIA CHIPMAN, b. 20 March 1763; living unm. Aug. 1817

    vi WILLIAM CHIPMAN, b. 14 Aug. 1764

    vii LEONA CHIPMAN (twin), b. 18 Feb. 1766

    viii DANIEL CHIPMAN (twin), b. 18 Feb. 1766; d.y.

    ix HANNAH CHIPMAN, b. 25 July 1769

    x DANIEL CHIPMAN, b. 9 July 1771

References: *VR Duxbury* p. 181(b. Hannah). *VR Kingston* pp. 39(b. son Benjamin), 40(b. Margaret thru Leona), 191(m.). *Bradford Desc* p. 53. Plymouth Co. LR 58:117(Benjamin Chipman). Cumberland Co. LR 10:406(Barnabas Winslow); 36:360(Josiah Little), 528(Hannah Chipman *et al.*). *Plymouth Co Ct Recs* Vol. 3; 15:91(Judah Alden *et al.*). *1771 Valuation* p. 642.

140. JAMES[5] BRADFORD (*William[4], John[3], William[2-1]*), b. Plymouth 2 July 1717; d. prob. Plainfield, Conn., 10 Dec. 1801 aged 84.

He m. (1) **PRISCILLA SPAULDING**, b. Plainfield, Conn., 17 Jan. 1718/9; d. there 11 Feb. 1743 aged 24; daughter of Josiah and Sarah (Warren) Spaulding. On 9 May 1743 James Bradford and his wife Persila, and Eleazer Cady and his wife Keziah of Plainfield sold to Samuel Shepard of Plainfield their right in the estate of Ziprah Spalding daughter of Josiah Spalding.

He m. (2) **ZERVIAH THOMAS**, b. Marshfield 3 Oct. 1715; d. Plainfield, Conn., 23 Nov. 1808 aged 93; daughter of John and Lydia (Waterman) Thomas, a descendant of Pilgrim **Richard Warren**. The will of John Thomas dated 12 May 1764 names daughter Zervah wife of James Bradford.

On 12 Dec. 1737 Samuel Bradford of Plymton, Gentleman, Robert Bradford of Kingston, yeoman, and George Partridge of Duxbury guardian of James Bradford, Samuel Bradford, Zadock Bradford, Eliphalet Bradford, and William Bradford grandsons of the Honorable John Bradford late of Plymouth, Esq., sold 1/9 part of land located near Muscongus in Lincoln Co., Maine. This deed was acknowledged in Boston on 27 Dec. 1737 but not recorded in Lincoln Co. until 25 Aug. 1763.

On 12 May 1746 James Bradford of Plainfield, Conn., sold to Samuel Foster land that belonged to his brother Zadock Bradford *et al.*

On 7 April 1783 James Bradford of Plainfield gave his son Anthony Bradford of Plainfield 35 acres.

James Bradford was listed in Plainfield, Conn., in the 1790 census, his household consisting of two men over 16, two boys under 16, and four females.

The will of James Bradford of Plainfield, Conn., "advanced in age," dated 17 May 1798, accepted 5 Jan. 1802, names wife Keziah [*sic*], also advanced in age; sons Anthony and Samuel; oldest daughter Persillah Dorrance; and daughter Keziah Clift.

Children of James and Zerviah (Thomas) Bradford:*

    i SAMUEL[6] BRADFORD, b. ca. 1744

    ii KEZIAH BRADFORD, b. 15 Oct. 1747

    iii ANTHONY BRADFORD, b. 6 Sept. 1749

    iv JAMES BRADFORD, b. 20 Jan. 1751; d. 3 Dec. 1777 ae 25; unm.

    v PRISCILLA BRADFORD, b. 20 Dec. 1752

    vi HANNAH BRADFORD, b. 8 Nov. 1756; d. 25 June 1778 ae 21; unm.

    vii JOSEPH BRADFORD, b. 30 Dec. 1758; d. 26 May 1759

* NOTE: No proof has been found for a son Josiah as given in *Bradford Desc.*

References: *MD* 8:176(b. Zerviah); 23:156. *Waterman Gen* 1:64-5, 627. *Bradford Desc* p. 53. Hale Cem Coll:Plainfield p. 184(d. James, Priscilla, son James, Zerviah, Hannah). Plainfield CT PR #230(James Bradford). *Marshfield VR* p. 42(b. Zerviah). Thomas Gen p. 165. Plymouth Co. LR 38:71(James Bradford). Plainfield CT VR 1:20(b. Priscilla). Plainfield CR LR 3:389; 6:530(James Bradford). Plainfield 1st Ch. Recs. 1:219(d. child 1759), 221(d. son James). Lincoln Co. ME LR 3:140(Samuel Bradford).

141. ELIPHALET[5] BRADFORD (*William[4], John[3], William[2-1]*), b. Plymouth 20 Jan. 1723; d. Duxbury 7 June 1795 in his 72nd year.

He m. (1) Duxbury 8 Aug. 1751 **HANNAH PRINCE**, b. Duxbury 22 Oct. 1730; d. there 11 July 1756 in her 26th year, daughter of Thomas and Judith (Fox) Prince, a descendant of Pilgrim **William Brewster**. On 18 Sept. 1755 Eliphalet Bradford of Duxbury, his wife Hannah, and Judith Prince of Duxbury, widow, sold to Freedom Chamberlain Jr. of Pembroke eight of the ten shares in a lot of cedar swamp.

He m. (2) Duxbury 9 Feb. 1758 **HANNAH OLDHAM** [poss. widow], b. 29 Oct. 1733; d. Duxbury 4 Nov. 1804 aged 71y 9d.

On 12 Dec. 1737 Samuel Bradford of Plymton, Gentleman, Robert Bradford of Kingston, yeoman, and George Partridge of Duxbury guardian of James Bradford, Samuel Bradford, Zadock Bradford, Eliphalet Bradford, and William Bradford grandsons of the Honorable John Bradford late of Plymouth, Esq., sold to 1/9 part of land located near Muscongus in Lincoln County, Maine. This deed was acknowledged in Boston on 27 Dec. 1737 but not recorded in Lincoln County until 25 Aug. 1763.

At the Sept. 1752 term of the court of General Sessions, Eliphalet Bradford was presented and fined for assaulting and striking Asa Soper. At the same term, Asa Soper was presented for assaulting and striking Eliphalet Bradford.

On 4 Sept. 1789 Eliphalet Bradford of Duxbury, yeoman, sold his right in his homestead of 23 acres, a 35-acre woodlot, and three pieces of salt marsh to Benjamin Freeman, Samuel Bradford, and Uriah Wadsworth all of Duxbury, yeomen. It was noted that Eliphalet would be "a tenent for life, the Reversion thereof belonging to" Hannah Freeman wife of Benjamin, Lydia Bradford wife of Samuel, and Eunice Wadsworth wife of Uriah.

Eliphalet Bradford's household in the 1790 census of Duxbury consisted of two men over 16 and two females.

No Plymouth County probate records were found for Eliphalet Bradford.

Children of Eliphalet and Hannah (Prince) Bradford, b. Duxbury:

    i   HANNAH[6] BRADFORD, b. 30 May 1752

   ii   LYDIA BRADFORD, b. 28 Jan. 1754

  iii   EUNICE BRADFORD, b. 8 May 1756

Children of Eliphalet and Hannah (Oldham) Bradford, b. Duxbury:

   iv   LUCY BRADFORD, b. 9 Nov. 1758

    v   ABIGAIL BRADFORD, b. 26 Dec. 1759

vi WILLIAM BRADFORD, b. 17 Nov. 1761

vii ZADOCK BRADFORD, b. 11 Aug. 1765

viii DEBORAH BRADFORD, b. 16 Dec. 1767

ix MARY BRADFORD, b. Sept. 1773; d. 16 May 1774

References: *MD* 9:160(d. wife Hannah); 11:237(b. Hannah Prince); 12:170(b. 1st 3 ch.); 16:168(int. 1st m.). *VR Duxbury* pp. 27-32(b. ch.), 222(both m.), 352(deaths), 353(d. Mary). *Bradford Desc* pp. 53-4. Lincoln Co. ME LR 3:140(Samuel Bradford). Plymouth Co. LR 43:233; 69:101(Eliphalet Bradford). *Plymouth Co Ct Recs* 3:28.

142. HANNAH⁵ BRADFORD (*William⁴, John³, William²⁻¹*), b. Plymouth 29 May 1724; d. Plainfield, Conn., 2 March 1755 aged 29y 9m.

She m. Plainfield, Conn., 20 Feb. 1745 **WILLARD SPAULDING**, b. Plainfield, Conn., 1 March 1716/7; d. Killingly, Conn., 19 Feb. 1766; son of Edward and Elizabeth (Hall) Spaulding. On 11 March 1746 Edward Spaulding of Plainfield gave his son Willard Spaulding of Plainfield land in Killingly.

On 15 March 1749/50 Willard Spaulding of Killingly, Conn., husbandman, and wife Hannah sold to John Brewster of Kingston land in Kingston that belonged "to our honoured father William Bradford."

The will of Willard Spaulding of Killingly, Conn., "sick and weak," dated 21 March 1765 with codicil 10 Dec. 1765, proved 4 March 1766, names only son Zadock, eldest daughter Mary, second daughter Hannah, and youngest daughter Elizabeth; brother Capt. James Bradford of Plainfield executor.

On 25 June 1774 Hannah Spaulding of Killingly sold to Zadock Spaulding of Killingly the land set off to her from the estate of her father Willard Spaulding. On 8 May 1776 Mary Spalding of Killingly sold to Zadock her share of her father's estate.

Children of Willard and Hannah (Bradford) Spaulding, 1st b. Plainfield, Conn.; rest b. Killingly, Conn.:

i ZADOCK SPAULDING⁶, b. 8 May 1746

ii MARY SPAULDING, b. 4 Sept. 1749

iii HANNAH SPAULDING, b. 29 June 1751

iv ELIZABETH SPAULDING, b. 18 Nov. 1753

References: *Bradford Desc* p. 54. Plymouth Co. LR 41:58(Willard Spaulding). Killingly CT PR #2013(Willard Spaulding). Plainfield CT VR 1:17(b. Willard); 2:13(m.; b. Zadock), 29(d. Hannah). Killingly CT VR 1:47(b. Mary, Hannah), 53(b. Elizabeth), 174(d. Willard).

Killingly CT LR 5:160(Edward Spaulding); 9:131(Hannah Spaulding), 161(Mary Spaulding). Plainfield 1st Ch. Recs. 1:218(d. Hannah).

143. LEMUEL BARNES[5] (*Alice*[4] *Bradford, William*[3-2-1]), b. Plymouth 16 Feb. 1707; d. there before 16 April 1751.

He m. Plymouth 21 May 1735 **LYDIA BARNES**, b. Plymouth 4 Dec. 1713; d. there 5 March 1774 (as Jonathan Samson's wife); daughter of John and Mary (Bartlett) Barnes, a descendant of Pilgrim **Richard Warren**. She may have m. (2) before 5 July 1756 JONATHAN SAMSON, though the church and land records below seem to indicate that they did not marry, but lived together. On 29 Aug. 1746 William Barnes, yeoman, Lemuel Barnes, shoreman, and Lydia Barnes, wife of Lemuel, sold to George Watson of Plymouth, Gentleman, 13 acres of woodland and another 17 acres; William Barnes and John Barnes had bought this land and now that John was deceased, his share belonged to Lydia.

At the September 1735 term of the Court of General Sessions, Lemuel Barnes of Plymouth and Lydia his wife confessed to fornication before marriage and were fined £4.

On 22 Feb. 1736 Lydia, wife of Lemuel Barnes, joined the Plymouth church.

At a Plymouth town meeting 12 Dec. 1743, Lemuel Barnes was chosen a constable; on 13 May 1734, 13 Dec. 1745, and 18 Dec, 1749 a juror; and on 11 March 1750 a surveyor of highways. On 25 March 1751 Jeremiah Howes was chosen a surveyor of highways "in the Room of Mr Leml Barnes now Deceasd."

On 16 April 1751 Lydia Barnes, widow of Lemuel Barnes, shoreman, late of Plymouth, gave her bond as administratrix on his estate.

On 5 July 1756 the Plymouth church chose a committee "to Enquire in to Affair of our Sister Lydia Barnes it being supposed that she was married to Jonathan Samson one that had been husband to her neice." On 3 Feb. 1757 "Sister Lydia Barnes Appeared & Acknowledged her Contempt of [?], Authority in the Chh & the Chh forgave Her in that Matter."

On 15 Oct. 1769 "ye Brethren of ye Chh [stayed after service] at ye Desire of our Sister Lydia Samson (once Barns) to lay her Case before them, being many Years ago suspended from Communion for ye Supposd Marrying Jonathan Samson, whose first Wife was her Niece – Said a few Things on it, but referd ye full & further Consideration of it to Wednesday after next." On 25 Oct. 1769 the Church met to:

... consider the Case of our Sister Lydia Samson alias Barnes, but there were so few of the Brethren who met, that, partly on that Account, but principally because twas judged best for her sake that the Affair should be entirely drop'd, as ye Consequence might otherwise be greatly to her Prejudice & Hurt, it appearing also that the Members of ye Chh were, the greater Part of them, by no means satisfy^d of ye Lawfulness of such a Marriage, but of the contrary Opinion. The Affair was accordingly drop^d.

On 21 Feb. 1759 Jonathan Samson and Lydia Barnes "(who by some is called by the name of Lydia Samson)" of Plymouth sold to Silvanus Bartlett of Plymouth, yeoman, salt marsh "which in the Division of the Estate of Mr John Barnes deceased (Father of the said Lydia) was assigned & set off to her." Lydia signed this deed as Lydia Barnes.

On 22 July 1777 John Barnes of Plympton, cordwainer, son of Lemuel Barnes and grandson of William Barnes both late of Plymouth, sold to Thomas Jackson of Plymouth, yeoman, land he had from the will of William Barnes; John's wife Margaret also signed this deed. On 1 June 1779 and 7 Feb. 1788 William Barnes, son of Lemuel and grandson of William, sold land to Thomas Jackson from the estate of William Barnes. And on 31 March 1781 Lemuel Barnes, son of Lemuel and grandson of William, sold land from the estate of William Barnes.

On 11 Dec. 1782 the heirs of Lemuel Barnes received their share of the estate of their grandfather William Barnes with William Barnes receiving two-sevenths; one-seventh each went to John and Lemuel Barnes, Hannah Thomas wife of James, Lydia Bartlett wife of Nathaniel, and Alice Finney wife of Josiah.

Children of Lemuel and Lydia (Barnes) Barnes, b. Plymouth; a child of Lemuel Barnes d. 18 Dec. 1761:

    i   HANNAH BARNES[6], b. 6 Aug. 1735, bp. 11 April 1736

   ii   LYDIA BARNES, b. 9 Sept. 1737, bp. 11 Sept. 1737

  iii   WILLIAM BARNES, b. 4 March 1740/1

  iv   LEMUEL BARNES, b. 30 March 1743; d. 29 July 1743

   v   ALICE BARNES, b. 30 June 1744

  vi   LEMUEL BARNES, b. 11 Aug. 1746

 vii   JOHN BARNES, b. 11 Sept. 1748, bp. 18 Sept. 1748

viii   ISAAC BARNES, b. 2 May 1750, bp. 6 May 1750; d. Oct. 1750

References: *MD* 2:20(b. Lydia); 5:53(d. Lemuel); 14:156(m.); 15:162(b. ch.). *Plymouth Ch Recs* 1:302-3, 331-2(m. to Jonathan), 391(d. child), 402(d. Lydia), 437(bp. Hannah, Lydia), 444(bp. John); 2:523(Lydia joined). *Bradford Desc* p. 54. Plymouth Co. PR 12:45,

123(Lemuel Barnes); 28:507(William Barnes). *Plymouth VR* pp. 16(b. Lydia), 99(m.), 125(b. 1st 3 ch.), 126(b.& d. rest of ch.). Plymouth Co. LR 38:103(William Barnes); 47:55(Jonathan Samson); 59:55(John Barnes), 250(William Barnes); 60:188(Lemuel Barnes); 67:134(William Barnes). *Plymouth Town Recs* 2:294; 3:7, 12, 33, 39,40.

144. MERCY BARNES⁵ (*Alice⁴ Bradford, William³⁻²⁻¹*), b. Plymouth 19 Dec. 1708; d. there 24 or 25 Dec. 1791 aged 83, "relict of Capt. Barnabas Hedge."

She m. (1) Plymouth 14 Nov. 1728 **SAMUEL COLE**, b. Plymouth 2 April 1709; d. Plymouth 18 Aug. 1731 in 23rd yr.; son of Ephraim and Rebecca (Gray) Cole.

She m. (2) int. Plymouth 21 Dec. 1733 **BARNABAS HEDGE**, b. Yarmouth 27 Dec. 1704; d. Plymouth 18 Jan. 1762 aged 56y 22d; son of John and Thankful (Lothrop) Hedge. He is called "Capt." on his death notice in the Church Records.

At a Plymouth town meeting 11 May 1730, Samuel Cole was chosen as a juror.

On 31 Jan. 1731[/2] Marcy Cole of Plymouth gave her bond as administratrix of the estate of her late husband Mr. Samuel Cole of Plymouth deceased. On 11 March 1733/4 Barnabas Hedge was appointed guardian of Samuel Cole, under 14, son of Samuel Cole late of Plymouth deceased.

At the March 1732/3 term of the Plymouth County Court of General Sessions, Mary Cole, administratrix of the estate of Samuel Cole, glazier, was paid for the mending Samuel had done on the "Court House Glass."

At the September 1725 term of the Court of Common Pleas, Lazarus Lebaron of Scituate, laborer, brought suit against James Cole and Samuel Cole both of Plymouth, minors and sons of Ephraim Cole, for entering Lazarus' land and throwing fence boards into his garden. The jury found for Lazarus.

Barnabas Hedge graduated from Harvard in 1724. *Harvard Grads* says "Hedge was evidently a mariner, which would explain his small participation in town affairs. He was once constable but seven times juryman, which would have been a convenient kind of public service for a man often absent at sea. Although his name does not appear on the list of members of the First Church, he served once on a committee to obtain a minister for that organization."

At Plymouth town meetings 3 March 1734/5, 15 Dec. 1740, 10 May 1742, 20 June 1748, 7 July 1752, and 18 June 1753, Barnabas Hedge was chosen as a juror, and on 2 March 1746 as a constable.

Barnabas Hedge of Plymouth, retailer, was granted a license to sell liquor from 1744 to 1747, 1752, 1753, 1757 to 1759, and 1761. At the March

1749/50 term of the Court of General Session, Barnabas was presented for "Bringing a Sloop to Sail on the Lord's Day in the Month of August last."

At the May 1745 term of the court of Common Pleas, Barnabas Hedge of Plymouth, mariner, brought suit against James Thomas "Indianman" of Middleborough, laborer. Barnabas said that on 17 Feb. 1743/4 James "shipt himself as an able sailor on Board the sloop *Betty* (whereof the pltf. was then master) to proceed on a Voidge from the port of Boston in New England to North Carolina and Back again," and that James had received one month's wages in advance. But James deserted the vessel.

On 18 Nov. 1762 Mercy Hedge of Plymouth gave her bond as administratrix on the estate of Barnabas Hedge late of Plymouth, gentleman. This is the only paper in the record books for this probate file.

In the 1771 Valuation List, Marcy Hedge appears in Plymouth with one shop, £36:12:6 of merchandise, £293:1:10 lent at interest, and two head of cattle. Barnabas Hedge is listed next to her.

On 19 Sept. 1792 John Davis Esq. and Barnabas Hedge Jr., merchants of Plymouth, were appointed administrators on the estate of Mercy Hedge late of Plymouth, widow.

On 10 Jan. 1795 Samuel Cole, Barnabas Hedge, yeomen, William Davis, merchant, John Davis Esq., Samuel Davis, goldsmith, and Wendell Davis, student, all of Plymouth, Thomas Davis Esqr., Isaac Davis, ropemaker, and Sarah Bradford, widow, all of Boston sold to Josiah Elles, Seth Swift, and Mordica Elles all of Sandwich, yeomen, 73 acres of woodland in Plymouth, part of the estate of Mercy Hedge late of Plymouth, widow, which had been devised to her by her father William Barnes in his will and was held by them as her heirs. On the same day they sold to Thomas Morton Jr., Ichabod Morton Jr., and Amasa Morton 31 acres of woodland that had been devised to Mercy by her father's will.

Children of Samuel and Mercy (Barnes) Cole, b. Plymouth:

    i JAMES COLE[6], b. 12 Sept. 1729; d. 10 Dec. 1729

    ii EPHRAIM COLE, b. 14 Nov. 1730; d. 25 Jan. 1730/1

    iii SAMUEL COLE, b. 14 Nov. 1731

Children of Barnabas and Mercy (Barnes) (Cole) Hedge, b. Plymouth:

    iv MERCY HEDGE[6], b. 27 Nov. 1734

    v LEMUEL HEDGE, b. 20 Sept. 1736; d. 3 Oct. 1736

    vi ABIGAIL HEDGE, b. 2 Dec. 1737; d. 9 Dec. 1763 ae 26 yrs; unm. No probate record.

vii   BARNABAS HEDGE, b. 3 May 1740

viii LEMUEL HEDGE, b. 25 June 1742; d. 7 July 1742

ix   LOTHROP HEDGE, b. 5 Nov. 1744; d. 20 Jan. 1745

x   SARAH HEDGE, b. 5 June 1746

xi   JOHN HEDGE*

xii   WILLIAM HEDGE, b. 1750*

* Note: These two sons are listed in *Bradford Desc* and *Harvard Grads*, but no proof has been found. A child of Barnabas Hedge d. 15 Oct. 1763.

References: *MD* 2:20(b. Samuel); 11:112(b. Barnabas); 14:72(1st m.), 240; 15:41, 114; 18:140. *(Plymouth) Burial Hill* pp. 36(d. Barnabas), 37(d. Abigail), 67(d. Mercy). *Bradford Desc* p. 54-5. Plymouth Co. PR 6:123, 435(Samuel Cole); 17:88(Barn. Hedge); 27:402(Mercy Hedge). *Yarmouth VR* 1:28(b. Barnabas). *Plymouth VR* pp. 16(b. Samuel), 95(1st m.), 105(b.&d. 1st 3 ch.), 113(b.&d. next 7 ch.), 169(int. 2nd m.). *Plymouth Ch Recs* 1:392(d. Barnabas), 393(d. Abigail, child), 419(d. Mercy). *Plymouth Co Ct Recs* 5:194(Lazarus LeBaron); 7:42(Barnabas Hedge). *1771 Valuation* p. 654. *Plymouth Ch. Recs* 1:392(d. Barnabas), 393(d. Abigail), 419(d. Mercy). *Harvard Grads* 7:356(Barnabas Hedge). Plymouth Co. LR 77:109, 111(Mercy's heirs). *Plymouth Town Recs* 2:269, 304, 336, 344; 3:19, 27, 48, 55.

145. BENJAMIN BARNES[5] (*Alice[4] Bradford, William[3-2-1]*), b. Plymouth 20 Dec. 1717; d. there 12 April 1760 in 43rd yr.

He m. Plymouth 14 June 1742 **EXPERIENCE RIDER**, b. Plymouth 13 Jan. 1724/5; living 9 Nov. 1778; daughter of Josiah and Experience (_____) Rider. She m. (2) Plymouth 19 July 1772 Elisha Corbin.

At Plymouth town meetings 2 March 1752, 3 March 1755, and 21 March 1757, Benjamin Barnes was chosen one of the surveyors of highways and on 20 March 1758, 26 March 1759, and 10 March 1760 a fence viewer and field driver.

At the July 1759 term of the Court of General Sessions, Benjamin Barnes and others were presented for "Riotous and Routous assembly and breaking open the common Pound in Plimouth."

On 24 July 1760 Experience Barnes of Plymouth, widow, gave her bond as administratrix on the estate of her husband Benjamin Barnes late of Plymouth deceased.

In the 1771 Valuation List, Experience Barnes appears in Plymouth with 2 polls, 1 house, 1 shop, £66:13:4 lent at interest, 1 horse, 4 oxen, 2 cattle, 16 goats or sheep, 1 swine, 20 acres of pasture, 1½ acres of tillage which produced 30 bushels of grain, 6 barrels of cider, 3 acres of upland which produced 1½ tons of hay, and 1 acre of fresh meadow which produced 1 ton of hay. Bradford Barnes is listed next to her.

On 17 Jan. 1775 dower was set off from Benjamin's estate to Experience Corban, wife of Elisha.

On 9 Nov. 1778 the following children and heirs of Benjamin Barnes gave their receipt to Elisha Corbin and wife Experience, "our mother": Samuel Battles and wife Alice, and Benjamin, Isaac, and Josiah Barnes, all of Plymouth, Elisha Corbin, Jr. and wife Experience, Bradford Barnes and Mercy Barnes, all of Dudley.

On 28 March 1787 the heirs of Benjamin Barnes divided the real estate set off to him from the estate of their grandfather William Barnes, with eldest son Bradford receiving a double share and single shares going to Benjamin, Josiah, and Isaac Barnes, Alice Battles wife of Samuel, Mercy Barnes deceased, Experience Corban wife of Elisha Jr., Sarah Barnes deceased, and the heirs of Benjamin Barnes.

Children of Benjamin and Experience (Rider) Barnes, b. Plymouth:

    i   ALICE BARNES[6], b. 2 April 1743

   ii MERCY BARNES, b. 8 July 1745; d. 16 Dec. 1783

  iii BRADFORD BARNES, b. 1 Aug. 1747

  iv BENJAMIN BARNES, b. 14 Jan. 1749/50

   v JOSIAH BARNES, b. 15 Jan. 1752

  vi ISAAC BARNES, b. 16 June 1754

 vii EXPERIENCE BARNES, b. 11 May 1756

viii SARAH BARNES, b. 13 June 1760 (not in 9 Nov. 1778 div.); may be the child of Benjamin Barnes' who d. 21 April 1764 or who d. 20 Aug. 1766 or who d. 13 Nov. 1772

References: *MD* 13:167(b. Experience); 14:159(m.); 15:161(b. ch.); 18:118; 27:45(2nd int.). *Bradford Desc* p. 55. Plymouth Co. PR 15:536; 21:413; 25:408(Benjamin Barnes); 30:128. *Plymouth VR* pp. 71(b. Experience), 102(m.), 125(b. ch.), 352(her 2nd m.). *Plymouth Ch Recs* 1:390(d. Benjamin), 393, 395, 401(d. child), 413(d. Mercy). *Plymouth Co Ct Recs* 3:132. *1771 Valuation* p. 650. *Plymouth Town Recs* 3:44, 66, 91, 107, 118.

146. SARAH[5] BRADFORD (*William[4-3-2-1]*), b. Plymouth 15 Dec. 1718; d. there 4 April 1794.

She m. Plymouth 23 Jan. 1738/9 **ZEPHANIAH HOLMES**, b. Plymouth 16 Jan. 1712/3; d. there 24 March 1774; son of Nathaniel and Joanna (Clark) Holmes.

On 27 Dec. 1739 Zephaniah Holmes of Plymouth, cordwainer, and wife Sarah sold to John Adams land in Kingston from the estate of her father William Bradford.

At a Plymouth town meeting 4 March 1744, Zephaniah Holmes was chosen one of the hogreeves and on 18 Dec. 1749, 10 Dec. 1753, and 3 Dec. 1766 a juror.

Sarah Holmes, wife of "Zeph," was listed as a member of the Plymouth Church on 30 Jan. 1760.

In the 1771 Valuation List, Zephaniah Holmes appears in Plymouth with one poll and one shop.

On 15 July 1778 Sarah Holmes, widow of Plymouth, was appointed administratrix on the estate of Elizabeth Bradford late of Plymouth, widow. On 21 Aug. 1779 Sarah Holmes, widow and administratrix of the estate of Elizabeth Bradford, having received permission to sell land to pay debts, sold to Elizabeth's part of a dwelling house.

No Plymouth County probate records have been found for Zephaniah Holmes.

Children of Zephaniah and Sarah (Bradford) Holmes, b. Plymouth:

    i   BRADFORD HOLMES[6], b. 9 Oct. 1739; d. 14 May 1740

   ii   ZEPHANIAH HOLMES, b. 30 July 1741

  iii   SARAH HOLMES, b. 23 Dec. 1743

  iv   LUCY HOLMES, b. 13 June 1747, bp. 21 June 1747

   v   DEBORAH HOLMES, b. 8 April 1750, bp. 15 April 1750

References: *MD* 2:80(b. Zephaniah); 14:158(m.); 15:162-3(b. ch.). *Bradford Desc* p. 55. *Plymouth Ch Recs* 1:403 (d. Zephaniah), 422(d. Sarah), 446(bp. Lucy, Deborah), 468(Sarah member). Plymouth Co. LR 33:74(Zephaniah Holmes); 60:19(Sarah Holmes). *Plymouth VR* pp. 19(b. Zephaniah), 101(m.), 126(b.&d. Bradford), 127(b. last 4 ch.). Plymouth Co. PR 23:186(Elizabeth Bradford). *1771 Valuation* p. 654. *Plymouth Town Recs* 3:10, 33, 55, 182.

147. JERUSHA[5] BRADFORD (*William[4-3-2-1]*), b. Plymouth 20 Dec. 1722; d. Middleboro 23 April 1820 in 98th yr.

She m. (1) Plymouth 16 April 1741 **EDWARD SPARROW**, b. England; d. at sea bet. 20 June 1744 and 5 June 1745.

She m. (2) Plymouth 22 Jan. 1746/7 **JOSIAH CARVER**, b. Plymouth 25 Sept. 1724, bp.4 Oct. 1724; d. Middleboro 5 April 1799 aged 74y 7m 17d; son of Josiah and Dorothy (Coole) Carver.

On 14 Nov. 1743 Edward Sparrow of Plymouth, mariner, and wife Jerusha sold to Thomas Adams land received from her father William Bradford.

On 5 June 1745 Jerusha Sparrow of Plymouth, widow of Edward late of Plymouth deceased, gave her bond as administratrix of his estate. On 27 April 1747 Jerusha Carver, late Jerusha Sparrow, reported that the estate was insolvent. At the May 1747 term of the Court of Common Pleas, Richard Waite of Plymouth, mariner, brought suit against Josiah Carver Jr. of Plymouth, blacksmith, and his wife Jerusha, administors of the estate of Edward Sparrow, for a debt. Josiah and Jerusha pleaded that the estate was insolvent.

On 23 May 1742 Jerusha Sparrow, wife of Edward, joined the Plymouth Church. Both Josiah and Jerusha Carver were listed as members of the church on 30 Jan. 1760, and in 1771 they were both dismissed to the Church of Christ in Wareham.

Josiah Carver was listed at Middleboro in the 1790 census, one man over 16 and one female.

The will of Josiah Carver of Middleboro dated 11 Feb. 1783, proved 2 May 1799, names wife Jerusha and appoints son-in-law [step-son] Edward Sparrow executor.

Child of Edward and Jerusha (Bradford) Sparrow, b. Plymouth:

    i EDWARD SPARROW[6], b. 2 April 1745, bp. 7 April 1745.

References: *MD* 12:142(d. Jerusha); 13:169(b. Edward), 173(b. Josiah); 16:254(1st m.); 17:5(2nd m.); 18:32(int. 1st m.); 25:26-7(deed). *Bradford Desc* p. 56. Plymouth Co. PR 9:46; 10:389(Edward Sparrow); 37:35(Josiah Carver). Plymouth Co. LR 36:77(Edward Sparrow). *Middleboro Deaths* pp. 34(Carver deaths), 173(d. Edward). *Plymouth VR* pp. 73(b. son Edward), 98(b. Josiah), 150(1st m.), 154(2nd m.). *Plymouth Ch Recs* 1:232(bp.Josiah), 443(bp. Edward), 468(members); 2:471(dismission), 527(Jerusha joins). *Plymouth Co Ct Recs* 7:81(Richard Waite).

148. JOSIAH[5] BRADFORD (*William[4-3-2-1]*), b. Plymouth 29 March possibly in 1724; d. there 26 April 1777.

He m. Plymouth 6 Nov. 1746 **HANNAH RIDER**, b. Plymouth 26 Nov. 1726; d. there 19 May 1790; daughter of Samuel and Mary (Sylvester) Rider, a descendant of Pilgrim **Richard Warren**. On 22 Nov. 1770 Josiah Bradford of Plymouth, mariner, and his wife Hannah, with other heirs of Samuel Rider, sold to Consider Barden of Middleboro, husbandman, four ninth parts of 21½ acres.

On 17 April 1745 Josiah Bradford of Plymouth, cordwainer, sold to Thomas Adams of Kingston, mariner, four acres from the division of William Bradford's estate. On 24 April 1747 Elizabeth Bradford, widow of William, sold to Thomas Adams her part of an old dwelling house where her husband dwelt. On 20 Oct. 1749 Josiah Bradford of Plymouth, cordwainer, sold to James Cobb Jr. of Kingston, seafaring man, 21 acres in Kingston from the estate of William Bradford. On 16 Aug. 1759 Elizabeth Bradford, widow, and Josiah Bradford, cordwainer, both of Middleborough sold to Thomas Adams land and garden that had been set off to Elizabeth as her dower and was now in the actual improvement of Thomas.

At Plymouth town meetings 7 May 1753, 23 Feb. 1757, and 15 March 1773, Josiah Bradford was chosen a juror

On 10 Jan. 1757 Josiah Bradford and family were warned from Middleboro. In 1763 Josiah Bradford and family, from Middleboro, were warned from Plymouth.

In the 1771 Valuation List, Josiah Bradford appears in Plymouth with 2 polls, and half of a shop. William Bradford is listed next to him.

On 21 Dec. 1772 Elizabeth Bradford of Plymouth, widow, sold land to her son Josiah Bradford which "was quit claimed to me and my two sisters by our Brothers Josiah Finney and John Finney."

Josiah Bradford became a member of the Plymouth Church on 23 May 1742 and was listed as a member on 30 Jan. 1760. On 26 Oct. 1777, Hannah Bradford, widow of Josiah, was admitted to the church.

On 30 Jan. 1797 Josiah Bradford, Samuel Bradford, Charles Bradford, Zepheniah Bradford, Ruth Bradford widow of William, Hannah Bradford, Lois Bradford, and Betsey Bradford, spinsters, all of Plymouth, and Thomas Perkins and wife Mercy of Halifax sold to Joshua Wright and Joseph Samson land that their grandmother Elizabeth Bradford deeded to their father Josiah Bradford.

No Plymouth County probate records were found for Josiah Bradford.

Children of Josiah and Hannah (Rider) Bradford, b. Plymouth:

    i WILLIAM[6] BRADFORD, b. 30 Oct. 1749, bp. 5 Nov. 1749

   ii HANNAH BRADFORD, b. 9 July 1751, bp. 21 July 1751

  iii JOSIAH BRADFORD, b. 7 Feb. 1754

  iv SAMUEL BRADFORD

   v CHARLES BRADFORD, bp. 29 Aug. 1756

  vi ZEPHANIAH BRADFORD

vii BETSEY BRADFORD; living unm. 30 Jan. 1797. She may be the Elizabeth Bradford, bp. in the Plymouth Ch. 6 July 1794 and who signed a petition to be dismissed from 1st Ch. to form a 3rd Ch. in Plymouth.

viii LOIS BRADFORD; living unm. 30 Jan.1797. She may be the Lois Bradford, maiden, bp. in the Plymouth Ch. 2 June 1793 and the "Lowis" Bradford who signed a petition to be dismissed from 1st Ch. to form a 3rd Ch. in Plymouth.

ix MERCY BRADFORD

References: *MD* 3:121(b. 1st 3 ch.); 15:38(b. Hannah); 17:5 (m.), 134(int.). *Bradford Desc* p. 55. *Plymouth Co Ct Recs* 3:75, 207. *Plymouth Ch Recs* 1:407(d. Josiah), 417(d. Hannah), 445(bp. William), 447(bp. Hannah), 451(bp. Charles), 468(Josiah member); 2:472(bp. Lois),473(Hannah admitted), 477(bp. Elizabeth), 524(Josiah admitted), 547(petition). Plymouth Co. LR 37:146(Josiah Bradford); 38:194(Elizabeth Bradford); 40:128(Josiah Bradford); 45:245(Elizabeth Bradford); 55:221(Josiah Bradford); 57:44(Elizabeth Bradford); 82:40(Josiah Bradford *et al.*). *Plymouth VR* pp. 30(b. 1st 3 ch.), 109(b. Hannah), 154 (m.). *1771 Valuation* p. 650. *Plymouth Town Recs* 3:53, 89, 271.

149. MERCY⁵ BRADFORD (*William⁴⁻³⁻²⁻¹*), b. Kingston 17 Jan. 1729; d. Plymouth 4 July 1762 in 34th yr.

She m. Plymouth 15 Dec. 1746 **SAMUEL HARLOW**, b. Plymouth 7 Sept. 1726, bp. 9 Oct. 1726; d. there 17 June 1767 in 41st yr.; son of William and Mercy (Rider) Harlow, a descendant of Pilgrim **Richard Warren**. He m. (2) Plymouth 9 Oct. 1763 Mary (or Mercy) Morton.

On 25 Oct. 1749 Samuel Harlow of Plymouth, mariner, and his wife Mercy, sold to Thomas Adams of Kingston, mariner, the 4th lot in the First Division, being four acres from the estate of William Bradford.

At a Plymouth town meeting 17 April 1761, Samuel Harlow was chosen a juror.

The will of Samuel Harlow of Plymouth, mariner, dated 26 Oct. 1765, with codicil dated 30 Oct. 1765, proved 4 Aug. 1767, names wife Mary, executor, to have all the goods she brought to the marriage; and children Samuel, Josiah, George, Mercy, and Jerusha Harlow. On 7 July 1772 James Hovey Esq. and wife Mary, executor of the will of Capt. Samuel Harlow late of Plymouth deceased, rendered an account on the estate. On 10 April 1787 John Davis of Plymouth was appointed administrator on Samuel's estate, his executrix having died before she could complete the administration.

On 8 Aug. 1767 Eleazer Stephens of Plymouth was appointed guardian to Samuel Harlow and Mercy Harlow, minor children of Samuel Harlow. On the same day Seth Harlow of Plymouth, housewright, was appointed guardian to Josiah Harlow, George Harlow, and Jerusha Harlow, children of Samuel.

On 8 Aug. 1767 land in Plymouth was set off to Mercy Harlow, widow, in a judgement against the estate of Samuel Rider late of Middleborough. On 17 April 1769 Mercy sold to this land to Eleazer Stephens of Plymouth, yeoman.

On 25 Aug. 1777 Josiah Harlow of Middleborough, blacksmith, sold to his brother Samuel Harlow of Plymouth, yeoman, all his right in the real estate of his father Samuel being part of a house, land, and a pew in the upper Meeting House, except for a small piece sold to Seth Harlow; Josiah's wife Olive also signed this deed.

Children of Samuel and Mercy (Bradford) Harlow, b. Plymouth:

  i   SAMUEL HARLOW[6], b. 22 Oct. 1747
  ii MERCY HARLOW, b. 20 Oct. 1749; d. 29 Sept. 1750 ae 13m 12d
  iii MERCY HARLOW, b. 10 April 1752
  iv JERUSHA HARLOW, b. 13 Feb. 1754
  v   JOSIAH HARLOW, b. 2 Jan. 1756
  vi JAMES HARLOW, b. 23 Nov. 1757; d. 10 Jan. 1758
  vii GEORGE HARLOW, b. 18 Jan. 1759

References: *MD* 7:177-8(b. ch.; d. 2 ch.); 12:87(b. Samuel); 17:5(m.); 18:119(int.). *Bradford Desc* p. 56. *(Plymouth) Burial Hill* pp. 28(d. dau. Mercy), 36(d. Mercy), 40(d. Samuel). Plymouth Co. PR 19:494, 498, 508, 512(guardianships), 511; 21:152; 27:511(Samuel Harlow). *Plymouth VR* pp. 43(b.&d. 1st 6 ch.), 44(b. George), 53(b. Samuel), 154(m.), 298(d. Mercy), 299(d. Samuel), 347(his 2nd m.). *Harlow Gen* pp. 90-1. Plymouth Co. LR 40:128(Samuel Harlow); 53:234; 54:241(Mercy Harlow); 59:64(Josiah Harlow). *Plymouth Ch Recs* 1:234(bp. Samuel), 392(d. Mercy), 396(d. Samuel). *Plymouth Town Recs* 3:126.

150.   SARAH BARNES[5] (*Sarah[4] Bradford, William[3-2-1]*), b. prob. Plymouth 9 Oct. 1709; d. Chatham 27 Dec. 1776.

She m. Plymouth 20 May 1729 **THOMAS DOANE**, b. Eastham 10 Jan. 1701/2; d. before 13 May 1747; son of Thomas and Patience (Mulford) Doane.

On 13 May 1747 Paul Sears, gentleman, and Sarah Doane, widow, both of Chatham, were appointed administrators on the estate of Thomas Doane Jr. late of Chatham, mariner, deceased.

The will of Thomas Doane's father Thomas Doane of Chatham, blacksmith, dated 17 March 1756, names grandson Nehemiah [son of Thomas] and grandchildren Reuben, Thomas, Mary, and Elizabeth Doane, children of son Thomas deceased, and daughter-in-law Sarah Doane, widow of son Thomas.

Children of Thomas and Sarah (Barnes) Doane, b. Chatham:

  i NEHEMIAH DOANE[6], b. 15 Feb. 1730

 ii REUBEN DOANE (named in grandfather's will). *Bradford Desc* says he d. abt. 1758; unm.

iii MARY DOANE (named in grandfather's will)

 iv THOMAS DOANE, b. March 1737

  v ELIZABETH DOANE, b. 18 April 1744

References: *MD* 5:142(b. Nehemiah); 9:8(b. Thomas); 14:72(m.); 18:140. *Bradford Desc* p. 56. Barnstable Co. PR 7:39(Thomas Doane); 9:237(Thomas Doane Sr.). *Plymouth VR* p. 95(m.).

151. REBECCA BARNES[5] (*Sarah[4] Bradford, William[3-2-1]*), b. prob. Plymouth 14 March 1711; living 21 Jan. 1772.

She m. Plymouth 22 Sept. 1730 **EBENEZER PHINNEY**, b. Barnstable 26 May 1708, bp. West Parish Church 27 June 1708; d. 2 Dec. 1772 aged 67; son of Ebenezer and Susanna (Linnell) Phinney, a descendant of Pilgrim **Thomas Rogers**.

On 29 Feb. 1732 Ebenezer Phinney Jr. recorded his ear mark, "a Crop of each ear and two half penny under ye left."

On 16 March 1741 Ebenezer Phinney Jr. of Barnstable, laborer, and his wife Rebecca, sold to Stephen Churchill Jr. of Plymouth, cooper, land he had bought at the vendue of father Jonathan Barnes' estate.

On 25 July 1742 Ebenezer Phinney Jr. was received into full communion with the East Parish Church in Barnstable. On 8 Aug. Jonathan, Lemuel, Sarah, Martha, and Lydia children of Ebenezer and Rebecca Phinney were baptised.

On 21 Jan. 1772 Ebenezer Phinney and wife Rebecca of Barnstable sold land that fell to them from their father Jonathan Barnes.

No Barnstable County probate records were found for Ebenezer or Rebecca Phinney.

Children of Ebenezer and Rebecca (Barnes) Phinney, b. Barnstable:

  i SARAH PHINNEY[6], b. 11 May 1732

 ii JONATHAN PHINNEY, b. 14 Sept. 1733

iii MARTHA PHINNEY, b. 16 July 1735

    iv LEMUEL PHINNEY, b. 24 April 1737

    v LYDIA PHINNEY, bp. with siblings 8 Aug. 1742

    v SETH PHINNEY, b. 9 June 1743, bp. 10 July 1743; d. 2 Jan. 1744/5 ae
        71m 23d, bur. Lothrop's Hill Cem.

    vi REBECCA PHINNEY, b. 16 March 1747, bp. 20 March 1747/8

References: *MD* 11:132(b. Ebenezer); 14:73(m.); 18:121(int.); 32:155-6(b. ch.). *MF* 19:117-8. *Bradford Desc* p. 56. Plymouth Co. LR 35:10; 56:175(Ebenezer Phinney). *Plymouth VR* p. 96(m.). Barnstable Co. Rec. on CD.

152. LYDIA BARNES[5] (*Sarah*[4] *Bradford, William*[3-2-1]), b. prob. Plymouth 30 Jan. 1714/5; d. there 20 May 1777.

    She m. Plymouth 2 May 1738 **JOSEPH SMITH**, b. Yarmouth 6 July 1711; d. there 1 Feb. 1792 aged 81; son of Elisha and Sarah (_____) Smith.

    On 25 Aug. 1749 Joseph Smith of Plymouth, fisherman, and his wife Lydia mortgaged a lot of land in Plymouth to Lemuel Barnes of Plymouth, shoreman; the mortgage was released 27 March 1771 by Lydia Barnes administrator of the estate of Lemuel Barnes.

    On 20 March 1771, acknowledged 27 March 1771, Joseph Smith of Plymouth, laborer, and wife Lydia sold to their daughter Sarah Smith of Plymouth, taylor, house and land in Plymouth "wherein we now dwell."

    No Plymouth County probate records were found for Joseph Smith.

    Children of Joseph and Lydia (Barnes) Smith, b. Plymouth; they are probably the "Maiden Sisters" who joined the Plymouth church on 18 Aug. 1793 and who were on the petition to set up the 3rd church in Plymouth:

    i SARAH SMITH[6], b. 9 Feb. 1738/9

    ii LYDIA SMITH, b. 23 May 1744

References: *MD* 13:225(b. Joseph); 14:158(m.); 15:113(b. ch.); 18:28(int.). *Bradford Desc* p. 57. *Plymouth Ch Recs* 1:407(d. Lydia), 419(d. Joseph); 2:476(maiden sisters), 547(petition). Plymouth Co. LR 40:104; 56:12(Joseph Smith). *Yarmouth VR* 1:37(b. Joseph). *Plymouth VR* pp. 100(m.), 120(b. ch.).

153. HANNAH BARNES[5] (*Sarah*[4] *Bradford, William*[3-2-1]), b. prob. Plymouth 1717; d. there 12 June 1793 "wife of Mr. Jeremiah Howes and widow of Mr. Stephen Churchill in 75th yr."

She m. (1) Plymouth 4 July 1738 **STEPHEN CHURCHILL**, b. Plymouth 24 Aug. 1717; d. there 5 Sept. 1751 in 36th yr.; son of Stephen and Experience (Ellis) Churchill.

She m. (2) Plymouth 3 May 1759 **JEREMIAH HOWES**, b. Yarmouth 26 April 1704; d. Plymouth 14 July 1783 aged 80; son of Prince and Dorcas (Joyce) Howes. He m. (1) Plymouth 24 Oct. 1734 MERIAH MORTON with whom he had Silvanus, Rebecca, Ebenezer, Meriah, Jerusha, and Sarah.

At a Plymouth town meeting 5 March 1749, Stephen Churchill Jr. was chosen one of the constables.

On 26 Sept. 1751 Hannah Churchill, widow, was appointed administratrix on the estate of Stephen Churchill late of Plymouth deceased. On 20 Aug. 1752 Hannah was appointed guardian of Stephen, Zadock, and Hannah, minor children of Stephen Churchill.

Jeremiah Howes served the town of Plymouth in several capacities including surveyor of highways, juror, grand juror, as one to take care of the beach, and fence viewer and field driver. On 27 Sept. 1756 he was one of the "Subscribers freeholders of the town of Plimouth Concieving Great Advantage would accrue to the town from a work house in it, under proper regulations, desire you to Insert a clause in Your warrant for Calling the next town meeting so as to bring a matter of Such Consequence to the Interest of the town."

"Hannah Howes Jer^h" is listed a member of the Plymouth Church on 30 Jan. 1760 when Rev. C. Robbins was ordained.

On 29 March 1754 Prence Howes of Stratford, Conn., yeoman, and Thomas Howes Jr. and Lot Howes of Yarmouth, yeomen, sold to their brother Jeremiah Howes of Plymouth, yeoman, all their right in the estate of their father Prence Howes late of Yarmouth.

The General Sessions court records show that Jeremiah Howes of Plymouth was granted a license to sell tea from 1762 to 1764. He was granted a license to sell liquor in 1768, from 1771 to 1773, and from 1779 to 1782.

On 16 April 1770 Jeremiah Howes of Plymouth, trader, sold to Jonathan Pratt of Bridgewater, yeoman, land in Bridgewater that had been laid out to his grandfather Jeremiah Howes deceased; Jeremiah's wife Hannah also signed this deed.

In the 1771 Valuation List, Jeremiah Howes appears in Plymouth with 1 poll, half of a shop, and £54:14 in merchandise.

On 17 Sept. 1783 Hannah Howes, widow, and Sylvanus Howes, fisherman, both of Plymouth, were appointed administrators on the estate of Jeremiah Howes late of Plymouth, trader.

Hannah Howes' household at Plymouth in 1790 consisted of herself and one boy under 16.

On 18 Oct. 1793 Stephen Churchill of Plymouth, gentleman, was appointed administrator on the estate of Hannah Howes late of Plymouth, widow.

Children of Stephen and Hannah (Barnes) Churchill, b. Plymouth:

    i SARAH CHURCHILL[6] (twin), b. 18 July 1739; d. 13 Aug. 1740

   ii MERCY CHURCHILL (twin), b. 18 July 1739; d. 13 July 1740

  iii STEPHEN CHURCHILL, b. 17 July 1741; d. 14 Sept. 1742

  iv STEPHEN CHURCHILL, b. 7 June 1743

   v HANNAH CHURCHILL, b. 14 Feb. 1744/5

  vi ZADOCK CHURCHILL, b. 16 July 1747, bp 21 June 1747 [sic]

 vii PELEG CHURCHILL, b. 9 July 1749; d. 5 Oct. 1750

Child of Jeremiah and Hannah (Barnes) (Churchill) Howes, b. Plymouth:

 viii MERIAH HOWES[6], b. 30 Jan. 1762, bp. 30 Jan. 1762; d. 2 Dec. 1776 in 15th yr.

References: *MD* 12:13(b. Stephen); 14:158(1st m.); 15:210(b. Churchill ch.; d. first 3 ch.); 18:29(int. 1st m.); 20:72(b. Meriah); 25:188(2nd m.). *Plymouth Ch Recs* 1:406(d. Meriah), 412(d. Jeremiah), 420(d. Hannah), 443(bp. Zadoc), 453(bp. Meriah), 469(Hannah member). *(Plymouth) Burial Hill* pp. 29(d. Stephen), 47(d. Meriah), 68(d. Hannah). *Bradford Desc* p. 57.   Plymouth Co. PR 12:356 (Stephen Churchill), 513(guardianships); 27:140(Jeremiah Howes), 452(Hannah Howes). *NEHGR* 119:266. *Plymouth VR* pp. 23(Jeremiah's 1st m.), 50(b. Stephen), 101(1st m.), 115(b. ch. Jeremiah & Meriah), 130(b.&d. ch.), 201(b. Meriah), 347(2nd m.). *Plymouth Co Ct Recs* Vol. 3, 4. Plymouth Co. LR 43:43(Prence Howes); 55:132(Jeremiah Howes). *1771 Valuation* p. 654. *Howes Fam* pp. 15, 24. *Plymouth Town Recs* 3:13, 19, 31,34-5, 44, 52, 57, 66-7, 101, 125, 143, 152, 161, 248, 316.

154. THOMAS[5] BRADFORD (*Joshua[4], Thomas[3], William[2-1]*), b. Canterbury, Conn., 14 Nov. 1712; bp. 12 July 1713; d. before 3 July 1781.

He m. Canterbury, Conn., 2 May 1733 **EUNICE ADAMS**, b. Canterbury, Conn., 25 July 1713; d. 5 Aug. 1804 aged 91y, bur. Canterbury; daughter of Joseph and Eunice (Spaulding) Adams. On 22 Feb. 1764 the division of the estate of Joseph Adams of Canterbury included one-sixth part to Eunice wife of Thomas Bradford of Canterbury.

On 11 Aug. 1734 Eunice and Thomas Bradford owned the covenant in the Canterbury First Church and were admitted members on 16 Nov. 1735.

On 31 March 1762 Thomas and William Bradford gave their bond as administrators on the estate of James Bradford late of Canterbury, deceased. In 1762 (acknowledged 8 May 1762) Thomas Bradford with the other heirs of James Bradford sold their right to land in Canterbury.

On 22 May 1771 Thomas Bradford of Canterbury gave to his son Samuel 41 acres of his home farm. On 19 Aug. 1775 Thomas gave to his son Thomas Jr. 15 acres and half of his upland, and to his son John Jr. 25 acres and the other half of the upland.

Thomas Bradford of Canterbury made his will on 19 March 1781, proved 3 July 1781, naming his wife Eunice; sons Samuel Bradford, Thomas Bradford, and John Bradford; and daughters Susanna Brown wife of Ebenezer and Submit Bradford. On 26 Jan. 1782 distribution of the estate of Thomas Bradford of Canterbury deceased named wife Eunice Bradford; eldest son Samuel, second son Thomas, and youngest son John; eldest daughter Susanna Brown wife of Ebenezer, and youngest daughter Submit Bradford.

On 28 Feb. 1782 Eunice Bradford of Canterbury gave to her daughter Submit Bradford of Canterbury several pieces of land.

Children of Thomas and Eunice (Adams) Bradford, b. Canterbury, Conn., bp. First Church there:

- i THOMAS[6] BRADFORD, b. 23 March 1734, bp. 11 Aug. 1734; d. 12 Feb. 1735/6
- ii JOHN BRADFORD, b. 1 July 1735; d. 18 May 1750
- iii SUSANNA BRADFORD, b. 12 Feb. 1736/7
- iv EUNICE BRADFORD, b. 6 April 1739, bp. 29 April 1739; d. 3 March 1749/50
- v EDITH BRADFORD, b. 23 Oct. 1741, bp. 11 Dec. 1741; d.y.
- vi LYDIA BRADFORD, b. 6 March 1744, bp. 2 June 1744; d. 24 May 1750
- vii JAMES BRADFORD, b. 4 Jan. 1746; d. 17 Sept. 1749
- viii SAMUEL BRADFORD, b. 25 July 1748
- ix SUBMIT BRADFORD, b. 24 Feb. 1750, bp. 27 Jan. 1751
- x THOMAS BRADFORD, b. 3 Jan. 1751/2, bp. 22 Sept. 1754
- xi JOHN BRADFORD, b. 27 July 1754

References: *Bradford Desc* pp. 57-8. Plainfield CT PR #238 (Thomas Bradford). Canterbury CT VR 1:54(b. Eunice), 69(m.), 75(b. John), 76(b. Susanna, Eunice), 77(b. Thomas), 78(b. Edith, Lydia, James, Samuel, John), 79(b. Submit, Thomas). Hale Cem Coll:Canterbury p. 101(d. Eunice). *Adams Gen* p. 95. Canterbury CT LR 5:209(James Bradford); 7:228(heirs of James Bradford); 8:393, 424-5(Thomas Bradford); 8:450(Eunice Bradford). Plainfield CT PR #22(Joseph Adams); #229(Thomas Bradford). Canterbury

1st Ch. Recs. pp. 9(admitted), 23(owned cov.), 75(bp. Thomas), 81(bp. Eunice), 85(bp. Edith), 86(bp. Lydia), 92(bp. Submit), 95(bp. John).

155. JERUSHA[5] BRADFORD (*James[4], Thomas[3], William[2-1]*), b. Canterbury, Conn., 27 June 1716; bp. 1 July 1716; d. after 4 Feb. 1795 when mentioned in daughter Edith's deed (1807 in *Bradford Desc*).

She m. Canterbury, Conn., 20 Feb. 1733 **JONATHAN PELLET**, b. Canterbury, Conn., 2 March 1704; d. there 4 Oct. 1782; son of Richard and Ann (Brooks) Pellet. On 22 Feb. 1727/8 Richard Pellet of Canterbury, innholder, gave his son Jonathan Pellet of Canterbury, 125½ acres as his full portion of Richard's estate.

On 23 Feb. 1735 Jonathan Pellet owned the covenant in the Canterbury First Church. His wife Jerusha owned the covenant on 25 Sept. 1746 and they both were admitted as members in Oct. 1745.

In 1762 (acknowledged 8 May 1762) Jonathan and Jerusha Pellet with the other heirs of James Bradford sold their right to land in Canterbury.

On 29 May 1769 Jonathan Pellet of Canterbury sold to his son Thomas Pellet two acres that were formerly his father Bradford's and "that I count towards his portion...with my wife Jerusha." On 2 April 1781 Jonathan and Jerusha gave Thomas another 23 acres. On the same day they gave land to their daughter Ede Pellet and their son Jonathan, and parts of the farm on which they were living to sons Hezekiah and Joseph, 32 acres to Hezekiah, and 48 acres to Joseph. On 4 July 1781 they gave away 25 more acres of the farm, to son Rufus.

On 7 Nov. 1782 Jonathan Pellet of Pomfret and Thomas Pellet of Canterbury gave their bond as administrators on the estate of Jonathan Pellet late of Canterbury deceased. A distribution of the estate dated 10 Dec. 1782 names widow Jerusha Pellet; Thomas the eldest son, second son Joseph, third son David, fourth son Jonathan, fifth son Hezekiah, and youngest son Rufus; and eldest daughter Edith Pellet and youngest daughter Jerusha Pierce, wife of Willard.

On 21 Nov. 1783 Jonathan Pellet of Pomfret, Conn., sold to Rufus Pellet of Canterbury land distributed to him as his portion of the real estate of his father, reserving to his mother Jerusha Pellet the improvement of the land during her natural life. On 25 Nov. 1783 Jonathan sold to Thomas Bradford of Canterbury two pieces of land, one bounded by Edith Pellet.

On 20 March 1784 Thomas Pellet of Canterbury sold to David Pellet of Canterbury land from the estate of his father Jonathan Pellet deceased, reserving the improvement to his mother Jerusha.

On 7 Feb. 1794 David Pellet of Canterbury sold to Rufus Pellet of Canterbury four acres set out to him from the estate of his father Jonathan Pellet deceased, reserving the improvement to his mother Jerusha.

On 4 Feb. 1795 Edith Pellet of Canterbury, singlewoman, sold to Rufus Pellet of Canterbury one acre bounded by Rufus Pellet and Hezekiah Pellet with part of a house set off to Edith from estate of Jonathan Pellet, reserving the improvement to her mother Jerusha.

On 13 Feb. 1799 David Pellet of Canterbury sold to Rufus Pellet of Canterbury 12 acres.

Children of Jonathan and Jerusha (Bradford) Pellet, b. Canterbury, Conn.; bp. First Church there:

  i JONATHAN PELLET[6], b. 20 June 1733 [*sic*], bp. 23 Feb. 1735; d. 8 March 1735/6

  ii EDITH PELLET, b. 25 March 1735, bp. 11 May 1735; d.y.

  iii EDITH PELLET, bp. 27 March 1739

  iv JAMES PELLET, b. 9 Feb. 1737; d. 13 May 1766

  v JONATHAN PELLET, b. 19 Oct. 1739, bp. 23 Dec. 1739; d.y.

  vi THOMAS PELLET, b. 20 April 1742, bp. 27 June 1742

  vii JERUSHA PELLET, b. 6 June 1744, bp. 9 Aug. 1744

  viii JOSEPH PELLET, b. 18 March 1748

  ix DAVID PELLET, b. 21 Feb. 1750, bp. 29 April 1751

  x JONATHAN PELLET, b. 12 July 1753, bp. 30 Sept. 1753

  xi HEZEKIAH PELLET, b. 25 Feb. 1757, bp. 23 Oct. 1757

  xii RUFUS PELLET, b. 25 May 1760

References: *Bradford Desc* p. 58. Canterbury CT PR #1644 (Jonathan Pellet). Canterbury CT VR 1:192(m.), 195(b. Jonathan), 198(b. ch. exc. Rufus), 199(b. Rufus), 207(d. Jonathan). Canterbury CT LR 3:402(Richard Pellet); 7:228(heirs of James Bradford); 7:525; 8:449; 9:254-5; 10:40-1, 63(Jonathan to sons), 111(Jonathan to Rufus), 115(Jonathan to Thomas), 155(David to Rufus), 156(Thomas to David); 13:44(Edith Pellet), 134(David Pellet). Canterbury 1st Ch. Recs. pp. 23(Jonathan owned cov.), 19(admitted ch.), 32(Jerusha owned cov.), 55(bp. Jerusha), 76(bp. Jonathan), 76(bp. 1st Edith), 79(bp. 2nd Edith), 82(bp. Jonathan), 85(bp. Thomas), 87(bp. Jerusha), 92(bp. David), 95(bp. Jonathan), 98(bp. Hezekiah).

156. WILLIAM[5] BRADFORD (*James[4]*, *Thomas[3]*, *William[2-1]*), b. Canterbury, Conn., 1 July 1718; bp. 10 Aug. 1718; d. there 19 June 1781.

He m. (1) Canterbury, Conn., 13 Dec. 1739 **ZERVIAH LOTHROP**, b. Norwich, Conn., 9 April 1718; d. Canterbury, Conn., 22 Oct. 1741; daughter of Joseph and Elizabeth (Waterhouse) Lothrop. An account dated 6 Sept. 1758 in the estate of Joseph Lothrop, late of Norwich, notes that he had five children and one deceased.

He m. (2) Canterbury, Conn., 6 April 1743 **MARY CLEVELAND**, b. Canterbury, Conn., 29 June 1720; d. there 6 Aug. 1765; daughter of Josiah and Abigail (Paine) Cleveland, a descendant of Pilgrim **Stephen Hopkins**. The will of Josiah Cleveland of Canterbury dated 28 Dec. 1750 names daughter Mary Bradford.

He m. (3) Canterbury, Conn., 24 March 1766 **MARTHA WARREN**, b. Plainfield, Conn., 22 Aug. 1735; d. Canterbury, Conn., 8 Sept. 1775; daughter of Joseph and Martha (Bateman) Warren.

He m. (4) by 31 Dec. 1777 **ABIGAIL (_____) STETSON** (or **STEDMAN**); prob. d. by 20 Oct. 1781 when she is not in the distribution of William's estate.

On 2 Sept. 1739 William Bradford, son of James, owed the covenant and became a member of the First Church of Canterbury.

On 27 March 1746 James Bradford of Canterbury gave to his son William Bradford of Canterbury 150 acres.

On 31 March 1762 Thomas and William Bradford gave their bond as administrators on the estate of James Bradford late of Canterbury, deceased.

In 1762 (acknowledged 8 May 1762) William Bradford with the other heirs of James Bradford sold their right to land in Canterbury.

On 8 Feb. 1776 William Bradford of Canterbury gave to his son John 50 acres. On 27 Jan. 1777 William gave to his son Joshua land in Canterbury.

On 31 Dec. 1777 William and Abigail Bradford sold to William Jr. 60 acres that William had given Abigail before their marriage.

On 23 March 1778 William Bradford Jr. gave his brother David Bradford 12 acres "by the desire & consult of my Father William Bradford." On 18 May 1778 William Bradford Sr. sold to his son Ebenezer Bradford of Danbury more than 76 acres in Canterbury.

On 14 July 1781 David Bradford and Joshua Bradford were appointed administrators of the estate of William Bradford. The distribution of the estate of William Bradford of Canterbury, Conn., on 20 Oct. 1781 names sons: eldest William, second Ebenezer, third David, fourth John, fifth Joshua, sixth Josiah, seventh Moses, and youngest Benjamin; and daughters: eldest

Mary Pellet wife of William, second Abigail Barton wife of Lewis, third Olive Barstow wife of Hezekiah, fourth Lydia Hebbard wife of Rufus, and youngest Beulah Bradford.

On 3 July 1781 Moses Worrin of Canterbury was appointed guardian of Benjamin Bradford son of William Bradford.

On 7 July 1782 David Bradford of Canterbury and his wife Rhoda sold to William Bradford of Canterbury 12 acres bounded on "lands reserved by the late William Bradford dec^d for a road."

On 22 May 1783 Joshua Bradford of Canterbury sold to Josiah Bradford of Canterbury part of the farm lately owned by William Bradford bounded on lands of Lewis and Abigail Barton, Rufus and Lydia Hebbard, and Benjamin Bradford.

On 22 Nov. 1783 William Bradford of Canterbury, Minister of the Gospel, sold to Josiah Bradford of Canterbury, husbandman, a house and six acres where Josiah lived.

On 10 Dec. 1798 Benjamin Bradford of Canterbury released all his right in the estate of William Bradford deceased to Ebenezer Bradford, David Bradford, Joshua Bradford, Mary Pellet, Abigail Barton, Olive Barstow, Lydia Hubbard, and Beulah Butterfield all of Canterbury.

On 8 April 1799 John Bradford of Canterbury sold to his brother William Bradford of Canterbury 50 perches bounded on his sister Butterfield and part of the house his father lived in.

Child of William and Zerviah (Lothrop) Bradford, b. Canterbury, Conn.:

    i   ZERVIAH[6] BRADFORD, b. 6 Sept. 1740, bp. 1st Ch. Canterbury 19 Oct. 1740; d. 22 Oct. 1740

Children of William and Mary (Cleveland) Bradford, b. Canterbury, Conn.:

   ii   MARY BRADFORD, b. 1 March 1744, bp. 1st Ch. Canterbury 2 June 1744

  iii WILLIAM BRADFORD, b. 4 March 1745

  iv EBENEZER BRADFORD, b. 25 May 1746

   v DAVID BRADFORD, b. 8 May 1748

  vi JOHN BRADFORD, b. 27 July 1750

 vii JOSHUA BRADFORD, b. 27 Oct. 1751

viii ABIGAIL BRADFORD, b. 2 Sept. 1753

  ix JAMES BRADFORD, b. 1 Feb. 1755; d. 17 Sept. 1775

   x OLIVE BRADFORD, b. 13 July 1756

  xi JOSIAH BRADFORD, b. 25 Nov. 1757

    xii [DAUGHTER] BRADFORD, d.y.

    xiii LYDIA BRADFORD, b. 2 July 1760

    xiv BEULAH BRADFORD, b. 3 Sept. 1763

    xv MOSES BRADFORD, b. 6 Aug. 1765

Children of William and Martha (Warren) Bradford, b. Canterbury, Conn.:

    xvi JOSEPH BRADFORD, b. 22 Jan. 1767; d. 23 Sept. 1775

    xvii BENJAMIN BRADFORD, b. 22 March 1768

    xviii KEZIAH BRADFORD (triplet), b. 12 June 1770; d. 20 June 1770

    xix ZERVIAH BRADFORD (triplet), b. 12 June 1770; d. 23 Sept. 1775

    xx MARTHA BRADFORD (triplet), b. 12 June 1770; d. 23 Sept. 1775

    xxi SAMUEL WARREN BRADFORD, b. 15 Nov. 1772; d. 13 Sept. 1775

References: *MD* 15:66(Bible rec.). *Bradford Desc* pp. 58-9. *Cleveland Fams* pp. 164-5. Plainfield CT PR 2:136, 139; 3:261-2(Josiah Cleveland); #229(James Bradford); #241, 6:436(Wm. Bradford), 434(guardianship). Canterbury CT VR 1:69(1st 2 m.), 70(3rd m.), 76(b.&d. 1st dau. Zerviah), 77(b. Wm., Ebenezer, David, John, Joshua, Abigail), 78(b. James), 80(b. Olive), 81(b. dau.), 82(b. Beulah, Moses), 83(b. Joseph), 84(b. Josiah, Lydia, Benjamin), 85(b. last 4 ch.), 95(d. 1st wife), 97(d. 2nd & 3rd wives), 104(b. Mary Cleveland). *Lo-Lathrop Gen* pp. 48, 63. *MF* 6:1171. Canterbury CT LR 6:100(James Bradford); 7:228(heirs of James Bradford); 8:253; 9:143, 189-90(William Bradford); 308(William to Josiah); 10:3(David to William), 98(Joshua to Josiah); 13:108(Benjamin Bradford), 123(John to William). Canterbury 1st Ch. Recs. pp. 11(William admitted Ch.), 24(owned cov.), 57 (bp. William), 84(bp. Zerviah), 87(bp. Mary). *Desc Arthur Warren* pp. 27, 48. Plainfield CT VR 1:64(b. Martha).

157.   SARAH⁵ BRADFORD (*James⁴, Thomas³, William²⁻¹*), b. Canterbury, Conn., 27 Aug. 1720; bp. 2 Oct. 1720; d. 20 March 1807 or 20 April 1807 aged 86.

    She m. Canterbury, Conn., in 1739 **JOSEPH ADAMS**, b. Canterbury, Conn., 6 Dec. 1715; d. there 6 Dec. 1780; son of Joseph and Eunice (Spaulding) Adams. On 10 May 1743 Joseph Adams 2nd of Canterbury gave his son Joseph 111 acres where his son "now lives" and on 18 Feb. 1746/7 Joseph sold to his son Joseph another 13 or 14 acres. The distribution of the estate of Joseph Adams, late of Canterbury, dated 22 Feb. 1764 does not include a son Joseph, but the 111 acres given him in 1743 may have been his share.

    In 1762 (acknowledged 8 May 1762) Joseph and Sarah Adams with the other heirs of James Bradford sold their right to land in Canterbury.

On 24 Aug 1765 Joseph Adams and his wife Sarah of Canterbury gave to their son John 60 acres. On 13 April 1773 Joseph gave to his son Joseph Jr. 42 acres, and to his son James 23 acres with a house and barn. On the same day Joseph sold to his son James 15 acres, part of the land laid out to his wife Sarah in the distribution of the estate of James Bradford.

Samuel Adams was made administrator of the estate of Joseph Adams of Canterbury on 9 Jan. 1781. Distribution on 20 March 1781 names widow Sarah; sons: eldest Samuel, second John, third Joseph, fourth James, fifth Bradford, and sixth Jesse; and daughters: eldest Sarah Hide wife of David and youngest Triphena Safford wife of Joseph.

On 10 April 1781 Jesse Adams of Canterbury sold to his brother James Adams of Canterbury three pieces of land one of which was bounded on Bradford Adams; and for 40 shillings annually Sarah Adams released her dower in this land to her son James. On the same day Samuel Adams 3rd of Canterbury sold to his brother James two pieces of land, one with a house and barn and bounded by land set out to Tryphena Safford and Bradford Adams.

On 10 May 1790 Sarah Adams of Canterbury sold to David Hide of Canterbury nine acres subject to her right of dower during her natural life. The land had been distributed to her from the estate of her late husband Joseph Adams.

Children of Joseph and Sarah (Bradford) Adams, b. Canterbury, Conn.:

    i   WILLIAM ADAMS[6], b. 4 March 1740; d. 5 July 1759

   ii   SAMUEL ADAMS, b. 30 March 1742

  iii   JOHN ADAMS, b. 17 Feb. 1743/4

  iv   JOSEPH ADAMS, b. 2 Feb. 1745/6

   v   JAMES ADAMS (twin), b. 7 June 1748

  vi   SARAH ADAMS (twin), b. 7 June 1748

 vii   BRADFORD ADAMS, b. 11 June 1750

viii   JESSE ADAMS (twin), b. 7 Dec. 1752; d.y.

  ix   ELISHA ADAMS (twin), b. 7 Dec. 1752; d. 12 Jan. 1753

   x   MARY ADAMS, b. 5 Dec. 1755; prob. d. by 20 March 1781 when not in division

  xi   JESSE ADAMS, b. 6 Feb. 1757

  xii   TRYPHENIA ADAMS, b. 17 July 1760

References: *Adams Gen* p. 106. *Bradford Desc* p. 59. Canterbury CT VR 1:52(m.), 54(b. Joseph), 55(b. 1st 3 ch., Jesse, Elisha), 56,(b. Joseph, James, Sarah, Bradford, Mary, Jesse), 57 (b. Tryphenia), 67(d. Joseph). Hale Cem Coll:Canterbury p. 24 (d. Sarah). Plainfield

CT PR #22(Joseph Adams); #23 (Joseph Adams). Canterbury CT LR 5:89, 161(Joseph Adams 2nd); 7:228(heirs of James Bradford); 7:291; 8:163(Joseph to son), 419(Jesse to James), 420(Samuel to James); 9:21-2(Joseph to sons), 528(Sarah Adams). Canterbury 1st Ch p. 59(bp. Sarah).

158.   ANN⁵ BRADFORD *(James⁴, Thomas³, William²⁻¹)*, bp. Canterbury, Conn., 10 July 1726; d. 1814.

She m. Canterbury, Conn., 25 April 1750 **ELEAZER CLEVELAND**, b. Canterbury, Conn., 26 May 1722; d. there bef. 23 May 1787; son of Samuel and Sarah (Buswell) Cleveland.

In 1762 (acknowledged 8 May 1762) Elezer and Anna Cleveland with the other heirs of James Bradford sold their right to land in Canterbury.

On 2 May 1770 Eleazer Cleveland and his wife Ann of Canterbury sold to Joseph Bacon 24½ acres of the farm they live on.

On 23 May 1787 Anne Cleveland of Canterbury, widow, sold to Perez Cleveland of Canterbury 21¼ acres reserving the improvement of the land for herself. On 16 May 1803 Ann sold to Perez another 89 rods with a house.

No Connecticut probate records have been found for Eleazer or Ann Cleveland.

Children of Eleazer and Ann (Bradford) Cleveland, b. Canterbury, Conn.:

    i ANNA CLEVELAND⁶, b. 3 Nov. 1750, bp. Canterbury 1st Ch. 24 March 1751

    ii SUSANNA CLEVELAND, b. 29 July 1752, bp. Canterbury 1st Ch. 9 Aug. 1752

    iii SQUIRES CLEVELAND, b. 29 July 1754

    iv MEHITABLE CLEVELAND, b. 14 July 1756

    v JOHN CLEVELAND, b. 29 June 1758; d. soon after 26 Dec. 1776 in Rev. War

    vi PEREZ CLEVELAND, b. 17 July 1760

    vii POLLY CLEVELAND, b. 19 Aug. 1762

    viii BRADFORD CLEVELAND, b. 9 Sept. 1764

    ix ALICE CLEVELAND, b. 16 Dec. 1767

    x WILLIAM CLEVELAND, b. 22 Feb. 1771, "10th child & 5th son"

References: *Bradford Desc* p. 59. *Cleveland Fams* pp. 128-9. Canterbury CT VR 1:100(m.), 104(b. Eleazer), 105 (b. Susanna), 107(b. Anna, Squires), 108(b. Mehitable), 109(b. John, Perez, Polly), 110(b. Bradford), 111(b. last 2 ch.). Canterbury CT LR 7:228(heirs of James Bradford); 8:126(Eleazer Cleveland); 10:260, 327(Anne Cleveland). Canterbury 1st Ch. Recs. pp. 60(bp. Ann), 92(bp. Anna), 94(bp. Susanna).

159. MARY⁵ BRADFORD (*James⁴*, *Thomas³*, *William²⁻¹*), bp. Canterbury, Conn., June 1729; d. Hanover, N.H., 1 July 1806.

She m. Canterbury, Conn., 31 May 1748 **JOSEPH WOODARD**, b. Canterbury, Conn., 26 Feb. 1725/6; d. Hanover, N.H., 10 May 1805; son of Joseph and Hannah (Richards) Woodard.

In 1762 (acknowledged 8 May 1762) Joseph and Mary Woodward with the other heirs of James Bradford sold their right to land in Canterbury.

On 24 Nov. 1762 Paul Davenport and Joseph and Mary Woodard of Canterbury sold to Asa Aspanwell of Canterbury land that was distributed to Mrs. Susanah Bradford, the mother of Mary Woodard, and to Mrs. Abigail Davenport, the mother of Paul Davenport, out of the estate of Mrs. Margaret Adams late of Canterbury.

On 27 Oct. 1774 Benoni Hurlburt of Castleton, Vt., sold land in Castleton to Joseph Woodward of Canterbury, Conn.

On 4 June 1785 Araunah Woodward of Castleton sold land to father Joseph Woodward. On the same day Joseph Woodward sold land to son Araunah Woodward.

On 1 April 1786 Joseph Woodward of Castleton gave land in Castleton to son James Woodward. On 28 May 1789 he gave land in Castleton to eldest daughter Welthean Foot of Castleton.

On 27 Feb. 1796 George Foot of Hanover sold two pieces of land to Joseph Woodward of Hanover. On 1 April 1801 Joseph Woodward sold to this land to Ebenezer Woodward of Hanover.

The will of Joseph Woodward dated 9 May 1803, proved 8 June 1805, names wife Mary; son Ebenezer; daughters Mary Davis and Susannah Plumb; and other children James Woodward, Araunah Woodward, Rufus Woodward, Asa Woodward, Sarah Mason and Wealthy Foot.

Children of Joseph and Mary (Bradford) Woodard, b. Canterbury, Conn.:

    i JAMES WOODARD⁶, b. 16 Feb. 1749

    ii RUFUS WOODARD, b. 21 April 1751, bp. 23 June 1751; d. 11 Sept. 1753

    iii ARUNNAH WOODARD, b. 27 Dec. 1753, prob. the child, bp. 17 March 1754

    iv WEALTHEAN WOODARD, b. 3 Jan. 1756

    v RUFUS WOODARD, b. 15 Feb. 1758, bp. 26 Feb. 1758

    vi ASA WOODARD, b. 15 Feb. 1760, bp. 24 Feb. 1760

   vii EBENEZER WOODARD, b. 2 July 1762, bp. 18 July 1762

  viii MARY WOODARD, b. 26 June 1764, bp. 1 July 1764

    ix SUSANNA WOODARD, bp. 12 July 1766, bp. 13 July 1766

     x SARAH WOODARD, b. 28 May 1768, bp. 5 June 1768

References: *Bradford Desc* pp. 59-60. Canterbury CT VR 1:236 (m.), 238(b. Joseph), 239(b. Rufus, Arunnah, Asa), 240(b. Wealthean, Rufus, Ebenezer, Mary, Susanna), 241(b. James Sarah), 246(d. Rufus). Genealogical Records of Hanover NH at Dartmouth College Library(d. Joseph, Mary). Castleton VT LR 1:53(Benoni Hurlburt); 2:71(Araunah Woodward), 106(to Araunah), 116(to James), 219(to Welthian). Grafton Co. NH LR 23:164, 165(George Foot); 32:95(to Ebenezer). Grafton Co. NH PR A:78(Joseph Woodward). *Woodward Gen* p. 269. Canterbury CT LR 7:107(Paul Davenport); 7:228(heirs of James Bradford). Canterbury 1st Ch. Recs. pp. 68(bp. Mary), 92(bp. Rufus), 95(bp. child), 98(bp. Rufus), 100(bp. 24 Feb. 1760), 102(bp. 18 July 1762), 104(bp. 1 July 1764), 105(bp. 13 July 1766), 107(bp. 5 June 1768).

160. ANN STRICKLAND[5] (*Ann[4] Bradford, Thomas[3], William[2-1]*), b. prob. New London, Conn., ca. 1704; d. Windham, Conn., 31 Jan. 1741/2.

She m. Windham, Conn., 13 Oct. 1726 **JOSEPH HEBARD**, b. Windham, Conn., 15 Jan. 1703/4; d. there 15 March 1751/2 aged 73y; son of Joseph and Abigail (Kendall) Hebard. He m. (2) MARTHA (SMITH) GOULD. On 2 May 1748 Joseph Hebard Jr. of Windham sold to his father two parcels of land. The next day Joseph sold the land back to his son and they made an indenture that Joseph Jr. would allow his father and mother, Joseph and Abigail, to have the use of the land for their lives.

On 7 April 1718/9 [*sic*] Ann, only daughter of Peter Strickland Jr. of New London, dec., chose her [great-]uncle Samuel Comstock to be her guardian.

On 20 July 1729 Joseph Hebard was admitted to the Windham Cong. Ch. and his wife Ann was admitted on 17 Aug. 1729. Martha Hebard wife of Joseph was admitted on 23 May 1743 from Ipswich.

Joseph Hebard was a physician.

Children of Joseph and Ann (Strickland) Hebard, b. Windham, Conn.:

    i JOSEPH HEBARD[6], b. 15 Sept. 1727; d. 3 Oct. 1727

   ii ANNA HEBARD, b. 22 June 1730, bp. 26 July 1730 (see #164)

  iii JOANNA HEBARD, b. 4 April 1732, bp. 9 April 1732

  iv JOSEPH HEBARD, b. 15 March 1733/4, bp. 24 March 1734

   v BENJAMIN HEBARD, b. 17 Feb. 1735/6, bp. 18 April 1736; d. 28 July 1737

v BENJAMIN HEBARD, b. 17 Feb. 1735/6, bp. 18 April 1736; d. 28 July 1737

vi ABIGAIL HEBARD, b. 9 June 1738, bp. 11 June 1738

vii JEMIMA HEBARD, b. 11 June 1740

References: Windham CT VR 1:96(b. Joseph; m.; b. ch.; d. Ann, 2 ch), 245(d. Joseph). *NEHGR* 51:320(his parents). Hale Cem Coll:Windham p. 281(d. Joseph). *Hibbard Fam* p. 34. New London CT PR #5201(Ann Strickland). Windham CT LR I:170-1, 180(Joseph Hebard). Windham Cong. Ch. Recs. pp. 13(bp. Anna), 15(Joanna), 17(Joseph), 19(bp. Benjamin), 21(bp. Abigail), 32(admitted members).

161. SILAS NEWCOMB[5] (*Jerusha*[4] *Bradford, Thomas*[3], *William*[2-1]), b. Lebanon, Conn., 2 Sept. 1717, bp. 2 March 1718; d. there 24 May 1773 in 56th yr or aged 55y.

He m. Lebanon, Conn., 1 March 1739 **SUBMIT PINNEO**, b. Lebanon 19 Oct. 1717; d. there 12 Feb. 1804 in 87th yr. "relict of Silas Newcomb" or aged 86y; daughter of James and Dorothy (Badcock) Pinneo.

On 25 Dec. 1742 Hezekiah Newcomb of Lebanon, yeoman, deeded land in Falltown [later called Bernardston] to son Silas Newcomb of Falltown.

On 12 March 1764 Silas Newcomb of Lebanon gave to his son Daniel Newcomb of Lebanon 100 acres in Bardnardston.

On 21 June 1774 Daniel Newcomb of Bernardston sold to Paul Newcomb of Lebanon land that had belonged to his father Silas Newcomb. On 2 Nov 1779 Calvin Newcomb of Lebanon sold to Jesse Newcomb of Lebanon land set out to him from the estate of his grandfather Hezekiah Newcomb. On 14 April 1781 Silas Newcomb of Somers, Conn., sold to Paul his right in his father's estate. On 7 Feb. 1782 Jesse sold to John Newcomb of Lebanon the land that he had bought from Calvin who was the son of Silas. On 26 Sept. 1787 Consider and Submit Cushman of Montague, Mass., sold to John Newcomb their rights in the land of Silas Newcomb assigned to Submit. And on 9 April 1788 Submit Newcomb, Paul Newcomb, Jesse Newcomb, and John Newcomb all of Lebanon sold two tracts of land, one being part of the farm lately belonging to Silas Newcomb; on the same day Paul sold to John nine acres set off to their sister Submit Cushman and 10 acres set off to their brother Bradford from Silas' estate under the incumbrances of the widow's thirds.

On 13 Nov. 1777 Peter Newcomb, James Newcomb, Paul Newcomb, Wadsworth Brewster and Jerutia [*sic*] his wife, Samuel Guild and Hannah his wife, and Jesse Newcomb all of Lebanon; Daniel Newcomb of Barnards Town; Silas Newcomb of Somers; Bradford Newcomb of Mansfield [Conn.]; and Roswell Bill and Hezekiah Coburn and Mary his wife of Windham [Conn.] sold to Charles Swift and William Swift of Lebanon their rights in a 100-acre farm in Lebanon.

In 1790 Submit Newcomb was head of a household in Mansfield, Conn., consisting of five females.

Children of Silas and Submit (Pinneo) Newcomb, b. Lebanon, Conn., exc. Daniel and Silas, b. Falltown:

    i   JERUSHA NEWCOMB[6], b. 6 Jan. 1740; bp. 8 Jan. 1740

    ii   DANIEL NEWCOMB, b. 18 Nov. 1741

    iii SILAS NEWCOMB, b. 29 Nov. 1743

    iv SUBMIT NEWCOMB, b. 7 Oct. 1745

    v   BRADFORD NEWCOMB, b. 9 Nov. 1747

    vi HANNAH NEWCOMB, b. March 1749/50; d. Aug. 1752

    vii PAUL NEWCOMB, b. 15 March 1752

   viii HANNAH NEWCOMB, b. 17 May 1754

    ix JESSE NEWCOMB, b. 26 May 1756

    x   CALVIN NEWCOMB, b. 22 May 1758

    xi JOHN NEWCOMB, b. 26 May 1760

    xii LUTHER NEWCOMB, b. 12 June 1762

References: *Newcomb Gen* pp. 70-2. *Bradford Desc* p. 60. *Conn Marr* 2:41. Lebanon CT VR 1:222(m.; b. ch.; d. Silas, Hannah), 244(b. Submit). Hale Cem Coll:Lebanon p. 65 (d. Silas, Submit). Hampshire Co. LR 5:183(Silas Newcomb). Lebanon CT LR 13:121(Hezekiah Newcomb), 122(Daniel Newcomb), 271(Silas Newcomb); 14:539(Calvin Newcomb), 540(Jesse Newcomb), 544(Consider Cushman), 546(Paul Newcomb); 19:123(Submit Newcomb *et al*), 339(Peter Newcomb *et al*). Lebanon 1st Ch. Recs. 4:33(bp. Silas), 27(bp. Jerusha), 169(m.).

162.   PETER NEWCOMB[5] (*Jerusha[4] Bradford, Thomas[3], William[2-1]*), b. Lebanon, Conn., 28 Nov. 1718, bp. 30 Nov. 1718; d. there 26 Sept. 1779 in 61st yr.

He m. Lebanon, Conn., 22 Nov. 1740 **HANNAH ENGLISH**, b. Lebanon, Conn., 19 Sept. 1722, bp. Columbia (Lebanon Crank) Church 23 Sept. 1722; d. there 9 Jan. 1796; daughter of Richard and Mary (Hinckman) English. The will of Richard English of Lebanon made 13 Aug. 1743, proved

20 May 1748, named his daughter "Hannah English alias Newcomb" to whom he gave a Bible.

On 25 Dec. 1742 Hezekiah Newcomb of Lebanon, yeoman, deeded land in Falltown [later called Bernardston] to his son Peter Newcomb of Falltown. Peter returned to Lebanon about 1744 because of troubles with the Indians. He served in an expedition against Canada in 1758.

Peter and Hannah Newcomb were admitted to the Columbia (Lebanon Crank) Church without a date. Their children were baptised but no dates are recorded.

Hezekiah Newcomb served the town of Lebanon as suveyor in 1748, collector of taxes in 1753, lister in 1760, lister and surveyor of highways in 1761, surveyor of highways in 1766 and 1772, and hayward in 1777.

On 1 May 1771 Hezekiah Newcomb Jr. of Lebanon traded land in Falltown [now Barnardston] with Simon Gager of Norwich. On 19 Dec. 1771 Simon Gager sold to this land to Peter Newcomb of Lebanon.

On 28 Feb. 1774 Joseph Newcomb of Lebanon sold to Hezekiah Newcomb of Barnardston several pieces of land in Barnardston given to him by the will of his grandfather Newcomb late of Lebanon.

On 13 Nov. 1777 Peter Newcomb, James Newcomb, Paul Newcomb, Wadsworth Brewster and Jerutia [sic] his wife, Samuel Guild and Hannah his wife, and Jesse Newcomb all of Lebanon; Daniel Newcomb of Barnards Town; Silas Newcomb of Sumers [Conn.]; Bradford Newcomb of Mansfield [Conn.]; and Roswell Bill and Hezekiah Coburn and Mary his wife of Windham [Conn.] sold to Charles Swift and William Swift of Lebanon their rights in a 100-acre farm in Lebanon.

The will of Peter Newcomb of Lebanon dated 9 Sept. 1779, proved 11 Oct. 1779, names wife Hannah; oldest son Hezekiah, second son Samuel, third son William, fourth son Joseph, and daughters Phebe Cushman and Jemima (no surname).

There are no Connecticut probates for this couple listed in the index.

Children of Peter and Hannah (English) Newcomb, b. Lebanon, Conn., not included in Barbour Index:

    i PHEBE NEWCOMB[6], b. 15 Sept. 1741

    ii HEZEKIAH NEWCOMB, b. 6 May 1747

    iii SAMUEL NEWCOMB, b. 23 Aug. 1749

    iv WILLIAM NEWCOMB, b. 19 March 1752

    v JEMIMA NEWCOMB, b. 24 Oct. 1756

    vi JOSEPH NEWCOMB, b. 3 May 1762

References: *Newcomb Gen* pp. 72-5.   *Bradford Desc* p. 60.   Lebanon CT VR 1:80(b. Hannah).   Hampshire Co. LR 14:53-4(with Simon Gager); 16:197(Joseph Newcomb). Lebanon CT LR 14:141(James Newcomb); 19:339(Peter Newcomb *et al.*).   Lebanon 1st Ch. Recs. 4:33(bp. Peter).   Columbia (Lebanon Crank) Ch. Recs. 1:11(bp. Hannah); 5:29(admitted ch.), 206(bp. ch.-no dates), 354(d. Peter).   Windham CT PR 3:496(Richard English).

163.   ANNE NEWCOMB[5]   *(Jerusha[4] Bradford, Thomas[3], William[2-1])*, b. Lebanon, Conn., 4 April 1720, bp. 13 March 1719/20; d. 30 July 1751 Canterbury, Conn., "wife of Joseph Smith Jr."

She m. **JOSEPH SMITH JR**, b. Canterbury, Conn., 14 Jan. 1716/7; d. after 1751; son of Joseph and Elizabeth (Burknap) Smith.   On 4 May 1749 Joseph Smith of Canterbury gave to his son Joseph Smith Jr. 50 acres.

Joseph Smith Jr. was admitted to the Canterbury Church 22 March 1741.

Children of Joseph and Anne (Newcomb) Smith, b. Canterbury, Conn.:*

  i   SAMUEL SMITH[6], b. 25 Dec. 1747
  ii DAN SMITH, b. 3 Feb. 1748/9 (a Dan Smith, son of Joseph Jr. and Zerviah, was bp. 3 Sept. 1749)
  iii ANNE SMITH, b. 26 July 1751; bp. 4 Aug. 1751

* Note: Joseph Jr. and Zerviah had a child, bp. 22 July 1750 and Daniel, son of Joseph Jr. was bp. 5 Oct. 1755.   A Joseph Smith d. in Canterbury 5 Sept. 1765.

References: *Newcomb Gen* p. 44.   *Bradford Desc* p. 60-1.   Canterbury CT VR 1:216(b. Joseph), 217(b. Samuel), 218 (b. Dan, Anne), 227(d. Anne).   Canterbury CT LR 5:298(Joseph Smith).   Canterbury 1st Ch. Recs. 4:33(bp. Anne).

164.   THOMAS NEWCOMB[5]   *(Jerusha[4] Bradford, Thomas[3], William[2-1])*, b. Lebanon, Conn., 3 Sept. 1724, bp. 8 Nov. 1724; d. there 26 Aug. 1753 in 29th yr.

He m. Lebanon, Conn., 26 March 1751 **ANN HEBARD**, b. Windham, Conn., 22 July 1730; d. Willington, Conn., 1 July 1785 aged 55 "wife of Lt. Francis Fenton Jr."; daughter of Joseph and Anne (Strickland) Hebard (see Family #160ii).   Distribution of the estate of Joseph Hebard of Windham on 15 April 1754 names daughter Anne Newcomb.   She m. (2) Willington, Conn., 31 Oct. 1754 FRANCIS FENTON of Willington.

On 7 Dec. 1773 Joseph Newcomb of Lebanon sold 36 acres in Lebanon; this deed was also signed by Francis Fenton Jr. and Anne Fenton Jr.

No Connecticut probate records for this couple were found in the index.

Child of Thomas and Ann (Hebard) Newcomb, b. Lebanon, Conn.:

 i JOSEPH NEWCOMB[6], b. 21 Aug. 1752

References: *Newcomb Gen* p. 44, 75. *Bradford Desc* p. 61. Windham CT PR #1853(Joseph Hebard). Lebanon CT VR 1:224 (m.; b. ch.). Windham CT VR 1:96(b. Ann). Willington CT VR A16(2nd m.). Hale Cem Coll:Lebanon p. 72(d. Thomas). Lebanon CT LR 12:258(Joseph Newcomb). Lebanon 1st Ch. Recs. 4:36(bp. Thomas).

165. JERUSHA NEWCOMB[5] *(Jerusha[4] Bradford, Thomas[3], William[2-1])*, b. Lebanon, Conn., 24 March 1726, bp. 27 March 1726; d. Burlington, Conn., 24 (or 25 or 28) Oct. 1804 aged 82.

She m. before May 1745 **EZRA CLEVELAND** bp. Canterbury, Conn., 27 March 1726; d. Bristol (now Burlington), Conn., 7 Jan. 1802 aged 80; son of Joseph and Sarah (Ensworth or Ainsworth) Cleveland. On 7 March 1753 Joseph Cleveland of Canterbury gave to his son Ezra Cleveland of Canterbury 85 acres.

In May 1745 Ezra and Jerusha Cleveland were admitted members of the First Church of Canterbury.

On 30 March 1771 Ezra Cleveland of Tolland sold to Joseph Adams of Canterbury 28 acres with a dwelling house and barn.

In 1772 they were "late of Tolland now of Worthing Mass." according to the Newcomb Genealogy.

On 21 Jan. 1789 Ezra Cleaveland and Newcom Cleaveland of Worthington, yeomen, sold Ephraim Parish of Worthington, yeoman, 23 acres being one-half of lot #106 where Ezra and Newcom live; Ezra's wife Jerusha released her dower rights.

In 1790 Ezra Cleveland's household in Bristol, Conn., consisted of one man, 2 boys under 16, and 4 females.

Children of Ezra and Jerusha (Newcomb) Cleveland, all except last child, b. Canterbury, Conn.:

 i EZRA CLEVELAND[6], b. 22 June 1748, bp. Canterbury 1st Ch. but no date given

 ii TYXHALL CLEVELAND, b. 26 April 1750, bp. Canterbury 1st Ch. but no date given

 iii THOMAS CLEVELAND, b. 25 March 1752, bp. Canterbury 1st Ch. 26 April 1752

 iv SARAH CLEVELAND, b. 29 Oct. 1754

   v NEWCOMB CLEVELAND, b. 6 Nov. 1756

  vi JERUSHA CLEVELAND, b. 31 Aug. 1758

 vii ARUNAH CLEVELAND, b. 16 May 1763

viii ZERVIAH CLEVELAND, b. 6 March 1765

  ix DOROTHY CLEVELAND, b. 14 Sept. 1767

   x FREDERICK CLEVELAND, b. Tolland, Conn., 11 April 1770

References: Hale Cem Coll:Burlington p. 29(d. Jerusha, Ezra). *Newcomb Gen* p. 44. *Bradford Desc* p. 61. Canterbury CT VR 1:107(b. Ezra, Tuxhall, Sarah), 108(b. Thomas, Newcomb), 109(b. Jerusha, Arunah), 110(b. Zerviah, Dorothy). Tolland CT VR 2:78(b. Frederick). *Cleveland Gen* 1:138. Canterbury CT LR 6:52(Joseph Clevelenad); 8:1(Ezra Cleveland). Canterbury 1st Ch. Recs. pp. 13(admitted ch.), 88(bp. Tyxhall), 90(bp. Ezra), 93(bp. Thomas). Lebanon 1st Ch. Recs. 4:36(bp. Jerusha). Hampshire Co. LR 2:285(Ezra Cleaveland).

166. ELIZABETH NEWCOMB⁵ (*Jerusha⁴ Bradford, Thomas³, William²⁻¹*), b. Lebanon, Conn., 19 Dec. 1727, bp. 24 Dec. 1727; d. Canterbury, Conn., 31 July 1801 aged 72y.

She m. Norwich, Conn., 21 April 1747 **JOHN BARSTOW**, b. Norwich, Conn., 31 Dec. 1724; d. Canterbury, Conn., 9 Feb. 1796 aged 71 or 9 Feb. 1806 [*sic*] aged 72y; son of Job and Rebecca (Bushnell) Barstow. Job Barstow of Norwich in his will dated 6 April 1756, proved 5 Nov. 1764, named his son John, and John is included in the distribution of Job's estate on 15 March 1765. Job added this personal note at the end of his will:

> ... as my fatherly advice to you my Children...that you use all possible prudence for a Loving agreement in yᵉ Division of yᵉ Estate Given you in sᵈ Will, and in your Division Let there Be a Spirit of Condosention So far toward those of you that have already Land that was formerly mine ... that their parts may Be Laid out to them adjoining to that they already have, if it may Be Done with any tolarable Conveniency So that none are Much hurt thereby.

On 17 Nov. 1751 Elizabeth Barstow wife of John was admitted a member of the First Church of Canterbury.

Administration was granted to Samuel Barstow on the estate of John Barstow of Canterbury. Samuel Barstow and Hezekiah Barstow each submitted bills for settling their father's estate on 1 March 1796.

On 22 Jan. 1798 Alpheus Barstow of Leyden, Mass., and John Barstow of Canterbury sold to Hezekiah Barstow of Canterbury land belonging to them as heirs of John Barstow, and on 15 Feb. 1798 Job Barstow of Dalton, Mass., sold his share to Hezekiah Barstow. On 3 April 1798 Samuel and Hezekiah Barstow as administrators of the estate of John Barstow sold land in Canterbury to John Barstow of Canterbury. On 22 Jan. 1799 Ebenezer Barstow of Shelborn, Vt., sold to John Barstow of Canterbury land in Canterbury bounded on land distributed and set out to Jerusha Palmer as her share in the real estate of his father John Barstow's estate. And on 1 Feb. 1802 William A. Barstow of Plainfield sold to Hezekiah Barstow 11 acres distributed to him from his father's estate.

Children of John and Elizabeth (Newcomb) Barstow, first two b. Norwich, Conn.; rest b. Canterbury, Conn., bp. First Church there::

    i   ALPHEUS BARSTOW[6], b. 6 Feb. 1747/8

   ii SAMUEL BARSTOW, b. 28 Dec. 1749

  iii JOHN BARSTOW, b. 2 Oct. 1751, bp. 17 Nov. 1751; d. 19 Dec. 1752

  iv JOHN BARSTOW, b. 21 Dec. 1752, bp. 4 Feb. 1753

   v HEZEKIAH BARSTOW, b. 28 Feb. 1755, bp. 13 April 1755

  vi EBENEZER BARSTOW, b. 7 Sept. 1756, bp. 31 Oct. 1756

 vii ANNA BARSTOW, b. 31 July 1759; d. 12 April 1773 ae 14

viii JOB BARSTOW, b. 5 March 1761, bp. 22 March 1761

  ix REBECCA ELIZABETH BARSTOW, b. 11 June 1763, bp. 19 June 1763

   x WILLIAM AUGUSTUS BARSTOW, b. 21 Feb. 1765, bp. 17 March 1765

  xi JERUSHA BRADFORD BARSTOW, b. 2 March 1767, bp. 5 April 1767

References: *Barstow-Bestor* pp. 16-7. *Bradford Desc* p. 61. *Norwich CT VR* 1:63(b. John); 1:253(m.; b. 1st 2 ch.). Canterbury CT VR 1:79(b. John, John, Hezekiah; d. John), 80(b. Jerusha). Hale Cem Coll:Canterbury pp. 80(d. Elizabeth, John), 24(d. Anna). Plainfield CT PR #151 (John Barstow). Canterbury CT LR 12:114(Ebenezer Barstow); 13:67(Alpheus Barstow), 68(Job Barstow), 80(Samuel & Hezekiah Barstow), 264(William A. Barstow). Canterbury 1st Ch. Recs. 14(admitted ch.), 93(bp. 1st John), 94(bp. 2nd John), 96(bp. Hezekiah), 97(bp. Ebenezer), 101(bp. Job), 103(bp. Rebecca), 105(bp. William), 106(bp. Jerusha). Lebanon 1st Ch. Recs. 4:37(bp. Elizabeth). Norwich, Conn., PD #797(Job Barstow).

167.   JEMIMA NEWCOMB[5] (*Jerusha*[4] *Bradford, Thomas*[3], *William*[2-1]), b. Lebanon, Conn., 14 Dec. 1730, bp. 27 Dec. 1730; d. Thetford, Vt., 25 June 1794 (or 20 Nov. 1790).

She m. (1) Norwich, Conn., 23 Nov. 1749 **JONATHAN LAMB**, d. Norwich, Conn., 13 Nov. 1754.

She m. (2) Preston, Conn., 12 June 1755 **JOSEPH KINNE**, b. Preston 17 Feb. 1717/8; bp. Preston First Church 4 May 1718; d. Cardigan (now Orange) N.H., 15 Oct. 1793 [*Kinne Gen.* says d. 1781 in Thetford, Vt., at home of son David]; son of Joseph and Keziah (Peabody) Kinne. He m. (1) Preston 10 June 1740 Sarah Blunt. On 22 Aug. 1745 Joseph Kinne and the other heirs of Joseph Kinne divided his estate in Preston.

The will of Jonathan Lamb of Norwich made 18 Sept. 1754, proved 21 Jan. 1755, names his wife Jemime, son Jeduthan, and daughter Charlotte.

On 30 May 1756 Joseph and Jemima Kinne were admitted to the Preston Church from the East Norwich Church, from which they were dismissed when they moved to Vermont. In 1761 Joseph was appointed Lt. Col. of the 1st Co. 8th Regt. and in 1763 he represented Preston in the General Assembly.

On 15 Sept. 1766 Jeduthan Lamb of Norwich, son of Jonathan Lamb late of Norwich, deceased, a minor over 14, chose Lt. Joseph Kinne of Preston as his guardian.

Joseph Kinne owned the covenant in the Plainfield Church 5 Sept 1768.

Children of Jonathan and Jemima (Newcomb) Lamb, b. Norwich, Conn.:

    i   JEDUTHAN LAMB[6], b. 15 July 1751
    ii   CHARLOTTE LAMB, b. 22 April 1753

Children of Joseph and Jemima (Newcomb) (Lamb) Kinne, first 10 b. and 7 bp. Preston, Conn., last 2 b. and bp. Plainfield, Conn.:

    iii   JOSEPH KINNE[6], b. 25 March 1756, bp. 30 May 1756
    iv   JONATHAN KINNE, bp. 22 Aug. 1757, bp. 22 Aug. 1757; d.y.
    v   DANIEL KINNE, b. 15 Oct. 1759, bp. 28 Oct. 1759
    vi   NEWCOMB KINNE, b. 18 Jan. 1761, bp. 1 March 1761
    vii   DAVID KINNE (twin), b. 9 June 1762, bp. 13 June 1762
    viii JONATHAN KINNE (twin), b. 9 June 1762, bp. 13 June 1762
    ix   BRADFORD KINNE, b. 2 Dec. 1764, bp. 15 Sept. 1765
    x   JEMIMA KINNE, b. 2 May 1766
    xi   PARELEY (or PERLEY) KINNE, b. 6 April 1768
    xii   SANFORD KINNE, b. 14 Aug. 1769

xiii GEORGE WHITEFIELD KINNE, b. 14 April 1771, bp. 25 Aug. 1771; d. 1790 ae 27; unm.

xiv WEALTHY KINNE, b. 11 April 1773, bp. 25 April 1773

References: Norwich CT VR 2:66(b. Lamb ch.; m.; d. Jonathan). Preston CT VR 1:38(b. Joseph); 2:49(m.; b. Joseph thru Sanford). Plainfield CT VR 2:81(b. last 2 ch.). *Newcomb Gen* pp. 44-5. *Bradford Desc* pp. 61-2. Norwich CT PR #6511 (Jonathan Lamb); #6507 (Jedutham Lamb). *Kinne Gen* p. 31. Preston CR LR 5:428(division). Preston 1st Ch. Recs. 1:50(bp. Joseph, Jonathan), 51(bp. Daniel, Newcomb, David, Jonathan), 52(bp. Bradford). Lebanon 1st Ch. Recs. 4:38(bp. Jemima). Plainfield CT Ch. Recs. 1:23(owned cov.), 136(bp. George), 137(bp. Wealthy).

168. JAMES NEWCOMB⁵ (*Jerusha⁴ Bradford, Thomas³, William²⁻¹*), b. Lebanon, Conn., 7 Feb. 1732/3, bp. 18 Feb. 1733; d. Stephentown N.Y., 14 Dec. 1799.

He m. (1) Lebanon, Conn., 11 Sept. 1755 **SUBMIT (DOWNER) DAVIS**, b. Norwich, Conn., ca. 1725; d. Mansfield, Conn., ca. 1820 aged 96; daughter of Samuel and Phebe (Bishop) Downer.

He may have married (2) **NELLIE ALLEN**. Claude Barlow wrote, "Submit's birth and 1st m. not in any, Conn., rec; think Submit d. before 1790 and he m. (2) Nellie Allen. Can prove nothing after 1771. Was there a divorce? Note James rem. Little Hoosac, Albany Co. by 1782; Stephentown: Rensselaer Co. 1785; last 3 ch., b. Petersburgh NY by Nellie Allen." Aspinwall stated, "He must have separated from her for the three last children were born at Petersburg N.Y. by Nellie Allen." The situation remains confusing, and it is suspected that it may have been the son James who married Nellie Allen and had the children listed. More research is needed.

On 8 Nov. 1774 James Newcomb of Lebanon sold to Paul Newcomb a barn standing on his father's farm that James had inherited by his father Hezekiah Newcomb's will. On 22 Sept. 1782 James Newcomb of Lebanon sold to Timothy Larrabee of Lebanon several parcels of land, some that fell to him from the estate of his father Hezekiah Newcomb and others that he had bought from his brother Peter Newcomb deceased.

On 13 Nov. 1777 Peter Newcomb, James Newcomb, Paul Newcomb, Wadsworth Brewster and Jerutia [*sic*] his wife, Samuel Guild and Hannah his wife, Jesse Newcomb all of Lebanon; Daniel Newcomb of Barnards Town; Silas Newcomb of Somers [Conn.]; Bradford Newcomb of Mansfield [Conn.]; and Roswell Bill and Hezekiah Coburn and Mary his wife of Windham

[Conn.] sold to Charles Swift and William Swift of Lebanon their rights in a 100-acre farm in Lebanon.

Children of James and Submit (Downer) (Davis) Newcomb, b. Lebanon, Conn.:

    i   JAMES NEWCOMB[6], b. 8 May 1756

    ii PHEBE NEWCOMB, b. 12 May 1757

    iii REBECCA NEWCOMB, b. 29 Dec. 1758

    iv THOMAS NEWCOMB, b. 12 May 1761

    v   DAVID NEWCOMB, b. 13 Feb. 1763

    vi SUBMIT NEWCOMB, b. 10 April 1765

    vii CLARISSA NEWCOMB, b. 8 Feb. 1767

    viii CYPRIAN NEWCOMB, b. 18 Nov. 1768; d. near Charlestown, S.C.; unm.

    ix DODDRIDGE NEWCOMB, b. 11 Feb. 1771

? Children of James and Nellie (Allen) Newcomb, b. Petersburgh N.Y.:*

    x   HEZEKIAH NEWCOMB, b. 3 Oct. 1791

    xi SILAS NEWCOMB d.y.

    xii WHEELOCK NEWCOMB d.y.

* Note: The last 3 children are in *Bradford Desc* and *Newcomb Gen.* Are they really children? Maybe grandchildren? Any proof for Nellie? and are these her children?

References: Lebanon CT VR 1:225(m.; b. 1st 9 ch.). *Newcomb Gen* pp. 45, 75-6. *Bradford Desc* p. 62. Lebanon CT LR 13:121; 14:141(James Newcomb); 339(Peter Newcomb *et al.*). Lebanon 1st Ch. Recs. 4:39(bp. James).

169. ANNE WHITING[5] (*Elizabeth Adams[4], Alice[3] Bradford, William[2-1]*), b. Windham, Conn., 2 Jan. 1698; d. there 18 Sept. 1778 or 23 Feb. 1778 aged 82.

    She m. Lebanon, Conn., 29 Dec. 1721 **JOSEPH FITCH**, b. Saybrook, Conn., in Nov. 1681; d. Lebanon, Conn., 9 May 1741 aged 59; son of James and Priscilla (Mason) Fitch. He m. (1) 2 Nov. 1703 SARAH MASON with whom he had Judith, Sarah, Mason, and Joseph.

    On 26 May 1734 Joseph Fitch Jr. was admitted a member of the First Church of Lebanon and Joseph Fitch was admitted a member on 28 Sept. 1734.

    On 27 April 1744 Nathan Fitch of Lebanon in consideration of a tract of land conveyed to him by Eleazer Fitch of Lebanon and for the settlement of a line between him and the lands that did formerly belong to Joseph Fitch deceased, quitclaimed to Azell Fitch and Ichabod Fitch, heirs of Joseph, 16 acres. On 1 June 1761 Ichabod Fitch of Lebanon sold to Azel Fitch of Lebanon 122 acres that had been devised to their brothers Eleaz[r] Fitch of Windham, Sam[ll] Fitch of Boston, and Thom[s] Fitch deceased; Ichabod's part was 1/5 of 1/3 lying undivided reserving their mother's thirds during her life. And on 3 June 1761 Azel sold to Ichabod his right in half a house, barn, and land that had belonged to their father Joseph.

On 27 Nov. 1751 William Whiting of Norwich, John Whiting of Stonington, Samuel Whiting of Hartford, Nathan Whiting of New Haven, and Ann Fitch of Lebanon together with the residue of the heirs of Eliphalet Whiting late of Windham, sold to John Abbe of Windham one acre of land, the deed signed also by David and Mary Wooster and Timothy and Tempe Pitkin.

Children of Joseph and Anne (Whiting) Fitch, b. Lebanon Conn.; bp. First Church:

  i   SAMUEL FITCH[6], b. 16 Jan. 1723/4, bp. 19 Jan. 1724
  ii   ELEAZOR FITCH, b. 29 Aug. 1726, bp. 4 Sept. 1726
  iii AZEL FITCH, b. 7 Nov. 1728, bp. 17 Nov. 1728 as Arel; d. ca. 1769; unm.
  iv   ICHABOD FITCH, b. 17 May 1734, bp. 26 May 1734
  v   ANN FITCH, b. 12 July 1737, bp. 17 July 1737
  vi   THOMAS FITCH, b. 11 June 1739, bp. 24 June 1739; d. 27 Feb. 1746/7 ae 7y

References: *Waterman Gen* 1:649, 655-6. Norwich CT VR 1:40(b. Joseph). Lebanon CT VR 1:102(m.; b. ch.; d. Thomas, Joseph). Windham CT VR 1:54(d. Anne). Hale Cem Coll:Lebanon p. 74 (d. Joseph, Thomas); Windham p. 285 (d. Anne). Lebanon CT LR 6:467(Nathan Fitch); 9:550(Azel Fitch); 11:134(Ichabod Fitch). Windham CT LR L:332(William Whiting *et al.*). Lebanon 1st Ch. Recs. 4:5(admitted members), 35(bp. Samuel), 36(bp. Eleazor), 38(bp. Arel), 40(bp. Ichabod), 42(bp. Ann), 43(bp. Thomas).

170. ELIZABETH WHITING[5] (*Elizabeth Adams[4], Alice[3] Bradford, William[2-1]*), b. Windham, Conn., 11 Feb. 1702; d. Lebanon 2 Sept. 1730 "having lived about 4 times 7 years."

She m. Lebanon, Conn., 1 Nov. 1725 **WILLIAM GAGER**, b. Norwich, Conn., 29 Dec. 1704; d. before 4 Sept. 1766; son of Samuel and Rebecca (Lay)

(Raymond) Gager. He m. (2) 1 June 1731 MEHITABLE TAYLOR with whom he had William, Mary, Mehetable, and William. He m. (3) Lebanon, Conn., 31 May 1737 MARY ALLEN with whom he had Samuel. William is mentioned in his father Samuel's will written on 18 April 1738 and proved 1 July 1740.

William Gager graduated from Yale in 1721. He settled in the pastoral office for the North Society in Lebanon (Lebanon Crank, now Columbia) on 27 Jan. 1724/5 and resigned on 4 Sept. 1734 because "much dissatisfaction and uneasiness had recently arisen in his church respecting himself, by reason of several scandalous reports of his drinking to excess."

William Gager of Lebanon in his will dated 25 Nov. 1763, proved 4 Sept. 1766, named his wife Mary, only son William, daughter Sarah wife of Elijah Edgerton, grandchildren William and Elizabeth Tupper (their mother now deceased), and daughter Mary. The inventory taken 4 Feb. 1767 included land in Lebanon and Winchester. On 21 May 1771 the personal estate of William Gager Sr. was given to Mary Gager his widow and "The Remainder of the Personal Estate ... Distributed to William Gager ju^r Deceased Who was the Executor to the Last Will & Testament of William Gager Senr He having in his lifetime Delivered to John [Henry/Hovey?] and Mary his Wife the Whole of her part of the Personal Estate and Taken their Receipt for the Same...."

Children of William and Elizabeth (Whiting) Gager, b. Lebanon, Conn.:

  i   SARAH GAGER[6], b. 10 Oct. 1726, bp.172[?]
  ii SAMUEL GAGER, b. 18 April 1728; d. 15 Dec. 1728 in 8th mo.
  iii ELIZABETH GAGER, bp. 27 May 1729

References: *Bradford Desc* p. 62. Norwich CT VR 1:59(b. William). Lebanon CT VR 1:121(m.; b. ch.; d. Samuel; 3rd m.), 124(d. Elizabeth). Columbia (Lebanon Crank) Ch. Recs. 1:10(bp. Elizabeth), 17(d. Samuel, bp. Sarah); 5:332(d. Elizabeth). *Yale Grads* pp. 1:252. New London CT PR #2132(Samuel Gager). Windham CT PR #1580(William Gager). *Gager Fam* pp. 10, 16-7.

171. WILLIAM WHITING[5] (*Elizabeth Adams[4], Alice[3] Bradford, William[2-1]*), b. Windham, Conn., 22 Jan. 1704; d. Bozrah, Conn., 25 May 1787.

He m. (1) Norwich, Conn., 5 March 1724 **ANNA RAYMOND**, b. New London, Conn., 1701 (or New Shoreham [Block Island] 1695 - *Raymond Gen*); d. Norwich, Conn., 26 Nov. 1773; dau. Joshua and Mercy (Sands) Raymond.

He m. (2) Norwich, Conn., 8 March 1774 **ALATHEA (SMITH) WOODWORTH**, b. 1714; prob. d. before 11 April 1791 when administration was granted on first wife's estate; perhaps daughter of Nehemiah and

Dorothy (Wheeler) Smith. She m. (1) Groton, Conn., 2 Oct. 1733 STEPHEN WOODWORTH.

William Whiting was at the Siege of Louisburg under Sir William Johnson.

On 27 Nov. 1751 William Whiting of Norwich, John Whiting of Stonington, Samuel Whiting of Hartford, Nathan Whiting of New Haven, and Ann Fitch of Lebanon together with the rest of the heirs of Eliphalet Whiting late of Windham, sold to John Abbe of Windham one acre of land, the deed signed also by David and Mary Wooster and Timothy and Tempe Pitkin.

On 18 April 1774 William Whiting of Norwich sold to his son Caleb Whiting of Norwich 26 acres, part of the farm where William lately dwelt. On 21 Feb. 1786 William sold to Caleb another 26 acres.

On 3 March 1789 Caleb Whiting of Bozrah was granted administration on the estate of William Whiting late of Bozrah. The inventory taken on 1 April 1789 included "a right or ½ right" in the Susquehannah Purchase.

On 11 April 1791 Caleb Whiting of Bozrah was granted administration on the estate of Anna Whiting late of Norwich (administration on Anna's estate may have had to wait until after the death of his second wife to clear title). The distribution on 17 May 1792 was to eldest son Caleb Whiting, daughter Mrs. Anne Dyar, and son William Whiting.

Children of William and Anna (Raymond) Whiting, b. Norwich, Conn.:

 i JOHN WHITING[6], b. 5 Aug. 1725; killed by Indians at Siege of Louisburg

 ii SAMUEL WHITING, b. 3 May 1727; apparently d. by 17 May 1792 dist.

 iii WILLIAM WHITING, b. 3 Aug. 1728; d. 6 Oct. 1728

 iv CALEB WHITING, b. 11 July 1729

 v WILLIAM WHITING, b. 17 April 1731

 vi ANNE WHITING, b. 16 Nov. 1732

References: *Bradford Desc* pp. 62-3. *DAR Patriot Index* p. 738. Bozrah CT VR 1:5(d. William). *Norwich CT VR* 1:103 (m.; b. ch.), 104(2nd m., d. Anna). Norwich CT PR #11450 (William Whiting); #11427 (Anna Whiting). *Raymond Gen* pp. 34-7. *Woodworth Gen* 1:42-3(d. John). Norwich CT LR 22:236; 26:98(William Whiting). Windham CT LR L:332(William Whiting *et al.*).

172. JOHN WHITING[5] (*Elizabeth Adams[4], Alice[3] Bradford, William[2-1]*), b. Windham, Conn., 20 Feb. 1705/6; d. there 28 March 1786 in 81st y.

He m. (1) Stonington, Conn., 3 Dec. 1729 **PHEBE (GREENMAN) HALLAM**, b. Stonington 29 Jan. 1691/2; d. Newport, R.I.,1 May 1763 in 76th yr; daughter of Edward and Margaret (Garthrot) Greenman. She m. (1)

Stonington 18 Dec. 1716 AMOS HALLAM with whom she had John, Phebe, and Prudence.

He m. (2) probably in early 1768 **MARY (TRACY) CLARK.**

John Whiting graduated from Yale in 1726. "He undertook to preach, soon after graduation, without being regularly licensed; and the Windham County Association of ministers summoned him ... for discipline ... having acknowledged his fault, and passed a satisfactory examination, he was formerly licensed ... however [he soon] left the ministry ... On the outbreak of the French War (1755) he entered service ... was made a Captain, and participated in several campaigns. At the battle of Lake George (July 1758), he was slightly wounded. In 1759 he was promoted to the rank of Major; in 1760, to that of Lieutenant Colonel; and in 1761, to that of Colonel." In 1775 he was appointed Judge of the Windham Probate District.

On 1 March 1729/30 Phebe Whiting was admitted a member of the First Church in Stonington and on 8 March John was admitted from the First Church of Windham.

On 21 May 1747 Nathan Whiting of New Haven sold to John Whiting of Stonington all his right in the estate of his father John Whiting late of Windham.

On 27 Nov. 1751 William Whiting of Norwich, John Whiting of Stonington, Samuel Whiting of Hartford, Nathan Whiting of New Haven, and Ann Fitch of Lebanon together with the remaining heirs of Eliphalet Whiting late of Windham, sold to John Abbe of Windham one acre of land, this deed also signed by David and Mary Wooster and Timothy and Tempe Pitkin.

Children of John and Phebe (Greenman) (Hallam) Whiting, b. Stonington, Conn., bp. First Church:

> i   AMOS WHITING[6], b. 1 Jan. 1730/1, bp. 3 Jan. 1730/1
>
> ii WEALTHEAN WHITING, b. 13 Aug. 1733, bp. 30 Sept. 1733
>
> iii MARY WHITING, b. 13 Aug. 1735, bp. 17 Aug. 1735.

References: *Bradford Desc* p. 63. *Stonington CT Hist* pp. 405, 412. Stonington CT VR 2:60(b. Phebe); 3:3(m.; b. ch.). *Greenman Fam* p. 5. *Harvard Grads* 1:341-2. Windham CT LR I:163(Nathan Whiting); L:332(William Whiting *et al.*). Stonington 1st Ch. Recs. 2:6(admitted ch.), 44(bp. Amos), 45(bp. Wealthean, Mary).

173. SYBIL WHITING⁵ (*Elizabeth Adams⁴, Alice³ Bradford, William²⁻¹*), b. Windham, Conn., 6 May 1708; d. there 7 Aug. 1755 aged 47y.

She m. Windham, Conn., 15 Jan. 1725 **JOHN BACKUS**, b. Windham, Conn., Jan. 1698; d. June 1769; son of John and Mary (Bingham) Backus. On 31 Oct. 1739 John Backus Sr. of Windham gave to his son John Backus Jr. of Windham several lots of land.

On 17 Sept. 1742 Samuel Whiting of Milford, Conn., sold to John Backus Jr. of Windham 3¼ acres.

On 30 May 1751 John Backus of Windham gave to his son John Backus of Stratford land in Windham. On 31 Jan. 1752 John sold to Ebenezer Backus of Norwich the land and dwelling house in Windham "where I formerly lived." On 7 July 1758 John gave his son Silvanus Backus of Windham 14 acres and on 8 Aug. 1758 he gave Silvanus another 9 or 10 acres. On 11 June 1767 John sold to Whiting Backus of Windham 25 acres which had been laid out to his father John Backus in May 1724. And on 2 Nov. 1768 John gave to his son Whiting two lots of 12 and 15 acres.

Inventories of the estate of John Backus of Windham were taken in May and June 1770. Ebenezer Backus was the administrator. Among the purchasers of estate sold to pay off debts were Whiting Backus who bought an old hat and Ebenezer Backus who bought 8 acres of cedar swamp.

Children of John and Sybil (Whiting) Backus, b. Windham, Conn., bp. Congregational Church there.:

    i   NATHANIEL BACKUS⁶, b. 5 Feb. 1726/7; d. 29 Nov. 1727 ae 1y 10m

    ii   JOHN BACKUS, b. 23 March 1728, bp. 24 March 1728

    iii SYBIL BACKUS, b. 1 March 1729/30, bp. 1 March 1730

    iv ELIZABETH BACKUS, b. 17 Feb. 1731/2, bp. 20 Feb. 1732; d. 21 Oct. 1747

    v   LUCRETIA BACKUS, b. 22 Feb. 1733/4, bp. 24 March 1734

    vi LYDIA BACKUS, b. 15 July 1736, bp. 18 July 1736

    vii SYLVANUS BACKUS, b. 5 April 1738, bp. 16 July 1738

    viii EBENEZER BACKUS, b. 31 May 1740, bp. 27 July 1740

    ix MARY BACKUS, b. 5 May 1742; d. 28 May 1744 ae 2y

    x   DELUCENA BACKUS (son), b. 2 Oct. 1744

    xi WHITING BACKUS, b. 28 Dec. 1747

    xii CHARLES BACKUS, b. 15 Aug. 1753; d. 7 Sept. 1776

References: *Bradford Desc* p. 63. Windham CT VR A:2(b. John); 1:72(m.; d. Sybil; b. 1ˢᵗ 5 ch.), 158(b. next 6 ch.), 159(b. Charles). Hale Cem Coll:Windham p. 263(d. Sybil, Nathaniel, Mary). Windham CT LR H:8(John Backus Sr.), 147(Samuel Whiting); K:6, 64;

L:137, 141; N:338; O:67(John Backus). Windham Cong. Ch. pp. 11(bp. John), 13(bp. Sybil), 15(bp. Elizabeth), 17(bp. Lucretia), 20(bp. Lydia), 21(bp. Sylvanus). Trumbull Cong. Ch. 1:174(bp. Ebenezer). Windham CT PR #153(John Backus).

174. MARY WHITING[5] (*Elizabeth Adams*[4], *Alice*[3] *Bradford, William*[2-1]), b. Windham, Conn., 24 Nov. 1712; d. there 9 Aug. 1736 in 24th yr.

She m. Windham, Conn., 23 Nov. 1727 Rev. **THOMAS CLAPP**, b. Scituate 20 June 1703; d. New Haven, Conn., 7 Jan. 1767 in 64th yr.; son of Stephen and Temperance (Gorham) Clapp, a descendant of Pilgrim **John Howland.** He m. (2) New Haven 5 Feb. 1740/1 MARY (HAYNES) (LORD) SALTONSTALL.

Thomas Clapp graduated from Harvard in 1728 and was President of Yale from 1741 to 1766.

Rev. Thomas Clapp had his negro Tamar baptized on 3 April 1737 and his negro child Sylan baptized 23 Sept. 1738.

On 10 Dec. 1739 Thomas Clapp was dismissed from the Windham Congregational Church, and he was installed as rector at Yale on 2 April 1740.

On 15 May 1741 Thomas Clapp of New Haven, Clerk, sold to Stephen White of Windham, Clerk, 36 acres reserving to Mrs. Elizabeth Niles of "Brantry," late the relict of Rev. Mr. Samuel Whiting of Windham, the use and improvement of part of the house.

On 2 March 1747 Thomas Clap of New Haven, Samuel Whiting of Stratford, and Nathan Whiting of New Haven, sold to Eleazer Fitch of Windham land with a dwelling house "lately belonging to our brother Eliphalet Whiting."

No Connecticut probate records have been found for Thomas Clapp.

Children of Thomas and Mary (Whiting) Clapp, b. Windham, Conn., bp. Congregational Church there:

    i   MARY CLAPP[6], b. 21 April 1729, bp. 27 April 1729

    ii TEMPERANCE CLAPP, b. 26 April 1731, bp. 2 May 1731; d. Enfield, Conn., 3 June 1731

   iii TEMPERANCE CLAPP, b. 29 April 1732, bp. 30 Feb. 1732

   iv ANNE CLAPP, b. 13 May 1734, bp. 19 May 1734; d. April 1735

    v [CHILD] CLAPP, b. and d. 25 July 1736

References: *Bradford Desc* p. 64. *Clapp Fam In Amer* by E. Clapp 1876. *New Haven Fams* p. 403. *VR Scituate* 1:75(b. Thomas). Windham CT VR 1:88(m.; b. ch.; d. Mary). New Haven CT VR 1:631(2nd m.). Windham CT LR H:89(Thomas Clapp); I:59(Thomas Clap *et al.*). Windham Cong. Ch. Recs. pp. 12(bp. Mary), 14(bp. 1st Temperance), 15(bp. 2nd Temperance), 17(bp. Anne), 20(bp. Tamar), 21(bp. Sylan), 26(dis. Thomas, d. Mary).

175. SAMUEL WHITING[5] (*Elizabeth Adams*[4], *Alice*[3] *Bradford, William*[2-1]), b. Windham, Conn., 15 March 1720; d. Stratford, Conn., 15 Feb. 1803 aged 82 called "Col."

He m. 1743 **ELIZABETH JUDSON**, b. Stratford, Conn., in 1723; d. there 5 Dec. 1793 aged 70; daughter of Daniel Judson.

On 17 Sept. 1742 Samuel Whiting of Milford, Conn., sold to John Backus Jr. of Windham 3¼ acres.

On 2 March 1747 Thomas Clap of New Haven, Samuel Whiting of Stratford, and Nathan Whiting of New Haven, sold to Eleazer Fitch of Windham land and a dwelling house "lately belonging to our brother Eliphalet Whiting."

On 27 Nov. 1751 William Whiting of Norwich, John Whiting of Stonington, Samuel Whiting of Hartford, Nathan Whiting of New Haven, and Ann Fitch of Lebanon together with the rest of the heirs of Eliphalet Whiting late of Windham, sold to John Abbe of Windham one acre of land, the deed signed also by David and Mary Wooster and Timothy and Tempe Pitkin.

On 25 April 1794 the name of Samuel Whiting, a soldier on the Connecticut line, appeared on a list of applicants for invalid pension. He was of Stratford, Conn.

Samuel Whiting's household in Stratford in 1790 consisted of two men, one boy under 16, and one female.

Children of Samuel and Elizabeth (Judson) Whiting, b. Stratford, Conn.:

    i SAMUEL WHITING[6], b. March 1744

    ii JUDSON WHITING, bp. March 1746; d. 16 Jan. 1777 as a prisoner. He served as a ensign in Capt. Elijah Abel's company, Col. Philip Burr Bradley's regiment which was taken prisoner at Ft. Washington 16 Nov. 1776.

   iii JOHN WHITING, bp. Nov. 1748

   iv ELIZABETH WHITING, bp. Nov. 1751

    v JOSEPH WHITING, bp. April 1754

   vi SARAH WHITING, bp. Sept. 1756

  vii MARTHA WHITING, b. 19 Aug. 1759

 viii MARY WHITING, b. 1760

   ix DAVID WHITING, bp. Mary 1762

    x WILLIAM NATHAN WHITING, bp. Sept. 1764

   xi SEYMOUR CONWAY WHITING, bp. July 1766; d. 26 July 1841 ae 71

References: *Bradford Desc* p. 64. *Stratford CT Hist* p. 1345. Wallingford CT VR V-1:86(d. Samuel). Windham CT LR H:147(Samuel Whiting); I:59(Thomas Clap *et al.*); L:332(William Whiting *et al.*). Hale Cem Coll:Stratford 497(d. Samuel, Elizabeth, Seymour). *Rev War Pensions* 3:3807(Samuel Whiting). *CT Men Rev War* p. 414(Judson Whiting).

176. NATHAN WHITING[5] (*Elizabeth Adams*[4], *Alice*[3] *Bradford, William*[2-1]), b. Windham, Conn., 4 May 1724; d. New Haven, Conn., 9 April 1771 aged 49.

He m. New Haven, Conn., 12 July 1750 **MARY SALTONSTALL**, d. after 23 Nov. 1784 (dist.); daughter of Roswell and Mary (Haynes) Saltonstall. She m. (2) Rev. WARHAM WILLIAMS.

Nathan Whiting graduated from Yale in 1743.

In 1745 Nathan, as an Ensign, accompanied the Connecticut troops in the Louisburg Expedition.

> [In] this service he so distinguished himself, that at the end of the campaign, a lieutenancy in the British army was given him by Sir William Pepperrell ... the French war began in 1755; and he was appointed ... Lieutenant-Colonel of the 2d Connecticut Regiment. He assisted in garrisoning Fort Edward; and on September 8, was with Colonel Ephraim Williams in the detachment sent against Baron Dieskau. On the fall of the Williams, the command devolved on Lieutenant Colonel Whiting, who conducted the retreat of the corps with a skill and coolness which did him high credit. When the next expedition was sent out, in 1756, he was promoted to a Colonelcy. He continued in the service throughout the war, and was esteemed by both British and Americans an officer of uncommon merit.

On 2 March 1747 Thomas Clap of New Haven, Samuel Whiting of Stratford, and Nathan Whiting of New Haven, sold to Eleazer Fitch of Windham land and dwelling house "lately belonging to our brother Eliphalet Whiting." On 21 May 1747 Nathan Whiting of New Haven sold to John Whiting of Stonington all his right in the estate of his father John Whiting late of Windham.

On 27 Nov. 1751 William Whiting of Norwich, John Whiting of Stonington, Samuel Whiting of Hartford, Nathan Whiting of New Haven, and Ann Fitch of Lebanon together with the rest of the heirs of Eliphalet Whiting late of Windham, sold to John Abbe of Windham one acre of land, the deed signed also by David and Mary Wooster and Timothy and Tempe Pitkin.

On 6 May 1771 Mary Whiting and Jonathan Fitch of New Haven were granted administration on the estate of Nathan Whiting late of New Haven. On 23 Nov. 1784 distribution was made to his widow, Nathan H. Whiting, Polly Hale, Gurding Whiting, and Samuel Whiting. The distribution included land in Whitingham, Vt.

Children of Nathan and Mary (Saltonstall) Whiting, b. New Haven, Conn.:

   i   MARY WHITING[6], b. 6 Jan. 1751; d. 27 Feb. 1752 ae 9m

  ii   ELIPHALET WHITING, b. 17 June 1753; d. 11 Sept. 1753[prob. 1758] ae 3y

 iii   [DAUGHTER] WHITING, b. 14 Oct. 1754; d. 26 Oct. 1754

 iv   [SON] WHITING, b. 27 Dec. 1756; d. 28 Dec. 1756

  v   NATHAN HAINS WHITING, b. 6 Nov. 1759

 vi   ELIZABETH MARY WHITING, b. 21 July 1761; d. 14 Oct. 1761

 vii MARY (or POLLY) WHITING, b. 14 Oct. 1763

viii GURDON SALTONSTALL WHITING, b. 10 Sept. 1766

 ix SAMUEL WHITING, b. 22 Feb. 1768

References: *Bradford Desc* p. 65. *New Haven Fams* p. 1971. New Haven CT VR 1:702(b. 1st Mary), 813(b. Eliphalet); 2:68(b. Nathan), 90(b. Gurdon), 99(b. Sybil), 107(b. Elizabeth, 158(m.), 207(b. dau., son), 235(d. dau., son). *Yale Grads* 1:750-1. New Haven CT PR #11395(Nathan Whiting). Windham CT LR I:59(Thomas Clap *et al.*), 163(Nathan Whiting); L:332(William Whiting *et al.*). Hale Cem Coll:New Haven 389(d. Nathan), 413(d. dau. Mary), 414(d. Eliphalet).

177. ANN COLLINS[5] (*Alice Adams[4], Alice[3] Bradford, William[2-1]*), b. Enfield, Conn., 20 Dec. 1702; d. there 10/18 Sept. 1778.

She m. Enfield, Conn., 13 Sept. 1723 **EPHRAIM TERRY**, b. Enfield 24 Oct. 1701; d. there 14 Oct. 1783; son of Samuel and Martha (Boardman) Terry. His gravestone calls him "Esq." and has a Rev. War marker.

On 4 Aug. 1760 Ephraim Terry of Enfield, Conn., sold to Ephraim Terry Jr. and Elijah Terry of Enfield, Conn., 186 acres.

On 21 Feb. 1763 Ephraim Terry of Enfield, Conn., sold to Elijah Terry of Enfield a houselot formerly owned by the Rev. Nathaniel Collins deceased.

On 30 Nov. 1770 Ephraim Terry and Nathaniel Terry of Enfield sold to Samuel Terry of Enfield 14¼ acres. On 27 Sept. 1773 Ephraim Terry of Enfield sold to six acres of his home lot to Nathaniel Terry of Enfield.

The will of Ephraim Terry of Enfield, Conn., dated 18 Aug. 1772, proved 6 Oct. 1787, names his wife Ann; sons Eliphalet, Samuel, Ephraim, and Elijah;

daughters Mary Pease, Lucy Barrett, and Sibbel Chapin; children of deceased daughter Ann Kellogg; and son Nathaniel.

Children of Ephraim and Ann (Collins) Terry, b. Enfield, Conn.:

   i   MARY TERRY[6], b. 1 Jan. 1723/4

   ii   SAMUEL TERRY, b. 18 Oct. 1725

   iii   EPHRAIM TERRY, b. 3 May 1728

   iv   NATHANIEL TERRY, b. 3 June 1730

   v   ANN TERRY, b. 17 Aug. 1732

   vi   LUCY TERRY, b. 22 June 1734

   vii   ELIJAH TERRY, b. [4] Aug. 1736

   viii   ALICE TERRY, b. 29 Aug. 1738; d. 10 Sept. 1743 ae 5y 12d

   ix   SYBIL TERRY, b. 8 Aug. 1740

   x   ELIPHALET TERRY, b. 24 Dec. 1742

   xi   ELIZABETH TERRY (not in will, Aspinwall, or *Enfield CT Hist*)

References: *Bradford Desc* p. 56. *Terry Fam* pp. 10, 16-8. *Enfield CT Hist* 1:38; 2:1590-1, 1606(b. Mary), 1609(b. Samuel), 1611(b. Ephraim), 1613(b. Nathaniel), 1616(b. Ann), 1619(b. Lucy), 1627(b. Elijah, Alice, Sybil, Eliphalet), 1768, 1869(d. Alice); 3:2243, 2384-6. Enfield CT LR 3:11, 409; 4:80, 270(Ephraim Terry). East Windsor CT PR #3050(Ephraim Terry). Hale Cem Coll:Enfield p. 61(d. Ann, Ephraim, Alice).

178. JOHN COLLINS[5] (*Alice Adams[4], Alice[3] Bradford, William[2-1]*), b. Enfield, Conn., 7 Nov. 1704/5; d. on Cape Breton Nova Scotia expedition 26 March 1746.

He m. Enfield, Conn., 22 Aug. 1728 **MARY MEACHAM**, b. Enfield 19 July 1706; d. Somers, Conn., 21 May 1766; daughter of Isaac and Mary (Root) Meacham. She m. (2) Somers, Conn., 2 March 1747/8 JOSEPH SEXTON.

On 14 April 1738 Nathaniel Collins of Glastonbury, Conn., sold 3 acres to his son John Collins of Enfield, Conn.

On 16 March 1746 Mary Collins of Enfield gave her bond as administratrix on the estate of John Collins late of Enfield, deceased; the estate was insolvent. On 6 Oct. 1746 John Collins, son of John late of Enfield, Conn., deceased, chose his mother as his guardian. On 19 May 1748 Joseph Saxton of Somers, Conn., gave bond, his wife Mary being guardian to Giles and Ariel Collins, both under 14, heirs of John Collins.

Children of John and Mary (Meacham) Collins, b. Enfield, Conn.:

   i   JOHN COLLINS[6], b. 9 March 1729/30

    ii MARY COLLINS, b. 22 Nov. 1732; d. 29 Dec. 1732

   iii GILES COLLINS, b. 3 Dec. 1734

   iv ARIEL COLLINS, b. 9 June 1737

    v ISAAC COLLINS, b. 21 Aug. 1741; d.y.

   vi AMBROSE COLLINS, b. 23 Dec. 1743; d.y.

  vii ELIJAH COLLINS, b. 12 June 1746; d. 27 Aug. 1747

References: *Bradford Desc* p. 65. *Enfield CT Hist* 2:1613(b. son John), 1617(b. Mary), 1629(b. Giles, Ariel, Isaac, Ambrose, Elijah), 1871(d. John, Elijah); 3:2221(John Collins' PR). *Harvard Grads* 5:345-9. Hampshire Co. PR Box 35 #22(John Collins). Somers CT VR 1:15(2nd m.), 55(d. Mary). Glastonbury CT LR 6:25(Nathaniel Collins).

179. NATHANIEL COLLINS⁵ (*Alice Adams⁴, Alice³ Bradford, William²⁻¹*), b. Enfield, Conn., 17 Aug. 1709; d. there 5 Dec. 1785 or 1787 in 79th yr.

He m. Enfield 17 July 1735 **ABIGAIL PEASE**, b. Enfield 7 June 1708; d. there 1 May 1792; daughter of James and Hannah (Hamm) Pease.

On 12 Feb. 1733/4 Nathaniel Collins of Enfield, clerk, sold to Nathaniel Collins Jr. of Enfield, husbandman, 60 acres reserving the use and improvement of this land during the natural lives of Nathaniel and his wife Alice.

Children of Nathaniel and Abigail (Pease) Collins, b. Enfield, Conn.:

     i ELIPHALET COLLINS⁶, b. 29 Oct. 1735; d. 20 Sept. 1737

    ii NATHANIEL COLLINS, b. 5 Aug. 1737; d. 11 May 1748

   iii ABIGAIL COLLINS, b. 15 March 1739

   iv ALICE COLLINS, b. 3 Dec. 1741

    v JERUSHA COLLINS, b. 5 Jan. 1742/3; d. 31 Oct. 1743

   vi ELIPHALET COLLINS, b. 11 July 1744

  vii JERUSHA COLLINS, b. 5 Feb. 1746/7

  viii MARY COLLINS, b. 3 Oct. 1748

   ix JOHN COLLINS [not in Aspinwall or *Enfield CT Hist*]

References: *Bradford Desc* pp. 65-6. *Enfield CT Hist* 2:1620(b. Eliphalet), 1629(b. Nathaniel, Abigail, Alice, Jerusha), 1630(b. 2nd Eliphalet, 2nd Jerusha, Mary), 1771(m.), 1868, 1871(d. Nathaniel, Jerusha), 1878. Enfield CT LR G:379(Nathaniel Collins).

180. WILLIAM COLLINS[5] (*Alice Adams*[4], *Alice*[3] *Bradford*, *William*[2-1]), b. Enfield, Conn., 24 June 1711; d. Somers, Conn., 5 May 1804 aged 93. His gravestone calls him "Deacon."

He m. Enfield 3 May 1734 **ANNE JONES**, b. Enfield 9 Sept. 1714; d. Somers 22 Sept. 1808 aged 94; daughter of Benjamin and Anne (____) Jones.

William Collins and his wife were admitted to full communion in the Somers Church on 13 July 1735.

William Collins served in the Revolutionary War in Capt. Samuel Chandler's company, Major General Phinehas Lyman's regiment from 20 March to 1 Dec. 1756.

On 23 May 1812 Jabez Collins of Somers gave to his son Oliver Collins of Somers land that his father William Collins had deeded to him.

Children of William and Anne (Jones) Collins, b. or bp. Somers, Conn.:

  i ANNE COLLINS[6], b. 16 March 1735, bp. 1st Ch. Somers 13 July 1735

  ii WILLIAM COLLINS, bp. 1 May 1737 1st Ch. Somers; d. 13 Dec. 1756

  iii LEVI COLLINS, b. 9 Aug. 1739

  iv ABI COLLINS, b. 21 May 1742, bp. 1st Ch. Somers 23 May 1742

  v JABEZ COLLINS, b. 3 Dec. 1744, bp. 1st Ch. Somers 9 Dec 1744

  vi JOSEPH COLLINS, b. 25 Dec. 1747

  vii JOHN COLLINS, b. 14 Sept. 1749

References: *Bradford Desc* p. 66. *Enfield CT Hist* 2:1599(b. Anne), 3:2180(bp. dau. Anne), 2181(bp. William), 2183(bp. Abi), 2184(bp. Jabez), 2188(admitted), 2194(m., b. Anne), 2205(b. Abi), 2208(b. Joseph), 2212(b. John), 2458(d. William, Anne), 2636(Rev. War service). Hale Cem Coll:Somers p. 7(d. William, Anne). Somers CT LR G:182(Jabez Collins).

181. EDWARD COLLINS[5] (*Alice Adams*[4], *Alice*[3] *Bradford*, *William*[2-1]), b. Enfield, Conn., 16 Nov. 1713; d. there 10 Oct. 1796.

He m. (1) Enfield 19 Feb. 1735/6 **TABITHA GEER**, b. Enfield 21 July 1712; d. there 30 Aug. 1746; daughter of Shubal and Sarah (Abbe) Geer.

He m. (2) Enfield 26 March 1747 **REBECCA HALE**, b. Enfield 1727; d. there 1 Aug. 1786 in 59th yr. "wife of Edward Esq."; daughter of John and Susannah (Risley) (Colt) Hale.

On 10 March 1735 Nathaniel Collins of Enfield sold to Edward Collins 18 acres; this deed was not recorded until 20 May 1751.

The household of Edward Collins Esq. in 1790 in Enfield consisted of one man and one female. Listed next to him was Nathaniel Collins with one man, one boy under 16, and 3 females.

On 15 July 1794 Edward Collins of Enfield sold to Nathaniel Collins of Enfield four acres.

Edward Collins in his will dated 3 Sept. 1796, proved 26 Feb. 1798, named his children John, Ebenezer, Nathaniel, Tabitha Ware, Rebecca Ellsworth, and Martha Bliss, and his grandson Edward Collins. He named John as his executor and bequeathed to him what was left of the estate after debts were paid since he had given his other children their portions and "therefore I Do Not give them any thing." His inventory taken 7 Nov. 1809 included an old mare, a colt, and just a few personal items.

Children of Edward and Tabitha (Geer) Collins, b. Enfield, Conn.:

    i   EDWARD COLLINS[6], b. 4 Jan. 1736/7; d. 4 Oct. 1743

   ii   ELISHA COLLINS, b. 17 Jan. 1738/9; d.y.

  iii   EBENEZER COLLINS, b. 17 April 1741

  iv   TABITHA COLLINS, b. 23 June 1743; d. 7 Aug. 1749

   v   ELIHU COLLINS d. 4 Oct. 1743 (not named in will)

  vi   stillborn child 30 Aug. 1746

Children of Edward and Rebecca (Hale) Collins, bp. Enfield, Conn.:

  vii   EDWARD COLLINS, b. 21 Feb. 1747/8; d. 8 Aug. 1749

 viii   TABITHA COLLINS, b. 30 May 1750

   ix   EDWARD COLLINS, b. 10 April 1752 (not named in will)

   x   EDWARD COLLINS, b. 1 July 1753 (not named in will)

  xi   REBECCA COLLINS, b. 22 March 1755

  xii   ALICE COLLINS, b. 16 Feb. 1757 (not named in will)

 xiii   MARTHA COLLINS, b. 28 Aug. 1759

 xiv   JOHN COLLINS, b. 12 Oct. 1761

  xv   SUSANNA COLLINS, b. 15 Sept. 1763

 xvi   NATHANIEL COLLINS, b. 5 Nov. 1766

References: *Bradford Desc* p. 66. *Enfield CT Hist* 2:1629(b. Elisha, Ebenezer, 1st Tabitha, 2nd Edward), 1630(b. 2nd Tabitha), 1665(b. 3rd Edward, 4th Edward, Rebecca, Alice), 1666(b. Martha, John, Susanna, Nathaniel), 1867(d. dau. Tabitha, 2nd son Edward), 1870(d. Tabitha, son Edward, Elihu, child), 1877(Rebecca), 1879(d. Edward); 3:2249(Edward's PR), 2329(d. Rebecca). *Hale House* p. 236. Hale Cem Coll:Enfield p. 37(d. Rebecca). Enfield CT LR 3:309(Nathaniel Collins); 6:127(Edward Collins).

182. ALICE COLLINS⁵ (*Alice Adams⁴, Alice³ Bradford, William²⁻¹*), b. Enfield, Conn., 14 March 1716; d. after 8 Nov. 1757.

She m. Enfield 15 Jan. 1735/6 **NATHANIEL PARSONS**, b. Enfield 15 March 1709/10; d. after 27 March 1781; son of Philip and Anna (_____) Parsons.

On 22 Nov. 1761 Nathaniel Parsons of Enfield, Conn., leased a farm of 30 acres lately belonging to his father Philip Parsons to his father for his use during his natural life.

On 30 Oct. 1765 Nathaniel Parsons of Enfield sold to 18 acres to Nathaniel Parsons Jr. of Enfield. On 6 Jan. 1767 he sold to Nathaniel Jr. another 8 acres.

On 17 March 1780 Nathaniel Parsons of Enfield sold to Ebenezer Parsons of Enfield part of his home lot. On the same day he sold to his son Shubael Parsons of Enfield his home lot with buildings reserving a room and half an acre to himself and the two acres conveyed to his son Ebenezer. On 27 March 1781 he sold to Shubael another 35 acres.

Children of Nathaniel and Alice (Collins) Parsons, b. Enfield, Conn.:

  i   NATHANIEL PARSONS⁶, b. 30 April 1736
  ii ALICE PARSONS, b. 10 June 1738
  iii ZERVIAH PARSONS, b. 8 Oct. 1740
  iv ASA PARSONS, b. 4 Feb. 1742/3
  v   EDWARD PARSONS, b. 25 April 1745
  vi EBENEZER PARSONS, b. 19 April 1748
  vii WILLIAM PARSONS, b. 13 March 1750
  viii SHUBAL PARSONS, b. ca. 1752 (d. 14 Oct. 1819, ae 67y)
  ix LUCIA PARSONS, b. 14 June 1755

Note: There is a Nathaniel Parsons who d. Somers, Conn., 29 Oct. 1792 in 90th year (Somers VR 1:110). That does not appear to be the above.

References: *Bradford Desc* pp. 66-7. *Enfield CT Hist* 2:1622(b. Nathaniel, Alice), 1623(b. Asa), 1654(b. Edward, Ebenezer, William), 1665(b. Lucia), 1885(d. Shubal); 3:2371. Enfield CT LR 3:151, 303, 387; 4:319, 327, 484(Nathaniel Parsons).

183. ABIEL METCALF⁵ (*Abiel Adams⁴, Alice³ Bradford, William²⁻¹*), b. Falmouth 15 Nov. 1709 (twin); d. Greenbush N.Y., before 2 Feb. 1778 (deed).

She m. Lebanon, Conn., 22 Nov. 1733 **JAMES FITCH**, b. Lebanon 15 Oct. 1709; d. Salisbury, Conn.,15 Nov. 1760; son of Nathaniel and Anne (Abel) Fitch. He m. (1) ANNE _____, with whom he had Ann and Elizabeth.

On 30 Jan. 1761 Abiel Fitch and John Hutchinson gave their bond as administrators on the estate of James Fitch late of Greenbush, and in June 1742 dower was set off to the widow.

On 2 Feb. 1778 William Fitch of Pollet [Paulet] in the State of Vermont; Robert Woodworth and Rachel, his wife, Joseph Fitch, and Nathaniel Fitch all of Greenbush, N.Y.; and Moses Marsh of Canaan, Conn., sold to Elias Herrick land in Salisbury, part of the estate of their mother Abiel Fitch, late of Greenbush, deceased.

Children of James and Abiel (Metcalf) Fitch, first, b. Lebanon, Conn.; rest, b. Salisbury, Conn.:

>   i   WILLIAM FITCH[6], b. 18 Sept. 1734
>   ii   RACHEL FITCH, b. 7 July 1736
>   iii   JABEZ FITCH, b. 11 Aug. 1738
>   iv   SYBIL FITCH, b. 13 Sept. 1743
>   v   JOHN FITCH, b. 17 March 1745
>   vi   JAMES FITCH, b. 18 Nov. 1747; d. Nov. 1776 (Bible rec. in *NYGBR*)
>   vii   JOSEPH FITCH, b. 17 Oct. 1749
> viii   NATHANIEL FITCH, b. 7 Aug. 1752

References: *Bradford Desc* p. 67. Sharon CT PR #1261(James Fitch). *Conn Marr* 2:40. Lebanon CT VR 1:101(b. James), 104(b. William). Salisbury CT VR 1:199(b. all ch. exc. Wm.). *NYGBR* 64:34-7(family rec.; deed).

184.   ALICE METCALF[5] (*Abiel Adams[4], Alice[3] Bradford, William[2-1]*), b. Falmouth 2 May 1712; d. Lebanon, Conn., 22 Oct. 1740 aged 28y.

She m. Lebanon 30 June 1736 **JOHN WILLIAMS**, b. Roxbury, Conn., 6 June 1706; d. Sharon, Conn., 14 March 1774 as "Colonel" in his 68th yr.; son of Parke and Priscilla (Payson) Williams. He m. (2) Lebanon 24 Aug. 1741 MARGARET METCALF. On 8 Oct. 1734 and 10 April 1742 Park Williams of Lebanon sold to his son John Williams more than 60 acres.

John Williams graduated from Harvard in 1725.

Children of John and Alice (Metcalf) Williams, b. Lebanon, Conn.:

>   i   EUNICE WILLIAMS[6], b. 11 June 1737
>   ii   ALICE WILLIAMS, b. 25 May 1739

Note: *Harvard Grads* says that this Alice Metcalf m. William Metcalf (5:223); this is corrected in Vol. 8:230: William Metcalf m. Abigail Edwards.

References: *Bradford Desc* p. 67. *Conn Marr* 2:41. Lebanon CT VR 1:331(both m.; b. ch.; d. Alice). Sharon CT VR LR 7:297(d. John); 2:23(b. ch.). *Harvard Grads* 5:223. Hale Cem Coll:Lebanon p. 81(d. Alice). Lebanon CT LR 5:78; 6:330(Park Williams).

185.   HANNAH METCALF[5] (*Abiel Adams[4], Alice[3] Bradford, William[2-1]*), b. Falmouth 2 May 1712; living 26 June 1774.

She m. ca. 1736 **TIMOTHY METCALF**, b. probably Lebanon, Conn., ca. 1711 (he is listed in the VRs without a date); d. Mansfield, Conn., 10 March 1773 aged 62; son of Ebenezer and Hannah (Abell) Metcalf.

On 10 Sept. 1745 Ebenezer Metcalf of Lebanon sold to Timothy Metcalf of Mansfield part of the farm he had bought from Moses Rogers and on 8 Jan. 1750/1 Ebenezer gave Timothy the rest of the farm.

Timothy Metcalf was admitted as a member of the First Church of Lebanon on 29 July 1733 and he and his wife Hannah owned the covenant 16 Oct. 1737.

Distribution of the estate of Timothy Metcalf on 26 June 1774 names widow Hannah; daughter Abiel, eldest son Ezra, sons Ebenezer, Timothy and Jabez, and daughters Alice, Abigail, and Anne.

On 22 July 1793 Ebenezer Metcalf of Mansfield sold to Jonathan and Nathaniel Dunham of Mansfield part of the farm of his father Timothy Metcalf late of Mansfield. On 2 Sept. 1793 in three separate deeds Alice Metcalf, Anne Metcalf, and Hannah Metcalf sold to Jonathan and Nathaniel part of their father's estate. On 5 Sept. 1793 Alice Metcalf of Mansfield sold to Hannah Metcalf of Mansfield three pieces of land laid out to her in the division of her father's estate on provision that Hannah take care of Alice and pay her debts after death. On 8 April 1796 Ezra Metcalf and Timothy Metcalf of Mansfield sold more land to Nathaniel Dunham. On 7 Nov. 1807 Hannah Metcalf of Mansfield sold to Jabez Metcalf of Mansfield land bounded on Timothy, Ezra, and Ebenezer Metcalf. On 22 Jan. 1822 Hannah and Anna Metcalf of Mansfield sold to William Metcalf of Tolland a farm with house and barn from the distribution of the estate of "Dean Tmothy Metcalf to Ezra and Timothy Metcalf."

Children of Timothy and Hannah (Metcalf) Metcalf, first five b. Stafford, Conn., rest, b. Mansfield, Conn.:

   i   EZRA METCALF[6], b. 21 May 1737; bp. Lebanon 1st Ch. 16 Oct. 1737

ii ABRIEL METCALF, b. 1 Jan. 1739; an Abigal was bp. Lebanon 1st Ch. 15 April 1739

iii JOSEPH METCALF, b. 3 Jan. 1741

iv HANNAH METCALF, b. 21 Feb. 1743

v ALLIS METCALF, b. 13 Dec. 1744

vi ABIGAIL METCALF, b. 25 Nov. 1746

vii EBENEZER METCALF, b. 26 Jan. 1748/9

viii ANN METCALF (twin), b. 8 Jan. 1753

ix TIMOTHY METCALF (twin), b. 8 Jan. 1753

x JABEZ METCALF, b. 9 Jan. 1755

xi JOSEPH METCALF; d. 18 Oct. 1760

References: *Bradford Desc* p. 67. Windham CT PR #2725(Timothy Metcalf). Stafford CT VR 1:27(b. 1st 4 ch.), 30(b. Allis). Mansfield CT VR D:128(b. Abigail thru Jabez), 332(d. Joseph). Lebanon 1st Ch. Recs. 4:5(Timothy a member), 42(bp. Ezra), 43(bp. Abigail), 86(owned cov.). Hale Cem Coll:Mansfield p. 95(d. Timothy). Mansfield CT LR 4:369; 5:320(Ebenezer Metcalf), 12:213(Ebenezer Metcalf), 472(Alice Metcalf), 473(Anne Metcalf), 474(Hannah Metcalf); 14:67(Ezra & Timothy Metcalf), 257(Hannah Metcalf); 18:509(Alice Metcalf); 23:235(Hannah & Anna Metcalf).

186. MARY METCALF⁵ (*Abiel Adams⁴, Alice³ Bradford, William²⁻¹*), b. Falmouth 17 Dec. 1715; living 28 Jan. 1784, poss. living 1790.

She m. Lebanon, Conn., 1 July 1745 **DANIEL RUDD**, b. Norwich, Conn., 12 March 1710; living 26 July 1781; son of Nathaniel and Abigail (Hartshorn) Rudd.

The will of Daniel Rudd dated 26 July 1781, proved 2 Oct. 1781, names wife Mary; sons Daniel and Asher; and daughters Eunice, Lucy and Elizabeth. A 28 Jan. 1784 distribution of the estate names widow Mary Rudd, Daniel Rudd, Eunice Rudd, Lucy wife of Jesse Brown, Elizabeth Rudd, and Asher Rudd.

On 23 April 1782 Daniel, Eunice, Elizabeth, and Asher Rudd, all of Norwich, sold land formerly of their father Daniel Rudd to Jesse Brown of Norwich. On the same day Daniel, Eunice, Elizabeth, and Asher Rudd as well as Jesse Brown and his wife Lucy sold more land of their father Daniel.

She may be the Mary Rudd listed in 1790 at New London Co. with a household consisting of one man, 2 boys under 16, and 5 females.

Children of Daniel and Mary (Metcalf) Rudd, b. Norwich, Conn.:

  i ELIZABETH RUDD[6], b. 23 March 1745/6; d. 25 Aug. 1753
 ii EUNICE RUDD, b. 20 March 1747/8
iii LUCY RUDD, b. 2 Jan. 1750
 iv DANIEL RUDD, b. 18 Jan. 1753; d. 18 Feb. 1753
  v DANIEL RUDD, b. 10 June 1754
 vi ELIZABETH RUDD, b. 3 Sept. 1757
vii ASHER RUDD, b. 10 Oct. 1759

Note: *Harvard Grads* incorrectly says Mary m. John Reed or Rudd of Lebanon (5:223).

References: *Bradford Desc* p. 67-8. Norwich CT PR #9519; 7:111, 113, 287(Daniel Rudd). *Conn Marr* 2:43. Norwich CT VR 1:54; 2:11(m.; b.&d. ch.), 65(b. Daniel Sr.). Norwich CT LR 24:126; 26:143(Daniel Rudd *et al.*).

187. ELIZABETH METCALF[5] (*Abiel Adams[4], Alice[3] Bradford, William[2-1]*), b. Falmouth 6 March 1716/7; d. Salisbury, Conn., 22 Feb. 1762.

She m. Lebanon, Conn., 3 Sept. 1744 Rev. **JONATHAN LEE**, b. Coventry, Conn., 10 July 1718; d. Salisbury, Conn., 8 Oct. 1788 in 71st yr.; son of David and Lydia (Strong) Lee. He m. (2) Salisbury 22 Nov. 1762 LOVE (GRAHAM) BRINKERHOFF with whom he had Chauncey, Robert Walker, and Love.

Jonathan Lee graduated from Yale in 1742 and was licensed July 1743. On 3 Jan. 1744 he received a call from Salisbury and was ordained there on 3 Nov. *Yale Grads* says "Mr. Lee was an animated and popular preacher, and exerted an important influence in the Connecticut churches during his long ministry." He was one of the chaplains in the expedition against Crown Point in 1756.

On 13 Feb. 1785 Jonathan Lee of Salisbury gave to son Samuel Lee 85 acres in Salisbury. In 3 deeds dated 15 Aug. 1787 he gave land to sons Chauncey Lee, Mylo Lee, Jonathan and Elisha Lee, all of Salisbury.

The will of Jonathan Lee of Salisbury dated 3 March 1785, proved 18 Nov. 1788, names wife Love; sons Jonathan, Samuel, Elisha, Mylo, and Chauncey; daughters Elizabeth Allen, Rhoda Ensign, and Salome Hale; son Robert Walker Lee; and daughter Love Lee.

Children of Jonathan and Elizabeth (Metcalf) Lee, b. Salisbury, Conn.:

  i JONATHAN LEE[6], b. 26 Oct. 1745

ii   ELIZABETH LEE, b. 4 Sept. 1747

iii   SAMUEL LEE, b. 27 Sept. 1749

iv   CHLOE (or CLOA) LEE, b. 20 Sept. 1751; d. 26 Nov. 1752

v   RHODA LEE, b. 26 Feb. 1753

vi   SALOME LEE, b. 15 Dec. 1754

vii   ELISHA LEE, b. 13 Feb. 1757

viii   MYLO LEE, b. 27 June 1760

References: Coventry CT VR D:75(b. Jonathan). Salisbury CT VR 1:148(b. Elisha), 209(b. 1st 6 ch. & Mylo), 236(d. Chloe), 238(d. Elizabeth), 240(1st m.), 250(2nd m.); 2:50(d. Jonathan). *Lee Desc* pp. 402, 405-8. *Yale Grads* pp. 716-7. *NEHGR* 9:127-8. Town Hall Cemetery, Salisbury CT(d. Jonathan, Elizabeth). Salisbury CT LR 7:163(to Samuel), 300(to Chauncey), 388(to Mylo), 411(to Jonathan, Elisha). Sharon CT PR #2060(Jonathan Lee).

188. DELIGHT METCALF[5] (*Abiel Adams*[4], *Alice*[3] *Bradford, William*[2-1]), b. Falmouth 1 May 1719; d. before 1753 (birth of child Thomas to second wife).

She m. Mansfield, Conn., 7 June 1737 **THOMAS WARNER**, b. Windham, Conn., in April 1705; d. Ashford, Conn., between 11 Feb. 1756 and 15 Dec. 1756 (inv.); son of Andrew and Deborah (Leffingwell) Warner. He m. (2) 1753 ELIZABETH (RUST) LADD with whom he had Thomas and Elisha.

On 2 May 1742 Delight Warner wife of Thomas was admitted a member of the First Church of Mansfield.

On 21 April 1752 Thomas Warner of Ashford sold to Joseph Warner of Windham 95 acres in Ashford. On 12 Jan. 1758 Joseph sold this land "bought of my uncle Thomas Warner," excepting 30 acres, to Samuel Hutchinson Jr. of Windham.

An inventory of the estate of Thomas Warner was taken 15 Dec. 1756, and William Warner was appointed administrator 23 Dec. 1756. On 5 May 1760 the estate was divided between Eleazer Warner, eldest son, and Abigail, Sarah, Elas [*sic*], and Delight Warner.

On 30 Oct. 1765 Alice Warner of Ashford sold to her brother Eleazer Warner of Ashford six acres with a barn that had been set off to her from her father Thomas' estate and was bounded by the land of her sisters Abigail Warner and Delight Warner.

Children of Thomas and Delight (Metcalf) Warner, b. Mansfield, Conn., last three bp. First Church:

 i   ELEAZER WARNER[6], b. 8 Feb. 1737/8
 ii SARAH WARNER, b. 9 May 1740
 iii ALICE WARNER, b. 11 Aug. 1742
 iv ELIPHALET WARNER, b. 11 Feb. 1743/4, bp. 15 April 1744; d.y.
 v   ABIGAIL WARNER, bp. 21 Dec. 1746
 vi DELIGHT WARNER, b. Wellington, Conn., 9 June 1749, bp. 23 July 1749

References: *Bradford Desc* p. 68. *Warner Desc* pp. 127-8. *TAG* 46:44. Windham CT VR 1:40(b. Thomas). Mansfield CT VR D:190(b. Eleazer, Sarah, Eliphalet, Delight), 294(m.). Pomfret CT PR #4236, B:115, 503(Thomas Warner). Ashford CT LR H:107(Thomas Warner); J:210(Joseph Warner); L:116(Alice Warner). Mansfield 1st Ch. Recs. A:17(admitted ch.), 47(bp. Eliphalet), 69(bp. Abigail), 71(bp. Delight).

189. SARAH METCALF[5] (*Abiel Adams[4], Alice[3] Bradford, William[2-1]*), b. Falmouth 10 Feb. 1720/1; d. 1 June 1779 aged 61y 4m 4d.

She m. Lebanon, Conn., 13 Feb. 1747/8 **JOSEPH FOWLER**, b. Suffield, Conn., 5 Dec. 1722; d. East Haddam, Conn., 10 June 1771 in 49th yr.; son of Joseph and Hannah (____) Fowler.

Joseph Fowler graduated from Yale in 1743. He was minister of the East Haddam Church from 15 May 1751 until his death.

On 3 Dec. 1759 Joseph Fowler of Lebanon for love gave his nephew Joseph Fowler of East Haddam four acres.

The will of Rev. Joseph Fowler of East Haddam dated 20 May 1771, proved 2 July 1771, names wife Sarah; sons Joseph, Elisha, and William; and daughters Sarah and Electa.

On 17 April 1781 Joseph Fowler and Elisha Adams Fowler of East Haddam sold to Joshua Cove of East Haddam two pieces of land totaling 14¾ acres.

Children of Joseph and Sarah (Metcalf) Fowler, b. East Haddam, Conn., last six, bp. First Church::

 i   JOSEPH FOWLER[6], b. 31 Dec. 1748
 ii ELIZABETH FOWLER, b. 19 Jan. 1750; d. 12 Feb. 1750
 iii ELIZABETH FOWLER, b. 17 Oct. 1751, bp. 27 Oct. 1751; d. 19 Sept. 1762
 iv SARAH FOWLER, b. 11 Nov. 1753, bp. 18 Nov. 1753

   v ELISHA ADAMS FOWLER, b. 29 Sept. 1755, bp. 19 Oct. 1755

   vi WILLIAM FOWLER, b. 27 Dec. 1757, bp. 1 Jan. 1758; d. 16 July 1759

   vii WILLIAM FOWLER, b. 27 Sept. 1761, bp. 4 Oct. 1761

   viii ELECTA FOWLER, b. 7 July 1767, bp. 12 July 1767

References: *Bradford Desc* p. 68-9. *Fowler Hist*, Christine Fowler, 1950, p. 605. *Conn Marr* 2:43. East Haddam CT VR 2:37(d. Joseph). East Haddam CT LR 8:3(m.; b. ch.). Suffield CT VR NB1:47(b. Joseph). Colchester CT PR #1236 (Joseph Fowler). East Haddam Church records 2:324-5. East Haddam 1st Ch. Recs. 1:40(bp. Elizabeth), 41(bp. Sarah), 43(bp. Elisha), 44(bp. 1st William), 46(bp. 2nd William), 65(bp. Electa). East Haddam CT LR 5:73; 11:161(Joseph Fowler).

190. AZUBA METCALF[5] (*Abiel Adams*[4], *Alice*[3] *Bradford, William*[2-1]), b. Falmouth ca. 1723; d. Sudbury, Vt., 15 Dec. 1803 aged 79y 17d.

She m. Union, Conn., 17 Feb. 1746/7 **WILLIAM WILLIAMS**, b. Newton 3 Aug. 1723; d. Willington, Conn., 3 Feb. 1800 in 77th yr. and buried there, "of Sudbury Vermont while on a visit to his friends at Willington Connecticut"; son of William and Experience (Wilson) Williams.

On 27 March 1767 Elisha, Amariah, Phinehas, and Jesse Williams; Joseph Hovey Jr. and wife Eunice, all of Mansfield; and Nathan Jennings and wife Esther of Willington sold two tracts in Union to William Williams of Union.

On 9 Jan. 1796 William Williams formerly of Union but now of Ashford sold 20 acres in Union to Benjamin James.

The inventory of the estate of William Williams of Sudbury, Vt., presented 19 Feb. 1801, included 104 acres in Union, Conn.

Children of William and Azuba (Metcalf) Williams, b. Union, Conn., last three bp. Congregational Church:

   i ANNA WILLIAMS[6], b. 9 Jan. 1747/8; d. 22 Nov. 1754

   ii SYBIL WILLIAMS, b. 11 Feb. 1748/9

   iii ABIJAH WILLIAMS, b. 24 Sept. 1750; d. 28 Nov. 1754

   iv WILLIAM WILLIAMS, b. 19 Aug. 1752

   v ELIPHALET WILLIAMS, b. 6 Nov. 1754

   vi ESTHER WILLIAMS, b. 15 Nov. 17--

   vii ASAHEL WILLIAMS, b. 7 Jan. 17-- (1760 based on age at d.)

   viii ABIJAH WILLIAMS, b. 23 May 1762

   ix JOSEPH WILLIAMS, b. 17 July 1764, bp. 2 Sept. 1764

   x ANNA WILLIAMS, b. 11 July 1767, bp. 31 May 1767

   xi ELIJAH WILLIAMS, b. 26 Nov. 1769, bp. 26 Nov. 1769

References: *Bradford Desc* p. 69. Union CT VR LR2:295(m.), 288(b. 1st 4 ch.), 295(b. Eliphalet), 267(b. Abijah), 269(b. Joseph), 293(b. Ashahel). *VR Newton* 215(b. William). Hale Cem Coll:Willington, p. 6(d. William). Stafford CT PR (inv. of William Williams). Sudbury VT VR 4:42(d. Azubah, Asahel). Union CT LR 4:165(Elisha Williams *et al.*), 194(William Williams). Union Cong. Ch. Recs. 1:43(bp. Joseph), 44(bp. Anna), 45(bp. Elijah).

191. SYBIL DYER[5] (*Abigail Fitch[4], Alice[3] Bradford, William[2-1]*), b. Canterbury, Conn., 26 Oct. 1714; d. Bozrah, Conn., after 29 May 1794.

She m. Canterbury, Conn., 27 Nov. 1735 **BENJAMIN THROOP**, b. Block Island, R.I., 9 June 1712; d. New Concord (Bozrah), Conn., 16 Sept. 1785 aged 74; son of William and Martha (Collye) Throop.

Benjamin Throop graduated from Yale in 1734 and was licensed to preach by the Windham County Association of Ministers on 31 Aug. 1736. He was ordained minister of the newly organized parish of New Concord (now Bozrah) on 3 Jan. 1738/9 and remained there until his death.

In 1755 he was appointed chaplain to the Crown Point expedition.

It is written of him in *Norwich History*, "He left behind him the reputation of a scholar and a gentleman; seasoning all his speech with a divine relish, yet genial, social, always diffusing good-humor, always thirsting for information, and ever ready to impart knowledge from his ample stores to others."

The will of Benjamin Throop of Norwich, Conn., dated 14 May 1784, proved 27 Sept. 1785, names wife Sybil; sons Dyar, Benjamin, and William; daughters Elizabeth, Sybil, Abigail, Octavia, and Sarah; and grandsons Dyar Throop Hinckley and Daniel Throop.

On 29 May 1794 widow Sibbel Throop of Bozrah wished to set free Shem, a negro man, servant for life to Sibbel. She stated that he was over 25 and under 45 and in good health. Her wish was allowed.

Children of Benjamin and Sybil (Dyer) Throop, b. Norwich, Conn.:

- i CHLOE THROOP[6], b. 20 Sept. 1736; d. 23 Dec. 1736
- ii ISABELLA THROOP, b. 25 Oct. 1737; d. same day
- iii DYER THROOP, b. 17 Sept. 1738
- iv ELIZABETH THROOP, b. 9 April 1741
- v BENJAMIN THROOP, b. 9 March 1743
- vi WILLIAM THROOP, b. 26 Dec. 1744
- vii SYBIL THROOP, b. 20 Jan. 1746/7
- viii ABIGAIL THROOP, b. 23 Aug. 1749

ix SARAH THROOP, b. 19 Dec. 1751; living 14 May 1784 (will)

x OCTAVIA THROOP, b. 7 July 1754

References: *Bradford Desc* p. 69. Norwich CT PR #10614(Benjamin Throop). *Conn Marr* 2:123. *Norwich CT VR* 1:184-5(b. ch.). *Yale Grads* 1:514-5. Hale Cem Coll:Bozrah p. 24(d. Benjamin). *Norwich Hist* p. 434. Bozrah CT LR 2:19(freedom for Shem).

192. ELIJAH DYER[5] (*Abigail Fitch*[4], *Alice*[3] *Bradford, William*[2-1]), b. Canterbury, Conn., 10 Sept. 1716; d. there 15 Feb. 1793 aged 76y.

He m. Plainfield, Conn., 16 Nov. 1752 **ELIZABETH WILLIAMS**, b. Plainfield 6 Feb. 1733; d. Canterbury, Conn., 1 May 1817 aged 84y; daughter of Ebenezer and Judeth (Brown) Williams. She m. (2) Canterbury 7 Oct. 1798, William Johnson.

On 4 May 1743 John Dyar of Canterbury gave his eldest son Elijah Dyar part of his home farm and 25 acres. On 25 Sept. 1759 John Dyer of Canterbury gave his son Elijah Dyer of Canterbury three pieces of land.

In 1790 Elijah Dyer was head of a household in Canterbury consisting of 5 men over 16, one boy, and 4 females.

Administration on the estate of Elijah Dyar of Canterbury was granted to Ebenezer and Elijah Dyar on 2 April 1793. Distribution was made on 4 April 1795 to widow Elizabeth; sons eldest Ebenezer, second Elijah, youngest Joseph; and daughters Alice Cleveland wife of Capt. Josiah, Sibbil Paine wife of Luther, and Eunice Johnson wife of Capt. Jedidiah. Two later distributions were made: the first on 11 June 1816 names Allice Cleveland wife of Josiah, Ebenezer Dyar, Sibbel Paine wife of Luther, heirs of Eunice Johnson late wife of Jedediah, Elijah Dyar, and Joseph Dyar; the second on 8 July 1816, which was to distribute the remaining lands set off to Mrs. Elizabeth Dyer, widow and relict of Elijah Dyer, names the following heirs: Alice Cleveland wife of Josiah, Ebenezer Dyar, Sibbil Paine wife of Luther, heirs of Eunice Johnson late wife of Jedidiah, and Elijah Dyer (who has bought Joseph Dyer's part).

On 27 Dec. 1794 Ebenezer Dyar and Elijah Dyar of Canterbury, Conn., administrators of the estate of their father Elijah Dyar with permission of the court sold to Jesse Ensworth of Canterbury 158 acres in Canterbury and Plainfield.

On 11 Nov. 1801 William and Elizabeth Johnson, Josiah and Alice Cleveland, Luther and Sibbel Paine, Jedediah and Eunice Johnson, and Elijah Dyer all of Canterbury, Ebenezer Dyer of Norwich, Vt., and Joseph Dyer of Stratford, N.H., sold to Josiah Rose of Canterbury land with one-half of a house, corn house, and barn, it being land set off to the widow Elizabeth Johnson as part of her dower in the estate of Elijah Dyer.

On 24 Feb. 1807 Joseph Dyer of Stewartstown, Coos Co., N.H., sold to Elijah Dyar of Canterbury, Conn., land that had descended to him from his father Elijah Dyar.

On 12 Sept. 1815 Ebenezer Dyer of Sharon, Vt., sold to Elijah Dyer of Canterbury, Conn., her right in the estate of Elijah Dyer dec.

Children of Elijah and Elizabeth (Williams) Dyer, b. Canterbury, Conn., except Sybil:

    i   ALICE DYER[6], b. 28 Feb. 1754

    ii EBENEZER DYER, b. 26 Aug. 1756

   iii WILLIAM DYER, b. 26 Sept. 1758; d. Canterbury, Conn., 14 Jan. 1777

   iv SYBIL DYER, b. Norwich, Conn., 29 Dec. 1761

    v ELIJAH DYER, b. 13 Feb. 1764

   vi EUNICE DYER, b. 2 Dec. 1766

  vii MEHITABLE DYER, b. 26 March 1769; d. 15 Oct. 1776 ae 6y

 viii JOSEPH DYER , b. 19 June 1772

Note: There is no proof for a dau. Elizabeth, twin to Joseph, as given in *Bradford Desc.* No such child is listed in Barbour, IGI-CT, or *Dyar Gen.*

References: *Bradford Desc* p. 69-70. *Dyar Gen* p. 9. *Conn Marr* 2:66. Plainfield CT VR 1:59(b. Elizabeth). Canterbury CT VR 1:120(m.), 123(b. Alice), 124(b. Ebenezer), 125(b. Sybil, Elijah), 127(b. Eunice, Mehitable, Joseph). Hale Cem Coll:Canterbury p. 24 (d. Elijah, Elizabeth, Mehitable). Plainfield CT PR #733(Elijah Dyar). Canterbury CT LR 5:158; 7:240(John Dyer); 11:189(Ebenezer Dyar); 13:322(William Johnson); 15:218(Joseph Dyar), 286(Ebenezer Dyer).

193. ABIGAIL DYER[5] (*Abigail Fitch[4], Alice[3] Bradford, William[2-1]*), b. Canterbury, Conn., 13 April 1718; d. Orwell, Vt., 10 Jan. 1808 aged 91y 7m 23d or 92y. She and her husband are buried in Mettowee Valley Cem.

She m. Canterbury, Conn., 5 Nov. 1739 **GIDEON COBB**, b. Stonington, Conn., 8 July 1718; d. Pawlet, Vt., 25 July 1798 aged 81y; son of Gideon and Margaret (Fish) Cobb.

On 20 April 1762 Gideon Cobb of Canterbury, Conn., sold to Joseph Marshall of Canterbury 39 acres with a house and barn.

On 9 Nov. 1778 John Cobb of Canterbury, Conn., bought land in Pawlet, Vt.; on 4 Feb. 1779 Joshua Cobb of Stillwater, N.Y., bought land in Pawlet;

and on 9 Nov. 1779 Ebenezer Cobb of Stillwater, N.Y., bought land in Pawlet.

In 1786 Gideon Cobb released his right in land that was sold to for back taxes.

Children of Gideon and Abigail (Dyer) Cobb, b. Canterbury, Conn.:

    i   GIDEON COBB⁶, b. 24 May 1740; d. Canterbury, Conn., 26 Dec. 1760

    ii WILLIAM COBB, b. 21 Oct. 1742

    iii JOHN COBB, b. 21 Oct. 1744

    iv ELKANAH COBB, b. 21 Jan. 1746/7

    v EBENEZER COBB, b. 16 March 1748/9

    vi JOSHUA COBB, b. 16 July 1751

    vii WEALTHY COBB, bp. 7 Oct. 1753

    viii ABIGAIL COBB, b. 7 Sept. 1756

    ix SARAH COBB, b. 12 Jan. 1759

References: *Bradford Desc* p. 70. *Dyar Gen* p. 9. *Conn Marr* 2:123(yr. only). Stonington CT VR 1:114(b. Gideon). Canterbury CT VR 1:100(m.), 106(b. Gideon, Wealthy), 108(b. Abigail), 109(b. Sarah), 118(b. Gideon); 2:20(b. William thru Joshua). Canterbury CT LR 7:12(Gideon Cobb). *Pawlet VT Cem Rec* p. 49(bur. Abigail, Gideon). Pawlet VR LR 1:69(John Cobb), 171(Joshua Cobb), 266(Ebenezer Cobb), 353(Gideon Cobb).

194. JAMES DYER⁵ (*Abigail Fitch⁴, Alice³ Bradford, William²⁻¹*), b. Canterbury, Conn., 16 Feb. 1719/20; d. there 27 May 1790.

He m. Canterbury, Conn., 8 Dec. 1753 **ANN WHITING**, b. Norwich, Conn., 16 Nov. 1732; d. after 7 June 1793; daughter of William and Ann (Raymond) Whiting.

On 10 May 1743 John Dyer of Canterbury sold to his son James Dyer of Canterbury land with a dwelling house and barn and on 23 March 1752 John sold to James another 55 acres.

Administration on the estate of James Dyer of Canterbury was granted to Anna Dyer and James Dyer on 3 April 1792. On 7 June 1793 Anne Dyer "sold to the whole of articles at privit sail to James Dyer of Canterbury" for £20:15:3.

Children of James and Ann (Whiting) Dyer, b. Canterbury, Conn.:

    i WILLIAM DYER⁶, b. 19 Jan. 1755; d. 22 July 1756

    ii JOHN DYER, b. 24 March 1757; d. Philadelphia, Penna., 17 Sept. 1777 or 1 Sept.

iii JAMES DYER, b. 25 Nov. 1759; d. 7 Jan. 1760

iv ABIGAIL DYER, b. 10 May 1761

v JAMES DYER, b. 10 Feb. 1764

vi ANNA DYER, b. 19 May 1766

vii SARAH DYER, bp. 27 May 1770; d. Canterbury, Conn., 25 Jan. 1790

viii SAMUEL DYER, b. 2 Feb. 1773

ix PAMELIA DYER, b. 21 June 1775; d. Canterbury, Conn., 27 Dec. 1789

References: *Bradford Desc* p. 70. *Conn Marr* 1:111. Norwich CT VR 1:109(b. Ann); 3:299(b. Pamelia). Canterbury CT VR 1:120(m.), 124(b.&d. 1st 3 ch., 2nd James), 125(b. Abigail), 126(b. Anna), 127(b. Samuel), 132(b. Pamelia). Plainfield CT PR #734 (James Dyer). *Dyar Gen* p. 10. Canterbury CT LR 5:165; 6:5(John Dyer).

195. JOHN DYER[5] (*Abigail Fitch[4], Alice[3] Bradford, William[2-1]*), b. Canterbury, Conn., 13 May 1722.

He m. Woodstock, Conn., 29 March 1753 **ANNA PAYSON**, b. Woodstock 17 Aug. 1726; d. Canterbury 15 Oct. 1776 aged 50y; daughter of Jonathan and Mary (Cook) Payson.

On 24 May 1749 John Dyer of Canterbury sold to his son John Dyer of Canterbury 35 acres.

Children of John and Anna (Payson) Dyer, first 4 b. Canterbury, Conn.:

i MOLLY DYER[6], b. 11 May 1754

ii OLIVE DYER, b. 31 Aug. 1756

iii ROGER DYER, b. 29 Dec. 1758

iv ELISHA DYER, b. 30 Oct. 1760

v BETSEY DYER, b. Woodstock, Conn., 22 July 1765

vi JOHN DYER, b. New London, Conn., 6 April 1771; d. Canterbury 17 Sept. 1776 ae 5y

References: *Woodstock CT By Bowen*. Canterbury CT VR 1:120(m.), 123(b. Molly), 124(b. Olive, Roger), 130(b. Elisha), 132(d. Anna; d. ch. John). Woodstock CT VR 1:41(b. Anna); 2:36(b. son John). New London CT VR 3:50(b. John). Hale Cem Coll:Canterbury p. 24(d. Anna, s. John). *Dyar Gen* p. 10. Canterbury CT LR 5:375(John Dyer).

196. JOSEPH DYER[5] (*Abigail Fitch[4], Alice[3] Bradford, William[2-1]*), b. Canterbury, Conn., 9 May 1724; d. there 8 Dec. 1781.

He m. Canterbury, Conn., 1 Feb. 1749 **MARTHA DARBE** (or **DERBY**), b. Canterbury 6 Feb. 1725; living 24 Dec. 1791; daughter of William and Elizabeth (Spaulding) Derby.

On 1 Oct. 1759 John Dyer of Canterbury gave to his son Joseph Dyer 100 acres with a dwelling house.

Administration on the estate of Joseph Dyar of Canterbury, Conn., was granted to Jareb Dyer of Canterbury on 30 Jan. 1782. His inventory was taken on 2 April 1782.

On 24 Dec. 1791 Jareb Dyer of Canterbury sold to Wyllys Dyer of Canterbury three pieces of land "excepting in the third described tract all lawful right & claim of Daniel West and Chloe his wife" of New London. On the same day Martha Dyer, Jesse and Lotilla Ensworth, Wyllys Dyer, and Annis Dyer of Canterbury, Conn., sold to Dr. Jareb Dyer of Canterbury their rights in the real estate of Capt. Joseph Dyer. On 16 Jan. 1786 Daniel and Chloe West of Canterbury sold to Wyllys Dyer their right in the estate of Capt. Joseph Dyer.

On 24 Dec. 1791 Wyllys Dyer of Canterbury and his mother Martha Dyer of Canterbury agreed on land for her use and improvement during her life.

Children of Joseph and Martha (Darbe) Dyer, b. Canterbury, Conn.:

    i CHLOE DYER[6], b. 16 Aug. 1750

    ii JEDD DYER, b. 17 Oct. 1752; d. York 20 Jan. 1777 in Rev. War. The list of Capt. Bacon's Co. in Chester's regiment raised in 1776 includes a Jada Dyar and the list of Non-Commissioned Officers and Privates taken prisoner at the surrender of Ft. Washington, N.Y., Island on 16 Nov. 1776 includes Jedediah Dyer from Chester's regiment. He died 20 Jan. 1777.

    iii JAREB DYER, b. 3 Oct. 1754

    iv LOTILLA DYER, b. 8 May 1757

    v WYLLYS DYER, b. 4 Aug. 1760

    vi MANSUR FITCH DYER, b. 4 Dec. 1762

    vii ANNICE DYER, b. 7 March 1766

References: *Bradford Desc* p. 70. *Dyer Gen* p. 10. *Conn Marr* 2:123. Canterbury CT VR 1:120(m.), 122(b. Martha), 124 (b.&d. 1st 4 ch.), 125(b. next 2 ch.), 126(b. Annice), 132(b. Pamelia; d. Joseph). Plainfield CT PR #736 (Joseph Dyar). Canterbury CT LR 7:61(John Dyer); 10:395(Jareb Dyer); 11:23(Martha Dyer), 24(Daniel West), 25(Jareb Dyer); 13:93(Wyllys Dyer). *CT Men Rev War* 123(list of prisoners), 412(Chester's regt.).

197. SARAH DYER[5] (*Abigail Fitch[4], Alice[3] Bradford, William[2-1]*), b. Canterbury, Conn., 14 Nov. 1727; d. New London, Conn., 27 May 1807.

She m. (1) Norwich, Conn., 23 Dec. 1757 **SAMUEL WHITING**, b. Norwich 3 May 1727; d. Bozrah, Conn., in March 1761; son of William and Ann (Raymond) Whiting.

She m. (2) New Concord (Bozrah), Conn., 7 Feb. 1765 **THOMAS HARRIS**, bp. New London, Conn., 19 Sept. 1725; d. in battle 24 Feb. 1778; son of Frank and Lucy (Smith) Harris.

Sarah Harris was listed in the 1790 census in New London Co., Conn., as head of a household consisting of one man over 16 and 3 females. Listed next to her was John Harris.

The will of Sarah Harris of New London, Conn., dated 20 March 1805, proved 13 July 1807, names son Dyer Harris and daughters Mary Fish and Lucy Smith.

Child of Samuel and Sarah (Dyer) Whiting, b. Norwich, Conn.:

    i JOHN WHITING[6], b. 20 Oct. 1758

Children of Thomas and Sarah (Dyer) (Whiting) Harris, b. Norwich, Conn.:

    ii DYER HARRIS, b. 25 Nov. 1765
    iii MARY HARRIS, b. 20 April 1767
    iv LUCY HARRIS, b. 15 Nov. 1769

References: *Bradford Desc* p. 71. *Dyar Gen* p. 10. New London CT PR #2485(Sarah Harris). *Conn Marr* 5:54(2nd m.). Norwich CT VR 1:196(b. Samuel); 2:210(1st m.; b. John). New London CT VR 2:78(2nd m.; b. Harris ch.).

198. ALICE FITCH[5] (*Ebenezer[4], Alice[3] Bradford, William[2-1]*), b. Windsor, Conn., 30 June 1713; d. 1796.

She m. Windham, Conn., 25 Jan. 1730/1 **JOHN FITCH**, b. Windham 18 March 1704/5; d. there 19 Feb. 1760 aged 54y 11m; son of John and Elizabeth (Waterman) Fitch.

John Fitch of Windham made his will on 13 Feb. 1760, proved 10 March 1760, and named his wife Alice; sons Ebenezer, James, Elijah, and Jabez; daughters Alice Wight, Meriam, Elizabeth, Eunice, and Lucy; and two grandchildren, Alice and John, children of son John, deceased. He mentioned several pieces of land located in Brimfield, Mass., and in Kent, Cornwall, and Salisbury, Conn., as well as in Windham. The first distribution was made on 25 Oct. 1764 and mentions widow Alice and children Alice, Ebenezer, James,

Miriam, Elizabeth, Elijah, Eunice, and Lucy. A second distribution made on 22 Aug. 1767 names the widow Alice and the above children, but also includes Jabez among the children.

Children of John and Alice (Fitch) Fitch, b. Windham, Conn., first 4 bp. Windham:

    i   JOHN FITCH[6], b. 14 July 1732, bp. 16 July 1732

    ii ALICE FITCH, b. 7 Oct. 1734, bp. 13 Oct. 1734

   iii EBENEZER FITCH, b. 30 Nov. 1736, bp. 5 Dec. 1736

   iv JAMES FITCH, b. 9 April 1739, bp. 15 April 1739

    v MIRIAM FITCH, b. 9 June 1741

   vi ELIZABETH FITCH, b. 4 Oct. 1743

  vii ELIJAH FITCH, b. 8 Jan. 1746

 viii JABEZ FITCH, b. 2 March 1747/8

   ix LUCY FITCH, b. 26 March 1753

    x EUNICE FITCH

References: *Bradford Desc* p. 71. *TAG* 46:44. *Waterman Gen* 1:50. Windham CT VR A:15(b. John); 1:119(m.; d. John; b. ch.). Windham CT PR #1376(John Fitch). Windham 1st Ch. Recs. 1:16(bp. John), 18(bp. Alice), 20(bp. Ebenezer), 22(bp. James).

199. JAMES FITCH[5] (*Ebenezer[4], Alice[3] Bradford, William[2-1]*), b. Windsor, Conn., 24 July 1715; living 17 Aug. 1782 (deed).

He m. Coventry, Conn., 6 Oct. 1738 **PHEBE MARAUGH**, who was living 17 Aug. 1782 (deed); daughter of Richard and Deliverance (_____) Maraugh. The will of Richard Maraugh of Coventry dated 29 March 1756 names daughter Phebe Fitch.

On 2 May 1741 James Fitch of Durham sold to Elijah Fitch of Ashford his two-sevenths share of the land of their father Ebenezer Fitch of Windsor. On 14 Aug. 1741 sons Eleazer, James, and Elijah Fitch and son-in-law John Fitch quitclaimed their rights to their father's land in Canterbury to their uncle Jabez Fitch.

On 9 July 1752 John French of Windsor sold to James Fitch of Coventry land in Windsor.

On 17 Aug. 1782 John Parker and wife Sarah of Coventry, Josiah Badcock and wife Mary of Mansfield, and James Fitch and wife Phebe of East Windsor sold to Levi Dow of Coventry 12 acres in Coventry formerly owned by Richard Marough, deceased.

Children of James and Phebe (Maraugh) Fitch, first 4 b. Coventry, Conn.; last 4 b. Windsor, Conn.:

    i   PHEBE FITCH[6], b. 23 Dec. 1738; d. 11 Jan. 1738/9

    ii RICHARD FITCH, b. 31 July 1742

    iii PHEBE FITCH, b. 4 March 1748

    iv JESSE FITCH, b. 11 March 1752

    v SARAH FITCH, b. 3 Feb. 1755

    vi HANNAH FITCH, b. 7 April 1757

    vii RUSSELL FITCH, b. 29 Sept. 1760

    viii JAMES FITCH, b. 2 May 1762

References: Coventry CT VR 1:409(m.); D42(b. 1st 4 ch.; d. Phebe); D139(m.). Windsor CT VR 2:335(b. last 4 ch.). Windham CT PR #2634(Richard Maraugh). Windsor CT LR 7:205(to Elijah); 9:187(John French). Coventry CT LR 7:48 (John Parker *et al.*). Canterbury CT LR 4:323(quitclaim).

200. ELIJAH FITCH[5] (*Ebenezer[4], Alice[3] Bradford, William[2-1]*), b. Windsor, Conn., 23 Feb. 1717/8; d. Chester, Nova Scotia, after 28 April 1778.

He m. (1) Windsor, Conn., 28 Oct. 1742 **MARY LOOMIS**, b. Windsor 12 Jan. 1720/1; d. there 5 May 1744; daughter of Joseph and Mary (Cooley) Loomis.

He m. (2) Ashford, Conn., 24 Sept. 1745 **ABIGAIL TAYLOR**, b. Windsor, Conn., 10 Feb. 1721/2; daughter of Nathaniel and Ruth (Stiles) Taylor.

In May 1741 James Fitch of Durham, Conn., sold to Elijah Fitch of Ashford, Conn., his right in land in Windsor that Ebenezer Fitch died seized of. On 14 Aug. 1741 sons Eleazer, James, and Elijah Fitch and son-in-law John Fitch quitclaimed their rights to their father's land in Canterbury to their uncle Jabez Fitch.

On 22 April 1742 Elijah Fitch of Ashford sold 160 acres in Ashford to Benjamin Russell Jr. On the same day Elijah was received into full communion with the Ashford Church.

On 31 Jan. 1761 Elijah Fitch of Canterbury sold land in Ashford to Daniel Bull.

Elijah Fitch moved to Chester, Nova Scotia, in 1763 with 2 males and 1 female. Ebenezer Fitch settled there in 1764 with 2 males and 4 females.

On 28 April 1778 Elijah Fitch of Chester, yeoman, sold William Knowlton of Chester, mariner, town lot #99. Ebenezer Fitch was one of the witnesses.

Child of Elijah and Mary (Loomis) Fitch, b. Ashford, Conn.:

    i   MARY FITCH[6], b. 25 April 1744

Children of Elijah and Abigail (Taylor) Fitch, b. Ashford, Conn.:

    ii   EBENEZER FITCH, b. 25 July 1746
    iii SOPHIAH FITCH, b. 21 June 1751; d. 4 July 1753
    iv ELIHU FITCH, b. 11 July 1753; d. 19 Sept. 1754
    v   KEZIAH FITCH, b. 4 April 1758

References: *Bradford Desc* pp. 71-2. Windsor CT VR 2:60(b. Mary Loomis), 108(b. Abigail), 152(1st m.), 234(d. Mary), 332(b. dau. Mary). Ashford CT LR D:69; K:180(Elijah Fitch). Ashford CT VR 2:52(2nd m.; b. last 4 ch.; d. 2 ch.). *Desc Rev James Fitch* pp. 96-7. Windsor CT LR 7:205(James Fitch). Canterbury CT LR 2:93(James Fitch); 4:323(quitclaim). Lunenburg Co. N.S. LR 3:17(Elijah Fitch). *Hist Co Lunenburg* p. 265.

201. ELEAZER FITCH[5] (*Ebenezer[4], Alice[3] Bradford, William[2-1]*), b. Windsor, Conn., 28 May 1720; d. there 2 May 1800.

He m. Windham, Conn., 11 May 1738 **ZERVIAH WALES**, b. Windham 11 Nov. 1719; d. ca. April 1797; daughter of Nathaniel and Mercy (West) Wales.

On 29 June 1741 Eleazer Fitch of Windham sold to Elijah Fitch of Ashford his one-seventh share of their father's land in Windsor. On 14 Aug. 1741 sons Eleazer, James, and Elijah Fitch and son-in-law John Fitch quitclaimed their rights to their father's land in Canterbury to their uncle Jabez Fitch.

In 1787 Eleaser Fitch was elected a Deacon in the Windham Congregational Church.

Eleaz[r] Fitch's household at Windham in 1790 consisted of one man over 16 and 2 females.

Children of Eleazer and Zerviah (Wales) Fitch, b. Windham, Conn.:

    i   ZERVIAH FITCH[6], b. 19 July 1739; d. same day
    ii   ZERVIAH FITCH, b. 9 March 1741
    iii ELEAZER FITCH, b. 20 April 1743

   iv NATHANIEL FITCH, b. 9 Aug. 1745

   v BRIDGET FITCH, b. 14 Feb. 1748; d. 4 Oct. 1759

   vi SHUBAEL FITCH, b. 22 Feb. 1750

   vii MARY FITCH, b. 17 May 1751

   viii ABNER FITCH, b. 16 Dec. 1753; d. 6 April 1754

   ix OLIVE FITCH, b. 5 Aug. 1755

   x LUTHER FITCH, b. 9 Dec. 1757

   xi JERUSHA FITCH, b. 2 Aug. 1761

References: *Bradford Desc* p. 72. Windham CT VR 1:11(b. Zerviah), 183(m.; b.&d. ch.). Windsor CT LR 7:205(Eleazer Fitch). *Desc Rev James Fitch* pp. 97-8. Canterbury CT LR 4:323(quitclaim).

202. MEDINA FITCH[5] (*Ebenezer*[4], *Alice*[3] *Bradford, William*[2-1]), b. Windsor, Conn., 20 Nov. 1722; d. Ellington, Conn., 14 Nov. 1792 aged 70.

He m. (1) Windsor, Conn., 19 Feb. 1744 **LYDIA AVERY**, b. Ashford, Conn., 6 Jan. 1727/8 (or Dedham, bp. Dedham 23 Feb. 1734); d. there (or Ellington), Conn., 16 Oct. 1762 aged 36; daughter of Jonathan and Lydia (Healy) Avery. In his will dated 19 June 1754, proved 6 July 1761, Jonathan Avery of Ashford named his daughter Lydia Fitch. She was included in two divisions on 30 April 1762 and 11 Oct. 1762 that gave her land in Ashford and Simsbury. On 5 July 1762 Medinah Fitch and his wife Lydia of Windsor sold to Abner Burroughs of Windsor, 80 arces in Simsbury that had come from her father Jonathan Avery. On 9 Sept. 1762 Medinah and Lydia sold to John Avery of Ashford, five acres with a barn and another seven acres in Ashford, part of the estate of Jonathan Avery.

He m. (2) **JERUSHA THOMSON**, who d. Ellington, Conn., 9 Aug. 1831; daughter of Robert and Rachel (_____) Thomson. The will of Robert Thomson of East Windsor dated 6 June 1785 names wife Rachel and daughter Jerusha Fitch.

On 11 Aug. 1744 Medinah Fitch purchased land in Ellington, Conn., from Alexander Allen. On 3 Feb. 1746 Medinah Fitch and his wife Lydia were dismissed to the church in Ellington.

Medinah Fitch was a First Lieutenant during the French and Indian Wars in 1755 and 1756.

The household of Medi[n] Fitch in 1790 in Ellington, Conn., consisted of 2 men over 16 and 2 females.

On 14 Oct. 1790 Medina Fitch of Ellington and wife Jerusha; John Thomson; Rachel Potwine, and Abigail Thomson, heirs of Rachel Thomson of East Windsor sold 43 acres in East Windsor to Israel Allen.

Children of Medina and Lydia (Avery) Fitch:

i JONATHAN FITCH[6], b. Windsor, Conn., 15 Feb. 1745

ii BRIDGET FITCH, b. 12 July 1746

poss iii ELNATHAN, b. Windsor, Conn., ca. 1758 [ae 60 on 29 May 1818 when applied for pension and 66 on 5 Dec. 1824 when he died]

poss. iv MEDINAH

References: *Bradford Desc* p. 72. Windsor CT VR 2:152(m.), 333(b. Jonathan). Ellington CT VR pp. 7(d. Medina, Jerusha). Ellington Center Cemetery p. 5(d. Medina, Lydia). Windsor CT LR 7:247(Alexander Allen). *Desc Rev James Fitch* pp. 1:98-100. East Windsor CT PR #3093(Robert Thomson). Ashford CT LR K:284(Medinah Fitch). Simsbury CT LR 9:186(Medinah Fitch).

203. EBENEZER FITCH[5] (*Ebenezer[4], Alice[3] Bradford, William[2-1]*), b. Windsor, Conn., 10 March 1724/5; d. prob. Wallingford, Conn., ca 1773 (or 1777).

He m. Wallingford, Conn., 16 May 1749 **LYDIA JOHNSON**, b. Wallingford, Conn., 4 Nov. 1730; d. there 27 Jan. 1812 in 82nd yr.; daughter of Abner and Charity (Dayon) Johnson.

On 3 Aug. 1756 Daniel Clark sold seven acres in Wallingford to Ebenezer Fitch. On 1 Dec. 1760 Ebenezer Fitch sold this land and his dwelling house to Isaac Johnson.

Lidia Fitch was head of a household consisting of 2 females in Wallingford in 1790.

Children of Ebenezer and Lydia (Johnson) Fitch, b. Wallingford, Conn.:

i LYDIA FITCH[6], b. 28 Dec. 1749; d. 8 Jan. 1750

ii JUSTUS JOHNSON FITCH, b. 12 April 1751

iii HEZEKIAH FITCH, b. 9 Nov. 1753

iv CYNTHIA FITCH, b. 31 July 17--

v LYDIA FITCH, b. 27 Jan. 1761; d. 1 June 1761

vi EBENEZER FITCH, b. 4 July 1762; d. 24 Aug. 1762

vii IRENE FITCH, b. 16 June 1771

References: *Bradford Desc* p. 72. Wallingford CT VR 5:525(b. Lydia), 5-1:B(d. Lydia); 9:561(m.); 11:546(b. Lydia), 552(b. Justus); 12:351(b. Hezekiah); 14:504(b.& d. Lydia);

15:3(b. Ebenezer), 696(b. Cynthia); 18:494(b. Irene). Wallingford CT LR 13:629(Daniel Clark); 15:179(Ebenezer Fitch). *Desc Rev James Fitch* pp. 1:100-1.

204. WILLIAM FITCH[5] (*Daniel*[4], *Alice*[3] *Bradford*, *William*[2-1]), b. Canterbury, Conn., Aug. 1720, bp. Canterbury 17 July 1720; d. Oneida Co., N.Y.

He m. Canterbury, Conn., 27 Jan. 1740/1 **MARY PAINE**, b. Canterbury 12 April 1723; d. Liverpool, Nova Scotia, 4 Feb. 1762; daughter of Elisha and Mary (Johnson) Paine. [VRs in *NEHGR* say Mary wife of William d. 4 July ____.]

William Fitch moved to Liverpool, Nova Scotia in 1759. On 4 June 1762 William Fitch of Liverpool, Gentleman, sold Simeon Perkins of Liverpool, merchant, his right in fish lot letter B number 5. On 25 Aug. 1762 he sold Israel Tupper of Liverpool, yeoman, his right in town lot letter D number 10; William Fitch Jr. was a witness. On 27 Aug. 1762 he sold Samuel Freeman, Cornelius Knowles, and Simeon Perkins all his right in the township of Liverpool both divided and undivided and a small dwelling house. On 13 Sept. 1772 William Fitch Sr. of Dudley, Gentleman, sold Joseph Barnaby of Liverpool his right in a fish lot.

He eventually moved to Oneida, N.Y.

Children of William and Mary (Paine) Fitch, b. Canterbury, Conn., except last:

    i   ANNA FITCH[6], b. 1 July 1742

   ii   WILLIAM FITCH, b. 14 Feb. 1744

  iii   ABIGAIL FITCH, b. 23 June 1745

   iv   MARY FITCH, b. 27 Oct. 1747

    v   ELISHA FITCH, b. 6 May 1749

   vi   ALICE FITCH, b. 18 Aug. 1751

  vii   RUFUS FITCH, b. 26 July 1755

 viii   OLIVE FITCH (twin), b. 21 Aug. 1757

   ix   PHEBE FITCH (twin), b. 21 Aug. 1757

    x   JAMES PAINE FITCH, b. 1758; bp. 23 Sept. 1758; killed in Rev. service in the Battle of Monmouth, N. J.

   xi   DANIEL FITCH, b. Liverpool, N.S., 6 Jan. 1762

References: *Bradford Desc* p. 72. Canterbury CT VR 1:138(m.), 141(b. 1st 2 ch.), 142(b. Mary, Elisha, Rufus, Olive, Phebe), 195(b. Mary Paine). *Desc Rev James Fitch* pp. 1:101-2. *NEHGR* 126:95(d. Mary, b. Daniel). Queens Co. N.S .LR 1:5, 55,195, 371(William Fitch).

205. EBENEZER[5] FITCH (*Daniel[4]*, *Alice[3]* *Bradford*, *William[2-1]*), b. Canterbury, Conn., 14 July 1724; d. Norwich, Conn., 13 Feb. (or Jan.) 1797 in his 72nd yr.

He m. Norwich, Conn., 3 Sept. 1750 **MARY HUNTINGTON**, b. Norwich 26 Nov. 1728; d. 4 Dec. 1798 in her 72nd yr.; daughter of Isaac and Rebecca (Lathrop) Huntington. On 6 June 1783 Ebenezer Fitch and his wife Mary of Norwich, along with other heirs, sold land that had belonged to Isaac Huntington; and on 20 Aug. 1784 Ebenezer and Mary sold land set off to them from the distribution of Isaac's estate.

Eben[r] Fitch was head of a household in New London Co., Conn., in 1790 consisting of 2 men over 16, one boy, and 3 females.

On 17 Aug. 1793 Ebenezer Fitch of Norwich and his wife Mary sold to Capt. Oliver Fitch of Norwich, mariner, two acres.

Children of Ebenezer and Mary (Huntington) Fitch, b. Norwich, Conn.:

   i   EUNICE FITCH[6], b. 23 March 1752; d. 31 Aug. 1753 ae 17m.
   ii GERARD FITCH, b. 14 July 1753
   iii EUNICE FITCH, b. 17 April 1755
   iv ABIGAIL (or NABBE) FITCH, b. 4 Aug. 1757
   v   EBENEZER FITCH, b. 29 Oct. 1759
   vi ROGER FITCH, b. 13 Sept. 1761
   vii MARY FITCH, b. 3 Jan. 1764
   viii OLIVER FITCH, b. 23 July 1766
   ix ELIZABETH FITCH, b. 10 Nov. 1768
   x   SARAH FITCH, b. 10 Aug. 1771
   xi CHARLES FITCH, b. 8 Nov. 1775; d. Norwich ca. Aug. 1801 ae 25

References: Norwich CT LR 25:29; 216; 29:165(Ebenezer Fitch). Norwich CT VR 1:104(b. Mary), 316(m., b. ch. thru Sarah), 348(b. Charles, d. Ebenezer). *Desc Rev James Fitch* pp. 1:102-3.

206. THEOPHILUS FITCH[5] (*Daniel[4]*, *Alice[3]* *Bradford*, *William[2-1]*), b. Canterbury, Conn., 14 July 1731; d. before 4 July 1781.

He m. **HANNAH ASHLEY**, b. Sheffield 3 Sept. 1735; d. Norwich, Conn., 22 Oct. 1814 aged 79; daughter of Ezekiel and Hannah (Griswold) Ashley.

Child of Theophilus and Hannah (Ashley) Fitch:

   i   HANNAH FITCH[6], b. ca. 1761 (in 50th yr. in 1810)

References: *Bradford Desc* p. 73. *NEHGR* 2:404(d. Hannah; dau. Hannah). Hale Cem Coll:Norwich p. 673(d. dau. Hannah Niles). *Desc Rev James Fitch* pp. 1:103-4. Hale Newspaper Coll: *Norwich Courier* 56:120(d. Hannah).

207. JABEZ BISSELL[5] (*Jerusha Fitch*[4], *Alice*[3] *Bradford, William*[2-1]), b. Windsor, Conn., 16 Feb. 1718; d. after 14 Feb. 1769 [or after 8 Dec. 1773 if he is the Jabez Bissell who owned the covenant in First Church, Somers].

He m. ca 1741 **DORCAS MARSH**, b. Windsor, Conn., 31 Aug. 1718; daughter of Rev. Jonathan and Margaret (Whiting) Marsh. The will of Jonathan Marsh of Windsor dated 7 Sept. 1747 names wife Margaret; daughter Dorcas Bissell, and others.

On 4 Jan. 1750/1 Jabez Bissell of Windsor sold to David Hayden of Windsor 120 acres in Harwinton including his dwelling house.

On 2 March 1764 Jabez Bissell of Windsor sold to Daniel Bissell of Windsor 14 acres with a house and barn.

On 14 Feb. 1769 Jabez Bissell of Somers sold to Ezekiel Schovel and his wife Mindwell of Harwinton 147 acres in Harwinton, acknowledging the deed the same day.

Children of Jabez and Dorcas (Marsh) Bissell:

 i DORCAS BISSELL[6], b. Harwinton, Conn., 26 April 1742; d. 14 Jan. 1749/50

 ii JERUSHA BISSELL, b. Harwinton, Conn., 22 Aug. 1743

 iii MARY BISSELL, b. Harwinton, Conn., 15 Feb. 1744/5

 iv JONATHAN MARSH BISSELL, b. Harwinton, Conn., 12 Aug. 1748; d. 14 Jan. 1749/50

 v WILLIAM BISSELL, b. Windsor, Conn., 26 July 1752

 vi ABIGAIL BISSELL, b. Windsor, Conn., 16 May 1756

 vii JONATHAN MARSH BISSELL, b. Somers, Conn., 21 Dec. 1761, bp. 21 March 1762 (Aspinwall)

References: *Bradford Desc* p. 73. Harwinton CT VR 1:5, 6(b. Dorcas), 23(b. next 3 ch.). Windsor CT VR 2:68(b. Dorcas), 305(b. William), 638(b. Abigail). Somers CT VR 1:54 (b. Jonathan). *Manwaring* 3:587(Jonathan Marsh). 1st Ch. Somers, Conn., 4:8(Jabez owned cov.). Harwinton CT LR 1:254; 2:216(Jabez Bissell). Windsor CT LR 14:5(Jabez Bissell).

208. JERUSHA BISSELL[5] (*Jerusha Fitch*[4], *Alice*[3] *Bradford, William*[2-1]), b. Windsor, Conn., 11 April 1721; d. Hartford 9 July 1803 aged 83.

She m. (1) Windsor, Conn., 22 Sept. 1743 **JOSEPH WADSWORTH** of Canterbury, Conn., b. 27 Feb. 1711/12; d. Windsor 2 Feb. 1750; son of Joseph and Lydia (Brown) Wadsworth.

She m. (2) 4 March 1762 **JOHN PALMER**; d. before 16 Oct. 1777; son of John and Deborah (Fille) Palmer. He m. (1) (as John Palmer 3rd.) at Windsor 3 Dec. 1748/9 Jerusha Allyn with whom he had John and Jerusha.

She m. (3) before 20 March 1786 **DANIEL SKINNER**, b. Hartford 1 April 1703/4; d. there 2 May 1796 aged 84; son of John and Rachel (Pratt) Skinner. He m. (1) Jerusha Whiting with whom he had Jerusha, Daniel, Sarah, Abigail, Theodore, Elisha, Abigail, William, and Sarah.

Joseph Wadsworth of Windsor, Conn., made his will 30 Jan. 1749/50 naming his wife Jerusha and son Joseph under age. He named his "father" Daniel Bissell as executor. The inventory taken on 7 March 1749/50 included a negro man named Hazard.

On 4 June 1770 Daniel Bissell of Windsor sold to his daughter Jerusha the wife of John Palmer Jr. of Windsor 33 acres. On 4 April 1774 John Palmer Jr. and Jerusha his wife of Windsor sold to Daniel Bissell and Eb: Fitch Bissell of Windsor 33 acres "Our Hon^d Father Daniel Bissell late of Windsor Dec^d Gave to the said Jerusha Palmer Wife of said John Palmer Junr said Thirty Three Acres Lyes in Common and undivided with the Heirs of Said Deceased."

Administration of the estate of John Palmer Jr. late of Windsor was granted on 16 Oct. 1777 to John Palmer Jr. and John Palmer of Windsor [this was the only paper in the file]. In two deeds on 14 Dec. 1779 John Palmer Jr. of Windsor and his sister Jerusha Palmer, the only heirs of the real estate of their father John Palmer, divided the real estate.

On 20 March 1786 Ebenezer Fitch Bissell of Windsor sold to Daniel Bissell of Windsor and Jerusha Skinner of East Windsor his right in two pieces of land from the estate of his father Daniel Bissell. On 29 Sept. 1786 Margaret Loomis of Windsor sold to Daniel Bissell of Windsor her right in two lots; the first was from her father Daniel Bissell's estate and the second was undivided with Daniel Bissell, Ebenezer Fitch Bissell, and Jerusha Skinner, all heirs of their sister Lucy Bissell late of Windsor. On 24 Jan. 1787 Jerusha Skinner late of East Windsor now of Ellington, Conn., sold to Daniel Bissell of Windsor her right in seven acres that had been part of her father's estate.

On 10 April 1792 Jerusha Skinner and James L. Wood of Ellington sold to Seth Dexter and Jabez Haskell their right in land in Windsor. [James L.

Wood had married Roxanna Wadsworth only child of Jerusha's son Joseph Wadsworth.]

On 21 June 1796 Jerusha Skinner and James L. Wood of Ellington leased to John Palmer of Windsor land with a house and barn that John Palmer and his sister Jerusha Palmer had conveyed to Jerusha Skinner for her use and improvement for life.

On 9 June 1798 the estate of Daniel Skinner late of Hartford was divided among his widow Jerusha and his children.

Child of Joseph and Jerusha (Bissell) Wadsworth:

      i   JOSEPH WADSWORTH[6], b. bet. 1743 and 1749

Note: John Palmer of Windsor made his will on 31 Jan. 1776 (proved 16 Sept. 1794), naming his son John Palmer and grandson John Palmer 3rd. His codicil made on 9 Jan. 1778 says that his son John is now dead, and names his grandson John Palmer, only son of son John, and granddaughter Jerusha Palmer, only daughter of son John. He mentions that these grandchildren have also been provided for by their grandparents Palatiah and Mary Allyn.

References: Hale Newspaper Coll: *Hartford Courant* 26:135(d. Jerusha). Windsor CT LR 15:236(Daniel Bissell), 236(John Palmer); 16:65(John Palmer), 112(Jerusha Palmer); 17:46(Margaret Loomis), 47(Ebenezer F. Bissel), 47(Jerusha Skinner); 19:57; 20:242(Jerusha Skinner). Hartford CT PR #4089(John Palmer), #4090(John Palmer), #4888(Daniel Skinner), #5591(Joseph Wadsworth). Horace Palmer Papers at NEHGS #6024. *Hartford By Barbour* pp. 535-6. *Hist Windsor* 2:80-1, 441, 774.

209. MARGARET BISSELL[5] (*Jerusha Fitch[4], Alice[3] Bradford, William[2-1]*), b. Windsor, Conn., 24 May 1723; d. Torrington, Conn., 16 Aug. 1803 aged 80, "consort of Deacon Nathaniel Loomis."

She m. Windsor, Conn., 15 Dec. 1745 **NATHANIEL LOOMIS**, b. Windsor 11 April 1719; d. East Windsor 14 June 1784 aged 65y, buried Windsor; son of Nathaniel and Ann (Allyn) Loomis.

On 6 Dec. 1750 Nathaniel Loomis of Windsor gave to his son Nathaniel Loomis 3rd of Windsor the houselot on which his son "now lives" and an acre with a barn. On the same day Nathaniel 3rd leased the land back to his father for his father's lifetime.

On 2 July 1770 Nathaniel Loomis of Windsor gave to his son Watson Loomis of Windsor five acres with the house in which Watson "now lives." On 11 Aug. 1784 Margaret Loomis gave to her son Watson his portion of her estate in a settlement with his brother Fitch. On the same day Fitch Loomis of

Torrington sold to Watson his right in two pieces of land in Windsor and Watson sold to Fitch his right in 11 acres in Windsor.

Nathaniel Loomis of Windsor made his will on 21 Oct. 1766, proved 11 Aug. 1784, naming his wife Margaret and his two sons Watson and Fitch.

On 29 Sept. 1786 Margaret Loomis of Windsor sold to Daniel Bissell of Windsor her right in two lots; the first was from her father Daniel Bissell's estate and the second was undivided with Daniel Bissell, Ebenezer Fitch Bissell, and Jerusha Skinner, all heirs of their sister Lucy Bissell late of Windsor.

On 6 March 1787 Margaret Loomis of Torrington sold to Watson Loomis of Windsor her right in the land belonging to her late husband.

Margaret Loomis of Torrington made her will on 12 July 1802, proved 21 Aug. 1804, naming her daughter[-in-law] Prudence Loomis of Windsor widow of Watson, son Fitch, Prudence Loomis, Molly Loomis, Rhoda Bissell wife of Capt. Elisha Bissell of Torrington, and Triphena Loomis daughter of George Loomis of Windsor.

Children of Nathaniel and Margaret (Bissell) Loomis, b. East Windsor, Conn.:

  i   WATSON LOOMIS[6], b. 1 Jan. 1746/7
  ii FITCH LOOMIS, b. 8 Dec. 1748; d. 9 Dec. 1748 or 20 Dec 1748
  iii FITCH LOOMIS, b. 14 May 1751
  iv TRIPHENA LOOMIS, b. 9 Oct. 1753; d. 4 July 1765 ae 11y

References: *Bradford Desc* p. 73. Windsor CT VR 2:59(b. Nathaniel), 173(m.), 250(d. Nathaniel), 383(b. Fitch); 3:380(b. Watson), 382(b. Fitch, Tryphena). Hale Cem Coll:Windsor p. 37(d. Nathaniel, Fitch, Triphena); Torrington(d. Margaret). Windsor CT LR 9:40(Nathaniel Loomis), 41(Nathaniel Loomis 3rd); 16:16(Nathaniel Loomis), 159; 17:46, 59(Margaret Loomis), 237(Fitch Loomis, 237(Watson Loomis). Hartford CT PR #3452(Nathaniel Loomis). Litchfield CT PR #3525(Margaret Loomis).

210. DANIEL BISSELL[5] (*Jerusha Fitch[4], Alice[3] Bradford, William[2-1]*), b. Windsor, Conn., 2 Feb. 1724; d. Randolph, Vt., 28 Dec. 1814 in his 90th yr.

He m. (1) Windsor, Conn., 11 Feb. 1746/7 **ELIZABETH NEWBURY**, b. Windsor, Conn., 28 June 1728; d. there 3/4 June 1749 or 9 Jun 1749 aged 21y; daughter of Roger and Elizabeth (Wolcott) Newbury.

He m. (2) Windsor, Conn., 9 April 1752 **ELIZABETH LOOMIS**, b. Windsor, Conn., 29 Nov. 1726; d. Randolph, Vt., 28 Feb. 1818 in 92nd yr.; daughter of David and Elizabeth (Norman) Loomis.

On 2 March 1764 Jabez Bissell of Windsor sold to Daniel Bissell of Windsor 14 acres with a house and barn.

On 22 Jan. 1770 Daniel Bissell of Windsor gave to his son Daniel Bissell of Windsor three pieces of land totaling more than 20 acres.

On 4 April 1774 John Palmer Jr. and Jerusha his wife of Windsor sold to Daniel Bissell and Eb: Fitch Bissell of Windsor 33 acres that "Our Hon^d Father Daniel Bissell late of Windsor Dec^d Gave to the said Jerusha Palmer Wife of said John Palmer Junr said Thirty Three Acres Lyes in Common and undivided with the Heirs of Said Deceased."

On 20 March 1786 Ebenezer Fitch Bissell of Windsor sold to Daniel Bissell of Windsor and Jerusha Skinner of East Windsor his right in two pieces of land from the estate of his father Daniel Bissell. On 29 Sept. 1786 Margaret Loomis of Windsor sold to Daniel Bissell of Windsor her right in two lots; the first was from her father Daniel Bissell's estate and the second was undivided with Daniel Bissell, Ebenezer Fitch Bissell, and Jerusha Skinner, all heirs of their sister Lucy Bissell late of Windsor. On 24 Jan. 1787 Jerusha Skinner late of East Windsor now of Ellington, Conn., sold to Daniel Bissell of Windsor her right in seven acres that had been part of her father's estate.

On 20 March 1790 Daniel Bissell of Windsor, Conn., sold to Josiah Bissell of Windsor 8 acres with a "mantion" house, barn, and other buildings being the lot where Daniel lives. On 7 Feb. 1792 Daniel Bissell of Randolph, Vt., sold 1½ acres in Windsor, Conn., to David Gibbs of Windsor.

No probate records were found for Daniel or Elizabeth in Randolph, Vt., Probate District.

Children of Daniel and Elizabeth (Newbury) Bissell, b. Windsor, Conn.:

    i ELIZABETH BISSELL⁶, b. 7 Feb. 1747/8

    ii NEWBURY BISSELL, b. 9 June 1749

Children of Daniel and Elizabeth (Loomis) Bissell, b. Windsor, Conn.:

    iii LUCINDA BISSELL, b. 10 March 1753

    iv DANIEL BISSELL, b. 30 Dec. 1754

    v ELIHU BISSELL, b. 13 Jan. 1757

    vi ELIAS BISSELL, bp. 7 June 1759

    vii SYBIL BISSELL, b. 1 June 1761

    viii EZEKIEL BISSELL, b. 22 April 1764

    ix PEREZ BISSELL, b. 18 June 1767

References: *Bradford Desc* pp. 73-4. Windsor CT VR 2:70(b. Eliz. Newbury), 132(1st m.), 133(2nd m.), 257(d. Eliz. Newbury), 302(b. 1st 2 ch.), 372(b. Eliz. Loomis), 536 (b. Lucinda, Daniel), 538(b. Elihu, Elias), 540(b. Sybil), 569(b. last 2 ch.). Bissell TSS #313 (d. Daniel, 2nd wife). Hale Cem Coll:Windsor p. 81(d. 1st wife). Windsor CT LR 14:5(Jabez Bissell);

15:236(John Palmer); 17:46(Margaret Loomis), 47(Ebenezer F. Bissell), 47(Jerusha Skinner); 18:40, 168(Daniel Bissell).

211.   EBENEZER FITCH BISSELL⁵ (*Jerusha Fitch⁴, Alice³ Bradford, William²⁻¹*), b. Windsor, Conn., 1736; d. 1814, bur. Windsor. His gravestone calls him Capt. with service in the 17th Conn. Regt.

He m. Windsor, Conn., 24 June 1756 **ESTHER HAYDEN**, b. Windsor, Conn., 28 Nov. 1736; d. 1815; daughter of Daniel and Esther (Moore) Hayden.

On 16 Dec. 1755 Daniel Bissell deeded half a lot in Windsor to son Ebenezer Fitch Bissell.

On 4 April 1774 John Palmer Jr. and Jerusha his wife of Windsor sold to Daniel Bissell and Eb: Fitch Bissell of Windsor 33 acres "Our Hon^d Father Daniel Bissell late of Windsor Dec^d Gave to the said Jerusha Palmer Wife of said John Palmer Junr said Thirty Three Acres Lyes in Common and undivided with the Heirs of Said Deceased."

Ebenezer Fitch Bissell served in the Revolutionary War as a Captain.

On 20 March 1786 Ebenezer Fitch Bissell of Windsor sold to Daniel Bissell of Windsor and Jerusha Skinner of East Windsor his right in two pieces of land from the estate of his father Daniel Bissell. On 29 Sept. 1786 Margaret Loomis of Windsor sold to Daniel Bissell of Windsor her right in two lots; the first was from her father Daniel Bissell's estate and the second was undivided with Daniel Bissell, Ebenezer Fitch Bissell, and Jerusha Skinner, all heirs of their sister Lucy Bissell late of Windsor.

In 1790 the household of Eben^r F. Bissel Windsor, Conn., consisted of 2 men over 16, a boy under 16, and one female. Eben^r F. Bissel Jr. was nearby.

Children of Ebenezer Fitch and Esther (Hayden) Bissell, first 3 b. Windsor, Conn.:

  i   ESTHER BISSELL⁶, b. 13 July 1757; d. 7 Sept. 1777 ae 20y
  ii EBENEZER FITCH BISSELL, b. 4 Jan. 1760
  iii RHODA BISSELL, b. 19 Dec. 1761
  iv JERUSHA BISSELL, b. 1764
  v   TITUS LUCRETIUS BISSELL, b. 22 Oct. 1766
  vi ELI BISSELL, b. ca. 1769; d. 15 Sept. 1773 ae 4y

References: *Bradford Desc* p. 74. Windsor CT VR 2:52(b. Esther), 133(m.), 537(b. 1st ch.), 540(b. next 2 ch). Hale Cem Coll:Windsor p. 81(d. Ebenezer F., Esther, Eli). *DAR Patriot*

Index p. 61. Windsor CT LR 11:152(Daniel Bissell); 15:236(John Palmer); 17:46(Margaret Loomis), 47(Ebenezer F. Bissell). *Ancient Windsor* 2:83.

212. WILLIAM CLEVELAND[5] (*Lucy Fitch*[4], *Alice*[3] *Bradford*, *William*[2-1]), b. Canterbury, Conn., 7 July 1719; d. prob. Windsor ca 1791 aged 72y.

He m. Plainfield, Conn., ca. 1739 **RACHEL WARREN**, b. Plainfield, Conn., 23 Aug. 1717; d. Mansfield, Conn. after 7 June 1791; daughter of Jacob and Abigail (Haines) Warren.

On 13 Feb. 1743/4 Nehemiah Cleveland of Mansfield, Conn., quit-claimed to his brother William Cleveland of Mansfield part of the farm they had bought together from Enoch Hunt.

On 21 Dec. 1749 Henry Cleveland sold land to his son William.

On 11 Dec. 1750 William Cleveland of Mansfield sold to his father Henry Cleveland his right in six acres.

On 7 June 1791 Rachel Cleveland petitioned that her son Jedediah Cleveland be appointed administrator for her husband's estate. The inventory for the estate of Wm. Cleveland late of Windsor was presented by Jeddidiah Cleveland.

Children of William and Rachel (Warren) Cleveland:

    i ALICE CLEVELAND[6], b. Canterbury, Conn., 21 July 1740

    ii RACHEL CLEVELANd bp. 19 Dec. 1741

    iii SYLVIA CLEVELAND

    iv LUCY CLEVELAND

    v HENRY CLEVELAND, b. Mansfield, Conn., 1 or 11 May 1746

    vi ABBY (or ABIJAH) CLEVELAND [female]

    vii JACOB CLEVELAND, b. ca. 1750

    viii WILLIAM CLEVELAND, b. ca. 1752 (d. Dalton 28 Dec 1799 in 53rd yr.)

    ix LYDIA CLEVELAND, b. Mansfield, Conn., 9 March 1755

    x JEDEDIAH CLEVELAND, b. 5 Sept. 1758

    xi ISRAEL CLEVELAND

References: *Bradford Desc* p. 76. Plainfield CT VR 1:17(b. Rachel). Canterbury CT VR 1:106(b. Alice). *Mansfield CT VR* p. 45(b. Henry, Lydia). *VR Dalton* pp. 17(b. Henry), 71 (d. son William). *Cleveland Gen* 1:179-80. Mansfield CT LR 4:352(Nehemiah Cleveland); 5:198(Henry Cleveland), 282(Nehemiah Cleveland). Berkshire Co. PR #1518(William Cleveland).

213. NEHEMIAH CLEVELAND[5] (*Lucy Fitch*[4], *Alice*[3] *Bradford*, *William*[2-1]), b. Canterbury, Conn., 30 July 1721; d. Williamsburg 27/29 Oct. 1792 aged 71y.

He m. Mansfield, Conn., 8 Nov. 1744 **DINAH BROWN**, b. Canterbury, Conn., 15 Jan. 1721; d. Williamsburg 1 or 15 Jan. 1805; daughter of Deliverance and Abigail (Wells) Brown. Deliverance Brown of Canterbury made his will on 7 Oct. 1763, proved 2 Feb.1768, naming his daughter Dinah Cleaveland. On 18 March 1768 the children agreed to divide Deliverance's estate and Dinah and Nehemiah Cleaveland signed this agreement.

On 20 March 1742/3 Henry Cleveland of Mansfield sold to his son Nehemiah Cleveland of Mansfield 20 acres in Canterbury. On 2 Feb. 1748/9 Henry sold to his son Nehemiah a large tract of land in Mansfield.

On 13 Feb. 1743/4 Nehemiah Cleveland of Mansfield quitclaimed to his brother William Cleveland of Mansfield part of the farm they had bought together from Enoch Hunt. On 24 Jan. 1755 Nehemiah sold to his father Henry Cleveland 20 acres, part of the farm they had bought from Prince Storrs; Henry sold to these 20 acres on 28 May 1763. On 15 Jan. 1759 Henry and Nehemiah sold to 20 acres of the farm on which Nehemiah lived to John Slapp.

In the 1771 Valuation List, Nehemiah Cleaveland appears in Williamsburg with 1 poll, 1 house, 1 horse, 1 cattle, 1 swine, 8 acres of tillage which produced 32 bushels of grain, and 1½ acre of fresh meadow which produced 1 ton of hay.

In 1790 Deacon Nehemiah Cleveland was head of a household in Williamsburg consisting of 2 men over 16 and 7 females. Also listed in Williamsburg were Amasa (1 man, 4 boys, 2 females), Nehemiah (2 men, 1 female), and Roswell (1 man, 4 females).

Nehemiah Cleveland of Williamsburgh made his will on 20 Oct. 1792, proved 1 April 1793, naming wife Dinah, son Azariah, daughter Deliverance, son Nehemiah, son Amasa, and son Roswell.

Children of Nehemiah and Dinah (Brown) Cleveland, b. Mansfield, Conn.:

    i AZARIAH CLEVELAND[6], b. 2 Dec. 1745; d. 1825 unm.

    ii DELIVERANCE CLEVELAND, b. 22 Aug. 1749

    iii NEHEMIAH CLEVELAND, b. 5 April 1753

    iv AMASA CLEVELAND, b. 16 June 1756

    v ROSWELL CLEVELAND, b. 2 July 1759

References: *Bradford Desc* p. 76. Canterbury CT VR 1:75(b. Dinah), 117(b. Nehemiah). *Mansfield CT VR* p.44(b. Azariah), 45(b. next 4 ch.), 222(m.). *Cleveland Gen* 1:180 (gives her mother's maiden name as Waldo). Canterbury CT LR 5:164(Henry Cleveland). Mansfield CT LR 5:150(Henry Cleveland); 4:352(Nehemiah Cleveland); 5:669(Nehemiah Cleveland); 6:180(Henry & Nehemiah); 7:41(Henry Cleveland). Plainfield CT PR #272(Deliverance Brown). *1771 Valuation* p. 408.

214.   LUCY CLEVELAND[5] (*Lucy Fitch*[4], *Alice*[3] *Bradford*, *William*[2-1]), b. Canterbury, Conn., 2 March 1724/5; d. after 27 March 1794.

She m. Mansfield, Conn., 3 Dec. 1743 **JUDAH STORRS**, b. Mansfield, Conn., 26 Sept. 1723; d. there 29 May 1791; son of Thomas and Mehitabel (_____) Storrs. On 7 March 1744/5 Thomas Storrs of Mansfield, Conn., for love and affection gave his son Judah Storrs of Mansfield land adjoining Judah's farm.

On 31 July 1754 Judah Storrs of Mansfield sold to his father Thomas Storrs and Amiziah Storrs of Mansfield nine acres.

Judah Storrs' household in Mansfield, Conn., in 1790 consisted of 3 men over 16, 5 females, and one other free person.

On 9 Oct. 1790 Judah Storrs of Mansfield for love and affection gave to his son Henry Storrs of Mansfield two-thirds of 100 acres and of the buildings, the farm on which Judah was living.

The will of Judah Storrs of Mansfield, made on 9 Oct. 1790, proved 10 June 1791, names his wife Lucy; sons Asahel, Justis, Berzaleel, Frederick, Henry, and Chester; and daughters Lucy Crafts and Zeruah.

On 27 March 1794 Lucy Storrs of Mansfield, widow, in exchange for her comfortable support during her natural life, give up her dower rights in the estate of her late husband Judah Storrs to her son Henry Storrs.

Children of Judah and Lucy (Cleveland) Storrs, b. Mansfield, Conn.:

    i   ASAHEL STORRS[6], b. 3 May 1745

    ii   LUCY STORRS, b. 3 May 1747; d. 11 Sept. 1751

    iii   OLIVE STORRS, b. 15 May 1749; prob. d.y. (not in father's will)

    iv   JUSTUS STORRS, b. 26 April 1751; d. 26 Oct. 1754

    v   HENRY STORRS, b. 14 Sept. 1753

    vi   JUSTUS STORRS, b. 11 Oct. 1755

    vii   WILLIAM FITCH STORRS, b. 3 July 1757

    viii   LUCY STORRS, b. 26 Oct. 1759

    ix   BEZALEEL STORRS, b. 6 Aug. 1761

    x   FREDERICK STORRS, b. 2 May 1764

    xi   CHESTER STORRS, b. 1767

    xii   ZERUAH STORRS (in father's will)

References: *Bradford Desc* p. 77. Mansfield CT VR D:169(b. Judah), 171(b. 1st 10 ch.), 286(m.), 343(d. Judah). *Cleveland Gen* 1:181. Mansfield CT PR #3614(Judah Storrs). Mansfield CT LR 4:371(Thomas Storrs); 5:423(Judah Storrs); 12:17(Judah Storrs), 168(Lucy Storrs). Canterbury CT VR 1:117(b. Lucy).

215. JABEZ CLEVELAND[5] (*Lucy Fitch[4], Alice[3] Bradford, William[2-1]*), b. Canterbury, Conn., 4 Nov. 1737; d. in the battle of Bunker Hill 17 June 1775 aged 38y.

He m. Mansfield, Conn., 30 July 1760 **JANE TRUMBULL**, b. Voluntown, Conn.; d. York Springs, Penna.; daughter of Walter and Jean or Jane (Campbell) Trumbull. She m. (2) Dr. JOHN ARNOLD with whom she had John Arnold.

On 10 April 1760 Henry Cleveland sold to his son Jabez several lots of land, it being the farm on which Henry lived. On 29 April 1761 Henry sold more land in Mansfield to his son Jabez. On 10 Oct. 1764 Jabez sold half of a home lot with a house to his father Henry.

On 19 June 1776 Judah Storrs was appointed the administrator for Jabez Cleveland's estate.

Children of Jabez and Jane (Trumbull) Cleveland, b. Mansfield, Conn.:

    i   RACHEL CLEVELAND[6], b. 3 July 1761; d. 10 Aug. 1763

   ii   SARAH CLEVELAND, b. 30 Sept. 1762

  iii   RACHEL CLEVELAND, b. 22 Nov. 1764; d. York Springs PA; unm.

  iv   FREDERICK CLEVELAND, b. 22 Oct. 1766

   v   CHARLOTTE CLEVELAND, b. 26 July 1768

References: *Bradford Desc* p. 77. Canterbury CT VR 1:117(b. Jabez). Mansfield CT VR pp. 45(b. ch.), 222(m.), 310(d. Rachel). *Cleveland Gen* 1:181-2. "The Ancestors and Descendants of Milton Elmer Trumbull," Connie Harrie Fraser (1988, typescript at NEHGS) p. 28. Mansfield CT LR 6:408; 7:55 (Henry Cleveland), 264(Jabez Cleveland). Windham CT PR #905, 9:199.

216. SAMUEL FITCH[5] (*Theophilus[4], Alice[3] Bradford, William[2-1]*), b. Stonington, Conn., 17 June 1735; d. after 1784.

He m. Stonington, Conn., 15 April 1756 **PRISCILLA HILLIARD**; d. after 1784; daughter of William and Priscilla (Irish) Hilliard.

On 28 Jan. 1757 William Hilliard of Stonington sold to Samuel Fitch of Stonington two acres with a house. On 29 May 1760 Samuel sold to William two acres with a house. In two deeds on 31 Oct. 1765 Samuel sold to William land with a house and cooper's shop and 12 rods with a mansion house.

On 7 July 1766 William Hilliard of Stonington sold to Samuel Fitch land with a house and cooper's shop, and on the same day Samuel sold this land to Jolly Allen of Boston, merchant.

Samuel Fitch served in the Revolutionary War.

On 23 Jan. 1770 Henry Hillard of Stonington for love and affection gave to his nephew Dyar Fitch of Richmond, "my sister's child," 100 acres, lot #30 in the second division in Richmond. On 6 April 1780 Dyer Fitch sold part of this lot to Joseph Talbutt of Richmond. On 6 Sept. 1784 Samuel Fitch and Dyer Fitch, late of Richmond, sold to Henry Van Schaack of Stockbridge part of lot #30 with a house and barn. And on 23 Nov. 1784 Samuel and Dyer, late of Richmond, sold more of lot #30 and another lot to Hezekiah Phelps; this deed was acknowledged at Albany Co.

There are no probate records in Berkshire Co. for Samuel Fitch.

Children of Samuel and Priscilla (Hilliard) Fitch, b. Stonington, Conn.:

    i LUCY FITCH[6], b. 2 Dec. 1756

    ii DYAR FITCH, b. 18 Oct. 1758

References: *TAG* 46:45. Stonington CT VR 3:189(m.; b. ch.). *Desc Rev James Fitch* pp. 1:104-5. Stonington CT LR 7:80(William Hillard), 278; 8:140(Samuel Fitch), 157(William Hilliard). Berkshire Co. LR 8:88(Henry Hillard); 17:436, 501(Samuel & Dyar); 22:68(Dyer Fitch).

217. THEOPHILUS FITCH[5] (*Theophilus[4], Alice[3] Bradford, William[2-1]*), b. Stonington, Conn., 8 May 1737; d. bet. 22 April 1774 (when the constable could not find enough estate to satisfy a debt) and 4 July 1781 (adm.).

He m. Stonington, Conn., 9 Nov. 1757 **HANNAH STEPHENS**, b. Stonington 16 May 1738; d. after 4 July 1781; daughter of Simeon and Mercy (Coates) Stevens.

Theophilus Fitch was a Private in the Revolutionary War.

On 4 July 1781 Hannah Fitch was granted administration on the estate of Theophilus Fitch.

Children of Theophilus and Hannah (Stephens) Fitch, b. Stonington Conn:

    i SARAH FITCH[6], b. 7 Nov. 1758

    ii PRENTICE FITCH, b. 18 Nov. 1760

    iii JAMES FITCH, b. 25 Dec. 1762

    iv CATHERINE FITCH, b. 22 Sept. 1767

    v THEOPHILUS FITCH, b. 10 Jan. 1770

    vi FREELOVE FITCH, b. 20 May 1773

References: Stonington CT TR 3:199(m.; b. ch.). Stonington CT PR #1313 (Theophilus Fitch). *Desc Rev James Fitch* pp. 1:105-6.

218. MARY FITCH[5] (*Theophilus*[4], *Alice*[3]*Bradford*, *William*[2-1]), b. Stonington, Conn., 22 April 1744.

Fitch Gen says she m. Stonington, Conn., 14 Feb. 1759 **AMOS FRINK**, b. Stonington 18 Jan. 1737; son of Benjamin and Tacy (Burdick) Frink. On 1 Feb. 1760 Benjamin Frink of Stonington sold to his son Amos Frink of Stonington five acres that Benjamin bought of his brother Thomas and that had been given to them by their father's will. On 29 Feb. 1764 Benjamin gave Amos two acres.

Mary would be only 14 years old at the time of this marriage. Proof is needed.

A list of inhabitants of the east part of the first Society in Stonington for the year 1770 includes Amos Frink and Mary Frink.

The household of Amos Frink in New London Co., Conn., in the 1790 census consisted of 3 men over 16, 2 boys, and 3 females.

No Connecticut probate records have been found for Amos Frink.

Children of Amos and Mary (Fitch) Frink, b. Stonington, Conn.:

    i AMOS FRINK[6], b. 18 Nov. 1760

    ii GILBERT FRINK, b. 12 Dec. 1762

poss iii OLIVER FRINK

poss iv EZRA FRINK

poss v CHARLES FRINK

References: Stonington CT VR 3:211(m.). *Frink Gen* p. 34(adds last 3 ch.). *Desc Rev James Fitch* p. 1:106. Stonington CT LR 7:375; 8:69(Benjamin Frink). *Hist Stonington CT* p. 380(b. Amos, Gilbert). Stonington 1st Ch 8:108(list of inhabitants).

219. JERUSHA FITCH[5] (*Jabez*[4], *Alice*[3] *Bradford*, *William*[2-1]), b. Stonington, Conn., 30 Jan. 1723; d. after 4 Feb. 1788.

She m. (1) Canterbury, Conn., 6 Dec. 1742 **TYXHALL ENSWORTH**, b. Canterbury, Conn., 19 Dec. 1717; d. there 6 Jan. 1776 aged 59; son of John and Elizabeth (Cleveland) Ensworth.

She m. (2) Preston, Conn., 11 Dec. 1776 **JACOB BROWN**, b. Preston, Conn., 6 July 1711; d. after 4 Feb.1788; son of John and ____ (____) Brown. He m. (1) Preston 11 Nov. 1742 DELIVERANCE BUMP with whom he had

Martha, Sarah, Rebekah, Elizabeth, Kezia, Deliverance, and Deliverance again. He m. (2) Preston 14 Dec. 1757 MARY PAYSON with whom he had Mary.

On 4 Feb. 1788 Jacob Brown and his wife Jerusha of Preston, Conn., sold to William Bingham of Canterbury, Conn., their right of dower in the real estate of her first husband Tyxhall Ensworth deceased, consisting of ¾ acre with a house and barn; Jedediah Ensworth was one of the witnesses.

Children of Tyxhall and Jerusha (Fitch) Ensworth, b. Canterbury Conn.:

   i   EPHRAIM ENSWORTH[6], b. 1 Dec. 1744; d. 23 June 1749
  ii   JERUSHA ENSWORTH, b. 6 May 1746
 iii   LYDIA ENSWORTH, b. 3 July 1748; d.y.
  iv   ELIZABETH ENSWORTH, b. 26 June 1750
   v   ALICE ENSWORTH, b. 21 July 1752
  vi   PERSIS ENSWORTH, b. 26 Nov. 1754; d. 1777
 vii   JEDEDIAH ENSWORTH, b. 1 Sept. 1758
viii   EPHRAIM ENSWORTH, b. 1 Dec. 1760; prob. d. in England as a prisoner of war during the Rev. War.
  ix   ABIGAIL ENSWORTH, b. 22 April 1768; d. 16 May 1773

References: *Bradford Desc* p. 74. Canterbury CT VR 1:133(m.), 134(b. Tyxhall, Jerusha, Lydia, Elizabeth, Alice, Persis), 135(b. last 3 ch.), 137(d. Tyxhall). Canterbury CT LR 9:485(Jacob Brown). *Desc Rev James Fitch* p. 1:107. Preston CT VR 1:119(his 1st m., children); 2:83(his 2nd & 3rd m., b. Mary).

220. ALICE FITCH[5] (*Jabez[4], Alice[3] Bradford, William[2-1]*), b. Stonington, Conn., 8 Jan. 1724/5; d. April 1772.

She m. Canterbury, Conn., 24 April 1745 **JAMES COGSWELL**, b. Saybrook, Conn., 6 Jan. 1720; d. Hartford, Conn., 2 Jan. 1807; son of Samuel and Ann (Mason) Cogswell. He m. (2) Hampton, Conn., 21 Jan. 1773 Mrs. MARTHA (LATHROP) DEVOTION, widow of Rev. Ebenezer Devotion. He m. (3) Cheshire, Conn., 5 May 1797 IRENE (RIPLEY) HEBARD, widow of Nathaniel Hebard.

James Cogswell graduated from Yale in 1742. He was licensed to preach by the Windham County Association on 15 May 1744. He was minister of the church in Canterbury, Conn., 1744–1771 and then was minister of the church in Scotland, Conn., for 33 years. *Yale Grads* says "In his religious views he was a decided 'Old Light,' observing to the last the half-way covenant, and alarmed at the growth of 'Hopkinsianism.' His natural mildness and geniality of manner were aided by respectable natural talents and good literary attainments."

Cogswell Fam says "Rev. Dr. Cogswell had a long, laborious, and useful ministry. His life was one of many and great afflictions; his ministry doubtless had its shady side, and his old age had its infirmities, but he kept the faith, was a faithful minister of Jesus Christ, and attained unto his crown of heavenly reward ... He was well-read student and a teacher of theology. He was called by contemporaries, 'The big theologian,' and students for the ministry resorted to him for instruction. Among his pupils were Josiah Whitney, afterwards pastor of Brooklyn Parish, and Naphtali Daggett, subsequently the President of Yale College."

No Connecticut probate records were found for James Cogswell.

Children of James and Alice (Fitch) Cogswell, b. Canterbury, Conn.:

    i JAMES COGSWELL⁶, b. 31 July 1746

    ii ALICE COGSWELL, b. 7 Dec. 1749; d. 9 May 1772; unm.

    iii SAMUEL COGSWELL, b. 23 May 1754

    iv MASON FITCH COGSWELL, b. 18 Sept. 1760

    v SEPTIMUS COGSWELL, b. 30 Aug. 1769; d. Oct. 1773

References: *Bradford Desc* pp. 74-5. Canterbury CT VR 1:100(m.), 106(b. 1ˢᵗ 3 ch.), 109(b. Mason Fitch). *Desc Rev James Fitch* pp. 1:108-9. *Yale Grads* 1:702. *Cogswell Fam* p. 117.

221. PEREZ FITCH⁵ (*Jabez⁴, Alice³ Bradford, William²⁻¹*), b. Canterbury, Conn., Dec. 1726; d. 6 Sept. 1775. He and his wife are both buried in North Street Cemetery, Stamford, Conn.

He m. Stamford, Conn., 4 Sept. 1753 **MARTHA COGGESHALL**, b. Milford, Conn., 25 June 1730; d. Stamford 12 Jan. 1812 aged 83; daughter of Freegift and Martha (Nettleton) Coggeshall. She m. (2) Stamford 8 Aug. 1776 ABRAHAM DAVENPORT. She m. (3) DR. AMOS MEAD. Her gravestone in North Street Cem. in Stamford, which is next to that of Dr. Perez Fitch, says Martha Coggeshall Fitch, wife of Dr. Perez.

Perez Fitch graduated from Yale in 1750. He settled in Stamford as a physician, and united with the Stamford church on 9 Sept. 1759.

The will of Perez Fitch dated 2 Aug. 1773, proved 22 Feb. 1775, names his wife Martha; two sons William and Samuel; and three daughters Martha, Abigail, and Betsey; Abraham Davenport was one of the witnesses to the will. The inventory taken on 14 Dec. 1775 included a servant man, Tom, and a servant woman, Cloe. On 13 Jan. 1776 Martha informed the court that the estate was insolvent.

On 17 Nov 1773 Jabez Fitch mortgaged 27 acres to his son Perez Fitch of Stanford.

On 6 May 1776 Martha Fitch, administratrix of the estate of Perez Fitch, sold to Isaac Hart of Stamford 17½ acres and on the same day she sold two pieces of land totaling 22 acres to Thadeus Hart of Stamford.

Abraham Davenport of Stamford made his will 22 Sept. 1789, proved 1 July 1790, naming his wife Martha, nephew John Davenport (son of John Davenport), granddau. Alice Cogswell (dau. of Elizabeth his dec. dau.), Mehitable Coggeshall (niece of "my present wife"); and sons John and James. Amos Mead was a witness to the will.

On 7 April 1812 Jeremiah Andreas was granted administration on the estate of Martha Mead late of Stamford. The inventory was taken 13 April 1812. No probate record could be found for Amos Mead, but at the end of this inventory is an application by Richard Mead, administrator of the estate of Amos Mead late of Greenwich, asking on 5 May 1808 that two men be appointed to set out to widow Martha Mead her widow's thirds.

Children of Perez and Martha (Coggeshall) Fitch, b. Stamford, Conn.:

  i MARTHA FITCH[6], b. 20 July 1754; bur. North St. Cem. no dates

 ii WILLIAM FITCH, b. 10 Oct. 1756

iii BETSEY FITCH, b. 4 Oct. 1756 [sic]; bur. North St. Cem. no dates

 iv ABIGAIL FITCH, b. 29 March 1760[Stamford VRs say 1766, the *Coggeshall Fam* says it should be 1760 since she m. in 1780]

  v KATE FITCH, b. 1763 [same as Catherine?]

 vi SAMUEL FITCH, b. 20 Aug. 1768; bur. North St. Cem. no dates

vii CATHERINE FITCH; d. bef. 2 Aug. 1773 (father's will), bur. North St. Cem. no dates

References: *TAG* 46:46. Stamford CT VR 1:108(m.; b. Martha), 124(b. William), 158(b. Betsey, Abigail), 171(b. Samuel). Milford CT VR 1:115(b. Martha). Canterbury CT LR 9:56(Jabez Fitch). *Desc Rev James Fitch* p. 1:109. Stamford CT PR 4:155; 5:284, 286(Perez Fitch). Stamford CT LR I:257-8(Martha Fitch). *Coggeshall Fam* p. 36. *Yale Grads* 2:232. Hale Cem Coll:Stamford(bur. Perez, Martha, dau. Martha, Betsey, Catherine). Stamford CT PR 7:184(Abraham Davenport); 10:523;11:158(Martha Mead), 159(application of Richard Mead).

222. JABEZ FITCH⁵ (*Jabez⁴, Alice³ Bradford, William²⁻¹*), b. Norwich (or Lisbon), Conn., 23 May 1729; d. Sheldon, Vt., 19 Dec. 1806 aged 78.

He m. Canterbury, Conn., 22 Aug. 1754 **LYDIA HUNTINGTON**, b. Norwich, Conn., 27 Oct. 1735; d. Vergennes, Vt., 3 April 1803 aged 68; daughter of Ebenezer and Sarah (Leffingwell) Huntington.

On 18 Aug. 1751 Jabez Fitch was admitted to the Canterbury Church. His wife was admitted on 27 Jan. 1760.

On 4 Feb. 1754 Jabez Fitch of Canterbury sold to his son Jabez Jr. "all his farm I now live on" and on 4 April 1758 they partitioned the farm. In an undated deed (ack. 27 March 1765) Jabez Fitch and Elizabeth Fitch, formerly the widow of William Darbee formerly of Pomfret and now the wife of Jabez, sold to Jabez Fitch Jr. half of a dwelling house where Jabez Jr. now lived and 10 acres. On 10 May 1774 Jabez sold 17 acres to Jabez Jr. reserving the right to cut wood and rails.

Jabez Fitch served as a Private in the Revolutionary War.

Jabez Fitch and Solomon Morgan were the administrators of his father's estate in 1784 and Jabez signed an additional inventory on 20 March 1786. On 10 May 1794 an execution against Solomon and Jabez calls Jabez "late of Canterbury now absconded and gone." On 15 Jan. 1798 Calvin Goddard wrote:

> The subscriber having been appointed Administrator de bonis non upon the Estate of Col Jabez Fitch decsd for the sole purpose of completing the settlement of said Estate by paying Creditors & the Inventory consisting only of an Execution against Doct Jabez Fitch to whom after paying Creditors the residue of Estate is given by Will the Subscriber does not think himself authorized to collect the Exe of Doct Fitch or Mr Morgan for the purpose of paying the ballance to Doct Fitch — he therefore prays this acct may [be] accepted & sd Estate closed.

He may be the Jabez Fitch in Hillsdale, Columbia Co., N.Y., in 1790 with 3 males over 16, 2 under 16, and 4 females in his household. He and his son Jabez G. Fitch are listed in the 1800 census in Vergennes, Vt.

Jabez Fitch of Sheldon, Vt., in his will dated 13 Dec. 1805, proved 4 Feb. 1807, named his sons Ebenezer, Jabez, Chancy, and Samuel; his daughters Sally Knowlton, Nancy Sanders, Lucy Williams, and Allice Coleman; and the heirs of his deceased daughter Lydia Perkins. The witnesses were all of Williamstown, Mass., and made their depositions in Berkshire Co. Chauncey Fitch was appointed administrator on 4 Feb. 1807.

Children of Jabez and Lydia (Huntington) Fitch, all but 2nd b. Canterbury, Conn.:

    i PEREZ FITCH[6], b. 5 Sept. 1755; d. 6 Sept. 1755

    ii EBENEZER FITCH, b. Norwich, Conn., 2 Sept. 1756

    iii ABIGAIL FITCH, b. ca. 1757; d. Canterbury 11 March 1759 ae 2

    iv LYDIA FITCH, b. 9 Oct. 1758; d. 2 Aug. 1759 ae 10m

    v LYDIA FITCH, b. 14 June 1760

    v ABIGAIL FITCH, b. 24 April 1762; d. March 1763 or 24 April 1763 ae 9m

    vi JABEZ GAILL FITCH, b. 20 Jan. 1764

    vii SARAH FITCH, b. 28 April 1766

    viii ANNA FITCH, b. 3 Feb. 1768

    ix CHAUNCEY FITCH, b. 17 Jan. 1771

    x SAMUEL FITCH, b. 3 March 1773

    xi LUCY FITCH, b. 24 Jan. 1777

    xii ALICE FITCH, b. 2 June 1781

References: *Bradford Desc* p. 75. Norwich CT VR 1:84(b. Lydia). Canterbury CT VR 1:138(m.), 142(b. Eben., Lydia, Lydia, Abigail), 143(b. Jabez Gaill, Sarah, Anna), 144(b. Chauncey, Samuel, Lucy), 145(b. Alice). Hale Cem Coll:Canterbury p. 30(d. Lydia, Abigail). Franklin CT PR B:23, E:354-9(Jabez Fitch). Canterbury CT LR 6:118, 297; 7:200; 9:194(Jabez Fitch). *Desc Rev James Fitch* p. 1:110.

223. LYDIA FITCH[5] (*Jabez[4], Alice[3] Bradford, William[2-1]*), bp. Canterbury, Conn., 24 June 1736; d. Norwich, Conn., 14 July 1820 aged 85y, buried Norwich.

She m. Canterbury, Conn., 31 Dec. 1751 **PHINEAS ADAMS**, b. Norwich, Conn., 7 Sept. 1726 (or 1729); d. there 1 Jan. 1779 or 7 Jan. 1779 aged 52y; buried Norwich; son of William and Susannah (Woodward) Adams.

Phineas Adams served during the Revolutionary War; his gravestone says he served in Capt. Ensign's Co.

In his will dated 30 Dec. 1778, proved 8 Feb. 1779, Phineas Adams of Norwich named his wife Lydia; six sons William, Asahel, Phinehas, Roger, Jabez, and Fitch; daughters Abigail, Welthey, Lydia, and Allice; and friend Benjamin Morse Jr.; he mentioned but did not name his mother. The division on 28 Sept. 1779 was among wife Lydia; sons William, Asail, Phineas, Roger, Jabez, and Fitch; and daughters Abigail, Welthey, Lydia, and Alice.

On 15 March 1779 Lydia Adams of Norwich and Jabez Fitch of Canterbury were made guardians of Lydia and Alice. William Adams of

Norwich and Jabez Fitch of Canterbury were made guardians of Jabez and
Fitch. On the same day Phineas and Roger Fitch made choice of their brother
William Fitch to be their guardian.

Children of Phineas and Lydia (Fitch) Adams, b. Norwich, Conn.:

   i   WILLIAM ADAMS[6], b. 17 Oct. 1752

   ii ASAHEL ADAMS, b. 13 Sept. 1754

  iii ABIGAIL ADAMS, b. 7 Dec. 1756

  iv LYDIA ADAMS, b. 22 Dec. 1758; d. 16 Feb. 1759

   v WEALTHEON ADAMS, b. 22 Feb. 1760

  vi PHINEAS ADAMS, b. 17 Aug. 1762

 vii ROGER ADAMS, b. 6 Nov. 1764

viii JABEZ ADAMS, b. 23 Feb. 1768

  ix FITCH ADAMS, b. 2 Jan. 1772

   x LYDIA ADAMS, b. 4 May 1774

  xi ALICE ADAMS, b. 8 Oct. 1776

References: *Bradford Desc* p. 75. Norwich CT VR 1:87(b. Phineas); 2:42(d. Phineas; b. last
6 ch.), 157(m.; b. 1st 5 ch.). Hale Cem. Coll.: Norwich p. 68(d. Lydia, Phineas). *Desc Rev
James Fitch* pp. 1:111-2. Canterbury 1st Ch p. 68(bp. Lydia), 169(m.). Norwich CT PR
#100(Phineas Adams), #58, 72, 77, 92, 101(guardianships).

224. LUCY FITCH[5] (*Jabez[4], Alice[3] Bradford, William[2-1]*), b. Canterbury, Conn.,
24 June 1736; bp. 27 June 1736; d. Mansfield, Conn., 27 Feb. 1814. She and
David are buried in the Old Mansfield Center Cem.

She m. Canterbury, Conn., 29 Oct. 1761 **DAVID ADAMS**, b. Canterbury
23 May 1731; d. Mansfield 26 March 1790 aged 59; son of David and
Katherine (Adams) Adams. David Adams of Canterbury made his will 17
June 1753, proved 17 Sept. 1753, naming David among the children of his
first wife Katherine.

Lucy wife of Dr. Adams was admitted to the Scotland Congregational
Church in 1762.

Dr. David Adams was a physician and served during the Revolutionary
War.

Lucy Adams of Pomfret, widow of Dr. David Adams, made her will 17
Sept. 1810, proved 5 April 1814, naming daughter Lucy Ensworth, widow;
dau. Lydia Grosvenor wife of Nathan; and daughter Polly Holt wife of Elijah
Holt who was in debt to Lucy. On 20 Feb. 1815 Elijah Holt of Buffalo,

Niagara Co., N.Y., signed a bond for his debt to Lucy's executor and accepts his wife Polly's part of the estate.

Children of David and Lucy (Fitch) Adams, b. Scotland, Conn., bp. Scotland Congregational Church:

    i LUCY ADAMS[6], b. 7 Aug. 1762, bp. 15 Aug. 1762

    ii DAVID AUGUSTUS ADAMS, bp. 29 Jan. 1764; d. Lake Francois, Santo Domingo W.I. 26 Aug. 1783

    iii LYDIA ADAMS, b. 16 Oct. 1768, bp. 23 Oct. 1768

    iv MARY ADAMS, b. 10 Dec. 1771, bp. Dec. 1771

References: *Bradford Desc* pp. 75-6. Canterbury CT VR 1:59(b. David). Windham CT VR 2:88(m.; b. Lucy, David, Mary). *Desc Rev James Fitch* pp. 1:112-3. Scotland Cong. Ch. Recs. 2:10(Lucy adm.), 34(bp. Lucy), 76(bp. David), 79(bp. Lydia), 80(bp. Mary). Canterbury 1st Ch p. 71(bp. Lucy). Hale Cem Coll:Mansfield p. 15(d. David, Lucy). Plainfield CT PR #9(David Adams). Pomfret CT PR #35(Lucy Adams).

225. ASHAEL FITCH[5] (*Jabez[4], Alice[3] Bradford, William[2-1]*), bp. Canterbury, Conn., 27 Aug. 1738; d. Redding, Conn., 31 March 1793 aged 55, buried Redding.

He m. (1) 24 June 1760 **RACHEL STRONG**, d. Redding, Conn., 13 April 1762.

He m. (2) Wilton, Conn., 4 Oct. 1764 **HANNAH LOCKWOOD**, b. Norwalk, Conn., 23 Sept. 1743; d. Redding, Conn., 13 March 1821, aged 77y, bur. Redding; daughter of Peter and Abigail (Hawley) Lockwood. Peter Lockwood named his daughter Hannah (without surname) in his will dated 26 Aug. 1775, proved 1 Nov. 1755. Hannah wife of Asahel Fitch received a share of Peter Lockwood's estate in a distribution of 5 April 1777.

Asael Fitch and his wife joined the Redding Congregational Church by profession on 5 June 1768.

Ashael Fitch served as a Surgeon's Mate during the Revolutionary War and was the first physician to settle in Redding.

Arael Fitch's household in Redding in 1790 consisted of 2 men over 16 and 5 females.

Administration on the estate of Dr. Ashael Fitch of Redding was granted to Hannah on 24 April 1793; the estate was insolvent. The inventory taken on 15 June 1793 lists 21 pairs of sheets, 16 pillowcases, 17 blankets or bedquilts, and 11 beds or underbeds. He must have taken patients into his own home to care for them.

Child of Ashael and Rachel (Strong) Fitch, b. Redding, Conn.:

    i ANNA FITCH[6], b. 24 March 1760

Children of Ashael and Hannah (Lockwood) Fitch, b. Redding, Conn.:

    ii CLARISSA FITCH, b. 25 Sept. 1768, bp. 21 Oct. 1768

    iii HANNAH FITCH, b. 28 April 1770, bp. 1 July 1770

    iv JAMES GALE FITCH, b. 31 Aug. 1773, bp. 3 Oct. 1773; d. 1 Aug. 1795

    v ABIGAIL ELLIS FITCH (twin), b. 8 Sept. 1776

    v ELLIS ABIGAIL FITCH (twin), b. 8 Sept. 1776; d. 3 March 1796

    vi MARTHA FITCH, bp. 10 Oct. 1779

Note: *Desc Rev James Fitch* says his name is spelled several ways: Ashbel, Asel, Asahel, Azahel. I have spelled the way it was in each of the different sources. Most of the dates are from a manuscript by Asa Fitch at NYG&B citing a family Bible.

References: *Bradford Desc* p. 76. Hale Cem Coll:Redding pp. 3(d. Ashael), 54(d. Hannah). *Lockwood Gen* pp. 86-8. Danbury CT PR #3059(Peter Lockwood). *Redding CT Ch* pp. 20(Aseal joins ch.), 24(d. Hannah). Danbury CT PR #1831(Ashael Fitch). *Hist Redding CT* p. 178. Redding Ch Recs 1:95(bp. James Gale), 99(b. Abigail Ellis, Ellis Abigail), 103(bp. Martha), 142(bp. Clarissa), 144(bp. Hannah). Redding CT VR p. 27(b. James Gale). *Desc Rev James Fitch* p. 1:113. Canterbury 1st Ch. p. 73(bp. Ashael).

226. JERUSHA STEELE[5] (*Thomas[4], Mercy[3] Bradford, William[2-1]*), b. Hartford, Conn., 1 July 1710, bp. Second Church 2 July 1710; d. between 10 April 1749 (sold land) and 21 Sept. 1756 (when not among Samuel Steele's heirs).

She m. West Hartford, Conn., 12 Feb. 1729/30 **DANIEL MILLS**; b. Windsor, Conn., 22 May 1706; d. after 25 Sept. 1751; son of Peter and Joanna (Porter) Mills. On 15 March 1733/4 Peter Mills Sr. of Windsor gave his son Daniel Mills of Windsor 55 acres.

In Jan. 1744 Daniel Mills of Windsor sold to Peletiah Mills of Windsor two pieces of land in Windsor. On 15 Oct. 1746 Daniel Mills of Simsbury and Isaac Skinner of Windsor sold to Edward Griswold of Windsor 22 acres.

On 21 March 1745 and 10 April 1749 Thomas Steele's children, including Jerusha Mills of Simsbury, sold two tracts of land laid out in the right of Samuel Steele in Farmington.

On 7 May 1751 Josiah Phelps 3rd of Windsor who had a well-excuted deed for 200 acres in Simsbury from Daniel Mills late of Simsbury now living in the Nine Partners in Dutchess Co., N.Y., sold the land back to Daniel. On

23 Aug. 1751 (ack. 25 Sept. 1751) Daniel Mills late of Simsbury now of Crum Elbow, Dutchess Co., N.Y., sold to Peletiah Mills of Windsor 200 acres; witnesses were Daniel Mills Jr. and Thomas Mills.

Children of Daniel and Jerusha (Steele) Mills, b. Windsor, Conn.:

    i   DANIEL MILLS[6], b. 19 Nov. 1730

    ii THOMAS MILLS, b. 3 April 1732

   iii JERUSHA MILLS, b. 27 Dec. 1734

   iv ANN MILLS, b. 24 March 1735/6; d. 1737

    v ANNA MILLS, b. 25 March 1737

   vi ISAAC MILLS, b. 18 April 1738

  vii SUSANNA MILLS, bp. 3 Jan. 1742

References: *W Hartford Fam* p. 1518. W. Hartford 1st Ch. p. 114(m.). *Bradford Desc* p. 77. *Windsor By Stiles* pp. 495-6. Windsor CT VR 2:63(b. Daniel), 177(m.), 253(b. Anna), 394(b. first 3 ch.), 395(b. Ann, Isaac). Windsor CT LR 6:180(Peter Mills); 8:37, 228(Daniel Mills). Simsbury CT LR 7:568(Josiah Phelps), 569(Daniel Mills). Farmington CT LR 7:125, 466, 486(Samuel Steel's heirs). *Hartford CT Second Ch* p. 319(bp. Jerusha). *Mills Gen.*

227. SAMUEL STEELE[5] (*Thomas[4], Mercy[3] Bradford, William[2-1]*), b. Hartford, Conn., 11 March 1712, bp. Second Ch. 16 March 1712; d. W. Hartford, Conn., 12 or 13 Sept. 1779 "of shortness of breath."

He m. (1) W. Hartford, Conn., 20 Dec. 1739 **ELIZABETH MERRY**.

He m. (2) **MARTHA** _____. Was she the Martha, widow, d. W. Hartford 14 Sept. 1801 aged 75y?

Samuel Steele owned the covenant on 4 May 1729.

Elizabeth wife of Samuel Steele was admitted to the W. Hartford church 5 Aug. 1742.

On 21 March 1745 and 10 April 1749 Thomas Steele's children, including Samuel Steel of Hartford, sold two tracts of land laid out in the right of Samuel Steele in Farmington.

On 21 Oct. 1751 Samuel Steele of Hartford sold to his brother John Steele of Hartford two pieces of land.

The will of Samuel Steele of Hartford dated 7 Feb. 1777, proved 6 Oct. 1777, names wife Martha; sons Allyn, Joel, and Thomas; and daughters Elizabeth, Mary, Martha, Lucrecia, and Sybil.

On 2 April 1792 Martha Steel and Joel Steel of Hartford sold to Jonathan Belden Black three acres with a house. On the same day Allyn Steel of

Hartford sold to Joel Steel of Hartford 50 acres. And on the same day Joel sold to Allen 25 acres.

Children of Samuel and Elizabeth (Merry) Steele, b. W. Hartford, Conn., with Elizabeth; a child of Samuel d. 8 Dec. 1760:

    i TIMOTHY STEELE⁶, bp. 8 Oct. 1739 [ch. rec. in chronological order says 1732; not in Aspinwall]

    ii SAMUEL STEELE, bp. 3 Feb. 1740; d.y.

    iii ELIZABETH STEELE, b. 1 Jan. 1741, bp. 1 Jan. 1741

    iv THOMAS STEELE, bp. 24 Oct. 1742

    v ANNA STEELE, b. 15 Sept. 1745; d. 16 Nov. 1762 ae 17y 2m "of a malignant fever"

    vi MARY STEELE (twin), b. 28 Sept. 1747, bp. 4 Oct. 1747; d.y.

    vii SARAH STEELE (twin), b. 28 Sept. 1747, bp. 4 Oct. 1747; d.y. (not in father's will)

    viii MARY STEELE (twin), b. 26 April 1749

    ix SARAH STEELE (twin), b. 26 April 1749

    x MARTHA STEELE, b. 13 April 1751, bp. 14 April 1751

    xi LUCRETIA STEELE, b. 13 Sept. 1753, bp. 16 Sept. 1753

    xii SAMUEL STEELE, b. 28 Feb. 1755, bp. 23 Feb. 1755 [sic]; d. 27 Dec. 1776 "of putred fever"

    xiii ALLYN STEELE, b. 21 July 1757

    xiv MARTIN STEELE, b. 11 Oct. 1760; d. 21 Oct. 1769 "of mortification of the bowels"

    xv SYBIL STEELE, b. 1763, bp. 22 Jan. 1764

    xvi JOEL STEELE, b. 27 March 1767, bp. 22 March 1767 [sic]

References: *W Hartford Fam* p. 1518. *Steele Fam* p. 14. *Bradford Desc* pp. 77-8. *Conn Marr* 2:73. *Hartford By Barbour* p. 579. W. Hartford Ch. 1:10(adm. Elizabeth), 24(d. child), 35(bp. Timothy), 39(bp. Samuel & Elizabeth), 41(bp. Thomas), 44(bp. Mary, Sarah), 46(bp. Martha), 48(bp. Lucretia), 49(bp. Samuel), 54(bp. Martin), 56(bp. Sybil), 61(bp. Joel), 114(m.), 100(Samuel owned cov.), 143(d. Anna), 145(d. Martin), 150(d. son Samuel), 152(d. Samuel-13 Sep), 159(d. Martha). Hartford CT PR #5201(Samuel Steele). Hartford CT LR 8:390(Samuel Steele); 18:273(Martha Steel); 19:16(Allyn Steel), 284(Joel Steel). Farmington CT LR 7:125, 466, 486(Samuel Steel's heirs). *Hartford CT Second Ch* p. 320(bp. Samuel).

228. WILLIAM STEELE[5] (*Thomas⁴, Mercy³ Bradford, William²⁻¹*), b. Hartford, Conn., 10 Dec. 1713, bp. Second Ch. 13 Dec. 1713; d. New Hartford, Conn., 1777.

He m. **LYDIA SEYMOUR**, b. Hartford, Conn., 11 May 1719; d. before 10 Feb. 1777; daughter of John and Lydia (Mason) Seymour. The will of John Seymour dated 11 July 1758, proved 19 Sept. 1758, names his daughter Lydia Steele.

On 25 Dec. 1739 Thomas Steele of Hartford gave to his son William Steele of New Hartford 33 acres in New Hartford.

On 21 March 1745 and 10 April 1749 Thomas Steele's children, including William Steel of Hartford, sold two tracts of land laid out in the right of Samuel Steele in Farmington.

On 8 Sept. 1768 William Steel of New Hartford gave to his son William Steel of New Hartford land in that town.

On 25 Jan. 1777 William Steel of New Hartford sold to Samuel Steel of Hartford half an acre with a mansion house in Hartford.

The will of William Steele of New Hartford dated 10 Feb. 1777, proved 22 April 1777, names the widow of his son Timothy deceased; sons William, Isaac, and Seth; children of son Timothy; and daughters Lydia and Huldah who were to have his "Deceased wife wearing apperrel." An undated distribution names Isaac Steel, Abigail Steel widow of Timothy, Seth Steel, and William Steel.

Children of William and Lydia (Seymour) Steele, b. New Hartford, Conn.:

    i   WILLIAM STEELE[6], b. 27 May 1742

   ii   TIMOTHY STEELE, b. 3 Nov. 1745

  iii   LYDIA STEELE, b. 26 March 1747/8

  iv   HULDA STEELE, b. 12 Aug. 1749

   v   ISAAC STEELE, b. 14 Oct. 1752

  vi   RODERICK STEELE, b. 4 Aug. 1755

 vii   SETH STEELE, b. 12 April 1757

References: New Hartford CT VR 1:21(b. 1ˢᵗ 3 ch.); 2:19(b. last 3 ch.). Hartford CT VR FFS:79(b. Lydia). *Steele Fam* pp. 13, 20. *Bradford Desc* p. 78. *Seymour Gen* p. 67. Farmington CT PR #2620(William Steele). Hartford CT LR 15:386(William Steel). New Hartford CT LR 1:12(Thomas Steele); 2:87(William Steel). Farmington CT LR 7:125, 466, 486(Samuel Steel's heirs). *Hartford CT Second Ch* p. 321(bp. William).

229. SUSANNA STEELE[5] (*Thomas[4], Mercy[3] Bradford, William[2-1]*), b. Hartford, Conn., 15 Dec. 1715; d. W. Hartford, Conn., 7 Oct. 1798 aged 83/84.

She m. W. Hartford, Conn., 18 July 1734 **THOMAS HOSMER**, b. Hartford, Conn., 28 Oct. 1701; d. W. Hartford 22/23 Jan. 1777 aged 75y; son of Thomas and Ann (Prentiss) Hosmer. The will of Thomas Hosmer dated 10 Jan. 1731/2, proved 5 May 1732, names his son Thomas to whom he gave his negro boy Haniball.

Thomas Hosmer and his wife were communicants in 1737 at the ordination of Nathaniel Hooker in the W. Hartford church. Thomas had his negro servants Hannibal, bp. 5 Nov. 1738, and Hercules, bp. 27 June 1742.

On 21 March 1745 and 10 April 1749 Thomas Steele's children, including Thomas Hosmer and his wife Susanna of Hartford, sold two tracts of land laid out in the right of Samuel Steele in Farmington.

On 27 Jan. 1768 Thomas Hosmer of Hartford sold to his son Eldad Hosmer of Hartford 20 acres. On 5 Aug. 1774 Thomas gave to his son Daniel Hosmer of Hartford seven acres.

The will of Thomas Hosmer of Hartford dated 1 Jan. 1777, proved 24 Feb. 1777, names wife Susannah; daughter Susannah Kellogg wife of Samuel; daughter Ruth Kellogg wife of Ephraim; daughter Jerusha; granddaughter Susannah Kellogg (under 18); six sons Thomas, Eldad, Daniel, Elisha, Simeon, and Ashbel; and his negro man Hannibal. The inventory taken 5 March 1777 included part of a saw mill.

On 24 May 1777 Susannah Hosmer, Eldad Hosmer, and Daniel Hosmer of Hartford sold to Timothy Seymour Jr. of Hartford 20 acres. On 16 May 1778 Thomas Hosmer of Hartford sold to Elisha Hosmer of Hartford two pieces of land one of which was bounded on Ashbel Hosmer. On 7 June 1781 Thomas Hosmer of Canaan, Eldad Hosmer, Daniel Hosmer, and Simeon Hosmer all of Hartford sold to Jeremiah Wadsworth of Hartford 17 acres that had come from their father Thomas Hosmer Esq. deceased.

On 20 March 1786 Thomas Hosmer and Ashbel Hosmer of Canaan, Eldad Hosmer, Daniel Hosmer, and Simeon Hosmer of Hartford sold to John Whitman Jr. several acres of land bounded on land set off to Mrs. Susanna Hosmer. On 19 June 1788 Eldad Hosmer of Mayfield, N.Y., and Daniel Hosmer of Hartford sold to Nathan Haynes Whiting of Hartford seven acres "under incumbrance of dower of the widow of Thomas Hosmer." On 21 April 1791 Eldad Hosmer and Daniel Hosmer of Coughnawago, Montgomery Co., N.Y., sold to Nathan H. Whiting of Hartford six acres also "under incumbrance" of the widow Susannah Hosmer.

Children of Thomas and Susanna (Steele) Hosmer, bp. W. Hartford, Conn.:

- i   SUSANNA HOSMER[6], bp. 29 May 1737
- ii THOMAS HOSMER, bp. 1 April 1739
- iii DEBORAH HOSMER, bp. 12 April 1741; d. 23 Oct. 1776
- iv ELDAD HOSMER, bp. 24 April 1743
- v RUTH HOSMER, b. 20 Sept. 1744, bp. 4 Aug. 1745
- vi DANIEL HOSMER, bp. 9 Aug. 1747
- vii JERUSHA HOSMER (named in will)
- viii ELISHA HOSMER, bp. 1 April 1753
- ix SIMEON HOSMER, bp. 11 May 1755
- x ASHBEL HOSMER, bp. 7 May 1758

References: *W Hartford Fam* p. 1518. *Steele Fam* p. 14. *Hosmer Gen* pp. 5, 7. *Bradford Desc* p. 78. *Hartford By Barbour* pp. 321-2. *Conn Marr* 2:73. Hartford CT VR FFS:31(b. Thomas), 33(m.). Hale Cem Coll:West Hartford, p. 7(d. Susanna & Thomas). W. Hartford Ch. 1:36(bp. Susanna), 38(bp. Thomas), 39(bp. Deborah), 41(bp. Eldad), 42(bp. Ruth), 44(bp. Daniel), 48(bp. Elisha), 49(bp. Simeon), 51(bp. Ashbel), 114(m.), 150(d. Thomas), 159(d. Susanna), 165(communicants). Hartford PR #2913(Thomas Steele), #2914(Thomas Steele). Hartford CT LR 12:190; 15:288(Thomas Hosmer); 14:156, 226(Thomas Hosmer the son); 17:59(Thomas Hosmer *et al.*); 18:190-1(Eldad Hosmer *et al.*). Farmington CT LR 7:125, 466, 486(Samuel Steel's heirs).

230. JAMES STEELE[5] (*Thomas[4], Mercy[3] Bradford, William[2-1]*), b. Hartford, Conn., 22 Dec. 1719; d. 1766.

He m. **LOIS** _____; d. after 30 April 1771.

On 21 March 1745 and 10 April 1749 Thomas Steele's children, including James Steele of Hartford, sold two tracts of land laid out in the right of Samuel Steele in Farmington.

On 18 May 1753 James Steel of New Hartford sold to Hezekiah Porter and Timothy Porter of Hartford all the right he has or could have in land in New Hartford.

Administration on the estate of James Steel of New Hartford was granted to Lois Steel and James Steel on 20 Jan. 1767. A distribution of 30 April 1771 names widow Lois Steal, eldest son James Steal, Sarah Nicholson, Loos Spencer, Elisabeth Steal, Susannah Steal, Ann Steal, John Steal, and Jesse Steal. An account dated 25 April 1771 says "there was one Child that was But one year and Eleven month old at the Deces[d] of the father and a Nother that was But three years and Six month old at the Descas[d] Death."

Children of James and Lois (_____) Steele, b. New Hartford, Conn.:

    i   JAMES STEELE[6], b. 7 July 1746, bp. 14 July 1746

    ii LOIS STEELE, b. 15 May 1748, bp. 22 May 1748

   iii SARAH STEELE, b. 18 Nov. 1750

   iv JOHN STEELE, b. 24 Oct. 1753

    v JESSE STEELE, b. 18 Aug. 1755

   vi SUSANNA STEELE, b. 30 May 1760

  vii ELIZABETH STEELE, b. 28 March 1765 [*sic.*, but prob.1763]

 viii ANNA STEELE, b. 5 Nov. 1764

References: *W Hartford Fam* p. 1518. *Steele Fam* pp. 14, 21. New Hartford CT VR 1:43(b. James, Lois, Sarah, John, Jesse), 55(b. Susanna), 57(b. Anna, Elizabeth). *Bradford Desc* pp. 78-9. Hartford CT PR #5184(James Steele). New Hartford CT LR 1:155(James Steel). W. Hartford Ch. 1:43(bp. James), 45(bp. Lois). Farmington CT LR 7:125, 466, 486(Samuel Steel's heirs).

231. NATHANIEL STEELE[5] (*Thomas[4], Mercy[3] Bradford, William[2-1]*), b. W. Hartford, Conn., 11 March 1721; d. Hartford, Conn., 15 Oct. 1789 or 5 Oct. 1787 aged 70.

He m. W. Hartford, Conn., 16 Oct. 1746 **SUSANNA OLMSTEAD**, b. W. Hartford, Conn., 19 Oct. 1719, bp. 1 Nov. 1719; living 1764; daughter of Thomas and Ann (Webster) Olmstead.

On 21 March 1745 and 10 April 1749 Thomas Steele's children, including Nathaniel Steele of Hartford, sold two tracts of land laid out in the right of Samuel Steele in Farmington.

Nathaniel Steele was admitted to the W. Hartford church on 23 Aug. 1746. Nathaniel Steele and his wife were communicants at the ordination of Nathaniel Hooker on the 21 Dec. 1757 at the W. Hartford church.

On 17 Oct. 1771 Moses Steel of Hartford, for land conveyed to him by his brother Nath[l] Steel Jr. of Hartford, sold to his brother his right in 18 acres with house and barn.

On 5 April 1784 Nathaniel Steel of Hartford sold to Hezekiah Steel of Hartford 12 acres of land bounded on Moses and Allen Steel; Josiah Steel Jr. was one of the witnesses. On the same day Moses Steel of Hartford sold to Hezekiah one acre with buildings bounded on Josiah Steel Jr., Allen Steel, and Nathaniel Steel. On 7 May 1784 Nathaniel Steel Jr. of Hartford sold to Hezekiah one quarter acre with buildings and tan vats used for tanning and shoemaking. On 14 May 1788 Moses Steel and Hezekiah Steel of Hartford sold to Frederick Steel of Hartford seven acres with buildings.

Children of Nathaniel and Susanna (Olmstead) Steele, b. W. Hartford, Conn.:

    i   SUSANNA STEELE[6], bp. 23 Aug. 1747; d.y.

    ii   NATHANIEL STEELE, bp. 23 Aug. 1747

    iii   MOSES STEELE, bp. 14 Oct. 1750

    iv   SUSANNA STEELE (twin?) , bp. 4 March 1753; d. 4 Sept. 1770 ae 17y 6m "of nervous fever"

    v   ANNA STEELE (twin?) , bp. 4 March 1753

    vi   ABIGAIL STEELE, bp. 9 March 1755

    vii   SARAH STEELE, bp. 9 April 1758

    viii   HEZEKIAH STEELE, bp. 10 Aug. 1760

    ix   FREDERICK STEELE, b. 16 June 1762, bp. 11 July 1762

    x   [CHILD] STEELE, stillborn. 26 Aug. 1764

References: *W Hartford Fam* p. 1518. *Steele Fam* pp. 14, 21. W. Hartford Ch. 1:10(Samuel adm.), 27(bp. Susanna), 44(bp. 1st Susanna), 46(bp. Moses), 48(bp. Susanna & Anna), 49(bp. Abigail), 51(bp. Sarah), 53(bp. Hezekiah), 55(bp. Frederick), 116(m.), 145(d. Susanna), 154(d. Nathaniel), 165(communicants). *Bradford Desc* p. 79. *Hartford By Barbour* p. 439. *Conn Marr* 2:74. Hartford CT VR D:16(b. Susanna). Hartford CT LR 14:89(Moses Steel); 17:258(Nathaniel Steel), 259(Moses Steel), 260(Nathaniel Steel); 18:232(Moses & Hezekiah). Farmington CT LR 7:125, 466, 486(Samuel Steel's heirs).

232. JOHN STEELE[5] (*Thomas[4], Mercy[3] Bradford, William[2-1]*), bp. W. Hartford, Conn., 17 Nov. 1723; d. there 5 Dec. 1760 aged 37.

He m. **LYDIA FRANCIS**, b. Wethersfield, Conn., 12 June 1729; d. Newtown, Conn., 17 July 1817; daughter of Thomas and Abigail (Griswold) Francis. Distribution of the estate of Thomas Francis of Wethersfield, Conn., dated 19 Sept. 1774, names [dau.] Lydia Sanford wife of Robert. She m. (2) in 1762 ROBERT STANFORD (or Sanford?).

On 21 March 1745 and 10 April 1749 Thomas Steele's children, including John Steele of Hartford, sold two tracts of land laid out in the right of Samuel Steele in Farmington.

On 21 Oct. 1751 Samuel Steele of Hartford sold to his brother John Steele of Hartford two pieces of land.

The will of John Steele Jr. of Hartford, Conn., "under bodily sickness," dated 4 Dec. 1760, proved 14 April 1761, names wife Lydia after whose decease the house and land were to go to "my brothers and sisters."

Possible children of John and Lydia (Francis) Steele, b. West Hartford, Conn.:

   i JOHN STEELE⁶, bp. W. Hartford, Conn., 27 Aug. 1749

  ii TIMOTHY STEELE, bp. W. Hartford, Conn., 20 May 1759

References: *W Hartford Fam* p. 1518. W. Hartford Ch pp. 1:46(bp. John), 52(bp. Timothy), 142(d. John). *Bradford Desc* p. 79. *Wethersfield CT By Stiles* p. 339. Wethersfield CT PR(Thomas Francis). Hartford CT PR #5190(John Steele Jr.). *Steele Fam* p. 14. Wethersfield CT VR 1:100(b. Lydia). Hale Cem Coll:W. Hartford, p. 6(d. John). Hartford CT LR 8:390(Samuel Steele). Farmington CT LR 7:125, 466, 486(Samuel Steel's heirs).

233. ELISHA WEBSTER⁵ (*Abiel Steele⁴, Mercy³ Bradford, William²⁻¹*), b. Hartford, Conn., 12 Nov. 1713, bp. 15 Nov. 1713; d. Southington, Conn., 29 Jan. 1788 in his 75th year.

He m. Wethersfield, Conn., 8 March 1749/50 **SARAH WARNER**, b. Wethersfield 2 Feb. 1707/8; d. Southington, Conn., 1 Feb. 1789; daughter of Daniel and Mary (Boardman) Warner.

Elisha Webster graduated from Yale in 1738.

On 13 Dec. 1742 John Webster of Southington in Farmington for love and affection gave to his second son Aaron Webster of Southington in Farmington 80 acres. On 17 Jan. 1742/3 Aaron Webster of Southington in Farmington sold to Elisha Webster, Pastor of the Church in Canaan, Conn., these 80 acres and on 6 June 1744 Elisha sold to the same property back to Aaron.

On 20 Oct. 1755 Elisha Webster of Wethersfield sold to Aaron Webster of Farmington two pieces of land in Farmington and one in Litchfield.

The will of Sarah Webster of Southington, Conn., dated 17 Jan. 1789, proved 5 March 1789, left everything to nephew William Warner 2nd of Wethersfield.

No Connecticut probate records have been found for Elisha Webster.

References: *Bradford Desc* p. 79. *Webster Fam* p. 79. *Hartford By Barbour* p. 649. *Wethersfield CT By Stiles* p. 730. *Conn Marr* 3:8(m). Wethersfield CT VR 1:23(b. Sarah). Hartford CT PR 24:70; #5781(Sarah Webster). Wethersfield First Ch. Rec. 2:302(d. Sarah). *Yale Grads* 1:611. Farmington CT LR 6:427(John Webster), 428(Aaron Webster); 7:64; 10:209(Elisha Webster). *Hartford CT Second Ch* (bp. Elisha).

234.   JERUSHA WEBSTER[5] (*Abiel Steele*[4], *Mercy*[3] *Bradford*, *William*[2-1]), b. Hartford, Conn., 8 Jan. 1714/5, bp. West Hartford Sept. 1714; d. Farmington, Conn., 4 Nov. 1752.

She m. (1) 11 Nov. 1736 **ISAAC COWLES**, b. Farmington, Conn., 21 April 1702; d. Southington, Conn., 29 Sept. 1737; son of Isaac and Mary (Andrews) Cowles. He m. (1) _____ _____ with whom he had Isaac and Mary.

She m. (2) Farmington, Conn., 4 July 1745 **ELDAD LEWIS**, b. Farmington 11 Feb. 1710/1; d. Southington, Conn., 29 July 1784; son of Isaac and Abigail (Little) Lewis of Farmington. On 7 Feb. 1760 Isaac Lewis of Farmington for love and affection gave his eldest son Eldad Lewis of Farmington 36 acres.

The will of Isaac Cowles Jr. of Southington in Farmington dated 24 Sept. 1737, proved 6 Dec. 1737, names wife Jerusha; mentions but does not name his first wife; son Isaac; unborn child by Jerusha; daughter Mary; and brother-in-law Samuel Root.

On 6 Dec. 1737 Samuel Root was appointed guardian of Isaac Cowles, son of Isaac Cowles and Capt. Isaac Cowles was appointed guardian of Mary Cowles, aged 6 years. On 17 March 1737/8 Jerusha Cowles, widow, was appointed guardian of Ruth Cowles, aged 6 months, posthumous child of Isaac Cowles.

On 30 March 1739 Samuel Root made an agreement with Jerusha Cowles concerning her dower.

On 4 Aug. 1752 Isaac Cowles, now 16 years of age, chose Samuel Root as guardian.

On 2 Oct. 1753 Ruth Cowles, 16 years of age, daughter of Isaac Cowles, chose Eldad Lewis as her guardian.

Child of Isaac and Jerusha (Webster) Cowles, b. Farmington, Conn.:

    i   RUTH COWLES[6], b. 8 Oct. 1737

Child of Eldad and Jerusha (Webster) (Cowles) Lewis, b. Farmington, Conn.:

    ii   JOHN LEWIS, bp. 20 April 1746

References: Farmington CT LR 1:4(b. Isaac); 23:99(b. John); 6:2(b. Ruth), 6:10(d. Isaac), 38(agree.); 7:46(2nd m.); 9:495(d. Jerusha). 1st Ch Southington Recs 1:28 (bp. John). *Cowles Fam* 1:66-7.   Hartford CT PR 13:57: 13A:17(Isaac Cowles). Farmington CT LR 11:490(Isaac Lewis). *Hartford by Barbour* p. 649.

235. AARON WEBSTER[5] (*Abiel Steele*[4], *Mercy*[3] *Bradford*, *William*[2-1]), b. Hartford, Conn., 24 Feb. 1716/7, bp. West Hartford March 1717; d. Southington, Conn., 21 March 1783.

He m. Farmington, Conn., 17 Nov. 1743 **LYDIA** _____.

On 13 Dec. 1742 John Webster of Southington in Farmington for love and affection gave to his second son Aaron Webster of Southington in Farmington 80 acres. On 17 Jan. 1742/3 Aaron Webster of Southington in Farmington sold to Elisha Webster, Pastor of the Church in Canaan, Conn., these 80 acres and on 6 June 1744 Elisha sold to the same property back to Aaron.

On 8 April 1755 and 11 June 1756 Aaron Webster of Farmington sold land to Ose Webster of Farmington.

On 20 Oct. 1755 Elisha Webster of Wethersfield sold to Aaron Webster of Farmington two pieces of land in Farmington and one in Litchfield.

On 7 Sept. 1757 Stephen and Abial Hopkins of Waterbury gave to "their son" Aaron Webster whatever interest they might have in Farmington land derived from her father Samuel Steele or her uncle, Benoni Steele.

On 12 Nov. 1777 Aaron Webster of Farmington gave to his son Robert Webster of Farmington a lot of land with one-third of the celler and of the well. On the same day Aaron sold to Robert 11 acres. And on the same day Aaron gave to his son Aaron Webster of Farmington 16 acres.

Administration on the estate of Aaron Webster of Southington was given on 23 April 1783 to Robert Webster. On 7 Dec. 1785 Lydia Webster, Jared Harrison and Hannah Harrison, Aaron Webster, Elisha Webster, and Daniel Barns and Sarah Barns, signed a receipt to Robert Webster that they had received the full amount due them from the personal estate of Aaron Webster.

Children of Aaron and Lydia (_____) Webster, b. Farmington, Conn.:

    i LYDIA WEBSTER[6], b. 20 July 1744 [not in Barbour], bp. 29 July 1744; d. 5 Sept. 1746

   ii LYDIA WEBSTER, b. 7 Oct. 1746

  iii HANNAH WEBSTER, b. 20 Oct. 1748

  iv ABIEL WEBSTER, b. 6 Feb. 1750; d. 20 July 1784

   v ROBERT WEBSTER, b. 14 Dec. 1752

  vi AARON WEBSTER, b. 2 Feb. 1755

 vii JERUSHA WEBSTER, b. 14 Dec. 1756

viii ELISHA WEBSTER, b. 22 Nov. 1758

  ix DANIEL WEBSTER, b. 1765; bp. & d. 14 April 1765 [not in Barbour]

   x SARAH WEBSTER, b. 7 Aug. 1767

References: *Southington CT By Timlon* p. cclii. *Webster Fam* p. 80. *Bradford Desc* pp. 79-80.
Farmington CT VR LR 14:11(b. 2nd Lydia, Hannah, Abiel, Robert, Aaron, Jerusha,
Elisha). Farmington CT PR #2865, 3:3(Aaron Webster). Farmington CT LR 6:427(John
Webster), 428(Aaron Webster); 7:64(Elisha Webster); 10:209(Elisha Webster); 315-
6(Aaron Webster); 12:450(Stephen Hopkins); 22:81, 88, 102(Aaron Webster). *Hartford by
Barbour* p. 649.

237.   SARAH WEBSTER[5] (*Abiel Steele*[4], *Mercy*[3] *Bradford, William*[2-1]), b.
Hartford, Conn., 17 April 1722, bp. West Hartford 22 April 1722; d.
Southington, Conn., 12 Feb. 1755 aged 32.

She m. **SAMUEL ROOT**, b. Farmington, Conn., 8 Jan. 1723/4; d. there
8 April 1782 aged 58; son of Samuel and Abigail (Cowles) Root. He m. (2)
Southington, Conn., 22 March 1757 CHLOE PALMER with whom he had
Moses, Ozias, Samuel, Samuel again, Ur, Selah, Aaron, Judah, and Elisha.

Children of Samuel and Sarah (Webster) Root, b. Farmington, Conn.:

i   OLIVER ROOT[6], b. 10 Feb. 1748; d. 24 Feb. 1749/50 ae 2

ii SARAH ROOT, b. 15 Dec. 1750; d. 2 Oct. 1808 (1809 in Aspinwall)

iii OLIVE/OLIVER ROOT, b. 7 Nov. 1754 [Farmington Barbour says
    "Olive d. Samuel," but the *Root Gen* carries on with an Oliver; Aspinwall
    says Oliver who m. Anna Holcomb and d. 6 Sept. 1797]

References: *Southington CT By Timlon* p. ccxvi. *Webster Fam* p. 80. *Bradford Desc* p. 80.
Farmington CT VR LR2:65(b. Samuel); 7:540(d. Oliver); 11:588(2nd m.; b. last 2 ch.). *Root
Gen* p. 132. *Hartford by Barbour* p. 649. *Gen Data Conn Cem, Southington* p. 45(d. Sarah,
Oliver).

238. ANN WEBSTER[5] (*Abiel Steele*[4], *Mercy*[3] *Bradford, William*[2-1]), b. Hartford,
Conn., 18 April 1724, bp. West Hartford 19 April 1724; d. 31 Dec. 1818.

She m. 15 Dec. 1757 **JOSEPH NICHOLS**, b. 1724; d. Waterbury,
Conn., 24 Jan. 1773; son of Joseph and Elizabeth (Wood) Nichols. He m. (1)
Waterbury, Conn., 1750 TAMAR BRONSON with whom he had Eunice and
Solomon/Simeon.

The will of Joseph Nichols of Waterbury dated 7 Jan. 1773, proved
1 March 1773, names wife Anna, son Simeon, and daughters Eunice and Lucy.
The distribution of 26 Feb. 1789 was signed by Anne Nichols, Simeon
Nichols, Michael Bronson, Eunice Bronson, Luke Adams, and Lucy Adams.

Lucy Nichols, daughter of Joseph Nichols late of Waterbury dec., being
more than 12 years of age, made choice of her mother Mrs. Anna Nichols as

her guardian. On 2 March 1773 Anna *Nichols* [crossed out at top of guardianship but listed later as guardian] and Ezra Bronson [only he signed the guardianship bond] were appointed guardians of Lucy.

Child of Joseph and Ann (Webster) Nichols, b. Waterbury, Conn.:

    i LUCY NICHOLS[6], b. 5 Dec. 1758

References: *Bradford Desc* p. 80. *Webster Fam* pp. 80-1. Waterbury CT VR 1:387(both m.; d. Tamor, Joseph; b. Lucy). Woodbury CT PR #3291(Joseph Nichols), #3292(Lucy Nichols). *Hartford by Barbour* p. 650.

239. SUSANNAH WEBSTER[5] (*Abiel Steele[4], Mercy[3] Bradford, William[2-1]*), b. Hartford, Conn., 8 July 1726, bp. West Hartford 10 July 1726; living 1755.

She m. Farmington, Conn., 1 Nov. 1746 **EBENEZER SCOTT**, b. Farmington 2 Aug. 1723; d. 1778; son of Samuel and Mary (Pinchon) Scott.

Children of Ebenezer and Susannah (Webster) Scott, b. Farmington, Conn.:

    i SAMUEL SCOTT[6], b. 2 Sept. 1747
    ii LUCY SCOTT, b. 20 April 1749
    iii ELISHA SCOTT, b. 8 Jan. 1751
    iv JERUSHA SCOTT, b. 10 March 1753
    v ASEL SCOTT, b. 19 Oct. 1755

References: *Bradford Desc* p. 80. *Webster Fam* p. 81. Farmington CT VR 2:46(b. Ebenezer). LR 8:8(b. Samuel, Lucy, Elisha, Jerusha), 10(m.). *Hartford by Barbour* p.650.

240. JOHN WEBSTER[5] (*Abiel Steele[4], Mercy[3] Bradford, William[2-1]*), b. Hartford, Conn., 4 Sept. 1728; d. Southington, Conn., before 8 May 1772.

He m. Farmington, Conn., 3 Nov. 1755 **RHODA LEWIS**, b. Farmington 20 March 1733; d. Southington 25 Dec. 1789; daughter of Nathan and Mary (Gridley) Lewis.

On 13 June 1752 John Webster of Southington gave to his son John Webster of Southington four acres.

On 18 May 1772 administration on the estate of John Webster of Farmington was granted to Nathan Lewis Jr. and Rhodah Webster. The distribution dated 9 Jan. 1778 names Vashti Webster, Rhoda Webster, widow Rhoda Webster, Theodosia Webster, Hannah Webster, Ursula Webster, and Philologus Webster, the only son.

On 20 April 1774 Rhoda Webster, administrator of the estate of John Webster, sold to Timothy Clark 6¾ acres.

On 24 April 1779 Theodosia Webster of Farmington sold to Philologus Webster of Farmington half of a saw mill and its "utensills."

The inventory of the estate of Rhoda Webster of Southington, deceased, was taken on 18 Aug. 1791. The distribution of the estate, dated 18 Aug. 1791, names Philologus Webster, the only son; representatives of Theodocia Cowles deceased.: Rhoda, Seba, and Theodocia Cowles; the representatives of Hannah Dutton deceased: Elesta and Rowlan Dutton; Ursula Sloper; Vashti Lankton; and Rhoda Howd.

Children of John and Rhoda (Lewis) Webster, b. Southington (now Farmington), Conn.:

    i THEODOSIA WEBSTER[6], b. 19 Aug. 1756

    ii PHILOLOGUS WEBSTER, b. 24 April 1759

    iii HANNAH LEWIS WEBSTER, b. 20 May 1762

    iv URSULA WEBSTER, b. 27 March 1765

    v VASHTI WEBSTER, b. 19 Dec. 1767

    vi RHODA WEBSTER, b. 3 Oct. 1769

References: *Southington CT By Timlon* p. ccliii. *Bradford Desc* p. 81. *Webster Fam* p. 81. Farmington CT VR LR5:5(b. Rhoda), LR9:286(m.), LR14:11(b. ch.). Southington CT VR(d. Rhoda). Farmington CT PR #2881(John Webster), #2889, 3:202, 309(Rhoda Webster). Farmington CT LR 8:408(John Webster); 20:429(Rhoda Webster); 23:94(Theodosia Webster). *Hartford by Barbour* p. 650.

241. ABIGAIL WEBSTER[5] (*Abiel Steele[4], Mercy[3] Bradford, William[2-1]*), b. Farmington, Conn., 23 Sept. 1731; d. Oxford, Conn., April 1824 aged 92.

She m. Farmington, Conn., 14 March 1754 **JOHN DUTTON**, b. Wallingford, Conn., 23 Jan. 1730; d. Oxford, Conn., 27 Aug. 1819 aged 90; son of Benjamin and Mary (Cone) Dutton. On 11 Jan. 1754 Benjamin Dutton of Wallingford gave to his son John Dutton of Farmington 20 acres in that town.

John Dutton was head of a household in Litchfield Co., Conn., in 1790 consisting of 2 men over 16, 2 boys under 16, and 5 females.

Children of John and Abigail (Webster) Dutton, first 4 b. Farmington, Conn.; rest b. Southington, Conn.:

    i OSEE (or HOSEA) DUTTON[6], b. 29 Dec. 1754

ii LUTHENA DUTTON, b. 31 July 1756

iii JOHN DUTTON, b. 25 Aug. 1758

iv LEVI DUTTON, b. 14 Feb. 1760

v SUSANNA DUTTON, bp. 8 Aug. 1762

vi ABIGAIL DUTTON, b. 10 May 1764

vii RHODA DUTTON, bp. 7 Jan. 1767

viii PRUDENCE DUTTON, bp. 15 Jan. 1769

References: *Bradford Desc* p. 81. *Webster Fam* pp. 81-2. *Oxford CT By Sharpe*, pp. 78-9. Wallingford CT VR 5:525(b. John). Oxford CT VR 2:110(d. John). Farmington CT VR LR9:286(m.), 9:7-8(b. Osee); LR11:58(b. Luthena, John, Levi). Hale Cem Coll:Oxford p. 18(d. John, Abigail). Farmington CT LR 9:498(Benjamin Dutton). *Hartford by Barbour* p. 650.

242.   OSEE WEBSTER⁵ (*Abiel Steele⁴, Mercy³ Bradford, William²⁻¹*), b. Hartford, Conn., 7 April 1734; d. bef. 5 March 1777.

He m. 12 May 1757 **MERCY BECKWITH**, b. Lyme, Conn., 13 July 1732; daughter of Raynold and Martha (Marvin) Beckwith. She m. (2) Farmington 17 April 1777 ABEL CARTER.

On 8 April 1755 and 11 June 1756 Aaron Webster of Farmington sold land to Ose Webster of Farmington. On 4 June 1756 John Webster of Farmington sold to 11 acres to Osee Webster of Farmington. On 30 Sept. 1756 Osee sold to John two acres with apple trees.

On 5 March 1777 administration on the estate of Ose Webster of Farmington was granted to Mercy Webster and Joshua Porter of Farmington. On 2 Feb. 1778 part of the estate was set out to the widow of Ose Webster, deceased, now Mercy Carter.

Children of Osee and Mercy (Beckwith) Webster, b. Farmington, Conn.:

i OSEE WEBSTER⁶, b. 20 Feb. 1763

ii CYRUS WEBSTER, b. 24 March 1765

iii SARAH WEBSTER, b. 6 May 1767

iv JOHN WEBSTER, b. 14 Aug. 1769

v ANNE WEBSTER, b. 28 May 1771; d.y.

vi SETH WEBSTER, b. 6 Feb. 1774

References: *Bradford Desc* p. 81. *Webster Fam* p. 82. *Southington CT By Timlon* p. ccliii. Farmington CT VR LR11:591(b. Osee); LR21:553(b. Cyrus, Sarah, John, Anne, Seth). Farmington CT PR #2887(Ose Webster). *Beckwith Notes* (Elkhorn WI, 1899), 1:11-2; 2:10. Farmington CT LR 10:315-6(Aaron Webster), 317(John Webster); 11:20(Osee Webster).

243. MARY STEELE[5] (*Daniel*[4], *Mercy*[3] *Bradford, William*[2-1]), bp. Hartford, Conn., 2 Feb. 1728/9; d. there 21 Nov. 1791 aged 63.

She m. **OZIAS GOODWIN**, b. Hartford, Conn., 6 June 1724, bp. 15 June 1729; d. there 12 Nov. 1789 aged 60; son of Ozias and Martha (Williamson) Goodwin.

On 15 Dec. 1761 Ozias Goodwin Jr. of Hartford sold to his father Ozias Goodwin of Hartford one acre of land.

Mary Goodwin was listed in the 1790 census as head of a household in Hartford consisting of three females. Asher Goodwin was living next to her with one man over 16, one boy under 16, and one female.

No Connecticut probate records were found for Ozias or Mary Goodwin.

Children of Ozias and Mary (Steele) Goodwin, bp. 1st Ch. Hartford, Conn.:

    i   MARY GOODWIN[6], b. 19 Jan. 1751; bp. 30 June 1751; d. 11 Aug. 1830; unm.

   ii   ROSWELL GOODWIN, b. 28 Jan. 1753; bp. same day; d. prison ship in Rev. War March 1778

  iii   OZIAS GOODWIN, b. 20 Jan. 1755; bp. 29 Dec. 1754 [*sic*]

  iv   JOB GOODWIN, b. 12 March 1757; bp. 20 March; d. 26 March 1757

   v   ABIGAIL GOODWIN, b. 9 Sept. 1758; bp. 10 Sept. 1758

  vi   DANIEL GOODWIN, b. 12 Jan. 1761; bp. 5 Jan. 1761[sic]; d. soon after being taken prisoner Feb. 1780

  vii   LUCY GOODWIN, b. 20 Jan. 1765; bp. 3 Feb. 1765

 viii   HORACE GOODWIN (twin), b. 15 May 1768; bp. 22 May 1768

  ix   ASHER GOODWIN (twin), b. 15 May 1768; bp. 22 May 1768

   x   BETSEY GOODWIN, b. 10 June 1770; bp. 1 July 1770; d. 11 July 1825, unm.

References: *NEHGR* 2:334. *Goodwins Of Hartford* pp. 681-2. *Bradford Desc* p. 82. *Hartford By Barbour* p. 275. Hartford CT VR D:13(b. Ozias). *Steele Fam* p. 14. Hartford CT LR 12:379(Ozias Goodwin).

244. WELTHIA STEELE[5] (*Daniel*[4], *Mercy*[3] *Bradford, William*[2-1]), bp. Hartford, Conn., 14 Feb. 1730; d. Branford, Conn., 13 March 1772.

She m. Branford, Conn., 22 Aug. 1751 **ASHER SHELDON**, b. Suffield, Conn., 16 Nov. 1728; d. Branford, Conn., 19 Feb. 1794; son of Josiah and Ann (Stanley) Sheldon.

Asher Sheldon was head of a household in Bradford in 1790 consisting of two men over 16 and one female.

On 9 Feb. 1795 Roswell Sheldon of Branford, administrator of the estate of Asher Sheldon late of Branford, sold to Solomon Tyler of Branford half an acre with a house and buildings reserving for himself the use of the shop.

Children of Asher and Welthia (Steele) Sheldon, b. Branford, Conn.:

  i ASHER SHELDON[6], b. 30 Jan. 1756
  ii DANIEL SHELDON, b. 11 Nov. 1760
  iii ROSWELL SHELDON, b. 28 Dec. 1763
  iv MARY SHELDON, b. 15 April 1766
  v ANN SHELDON, b. 3 Dec. 1768
  vi ABIGAIL SHELDON, b. 28 Nov. 1771; d. 9 April 1773
  vii WEALTHY SHELDON, b. 17 March 1773

References: *Bradford Desc* p. 82. Branford CT VR 3:268(m.; b. ch.; d. Abigail, Welthia), 402(d. Asher). Suffield CT VR NB1:67(b. Asher). *Steele Fam* p. 14. Branford CT LR 12:342(Roswell Sheldon).

245. TIMOTHY STEELE[5] (*Daniel*[4], *Mercy*[3] *Bradford, William*[2-1]), bp. 2nd Ch. Hartford, Conn., 19 June 1736; d. there 16 June 1806 in 70th yr.

He m. **SARAH SEYMOUR**, b. Harwinton, Conn., 20 Jan. 1740/1; d. Albany, N.Y., 27 Dec. 1808 aged 68; daughter of Zachariah and Sarah (Steele) Seymour.

Timothy Steele's household in Hartford in the 1790 census consisted of 2 men over 16, a boy under 16, and 4 females.

On 14 Nov. 1804 Timothy Steele of Hartford gave to his son Oliver Steele of Danbury two pieces of land in Hartford.

The will of Timothy Steele of Hartford, Conn., signed 16 June 1806, proved 4 Aug. 1807, names wife Sarah; sons Daniel and Oliver; daughter Mittie Benton wife of George; grandchildren George, Lucy, and Julia Beach; grandchildren Nathaniel and Rufus White; granddaughter Sally White;

grandson Augustus Seymour Porter; grandson Elnathan William Whitman; and son Roswell Steele.

On 6 June 1812 James Wells of Hartford administrator of the estate of Roswell Steel of Hartford sold to Daniel Steel of Albany, N.Y., and Oliver Steel of New Haven one-eighth part of an acre in Hartford.

Children of Timothy and Sarah (Seymour) Steele:

     i ROSWELL STEELE[6], b. ca. 1765; d. 21 April 1809 ae 44; unm. The will of Roswell Steele of Hartford dated 17 April 1809, proved 15 May 1809, names brothers Daniel and Oliver Steele; sister Mittie Benton wife of George; children of sister Lucy dec.: George, Lucy and Julia Beach; James Wells and George Benton executors. Distribution was made 13 April 1811 to Oliver Steele, Daniel Steele, Lucy Beach, Mittle Benton wife of George, Sally Meacham wife of Hosea, Nathaniel White, Rufus White, George Beach, and Julia Beach.

    ii SARAH STEELE, b. ca. 1766

   iii LUCY STEELE, b. ca. 1769

   iv DANIEL STEELE, b. 20 March 1772

    v LAVINIA STEELE, b. 1772; d.y.

   vi LAVINIA STEELE, b. ca. 1775 [*Seymour Gen* and *Hartford by Barbour* have only one Lavinia as does Aspinwall]

   vii MITTIE STEELE, b. 14 Dec. 1777

  viii OLIVER STEELE, b. ca. 1781

References: *Hartford By Barbour* p. 54. *Bradford Desc* p. 82. *Seymour Fam* p. 87. Hartford CT PR (Timothy Steele), (Roswell Steele). *Steele Fam* pp. 14, 21-2. Hartford CT LR 24:401(Timothy Steele); 29:484(James Wells).

246.   ROSWELL STEELE[5] (*Daniel[4], Mercy[3] Bradford, William[2-1]*), bp. Hartford, Conn., 4 Feb. 1738/9; d. prob. before 7 July 1785 (not in father's will).

He m. **EMMA _____**.

Poss. child of Roswell and Emma (_____) Steele:

     i EMMA STEELE[6]

References: *Steele Fam* p. 14. *Bradford Desc* p. 82.

247. THOMAS STEELE⁵ (*Daniel⁴, Mercy³ Bradford, William²⁻¹*), b. Hartford, Conn., 1740; d. there Aug. 1828 aged 87.

He m. (1) Hartford, Conn., **EUNICE CLAPP**, b. 27 Dec. 1745; d. Hartford 13 Aug. 1804 aged 59; daughter of Elijah and Mary (Benton) Clapp.

He m. (2) *Hartford Courant* of 9 Nov. 1808 Mrs. **OLIVE RODGERS**, who d. 24 May 1846 aged 90.

On 16 July 1782 Lemuel Steel and his wife Mary and Thomas Steel and his wife Eunice of Hartford, with the other heirs, sold their right in the homestead formerly belonging to Elijah Clapp.

Thomas Steele's household in Hartford in the 1790 census consisted of 4 men over 16, 4 boys under 16, and 4 females.

On 17 Oct. 1826 Thomas Steele of Hartford gave to Horace Steele of Berlin, Conn., and Hezekiah Steele of Hudson, N.Y., land bounded on a brick house owned and occupied by his daughter Anna Smith. On 21 Oct. 1829 Horace and Hezekiah mortgaged this property and then sold to it on 20 April 1835.

On 20 Oct. 1826 Thomas Steel of Hartford for love and affection gave 14 acres to Edward Thomas Day of Hartford, "son of my grandson Edward Day." On 12 April 1727 "I Thomas Steel do agree to Lett Edward Day have the part of the House now occupied by Mʳ Pearl for Five years at the rate of Thirty five dollars pʳ year commencing the 15ᵗʰ day of April 1827."

The will of Thomas Steele of Hartford, Conn., dated 12 Jan. 1827, proved 16 Aug. 1828, gives all his estate to Laertes Chapin for support of his wife Olive Steele. On 15 April 1846 Laertes Chapin asked to be discharged as executor. Inventory at that time included shares for support of Thomas Steele's widow, she being lately deceased. On 27 Aug. 1847 distribution of intestate estate was made among: Mrs. Anne Pomeroy of Buffalo, N.Y.; Mrs. Nancy Cook of Hartford, Conn.; heirs of Eunice Sheldon: Caleb Sheldon of Windsor, Vt., Charles Sheldon of Natchez, Miss., and heirs of Nahum Sheldon; heirs of Rhoda Day late of Hartford, Conn.: Joseph Day of Amsterdam, Ind., Amelia Peck wife of P. Peck of Albany, N.Y., Horace Day of Schenectady, N.Y.; and heirs of Edward Day late of Hartford, Conn.: Edward Thomas Day of Hartford, Amelia J. Williams wife of John, Harriet Roberts wife of Moseley, Catharine Day wife of Horace H. Day of N.Y., Aurelia R. Day of Hartford, and Wheaton Day of Hartford.

On 29 July 1846 administration on the estate of Olive Steel of Hartford was granted to William D. Ely. On 19 Sept. 1846 William D. Ely reported "That he has made diligent inquiry after the goods & estate of said deceased but can find <u>none</u>, unless the said Court should be of opinion, that an interest in the estate of her late husband Thomas Steele, held in trust for her maintainence and support ... is intestate estate."

Children of Thomas and Eunice (Clapp) Steele:

  i   HORACE STEELE[6], b. 1775
  ii THOMAS STEELE, b. 1777 (d. 17 Aug. 1817 ae 38)
  iii HEZEKIAH STEELE, b. 4 March 1785
  iv EUNICE STEELE
  v   RHODA STEELE
  vi ANN STEELE
  vii NANCY STEELE, b. ca. 1782 (d. 29 March 1863 ae 81 wife John Cook)

Deaths of ch. rec. Oct. 1775 aged 1 and April 1775 aged 6 yrs.

References: *Steele Fam* pp. 14, 22. *Bradford Desc* p. 83. *Clapp Fam In Amer* p. 40. Hartford CT PR(Thomas Steele), (Olive Steele). Hale Cem Coll:Hartford(d. Nancy Cook). Hartford CT LR 12:537(Lemuel Steel); 45:18(Horace & Hezekiah), 24, 43(Thomas Steele); 48:275; 54:371(Horace & Hezekiah).

248. LEMUEL STEELE[5] (*Daniel[4], Mercy[3] Bradford, William[2-1]*), b. Hartford, Conn., ca. 1742; d. there 22 Nov. 1815 from a fall, aged 73.

He m. Hartford, Conn., 1764 **MARY CLAPP**, b. 1747; d. Hartford, Conn., 1 Feb. 1816 aged 69; daughter of Elijah and Ann (Benton) Clapp.

On 16 July 1782 Lemuel Steel and his wife Mary and Thomas Steel and his wife Eunice of Hartford, with the other heirs, sold their right in the homestead formerly belonging to Elijah Clapp.

Lemuel Steele's household in Hartford in the 1790 census consisted of one man over 16, 3 boys, and 7 females.

On 6 May 1808 Lemuel Steel of Hartford sold to Henry Steel of Hartford 18 acres.

The will of Lemuel Steele of Hartford, Conn., signed 2 Nov. 1815, proved 11 Jan. 1816, names wife Mary; sons Frederick, Levi, Henry, and Lemuel; daughters Wealthy, Mary, Elizabeth, Chloe, Dorothy, Martha, Harriet, Lucy, and Hepzibah; and grandson George Smith (under 21).

On 19 Feb. 1817 Henry Steele of Hartford mortgaged five acres to Levi Steele and Lemuel Steele of Albany, N.Y., that had been part of their father's homestead. On the same day Henry mortgaged three acres to Frederick Steele of Litchfield that had been part of their father's homestead. And on the same day Frederick, Levi, and Lemuel sold to Henry 8½ acres with buildings that was part of the homestead of their father Lemuel Steele, and another 8½ acres.

On 25 Aug. 1821 Levi and Lemuel Steel of Albany sold to Henry Steel of Hartford 5 acres.

Children of Lemuel and Mary (Clapp) Steele, b. Hartford, there is a gap in the 2nd Ch. baptisms from 1730 to 1791 [dates in brackets from *Steele Fam*]:

    i   WELTHIE STEELE[6], b. 1 Aug. 1765 [22 Aug]

   ii   MARY STEELE, b. 18 July 1767

  iii   ELIZABETH STEELE, b. 16 Oct. 1769

  iv   CHLOE STEELE, b. 2 Oct. 1771 [26 Oct.]

   v   FREDERICK STEELE, b. 6 June 1774

  vi   LEVI STEELE, b. 17 Nov. 1776

 vii   DOLLY (or Dorothy) STEELE, b. 1 Dec. 1778

viii   PATTY (or Martha) STEELE, b. 15 Jan. 1781

  ix   HENRY STEELE, b. 21 Dec. 1783

   x   HARRIET STEELE, b. 12 Feb. 1785

  xi   LEMUEL STEELE, b. 2 Aug. 1785 [22 Aug 1787]

 xii   LUCY STEELE, b. 11 June 1790; bp. 2nd Ch. Hartford 8 May 1791

xiii   HEPSIBLE (or Heppy) STEELE, b. 9 March 1794; bp. 2nd Ch. Hartford 13 April 1794

References: *Steele Fam* pp. 14, 23. *Bradford Desc* p. 83. *Clapp Fam In Amer* p. 40. Hartford CT PR(Lemuel Steele). *Hartford By Barbour* p. 581(ds, b. Elizabeth, bp. Lucy, Heppy). Hartford CT LR 12:537(Lemuel Steel); 36:76-7(Henry Steele), 83(Frederick Steele); 26:454(Lemuel); 40:339(Levi Steel). *Hist 2nd Ch Hartford* pp. 329(bp. Lucy), 332(bp. Hepsible), 396(d. Lemuel, Molly).

249. SUBMIT (MITTIE) STEELE[5] (*Daniel[4], Mercy[3] Bradford, William[2-1]*), b. Hartford, Conn., ca. 1746; d. there 26 Aug. 1773 aged 26.

She m. **WILLIAM BURR**, b. Hartford, Conn., ca. 1747; d. 30 Oct. 1800 aged 53; son of Thomas and Sarah (King) Burr. He m. (2) Hartford, Conn., 29 July 1784 LYDIA (BARNARD) OLCOTT, widow of George Olcutt, with whom he had Harry and John.

On 4 Nov. 1800 administration of the estate of William Burr of Hartford was granted to Lydia Burr and James Burr with Joseph Burr, Timothy Burr, and Lemuel Burr as sureties.

On 31 March 1814 Harry Burr and John Burr of Hartford sold to Horace Burr of Hartford land in Hartford.

Child of William and Submit (Steele) Burr:

    i   WILLIAM BURR[6], b. ca. 1772; d. 16 Oct. 1792 ae 19

References: *Steele Fam* p. 14. *Bradford Desc* p. 82. *Hartford By Barbour* pp. 132-3. Hartford CT LR 34:163(Harry Burr).   Hartford, Conn., PD [no number on docket envelope](William Burr). Hale Cem Coll:Hartford, 1st Cem. p. 4(d. William, son William, Mittie).

250.   JOSIAH STEELE[5] (*Eliphalet[4], Mercy[3] Bradford, William[2-1]*), b. W. Hartford, Conn., 24 Feb. 1723/4; d. there 11 March 1801.

He m. Hartford, Conn., 2/11 Dec. 1753 **ELIZABETH COLTON**, b. Hartford, Conn., 28 Nov. 1728 or 9 Dec. 1728; d. in Vermont 18 July 1812; daughter of Benjamin Colton and his second wife Elizabeth.

On 8 Nov. 1752 Eliphalet Steele gave seven acres in Hartford to his son Josiah.

On 12 March 1767 Josiah Steel of Hartford sold to Peletiah Pierce and Ashbel Steel of Hartford nine acres with his house and barn.

On 21 Feb. 1786 Catharine Steel, Josiah Steel, and Eliphaz Steel of Hartford sold to Caleb Perkins of Hartford 11 acres.

Children of Josiah and Elizabeth (Colton) Steele, b. Hartford, Conn.:

    i   ELIZABETH STEELE[6], b. 9 Oct. 1754

    ii AMANDA STEELE, b. 27 July 1756

   iii ELIPHAZ STEELE, b. 4 March 1758

   iv JOSIAH STEELE, b. 24 Aug. 1760

    v MARSHFIELD STEELE, b. 12 Oct. 1762; d. 24 June 1770 ae 7y 7m

   vi RACHEL STEELE, b. 12 Aug. 1764

  vii CATHERINE STEELE, b. 2 Oct. 1766

 viii GEORGE STEELE, b. 18 Dec. 1768

   ix MARSHFIELD STEELE, b. 10 Aug. 1771

References: *Bradford Desc* p. 83. *Steele Fam* pp. 14, 24. *Hartford By Barbour* p. 581(m.). Hartford CT VR FFS:67(b. Eliz.); 22:40(b. Josiah, Elizabeth, Rachel; d. Josiah, Elizabeth; m.).   W Hartford Ch 1:145(d. Marshfield).   Hartford CT LR 8:498(Eliphalet Steele); 10:541(Josiah Steel); 17:343(Catharine Steel).

251.   MERCY STEELE⁵ (*Eliphalet⁴, Mercy³ Bradford, William²⁻¹*), b. W. Hartford, Conn., 8 Oct. 1727, bp. 8 Oct. 1727; d. there 5 Oct. 1794 aged 67.

She m. W. Hartford, Conn., 12 Jan. 1749 **NOAH WEBSTER**, b. W. Hartford, Conn., 25 March 1722; d. there 9 Nov. 1813 aged 90y 7m 14d, or 96y 7m; son of Daniel and Miriam (Cooke) Webster. He m. (2) W. Hartford, Conn., 1806 SARAH (OLMSTEAD) HOPKINS, widow of Stephen.

On 1 July 1777 Noah Webster of Hartford gave to his son Abram Webster of Hartford half an acre with buildings, and on 7 July 1777 Noah gave Abraham another 10 acres.

Noah Webster served in the Revolutonary War.

On 3 Dec. 1789 Noah Webster of Hartford sold to Charles Webster of Hartford 15 acres of land. On 11 Jan. 1790 Abraham Webster and Charles Webster of Hartford sold one-third of 12 acres to Mercy Griswold and two-thirds of the same 12 acres to Josiah Griswold; they also sold another 3 acres to Josiah.

Noah Webster's household in Hartford in the 1790 census consisted of 2 men over 16, 3 boys under 16, and 3 females.

On 15 April 1807 Noah Webster and his wife Sarah of Hartford sold to Noah Webster Jr. of New Haven, Conn., their right in dower lands in Hartford and Farmington, Conn., belonging to Stephen Hopkins deceased set off to Sarah Webster during her natural life.

The will of Noah Webster of Hartford, Conn., dated 9 March 1813, proved 29 Nov. 1813, names wife Sarah; son Charles executor; children Mercy Belden, Jerusha Lord, Abram Webster, Noah Webster, and Charles Webster.

Children of Noah and Mercy (Steele) Webster, b. Hartford, Conn.:

  i   MERCY WEBSTER⁶, b. 8 Nov. 1749
 ii   JERUSHA WEBSTER, b. 22 Jan. 1756
iii   NOAH WEBSTER, b. 16 Oct. 1758 (compiler of Webster's Dictionary)
 iv   ABRAM WEBSTER, b. 17 Sept. 1761 [Abraham, b. 17 Sept. 1751 in *Steele Fam*]
  v   CHARLES WEBSTER, b. 2 Sept. 1762
 vi   [CHILD] WEBSTER, d.y.

References: Hale Cem Coll:W. Hartford p. 2(d. Mary, Noah). *Bradford Desc* p.84. *Steele Fam* pp. 14. Hartford CT PR(Noah Webster). *Conn Marr* 2:74. *Hartford By Barbour* p. 655. Hartford CT VR D:16(b. Noah); FFS:84(m.), 86(b. ch.). Hartford CT LR 13:309; 14:135; 17:361(Noah Webster), 382(Abraham Webster); 22:430(Noah Webster). W. Hartford Ch. Recs. 1:31(bp. Mercy).

252. THEOPHILUS STEELE[5] (*Eliphalet*[4], *Mercy*[3] *Bradford, William*[2-1]), bp. W. Hartford, Conn., 31 May 1730; d. W. Hartford, Conn., 10 July 1775 aged 45.

He m. 1760 **MARIANNE HOSMER**, b. Hartford, Conn., 2 Feb. 1734/5; living 27 Sept. 1781 (adm. of son's estate); daughter of Stephen and Deliverance (Graves) Hosmer. She m. (2) West Hartford, Conn., 11 Feb. 1788 ZACHARIAH GARYWICK. She was called Margaret Steele on this county marriage record and he was called of Leasingburgh [prob. Lansingburgh in Rensselaer Co., N.Y., four miles north of Troy and bounded by Brunswick]. A Mr. Garruyck of "ye N--- city above Albanna" m. West Hartford 11 Dec. 1787 Mary Webster. In the N.Y. 1800 census Zachariah Garnrite is listed in Troy, Rensselaer Co., and in 1810 Z. Garniex is listed in Brunswick, Rensselaer Co.

The will of Theophilus Steele of Hartford dated 19 June 1775, inventory taken 19 Aug. 1775, mentions "my beloved wife" and son Theophilus under 21. Marianne Steele, widow and executrix, made oath to the inventory.

Child of Theophilus and Marianne (Hosmer) Steele, b. W. Hartford, Conn.:

    i THEOPHILUS STEELE[6], bp. 20 Dec. 1761; drowned 10 March 1779. On 27 Sept. 1781 administration on his estate was granted to his mother Marianne Steele; he is described as the son and heir of Theophilus Steele late of Hartford, dec.

References: *Bradford Desc* p. 84. *Steele Fam.* p. 25. Hartford CT PR #5206(Theophilus Steele). *Hartford By Barbour* p. 581. Hartford CT VR FFS:79(b. Marianne). Hartford CT PR #5207(Theophilus Steele Jr.). W. Hartford Ch. Recs. 1:33(bp. father), 54(bp. son). CT *Marr* 2:81(Zachariah's 1st m.), 82(m. to Margaret).

253. ELIJAH STEELE[5] (*Eliphalet*[4], *Mercy*[3] *Bradford, William*[2-1]), bp. W. Hartford, Conn., 20 April 1735; d. Cornwall, Conn., after 23 Nov. 1804 (deed).

He m. (1) Cornwall, Conn., 18 Jan. 1759 **ESTHER MILLARD**, b. Cornwall, Conn., 11 Oct. 1742; d. Cornwall, Conn., 20 April 1771 aged 29y; daughter of Matthew and Mary (_____) Millard. Matthew Millard of Cornwall made his will on 6 Sept. 1749, proved 6 Nov. 1749, naming his wife Marey and daughter Esther.

He m. (2) Cornwall, Conn., 4 Aug. 1773 **SARAH ANDREWS**, b. Wallingford, Conn., 5 April 1750; d. Cornwall, Conn., 28 Sept. 1808; daughter of Stephen and Mabel (_____) Andrews. Stephen Andrews of Wallingford made his will 9 May 1792, proved 25 April 1795, naming his daughter Sarah and her son William. In the distribution in Oct. 1795 they are called Sarah Steele and William Andrews and on 30 April 1800 the court was informed that William Andrews had died. On 15 Jan. 1798 John Sedgewick was appointed administrator of the estate of William Andrews, who was the natural son of Sarah Steele wife of Elijah Steele. William died without heirs so a trust was set up to pay Sarah an annual payment; an account in William's file lists payments made to Sarah until 28 Sept. 1808 "it being the day of the death of Mrs. Steele."

At a Cornwall town meeting of 18 Sept. 1759 the town voted that Elijah Steele be admitted as a town inhabitant. Elijah served the town in many capacities such as surveyor of highways, leather sealer, tithingman, fence viewer, grand juror, constable, and selectman. He also served on many committees including one to provide for the families of the soldiers in 1777.

On 8 Jan. 1771 Elijah Steele of Cornwall and his wife Esther sold to William Douglass of Cornwall 8¾ acres.

On 24 June 1773 Elijah Steele became a Deacon, although he resigned on 20 June 1776.

On 4 March 1780 Elijah Steele of Cornwall sold to Samuel Butler Jr. of Cornwall the second piece of land laid out to the heirs of Matthew Millard late of Cornwall.

On 19 April 1783 Elijah Steele and Matthew Millard Steele were appointed administrators of the estate of Esther Steele late of Cornwall. On 25 June 1783 the land she had inherited from her father was divided between her sons Matthew Millard Steele, Elijah Steele Jr., and Eliphalet Mashfield or Marshfield Steele.

On 28 June 1783 Matthew Millard Steele of Cornwall sold to Nathan Bristol of Cornwall 140 acres and 21 acres which land had been set off to Matthew in the distribution of the estate of his mother Esther Steele. On 6 Feb. 1802 Matthew sold to Isaac Doty of Cornwall more of the land set off from his mother's estate.

The 1790 census listed Elijah Steel in Cornwall with a household consisting of one man, one boy, and 2 females. Listed next to him was Elijah 2d (a man and 4 females), and nearby were Mathew M. (a man, a boy, 4 females) and Eliphet "Sleet" (living alone).

On 23 Nov. 1804 Eliphalet Steel of Hartford sold to his father Elijah Steel of Hartford nine acres, and to his mother Sarah Steel of Hartford another nine acres.

On 7 Nov. 1808 Benjamin Sedgwick and John Sedgwick were appointed administrators of the estate of Sarah Steele late of Cornwall. The inventory includes real estate in Cornwall and Wallingford and cash in the hands of the trustees of the estate of William Andrews.

Children of Elijah and Esther (Bullard) Steele, b. Cornwall, Conn.:

    i   MATTHEW STEELE[6], b. 23 March 1760; d. 29 March 1760
    ii MATTHEW MILLARD STEELE, b. 10 Nov. 1761
    iii ELIJAH STEELE, b. 6 Feb. 1764
    iv ELIPHALET MOSEFIELD STEELE, b. 20 Jan. 1766
    v   ORLO STEELE, b. 21 Feb. 1768; d. 22 March 1768

References: *Bradford Desc* p. 84. *Steele Fam* pp. 15, 25. Cornwall CT VR 1:36(m.; b. Matthew), 44(b. Matthew), 54(b. Elijah), 87(b. Elijah, Eliphalet, Orlo), 105(d. Esther); 3:5(2nd m.). Hartford CT LR 25:57-8(Eliphalet Steel). W. Hartford Ch. Recs. 1:57(bp. Elijah). *Cornwall Documents* pp. 28(inhabitant *et al.*). *Cornwall CT Hist* p. 510(deacon, Easter's ae at d.). Litchfield CT PR #3910(Matthew Millard); #5472(Esther Steele), #115(William Andrews), #5475(Sarah Steele). Wallingford CT PR #41(Stephen Andrews).

254. RACHEL STEELE[5] (*Eliphalet[4], Mercy[3] Bradford, William[2-1]*), bp. W. Hartford, Conn., 4 Sept. 1737; d. Hartford, Conn., 5 (or 6) June 1763.

She m. W. Hartford, Conn., 27 April 1758 **BENJAMIN HOPKINS**, b. 19 May 1734; d. Hartford, Conn., 5 (or 6) March 1764; son of Thomas and Mary (Beckley) Hopkins. This is not a *Mayflower* Hopkins line.

On 4 Sept. 1764 Stephen Hopkins, Thomas Hopkins, and Moses Hopkins refused to administer the insolvent estate of Benjamin Hopkins late of Hartford. On the same day administration was granted to Elisha Hopkins.

Children of Benjamin and Rachel (Steele) Hopkins:

    i   SALLY HOPKINS[6], bp. 27 Jan. 1759
    ii CATHERINE HOPKINS, bp. 10 April 1763; d. 23 March 1764

References: *Bradford Desc* p. 84. *Hopkins Gen* pp. 104-5. *Steele Fam* p. 14. Hartford CT PR #2852(Benjamin Hopkins). Conn *Marr* 2:75(m.). *Hartford By Barbour* p. 317. W. Hartford Ch. Recs. 1:37(bp. Rachel), 116(m.).

255. KATHERINE STEELE[5] (*Eliphalet[4], Mercy[3] Bradford, William[2-1]*), b. ca. 1734, bp. Hartford, Conn., 27 Jan. 1740; d. W. Hartford 12 Nov. 1774 aged 40.

She m. int. W. Hartford, Conn., 1758 **ELIJAH ENSIGN**, b. Hartford, Conn., 18 Dec. 1734; d. 12 Jan. 1793 aged 59; son of John and Elizabeth

(Dickinson) Ensign. He m. (2) W. Hartford, Conn., 30 April 1778 LOIS OLMSTEAD with whom he had Lois and Lucretia.

Elijah Ensign was listed in the 1790 census in Hartford with a household consisting of 2 men over 16 and 3 females.

Children of Elijah and Katherine (Steele) Ensign, bp. W. Hartford, Conn.:

   i KATHERINE ENSIGN[6], bp. 9 April 1758

  ii ELIZABETH ENSIGN, bp. 2 Jan. 1760

 iii CYNTHIA ENSIGN, bp. 17 June 1762

  iv ELIJAH ENSIGN, bp. 1 April 1764

   v CELIA ENSIGN, bp. 26 Jan. 1766

  vi ELI ENSIGN, bp. 3 April 1768

References: W. Hartford Ch. rec. *Bradford Desc* p. 83. *Steele Fam* p. 14. *Ensign Desc* pp. 20, 30-1. *Conn Marr* 2:78(his 2nd m.). *Hartford By Barbour* p. 240. W. Hartford Ch. Recs. 1:38(bp. Katherine).

256. ELIPHALET STEELE[5] (*Eliphalet⁴, Mercy³ Bradford, William²⁻¹*), bp. W. Hartford, Conn., 27 June 1742; d. Paris, Oneida Co., N.Y., 7 Oct. 1817 aged 75. The records of the Paris, N.Y., Religious Society say "Departed this life in strong faith and in the greatest composure Rev. Eliphalet Steele Age 75 years. In the 47th year of his ministry; and having been 22 years the pastor of this Church."

He m. (1) New Marlborough 4 Dec. 1771 **ELIZABETH STRONG**, b. there 12 Dec. 1748; d. Egremont, Mass., 4 Feb. 1793 aged 44; daughter of Thomas and Elizabeth (Barnard) Strong.

He m. (2) Feb. 1797 **CHLOE (FLINT) CHAPMAN**, b. Windham, Conn., 26 July 1752; d. Paris, N.Y., 10 Jan. 1833; daughter of James and Jemima (Jennings) Flint.

Eliphalet Steele graduated from Yale in 1764.

On 12 March 1767 Eliphalet Steel of Hartford sold to Pelatiah Pierce and Ashbel Steel of Hartford 50 acres with his house and barn.

On 28 June 1770 Eliphalet Steele was ordained pastor of the Egremont Congregational Church or First Church of Christ. Elizabeth, wife of Eliphalet, was admitted on 30 Aug. 1772 from the New Marlboro Church.

On 15 July 1795 Eliphalet Steele was installed as the minister of the Paris, N.Y., Religious Society (later known as the United Presbyterian Congregational Church.). On 29 Jan. 1798 Chloe, wife of Rev. E. Steele, was admitted from the Secind Church of Hartford.

Eliphalet Steel of Paris made his will on 8 March 1817, proved 16 Dec. 1817, naming his wife Chloe; son-in-law Gurdin Thompson and his wife Betsey; daughters Caty wife of Roswell Harrison, Louisa wife of Daniel P. Handy, Pamela wife of B. Harrison, and Nancy wife of Timothy Hopkins; and son Theophilus.

Children of Eliphalet and Elizabeth (Strong) Steele, some, b. Egremont MA:

   i   ELIZABETH STEELE⁶, b. 24 Oct. 1772
  ii   CATHERINE STEELE, b. 19 Nov. 1774; d. 4 May 1776
 iii   CATHERINE STEELE, b. 15 Nov. 1776, bp. Egremont 1776
  iv   LOUISA STEELE, b. 11 Nov. 1778, bp. Egremont 1778
   v   JERUSHA STEELE, b. 25 Aug. 1780, bp. Egremont 1780
  vi   NANCY STEELE, b. 17 Aug. 1782, bp. Egremont 1782
 vii   THEOPHILUS STEELE, b. 10 Aug. 1784
viii   PAMELIA STEELE, b. 18 Sept. 1786
  ix   SOPHIA STEELE, b. 14 June 1789; d. 18 Feb. 1792

References: *Bradford Desc* p. 85. *Steele Fam. Strong Desc* pp. 1249-50(desc. of Elder Eben Strong, son of ditto, both of Northampton). *Hartford By Barbour* p. 581. Windham CT 1:316(b. Chloe). Hartford CT LR 10:540(Eliphalet Steele). Paris NY Religious Soc. 1:flyleaf(Eliphalet installed), 11(Chloe admitted), 38(d. Eliphalet); 2:635(d. Chloe). Onieda Co. NY PR will book 2:97(Eliphalet Steele). Egremont Cong. Ch. pp. 136(Eliphalet ordained), 137(Elizabeth admitted), 139(4 daus., bp. years only). W. Hartford Ch. Recs. 1:40(bp. Eliphalet).

257. SAMUEL EDGERTON⁵ (*Alice Ripley⁴, Hannah³ Bradford, William²⁻¹*), b. Norwich, Conn., 15 March 1704; d. there 21 Sept. 1780.

He m. Norwich, Conn., 20 Dec. 1727 **MARGARET ABEL**, b. Norwich, Conn., 27 Feb. 1700; d. there 3 Nov. 1768; daughter of Samuel and Elizabeth (Sluman) Abel. Samuel Abell of Norwich made his will on 23 Dec. 1757, proved 16 Dec. 1761, naming his daughter Margaret wife of Samuel Edgerton.

Samuel Edgerton gave or sold to his son Samuel 13 acres on 19 May 1727, 70 acres on 11 Nov. 1730, two acres on 7 May 1742, and a final piece of land on 17 April 1745.

On 19 Sept. 1752 Samuel Edgerton of Norwich gave to his son Zebulon Edgerton of Norwich 20 acres "reserving liberty for my heirs & heirs of my father Samuel Edgerton to pass." On the same day Samuel gave to his son John Edgerton the third of the Norwich 20 acres with the same reservation. On 9 Aug. 1774 Samuel sold to his son John two pieces of land including a dwelling house and barn where Samuel dwelt. And on the same day he sold to his son Zebulon 22 acres with the dwelling house where Zebulon lived. Both these deeds include the same reservation as the earlier deeds.

Children of Samuel and Margaret (Abel) Edgerton, b. Norwich, Conn.:

    i   ZEBULON EDGERTON⁶, b. 14 Nov. 1728

   ii JOHN EDGERTON, b. 6 June 1731

  iii ANNE EDGERTON, b. 14 Nov. 1733

References: *Bradford Desc* p. 85. *Norwich CT VR* 1:36(b. Marg.), 60(b. Samuel), 105-6(m.; b. ch.; deaths). Norwich CT LR 6:6, 221; 8:409; 9:546; 12:284, 287; 21:411, 426(Samuel Edgerton). Norwich CT PR #41(Samuel Abell).

258. PETER EDGERTON⁵ (*Alice Ripley⁴, Hannah³ Bradford, William²⁻¹*), b. Norwich, Conn., 14 Jan. 1705; d. there 12 Feb. 1778 aged 66. He and both wives are buring in Gagertown Cem. in Franklin, Conn.

He m. (1) Norwich, Conn., 2 Jan. 1732 **HANNAH RIPLEY**, b. Norwich 21 June 1707; d. there 23 July 1751 aged 48; daughter of Jeremiah and Mary (Gager) Ripley.

He m. (2) Norwich, Conn., 2 May 1753 **HANNAH WEBB**, b. Windham, Conn., 29 Jan. 1715; d. Franklin, Conn., 18 Jan. 1817 aged 101y 6m 8d; daughter of Samuel and Hannah (Ripley) Webb, a descendant of Pilgrim **William Bradford** (see #264).

Samuel Edgerton gave or sold to his son Peter 30 acres of his farm on 13 Jan. 1728/9 and 21 acres on 11 Nov. 1730.

On 10 June 1745 Elijah Edgerton of Norwich sold to Peter Edgerton of Norwich five acres.

On 21 June 1773 administration on the estate of Peter Edgerton of Norwich was granted to John Edgerton Jr. of Norwich. Distribution was made to the widow Hannah on 12 March 1774 and on 13 Oct. to the other heirs: Nathan, only son; daughters Hannah, Sarah, Mary, Huldah, Jerusha, and Abigail Edgerton; and the the heirs of daughter Miriam Edgerton.

On 11 Nov. 1774 Nathan Edgerton of Norwich sold to Obadiah Kingsbury of Norwich one acre with the east half of the house formerly of Peter Edgerton late of Norwich, under an incumbrance of Hannah Edgerton widow of Peter, and a blacksmith shop.

Children of Peter and Hannah (Ripley) Edgerton, b. Norwich, Conn.:

    i NATHAN EDGERTON⁶, b. 8 Jan. 1733

    ii HANNAH EDGERTON, b. 18 Jan. 1736; d.y.

   iii ABIGAIL EDGERTON, b. 28 Dec. 1739

   iv MARY EDGERTON, b. 10 April 1744

    v MERIAM EDGERTON, b. 20 Oct. 1746

   vi SARAH EDGERTON, b. 10 May 1749; d. 10 Dec. 1754

  vii HANNAH EDGERTON, b. 23 July 1751

Children of Peter and Hannah (Webb) Edgerton, b. Norwich, Conn.:

  viii SARAH EDGERTON, b. 3 Feb. 1754

   ix HULDAH EDGERTON, b. 4 April 1756

    x JERUSHA EDGERTON, b. 20 May 1758

References: *Bradford Desc* p. 85. *Norwich CT VR* 1:60(b. Peter),149(1st m.; b. 1st 9 ch.; d. Hannah, Sarah); 2:163(d. Peter; 2nd m.; b. last 3 ch.). Windham CT VR 1:7(b. 2nd wife); A:17(b. 1st wife). Franklin CT VR(d. Hannah Webb). Norwich CT PR #3593(Peter Edgerton). Norwich CT LR 6:9, 249(Samuel Edgerton); 9:547(Elijah Edgerton); 21:48(Nathan Edgerton). Hale Cem Coll:Franklin (d. Peter, both Hannahs).

259. JOSHUA EDGERTON[5] (*Alice Ripley*[4], *Hannah*[3] *Bradford*, *William*[2-1]), b. Norwich, Conn., 26 Feb. 1707/8; d. there 6 March 1779 in 71st yr. He and Ruth are buried in the Old Franklin Plains Cem.

He m. Norwich, Conn., 28 Jan. 1734 **RUTH KINGSBURY**, b. Norwich, Conn., 24 Feb. 1712/3; d. there 13 Nov. 1769 in 57th yr.; daughter of Joseph and Ruth (Denison) Kingsbury.

Samuel Edgerton gave or sold land to his son Joshua on 11 Nov. 1730, five acres on 6 April 1736, four acres on 13 July 1742, and one acre on 14 April 1743.

On 10 June 1745 Elijah Edgerton of Norwich sold to Joshua Edgerton of Norwich 6 acres and on 9 June 1747 Elijah sold to Joshua ¾ of an acre. On 9 March 1747/8 David Edgerton of Norwich sold to Joshua 2 acres.

On 16 April 1771 Joshua Edgerton of Norwich sold to his son Samuel Edgerton Jr. of Norwich 17½ acres "part of the farm where Joshua lives."

The will of Joshua Edgerton of Norwich dated 25 June 1776, proved 17 March 1779, names daughter Anne Edgerton; youngest son Joseph Kingsbury Edgerton; oldest surviving son Sims; other sons Samuel, Eleazer, and Uriah; and grandchildren, children of son Joshua, deceased: James, Deliverance, Elisabeth and Anne Edgerton. On 28 April 1779 distribution was made to sons Sims, Samuel Jr., Eleaser, Uriah, and Joseph Kingsbury; Anne Edgerton, only daughter; and children of son Joshua: Elisabeth, Deliverance, James, and Anne Edgerton.

On 19 Oct. 1779 Sims Edgerton of Norwich sold to James Edgerton of Norwich 7 acres set out to him in the division of the estate of his father Joshua Edgerton, the land bounded by land set out to Sam[ll] Edgerton Jr. and Deliverance Edgerton.

Children of Joshua and Ruth (Kingsbury) Edgerton, b. Norwich, Conn.:

    i   RUTH EDGERTON[6], b. 12 Nov. 1735; d. 8 Oct. 1762 (not in will)

   ii   JOSHUA EDGERTON, b. 27 Oct. 1737

  iii   SIMS EDGERTON, b. 14 Feb. 1739

  iv   SAMUEL EDGERTON, b. 9 May 1742

   v   DELIVERANCE EDGERTON, b. 18 May 1744; d. Norwich, Conn., 8 Oct. 1762 ae 18

  vi   MARGARET EDGERTON, b. 14 May 1746; d. Norwich, Conn., 14 Jan. 1765 (just a footstone)

 vii   ELEAZER EDGERTON, b. 8 Aug. 1748

viii   ANNE EDGERTON, b. 28 Nov. 1750

  ix   ANDREW EDGERTON, b. 18 Jan. 1753; d. Norwich, Conn., 30 May 1768

   x   ALPHEUS EDGERTON, b. 3 March 1755; d. Norwich, Conn., 13 May 1776 (just a footstone)

  xi   URIAH EDGERTON, b. 12 July 1757

 xii   JOSEPH KINGSBURY EDGERTON, b. 4 Aug. 1759

References: *Bradford Desc* p. 86. *Norwich CT VR* 1:60(b. Joshua), 66(b. Ruth), 161(m.; b. ch.); 397(deaths). Norwich CT PR #3588(Joshua Edgerton). Norwich CT LR 6:224; 7:245; 8:403, 505(Samuel Edgerton); 9:546; 10:77(Elijah Edgerton), 78(David Edgerton); 19:236(Joshua Edgerton); 23:310(Sims Edgerton). Hale Cem Coll:Franklin p. 78(d. Joshua, Ruth, Deliverance, Margaret, Alpheus).

260. WILLIAM EDGERTON[5] (*Alice Ripley[4], Hannah[3] Bradford, William[2-1]*), b. Norwich, Conn., 25 March 1710; d. Franklin, Conn., 1 Dec. 1760 aged 50. He and Lydia are both buried in the Old Franklin Plains Cem.

He m. Norwich, Conn., 6 Nov. 1733 **LYDIA BARSTOW**, b. Norwich 27 May 1715; d. there 7 May 1769 in 54th yr.; daughter of Job and Rebecca (Bushnell) Barstow. Job Barstow of Norwich in his will dated 6 April 1756, proved 5 Nov. 1764, named his daughter Lydia Edgerton and Lydia is also included in the distribution of Job's estate on 15 March 1765. Job added at the end of his will:

... as my fatherly advice to you my Children...that you use all posible prudence for a Loving agreement in ye Division of ye Estate Given you in s^d Will, and in your Division Let there Be a Spirit of Condosention So far toward those of you that have already Land that was formerly mine...that their parts may Be Laid out to them adjoyning to that they already have, if it may Be Done with any tolarable Convenency So that none are Much hurt thereby.

Samuel Edgerton gave or sold to his son William 70 acres on 11 Nov. 1730, three acres on 25 Jan. 1736/7, another piece of land on 9 Jan. 1737/8, and three more acres on 27 May 1742.

The will of William Edgerton of Norwich dated 19 Nov. 1760, proved 17 Dec. 1760, names wife Lydia; children Asa Edgerton, Martha Willes, Zerviah, Alice, Rebekah, Lebeus, Ezra, Lavinia, and Ariel Edgerton; and father-in-law Job Barstow and his wife Rebekah. The distribution dated 21 Nov. 1761 was to widow Lydia; sons Asa, Lebbeus, Ezra, and Ariel; and daughters Martha Willes, Zerviah, Alice, Rebekah, and Lavinia Edgerton.

On 12 June 1769 administration on the estate of widow Lydia Edgerton was granted to Asa Edgerton. On 18 March 1771 distribution was made to Asa Edgerton, Ezra Edgerton, Ariel Edgerton, Alice Lothrop, and Lavinia Edgerton. An account dated 4 Feb. 1771 included a payment for gravestones for Lebbeus Edgerton and Zerviah Edgerton.

On 23 Jan. 1781 Asa Edgerton of Mansfield, Conn., sold to Alice Lothrop of Lebanon 2½ acres in Norwich which fell to him as an heir of Zerviah Edgerton deceased.

On 16 April 1791 Asa Edgerton, Ezra Edgerton, Rebecca Hide wife of Azariah of Randolph, Vt., Allice Lathrop wife of Zebulon of Lebanon, Ariel Edgerton, and Lavinia Sanford wife of Kingsbury of Franklin, Conn., sold land to Adam Driscoll of Norwich.

Children of William and Lydia (Barstow) Edgerton, b. Norwich, Conn.:

    i ASA EDGERTON[6], b. 28 March 1736

   ii SUBMIT EDGERTON, b. 15 May 1738; d. same day

  iii MARTHA EDGERTON, b. 2 April 1739

  iv ZERVIAH EDGERTON, b. 8 Aug. 1741; d. 30 March 1767 ae 24. On 5 June 1768 administration on the estate of Zerviah Edgerton was granted to Asa Edgerton. On 20 Jan. 1768 distribution was made to Asa, Lebbeus, Ezra, Ariel, Rebekah, and Lavinia Edgerton, and Alice Lothrop.

   v ALICE EDGERTON, b. 23 Aug. 1744

  vi REBECCA EDGERTON, b. 3 April 1747

vii LEBBEUS EDGERTON, b. 12 July 1749; d. 12 May 1768 ae 18. On 28 Nov. 1768 administration on the estate of Lebbeus, a minor, was granted to Asa Edgerton. On 2 Jan. 1769 distribution was made to his brothers and sisters: Asa, Rebecca, Ezra, Ariel, and Lavina Edgerton, and Alice the wife of Zebulon Lothrop Jr.

viii EZRA EDGERTON, b. 17 Jan. 1752

ix LAVINIA EDGERTON, b. 6 July 1754

x ARIEL EDGERTON, b. 8 Aug. 1757

References: *Bradford Desc* p. 86. *Norwich CT VR* 1:60(b. William), 63(b. Lydia), 152(m.; b. 1st 7 ch.), 300(b. last 3 ch.). Norwich CT PR #797(Job Barstow); #3600(William Edgerton), #3603(Zerviah Edgerton), #3589(Lebbeus Edgerton), #3592(Lydia Edgerton). Norwich CT LR 6:219; 7:365; 8:131, 447(Samuel Edgerton); 23:457; 29:32(Asa Edgerton *et al.*). Hale Cem Coll:Franklin p. 66(d. William, Lydia, Zerviah, Lebbeus).

261. MARY EDGERTON⁵ (*Alice Ripley⁴, Hannah³ Bradford, William²⁻¹*), b. Norwich, Conn., 17 May 1713; d. Willington, Conn., 22 Feb. 1784 aged 70y.

She m. Willington, Conn., 26 Oct. 1742 **DANIEL FULLER**, poss. b. Windham, Conn., 1 March 1702; d. Willington 6 Dec. 1758 of small pox, aged 59, son of Daniel and Mary (_____) Fuller; or poss. b. Dedham, 20 April 1699, son of Thomas and Esther (Fisher) Fuller. He m. (1) Wethersfield, Conn., 7 Aug. 1723 LUCY GOODRICH with whom he had Daniel, Rebecca, Jonathan, Abigail, Hester, and Lucy.

Daniel Fuller graduated from Yale in 1721 and in April 1725 was called to preach at Poquonnoc in Windsor, Conn. In 1727 the township of Willington was constituted and Daniel was ordained there in Sept. 1728.

On 25 July 1748 Daniel and Mary Fuller gave receipt for their share of the estate of Samuel Edgerton.

The will of Daniel Fuller of Willington, clark, dated 2 Dec. 1758, proved 5 Feb. 1759, names wife Mary; sons Daniel, Jonathan, and Samuel (under 21); and daughters Abigail [Noyes?], Lucy, Mary, and Allias. On 21 April 1760 dower was set off to Mary Fuller widow and relict of Revd. Mr. Daniel Fuller.

Children of Daniel and Mary (Edgerton) Fuller, b. Willington, Conn.:

i LUCIE FULLER⁶, b. 12 July 1744

ii MARY FULLER, b. 6 Feb. 1747/8

iii SAMUEL FULLER, b. 22 Dec. 1749

iv ALICE FULLER, b. 17 Dec. 1751

References: New London CT PR #1884(Samuel Edgerton). Willington CT VR A-23(m.; b. ch.); A-24(d. Mary, Daniel). Windham CT VR A:26(b. Daniel). Wethersfield CT VR 1:17(his 1st m.). Hartford CT PR #2078(Daniel Fuller). *Yale Grads* 1:251-2. *VR Dedham* p. 94. Hale Cem Coll:Willington p. 30. *Norwith CT VR* 1:60(b. Mary).

262. ELIJAH EDGERTON[5] (*Alice Ripley*[4], *Hannah*[3] *Bradford, William*[2-1]), b. Norwich, Conn., 1 Dec. 1715.

He m. (1) Norwich, Conn., 21 Feb. 1742/3 **SARAH GAGER**, b. Lebanon, Conn., 10 Oct. 1726; d. Norwich, Conn., 18 Jan. 1766 aged 39; daughter of William and Elizabeth (Whiting) Gager; a descendant of Pilgrim **William Bradford** (see #170). She is buried in Old Franklin Plains Cem.

He m. (2) Norwich, Conn., 1 Sept. 1766 **BETHIA (MUNSIL) WALDEN**.

Samuel Edgerton gave or sold to his son Elijah 17 acres on 9 Sept. 1740, 50 acres on 27 May 1742, and 36 acres and 20 acres on 15 March 1743/4.

On 15 March 1743/4 Samuel Edgerton and Elijah Edgerton of Norwich agreed that Samuel and his wife Alice would pay a yearly rent for living on a farm which would go to Elijah after their deaths. The rent was "one Indian Kernel of Corn, or Corn of wheat" paid on the first of April each year.

On 10 June 1745 Elijah Edgerton of Norwich sold to Joshua Edgerton of Norwich six acres. On 17 Jan. 1745/6 Elijah sold to Peter Edgerton of Norwich five acres, and on 9 June 1747 Elijah sold to Joshua ¾ of an acre.

Children of Elijah and Sarah (Gager) Edgerton, b. Norwich, Conn.:

    i EBENEZER EDGERTON[6], b. 8 March 1744/5

    ii ELIPHALET EDGERTON, b. 1 March 1747/8

    iii LUTHER EDGERTON, b. 9 Aug. 1750

    iv CYNTHIA EDGERTON; d. 11 Sept. 1764 ae 4d

Children of Elijah and Bethia (Munsil) (Walden) Edgerton, b. Norwich, Conn.:

    v SARAH EDGERTON, b. 27 May 1767

    vi BRADFORD EDGERTON, b. 11 Feb. 1769

References: *Bradford Desc* p. 86. *Norwich CT VR* 1:60(b. Elijah); 219(m.; b. ch.; d. Sarah). Lebanon CT VR 1:121(b. Sarah). Norwich CT LR 8:310, 503; 9:345, 543(Samuel Edgerton), 544(indenture), 546, 547; 10:77(Elijah Edgerton). Hale Cem Coll:Franklin p. 68(d. Sarah, Cynthia).

263. DAVID EDGERTON[5] (*Alice Ripley*[4], *Hannah*[3] *Bradford, William*[2-1]), b. Norwich, Conn., 28 Aug. 1718; d. there 12 June 1771 aged 52. He is buried in the Gagertown Cem. in Franklin, Conn.

He m. Norwich, Conn., 20 Sept. 1744 **SILENCE FALES/FALLS**, b. Norwich 15 Oct. 1724; d. after 18 March 1769; dau. Samuel and Abigail (Elderkin) Falls.

Samuel Edgerton gave or sold to his son David 50 acres on 27 May 1742.

On 9 March 1747/8 David Edgerton of Norwich sold two acres to Joshua Edgerton of Norwich.

In his will dated 18 March 1769, proved 2 July 1771, David Edgerton of Norwich left everything to his wife Silence and after her death to the West or Second Society.

David and Silence evidently had no surviving children.

References: *Bradford Desc* p. 86. *Norwich CT VR* 1:60(b. David), 91(b. Silence); 243 (m.; d. David). Norwich CT PR #3573(David Edgerton). Norwich CT LR 8:501(Samuel Edgerton); 10:78(David Edgerton). Hale Cem Coll:Franklin p. 44(d. David).

264. HANNAH WEBB[5] (*Hannah Ripley*[4], *Hannah*[3] *Bradford, William*[2-1]), b. Windham, Conn., 29 Jan. 1715; d. Franklin, Conn., 18 Jan. 1817, aged 101y 6m 8d.

She m. Norwich, Conn., 2 May 1753 **PETER EDGERTON**, b. Norwich, Conn., 15 Jan. 1705/67; d. there 12 Feb. 1773; son of Samuel and Alice (Ripley) Edgerton, a descendant of Pilgrim **William Bradford**.

See #258 for an account of this family.

References: Windham CT VR 1:7(b. Hannah). Norwich CT VR 1:63(b. Peter); 2:163(m.; d. Peter). Franklin CT VR 1:191(d. Hannah).

265. EBENEZER WEBB[5] (*Hannah Ripley*[4], *Hannah*[3] *Bradford, William*[2-1]), b. Windham, Conn., 12 Jan. 1718/9; d. there 11 Feb. 1803 aged 85; buried Scotland, Conn.

He m. Windham, Conn., 3 Dec. 1740 **RUTH CRANE**, b. Windham 12 April 1718; d. there 28 Feb. 1796 aged 77; buried Scotland, Conn.; daughter of Isaac and Ruth (Waldo) Crane.

On 1 April 1743 Samuel Webb gave land in Windham to his son Ebenener Webb.

On 2 May 1736 Ebenezer Webb was admitted to the First Congregational Church of Windham and his wife Ruth was admitted on 23 May 1742.

Ebenezer Webb's household in Windham in 1790 consisted of one man over 16 and 2 females.

Children of Ebenezer and Ruth (Crane) Webb, b. Windham, Conn.:

    i   DARIUS WEBB[6], b. 28 July 1742

    ii JERUSHA WEBB, b. 17 April 1744; d. 25 Nov. 1827; unm.

   iii ANN WEBB, b. 13 March 1745/6, bp. 16 March 1746

   iv JONATHAN WEBB, b. 2 Oct. 1747, bp. 11 Oct. 1747

    v ALICE WEBB, b. 3 Aug. 1749, bp. 6 Aug. 1749

   vi RUTH WEBB, b. 22 Feb. 1750/1, bp. 24 Feb. 1751

  vii ELIZABETH WEBB, b. 19 Feb. 1753, bp. 4 March 1753

 viii CHRISTOPHER WEBB, b. 14 June 1755, bp. 20 July 1755

   ix EBENEZER WEBB, b. 29 May 1757, bp. 5 June 1757

    x HANNAH WEBB, b. 31 Aug. 1759

References: *Bradford Desc* p. 87.   Windham CT VR 1:7(b. Ebenezer), 132(b. Ruth), 210(m.; b. ch.; d. Ruth).   Windham CT LR H:191(Samuel Webb).   Windham 1st Ch. Recs. 1:7(adm. Ebenezer), 32(adm. Ruth).   Scotland Cong. Ch. Recs. 2:23(bp. Ann), 24(bp. Jonathan), 25(bp. Alice), 26(bp. Ruth), 28(bp. Elizabeth), 30(bp. Christopher), 31(bp. Ebenezer).   Hale Cem Coll:Scotland p. 17(d. Ebenezer, Ruth).

266. JOSHUA WEBB[5] (*Hannah Ripley[4], Hannah[3] Bradford, William[2-1]*), b. Windham, Conn., 9 Feb. 1721/2; d. Rockingham, Vt., 17 April 1808 in his 87th y.

He m. Windham, Conn., 28 May 1744 **HANNAH ABBE**, b. Windham 17 Sept. 1724; d. Rockingham, Vt., 12 Feb. 1815 aged 90y 4m 25d; daughter of John and Mary (Palmer) Abbe. John Abbe of Windham made his will on 6 June 1767, proved 31 Jan. 1770, giving his daughter Hannah movable estate to the value of £10 and to her husband Joshua Webb "all that he owes me by Bond Book Note Judgment or otherwise being about three hundred pounds."

On 3 Sept. 1738 Joshua Webb was admitted to Windham First Congregational Church.

On 15 July 1743 Samuel Webb gave his son Joshua Webb land in Windham and on 26 Feb. 1749/50 sold to Joshua another 10 acres lying in partnership between them.

The will of Joshua Webb of Rockingham, Vt., dated 11 Feb. 1808 names wife Hannah; daughter Hannah Carpenter; daughter Ann Ripley; daughters Eunice and Mary Webb; and son Joshua R. Webb; and mentions other sons but does not name them. On 15 April 1809 Abiel Carpenter, husband of

Hannah, signed a receipt for her share in her father's estate and on 28 April Hannah Webb, widow, Eunice Webb, Mary Webb, and Epaphras Ripley, husband of Anna, signed receipts for their shares.

Children of Joshua and Hannah (Abbe) Webb, first 5 b. Windham, Conn.:

  i JEHIAL WEBB⁶, b. 23 Jan. 1745

 ii JOSEPH WEBB, b. 8 May 1746

iii AZARIAH WEBB, b. 11 Oct. 1748

 iv CHARLES WEBB, b. 19 Aug. 1750

  v HANNAH WEBB, b. 19 June 1753; d. Oct. 1817 (Aspinwall)

 vi EUNICE WEBB, b. 28 Nov. 1755; d. Rockingham VT 26 June 1845 in 90th yr.; unm.

vii CALVIN WEBB, b. 31 July 1757

viii MARY WEBB, b. Union, Conn., 27 Jan. 1760; d. 30 July 1841

 ix ANN WEBB, b. Union, Conn., 21 Aug. 1761

  x LUTHER WEBB, b. Union, Conn., 23 Oct. 1763

 xi JOSHUA R[IPLEY] WEBB, b. Westminster VT 7 July 1766

References: *Bradford Desc* p. 87. Windham CT VR 1:7(b. Joshua), 59(b. Hannah), 244(m.; b. Jehiel, Joseph, Azariah, Hannah). Union CT VR LR:268(b. Luther, 293(b. Mary), 294(b. Anna). *Rockingham VT Hist* pp. 774-5(acct. of fam.; d. Joshua). Gravestone photos with General Society #61116(d. Joshua, Hannah). Winchester VT PR C:60-1, 279(Joshua Abbe). *Abbe-Abbey Gen* p. 29. Windham CT PR H:266; I:408(Samuel Webb). Windham Cong. Ch. Recs. 1:8(Joshua adm.). Windham CT PD #16(John Abbe). VTVR Cem. card(d. Hannah, Eunice).

267. JERUSHA BINGHAM⁵ (*Faith Ripley⁴, Hannah³ Bradford, William²⁻¹*), b. Windham, Conn., 2 Feb. 1708; d. Stafford, Conn., 29 April 1774.

She m. Scotland, Conn., 4 March 1728/9 **BENJAMIN ROBINSON**, b. Tisbury 23 Feb. 1703/4; d. Stafford, Conn., 12 April 1772; son of Peter and Experience (Morton) Robinson. On 14 Feb. 1727/8 Peter Robinson of Windham gave to his son Benjamin Robinson of Windham land in Windham.

Jerusha Robinson was admitted to the Windham First. Congregational Church on 24 Aug. 1729 and Benjamin Robinson was admitted on 25 July 1734.

On 5 Dec. 1771 Benjamin Robinson of Stafford gave to his son Eliphalet Robinson of Stafford 24 acres of his homestead.

The will of Benjamin Robinson of Stafford dated 19 March 1772, proved 4 May 1772, names wife Jerusha; sons Elijah, Benjamin, and Eliphalet; and daughters Jerusha Robinson, Eunice White, Irene Blogget, and Lydia Blogett.

On 25 March 1778 Benjamin Robinson of Willington, Conn., sold to Elijah Robinson of Stafford 50 acres in Stafford.

Children of Benjamin and Jerusha (Bingham) Robinson, first 5 b. Windham, Conn., next 2 b. Lebanon, Conn.:

> i   EUNICE ROBINSON[6], b. 16 Nov. 1731, bp. Windham 1st Ch. 21 Nov. 1731
>
> ii IRENE ROBINSON, b. 1 Nov. 1733, bp. Windham 1st Ch. 11 Nov. 1733
>
> iii ELIJAH ROBINSON, b. 1 Oct. 1735, bp. Scotland Cong. Ch. [no date]
>
> iv ELIPHALET ROBINSON, b. 5 Dec. 1739, bp. Scotland Cong. Ch. 16 Dec. 1739
>
> v   LYDIA ROBINSON, b. 5 Feb. 1741/2, bp. Scotland Cong. Ch. 14 Feb. 1742
>
> vi JERUSHA ROBINSON, b. 8 Aug. 1746
>
> vii BENJAMIN ROBINSON, b. 24 April 1749

References: *Bradford Desc* pp. 87-8. Windham CT VR 1:3(b. Jerusha), 110(m.; b. 5 ch.). Lebanon CT VR 1:268(b. Jerusha, Benjamin). Stafford CT VR 2:174(d. Benjamin). Stafford CT LR 4:197; 5:276(Benjamin Robinson). Stafford CT PR #1802 (Benjamin Robinson). Windham CT LR F:417(Peter Robinson). Windham 1st Ch. Recs. 1:7(adm. Jerusha, Benjamin), 15(bp. Eunice), 17(bp. Irene). Scotland Cong. Ch. Recs. 2:15(bp. Elijah), 17(bp. Eliphalet), 19(bp. Lydia).

268. ABISHA BINGHAM[5] (*Faith Ripley[4], Hannah[3] Bradford, William[2-1]*), b. Windham, Conn., 29 Jan. 1709/10; living 17 April 1764 (deed).

He m. Lyme, Conn., 28 Dec. 1731 **MARY TUBBS**, b. Lyme 2 April 1710; daughter of Isaac and Martha (Smith) Tubbs.

Abisha Bingham and his wife owned the covenant in the Windham First Church on 25 Feb. 1733.

On 17 April 1764 Abisha Bingham of Windham sold two acres in Windham to Ebenezer Fitch.

No Connecticut probate records have been found for Abisha or Mary Bingham.

Children of Abisha and Mary (Tubbs) Bingham, b. Windham, Conn.:

> i   JERUSHA BINGHAM[6], bp. Windham 1st Ch. 25 Feb. 1733

   ii ABISHA BINGHAM, bp. Windham 1st Ch. 26 May 1734; d.y.

  iii ABISHA BINGHAM, bp. 28 Feb. 1735 [bp. not found in either ch.]

  iv REUBEN BINGHAM, bp. Scotland Cong. Ch. 9 April 1738

   v ABNER BINGHAM, bp. Scotland Cong. Ch. [no date] 1739

  vi MARTHA BINGHAM, bp. 15 Aug. 1741 [Martha dau. Abishai, bp. Scotland Cong. Ch. 10 Aug. 1740. Same or two Marthas?]

 vii ABIGAIL BINGHAM, bp. 13 March 1743 [an Abigail Bingham was admitted to the Windham Ch. on 13 March 1743. Is there a confusion here?]

References: *Bradford Desc* p. 88. Lyme CT VR pp. 266(b. Mary). Windham CT VR 1:3(b. Abisha). Windham CT LR N:175(Abisha Bingham). Windham 1st Ch. Recs. 1:8(owed cov.), 16(bp. Jerusha), 17(bp. 1st Abisha), 32(Abigail adm). Scotland Cong. Ch. Recs. 2:15(bp. Abner), 16(bp. Reuben), 18(bp. Martha).

269. LEMUEL BINGHAM[5] (*Faith Ripley*[4], *Hannah*[3] *Bradford, William*[2-1]), b. Windham, Conn., 20 Sept. 1713; d. there 3 Nov. 1788 aged 76.

He m. Norwich, Conn., 28 April 1737 **HANNAH PERKINS**, b. Norwich, Conn., 15 Dec. 1717; d. 21 Oct. 1793 aged 76; daughter of Joseph and Martin (Morgan) Perkins.

On 1 March 1774 Lemuel Bingham and wife Hannah of Windham gave land in Windham to son Jedediah.

The will of Lemuel Bingham dated 25 May 1787, proved 26 Feb. 1789, names wife Hannah and sons Jedediah and Elias; and mentions four unmarried daughters.

Children of Lemuel and Hannah (Perkins) Bingham, b. Windham, Conn.:

   i HANNAH BINGHAM[6], b. 26 April 1738, bp. 24 Sept. 1738

  ii ZERVIAH BINGHAM, b. 5 March 1740, bp. 9 March 1740

 iii LUCY BINGHAM, b. 14 Sept. 1742, bp. 26 Sept. 1742; d. 7 Feb. 1777; unm.

  iv FAITH BINGHAM, b. 27 Jan. 1745, bp. 27 Jan. 1745

   v JEDEDIAH BINGHAM, b. March 1748

  vi ANNA BINGHAM, b. 12 Sept. 1750

 vii ELIAS BINGHAM, b. 28 Sept. 1753

viii JERUSHA BINGHAM, b. 3 July 1756; d. 10 July 1756

References: *Bradford Desc* p. 88. Windham CT VR 1:3(b. Lemuel), 162(d. Lemuel, Hannah, Lucy, Jerusha; b. all ch. exc. Faith). Norwich CT VR 1:60(b. Hannah). Windham CT PR 12:345; #382(Lemuel Bingham). Windham CT LR P:167(Lemuel

Bingham). (Lisbon) Newent Cong. Ch. Recs. 1:82(m.). (Scotland) Brunswick Separate Ch. 1:207(d. Lemuel, Hannah). Scotland Cong. Ch. 2:16(bp. Hannah), 17(bp. Zerviah), 20(bp. Lucy), 22(bp. Faith).

270. ANNE BINGHAM[5] (*Faith Ripley*[4], *Hannah*[3] *Bradford, William*[2-1]), b. Windham, Conn., Nov. 1716; d. 22 Feb. 1760.

She m. Windham, Conn., 3 May 1739 **SAMUEL FOLSOM**, b. Exeter, N.H., ca 1716; d. Ohio ca. 1800; son of Israel and Rachel (Berry) Folsom.

On 20 May 1762 Theop[s] Nichols of Stratford, Conn., sold to Sam[l] Fulsom of Stratford one quarter of an acre right of commonage. On 1 June 1762 land was laid out to Samuel Fulsom.

In 1760 Samuel was quite active in buying land in Stratford, but in 1769 there were several judgements against him. On 5 July 1771 Samuel sold to John Starling of Stratford his right in a house, barn, and ½ acre "being my late dwelling house," also his right in another house and shop with ½ acre, his right in Blackman's lot, and to lands "lying by Delaware River."

He may be the Samuel Fulsome or Samuel Folsom who appears in Marietta, Ohio in 1800 and 1803.

Children of Samuel and Anne (Bingham) Folsom, b. Stratford, Conn.:

    i ANNA FOLSOM[6], b. 19 Aug. 1740

    ii SAMUEL FOLSOM, b. 9 May 1742

    iii DARIUS FOLSOM, b. 24 Dec. 1743

    iv CYRUS FOLSOM, b. 4 Dec. 1745

    v ABIGAIL FOLSOM, b. 15 Oct. 1747

    vi MARY FOLSOM, b. 4 March 1750

    vii NATHANIEL FOLSOM, b. 6 July 1752

    viii ANNAH (or GLORIANNA) FOLSOM, b. 24 Dec. 1753

    ix JOHN FOLSOM, b. 17 May 1756

References: *Bradford Desc* p. 88. Windham CT VR 1:3(b. Anne), 193(m.; b. 1st 2 ch.). Stratford CT VR LR 5:38(b. ch.). Stratford CT LR 13:84(Theos. Nichols, land laid out); 17:49(Samuel Folsom). *Early Ohio Census Records.*

271. MARY RIPLEY[5] (*Joshua*[4], *Hannah*[3] *Bradford*, *William*[2-1]), b. Windham, Conn., 18 Nov. 1714; d. there 13 Oct. 1769 or 13 Oct. 1770 aged 53y.

She m. Windham, Conn., 14 April 1736 **JOSHUA ABBE**, b. Mansfield, Conn., 20 Jan. 1710; d. Windsor, Conn., 13 Jan. 1807 aged 96y; son of Ebenezer and Mary (Allen) Abbe.

On 2 Jan. 1737 Joshua Abbe and his wife Mary were admitted to the Windham First Church.

In Nov. 1751 Joshua Ripley and his wife Mary; Joshua Abbe and his wife Mary; Nathaniel Ripley; and Ebenezer Ripley all of Windham; and John Alden and his wife Elizabeth of Lebanon quitclaimed to Joshua Ripley Jr. of Windham their rights in land conveyed to Mary Ripley for life and then to her daughter Hannah Ripley now deceased.

Joshua Abbe's household in Windham in the 1790 census consisted of 2 men over 16, 4 boys under 16, and 3 females. Listed next to him was Joshua Abbe Jr. with 2 men, 3 boys, and 8 females.

The will of Joshua Abbe of Mansfield dated 7 April 1804, proved 21 Jan. 1807, names daughters Zibah Wales, Mary Hebard, Zerviah Webb, and Lucretia Badger; his other children were not named, he "having given a due proportion of my Estate to my other children."

According to the *Abbe-Abbey Gen* in 1803-4 he had nine children, 88 grandchildren, 120 great-grandchildren, and one great-great-grandchild.

Children of Joshua and Mary (Ripley) Abbe, b. Windham, Conn.:

   i ZIRUIAH ABBE[6], b. 11 June 1737, bp. 17 July 1737
   ii RACHEL ABBE, b. 6 Feb. 1739, bp. 18 Feb. 1739
   iii MARY ABBE, b. 21 Dec. 1740
   iv ZERVIAH ABBE, b. 7 Jan. 1743
   v SHUBAEL ABBE, b. 9 Nov. 1744
   vi PHINEAS ABBE, b. 22 Nov. 1746
   vii LUCRETIA ABBE, b. 10 March 1749
   viii JOSHUA ABBE, b. 9 Jan. 1751
   ix ELISHA ABBE, b. 15 May 1753
   x ELIZABETH ABBE, b. 6 Dec. 1758; d. 20 Jan. 1759

References: *Bradford Desc* p. 89. Windham CT VR 1:35(b. Joshua), 39(b. Mary), 161(m.; b. ch.). Windham CT PR #21, 15:280(Joshua Abbe). Hale Cem Coll:Windham pp. 280, 317. *Abbe-Abbey Gen* p. 35. Windham CT LR K:128(quitclaim). Windham 1st Ch. Recs. 1:8(Mary adm.), 20(bp. Ziruiah), 22(bp. Rachel), 352(Joshua adm.).

272. NATHANIEL RIPLEY⁵ (*Joshua⁴, Hannah³ Bradford, William²⁻¹*), b. Windham, Conn., 30 June 1721; d. after 6 Feb. 1752.

He m. Windham, Conn., 31 Oct. 1745 **ANN RIPLEY**, b. Windham 24 Aug. 1726; d. Scotland, Conn., 6 Sept. 1792 aged 65; daughter of David and Lydia (Cary) Ripley, a descendant of Pilgrim **William Bradford** (see #295). She m. (2) Scotland, Conn., 17 May 1769 SAMUEL BINGHAM.

On 19 July 1749 Joshua Ripley Jr. sold to Nathaniel Ripley his right in land then in the improvement of his father Joshua on which he dwelt that his late brother Phineas in his will bequeathed to his father during his life. On 7 July 1750 Ebenezer Ripley also sold his right to this land to Nathaniel.

In Nov. 1751 Joshua Ripley and his wife Mary; Joshua Abbe and his wife Mary; Nathaniel Ripley and Ebenezer Ripley all of Windham; and John Alden and his wife Elizabeth of Lebanon quitclaimed to Joshua Ripley Jr. of Windham their rights in land conveyed to Mary Ripley for life and then to her daughter Hannah Ripley now deceased.

On 6 Feb. 1752 Nathaniel Ripley of Windham sold to John Ripley Jr. of Windham his share of the land of Phinehas Ripley.

No Connecticut probate record, nor any further record, has been found for Nathaniel Ripley.

Children of Nathaniel and Ann (Ripley) Ripley, b. Windham, Conn.:

 i PHINEHAS RIPLEY⁶, b. 20 March 1746/7

 ii ANN RIPLEY, b. 20 Aug. 1749

 iii AMY RIPLEY, b. 20 Nov. 1751

References: *Bradford Desc* p. 89. Windham CT VR 1:39(b. Nathaniel), 61(b. Ann), 273(m.; b. ch.). Scotland CT Cong. Ch. Rec. 2:72(Ann's 2ⁿᵈ m.). Old Scotland CT Cemetery Rec. p.15(d. Ann). Windham CT LR K:63(Nathaniel Ripley), 128(quitclaim).

273. ELIZABETH RIPLEY⁵ (*Joshua⁴, Hannah³ Bradford, William²⁻¹*), b. Windham, Conn., 4 Nov. 1724; d. Lebanon, Conn., 26 March 1789 aged 64.

She m. Lebanon, Conn., 9 Oct. 1744 **JOHN ALDEN**, b. Duxbury 23 July 1716; d. Lebanon 2 May 1764 in 45th yr.; son of Andrew and Lydia (Stanford) Alden, a descendant of Pilgrim **John Alden**. On 2 Feb. 1737/8 Andrew Alden of Lebanon sold to his son John Alden of Lebanon the farm on which Andrew lived and all other land in Lebanon. On 30 June 1739 Andrew and John Alden sold to Abial Stark of Lebanon three pieces of land with buildings.

John Alden was admitted to the Goshen (Lebanon), Conn., church 28 March 1742 and Elizabeth was admitted on 21 April 1745.

In Nov. 1751 Joshua Ripley and his wife Mary; Joshua Abbe and his wife Mary; Nathaniel Ripley and Ebenezer Ripley all of Windham; and John Alden and his wife Elizabeth of Lebanon quitclaimed to Joshua Ripley Jr. of Windham their rights in land conveyed to Mary Ripley for life and then to her daughter Hannah Ripley now deceased.

On 8 June 1765 widow Elizabeth Alden was named administratrix on the estate of John Alden, late of Lebanon. On 2 July 1766 the estate was declared insolvent.

The will of Elizabeth Alden dated 13 Dec. 1784, proved 27 April 1789, names daughter Violette wife of Isaac Fitch; son Roger Alden; daughter Elizabeth Alden Jr.; daughter Parthenia wife of Woodbridge Little; and daughters of Violette.

Children of John and Elizabeth (Ripley) Alden, b. Lebanon, Conn.:

    i   PERTHENA ALDEN[6], b. 5 Sept. 1745

   ii   VIOLETTA ALDEN, b. 8 April 1748, bp. 10 April 1748

  iii   JOHN ALDEN, b. 18 June 1750, bp. 24 June 1750

  iv   JUDAH ALDEN, b. 10 March 1752; killed during the Rev. War in the battle near White Plains 22 Aug. 1777. He was a Captain in the Continental Army. Roger Alden was appointed administrator of his estate on 25 April 1785 which was handled with the estate of his brother John. On 14 July 1785 the estates of both brothers were declared insolvent.

   v   ROGER ALDEN, b. 11 Feb. 1754, bp. 17 Feb. 1754

  vi   ELIZABETH ALDEN, b. 23 Dec. 1757; d. 25 May 1758 ae 5m

  vii   [TWIN SON] ALDEN, b. Aug. 1759; d. instantly

 viii   [TWIN SON] ALDEN, b. Aug. 1759; d. next morning

  ix   ELIZABETH ALDEN, b. 17 May 1762

References: *Bradford Desc* p. 89. Windham CT VR 1:3(m.), 39(b. Elizabeth). Lebanon CT VR 1:3(m.; b. 8 ch.), 5(b. dau. Elizabeth). *MD* 10:185(b. John). *VR Duxbury* p. 16(b. John). Hale Cem Coll:Lebanon CT p. 82 (deaths). Windham CT PR #63-5(John Alden); #63-3, 12:375(Elizabeth Alden); #67-7, 5:86, 161, 234(Judah and John Alden). Lebanon CT LR 5:417(Andrew Alden); 6:63(Andrew & John). Windham CT LR K:128(quitclaim). Lebanon 1st Ch. Recs. 4:50(bp. Violetta), 51(bp. John), 54(bp. Roger); 5:153; 7:35(d. wife Elizabeth). MF 16:1:446-7.

274. JOSHUA RIPLEY[5] (*Joshua*[4], *Hannah*[3] *Bradford, William*[2-1]), b. Windham, Conn., 30 Oct. 1725, bp. 13 Nov. 1726; d. there 17/19 Dec. 1787 aged 61y.

He m. (1) Windham, Conn., 26 March 1748 **ELIZABETH LATHROP**, b. Barnstable 9 March 1731; d. Windham, Conn., 30 June 1778, aged 47y; daughter of Benjamin and Mary (Baker) Lathrop.

He m. (2) 25 Nov. 1779 **DEBORAH BINGHAM**, b. Windham, Conn., 4 May 1729; d. 30 Aug. 1810; daughter of Samuel and Elizabeth (Manning) Bingham.

On 19 July 1749 Joshua Ripley Jr. sold to Nathaniel Ripley his right in land then in the improvement of his father Joshua on which Joshua Sr. dwelt, that his late brother Phineas in his will bequeathed to their father during his life.

In Nov. 1751 Joshua Ripley and his wife Mary; Joshua Abbe and his wife Mary; Nathaniel Ripley and Ebenezer Ripley all of Windham; and John Alden and his wife Elizabeth of Lebanon quitclaimed to Joshua Ripley Jr. of Windham their rights in land conveyed to Mary Ripley for life and then to her daughter Hannah Ripley now deceased.

The will of Joshua Ripley of Windham, Conn., dated 10 Nov. 1787, proved 17 Jan. 1788, names wife Deborah; sons Eliphalet, Ralph, Nathaniel and Erastus; and daughters Polly, Elizabeth, Olive, and Lydia (without surnames). On 6 April 1789 widow Deborah sold her interest in her husband's estate for £51. On 14 April 1789 distribution was made to Ralph, Nathaniel, Erastus, and Polly Ripley.

Children of Joshua and Elizabeth (Lathrop) Ripley, b. Windham, Conn., with first wife:

    i   ELIPHALET RIPLEY[6], b. 28 Oct. 1749

   ii   RALPH RIPLEY, b. 25 Oct. 1751

  iii   ELIZABETH RIPLEY, b. 22 May 1754

  iv   OLIVE RIPLEY, b. 13 Sept. 1756

   v   ROGER RIPLEY, b. 16 April 1759; lost at sea

  vi   JOSHUA RIPLEY, b. 16 May 1761; lost at sea

 vii   LYDIA RIPLEY, b. 30 July 1763

viii   NATHANIEL RIPLEY, b. 14 Feb. 1768

  ix   ERASTUS RIPLEY, b. 17 Jan. 1770

   x   MARY RIPLEY, b. 14 Oct. 1774

References: *Bradford Desc* pp. 89-90. Windham CT VR 1:39(b. Joshua), 69(b. Deborah), 290(1st m.; b. ch.). Windham CT PR #3173, 12:208(Joshua Ripley). Hale Cem

Coll:Windham p. 283.   Windham CT LR I:295(Joshua Ripley); K:128(quitclaim).
Windham 1st Ch. Recs. 1:9(bp. Joshua).   Scotland Cong. Ch. Recs. 2:74(2nd m.).

275.   EBENEZER RIPLEY⁵ *(Joshua⁴, Hannah³ Bradford, William²⁻¹)*, b.
Windham, Conn., 22 [27 in Bible] June 1729, bp. 29 June 1729; d. there 11
June 1811 aged 82.

He m. Suffield, Conn., 11 June 1752 **MEHITABLE BURBANK**, b.
Suffield, Conn., 28 July 1729; d. Windham, Conn., 20 May 1813 aged 84;
daughter of Abraham and Mehitable (Dwight) Burbank. In his will dated 24
Oct. 1767, proved 30 Jan. 1768, Abraham Burbank of Suffield named his
daughter Mehitabel Ripley and gave her £130 worth of land in Springfield.

On 19 July 1749 Joshua Ripley Jr. sold to Nathaniel Ripley his right in
land now in the improvement of his father Joshua on which Joshua Sr. dwells
that his late brother Phineas in his will bequeathed to their father during his
life. On 7 July 1750 Ebenezer Ripley also sold his right to this land to
Nathaniel.

In Nov. 1751 Joshua Ripley and his wife Mary; Joshua Abbe and his wife
Mary; Nathaniel Ripley; and Ebenezer Ripley all of Windham; and John Alden
and his wife Elizabeth of Lebanon quitclaimed to Joshua Ripley Jr. of
Windham their rights in land conveyed to Mary Ripley for life and then to her
daughter Hannah Ripley now deceased.

Ebenezer Ripley's household in Windham in 1790 consisted of 2 men
over 16 and 2 females.

On 1 Jan. 1803 Ebenezer Ripley of Windham sold land in Windham to
his son John Ripley.

On 10 July 1811 his son Dwight Ripley of Norwich posted bond as
administrator of the estate of Ebenezer Ripley.

Children of Ebenezer and Mehitable (Burbank) Ripley, b. Windham, Conn.:

   i   HANNAH RIPLEY⁶, b. 28 April 1753
  ii   ELEANOR RIPLEY, b. 16 Aug. 1754
 iii   JERUSHA RIPLEY, b. 28 May 1756
  iv   JULIANA RIPLEY, b. 31 July 1757; d. 18 July 1759 ae 2y
   v   JUSTIN RIPLEY, b. 1 Jan. 1759; d. 26 Oct. 1761 or 23 Oct. ae 2y 2m
  vi   ABRAHAM RIPLEY, b. 25 Feb. 1760
 vii   ABIAH RIPLEY, b. 12 Dec. 1762
viii   DWIGHT RIPLEY, b. 7 Aug. 1764
  ix   EBENEZER RIPLEY, b. 26 March 1766

x   THADDEUS RIPLEY, b. 22 Oct. 1767

xi ANNA RIPLEY, b. 20 June 1770

xii HORACE RIPLEY, b. 20 Aug. 1772

References: *Bradford Desc* p. 90.   Windham CT VR 1:39(b. Ebenezer); 2:11(b. ch.). Suffield CT VR 1:93(b. Mehitable); NB1:128(m.).   Windham CT Cem p. 271(d. Ebenezer). Windham CT PR #3161(Ebenezer Ripley). Windham CT LR I:444(Ebenezer Ripley); K:128(quitclaim); W:154(Ebenezer Ripley).   Hale Cem Coll:Windham p. 280. Windham 1st Ch. Recs. 1:12(bp. Ebenezer), 358(d. Ebenezer).   Ripley Bible with GS#58617. Hartford CT PR #925 20:240(Abraham Burbank).

276. WILLIAM RIPLEY[5] (*Joshua*[4], *Hannah*[3] Bradford, *William*[2-1]), b. Windham, Conn., 12 Feb. 1734, bp. 31 March 1734/5; d. Cornish, N.H., 17 Feb. 1818.

He m. Windham, Conn., 11 Jan. 1757 **LYDIA BREWSTER**, b. Windham, Conn., 18 March 1739/40; d. Cornish 2 Nov. 1829; daughter of James and Faith (Ripley) Brewster, a descendant of Pilgrims **William Bradford** and **William Brewster.**

On 29 Jan. 1762 William Ripley and wife Lydia sold their rights in the land of her father Capt. James Brewster of Windham deceased to David Adams.

The Ripley Bible says "We moved from Connecticut with our family June 5, and arrived at Cornish the 14, 1775."

William Ripley served as a sergeant in the Revolutionary War.

On 20 April 1776 David Chase of Cornish sold 10 acres in Cornish to William Ripley of Cornish, cordwainer. On 25 Oct. 1791 William Ripley Esq. of Cornish and wife Lydia sold 80 acres in Cornish to James Ripley of Cornish, yeoman.

No Cheshire Co., N.H., probate records have been found for William Ripley.

Children of William and Lydia (Brewster) Ripley, b. Windham, Conn.:

i   FAITH RIPLEY[6], b. 13 Oct. 1757

ii   ALETHEA RIPLEY, b. 23 Aug. 1759; d. 5 Sept. 1759

iii ALATHEA RIPLEY, b. 11 Jan. 1761

iv   JAMES RIPLEY (twin), b. 4 April 1763

v   SELINDA RIPLEY (twin), b. 4 April 1763

References: *Bradford Desc* p. 90.   Windham CT VR 1:39(b. William), 160(b. Lydia); 2:24(m.; b. 1st 4 ch.). Windham CT LR M:285(William Ripley). Cheshire Co. NH LR 5:67(Dudley Chase); 26:463(William Ripley).   *Cornish NH Hist* 2:314.   Hale Cem

Coll:Scotland p. 25(d. Alethea). Windham 1st Ch. Recs. 1:17(bp. William). Scotland Cong. Ch. 2:70(m.). Ripley Bible with GS#58617.

277. JOHN RIPLEY⁵ (*Joshua⁴, Hannah³ Bradford, William²⁻¹*), b. Windham, Conn., 31 March 1738, bp. 2 April 1738; d. Hartford, Conn., 27 June 1823 aged 85.

He m. Windham, Conn., 7 June 1769 **ABIGAIL MARSH**, b. Norwich, Conn., 8 April 1751; d. Hartford, Conn., 3 [21 in Bible] July 1805 aged 54; daughter of Jonathan and Sarah (Hart) Marsh.

John and Abigail Ripley were admitted to the Windham First Church on 15 Aug. 1773.

John Ripley served in the Revolutionary War as a major.

On 22 May 1786 John Ripley of Windham and wife Abigail sold to five tracts of land in Windham and their dwelling house to John Brown of Providence.

John Ripley's household in Windham in 1790 consisted of a man over 16, 3 boys under 16, and 3 females.

On 16 Nov. 1821 John Ripley of Hartford sold land in Hartford to Jabez Ripley of Hartford.

Children of John and Abigail (Marsh) Ripley, b. Windham, Conn.:

    i   HENRIETTA RIPLEY⁶, b. 13 March 1770; d. Windham, Conn., 23 Oct. 1795 ae 25y 5m; unm.

    ii   ELISHA PAINE RIPLEY, b. 12 Dec. 1771; d. 26 May 1773 [1777 in Hale Cem Coll] ae 1y

    iii   ABIGAIL RIPLEY, b. 28 Sept. 1773; d. 24 Nov. 1777 ae 5

    iv   POLLY RIPLEY, b. 3 [2 in Bible] Nov. 1775; d. 22 Nov. 1777 ae 2y 20d

    v   HANNAH RIPLEY, b. 7 Oct. 1777; d. 10 Oct. 1777 ae 3d

    vi   LUCY RIPLEY, b. 12 Sept. 1778; d. Hartford, Conn., 23 Jan. 1853 ae 84; unm.

    vii   JOHN BRADFORD RIPLEY, b. 6 July 1780

    viii   WILLIAM BRADFORD RIPLEY, b. 14 Aug. 1784; d. 15 Sept. 1785 (Hale Cem Coll:Hartford: d. 15 Sept. 1765 [*sic*] ae 1y 1m 8d)

    ix   JABEZ RIPLEY, b. 24 May 1786

    x   OLIVER RIPLEY, b. 14 [12 in Bible] Nov. 1788

    xi   JULIA RIPLEY, b. 16 May 1792

References: *Bradford Desc* pp. 90-1. Windham CT VR 1:39(b. John); 2:124(b. Abigail), 155(m.; b. ch.). Old North Cemetery, Hartford CT p. 175(d. John, Abigail, Lucy). *DAR*

Patriot Index p. 572. Windham CT LR S:228(John Ripley). Hartford CT LR 42:100(John Ripley). Hale Cem Coll:Windham pp. 278(d. Henrietta, Bradford), 280(d. Elisha Paine, Polly, Hannah), 281(d. Abigail). Windham 1st Ch. Recs. 1:21(bp. John), 35(adm.). Ripley Bible with GS#58617. Hale Cem Coll:Hartford p. (d. William).

278. SAMUEL SEABURY⁵ (*Margaret Ripley⁴, Hannah³ Bradford, William²⁻¹*), b. Lebanon, Conn., ca 1718; d. there 16 March 1800 in 83rd year.

He m. Lebanon, Conn., 22 Feb. 1738/9 **ANN TERRY**, b. Lebanon 12 Sept. 1716; d. there 13 Feb. 1792 aged 75; daughter of Ephraim and Hannah (Eggleston) Terry.

On 3 Jan. 1758 Benjamin Seabury of Lebanon gave to his son Samuel Seabury of Lebanon 100 acres.

Samuel Seabury's household in Lebanon in 1790 consisted of 2 men over 16, 1 boy, and 2 females.

The will of Samuel Seabury of Lebanon, Conn., dated 11 Sept. 1792; codicil dated 25 Feb. 1800, proved 31 March 1800, names nephew John Manning, nephew Benjamin Seabury, and friend Zelinda Morgan. The codicil includes bequests to the children of sister Sarah Manning. The 16 April 1800 distribution names Sarah's children as John, Andrew, Benjamin, Seabury, Barnabas, and Gamaliel Manning and Alathea Welch, wife of Eleazer Welch.

Samuel and Ann apparently had no children.

References: Lebanon CT VR 1:284(m.), 305(b. Ann). First Church, Lebanon CT rec. 5:157(d. Ann), 164(d. Samuel). Windham CT PR 14:382(Samuel Seabury). Hale Cem Coll:Lebanon(d. Samuel & Ann). Lebanon CT LR 8:342(Benjamin Seabury). *Terry Fam* p. 12.

279. ELISHA SEABURY⁵ (*Margaret Ripley⁴, Hannah³ Bradford, William²⁻¹*), b. prob. Lebanon, Conn., 1721; d. Lebanon, Conn., 3 Nov. 1776 aged 55.

He m. Martha's Vineyard 13 Sept. 1744 **HEPZIBAH ATHEARN**, b. ca 1720; d. Lebanon, Conn., 5 May 1786 aged 67; daughter of Solomon and Sarah (Skiff) Athearn.

On 3 Jan. 1758 Benjamin Seabury of Lebanon gave to his son Elisha Seabury of Lebanon 100 acres. On 10 April 1773 Benjamin deeded 16 acres in Lebanon to his grandson Benjamin Seabury.

Children of Elisha and Hepzibah (Athearn) Seabury, b. Lebanon, Conn.:

    i EUNICE SEABURY⁶, b. 9 Dec. 1745, bp. 15 Dec. 1745

   ii JEDEDIAH SEABURY, b. 12 May 1747, bp. 24 May 1747

iii SUBMIT SEABURY, b. 29 April 1749, bp. 18 June 1749; d. 10 Dec. 1751

iv REBECCA SEABURY, b. 18 Jan. 1751, bp. 27 Jan. 1751

v BENJAMIN SEABURY, b. 3 Feb. 1753

vi LUCRETIA SEABURY, b. 5 May 1755, bp. 11 May 1755

vii MARY SEABURY, b. 4 April 1759, bp. 21 Oct. 1759

References: *Bradford Desc* p. 91. Lebanon CT VR 1:290(d. Elisha, Hepzibah; m.; b. ch.). *Martha's Vineyard By Banks* 3:22(parents of Hepzibah). Norwich CT LR 9:343; 12:227(Benjamin Seabury). Lebanon 1st Ch. Recs. 4:48(bp. Eunice), 49(bp. Jedediah), 50(bp. Submit), 51(bp. Rebecca), 55(bp. Lucretia), 57(bp. Mary); 5:151; 7:33(d. Hepzibah). Hale Cem Coll:Lebanon p. 69(d. Elisha).

280. SARAH SEABURY[5] (*Margaret Ripley*[4], *Hannah*[3] *Bradford, William*[2-1]), bp. Lebanon, Conn., 29 Jan. 1723; d. Scotland, Conn., 21 Dec. 1817 aged 92. [See #309]

She m. Windham, Conn., 27 Jan. 1752 **JOHN MANNING**, b. Cambridge 10 July 1720; d. Scotland, Conn., 6 Oct. 1779 aged 59; son of John and Abigail (Winship) Manning. He m. (1) SARAH _____, who d. 29 April 1751 aged 31. (Was she #309. SARAH WHEAT[5]?) They had a daughter Sarah who d. 8 July 1750 aged 9m.

His son John Manning was head of a household in Lebanon in 1790 consisting of a man over 16, 3 boys, and 2 females.

No Connecticut probate records were found for John Manning. However, the probate record of Sarah's brother Samuel Seabury names her children.

Children of John and Sarah (Seabury) Manning, b. Windham, Conn.:

i BENJAMIN MANNING[6] (twin), b. 20 March 1753, bp. 20 May 1753; d. 18 Feb. 1755 ae 1

ii JOHN MANNING (twin), b. 20 March 1753, bp. 20 May 1753; prob. d.y.

iii ANDREW MANNING, b. 8 July 1755, bp. 13 July 1755

iv BENJAMIN MANNING, b. 16 Oct. 1757, bp. 23 Oct. 1757

v ALATHEA MANNING, b. 25 Jan. 1760, bp. 27 Jan. 1760

vi SEABURY MANNING, b. 3 July 1763, bp. 11 July 1762; d. 14 Dec. 1843 ae 81; unm.

vii JOHN MANNING, b. 10 Feb. 1765; d. 23 July 1851; unm.

viii BARNABAS MANNING, b. 14 Sept. 1768, bp. 30 Oct. 1768

References: *Bradford Desc* p. 91. Windham CT VR 1:234(b. Alathea), 265(m.; b. 1st 7 ch. exc. Alathea); 2:139(b. Barnabas). *Cambridge Hist* p. 602(b. John). *VR Cambridge* 1:461(b. John). Lebanon 1st Ch. Recs. 4:158(m.). Scotland Cong. Ch. Recs. 2:28(bp. Benjamin, John), 30(bp. Andrew), 31(bp. Benjamin), 33(bp. Alathea), 34(bp. Seabury), 79(bp. Barnabas). Hale Cem Coll:Scotland pp. 13(d. Seabury), 21(d. John, Sarah, Benjamin).

281. PEREZ TRACY[5] (*Rachel Ripley[4], Hannah[3] Bradford, William[2-1]*), b. Norwich, Conn., 13 Nov. 1716; d. there 12 Feb. 1801.

He m. Norwich, Conn., 7 Aug. 1740 **ELIZABETH HYDE**, b. Norwich 23 Aug. 1724; d. there 24 April 1805; daughter of William and Anne (Bassett) Hyde.

Peres Tracy was head of a household in New London Co. in 1790 consisting of 2 men over 16 and 2 females.

Children of Perez and Elizabeth (Hyde) Tracy, b. Norwich, Conn.:

　　i　JOSHUA TRACY[6], b. 7 June 1741

　　ii　RACHEL TRACY, b. 17 Sept. 1743; d. Norwich, Conn., 12 July 1764; unm.

　　iii　ELIZABETH TRACY, b. 23 June 1746

　　iv　WILLIAM TRACY, b. 2 May 1750

　　v　BENJAMIN TRACY, b. 4 Nov. 1756

References: *Bradford Desc* p. 91. *Norwich CT VR* 1:94(b. Elizabeth), 202(m.; b. ch.). *Tracy Gen* p. 41. *Hyde Gen* pp. 29, 112-3.

282. JOSIAH TRACY[5] (*Rachel Ripley[4], Hannah[3] Bradford, William[2-1]*), b. Norwich, Conn., 10 May 1718. He is probably the man of that name who d. Franklin, Conn., 26 March 1803 aged 85.

He m. (1) Norwich, Conn., 3 Nov. 1740 **RACHEL ALLEN**, b. Norwich 10 June 1719; d. there 28 Aug. 1761; daughter of Timothy and Rachel (Bushnell) Allen.

He m. (2) Norwich, Conn., 28 June 1762 **ESTHER (RICHARDS) PRIDE**, who d. Franklin, Conn., 30 Aug. 1799. She m. (1) Norwich 10 Aug. 1742 MICAJAH PRIDE with whom she had Asa, Abner, James, Elijah, Ruben, Jerusha, Jonathan, and Amasai Pride.

Winslow Tracy gave or sold to his son Josiah 20 acres on 22 Dec. 1744, 39 acres on 14 May 1752, one acre on 8 April 1751, and 22 acres on 21 Nov. 1752.

Josiah Tracy's household in New London Co. in the 1790 census consisted of a man and 2 females; listed next to him was Calvin Tracy with a man, 2 boys, and 3 females.

No Connecticut probate records were found for Josiah Tracy.

Children of Josiah and Rachel (Allen) Tracy, b. Norwich, Conn.:

    i   IRENE TRACY[6], b. 21 Dec. 1741

    ii NEHEMIAH TRACY, b. 23 March 1744

   iii DANIEL TRACY, b. 8 Nov. 1746; d. 19 Jan. 1747/8

   iv DANIEL TRACY, b. 19 Jan. 1747/8; d.y.

    v ANNE TRACY, b. 22 Dec. 1748

   vi JERUSHA TRACY, b. 26 April 1751

  vii CALVIN TRACY, b. 14 Sept. 1753; d. 1 Jan. 1755

 viii CALVIN TRACY, b. 7 June 1755; d.y.

   ix DANIEL TRACY, b. 23 Oct. 1756

    x CALVIN TRACY, b. 7 June 1759

Children of Josiah and Esther (Richards) (Pride) Tracy, b. Norwich, Conn.:

   xi RACHEL TRACY, b. 8 June 1763; d. 20 Dec. 1777

  xii MEHITABLE TRACY, b. 28 Oct. 1765

References: *Bradford Desc* pp. 91-2. Franklin CT VR 1:19(d. Josiah, Esther). *Norwich CT VR* 1:11(b. Rachel), 202(1st m.; d. Rachel; b. Irene through 3rd Calvin), 370(2nd m.; b. Rachel, Mehitable), 371(d. Rachel, Esther's 1st m.). Norwich CT LR 9:317; 12:16, 22, 253(Winslow Tracy). *Tracy Gen* p. 42.

283. ELIPHALET TRACY[5] (*Rachel Ripley[4], Hannah[3] Bradford, William[2-1]*), b. Norwich, Conn., 14 Nov. 1720; d. Franklin, Conn., 21 March 1807 aged 86.

He m. Lebanon, Conn., 28 Nov. 1743 **SARAH MANNING**, b. Windham, Conn., 22 Feb. 1724; d. Franklin, Conn., 3 May 1809 aged 86; daughter of Samuel and Irene (Ripley) Manning, a descendant of Pilgrim **William Bradford** (see #306).

Winslow Tracy gave or sold to his son Eliphalet 20 acres on 22 Dec. 1744, four acres on 28 Feb. 1752, 23 acres on 14 May 1752, and 23 more acres on 21 Nov. 1752.

On 25 Jan. 1775 Eliphalet Tracy of Norwich sold 38 acres in Norwich to son Elisha Tracy Jr. of Norwich; Uriah Tracy Jr. was a witness.

Eliphalet Tracy's household in New London Co. in the 1790 census consisted of one man and 2 females.

On 22 July 1803 Eliphalet Tracy of Franklin sold land in Franklin to son Elisha Tracy and his son Gurdon Tracy.

No Connecticut probate records have been found for Eliphalet Tracy.

Children of Eliphalet and Sarah (Manning) Tracy,* b. Norwich, Conn.:

    i   ELISHA TRACY[6], b. 23 Feb. 1743/4

   ii   ALATHEA TRACY, b. 28 Jan. 1746/7

  iii   LUCY TRACY, b. 26 Sept. 1749

  iv   URIAH TRACY, b. 3 Feb. 1755

* *Tracy Genealogy* includes a Martha, b. ca. 1748 Franklin, Conn., m. Jasper Smith.

References: *Bradford Desc* p. 92. Franklin CT VR 1:10(d. Eliphalet, Sarah). *Norwich CT VR* 1:2251(m.; b. ch.). Windham CT VR 1:77(b. Sarah). Norwich CT LR 9:318; 12:34-5, 334(Winslow Tracy); 21:516(Eliphalet Tracy). Franklin CT LR 2:241(Eliphalet Tracy). *Tracy Gen* p. 42. *Manning Fam* pp. 189-90. Hale Cem Coll:Franklin p. 77(d. Eliphalet, Sarah).

284. NEHEMIAH TRACY[5] (*Rachel Ripley[4], Hannah[3] Bradford, William[2-1]*), b. Norwich, Conn., 18 March 1722; d. 9 Sept. 1776.

He m. Windham, Conn., 19 June 1744 **SUSANNAH SMITH**, b. 1725; d. 29 April 1806; daughter of Matthew and Sarah (Mack) Smith.

On 13 May 1785 Nehemiah Tracy and Gamaliel Ripley Tracy of East Haddam sold to Hezekiah Mack of East Haddam a lot in East Haddam. On 29 Nov. 1785 Nehemiah sold to Gamaliel his right in three pieces of land and on 30 Dec. 1790 Gamaliel sold to Nehemiah his right in the same three pieces plus a fourth.

Susanna Tracy's household in East Haddam in the 1790 census consisted of a boy under 16 and 4 females.

On 18 April 1798 Susannah Tracy, Nehemiah Tracy, Samuel Crowell and his wife Jerusha, Elisha Cone and his wife Elizabeth, and Sarah Tracy all of East Haddam, and Daniel Tracy of Colchester, Elijah Selden and his wife Hannah of Windsor, and Lament Peck and his wife Rachel of Bristol, sold to Gamaliel Ripley Tracy of East Haddam two lots of land. The first was 70 acres with a house and barn that had been the home lot of Nehemiah Tracy deceased, and the second was 30 acres. Samuel Crowell did not sign or acknowledge the deed.

On 6 May 1806 Gamaliel R. Tracy was granted administration on the estate of Susanna Tracy of East Haddam. The inventory included notes from Gamaliel R. Tracy, Daniel Tracy, and Nehemiah Tracy.

No Connecticut probate records have been found for Nehemiah Tracy.

Children of Nehemiah and Susannah (Smith) Tracy, first b. Windham, Conn., rest b. East Haddam, Conn.:

    i   SUSANNA TRACY[6], b. 14 March 1745

   ii   TRYPHENA TRACY, b. 19 Jan. 1747; d. same day

  iii   TRYPHENA TRACY, b. 14 April 1748

  iv   JERUSHA TRACY, b. 23 Oct. 1751

   v   NEHEMIAH TRACY, b. 8 Nov. 1753

  vi   SARAH TRACY, b. 15 June 1755

 vii   RACHEL TRACY, b. 18 March 1757

viii   GAMALIEL RIPLEY TRACY, b. 17 Feb. 1759

  ix   HANNAH SMITH TRACY, b. 26 Oct. 1760

   x   JEDEDIAH TRACY, b. 16 Oct. 1762

  xi   DANIEL TRACY, b. 9 June 1765

 xii   ELIZABETH TRACY, b. 6 July 1767

xiii   ELIPHAS TRACY, b. 1 May 1772; d. 29 Aug. 1776

References: *Bradford Desc* p. 92. Windham CT VR 1:145(b. dau. Susanna), 245(m.). East Haddam CT VR 2:23(d. Nehemiah); LR 4:446(b. Tryphena thru Elizabeth exc. Jedediah). Colchester CT PR #3035(Susanna Tracy). *Tracy Gen* pp. 42-3. East Haddam CT LR 10:203, 221(Nehemiah Tracy); 11:203(Gamaliel Tracy); 13:178(Susannah Tracy *et al.*).

285. SOLOMON TRACY[5] (*Rachel Ripley[4], Hannah[3] Bradford, William[2-1]*), b. Norwich, Conn., 23 May 1728; d. after 1773.

He m. Norwich, Conn., 1 Sept. 1755 **ANN EDGERTON**, b. Norwich, Conn., 14 Nov. 1733; d. after 1773; daughter of Samuel and Margaret (Abell) Edgerton, a descendant of Pilgrim **William Bradford** (see #257iii).

Winslow Tracy gave or sold to his son Solomon 20 acres on 26 July 1749 and 15 acres on 21 Nov. 1752.

No Connecticut probate records have been found for Solomon Tracy.

Children of Solomon and Ann (Edgerton) Tracy, b. Norwich, Conn.:

   i   SIBIL TRACY[6], b. 5 Aug. 1756

  ii   SAMUEL TRACY, b. 4 March 1758

 iii   SARAH TRACY, b. 3 June 1761

    iv ELEAZER TRACY, b. 12 July 1763

    v LAVISSA TRACY, b. 29 May 1765

    vi WINSLOW TRACY, b. 13 March 1768

    vii MARGARET TRACY, b. 10 April 1770

    viii CLARISA TRACY, b. 18 April 1773

    ix SOLOMON TRACY

References: *Bradford Desc* p. 72. *Norwich CT VR* 1:106(b. Ann), 329(m.; b. ch. exc. Solomon). Norwich CT LR 10:230(Winslow Tracy). *Tracy Gen* pp. 43-4.

286.   REBECCA COOK⁵ (*Leah Ripley⁴, Hannah³ Bradford, William²⁻¹*), b. Windham, Conn., 26 Nov. 1718; d. Sharon, Conn., 15 July 1764.

She m. Norwich, Conn., 19 Nov. 1735 **CALEB JEWETT**, b. Norwich 25 June 1710; d. Sharon, Conn., 18 Jan. 1778; son of Eleazer and Mary (Amstrong) Jewett. He m. (2) Sharon, Conn., 26 May 1766 FAITH (RIPLEY) BREWSTER (see #289). On 14 Jan. 1735/6 Eleazer Jewett of Norwich gave to his son Caleb Jewett of Norwich 70 acres and on 8 Nov. 1740 sold to his son Caleb all the land he had in Norwich.

Caleb Jewett gave or sold land to several of his children. On 9 Oct. 1765 he deeded 60 acres each to Eliezer and Caleb Jr.; on 9 April 1768, 61 acres to Thaddeus; on 12 April 1768 more land to Eliezer; on 29 June 1769 more to Caleb Jr., and on 4 March 1776 59 more acres to Caleb; and on 19 March 1773 eight acres to Rebecca Calkin wife of John Jr. In October 1769 Thaddeus sold to Eliezer 60 acres and on 18 Dec. 1775 Eliezer sold to his father Caleb his right in seven rods of land.

Caleb Jewett served as a selectman for 12 years and a member of the Colonial Legislature for 11 sessions.

Children of Caleb and Rebecca (Cook) Jewett, first two b. Norwich, Conn., rest b. Sharon, Conn.:

    i JERUSHA JEWETT⁶, b. 6 April 1736

    ii IRENE JEWETT, b. 6 Jan. 1737/8; d. 1 Oct. 1739

    iii CALEB JEWETT, b. 15 Jan. 1739/40

    iv MARY JEWETT, b. 27 Feb. 1741; d. 12 March 1742

    v ELEAZER JEWETT, b. 13 March 1743

    vi NATHAN JEWETT, b. 3 Dec. 1744

    vii THADDEUS JEWETT, b. 17 Dec. 1746

    viii REBECCA JEWETT, b. 16 Jan. 1748/9

    ix IRENE JEWETT, b. 27 Dec. 1750

x   MARY JEWETT, b. 13 Aug. 1753

xi   ALPHEUS JEWETT, b. 15 Jan. 1756

xii   SYBIL JEWETT, b. 22 April 1760

References: *Bradford Desc* pp. 92-3. *Norwich CT VR* 1:52(b. Caleb); 187(m.; b. 1st 3 ch.; d. 1st Irene). Sharon CT VR LR2:24(b. Thaddeus), 219(b. Mary, Eleazer, Nathan); 3:101(b. Irene), 333(b. 2nd Mary); 4:320(b. Sybil); 5:151(b. Rebecca; d. mother Rebecca), 255(2nd m.); 7:303(b. Alpheus). *Sharon CT Bury Gr* p. 34(d. Caleb). *Jewett Gen* 1:94. Norwich CT LR 7:276; 8:407(Eleazer Jewett). Sharon CT LR 5:448; 6:73, 119, 229, 314; 7:120, 260(Caleb to children); 6:403(Thaddeus Jewett); 7:405(Eliezer Jewett).

287.   JERUSHA COOK⁵ (*Leah Ripley⁴, Hannah³ Bradford, William²⁻¹*), b. Windham, Conn., 20 Feb. 1721/2; d. Newton 1749.

She m. Newton 28 July 1745 **JOHN ALLEN**, b. Boston 27 Oct. 1718; d. Newton 27 July 1758; son of John and Mary (_____) Allen.

Children of John and Jerusha (Cook) Allen, b. Newton:

i   JERUSHA ALLEN⁶, b. 20 Aug. 1746

ii   JOHN ALLEN, b. 16 Dec. 1747; d. 27 May 1748

References: *Bradford Desc* p. 93. *BRC*: 24:127(b. John). *VR Newton* pp. 12(b. Jerusha, John), 420(d. John).

288.   WEALTHEAN COOK⁵ (*Leah Ripley⁴, Hannah³ Bradford, William²⁻¹*), b. Windham, Conn., 20 Aug. 1724; d. Sharon, Conn., 19 Nov. 1804.

She m. Sharon, Conn., 24 Nov. 1743 **THOMAS PARDEE**, b. Norwich, Conn., 31 Oct. 1722 [not in VR]; d. Sharon, Conn., 1 Aug. 1806; son of John and Betsy (Horne) Pardee.

On 20 April 1789 Thomas Pardee of Sharon gave to his son Samuel Pardee of Sharon three pieces of land totaling more than 69 acres. On 15 March 1797 Thomas sold to Samuel another 14 acres bounded on land he had given to his daughter Withly Dorman. On 25 March 1797 Samuel sold to 10 acres back to Thomas.

Children of Thomas and Wealthean (Cook) Pardee, b. Sharon, Conn.;

i   IRENE PARDEE⁶, b. 25 Dec. 1744; d. 12 April 1745

ii   SAMUEL PARDEE, b. 7 March 1746

iii   WEALTHEON PARDEE, b. 25 Dec. 1748

iv   GAMALIEL PARDEE, b. 26 Nov. 1750; d. 8 Dec. 1750

v   GAMALIEL PARDEE, b. 31 May 1752

    vi WILLIAM PARDEE, b. 3 March 1754; d. 1 Jan. 1767

    vii AUGUSTUS PARDEE (twin), b. 22 April 1756; d. May 1756

    viii PARTHENA PARDEE (twin), b. 22 April 1756; d. May 1756

    ix CALVIN PARDEE, b. 26 July 1757

    x ASENA PARDEE, b. 24 Feb. 1759; d. 7 June 1777

References: *Bradford Desc* p. 93. Sharon CT VR LR2:20(m.), 24(b. Wealtheon), 167(b. 1st 2 ch.); LR3:101(b.&d. both Gamaliel); LR5:106(b. William, Calvin, Asena). *Sharon CT Bur Gr* p. 43(d. Thomas, Wealthean). Sharon CT LR 11:459; 12:64(Thomas Pardee), 215(Samuel Pardee).

289. MARY COOK[5] (*Leah Ripley[4], Hannah[3] Bradford, William[2-1]*), b. Windham, Conn., 25 July 1729; d. Franklin, Conn., 28 Nov. 1796 aged 67.

She m. Scotland, Conn., 13 Oct. 1746 **JOSIAH MANNING**, bp. Hopkinton 20 June 1725; d. Windham, Conn., 16 Dec. 1806 aged 81; son of John and Abigail (Winship) Manning.

Josiah Manning's household in Windham in the 1790 census consisted of 2 men over 16 and 5 females.

Children of Josiah and Mary (Cook) Manning:

    i TRIPHENA MANNING[6] (twin), b. Dec. 1748; bp. Windham 7 Oct. 1750.

    ii CALEB MANNING (twin), b. Dec. 1748; d. 3 March 1749 in 4th m.

    iii MARTHA MANNING, b. Norwich, Conn., 15 Jan. 1749/50

    iv JOHN MANNING, b. 1751; d. 9 May 1761 ae 10y

    v FREDERICK MANNING, b. 1753; d. 23 June 1756 ae 3y

    vi LEAH MANNING (twin), b. 15 Feb. 1756; d. 15 March 1756 ae 4w

    vii RACHEL MANNING (twin), b. 15 Feb. 1756; d. 20 March 1756 ae 4w 5d

    viii JUNIUS MANNING (twin), b. 14 May 1757; d. 15 May 1757 ae 1d.

    ix TRIMELIUS MANNING (twin), b. 14 May 1757; d. 15 May 1757 ae 1d.

    x FREDERICK MANNING, b. ca. 1758

    xi ROCKWELL MANNING, b. ca. 1760

    xii MARY MANNING, b. 23 Nov. 1762

    xiii JARED MANNING, b. 23 May 1765; d. June or 25 May 1765 ae 4 weeks

    xiv COOK MANNING, b. 26 Aug. 1766; d. Oct. or 26 Aug. 1766 ae 7 weeks

    xv JIMIAS MANNING (twin); d. 13 May 1767 ae 1d

    xvi TRINE MANNING (twin); d. 13 May 1767 ae 1d

xvii NANCY MANNING

xviii FAITH MANNING

References: *VR Hopkinton* p. 129(bp. Josiah). *Bradford Desc* pp. 93-4. *CT Marr* 3:44(m.). Hale Cem Coll:Windham pp. 262(d. Mary, Josiah), 279(d. John, Frederick, Jared, Cook, Jimias, Trine). *Manning Fam* pp. 153, 197-9. *Norwich CT VR* 1:278(b. Martha). Hale Cem Coll:Franklin p. 44(d. Caleb, Leah, Rachel).

290. SAMUEL COOK⁵ (*Leah Ripley⁴, Hannah³ Bradford, William²⁻¹*), b. Windham, Conn., 8 Oct. 1732; d. Newton 9 April 1758.

He m. Windham, Conn., 31 Mach 1751 **EUNICE WEBB**, b. 25 Jan. 1732; d. Feb. 1820 Canterbury, Conn.; daughter of Timothy and Sarah (Howard) Webb.

On 26 June 1755 Samuel Cook of Windham sold to Joseph Allen of Windham part of a farm partly in Windham and partly in Canterbury that his father Samuel Cook willed to "me and my brother Phineas Cook," excepting the widow Leah's thirds.

Children of Samuel and Eunice (Webb) Cook, first 2 b. Windham, Conn., last b. Plainfield, Conn.:

i SYBEL COOK⁶, b. 3 Sept. 1751

ii SAMUEL COOK, b. 28 Feb. 1754

iii LEAH COOK, b. 26 Jan. 1758

References: *Bradford Desc* p. 94. *Windham CT VR* 1:311(m.; b. 2 ch.). Plainfield CT VR 2:38(d. Samuel; b. Leah). Windham CT LR L:306(Samuel Cook).

291. PHINEAS COOK⁵ (*Leah Ripley⁴, Hannah³ Bradford, William²⁻¹*), b. Windham, Conn., 7 June 1736; d. Newton 12 Jan. 1784 aged 47½y.

He m. Newton 1 March 1759 **ABIGAIL DURANT**, b. Newton 5 Jan. 1735/6; d. Watertown ca. 1830 aged about 89y; daughter of Edward and Ann (Jackson) Durant.

On 26 June 1755 Samuel Cook of Windham sold to Joseph Allen of Windham part of a farm partly in Windham and partly in Canterbury that his father Samuel Cook willed to "me and my brother Phineas Cook," excepting the widow Leah's thirds.

On 8 Oct. 1757 James Bradford and his wife Leah for love and affection gave to Phineas Cook of Newtown, Mass., son of Samuel Cook late of

Windham and of Leah, their right in the lands of Samuel Cook partly in Windham and partly in Canterbury.

Phineas served the town of Newton as a hogreeve in 1761, tithingman 1762, deer reeve 1764, fish reeve 1764 and 1768, surveyor of highways 1767, hayward 1770, assessor 1772–1775, and clerk of the market 1775.

Phineas was a captain in the Revolutionary War and he served on several committees in Newton on war-related matters.

On 5 May 1784 William Hunt was appointed administrator on the estate of Phinehas Cook late of Newton, Gentleman. The estate was insolvent and the dower was set off to the widow Abigail on 27 Sept. 1784. On 2 Nov. 1784 the following persons signed an agreement to the dower: Abigail Cook, Nancy Cook, John [Fowles?], and Aaron Richardson as guardian of Daniel Cook.

On 4 July 1784 Daniel Cook, age 18, son of Phinehas Cook, chose Aaron Richardson of Newton, Gentleman, as his guardian.

Abigail Cook's household in Newton in the 1790 census consisted of 2 men over 16 and 2 females.

Children of Phineas and Abigail (Durant) Cook, b. Newton:

    i   MARY COOK[6], b. 18 May 1759

   ii   DANIEL COOK, b. 13 Sept. 1761; d. 9 May 1763

  iii   ARTEMAS COOK d.y.*

  iv   ANN (or NANCY) COOK, b. 8 May 1764

   v   DANIEL COOK, b. 18 May 1766*

  vi   ABIGAIL COOK

 vii   SARAH COOK*

viii   SUSANNAH (or SUKEY) COOK, b. 1776*

  ix   ARTEMAS COOK d.y.*

* Newton VRs has only one Artemas born before 1773, and only Sukey (no Susannah), who m. Walter Hunnewell and died Watertown 9 Oct 1841 ae 65y. The second Daniel is not in VR; he d. Corinth, Vt., 25 Sept. 1839 ae 73y 4m. *Durant Gen* adds Sarah, b. ca. 1773, d. ca. 1812 ae 39y Corinth, Vt. but not in VT VR cards.

References: *Bradford Desc* p. 94. *VR Newton* pp. 41(b. Daniel, Artemas, Ann, Abigail), 42(b. Mary), 43(b. Sukey), 262(m.), 435(d. Daniel, Phineas). *MSSR* 3:939. *Durant Gen* 1:44; 2:7, 8. *Hist Newton* p. 249. Windham CT LR L:306(Samuel Cook); M:85(James Bradford). Middlesex Co. PR #5036(Phinehas Cooke); #5037(guardianship). *Newton Bio Dir* pp. 19-20.

292. HEZEKIAH RIPLEY⁵ (*Hezekiah⁴, Hannah³ Bradford, William²⁻¹*), b. Windham, Conn., 25 Sept. 1748 [6 Oct. on g.s.]; d. there 11 Nov. 1836 aged 88y.

He m. Windham, Conn., 29 April 1784 **EUNICE (CHESTER) DUMONT**, d. Windham, Conn., 4 May 1823 aged 64; daughter of Jonathan and Freelove (Waterman) Chester. (Windham 1st Ch. says: "Mrs. Hezekiah Ripley d. April 1826 aged 66."] She m. (1) before 1780 MICHAEL CLAUDIUS DUMONT with whom she had Freelove Dumont. On 9 Aug. 1780 the other heirs of Jonathan Chester sold their rights in 129 rods with a house and other buildings to Claudius Michel Dumont. On 2 Feb. 1784 Eunice Dumont sold to 1/5th of a house and land which "my father Capt. Jonathan Chester ... died siezed of" together with the 4/5ths which her husband had purchased.

On 26 March 1788 Hezekiah Ripley of Windham was granted the guardianship of Freelove Dumont daughter of Michael Dumont late of Norwich, deceased. An account of 11 April 1788 in the probate file of Michael C. Dumont included a payment to the widow Eunice Dumont and a balance paid to Hezekiah Ripley as guardian of the only child.

Hezekiah Ripley's household in Windham in the 1790 census consisted of a man over 16, 3 boys, and 5 females.

On 8 Dec. 1812 Hezekiah Ripley of Windham sold to George Ripley of Windham 7 acres at the east end of his home lot. In the acknowledgement he is called Hezekiah Ripley Esq. Lucy Ripley was one of the witnesses.

Children of Hezekiah and Eunice (Chester) (Dumont) Ripley, b. Windham, Conn.:

    i HEZEKIAH RIPLEY⁶, b. 17 May 1785

   ii MARIAN RIPLEY, b. 29 Dec. 1786

  iii EUNICE RIPLEY, b. 6 Jan. 1789

  iv GEORGE RIPLEY, b. 7 March 1792; d. 19 May 1817 at sea ae 25y; unm.

   v LUCY RIPLEY, b. 10 May 1794

References: *Bradford Desc* pp. 94-5. Windham CT VR 2:253(m.; b. 4 ch.); 3:1(m.; b.&d. George; d. parents). Hale Cem Coll:Windham p. 314(d. Hezekiah, Eunice, George). *Waterman Gen* pp. 225-7. Norwich CT PR #3467(guard. Freelove); #3468(Michael Dumont). Norwich CT LR 23:388(Michael Dumont buys); 24:370(Eunice Dumont). Windham CT LR Z:439(Hezekiah Ripley). Windham 1st Ch. 1:368(d. Mrs. Ripley).

293. FAITH RIPLEY⁵ (*David⁴, Hannah³ Bradford, William²⁻¹*), b. Windham, Conn., 6 May 1722; d. Sharon, Conn., 8 March 1787.

She m. (1) Windham, Conn., 15 March 1738/9 **JAMES BREWSTER**, b. Duxbury about May 1715; d. Sharon, Conn., 2 Oct. 1755 aged 40 last May (Aspinwall), son of Jonathan and Mary (Partridge) Brewster, a descendant of Pilgrim **William Brewster**.

She m. (2) Sharon, Conn., 26 May 1766 **CALEB JEWETT**, b. Norwich, Conn., 25 June 1710; d. Sharon 18 Jan. 1778; son of Eleazer and Mary (Armstrong) Jewett. He m. (1) Norwich, Conn., 2 Nov. 1735 REBECCA COOK. (See #286).

The 15 Dec. 1761 division of the estate of James Brewster late of Windham names widow Faith; sons James and David; daughters Lydia Ripley, Olive, Faith, and Mary Brewster.

On 1 July 1765 Olive Brewster of Windham sold to David Adams of Windham part of the estate of her father Capt. James Brewster "In Compliance with the Conditions of a Certain Bond entered Into ... by my Mother Mrs. Faith Brewster together with Willm Ripley and Gamaliel Ripley to the s^d Adams [Olive] being Now arrived at the Age of Twenty One Years." On 12 April 1768 Faith Brewster, now 21, sold her part to David Adams. On 25 Aug. 1772 Mary Brewster late of Windham now of Sharon, Conn., sold 1/7th part of her father's estate to David Adams. And on 6 Feb. 1775 David Brewster of Pomfrett sold to Dr. David Adams of Pomfrett his share of his father's estate.

Children of James and Faith (Ripley) Brewster, b. Windham, Conn.:

    i   LYDIA BREWSTER⁶, b. 18 March 1739/40, bp. 23 March 1740

   ii FAITH BREWSTER, b. 30 May 1742, bp. 6 June 1742; d. 28 Sept. 1745

  iii OLIVE BREWSTER, b. 18 June 1744, bp. 24 June 1744

  iv FAITH BREWSTER, b. 18 Nov. 1746, bp. 24 Nov. 1746

   v JAMES BREWSTER, b. 8 Jan. 1748/9; d. 22 Feb. 1777; unm.

  vi MARY BREWSTER, b. 30 June 1751, bp. 30 June 1752

 viii DAVID BREWSTER, b. 21 Dec. 1753, bp. 23 Dec. 1753

References: *Bradford Desc* p. 95. Windham CT VR 1:160(m.; b. 1st 3 ch.), 263(d. both James, Faith; b. last 4 ch.). Sharon CT VR LR 5:255(2nd m.). Windham CT PR #472(James Brewster). Windham CT LR O:372(Mary Brewster); P:23(Olive Brewster), 373(Faith Brewster); Q:142(David Brewster). Scotland Cong. Ch. Recs. 2:17(bp. Lydia), 19(bp. Faith), 21(bp. Olive), 23(bp. Faith), 25(bp. James), 27(bp. Mary), 28(bp. David).

294. LYDIA RIPLEY⁵ (*David⁴, Hannah³ Bradford, William²⁻¹*), b. Windham, Conn., 20 Feb. 1723/4; d. after 18 April 1761.

She m. Union, Conn., 11 Jan. 1749/50 **SAMUEL WOOD**, b. Boxford 4 June 1724; d. 1777; son of David and Mary (Spofford) Wood.

On 15 Nov. 1745 Samuel Wood of Boxford sold to Nathaniel Sessions of Pomfret, Conn., land in Union, Conn., that Nathaniel had conveyed to Samuel's father David Wood of Boxford deceased. On the same day Nathaniel sold to Samuel 232½ acres in Lot #7 and 92 acres in Lot #13 in Union. On 22 Sept. 1746 Nathaniel sold to Samuel half of Lot #8, it being 294¾ acres.

Samuel Wood served the town of Union, Conn., as a selectman in 1754, 1755-7, and 1759. Samuel Wood and his wife Lydia are on a list of people who were church members before 14 June 1759.

On 18 April 1761 Samuel Wood of Union, Esq., sold to David Wood and Jnoᵃ Wood of Boxford, yeomen, part of Lot #8.

No Connecticut probate records have been found for Samuel or Lydia Wood.

Children of Samuel and Lydia (Ripley) Wood, b. Union, Conn.:

    i   DAVID WOOD⁶, b. 13 Nov. 1750
    ii LYDIA WOOD, b. 26 March 1752
    iii IRENEY WOOD, b. 7 June 1754
    iv FAITH WOOD, b. 7 June 1756
    v   SAMUEL WOOD, b. 12 April 1758
    vi ALATHEA WOOD, b. 17 Aug. 17--
    vii [CHILD] WOOD, d.y.

References: *Bradford Desc* p. 95. Union CT VR 2LR:288(b. David), 288(b. Lydia, Ireney), 293(b. Faith, Samuel, Alathea), 295(m.). *VR Boxford* p. 107(b. Samuel). Union CT LR 2:8(Samuel Wood), 15, 24(Nathaniel Sessions),181(Samuel Wood). *Union CT Hist* 503(selectman).

295. ANN RIPLEY⁵ (*David⁴, Hannah³ Bradford, William²⁻¹*), b. Windham, Conn., 24 Aug. 1726, bp. 23 Oct. 1726; d. 6 Sept. 1792.

She m. Windham, Conn., 31 Oct. 1745 **NATHANIEL RIPLEY**, b. Windham 30 June 1721; son of Joshua and Mary (Backus) Ripley, a descendant of Pilgrim **William Bradford** (see #272).

References: Windham CT VR 1:39(b. Nathaniel), 273(m.; b. ch.). Windham 1ˢᵗ Ch. Recs. 1:9(bp. Ann).

296. IRENE RIPLEY[5] (*David[4], Hannah[3] Bradford, William[2-1]*), b. Windham, Conn., 11 Feb. 1728/9, bp. 6 April 1729; d. 24 Feb. 1804.

She m. (1) Windham, Conn., 11 Jan. 1749/50 **TIMOTHY WARNER**, b. Lebanon, Conn., 1 Dec. 1724; d. Windham 8 April 1760; son of Ichabod and Mary (Metcalf) Warner.

She m. (2) Windham, Conn., 4 Dec. 1764 **NATHAN HIBBARD**, b. Windham 6 Nov. 1715; d. Windham bet. 19 Dec. 1789 and 26 Feb. 1791; son of Ebenezer and Margaret (Morgan) Hibbard. He m. (1) 14 Dec. 1738 ZIPPORAH BUSHNELL with whom he had Nathan, Zipporah, Elizabeth, Dan, Charity, Andrew, Prudence, Abigail, Althea, Ebenezer, Bushnell, and Charity Hibbard.

She m. (3) 5 May 1797 **JAMES COGSWELL**, b. Saybrook, Conn., 6 Jan. 1720; d. Hartford, Conn., 2 Jan. 1807 aged 87y; son of Samuel and Anne (Mason) Cogswell. He m. (1) Canterbury, Conn., 24 April 1745 ALICE FITCH (see #220) with whom he had James, Alice, Samuel, Mason, and Septimus Cogswell. He m. (2) Chesire, Conn., in 1773, MARTHA (LOTHROP) DEVOTION.

In 1750 Mrs. Irene Warner wife of Dr. Warner was admitted to the Scotland Congregational Church.

In Oct. 1755 Timothy Warner was appointed physician to the army going to Crown Point.

On 1 Dec. 1763 Gamaliel Ripley of Windham sold to William Ripley of Windham 21 acres that was part of the real estate of his brother Dr. Timothy Warner of Windham deceased and his wife Irena Warner.

In 1766 the distribution of Dr. Timothy Warner's estate was made to Mrs. Ireny Hibberd the widow, Jared eldest son, Hannah eldest daughter, and daughter Ireney.

Nathan Hibbard of Windham made his will on 19 Dec. 1789, proved 26 Feb. 1791, naming his wife Irena; sons Nathan, Dan, Bushnell, Warner, and Ebenezer; heirs of deceased daughters Ziporah, Elizabeth, and Prudence; and daughters Abigail, Allethea, Charrity, Elizabeth, and Lydia.

James Cogswell graduated from Yale in 1742, was ordained in 1744, and became the pastor of the church in Canterbury, Conn. After 27 years he resigned and became the pastor of the Scotland Parish, Windham, church where he served until 1804.

James Cogshall's household in Windham in the 1790 census consisted of a man over 16, a boy, 2 females, and a slave.

Children of Timothy and Irene (Ripley) Warner, b. Windham, Conn.:

    i   HANNAH WARNER[6], b. 23 Nov. 1751, bp. 25 Nov. 1750

    ii IRENE WARNER, b. 30 Jan. 1753, bp. 25 Nov. 1752

   iii JARED WARNER, b. 10 Sept. 1754, bp. 29 Sept. 1754; d. 15 Oct. 1755

   iv JARED WARNER, b. 17 Sept. 1756, bp. 19 Sept. 1756

    v LYDIA WARNER, b. 1 March 1759, bp. 8 April 1759; d. 6 Dec 1764 in 6th y.

Children of Nathan and Irene (Ripley) (Warner) Hibbard, b. Windham, Conn.:

   vi TIMOTHY WARNER HIBBARD, b. 22 Oct. 1764, bp. 4 Nov. 1764

  vii ELIZABETH HIBBARD, b. 17 May 1767, bp. 24 May 1767

 viii LYDIA HIBBARD, b. 9 Nov. 1769, bp. 19 Nov. 1768; d. 6 Feb. 1770

References: *Bradford Desc* pp. 95-6. Windham CT VR 1:47(b. Nathan), 300(1st m.; b. Warner ch.), 326(b.&d. Timothy); 2:103(2nd m.; b. Hibbard ch.). Windham CT LR N:153(Gamaliel Ripley). *Cogswell Desc* pp. 51-3. *Warner Desc* pp. 136-7. *Hibbard Fam* pp. 27, 38. *Yale Grads* 1:701-3. Windham 1st Ch. Recs. 1:12(bp. Irene). Scotland Cong. Ch. 2:12(Irene adm.), 26(bp. Hannah), 27(bp. Irene), 29(bp. Jared), 30(bp. Jared), 32(bp. Lydia), 71(2nd m.), 77(bp. Timothy), 78(bp. Elizabeth), 79(bp. Lydia), 289(3rd m.).

297. DAVID RIPLEY[5] (*David[4], Hannah[3] Bradford, William[2-1]*), b. Windham, Conn., 7 Feb. 1730/1; d. Abington, Conn., 2 Sept. 1785 aged 54y.

He m. Lebanon, Conn., 12 Dec. 1758 **BETSY ELLIOT**, b. Lebanon 16 March 1736; d. 1 Aug. 1807 in her 72nd y; daughter of Jacob and Betty (Robinson) Elliot.

On 21 Dec. 1752 at a meeting of the Abington Church (the 2nd Society in Pomfret) "it was put to vote wheather they would call Mr David Ripley to the work of the gospel ministry in this place and it passed in the affirmative by a very great majoority." On 15 Jan. 1776 the church voted whether to do anything "in the time of the Revd Mr Ripley's confinment by sickness." On 26 April 1776 they voted to give him annual payments after "being dismissed from his Pastoral Relation to this Church and People."

On 10 Oct. 1785 Betty Ripley and Jared Warner were appointed administrators of the estate of David Ripley late of Pomfret. The inventory taken 5 Dec. 1785 included a library of over 70 books. On 20 Nov. 1792 the estate was distributed among the widow Betsey, David Bradford Ripley, eldest daughter Polly Ripley, and youngest daughter Betsey Ripley.

On 13 Nov. 1792 David Bradford Ripley chose Daniel Goodell of Pomfret as his guardian; Daniel was appointed guardian on 17 April 1793.

On 29 April 1793 Betsey Ripley Jr. of Pomfret, Conn., sold to Jared Warner of Pomfret two pieces of land one of which was bounded on land set off to the widow Betsey Ripley. On 10 June 1800 David Bradford Ripley of Pomfret sold to Jared Warner land distributed to him from the estate of his father David Ripley.

Children of David and Betsy (Elliot) Ripley, b. Pomfret, Conn.; bp. Abington Church:

-   i   DAVID RIPLEY[6], b. 11 July 1761, bp. 12 July 1761; d. 9 Sept. 1764
-   ii   MARY RIPLEY, b. 26 Aug. 1763, bp. 28 Aug. 1763
-   iii   AUGUSTUS RIPLEY, b. 1 Nov. 1765, bp. 3 Nov. 1765; d. 24 March 1769
-   iv   ELIZABETH RIPLEY, b. 5 Sept. 1767, bp. 11 Sept. 1768; d. Oct. 1843; unm.
-   v   DAVID WILLIAM RIPLEY, b. 17 July 1770, bp. 22 July 1770; d. 2 Aug. 1771
-   vi   DAVID BRADFORD RIPLEY b., Conn., 11 Feb. 1777, bp. 16 Feb. 1777

References: *Bradford Desc* p. 96. Lebanon CT VR 1:81(b. Betsy), 271(m.). Pomfret CT VR 1:87(b.&d. ch.). Abington Ch (2nd Society in Pomfret) 1:15, 48; 3:217(d. David), 225(d. Betty), 280(bp. David), 282(bp. Mary), 284(bp. Augustus), 287(bp. Elizabeth), 288(bp. David William), 291(bp. David Bradford). Pomfret CT LR 8:21(Betsey Ripley); 9:169(David Bradford Ripley). Pomfret CT PR #3416(David Bradford Ripley); #3418(David Ripley).

298. WILLIAM RIPLEY[5] (*David[4], Hannah[3] Bradford, William[2-1]*), b. Windham, Conn., 12 July 1734, bp. 25 Aug. 1734; d. 11 Nov. 1811.

He m. Windham, Conn., 10 March 1757 **REBECCA MARCY**, b. Woodstock, Conn., 10 Nov. 1735; d. Scotland, Conn., 6 Nov. 1818 aged 83; daughter of Joseph and Mary (Throop) Marcy. Mrs. Rebecca Ripley shared in the 1 Feb. 1791 division of the estate of Joseph Marcy late of Woodstock, Conn.

On 10 June 1757 David Ripley of Windham gave 40 acres in Windham to his son William Ripley and on 11 May 1760 he gave William 50 more acres. On 7 May 1762 William sold to David 40 acres "being the part of the land which my father gave me and part of the house in which he now dwells."

Rebecca wife of William Ripley was admitted to the Scotland Congregational Church in 1762.

On 1 Dec. 1763 Gamaliel Ripley of Windham sold to William Ripley of Windham 21 acres that was part of the real estate of his brother Dr. Timothy Warner of Windham deceased and his wife Irena Warner.

William Ripley's household in Windham in the 1790 census consisted of 2 men over 16, 2 boys, and 3 females.

Child of William and Rebecca (Marcy) Ripley, b. Windham, Conn.:

    i FAITH RIPLEY[6], bp. 30 April 1758

    ii DAVID RIPLEY, b. 18 Jan. 1761, bp. 28 Feb. 1762; d. 11 June 1782

References: *Bradford Desc* p. 96. Windham CT VR 2:27(m.; b.&d. David). Windham CT LR L:287; N:74(David Ripley; M:208(William Ripley); N:153(Gamaliel Ripley). Pomfret CT PR #2777(Joseph Marcy). *Marcy Gen* p. 288. Windham 1st Ch. Recs. 1:18(bp. William). Scotland Cong. Ch. Recs. 2:31(bp. Faith), 33(bp. David); 3:2(Rebecca adm.).

299. ALATHEA RIPLEY[5] (*David[4], Hannah[3] Bradford, William[2-1]*), b. Windham, Conn., 24 April 1738, bp. 30 April 1738; d. Pomfret, Conn., 24 May 1762.

She m. Pomfret, Conn., 18 Jan. 1759 **ELISHA LORD**, b. Preston, Conn., 18 July 1733; d. bet. 15 May 1809 and 12 Feb. 1810; son of Hezekiah and Sarah (Fish) Lord. He m. (2) Pomfret, Conn., 16 Nov. 176- TAMASINE (KIMBALL) COIT with whom he had Experience, Hezekiah, Alletheiah, Sarah, Mary, and Pamlia.

Elisha Lord's household in Pomfret in the 1790 census consisted of 3 men over 16, 2 boys, 9 females, and 2 other free persons.

Elisha Lord of Pomfret in his will dated 15 May 1809, proved 12 Feb. 1810, named his wife Tamerson, only son Elisha, and daughters Experience, Alathea, Sarah, Mary, and Pamlia. On 17 Feb. 1810 Capt. Elisha Lord was granted executorship on the estate of Dr. Elisha Lord late of Pomfret.

Child of Elisha and Alathea (Ripley) Lord, b. Pomfret, Conn.:

    i ELISHA LORD[6], b. 20 Dec. 1759

References: Preston CT VR 1:66(b. Elisha). Pomfret CT VR 1:83 (b. ch.), 84(d. Alathea), 107(m.), 111(2nd m.). Pomfret CT PR #2625(Elisha Lord). Windham 1st Ch. Recs. 2:16(bp. Alathea).

300. GAMALIEL RIPLEY[5] (*David*[4], *Hannah*[3] *Bradford, William*[2-1]), b. Windham, Conn., 20 Oct. 1740, bp. 26 Oct. 1740; d. there 15 April 1799.

He m. (1) Windham, Conn., 15 Dec. 1764 **ELIZABETH HIBARD**, b. Scotland, Conn., 9 Jan. 1743; d. Windham, Conn., 10 Jan. 1766; daughter of Nathan and Zipporah (Bushnell) Hibbard (see #296).

He m. (2) Windham, Conn., 23 Jan. 1772 **JUDITH PERKINS**, b. Norwich, Conn., 14 April 1747; d. Windham, Conn., 6 July 1803; daughter of Jacob and Jemima (Leonard) Perkins.

On 1 Dec. 1763 Gamaliel Ripley of Windham sold to William Ripley of Windham 21 acres that was part of the real estate of his brother Dr. Timothy Warner of Windham deceased and his wife Irena Warner.

On 5 Jan. 1779 David Ripley sold 60 acres in Windham to his son Gamaliel of Windham.

Gamaliel Ripley's household in Windham in the 1790 census consisted of 2 men over 16, 4 boys, 4 females, and a slave.

The will of Gameliel Ripley of Windham dated 13 April 1799, proved 18 June 1799, names wife Judith and children Hervey, Betsey, Bradford, Zephaniah, and William. On 15 April 1800 David B. Ripley, Hervey Ripley, and Elizabeth and John Adams Jr. of Canterbury signed receipts for their shares in the estate.

The will of Judith Ripley of Windham dated 1 July 1803, proved 2 Aug. 1803, names son Harvey Ripley and other children Betsey Adams, Bradford Ripley, Zephaniah Ripley, and William Ripley. The distribution on 9 Dec. 1803 went to the same children. On 10 Dec. 1803 a receipt was signed by John and Elizabeth Adams; on 2 April 1804 by Zephaniah Ripley; on 4 April 1804 by David B. Ripley; and on 17 Sept. 1804 by Harvey Ripley.

On 15 April 1800 Bradford Ripley of Windham was made the guardian of Lois Ripley, grandchild of Gamaliel Ripley, deceased, aged about 10. On 11 March 1807, when she was 17, Lois chose Veniah Parker of Windham for her guardian.

Child of Gamaliel and Elizabeth (Hibard) Ripley, b. Windham, Conn.:

   i ROSWELL RIPLEY[6], b. 31 Dec. 1765; d. Windham 4 Oct. 1791.

Children of Gamaliel and Judith (Perkins) Ripley, b. Windham, Conn.:

   ii HARVEY RIPLEY (twin), b. 25 Oct. 1772; d. Ellsworth, Ohio, 7 March 1813 ae 39, formerly of Windham.

   iii JUDITH RIPLEY (twin), b. 25 Oct. 1772; d. 25 Oct. 1772

   iv GAMALIEL RIPLEY, b. 8 Feb. 1774; d. 11 July 1795 ae 21y 5m

    v ELIZABETH RIPLEY, b. 19 March 1776

   vi DAVID BRADFORD RIPLEY, b. 19 April 1778

  vii ZEPHANIAH RIPLEY, b. 17 Oct. 1779

 viii LYDIA RIPLEY, b. 4 Dec. 1780; d. 10 May 1789

   ix WILLIAM RIPLEY, b. 27 May 1782

    x JABEZ PERKINS RIPLEY, b. 25 March 1788; d. 18 Feb. 1790

References: *Bradford Desc* pp. 96-7. *Norwich CT VR* 1:244(b. Judith). Windham CT VR 2:84(m.; b. ch.; d. Gamaliel, Elizabeth, Judith, Roswell, Lydia, Jabez). Windham CT PR #3167(Gamaliel Ripley), #3175(Judith Ripley), #3176(Lois Ripley). Windham CT LR N:153(Gamaliel Ripley); Q:293(David Ripley). *Hibbard Fam* p. 38. Windham 1st Ch. Recs. 2:18(bp. Gamaliel). Hale Coll, *Connecticut Mirror*, 26 April 1813(d. Harvey).

301. HEZEKIAH RIPLEY⁵ (*David⁴, Hannah³ Bradford, William²⁻¹*), b. Windham, Conn., 3 Feb. 1742/3, bp. 6 Feb. 1743; d. Westport, Conn., 29 Nov. 1831 aged 88y 2m 15d.

He m. New Haven, Conn., 9 Jan. 1765 **DOLLY** (or **DOROTHY**) **BRINTNALL**, b. New Haven, Conn., 13 July 1736; d. Fairfield, Conn., 19 Aug. 1831 aged 94y; daughter of William and Zerviah (Buckminster) Brintnall.

Hezekiah Ripley graduated from Yale College in 1763 and was ordained a minister at Greens Farms, Fairfield, 11 Feb. 1767. He resigned in August 1821.

Hezekiah Ripley served as Chaplain in Gen. Gold S. Silliman's brigade in 1776.

Hezekiah Ripley's household in Fairfield as listed in the 1790 census consisted of 2 men over 16, 1 boy, 3 females, and a slave.

The will of Hezekiah Ripley dated 20 June 1831, proved 1 March 1832, names his wife; the heirs of Joseph Disbrow of New Fairfield, coming from their aunt Deborah; heirs of his deceased son William; son David; daughter Alethea Bartlett; and granddaughters Alethea and Dolly Bartlett.

Children of Hezekiah and Dolly (Brintnall) Ripley:

    i ANN RIPLEY⁶, b. 1765; d. Westport, Conn., 26 Dec. 1830 ae 66y, unm.

   ii ALATHEA RIPLEY, b. 11 Nov. 1766

  iii WILLIAM RIPLEY, b. 3 Aug. 1768

  iv HEZEKIAH AUGUSTUS RIPLEY, bp. 27 May 1770

   v BRADFORD RIPLEY, b. 7 May 1773; d. 19 April 1774

  vi DAVID BRADFORD RIPLEY, b. 20 March 1775; d. 7 Oct. 1776

  vii DAVID RIPLEY, b. 20 March 1780

References: *Bradford Desc* p. 97., *Conn. Marr* 1:9(m.). *Fairfield Fams* 3:784. *New Haven Fams* 1:308. Windham 1ˢᵗ Ch. Recs. 2:20(bp. Hezekiah). Fairfield PR #5221(Hezekiah).

302. HANNAH RIPLEY⁵ (*David⁴, Hannah³ Bradford, William²⁻¹*), b. Windham, Conn., 23 Feb. 1750; d. Dutchess Co. NY 27 July 1813 aged 63; bur. in Spencer's Corner, North East, N.Y.

She m. **CYPRIAN (or ZEPORAN) WALDO**, b. Windham, Conn., 13 Nov. 1747; d. Sharon, Conn., 8 July 1797; son of Zacheus and Tabitha (Kinsbury) Waldo. Zacheus Waldo of Windham made his will 12 Feb. 1795, proved 17 Sept. 1810, naming his son Cyprian.

On 17 Dec. 1771 Cyprian Waldow bought a farm or homelot in Sharon and on 3 May 1797 gave it to his son Bradford Waldow. On 10 Feb. 1800 Hannah Waldo quitclaimed to Bradford Waldo all her right in the farm whereon they lived for "which a lease for life was heretofore excuted by said Bradford to me and my late Husband Cyprian Waldo dec."

Syprean Waldo's household in Litchfield Co. as listed in the 1790 census consisted of 3 men over 16, 2 boys, and 3 females.

Cyprian Waldo of Sharon in his will dated 6 May 1797, proved 30 Aug. 1797, named his sons Alfred, Bradford, David, Zacheus (under 21); daughter Ora Waldo (under 18); and wife Hannah.

Children of Cyprian and Hannah (Ripley) Waldo, b. Sharon, Conn.:

   i ALFRED WALDO⁶, b. 14 April 1772

   ii BRADFORD WALDO, b. 30 Dec. 1773

   iii LYDIA WALDO, b. 28 Nov. 1775; d. 4 May 1790; unm.

   iv DAVID WALDO, b. 24 July 1778

   v ZACHEUS WALDO, b. 27 Nov. 1780

   vi HARRIET WALDO, b. 1783; d. 18 Dec. 1784 ae 1y

   vii ORA WALDO, b. 1 April 1788

References: *Bradford Desc* p. 97. Windham CT VR 1:268(b. Cyprian). Sharon CT VR LR 6:128(b. Alfred); 7:301(b. Lydia, David, Zacheus), 306(b. Bradford); 10:143(b. Ora), 12:66(Cyprian Waldow); 13:522(Hannah Waldo). *Sharon CT Bury Gr* pp. 55(d. Lydia, Harriet), 169(d. Hannah). *Waldo Fam* pp. 142, 238-9. Windham CT PR #3933(Zacheus Waldo).

303. JOSIAH MANNING⁵ (*Irena Ripley⁴, Hannah³ Bradford, William²⁻¹*), b. Windham, Conn., 18 March 1719/20; d. there 31 Oct. 1800.

He m. Windham, Conn., 6 May 1742 **MARY KINGSLEY**, b. Windham, Conn., 11 Oct. 1719; d. after 20 Jan. 1808; daughter of Josiah and Dorothy (Bingham) Kingsley.

Josiah Manning was admitted to the Scotland Congregational Church on 22/23 Aug. 1751. Mrs. Mary Manning was admitted to the church in 1750. Mary Manning widow was a church member on a list of 20 Jan. 1808.

On 6 March 1749/50 Samuel Manning of Windham for love and affection gave to his sons Hezekiah Manning and Josiah Manning of Windham all his farm "on which he now dwells."

Josiah Manning served Windham, Conn., as a fence viewer in 1745, highway surveyor in 1754, and tithingman in 1747, 1753, 1755, and 1765. He was a grand juror in 1762.

Josiah Manning's household in Windham as listed in the 1790 census consisted of 2 men 16 or older, 5 females, and a slave.

No Connecticut probate records were found for Josiah Manning.

Children of Josiah and Mary (Kingsley) Manning, b. Windham, Conn.:

    i   CYRUS MANNING⁶, b. 15 May 1743, bp. 15 May 1743

    ii   MARY MANNING, b. 20 Jan. 1744/5, bp. 27 Jan. 1745

    iii IRENA MANNING, b. 25 July 1747, bp. 26 April 1747

    iv ELEAZER MANNING, b. 25 July 1749, bp. 30 July 1749

    v   HANNAH MANNING, b. 22 May 1751, bp. 26 May 1751; d. Oct. 1753

    vi ALATHEA MANNING, b. 23 Feb. 1753, bp. 25 Feb. 1753

    vii ELIJAH MANNING, b. 3 April 1755, bp. 6 April 1754; d. in the Army latter part of 1777 or beginning of 1778

   viii HANNAH MANNING, b. 18 May 1757, bp. 29 May 1757

    ix MARTHA MANNING, b. 23 March 1759, bp. 1 April 1759

    x   INCREASE MANNING, b. 18 Jan. 1761, bp. 25 Jan. 1761

References: *Bradford Desc* pp. 97-8. Windham CT VR 1:28(b. Mary), 234(m.; b. ch.; d. Hannah, Elijah). Windham CT LR I:402(Samuel Manning). *Manning Fam* pp. 116, 186-7. *Kingsley Fam* p. 63(wrongly says that she m. Samuel Hibbard). Scotland Cong. Ch. Recs. 2:6(Josiah adm.), 20(bp. Cyrus), 22(bp. Mary), 23(bp. Irena), 25(bp. Eleazer), 27(bp. Hannah), 28(bp. Alathea), 29(bp. Elijah), 31(bp. Hannah), 32(bp. Martha), 33(bp. Increase); 3:1(1808 list); 4:9(Mary adm.).

304. HEZEKIAH MANNING⁵ (*Irena Ripley⁴, Hannah³ Bradford, William²⁻¹*), b. Windham, Conn., 8 Aug. 1721; d. there 20 April 1802.

He m. (1) Windham, Conn., 22 Sept. 1745 **MARY WEBB**, b. Windham 23 Dec. 1725; d. there 20 Dec. 1785; daughter of Nathaniel and Elizabeth (Fitch) Webb. Nathaniel Webb of Windham made his will on 12 Sept. 17[*illegible in fold*], proved 9 Nov. 1750, naming his daughters Mary Manning and Ann Webb.

He m. (2) **ANNA WEBB**, b. Windham, Conn., 13 June 1728; d. there Jan. 1804; sister of his first wife.

On 6 March 1749/50 Samuel Manning of Windham for love and affection gave to his sons Hezekiah Manning and Josiah Manning of Windham all his farm on which "I now dwell."

Mary wife of Hezekiah Manning was admitted to the Scotland Congregational Church in March 1753.

Hezekiah served the town of Windham as tithingman in 1745 and 1746, assessor in 1754 and 1755, grand juror in 1747 and 1753, constable from 1758 to 1766, and deputy or representative from Windham six times between 1764 and 1767. He was a justice of the peace from 1767 to 1780. He served on a Committee of Correspondence in 1774.

Hezekiah Manning's household in Windham as listed in the 1790 census consisted of 2 men 16 or older, 2 boys, and 4 females.

No Connecticut probate records were found for Hezekiah Manning.

Children of Hezekiah and Mary (Webb) Manning, b. Windham, Conn., 1ˢᵗ 4 bp. 1 July 1753:

    i   CALVIN MANNING⁶, b. 4 May 1746
   ii LUTHER MANNING, b. 5 Jan. 1748
  iii JERUSHA MANNING, b. 19 Dec. 1750
  iv LUCY MANNING, b. 1 Feb. 1753
   v ELIZABETH MANNING, b. 7 July 1755, bp. 7 Sept. 1755
  vi OLIVE MANNING, bp. 6 Nov. 1757
 vii NATHANIEL MANNING, bp. 16 March 1760
viii MARY MANNING, bp. 13 June 1762
  ix EUNICE MANNING, bp. 26 Aug. 1764
   x AMELIA MANNING, bp. 7 Sept. 1766; d.y.
  xi AMELIA MANNING, bp. 14 May 1768

References: *Bradford Desc* p. 98. Windham CT VR 1:33(b. both wives), 229(m.; b. 1ˢᵗ 5 ch.). Windham CT LR I:402(Samuel Manning). *Manning Fam* pp. 187-8. Windham CT PR #4035(Nathaniel Webb). Scotland Cong. Ch. 2:12(Mary adm.), 28(bp. 1ˢᵗ 4 ch.),

30(bp. Elizabeth), 31(bp. Olive), 33(bp. Nathaniel), 34(bp. Mary), 76(bp. Eunice), 78(bp. Amelia), 79(bp. Amelia).

305. ABIGAIL MANNING[5] (*Irena Ripley*[4], *Hannah*[3] *Bradford*, *William*[2-1]), b. Windham, Conn., 25 Nov. 1722; d. there 6 Jan. 1794 (TR) or 6 Feb. 1794 (g.s.) aged 71.

She m. Windham, Conn., 27 Oct. 1745 **JOHN WELCH**, b. Windham, Conn., 8 July 1717; d. there 4 March 1802 aged 84; son of Thomas and Hannah (Abbe) Welch.

On 23 Jan. 1802 John Welch of Windham gave to Ashbel Welch and John Welch Jr. land reserving the use and improvement of the land. On 11 Jan. 1805 John Welch sold to Ashbel Welch his half of the undivided land that had been their father's.

Children of John and Abigail (Manning) Welch, b. Windham, Conn.:

    i   IRENAH WELCH[6], b. 7 Sept. 1746

    ii JERUSHA WELCH, b. 4 Sept. 1748

    iii JOHN WELCH, b. 3 Feb. 1750/1

    iv ASENATH WELCH, b. 4 April 1753

    v ASHBALL WELCH, b. 21 April 1764

References: *Bradford Desc* p. 98. Windham CT VR 234, cert. by Windham Town Clerk ("John Welch's Family," m., b. ch., Abigail's d.). Hale Cem Coll:Windham p. 266(d. Abigail, John). *Manning Fam* pp. 188-9. Windham CT LR W:145, 199(John Welch).

306. SARAH MANNING[5] (*Irena Ripley*[4], *Hannah*[3] *Bradford*, *William*[2-1]), b. Windham, Conn., 22 Feb. 1723/4; d. Franklin, Conn., 3 May 1809 aged 86.

She m. Lebanon, Conn., 28 Nov. 1743 **ELIPHALET TRACY**, b. Norwich, Conn., 14 Nov. 1720; d. Franklin, Conn., 21 March 1807 aged 86; son of Winslow and Rachel (Ripley) Tracy; a descendant of Pilgrim **William Bradford** (see #283).

References: Norwich CT VR 1:25(b. Eliphalet); 2:31(m.). Franklin CT VR 1:10(d. Eliphalet, Sarah). Hale Cem Coll:Franklin p. 77(d. Eliphalet, Sarah). *Manning Fam* pp. 189-90.

307. SAMUEL MANNING[5] (*Irena Ripley*[4], *Hannah*[3] *Bradford*, *William*[2-1]), b. Windham, Conn., 22 Oct. 1725; d. Huntington, Conn., after 8 April 1796.

He m. (1) Stratford, Conn., 26 Jan. 1748 **ABIGAIL CLARK**, b. Stratford, Conn., 3 April 1728; d. 3 Sept. 1758; daughter of John and Jane (___) Clark.

He m. (2) 2 Aug. 1759 **EUNICE FRINK**, b. 1734; d. 19 Jan. 1829 aged 95.

He probably served in the Revolutionary War under Capt. Abraham Mead and Capt. Thomas Hobby.

Samuel Mannon's household in Huntington as listed in the 1790 census consisted of a man 16 or older and 2 females.

On 8 April 1796 Samuel Manning sold to Elisha Mills one acre.

No Connecticut probate records have been found for Samuel Manning

Children of Samuel and Abigail (Clark) Manning, b. Stratford, Conn.:

  i   SAMUEL MANNING⁶, b. 13 Dec. 1749; d. 3 Feb. 1759
  ii   JERUSHA MANNING, b. 16 Oct. 1751
  iii   SARAH MANNING, b. 2 Sept. 1756

Children of Samuel and Eunice (Frink) Manning, b. Stratford, Conn.:

  iv   JOSEPH MANNING, b. 7 June 1761
  v   SAMUEL MANNING, b. 22 March 1763; d. Yorktown VA 15 Oct 1781
  vi   EUNICE MANNING, b. 3 April 1765
  vii   ELIAS MANNING, b. 7 Sept. 1767; d. 12 Jan. 1769
  viii   ELIAS MANNING, b. 5 March 1772

References: *Bradford Desc* pp. 98-9. Stratford CT VR LR 5:28(b. Abigail), 51(1ˢᵗ m.; b. 1ˢᵗ 3 ch.). *Manning Fam* pp. 190-1.

308. DAVID MANNING⁵ (*Irena Ripley⁴, Hannah³ Bradford, William²⁻¹*), b. Windham, Conn., 14 Jan. 1726; bp. First Ch. 22 Jan. 1727; d. Lisle, N.Y., 29 Sept. 1807; buried Yorkshire Manningville Cemetery.

He m. (1) Sharon, Conn., 1 Aug. 1751 **ANNE HAMILTON**, d. bef. 1768; daughter of David Hamilton. David Hamilton's 1780 will gives "to the heirs of my daughter Anne Manning 30 acres of land in my right at ye Susquehannah."

He m. (2) before 1768 **MIRIAM SIMMONS**, b. Dec. 1735; d. Owego, N.Y., 7 June 1808 aged 73½y.

David Manning served under Capt. Samuel Elmer [or Elmore] in 1758 in the French and Indian War.

No probate records were found in Tioga or Broome counties for David Manning.

Children of David and Anne (Hamilton) Manning:

  i   JOSEPH MANNING⁶

    ii JOHN MANNING

   iii SARAH MANNING, b. ca. 1753

   iv DAVID MANNING, b. ca. 1759

    v ANNA MANNING, b. ca. 1762

Children of David and Miriam (Simmons) Manning:

   vi RIPLEY MANNING, bp. Sharon 11 Sept. 1768

  vii EUNICE MANNING, b. 31 July 1776; bp. Sharon 2 Sept. 1776

References: *Bradford Desc* p. 99. Sharon CT VR LR 3:261(m.). *Manning Fam* pp. 192-3. Sharon 1st Ch Recs pp. 34(bp. Ripley), 35(bp. Eunice).

309.   SARAH WHEAT[5] (*Anna Ripley*[4], *Hannah*[3] *Bradford, William*[2-1]), bp. Windham, Conn., 3 Oct. 1731.
    She m. **JOHN MANNING** (see #280).

References: *Bradford Desc* p. 99. *Wheat Gen* p. 14.

310.   MARY WHEAT[5] (*Anna Ripley*[4], *Hannah*[3] *Bradford, William*[2-1]), bp. Old Lyme, Conn., 1 July 1733; d. after 18 Feb. 1780 if she is the Mary Aldrich who witnessed a deed.
    She apparently m. Mendon 1 May 1752 **AARON ALDRICH**, b. Mendon 3 Jan. 1733/4; d. poss. after 1 Oct. 1792; son of Moses and Hannah (White) Aldrich.
    On 18 Feb. 1780 Eleazer Martin of Richmond, N.H., sold to Aaron Aldrich of Richmond, physician, 40 acres, the north half of lot 17; Mary and Solomon Aldrich were witnesses.
    On 31 Aug. 1787 Royal Aldrich of Richmond, yeoman, sold to Solomon Aldrich of Richmond, laborer, 80 acres in the 7th lot 2nd range.
    On 16 April 1790 Aaron Aldrich of Richmond, yeoman, sold to Nathan Aldrich of Richmond, gentleman, 36 acres in lot 17 3rd range and on 15 Sept. 1792 (acknowledged 1 Oct. 1792) Aaron Aldrich of Richmond, yeoman, sold to Jonathan Cass of Richmond, husbandman, 6¼ acres in lot 7 of the 3rd range. (These two deeds may be for his son Aaron.)
    They possibly moved to Mt. Holly, Vt. No records of them have been found in Vermont Vital Records or the Mt. Holly Land Records, which begin in 1792.

Children of Aaron and Mary (Wheat) Aldrich:

    i   SOLOMON ALDRICH[6], b. Mendon 18 Dec. 1753

   ii   ROYAL ALDRICH

  iii   CALEB ALDRICH, b. Massachusetts 1760

  iv WAILES ALDRICH, b. Massachusetts 1769

   v   AARON ALDRICH, b. Massachusetts 1771

References: *VR Mendon* pp. 13(b. Aaron), 229(m.). *History Of The Town Of Richmond NH* p. 257. *Aldrich Gen* 1:47-8, 66; 5:23. *Wheat Gen* p. 14. Cheshire Co. NH LR 10:244(Royal Aldrich); 22:72; 55: 232(Aaron Aldrich), 231(Eleazer Martin).

311.   ANNA WHEAT[5] (*Anna Ripley[4], Hannah[3] Bradford, William[2-1]*), b. Windham, Conn., 8 July 1736; d. after 19 Dec. 1772 when she acknowledged a deed.

She m. Uxbridge 1 May 1755 **JOHN BURNAP** of Hopkinton, b. Hopkinton 20 Sept. 1731; d. after 1790; son of Benjamin & Hannah (_____) Burnap. He m. (2) Barre 10 April 1788 LYDIA (KENT) RIPLEY.

On 16 Sept. 1751 Benjamin Burnap, Jr., of Hopkinton, husbandman, sold John Burnap of Westboro, cooper, 12 acres in Hopkinton. On 20 Dec. 1765 Benjamin sold to John one half of his land and buildings in Hopkinton and Westboro; Benjamin's wife Hannah released her dower rights.

In the 1771 Valuation List, John Burnap was listed in Hopkinton with 1 poll, 1 horse, 2 oxen, 2 cattle, 5 goats or sheep, 6 acres of tillage which produced 50 bushels of grain, 1 barrel of cider, 6 acres of upland which produced 3 tons of hay, and 3 acres of fresh meadow which produced 2 tons of hay.

On 19 Dec. 1772 John Burnett of Hopkinton, gentleman, sold land in Hopkinton to Marachias Morse; wife Anna Burnett acknowledged the deed.

He may be the John Burnap whose name appears on a muster roll of Worcester Co. for service in Rhode Island.

On 26 Nov. 1785 Benjamin Burnett [*sic*] of Hopkinton, yeoman, sold to John Burnett of Barre land in Hopkinton. On the same day Benjamin sold to John land in Westboro.

On 26 Jan. 1789 John Burnett of Barre sold to Jacob Parker of Hopkinton, yeoman, land in Hopkinton that had been part of the farm formerly belonging to Dea. Benjamin Burnett, deceased; witnesses were Nathaniel Burnett and Charles R. Burnett.

John Burnet's household as listed in the 1790 census of Barre consisted of 2 men 16 or older and 1 female. Listed next to him was Charles R. Burnet with 1 man, a boy, and 3 females.

No Worcester County probate records were found for John Burnap.

Children of John and Anna (Wheat) Burnap, b. Hopkinton:

    i   ANNIS BURNAP[6], b. 14 Aug. 1756

    ii HANNERETTA BURNAP, b. 2 July 1758

    iii CHARLES RIPLEY BURNAP, b. 15 July 1760

    iv BENJAMIN BURNAP, bp. 23 May 1762

    v JOHN BURNAP, bp. 12 April 1767

    vi NATHANIEL BURNAP, bp. 7 April 1771

    vii ABNER BURNAP, bp. 12 Dec. 1774

References: *VR Hopkinton* pp. 41-2(b. John; b. &, bp. ch.). *VR Uxbridge* p. 221(m.). *Burnap-Burnett* pp. 115-7. Middlesex Co. LR 65:553(Benjamin Burnap); 73:525 (John Burnap); 91:471; 93:745(Benjamin Burnett); 101:234(John Burnett). *Wheat Gen* p. 14, 47. *1771 Valuation* p. 222. Worcester Co. LR 55:33(Benjamin Burnap). *Burnap-Burnett* pp. 83-4, 115-7.

312. HANNAH WHEAT[5] (*Anna Ripley[4], Hannah[3] Bradford, William[2-1]*), b. Windham, Conn., 16 July 1738; d. Hartford, N.Y., 3 April 1815 aged 75y, widow, **bur. Old Hartland Cem.**

She m. int. Uxbridge 18 Aug. 1758 **JOSEPH TAYLOR**, b. Concord 26 March 1734; d. after 1769; son of Joseph and Elizabeth (_____) Taylor.

On 26 Jan. 1769 Joseph Taylor of Concord, cooper, sold land in Concord to Timothy and Isaac Wilkins with wife Hannah releasing dower.

Wheat Gen says he moved to Hartford, Washington Co., N.Y., and later to Bristol near Canandaigua, N.Y.

Children of Joseph and Hannah (Wheat) Taylor, b. Concord:

    i   ANNA TAYLOR[6], b. 14 Oct. 1759

    ii NATHAN TAYLOR, b. 11 Feb. 1761

    iii SAMUEL TAYLOR, b. 7 Jan. 1763

    iv HANNAH TAYLOR, b. 31 Dec. 1764

    v JOSEPH TAYLOR, b. 5 April 1767

    vi SARAH TAYLOR, b. 10 Sept. 1769

poss. vii ELIZABETH TAYLOR

References: *VR Concord* pp. 150(b. Joseph), 202(b. Anna), 210(b. Nathan), 225(b. Samuel, Hannah, Joseph), 230(b. Sarah). *VR Uxbridge* p. 322(int.). Middlesex Co. LR 68:542 (Joseph Taylor). *Bradford Desc* p. 100. *Cemetery Records, The Township of Hartford, Washington Co, NY* (1992) p. 74(d. Hannah). *Wheat Gen* pp. 14, 48.

313. JEMIMA WHEAT⁵ (*Anna Ripley⁴, Hannah³ Bradford, William²⁻¹*), bp. Ashford, Conn., 28 July 1740; d. after 7 May 1781.

She m. (1) Hopkinton 29 Nov. 1759 **JOSEPH MORSE**, b. Holliston 15 Sept. 1738; d. Stillwater, N.Y., 18 Sept. 1777 in Revolutionary War service in the fight at Stillwater (rec. at Athol); son of Seth and Abigail (Battle) Morse.

She m. (2) 5 June 1794 **BENJAMIN STREETER** Sr. and moved to Phelps, Ontario Co., N.Y.

On 20 Aug. 1765 Joseph Morse, wife Jemima and three children were warned from Westboro.

On 4 Feb. 1778 widow Jemima Morse posted bond as administratrix of the estate of Joseph Morse of Athol. Amasa Morse was appointed guardian of Irena, James, Eunice, Ann Ripley, and Mima; Samuel Hazen was guardian to Alathear and James Morse was guardian to Joseph Wheat, Luther, and Amasa. Distribution of the estate on 7 May 1781 went to widow; Eunice third daughter; Joseph double share, Amassa, Luther, James, and Mima.

Children of Joseph and Jemima (Wheat) Morse:

    i   IRENE MORSE⁶, b. Hopkinton 7 Oct. 1760

    ii ALITHEA MORSE, b. Hopkinton 10 Feb. 1762

   iii JOSEPH WHEAT MORSE, b. or bp. Brookfield 1 Dec. 1763

   iv AMASA MORSE, b. Westboro 12 Aug. 1765

    v LUTHER MORSE, b. Westboro 5 May 1767

   vi JAMES MORSE, b. Barre 14 May 1769

  vii DENISON MORSE (twin), b. Barre 20 May 1772; d. Athol 14 Aug. 1773

 viii EUNICE MORSE (twin), b. Barre 20 May 1772

   ix ANN RIPLEY MORSE, b. Athol 8 April 1774

    x MIMA/JEMIMA MORSE, b. Athol 28 March 1776

References: *VR Athol* pp. 61-2(b. Ann Ripley, Mima); 210(d. Joseph, Denison). *VR Brookfield* p. 160(b. Joseph Wheat). *VR Hopkinton* pp. 136(b. Alithea), 138(b. Irene), 330(m.). *VR Holliston* p. 111(b. Joseph). *VR Westboro* p. 76(b. Joseph W., Amasa, Luther). *DAR Patriot Index* p. 482. *Worcester Co Warnings* p. 82. Worcester Co. PR A 41940(Joseph Morse). *NEHGR* 95:202(family rec.). *Wheat Gen* pp. 14, 48-9.

314. JOHN SHEPHARD[5] (*Bethia Steele*[4], *Melatiah*[3] *Bradford, William*[2-1]), b. Hartford, Conn., 28 April 1710, bp. Second Ch. 30 April 1710; d. there 14 April 1789 aged 80; buried in Center Church Cemetery.

He m. ca. 1737 **REBECCA [BUTLER?]*, poss., bp. Hartford, Conn., 8 Dec. 1706; d. there 10 June 1777 aged 68; poss. daughter of Joseph and Esther (Hubbard) Butler. The daughter of Joseph and Esther was still single on 2 March 1735/6 when she signed a receipt for her share in her father's estate. Nothing has been found to confirm that John Shephard's wife was Rebecca Butler, but John's father married Rebecca's sister Eunice as his second wife, so the families did know each other.

On 18 Aug. 1768 John Shepard of Hartford sold to his son John Shepard of Hartford one rod of land.

On 17 Dec. 1784 John Shepard of Hartford gave to his son John Shepard of Hartford 18 acres reserving the use and improvment of the land for himself.

The will of John Shepard dated 7 June 1785, proved 7 July 1789, names son John; unmarried daughters Jerusha and Rebecca; children of son Aaron deceased; son Eldad; daughters Anna wife of Hubbel Stephens, Eunice wife of Joshua Boles, and Huldah wife of William Adams.

On 9 Aug. 1794 Jerusha and Rebecca Shepard of Hartford, Conn., sold to (their brother) John Shepard land they received from their father's will.

Children of John and Rebecca (Butler?) Shephard, b. Hartford, Conn.; bp. First Church:

    i   JOHN SHEPHARD[6], bp. 29 Jan. 1737/8

    ii AARON SHEPHARD, bp. 18 Feb. 1738/9

    iii ELDAD SHEPHARD, bp. 30 Nov. 1740

    iv ANNA SHEPHARD perhaps, b. 1742 (in will)

    v EUNICE SHEPHARD, bp. 29 July 1744

    vi HULDAH SHEPHARD, bp. 10 Aug. 1746

    vii JERUSHA SHEPHARD, bp. 6 Aug. 1749; living 1794 unm.

    viii REBECCA SHEPHARD, bp. 22 April 1753; living 1794 unm.

* His wife is called REBECCA BEAMAN in *Mayflower Index*, but this identification is unlikely.

References: *Hartford By Barbour* pp. 136, 524-5. *Shepard Fam* 2:32-3. *NEHGR* 150:157-61(dau. Anna).   Hartford CT PR #1016(Joseph Butler).   Hartford CT LR 11:184; 16:198(John Shepard); 19:285(Jerusha Shepard). *Hartford CT Second Ch* (bp. John).

315.   JAMES SHEPHARD[5] (*Bethia Steele*[4], *Melatiah*[3] *Bradford, William*[2-1]), b. Hartford, Conn., 27 April 1714, bp. Second Ch. 2 May 1714; d. Northampton 11 Aug. 1790.

He m. (1) Hartford, Conn., 22 Nov. 1739 **SARAH HOPKINS**, b. Hartford, Conn., 28 Oct. 1719; d. there 13 Jan. 1762, buried in Center Church Cemetery; daughter of Thomas and Mary (Beckley) Hopkins.

He m. (2) Hartford, Conn., 9 Feb. 1764 **OBEDIENCE (BELDEN) TRUMBULL**, b. Norwich, Conn., 17 April 1722; d. Hartford, Conn., 12 Feb. 1804; daughter of Stephen and Obedience (Copp) Belden. She m. (1) JOSEPH TRUMBULL with whom she had Joseph.

On 5 Nov. 1740 Samuel Shepherd of Hartford gave to his son James Shepherd of Hartford three acres reserving to himself two acres for his use during his life and if his wife Eunice should survive him, James was to pay her one-third of the yearly value. On 17 Dec. 1745 Samuel sold to James half of a lot lying undivided with the heirs of John Shepherd.

On 22 Sept. 1790 administration on the estate of James Shepard of Hartford, Conn., was granted to Levi Shepard of Northampton. Dower was set off to the widow. On 13 May 1791 Obedience Shepard of Hartford, widow of James Shepard deceased, sold all her right in the estate of James to Levi Shepard of Northampton.

Children of James and Sarah (Hopkins) Shephard, b. Hartford, Conn.; bp. First Church:

    i   LUCY SHEPHARD[6], bp. 6 Dec. 1741

    ii   LEVI SHEPHARD, bp. 15 Jan. 1743/4

    iii   JAMES SHEPHARD, bp. 25 May 1746; d. 10 May 1818; unm.

    iv   RUTH SHEPHARD, bp. 5 Sept. 1748; d. 1 Feb. 1790 ae 42; unm. She had a dau. Elizabeth Phillips.

    v   ASHER SHEPHARD, b. 2 April 1751

    vi   WEALTHY SHEPHARD, bp. 6 May 1753

    vii   [CHILD] SHEPHARD, d. 15 Feb. 1756

    viii   EPAPHRAS SHEPHARD, bp. 6 June 1757; d. 27 March 1759

    ix   CHLOE SHEPHARD, bp. 15 Dec. 1759; d. 18 April 1761 ae 2 yrs.

Child of James and Obedience (Belden) Shephard, b. Hartford, Conn.:

    x   THEODORE SHEPHARD, bp. 20 Sept. 1767

References: *Bradford Desc* p. 100. *Hartford By Barbour* p. 525. Hartford CT VR 5:60(b. James). *Shepard Fam* 2:33-4. Norwich CT VR 1:6(b. Obedience). Hartford CT LR 8:53, 66(Samuel Shepherd); 18:494(Obedience Shepard). *Hartford CT Second Ch* (bp. James).

316. JOHN STEELE[5] (*Ebenezer*[4], *Melatiah*[3] *Bradford, William*[2-1]), bp. Hartford, Conn., 22 Feb. 1718; d. Washington, Mass., between 1 Jan. and 5 April 1785 (probate).

He m. **CHRISTIAN [? FLOWER]**, who d. Washington, Mass., 8 Jan. 1799.

On 5 Sept. 1769 John Steel, Daniel Steel Jr., and Elisha Steel of Hartford, and Bradford Steel of Derby, Conn., sold to Joseph Steel of Hartford their right in 38 acres of land laid out to the heirs of James Steel deceased. On 29 May 1785 Bradford Steel of Derby, Conn., and Elisha Steel of South Hadley sold to Moses Steel of Washington three acres in Hartford with buildings.

John Steel of Washington, yeoman, made his will 1 Jan. 1785, proved 5 April 1785, naming his wife Christian; sons Ebenezer, Moses, Timothy, Aaron, and Pitt; and daughters Christian and Ruth.

On 24 Oct. 1798 Pitt Steel of Washington, yeoman, and Aaron Steel of Lenox, yeoman, sold to Christian Steel of Washington, widow, 50 acres they had from the will of their father John Steel deceased.

Christian Steel, widow of the late John Steel, made her will on 9 Nov. 1798, proved 2 April 1799, naming her children Ebenezer, Moses, Aaron, Pitt, Christian, Ruth, and Timothy. An account dated 3 Sept. 1799 includes a payment to her son Pitt for digging her grave.

On 2 April 1799 John Lankton was appointed the guardian of Christian, Ruth, and Timothy Steel *non-compos-mentis* persons.

On 1 April 1800 Ebenezer Steel of Hartford, cordwainer, Moses Steel of Northampton, yeoman, Pitt Steel of Washington, innholder, and Aaron Steel of Chenango, N.Y., laborer, sold to Ruth Steel, singlewoman, and Timothy Steel, yeoman, both of Washington 40 acres in Washington held in common with Ruth and Timothy as heirs of Christian Steel, spinster, deceased.

Children of John and Christian (Flower) Steele, bp. in West Hartford Church; b. dates from *Steele Fam.*

    i CHRISTIAN STEELE[6], b. 31 May 1747, bp. 1 June 1746; d. Washington 5 Feb. 1800; unm.

    ii RUTH STEELE, bp. 28 Nov. 1748, bp. 29 Nov. 1747; d. Washington 9 July 1822; unm.

    iii JOHN STEELE, b. 20 Aug. 1749, bp. 27 Aug. 1749

    iv EBENEZER STEELE (triplet), b. 15 April 1752, bp. 27 April 1752; d.y.

    v AARON STEELE (triplet), b. 15 April 1752, bp. 27 April 1752; d.y.

    vi MOSES STEELE (triplet), b. 15 April 1752, bp. 27 April 1752; d.y.

    vii EBENEZER STEELE, b. 5 Aug. 1753, bp. 27 April 1753

viii MOSES STEELE, bp. 19 Oct. 1755

viii MOSES STEELE, b. 10 Dec. 1757, bp. 30 Jan. 1757

ix TIMOTHY STEELE, b. 16 May 1759, bp. 20 May 1759

x AARON STEELE, b. 8 Jan. 1761, bp. 11 Jan. 1761

xi LUCY STEELE, b. 13 Oct. 1762, bp. 17 Oct. 1762; d. 17 May 1768 ae 5y 7m

xii PITT STEELE, b. 23 Oct. 1767, bp. 26 Oct. 1766; d. 26 Feb. 1770 ae 3y 4m

xiii PITT STEELE, b. 4 Feb. 1770, bp. 29 April 1770

References: *Bradford Desc* p. 102. *VR Washington* p. 56(d. both Christians). *Steele Fam* pp. 17, 30-1. Berkshire Co. LR 37:462(Pitt Steel); 52:162(Ebenezer Steel). Berkshire Co. PR 5:147(John Steel); 10:2, 94, 177(Christian Steel). Hartford CT LR 12:398(John Steel); 17:450(Bradford Steel). West Hartford Ch. Recs. 1:43(bp. Christian), 44(bp. Ruth), 46(bp. John), 47(bp. triplets), 48(bp. Ebenezer), 50(bp. both Moses), 52(bp.Timothy), 54(bp. Aaron), 55(bp. Lucy), 60(bp. Pitt), 64(bp. Pitt), 144(d. Lucy), 145(bp. Pitt).

317. MARY STEELE⁵ (*Ebenezer⁴, Melatiah³ Bradford, William²⁻¹*), bp. Hartford, Conn., 1 Jan. 1721; d. 13 April 1813. Goshen, Conn., VR say that the widow of Samuel Kellogg d. there 12 June 1813 aged 95.

She m. West Hartford, Conn., 8 Jan. 1741 **SAMUEL KELLOGG**, b. New Hartford, Conn., 15 Nov. 1718; d. Poultney, Vt., in 1770; son of Isaac and Mary (Webster) Kellogg.

Children of Samuel and Mary (Steele) Kellogg, b. Enfield, Conn., exc. Helmont:

i RUTH KELLOGG⁶, b. 20 March 1742; d. 3 Sept. 1746

ii RHODA KELLOGG, b. 24 Feb. 1744/5

iii RUTH KELLOGG, b. 13 Feb. 1746/7

iv SAMUEL KELLOGG, b. 3 Feb. 1748/9; d. ca. 1751

v EBENEZER KELLOGG, b. 6 Sept. 1751

vi LEVERETT KELLOGG, b. 28 June 1753; d. 1777 in Rev. War

vii SAMUEL KELLOGG, b. 20 July 1755

viii ASAPH KELLOGG, b. 20 Aug. 1757; d. 1790; unm.

ix BRADFORD KELLOGG, b. 9 July 1760

x HELMONT KELLOGG, b. New Hartford, Conn., 17 March 1762

References: *Bradford Desc* p. 102. Hartford CT VR FFS:69(b. Samuel). Goshen CT VR 2:396(d. widow). New Hartford CT VR 1:54(b. Helmont). *Conn Marr* 2:74. *The Kelloggs* pp. 66, 107-8. *Enfield CT Hist* 2:1650(b. ch.), 1870(d. Ruth).

318. SUSANNA STEELE[5] (*Ebenezer*[4], *Melatiah*[3] *Bradford, William*[2-1]), bp. Hartford, Conn., 30 June 1720.

She m. West Hartford, Conn., 14 July 1747 **REUBEN FLOWER**, b. New Hartford, Conn., 27 May 1722, bp. West Hartford 27 May 1722; d. in camp 2 Nov. 1776; son of John and Elizabeth (Baker) Flower.

On 14 Aug. 1748 Reuben Flower and his wife were admitted to the West Hartford Church.

No Connecticut probate records were found for this family and they are not included in the Hale Cemetery Collection.

References: *Bradford Desc* p. 102. *Conn Marr* 2:74. New Hartford CT VR 1:26(b. Reuben). West Hartford Ch. Recs. 1:28(bp. Reuben), 10(admitted), 116(m.), 149(d. Reuben).

319. HULDAH STEELE[5] (*Ebenezer*[4], *Melatiah*[3] *Bradford, William*[2-1]), bp. Killingworth, Conn., 8 March 1729/30; d. Roxbury, Conn., 17 June 1822.

She m. West Hartford, Conn., 30 Sept. 1745 **NATHANIEL FLOWER**, b. West Hartford, Conn., 31 July 1720; d. West Hartford, Conn., 1800; son of John and Elizabeth (Baker) Flower.

On 5 Jan. 1746 Nathaniel Flower and his wife Hulda owned the covenant in the West Hartford Church.

No Connecticut probate record or Hale Cemetery record was found for Nathaniel or Huldah Flower.

Children of Nathaniel and Huldah (Steele) Flower, b. West Hartford, Conn.; bp. West Hartford Church:

- i HULDA FLOWER[6], b. 5 Jan. 1746, bp. 2 March 1746
- ii SABRA FLOWER, bp. 27 Nov. 1748
- iii GABRIEL FLOWER, bp. 25 Nov. 1750
- iv NATHANIEL FLOWER, bp. 8 July 1753
- v ZTHURIEL (or JTHURIEL) FLOWER, bp. 18 June 1758
- vi CHRISTIAN FLOWER, bp. 26 Feb. 1760; d. 27 Feb. 1760 ae 2d
- vii [CHILD] FLOWER, stillborn 10 Feb. 1761
- viii PHILOMELA FLOWER, bp. 12 Dec. 1762
- ix ZEPHON FLOWER (twin), b. 30 Nov. 1765, bp. 6 Nov. 1774
- x ZILEMA (or AULIMENA) FLOWER (twin), b. 30 Nov. 1765, bp. 6 Nov. 1774
- xi RAPHAEL FLOWER, bp. 30 July 1773
- xii CASSANDRA FLOWER, bp. 6 Nov. 1774

References: *Bradford Desc* p. 103. *Conn Marr* 2:74. New Hartford CT VR 1:26(b. Nathaniel). West Hartford Ch. Recs. 1:43(bp. Hulda), 45(bp. Sabra), 46(bp. Gabriel), 48(bp. son Nathaniel), 52(bp. Jthuriel), 53(bp. Christian), 55(bp. Philomena), 67(bp. Raphael), 69(bp. Zephon, Zilema, Cassandra), 115(bp. Nathaniel), 100(owned cov.), 142(d. Christian, d. stillborn ch.).

320. BRADFORD STEELE[5] (*Ebenezer*[4], *Melatiah*[3] *Bradford, William*[2-1]), bp. Hartford, Conn., 22 Sept. 1734; d. Derby, Conn., 10 April 1804.

He m. (1) Enfield, Conn., 19 Dec. 1754 **MARY PERKINS**, b. Enfield, Conn., 11 Oct. 1732; d. Derby, Conn., 16 Oct. 1788; daughter of Thomas and Mary (Allen) Perkins.

He m. (2) **SARAH (BALDWIN) WHEELER**, d. after 9 Feb. 1805; daughter of James and Sarah (Johnson) Baldwin. She m. (1) SIMEON WHEELER.

On 5 Sept. 1769 John Steel, Daniel Steel Jr., and Elisha Steel of Hartford, and Bradford Steel of Derby, Conn., sold to Joseph Steel of Hartford their right in 38 acres of land laid out to the heirs of James Steel deceased. On 29 May 1785 Bradford Steel of Derby, Conn., and Elisha Steel of South Hadley sold to Moses Steel of Washington three acres in Hartford with buildings.

Bradford Steele performed private service during the Revolutionary War.

Bradford Steel's household as listed in Derby in the 1790 census consisted of 2 men over 16, 2 females, and a slave; living near him was Bradford Steel 2nd with 1 man, 1 boy, and 1 female.

On 7 May 1804 administration was granted to George Steele on the estate of Bradford Steele of Derby with Nathan Wheeler and William Kenney as sureties. On 9 Feb. 1805 the estate was divided among the widow Sarah Steel, Ashbel [*sic*] Steel, Bradford Steel, Daniel Steel, George Steel, heirs of Susanah Flowers, Mille wife of William Keney, Mary wife of Edward Warren, and widow Hannah Whitney.

Children of Bradford and Mary (Perkins) Steele, b. Derby, Conn. (not in Barbour):

    i [INFANT] STEELE[6] (twin), b. 14 Dec. 1756; d.y.

    ii SUSANNA STEELE (twin), b. 14 Dec. 1756; d.y.

    iii ASHER STEELE, b. 3 Aug. 1757

    iv MELATIAH STEELE, b. 9 March 1760

    v BRADFORD STEELE, b. 31 Aug. 1762

    vi MARY STEELE, bp. 9 Sept. 1764

    vii HANNAH STEELE, b. 4 Aug. 1766

viii DANIEL STEELE, b. 14 July 1768

ix GEORGE STEELE, b. 5 Sept. 1770

References: *Bradford Desc* p. 103. *Hist Enfield Conn* 2:1618(b. Mary), 1776(1st m.). *Steele Fam* pp. 17, 31. Hartford CT LR 12:398(John Steel); 17:450(Bradford Steel).

321. ELISHA STEELE[5] (*Ebenezer[4], Melatiah[3] Bradford, William[2-1]*), b. ca. 1737; d. 1805.

He m. (1) Hartford, Conn., 17 April 1760 **MARY MERRILLS**, b. ca. 1745; d. Hadley 1805; daughter of Gideon and Mary (Bigelow) Merrills.

He m. (2) after 10 Dec. 1783 **EUNICE (BOTSFORD) PRICHARD**, b. Derby, Conn., 26 April 1739; d. after 1 July 1805; daughter of Samuel and Hannah (Smith) Botsford. She m. (1) JABEZ PRICHARD. Samuel Botchford of Derby in his will dated 5 April 1780, proved 10 Dec. 1783, named his daughter Eunice Pritchard.

On 30 Jan. 1763 Elisha and Mary Steele were admitted to the West Hartford Church. On 15 Dec. 1763 Elisha was chosen a collector.

On 5 Sept. 1769 John Steel, Daniel Steel Jr., and Elisha Steel of Hartford, and Bradford Steel of Derby, Conn., sold to Joseph Steel of Hartford their right in 38 acres of land laid out to the heirs of James Steel deceased. On 29 May 1785 Bradford Steel of Derby, Conn., and Elisha Steel of South Hadley sold to Moses Steel of Washington three acres in Hartford with buildings.

Elisha Steel's household in Derby as listed in the 1790 census consisted of 2 men over 16, a boy, and 1 female.

On 1 June 1805 Norman Steel was granted administration of the estate of Elisha Steel late of Derby. On 1 July 1805 the widow Eunice Steel quitclaimed all her right in the estate of Elisha to Norman Steel.

Children of Elisha and Mary (Merrills) Steele; first 5 bp. West Hartford, Conn.:

i MARY STEELE[6], b. 25 Jan. 1763, bp. 5 Feb. 1763

ii CANDICE STEELE, bp. 6 Jan. 1765; d.y.

iii CLARISSA STEELE, b. 9 Feb. 1766, bp. 9 Feb 1767

iv LUCY STEELE, b. 28 May 1769, bp. 28 May 1769

v ELISHA STEELE, bp. 3 Feb. 1771

vi NORMAN STEELE, b. 1780

References: *Bradford Desc* pp. 103-4. *Hartford By Barbour* p. 399. Derby CT VR 4:A5(b. Eunice). *Steele Fam* pp. 17, 31-2. Hartford CT LR 12:398(John Steel); 17:450(Bradford Steel). West Hartford Ch. Recs. 1:12(admitted), 56(bp. Mary), 58(bp. Candice), 61(bp.

Clarissa), 63(bp. Lucy), 65(bp. Elisha). Hartford 1st Soc:37(collector). New Haven CT PR #1472(Samuel Botchford); #9844(Elisha Bradford).

322. LEVERETT HUBBARD[5] (*Elizabeth Stevens*[4], *Melatiah*[3] *Bradford, William*[2-1]), b. Killingworth, Conn., 21 July 1725; d. there 1 Oct. 1794 aged 70.

He m. (1) New Haven, Conn., 22 May 1746 **SARAH WHITEHEAD**, b. New Haven, Conn., 27 Oct. 1729; d. there 5 Dec. 1769 aged 40, buried in Grove St. Cemetery; daughter of Stephen and Mary (Miles) Whitehead.

He m. (2) New Haven, Conn., 13 Feb. 1771 **HESTER ROBINSON**, b. ca. 1749; d. New Haven, Conn., 19 Oct. 1800 aged 51; daughter of Benjamin and Katherine (Durand) Robinson.

Leverett Hubbard graduated from Yale College in 1744.

On 21 May 1746 Leverett Hubbard was admitted to the First Church of Christ in New Haven, on 26 June 1757 Sarah was admitted, and on 24 Nov. 1771 Hester was admitted.

On 5 July 1755 Leverett Hubbard and his wife Sarah of New Haven sold to John Hubbard Jr. of New Haven land laid out in the names of Samuel and Stephen Whithead; one of the witnesses was Mary Whithead.

On 3 April 1765 John Hubbard of New Haven sold to his son Leverett Hubbard of New Haven 19½ acres.

Leveret Hubbard's household in New Haven as listed in the 1790 census consisted of 2 men over 16, 1 boy, 3 females, a slave, and one other free person.

On 4 Jan. 1791 John Hubbard of Hamden, Conn., and Isaac Hubbard of Wallingford, Conn., sold to their uncle Col. Leveret Hubbard of New Haven several pieces of land that had been the estate of their grandfather Col. John Hubbard of New Haven.

Children of Leverett and Sarah (Whithead) Hubbard, b. New Haven, Conn.:

    i STEPHEN WHITEHEAD HUBBARD[6], b. 16 June 1747; d. Sept. 1771

   ii LEVERETT HUBBARD, b. 7 Sept. 1749

  iii MARY HUBBARD, bp. 5 April 1752

  iv WYLLYS HUBBARD, b. 25 Feb. 1755; d. 29 March 1774 ae 19y

   v SARAH HUBBARD, b. 31 May 1758

  vi BRADFORD HUBBARD, bp. 23 Aug. 1761

 vii NATHANIEL HUBBARD, b. 11 Aug. 1765

Children of Leverett and Hester (Robinson) Hubbard, b. New Haven, Conn.:

    viii ELIZABETH HUBBARD, bp. 1 Dec. 1771; d. 3 Dec. 1771 ae 5d

    ix ELIZABETH HUBBARD, bp. 11 April 1773; d. 18 Jan. 1787 ae 14y, bur. Grove St. Cem.

    x JULIANNA HUBBARD, bp. 8 Oct. 1775; d. 22 Jan. 1778 ae 24y[sic] 2m

    xi JULIANNA HUBBARD, bp. 14 Feb. 1779; d. 29 March 1794 ae 16y

    xii LUCRETIA HUBBARD, bp. 12 Aug. 1781

    xiii WYLLYS HUBBARD, bp. 28 March 1784

References: *Bradford Desc* p. 104. *Conn Marr* 1:11(2nd m.). New Haven CT VR 1:356(b. Sarah), 547(m.), 642(b. Stephen), 660(b. Leverett); 2:10(b. Wyllys), 51(b. Sarah). *New Haven Fams* 4:864-5. New Haven CT LR 19:124(Leverett Hubbard); 27:131(John Hubbard); 44:192(John & Isaac). *New Haven CT 1st Ch* pp. 88(Leverett admitted), 91(Sarah admitted), 101(Hester admitted). Hale Cem Coll:New Haven pp. 392(d. Sarah, Elizabeth, 2nd Julianna), 405(1st Julianna). *Yale Grads* 2:100(d. Stephen).

323. JOHN HUBBARD[5] (*Elizabeth Stevens*[4], *Melatiah*[3] *Bradford*, *William*[2-1]), b. New Haven, Conn., 24 Jan. 1727; d. Meriden, Conn., 18 Nov. 1786 aged 60y.

He m. (1) New Haven 25 Jan. 1749 **REBECCA DICKERMAN**, b. there 2 July 1726; d. there 24 Nov. 1768 aged 42y; daughter of Isaac and Mary (Atwater) Dickerman.

He m. (2) Wallingford, Conn., 20 Sept. 1770 **MARY (RUSSELL) FROST**; b. Tiverton 16 July 1735; d. 2 March 1806 aged 70y; daughter of John and Abigail (_____) Russell. She m. (1) GEORGE FROST.

John Hubbard graduated from Yale in 1744 and was licensed to preach by the New Haven Association on 27 May 1746. He preached occasionally, but was also in a mercantile business with Chauncey Whittelsey. He was called to become the pastor of the Meriden parish (which later became the town of Meriden) in Wallingford in 1767. There was a minority in the church which did not want him, but he was finally ordained on 22 June 1769. "Mr. Hubbard's good qualities of heart and power as a preacher gradually won back the opposing element, and he grew in favor with the society, until he was disabled from service in the winter of 1783-84 by being thrown from his sleigh."

On 29 June 1745 Rebecca Hubbard was admitted to the First Church of Christ in New Haven and John was admitted on 21 May 1746.

Mary Hubbard was head of a household consisting of 2 females in New Haven in the 1790 census.

On 4 Jan. 1791 John Hubbard of Hamden, Conn., and Isaac Hubbard of Wallingford, Conn., sold to their uncle Col. Leveret Hubbard of New Haven several pieces of land that had been the estate of their grandfather Col. John Hubbard of New Haven.

Children of John and Rebecca (Dickerman) Hubbard, b. New Haven, Conn.:

    i JOHN HUBBARD[6], b. 3 Jan. 1750

    ii ISAAC HUBBARD, b. 23 Nov. 1752

References: *Bradford Desc* p. 104. New Haven CT VR 1:335(b. Rebecca), 691(b. John); 2:20(b. Isaac). Wallingford CT VR 17:200(2nd m.). *New Haven Fams* 4:865. New Haven CT LR 44:192(John & Isaac). *New Haven CT 1st Ch* pp. 88(John admitted), 93(Rebecca admitted). *Yale Grads* 1:759.

324. DANIEL HUBBARD[5] (*Elizabeth Stevens[4], Melatiah[3] Bradford, William[2-1]*), b. New Haven, Conn., 24 Dec. 1729; d. there 28 Aug. 1765 aged 36y.

He m. (1) New Haven, Conn., 13 Sept. 1750 **MARTHA WOODIN**, b. New Haven 11 March 1729/30; d. there 17 May 1760 aged 30y; daughter of John and Desire (Cooper) Woodin.

He m. (2) prob. **RACHEL WATTS**, bp. Marblehead 13 July 1742; d. Marblehead 1773*; daughter of Alexander and Rachel (Coose) Watts. She m. (2) Marblehead 30 Oct. 1768 JEREMIAH PROCTOR and had Mary Proctor and Rachael Watt Proctor.

Daniel Hubbard graduated from Yale in 1748 and was in business in New Haven as a druggist.

On 5 Feb. 1759 John Hubbard of New Haven sold to his son Daniel Hubbard of New Haven half of a house and one and a half acres.

On 28 Sept. 1760 Daniel Hubbard was admitted to the First Church of Christ in New Haven.

Children of Daniel and Martha (Woodin) Hubbard, b. New Haven, Conn.:

    i DANIEL HUBBARD[6], b. 26 May 1756

    ii [INFANT] HUBBARD, d.y.

    iii [INFANT] HUBBARD, d.y.

    iv [INFANT] HUBBARD, d.y.

* The death date of 1773 cannot be verified. It traces back to a footnote in "Inscriptions on Tombstones in New Haven" in 1882 in *New Haven Colony Hist. Society Papers*, 3:538 and has been copied in other sources.

Note: On 6 Jan. 1763 Alexander Watts of Marblehead made his will naming his wife Rachel and kinsman Alexander Watts. There was no mention of children. Rachel Watts left an administration and in account of 6 Aug. 1781 includes "due to M' Jeremiah Proctor which the said adm' is to pay."

References: *Bradford Desc* pp. 104-5. New Haven CT VR 1:371(b. Mary), 750(m.); 2:21(b. Daniel). *New Haven Fams* 4:866. New Haven CT LR 22:67(John Hubbard). *New Haven CT 1st Ch* p. 93 (Daniel admitted). *Marblehead VR* 1:541(bp. Rachel), 228(m. to Proctor). Essex Co. PR 348:356(will Alexander Watts); 354:512(Rachel Watts). *Yale Grads* 2:165.

325. ELIZABETH HUBBARD[5] (*Elizabeth Stevens*[4], *Melatiah*[3] *Bradford, William*[2-1]), b. New Haven, Conn., 3 July 1731; d. Newport, R.I., 29 May 1775 in 44th yr.

She m. Newport, R.I., 10 Feb. 1757 **EZRA STILES**, b. New Haven, Conn., 29 Nov. 1727; d. there 12 May 1795 aged 68; son of Isaac and Keziah (Taylor) Stiles. He m. (2) Newport, R.I., 2 Nov. 1782 MARY (CRANSTON) CHECKLEY.

Ezra Stiles graduated from Yale in 1746 and eventually was ordained as paster of the Second Congregational Church in Newport, R.I., where he spent 20 years. He preached for a short time in both Dighton, Mass., and Portsmouth, N.H. In 1778 he was invited to become President of Yale and on 8 July he was installed as President and Professor of Ecclesiastical History. He remained President for 18 years until his death.

Rev. Ezra Stiles' household in New Haven in the 1790 census consisted of 2 men over 16, 1 boy, 6 females, and 1 other free person.

The will of Ezra Stiles, president of Yale College, dated 16 Sept. 1793, proved 8 June 1795, names wife Mary; son Isaac; daughters Elizabeth, Emilia, and Ruth Stiles; daughter Mary Holmes; daughters of deceased son Ezra: Elizabeth Hubbard Stiles and Emilia Harriet Stiles; and [son-in-law] Rev. Abiel Holmes. The 30 June 1796 distribution shows that Mary Holmes was dead by then and daughter Amelia had married Jonathan Leavitt.

Children of Ezra and Elizabeth (Hubbard) Stiles, b. Newport, R.I.:

    i   ELIZABETH STILES[6], b. 17 April 1758; d. Cambridge 16 Nov. 1795 ae 38; unm.

   ii   EZRA STILES, b. 11 March 1759

  iii   KEZIA T. STILES, b. 27 Sept. 1760 (not in will)

  iv   EMILY (or AMELIA) STILES, b. 21 April 1762

   v   ISAAC STILES, b. 10 Aug. 1763

vi RUTH STILES, b. 20 Aug. 1765

vii MARY STILES, b. 25 Aug. 1767

viii SARAH STILES, b. 14 June 1769; d. unm. before 16 Sept. 1793

References: *Bradford Desc* p. 105. New Haven CT VR 1:368(b. Ezra). *RIVR* Newport 4:2:39(m.), 116(b. 1st 6 ch.). *RIVR* 12:31(2nd m.). *New Haven Fams* 7:1705. New Haven PR #9904(Ezra Stiles). *Cambridge VR* 2:750(d. dau. Elizabeth). *Yale Grads* 1:92.

326. WILLIAM ABDIEL HUBBARD[5] (*Elizabeth Stevens*[4], *Melatiah*[3] *Bradford, William*[2-1]), b. New Haven, Conn., 15 Dec. 1736; d. Killingworth, Conn., 25 April 1772 aged 36y; buried New Haven. He and his wife were buried in Grove St. Cemetery.

He m. New Haven, Conn., 14 Feb. 1759 **SARAH GILBERT**, b. ca 1732; d. New Haven, Conn., 14 Sept. 1776 aged 44y; daughter of Thomas and Ruth (Hotchkiss) Gilbert.

Children of William Abdiel and Sarah (Gilbert) Hubbard, b. New Haven, Conn.:

i ELIJAH HUBBARD[6], b. 14 Sept. 1761; d. 1 Sept. 1776 ae 17y

ii RACHEL LORANA HUBBARD, bp. 29 May 1763

References: *Bradford Desc* p. 105. New Haven CT VR 2:57(b. Elijah), 148(m.). *New Haven Fams* 4:866. Hale Cem Coll:New Haven p. 404(d. William, Sarah, Elijah). *New Haven CT 1st Ch* p. 98(Hezekiah & Emelia admitted).

327. AMELIA HUBBARD[5] (*Elizabeth Stevens*[4], *Melatiah*[3] *Bradford, William*[2-1]), bp. New Haven 24 Oct. 1742 and bp. Killingworth, Conn., 25 Oct. 1742; d. after 15 July 1807.

She m. New Haven, Conn., 1 Jan. 1765 **HEZEKIAH SILLIMAN**, b. Fairfield, Conn., 11 March 1738/9; d. Huntington, Conn., between 13 Dec. 1803 and 9 Feb. 1804; son of Ebenezer and Abigail (Selleck) Silliman.

On 30 June 1765 Hezekiah and Emelia Silliman were admitted to the First Church of Christ in New Haven. They were admitted to the First Church of Fairfield 5 Feb. 1769.

The will of Hezekiah Silliman of Huntington dated 13 Dec. 1803, proved 9 Feb. 1804, names wife Emelia; sons Isaac, Hezekiah, Wyllys, John Hubbard, Ebenezer Hinsdale, and Leverit Stiles; daughters Polly, Abigail, and Emelia; and children of deceased daughter Malissa (Jemima, Emelia, Sally, Betsey, William). In an account dated 18 June 1807, Emelia Silliman, executrix of Hezekiah's estate, included the expenses for her removal to the state of Ohio to live with her son. On 15 July 1807 Emelia Silliman reported that she had sold the whole of the estate to David Lyon.

Children of Hezekiah and Amelia (Hubbard) Silliman, first 3 bp. First Cong. Ch. New Haven; next 6 bp. First Ch. Fairfield; last 6 bp.Trumball Ch.:

    i   NATHANIEL SILLIMAN[6], bp. 6 Oct. 1765

   ii MALISSA SILLIMAN, bp. 19 Oct. 1766

  iii ELIZABETH SILLIMAN, bp. 13 Dec. 1767

  iv ABIGAIL SILLIMAN, bp. 5 March 1769; d.y.

   v ISAAC SILLIMAN, bp. 8 July 1770

  vi FANNY SILLIMAN, bp. 1 Dec. 1771

 vii SALLY SILLIMAN, bp. 28 Feb. 1773

viii HEZEKIAH SILLIMAN, bp. 25 Feb. 1776

  ix WILLIAM SILLIMAN, b. 8 Oct. 1777, bp. 16 Nov. 1777

   x ABIGAIL SILLIMAN, b. 8 March 1779, bp. 18 April 1779

  xi JOHN HUBBARD SILLIMAN, b. Aug. 1780, bp. 22 Oct. 1780

 xii AMELIA SILLIMAN (bp. as Emelia), b. 26 April 1782, bp. 16 June 1782

xiii EBENEZER HINSDALE SILLIMAN, b. 30 Aug. 1784, 31 Oct. 1784

xiv LEVERIT STILES SILLIMAN, bp. 24 June 1787

References: *Bradford Desc* p. 105. Fairfield CT VR 1:66(b. Hezekiah). *Conn Marr* 1:8. *Fairfield Fams* 3:871, 876-7. *New Haven Fams* 4:866. *New Haven CT 1st Ch* p. 98(Hezekiah & Emelia admitted). New Haven 1st Cong. Ch. 9:9(Hezekiah & Emelia admitted), 34(bp. Nathaniel), 36(bp. Malissa), 38(bp. Elizabeth). Fairfield 1st Ch. pp. 11(admitted), 53(bp. Abigail), 54(bp. Isaac), 55(bp. Fanny, Sally), 65(bp. Hezekiah). Turmbull Ch. 1:109(bp. William), 111(bp. Abigail), 113(bp. John), 114(bp. Emelia), 117(bp. Ebenezer), 118(bp. Leverit). Stratford CT PR #1696(Hezekiah Silliman).

328. WILLIAM STEVENS[5] (*William[4], Melatiah[3] Bradford, William[2-1]*), b. Killingworth, Conn., 1 Sept. 1736; d. Hartford, Conn., before 4 March 1763 (adm.).

He m. West Hartford 9 July 1761 **ELISABETH SEDGWICK**, bp. there 5 July 1741; d. Hartford, Conn., 24 Nov. 1802 aged 61; daughter of William and Elizabeth (Brace) Sedgewick. She m. (2) Hartford, Conn., 23 Jan. 1766 JAMES TAYLOR. She m. (3) EBENEZER KNEELAND.

On 4 March 1763 John Steel was appointed administrator of the estate of William Stevens late of Hartford with Elisha Steel as surety. The inventory of personal estate was taken 17 March 1763.

Child of William and Elisabeth (Sedgwick) Stevens:

    i   ELIZABETH STEVENS[6], bp. 13 June 1762

References: *NEHGR* 129:20. Hartford CT PR #5219(Wm. Stevens). *Conn Marr* 2:75. *Hartford By Barbour* pp. 359, 599. Hale Cem Coll:Hartford (d. Elizabeth).

329. CHRISTOPHER STEVENS[5] (*William[4], Melatiah[3] Bradford, William[2-1]*), b. Killingworth, Conn., 13 Sept. 1738; d. there 4 Sept. 1787.

He m. Killingworth, Conn., 27 Sept. 1764 **NAOMI STEVENS**, b. Killingworth, Conn., 23 April 1737; d. after 16 March 1777; daughter of Amos and Mary (Stannard) Stevens.

Children of Christopher and Naomi (Stevens) Stevens, b. Killingworth, Conn.:

    i   WILLIAM STEVENS[6], b. 22 Feb. 1767
    ii   RUHAMAH STEVENS, b. 25 Oct. 1768
    iii   EUNICE STEVENS, b. 24 Aug. 1770
    iv   LUCINDA STEVENS, b. 31 Aug. 1772; d. "10 weeks after"
    v   MOSES STEVENS, b. 12 May 1774
    vi   LUCINDA STEVENS, b. 16 March 1777

References: *NEHGR* 129:20-1. Killingworth CT VR 2;75(m.), 88(b. ch.), 142(b. Naomi).

330. LEVERETT STEVENS[5] (*William[4], Melatiah[3] Bradford, William[2-1]*), b. Killingworth, Conn., 19 Sept. 1742; "last seen on the coast of Florida" 24 Oct. 1799. His gravestone in the Grove St. Cemetery says he d. 21 Oct. 1799 aged 37, "lost at sea."

He m. New Haven, Conn., 24 Oct. 1771 **ESTHER MACUMBER**, bp. New Haven 2 Sept. 1750; d. there 14 Aug. 1829 aged 79; daughter of Jeremiah and Sarah (Cooper) Macumber.

Leveret Stevens' household in New Haven as listed in the 1790 census consisted of 1 man, a boy, and 4 females.

Esther Stevens of New Haven made her will in April 1822, proved 24 Aug. 1829, naming her sons Leveret, Earl, and Isaac and daus. Hannah, Sarah Hall, and Esther. On 18 Aug. 1829 Earl Stevens declined to be executor (this is dated "at New York") and Stephen D. Pardee, Jr., was appointed in his place.

Children of Leverett and Esther (Macumber) Stevens, b. New Haven, Conn.:

   i   LEVERETT STEVENS[6], b. 4 July 1773

   ii EARL STEVENS, b. 3 Oct. 1775

  iii DANIEL STEVENS, bp. 8 Feb. 1778; d. 4 July 1796

  iv SARAH STEVENS, bp. 12 Nov. 1780

   v JOHN STEVENS, b. 16 Feb. 1785

  vi ESTHER STEVENS, bp. 28 May 1786

 vii HANNAH STEVENS, bp. 1 March 1789

viii ISAAC STEVENS, b. 17 Aug. 1793

References: *NEHGR* 129:21-2. *Conn Marr* 1:11. New Haven CT VR 2:194(b. Leverett, Earl); 3:6(b. John, Isaac). Hale Cem Coll:New Haven p. 109(d. Leverett). New Haven CT PR #9860(Esther Stevens).

331. HANNAH GILBERT[5] (*Hannah[4] Bradford, Samuel[3], William[2-1]*), b. Taunton 9 Feb. 1711/2; d. there 10 Aug. 1747 in 36th yr.

She m. Taunton 26 Nov. 1730 **EBENEZER SMITH**, d. before 26 Nov. 1746; son of John and Mary (Godfree) Smith. The 3 Feb. 1740 will of John Smith of Taunton names among others his wife Mary and son Ebenezer. A 1748 codicil mentions that son Ebenezer is dead.

On 26 Nov. 1746 Nathaniel Gilbert of Berkley, deeded four acres in Taunton to his daughter Hannah Smith of Taunton, widow of Ebenezer Smith.

The will of Hannah Smith of Taunton, widow, dated 8 Aug. 1747, proved 6 Oct. 1747, names sons Lemuel, John, and Ebenezer Smith; daughters Mary Smith, Sible Smith, Hannah Smith, and Abigail Smith (all under 18); father Nathaniel Gilbert; brother Nathaniel Gilbert; and brother[-in-law] Job Smith.

On 4 July 1749 Nathaniel Gilbert of Taunton, yeoman, was appointed guardian of John Smith (over 14) and Mary Smith, Sybel Smith, Abigail Smith, Hannah Smith, and Ebenezer Smith (all under 14).

Children of Ebenezer and Hannah (Gilbert) Smith, all named in will:

   i LEMUEL SMITH[6]

  ii JOHN SMITH

 iii EBENEZER SMITH

 iv MARY SMITH

  v SIBLE SMITH

 vi HANNAH SMITH

vii ABIGAIL SMITH

References: *Gilberts of NE* p. 86. Bristol Co. PR 11:332-4(Hannah Smith), 606-7(John Smith); 12:15:6 (gdns.). *VR Taunton* 2:438(m.); 3:185(d. Hannah). Bristol Co. LR 36:403(Nathaniel Gilbert).

332. THOMAS GILBERT⁵ (*Hannah⁴ Bradford, Samuel³, William²⁻¹*), b. Taunton 28 Nov. 1714; d. Gagetown, New Brunswick, 2 July 1797.

He m. int. Berkley 13 Aug. 1737 **MARY GODFREY**, b. Freetown 7 Oct. 1719; d. Gagetown, N.B., 17 Jan. 1804; daughter of Richard and Bathsheba (Walker) Godfrey. The will of Richard Godfree of Taunton dated, 21 Feb. 1742, names among others his wife Bathsheba and daughter Mary Guilbert. The will of Bathsheba Godfrey of Taunton, widow, dated 13 Dec. 1753, names among others daughter Mary Gilbert, wife of Thomas Gilbert.

On 17 Sept. 1736 Nathaniel Gilbert of Berkley deeded to his son Thomas Gilbert of Berkley, husbandman, the westerly part of his homestead lying partly in Taunton and partly in Berkley. Thomas (with wife Mary signing) deeded it back to his father on 25 Dec. 1740. On 28 Feb. 1745 Nathaniel gave to his son Thomas 100 acres of his farm and on 1 Dec. 1749 he gave Thomas 150 more acres of his farm with the dwelling house where Nathaniel was living. On the same day Thomas sold to his father 88 acres. Finally, on 15 April 1763 Nathaniel of Berkley gave to his son Thomas of Freetown 20 acres with a dwelling house.

Col. Thomas Gilbert moved to Freetown 28 April 1760. He was a Loyalist and sailed with the Loyalists from New York to Nova Scotia in 1783.

The will of Thomas Gilbert Esq. of Gage Town dated 29 Oct. 1795, proved 5 Sept. 1797, names wife Mary; sons Thomas of Sunbury, Peres of Gage Town, and Bradford of St. John; heirs of deceased daughter Molly, wife of Thomas Hathaway; Bathsheba, wife of Samuel Crane; Hannah, wife of Ephraim Winslow; and unmarried daughter Deborah Gilbert.

In her will dated 23 Sept. 1797, proved 11 Feb. 1804, Mary Gilbert, widow of Thomas Gilbert, Esq. of Gage Town, left all to her daughter Deborah. She is called Deborah Scovil, formerly Gilbert in the probate papers.

Children of Thomas and Mary (Godfrey) Gilbert, first 6 b. Berkley:

  i   THOMAS GILBERT⁶, b. 9 Aug. 1738
  ii MOLLY GILBERT, b. 2 Dec. 1739
  iii BATHSHEBA GILBERT, b. 17 Aug. 1741
  iv PERES GILBERT, b. ca. 1742

v   BRADFORD GILBERT, b. 27 Jan. 1746

vi   HANNAH GILBERT, b. 13 Dec. 1751

vii   DEBORAH GILBERT, b. prob. Freetown 19 July 1760

References: *Gilberts of NE* pp. 108-14. Index to Births, Berkley p. 13(b. 1st 3 ch. & Bradford). Index to Mar. Int. Berkley p. 4(int.). Queens Co. NB PR #A59(Thomas Gilbert); A:134(Mary Gilbert). Bristol Co. LR 5:46, 48; 13:554(Thomas Gilbert); 20:76; 25:148; 36:512; 37:130(Nathaniel Gilbert). Bristol Co. PR 13:478-80(Richard Godfree); 14:657-8(Bathsheba Godfrey).

333. MARY GILBERT⁵ (*Hannah⁴ Bradford, Samuel³, William²⁻¹*), b. Taunton 17 Feb. 1717; d. Norton 7 Nov. 1811 aged 95.

She m. Berkley 17 Feb. 1737 **JAMES GODFREY**, b. Taunton ca 1715; d. Norton 3 April 1795 in 80th yr; son of Richard and Bathsheba (Walker) Godfrey.

On 13 July 1759 Nathaniel Gilbert of Berkley, Gentleman, and his wife Hannah deeded to their children James Godfrey of Norton and his wife Mary one quarter of a house and lot in Boston given to Hannah by her mother Hannah Bradford. On 30 Dec. 1760 James and Mary Godfrey sold to this property to Martin Gay of Boston.

In the 1771 Valuation List, James Godfrey appears in Norton with 1 poll, 1 house, 1 tanhouse, 1 horse, 2 oxen, 3 cattle, 20 goats or sheep, 2 swine, 20 acres of pasture, 20 acres of tillage which produced 140 bushels of grain, 30 acres upland which produced 15 tons of hay, and 10 fresh meadow which produced 5 tons of hay.

James Godfrey's household in Norton in the 1790 census consisted of 1 man and 2 females. Listed next to him were James Godfrey Jr., with 1 man, 1 boy, and 1 female; and Samuel Godfrey with 2 men, 1 boy, and 4 females.

On 4 Dec. 1795 an inventory was ordered on the estate of James Godfrey of Norton. On 24 Jan. 1794 [*sic*] Mary Godfrey administratrix of the estate swore to the inventory.

Children of James and Mary (Gilbert) Godfrey, b. Norton:

i   BARSHEBA GODFREY⁶, b. 9 May 1738

ii   MARY GODFREY, b. 4 May 1740

iii   JAMES GODFREY, b. 19 March 1742; d. 18 May 1754

iv   GERSHOM GODFREY, b. 29 Feb. 1744

v   SAMUEL GODFREY, b. 7 July 1746

vi   RACHEL GODFREY, b. 2 Sept. 1748

vii ABBE GODFREY, b. 10 March 1752

viii HANNAH GODFREY, b. 5 July 1754; d. 19 Dec. 1758

References: *Gilberts of NE* p. 86. *VR Norton* pp. 63(b. ch.), 371-2(deaths). Index of Marriages, Berkley(m.). Bristol Co. PR 34:352(James Godfrey). *1771 Valuation* p. 584. Suffolk Co. LR 95:196(Nathaniel Gilbert), 195(James Godfrey).

334. NATHANIEL GILBERT[5] (*Hannah[4] Bradford, Samuel[3], William[2-1]*), b. Taunton; Capt. Gilbert was killed in action at Lake George, N.Y., 8 Sept. 1755.

He m. int. Dartmouth 20 Sept. 1745 **DEBORAH POPE**, b. Dartmouth 9 Dec. 1721; living 1781, prob. d. Lebanon, Conn., where her second husband d.; daughter of Lemuel and Elizabeth (Hunt) Pope. She m. (2) Lebanon, Conn., 10 June 1762 EBENEZER TISDALE.

On 28 Feb. 1745/6 Nathaniel Gilbert deeded land and a house in Taunton to his son Nathaniel Gilbert.

The will of "Nathaniel Guilbert of Taunton, gentleman, going forth to war," dated 18 June 1755, proved 7 Oct. 1755, names wife Deborah; sons Nathaniel and George; and daughters Welthea, Abigail, and Joanna.

On 15 June 1762 Deborah Tisdale, late Deborah Gilbert, widow of Nathaniel Gilbert of Taunton rendered an account, she being guardian of Joanna, Wealthy, Abigail, Nathaniel, and George Gilbert.

Children of Nathaniel and Deborah (Pope) Gilbert:

    i WELTHEA GILBERT[6], b. ca. 1746

    ii ABIGAIL GILBERT, b. 16 May 1748

    iii JOANNA GILBERT, b. ca. 1750

    iv NATHANIEL GILBERT, b. ca. 1752; d. Taunton 14 Oct. 1771 in 20th yr.

    v GEORGE GILBERT, b. 14 July 1755

References: *Gilberts of NE* pp. 114-6. *VR Dartmouth* 1:183(b. Deborah); 2:208(int.). *VR Taunton* 3:88(d. son Nathaniel). Bristol Co. PR 14:555-8(Nathaniel Gilbert). Bristol Co. PR 18:97(acct.). *MD* 45:18(acct.). Bristol Co. LR 36:403(Nathaniel Gilbert). *MA Sold French & Indian War* p. 78(d. Nathaniel).

335. SAMUEL GILBERT[5] (*Hannah[4] Bradford, Samuel[3], William[2-1]*), b. Taunton ca. 1723; d. there 7 Aug. 1796 in 73rd yr.

He m. int. Dighton 2 Nov. 1752 **SARAH DEAN**, b. Dighton 14 Oct. 1724; d. Taunton 17 Dec. 1806; daughter of Joseph and Sarah (Burt) Dean.

On 30 July 1752 Nathaniel Gilbert deeded 134 acres in Norton to his son Samuel Gilbert of Berkley.

In the 1771 Valuation List, Samuel Gilbert appears in Berkley with 1 poll, 3 houses, 2 horse, 4 oxen, 6 cattle, 11 goats or sheep, 3 swine, 10 acres of pasture, 10 acres of tillage which produced 120 bushels of grain, 10 barrels of cider, 24 acres of upland which produced 12 tons of hay, and 24 acres of fresh meadow which produced 8 tons of hay.

On 20 April 1778 an inventory was taken of the estate of Samuel Gilbert late of Berkley, but now an absentee. One-third was set off to Sarah Gilbert wife of Samuel Gilbert.

Samuel Gilbert was a Loyalist. In 1783 he took up land on St. Mary's Bay, Nova Scotia. A year or two later he returned to Berkley. He went to Nova Scotia in 1786 and to St. John in 1788.

The division of the estate of widow Sarah Gilbert of Berkley went to Jerusha Chase wife of Ezra and Sally Pierce wife of Ebenezer Pierce.

A Samuel Gilbert was listed at Berkley in the 1790 census with a household consisting of 1 man and 2 females.

Children of Samuel and Sarah (Dean) Gilbert, first 3 b. Taunton:

 i JEMIMA GILBERT[6], b. 27 Sept. 1755; d. 4 Oct. 1755
 ii SARAH GILBERT, b. ca. 1757; d. 10 June 1759 in 2nd yr.
 iii JERUSHA GILBERT, b. ca. 1759 (named in division)
 iv SALLY GILBERT, b. Freetown ca. 1760 (named in division)

References: *Gilberts of NE* pp. 116-7. *VR Taunton* 3:87(d. Jemima), 88(d. Samuel, Sarah, dau. Sarah). Bristol Co. PR 25:359, 479, 572(Samuel Gilbert); 43:311(Sarah Gilbert). Dighton VR 1:78(b. Sarah), 195(int.). Bristol Co. LR 36:403(Nathaniel Gilbert). *1771 Valuation* p. 554.

336. WELTHIA GILBERT[5] (*Hannah[4] Bradford, Samuel[3], William[2-1]*), b. Taunton ca. 1725; d. after 12 March 1792.

She m. Berkley 17 April 1744 **EBENEZER HATHAWAY**, b. Freetown 13 July 1718; d. there 16 June 1791; son of Ebenezer and Hannah (Shaw) Hathaway.

On 13 July 1759 Nathaniel Gilbert of Berkley and his wife Hannah deeded to their children Ebenezer Hathaway of Freetown and his wife Welthean one-quarter of a tract of land in Kingston devised to Hannah by her mother Hannah Bradford.

In the 1771 Valuation List, Ebenezer Hathaway appears in Berkley with 28 acres of pasture, and 2 acres of fresh meadow which produced 2 tons of hay.

On 25 July 1787 Ebenezer Hathaway of Freetown, gentleman, sold to Ebenezer Hathaway of Burton, N.B., land and part of a house in Freetown.

On 4 Aug. 1790 Ebenezer Hathaway of Freetown, gentleman, gave to daughter Hannah Hathaway of Freetown, single, half of a gristmill in Freetown.

Ebenezer Hathaway's household in Freetown in the 1790 census consisted of 1 man, 1 boy, and 2 females; listed next to him was Gilbert Hathaway with 1 man, 4 boys, and 6 females.

On 12 March 1792 Welthea Hathaway petitioned the court for her dower rights to the estate of her late husband Ebenezer Hathaway, late of Freetown. On 15 March 1792 her son Gilbert Hathaway supported the petition.

Children of Ebenezer and Welthia (Gilbert) Hathaway, all, b. prob. Freetown:

  i   GILBERT HATHAWAY[6] (twin), b. 6 Feb. 1745/6
  ii TRYPHENA HATHAWAY (twin), b. 6 Feb. 1745/6
  iii EBENEZER HATHAWAY, b. 25 July 1748
  iv WELTHEA HATHAWAY, b. 1 Sept. 1750
  v   SHADRACH HATHAWAY (twin), b. 9 June 1752
  vi CALVIN HATHAWAY (twin), b. 9 June 1752
  vii LUTHER HATHAWAY, bp. 1754
  viii HANNAH HATHAWAY, b. ca. 1758, a dwarf. She d. Berkley 12 Nov. 1823; unm. Her will dated 12 Nov. 1823, proved 9 Jan. 1824, mentions ten children of dec. sister Tryphena; brothers Gilbert, Calvin, and Luther; sister Welthea Ruggles; nephews Ebenezer and Shadrach.

References: *Gilberts of NE* pp. 86-7. *Hathaway Gen (1970)* p. 125. Bristol Co. PR 32:312(Ebenezer Hathaway); 61:224(Hannah Hathaway). Bristol Co. LR 47:69(Nathaniel Gilbert); 66:243; 70:52(Ebenezer Hathaway). *VR Freetown*(b. 1st 5 ch.). *1771 Valuation* p. 554.

337. PRISCILLA[5] BRADFORD (*Gershom[4], Samuel[3], William[2-1]*), b. ca. 1716; d. Newport, R.I., 18 Nov. 1811 aged 93.

She m. Newport, R.I., 26 July 1750 **MOSES NORMAN**, b. Boston 25 June 1717; d. Newport, R.I., 8 July 1776; son of Moses and Ann (Bullfinch) Norman.

Priscilla was blind for 50 years.

No land or probate records were found for them in Newport.

Children of Moses and Priscilla (Bradford) Norman, b. Newport, R.I.:

    i   MOSES NORMAN[6], b. 1751

    ii ANN NORMAN, b. 1753

    iii HOPE NORMAN, b. 1762

    iv JOHN BRADFORD NORMAN, b. 1765

    v PRISCILLA NORMAN, b. 1767

References: *Bradford Desc* pp. 106-7. *RIVR* Newport 4:2:51(m.); 8:423(m.). *NEHGR* 110:479(family rec.). Island Cemetery, Newport RI(d. Priscilla, Moses). *BRC*: 24:173(b. Norman). *MD* 22:124(family record).

338. DANIEL[5] BRADFORD (*Gershom[4], Samuel[3], William[2-1]*), b. ca. 1720; d. Bristol, R.I., 22 July 1810 aged 89.

He m. (1) Bristol, R.I., 1 Oct. 1749 **MARY (REYNOLDS) CHURCH**, bp. Bristol 20 Nov. 1716; d. there 16 April 1772; daughter of Peter and Mary (Giles) Reynolds. She m. (1) Bristol 25 Jan. 1732 CONSTANT CHURCH with whom she had Constant, Charles, Peter, and Mary Church.

He m. (2) Bristol, R.I., 25 Sept. 1771 **SUSANNA JARVIS**, b. Boston ca. 1740; d. Bristol, R.I., 31 Dec. 1815 in 75th yr.; daughter of Leonard and Susanna (Condy) Jarvis.

On 28 Sept. 1749 Gershom Bradford of Bristol deeded land to his son Daniel Bradford of Bristol. On 25 May 1769 Daniel Bradford of Bristol, Esq., sold his share of his father's estate to [his brother-in-law] Joseph Nash.

Daniel Bradford's household in Bristol as listed in the 1790 census consisted of 2 men, 3 boys, and 2 females.

The will of Daniel Bradford Esq. was exhibited 6 Aug. 1810 and was declared insolvent. The inventory taken 7 Jan. 1811 included a pew in the Congregational Church.

Children of Daniel and Mary (Reynolds) (Church) Bradford, b. Bristol, R.I.:

    i ELIZABETH[6] BRADFORD, b. 5 June 1750

    ii PRISCILLA BRADFORD, b. 1 March 1752

Children of Daniel and Susanna (Jarvis) Bradford, b. Bristol, R.I., except Daniel:

    iii DANIEL BRADFORD, b. Attleboro 27 June 1778

    iv LEONARD JARVIS BRADFORD, b. 22 May 1780

    v SAMUEL BRADFORD, b. 6 May 1783

vi HANNAH BRADFORD, b. 29 July 17--; d. 26 Dec. 1799; unm. [not in Aspinwall]

References: *NEHGR* 110:48-50.   *Bradford Desc* p. 107.   *RIVR* Bristol 6:1:9(both m.), 14(1st m. Mary), 65(b. 1st 5 ch), 119(d. Daniel, Susanna).   Bristol RI PR 2:737-8(Daniel Bradford).   Bristol RI LE 1:176(Gershom Bradford).   Plymouth Co. LR 48:166; 49:34(Daniel *et al.*).

339. NOAH⁵ BRADFORD (*Gershom⁴, Samuel³, William²⁻¹*), b. prob. Plymouth about 1722-1724; d. before 3 March 1746.

He m. Plymouth 10 March 1743 **HANNAH CLARKE**, b. Plymouth Middle of Oct. 1721; d. there 29 May 1770; daughter of Samuel and Mary (Phinney) Clarke. She m. (2) int. Plymouth 11 March 1748/9 LEVI POTTER.

Noah Bradford of Plymouth, mariner, made his will on 16 April 1746, proved 3 March 1746/7, leaving all his real and personal estate to his wife Hannah.   On 3 March 1746 Hannah Bradford of Plymouth was appointed administratrix of the estate of her deceased husband Noah Bradford, mariner. On 22 July 1749 Hannah Potter, late Hannah Bradford, submitted an account recording the sale of the real estate.

On 20 Dec. 1748 Hannah Bradford of Plymouth, widow and executor of the will of Noah Bradford, sold land to pay debts including a garden spot with buildings except for the improvement of that part set to the widow during her life.

Child of Noah and Hannah (Clarke) Bradford:

i NOAH⁶ BRADFORD prob. d.y.

References: *NEHGR* 110:47.   *MD* 14:160(m.).   *Clark Fam* pp. 13-4.   Plymouth Co. PR 10:363-4, 424, 426; 11:168, 265; 12:368(Noah Bradford).   *Plymouth VR* pp. 58(b. Hannah), 103(m.), 156(int. her 2nd m.).   *Plymouth Ch Recs* 1:399(d. Hannah).   Plymouth Co. LR 39:251(Hannah Bradford).

340. JOB⁵ BRADFORD (*Gershom⁴, Samuel³, William²⁻¹*), b. ca. 1726; d. Boston 29 April 1790 aged 63.

He m. Duxbury 26 Jan. 1758 (also recorded in New North Church, Boston) **ELIZABETH PARKMAN**, b. Boston 30 April 1732, bp. New North Church 30 April 1732; d. there 8 May 1787 aged 55 yrs.; daughter of Samuel and Dorcas (Bowes) Parkman.

"February 1st 1757 Capt Job Bradford in the Schooner *Loranio* from Philadelphia being Stopd at the Castle on Accot of the Small Pox being in

Philadelphia Sent one of his men to Town who on Examination by the Selectmen says that they have been on their Passage from thence one Month that they have no goods on Board Liable to Infection therefore Voted that the Vessell be permitted to Come up to Town."

On 4 March 1759 Elizabeth Bradford was admitted to the New North Church in Boston and on 3 Feb. 1760 Job Bradford was admitted.

On 21 May 1763 Capt. Job Bradford, mariner, arrived in the port of Boston on the schooner *Tryal* from Martinico. On 26 Dec. 1766 he arrived on the sloop *Olive* from North Carolina.

In the 1771 Valuation List, Job Bradford appears in Boston with 1 poll, £1000 in merchandise, renting a house from Samuel Parkman.

On 24 April 1775 Job Bradford appears on "A List of the Persons Names who lodge their Arms with the Selectmen pursuant to a Vote by them passed yesterday." He lodged one gun with them.

On 18 Dec. 1784 Job Bradford of Boston, mariner, sold to William Bowes Bradford of Boston, tailor, one undivided half of a house and land on Union Street. On 6 May 1785 William sold to his mother 1/3 of this half of the house and land, and on 22 Nov. 1785 Elizabeth Bradford released her dower rights. Then on 28 April 1790 Silas Noyes of Newburyport, merchant, and his wife Dorcas, William Bowes Bradford of Boston, tailor, and Abigail Bradford of Boston, spinster, sold this half house and land to Edward Powers of Boston, blacksmith; Mary the wife of William released her dower rights. On 29 May 1793 Joseph Nash Bradford of Boston, yeoman, sold to Edward Powers his share of this property that had come to him after the death of his brother Rufus Bradford.

On 22 July 1791 Silas Noyes of Newburyport, trader, and his wife Dorcas, and John Allyn of Duxbury and his wife Abigail, sold to William Bowes Bradford 2/9 and 1/18 part of a house and land in Boston; on 21 March 1793 Joseph Nash Bradford sold to William 1/9 and 1/36 part of the same property.

On 23 Sept. 1791 William Bowes Bradford and Joseph Nash Bradford sold to John Faunce of Kingston the 1/8 share of the Jones River Meadow that had in turn belonged to Samuel Bradford, Gershom Bradford, and their deceased father Job Bradford of Boston.

Children of Job and Elizabeth (Parkman) Bradford, b. Duxbury, bp. New North Church, Boston:

    i ELIZABETH[6] BRADFORD, b. 30 June 1759, bp. 1 July 1759

    ii DORCAS BRADFORD, b. 19 June 1760, bp. 22 June 1760

    iii SAMUEL BRADFORD, bp. 9 Aug. 1761

  iv WILLIAM BOWES BRADFORD, b. 2 Aug. 1762, bp. 8 Aug. 1762

  v ABIGAIL BRADFORD, b. 20 July 1765, bp. 24 July 1765

  vi JOB BRADFORD, bp. 18 Oct. 1767

  vii RUFUS BRADFORD, b. 18 June 1769, bp. 18 June 1769; d. Swansbury, N.C., 10 Oct. 1790

  viii JOSEPH NASH BRADFORD, b. 29 Sept. 1770, bp. 30 Sept. 1770

References: *Bradford Desc* p. 108. *NEHGR* 110:47. *VR Duxbury* pp. 28-31(b. ch.), 222(m.), 353(d. Rufus). *Boston News Obits* 1:36(d. Job, Elizabeth). *BRC* 24:209(b. Elizabeth). *RIVR* Bristol 6:1:119(d. William). Plymouth Co. LR 72:185(William Bowes Bradford). Suffolk Co. LR 152:118-9(Job Bradford); 170:57(Silas Noyes *et al.*); 176:88(Joseph Nash Bradford); 178:246-7(Silas Noyes *et al.*). *New North Ch Recs* pp. 15(Job & Elizabeth adm., m., bp. ch.), 90(bp. Elizabeth). *1771 Valuation* p. 22. *BRC* 19:53(arrival of *Loranio*); 29:246, 290(arrival), 324(lodged gun).

341. ALEXANDER[5] **BRADFORD** (*Gershom*[4], *Samuel*[3], *William*[2-1]), b. ca. 1713; d. Stonington, Conn., before 14 July 1785 when he was called deceased in his son's marriage record.

  He m. Pembroke 15 Dec. 1748 **HANNAH BRIGGS**, b. Aug. 1720; daughter of Cornelius and Ruth (Barker) Briggs.

  On 16 Feb. 1760 Alexander Bradford of Newport, R.I., blacksmith, sold an undivided 6th part of 45 acres in Hanover.

  On 4 Nov. 1763 Alexander Bradford of Stonington, Conn., Gentleman, sold his share of his father's estate.

  On 4 June 1764 Alexander Bradford and his wife Hannah of Stonington, Conn., signed a deed as heirs of Cornelius Briggs.

  On 6 Feb. 1786 Alexander Bradford Jr. was appointed administrator of the estate of Alexander Bradford, late of Stonington.

  Children of Alexander and Hannah (Briggs) Bradford, b. prob. Stonington, Conn:

  i RACHEL[6] BRADFORD, b. 1753

  ii ALEXANDER BRADFORD, b. ca. 3 March 1761; d. Stonington, Conn.

  iii HANNAH BRADFORD, b. ca. 1761; d. Stonington, Conn., 3 March 1791 ae 30; unm.

Note: The claim that Alexander's second wife was Hannah *Stanton* is not valid. The marriage record and probate record prove Hannah was his wife from 1748 to at least 4 June 1764. William Stanton of Stonington did call Alexander Bradford Jr. his nephew in a deed dated 3 March 1781 (Stonington LR 10:287-8). His wife was Lucy Briggs, sister of Hannah Briggs, therefore Alexander Bradford Jr. was his nephew (*NEHGR* 101:296-303).

References: *Bradford Desc* pp. 107-8. *VR Pembroke* p. 245(2nd m.). *NEHGR* 101:296-303; 110:47. Plymouth Co. LR 46:24; 49:34; 50:207-8(Alexander Bradford *et al.*). Stonington CT PR 5:19-20(Alexander Bradford).

342. SOLOMON[5] BRADFORD (*Gershom[4], Samuel[3], William[2-1]*), b. prob. Kingston ca. 1727 or 1728; d. Providence, R.I., 8 April 1795 in 68th yr.

He m. (1) Rehoboth 5 Nov. 1749 **BETTE GREENWOOD**, b. Rehoboth 8 Feb. 1731/2; d. there 22 April 1759; daughter of John and Lydia (Holmes) Greenwood.

He m. (2) Providence, R.I., 9 Nov. 1769 **MARY (RUTTENBURG) (TRIPP) OWENS**, b. 1732; d. Providence, R.I., 21 May 1816 in 84th yr.; daughter of Solomon and Mercy (Fenner) Ruttenburg. She m. (1) ANTHONY TRIP with whom she had Arthur Trip. She m. (2) JOSEPH OWENS.

On 2 July 1762 Solomon Bradford of Bristol, R.I., sold his share of his father's estate to Joseph Nash.

On 9 May 1770 Solomon Bradford of Providence, yeoman, guardian of Arthur Tripp, son of Anthony Tripp, in consideration of 200 Spanish milled dollars paid by Thomas Owen of Glocester, R.I., Esq., and Aaron Mason of Providence, yeoman, administrators of the estate of Joseph Owen "late of said Providence Marriner supposed to be lost at Sea," gave up any claim to "personal Estate of the said Arthur which came to the Hands of the said Joseph Owen." At the end of the deed it says that Soloman had married Mary the administratrix of the estate of Anthony Tripp.

"Tolloman" Bradford's household in 1790 in Providence consisted of one man and 3 females.

On 1 June 1795 Mary Bradford was appointed adiministrix for the estate of Solomon Bradford late of Providence.

Children of Solomon and Bette (Greenwood) Bradford, b. Rehoboth:

    i NOAH[6] BRADFORD, b. 26 Oct. 1750

    ii SOLOMON BRADFORD, b. 11 Nov. 1751; d. 23 Nov. 1751

    iii BETTE BRADFORD, b. 6 Oct. 1752; d. 5 June 1753

    iv HULDAH BRADFORD, b. 7 May 1754

    v BETTE GREENWOOD BRADFORD, b. 26 June 1756; d. 21 June 1759

    vi SOLOMON BRADFORD

References: *NEHGR* 110:47. *Bradford Desc* p. 108. *Rehoboth VR* pp. 55(1st m.), 553(b. ch.), 803(d. Phebe, 3 ch.). *RIVR* Providence 2:1:22(2nd m.). *RIVR* 13:200(d. Solomon); 18:287; 20:601(d. Mary). Plymouth Co. LR 48:166; 49:34(Solomon Bradford).

Providence RI PR, will book, 7:762(Solomon Bradford). Providence RI LR 19:239(Solomon Bradford).

343. HOPESTILL⁵ BRADFORD (*Gershom⁴, Samuel³, William²⁻¹*) drowned in the Mississippi River.

She m. Bristol, R.I., 9 Jan. 1756 **JOSEPH NASH** of Providence, bp. Abington 6 Jan 1723/4; d. "at the Mississippi" before 14 Feb. 1781; the son of Simeon and Ann (West) Nash. He m. (1) Rehoboth 3 May 1750 SARAH CARPENTER with whom he had Jacob.

On 2 July 1762, 4 Nov. 1763, and 25 May 1763 Solomon, Alexander, and Daniel Bradford each sold their share of their father's estate to [their brother-in-law] Joseph Nash and on 9 June 1763 Joseph Nash and his wife Hopestill sold half a lot (4 shares) of land that had been their father's Capt. Gershom Bradford late of Bristol.

Richard Benson, in *Nash Family*, relates:

> [Joseph] served as the cornet of a mounted horse company at Providence in 1754 and was a deputy to the legislature from Providence in 1762 and 1769. In 1762, he was named one of the directors of a lottery established by the legislature to raise funds to repair the church in Providence and build a new steeple...Joseph was a shipmaster and owner. In 1774, Joseph Nash and Christopher Whipple, who were owners of the sloop *Two Pollies*, shipped a cargo of goods to sell to settlers on the Mississippi River. They sailed on the sloop *Hope* in November and reached the *Two Pollies* in New Orleans. While the *Two Pollies* was lying at anchor, about two miles above the town of New Orleans, early on Sunday morning 20 February 1774, the sloop was boarded by a party of Spanish soldiers, with their swords drawn and bayonets fixed. They declared they had orders from the Spanish governor and sailed the sloop to New Orleans. They then stripped it of its riggings and unloaded the cargo. Joseph Nash, who was on board, the ship's captain, Ephraim Carpenter, and the ship's mate, Benjamin Pitcher, were sent to prison, where they remained a considerable time.

Child of Joseph and Hopestill (Bradford) Nash:

    i   [SON] NASH⁶ (or was he a child of the first m.?)

References: *Bradford Desc* p. 107. R*IV*R Bristol 6:1:9(m.); 14:31; 16:137(d. Joseph). Plymouth Co. LR 48:166; 49:34; 72:185(Gershom's shares). Richard H. Benson, *The Nash Family of Weymouth Massachusetts* (1998) pp. 122-3. *NEHGR* 110:48. *Abington VR* 1:145(bp. Joseph).

344. JEREMIAH⁵ BRADFORD (*Gershom⁴, Samuel³, William²⁻¹*), b. Kingston 1734; d. Chatham, Conn., 1817.

He m. Chatham, Conn., 3 June 1756 **REBECCA DART**, b. Bolton, Conn., 24 Nov. 1728; d. after 4 April 1811; daughter of Ebenezer and Ruth (Loomis) Dart.

Jeremiah Bradford was a physician in Middle Haddam. "Where Dr. Bradford studied medicine is not ascertained. He settled in Middle Haddam probably as early as 1754 or 5, and practised until old age, dying in 1814, aged 80. He was a man of good sense and an able practitioner."

Jeremiah Bradford's household in Chatham in the 1790 census consisted of two men and two females; listed near him was Jeremiah Bradford Jr. with one man and three females.

On 28 Oct. 1807 Jeremiah Bradford and Joel Bradford of Chatham, William Bradford of Wethersfield, Conn., and Jeremiah Bradford Jr. of Berlin, Vt., sold to Barnabas Dunham of Berlin, Conn., one-quarter of an acre in Chatham.

On 4 April 1811, acknowledged same day, Jeremiah Bradford of Chatham, Conn., quitclaimed to wife Rebecca and third son Joel land in Chatham.

No Connecticut probate records have been found for Jeremiah Bradford.

Children of Jeremiah and Rebecca (Dart) Bradford:

    i   VIENNA⁶ BRADFORD, b. 5 Nov. 1757
    ii JEREMIAH BRADFORD, bp. 29 Oct. 1758
    iii WILLIAM BRADFORD, b. 10 Nov. 1758
    iv JOEL BRADFORD, b. 17 June 1764

References: *Bradford Desc* p. 108. *NEHGR* 110:48. Chatham CT LR 13:483(Jeremiah Bradford). Haddam Neck, Conn., Cong. Ch recs 1:38(m.). Bolton CT VR 1:22(b. Rebecca). Chatham CT LR 14:157(Jeremiah Bradford *et al*.). *Centenial Address With Sketches Of Middletown And Its Parishes* , David Field (1853) p. 278(quote re Jeremiah).

345. ABIGAIL⁵ BRADFORD (*Perez⁴, Samuel³, William²⁻¹*), b. Dedham 15 May 1721; d. 15 Nov. 1804.

She m. Swansea 31 Dec. 1741 **SAMUEL LEE**, b. Swansea 9 Dec. 1717; d. after April 1772; son of Samuel and Sarah (_____) Lee.

On 24 Oct. 1749 Abigail's siblings sold to Samuel Lee Jr. of Swanzey 11 acres in Swanzey, "the homestead on which Samuel Lee dwells with a dwelling house and orchards from the estate of Perez Bradford dec." On 21 March

1750 Samuel and Abigail, with her siblings, heirs of Perez Bradford, sold three pieces of land in Attleboro.

On 27 Feb. 1760 Samuel Lea Jr. of Swanzey and his wife Abigal, with John Bradford, sold two-eighths of the land their brother Joel Bradford died siezed of.

In the 1771 Valuation List, Samuel Lee appears in Swansey with 1 poll, 1 house, 1 tanhouse, 1 servant for life, 1 horse, 1 cattle, 4 acres of pasture, and 4 acres of upland which produced 2 tons of hay.

At the April 1772 term of the Bristol Co. Court of Common Pleas, suit was brought against Samuel Lee of Swanzey, shipwright.

Children of Samuel and Abigail (Bradford) Lee, b. Swansea:

    i   CHARLES LEE[6], b. 15 Sept. 1742

    ii ABIGAIL LEE, b. 10 June 1744

  iii MARGARET LEE, b. 1 Feb. 1744/5; d.y.

  iv SAMUEL LEE, b. 10 Feb. 1745/6; d.y.

    v ELIZABETH LEE, b. 7 March 1747/8

  vi MARGARET LEE, b. 1 Feb. 1749

 vii SAMUEL LEE, b. 7 June 1753

viii MARY LEE, b. 5 Aug. 1755

  ix WILLIAM LEE, b. 9 May 1758

    x REBECCA LEE, b. 16 April 1760

  xi BELCHER LEE, b. 3 Feb. 1763

References: *Bradford Desc* p. 109. *Swansea VR* pp. 37(b. Abigail), 43(b. Belcher), 49(b. Charles), 66(b. Elizabeth), 118(b. Margaret), 119(b. Mary), 120(b. Margaret), 142(b. Rebecca), 153(b. Samuel), 155(b. Samuel), 164(b. William), 203(m.).   Bristol Co. LR 41:278(Samuel Lee); 44:517-8(Joel's heirs); 48:368(Jabez Gay *et al.*).   *Plymouth Co Ct Recs* 8:405. *1771 Valuation* p. 604.

346. MARY[5] BRADFORD (*Perez[4], Samuel[3], William[2-1]*), b. ca. 1723; d. after 18 May 1784 (deed).

She m. (1) int. Attleboro 12 April 1746 **JABEZ GOULD** of Wrentham; son of Jabez Gould.

She m. (2) int. Attleboro 8 Feb. 1754 **DANIEL SEARLE**, b. Little Compton 8 Sept. 1730; d. there 31 May 1779 in 49th yr.; son of Nathaniel and Elizabeth (Kinnecut) Searle. On 13 April 1763 Nathaniel Searle Esq. of Little Compton sold to his son Daniel Searle of Little Compton, taylor, half an acre of land with a house.

On 8 Nov. 1748 widow Mary Gould was named administratrix of the estate of Jabez Gould.

On 24 Oct. 1749 Mary Gould of Cumberland, R.I., with her siblings, sold to Samuel Lee Jr. of Swanzey 11 acres in Swanzey, the homestead on which Samuel Lee lived with a dwelling house and orchards from the estate of Perez Bradford deceased. On 21 March 1750 Mary Gould, widow, with her siblings, heirs of Perez Bradford sold three pieces of land in Attleboro.

No probate records have been found for Daniel Searle.

On 18 May 1784 Sarah Jonson/Johnson of Little Compton, widow and daughter of Daniel Searle late of Little Compton, sold to Nathaniel Searle Esq. of Little Compton three-quarters of half an acre with three-quarters of the house; Mary Searle, widow of Daniel Searle gives up her dower rights.

Child of Jabez and Mary (Bradford) Gould, b. Cumberland, R.I.:

    i   JABEZ GOULD[6], b. 24 March 1748/9

Children of Daniel and Mary (Bradford) (Gould) Searle, b. Little Compton, R.I.:

    ii   BETTY SEARLE, b. 15 June 1755

    iii SARAH SEARLE, b. 5 May 1757

    iv JOEL SEARLE, b. 6 Feb. 1759

    v   JOHN SEARLE, b. ca. 1766; d. 12 June 1779 ae 13.

References: *VR Attleboro* pp. 442(int. 1st m.), 548(int. 2nd m.). *RIVR* Little Compton 4:6:157(b. Daniel, 1st 3 ch.). *NEHGR* 115:261(d. Daniel). *Little Compton Fams* p. 551. Cumberland RI Town Council and PR Rec. 3:12-3(Jabez Gould). *RIVR* Cumberland 3:5:100(b. Jabez). Bristol Co. LR 41:278(Samuel Lee *et al.*); 44:517-8(Joel's heirs); 48:368(Jabez Gay *et al.*). Little Compton RI LE 1:442(Nathaniel Searle); 3:25(Sarah Johnson).

347. HANNAH[5] BRADFORD (*Perez[4], Samuel[3], William[2-1]*), b. ca. 1724; d. Attleboro 10 Sept. 1778 in 55th yr.

She m. Attleboro 30 April 1747 **JABEZ GAY**, b. Dedham 16 Dec. 1721; d. Attleboro 4 Oct. 1801; son of Lusher and Mary (Ellis) Gay.

On 24 Oct. 1749 Jabez Gay and his wife Hannah, with her siblings, sold to Samuel Lee Jr. of Swanzey 11 acres in Swanzey, the homestead on which Samuel Lee lived with a dwelling house and orchards from the estate of Perez Bradford deceased. On 21 March 1750 Jabez Gay and Hannah, with her siblings, heirs of Perez Bradford, sold three pieces of land in Attleboro.

On 27 Feb. 1760 Jabez Gay and his wife Hannah, with Samuel Sweetland and his wife Elizabeth, sold two-eighths of the land their brother Joel Bradford had died siezed of.

In the 1771 Valuation List, Jabez Gay appears in Attleboro with 2 polls, 1 house, £100 lent at interest, 1 horse, 2 oxen, 6 cattle, 17 goats or sheep, 2 swine, 24 acres of pasture, 6 acres of tillage which produced 60 bushels of grain, 15 barrels of cider, 10 acres of upland which produced 5 tons of hay, and 2 acres of fresh meadow which produced 2 tons of hay.

In 1790 Jabez Gay's household in Attleboro consisted of 4 men 16 or older, 2 boys under 16, and 5 females.

The will of Jabez Gay of Attleborough dated 9 Jan. 1796, proved 26 Oct. 1801, names daughters Hannah Church and Selah Gay; and mentions the children of Filena Whitaker, Monica Baker, Molly Metcalf, and Lucy Metcalf, and the heirs of Eleanor Bacon. On 5 Jan. 1802 the executor Ebenezer Bacon reported payments of $100 each to Hannah Church, Selah Gay, Monorchy Baker, the heirs of Philena Whitaker, Molly Metcalf, and Lucy Metcalf, and the heirs of Eleanor Bacon.

Children of Jabez and Hannah (Bradford) Gay, b. Attleboro:

    i   HANNAH GAY[6], b. 4 Feb. 1747/8

    ii SELAH GAY, b. 13 July 1750; d. unm.

   iii PHILENA GAY, b. 8 April 1752

   iv MONICA GAY, b. 19 Feb. 1754

    v MOLLY GAY, b. 29 Nov. 1755

   vi JABEZ GAY, b. 12 Feb. 1758; not in father's will

   vii LUCY GAY, b. 31 Oct. 1759

  viii HOPE GAY, bp. 29 Nov. 1761; not in father's will

   ix ELEANOR GAY, b. 14 Dec. 1763

    x LYDIA GAY, bp. 20 July 1766; not in father's will

References: *Bradford Desc* p. 100. *VR Attleborough* pp. 137(b. ch.), 439(m.), 678(d. Hannah, Jabez). Bristol Co. PR 38:392 and loose files (Jabez Gay). *Dedham VR* 1:150(b. Jabez). Bristol Co. LR 41:278(Samuel Lee *et al.*); 44:517-8(Joel's heirs); 48:368(Jabez Gay *et al.*). *1771 Valuation* p. 546.

348. ELIZABETH⁵ BRADFORD (*Perez⁴, Samuel³, William²⁻¹*), bp. Milton 1728; living 7 Oct. 1766.

She m. Attleboro 28 Dec. 1749 **SAMUEL SWEETLAND**, bp. Marblehead 4 Dec. 1726; d. before 11 Sept. 1766 (inv.); son of William and Mary (Cruff) Sweetland.

On 8 Jan. 1749/50 William Sweetland of Marblehead and James, Benjamin, and Samuel Sweetland of Attleboro, yeomen, quitclaimed to Philip Hammond a small tract of land in Marblehead owned by their late father.

On 21 March 1750 Samuel Sweetland and his wife Elizabeth, with her siblings, heirs of Perez Bradford, sold three pieces of land in Attleboro.

On 27 Feb. 1760 Samuel Sweetland and his wife Elizabeth, with Jabez Gay and his wife Hannah, sold two-eighths of the land their brother Joel Bradford had died siezed of.

The inventory of the estate of Samuel Sweetland was taken 11 Sept. 1766.

Children of Samuel and Elizabeth (Bradford) Sweetland, first b. Attleboro; rest b. prob. Marblehead:

  i WILLIAM SWEETLAND⁶, b. 14 Aug. 1750
  ii GEORGE SWEETLAND
  iii ELIZABETH SWEETLAND
  iv ABIGAIL SWEETLAND, bp. 21 Nov. 1756; d.y.
  v ABIGAIL SWEETLAND, bp. 17 Nov. 1759
  vi MARY SWEETLAND, bp. 24 Jan. 1762
  vii SAMUEL SWEETLAND, bp. 30 Sept. 1764

References: *Bradford Desc* p. 110. *VR Attleboro* pp. 258(b. son Samuel), 574(m.). *VR Marblehead* 1:498(bp. Samuel). Essex Co. PR 343:240(Samuel Sweetland *et al.*). Essex Co. LR 100:186(William Sweetland *et al.*). Bristol Co. LR 44:517-8(Joel's heirs); 48:368(Jabez Gay *et al.*).

349. PEREZ⁵ BRADFORD (*Perez⁴, Samuel³, William²⁻¹*), bp. Milton 5 Jan. 1728/9; d. 1763.

He m. Cumberland, R.I., 24 Jan. 1750 **MARY JACKSON**, b. there 15 May 1732; daughter of Joseph and Zipporah (Tower) Jackson.

On 24 Oct. 1749 Perez Bradford of Attleboro, with his siblings, sold to Samuel Lee Jr. of Swanzey 11 acres in Swanzey, the homestead on which Samuel Lee was living, with a dwelling house and orchards from the estate of Perez Bradford deceased. On 21 March 1750 Perez Bradford, with his siblings, heirs of Perez Bradford, sold three pieces of land in Attleboro.

Children of Perez and Mary (Jackson) Bradford, b. Attleboro:

    i   PEREZ[6] BRADFORD, b. 13 Aug. 1751

    ii ELIZABETH BRADFORD, b. 17 Sept. 1753

    iii MARY BRADFORD, b. Oct. 1755

References: *Bradford Desc* p. 109. *VR Attleboro* p. 45(b. 1st 2 ch.). *RIVR* Cumberland 3:5:15(m.), 105(b. Mary). Bristol Co. LR 41:278(Samuel Lee *et al.*); 48:368(Jabez Gay *et al.*).

350. GEORGE[5] BRADFORD (*Perez[4], Samuel[3], William[2-1]*), bp. Milton 22 Oct. 1732; d. Woodstock, Conn., 11 May 1795.

He m. int. Attleboro 28 April 1756 **SARAH CARPENTER**, b. Attleboro 22 Feb. 1736/7; d. Cooperstown, N.Y., 1836; daughter of Dan and Mary (Wiswell) Carpenter. The will of Mary Carpenter of Attleboro, widow of Dan Carpenter, dated 16 Feb. 1757 names daughter Sarah Bradford.

On 24 Oct. 1749 George Bradford of Attleboro, with his siblings, sold to Samuel Lee Jr. of Swanzey 11 acres in Swanzey, it being the homestead "on which Samuel Lee dwells" with a dwelling house and orchards from the estate of Perez Bradford deceased.

On 16 Feb. 1757 George Bradford and wife Sarah signed a receipt for her legacy from estate of her father Dan Carpenter of Attleboro. On 5 April 1757 Sarah Bradford, a minor over 14, daughter of Dan Carpenter, chose her husband, George Bradford, to be her guardian.

On 27 March 1771 Joseph Bradford of Attleborough, yeoman, sold to George Bradford of Cumberland, R.I., shop joyner, 12 acres in Attleborough.

On 12 April 1774 George Bradford of Cumberland, R.I., shop joyner, sold to Jeremiah Whipple Esq. of Cumberland one-half of 16 acres with a small house; George's wife Sarah also signed this deed.

There are two George Bradfords listed in Woodstock in the 1790 census; one with a household consisting of one man and 2 females, the other with a household of 3 men, 1 boy under 16, and 4 females. Listed near the second one was Essick Bradford with one man and 2 females.

Children of George and Sarah (Carpenter) Bradford, first 4 b. Attleboro:

    i   GEORGE[6] BRADFORD, b. 11 May 1757

    ii SARAH BRADFORD, b. 2 Dec. 1759

    iii CARPENTER BRADFORD, b. 7 March 1762

    iv PEREZ BRADFORD, b. 25 July 1764

    v HANNAH BRADFORD, b. 20 Nov. 1766

    vi ESECK BRADFORD, b. 21 May 1768

   vii BETSEY BRADFORD, b. 21 Sept. 1771

  viii MATILDA BRADFORD, b. 8 Nov. 1774

    ix SYLVESTER BRADFORD, b. 19 July 1780

References: *Bradford Desc* p. 109. *VR Attleboro* pp. 45(b. 1st 4 ch.), 67(b. Sarah), 342(int.). Bristol Co. PR 15:270-1(receipt), 271-2(Mary Carpenter), loose files(guard.). Bristol Co. LR 48:368(Jabez Gay *et al.*); 53:476(Joseph Bradford); 60:269(George Bradford). *Woodstock By Bowen* p. 620(d. George).

351. JOHN⁵ BRADFORD (*Perez⁴, Samuel³, William²⁻¹*), b. Attleboro 1734; d. Rehoboth 25 April 1781.

He m. (1) Attleboro 10 June 1761 **PHEBE STEARNS**, b. Dedham 23 Feb. 1738/9; d. Rehoboth 23 May 1770; daughter of John and Rebecca (Deane) Stearns.

He m. (2) Rehoboth 28 Nov. 1771 **SARAH DAGGETT**, b. Rehoboth 23 April 1742; living 30 Jan. 1794; daughter of Israel and Hannah (Daman) Daggett.

On 24 Oct. 1749 John Bradford of Attleboro, with his siblings, sold to Samuel Lee Jr. of Swanzey 11 acres in Swanzey, it being the "homestead on which Samuel Lee dwells" with a dwelling house and orchards from the estate of Perez Bradford deceased.

In the 1771 Valuation List, John Bradford appears in Rehoboth with 1 poll, 1 house, 1 tanhouse, 1 cattle, 5 acres of pasture, 2 acres of tillage which produced 16 bushels of grain, 7 barrels of cider, and 3 acres fresh meadow which produced 1 ton of hay.

The inventory of the estate of John Bradford, late of Rehoboth, was taken 10 May 1781. On 7 Aug. 1781 Sarah Bradford, administratrix of the estate, swore to the inventory. On the same day she was appointed guardian to Walter Bradford, son of John. On 27 March 1793 Sarah Bradford petitioned to sell the house.

On 24 Aug. 1782 Sarah Bradford of Rehoboth, widow and administratrix of the estate of her husband John Bradford, sold to Capt. Stephen Jenks of North Providence 65½ acres that had been set off as part of her dower. On the same day she sold more of John's estate to Oliver Starkweather of Rehoboth. On 24 Oct. 1782 she sold more to Solomon Smith of Rehoboth; to Doley Sabin of Providence on 31 July 1793; and to Mary Travers of Providence, widow; and Dorothy Sabin of Rehoboth on 30 Jan. 1794.

Children of John and Phebe (Stearns) Bradford, b. Rehoboth:

    i JOHN[6] BRADFORD, b. 24 June 1762

    ii WILLIAM BRADFORD, b. 23 April 1763

    iii MARY BRADFORD, b. 20 Nov. 1764

    iv PHEBE BRADFORD, b. 9 June 1767

    v WALTER BRADFORD, b. 11 Dec. 1769

Children of John and Sarah (Daggett) Bradford, b. Rehoboth:

    vi HANNAH BRADFORD, b. 11 July 1772

    vii ISRAEL BRADFORD, b. 3 May 1775

    viii JOEL BRADFORD, b. 17 May 1777

References: *Bradford Desc* p. 110. *VR Attleboro* p. 342(1st. m.). *Rehoboth VR* pp. 445(Sarah's par.), 553(b. ch.), 599(b. Sarah), 803(d. John, Phebe). *Dedham VR* p. 67(d. Phebe). Bristol Co. PR 26:456-7; 27:477; 32:86-7(John Bradford); loose files(guard. Walter). Bristol Co. LR 48:368(Jabez Gay *et al.*); 61:113, 158, 183; 72:108, 372, 541(Sarah Bradford). *1771 Valuation* p. 594.

352. JOSEPH[5] BRADFORD (*Perez[4], Samuel[3], William[2-1]*), b. Attleboro 1737; d. Providence, R.I., 18 March 1797.

He m. int. Attleboro 14 Jan. 1758 **BEULAH MORSE**, b. Attleboro 13 Nov. 1738; d. Providence, R.I., 25 Dec. 1818; daughter of Henry and Mary (Follett) Morse.

On 24 Oct. 1749 Joseph Bradford of Attleboro, with his siblings, sold to Samuel Lee Jr. of Swanzey 11 acres in Swanzey, it being the homestead "on which Samuel Lee dwells" with a dwelling house and orchards from the estate of Perez Bradford deceased.

On 27 March 1771 Joseph Bradford of Attleborough, yeoman, sold to George Bradford of Cumberland, R.I., shop joyner, 12 acres in Attleborough.

In the 1771 Valuation List, Joseph Bradford appears in Attleboro with 1 poll, and 1 house.

Administration was granted on the estate of Joseph Bradford on 5 Feb. 1798 and the estate was declared insolvent.

Children of Joseph and Beulah (Morse) Bradford:

    i JOEL[6] BRADFORD, b. 1758

    ii SARAH BRADFORD

    iii HENRY BRADFORD

    iv CHLOE BRADFORD, b. 1763

    v ABIGAIL BRADFORD

    vi PHILENA BRADFORD

    vii JOSEPH BRADFORD, b. 1777

    viii MARY BRADFORD

References: *Bradford Desc* p. 109. *VR Attleboro* pp. 183(b. Beulah), 342(int.). *RIVR* 13:201(d. Beulah); 14:201(d. Joseph). Bristol Co. LR 48:368(Jabez Gay *et al.*); 53:476(Joseph Bradford). Providence RI PR A1621, TC 7:216(Joseph Bradford). *1771 Valuation* p. 544.

353. MARY WHITING[5] (*Elizabeth*[4] *Bradford, Samuel*[3], *William*[2-1]), bp. New London, Conn., 2 March 1717.

    She m. _____ **GARDNER** of Hingham.*

    On 9 Oct. 1780 the heirs of Elizabeth Noyes, dec., sold land in Kingston that had been given to her and [her sisters] Jerusha Gay, Hannah Gilbert, and Wealthea Lane. These heirs included Mary Gardner of Hingham.

* Note: Perhaps she m. Hingham 15 Nov. 1736 HOSEA GARDNER and had 4 ch. but *Hingham Hist* 2:247 says the parents of that Mary Whiting were John and Mary (Tower) Whiting.

References: *Bradford Desc* p. 110. Plymouth Co. LR 60:112(heirs Elizabeth Noyes).

354. JOHN WHITING[5] (*Elizabeth*[4] *Bradford, Samuel*[3], *William*[2-1]), b. New London, Conn., 3 Aug. 1719; d. there bef. 11 Dec. 1770. His death notice appeared in the 1 Jan. 1771 issue of the *Hartford Courant*.

    He m. Newport, R.I., **PHILENA (PHOEBE) COGGESHALL**, b. Newport, R.I.; d. New London, Conn., 7 July 1776 aged 51, bur. Old Norwich Town Cemetery; daughter of William and Philemon (Freeman) Coggeshall.

    On 11 Dec. 1770 Philenah Whiting was appointed administratrix of the estate of John Whiting late of New London.

    On 9 Oct. 1780 the heirs of Elizabeth Noyes, deceased, sold land in Kingston that had been given to her and [her sisters] Jerusha Gay, Hannah Gilbert, and Wealthea Lane. These heirs included the heirs of John Whiting: James Houghton and his wife Philena, Elizabeth Leffingwell, Mary Whiting, and James Woolf Whiting of Norwich.

Children of John and Philena (Coggesweld) Whiting:

  i JAMES [WOLF] WHITING[6], b. 1746

  ii ELIZABETH WHITING, b. ca. 1750

  iii PHILENA WHITING, b. prob. by 1752 (m. in 1768)

  iv MARY (or POLLY) WHITING

References: *Bradford Desc* pp. 110-1. Plymouth Co. LR 60:112(heirs Elizabeth Noyes). New London CT PD #5692(John Whiting). Hale Cem Coll:Norwich p. 600(d. Philena).

355. SYBIL WHITING[5] (*Elizabeth[4] Bradford, Samuel[3], William[2-1]*), bp. New London, Conn., 29 July 1722; d. 27 April 1790.

 She m. Stonington, Conn., 18 Dec. 1739 **WILLIAM NOYES**, b. Stonington, Conn., 2 March 1715; d. 1809; son of John and Mary (Gallup) Noyes.

 On 9 Oct. 1780 the heirs of Elizabeth Noyes, deceased, sold land in Kingston that had been given to her and [her sisters] Jerusha Gay, Hannah Gilbert, and Wealthea Lane. These heirs included Sibel Noyes of Groton, Conn.

 Children of William and Sybil (Whiting) Noyes, b. Groton and Canaan, Conn. [iv - x not in Barbour]:

  i WILLIAM NOYES[6], b. 13 April 1743

  ii SYBIL NOYES, b. 19 Nov. 1745

  iii SAMUEL NOYES, b. 9 Nov. 1747

  iv JOHN NOYES, b. 6 Nov. 1750

  v MARY NOYES, b. 22 July 1754

  vi TEMPERANCE NOYES, b. 26 July 1755

  vii NATHAN NOYES

  viii LUCY NOYES

  ix ELIZABETH NOYES, b. 1762

  x NATHANIEL NOYES

  xi CHARLES WHITING NOYES, b. 1 March 1765

References: *Bradford Desc* p. 111. Stonington CT VR 2:31(b. William); 3:107(m.). Groton CT VR 1:157(b. 1st 3 ch., Charles). Plymouth Co. LR 60:112(heirs Elizabeth Noyes).

356. CHARLES WHITING⁵ (*Elizabeth⁴ Bradford, Samuel³, William²⁻¹*), bp. New London, Conn., 8 Aug. 1725; d. bef. 1 April 1765 when his death notice appeared in the *Hartford Courant*.

He m. ca. 1750 **HONOR GOODRICH**, b. Wethersfield, Conn., 22 Feb. 1732; d. there 21 Aug. 1801; daughter of Hezekiah and Honor (Deming) Goodrich. She m. (2) Wethersfield, Conn., 14 Nov. 1774 JOSHUA BELDING.

On 6 Aug. 1765 Honor Whiting was appointed administratrix to the estate of Charles Whiting late of Norwich. The inventory was taken on the same day.

On 9 Oct. 1780 the heirs of Elizabeth Noyes, deceased, sold land in Kingston that had been given to her and [her sisters] Jerusha Gay, Hannah Gilbert, and Wealthea Lane. These heirs included Honor Belding of Wethersfield, Conn., administratrix of Charles Whiting late of Norwich, deceased.

Children of Charles and Honor (Goodrich) Whiting, b. Norwich, Conn.:

i   CHARLES WHITING⁶, b. 5 April 1751
ii HONOR WHITING, b. 5 July 1753; d.y.
iii HEZEKIAH WHITING, b. 22 June 1755; d. at sea; unm.
iv MARY WHITING, b. 17 Oct. 1757
v   HONOUR WHITING, b. 29 June 1760 (given by Aspinwall as ELIZABETH)
vi JEFFERY WHITING, b. 18 Dec. 1762; d. Bath NC 1 Sept. 1790 ae 26. His death notice appeared in the 18 Oct. 1790 issue of the *Hartford Courant*.

References: *Bradford Desc* p. 111. *Norwich CT VR* 1:312(b. ch.). Plymouth Co. LR 60:112(heirs Elizabeth Noyes). Wethersfield CT VR 1:27(b. Honor); 2:79(2ⁿᵈ m.; d. Honor). Norwich CT PD #11430(Charles Whiting).

357. ELIZABETH WHITING⁵ (*Elizabeth⁴ Bradford, Samuel³, William²⁻¹*), bp. New London, Conn., 8 Aug. 1725; living 16 Oct 1780 Hebron, Conn., when she acknowledged a deed with other heirs of her mother.

She m. Wethersfield, Conn., 10 June 1741 **SAMUEL GOODRICH**, b. Wethersfield 1 Nov. 1721; d. Hebron, Conn., 16 Nov 1773; son of Josiah and Sarah (Parker) Goodrich. On 9 July 1750 Samuel Goodrich of Wethersfield, tailor, sold to Samuel Chapman of Tolland one-fifth part of 88 acres formerly held by "my father Josiah Goodrich Esq., deceased."

On 15 Nov. 1751 Samuel Goodrich of Wethersfield sold to John Chester of Wethersfield an undivided one half of 73+ acres, the other half of which belonged to David Goodrich, son of Josiah Goodrich Esq., deceased.

On 1 Feb. 1774 widow Elizabeth Goodrich posted bond as administratrix of the estate of Samuel Goodrich.

On 9 Oct. 1780 the heirs of Elizabeth Noyes, deceased, sold land in Kingston that had been given to her and [her sisters] Jerusha Gay, Hannah Gilbert, and Wealthea Lane. These heirs included Elizabeth Goodrich of Hebron, Conn.

Children of Samuel and Elizabeth (Whiting) Goodrich, b. Wethersfield, Conn.:

  i   SAMUEL GOODRICH[6], b. 17 July 1748
  ii WELTHEAN GOODRICH, b. 24 Sept. 1750
  iii MILLICENT GOODRICH, b. 29 Nov. 1752
  iv ELIZABETH GOODRICH, b. 28 Feb. 1755
  v   PORTER GOODRICH, b. 11 May 1757
  vi SOLOMON GOODRICH, b. 28 Feb. 1760
  vii ANNE GOODRICH, b. 16 April 1762
  viii ELIPHALET GOODRICH, b. 30 Sept. 1764

References: *Bradford Desc* p. 111. Wethersfield CT VR 1:83(b. Samuel); 2:74(m.; b. ch.). Plymouth Co. LR 60:112(ack. deed). Colchester CT PR Dist. #1480(Samuel Goodrich). Wethersfield CT LR 9:147(Samuel to John Chester). Tolland CT LR 4:391(Samuel to Samuel Chapman). Plymouth Co. LR 60:112(heirs Elizabeth Noyes).

358. GAMALIEL WHITING[5] (*Elizabeth[4] Bradford, Samuel[3], William[2-1]*), bp. New London, Conn., 14 Sept. 1717; d. Great Barrington 27 Nov. 1790 aged 76; "Gam buried 30 Nov. 1790."

He m. Canaan, Conn., 18 June 1752 **ANNIE GILLETTE**, b. Canaan 18 Feb. 1738; d. Great Barrington 27 Feb. 1808.

On 9 Oct. 1780 the heirs of Elizabeth Noyes, deceased, sold land in Kingston that had been given to her and [her sisters] Jerusha Gay, Hannah Gilbert, and Wealthea Lane. These heirs included Gamaliel Whiting of Great Barrington.

Gamaliel Whiting's listing in the 1790 census of Great Barrington was 4 men 16 or older, 1 boy, and 4 females. Living next to him was William Whiting 2nd with 1 man, 1 boy, and 7 females.

Children of Gamaliel and Annie (Gillette) Whiting, b. Canaan, Conn., not all recorded there:

    i   ELIZABETH WHITING[6], b. 19 May 1753; d. 11 Nov. 1772

   ii ANNA WHITING, b. 8 Nov. 1754

  iii WILLIAM WHITING, b. 16 Feb. 1757

  iv MARY WHITING, b. 11 Dec. 1758

   v EBENEZER WHITING, b. 30 June 1760

  vi SARAH WHITING, b. 26 April 1762

 vii GAMALIEL WHITING, b. 7 Feb. 1764

viii CHARLES WHITING, b. 6 Jan. 1766

  ix BERNICE WHITING, b. 14 April 1769

   x JOHN WHITING, b. 3 Jan. 1771

  xi ELIZABETH WHITING, b. 17 March 1773

References: *Bradford Desc* pp. 111-2. Canaan CT VR LR 1:427(m.). Canaan CT LR 2:228(b. Mary), 232(b. William), 238(b. Anna), 239(b. Elizabeth): VR A:3(b. Sarah), A:4(b. Gamaliel). Plymouth Co. LR 60:112(heirs Elizabeth Noyes). *Great Barrington VR* p. 88(bur. Gam).

359. WILLIAM BRADFORD WHITING[5] (*Elizabeth[4] Bradford, Samuel[3], William[2-1]*), bp. New London, Conn., 11 April 1731; d. Canaan, N.Y., 13 Oct. 1796.

He m. (1) Norwich, Conn., 10 April 1754 **ABIGAIL CARREW**, b. Norwich, Conn., 28 Feb. 1728/9; d. there 20 May 1756 aged 27; daughter of Thomas and Abigail (Huntington) Carrew.

He m. (2) Norwich, Conn., 24 July 1757 **AMY LOTHROP**, b. Norwich, Conn., 13 Aug. 1735; d. 20 Jan. 1815; daughter of Nathaniel and Ann (Backus) Lothrop.

On 15 May 1771 William Bradford Whiting of New Canaan, N.Y., sold to Azariah Lothrop of Norwich three-quarters of an acre with buildings.

On 9 Oct. 1780 the heirs of Elizabeth Noyes, deceased, sold land in Kingston that had been given to her and [her sisters] Jerusha Gay, Hannah Gilbert, and Wealthea Lane. These heirs included William B. Whiting of New Canaan, Albany Co., N.Y.

It is written of him in *Canaan NY Reflections:*

    His brother Gamaliel was a proprietor on the Indian Deed and he came to Canaan in 1763. Life here was too rugged for him, so in 1765 he turned his interests over to William. It was then that a grist mill was erected at the outlet of the pond which was to bear the family's name. William was elected first supervisor of the King's District and served two terms. In 1775 he was appointed clerk of the Committee of Correspondence and Safety. On June 24, 1776 he was chairman at the meeting to elect delegates to the Continental Congress and to direct these delegates to vote for independence. He was commissioned and he served as Colonel of the 17th Regiment of Albany County Militia during the entire revolution. His Regiment was under General Horatio Gates and they were present at the Battle of Saratoga and the surrender of Burgoyne. His mill, filled with government grain, was burned by the Loyalists at that time. He was State Senator from 1781 – 1785. He was appointed a judge at the formation of Columbia County in 1786. In 1792 he was one of the judges who found the men who were tried, not guilty, of the murder of Cornelius Hogeboom, the high sheriff who was killed by the anti-renters when he was preforming the duties of his office.

Child of William Bradford and Abigail (Carrew) Whiting, b. Norwich, Conn.:

  i ABIGAIL WHITING⁶, b. 12 May 1756; d. Norwich, Conn., 20 March 1757

Children of William Bradford and Amy (Lothrop) Whiting, first four b. Norwich, Conn.:

  ii   WILLIAM WHITING⁶, b. 29 May 1758; d. 4 May 1759

  iii ABIGAIL WHITING, b. 4 Feb. 1759

  iv   ANNA WHITING, b. 8 Feb. 1762

  v   JOHN WHITING, b. 4 Feb. 1764

  vi   WILLIAM B. WHITING, b. 17 April 1766

  vii DANIEL WHITING, b. 23 May 1768

  viii HANNAH WHITING, b. 8 May 1770; d. 1781

  ix   NATHAN WHITING, b. 16 May 1772

  x   SAMUEL WHITING, b. 10 Oct. 1776

  xi   HARRIET WHITING, b. 14 Sept. 1779; d. 13 July 1804

  xii CHARLES WHITING, b. 13 Jan. 1783; d. 1783

References: *Bradford Desc* p. 112. *VR Of Eastern NY* by Bowman p. 282(d. William). *Norwich CT VR* 1:94(b. Abig.), 112(b. Amy); 334(both m.; b. 1ˢᵗ 3 ch.; d. Abigail), 397(b. Anna, John). Norwich CT LR 19:271. Plymouth Co. LR 60:112(heirs Elizabeth Noyes). *Canaan NY Reflections* p. 8(quote).

360. EBENEZER WHITING⁵ (*Elizabeth⁴ Bradford, Samuel³, William²⁻¹*), b. New London, Conn., 18 May 1735; d. Norwich, Conn., 6 Sept. 1794.

He m. Windham, Conn., 29 Nov. 1767 **ANN FITCH**, b. Windham, Conn., 18 April 1747; d. 27 June 1827 aged 80 (Aspinwall), bur. Norwich City Cemetery; daughter of Eleazer and Amy (Bowen) Fitch.

On 9 Oct. 1780 the heirs of Elizabeth Noyes, deceased, sold land in Kingston that had been given to her and [her sisters] Jerusha Gay, Hannah Gilbert, and Wealthea Lane. These heirs included Ebenezer Whiting of Norwich.

Ebenʳ Whiting's household as listed in New London Co. in the 1790 census consisted of 3 men over 16, 4 boys, 6 females, and 2 slaves.

On 16 Sept. 1794 Nancy Whiting and Augustus Whiting were appointed administrators of the estate of Major Ebenezer Whiting. An account of 25 Nov. 1794 listed a bill to [outfit?] daughters Bernice and Charlotte. An account of 30 March 1795 listed a bill for making a coffin for Charlotte. In the estate papers is a copy of a bond dated 1 Jan. 1794 in which Ebenezer Whiting and Benadam Dennison are bound to the United States of America; they agree to remove distilled spirits from "a certain Distillery situated at Norwich now belonging to Ebenezer Whiting & under the superintendance or Management of sᵈ Whiting" within 3 months.

On 7 Oct. 1794 Hezekiah Perkins was appointed guardian of Bowen Whiting, Charles Whiting, Edward Whiting, Elizabeth Whiting, Henry Whiting, and Nancy Whiting, children of Major Ebenezer Whiting. On 10 Oct. 1794 Hezekiah Perkins, as guardian to the children, "that the sᵈ Deceased died possessed of about three acres of Improved Land with a Dwelling House thereon, a Distillery & about thirty Acres of woodland Lying in sᵈ Norwich – that said Decᵈ a short time before his Death had agreed to purchase a Farm of about three hunᵈ Acres of Land in Kinderhook in the State of New York ... & for the purpose of making payment therefor it is necessary to make Sale of sᵈ Houses & Land at Norwich ... & to Invest the avails thereof in sᵈ Farm at Kinderhook for the Benefit of sᵈ Minors." The General Assembly of Connecticut agreed.

Children of Ebenezer and Ann (Fitch) Whiting, b. Norwich, Conn., (ii-ix from Aspinwall):

    i   AUGUSTUS WHITING⁶, b. 18 Nov. 1768

   ii   EDWARD WHITING

  iii   HENRY WHITING

  iv   NANCY WHITING

    v   CHARLES WHITING

    vi BOWEN WHITING

    vii BETSEY WHITING

    viii CHARLOTTE WHITING, b. ca. 1771; d. 15 Oct 1794 ae 23, bur. Old
         Norwich Town Cemetery.

    ix BERNICE WHITING

References: *Bradford Desc* p. 112. Windham CT VR 2:26(b. Ann); 3:35(b. Augustus), 43(m.). *Norwich CT VR* 1:449(m., b. Augustus). Plymouth Co. LR 60:112(heirs Elizabeth Noyes). Hale Cem Coll:Norwich p. 600(d. Charlotte); 639(d. Ann). Norwich CT PD #11434(Ebenezer Whiting); #11428(guard.).

361.   CALVIN GAY[5] (*Jerusha*[4] *Bradford, Samuel*[3], *William*[2-1]), b. Hingham 1 Sept. 1724; d. Quebec 11 March 1765 aged 40 yrs, d. of small pox; buried Quebec on the north side of the Cathedral.

He m. Hingham 2 April 1752 **MARY SMITH** of Sandwich.

On 11 May 1765 Martin Gay of Boston, gentleman, was appointed administrator of the estate of Calvin Gay late of Quebec in the Province of Canada, formerly of Boston, merchant. The inventory of 7 Aug. 1765 mentions goods in the possession of his widow Mary.

    Child of Calvin and Mary (Smith) Gay:

    i   CHRISTIANA GAY[6], b. 1752

References: *Bradford Desc* p. 112. *Hingham Hist* 2:265. Suffolk Co. PR #13626(Calvin Gay). *Boston News Obits* 1:418(d. Calvin).

362.   MARTIN GAY[5] (*Jerusha*[4] *Bradford, Samuel*[3], *William*[2-1]), b. Hingham 29 Dec. 1726; d. Boston 13 Feb. 1809 aged 82 yrs.

He m. (1) Boston 27 Feb. 1749 [or 13 Dec. 1750 in New North Ch.] **MARY PINCKNEY**, b. Boston 7 March 1729; d. there 15 Nov. 1764; daughter of John and Elizabeth (Gretian) Pinckney.

He m. (2) Boston 24 Oct. 1765 **RUTH ATKINS** of Hingham, b. ca. 1736; d. 12 Sept. 1810 aged 74 yrs.

At a Boston Selectmen's meeting on 17 Jan. 1749, Martin Gay was admitted to the North Engine. At a meeting 7 April 1758, "the Governer having upon application made to Him been pleased to Excuse One hundred men from Military duty for the Service of the Several Engines in the Town." Martin Gay was one of the nine men approved for Engine No. 2.

At Boston town meetings on 13 March 1758, 9 March 1761, and 8 March 1762, Martin Gay was chosen as a hayward.

On 30 Sept. 1760 Ebenezer Gay and his wife Jerusha sold to their son Martin Gay of Boston her one-quarter interest in a Union Street property that had been devised to her by her mother Hannah Bradford.

Martin Gay was chosen a member of the Ancient and Honourable Artillery Company in 1761, lieutenant in 1770, and captain in 1772.

At Boston town meetings on 14 March 1763, 20 Feb. 1764, 12 March 1765, and 10 March 1766, Martin Gay was chosen as an assay master.

On 4 Nov. 1765 William Edwards, servant to Martin Gay, arrived in the port of Boston on the sloop *Salley* from Quebec.

At Boston town meetings on 9 March 1767 and 14 March 1768, Capt. Martin Gay was chosen as a fireward and at the same meetings as well as 13 March 1769, he was also chosen as an assay master.

At a selectmen's meeting in June 1770, it was "Voted, that there be a visitation of the Free Schools in this Town on Wednesday the 4th of July next, & that the following Gentlemen be invited to accompany the Selectmen..." Martin Gay was one of the gentlemen. On 25 June 1772 and 5 May 1773, Capt. Martin Gay, an overseer of the poor, again was chosen to accompany the selectmen on a visit to the Free Schools.

At a Boston town meeting on 15 Oct. 1770, Martin Gay was chosen one of the 12 wardens of the town. At the same meeting he was chosen a surveyor of wheat. On 9 March 1772 and 8 March 1773, he was chosen one of the 16 firewards and a surveyor of wheat. On 14 March 1774 he was chosen as a fireward and as an assay master.

In the 1771 Valuation List, Martin Gay appears in Boston with 3 polls, 1 house, 1 tanhouse, £420:14:2 in merchandise, and 1 head of cattle.

On 26 April 1775 M. Gay appears on "A List of the Persons Names who lodge their Arms with the Selectmen pursuant to a Vote by them passed yesterday." He lodged two guns with them.

He was a Loyalist and was captured in November 1775 on the sloop *Polly* and taken prisoner. He returned to Boston in 1792.

On 3 May 1790 Martin Gay, Esq., of Westmoreland N.B. (now residing in Boston) sold to Jotham Gay of Hingham, Esq., his interest in one-quarter part of the real estate that Ebenezer Gay had given in his will equally to his four children, Martin, Jotham, Abigail, and Jerusha.

In the 1798 Direct Tax, Martin Gay is listed as the owner of a lot of land with copper works and shop situated at the back of the Gay house on Union

Street valued at $1,000 and of a 3-story brick house with 34 windows on Union Street valued at $3,500.

The will of Martin Gay of Boston, gentleman, proved 13 Feb. 1809, names son Samuel Gay of Westmorland in the Province of New Brunswick; daughter Mary Black wife of Rev. William Black of Halifax, N.S.; daughter Frances Winslow wife of Isaac Winslow of Marshfield; grandson Martin Black, son of William and Mary; grandson Martin Gay son of Ebenezer Gay and Mary Alline Gay; and his wife. Widow Ruth Gay refused to be executrix 13 Feb. 1809.

Children of Martin and Mary (Pinckney) Gay, b. prob. Boston and Hingham:

  i CELIA GAY[6], b. ca. 1752 (ae 20 at m. in 1772)

  ii SAMUEL GAY, b. ca. 1754

 iii MARY GAY, b. 7 Jan. 1755; bp. Brattle St. Church 13 Jan. 1754(?)

 iv ELIZABETH GAY, bp. Brattle St. Church 19 Feb. 1758

  v MARTIN GAY, b. 1760, bp. Brattle St. Church 20 July 1760; d. 17 April 1778 ae 18 yrs.

 vi FRANCES GAY (dau.) , bp. West Church April 1763

 vii PINCKNEY GAY, bp. West Church 18 Nov. 1764; d. April 1773

Children of Martin and Ruth (Atkins) Gay, b. prob. Boston and Hingham:

 viii EBENEZER GAY, bp. Brattle St. Ch. and West Ch. 21 Sept. 1766; d.y.

 ix EBENEZER GAY, bp. West Ch. 24 Feb. 1771

  x PINCKNEY GAY, bp. 2 July 1775; d. ae 2 weeks

References: *Bradford Desc* pp. 112-3. *Hingham Hist* 2:265. *NEHGR* 84:144(m. Celia), 167, 171(2nd m.), 268, 363; 85:21, 119. *BRC* 24:194(b. Mary); 28:247(1st m.); 30:424(2nd m.). *Hist A.&H.A.C.* 2:106. *The Loyalists of Mass* p. 143. Suffolk Co. LR 95:198(Ebenezer Gay); 180:14(Martin Gay). Brattle St. Ch. pp. 175(bp. Mary), 177(bp. Elizabeth), 179(bp. Martin), 183(bp. Ebenezer). West Ch. pp. 268(bp. Frances), 269(bp. Pinkney), 272(bp. Ebenezer), 277(bp. Ebenezer). *1771 Valuation* p. 22. *BRC* 17:232; 16:3, 50, 70(hayward), 84, 110, 136, 168, 204, 236, 270(assay master), 199, 233(fireward); 18:40(warden), 43, 65, 68, 111, 114, 130,151, 156(fireward, surveyor of wheat, assay master); 19:79(Engine Co.); 22:27, 239(1798 Direct Tax); 23:63, 132(school visits), 132(overseer of the poor); 29:272(William Edwards), 328(lodged guns).

363.   JERUSHA GAY[5] (*Jerusha[4] Bradford, Samuel[3], William[2-1]*), b. Hingham 17 March 1734/5; d. Boston Jan. 1812 aged 76.

She m. Hingham 29 Nov. 1790 **SIMEON HOWARD**, b. Bridgewater 29 April 1733; d. Boston 13 Aug. 1804 aged 71; son of David and Bethiah

(Leonard) Howard. Simeon m. (1) Boston 3 Dec. 1771 ELIZABETH (CLARKE) MAYHEW with whom he had John Clark, Algernon Sidney, and Jonathan Mayhew.

Simeon Howard graduated from Harvard in 1758 and first taught school in Dedham and Hingham. On 6 May 1767 he became the third minister at Boston's West Church. He was a member of the American Academy of Arts and Sciences, the Society for the Propagation of the Gospel in North America, the Massachusetts Humane Society, the Massachusetts Congregational Charitable Society, and the Massachusetts Convention of Congregational Ministers, and he served on the editorial board of the *Boston Magazine*.

Simeon Howard's household in 1790 in Boston consisted of 2 men 16 or older, 1 boy, 1 female, and 1 other free person.

Simeon and Jerusha Howard had no children.

References: *Bradford Desc* p. 113. *VR Bridgewater* 1:141(b. Simeon). *BRC* 30:301(m.). *Hingham Hist* 2:386(m.; b. ch.). *Harvard Grads* 14:279-89. *Dexter's Memorandum* p. 276(d.Jerusha).

364. HANNAH LANE⁵ (*Welthea⁴ Bradford, Samuel³, William²⁻¹*), b. Hingham 27 May 1724; living 11 Nov. 1780.

She m. Hingham 18 Feb. 1744/5 **SAMUEL JOHNSON**; living 11 Nov. 1780.

On 13 May 1760 Peter Lane, yeoman, George Lane, Gentleman, Samuel Johnson, mariner, and his wife Hannah, Syble Lane and Sarah Lane, both singlewomen, all of Hingham, Ebenezer Wisweall and his wife Irania, and Daniel Johnson and his wife Lucie, all of Worcester, all children and heirs of Welthian Lane, deceased, late wife of Peter Lane, sold to Martin Gay of Boston their share of land in Boston. On 19 May 1760 the same grantors sold their right in 20 acres sold by Gershom Bradford and one-quarter part of 10 acres bought of Gershom.

On 27 March 1764 Ebenezer Wiswall, glazier, and his wife Irana; Daniel Johnson, yeoman, of Worcester; John Holbrook and his wife Sibyl; and Sarah Lane, spinster, of Hingham quitclaimed to Samuel Johnson of Hingham their interests in land in Scituate, formerly owned by Peter Lane, deceased.

On 11 Nov. 1780 Samuel Johnson of Hingham, taylor, and his wife Hannah sold to Levi Lincoln of Hingham, Gentleman, 8 acres at Broad Cove.

Children of Samuel and Hannah (Lane) Johnson, b. Hingham:

    i HANNAH JOHNSON⁶, b. 16 Jan. 1745/6

    ii CELIA JOHNSON, b. 8 April 1748; d. 15 Feb. 1751/2

   iii ESTHER JOHNSON, b. 22 Jan. 1749/50

   iv CELIA JOHNSON, b. 5 Aug. 1752; d. 9 April 1754

   v PEREZ JOHNSON, b. 10 Dec. 1754; d. 8 Dec. 1757

   vi CELIA JOHNSON, b. 28 Oct. 1756

   vii BENOIS (alias ADRIANENSENS) JOHNSON, bp. 13 June 1762

References: *Bradford Desc* p. 113. *Hingham Hist* 2:386. Suffolk Co. LR 95:197(heirs of Welthea Lane); 139:130(Samuel Johnson). Plymouth Co. LR 57:3(heirs Peter Lane).

365. IRENE LANE[5] (*Welthea*[4] *Bradford, Samuel*[3], *William*[2-1]), b. Hingham 6 Jan. 1725/6; d. Worcester 31 Dec. 1792 aged 76y.

She m. Hingham 10 Oct. 1748 **EBENEZER WISWELL**, b. Dorchester 10 June 1722; d. Worcester 19 March 1809 aged 87y; son of Ebenezer and Ann (Copen) Wiswell.

On 13 May 1760 Peter Lane, yeoman, George Lane, Gentleman, Samuel Johnson, mariner, and his wife Hannah, Syble Lane and Sarah Lane, both singlewomen, all of Hingham, Ebenezer Wisweall and his wife Irania, and Daniel Johnson and his wife Lucie, all of Worcester, all children and heirs of Welthian Lane, deceased, late wife of Peter Lane sold to Martin Gay of Boston their share of land in Boston. On 19 May 1760 the same grantors sold their right in 20 acres sold by Gershom Bradford and one-quarter part of 10 acres bought of Gershom.

On 27 March 1764 Ebenezer Wiswall, glazier, and his wife Irana; Daniel Johnson, yeoman, of Worcester; John Holbrook and his wife Sibyl; and Sarah Lane, spinster, of Hingham quitclaimed to Samuel Johnson of Hingham their interests in land in Scituate, formerly owned by Peter Lane, deceased.

Ebenezer Wiswell served as a private in Capt. Timothy Bigelow's company, Col. Artemas Ward's regiment which marched on the alarm on 10 April 1775. He also served in Capt. Jonas Hubbard's company, Col. Jonathan Ward's regiment; he enlisted on 24 April 1775 and served until 1 Aug. 1775.

Ebenezer Wiswall's household in Worcester in 1790 consisted of 4 men 16 or older, 2 boys, and 2 females.

Children of Ebenezer and Irene (Lane) Wiswall, b. Worcester:

   i SARAH WISWALL[6], b. 15 Dec. 1749

   ii SAMUEL WISWALL, b. 13 April 1752

   iii EBENEZER WISWALL, b. 17 Oct. 1754

   iv IRENE WISWALL, b. 18 March 1757

v DAVID WISWALL, b. 8 May 1759

vi HANNAH WISWALL, b. 12 Aug. 1761

vii DANIEL WISWALL, b. 13 Oct. 1763

viii JOHN WISWALL, b. 26 April 1770

References: *Bradford Desc* p. 113. *VR Worcester* pp. 284(b. ch.). *Worcester Inscrip* p. 67(d. Ebenezer, Irene). Suffolk Co. LR 95:197(heirs of Welthea Lane). Plymouth Co. LR57:3(heirs Peter Lane). *MSSR* 17:663(Ebenezer Wiswell).

366. GEORGE LANE⁵ (*Welthea⁴ Bradford, Samuel³, William²⁻¹*), b. Hingham 6 June 1731; d. there 12 May 1790 aged 59.

He m. Hingham 14 May 1752 **ELIZABETH THAXTER**, b. Hingham 6 Sept. 1732; d. there 29 Dec. 1801 aged 69 yrs.; daughter of John and Grace (Stockbridge) Thaxter.

On 13 May 1760 Peter Lane, yeoman, George Lane, Gentleman, Samuel Johnson, mariner, and his wife Hannah, Syble Lane and Sarah Lane, both singlewomen, all of Hingham, Ebenezer Wisweall and his wife Irania, and Daniel Johnson and his wife Lucie, all of Worcester, all children and heirs of Welthian Lane, deceased, late wife of Peter Lane, sold to Martin Gay of Boston their share of land in Boston. On 19 May 1760 the same grantors sold their right in 20 acres sold by Gershom Bradford and one-quarter part of 10 acres bought of Gershom.

On 20 May 1760 Peter Lane of Hingham, yeoman, sold to George Lane of Hingham, Gentleman, a tract near his dwelling house with a house occupied by George.

On 25 April 1768 John Holbrook of Boston, husbandman, and his wife Sybil sold to George Lane of Hingham 35 acres of land.

The inventory of Capt. George Lane of Hingham, yeoman, taken on 1 Sept. 1790 included a pew in the North Meetinghouse. On 2 Nov. 1790 the estate was declared insolvent and the widow Elizabeth was allowed £30 in personal estate.

On 21 July 1792 George Bradford Lane formerly of Hingham now of Hillsborough, N.B., shipwright, gives his power of attorney to Martin Gay of Boston now a resident of Westmoreland, N.B., to sell all real and personal estate from the estate of his father Capt. George Lane late of Hingham deceased. On 15 April 1794 George Bradford Lane by his attorney Martin Gay, William Cushing, leather dresser, of Hingham and his wife Elizabeth, and Lucy Lane of Hingham, preceptress, heirs of their father George Lane, sold to Benjamin Lincoln of Hingham three-fifths of 28 acres bounded on land that

Ferdinand Lane died siezed of. On 12 April 1794 William Cushing administrator of the estate of Ferdinand Lane sold to Benjamin Lincoln another one-fifth. On 1 May 1794 George B. Lane by his attorney Martin Gay, William Cushing and his wife Elizabeth, Lucy Lane, and William Cushing as guardian of Conway Lane a minor son of Capt. George Lane sold one acre of salt meadow to Benjamin Lincoln and two pieces of property to Jotham Lincoln.

Children of George and Elizabeth (Thaxter) Lane, b. Hingham:

  i   GEORGE LANE[6], b. 4 Jan. 1754
  ii PETER LANE, bp. 21 March 1756; d. 5 Jan. 1758
  iii PETER LANE, b. 30 May 1758; d. at sea 1779
  iv GEORGE BRADFORD LANE, b. 20 July 1763
  v   LUCY LANE, b. 30 Nov. 1765
  vi FERDINAND LANE, bp. 16 Oct. 1768; d. 10 Sept. 1793
  vii CONWAY LANE, b. 25 Sept. 1778

References: *Bradford Desc* p. 114. *Hingham Hist* 2:416-7(m.; b. ch.; deaths). Suffolk Co. LR 94:143(Peter Lane); 95:197(Peter Lane *et al.*); 119:57(John Holbrook); 178:91(power of attorney), 92(George B. Lane *et al.* and William Cushing); 178:122, 124(George B. Lane *et al.*). Suffolk Co. Admin. #19520, 89:620(George Lane).

367. LUCY LANE[5] (*Welthea[4] Bradford, Samuel[3], William[2-1]*), b. Hingham 16 March 1734/5; buried Worcester 5 Dec. 1762.

She m. Hingham 19 Nov. 1754 **DANIEL JOHNSON**, b. 1725; d. 1802; son of Solomon Johnson.

On 13 May 1760 Peter Lane, yeoman, George Lane, Gentleman, Samuel Johnson, mariner, and his wife Hannah, Syble Lane and Sarah Lane, both singlewomen, all of Hingham, Ebenezer Wisweall and his wife Irania, and Daniel Johnson and his wife Lucie, all of Worcester, all children and heirs of Welthian Lane, deceased, late wife of Peter Lane, sold to Martin Gay of Boston their share of land in Boston. On 19 May 1760 the same grantors sold their right in 20 acres sold by Gershom Bradford and one-quarter part of 10 acres bought of Gershom.

On 27 March 1764 Ebenezer Wiswall, glazier, and his wife Irana; Daniel Johnson, yeoman, of Worcester; John Holbrook and his wife Sibyl; and Sarah Lane, spinster, of Hingham quitclaimed to Samuel Johnson of Hingham their interests in land in Scituate, formerly owned by Peter Lane, deceased.

In the 1771 Valuation List, Daniel Johnson appears in Worcester with 1 poll, 1 horse, 2 oxen, 2 cattle, 2 goats or sheep, 2 swine, 3 acres of pasture, 4 acres of tillage which produced 40 bushels of grain, and 4 acres of upland which produced 4 tons of hay.

On 26 Aug. 1783 Daniel Johnson of Worcester, miller, sold to his son John Johnson of Worcester, laborer, three parcels of land totaling more than 30 acres that "I hold by deed from Gardner Chandler."

Children of Daniel and Lucy (Lane) Johnson, b. Worcester:

    i   WEALTHEAN JOHNSON[6], b. 25 Jan. 1756

   ii   DANIEL JOHNSON, b. 29 May 1757

  iii   NATHAN JOHNSON, b. 14 Jan. 1759

  iv JOHN JOHNSON, b. 28 Dec. 1760

   v   LUCY JOHNSON (twin), b. 21 Nov. 1762

  vi LYDIA JOHNSON (twin), b. 21 Nov. 1762

References: *Bradford Desc* p. 114. *Hingham Hist* 2:385(m.). *VR Worcester* pp. 148-52(b. ch.), 150(d. Lucy); 370(m.). Suffolk Co. LR 95:197(heirs of Welthea Lane). Plymouth Co. LR 57:3(heirs Peter Lane). Worcester Co. LR 89:295(Daniel Johnson). *1771 Valuation* p. 374.

368. SYBIL LANE[5] (*Welthea[4] Bradford, Samuel[3], William[2-1]*), b. Hingham 26 July 1741; buried Franklin, Vt., 6 June 1819 aged 74.

She m. Hingham 17 Nov. 1760 **JOHN HOLBROOK**, b. Weymouth 7 June 1730; bur. Franklin, Vt., 15 Jan. 1815 aged 84; son of John and Sarah (Hunt) Holbrook.

On 13 May 1760 Peter Lane, yeoman, George Lane, Gentleman, Samuel Johnson, mariner, and his wife Hannah, Syble Lane and Sarah Lane, both singlewomen, all of Hingham, Ebenezer Wisweall and his wife Irania, and Daniel Johnson and his wife Lucie, all of Worcester, all children and heirs of Welthian Lane, deceased, late wife of Peter Lane, sold to Martin Gay of Boston their share of land in Boston. On 19 May 1760 the same grantors sold their right in 20 acres sold by Gershom Bradford and one-quarter part of 10 acres bought of Gershom.

On 27 March 1764 Ebenezer Wiswall, glazier, and his wife Irana; Daniel Johnson, yeoman, of Worcester; John Holbrook and his wife Sibyl; and Sarah Lane, spinster, of Hingham quitclaimed to Samuel Johnson of Hingham their interests in land in Scituate formerly owned by Peter Lane, deceased.

On 25 April 1768 John Holbrook of Boston, husbandman, and his wife Sybil sold to George Lane of Hingham 35 acres of land.

In the Revolutionary War, John Holbrook served as a sergeant in Capt. Thomas White's company, Col. Joseph Palmer's regiment in March 1776 and in Capt. Samuel Holbrook's company, Col. Bass' regiment in June 1776. He was a First Lieutenant in Capt. Silas Wild's company, Col. Ebenezer Thayer's regiment in July 1777.

Children of John and Sybil (Lane) Holbrook, first b. Weymouth; rest b. Newfane, Vt.:

   i   JOHN HOLBROOK[6], b. 10 July 1761

   ii   SALLY HOLBROOK, b. 1763

   iii   SYLVANUS HOLBROOK, b. 1770

   iv   WEALTHEA HOLBROOK, b. 1772

   v   JOANNA HOLBROOK, b. 12 Aug. 1778

   vi   GEORGE BRADFORD HOLBROOK, b. 11 Sept. 1782; Bible abstract says, b. 1781; g.s. says, b. 12 Sept. 1790

References: *Bradford Desc* p. 114. *VR Weymouth* 1:132(b. both John), 2:111(int.). *Hingham Hist* 2:414-5(b. Sybil). Suffolk Co. LR 95:197(heirs of Welthea Lane); 119:57(John Holbrook). Plymouth Co. LR 57:3(heirs Peter Lane). GS#60857(Bible abstract; g.s. photo). *MSSR* 8:80.

369. SARAH LANE[5] (*Welthea[4] Bradford, Samuel[3], William[2-1]*), b. Hingham 6 Oct. 1745; d. there 17 April 1821 aged 76 yrs.

She m. Hingham 15 Sept. 1765 **THOMAS JONES**, b. Hingham 4 Nov. 1742; d. there 19 Feb. 1808 aged 65 yrs; son of Thomas and Mary (Marsh) Jones.

On 13 May 1760 Peter Lane, yeoman, George Lane, Gentleman, Samuel Johnson, mariner, and his wife Hannah, Syble Lane and Sarah Lane, both singlewomen, all of Hingham, Ebenezer Wisweall and his wife Irania, and Daniel Johnson and his wife Lucie, all of Worcester, all children and heirs of Welthian Lane, deceased, late wife of Peter Lane, sold to Martin Gay of Boston their share of land in Boston. On 19 May 1760 the same grantors sold their right in 20 acres sold by Gershom Bradford and one-quarter part of 10 acres bought of Gershom.

On 27 March 1764 Ebenezer Wiswall, glazier, and his wife Irana; Daniel Johnson, yeoman, of Worcester; John Holbrook and his wife Sibyl; and Sarah Lane, spinster, of Hingham quitclaimed to Samuel Johnson of Hingham their interests in land in Scituate, formerly owned by Peter Lane, deceased.

Thomas Jones served as a sergeant in Capt. Peter Cushing's company, Col. David Cushing's regiment for 6 days; the company assembled at Hull 27 Feb. 1778. He also served in Capt. Theophilus Wilder's company, Col. David Cushing's regiment; engaged 4 March 1778 and discharged 4 April 1778.

Children of Thomas and Sarah (Lane) Jones, b. Hingham:

    i   THOMAS JONES[6], b. 11 Dec. 1765

    ii BELA JONES, b. 6 Sept. 1767; d. 20 Oct. 1768

    iii SARAH JONES, b. 27 April 1769; d. 28 March 1790; unm.

    iv MARY JONES, b. 18 Jan. 1771

    v   LUCY JONES, b. 27 Oct. 1772; d. 7 March 1777

    vi EMMA JONES, b. 29 Dec. 1774

    vii LUCY JONES, b. 26 May 1777

   viii KATY JONES, b. 7 Jan. 1780

    ix BELA JONES, b. 22 Aug. 1785

    x   SARAH JONES, b. 26 Oct. 1790

References: *Bradford Desc* pp. 114-5. *Hingham Hist* 2:389-91. Suffolk Co. LR 95:197(heirs of Welthea Lane). Plymouth Co. LR 57:3(heirs Peter Lane). *MSSR* 8:964(Thomas Jones).

370. ABIGAIL[5] BRADFORD (*Gamaliel[4], Samuel[3], William[2-1]*), b. Duxbury 24 Sept. 1728; living 20 April 1784 (deed).

She m. Kingston 15 Dec. 1748 **WAIT WADSWORTH**, b. Duxbury 23 Oct. 1714; d. there 5 June 1799 aged 84y 7m 2d (called "Capt. Waight"); son of Elisha and Elizabeth (Wiswall) Wadsworth.

On 18 June 1756 Abiah Wadsworth of Meduncook; Wait Wadsworth, husbandman, and Elizabeth Wadsworth, spinster, both of Duxborough divided land that was the homestead farm of their father Mr. Elisha Wadsworth, deceased.

The court records show that Wait Wadsworth served the town of Duxbury as a selectman at least eight times from 1759 to 1773. He was granted a license to sell tea from 1760 to 1764 and to sell liquor from 1761 to 1764.

On 4 July 1764 Wait Wadsworth of Duxbury, Gentleman, sold land in Duxbury to Samuel Drew; wife Abigail also signed. On 28 April 1777 Wait Wadsworth of Duxborough, husbandman, sold his farm in Duxborough to John Faunce; wife Abigail also signed.

Both Wait Wadsworth and his son Wait had service in the Revolutionary War. Wait Sr. served as a private in Capt. Nehemiah Allen's company, Col. Theophilus Cotton's regiment on a secret expedition to Rhode Island in September and October 1777. Wait Jr. was a private in Capt. Bildad Arnold's company, Col. Thomas Lothrop's regiment which marched to Rhode Island on the alarm of 10 Dec. 1776.

On 20 April 1784 Wait Wadsworth of Duxborough, Gentleman, sold land in Duxborough to John Samson; wife Abigail also signed.

Wait Wadsworth's household in Duxbury in 1790 consisted of 3 men 16 or older and one female.

No Plymouth County probate records have been found for Wait Wadsworth or deeds from him to his children.

Children of Wait and Abigail (Bradford) Wadsworth, b. Duxbury (first 5 bp. 5 Sept. 1756):

   i   ABIGAIL WADSWORTH[6], b. 3 June 1749

   ii   JOSEPH WADSWORTH, b. 7 July 1750

   iii   AHIRA WADSWORTH, b. 1 Nov. 1751

   iv   SENECA WADSWORTH, b. 9 April 1753

   v   WAIT WADSWORTH, b. 7 Oct. 1754

   vi   CYNTHIA (or CLEANTHOS) WADSWORTH, b. 25 March 1756

   vii   ROBERT WADSWORTH, b. 26 Sept. 1757; d. 25 April 1760 ae 2y 7m

   viii   EDEN WADSWORTH, b. 12 May 1759; drowned 30 April 1818 ae 59y; unm. No probate record..

   ix   BEULAH WADSWORTH, b. 18 June 1762

   x   CELANNA M. WADSWORTH, b. 9 Dec. 1763

   xi   ELISHA WADSWORTH, b. 15 June 1765; drowned at sea 1786. No PR.

   xii   ZILPAH (or ZEPETH) WADSWORTH, b. 5 Oct. 1766

   xiii   WISWALL WADSWORTH, b. 25 Oct. 1768

References: *Bradford Desc* p. 115. *VR Duxbury* pp. 179-84(b. Wait, b. ch.); 221(m.); 431-3(d. Wait, Robert, Eden). *VR Kingston* p. 179(m.). Plymouth Co. LR 43:248(division); 49:137; 59:209: 62:212(Wait Wadsworth). *MD* 11:148(b. Wait). *MSSR* 16:383. *1790 Census MA* p. 169. *Wadsworth Fam* pp. 178, 241. *Plymouth Co Ct Recs* Vol. 3. *MSSR* 16:383(Wait Wadsworth).

371. SAMUEL⁵ BRADFORD (*Gamaliel⁴, Samuel³, William²⁻¹*), b. Duxbury 2 Jan. 1729/30; d. there 17 Feb. 1777 aged 47y 1m 26d.

He m. Kingston 1 Nov. 1749 **GRACE RING**, b. Kingston 6 April 1730; d. Duxbury 20 April 1793 in 64th year [under *Brewster*]; daughter of Samuel and Ruth (Sylvester) Ring, a descendant of Pilgrim **Stephen Hopkins**.

Samuel Bradford was a captain in the Revolutionary War serving in the 1st Duxbury company in Col. Warren's regiment which marched on the alarm of 19 April 1775. He enlisted again on 13 May 1775 and was named on a bounty coat list of 30 Oct. 1775.

On 1 Feb. 1779 son Samuel Bradford posted bond as administrator of the estate of Samuel Bradford; warrants of 4 May 1803 directed the setting off to Isaiah Bradford and Grace Bradford of their shares in both father's and grandfather's estates.

On 1 July 1782 Samuel Bradford of Duxbury, yeoman, as legal representative of his father Samuel Bradford deceased with his uncles, Gamaliel, Seth, Peabody, Peter, and Andrew, agreed to divide 90 acres in Winslow, Maine, that had been given to them by their father or grandfather Gamaliel Bradford, late of Duxbury, deceased. Samuel received two lots of land. On 7 Sept. 1790 his son George Bradford of Bath quitclaimed property in Lincoln County, Maine, to another son, William Bradford of Winslow.

Children of Samuel and Grace (Ring) Bradford, b. Duxbury:

- i DEBORAH⁶ BRADFORD, b. 11 Dec. 1750, bp. 23 May 1756
- ii SAMUEL BRADFORD, b. 27 March 1752, bp. 23 May 1756
- iii LYDIA BRADFORD, b. 6 April 1754, bp. 23 May 1756; d. 7 May 1769 ae 15 yrs.
- iv WILLIAM BRADFORD, b. 25 Nov. 1755
- v WELTHEA BRADFORD, b. 15 Nov. 1757
- vi LYMAN BRADFORD, b. 1 Oct. 1760; d. N.Y. 1776 ae 15; a pvt. in the Revolution
- vii GRACE BRADFORD, bp. 19 June 1763; d.y.
- viii ELIHU BRADFORD, bp. 16 June 1765; d. 1781 in Philadelphia, Pa.; unm.
- ix GRACE BRADFORD, b. 6 April 1765
- x GEORGE BRADFORD, b. 20 Nov. 1767; d. 1791 West Indies.
- xi ISAIAH BRADFORD, b. 25 Nov. 1769

References: *VR Duxbury* pp. 28-32(b. ch.), 353(d. Samuel, Lydia). *VR Kingston* pp. 121(b. Grace), 182(m.). *Bradford Desc* p. 115. Plymouth Co. PR #2600(Samuel Bradford). *MF*

6:514-5. *MSSR* 2:407. Kennebec Co. LR 5:206(Samuel Bradford, copy of Lincoln Co. LR). Lincoln Co. LR 5:208-9(George Bradford).

372. GAMALIEL[5] BRADFORD (*Gamaliel[4], Samuel[3], William[2-1]*), b. Duxbury 2 Sept. 1731; d. there 4 Jan. 1807 aged 75.

He m. (1) Duxbury 10 March 1757 **SARAH ALDEN**, b. Duxbury 2 Dec. 1731; d. there 4 Aug. 1788; daughter of Samuel and Sarah (Sprague) Alden, a descendant of Pilgrim **John Alden**. The will of Samuel Alden dated 10 Nov. 1779 names daughter Sarah Bradford, wife of Gamaliel.

He m. (2) Boston 24 Nov. 1790 **MARY (TILESTON) COOPER**, b. ca. 1751; bp. Boston 10 Nov. 1751; d. Duxbury 25 Feb. 1833 aged 82; daughter of Onesiphorous and Judith (Peirce) Tileston. She m. (1) Boston 24 June 1773 JACOB COOPER. In Oct. 1801 Onesiphorus Tileston of Dorchester, Sarah Clap of Boston, widow, and Gamaliel Bradford of Duxbury and his wife Mary, sold all their right in a mansion house in Boston formerly owned by their father Onesiphorus Tileston and all right in the estate of Benjamin Tileston late of Boston.

Gamaliel Bradford was a colonel in the Revolutionary War. He was a private in Col. Thomas Marshall's regiment from 28 May 1776 to 1 Dec. 1776. He was paid for service in the Continental Army from 1 Jan. 1777 to 31 Dec. 1779. On 28 Dec. 1779 he was commissioned an ensign and a Lieutenant on 16 April 1780. On 18 Oct. 1782 he was granted leave by Gen. Washington to go to Duxbury. He was granted bounty land 5 Sept. 1789.

On 1 July 1782 Gamaliel Bradford, Esq., Seth Bradford, Gentleman, Peabody Bradford, yeoman, Peter Bradford, yeoman, all of Duxbury, Andrew Bradford of Pembrook, Gentleman, and Samuel Bradford of Duxbury, yeoman, as legal representative of his father Samuel Bradford deceased, agreed to divide 90 acres in Winslow, Me., given to them by their father or grandfather Gamaliel Bradford. Gamaliel received two lots.

Gam[l] Bradford was listed as head of a household consisting of 6 men 16 or older, 1 boy, and 3 females in Duxbury in the 1790 census.

In the 1798 Direct Tax for Boston, Gamaliel is listed as the owner and occupier of a 2-story wooden dwelling with 26 windows on South St. valued at $3,000.

The will of Gamaliel Bradford of Duxbury dated 7 March 1796, proved 31 Jan. 1807, names wife; sons Perez and Gamaliel Bradford, executors; son Alden; and daughters Sophia Bradford, Sarah Bradford, and Jerusha Weston. A codicil dated 15 June 1802 states that Perez is dead and adds bequests to grandchildren Samuel Cooper Bradford and Judith Cooper Bradford children of son Perez, deceased.

On 4 Oct. 1808 Daniel Bradford of Duxbury, mariner, attorney for Gamaliel Bradford of Boston, Gentleman and executor of the last will and testament of Gamaliel Bradford Esq. late of Duxbury, sold to Gershom Bradford of Dorchester, mariner, the homestead farm and several other pieces of land from the estate of Gamaliel Bradford. On 10 Nov. 1809 Gamaliel Bradford sold to Daniel Bradford woodland near little pond.

On 3 June 1816 Gamaliel Bradford of Charlestown, Alden Bradford of Boston, Sophia Bradford and Sarah Hickling of Boston, Gershom Bradford, Ezra Weston Jr. and his wife Jerusha of Duxbury, and Daniel Bradford of Keene, N.H., heirs of the estate of Gamaliel Bradford late of Duxbury, sold to George Colburn and John Crowell Jr. of Winslow, Me., land in Winslow "called No. 2 of the Bradford right." Gamaliel's wife Elizabeth, Alden's wife Margaret, Gershom's wife Sarah, and Daniel's wife Sarah also signed the deed.

See Alden family #373.

Children of Gamaliel and Sarah (Alden) Bradford, b. Duxbury:

  i   PEREZ[6] BRADFORD, b. 14 Nov. 1758

  ii SOPHIA BRADFORD, b. 16 Nov. 1761; living unm. 3 June 1816 (see above deed).

  iii GAMALIEL BRADFORD, b. 4 Nov. 1763

  iv ALDEN BRADFORD, b. 19 Nov. 1765

  v   SARAH BRADFORD, b. 24 Feb. 1768

  vi JERUSHA BRADFORD, b. 3 Nov. 1770

  vii DANIEL BRADFORD, b. 27 Dec. 1771

  viii GERSHOM BRADFORD, b. 3 Feb. 1774

References: *VR Duxbury* pp. 18(b. Sarah), 353(d. Sarah), 352(d. Gamaliel), 28-32(b. all ch.). *Bradford Desc* pp. 115-6. Plymouth Co. PR 42:19-22(Gamaliel Bradford); #2590(Perez Bradford). *NEHGR* 13:122(bp. Mary). *BRC* 30:114(2nd m.), 330 (her 1st m.). *MD* 20:76-8(will of Samuel Alden). *MSSR* 2:402-3. Kennebec Co. ME LR 5:206(Gamaliel *et al.*). Plymouth Co. LR 114:95(Gamaliel Bradford); 115:235(Daniel Bradford). Suffolke Co. LR 199:68(Onesiphorus Tileston). *BRC* [1798 Direct Tax] 22:358. *Rev. War Pensions* 1:356(Gamaliel Bradford).

373. SETH[5] BRADFORD (*Gamaliel[4], Samuel[3], William[2-1]*), b. Duxbury 14 Sept. 1733; d. there 8 Feb. 1823 aged 89y 10m.

He m. Duxbury 7 Feb. 1760 **LYDIA SOUTHWORTH**, b. Duxbury 11 Oct. 1738; d. there 26 Aug. 1802 aged 63y 10m; daughter of Jedediah and Hannah (Scales) Southworth, a descendant of Pilgrim **John Alden**.

On 21 Jan. 1762 Seth Bradford of Duxbury, joiner, and his wife Lydia sold to Nicholas Loring of North Yarmouth, Me., clerk, one-third of half of "Equivalent Lot number Ten" in North Yarmouth, "the same is now divided between the heirs of Jedidiah Southworth, dec., and James Mason Esq.; the other half of the lot is set off to the widow of the dec." On 22 March 1773 Seth and Lydia sold to Edward Brewer of North Yarmouth, yeoman, eight and one-third acres which was one-sixth part of Equivalent Lot number 56 drawn in the right of Thomas Southworth. On 4 June 1793 James Southworth of Duxbury with Seth and Lydia sold to Richmond Loring of North Yarmouth, yeoman, their share of a ten-acre lot. And on 6 Sept. 1796 Seth and Lydia sold to Joseph Humphrey of North Yarmouth, yeoman, 23 acres, it being an undivided sixth part of lot number 17.

Seth was a private in the Revolutionary War serving in Capt. Benjamin Wadsworth's company in Col. James Warren's regiment which marched on the alarm of 19 April 1775.

On 1 July 1782 Gamaliel Bradford, Esq., Seth Bradford, Gentleman, Peabody Bradford, yeoman, Peter Bradford, yeoman, all of Duxbury, Andrew Bradford of Pembrook, Gentleman, and Samuel Bradford of Duxbury, yeoman as legal representative of his father Samuel Bradford deceased, agreed to divide 90 acres in Winslow, Me., given to them by their father or grandfather Gamaliel Bradford. Seth received two lots, and on 22 April 1797 he sold to them to Peter.

Seth Bradford was listed as head of a household consisting of one man, 4 boys, and 5 females in Duxbury in the 1790 census.

On 3 March 1814 Seth Bradford of Duxbury for love and affection gave to his three children, Seth Bradford of Medford, carpenter, James Bradford of Duxbury, mariner, and Abigail Bradford of Duxbury, singlewoman, all his homestead farm with dwelling house and other buildings with 16 acres of upland, a piece of salt meadow, and the woodlot on Island Creek given him in the will of his father, reserving the use and improvement of the farm for his lifetime. On 6 June 1825 Seth sold to Abigail his right in the land conveyed to them by their father Seth Bradford, deceased, being six acres of the homestead with half the house and barn, three and a half acres of salt marsh, and six acres of woodland; Seth's wife Betsey released her dower rights.

Children of Seth and Lydia (Southworth) Bradford, b. Duxbury:

    i   JOEL[6] BRADFORD, bp. 30 Nov. 1760; d. NY 1776 in Rev. War

   ii   ISAAC BRADFORD, bp. 15 May 1763

  iii   LYDIA BRADFORD, b. 6 Aug. 1765, bp. 15 Sept. 1765

  iv   ABIGAIL BRADFORD (twin), b. 20 March 1768, bp. 22 May 1768; d. Duxbury 20 Oct. 1846/7 ae 79y 6m; unm.

   v   HANNAH BRADFORD (twin), b. 20 March 1768, bp. 22 May 1768

  vi   SETH BRADFORD, bp. 13 May 1770

 vii   SARAH BRADFORD, bp. 19 Sept. 1773

viii   SUSANNAH BRADFORD, bp. 19 Sept. 1773

  ix   JOHN BRADFORD, b. 15 May 1776; d. 14 Oct. 1777 (neither date in VRs; this child not included in Alden or in Aspinwall)

   x   JOHN BRADFORD, bp. 6 Sept. 1778; d. 14 Oct. 1793 ae 15

  xi   SOUTHWORTH/SOUTHWARD BRADFORD, bp. 10 Oct. 1780; d. at sea 1804

 xii   JAMES BRADFORD, b. 2 Nov. 1784

References: *VR Duxbury* pp. 27-32(b. ch.), 167(b. Lydia), 223(m.), 353-4(d. Seth, Lydia, Abigail). *Bradford Desc* p. 116. *MSSR* 2:407. Kennebec Co. ME LR 5:206(Gamaliel *et al.*); 8:413(Seth Bradford). Plymouth Co. LR 124:62; 180:150(Seth Bradford). Cumberland Co. LR 13:520; 14:133(Seth Bradford); 24:486(James Southworth); 3:70(Seth Bradford).

374. PEABODY[5] BRADFORD (*Gamaliel[4], Samuel[3], William[2-1]*), b. Duxbury 8 March 1734/5; d. Kingston 5 Sept. 1782 aged 46y 5m.

Peabody Bradford had an illegitimate son with LYDIA FREEMAN.

He m. int. Kingston 14 March 1760 **WELTHEA DELANO**, b. Duxbury 7 Dec. 1741; d. Kingston 27 April 1783 aged 40y 4m 20d; daughter of Joshua and Hopestill (Peterson) Delano, a descendant of Pilgrims **John Alden** and **George Soule**.

Peabody Bradford of Duxbury, retailer, was granted a license to sell liquor in 1771.

On 1 July 1782 Gamaliel Bradford, Esq., Seth Bradford, Gentleman, Peabody Bradford, yeoman, Peter Bradford, yeoman, all of Duxbury, Andrew Bradford of Pembrook, Gentleman, and Samuel Bradford of Duxbury, yeoman, as legal representative of his father Samuel Bradford deceased, agreed to divide 90 acres in Winslow, Me., given to them by their father or grandfather Gamaliel Bradford. Peabody received two lots.

The 31 March 1792 distribution of the estate of Peabody Bradford of Duxbury, yeoman, names eldest son Lewis; Pamela Little, wife of Nathaniel Little, Jr.; Cynthia, Charles, Joah [later written as Joanna], Sylvia, Lucy Foster, and Ira Bradford.

Illegitimate child of Lydia Freeman and Peabody Bradford:

  i PEABODY[6] BRADFORD, b. 1 March 1757 (Bible rec.; ae 19 in 1777 and ae 74 in 1832)

Children of Peabody and Welthea (Delano) Bradford, ii–v, ix, and x rec. Kingston:

  ii LEWIS BRADFORD, b. 24 Aug. 1761

  iii IRA BRADFORD, b. 27 June 1763; d. bef. 17 April 1783

  iv PAMELA BRADFORD, b. 30 Nov. 1764

  v CHARLES BRADFORD, b. 2 Aug. 1767

  vi CYNTHIA BRADFORD, b. 29 March 1770

  vii JOAH [or JOANNA] BRADFORD, b. 17 Feb. 1772; d. Portland, Me., 26 April 1828 ae 56.

  viii SYLVIA BRADFORD, b. 8 Feb. 1774; d. 19 Jan. 1778

  ix WELTHEA BRADFORD, b. 9 April 1776; d. Duxbury 19 Jan. 1778 ae 9m.

  x LUCY FOSTER BRADFORD, b. 28 Oct. 1778

  xi IRA BRADFORD, b. 17 April 1783

Note: Deborah dau. Wealthier, bp. Sept. 1777 (*Duxbury VR* 26) may be another child.

References: *VR Duxbury* p. 69(b. Welthea), 354(d. dau. Welthea). *VR Kingston* pp. 27-9(b. ch.), 181(m.), 321-2(d. Peabody, Welthea). *MF* 3:321. *Bradford Desc* p. 116. Plymouth Co. PR 33:36(Peabody Bradford). *MD* 7:23(deaths); 11:238(b. Welthea). Kennebec Co. ME LR 5:206(Gamaliel *et al*). ME VR(d. Joah). *Pension Abstracts* 1:3571(ae Peabody). *MSSR* 2:405(ae Peabody Jr.). *Plymouth Co Ct Recs* 3:309. *Rev War Pensions* 1:357(Peabody Bradford Jr.).

375. HANNAH[5] BRADFORD (*Gamaliel[4], Samuel[3], William[2-1]*), b. Duxbury 30 July 1740.

She m. **JOSHUA STANFORD**, b. Duxbury 30 Nov. 1729; son of Robert and Fear (Wadsworth) Stanford, probably a descendant of Pilgrim **William Brewster**. On 28 Jan. 1757 Robert Stanford of Duxborough, Gentleman, gave to his oldest son Joshua Stanford of Duxborough, yeoman, his homestead farm consisting of 66 acres and 12 acres of upland and on 25 Oct. 1765 Robert sold to Joshua two-thirds of an acre of cedar swamp.

Joshua Stanford responded to the alarm of 19 April 1775 with service of three days as a private in Capt. Samuel Bradford's (1st Duxbury) company of militia in Col. Warren's regiment.

On 8 Oct. 1778 Joshua Stanford of Duxbury, gentleman, sold his homestead farm to Zebdiel Weston. Fear Stanford, widow of Robert Stanford and Hannah Stanford, wife of Joshua Stanford released their dower rights.

Joshua Stanford and Joshua Stanford Jr. were in Egremont in 1790 with households consisting of 1 man, 1 boy, and 2 females, and 1 man and 2 females respectively.

No probate records were found for Joshua Stanford in Plymouth or Berkshire counties.

Children of Joshua and Hannah (Bradford) Stanford, bp. Duxbury:

    i   ROBERT STANFORD[6], bp. 19 July 1760
    ii FREDERICK STANFORD, b. July 1760; d. 3 Oct. 1760 ae 3m
    iii REBECCA STANFORD, bp. 11 April 1762
    iv HANNAH STANFORD, bp. 17 July 1763
    v   JOSHUA STANFORD, bp. 30 Nov. 1766
    vi SAMUEL BRADFORD STANFORD, bp. 3 Aug. 1777

NOTE: Are Robert and Frederick the same child? *Bradford Desc* p. 117 says the family moved to Connecticut and New York.

References: *VR Duxbury* pp. 170-1(b. Joshua, b. ch.), 427(d. Frederick). *MD* 12:126(b. Robert). *Bradford Desc* pp. 116-7. NGSQ 71:87-8. Plymouth Co. LR 52:36-7(Robert Stanford); 59:190(Joshua Stanford). *MSSR* 14:821.

376. RUTH[5] BRADFORD (*Gamaliel⁴, Samuel³, William²⁻¹*), b. Duxbury 5 July 1743; d. there 19 or 22 April 1812 in her 69th yr.

She m. Duxbury 3 Sept. 1761 **ELIJAH SAMSON**, b. Duxbury 7 June 1734; d. there 12 or 16 March 1805 in 72nd yr.; son of John and Priscilla (Bartlett) Samson, a descendant of Pilgrims **John Alden, William Brewster, Henry Samson** and **Richard Warren**.

Elijah Samson's household consisted of 4 men 16 or older, 3 boys, and 7 females in Duxbury in the 1790 census.

On 28 March 1797 Elijah Samson of Duxbury, yeoman, sold four acres to Stephen Samson of Duxbury, yeoman, and ten acres of woodland to Bradford

Samson. In March 1801 Elijah Samson of Duxbury gave land to his son Bradford Samson of Duxbury, mariner; wife Ruth released her dower.

On 20 April 1804 Elijah Samson of Duxbury, yeoman, sold to Stephen Samson of Duxbury, mariner, his homestead farm with buildings reserving the right to live in the dwelling house for one year rent free and after that in one room for rent, and to have two horses and a cow pastured.

On 8 May 1805 Stephen Samson of Duxbury, mariner, was appointed administrator of the estate of Elijah Samson of Duxbury, yeoman, deceased, after the widow had refused administration.

Children of Elijah and Ruth (Bradford) Samson, b. Duxbury; first ten bp. Duxbury 27 April 1777:*

　i   PRISCILLA SAMSON[6], b. 18 Oct. 1762

　ii   ABIGAIL SAMSON, b. 16 Jan. 1764

　iii RUTH SAMSON, b. 24 April 1767

　iv   STEPHEN SAMSON, b. 23 Sept. 1768

　v   WELTHEA SAMSON, b. ca. 1770 (Aspinwall has 22 April 1773-1774)

　vi   BRADFORD SAMSON, b. 11 Nov. 1772

　vii ELIJAH SAMSON, bp. 27 April 1777; d. unm.

　viii ZOPHAR SAMSON, bp. 27 April 1777; d. England, unm.

　ix   DEBORAH SAMSON, b. ca. July 1776; d. 8 Sept. 1778 ae 2y 2m

　x   BARTLETT SAMSON, b. ca. 1777; bp. 27 April 1777

　xi   DORCAS SAMSON (twin), b. 4 April 1778; d. 18 April 1778 ae 14d

　xii ELIZABETH SAMSON (twin), b. 4 April 1778, bp. 17 May 1778; d. Duxbury 18 March 1815 ae 27; unm.

　xiii DEBORAH SAMSON, b. 7 Feb. 1780, bp. 16 April 1780

　xiv ELISHA SAMSON, b. ca. June 1782

　xv   SYLVIA SAMSON, b. 26 Oct. 1784

*Note:: Some full birth dates are from *Giles Mem* and not in VR.

References: *VR Duxbury* pp. 137(b. Bradford),145(b. Elijah), 145-8(bp. 1st 13 ch.), 298(m.), 409 (d. Elijah; d. ch. Deborah, Dorcas, Elizabeth), 411(d. Ruth). *Giles Mem* pp. 392/3. *MF* 19:156. *Bradford Desc* p. 117. Plymouth Co. PR 39:8(Elijah Samson). Plymouth Co. LR 81:160; 84:58; 89:243; 99:155(Elijah Samson).

377. PETER⁵ BRADFORD (*Gamaliel⁴, Samuel³, William²⁻¹*), b. Duxbury 2 June 1745; d. Readfield, Me., Dec. 1833.

He m. Duxbury 18 Jan. 1770 **ABIGAIL LORING**, b. Pembroke 15 March 1749; d. after 25 Aug. 1800 (released dower rights) and before 4 June 1818 when not included in husband's pension application; daughter of Nathaniel and Priscilla (Gray) Loring.

Peter Bradford was a sergeant in the Revolutionary War serving in Capt. Samuel Bradford's company in Col. Theophilus Cotton's regiment. He enlisted on 1 May 1775 and appears on a bounty coat list on 30 Oct. 1775.

On 23 June 1777 and 22 Aug. 1782 Peter Bradford was of Duxbury when he and other heirs of Nathaniel Loring sold land.

Peter Bradford of Duxbury, retailer, was granted a license to sell liquor in 1782.

On 1 July 1782 Gamaliel Bradford, Esq., Seth Bradford, Gentleman, Peabody Bradford, yeoman, Peter Bradford, yeoman, all of Duxbury, Andrew Bradford of Pembrook, Gentleman, and Samuel Bradford of Duxbury, yeoman, as legal representative of his father Samuel Bradford deceased, agreed to divide 90 acres in Winslow, Me., given to them by their father or grandfather Gamaliel Bradford. Peter received two lots, and on 22 April 1797 Seth sold his lots to Peter.

Peter Bradford was listed as head of a household in Duxbury consisting of 1 man, 3 boys, and 5 females in the 1790 census. The 1800 census listed him in Kennebec County, Me.

Peter Bradford is listed in Winslow, Me., in the 1798 Direct Tax List of Mass.

On 23 Aug. and 25 Aug. 1800 Peter Bradford of Winslow, Me., sold land in Duxbury; his wife Abigail released her dower rights on the first deed.

Peter Bradford was a resident of Vassalborough, Me., aged 72, when he applied for a pension on 4 June 1818 and a resident of Readfield, Me., in June 1833.

Children of Peter and Abigail (Loring) Bradford, first 3 b. Duxbury; rest b. prob. in Maine:

- i JUDITH⁶ BRADFORD, b. 27 April 1770
- ii PRISCILLA BRADFORD, b. 16 Jan. 1773
- iii ALEXANDER BRADFORD, b. 8 Dec. 1776
- iv NATHANIEL BRADFORD, b. 18 Feb. 1779
- v POLLY BRADFORD, b. 24 March 1782 (g.s.)
- vi ELIZABETH BRADFORD, b. 1785

vii MARTIN BRADFORD, b. 9 Sept. 1790

viii ANDREW BRADFORD

References: *VR Duxbury* pp. 28(b. Alexander), 30(b. Judith), 31(b. Priscilla), 223(m.). *Bradford Desc* p. 177. *MSSR* 2:406(Peter Bradford). Plymouth Co. LR 63:69; 64:127(Loring heirs); 85:73; 114:108(Peter Bradford). *Rev War Pensions* 1:357, S15761(Peter Bradford). Kennebec Co. ME LR 5:206(Gamaliel *et al.*); 8:413(Seth Bradford). GS#67492(g.s. photo for Polly). *Plymouth Co Ct Recs* 4:7.

378. ANDREW[5] BRADFORD (*Gamaliel[4], Samuel[3], William[2-1]*), b. Duxbury 2 June 1745; d. there 1 Jan. 1837 aged 91.

He m. Pembroke 23 Nov. 1775 **MARY TURNER**, b. Pembroke 8 Oct. 1746; d. Marshfield 10 June 1825 aged 78; daughter of Benjamin and Mary (_____) Turner.

Andrew Bradford graduated from Harvard College in 1771 and taught school in Duxbury and probably in Pembroke.

Andrew Bradford served as paymaster in Col. Gamaliel Bradford's regiment from 1777 to 1779 and for the Continental Army in 1780. He later served as an ensign and lieutenant. He was granted a leave on 9 Jan. 1781 to go to Pembroke until 1 April 1781, but he overstayed his leave by 367 days, and finally resigned his commission in 1782 due to illness.

On 1 July 1782 Gamaliel Bradford, Esq., Seth Bradford, Gentleman, Peabody Bradford, yeoman, Peter Bradford, yeoman, all of Duxbury, Andrew Bradford of Pembrook, Gentleman, and Samuel Bradford of Duxbury, yeoman as legal representative of his father Samuel Bradford deceased, agreed to divide 90 acres in Winslow, Me., given to them by their father or grandfather Gamaliel Bradford. Andrew received two lots.

Andrew Bradford is listed in Pembroke in 1790 with a household consisting of 1 man, 1 boy, and 2 females.

On 29 Feb. 1792 Andrew Bradford of Pembroke, Gentleman, with others sold land; his wife Polly released her dower rights. On 26 April 1796 Andrew of Pembroke with others sold more land; his wife Mary released her dower rights. And on 3 Jan. 1798 Andrew of Pembroke, Gentleman, with others sold two pieces of land; his wife Mary released her dower rights.

On 23 Aug. 1803 Andrew Bradford of Hingham, Gentleman, sold land in Pembroke and his wife Mary released her dower rights. On 22 May 1804 Andrew Bradford of Hingham bought land in Keene, N.H., and sold the land eight days later to George Turner of Pembroke; Andrew's wife Mary released her dower rights.

On 3 April 1818 as a resident of Boston, Andrew Bradford applied for a pension. In 1820 he was a resident of Marshfield, aged 75, and his wife was aged 74. His only son James H. Bradford applied from Suffolk County on 17 April 1843 for his pension.

No Plymouth County probate records have been found for Andrew Bradford.

Children of Andrew and Mary (Turner) Bradford, b. prob. Pembroke:

    i   JAMES HERVEY[6] BRADFORD, b. 27 March 1778
   ii   [CHILD] BRADFORD, d.y.

References: *VR Duxbury* p. 352(d. Andrew). *VR Pembroke* pp. 213(b. Mary), 245(m.). *Marshfield VR* p. 387(d. Mary). *Bradford Desc* p. 117. Kennebec Co. ME LR 5:206(Gamaliel *et al.*). *Harvard Grads* 17:500. *MSSR* 2:400-1. Plymouth Co. LR 72:208; 84:62; 91:11; 97:112(Andrew Bradford). Cheshire Co. LR 43:314, 359(Andrew Bradford). *Pension Abstracts* 1:356.

379. REBECCA KNOWLES[5] (*Mary Hunt[4], Mary[3] Bradford, William[2-1]*), b. Martha's Vineyard 30 Jan. 1710/11.

She m. Branford, Conn., 10 Jan. 1753 **GEORGE HUBBARD**, b. Guilford, Conn., b. 30 May 1717 (not in Barbour); d. Branford, Conn., 2 Nov. 1762; son of Ebenezer and Elizabeth (Lord) Hubbard.

No known issue.

References: *Bradford Desc* p. 118. Branford CT VR 3:178(m.; d. George). *Desc Richard Knowles* p. 27. *Desc Thomas Lord* p. 355. *Desc Richard Knowles* p. 27.

380. MARY KNOWLES[5] (*Mary Hunt[4], Mary[3] Bradford, William[2-1]*), b. Windham, Conn., Sept. 1713; d. Branford, Conn., 16 April 1759.

She m. Branford, Conn., 5 Nov. 1730 **WILLIAM LUDDINGTON**, b. New Haven, Conn., 6 Sept. 1703; son of Henry and Sarah (Collins) Luddington. He m. (2) Branford, Conn., 17 April 1760 MARY WILKENSON.

No Conn. probate records were found for William Luddington.

Children of William and Mary (Knowles) Luddington, b. Branford, Conn.:

    i   SUBMIT LUDDINGTON[6], b. 10 Feb. 1732/3
   ii   MARY LUDDINGTON, b. 20 May 1736
  iii   HENRY LUDDINGTON, b. 25 May 1739
  iv   LYDIA LUDDINGTON, b. 25 July 1741

    v SAMUEL LUDDINGTON, b. 30 April 1744

    vi REBECCA LUDDINGTON, b. 10 May 1747; d. 24 May 1754

    vii ANNE LUDDINGTON, b. 20 June 1750; d. 24 May 1754

    viii STEPHEN LUDDINGTON, b. 18 Oct. 1753

References: *Bradford Desc* p. 118. New Haven CT VR TMI:30, 1:141(b. William). Branford CT VR 3:70(m.), 78(b. Submit), 109(b. Mary thru Samuel), 112(b.&d. Rebecca), 133 (b.&d. Anne), 136(b. Stephen), 160(d. Mary; 2nd m.). *New Haven Fams* 5:112. *Desc Richard Knowles* p. 28. *Luddington-Saltus* pp. 144, 152.

381. JANE HUNT[5] (*William⁴, Mary³ Bradford, William²⁻¹*), bp. Martha's Vineyard 18 Aug. 1723; d. by 1754 when Samuel had a child with his second wife.

    She m. Chilmark 5 July 1744 **SAMUEL NICKERSON**, b. Chatham; d. probably Chilmark before 12 Aug. 1771 when his estate was proved; son of Nathaniel and Experience (Parker) Nickerson. He m. (2) ABIGAIL (BURGESS) PEASE with whom he had Abigail and Samuel.

    Samuel Nickerson was an innkeeper on Martha's Vineyard from 1749 to 1753, after which he moved to Boston.

    On 29 Aug. 1769 Robert Thomson and his wife Jean of Chilmark, and the other heirs of William Hunt, sold a dwelling house reserving the use and improvement of it during the natural life of Sarah Hunt, widow of Chilmark.

    Children of Samuel and Jane (Hunt) Nickerson, in grandfather's will:

    i. BERIAH NICKERSON[6]

    ii. JANE NICKERSON; m. 15 Jan. 1768 Robert Thompson

    iii. NATHANIEL NICKERSON, bp. Rochester 24 Feb. 1751

References: *Bradford Desc* p. 118. *VR Chilmark* p. 56(m.). Dukes Co. LR 9:674(Robert Thomson *et al.*). Dukes Co. PR 6:14(William Hunt). *VR Rochester* 1:222(bp. Nathaniel). *Nickerson Fam* 1:62.

383. SARAH HUNT[5] (*William⁴, Mary³ Bradford, William²⁻¹*), bp. Chilmark 10 July 1723.

    She m. int. Rochester 24 June 1751 **TIMOTHY HATCH**, bp. Falmouth 16 Jan. 1731/2; son of Nathaniel and Bethia (_____) Hatch.

    On 29 Aug. 1769 Timothy Hatch and his wife Sarah of Chilmark, and the other heirs of William Hunt, sold a dwelling house reserving the use and improvement of it during the natural life of Sarah Hunt, widow of Chilmark.

In the 1771 Valuation List, Timothy Hatch appears in Chilmark as a non-rateable poll and with 1 house.

Child of Timothy and Sarah (Hunt) Hatch, b. Rochester:

    i   [DAUGHTER] HATCH[6], bp. 19 July 1752

References: *Bradford Desc* pp. 118-20. *VR Falmouth* p. 72(bp. Timothy). *VR Rochester* 1:172(bp. dau.); 2:187(int.). Dukes Co. LR 9:674(Timothy Hatch *et al.*). *1771 Valuation* p. 692.

384. SAMUEL HUNT[5] (*William[4], Mary[3] Bradford, William[2-1]*), b. 1727; d. Liverpool, N.S., 15 Jan. 1800.

He m. Chilmark 7 Jan. 1747 **LOIS MAYHEW**, b. ca. 1712; daughter of John and Mehitable (Higgins) Mayhew.

On 29 Aug. 1769 Samuel Hunt of Liverpool, N.S., and the other heirs of William Hunt, sold a dwelling house reserving the use and improvement of it during the natural life of Sarah Hunt, widow of Chilmark. On 29 Nov. 1771 Samuel Hunt of Liverpool, N.S., Gentleman, sold land to Jeremiah Mayhew of Chilmark.

Children of Samuel and Lois (Mayhew) Hunt, b. Chilmark:

    i   WILLIAM HUNT[6], b. 29 Nov. 1748
    ii OLIVER HUNT, b. 6 Feb. 1749/50; d. Liverpool NS 7 March 1763
    iii SAMUEL HUNT, b. 5 Oct. 1751; d. at sea 1 Nov. 1773
    iv LOIS HUNT, b. 5 June 1753
    v EPHRAIM HUNT, b. 28 Sept. 1756

References: *Bradford Desc* p. 119. *Martha's Vineyard By Banks* 3:306. *NEHGR* 126:98-9(b.&d. ch.; d. Samuel). *VR Chilmark* p. 56(m.). Dukes Co. LR 9:674(Samuel Hunt *et al.*); 10:35(Samuel Hunt).

385. SARAH SHERMAN[5] (*Sarah Baker[4], Sarah[3] Bradford, William[2-1]*), b. Rochester 15 Aug. 1714; d. before 16 Aug. 1750.

She m. int. Rochester 3 Nov. 1746 **BARZILLA HAMMOND**; d. before 9 March 1779; son of Benjamin and Elizabeth (___) Hammond. He m. (1) Rochester 18 June 1725 MARY BARLOW with whom he had Nathaniel, Elizabeth, Benjamin, Moses, Stafford, Hannah, Micah, Lucie, and Sarah. He m. (3) Rochester 16 Aug. 1750 ANNA TOBEY with whom he had Elisha and Mary. He m. (4) Rochester 25 March 1759 SARAH DOTY.

On 9 March 1779 one third of the estate of Barzilla Hammond was set off to his widow. On 15 Dec. 1779 it was decided that the estate was too small to divide among his heirs so his eldest son Benjamin was to get the homestead and to pay his siblings their portions: Moses, Stafford, Micah, Elisha, Hannah wife of Jonathan Wing of Newfield, Conn., Lucy, Sarah wife of Hazel Jenney of Dartmouth, and Molly wife of Nathaniel Briggs of Rochester.

If this marriage took place, there were no children.

References: *VR Rochester* 2:269(m. int.). *Bradford Desc* p. 119. *Hammond Gen* pp. 254-5. Plymouth Co. PR 25:295, 407(Barzilla Hammond).

386.   JANE SHERMAN[5] (*Sarah Baker[4], Sarah[3] Bradford, William[2-1]*), b. Rochester 2 Oct. 1716.

She m. Rochester 20 June 1745 **JUSTUS WHITE**, b. Rochester 28 Feb. 1707; son of John and Martha (_____) White, a descendant of Pilgrim **William White**.

On 6 June 1753 Justis and Silvanus White of Rochester sold the house and farm of their father John White, deceased; Jean [*sic*] surrendered her dower 7 June 1753.

Justus White was head of a household consisting of 1 man, 1 boy, and 4 females in Rochester in the 1790 census.

No Plymouth County probate records were found for Justus White.

Children of Justus and Jane (Sherman) White, b. Rochester:

  i   RESOLVED WHITE[6], b. 18 April 1746
  ii EDWARD WHITE, b. 17 Feb. 1748
  iii JUSTICE WHITE, b. 10 April 1751
  iv MAJOR WHITE, bp. 7 Oct. 1753
  v   JANE WHITE, b. 17 Oct. 1758

References: *VR Rochester* 1:320-4(b. ch., b. Justus); 2:269(m.). *MF* 13:51-2. *Bradford Desc* p. 119. Plymouth Co. LR 44:9(Justus & Sylvanus White). *Sherman Gen* pp. 39, 68.

387 ALICE SHERMAN[5] (*Sarah Baker[4], Sarah[3] Bradford, William[2-1]*), b. Rochester 29 July 1719; d. Barre, Mass., in 1801 aged 79.

She m. Rochester 25 June 1738 **SAMUEL RUGGLES**, b. Rochester 5 July 1715; d. June 1802 aged almost 87; son of Timothy and Mary (White) Ruggles.

Samuel Ruggles of Rochester, retailer, was granted a license to sell liqour in 1743, 1744/5, 1746, and 1747.

At the May 1754 term of the Plymouth Co. Court of Common Pleas, Samuel Ruggles of Rochester, blacksmith, sued Josiah Wood of Middleborough, blacksmith. Samuel had a note dated 26 Oct. 1752 for "Seven hundred and Seventy five pound weight of Good Tough Deck nails under Twelve to the pound of Good Bloomery Iron at said Rochester by the First of April." Josiah says he never promised to deliver. The jury found for Samuel.

On 8 March 1758 Timothy Ruggles of Rochester, Clerk, gave to his son Samuel Ruggles of Hardwick five acres in Hardwick; recorded 9 May 1764.

A Sam¹ Ruggles was head of a household of 2 men, 3 boys, and 3 females in Orange in the 1790 census.

Children of Samuel and Alice (Sherman) Ruggles, first eight b. Rochester, last two bp. Hardwick:

    i SARAH RUGGLES⁶, b. 27 April 1739; bp. 3 Aug. 1740

    ii JOHN RUGGLES, b. 6 Jan. 1740/1

    iii SAMUEL RUGGLES, b. 17 March 1742/3

    iv TIMOTHY RUGGLES, b. 17 May 1745

    v EDWARD RUGGLES, b. 31 Dec. 1746

    vi ALICE RUGGLES, bp. 15 Jan. 1748

    vii NATHANIEL RUGGLES, bp. 6 Jan. 1750

    viii MARY RUGGLES, bp. 7 Jan. 1753

    ix KEZIAH RUGGLES, bp. 5 Oct. 1755; d. Barre Dec. 1820 ae 65

    x LUCY RUGGLES, bp. 4 Dec. 1757

References: *VR Rochester* 1:254-6(b. ch., b. Samuel); 2:272(m.). *Bradford Desc* p. 117. Worcester Co. LR 49:381(Timothy Ruggles). *VR Hardwick* p. 99(bp. Keziah, Lucy). *VR Barre* p. 265(d. dau. Keziah). *Ruggles Gen* pp. 55, 102-3. *Hardwick Hist* p. 483(d. Samuel, Keziah). *Sherman Gen* pp. 39, 69.

388. JOHN SHERMAN⁵ (*Sarah Baker⁴, Sarah³ Bradford, William²⁻¹*), b. Rochester 27 July 1721; d. there 5 Nov. 1802.

He m. (1) Rochester 15 March 1743/4 **DEBORAH WINSLOW**, b. Rochester 8 Feb. 1724; d. there April 1755; daughter of John and Bethia (Andrews) Winslow.

He m. (2) Sandwich 31 Oct. 1755 **MERCY (BLACKWELL) BUMPAS**, b. Sandwich 28 Oct. 1721; daughter of Samuel and Mary (Smith) Blackwell. She m. (1) Sandwich 7 Dec. 1752 SETH BUMPAS. The will of

Samuel Blackwell made 15 Aug. 1754, proved 4 Feb. 1755, named his daughter Mercy, but no surname. In distributions of the estate of Samuel Blackwell on 10 May 1756 and again on 5 Oct. 1756, she was called Mercy Sherman.

On 26 July 1765 John and Sarah Sherman of Rochester, for love and affection, deeded their homestead farm to sons John, William, and Samuel Sherman, all of Rochester.

John Sherman was head of a household consisting of 1 man, 2 females, and 1 other free person in Rochester in the 1790 census. Listed next to him was Joshua Sherman with 1 man, 1 female, and 1 other free person.

No Plymouth County probate records were found for John Sherman.

Children of John and Deborah (Winslow) Sherman, b. Rochester:

   i   JOHN SHERMAN[6], b. 26 April 1746

   ii WILLIAM SHERMAN, b. 4 July 1748

  iii SAMUEL SHERMAN, b. 18 Aug. 1750

  iv BETHIAH SHERMAN, b. 1 Jan. 1753

   v NATHANIEL SHERMAN, b. 24 April 1755

Children of John and Mercy (Blackwell) (Bumpas) Sherman, b. Rochester:

  vi THOMAS SHERMAN, b. 26 Sept. 1756

 vii MICAH SHERMAN, b. 3 March 1758

viii JOSHUA SHERMAN, b. 2 April 1760

  ix DEBORAH SHERMAN, b. 10 Feb. 1763

   x MERCY SHERMAN, b. 19 Feb. 1765

References: *VR Rochester* 1:262(b. John, William), 263(b. Bethiah, Nathaniel), 264(b. Micah), 265(b. ch. Deborah), 266(b. Mercy), 267(b. Samuel), 268(b. Thomas), 269(b. Joshua), 313(b. Deborah); 2:271(1st m.), 429(d. Deborah). *Bradford Desc* pp. 119-20. *TAG* 43:214-5(Bumpas). *NEHGR* 117:298-9(Blackwell). *Sandwich VR* 1:116(b. Mercy), 185(1st m. Mercy), 190(2nd. m.). Plymouth Co. LR 50:235(John Sherman). *Winslow Mem* 1:96-7. Barnstable Co. PR 9:124(Samuel Blackwell). *Sherman Gen* pp. 39, 70.

389. ABIGAIL SHERMAN[5] (*Sarah Baker*[4], *Sarah*[3] *Bradford*, *William*[2-1]), b. Rochester 27 July 1721.

She m. Dartmouth 18 Feb. 1745 **SYLVANUS COTTLE** of Chilmark; b. 9 May 1704; son of John and Jane (Look) Cottle. He m. (1) Chilmark 9 Dec. 1725 MARTHA HATCH with whom he had Isaac, Edward, Benjamin, Ann, Lydia, Jane, Keziah, and Mary.

Silvanus Cottle served the town of Tisbury as fenceviewer in 1727, 1737, 1748, 1750, and 1754; as constable in 1733; as hogreve in 1735; as surveyor of highways in 1737, 1752, and 1758; as moderator at town meetings in 1752 and 1755; as tithingman in 1755; and as overseer of the poor in 1759.

In 1743 the town records show that he had received one-third of lot #3 and half of lot #6 in the First Division of land, half of lot #14 and one-third of lot #9 in the Second Division, half of lot #14 and part of lot #13 in the Third Division. In a division in 1750, he received part of lots #7 and #15.

Children of Sylvanus and Abigail (Sherman) Cottle, b. Tisbury:

    i JABEZ COTTLE⁶, b. 22 Feb. 1747

    ii SYLVANUS COTTLE, b. 15 June 1750

    iii JOSEPH COTTLE, b. 28 July 1753

References: *VR Chilmark* p. 48(1ˢᵗ m.; his 2ⁿᵈ m.). *VR Dartmouth* 2:134(m.). *VR Tislbury* p. 31(b. ch.). *Bradford Desc* p. 120. *Martha's Vineyard By Banks* 3:109. *Tisbury* TR pp. 91, 96,100, 104, 114, 128, 133, 135, 137, 144, 146, 149, 150, 162, and 168. *Sherman Gen* p. 39.

390. BETHIAH SHERMAN⁵ *(Sarah Baker⁴, Sarah³ Bradford, William²⁻¹)*, b. Rochester 26 Jan. 1724; living 6 Feb. 1788 and prob. as late as 14 July 1794.

She m. Rochester 28 Nov. 1745 **JOHN WINSLOW**, b. Rochester 31 Oct. 1722; d. there 17 June 1774 [VR says 1777 but will proved in 1774] in 49th yr; son of John and Bethiah (Andrews) Winslow.

On 10 Feb. 1772 John Winslow of Rochester, Gentleman, sold to his son Stephen Winslow of Rochester, blacksmith, 46 acres. On 2 July 1773 John sold to Stephen four acres of cedar swamp.

John Winslow of Rochester, Gentleman, in his will dated 13 Jan. 1772, proved 2 May 1774, named his wife Bethiah, sons Stephen, John, Lemuel, Micah, and daughters Bethia wife of Increase Clap, Keziah wife of Elijah Dexter, Abigail Winslow, Deborah Winslow, Elizabeth Winslow, and Sarah Winslow. Dower was set off to the widow Bethiah on 27 May 1776.

On 6 Feb. 1788 Seth Dexter of Rochester, Gentleman, administrator of the estate of John Winslow, since the estate was not sufficient to pay the debts without disposing of the dwelling house and land set off to the widow, sold what estate remained at the widow's death to Lemuel and Micah Winslow, sons of John Winslow. Bethiah Winslow signed her agreement to this arrangement. On 14 July 1794 Lemuel Winslow, Micah Winslow, and Joseph Hammond established a boundary between their land which was bounded on land assigned to the widow Bethia Winslow as her dower in the estate of John Winslow late of Rochester her late husband deceased.

Children of John and Bethia (Sherman) Winslow, b. Rochester:

  i   STEPHEN WINSLOW[6], b. 21 Aug. 1747

  ii   BETHIA WINSLOW, b. 23 Feb. 1748

  iii ABIGAIL WINSLOW, b. 1 Aug. 1750; d. Rochester 24 Jan. 1825 ae 75; unm.

  iv   KEZIAH WINSLOW, b. 26 July 1752

  v   DEBORAH WINSLOW, b. 27 Jan. 1754; d. 20 Oct. 1754

  vi   JOHN WINSLOW, b. 23 Aug. 1755

  vii LEMUEL WINSLOW, b. 12 March 1757

  viii [CHILD] WINSLOW, d. soon after birth.

  ix   ZEPHANIA WINSLOW, b. 12 March 1760; not in father's will

  x   MICAH WINSLOW, b. 12 Nov. 1761; bp. 27 April 1760 [sic]

  xi   DEBORAH WINSLOW, b. 22 March 1763

  xii ELIZABETH WINSLOW, b. 9 July 1764; d. 13 Nov. 1764

  xiii ELIZABETH WINSLOW, bp. 17 Aug. 1766

  xiv SARAH WINSLOW, b. 6 Sept. 1768

References: *VR Rochester* 1:113-115(b. ch.), 314(b. John); 2:329(m.), 447(d. Abigail), 448(d. Deborah, Elizabeth). *Bradford Desc* p. 120. *Winslow Mem* 1:96-7, 162. Plymouth Co. LR 57:36, 197(John Winslow); 79:88(Seth Dexter); 75:161(Lemuel Winslow *et al.*). Plymouth Co. PR 21:458(John Winslow). *Sherman Gen* pp. 39, 73.

391. WILLIAM SHERMAN[5] (*Sarah Baker[4], Sarah[3] Bradford, William[2-1]*), b. Rochester 11 Jan. 1726; d. there 3 March 1800 in 74th yr.

He m. Sandwich 4 June 1752 **ABIGAIL HANDY**, b. Sandwich 13 Feb. 1732/3; d. between March 1809 and March 1810; daughter of Cornelius and Abigail (Saunders) Handy.

On 26 July 1765 John and Sarah Sherman of Rochester, for love and affection, deeded their homestead farm to sons John, William, and Samuel Sherman, all of Rochester.

William Sherman served in the Revolutionary War as a private in Capt. Nathaniel Hammond's company which responded to the alarm of 19 April 1775.

Wm. Shirman [*sic*] was head of a household of 3 men, 1 boy, 5 females, and 1 other free person in Rochester in the 1790 census. Listed near or next to him were Wm. Shirman 3rd (1 man, 4 boys, 2 females), Jabez Shirman (1 man, 3 boys, 2 females), and Cornelius Shirman (1 man, 1 boy, 3 females).

On 16 May 1800 Jabez Sherman, Jonathan Sherman, William Sherman all of Easton, Washington Co., yeomen, Abraham Tabor and his wife Sally of Chester, Washington Co., William Dailey and his wife Alice of Chester, Edmond Snow of New York City and his wife Abigail all in the state of New York, Cornelius Sherman, yeoman, Zebulon Haskell and his wife Sukey, Kezia Sherman, singlewoman, and Jenny Sherman, singlewoman, all of Rochester, sold to Lemuel Sherman of Rochester their rights in the estate of their father William Sherman.

On 10 April 1807 Lemuel Sherman of Rochester, yeoman, sold to Isaac Vincent of New Bedford, yeoman, all the lands and buildings of which his late father William Sherman had died seized.

No Plymouth County probate records were found for William or Abigail Sherman.

Children of William and Abigail (Handy) Sherman, b. Rochester:*

    i JABEZ SHERMAN6, b. 21 May 1754
   ii CORNELIUS SHERMAN, b. 15 May 1756
  iii ABIGAIL SHERMAN, b. 20 Aug. 1758
  iv ALICE SHERMAN, b. 9 May 1761
   v SARAH SHERMAN, bp. 12 Aug. 1764
  vi WILLIAM SHERMAN (twin) , bp. 9 Nov. 1766
 vii JONATHAN SHERMAN (twin) , bp. 9 Nov. 1766
viii SUSANNAH SHERMAN, bp. 6 Nov. 1768
  ix KEZIAH SHERMAN, bp. 11 Aug. 1771; unm.. in 1813
   x JANE SHERMAN, bp. 13 March 1774; unm. in 1813
  xi LEMUEL SHERMAN, bp. 25 Oct. 1778

* Note: *Bradford Desc* lists twins Lemuel and Rachel, b. 23 June 1762 who are not in VR and the date seems too close to the birth of Alice. Also listed is a daughter Jerusha born after Lemuel.

References: *VR Rochester* 1:262-268(b. ch.); 2:431(d. William). *NEHGR* 25:192-3(Handy). *Bradford Desc* p. 120. *Sandwich VR* 1:134(b. Abigail), 185(m.). Plymouth Co. LR 50:235(John Sherman); 105:221(Jabez Sherman *et al.*), 221(Lemuel Sherman). *MSSR* 6:146(William Sherman). *Sherman Gen* pp. 39, 74.

392. KEZIAH SHERMAN[5] *(Sarah Baker[4], Sarah[3] Bradford, William[2-1])*, b. Rochester 28 Oct. 1728.

She m. Rochester 3 April 1755 **GEORGE LINCOLN** of Taunton; living 1790; son of Benjamin and [poss. Elizabeth] (____) Lincoln.

On 31 Oct. 1753 Benjamin Linkon of Taunton asks that his son George Linkon be appointed administrator on the estate of "my son Benjamin" late of Taunton deceased. On 2 Nov. 1753 George Linkon "ye Second" of Taunton, husbandman, was appointed adminstrator of the estate of Benjamin Linkon Jr. of Taunton.

On 12 June 1754 George Linkon of Taunton, son of Benjamin Linkon of Taunton, sold to his father Benjamin eight acres given to him by his father on 2 July 1751; he signed the deed as George Linkon 2d. On 10 Dec. 1756 George Linkon "ye second" of Taunton, yeoman, sold to James Andrews of Taunton, Gentleman, ten acres in Taunton; George's wife Keziah released her dower on 11 Jan. 1757.

On 18 Feb. 1785 George Lincoln of Rochester, yeoman, sold to Sherman Lincoln of Rochester nine acres; one of the witnesses was William Sherman.

In 1790 George Lincoln is listed in Rochester with a household consisting of 2 men, 1 boy, and 3 females.

Poss. children of George and Keziah (Sherman) Lincoln (b. dates from *Sherman Gen*):

> i KEZIAH LINCOLN[6], b. 1 April 1756, bp. Rochester 10 July 1785 ae. about 30
>
> ii SHERMAN LINCOLN, b. Dec. 1763 (in above deed)

References: *VR Rochester* 1:203(bp. Keziah); 2:203(m.). *VR Taunton* 3:133(d. George). *Bradford Desc* p. 120. Bristol Co. LR 40:393; 42:139(George Linkon). Plymouth Co. LR 63:175(George Lincoln). Bristol Co. PR 13:484 & file papers(Benjamin Linkon Jr.). *Sherman Gen* pp. 39, 76.

393. SAMUEL SHERMAN[5] *(Sarah Baker[4], Sarah[3] Bradford, William[2-1])*, b. Rochester 2 Jan. 1730/1; d. after 1779.

He m. (1) Rochester 6 Nov. 1755 **RACHEL HATCH**, b. Rochester 27 March 1725; d. before 23 Feb. 1758; daughter of Elisha and Patience (Keen) Hatch, a descendant of Pilgrim **Edward Doty**.

He m. (2) Rochester 23 Feb. 1758 **LYDIA POPE**, b. Dartmouth 3 March 1736/7; d. after 5 Dec. 1818 (deed).

On 26 July 1765 John and Sarah Sherman of Rochester, for love and affection, deeded their homestead farm to sons John, William, and Samuel Sherman, all of Rochester.

Samuel Sherman of Rochester, innholder, was granted a license to sell liquor in 1782 and 1783.

On 8 Dec. 1788 Samuel Sherman of Rochester, yeoman, sold to Earl Clap "my homestead farm on which I now Dwell with my house"; Samuel's wife Lydia released her dower rights.

On 5 March 1808 Isaac Sherman, Seth Sherman, and Samuel Sherman all of York [Maine] sold Lemuel Sherman of Rochester, all the land descended to them from the estate of their father Samuel Sherman. On 5 Dec. 1818 Samuel Sherman, Thomas B. Sherman, Joseph Bramhall, cabinet maker, and his wife Lydia all of Plymouth sold to Lydia Sherman of Plymouth, widow, the house and land of which Samuel Sherman had died seized.

Children of Samuel and Lydia (Pope) Sherman, b. Rochester:

    i   ISAAC SHERMAN[6], b. 7 Aug. 1758

   ii   RACHEL SHERMAN, b. 25 Nov. 1760

  iii   EDWARD SHERMAN, b. 4 Jan. 1763

  iv   SETH SHERMAN, b. 16 April 1765

   v   LYDIA SHERMAN, b. 8 April 1768

  vi   SAMUEL SHERMAN, bp. 12 Aug. 1770

 vii   SUSANNA POPE SHERMAN, bp. 13 Dec. 1772

viii   SARAH BAKER SHERMAN, bp. 21 Feb. 1779

References: *VR Rochester* 1:265-269(b. ch.), 172(b. Rachel); 2:74(both m.). *Bradford Desc* p. 121. Plymouth Co. LR 50:235(John Sherman); 61:14(Samuel Sherman); 106:275(Isaac Sherman *et al.*); 138:232(Samuel Sherman *et al.*). *Plymouth Co Ct Recs* vol. 4. *Sherman Gen* pp. 39, 76.

394. JEREMIAH PHILLIPS[5] (*Eleanor Baker[4], Sarah[3] Bradford, William[2-1]*), b. Marshfield 17 Nov. 1717; d. there 2 Oct. 1789 in 72nd yr.

He m. Milton 1751 **HANNAH GLOVER**, b. Milton 29 June 1721; daughter of Edward and Sarah (Gill) Glover.

In the 1771 Valuation List, Jeremiah Phillips appears in Marshfield with 2 polls, 1 house, 1 shop, 4 oxen, 3 cattle, 15 goats of sheep, 4 swine, 10 acres of pasture, 4 acres of tillage which produced 80 bushels of grain, and 1 acre of upland which produced 1 ton of hay.

On 27 Jan. 1789 Jeremiah Phillips of Marshfield, yeoman, sold to his grandson Joseph Phillips Cushman his new house and ten acres; to his daughter Percis Cushman of Marshfield his new farm excepting ten acres; to his daughter Hannah Hatch of Marshfield all his home farm "where he now dwells" except 30 acres with a lease for his natural life; and to Prince Hatch of Marshfield, yeoman, 30 acres of his homestead.

No Plymouth Co. probate records were found for Jeremiah Phillips.

Children of Jeremiah and Hannah (Glover) Phillips, b. Marshfield:

  i JOSEPH PHILLIPS[6], b. 18 April 1753
 ii HANNAH PHILLIPS, b. 28 July 1759
iii PERSIS PHILLIPS, b. 27 Sept. 1760

References: *Bradford Desc* p. 121. *Marshfield VR* pp. 59(b. ch.), 406(d. Jeremiah). *VR Milton* pp. 28(b. Hannah), 125(m.). Plymouth Co. LR 67:248-50(Jeremiah Phillips). *1771 Valuation* p. 648.

395. BENJAMIN PHILLIPS[5] (*Eleanor Baker[4], Sarah[3] Bradford, William[2-1]*), b. Marshfield 3 Aug. 1719.

He m. (1) Marshfield 15 Nov. 1743 **ALICE THOMAS**, b. Marshfield 25 Dec. 1722; d. before 15 Sept. 1752 (2nd m.); daughter of Nathan and Sarah (Foster) (Bartlett) Thomas.

He m. (2) Marshfield 10 Sept. 1752 **ELIZABETH BOURNE**, prob. the one, b. Marshfield 18 Feb. 1725; daughter of John and Abigail (_____) Bourne.

No Plymouth Co. probate records were found for Benjamin Phillips.

Children of Benjamin Phillips:

  i ALICE PHILLIPS[6], b. Marshfield 24 Feb. 1744
 ii BENJAMIN PHILLIPS
iii NATHAN PHILLIPS

References: *Marshfield VR* pp. 75(b. dau. Alice), 84(b. Alice), 87(b. Elizabeth), 152(2nd m. int.), 159(1st m.), 161(2nd m.). Thomas Gen p. 165. *Bradford Desc* p. 121.

396. ABIGAIL THOMAS[5] (*Abigail Baker[4], Sarah[3] Bradford, William[2-1]*), b. Marshfield 4 Dec. 1722; d. Duxbury 14 Nov. 1743 aged 20y 11m 10d.

She m. Duxbury March 1739/40 **ELEAZER HARLOW**, b. Plymouth 17 Oct. 1719; d. Duxbury 8 Aug. 1812*; son of John and Hannah (Delano)

Harlow. He m. (2) Duxbury 11 Sept. 1745 ABIGAIL CLARK with whom he had Thomas, Asaph, Abigail, and William. He m. (3) int. Boston 23 Feb. 1758 ELIZABETH (GARDNER) DABNEY.

At the November 1808 term of the Plymouth Co. Court of Common Pleas, Eleazer Harlow of Duxbury, Physician, sued Ichabod Weston of Duxbury, for breaking and entering his close and carrying away his soil. The jury found for Eleazer.

On 31 Aug. 1812 Asaph Harlow was appointed executrix of the estate of Eleazer Harlow of Duxbury, physician.

Children of Eleazer and Abigail (Thomas) Harlow, b. Duxbury:

    i   ARAUNAH HARLOW[6], b. 7 Oct. 1741; d.y.

   ii   GIDEON HARLOW, b. 27 Oct. 1743

* Note: Eleazer Harlow d. Duxbury, not Plymouth as in Plymouth Co. PR 39:369, 44:360.

References: *VR Duxbury* pp. 87, 88(b. ch.), 261(his 2nd m.), 382(d. Abigail, Eleazer). *Marshfield VR* p. 402(d. Abigail). *Bradford Desc* p. 121. Plymouth Co. PR 39:369; 44:360 (Eleazer Harlow). *Plymouth VR* pp. 62(b.&d. Eleazer), 160(int. his 2nd m.), 299(b.&d. Eleazer). *BRC* 30:28(int. 3rd m.). *Harlow Gen* pp. 100-1. *Plymouth Co Ct Recs* 12:73(Eleazer Harlow).

397. MERCY THOMAS[5] (*Abigail Baker[4], Sarah[3] Bradford, William[2-1]*), b. Marshfield 27 June 1725; d. there 27 May 1808 in 83rd yr.

She m. Marshfield 29 Dec. 1748 **BENJAMIN WHITE**, b. Marshfield 23 Jan. 1724/5; d. there 8 Sept. 1783 in 59th yr.; son of Benjamin and Faith (Oakman) White, a descendant of Pilgrims **Edward Doty** and **William White**.

In the 1771 Valuation List, Benjamin White appears in Marshfield with 3 polls, 1 house, 1 shop, 1 horse, 2 oxen, 3 cattle, 15 goats or sheep, 2 swine, 50 acres of pasture, 6 acres of tillage which produced 70 bushels of grain, and 3 barrels of cider.

Benj[n] White was head of a household of 1 man and 1 female in Mansfield in the 1790 census and listed next to him was Luther White with 1 man, 1 boy, and 2 females.

On 9 April 1793 Benjamin White of Marshfield, gentleman [the son], and Mercy White, widow of Benjamin White, divided a farm in Marshfield that had been the homestead of Gideon Thomas deceased.

No Plymouth Co. probate records were found for Benjamin or Mercy White.

Children of Benjamin and Mercy (Thomas) White, b. Marshfield:

  i   BENJAMIN WHITE[6], b. 18 Dec. 1749
  ii TOBIAS WHITE, b. 1 May 1753
  iii GIDEON THOMAS WHITE, b. 15 June 1755
  iv LUTHER WHITE, b. 31 May 1758

References: *MF* 13:111-2. *Marshfield VR* pp. 80(b. Benjamin), 99(b. ch.), 413(d. Mercy, Benj.). *Bradford Desc* pp. 121-2. Plymouth Co. LR 88:254(Benjamin White *et al.*). *1771 Valuation* p. 644.

398. ANNA THOMAS[5] (*Abigail Baker[4], Sarah[3] Bradford, William[2-1]*), b. Marshfield 7 Aug. 1726; d. Pembroke 1 Oct. 1812 aged 88.

She m. (1) Duxbury 26 Dec. 1747 **NATHANIEL OLDS/OTIS**. There is some confusion over Nathaniel's last name. The Duxbury m. calls him Nathaniel Oals of Boston. The intention record in Boston is for Nathaniel Otis. When Anna remarried, she was Anna Oldes in both marriage and intention. And in the deed below, his son is named as Nathaniel Otis.

She m. (2) Marshfield 17 May 1753 **ELIJAH DAMON**, d. Pembroke 4 July 1810 aged 81; son of Ebenezer and Abigail (Thomas) Damon.

On 14 Feb. 1755 Gideon Thomas of Marshfield, yeoman, sold Elijah Damon of Marshfield, cooper, 30 acres in the 76th lot of the Second division of common land in Duxbury.

On 17 March 1780 Elijah Dammon of Pembroke and his wife Anna, yeoman and seamster, sold to Benjamin White Jr. of Marshfield, tanner, a salt meadow given by Gideon Thomas of Marshfield to his grandson Nathaniel Otis; Rueben Dammon and Anne Dammon were witnesses. This deed was not recorded until 28 Jan. 1802.

Elijah Damon was head of a household consisting of 1 man and 1 female in Pembroke in the 1790 census and listed next to him was Elijah Damon Jr. also with 1 man and 1 female.

On 1 Oct. 1810 one-third of the estate of Elijah Damon was set off to widow Anna Damon. On 1 May 1813 the estate of Elijah Damon Sr., late of Pembroke, yeoman, was divided among the heirs of his son Elijah Damon deceased; the heirs of Abigail Holmes deceased; the heirs of Nancy Holmes deceased; the heirs of Mercy Briggs; and Elizabeth the wife of Joshuah Eldridge of Salem.

No Plymouth County probate records were found for Nathaniel Olds.

Child of Nathaniel and Anna (Thomas) Olds:

    i NATHANIEL OLDS[6]

Children of Elijah and Anna (Thomas) (Olds) Damon, first 4 b. Marshfield:

    ii ABIGAIL DAMON, b. 15 July 1754

    iii MARY DAMON, b. 13 Feb. 1756

    iv ELIZABETH DAMON, b. 5 March 1758

    v REUBEN DAMON, b. 30 Nov. 1759

    vi NANCY (or ANN) DAMON, bp. Pembroke 30 May 1762 [not in VR]

    vii MERCY DAMON, b. ca. 1766 [d. 19 July 1806 ae 40y 6m, wife of Samuel Briggs]

    viii ELIJAH DAMON, b. ca. 1768 [d. 15 Nov. 1811 ae 41 or 43]

References: *MD* 11:78(m.). *VR Duxbury* p. 319(m.). *VR Pembroke* p. 400(d. Anna, Elijah, son Elijah). *Marshfield VR* pp. 106(b. 4 ch.), 141(m.). Plymouth Co. PR 43:353; 45:52(Elijah Damon). *Bradford Desc* p. 122. *BRC* 28:286(m. int.). Plymouth Co. LR 44:18(Gideon Thomas); 92:106(Elijah Dammon). *Middleboro Deaths* p. 25(d.Mercy). *John Damon, Scituate* 1:24, 72.

399. SARAH THOMAS[5] (*Abigail Baker[4], Sarah[3] Bradford, William[2-1]*), b. Marshfield 10 Feb. 1732/3; d. after 5 April 1815 (deed).

She m. Marshfield 19 April 1757 **JEREMIAH LOW**, b. Marshfield 25 July 1735; d. there 27 Feb. 1823 aged 89 yrs.; son of Arthur and Elizabeth (Crocker) Low.

In the 1771 Valuation List, Jeremiah Low appears in Marshfield with 1 poll, 1 house, 1 shop, 2 oxen, 2 cattle, 8 goats or sheep, 12 acres of pasture, 5 acres of tillage which produced 75 bushels of grain, and 9 acres of salt marsh which produced 6 tons of hay.

Jeremiah Low was head of a household of 3 men and 3 females in Marshfield in the 1790 census.

On 30 April 1800 Jeremiah Low of Marshfield, yeoman, sold to his son Thomas Low of Marshfield, yeoman, one acre of land.

On 6 March 1815 Jeremiah Low of Marshfield, yeoman, and his wife Sarah sold to Joseph Baker of Marshfield, laborer, nine acres of salt meadow given to Sarah in the will of her father Gideon Thomas; Sarah also acknowledged this deed with her husband on 5 April 1815. On 24 June 1816 Jeremiah sold to Joseph his homestead and 50 acres. Jeremiah reserved the use and improvement of the land in both these deeds for the natural lives of him and his wife.

No Plymouth Co. probate records were found for Jeremiah Low.

Children of Jeremiah and Sarah (Thomas) Low, b. Marshfield:

    i   JONATHAN LOW[6], b. 31 Jan. 1758

    ii HANNAH LOW, b. 22 Aug. 1760

    iii ABIGAIL LOW, b. 10 June 1764

    iv THOMAS LOW, b. 22 June 1768

    v SAMUEL LOW, b. 7 March 1773

References: *Marshfield VR* pp. 82(b. Jeremiah), 106(b. ch.), 139(int.), 140(m.), 205(d. Jeremiah). *Bradford Desc* p. 122. Plymouth Co. LR 102:256; 127:266-7(Jeremiah Low). *1771 Valuation* p. 644.

400. ELEANOR THOMAS[5] (*Abigail Baker*[4], *Sarah*[3] *Bradford, William*[2-1]), b. Marshfield 10 Feb. 1732/3; d. there 6 Feb. 1814 in 81st yr.

She m. Marshfield 7 May 1753 **ELIJAH FORD**, b. Marshfield 2 May 1731; d. there 19 Nov. 1792 aged 62y 6m 9d; son of William and Hannah (Barstow) Ford.

In the 1771 Valuation List, Elijah Ford appears in Marshfield with 1 poll, 1 horse, 2 cattle, 12 goats or sheep, 2 swine, and 10 acres of salt marsh which produced 7 tons of hay.

Elijah Foord was head of a household of 4 men 16 or older and 2 females in Marshfield in the 1790 census.

The will of Elijah Ford of Marshfield, yeoman, dated 14 Oct. 1792, proved 17 Dec. 1792, names wife Eleanor; sons Arunah, Elijah, and Joseph Ford; daughter Abigail who was to be given maintenance as long as she remained unmarried; and daughter Hannah Wright, wife of Jesse Wright.

On 25 Nov. 1814 Araunah Ford of Marshfield, yeoman, and Elijah Ford of Marshfield, yeoman, divided land they held in common from their father Elijah Ford deceased; Anna the wife of Araunah and Jane the wife of Elijah released their dower rights.

Children of Elijah and Eleanor (Thomas) Ford, b. Marshfield:*

    i   HANNAH FORD[6], b. 23 April 1756

    ii ARAUNAH FORD, b. 12 Aug. 1762

    iii ELIJAH FORD, b. 22 Nov. 1765

    iv ABIGAIL FORD, b. 12 Oct. 1768; unm. 14 Oct. 1792

v JOSEPH FORD, b. 17 Dec. 1775

* **Note:** No proof found for daughter Ann who m. Marlboro or daughter Eleanor who m. Eli Josselyn according to *Bradford Desc.* pp. 122, 435. They are not named in the will and appear to belong to other families. *Bradford Desc* also says Hannah d. 1842 unmarried. Her father's will, however, indicates that she married.

References: *Marshfield VR* pp. 72(b. Hannah), 90(b. Elijah), 152(int.), 156(b. Araunah, Elijah, Abigail, Joseph), 162(m.), 401(d. Eleanor, Elijah). Thomas Gen p. 166. *Bradford Desc* p. 122. Plymouth Co. PR 33:234-5(Elijah Ford). Plymouth Co. LR 141:246(Araunah Ford). *1771 Valuation* p. 646.

401. JOHN BAKER[5] (*Kenelm*[4], *Sarah*[3] *Bradford. William*[2-1]), b. Marshfield 18 Oct. 1719; d. there 1 July 1804 in 85th yr.

He m. Marshfield 24 Feb. 1742/3 **RUTH BARKER**, b. ca. 1715–1720; d. after 24 March 1794 (deed) [she is not the Ruth Baker, wife of John who died in Pembroke in 1783 as stated in *MF 11*:1:61; that Ruth would have been born in 1738 according to her age at death]; daughter of Ebenezer and Deborah (Randall) Barker. Ebenezer Barker died in 1781 intestate and insolvent and no children were named in his probate records.

In the 1771 Valuation List, John Baker appears in Marshfield with 1 poll, 1 house, 1 shop, ¼ of a grist mill, £6:13:4 lent at interest, 1 horse, 2 oxen, 3 cattle, 20 goats or sheep, 1 swine, 30 acres of pasture, 5 acres of tillage which produced 75 bushels of grain, 2 barrels of cider, 4 acres of salt marsh which produced 4 tons of hay, 4 acres of upland which produced 4 tons of hay, and 4 acres of fresh meadon which produced 5 tons of hay.

John Baker was head of a household of 4 men 16 or older and 2 females in Marshfield in the 1790 census.

On 22 March 1794 John Baker of Marshfield, Gentleman, sold to Elisha Ford of Marshfield, yeoman, ten acres of his homestead; John's wife Ruth also signed this deed. On 24 March 1794 John Baker gave to his son Scollay Baker of Marshfield, laborer, all his estate in Marshfield in exchange for the maintainance of John and his wife Ruth for their natural lives.

On 21 May 1803 John Baker of Marshfield, Gentleman, sold to his son Scollay Baker of Marshfield, laborer, all his real estate in Marshfield including a 45-acre homestead with dwelling house and barn bounded on land owned by widow Tabitha Baker and Bradford Baker, one-third part of a grist mill, and a pew in the south meeting house.

No Plymouth County probate records were found for John Baker.

Children of John and Ruth (Barker) Baker, b. Marshfield:

 i   JOHN BAKER[6], b. 14 Oct. 1743 [MF 11:1:61 says John died in Marshfield 22 Feb. 1813 with no record of a m. or ch., but there is a will proved 1 March 1813 for John Baker which names a wife, children, and grandchildren]

 ii   RUTH BAKER, b. 2 May 1745; d. y.

 iii ALICE BAKER, b. 25 Nov. 1747

 iv   PATIENCE BAKER, b. 14 Nov. 1759

 v   SARAH BAKER, b. 23 July 1751

 vi   ELIZABETH BAKER, b. 10 Nov. 1753

 vii RUTH BAKER, b. 10 Oct. 1755

 viii BARKER BAKER, b. 10 Sept. 1761

 ix   LUCY BAKER, b. 22 Sept. 1763

 x   EDWARD DOTEN BAKER, b. 10 Jan. 1765

 xi   SCOLLAY BAKER, b. 1768, according to Aspinwall.

References: *Marshfield VR* pp. 95(b. 1st 8 ch.), 96(b. last 2 ch.), 172(m.), 398(d. John). *Bradford Desc* pp. 122-3. Plymouth Co. LR 76:98, 118; 97:21(John Baker). *Barker Gen* p. 170. *1771 Valuation* p. 644.

402. ALICE BAKER[5] (*Kenelm[4], Sarah[3] Bradford, William[2-1]*), b. Marshfield 26 Jan. 1722; d. there 2 Jan. 1791 aged 69 yrs.

She m. ca. 1739 **EPHRAIM LITTLE**, b. Marshfield 15 April 1718; d. there 22 Oct. 1808 aged 90y 6m; son of John and Constant (Fobes) Little, a descendant of Pilgrims **John Alden** and **Richard Warren**.   He m. (2) Marshfield 1 Oct. 1795 SARAH (HALL) PORTER.

At the April 1761 term of the Plymouth Co. Court of Common Pleas, Simeon Keen of Marshfield, yeoman, sued "John Thomas, junr., Esqr., Nathaniel Little, Gentleman and Deputy Sheriff...and Ephraim Little, Husbandman, all of Marshfield," for falsely causing Simeon to be imprisoned for three hours on 5 July 1760 until he paid a fine. Simeon claimed,

> ... the Defts. were assessors of Taxes for the same Town of Marshfield for the year of our Lord 1758, and the plantf. was a Collector of the same yeare as such by Law Obliged to Collect and pay into the Treasurer of this Province whatever taxes or Duties of Tonnage should persuant to Law be assessed by said Assessors ... [on 6 Dec. the defendants] utterly Neglected to make any such Assesment of said Tonnage Duty and Deliver the same to the plantf. but ... made, Subscribed, signed, and Delivered to said Treasurer a Certificate directed to said Treasurer

therein falsely Certyfieing him that agreeable to a law of this Province passed in the year 1756 for raizing sixpence per Ton on all Shipping within the province towards Supporting two Armed vessells for Guarding the Fisherey etc ... Now the pltf. in fact says said Certificate and matters therein Contained are false, that no assessment was then made or Delivered of at any time dureing said year 1758.

The jury found in Simeon's favor.

In the 1771 Valuation List, Ephraim Little appears in Marshfield with 1 poll, 1 house, 1 shop, 1 horse, 2 oxen, 5 cattle, 25 goats or sheep, 3 swine, 40 acres pasture, 6 acres of tillage which produced 100 bushels of grain, 30 acres of salt marsh which produced 18 tons of hay, and 7 acres of upland which produced 3 tons of hay.

Ephraim Little gave or sold land to his son John on 27 Oct. 1783 one acre with a house, on 26 Nov. 1783 all rights to the farm where John lived, 17 acres of woodland, and four acres of salt meadow, and on 5 June 1794 sixty acres of woodland and pasture. Ephraim's wife Elice [Alice] signed two of these deeds. On 13 March 1787 Ephraim gave to his son Peabody four pieces of land and salt meadow. On 15 Oct. 1787 Ephraim and Peabody Little of Marshfield, yeomen, sold to George Little of Marshfield, Gentleman, one-half of Little's Island that had been assigned to Ephraim in the division of the estate of his father John Little; Ephraim's wife Alice and Peabody's wife Ruth also signed this deed. On 17 Feb. 1806 Ephraim gave to Ephraim Jr. part of his homestead, half the house and barn, and 25 acres of woodland. And on 9 Sept. 1806 Ephraim gave to his daughter Alice Hatch of Marshfield two acres of salt marsh.

Ephm Little was head of a household of 3 men, 1 boy, and 4 females in Marshfield in the 1790 census. Listed next to him was John Little with 2 men, 2 boys, and 3 females.

On 6 March 1805 Ephraim Little of Marshfield, yeoman, sold to Lucy Vinal of Marshfield, widow, two acres of salt marsh. On 29 Aug. 1805 Ephraim gave to his daughter Anna Little of Marshfield the southerly part of his house, half of the barn, and four and a half acres of land. On 21 Oct. 1808 Ephraim gave to his daughter Ann one acre of salt marsh "for her kindness to me in takeing care of me in my last sickness"; this acre was bounded by land given to the children of his daughter Cela Young.

On 5 Dec. 1808 John Little of Marshfield was made administrator for the estate of Ephraim Little of Marshfield, Gentleman. On 23 Sept. 1809 the estate was declared insolvent. Among the creditors were Patience Rogers, widow Zintha Tilden, and the children of Selah Young.

Children of Ephraim and Alice (Baker) Little, b. Marshfield:

    i   ZINTHIA LITTLE[6], b. 24 Dec. 1740

   ii MARY LITTLE, b. 22 March 1742/3

  iii ALICE LITTLE, b. 8 Jan. 1745

  iv JOHN LITTLE, b. 1 March 1747

   v CONSTANT LITTLE, b. 27 March 1749; d. Halifax, N.S., 24 Dec. 1784 in his 35th yr.

  vi ANNA LITTLE, b. 9 Feb. 1751; d. Marshfield 10 Dec. 1832 ae 81y. On 14 Jan. 1826 Luther Little of Marshfield, a friend of Anna Little, single-woman, told the probate court that she was *non compos* and not capable for taking care of herself. On 16 Feb. 1826 Major Charles Hatch Jr. was appointed her guardian.

  vii CELIA LITTLE, b. 20 Dec. 1753

 viii LUCE LITTLE, b. 11 Nov. 1755

  ix PEBODY LITTLE, b. 9 Dec. 1757

   x PATIENCE LITTLE, b. 31 Aug. 1761

  xi EPHRAIM LITTLE, b. 25 July 1765; d. 8 Oct. 1765 ae 3m.

  xii EPHRAIM LITTLE, b. 22 July 1766; d. Marshfield 23 March 1859 ae 93y. On 3 March 1809 George Little was made guardian of Ephraim Little of Marshfield "an intemperate person." On 17 Oct. 1800 Constant F. Oakman took over as Ephraim's guardian and on 20 Feb. 1826 he was succeeded by Charles Hatch Jr.

References: *Marshfield VR* p. 33(b. Ephraim), 56(b. 7 ch.), 57(b. Celia, Luce), 77(b. Mary), 79(b. Zinthia), 105(b.&d. 1st Ephraim), 137(Ephraim's 2nd m.), 206(deaths), 395(deaths). *Bradford Desc* p. 123. Plymouth Co. LR 66:225-7; 67:88; 75:152; 102:176, 177; 104:41; 109:225, 268(Ephraim Little). Plymouth Co. PR 39:171; 43:74, 77(Ephraim Little); 41:56; 42:520; 60:134(son Ephraim Little); 60:133(Anna Little). *1771 Valuation* p. 646.

403. SARAH BAKER[5] (*Kenelm[4], Sarah[3] Bradford, William[2-1]*), b. Marshfield 21 April 1726; d. there 29 Nov. 1792 in 67th yr.

    She m. Marshfield 21 April 1750 **THOMAS LITTLE**, b. Marshfield 16 June 1719; d. there 11 Dec. 1814 aged 93y 5m; son of John and Constant (Fobes) Little, a descendant of Pilgrims **John Alden** and **Richard Warren**. He m. (1) Marshfield 9 March 1742 ABIGAIL HOWLAND. He m. (3) Marshfield 21 Nov. 1793 LUCY (DINGLEY) BOURN.

    In the 1771 Valuation List, Thomas Little appears in Marshfield with 2 polls, 1 house, 1 shop, 1 horse, 4 oxen, 5 cattle, 19 goats or sheep, 4 swine, 45 acres of pasture, 6 acres of tillage which produced 120 bushels of grain, 30 acres of salt marsh which produced 20 tons of hay, and 3 acres of upland which produced 2 tons of hay.

Thomas Little was head of a household of 5 men over 16, 3 females, and 1 other free person in Marshfield in the 1790 census.

The will of Thomas Little of Marshfield, yeoman, dated 16 March 1809, proved 11 March 1815, names wife Lucy; granddaughter Abigail Little Rogers; daughter Abigail Tilden; sons Thomas Little and William Henry Little; grandson Thomas Little son of William Henry Little; sons Doty Little and Otis Little; daughters Abigail Tilden, Ruth Waterman, and Betsey Trevant; and grandchildren Joseph Bryant and Sarah Bryant.

On 10 June 1814 Thomas Little of Marshfield, yeoman, gave to his grandsons Thomas Little 3rd and Avery Little of Marshfield, laborers, ten acres of salt marsh that had been his father John Little's; Thomas' wife Lucy released her dower rights.

On 29 May 1824 Doty Little of Castine, Me., gentleman, sold to Otis Little Esq. of Castine all his right in land in Marshfield conveyed to him by the will of Thomas Little; Hannah Little wife of Doty released her dower rights.

Children of Thomas and Sarah (Baker) Little, b. Marshfield:

    i   CHARLES LITTLE[6], b. 28 May 1751; lost at sea Sept. 1779 in 29th yr.

    ii ABIGAIL LITTLE, b. 20 Jan. 1753

   iii SARAH LITTLE, b. 8 June 1755

   iv RUTH LITTLE, b. 19 Aug. 1757

    v THOMAS LITTLE, b. 1 Nov. 1759

   vi WILLIAM HENRY LITTLE, b. 21 Dec. 1761

  vii BETSA LITTLE, b. 25 March 1764

 viii DOTY LITTLE, b. 3 Oct. 1766

   ix OTIS LITTLE, b. 27 March 1769

    x AVERY LITTLE, b. 29 Dec. 1771; lost at sea April 1797; unm.

References: *Marshfield VR* pp. 33(b. Thomas), 105(b. ch.), 136(3rd m.), 159(1st m.), 395(d. Charles), 396(d. Sarah). Plymouth Co. PR 47:98-100(Thomas Little). Plymouth Co. LR 124:123(Thomas Little); 153:229(Doty Little). *1771 Valuation* p. 646.

404. KENELM BAKER[5] (*Kenelm*[4], *Sarah*[3] *Bradford, William*[2-1]), b. Marshfield 1 July 1728; d. before 26 March 1777 when his estate was inventoried.

He m. Marshfield 29 May 1753 **TABITHA HEWETT**, b. Marshfield 11 March 1733/4; d. after 21 May 1803 when mentioned in deed and before 10 Oct. 1808 when the children divided the land set to her from her husband's estate; daughter of Joseph and Sarah (Dingley) Hewett.

In the 1771 Valuation List, Kenelm Baker appears in Marshfield with 1 poll, 1 house, 1 shop, ½ of a grist mill, 1 horse, 2 oxen, 3 cattles, 7 goats or sheep, 8 acres of pasture, 2 acres of tillage which produced 40 bushels of grain, 1 barrel of cider, 3½ acres of salt marsh which produced 2 tons of hay, and 1 acre of fresh meadow which produced ½ ton of hay.

On 6 Jan. 1777 Joseph Hewitt was granted administration on the estate of Kenelm Baker. On 26 March 1777 the inventory was taken.

Also on 6 Jan. 1777 Tabitha Baker of Marshfield, widow, was made guardian to Tabitha Baker Jr., age 12, and Olive Baker, age 10, daughters of Kenelm Baker.*

On 21 May 1803 John Baker of Marshfield, Gentleman, sold to his son Scollay Baker of Marshfield, laborer, all his real estate in Marshfield including a 45-acre homestead with a dwelling house and barn bounded on land owned by widow Tabitha Baker and Bradford Baker, one third part of a grist mill, and a pew in the south meeting house.

On 10 Oct. 1808 Kenelm Baker of Pembroke, yeoman, Bradford Baker, Tabithy Lapham and Adam Lapham, and Olive Ford and Waterman Ford all of Marshfield, yeomen, sold to Henry Baker of Marshfield land in Marshfield that had been set off to Tabithy Baker, widow, from the estate of Kenelm Baker, and a pew in Mr. Shaw's meeting house; Kenelm reserved two-fifths of a salt marsh and Bradford reserved two-fifths of the pew.

Children of Kenelm and Tabitha (Hewett) Baker, b. Marshfield:

    i   KENELM BAKER[6], b. 29 Nov. 1753
   ii   BRADFORD BAKER, b. 2 Oct. 1755
  iii   HENRY BAKER
  iv   TABITHA BAKER, b. ca. 1765
   v   OLIVE BAKER, b. ca. 1767

* Note: The docket index says that there are guardianships for Henry, Tabitha, and Olive, but just two page numbers are given and they are for Tabitha and Olive.

References: *Marshfield VR* pp. 80(b. Sarah), 106(b. ch.), 141(m.). *Bradford Desc* p. 123. Plymouth Co. LR 97:21(John Baker). *1771 Valuation* p. 646.

405.   ELIZABETH BAKER⁵ (*Kenelm⁴, Sarah³ Bradford, William²⁻¹*), b. Marshfield 29 July 1730; d. after 11 Jan. 1781 (deed).

She m. **ABNER TURNER**, bp. Scituate 1 Sept. 1734; d. there 25 Jan. 1810 aged 77; son of Caleb and Rachel (Dwelly) Turner.   On 28 Feb. 1775 Caleb Turner of Scituate, yeoman, sold to Abner Turner of Scituate, calker, eleven acres with a house; Caleb's wife Rachel also signed this deed.

On 5 May 1780 Abner Turner of Scituate, yeoman, sold to William Copland of Scituate, housewright, five acres; Abner's wife Betty also signed this deed.   On 11 Jan. 1781 Abner sold to William six acres with a house, and Betty again signed the deed.

Abner Turner was head of a household of 1 man and 4 females in Scituate in the 1790 census.

No Plymouth Co. probate records were found for Abner or Elizabeth Turner.

References: *VR Scituate* 1:369(bp. Abner); 2:455(d. Abner).   Plymouth Co. LR 59:77(Caleb Turner); 60:104-5(Abner Turner).

406. WILLIAM BAKER⁵ (*Kenelm⁴, Sarah³ Bradford, William²⁻¹*), b. Marshfield 16 Oct. 1734; d. there 22 Sept. 1807 in 73ʳᵈ yr.

He m. Scituate 2 Nov. 1758 **HANNAH LINCOLN**, b. Scituate 2 Dec. 1734; d. after 17 Jan. 1814 when she acknowledged a deed; daughter of Joshua and Mercy (Dwelly) Lincoln.

In the 1771 Valuation List, William Baker appears in Marshfield with 1 poll, 1 house, 1 shop, ¼ of a sawmill, 1 horse, 2 oxen, 4 cattle, 13 goats or sheep, 4 swine, 20 acres of pasture, 3 acres of tillage which produced 36 bushels of grain, 3½ acres of salt marsh which produced 2 tons of hay, and 1 acre of fresh meadow which produced ½ ton of hay.

The court records show that William Baker served the town of Marshfield as a constable in 1772, and that William Baker of Marshfield, innholder, was granted a license to sell liquor from 1776 to 1793.

Wm. Baker was head of a household of 3 men, 2 boys under 16, and 3 females in Marshfield in the 1790 census.

On 19 Dec. 1798 William Baker of Marshfield, yeoman, sold to his son Joshua Baker of Marshfield, gentleman, four acres, the east part of his farm; William's wife Hannah released her dower rights.

On 2 Aug. 1807 William Baker of Marshfield, yeoman, sold to his two sons William Baker Jr., yeoman, and Joshua Baker, Gentleman, both of Marshfield, all his real estate including homestead, meadow, and woodland,

and his pew and part of a saw mill. He reserved the use and improvement of the estate for his life and the life of his wife and a right for his daughter Hannah Hunt "as long as her present Husband does not provide for her."

On 7 Dec. 1807 William Baker of Marshfield was appointed executor of the estate of William Baker of Marshfield, yeoman.

On 23 Nov. 1813 William Baker of Marshfield, yeoman, and Hannah Baker of Marshfield, widow, sold to Jonathan Stetson of Marshfield, yeoman, one-eighth of a saw mill; Abigail the wife of William also signed the deed and it was acknowledged by all three on 17 Jan. 1814.

Children of William and Hannah (Lincoln) Baker, b. Marshfield:*

    i WILLIAM BAKER[6], b. 10 Sept. 1759

    ii JOSHUA BAKER, b. 23 April 1764

    iii MERCY LINCOLN BAKER, b. 6 April 1766

    iv HANNAH BAKER, b. 28 Oct. 1767

    v NATHANIEL BAKER, b. 2 Feb. 1770

    vi BENJAMIN BAKER, b. 10 June 1773

* Aspinwall includes a son John, b. 23 April 1754 (before the m.) and dau. Mercy, b. April 1756

References: *Marshfield VR* pp. 51(b. ch.), 179(int.), 354(m.), 415(d. William). *VR Scituate* 1:220(b. Hannah); 2:17(m.). *Baker Desc* pp. 123-4. Plymouth Co. PR 39:144; 42:227(William Baker). Plymouth Co. LR 86:106; 107:74(William Baker). *Plymouth Co Ct Recs* Vol. 3, 4. *1771 Valuation* p. 646.

407. LUCY BAKER[5] (*Kenelm⁴, Sarah³ Bradford, William²⁻¹*), b. Marshfield 15 May 1737; d. 1814 according to Aspinwall.

She m. Marshfield 9 Dec. 1762 **DANIEL FISHER** of Duxbury.

On 29 March 1769 Daniel Fisher of Marshfield, Physician, and his wife Lucy, sold to Sybilline White of Marshfield, mariner, his whole farm of 40 acres.

In the 1771 Valuation List, Daniel Fisher appears in Marshfield with 1 poll and £13:6:8 lent at interest.

No Plymouth Co. probate records were found for Daniel or Lucy Fisher.

Children of Daniel and Lucy (Baker) Fisher, b. Marshfield:

    i DANIEL COWELL FISHER[6], b. 5 May 1764

    ii LUCE BAKER FISHER, b. 18 Dec. 1765

iii JOSEPH FISHER, b. 24 Nov. 1767

iv CHARLES FISHER, b. 10 Nov. 1772 (Aspinwall)

References: *Marshfield VR* pp. 152(m.), 177-8(b. ch.). Plymouth Co. LR 55:20(Daniel Fisher). *1771 Valuation* p. 646.

408. LUCY SPRAGUE[5] (*Keziah Baker*[4], *Sarah*[3] *Bradford*, *William*[2-1]), b. Rochester 23 Feb. 1731/2; d. there 19 Oct. 1800 aged 68y 7m.

She m. (1) Rochester 27 May 1762 **EBENEZER CLAP**, b. Rochester 2 Aug. 1734; d. there 20 Sept. 1769 in 35th yr.; son of Ebenezer and Mary (Winslow) Clap.

She m. (2) Rochester 15 Dec. 1774 **MICAH HASKELL**, b. Rochester 20 Nov. 1735; d. there 2 Aug. 1807 in 72nd yr.; son of Mark and Mary (_____) Haskell. On 21 Feb. 1806 Micah Haskell of Rochester, yeoman, sold to Robert Rider of Middleboro, yeoman, an undivided right in a lot of cedar swamp from his father Mark Haskell and grandfather Roger Haskell.

On 5 Dec. 1769 widow Keziah Clap was appointed administratrix of the estate of Ebenezer Clap, Jr.

On 4 Dec. 1788 Nathaniel Sprague of Rochester, Esq., and Micah Haskell of Rochester, taylor, and his wife Lucy, heirs of Nathaniel Sprague divided the homestead farm of their grandfather Samuel Sprague.

Micah Haskell was head of a household of 3 men 16 or older and 2 females in Rochester in the 1790 census.

Michal Haskell of Rochester, taylor, made his will on 28 July 1807 with a codicil on the same day, and it was proved 15 Aug. 1807. He named Nathaniel Clapp (executor); Zebulon Haskell and Job Haskell, both of Rochester, sons of Seth Haskell; Nathaniel Haskell of Hardwick; Samuel Haskell of Brookfield; Roger Haskell of Oakham; Zebulon Haskell of Middleborough; Elisha Haskell of Middleborough; Lydia Hammond wife of Benjamin of Rochester, daughter of Seth Haskell; Abiah Peeking wife of Benjamin of Rochester, daughter of Seth; Micah Haskell Ruggles, son of Elisha Ruggles of Rochester; and Henry Ruggles, James Ruggles, and William Ruggles, sons of Elisha.

Micah Haskell and Lucy Sprague had no children.

Children of Ebenezer and Lucy (Sprague) Clap, b. Rochester:

i KEZIAH CLAP[6], b. ca. 1765; bp. 20 Sept. 1772

ii NATHANIEL CLAP, b. ca. 1766; bp. 20 Sept. 1772

iii EBENEZER CLAP, b. ca. 1768; d. 12 May 1771 ae 2y 8m

References: *VR Rochester* 1:75(b. Ebenezer), 75-6(bp. Keziah, Nathaniel), 162(b. Micah); 2:76(2nd m.), 289(1st m.), 361(d. both Ebenezers), 394(d. Lucy, Micah). Plymouth Co. PR 20:310(Ebenezer Clapp); 42:150(Micah Haskell). Plymouth Co. LR 67:219(Nathaniel Sprague); 113:186(Micah Haskell).

409. NATHANIEL SPRAGUE[5] (*Keziah Baker*[4], *Sarah*[3] *Bradford, William*[2-1]), b. Rochester 21 May 1738; d. there 9 Jan. 1797 in 59th yr.

He m. (1) Rochester 28 May 1769 **MARY** or **POLLY BASSETT**, b. ca. 1747; d. Rochester 9 June 1770 in 23rd yr.

He m. (2) int. Rochester 12 Dec. 1772 **ELIZABETH HAMMOND**, b. Newport, R.I., 25 May 1743; d. Rochester 10 March 1805 in 63rd y; daughter of Elnathan and Mary (Wignal) Hammond of Newport, R.I.

Nathaniel Sprague of Rochester served as a Justice of the Peace.

On 20 Dec. 1768 Keziah Sprague of Rochester, widow, gave to son Nathaniel Sprague of Rochester, mariner, all her right to her son Micah's lands. On 4 Dec. 1788 Nathaniel Sprague of Rochester, Esq., and Micah Haskell of Rochester, taylor, and his wife Lucy, heirs of Nathaniel Sprague, divided the homestead farm of their grandfather Samuel Sprague.

At the October 1773 term of the Court of Common Pleas, Nathaniel Sprague of Rochester, Gentleman, sued William Nicols of Chilmark, clothier, for damaging a chaise. On 25 June 1773, Nathaniel

> … had acomodated, provided, and delivered to him the said William a certain horse and chaise of his the said Nathaniel's of the value of thirty pounds, to ride from Rochester aforesaid to a place called Bedford in the town of Dartmouth … William then and there promised the said Nathaniel that he would carefully and prudently drive said horse and chaise, and would not over-ride said horse or in any respect hurt or injure either the said horse or chaise in the same journey but would deliver both said horse and chaise safe and sound to the said Nathaniel when he had performed said journey … Nevertheless the said William … did so carelessly, imprudently and violently drive said horse and chaise that one side of said chaise and the box was broken and destroyed, and the said horse by the fatigue and undue riding of him was so injured, hurt and abused as to be rendered of little or no value.

The jury found William guilty.

At the Oct. 1787 term of the Court of Common Pleas, Nathaniel Sprague Esq. of Rochester sued Jabez Benson of Wareham, yeoman, for a broken covenant. On 22 Feb. 1786 Jabez had made an indenture and "did put his son Jabez an apprentice to the said Nathaniel faithfully to serve him until he should arrive to the Age of twenty one years, and the aforesaid Jabez (the

Father) did thereby Covenant and agree ... in Consideration of the several Matters and Things in the said Indenture mentioned by the said Nathaniel." Nathaniel claimed that he had fulfilled his part of the agreement, but that Jabez had not and that on 11 April 1787 his son "did absent himself from the said Nathaniel nor has he since returned to the same; and further ... the said Apprentice did purloin and carry away sundry articles of the said Nathaniel." The court found in Nathaniel's favor.

At the October 1788 term of the Court of Common Pleas, Nathaniel Sprague Esq. of Rochester sued Samuel Rider of Rochester and Robert Rider of Middleborough, both yeomen. Nathaniel said that on 28 April 1787 he "was possessed of a certain Close of Swamp ground lying and being in the Town of Rochester aforesaid containing Seventeen Acres," and the Riders "enkindled a Fire on a Close next adjoining the Close of the said Nathaniel and then and there so negligently and carelessly kept their Fire in said Close in which they had enkindled the same, that for want of due Care the said Fire Escaped into the Swamp of the Nathaniel and the Timber and Wood ... growing was then and there ... burnt down." The jury found in the Riders' favor.

Nath¹ Sprague Esq. was head of a household of 2 men, 1 boy under 16, and 2 females in Rochester in the 1790 census.

At the August 1791 term of the Court of General Sessions, Nathaniel Sprague, Ephraim Spooner, Isaac Tomson, and Ebenezer Washburn, as "a Committee to consider of the expediency of erecting an House of Correction in the County of Plymouth for keeping, correcting, and fitting to work of Rogues, Vagabonds *et al.*," reported "that the Prison of the County has better be appropriated at this Time for an House of Correction, vizt, such part of it as may be convenient," and that the selectmen of any town from which any persons are sent there "should take effectual care that proper materials for them to labour on be sent forward to the Prison Keeper that they may be properly employed and not chargeable to others; also that proper Utensils to work with should be procured by the County." At the April 1793 term, Daniel Howard, Nathaniel Sprague, and Abraham Holmes, Esqs., "a Committee to examine the State of the Goal," recommended that "the Glass Windows be repaired, that a new floor be laid down in the Kitchen, that the Room called the Debtors Room be ceiled with good pine boards of a full inch thick plained and jointed, that the roof and walls of said building be painted with some cheap kind of oil and paint for the preservation of the covering, and that such other small repairs be made as shall be unavoidably necessary."

The will of Nathaniel Sprague of Rochester dated 4 Jan. 1797, proved 20 Jan. 1797, names wife Elizabeth; nephew Nathaniel Clapp; sister Lucy, wife of Micah Haskell; kinsman Theophilus Pitcher; Nathaniel Sprague Spooner, son of Seth Spooner; Nathaniel Sprague Ruggles, son of Major Elisha Ruggles; Nathaniel Sprague, son of Peleg Sprague of Keene, N.H.; Polly Ruggles, wife of Major Elisha Ruggles; and Keziah Luce, wife of Stephen Luce.

Child of Nathaniel and Mary (Bassett) Sprague, b. Rochester:

> i   FRANCIS SPRAGUE[6], b. 4 April 1770; d. same day

Children of Nathaniel and Elizabeth (Hammond) Sprague, b. Rochester:

> ii   POLLY B. SPRAGUE d. 2 March 1784 ae 11
> iii RUTH SPRAGUE d. 25 Oct. 1775 ae 5w

References: *VR Rochester* 1:283(b. Francis); 2:290(both m), 436(d. Nathaniel, Polly, Elizabeth, Polly B.), 437(d. Ruth). Plymouth Co. PR 36:43(Nataniel Sprague). *RIVR* Newport 4:2:99(b. Elizabeth). Plymouth Co. LR 54:225(Keziah Sprague); 67:219(Nathaniel Sprague). *Plymouth Co Ct Recs* 4:89(Nathaniel Sprague *et al.*), 108(Daniel Howard *et al.*); 9:24; 10:79,113(Nathaniel Sprague).

410. ELEANOR BAKER[5] *(Samuel[4], Sarah[3] Bradford, William[2-1])*, b. Marshfield 21 Sept. 1727; d. 24 June 1823.

She m. Marshfield 7 Nov. 1754 **JOSEPH THOMAS**, b. Marshfield 2 Nov. 1719; d. before 13 Feb. 1758 (father's will); son of Joseph and Lydia (Winslow) Thomas.

The will of Joseph Thomas of Marshfield dated 13 Feb. 1758 names wife Lideah; grandson Joseph Thomas, the heir of son Joseph Thomas deceased, "If my son deceased should have an other heir yet unborn if it is a son to share equally with my grandson Joseph." (This would be Ichabod.)

On 3 April 1758 the court appointed Samuel Baker of Duxbury as guardian of Joseph Thomas, minor son of Joseph Thomas, Jr., late of Marshfield, dec. On 5 May 1758 he was appointed guardian of Ichabod.

Thomas Baker of Duxbury in his will dated 20 June 1827, probated 4 Sept. 1827, named his wife Hannah C. Baker, widow Celia Baker, Nancy and Polly F. Baker, Elijah Baker, Thomas Baker of Marshfield, George and Daniel Baker, Charles and Daniel Baker, Joseph and Ichabod Thomas of Maine, and Hannah B. McGlathlan. Except for his wife, there are no relationships given in his will.

Children of Joseph and Eleanor (Baker) Thomas, b. Marshfield:

  i JOSEPH THOMAS⁶, b. 13 May 1756
 ii ICHABOD THOMAS, b. 14 March 1758

References: *Marshfield VR* pp. 84(b. Joseph), 110(b. ch.), 142(m.), 151(int.). Thomas Gen p. 171. Plymouth Co. PR 15:31(gdns.); 272-3(Joseph Thomas); 64:229(Thomas Baker).

411. HANNAH BAKER⁵ (*Samuel⁴, Sarah³ Bradford, William²⁻¹*), b. Marshfield 25 Feb. 1729.

She m. Marshfield 29 July 1767 **SAMUEL SMITH** of Great Partners, N.Y.

On 4 Feb. 1767 Samuel Smith "a transient man...who came from Marshfield some time last fall" was warned out of Duxbury.

In the 1771 Valuation List, Samuel Smith appears in Marshfield with 1 poll, 1 house, 1 cattle, and 1 swine.

Child of Samuel and Hannah (Baker) Smith, b. Marshfield:

  i JOHN SMITH⁶, b. 15 Dec. 1769

References: *Marshfield VR* pp. 62(b. John), 141(m.). *Plymouth Co Ct Recs* 3:238. *1771 Valuation* p. 644.

412. BETHIAH BAKER⁵ (*Samuel⁴, Sarah³ Bradford, William²⁻¹*), b. Marshfield 11 May 1733; d. Hanover 20 Jan. 1822.

She m. Duxbury 25 Dec. 1760 **HENRY PERRY**, bp. Marshfield 28 May 1738; d. Pembroke 23 March 1815 in 80th yr.; son of Samuel and Eunice (Witherell) Perry.

Henry Perry served in the Revolutionary War as a private in Capt. Elijah Cushing's company of militia which marched in response to the alarm of 19 April 1775. He also served in Capt. Josiah Cushing's company, Col. John Cushing's regiment from 10 Dec. to 24 Dec. 1776. And he served in Capt. John Turner's company, Col. Eleazer Brooks' regiment with service from 6 Nov. 1777 to 2 April 1778.

Henry Perrey was head of a household of 4 men over 16 and 1 female in Pembroke in the 1790 census.

The will of Henry Perry of Pembroke, yeoman, dated 23 June 1812, proved 4 April 1815, names wife Bethiah and sons Samuel Baker Perry, James Perry, John Perry, and Henry Perry.

On 6 March 1820 Samuel Perry asked the judge to declare his mother *non-compos*. On 4 April 1820 she was so declared.

Children of Henry and Bethiah (Baker) Perry, b. Pembroke:

    i SAMUEL BAKER PERRY[6], bp. 25 April 1762

    ii HENRY PERRY, b. 25 April 1764

    iii JOHN PERRY (twin) , bp. 10 May 1768

    iv JAMES PERRY (twin) , bp. 10 May 1768

References: *Marshfield VR* p. 138(int.). *VR Duxbury* p. 215(m.). *VR Pembroke* pp. 162-3(b. ch.), 437 (d. Henry). *Bradford Desc* p. 124. Plymouth Co. PR 47:124-5(Henry Perry); 51:94(Bethiah Perry). *MSSR* 12:202(Henry Perry).

413. JAMES BAKER[5] (*Samuel[4], Sarah[3] Bradford, William[2-1]*), b. Marshfield 4 Jan. 1737; d. there 3 Aug. 1798 in 62nd yr.

He m. ca. May 1769 **CELIA ADAMS**, b. Kingston 8 Dec. 1747; d. Marshfield May 1839; daughter of Richard and Mary (Carver) Adams.

In the 1771 Valuation List, James Baker appears in Marshfield with 1 poll, 1 house, 1 shop, 2 cattle, 4 goats or swine, 5 acres of pasture, 1 acre of tillage which produced 20 bushels of grain, 10 acres of salt marsh which produced 8 tons of hay, and 2 acres of fresh meadow which produced 1 ton of hay.

James Baker was head of a household of 2 men, 1 boy under 16, and 3 females in Marshfield in the 1790 census.

On 13 April 1796 James Baker of Marshfield, yeoman, Charles Baker of Marshfield, yeoman, Thomas Baker of Duxbury, yeoman, and Elijah Baker of Duxbury, Gentleman, equal owners of the real estate their father Samuel Baker late of Duxbury, yeoman, deceased, had given to them by his will agreed to divide the land.

On 21 Aug. 1798 Samuel Baker of Marshfield was appointed executor of the estate of James Baker of Marshfield, yeoman. On 3 Dec. 1798 the court divided the real estate of James Baker with widow Celia Baker receiving her thirds and the rest divided between Samuel Baker, oldest son; Celia Baker; Polly Baker; and Thomas Baker.

On 20 Feb. 1799 Selah Baker Jr. and Polly Baker both of Marshfield, seamsters, sold to Charles Baker of Marshfield, yeoman, 30 acres in Duxbury "being part of the farm of our grandfather Samuel Baker in division to our father James Baker deceased and his brothers."

Thomas Baker of Duxbury in his will dated 20 June 1827, proved 4 Sept. 1827, named his wife Hannah C. Baker, widow Celia Baker, Nancy and Polly

F. Baker, Elijah Baker, Thomas Baker of Marshfield, George and Daniel Baker, Charles and Daniel Baker, Joseph and Ichabod Thomas of Maine, and Hannah B. McGlathlan. Except for his wife, there are no relationships stated in his will.

On 12 March 1830 Celia Baker of Marshfield, widow, appointed Bourne Thomas of Marshfield, yeoman, her attorney to sell land she received from the will of Thomas Baker late of Duxbury. On the same day her attorney sold two pieces of salt marsh from Thomas's will.

On 7 Aug. 1839 Thomas Baker of Marshfield, yeoman, sold to James Baker of Marshfield, yeoman, all his right to the part of the estate of his father James Baker set off to his widow.

Children of James and Celia (Adams) Baker, b. Marshfield (named in 3 Dec. 1798 division):*

    i   SAMUEL BAKER[6]

    ii CELIA BAKER, b. 3 Nov. 1772

    iii POLLY BAKER

    iv THOMAS BAKER, b. 1 May 1785

* Aspinwall adds a son James but he is not mentioned in the brother's will.

References: *Marshfield VR* pp. 157(b. Thomas), 201(d. Celia), 228(b. Celia), 398(d. James). Plymouth Co. PR 34:193; 36:464, 503(James Baker); 64:229(Thomas Baker). *VR Kingston* p. 15 (b. Celia/Selah). Plymouth Co. LR 86:175(James Baker *et al*); 88:206(Selah & Polly Baker); 167:166(Celia Baker); 194:223(Thomas Baker). *1771 Valuation* p. 646.

414. THOMAS BAKER[5] (*Samuel[4], Sarah[3] Bradford, William[2-1]*), b. Marshfield 24 Jan. 1739; d. between 20 June and 4 Sept. 1827 (probate).

He m. (1) Marshfield 8 Feb. 1795 **SARAH THOMAS**, b. Marshfield 21 Jan. 1753; d. 6 Jan. 1822; daughter of William and Mary (Hill) Thomas.

He m. (2) Marshfield 26 May 1822 **HANNAH COWIN SIMMONS** of Marshfield.

On 13 April 1796 James Baker of Marshfield, yeoman, Charles Baker of Marshfield, yeoman, Thomas Baker of Duxbury, yeoman, and Elijah Baker of Duxbury, Gentleman, equal owners of the real estate their father Samuel Baker late of Duxbury, yeoman, deceased, had given to them by his will, agreed to divide the land.

Thomas Baker of Duxbury in his will dated 20 June 1827, probated 4 Sept. 1827, named his wife Hannah C. Baker, widow Celia Baker, Nancy and Polly F. Baker, Elijah Baker, Thomas Baker of Marshfield, George and Daniel

Baker, Charles and Daniel Baker, Joseph and Ichabod Thomas of Maine, and Hannah B. McGlathlan. Except for his wife, there are no relationships stated in his will.

No children.

References: Thomas Gen p. 170. *Marshfield VR* pp. 102(b. Sarah), 169(m.). *Bradford Desc* p. 124. Plymouth Co. LR 86:175(James Baker *et al.*). Plymouth Co. PR 64:229(Thomas Baker).

415. CHARLES BAKER⁵ (*Samuel⁴, Sarah³ Bradford, William²⁻¹*), b. Duxbury 26 April 1741; d. Marshfield 11 Jan. 1817.

He m. Marshfield 21 Jan. 1768 **DEBORAH WILLIAMSON**, b. Marshfield 13 Jan. 1741; d. 16 Jan. 1834; daughter of Samuel and Elizabeth (Eames) Williamson.

In the 1771 Valuation List, Charles Baker appears in Marshfield with 1 poll, 1 house, 1 shop, 10 goats or sheep, and 3 acres of tillage which produced 15 bushels of grain.

Charles Baker was head of a household of 2 men, 2 boys under 16, and 3 females in Marshfield in the 1790 census.

On 13 April 1796 James Baker of Marshfield, yeoman, Charles Baker of Marshfield, yeoman, Thomas Baker of Duxbury, yeoman, and Elijah Baker of Duxbury, Gentleman, equal owners of the real estate their father Samuel Baker late of Duxbury, yeoman, deceased, had given to them by his will, agreed to divide the land.

On 16 March 1812 Charles Baker of Marshfield, yeoman, and his wife Deborah sold to their two sons Charles Baker Jr. and Samuel Baker Jr. of Marshfield seven acres given to Deborah by her late father Samuel Williamson.

The will of Charles Baker of Marshfield, yeoman, dated 16 March 1812, proved 26 Feb. 1817, names wife; daughter Deborah Weston (apparently a widow); sons Charles Baker and Samuel Baker; and daughters Eleanor Chandler and Abigail Walker.

On 22 Sept. 1826 Charles Baker and Samuel Baker Jr. agreed to divide the land their father died siezed of; Marian the wife of Charles and Eunice the wife of Samuel also signed the deed.

Thomas Baker of Duxbury in his will dated 20 June 1827, probated 4 Sept. 1827, named his wife Hannah C. Baker, widow Celia Baker, Nancy and Polly F. Baker, Elijah Baker, Thomas Baker of Marshfield, George and Daniel Baker, Charles and Daniel Baker, Joseph and Ichabod Thomas of Maine, and

Hannah B. McGlathlan. Except for his wife, there are no relationships stated in his will.

Children of Charles and Deborah (Williamson) Baker, b. Marshfield:*

 i ELEANOR BAKER⁶, b. 21 Jan. 1769
 ii ABIGAIL BAKER, b. 18 May 1770
 iii CHARLES BAKER, b. 28 Dec. 1771
 iv SAMUEL BAKER, b. 24 March 1774
 v DEBORAH BAKER, b. 10 Jan. 1781
 vi JOHN BAKER, b. 28 March 1788; d. Marshfield 10 June 1808 in 21st yr.

* **Note:** No record has been found for a son CHARLES, b. Sept. 1776; d. in 1778 as stated in *NEHGR* 81:292-3. Aspinwall adds John, b. 1776; d. 1778

References: *Marshfield VR* pp. 52(b. 1st 5 ch.), 53(b. John), 75(b. Deborah), 129(int.), 163(m.), 398(d. John). *Bradford Desc* pp. 124-5. Plymouth Co. PR 48:355-6(Charles Baker); 64:229(Thomas Baker). Plymouth Co. LR 86:75(James Baker *et al.*); 118:265(Charles Baker); 158:66(Charles & Samuel). *NEHGR* 81:292-3. *1771 Valuation* p. 646.

416. ELIJAH BAKER⁵ (*Samuel⁴, Sarah³ Bradford, William²⁻¹*), b. Duxbury 1 July 1744; d. there 7 or 17 May 1827 in 83rd yr.

He m. Pembroke 13 Jan. 1777 **POLLY / MARY WHITEMORE**, b. ca. 1751; d. Duxbury 7/20 Sept. 1832 in 81st yr; daughter of Jabez and Elizabeth (Howland) Whitemore.

Elijah Baker served in the Revolutionary War as a private in Capt. Benjamin Wadsworth's company, Col. James Warren's regiment which marched on the alarm of 19 April 1775. He served as a sergeant in Capt. Elijah Crooker's company, Brig. Gen. John Thomas' regiment; he enlisted 20 April 1775 and served for 3 months and 2 weeks. He served as a First Lieutenant in Capt. Calvin Partridge's company, Col. Joseph Cushing's regiment in 1776 and in Col. Theophilus Cotton's regiment in 1778.

The court records show that Elijah Baker served the town of Duxbury as a selectman in 1783 and 1784.

Elijah Baker was head of a household of 1 man, 3 boys under 16, and 3 females in Duxbury in the 1790 census.

On 13 April 1796 James Baker of Marshfield, yeoman, Charles Baker of Marshfield, yeoman, Thomas Baker of Duxbury, yeoman, and Elijah Baker of Duxbury, Gentleman, equal owners of the real estate their father Samuel

Baker late of Duxbury, yeoman, deceased, had given to them by his will agreed to divide the land.

On 24 May 1823 Elijah Baker of Duxbury, Gentleman, sold to George Baker of Marshfield, Gentleman, land in Duxbury. On 26 May 1823 Elijah sold land to Daniel Baker of Duxbury, mariner, bounded by George Baker. On 4 June 1825 Elijah sold to Elijah Baker Jr. of Duxbury, mariner, three and three-quarters acres and to Daniel one and three-quarters acres where Daniel's house stood. Elijah's wife Mary signed all four of these deeds.

Thomas Baker of Duxbury in his will dated 20 June 1827, probated 4 Sept. 1827, named his wife Hannah C. Baker, widow Celia Baker, Nancy and Polly F. Baker, Elijah Baker, Thomas Baker of Marshfield, George and Daniel Baker, Charles and Daniel Baker, Joseph and Ichabod Thomas of Maine, and Hannah B. McGlathlan. Except for his wife, there are no relationships stated in his will.

On 3 July 1827 George Baker was appointed administrator of the estate of Elijah Baker of Duxbury. On 28 Feb. 1829 George Baker, administrator of Elijah Baker's estate, was licensed to sell land to pay the debts; Ann W. Baker of Duxbury, singlewoman, being the highest bidder got the right of reversion in part of the dower set off to Mary Baker widow of Elijah, it being 70 rods of land, half of the house, and one-third of the barn.

Children of Elijah and Polly (Whitemore) Baker, b. Duxbury:

    i ANNE WHITEMORE BAKER[6], b. 29 April 1778

    ii ELIJAH BAKER, b. 8 Oct. 1782

    iii JABEZ WHITEMORE BAKER, b. 7 June 1786

    iv GEORGE BAKER, b. 14 Nov. 1787

    v POLLY BAKER, b. bet. 14 Nov. 1787 and 2 July 1790; d. ca. 1860

    vi DANIEL BAKER, b. 2 July 1790

References: *Bradford Desc* p. 125. *VR Duxbury* pp. 21-2(b. ch.), 349(d. Elijah, Polly, Anne [with no date]). Plymouth Co. PR 61:115(Elijah Baker); 64:229(Thomas Baker). Plymouth Co. LR 86:175(James Baker *et al.*); 151:102, 167; 159:1; 161:149(Elijah Baker); 179:204(George Baker). *NEHGR* 107:260(Whittemore gen.). *VR Pembroke* p. 229(m.). *MSSR* 1:475(Elijah Baker).

417. ABIGAIL BAKER[5] (*Samuel[4], Sarah[3] Bradford, William[2-1]*), b. Duxbury 24 Sept. 1746; d. Hanover 11 Dec. 1807 aged 61 yrs.

She m. Duxbury 15 Oct. 1769 **ISRAEL PERRY**, b. ca. 1744; d. Hanover 18 Feb. 1817 aged 74 yrs. He m. (2) Hanover 17 Dec. 1809 RELIEF SOPER.

The court records show that Israel Perry served the town of Hanover as a constable in 1773 and 1785 and that he was a county sheriff in 1782, 1784, 1788, and 1792.

Izrael Perrey was head of a household of 3 men, 4 boys under 16, and 4 females in Hanover in the 1790 census.

On 3 March 1817 Paul Perry was appointed to administer the estate of Israel Perry of Hanover, deceased. On 2 June 1817 the court gave widow Relief Perry one-third of the estate, with the remainder divided between heirs Israel Perry, Hannah Stetson, Eunice Baker, Ittai Perry, Oakes Perry, Horatio Perry, Paul Perry, Nabby Baker Perry, and the heirs of Thomas Perry, deceased.

On 8 Sept. 1819 Israel Perry late of Scarborough now resident of Boston, yeoman, sold to Paul Perry of Hanover, administrator of the estate of Israel Perry, all his right in the estate of Israel Perry.

On 17 Sept. 1824 Ittai Perry of Salem, Oakes Perry of Camden, Me., Horatio Perry of Salem, Paul Perry of Camden, Me., Samuel Baker of Marshfield and his wife Eunice, Samuel [later given as Edward] Stetson and his wife Hannah, and Nabby Baker Perry of Marshfield, all heirs of Israel Perry late of Hanover, made Edward Stetson their attorney; Abigail the wife of Ittai, Nancy the wife of Oakes, Harriet the wife of Horatio, and Chloe the wife of Paul released their dower rights.

Children of Israel and Abigail (Baker) Perry, b. Hanover:

  i ISRAEL PERRY[6], bp. 28 April 1771
 ii THOMAS PERRY, bp. 30 Aug. 1772
iii HANNAH PERRY, bp. 18 June 1775
 iv EUNICE PERRY, bp. 6 July 1777
  v HORATIO PERRY, bp. 3 Oct. 1784
 vi PAUL PERRY, b. 25 June 1786
vii OAKES PERRY (named in deed)
viii NABBY BAKER PERRY, bp. 6 Sept. 1789
 ix HAYTI (or ITTAI) PERRY (named in deed)

References: *VR Duxbury* p. 215(m.). *Hanover First Ch* pp. 105(2nd m.), 144(bp. Israel), 145(bp. Thomas), 147(bp. Hannah), 149(bp. Eunice), 152(bp. Horatio), 154(bp. Nabby), 205(d. Abigail), 208(d. Israel). *Bradford Desc* p. 125. Plymouth Co. PR 46:209; 50:421-5(Israel Perry). *Hanover VR* pp. 136(2nd m.), 204(d. Israel). Plymouth Co. LR 139:173(Israel Perry); 153:63(Ittai Perry *et al.*).

418. WILLIAM BAKER⁵ (*William⁴, Sarah³ Bradford, William²⁻¹*), b. Boston 13 June 1741; d. Stoughton 6 April 1785 aged 44 yrs.

He m. Boston 7 Jan. 1768 **ALICE PHILLIPS**, probably the one, b. Marshfield 24 Feb. 1744; d. Boston 2 Jan. 1824 aged 81, buried Granary Burial Ground. 4 Jan. 1823; daughter of Benjamin and Alice (Thomas) Phillips (see #395i).

In the 1771 Valuation List, William Baker Jr. appears in Boston with 1 poll and 1 house.

At a Selectmen's meeting on 1 Dec. 1779, William Baker was appointed Constable of the Watch at the South End. At a meeting on 7 Jan. 1784, he applied for a license as an auctioneer for the town and it was granted on 15 Jan. At a meeting on 25 July 1785, "Constable Wendell complains that two of his Compʸ viz. Thomˢ Pitcher and John Rennery, are deficient in their Duty – and proposes William Baker & John Frank as Watchmen in their room."

In Dec. 1785 Alice Baker of Boston, widow, was appointed guardian to William Baker and Elizabeth Baker, minors over 14, and Alice Baker and Phillips Baker, minors under 14, children of William Baker, late of Boston, deceased.

The will of William Baker of Boston dated 19 April 1785, proved 20 Dec. 1785, names the children of his son William: William, Betsey, Else, and Phillips.

At a Selectmen's meeting on 13 Sept. 1786 "Alice Baker approved of as a Retailer of Rum &c. at her Shop the Granary."

Children of William and Alice (Phillips) Baker, b. Boston, bp. Brattle St. Church:

  i   ELIZABETH BAKER⁶, b. 5 May 1769, bp. 14 May 1769
  ii WILLIAM BAKER, b. 27 Aug. 1770, bp. 2 Sept. 1770
  iii SARAH BAKER, b. 22 Feb. 1777, bp. 2 March 1777 (not named in grandfather's will
  iv ALICE BAKER, bp. 3 May 1778
  v   PHILLIPS BAKER, bp. 1 Aug. 1784

References: *Boston News Obits* 2:46(d. William).   BRC 24:318(b. Elizabeth), 320(b. William), 327(b. Sarah); 30:427(m.).   Suffolk Co. PR #18927-#18930(gdn.), #18583 84:719(William Baker). *Marshfield VR* p. 75(b. Alice). *Boston Cems* p. 427(bur. Alice). *Brattle St Ch Recs* pp. 186(bp. Elizabeth, William), 190(bp. Sarah, Alice), 191(bp. Phillips). *1771 Valuation* p. 42.   BRC 25:105(constable), 231, 235(auctioneer), 274(watchman), 325(Alice retailer).

419. SARAH BAKER[5] (*William[4], Sarah[3] Bradford, William[2-1]*), b. Boston 7 July 1742; d. there 30 Oct. 1825 aged 84y, buried Granary Burial Ground.

She m. Boston 23 May 1771 **HENRY BASS**, b. Boston 9 March 1740; d. there 5 June 1813 aged 74y; son of Moses and Hannah (Butler) Bass. He m. (1) Weston 16 April 1767 FAITH SAVAGE with whom he had Sarah.

Henry Bass owned the covenant in the Hollis Street church on 1 May 1768. His second wife may be the Sarah Bass who was admitted to the church on 5 July 1795.

At Boston town meetings on 10 March 1782 and 14 March 1777, Henry Bass was chosen as a warden.

In the 1771 Valuation List, Henry Bass appears in Boston with 1 poll, 1 house, 40 tons of vessels, and £30 in merchandise.

Henry Bass took part in the Boston Tea Party 16 Dec. 1773. At a town meeting on 7 Dec. 1774, he was chosen as a member of a "Committee of Inspection, & to carry the Resolutions of the Continental Congress into Execution" and on 10 March 1777, he was chosen for a "Committee of Correspondence Inspection & Safety." At a Selectmen's meeting on 18 Dec. 1776 he was one of the "Persons [to] be draughted as our proportion of the Militia, ordered by the Gen[l] Court as a reinforcement for the Continental Army at or near New York." Henry's name was marked with a "*" indicating he had paid a fine in lieu of serving. At a meeting on 11 March 1782, he was appointed to a committee to "Assist the Assessors in carrying the Resolve of the General Court for raising this Towns proportion of Men for the Continental Army."

At a Selectmen's meeting on 28 Aug. 1782, Henry Bass was listed as a retailer on Orange Street.

At a Boston town meeting on 11 March 1782, Henry Bass was chosen as a hayward. At town meetings on 14 March 1785, 22 March 1785, 12 March 1787, 10 March 1788, Henry Bass was chosen one of the sixteen firewards and at a meeting on 17 March 1789, he was one of four men "Voted, that the Thanks of the Town be & hereby are given ... for their good & faithful service in the Office of Fire Wards a Number of Years Past." On 12 March 1792, Henry Bass was appointed to a committee to "Consider the By Laws of the Town." On 2 March 1803, he was appointed to a committee "to receive correct and complete the list of qualified voters" in Ward 12.

Henry Bass was head of a household of 3 men, 4 boys under 16, and 4 females in Boston in the 1790 census.

In the 1798 Direct Tax for Boston, Henry Bass is listed as the owner and occupier of a two-story wooden dwelling with 25 windows on Rainsford's Lane with a barn and wood house valued at $1,500.

The will of Henry Bass of Boston, merchant, dated 19 May 1803, proved 21 June 1813, names wife Sarah; children Henry, George, Horatio, William, and Anna; and daughter Sarah, wife of Amos Bancroft of Weston.

Children of Henry and Sarah (Baker) Bass, bp. Hollis Street Church, Boston:

 i   HENRY BASS[6], bp. 1 March 1772 (also rec. Brattle St. Church)

 ii GEORGE BASS, bp. 22 Feb. 1779

 iii HORATIO BASS, bp. 22 Feb. 1779

 iv WILLIAM BASS (named in will)

 v   ANNA BASS, bp. 12 Feb. 1786

References: *BRC* 30:322(1st m.), 330(m.).   Suffolk Co. PR #24221(Henry Bass). *Descendants Of Samuel And Ann Bass*, Clarissa T. Bass, Freeport IL 1940 pp. 50-1. *VR Weston* p. 124(Henry's 1st m.). *Hollis St Ch* pp. 13-4. *Boston Cems* p. 493(d. Sarah). *Brattle St Ch Recs* p. 188(bp. Henry). *1771 Valuation* p. 32. BRC 18:74, 275(warden), 206, 271(committees);   22:399(1798   Direct   Tax);   25:23(militia);   25:191(retailer); 26:230(hayward), 236(militia committee); 31:54, 101, 134, 161(fireward), 190(thanks), 281-2(bylaws); 35:140(qualified voters).

420. BETHIAH BAKER[5] (*William[4], Sarah[3] Bradford, William[2-1]*), b. Boston 30 March 1744; d. there 29 June 1833 aged 90, buried in Granary Burial Ground.

She m. Boston 17 Nov. 1788, as his third wife, **EPHRAIM COPELAND**, b. Boston 5 Feb. 1726; d. there 11 Nov. 1810, bur. Granary Burial Ground 15 July 1810 aged 84y; son of Ephraim and Mercy (Verien) Copeland, a descendant of Pilgrim **John Alden**. He m. (1) Boston 20 Aug. 1755 ANNA CAZNEAU with whom he had Mercy, Ephraim, and William. He m. (2) Boston 13 July 1777 MARTHA HARVEY.

Ephraim Copeland was head of a household of 1 man, 1 boy under 16, and 2 females in Boston in the 1790 census.

The will of Bethiah Copeland of Boston, widow, dated 10 Dec. 1817, proved 29 July 1833, names Sarah Bass, widow of Henry Bass of Boston; Ann Bass, daughter of Sarah; Ephraim Copeland Bass, son of William; Elizabeth Tilden, widow, daughter of William Baker deceased; Hannah Perkins, daughter of Houghton Perkins deceased; Mrs. Winslow, widow and sister of late Mrs. Copeland; Mary Lincoln, widow, formerly Mary Carter; George Bass of Boston; Henry Bass of Boston; and Horatio Bass of Boston.

Bethiah had no children.

References: *BRC* 30:16(1st m.), 161(3rd m.), 405(2nd m.). Suffolk Co. PR #30285(Bethiah Copeland). *The Copeland Family*, Warren T. Copeland, Rutland VT 1937 pp. 36-7. *Boston News Obits* 2:1070. *Granary Bur Gr* p. 67. *Boston Cems* p. 427(bur. Bethiah, Ephraim). *Dexter Memorandum* p. 121 (d. Ephraim).

421. EDWARD BAKER⁵ (*Edward⁴, Sarah³ Bradford, William²⁻¹*), b. Boston 6 March 1748/9, bp. New South Church 12 March 1748; d. after 23 Oct. 1795 (deed). He may be the Edward Baker of Boston who d. Dorchester Sept. 1799.

He m. Boston at King's Chapel 30 May 1771 **LUCY MATHER**, bp. Middletown, Conn., First Church 8 Nov. 1752; dau. Eliakim and Ruth (Roper) Mather. Dr. Thomas Mather of Pomfret, Conn., formerly of Boston, made his will 13 March 1759, proved 20 July 1764, naming his neice Lucy Mather and her sisters Ruth and Sarah. Ruth and Sarah were also married in King's Chapel.

On 23 Oct. 1795 Edward Baker of Boston, tobacconist, sold to John Doyle of Boston, yeoman, half of a tomb in the Common Burying Ground "marked on the Slate in the Wall John and William Gibbons."

On 1 April 1800 Anna Durivage, widow, Letitia Baker and Hannah Baker, singlewomen, and William Baker, tobacconist, all of Boston mortgaged a house and land on Gibbons Court to John Freeland of Boston, tobacconist.

On 21 Nov. 1803 William Baker of Boston, tobacconist, sold to Hannah Baker of Boston, spinster, half a house and land on Gibbons Court; William's wife Hannah released her dower rights. On the same day Hannah Baker, spinster, sold the ½ house and land to Samuel Morse of Boston, retailer.

Children of Edward and Lucy (Mather) Baker, named in grandmother's will:

    i HANNAH MATHER BAKER⁶, bp. 22 April 1772

    ii WILLIAM BAKER

References: *BRC* 9:265(b. Edward); 30:363(m.). *New South Ch Recs* on *Boston Churches* CD (bp. Edward). Suffolk Co. LR 194:118(Anne Durivage); 207:147(Edward Baker), 148(Hannah Baker); 229:171(Edward Baker). *Boston Ch Recs* on CD(bp. Edward, Hannah). Suffolk Co. PR #13476, 63:51(Thomas Mather). Middletown CT 1st Ch. 1:87(bp. Lucy). *Dexter Memorandum* p. 27(d. Edward).

422. ANNA BAKER[5] (*Edward[4], Sarah[3] Bradford, William[2-1]*), b. Boston 16 March 1761; bp. New South Church 29 March 1761; d. there 16 Sept. 1828 aged 66, buried 18 Sept. Granary Burial Ground.

She m. Dedham 23 Jan. 1788 **NICHOLAS CAILLIAU DuRIVAGE**, b. ca. 1743; d. New London, Conn., 5 Oct. 1794 aged 51 yrs.

On 17 Oct. 1788 Nicholas DuRivage of Dedham, merchant, sold to James Hayman of Boston, merchant, two lots of land in Dedham; Nicholas' wife Anne also signed this deed.

Nicholas Durivage was head of a household consisting of 4 men, 3 boys under 16, 3 females, and a slave in New London Co., Conn., in the 1790 census.

The will of Nicholas Durivage dated 3 Oct. 1794, proved 10 Nov. 1794, names wife Anne Durivage and mentions but does not name "my children." A 1795 record mentions three small children. On 24 Oct. 1803 Anna wrote the Judge of Probate about the chance of collecting on the estate in England of her deceased husband, consisting of property in the West Indies taken from him by the "British spoilation."

In the 1798 Direct Tax for Boston, Anna "Durwerge" is listed as the owner and occupier of a three-story brick dwelling with 15 windows on Newbury Street valued at $1,500.

On 1 April 1800 Anna Durivage, widow, Letitia Baker and Hannah Baker, singlewoman, and William Baker, tobacconist, all of Boston mortgaged a house and land on Gibbons Court to John Freeland of Boston, tobacconist.

On 13 Oct. 1819 Anne Durivage of Boston, widow, sold to Letitia Baker of Boston, singlewoman, half of land and a house on Newbury St., her share in the estates of Hannah Baker, deceased, and Mehitable Baker, deceased.

Children of Nicholas Cailliau and Anna (Baker) DuRivage, first two named in the 17 May 1839 will of their aunt Letitia Baker (see #83vi):

    i   FRANCIS SHUTE DURIVAGE[6], bp. Trinity Church 10 May 1789
   ii   ANNE LETITIA DURIVAGE, b. before 1792
  iii   [CHILD], prob. HANNAH DURIVAGE, b. prob. 1792-93 (ae 2 at father's death); prob. d. Boston 18 Dec. 1821 ae 28

References: *Dedham VR* p. 204(m.). New London CT PR #1859 (Nicholas Durivage). *Boston Cems* p. 427(d. Anna, Hannah). *Trinity Ch Recs* p. 628(bp. Francis). Suffolk Co. LR 164:26(Nicholas Durivage); 194:118; 264:66(Anne Durivage). *Columbian Centinel* 15 Oct. 1794(d. Nicholas); 22 Dec. 1821(d. Hannah). Boston Ch Recs on CD(bp. Anna). *BRC* [1798 Direct Tax] 22:406.

423. ANN DIMMICK[5] (*Ann⁴ Bradford, Joseph³, William²⁻¹*), b. Mansfield, Conn., 23 May 1724; d. there 15 Feb. 1779.

She m. Mansfield, Conn., 2 Sept. 1740 **EBENEZER CLARK**, b. Rowley 19 Dec. 1717; d. Ellington, Conn., 5 Nov. 1807; son of Richard and Abigail (Wicom) Clark.

On 5 Oct. 1741 Timothy Dimmock of Mansfield sold to Ebenezer Clark of Mansfield 21 acres. On 23 Jan. 1748/9 Timothy sold land in Mansfield to his daughter Anna Clark. And on 10 July 1753 Timothy gave his eldest daughter Anne Clark 28 acres that he had bought from Ebenezer Clark. On 14 June 1777 Wycom Clark of Mansfield sold to his father Ebenezer Clark land that his grandfather Timothy Dimmock had given to his mother Anne Clark.

Children of Ebenezer and Ann (Dimmick) Clark, b. Mansfield, Conn.:

- i TEMPERANCE CLARK[6], b. 21 April 1741
- ii SIMON CLARK, b. 11 March 1744
- iii TIMOTHY CLARK, b. 26 Dec. 1745
- iv JOANNAH CLARK, b. 23 Jan. 1747/8
- v WYCOM CLARK, b. 8 April 1750
- vi ABIGAIL CLARK, b. 28 Feb. 1752
- vii EBENEZER CLARK, b. 10 March 1754
- viii DANIEL CLARK, b. 6 May 1756
- ix ANNA CLARK, b. 9 May 1759; d. 10 July 1786; unm.
- x EUNICE CLARK, b. 11 May 1761
- xi JONATHAN CLARK, b. 20 May 1763
- xii MARY CLARK, b. 7 May 1765
- xiii SALOMON CLARK, b. 7 Oct. 1767

References: *Bradford Desc* pp. 125-6. Mansfield CT VR pp. 42(b. 1st 10 ch.), 43(b. last 3 ch.), 221(m.). *VR Rowley* p. 48(b. Ebenezer). Mansfield CT LR 4:37; 5:116, 133, 550; 9:245.

424. TIMOTHY DIMMICK[5] (*Ann⁴ Bradford, Joseph³, William²⁻¹*), b. Mansfield, Conn., 8 April 1726; d. Coventry, Conn., 5 Feb. 1795.

He m. Coventry, Conn., 11 March 1749/50 **DESIRE DIMMICK**, b. Mansfield, Conn., 23 Jan. 1732; d. Coventry, Conn., 9 May 1802 aged 70; daughter of Thomas and Ann (Mason) Dimmick. On 12 June 1749/50 the distribution of the estate of Thomas Dimmock of Mansfield included one-sixth part set off to his daughter Desire Dimmock.

On 12 June 1753 Timothy Dimmock of Coventry and his wife Desiah sold to Timothy Dimmock of Mansfield 32 acres, part of the farm of Thomas Dimmock deceased set off to Desiah. On 2 July 1753 Timothy Dimmock of Mansfield gave to his son Timothy Dimmock Jr. 43½ acres.

Tim° Dimock was head of a household of 3 men, 1 boy under 16, and 3 females in Coventry in the 1790 census and listed next to him was Dan¹ Dimock (1 man, 4 females) and near him was Tim° Dimock Jr. (1 man, 4 females).

Children of Timothy and Desire (Dimmick) Dimmick, b. Coventry, Conn.:

 i DESIRE DIMMICK⁶, b. 22 Jan. 1751

 ii EUNICE DIMMICK, b. 9 Feb. 1753

 iii ANN DIMMICK, b. 15 Sept. 1754

 iv LOIS DIMMICK, b. 12 May 1756

 v SYBIL DIMMICK, b. 18 March 1758

 vi LUCY DIMMICK, b. 22 May 1760; d. July 1779

 vii TIMOTHY DIMMICK, b. 22 Aug. 1762

 viii DANIEL DIMMICK, b. 20 Feb. 1765

 ix MASON DIMMICK, b. 22 June 1767

 x RHODA DIMMICK, b. 10 Aug. 1770

 xi ROGER DIMMICK, b. 5 Aug. 1772

References: *Bradford Desc* p. 126. Coventry CT VR pp. 36(b. ch.), 138(m.), 224(d. Lucy-no parents), 232(d. Desire). Mansfield CT VR p. 63(b. Desire). Mansfield CT LR 5:525-6(Timothy Dimmock). Windham CT PR #1152(Thomas Dimmock).

425. JOHN DIMMICK⁵ (*Ann⁴ Bradford, Joseph³, William²⁻¹*), b. Mansfield, Conn., 24 March 1727/8; d. Stafford, Conn., 1800.

He m. Mansfield, Conn., 17 Jan. 1753 **HANNAH SMITH**, b. Lebanon, Conn., 31 July 1734; d. Stafford, Conn., 26 May 1777; daughter of Mathew and Mary (_____) Smith.

On 29 March 1749 Timothy Dimmock of Mansfield gave to his son John Dimmock of Mansfield 90 acres, part of the farm on which Timothy lived. On 24 May 1764 John Dimmock late of Mansfield now of Stafford sold to his father the 90 acres and another 15 acres he had sold to John.

On 9 Feb. 1778 John Dimmock of Stafford gave to his sons John Dimmock, Simeon Dimmock, and Timothy Dimmock of Stafford 50 acres each. On 7 Aug. 1780 he sold to Timothy another 20 acres. On 19 Nov. 1784

John gave to his son Amasa Dimmock 25 acres. On 11 April 1793 he gave to his sons Ephraim and Matthew land that would be theirs from his estate. And on 6 Feb. 1794 he gave to his son Abner land that would be his from his estate.

Jnº Dimock was head of a household of 3 men and 1 female in Stafford in the 1790 census and listed near him were Amasa Dimock (2 men, 1 boy, 4 females), Timº Dimock (1 man, 1 boy, 1 female), Jnº Dimock Jr. (1 man, 2 boys, 2 females), and Sylvanus Dimock (2 men, 1 boy, 2 females).

Children of John and Hannah (Smith) Dimmick,*, b. Stafford, Conn., except John:

    i JOHN DIMMICK[6], b. Mansfield, Conn., 18 Nov. 1753

    ii TIMOTHY DIMMICK, b. 2 April 1755

    iii SIMEON DIMMICK, b. 19 Oct. 1756

    iv HANNAH DIMMICK, b. 5 July 1758

    v SILVANUS DIMMICK, b. 23 March 1760

    vi AMASA DIMMICK, b. 17 Nov. 1761

    vii WILLIAM DIMMICK, b. 27 June 1763

    viii MERRIAM DIMMICK, b. 18 Sept. 1765

    ix ABNER DIMMICK, b. 8 Aug. 1767

    x EPHRAIM DIMMICK, b. 8 Oct. 1769

    xi MATHEW DIMMICK, b. 2 Nov. 1771

    xii JOSEPH DIMMICK, b. 21 Oct. 1773

* **Note**: *Bradford Desc* lists a dau. Mary, b. 11 May 1768, but there is no record of her and the birth dates of Abner and Ephraim make her existence very unlikely.

References: *Bradford Desc* p. 126. Lebanon CT VR 1:281(b. Hannah). Mansfield CT VR p. 64(b. John), 232(m.). Stafford CT VR 2:22(b. Timothy, Simeon, Amasa, William, Silvanus, Merriam, Abner, Ephraim). Mansfield CT LR 5:133(Timothy Dimmock); 7:87(John Dimmock). Stafford CT LR 5:62, 272-3, 419; 6:169; 7:237, 363, 365(John Dimmock).

426. JOANNA DIMMICK[5] (*Ann[4] Bradford, Joseph[3], William[2-1]*), b. Mansfield, Conn., 28 Aug. 1730.

She m. Mansfield, Conn., 19 Jan. 1748/9 **JOHN BADCOCK** or **BABCOCK**, b. Windham, Conn., 22 June 1728; son of John and Martha (Storrs) Badcock. He m. (2) KEZIAH _____ with whom he had Alathea. On

7 Dec. 1747 John Badcock of Mansfield and others sold land from the estates of their father and grandfather Samuel Storrs.

John Badcock was head of a household of 2 men, 1 boy under 16, and 3 females in Mansfield in the 1790 census.

On 6 July 1802 Jeduthan Badcock with Eliphalet Dimmock were granted administration on the estate of John Badcock of Mansfield. The distribution on 3 May 1803 listed the widow Kezia; sons Timothy, Ebenezer, Sylvanus, and Jeduthan; and daughters Martha Badcock, Joanna Pierce, Thankful Southworth, and Alathea (no surname).

On 3 Feb. 1804 Jeduthan Badcock of Mansfield sold to Jesse Spafford of Mansfield two pieces of land, part of the farm lately belonging to John Badcock deceased with a small dwelling house. On the same day Timothy Badcock, Jeduthan Badcock, and Martha Badcock, children and heirs of John Badcock deceased, sold to Jesse Williams three pieces of land set off to Timothy and Martha and three and a half acres of woodland set off to Jeduthan in the distribution of John's estate. On 21 Feb. 1804 Samuel Paine of Deruyter, Chenango Co., N.Y., and Ebenezer Badcock of Clinton, Dutchess Co., N.Y., sold to Jesse Williams thirteen acres bounded by land belonging to the heirs of John Badcock. On 15 Feb. 1808 Timothy Babcock, Jeduthan Babcock, and Martha Babcock all of Hudson, Columbia Co., N.Y., Ebenezer Babcock of Kinderhook, Columbia Co., N.Y., Sylvanus Babcock of Berlin, Rensselaer Co., N.Y., Samuel and Joanna Pierce, Edward and Thankfull Southworth all of German, Chenango Co., N.Y., and Zachariah and Alithea Decker of [Shadertynak?], Ulster Co., N.Y., sold to Gerry Russ of Mansfield sixteen acres with a dwelling house in Mansfield.

Children of John and Joanna (Dimmick) Badcock, b. Mansfield, Conn.:

    i TIMOTHY BADCOCK[6], b. 23 Oct. 1749

    ii MARTHA BADCOCK, b. 21 June 1751

    iii ANNE BADCOCK, b. 9 Oct. 1753

    iv JOANNA BADCOCK, b. 18 Nov. 1755

    v THANKFUL BADCOCK, b. 20 Jan. 1758

    vi JEDUTHAN (JONATHAN in VRs) BADCOCK, b. 12 March 1760

    vii SARAH BADCOCK, b. 9 June 1762

    viii EBENEZER BADCOCK, b. 8 Dec. 1763

    ix SYLVANUS BADCOCK, b. 12 Aug. 1765

References: *Bradford Desc* p. 126. *Mansfield CT VR* pp. 13(b. ch.), 205(m.). Windham CT VR 1:80(b. John). Windham CT PR #124(John Badcock). Mansfield CT LR 5:59(John

Badcock); 14:156(Jeduthan Badcock), 251(Timothy Badcock); 18:381-2(Timothy Babcock *et al.*).

427. OLIVER DIMMICK[5] (*Ann[4] Bradford, Joseph[3], William[2-1]*), b. Mansfield, Conn., 31 Dec. 1740; d. there 10 Feb. 1837.

He m. (1) Mansfield, Conn., 27 April 1764 **SARAH GURLEY**, b. Mansfield, Conn., 27 Aug. 1744; d. there 22 July 1790; daughter of Samuel and Hannah (Baker) Gurley. On 20 Sept. 1797 the distribution of the estate of Samuel Gurley late of Mansfield included five acres to the children (unnamed) of his daughter Sarah (no surname).

He m. (2) 17 Sept. 1792 **LUCY (LEONY) DIMOCK**, b. 1758; d. 5 Jan. 1820. She m. (1) LOT DIMOCK.

On 14 June 1774 Timothy Dimmock of Mansfield gave 130 acres "I now live on" to son Oliver Dimmock. On 8 Feb. 1775 he gave more land to son Oliver.

Oliver was called Deacon on the baptisms of his children in 1784 and 1787.

On 23 Jan. 1789 Dan Dimmock of Mansfield sold to Oliver Dimmock of Mansfield his right in land which fell to the children of Oliver by heirship from the estate of Capt. Samuel Gurley deceased. On the same day Samuel Dimmock of Mansfield sold to Oliver his right in this land. On 4 May 1809 Oliver Dimmock, Oliver W. Dimmock, and Roderick Dimmock sold to Nathaniel Dunham of Mansfield two pieces of land that fell to the children of Oliver from the estate of Capt. Samuel Gurley; Oliver held the right in this land by two deeds from Samuel and Dan Dimmock and Oliver W. and Roderick held their right by heirship from Capt. Samuel Gurley.

Oliver Dimmock was head of a household of 2 men, 4 boys under 16, and 4 females in Mansfield in the 1790 census.

On 19 Nov. 1804 Oliver Dimmock of Mansfield sold to Oliver W. Dimmock of Mansfield six acres. On 15 May 1805 Oliver sold to Roderick Dimmock of Mansfield eight acres.

On 22 March 1809 Roderick Dimmock of Mansfield sold to Oliver W. Dimmock of Mansfield all his right in the estate of Oliver Dimmock. On 6 April 1822 Oliver Dimmock sold to Oliver W. Dimmock land, dwelling house, barn, and out houses, all the real estate Oliver then owned and lived on.

Children of Oliver and Sarah (Gurley) Dimmick, b. Mansfield, Conn.:*

    i OLIVER W. DIMMICK[6], b. 13 June 1766; d. May 1777

    ii LUCINDA DIMMICK, b. 25 June 1768; d. 30 Jan. 1790

  iii SARAH DIMMICK, b. 6 June 1770; d. 1 March 1795

  iv SAMUEL DIMMICK, b. 2 March 1773

   v DAN DIMMICK, b. 1 March 1775

  vi EUNICE DIMMICK, b. 26 Nov. 1776

 vii OLIVER WARD DIMMICK, b. 20 June 1780

viii SOPHIA DIMMICK, b. 30 April 1782

  ix RODERICK DIMMICK, bp. Mansfield 2nd Ch. 20 June 1784

   x ALPHEUS DIMMICK, b. 22 March 1787; bp. Mansfield 2nd Ch. 20 May.

* **Note::** No evidence found for Mary and dau. listed in *Bradford Desc* p. 127.

References: *Bradford Desc* p. 127. *Mansfield CT VR* pp. 64(b. 1st 8 ch.), 88(b. Sarah Gurley), 232(m.), 436(bp. Roderick), 437(bp. Alpheus). Windham CT PR #1735(Samuel Gurley). Mansfield CT LR 9:71, 307(Timothy Dimmock); 13:81(Dan and Samuel Dimmock); 14:129, 163(Oliver Dimmock); 18:422(Roderick Dimmock); 19:525(Oliver Dimmock *et al.*); 23:279(Oliver Dimmock). *Yale Grads* 6:308(b. Alpheus).

428. DAN DIMMICK[5] (*Ann[4] Bradford, Joseph[3], William[2-1]*), b. Mansfield, Conn., 13 May 1743; d. before 6 June 1774.

He m. Mansfield, Conn., 3 May 1764 **PHOEBE TURNER**, b. Mansfield, Conn., 9 Jan. 1743/4; d. before 19 April 1791; daughter of Stephen and Mary (Jennings) Turner.

On 6 June 1774 Oliver Dimmock was appointed to administer the estate of his brother Dan Dimmock. On 6 Feb. 1775 widow Phebe Dimmock was appointed guardian to the four daughters. On 14 April 1775 a division was made to widow Phebe and daughters Molly, Eunice, Levina, and Diantha.

On 8 Dec. 1780 Timothy Dimmock of Mansfield gave to Mary, Eunice, Lavina, and Diantha Dimock of Mansfield, children of his deceased son Dan Dimock, land in Mansfield.

On 19 April 1791 Jesse Spafford was granted administration on the estate of Phebe Dimmock late of Mansfield. Receipts were signed by Lavina and Zenas Gurley on 20 May 1791, Diantha Dimmock on 5 Nov. 1791, and Eunice and Ephraim Wade on 1 Oct. 1792.

Children of Dan and Phoebe (Turner) Dimmick, b. Mansfield, Conn.:

  i MOLLY DIMMICK[6], b. 28 March 1765

 ii EUNICE DIMMICK, b. 10 Nov. 1766

iii LEVINA DIMMICK, b. 1 June 1769

 iv DIANTHA DIMMICK, b. 7 May 1772

References: *Bradford Desc* p. 127. *Mansfield CT VR* pp. 64(b. ch.), 232(m.). Windham CT PR #1137, 4:266(Dan Dimmock), 278(div.); 4:284(gdn); #1147(Phebe Dimmock). Mansfield CT LR 10:277(Timothy Dimock).

429. ELIZABETH⁵ BRADFORD (*Joseph⁴⁻³, William²⁻¹*), b. New London, Conn., 17 Jan. 1731; d. Haddam, Conn., 22 July 1796 aged 65.

She m. Chatham, Conn., 3 May 1773 **RICHARD MAYO**, b. Eastham 22 Oct. 1729; d. Haddam, Conn., 25 May 1813 aged 84; son of Richard and Rebecca (Sparrow) Mayo. He m. (1) Haddam, Conn., 2 June 1757 RUTH GIBBS with whom he had Richard.

Richard Mayo was head of a household of 2 men, 2 boys, and 4 females in Chatham in the 1790 census.

No Connecticut probate records have been found for Richard or Elizabeth Mayo.

Child of Richard and Elizabeth (Bradford) Mayo, b. Chatham, Conn.:

    i RUTH ELIZABETH MAYO⁶, b. 9 Feb. 1775

References: *MD* 16:203(b. Richard). Chatham CT VR 1:123(m. & b. Ruth). *Bradford Desc* p. 127. Haddam Neck Church Rec. 1:20(bp. son Richard), 38(Richard's 1ˢᵗ m.). Hog Hill Cemetery, Haddam, Conn., pp. 97(d. Richard), 98(d. Elizabeth).

430. ANNA⁵ BRADFORD (*Joseph⁴⁻³, William²⁻¹*), b. New London, Conn.; d. after 19 Sept. 1769.

She m. Mansfield, Conn., 15 June 1758 **RICHARD LYMAN**, b. Lebanon, Conn., 23 March 1721/2; living 6 Oct. 1781 (deed); son of Richard and Mary (Woodward) Lyman.

On 27 June 1746 John, David and Richard Lyman of Lebanon quitclaimed their interest in the estate of their father Richard Lyman of Lebanon to Ebenezer Lyman of Lebanon.

On 13 Dec. 1753 Benjamin Corey of Mansfield sold land in Mansfield to Richard Lyman of Lebanon.

On 2 Jan. 1755 Richard Lyman late of Lebanon, but now of Mansfield, sold all rights in the lands of his father Richard Lyman to John Lyman of Lebanon.

On 8 Nov. 1768 Benjamin Strong of Hartford, N.Y., sold a house and land in Lebanon to Richard Lyman late of Mansfield, but now of Lebanon.

On 26 Dec. 1768 Richard Lyman late of Mansfield, but now of Lebanon, sold land in Mansfield to James Allen Jr. of Mansfield.

On 6 Oct. 1781 Richard Lyman of Lebanon sold land in Lebanon to Asael Gray.

No Connecticut probate records have been found for Richard or Anna Lyman.

Children of Richard and Anna (Bradford) Lyman:

    i ANN LYMAN[6], b. Mansfield, Conn., 13 April 1759
    ii RICHARD LYMAN, b. Mansfield, Conn., 22 Sept. 1761
    iii JOSEPH BRADFORD LYMAN, b. Lebanon, Conn., 1 Sept. 1767
    iv RACHEL LYMAN, b. Lebanon, Conn., 19 Sept. 1769

References: Lebanon CT VR 1:176(b. Richard), 183(b. Joseph, Rachel). *Mansfield CT VR* pp. 126(b. first 2 ch.), 262(m.). Lebanon CT LR 8:342(to John Lyman); 9:292(John, David and Richard Lyman); 11:161(Benajah Strong); 13:175(to Asael Gray). Mansfield CT LR 5:546(Benjamin Corey); 7:425(Richard Lyman).

431. WILLIAM[5] BRADFORD (*Joseph[4-3], William[2-1]*), b. New London, Conn., 13 April 1734; d. after 10 July 1782.

He m. Chatham, Conn., 18 April 1762 **SARAH RICH**, b. Middletown, Conn., 30 Jan. 1739/40; daughter of Thomas and Thankful (Mayo) Rich.

On 4 May 1781 William Bradford of Chatham and Robert Bradford of Haddam sold 70 acres in Haddam, abutting land of Hannah Russell and Henry Bradford, to Solomon Hubbard of Middletown.

On 10 July 1782 William Bradford of Chatham sold 20 acres in Chatham to Benjamin Goff of Chatham.

No Connecticut probate records have been found for William or Sarah Bradford.

Children of William and Sarah (Rich) Bradford, b. Chatham, Conn.:

    i AMOS[6] BRADFORD, b. 24 Aug. 1763
    ii HENRIETTA BRADFORD, b. 4 Oct. 1765
    iii MERCY BRADFORD, b. 19 May 1769; d. 16 March 1770
    iv WILLIAM BRADFORD, bp. Haddam Neck Church 27 June 1779
    v WILLIAM BRADFORD, b. 17 June 1786 [sic]

References: Chatham CT VR 1:59(m.; b. ch.; d. Mercy). Middletown CT VR 1:121(b. Sarah). *Bradford Desc* pp. 127-8. Haddam Neck, Conn., Church rec. 2:12(bp. William). Chatham CT LR 6:33(William Bradford). Haddam CT LR 10:304(William Bradford).

432. HENRY SWIFT⁵ BRADFORD (*Joseph⁴⁻³, William²⁻¹*), b. New London, Conn., 21 Aug. 1736; d. probably Blenheim, Schoharie Co., N.Y., between 8 Aug. 1812 and 7 Oct. 1815.

He m. (1) **PRUDENCE GLOVER,** b. Newtown, Conn., 5 June 1742; d. after 5 July 1808; daughter of Henry and Prudence (Stoddard) Glover.

He m. (2) **MARY ANN** _____, living 8 Aug. 1812.

On 30 March 1763 Jacob Tomlinson of Derby sold land in Derby to Henry Bradford of Derby. On 6 Sept. 1774 Henry Bradford of Derby sold land in Derby to Capt. Thomas Horsey of Derby.

On 26 Sept. 1774 Elijah Elmor of Stratford sold 90 acres in Stepney in Stratford to Henry Bradford of Derby.

On 10 Feb. 1783 Henry Glover of Stratford gave to daughter Prudence Bradford land in North Stratford.

Hennery Bradford was head of a household of 3 men, 1 boy, and 4 females in Huntington in the 1790 census.

On 5 April 1793 Henry Bradford of Huntington sold ten acres in Stepney to Henry Beardslee of Huntington. On the same day Henry Bradford and wife Prudence sold fifteen acres in Stepney to Henry Beardslee; Simeon Bradford witnessed both deeds.

On 13 June 1794 Henry Bradford and wife Prudence of Stanford, Ulster Co., N.Y., sold the last of their land in Huntington to Aaron Hand of Reading.

In the 1800 census of Blenheim, N.Y., Henry Bradford and his wife were over 45.

On 5 July 1808 Henry S. and Prudence Bradford deeded land to son Silas Bradford.

The will of Henry S. Bradford of Blenheim, Schoharie Co., N.Y., dated 8 Aug. 1812, sworn 7 Oct. 1815, names wife Mary Ann; children Simeon Bradford, Anna Bennet, Cynthia Camfield's heirs, Polly Simonson, Priscilla Clark's heirs, and Silas Bradford; mention is made of son John S. Bradford and "my first wife."

Children of Henry Swift and Prudence (Glover) Bradford, first four bp. St. James, Derby, Conn.:

    i HENRIETTA⁶ BRADFORD, bp. 28 June 1767; d. Derby, Conn., 3 April 1790

    ii ANNA BRADFORD, bp. 30 April 1769

    iii SIMEON BRADFORD, bp. 9 Dec. 1770

    iv CYNTHIA BRADFORD, bp. 2 Feb. 1772

    v JOHN STODDARD BRADFORD, bp. Shelton, Conn., 24 July 1774

vi   POLLY BRADFORD, bp. Shelton, Conn., 21 July 1776
vii   SILAS BRADFORD, bp. Shelton, Conn., 14 May 1780
viii   PRISCILLA BRADFORD, bp. Shelton, Conn., 25 Nov. 1781

References: *Bradford Desc* p. 128. *Newtown CT VR* 1:80(b. Prudence). Schoharie Co. NY deed book C, p. 30(Henry S. Bradford *et al.*). Schoharie Co. NY will book B, p. 65(Henry S. Bradford). *NEHGR* 82:140-2(bp. 1st 4 ch.). Shelton, Conn., Episcopal Ch. rec. pp. 23(bp. John), 29(bp. Polly), 36(bp. Silas), 39(bp. Priscilla). Derby CT LR 7:407(Jacob Tomlinson); 10:14(Henry Bradford). Stratford CT LR 18:321(Elijah Elmor); 20:454 (Henry Glover). Shelton CT LR 1:625-6; 2:92(Henry Bradford).

433. ROBERT⁵ BRADFORD (*Joseph⁴⁻³, William²⁻¹*), b. New London, Conn., 21 July 1739; d. Haddam, Conn., 20 Jan. 1808 aged 77.

He m. Haddam, Conn., 15 Aug. 1768 **PENELOPE (BONFOY) RICH**, b. Middletown, Conn., 15 Nov. 1742; d. shortly before 29 Jan. 1822; daughter of Permot and Hannah (Butler) Bonfoy. She m. (1) PETER RICH with whom she had Penelope.

On 23 Sept. 1772 Joseph Bradford of Haddam gave to his son Robert Bradford of Haddam land and half of his house.

On 4 May 1781 William Bradford of Chatham and Robert Bradford of Haddam sold 70 acres in Haddam, abutting land of Hannah Russell and Henry Bradford, to Solomon Hubbard of Middletown.

Robert Bradford was head of a household of 3 men and 2 females in Haddam in the 1790 census.

The will of Robert Bradford of Haddam, Conn., dated 3 Sept. 1803, proved 7 Feb. 1808, names wife Penelope; eldest son Joseph Bradford of Westfield; and second son Peres Bradford.

On 29 Jan. 1822 Perez Bradford posted bond to administer the estate of his mother Penelope Bradford.

Children of Robert and Penelope (Bonfoy) (Rich) Bradford, b. Haddam, Conn.:

i   HENRIETTA⁶ BRADFORD (not in will)
ii   JOSEPH BRADFORD, b. 12 June 1771
iii   PEREZ BRADFORD, b. 9 Dec. 1773
iv   SUSANNA BRADFORD, b. 12 May 1776; d. 1793; unm.

References: *Bradford Desc* p. 128. Haddam CT VR LR 5:272(m.); LR 9:20(b. 3 ch.). Middletown CT VR 2:1(b. Penelope). Middletown CT PR #496; 9:61, 65(Robert Bradford); #495; 12:239, 268, 296(Penelope Bradford). Haddam, Conn., First Ch. Rec. 6:84(d. Robert). Haddam CT LR 9:203(Joseph Bradford); 10:304(William Bradford).

434. HANNAH⁵ BRADFORD (*Joseph⁴⁻³, William²⁻¹*), b. New London, Conn., 10 March 1740/1.

She m. _____ **RUSSELL** (father's will).

In November 1778 Hannah Russell, widow, was admitted to the First Church of Haddam, Conn.

On 10 May 1784 Hannah Russell of Haddam sold land in Haddam to Edward Brine. The land included seven acres on which her dwelling house stood, and part was land formerly belonging to her father Capt. Joseph Bradford.

The only Russell in Haddam in the 1790 census was Stephen Russell with 3 men, 4 boys, and 5 females.

No Connecticut probate records have been found for Hannah Russell.

Children of _____ and Hannah (Bradford) Russell, bp. First Church of Haddam, Conn., in April 1779 as children of Widow Russell:

    i   ESTHER RUSSELL⁶
    ii JOHN RUSSELL
    iii WILLIAM RUSSELL

References: Haddam, Conn., First Ch. Recs 5:8(Hannah adm.), 30(bp. ch.). Haddam CT LR 10:416(Hannah Russell).

435. SAMUEL HYDE⁵ (*Priscilla⁴ Bradford, Joseph³, William²⁻¹*), b. Lebanon, Conn., 24 Oct. 1725, bp. 24 Oct. 1725; d. Greenwich, Conn. [Lebanon, Conn., VR], (or in N.Y.) 12 (or 2) Oct. 1776.

He m. Lebanon, Conn., 2 (1 per Aspinwall) Jan. 1749/50 **ANNE FITCH**, daughter of Adonijah and Sarah (Fitch) Fitch.

On 27 April 1741 Samuel Hide of Lebanon sold to his son Samuel Hide Jr. of Lebanon his right in his whole farm, partly in Lebanon and partly in Norwich, on which his son was living.

On 23 Feb. 1752 Samuel Hyde Jr. and his wife Anne were admitted to the First Church in Lebanon.

On 3 June 1762 Samuel Hide Jr. of Lebanon sold to his brother Dan Hide of Lebanon his right in 60 acres in Lebanon and Norwich that they had bought of Ebenezer Fitch.

On 17 Aug. 1772 Samuel Hide Jr. of Lebanon sold to Samuel Hide of Lebanon 34 acres described as being northwesterly from a house where Dan Hide deceased had lived.

Samuel Hide of Lebanon in his will dated 16 Aug. 1776, proved 11 Dec. 1776, named his wife Ann; three daughters Sarah, Ann, and Elizabeth; and three sons Samuel, Joseph, and Azel. The distribution made on 12 Dec. 1785 names his widow Ann, eldest son Samuel, sons Joseph and Azel, eldest daughter Sarah Hyde, 2nd daughter Anna, and 3rd daughter Betsey. The distribution reserved part of the house for the life of Abigail Hyde sister of Samuel deceased.

Children of Samuel and Anne (Fitch) Hyde, b. Lebanon, Conn.:

    i   SAMUEL HYDE⁶, b. 1 Dec. 1750; d. 11 Aug. 1753

   ii   SARAH HYDE, b. 20 Aug. 1752, bp. [worn] 1752; d. Lebanon, Conn, 10 March 1797 "Sarah, sister of Joseph, & her d. Harriet d. Mar. 10, 1797, being burned in Joseph Hyde's dwelling."

  iii   SAMUEL HYDE, b. 15 Oct. 1754, bp. 20 Oct. 1754

  iv   JOSEPH HYDE, b. 7 Aug. 1757, bp. 14 Aug. 1757

   v   ASAEL HYDE, b. 11 May 1762, bp. 16 May 1762

  vi   ANN HYDE, b. 24 Feb. 1764, bp. 26 Feb. 1764

  vii   MASON HYDE, b. 24 Feb. 1766; d. 2 June 1769 ae 2, bur. Trumbull Cem.

viii   ELIZABETH HYDE, b. 1774; d. 24 Aug. 1844 ae 71, bur. Lebanon Center Cem.; unm.

References: *Bradford Desc* p. 129. Lebanon CT VR 1:151(m.; b. 6 ch.; d. Samuel, son Samuel, Sarah, Harriet). Lebanon CT LR 6:179; 9:517; 12:233(Samuel Hide). Windham CT PR #2146(Samuel Hide). Hale Cem Coll:Lebanon p. 51(d. Miss Betsey Hyde). Lebanon 1st Ch. 4:10(Samuel & Ann adm.), 36(bp. Samuel),53(bp. Sarah), 54(bp. son Samuel), 56(bp. Joseph), 59(bp. Azel), 60(bp. dau. Ann). *Desc Rev James Fitch* pp. 51, 135.

436. ANNE HYDE⁵ (*Priscilla⁴ Bradford, Joseph³, William²⁻¹*), b. Lebanon, Conn., 22 Oct. 1727, bp. 29 Oct. 1727; d. there 12 March 1783 aged 55. She and her husband are both buried in the Goshen Cemetery in Lebanon.

She m. Lebanon, Conn., 2 Oct. 1755 **JARED HINCKLEY**, b. Lebanon, Conn., 8 Oct. 1731; d. 15 Feb. 1820 aged 88y; son of Gershom and Mary (Buel) Hinckley. He m. (2) Lebanon, Conn., 26 Nov. 1783 MARY SHERMAN (or SHUNAN or NEWMAN). He m. (3) HANNAH _____, who is buried with him.

Jared Hinckley was head of a household of 4 men, 1 boy and 5 females in Lebanon in the 1790 census.

Children of Jared and Anne (Hyde) Hinckley, b. Lebanon, Conn.:

    i DANIEL HINCKLEY[6], b. 20 Sept. 1756; d. 16 Feb. 1759 ae 2y 5m, bur. Goshen Cem.

    ii JARED HINCKLEY, b. 8 Nov. 1758

    iii DAN HINCKLEY, b. 28 March 1761; d. 20 April 1761 ae 18d, bur. Goshen Cem.

    iv PRISCILLA HINCKLEY, b. 21 July 1763

    v ANNE HINCKLEY, b. 28 June 1765; d. 30 April 1814 ae 49, bur. Goshen Cem.; unm.

    vi TIMOTHY HINCKLEY, b. 25 Oct. 1767

References: *Bradford Desc* p. 129. Lebanon CT VR 1:150(b. Jared), 156(m.; b. Daniel, Jared, Priscilla, Anne, Timothy; d. mother Anne). Hale Cem Coll:Lebanon pp. 106(d. dau. Anne), 107(d. Ann, both Dans). Lebanon 1st Ch. 4:37(bp. Anne).

437. SYBIL HYDE[5] (*Priscilla[4] Bradford, Joseph[3], William[2-1]*), b. Lebanon, Conn., 16 April 1731, bp. 25 April 1731; d. there 5 Nov. 1790 aged 59. She and her husband are both buried in the Old Cemetery in Lebanon.

She m. Lebanon, Conn., 11 Dec. 1753 **JABEZ METCALF**, b. Lebanon, Conn., 30 Nov. 1718; d. there 15 Nov. 1794 aged 75; son of Ebenezer and Hannah (Abel) Metcalf. On 5 Nov. 1750 Ebenezer Metcalf of Lebanon gave to his son Jabez Metcalf of Lebanon 100 acres. Ebenezer Metcalf in his will dated 3 April 1755, proved 19 Nov. 1755, named his wife Hannah and son Jabez.

He served on the Lexington Alarm and in the Revolutonary War.

Jabez Metcalf was head of a household of one man and one female in New London Co., Conn., in the 1790 census.

Children of Jabez and Sybil (Hyde) Metcalf, b. Lebanon, Conn.:

    i JOSEPH METCALF[6], b. 12 June 1763

References: *Bradford Desc* p. 129. Lebanon CT VR 1:200(b. Jabez), 203(m.; b. Joseph). Lebanon CT LR 7:351(Ebenezer Metcalf). Windham CT PR #2711(Ebenezer Metcalf). Hale Cem Coll:Lebanon p. 66(d. Sybil, Jabez). Lebanon 1st Ch. 4:38(bp. Sybil).

438. DAN HYDE[5] (*Priscilla[4] Bradford, Joseph[3], William[2-1]*), b. Lebanon, Conn., 7 May 1733, bp. 13 May 1733; d. there 15 Nov. 1770.

He m. Lebanon, Conn., **MARY WATTLES**, b. Lebanon, Conn., 14 Oct. 1744; daughter of William and Abigail (Dennison) Wattles.

On 8 Nov. 1761 Dan Hyde and his wife Mary owned the covenant in the First Church in Lebanon.

On 3 June 1762 Samuel Hide Jr. of Lebanon sold to his brother Dan Hide of Lebanon his right in 60 acres in Lebanon and Norwich that they had bought of Ebenezer Fitch.

Samuel Hyde and Mary Hyde were appointed administrators of the estate of Dan Hyde of Lebanon. The inventory was taken on 26 March 1771, the widow's thirds were set off on 30 April 1773, and the estate was declared insolvent on 23 April 1774.

On 26 Sept. 1782 Samuel Hyde of Lebanon was chosen guardian of Priscilla Hyde, daughter of Dan Hyde, about 16 years of age. On 31 Oct. 1778 Samuel, as guardian to Mary and Priscilla, signed a receipt for a share of the estate of their grandmother Priscilla Hyde.

Children of Dan and Mary (Wattles) Hyde, named in the 30 Jan. 1775 will of their grandfather Samuel Hide and the 7 Dec. 1777 will of their grandmother Priscilla Hyde:

 i MARY HYDE[6]

 ii PRISCILLA HYDE, bp. Lebanon, Conn., 12 April 1767

References: *Bradford Desc* p. 129. Lebanon CT VR 1:331(b. Mary). Lebanon CT LR 9:517(Samuel Hide). Windham CT PR #2125(Dan Hyde); #2142(gdn. Priscilla); #2141(Priscilla Hyde). Lebanon 1st Ch. 4:38(bp. Dan), 62(bp. Priscilla), 89(Dan & Mary o. cov).

439. HANNAH HYDE[5] (*Priscilla[4] Bradford, Joseph[3], William[2-1]*), b. Lebanon, Conn., 19 July 1738, bp. 23 July 1738; d. before 2 May 1769.

She m. Mansfield, Conn., 4 Nov. 1760 **DANIEL MOULTON**, b. Ipswich May 1735; d. Mansfield, Conn., 17 April 1767; son of James and Mehitable (Hovey) Moulton.

Daniel Moulton of Mansfield in his will dated 19 March 1767, proved 5 May 1767, named his wife Hannah, sons Gurdon and Daniel, and mother Mehitable Moulton. The inventory was taken on 27 May 1767.

On 2 May 1769 an inventory was taken of the estate of Hannah Moulton late of Mansfield.

On 31 Oct. 1778 Jared Hinckley, as guardian of Gurdon and Daniel, sons of Hannah Moulton, signed a receipt for a share of the estate of their grandmother Priscilla Hyde.

On 5 April 1787 Daniel Moulton signed a receipt that he had received his share of his father's estate from his guardian Jared Hinckley.

Children of Daniel and Hannah (Hyde) Moulton, b. Mansfield, Conn.:

   i GURDON MOULTON[6], b. 29 Sept. 1763

  ii DANIEL MOULTON, b. 18 Dec. 1765

References: *Bradford Desc* pp. 129, 130. Mansfield CT VR D:129(b. Gurdon), 130(b. son Daniel), 265(m.), 333(d. Daniel). *VR Ipswich* 1:271(b. & bp. Daniel). Windham CT PR #2141(Priscilla Hyde); #2788(Daniel Moulton); #2789(gdn. Daniel Moulton); #2793(Hannah Moulton). Lebanon 1st Ch. 4:42(bp. Hannah).

440. ZERVIAH HYDE[5] (*Priscilla[4] Bradford, Joseph[3], William[2-1]*), b. Lebanon, Conn., 15 Dec. 1740, bp. 21 Dec. 1740; d. there 14 Jan. 1829 aged 88. She and her husband are both buried in Goshen Cemetery in Lebanon.

She m. Lebanon, Conn., 20 Sept. 1758 **ANDREW METCALF**, b. Lebanon, Conn., 5 Dec. 1736; d. there 4 July 1828 aged 91; son of Benjamin and Sarah (_____) Metcalf.

The will of Dr. Andrew Metcalf of Lebanon dated 17 March 1807, proved 27 Dec. 1828, names his wife Zerviah, daughter Priscilla Robinson, son Luke, son Jabez deceased, daughter Salome Metcalf, daughter Hannah H. Woodworth wife of Chandler, and grandson Andrew Robinson (under age). A codicil dated 2 Dec. 1811 indicates that his daughter Hannah had died.

On 21 Feb. 1829 the distribution of the estate of Zerviah Metcalf of Lebanon was made to Priscilla Robinson, Luke Metcalf, and Saloam Metcalf.

Children of Andrew and Zerviah (Hyde) Metcalf, first three b. Lebanon, Conn.:

    i PRISCILLA METCALF[6], b. 29 Jan. 1759

   ii JABEZ METCALF, b. 26 Aug. 1761; d. 14 Oct. 1792 ae 31

  iii LUKE METCALF, b. 4 May 1764

  iv SALOME METCALF d. after 21 Feb. 1829; unm. (dist.)

   v HANNAH METCALF, b. Bozrah, Conn., 8 June 1774; d. before 2 Dec. 1811 (codicil); unm.

References: *Bradford Desc* p. 130. Bozrah CT VR 1:66(b. Hannah). Lebanon CT VR 1:208(b. Andrew; m.; b. first 3 ch.). Hale Cem Coll:Lebanon(d. Zerviah, Andrew, Jabez). Lebanon CT PR #893(Andrew Metcalf); #905(Zerviah Metcalf). Lebanon 1st Ch. 4:44(bp. Zerviah).

441.   PRUDENCE LATHROP⁵ (*Sarah⁴ Bradford, Joseph³, William²⁻¹*), b. Norwich, Conn., 16 March 1748.

She m. Norwich, Conn., 28 Dec. 1768 **JAMES CROCKER**, b. Norwich, Conn., 4 Aug. 1747; d. Lebanon, N.H. between 14 Nov. 1815 and 17 March 1817; son of Jabez and Experience (Fox) Crocker. He m. (2) PRUDENCE ROBBINS. On 5 Dec. 1780 in the distribution of the estate of Jabez Crocker, his fifth son James received land with part of a house and corn house.

James Crocker of Lebanon, N.H., made his will 14 Nov. 1815, proved 17 March 1817, naming Ruth Crocker, widow of his late son Israel, and their children Ziba, Rutilla, Ezra Dyer, and James, who were to receive one-third of his estate in Moretown, Vt.; Daniel G. Crocker and Prudence Crocker, children of his late son John; daughters Sarah and Irena; and sons Joseph, Russell, and James.

Without a second marriage date or a date of death for Prudence Lathrop, it is not certain that some of James' children were not with second wife Prudence Robbins. The spacing of the births, however, suggests that only one mother was involved.

Children of James and probably first wife, Prudence (Lathrop) Crocker, first 5 b. Norwich, Conn., rest b. Lebanon, N.H.:

    i   ISRAEL CROCKER⁶, b. 28 Sept. 1769
    ii   JAMES CROCKER, b. 4 Aug. 1771; d. 17 Oct. 1779
    iii   JOHN CROCKER, b. 27 June 1773
    iv   JOSEPH CROCKER, b. 22 Aug. 1775; d. 14 Sept. 1779
    v   RUSSEL CROCKER, b. 6 Oct. 1777; d. 11 Sept. 1779
    vi   SARAH CROCKER, b. 31 Dec. 1779
    vii   JAMES CROCKER, b. 14 Nov. 1782; d. 20 June 1783
    viii   LYDIA CROCKER, b. 14 July 1784; d. 2 June 1805
    ix   JAMES CROCKER, b. 8 April 1786
    x   JOSEPH CROCKER, b. 5 Aug. 1788
    xi   IRENA CROCKER, b. 15 Sept. 1790
    xii   RUSSELL CROCKER, b. 5 Feb. 1794

References: *Bradford Desc* p. 130. Norwich CT VR 2:21(b. James); 3:59(m.; b. 5 ch.). Norwich CT PR #2971(Jabez Crocker). Grafton Co. NH PR 8:787(James Crocker). Lebanon NH TR 1:176(b. 2ⁿᵈ Russel through Joseph, d. Russel, Joseph, James); 2:52(b. Irena, Russell, d. Lydia).

442. TIMOTHY BUELL[5] (*Hannah*[4] *Bradford, Joseph*[3], *William*[2-1]), b. Hebron, Conn., 20 Nov. 1732; d. Elizabethtown, Ontario, Canada, in March 1789 aged 56.

He m. Hebron, Conn., 24 Jan. 1750/1 **MERCY PETERS**, b. Hebron, Conn., 26 March 1730; d. Tincap, Ontario 25 Dec. 1813; daughter of John and Mary (Marks) Peters.

Timothy Buell was a Loyalist and moved to Ontario Canada in 1781. "Timothy Buell, the head of the family in this province, was for a time a pensioner, and also held some situation in the Quartermaster's Department in the British Forces. At the close of the war, after residing a couple of years at Lachine, in Lower Canada, he emigrated with many others to the Township of Elizabethtown in Upper Canada."

Children of Timothy and Mercy (Peters) Buell, first two b. Hebron, Conn.:*

  i   WILLIAM BUELL[6], b. 24 Sept. 1751
  ii MERCY BUELL, b. 15 Oct. 1753
  iii TIMOTHY BUELL, b. Kent, Conn., 20 June 1760
  iv JONATHAN BUELL, b. 1762
  v   BENTSLEY BUELL, b. 22 Sept. 1765
  vi SAMUEL BUELL, b. 1767
  vii SABRINA BUELL, b. ca. 1770
  viii HANNAH BUELL, b. 1775

* **Note:** See *The Loyalists In Ontario* pp. 39-40 for an account of the children.

References: *Bradford Desc* p. 130. Hebron CT VR 2:4(m.), 146(b. 2 ch.). Kent CT VR 1:85(b. Timothy). *Buell Fam* p. 99.

443. ELIJAH BUELL[5] (*Hannah*[4] *Bradford, Joseph*[3], *William*[2-1]), b. Hebron, Conn., 9 Nov. 1735; d. Marlborough, Conn., 27 July 1808 aged 73y.

He m. Hebron, Conn., 15 April 1756 **TAMAR PHELPS**, b. Hebron, Conn., 18 Feb. 1733/4; d. Marlborough, Conn., 19 Feb. 1823 aged 90y; daughter of Cornelius and Margaret (Dewey) Phelps.

Elijah Buell was called "Capt." on his gravestone.

On 25 April 1786 Elijah Buell of Colchester sold to Elijah Buell Jr. of Colchester one quarter part of the iron works in Chatham, Conn.

Elijah Buell was head of a household of 3 men 16 or older and 3 females in New London Co., Conn., in the 1790 census; listed near him were Elijah Buell Jr. (2 men, 1 boy, 3 females) and Elisha Buell (2 men, 2 boys, 3 females).

Children of Elijah and Tamar (Phelps) Buell:

    i ELIJAH BUELL[6], b. Colchester, Conn., 27 Jan. 1757 (*Bradford Desc* p. 459)

    ii ELISHA BUELL, b. ca. 1764 (d. 24 May 1842 ae 80y)

    iii ELI BUELL, b. ca. 1765

References: *Bradford Desc* pp. 130-1. Hebron CT VR 1:19(b. Tamar), 38(b. Elijah); 2:4(m.). Hale Cem Coll:Marlborough p. 6(d. Elisha), 8(d. Elijah, Tamar). Chatham CT LR 4:439(Elijah Buell). *Buell Fam* p. 100.

444. HANNAH BUELL[5] (*Hannah[4] Bradford, Joseph[3], William[2-1]*), b. Hebron, Conn., 9 Nov. 1735; d. Marlborough, Conn., 5 April 1774 aged 38y.

She m. Colchester, Conn., 18 Oct. 1753 **JARED FOOTE**, b. Colchester, Conn., 28 Aug. 1728; d. Cornwell, Vt. 28 Jan. 1806 aged 76, bur. in Church Cemtery; son of Nathaniel and Mercy (Heecock) Foote. *DAR Patriot Index* says he m. (2) HEBZIBAH PHELPS and (3) JOANNA JENNINGS.

Buell Family says they removed to Pittsfield, Me., and in 1798 to Cornwall, Vt.

Children of Jared and Hannah (Buell) Foote, b. Colchester, Conn.:

    i HANNAH FOOTE[6], b. 19 Nov. 1754

    ii RHODA FOOTE, b. 3 Jan. 1757; d. 1812; unm.

    iii LUCY FOOTE, b. 1758; d. 1766

    iv MERCY FOOTE, b. 6 July 1760

    v JARED FOOTE, b. 5 April 1763

    vi LUCY FOOTE, b. 6 Dec. 1767

    vii JARED FOOTE, b. 30 Sept. 1770

References: *Bradford Desc* p. 131. Colchester CT VR 1:117(b. Jared), 150(m.; b. Hannah, Mercy, Jared, Lucy). Hebron CT VR 1:38(b. Hannah). Hale Cem Coll:Marlborough p. 8(d. Hannah). *Buell Fam* p. 100. VTVR(d. Jared Foot).

445. DEBORAH BUELL[5] (*Hannah[4] Bradford, Joseph[3], William[2-1]*), b. Hebron, Conn., 13 Sept. 1738; d. Rupert, Vt., 20 Jan. 1813 aged 74, bur. in West Rupert Cemetery.

She m. Hebron, Conn., 29 Jan. 1756 **JOSEPH DEWEY**, b. Hebron, Conn., 10 May 1733; d. 24 Feb. 1778; son of Charles and Abigail (Dewey) Dewey.

On 31 Oct. 1765 Charles Dewey of Hebron gave to his son Joseph Dewey of Hebron 80 acres.

Dewey Gen says that they went to Columbia Co., N.Y., and then to Rupert, Vt.

Children of Joseph and Deborah (Buell) Dewey, b. Hebron, Conn.:

    i   DEBORAH DEWEY[6], b. 11 Aug. 1756

    ii JOSEPH DEWEY, b. 16 Feb. 1758

   iii MARY DEWEY, b. 13 May 1760

   iv LYDIA DEWEY, b. 16 March 1762

    v ANNA DEWEY, b. 3 Feb. 1764

   vi JERUSHA DEWEY, b. 30 April 1766

  vii ELIAS DEWEY, b. 26 April 1768

 viii CHESTER DEWEY, b. 6 Sept. 1770

   ix SALLY DEWEY, b. 3 Dec. 1772

    x HANNAH DEWEY, b. 23 Oct. 1774

   xi MARCIA DEWEY, b. 22 Sept. 1776

References: *Bradford Desc* p. 131. Hebron CT VR 1:29(b. Joseph), 38(b. Deborah); 2:18(m.), 167(b. Deborah, Mary), 168(b. Joseph). Hebron CT LR 5:117(Charles Dewey). *Dewey Gen* p.736. VRVT cards(d. Deborah).

446. ICHABOD BUELL[5] (*Hannah[4] Bradford, Joseph[3], William[2-1]*), b. Hebron, Conn., 15 Feb. 1741; d. after 25 Aug. 1792.

He m. Hebron, Conn., 17 Nov. 1763 **HEPSIBAH DEWEY**, b. Lebanon, Conn., 20 Aug. 1736; daughter of Jonathan and Mary (Collier) Dewey.

On 9 April 1787 Ichabod Buell of Hebron and Ichabod Buell Jr. of Hebron sold to Timothy Dutton 17 acres with a dwelling house, barn, and horse shed where Bethuel Phelps was then living.

On 23 Feb. 1791 Ichabod Buell of Hebron sold to Amos Strong of Colchester three and a quarter acres, the lot that Ichabod lived on. On 25 Aug. 1792 Ichabod Buell of New Concord, Columbia Co., N.Y., sold to John Wass of Hebron his right in land and a house.

Children of Ichabod and Hepsibah (Dewey) Buell, b. Hebron, Conn.:

    i JEMIME BUELL[6], b. 9 June 1764

   ii ICHABOD BUELL, b. 22 July 1765

References: *Bradford Desc* p. 131. Hebron CT VR 1:38(b. Ichabod); 2:5(m.), 150(b. ch.). Lebanon CT VR 1:61(b. Hepsibah). Hebron CT LR 7:211; 8:183; 9:207(Ichabod Buell). *Dewey Gen* p. 399.

447. OLIVER BUELL[5] (*Hannah*[4] *Bradford, Joseph*[3], *William*[2-1]), b. Hebron, Conn., 6 May 1746; d. Canaan, N.Y., 6 June 1790.

He m. (1) Colchester, Conn., 15 Dec. 1768 **JUDITH TILDEN**, b. Hebron, Conn., 20 April 1749; d. Canaan, N.Y., 9 Nov. 1788; daughter of Isaac and Irene (Phelps) Tilden, a descendant of Pilgrim **Richard Warren**.

He m. (2) 6 May 1789 **SARAH DEWEY**, b. 29 Jan. 1750.

Oliver Buell was a lieutenant. in the Revolutionary War.

On 2 May 1812 and 22 June 1812 Bradford Buel of Canaan sold to Timothy Buel of Canaan an undivided third part of land that Oliver Buel of Canaan had died siezed of.

Children of Oliver and Judith (Tilden) Buell, b. Richmond:

  i   JUDAH BUELL[6], b. 7 Oct. 1769; d. 16 Nov. 1769

  ii OLEDINE BUELL, b. 7 Nov. 1773 [*sic*]; d. 27 Jan. 1774

  iii OLIVER BUELL, b. 13 May 1774 [*sic*]; d. Canaan, N.Y., 11 May 1797. Oliver Buel of Canaan, blacksmith, in his will dated 10 April 1797, proved 27 June 1797, named his brothers Timothy Buel and Bradford Buel and sister Olidine Buel.

  iv OLEDINE BUELL, b. 9 July 1776

  v   TIMOTHY BUELL, b. 15 April 1779

  vi BRADFORD BUELL, b. 30 Oct. 1783; d. 9 Sept. 1812; unm.

  vii ELISHA BUELL, b. 7 Dec. 1785; d. 6 March 1786

References: *Bradford Desc* p. 132. Hebron CT VR 1:45(b. Oliver), 83(m.); 2:356(b. Judith). Columbia Co. NY PR Will book A:397. Columbia Co. NY LR C:433, 459. *Buell Fam* p. 102. Colchester CT VR 1:63(1st m.). *MF* 18:2:120-1.

448. JOSEPH BUELL[5] (*Hannah*[4] *Bradford, Joseph*[3], *William*[2-1]), b. Hebron, Conn., 29 May 1749; d. Chatham, Conn., 24 July 1828 aged nearly 80.

He m. **HOPE LOVELAND**, b. Glastonbury, Conn., 7 June 1751; d. 21 April 1810 aged 59; daughter of John and Comfort (Talcott) Loveland.

He moved about 1775 to Glastonbury, Conn., about 1798 to Colchester, Conn., then to Chatham, Conn.

On 14 Feb. 1791 Elijah Buell of Canaan, Columbia Co., N.Y., sold to Joseph Buell of Chatham one-quarter right in the iron works.

Children of Joseph and Hope (Loveland) Buell:

    i SALLY BUELL⁶, b. 26 Aug. 1773; d. 17 April 1796

    ii JOSEPH BUELL, b. Colchester, Conn., 14 July 1775

    iii DAVID BUELL, b. 10 Jan. 1778

References: *Bradford Desc* p. 132. Glastonbury CT VR 1:114(b. Hope). Colchester CT VR 2:246(b. Joseph). Chatham CT LR 5:505(Elijah Buell). *Buell Fam* p. 102.

449. WILLIAM LISK⁵ (*Elizabeth⁴ Bradford, Joseph³, William²⁻¹*), b. Lebanon, Conn., 17 Dec. 1738; d. there 27 June 1808.

He m. **LYDIA HYDE**, daughter of Ebenezer Hyde.

On 13 April 1791 William Lisk and his wife Lydia of Lebanon sold to David Trumbull of Lebanon two tracts of land that Lydia's father Ebenʳ Hyde had died seized of and subject to the dower rights of Ebenʳ's widow. On 1 June 1805 William and Lydia of Lebanon sold to David Trumbull two tracts set out to the widow of Ebenezer Hyde who was now deceased.

On 30 June 1808 Ebenezer Fitch was appointed administrator of the estate of William Lisk late of Lebanon; the estate was insolvent.

On 5 Oct 1809 Ebenezer Fitch, administrator of the estate of William Lisk, sold two acres to pay debts.

It is claimed that Lydia separated from William and was living with some of their children near Cooperstown, N.Y.

Children of William and Lydia (Hyde) Lisk:

    i DAN LISK⁶

    ii ANNA LISK

    iii EBENEZER LISK, b. Lebanon, Conn., 17 June 1761

References: *Hyde Gen* pp. 79-80. Lebanon CT LR 17:8; 19:138(William Lisk); 24:339(Ebenezer Fitch). Windham CT PR #2462(William Lisk). Lebanon VR 1:182(b. William).

450. ANN LISK⁵ (*Elizabeth⁴ Bradford, Joseph³, William²⁻¹*), b. Lebanon, Conn., 24 March 1740.

She m. East Haddam, Conn., 12 Dec. 1765 **DAVID BELDEN**. (Did he m. (1) East Haddam 17 April 1760 MARY ACKLEY with whom he had Stephen and David Ackley and m. (3) East Haddam 10 Jan. 1776 MARGET CLARK of Lyme with whom he had Elizabeth, Henry, Obedience, and James?)

On 22 May 1786 David Belding of East Haddam sold two pieces of land to Jabez Chapman, Sylvanus Tinker, Amos White, Sarah Johnson administratrix of the estate of Edward Johnson, and Epophroditus Champion.

References: *Conn Marr* 6:122. East Haddam CT VR LR6:504(1st m.); 2:136(3rd m.). East Haddam CT LR 11:84(David Belding). Lebanon VR 1:182 (b. Ann).

451. MARTHA LISK⁵ (*Elizabeth⁴ Bradford, Joseph³, William²⁻¹*), b. Lebanon, Conn., 30 May 1742.

She m. _____ **FLINT** (father's will).

On 28 Jan. 1788 Dijah Fowler of Lebanon sold to Martha Flint of Lebanon a quarter of an acre beginning at a well near Abel Flint's. On 27 Jan. 1792 Martha Flint of Lebanon sold to Andrew Metcalf of Lebanon two pieces of land with a dwelling house.

Martha Flint was head of a household consisting of 1 boy under 16 and 3 females in Lebanon in the 1790 census.

References: Lebanon CT LR 15:315(Dijah Fowler); 16:47(Martha Flint). Lebanon VR 1:182 (b. Martha).

452. BETTY LISK⁵ (*Elizabeth⁴ Bradford, Joseph³, William²⁻¹*), b. Lebanon, Conn., 22 Nov. 1746, bp. 30 Nov. 1746; d. Vienna, N.Y., between 1826 and 1829.

She possibly m. Lebanon, Conn., ca. 1771 **JONATHAN GRAVES**, poss., b. Lebanon, Conn., ca. 1743; d. Vienna, N.Y., between 1826 and 1829.

Jonathan Graves served in the Revolutionary War in 1779.

Possible children of Jonathan and Betty (Lisk) Graves:

    i   SALLIE/SALLY GRAVES, b. 1768
    ii ANNA GRAVES, b. 1770
    iii STERLING GRAVES, b. 9 Sept. 1772
    iv BETSEY GRAVES, b. 30 Sept. 1774
    v   JONATHAN GRAVES, b. 7 May 1777
    vi ROSWELL GRAVES, b. ca. 1780
    vii ELIJAH GRAVES, b. perhaps Shelburne 17 Aug. 1782

References: Lebanon 1st Ch. 4:49(bp Betty). *Hazen Fam* p. 378. *John Graves* p. 53. Lebanon VR 1:182 (b. Betty).

453. AMY LISK⁵ (*Elizabeth⁴ Bradford, Joseph³, William²⁻¹*), b. Lebanon, Conn., 15 Jan. 1752.

She m. _____ **PALMER** (father's will). (A Silvester Palmer was a creditor to the estate of Dan Hyde.)

The 1790 census for Lebanon included Jabez Palmer (1 man, 1 boy, 2 females), Nehemiah Palmer (2 men, 2 females), and Amos Palmer (1 man, 2 boys, 4 females).

References: Lebanon VR 1:182 (b. Amy). Windham CT PR #2461(William Lisk).

454. HULDAH LISK⁵ (*Elizabeth⁴ Bradford, Joseph³, William²⁻¹*), b. Lebanon, Conn., 18 Aug. 1754, bp. 25 Aug. 1754; d. East Haddam, Conn., 10 May 1841 aged 87, buried Haddam.

She m. East Haddam, Conn., 20 March 1776 **GIDEON COOK**, b. East Haddam, Conn., 10 Jan. 1750; d. there 12 April 1806 aged 54 (or 57), buried Moodus Cemetery; son of Ebenezer and Marcy (Paine) Cook; a descendant of Pilgrim **Stephen Hopkins**.

On 24 Oct. 1772 Ebenezer Cook of Richmond, Mass., sold to his brother Gideon Cook of East Haddam one-quarter part of land in East Haddam that had been deeded by Jeremiah Gates to John Cook deceased.

Gideon Cook was head of a household of 2 men, 5 boys under 16, and 2 females in East Haddam in the 1790 census.

The 1806 distribution of the estate of Gideon Cook names widow Huldy; Anna, wife of Henry Snow; John Cook; Gideon Cook of Stockbridge; David Cook; William Cook; Andrew Cook; Azel Cook; Fanny Cook; and Ebenezer Cook. On 28 Jan. 1808 John Cook and Becklay Rowley gave bond as guardians of Fanny and Ebenezer Cook, 12 and 14 years old.

Gideon's widow applied for a pension for his Revolutionary War service from Connecticut on 16 Jan. 1837. On 18 Aug. 1836 she was aged 82 and a resident of East Haddam.

Children of Gideon and Huldah (Lisk) Cook, b. East Haddam, Conn.:

    i ANNA COOK⁶, b. 14 March 1777

    ii JOHN COOK, b. 11 Dec. 1778

    iii GIDEON COOK, b. 28 Nov. 1780

    iv DAVID COOK, b. 25 Nov. 1782

    v WILLIAM COOK, b. 11 Feb. 1785

    vi ANDREW COOK, b. 19 May 1787

    vii HULDAH COOK, b. 11 Sept. 1789

    viii [CHILD] COOK, b. & d. 1790 ae 3 mos.

    ix AZEL COOK, b. 17 Oct. 1791

    x FANNY COOK, b. 22 Dec. 1793

    xi EBENEZER COOK, b. 23 Feb. 1796

References: *Conn Marr* 6:124. *NEHGR* 126:93. Colchester CT PR #907(gdn.), #908(Gideon Cook). East Haddam CT VR 2:116(m.; b. first 3 ch.), 303(b. William). East Haddam First Congregational Church Records(d. Gideon). Lebanon 1st Ch. 4:54(bp. Huldah). Hale Cem Coll:East Haddam p. 43(d. Gideon); Haddam p. 103(d. Huldah). East Haddam CT LR 9:99(Ebenezer Cook). MF 6:186. *Rev War Pensions* 1:745. Lebanon VR 1:182 (b. Huldah).

455. ELEANOR HIDE[5] (*Althea*[4] *Bradford, Joseph*[3], *William*[2-1]), bp. Lebanon, Conn., 16 March 1739/40; d. there 10 Oct. 1804 aged 86 yrs [*sic*].

    She m. Sharon, Conn., 21 Dec. 1758 **DAVID COLE**, b. Sharon, Conn., 15 Aug. 1731; d. there 29 Aug. 1807 aged 77 yrs; son of Caleb and Rebecca (_____) Cole. On 22 Nov. 1755 Caleb Cole of Sharon gave to his son David Cole of Sharon 20 acres and on 19 Dec. 1769 Caleb sold to David another 20 acres.

    On 15 Feb. 1803 David Cole deeded 60 acres of land in Sharon, Conn., to his son David Cole.

    On 17 Nov. 1823 Richard Cole of Trumble [Trumbull] Co., Ohio, sold to David Cole of Sharon all his right, being one-fourth part, in the estate of his father David Cole deceased.

    No Connecticut probate records have been found for David Cole.

    Children of David and Eleanor (Hide) Cole, b. Sharon, Conn.:*

    i ANNA COLE[6], b. 22 June 1760

    ii POLLY COLE, b. ca. 1761; d. Sharon, Conn., 30 March 1805 ae 44 unm.

    iii DAVID COLE, b. ca. 1765 (based on age at d.)

    iv CALEB COLE, b. ca. 1767 (based on age at d.). Named in will of his Uncle Azel Hyde.

    v RICHARD B. COLE Named in will of his Uncle Azel Hyde.

* Note: The *Boston Evening Transcript* of 24 March 1915 (#4587) says they had seven children.

References: First Church, Sharon, Conn., Record 1:14(m.). Sharon CT LR 5:106(b. Anna); 3:404; 6:374(Caleb Cole); 14:183(David Cole); 20:26(Richard Cole). Hillside, Conn., Cemetery Rec. p. 6(d. David), 7(d. Polly), 30(d. Caleb).

456. SIMEON HIDE[5] (*Althea[4] Bradford, Joseph[3], William[2-1]*), b. Lebanon, Conn., 14 or 15 Sept. 1742; d. Walton, N.Y., in September (per Aspinwall) 1789.

He m. Sharon, Conn., 1764 **DOROTHY ST. JOHN**, b. Wilton, Conn., 14 Nov. 1742; d. Skaneateles, N.Y., 8 Feb. 1839; daughter of Mark and Hannah (Brown) St. John.

No Connecticut probate records have been found for Simeon Hide. Aspinwall says they went to Willkes Barre, Pa., then to Sharon, Conn., and then to New York. Simeon Hide does not appear in the grantor-grantee indexes of Sharon, Conn., or Delaware, Ulster, or Otsego counties, N.Y.

Children of Simeon and Dorothy (St. John) Hide, b. prob. Sharon, Conn.:

    i   DAN HIDE[6], b. 14 Dec. 1766

   ii   WALTER HIDE, b. 16 Jan. (June-as) 1768

  iii   JOHN HIDE, b. 22 Aug. 1774; d. unm. 1794-as

  iv   SARAH HIDE, b. 7 April 1777

   v   ALTIE HIDE, b. 13 June 1779; d. ae 7y-as

  vi   DAVID HIDE, b. 27 May 1783

 vii   LAURA HIDE, b. 22 March 1786

References: *St. John Gen* p. 104.

457. AVIS HIDE[5] (*Althea[4] Bradford, Joseph[3], William[2-1]*), bp. Lebanon, Conn., 28 Feb. 1747/8; living 14 May 1801 (Gen. Assembly Rec.).

She m. East Haddam, Conn., 3 March 1792 Colonel **DAVID BRAINERD SPENCER**, b. East Haddam, Conn., 22 Jan. 1744/5; d. there 2 May 1795 aged 51, buried in Goodspeed's or Nathan Hale Cemetery; son of Samuel and Jerusha (Brainerd) Spencer. He m. (1) East Haddam, Conn., 2 Feb. 1769 HULDAH BRAINERD with whom he had Dorothy and Samuel. He m. (2) East Haddam 24 June 1783 MARY FULLER with whom he had Hulda, Mary, David, Jerusha, and Oliver.

On 12 May 1795 Samuel Spencer was appointed administrator of the estate of David Brainerd Spencer. On 24 April 1796 dower was assigned to the widow. The distribution on 29 March 1797 included 100 acres of land in Ohio and Virginia. On 14 May 1801 The General Assembly approved the sale of a tract of David's homestead, now owned by his orphans, subject to the incumbrance of a dower.

On 6 July 1802 having received authorization from the General Assembly, John Brainerd, as guardian of Robert, and Samuel Spencer, as guardian of Huldah, Mary, David B., Jerusha, and Oliver, sold their interest in the family home to William Gilbert.

Child of David Brainerd and Avis (Hyde) Spencer, b. East Haddam, Conn.:

    i   ROBERT SPENCER[6], b. 8 Aug. 1793

References: East Haddam CT VR LR 3:12(b. David), VR 2:38(1st m.; b. Robert), 39(both m.). Colchester Co. PR #2808(David, b. Spencer), #2847(gdn.). East Haddam CT LR 14:127(John Brainerd *et al*). Hale Cem Coll:East Haddam p. 83(d. David). East Haddam 1st Ch. Recs. 1:162(1st m.), 170(2nd m.).

458. ANN HIDE[5] (*Althea[4] Bradford, Joseph[3], William[2-1]*), b. probably Sharon, Conn., ca. 1753; d. Lanesboro 31 Jan. 1831 in 78th yr.

She m. (1) Sharon, Conn., 1 Oct. 1769 **FRANCIS GRISWOLD**, bp. Norwich, Conn., 10 July 1737; d. Sharon, Conn., 6 Nov. 1779 aged 43, buried Hillside Cem.; son of Francis and Abigail (Bingham) Griswold.

She m. (2) Sharon, Conn., 1 Feb. 1785 **EBENEZER STEARNS**, b. Plainfield, Conn., 19 Jan. 1747; d. Lanesboro May 1833 (from PR); son of Ebenezer and Mary (_____) Stearns. He m. (1) 1 Dec. 1782 RACHEL JONES with whom he had Samuel.

Ebenezer Stearns served in the Revolutionary War as a sergeant in Capt. David Wheler's company with service of 6 days when the company marched from Lanesboro to Meloomscuyck on an alarm of 14 Aug. 1777.

The will of Francis Griswold dated 20 Oct. 1779, proved 12 April 1780, names wife and children Abigail, Anna, Polly, and Francis.

Ebenezer Stearns was head of a household of 1 man, 2 boys, and 5 females in Lanesboro in the 1790 census.

On 13 Jan. 1798 Ebenezer Sterne and his wife Anna of Lanesborough sold to Jonathan Reed of Sharon, Conn., what right Anna had in the farm of Francis Griswold deceased.

Ebenezer Stearns of Lanesboro in his will dated 25 June 1827, proved 8 Oct. 1833, mentioned but did not name his wife. He named his daughters Beulah, Avis, Abilene, Rachel deceased, and Cynthia; oldest son Samuel and youngest son Ebenezer; daughter-in-law [stepdaughter] Polly Griswold; and son Cyrus as executor. The distribution on 4 June 1833 states that Ebenezer left no widow and the children or their representative heirs were: Cyrus Stearns of Lanesboro, Ebenezer Stearns of N.Y., Bulah Stearns of N.Y., Avis wife of Joshua Cady of Vermont, Abilene Smith of Lanesboro, heirs of Rachel Phelps deceased, and Cynthia Stearns of Lanesboro.

Children of Francis and Ann (Hide) Griswold, b. Sharon, Conn.:

    i ABIGAIL GRISWOLD[6], b. 2 June 1770

    ii ANNA GRISWOLD, b. 7 March 1772

    iii POLLY GRISWOLD, b. 22 May 1774

    iv FRANCIS GRISWOLD, b. 28 March 1776

Children of Ebenezer and Ann (Hide) (Griswold) Stearns, b. Lanesboro:

    v RACHEL STEARNS, b. 12 Oct. 1785

    vi CYRUS STEARNS, b. 21 Jan. 1788 (not in father's will)

    vii CYNTHIA STEARNS, b. 21 Feb. 1790

    viii BEULAH STEARNS, b. 30 April 1792

    ix AVIS STEARNS, b. 25 Aug. 1794

    x ABILENE STEARNS (dau.), b. 27 Oct. 1796

    xi EBENEZER STEARNS, b. 3 March 1799

References: First Church, Sharon, Conn., Records 1:16(1st m.). Sharon CT VR LR 6:127(b. Abigail), 128(b. Anna); 7:143(b. Polly), 413(b. Francis). Lanesboro Cemetery Inscriptions p. 42(d. Ann). Hale Coll:Sharon p. 10(d. Francis). First Church of Norwich, Conn., Records 2:110(bp. Francis). *Lanesboro Hist* p. 104(b. Stearns ch.). Sharon CT PR E5:141, 360(Francis Griswold). Berkshire Co. PR #5400, 37:282, 453(Eben. Stearns). *Stearns Gen* 2:350. Sharon CT LR 13:488(Ebenezer Sterne). *MSSR* 16:873.

459. ELIZABETH HIDE[5] (*Althea[4] Bradford, Joseph[3], William[2-1]*), b. 8 Sept. 1758; d. Georgia, Franklin Co., Vt., 8 April 1818 aged 59y 7m.

She m. Lebanon, Conn., April 1779 **IRA HINCKLEY**, b. Middletown, Conn., 16 March 1756; d. Georgia, Vt., 21 Aug. 1825 aged 69y 5m 5d; son of John and Ruth (Gillette) Hinckley.

Ira Hinkley was head of a household of 2 men, 1 boy, and 4 females in Saybrook in the 1790 census.

Children of Ira and Elizabeth (Hide) Hinckley, first five b. Westbrook, Conn.; last two b. Georgia Twp., Vt.:

    i PHILENA HINCKLEY[6], b. 11 Feb. 1780

    ii LUCY HINCKLEY, b. 14 April 1782

    iii IRA HYDE HINCKLEY, b. 12 Aug. 1785

    iv JULIA HINCKLEY, bp. 10 July 1791

     v AVIS HINCKLEY, bp. 4 Nov. 1793

    vi ELIZABETH HINCKLEY, b. 2 Feb. 1799

   vii ANNA HINCKLEY, b. 31 July 1801

Note: IGI VT calls mother of children Elizabeth *Keyes* but shows marriage to Elizabeth *Hyde.*

References: Middletown CT VR 2:324(b. Ira). *Westbrook CT Ch Recs* p. 77(bp. first 5 ch). Georgia VT VR 1:41(b. last 2 ch.). VTVR (d. Ira, Elizabeth).

460. DAVID JANES[5] (*Irena*[4] *Bradford, Joseph*[3], *William*[2-1]), b. Lebanon, Conn., 23 Dec. 1736.

He m. Brimfield 10 Feb. 1762 **JEMIMA VORCE.**

Children of David and Jemima (Vorce) Janes, b. Brimfield:*

      i THOMAS JANES[6], b. 9 Aug. 1762

     ii DAVID JANES, b. 17 May 1764

    iii PHEBE JANES, b. 26 Feb. 1766

    iv TIMOTHY JANES, b. 13 May 1768; d.y.

     v SUSANNA JANES, b. 6 Aug. 1770

    vi IRENE JANES, b. 22 Jan. 1774

   vii JEMIMA JANES, b. 16 July 1776

  viii TIMOTHY JANES, b. 31 Jan. 1779

***Note:** No evidence found for son Bradford listed in *Bradford Desc.*

References: *Bradford Desc* p. 133. *VR Brimfield* pp. 80(b. David), 81(b. Jemima), 82(b. Thomas, Phebe, Timothy, Susanna, Irene, Timothy), 207(m.). *Brimfield Hist* p. 423(does not list son Bradford).

461. ELIPHALET JANES[5] (*Irena*[4] *Bradford, Joseph*[3], *William*[2-1]), b. Lebanon, Conn., 23 Feb. 1742/3; d. Sturbridge 5 June 1835 aged 93.

He m. ca. 1768 **ALFLEDA LYON**, b. Woodstock, Conn., 12 June 1749; d. Sturbridge 1 March 1792; daughter of Moses and Grace (Child) Lyon.

On 25 Dec. 1773 Jonathan Janes and Eliphalet Janes of Brimfield, yeomen, sold to Solomon Janes and Daniel Janes of Brimfield, clothiers, fifteen acres.

Eliphalet Janes served in the Revolutionary War as a private in Capt. James Sherman's company, Col. Pyncheon's regiment which marched on the alarm of 19 April 1775.

Eliphalet Janes was head of a household of 1 man, 1 boy under 16, and 3 females in Holland in the 1790 census.

Children of Eliphalet and Alfleda (Lyon) Janes, first five b. Brimfield:

 i LUCINDA JANES[6], b. 11 March 1769
 ii ROXEYLINA JANES, b. 29 Nov. 1770
 iii MAVISILY/MARSILVA JANES, b. 14 June 1772
 iv ALFRED JANES, b. 7 March 1775
 v WALTER JANES, b. 27 Feb. 1778
 vi ALMARIN JANES, b. 11 May 1781
 vii BRADFORD JANES, b. 1784
 viii SALLY JANES, b. 1 Dec. 1788

References: *Bradford Desc* p. 133. *VR Brimfield* pp. 80(b. Alfred), 81(b. Lucinda, Mavisily), 82(b. Roxeylina, Walter). *VR Sturbridge* p. 346(d. Eliphalet). *Hist Brimfield* p. 423. Hampden Co. LR 12:562(Eliphalet Janes). *MSSR* 8:715(Eliphalet Janes).

462. IRENE JANES[5] (*Irena[4] Bradford, Joseph[3], William[2-1]*), b. Lebanon, Conn., 30 July 1745; d. Holland 28 June 1819.

She m. Brimfield 27 Nov. 1766* **DAVID ANDERSON**, b. South Brimfield 24 Jan. 1744; d. Holland 5 March 1817; son of James and Mary (_____) Anderson.

David Anderson is listed in Holland in 1790 as head of a household of 1 man, 2 boys, and 5 females.

On 25 Oct. 1802 David Anderson of Holland, yeoman, sold to John Anderson of Holland, yeoman, the 85-acre farm on which David was then dwelling.

Children of David and Irene (Janes) Anderson, b. Holland:

 i TIRZAH ANDERSON[6], b. 25 Oct. 1767
 ii ELIZABETH ANDERSON, b. 28 March 1769
 iii IRENE ANDERSON, b. 10 Oct. 1771
 iv LUCY ANDERSON, b. 2 March 1774
 v JOHN ANDERSON, b. 4 June 1779
 vi LYMAN ANDERSON, b. 2 April 1789

* **Note:** The marriage date of 27 Nov. 1776 in the published VR is wrong. The original VR and the church record show the marriage was in 1766.

References: *Bradford Desc* p. 133. *VR Brimfield* p. 157(m.). *Holland Hist* pp. 430-1. Hampden Co. LR 38:674(David Anderson).

463. SOLOMON JANES[5] (*Irena[4] Bradford, Joseph[3], William[2-1]*), b. Lebanon, Conn., 20 June 1748; d. Calais, Vt., 4 April 1812 aged 63, buried East Hill Cemetery.

He m. Sturbridge 27 Jan. 1780 **BEULAH FISK**, b. Sturbridge 16 April 1757; d. Calais, Vt., 28 Feb. 1848 aged 91, buried East Hill Cemetery; daughter of Henry and Mary (Stone) Fisk.

On 25 Dec. 1773 Jonathan Janes and Eliphalet Janes of Brimfield, yeomen, sold to Solomon Janes and Daniel Janes of Brimfield, clothiers, fifteen acres. On 19 Feb. 1783 Solomon Janes of Templeton, clothier, sold to Daniel Janes of Monson all his right in the piece of land that he and Daniel had bought.

Solomon Janes served in the Revolutionary War as a private in Capt. James Sherman's company, Col. Pyncheon's regiment which marched on the alarm of 19 April 1775. He served as a corporal in Capt. Joseph Thompson's company, Col. Timothy Danielson's regiment; he enlisted on 29 April 1775 with service of 3 months and 10 days. He served as a sergeant in the same company and regiment later in 1775. He also served as a sergeant in Capt. Reuben Munn's company, Col. David Leonard's regiment; he entered service 1 March 1777 and was discharged 11 April 1777; this company was detached to reinforce the army at Ticonderoga.

Children of Solomon and Beulah (Fisk) Janes:

    i   NATHAN JANES[6], b. Sturbridge 12 Jan. 1781

    ii BEULAH JANES, b. Monson 9 Aug. 1784

    iii PARDON JANES, b. ca. 1788 (d. Feb 1870 ae 82, bur. East Hill Cem.)

    iv HENRY JANES, b. 18 Oct. 1792

    v   LORENZO JANES

    vi POLLY JANES, b. ca. 1790 (d. Dec 1869 ae 79, bur. East Hill Cem.)

    vii LORINDA JANES

    viii LUCRETIA JANES

References: *Bradford Desc* p. 134. *VR Sturbridge* pp. 49(b. Beulah), 74(b. Nathan), 220(m.), 346(d. Solomon). Hampden Co. LR 12:562; 26:241. Monson VR 1755-1837 p. 96(b. Beulah). VTVR(d. Solomon, Beulah, Pardon, Polly). *MSSR* 8:716.

464.   DANIEL JANES⁵ (*Irena⁴ Bradford, Joseph³, William²⁻¹*), b. Lebanon, Conn., 17 March 1751; d. Richford, Vt., 20 March 1809.

He m. Brimfield 25 June 1776 **ANNA SANDERS**, b. Charlestown 24 Jan. 1757.

On 25 Dec. 1773 Jonathan Janes and Eliphalet Janes of Brimfield, yeomen, sold to Solomon Janes and Daniel Janes of Brimfield, clothiers, fifteen acres.

On 4 April 1783 Daniel Janes of Monson, clothier, sold to Jonathan Janes of Brimfield, cordwainer, three pieces of land totaling 50 acres in Monson.

Children of Daniel and Anna (Sanders) Janes, first two b. Brimfield (first five rec. Monson):

- i   RACHEL JANES⁶, b. 2 May 1777
- ii   CHARLES JANES, b. 5 June 1779; d. 1785
- iii   ANNIE JANES, b. 10 Oct. 1782
- iv   JEREMIAH JANES, b. 2 Jan. 1785
- v   CHARLES JANES, b. 14 March 1785; d. 18 Aug. 1785
- vi   DANIEL JANES, b. 25 Sept. 1789
- vii   IRA JANES, b. 30 March 1794
- viii   IRENE JANES
- ix   LYDIA JANES, b. Feb. 1799

References: *Bradford Desc* p. 134.   *VR Brimfield* pp. 80(b. Charles), 82(b. Rachel), 207(m.). Hampden Co. LR 12:562; 25:400.   Monson VR 1755-1837 pp. 54(b. 1ˢᵗ 5 ch.), 71(d. Charles). *Hist Brimfield* p. 423.

465.   MARY JANES⁵ (*Irena⁴ Bradford, Joseph³, William²⁻¹*), b. Brimfield 28 April 1753; d. 1 Oct. 1813 aged 61.   She and her husband are buried in Troy St. Cemetery, Richford, Vt.

She m. 1773 **ROWLAND POWELL**, b. Lebanon, Conn., 16 Nov. 1751; d. 1838 aged 87; son of Rowland and Mary (Richardson) Powell.

On 5 Feb. 1777 Thomas Warner of Stafford sold to Rowland Powell of Stafford 54 acres.

Rowland Powell served in the Revolutionary War in Wood's 3ʳᵈ Regiment of Vermont Militia.

Rowland Powell is listed in 1800 and 1810 in Richford, Vt.

Children of Rowland and Mary (Janes) Powell, first two b. Stafford, Conn.:

- i   BRADFORD POWELL⁶, b. 5 Aug. 1775

    ii JOHN POWELL, b. 9 Dec. 1776

    iii ANNA POWELL (m. 1801)

    iv HORATIO POWELL

    v LUCY POWELL (m. 1804)

    vi ELFLEDA POWELL

    vii CHESTER POWELL

    viii HORACE POWELL

    ix CYNTHIA POWELL, b. poss. Hartford, Vt., ca 31 Oct 1793 (d. 9 Dec. 1853 ae 60y 1m 9d)

    x PROSPER POWELL, b. 7 Sept. 1795 (ae 65 in 1860; d. 1881 ae 86)

References: *Bradford Desc* p. 134. Lebanon CT VR 1:251(b. Rowland). Stafford CT VR 2:30(b. Bradford), 31(b. John). VTVR(m. ch.). Stafford CT LR 5:13(Thomas Warner). *Pension Abstracts* 3:2167(Rowland Powell). *Richford, VT, Area Cemeteries*, Marlene Simmons (1994), pp. 115, 170. *Lawrence Co IL Cem* p. 427(d. Cynthia). *Janes Fam* p. 112. *Early Settlers of Richford* p. 3, 7.

466. JONATHAN JANES[5] (*Irena*[4] *Bradford, Joseph*[3], *William*[2-1]), b. Brimfield 8 Jan. 1756; d. St. Albans, Vt., 31 June 1825 aged 69, buried Greenwood Cemetery.

He m. Sturbridge 4 March 1781 **PATTEE** (or **MARTHA**) **PLYMTON**, b. Sturbridge 29 March 1764; d. St. Johns, Lower Canada 29 July 1834, buried 29 July 1834 aged 73 Greenwood Cem. ("Martha wife of Jonathan"); daughter of Gershom and Martha (Marcy) Plymton.

On 25 Dec. 1773 Jonathan Janes and Eliphalet Janes of Brimfield, yeomen, sold 15 acres to Solomon Janes and Daniel Janes of Brimfield. On 4 April 1783 Daniel Janes of Monson, clothier, sold to Jonathan Janes of Brimfield, cordwainer, three pieces of land totaling 50 acres in Monson.

Jonathan Janes served in the Revolutionary War and applied for a pension on 8 April 1818 at Canandaigua, Ontario Co., N.Y., when he was aged 63. In June 1818 he was living in St. Albans, Vt., and had moved to Montgomery, Vt., in 1820 with his wife Martha aged 58, youngest child Fanney aged 15, and an orphaned grandchild Martha Hubbard aged 11.

On 15 Aug. 1823 Martha Janes was appointed administratrix of the estate of Jonathan Janes late of St. Albans. The estate was insolvent.

Children of Jonathan and Pattee (Plymton) Janes, first 3 rec. Monson, last 2 b. Richford, Vt.:

    i HORACE JANES[6], b. Brimfield 18 Sept. 1781

    ii CYNTHIA JANES, b. 18 July 1783

    iii RUBY JANES, b. 9 May 1785

    iv MARTHA JANES, b. 2 Jan. 1787

    v JONATHAN JANES, b. 23 March 1789; d. St. Albans, Vt., 13 July 1816 ae 17.

    vi GERSHOM PLIMPTON JANES, b. 3 Oct. 1790; d. Richford, Vt., 15 June 1801

    vii HENRY JANES, b. 1 Jan. 1792

    viii JULIA JANES, b. 15 Oct. 1794

    ix CHARLOTTE JANES, b. 22 May 1796; d. 15 June 1801

    x LEWIS JANES, b. 6 Feb. 1798

    xi DWIGHT PLIMPTON JANES, b. 31 July 1801

    xii FRANCES REBECCA JANES, b. 24 Jan. 1803

References: *Bradford Desc* pp. 134-5. *VR Sturbridge* pp. 107(b. Pattee), 220(m.). Hampden Co. LR 12:562; 25:400. Monson VR 1755-1837 p. 84(b. 1st 3 ch.). VTVR(d. Jonathan, Pattee, son Jonathan, Gershom; b. last 2 ch.). *Pensions Abstracts* 2:1822(Jonathan Janes). Franklin VT PR N:61-75(Jonathan Janes).

467. SAMUEL[5] BRADFORD (*John[4], Joseph[3], William[2-1]*), b. Montville, Conn., 4 Jan. 1736; d. there 29 July 1807 aged 69. He and his wife are buried in Raymond Hills Cemetery.

He m. **BRIDGET COMSTOCK**, b. Montville, Conn., 20 June 1738; d. there 15 July 1830 aged 92; daughter of Nathaniel and Margaret (Fox) Comstock. In his will written 4 June 1788, proved 22 Nov. 1791, Nathaniel Comstock of Montville named his wife Margaret and daughter Bridget Bradford. Bridget Bradford signed a receipt on 2 Jan. 1796 and Samuel and Bridget Bradford signed another receipt on 4 Nov. 1801.

John Bradford of New London conveyed land to his son Samuel on 31 Aug. 1765 and 28 Sept. 1765

On 14 March 1776 Samuel Bradford of New London, yeoman, sold to Dr. Seth Wymond Holmes of New London, 26 acres in two pieces.

Sam[l] Bradford was head of a household of 2 men over 16 and 4 females in New London Co. in the 1790 census and listed near him was Nath[l] Bradford with 1 man and 1 female.

On 14 Nov. 1807 Bridget Bradford, Samuel Bradford, and Mulford Raymond were granted administration on the estate of Samuel Bradford of Montville. The inventory was taken 14 Dec. 1807.

Children of Samuel and Bridget (Comstock) Bradford, b. Montville, Conn. (not in Barbour):

  i   BRIDGET BRADFORD⁶, b. 8 March 1760
  ii ELEANOR BRADFORD, b. 11 Feb. 1762
  iii SAMUEL BRADFORD, b. 27 March 1764
  iv NATHANIEL BRADFORD, b. 13 Oct. 1766
  v   MARGARET BRADFORD, b. 31 May 1769
  vi WILLIAM BRADFORD, b. 30 Jan. 1772
  vii SARAH BRADFORD, b. 1 Feb. 1774
  viii ESTHER BRADFORD, b. 2 Dec. 1782

References: *Bradford Desc* p. 135. *Montville CT Hist* p. 396. New London CT PR New London CT PR #671(Samuel Bradford); #1437(Nathaniel Comstock). Montville CT LR 1:94(Samuel Bradford). New London CT LR 18:97, 106(John Bradford). Hale Cem Coll:Montville p. 66(b. Samuel, Bridget).

468. JOHN⁵ BRADFORD (*John⁴, Joseph³, William²⁻¹*), b. Montville, Conn., 7 Dec. 1739; d. Cornwell, Conn., 5 June 1818 aged 80.

He m. (1) Norwich, Conn., ca. 1764 **MARY FITCH**, b. Norwich, Conn., July 1744; d. Montville, Conn., 5 Nov. 1780 aged 35; daughter of Daniel and Sarah (Sherwood) Fitch. On 25 April 1767 John Bradford of New London and his wife Mary, with others sold their right in the land of her brother James Fitch deceased that he had received from the will of his father Daniel Fitch. On 3 Feb. 1772 John Bradford Jr. of New London and his wife Mary sold to Samuel Sherwood Fitch of New London the 20 acres set off to Mary in the distribution of her father's estate; the land was partly in New London and partley in Norwich.

He m. (2) Cornwall, Conn., **MARY ROGERS**; d. Cornwall, Conn., 18 Feb. 1808 aged 63; daughter of Samuel and Lucy (Dennison) Rogers.

John Bradford of New London conveyed land to his son John on 31 Aug. 1765, 28 Sept. 1765, and 2 Feb. 1770.

John Bradford served in the Revolutionary War.

John Bradford was of New London 17 April 1783 when he purchased Cornwall real estate and was of Cornwall by 9 Feb. 1784.

John Bradford was head of a household of 1 man and 3 females in Cornwall in the 1790 census and listed next to him was James F. Bradford whose household also consisted of 1 man and 3 females.

Children of John and Mary (Fitch) Bradford, by first wife, b. Montville, Conn. (not in Barbour):

    i   JAMES [FITCH?] BRADFORD⁶, b. 1 May 1767

    ii RACHEL BRADFORD, b. ca. 1769

    iii REBECCA BRADFORD, b. ca. 1775 (based on age at d.)

    iv ABIGAIL BRADFORD, b. 18 July 1775 (or 1773)

    v MARY (or MOLLY) BRADFORD, b. 14 July 1777 (or 1771)

    vi ELEANOR BRADFORD, b. ca. 1777

    vii JOHN BRADFORD (not in Aspinwall)

References: *Bradford Desc* p. 135. *Montville CT Hist* p. 397. Montville CT LR 1:250(John Bradford). New London CT LR 18:99, 100, 184; 19:299(John Bradford). Hale Coll: Montville p. 61 (d. Mary); Cornwall CT VR p. 21(d. John, 2nd wife Mary, Rebecca). *Desc Rev James Fitch* pp. 142-3. Cornwall CT LR 4:367, 415(John Bradford).

469. JOSEPH⁵ BRADFORD (*John⁴, Joseph³, William²⁻¹*), b. Montville, Conn., 17 June 1742; d. there 21 March 1815 aged 73. He and his wife are both buried in Raymond Hills Cemetery.

He m. **EUNICE MAPLES**, b. ca. 1750; d. Montville, Conn., 22 Oct. 1821 aged 70; daughter of Stephen and Eunice (Way) Maples.

John Bradford of New London conveyed land to his son Joseph Bradford on 31 Aug. 1765.

Joseph Bradford was head of a household of 4 men, 1 boy under 16, and 5 females in New London Co. in the 1790 census.

Joseph Bradford of Montville in his will dated 25 March 1811, proved May 1815, named his wife Eunice, sons Joseph ("he has been absent many years from me"), Stephen, and Benjamin, daughters Sarah (under 18) and Patience (Benjamin was to support his "unfortunate" sister Patience), and granddaughter Eunice Way Bradford.

On 3 Oct. 1790 Joseph Bradford and his wife were admitted to the Montville Church. On 7 Nov. their children Sherred, Joseph, Steven, William, Patience, and Burissa were baptized. On 22 Nov. their children John, Eunice, Benjamin, and Sarah were baptized. On 5 June 1808 Eunice Way Bradford, grandchild of Joseph Bradford, was baptized.

On 16 March 1816 Benjamin Bradford 2nd of Montville sold to Eunice Bradford of Montville a farm partly in Montville and partly in Bozrah that had been given to Benjamin by the will of his father Joseph; Eunice agreed to support and maintain Benjamin's sister Patience. At the bottom of the deed is written "I hereby approve of the within conveyance & sale of the within described property or land by Benjamin Bradford 2[2] to whom I am overseer - Christopher Chapman."

Eunice Bradford of Montville in her will dated 27 Nov. 1819, proved 27 Nov. 1819, named her granddaughter Eunice Way Bradford and daughter Sarah Hilhouse who was to support the daughter Patience, and appointed Nathaniel and Sarah Hilhouse executors.

Children of Joseph and Eunice (Maples) Bradford (not in Montville in Barbour):

   i   JOSEPH BRADFORD[6] (named in will)
  ii   SHERWOOD BRADFORD, b. 1776; d. 16 Nov. 1805; unm.
 iii   WILLIAM BRADFORD, b. 1780
  iv   PATIENCE BRADFORD, b. 18 Feb. 1785
   v   JOHN BRADFORD, b. 7 Dec. 1787
  vi   EUNICE BRADFORD, b. 26 April 1789
 vii   BENJAMIN BRADFORD, b. 11 April 1791
viii   SARAH BRADFORD, b. 17 April 1796
  ix   STEPHEN BRADFORD, b. 8 Sept. 1798

References: *Bradford Desc* pp. 135-6. *Montville CT Hist* pp. 397-8. Montville CT LR 6:444(Benjamin Bradford). New London CT PR #665(Eunice Bradford), #667(Joseph Bradford). New London CT LR 18:97(John Bradford). Hale Cem Coll:Montville p. 60(d. Joseph, Eunice). Montville Ch. Rec. 3:28(admitted), 98(bp. of children), 131(bp. Eunice Way).

470. SARAH[5] BRADFORD (*John[4], Joseph[3], William[2-1]*), b. Montville, Conn., 27 July 1744; d. there 17 March 1768 aged 23. She and her husband are both buried in Raymond Hills Cemetery.

She m. **NATHANIEL COMSTOCK**, b. Montville, Conn., 5 July 1740; d. there 17 Dec. 1829, aged 90; son of Nathaniel and Margaret (Fox) Comstock. He m. (2) ANNA STARK with whom he had Nathaniel, Anna, Charlotte, Peggy, Mary, and Sophia. In his will written 4 June 1788, proved 22 Nov. 1791, Nathaniel Comstock of Montville named his wife Margaret and son Nathaniel. On 24 Sept. 1792 Nathaniel signed a receipt that he had received his portion of his father's estate.

On 1802 and 1805 Nathaniel Comstock of Montville freed two slaves, Peter aged 26 and Miriam aged 25.

Nathaniel Comstock of Montville in his will dated 14 July 1827, proved 4 Jan. 1830, named his wife Ana, sons Nathaniel and Perez of East Hartford, and daughters Sarah Hilhouse, Anna Ransom, Charlotte Raymond, Peggy Bradford, Mary Raymond, and Sophia Comstock.

Children of Nathaniel and Sarah (Bradford) Comstock [not in Montville in Barbour]:

    i SARAH COMSTOCK[6], b. ca. 1762
    ii PEREZ COMSTOCK, b. 8 May 1764

References: *Bradford Desc* p. 136. New London CT PR #1437(Nathaniel Comstock), #1438(Nathaniel Comstock). Montville CT LR 5:13, 400(freed slaves). Hale Cem Coll:Montville p. 68(d. Sarah, Nathaniel).

471. PEREZ[5] BRADFORD (*John[4], Joseph[3], William[2-1]*), b. Montville, Conn., 10 Oct. 1746; d. there 8 May 1817 aged 71, bur. in Raymond Hills Cem.

He m. Montville, Conn., 22 Feb. 1770 **BETSEY ROGERS**, b. 25 Nov. 1751; d. 25 May 1823; daughter of Thomas and Sarah (Fitch) Rogers.

John Bradford of New London conveyed land to his son Perez Bradford on 2 Feb. 1770, 29 March 1781, and 28 March 1785.

Peres Bradford was head of a household of 3 men 16 or older and 2 females in New London Co. in the 1790 census.

On 9 June 1817 Azel Rogers and Betty Bradford were granted administration on the estate of Perez Bradford late of Montville. The inventory was taken on 30 May 1817 and distribution of the widow's thirds was made on 4 July 1817.

Betty Bradford of Montville in her will dated 12 Oct. 1818, proved 7 June 1823, named her granddaughters Betsey R. Bradford, Mary D. Bradford, and Parthenia Church. On 31 Jan. 1824 a receipt was signed by Adon. F. Bradford as agent for Betsey R. and Mary D. Bradford. On 3 July 1824 Henry and Parthenia Church signed a receipt.

Children of Perez and Betsey (Rogers) Bradford, b. Montville, Conn.:

    i ADONIJAH FITCH BRADFORD[6], b. 9 Aug. 1771
    ii PARTHENIA BRADFORD, b. 13 Aug. 1773

References: Montville CT VR p. 11(m.; b. ch.). *Bradford Desc* p. 136. *Montville CT Hist* p. 398. New London CT PR #670(Perez Bradford), #662(Betty Bradford). New London

CT LR 20:198; 21:143; 22:60; 25:96(John Bradford). Hale Cem Coll:Montville p. 66(d. Perez). *Desc Rev James Fitch* p. 134.

472. BENJAMIN[5] BRADFORD (*John[4], Joseph[3], William[2-1]*), b. Montville, Conn., 8 Oct. 1748.

He m. ca. 1775 **PARTHENA ROGERS**, b. New London 8 Nov. 1752; daughter of Thomas and Sarah (Fitch) Rogers.

John Bradford of New London conveyed land to his son Benjamin Bradford on 2 Feb. 1770, 29 March 1781, and 28 March 1785.

Benjamin Bradford's household consisted of 1 man, 1 boy, and 1 female in New London Co. in the 1790 census.

Child of Benjamin and Parthena (Rogers) Bradford:

    i THOMAS BRADFORD[6], b. 6 Nov. 1776

References: *Bradford Desc* p. 136. *Montville CT Hist* p. 398. New London CT LR 20:198; 21:144; 22:60; 25:96(John Bradford). *Desc Rev James Fitch* p. 134.

473. REBECCA[5] BRADFORD (*John[4], Joseph[3], William[2-1]*), b. Montville, Conn., 17 Jan. 1754; d. there 17 Sept. 1839 aged 86.

She m. **JOSEPH FORD**, b. Norwich 16 Aug. 1737; d. 18 May 1812 aged 74; son of James and Elizabeth (Bartlett) Ford. He m. (1) Norwich, Conn., 18 Feb. 1761 MARY LILLEY with whom he had Charles, John, Roswell, Elisha, Joseph, Molly, and Philene.

Joseph Ford of Bozrah in his will dated 8 May 1812, proved 27 May 1812, named his wife Rebecca; eldest son Charles; sons John, Roswell, Joseph, Benjamin, and Samuel; Mary Ford daughter of his son Elisha deceased; seven daughters Mary Lamphier, Sarah Lefingwell, Eunice Lefingwell, Hannah Ford, Parthena Avery, Pamela Ford, and Eleanor Ford. The distribution dated 9 April 1813 included the widow and children Charles, John, Roswell, Joseph B., Benjamin, Samuel, Mary, Sarah, Eunice, Hannah, [Philomese?], Partene, and Elenor (surnames not included for the daughters). On 13 Dec. 1839 the land that had been set off to the widow was distributed to Joseph B. Ford, Charles Ford, Eunice Leffingwell, Sarah Leffingwell, Philena Gardner, Hannah Ford, Benjamin Ford, Eleanor Ford, John Ford, Samuel Ford, the heirs of Mary Lamphere, the heirs of Parthena Avery, and Roswell Ford.

Children of Joseph and Rebecca (Bradford) Ford:

    i LUTHER FORD[6], b. 23 May 1779 (not in father's will)

   ii SARAH FORD, b. 18 June 1780, bp. Bozrah 10 Sept. 1780

  iii EUNICE FORD, b. 25 April 1782

  iv HANNAH FORD, b. 10 July 1784; poss. d. Bozrah 7 Aug. 1853 ae 63

   v JOSEPH B. FORD, b. 10 Sept. 1786

  vi PARTHENIA FORD, b. 26 Aug. 1791

  vii SAMUEL FORD, b. May 1796

 viii ELEANOR FORD, b. 28 May 1799

  ix BENJAMIN FORD

References: *Bradford Desc* pp. 136-7. Hale Cem Coll:Bozrah p. 42(d. Rebecca, Joseph, Hannah). Bozrah Cong. Ch. Recs. 3:2, 10-13(bp. ch. 1st wife), 14(bp. Sarah); 4:80(d. Rebecca). *Norwich CT VR* 1:168(b. Joseph), 392(Joseph's 1st m.), 393(1st 3 ch. by 1st wife). Norwich CT PR #3936(Joseph Ford).

474. MARY⁵ BRADFORD (*John⁴, Joseph³, William²⁻¹*), b. Montville, Conn., 17 Jan. 1756; d. there March 1836. She and her husband are both bur. in Comstock Cem.

She m. ca. 1779 **SETH WYMOND HOLMES**, b. 2 Feb. 1738; d. 12 Dec. 1821; son of Alpheus and Delight (Harris) Holmes. He m. (1) SARAH ROGERS with whom he had James Wymond, Selina Matilda, and Almira.

On 14 March 1776 Samuel Bradford of New London, yeoman, sold to Dr. Seth Wymond Holmes of New London, 26 acres in two pieces.

Seth Homes' household consisted of 2 men, 2 boys under 16, and 3 females in New London Co. in the 1790 census.

Seth Wymond Holmes of Montville in his will dated 27 July 1821, proved 10 Jan. 1822, named his wife Mary, sons James Wymond Holmes and John Bradford Holmes, daughters Selina Matilda Loomis, Sally Teresa Holmes, Betsy R. Greene, and Almira Holmes, and grandson William Henry Greene (under 21). On 30 Dec. 1824 the land was distributed to his widow and daughter Sally T. Sheffield.

Children of Seth Wymond and Mary (Bradford) Holmes, b. Montville, Conn.:

   i JOHN BRADFORD HOLMES⁶, b. 23 June 1780; d. Montville 1824 ae 44, bur. Comstock Cem.

  ii BETSEY ROSALIE HOLMES, b. ca. 1782 (named in will)

 iii HENRY HOLMES d. at sea ae 23 yrs.

 iv SALLY TERESA HOLMES (named in will)

References: *Bradford Desc* p. 137. *Montville CT Hist* p. 332. Montville CT VR p. 27(b. John B.). New London CT PR #2678(Seth W. Holmes). New London CT LR 1:94(Samuel Bradford). Hale Cem Coll:Montville p. 30(d. Mary, Seth, John B.).

475. SARAH ADAMS[5] (*Bathsheba*[4] *Bradford, Israel*[3]*, William*[2-1]), b. Kingston 3 Dec. 1732; d. there 27 April 1818 aged 84y.

She m. (1) Kingston 11 Dec. 1753 **CALEB COOKE**, b. Kingston 4 July 1727; d. there 26 Sept. 1756; son of Caleb and Hannah (Shurtleff) Cooke, a descendant of Pilgrim **Francis Cooke**.

She m. (2) Kingston 19 Nov. 1766 **GERSHOM COBB**, b. Plymouth 16 March 1716/7; d. Kingston April 1799 aged 82y; son of James and Patience (Holmes) Cobb.

Gershom Cobb of Kingston, retailer, was granted a license to sell liquor in 1761 and 1763.

Administration of the estate of Caleb Cooke, gentleman of Kingston, dated 28 March 1757, names widow Sarah. On 7 Dec. 1762 Thomas Adams was appointed guardian to Amos and Bartlett Cooke. On 23 Aug. 1769 Gershom Cobb was appointed guardian to Bartlett Cooke and Amos Cooke.

In the 1771 Valuation List, Gershom Cobb appears in Kingston with 2 polls, 1 house, 2 cattle, 15 goats or sheep, 1 swine, 4 acres of pasture, and 5 acres of upland which produced 2 tons of hay.

On 11 Dec. 1771 Gershom Cobb, joyner, and his wife Sarah of Kingston, and the other heirs of Thomas Adams, sold to John Adams of Kingston some cedar swamp.

On 27 March 1773 Joshua Adams, mariner, Gershom Cobb, joyner, and his wife Sarah, and Deborah Adams, weaver, all of Kingston, sold to Ebenezer Adams of Kingston, mariner, land in Kingston bounded on the land of widow Bathsheba Adams; this deed was not recorded until 6 April 1833.

Gershom Cobb's household consisted of 1 man and 2 females in Kingston in the 1790 census.

Children of Caleb and Sarah (Adams) Cooke, b. Kingston:

  i BARTLETT COOKE[6], b. 9 Sept. 1754; d. aged 3
  ii AMOS COOKE, b. 12 March 1756

References: *VR Kingston* pp. 47(b. ch., Caleb), 167(1st m.), 199(2nd m.), 328(d. Gershom), 329(d. Sarah), 333(d. Caleb). Plymouth Co. PR #4851(gdn.), #4859(Caleb Cooke). *MD* 4:112(b. Gershom). *Bradford Desc* p. 137. *Plymouth VR* p. 34(b. Gershom). Plymouth Co. LR 56:193-4(Gershom Cobb *et al.*); 177:59(Joshua Adams *et al.*). *MF* 12:447. *Plymouth Co Ct Recs* Vol. 3. *1771 Valuation* p. 640.

476. JOSHUA ADAMS[5] (*Bathsheba*[4] *Bradford, Israel*[3]*, William*[2-1]), b. Kingston 21 Nov. 1735; d. in Rev. War 1782 according to Aspinwall.

He m. Chatham 12 Oct. 1757 **MARY GODFREY** of Chatham, b. ca. 1732; living 22 July 1788; d. Kingston 18 Dec. 1809 aged 72; daughter of Samuel and Thankful (_____) Godfrey; a descendant of Pilgrim **Stephen Hopkins**. She m. (2) Kingston 22 Jan. 1781 SILVANUS COOKE. Samuel Godfrey made his will 4 Feb. 1765, proved 30 Aug. 1768, naming among others his daughter Mary Adams.

On 1 Dec. 1762 Thomas Adams of Kingston, gentleman, sold to Joshua Adams of Kingston, mariner, one acre and a house near the house Thomas lived in.

In the 1771 Valuation List, Joshua Adams appears in Kingston with 1 poll, one-half of a house, 2 cattle, 4 goats or sheep, 3 acres of pasture, 1 acre of tillage which produced 10 bushels of grain, and 2 acres of fresh meadow which produced 1 ton of hay.

On 11 Dec. 1771 Joshua Adams, mariner, of Kingston, and the other heirs of Thomas Adams, sold to John Adams of Kingston some cedar swamp.

On 4 March 1782 Sylvanus Cook, housewright, and Mary Cook his wife, late wife of Joshua Adams, late Kingston, mariner, were appointed to administer the estate of Joshua Adams. On 22 July 1788 the estate was divided between Mary Cook (the widow) and Joshua Adams the eldest son; daughter Sally Perkins, wife of John Perkins of Plympton; daughter Saba Cushman, wife of Zachariah Cushman of Plympton; and children Thomas Adams, Polly Adams, and Barsheba Adams.

Children of Joshua and Mary (Godfrey) Adams, b. Kingston:

- i SARAH ADAMS[6], b. 16 Dec. 1757; d. 21 July 1759
- ii SARAH ADAMS, b. 28 April 1760
- iii SABA ADAMS, b. 24 June 1762
- iv JOSHUA ADAMS, b. 8 July 1767 (not in VR)
- v THOMAS ADAMS, b. 13 Feb. 1770 (not in VR)
- vi MARY ADAMS, b. 23 July 1772 (not in VR or division)
- vii BATHSHEBA ADAMS, b. 1 Jan. 1775 (no parents in VR)

References: *VR Kingston* pp. 15(b. ch.), 313(d. Sarah). *Bradford Desc* p. 137. Plymouth Co. PR 30:402-5(Joshua Adams). *MF* 6:412-3. Plymouth Co. LR 54:77(Thomas Adams); 56:193-4(Joshua Adams *et al.*). Queens Co. N.S. PR 1:7, File A-4(Samuel Godfrey). *Adams Fam* (1861) p. 20. *1771 Valuation* p. 640.

477. LYDIA⁵ BRADFORD (*Benjamin⁴, Israel³, William²⁻¹*), b. Kingston 7 June 1749; living 30 Aug. 1790.

She m. Kingston 19 April 1770 **LEVI HOLMES**, b. Kingston 28 Nov. 1747; d. there 6 May 1795 aged 47y 4m 9d or 7 May 1795 aged 42y; son of Ephraim and Sarah (Tilden) Holmes. On 10 Nov. 1772 Ephraim Holmes of Kingston, yeoman, sold to his son Levi Holmes of Kingston, yeoman, two acres of the farm where Ephraim lived. On 4 Dec. 1778 Ephraim gave to his son Levi six acres in Kingston.

In the 1771 Valuation List, Levi Holmes appears in Kingston with 1 poll and 6 goats or sheep.

Levi Holmes served in the Revolutionary War as a private in Capt. Ebenezer Washburn's company, Col. Thomas Lothrop's regiment, which marched to Bristol, R.I., on an alarm in December 1776. He also served in Capt. James Harlow's company, Col. Ezra Wood's regiment; he enlisted on 5 June 1778 and served 8 months and 4 days. And he served in Capt. Benjamin Rider's company, Col. John Jacob's regiment; this company was raised to reinforce the Continental Army; he enlisted 25 Aug. 1780 and was discharged 1 Nov. 1780.

On 7 Dec. 1785 Levi Holmes of Kingston, yeoman, and wife Lydia, sold to Thomas Brewer land in Kingston which Benjamin Bradford late of Kingston died seized of, with reference to the division deeds of the estate of Israel Bradford, late of Kingston. The deed states that Lydia was sole heir of Benjamin Bradford.

On 17 July 1790 Levi Holmes of Kingston, yeoman, and his wife Lydia, sold to Jedidiah Holmes of Kingston, Gentleman, a salt meadow that was assigned to "our father Benjamin Bradford" in the division of his father's estate between him and his brother Elisha, part of the estate that came to Lydia.

Levi Holmes' household consisted of 1 man, 2 boys, and 7 females in Kingston in the 1790 census.

On 28 March 1810 James Polden of Duxbury and his wife Lucy sold to Bradford Holmes and Levi Holmes of Duxbury, blockmakers, an undivided one-eighth part of 80 acres in Kingston that had belonged to her father Levi Holmes. On the same day Nathan Delano of Duxbury and his wife Marcy and Sarah Holmes of Duxbury, singlewoman, sold their rights to Bradford and Levi. On 7 April 1812 Sylvester Holmes of Kingston, singlewoman, sold her right. And on 7 Dec. 1813 Charlotte Holmes of Kingston, singlewoman, sold her right.

Children of Levi and Lydia (Bradford) Holmes, b. Kingston:

    i ZERESH HOLMES[6], b. 23 Jan. 1772

   ii SARAH HOLMES, b. 13 Dec. 1773; d. May 1843 (not in VR); unm.

  iii BRADFORD HOLMES, b. 1 March 1776

  iv LYDIA HOLMES, b. 26 April 1779

   v MERCY HOLMES, b. 10 Sept. 1781

  vi LEVI HOLMES, b. 8 Feb. 1784

 vii LUCY HOLMES, b. 12 May 1787

viii SYLVESTER HOLMES (daughter), b. 19 Nov. 1789

  ix CHARLOTTE HOLMES, b. 30 Oct. 1792

References: *VR Kingston* pp. 90(b. Bradford, Charlotte), 94(b. Levi Jr. & Sr.), 95(b. Lydia, Mercy, Lucy), 98(b. Sarah), 99(b. Sylvester), 100(b. Zeresh), 181(m.), 359(d. Levi). *Bradford Desc* pp. 137-8. *MD* 7:89(d. Levi); 16:140(deed). Plymouth Co. LR 59:23; 60:89(Ephraim Holmes); 72:12(Levi Holmes); 137:111(James Polden), 112(Nathan Delano), 112(Sarah Holmes), 112(Sylvester Holmes), 113(Charlotte Holmes). *1771 Valuation* p. 644. *MSSR* 8:171(Levi Holmes).

478. ELIJAH[5] BRADFORD (*Abner[4], Israel[3], William[2-1]*), b. Kingston 11 April 1735; d. Cheshire 1809.

    He m. **HULDAH BASSETT**, b. Kingston 31 June 1739.

    Elijah Bradford's household consisted of 1 man, 4 boys, and 3 females in Camden, Me., in the 1790 census.

    He resided in Belmont, Me.

Children of Elijah and Huldah (_____) Bradford:

    i ELIJAH BRADFORD[6], b. 1756 (ae 64 in 1820)

   ii ABRAHAM BRADFORD, b. 1758

References: *Bradford Desc* p. 138. 1790 Census ME p. 26. *Rev War Pensions* 1:356(Elijah Bradford Jr.).

479. MARY[5] BRADFORD (*Abner[4], Israel[3], William[2-1]*), b. Kingston 13 June 1742; d. Montgomery 20 May 1806 (not in VR).

    She m. **ISAAC CHAPMAN**, b. Groton, Conn., 18 Dec. 1740; d. Montgomery 13 March 1826; son of William and Mary (Stoddard?) Chapman.

    Isaac Chapman's household consisted of 3 men, 4 boys, and 3 females in Montgomery in the 1790 census.

On 9 Jan 1802 Isaac Chapman of Montgomery, yeoman, sold to Abner Chapman of Montgomery, yeoman, 62 acres. On the same day he sold to Nathan Chapman of Montgomery, yeoman, two pieces of land, one with a house, barn, and other buildings.

On 14 July 1806 the heirs of Simeon Potter who hold land in common in nine shares divided the estate. One of the shares belonged to Levi Bradford, Mary Chapman, Lucy Sheldon, Elisha Bradford, Margaret Ripley, Lydia Orcutt, and Hannah Bates.

On 26 Nov. 1806 Isaac Chapman, yeoman; Isaac Chapman, Jr., yeoman; Elisha Chapman, yeoman; Nathan Chapman, yeoman; Bradford Chapman, yeoman; Ephraim Avery and wife Susanna; Samuel Avery and wife Molly; David R. Cooley and wife Sarah, all of Montgomery, Hampshire Co., Mass., and Phinehas Leonard and wife Content of West Springfield in the same county granted power of attorney to Abner Chapman of Montgomery, yeoman, to demand of Levi Bradford of South Kingston, Washington Co., R.I., gentleman, their right to the estate of Mary Chapman, wife of Isaac Chapman, which came to her as heir to Simeon Potter, Esquire of Swansea.

Children of Isaac and Mary (Bradford) Chapman, b. poss. Groton, Conn.:

    i CONTENT CHAPMAN⁶, b. 8 Aug. 1763

   ii SUSANNA CHAPMAN, b. 11 Aug. 1765

  iii ISAAC CHAPMAN, b. 19 Oct. 1767

  iv MARY (or MOLLY) CHAPMAN, b. 3 April 1770

   v ABNER CHAPMAN, b. 20 June 1772

  vi ELISHA CHAPMAN, b. 26 Aug. 1774

 vii NATHAN CHAPMAN, b. 12 Oct. 1776

viii BRADFORD CHAPMAN, b. 5 May 1779

  ix SARAH CHAPMAN, b. 10 April 1781

References: *Bradford Desc* p. 138. Hampshire Co. LR 43:566(Isaac Chapman, Esq.). Groton CT VR 1:155(b. Isaac). *VR Montgomery* p. 60(d. Isaac). Bristol Co. LR 86:439(division). Hampden Co. LR 41:329; 51:508(Isaac Chapman). GS#52594(Bible abstract, b. ch.).

480. LYDIA⁵ BRADFORD (*Abner⁴, Israel³, William²⁻¹*), b. Kingston 20 Dec. 1749; d. after 9 March 1807.

She m. Kingston 17 May 1770 **CONSIDER ORCUTT**; b. Randolph 1746; d. after 19 Jan 1788; son of Benjamin and Tabitha (Crane) Orcutt.

In the 1771 Valuation List, Consider Orcutt appears in Kingston with 1 poll, 1 oxen, 1 swine, and 1 acre of tillage which produced 10 bushels of grain.

On 19 Jan. 1788 Consider Orcutt of Plymouth, yeoman, sold to Levi Bradford of Kingston, housewright, several tracts of land in Kingston; Lydia made her mark to sign the deed.

On 14 July 1806 the heirs of Simeon Potter who hold land in common in nine shares divided the estate. One of the shares belonged to Levi Bradford, Mary Chapman, Lucy Sheldon, Elisha Bradford, Margaret Ripley, Lydia Orcutt, and Hannah Bates. On 5 Feb. 1807 Elisha Bradford, John Sheldon and his wife Lucy all of Cheshire, Calvin Ripley and his wife Margaret of Kingston, Lydia Orcutt of Boston widow appointed Levi Bradford their attorney in the matter of the estate of Simeon Potter.

No Plymouth Co. probate records were found for Consider Orcutt.

Children of Consider and Lydia (Bradford) Orcutt, bp. Kingston:

    i   ELIZABETH ORCUTT[6], bp. 14 July 1771

    ii HANNAH ORCUTT, bp. 22 Aug. 1773

    iii CONSIDER ORCUTT, bp. 25 Sept. 1775

    iv PRISCILLA ORCUTT, bp. 12 July 1778

References: *VR Kingston* pp. 113(bp. ch.), 181(m.). *Bradford Desc* p. 138. Plymouth Co. LR 67:141(Consider Orcutt). Bristol Co. LR 86:439(division); 87:163(power of attorney). *1771 Valuation* p. 644.

481. HANNAH[5] BRADFORD (*Abner[4], Israel[3], William[2-1]*), b. Kingston 28 Feb. 1751; d. Martinsburg, N.Y., 13 Dec. 1831 [*Hist. Lewis Co.* says Mrs. Arthur d. Martinsburg 1815].

She m. (1) 1771 **RICHARD ARTHUR**, b. 1749; d. Westfield 2 Sept. 1790 aged 41; son of Barnabas and Mercy (_____) Arthur.

She m. (2) by 14 July 1806 _____ **BATES**. [Could this be Elijah Bates who witnessed Isaac Chapman deeds in 1802?]

Richard Arthur's household is listed in Westfield in 1790 with 2 men, 5 boys, and 6 females.

On 31 Oct. 1796 Hannah Arthur of Westfield, widow woman, sold to John Topliff of Westfield, shoemaker, ten acres in Westfield.

On 19 Nov. 1801 Hannah Arthur, Levi Arthur, Elisha Arthur, Russell Arthur, Clarissa Arthur, Joseph Arthur, Lucy Arthur, and Polly (or Sally) Arthur all of Westfield, Richard Arthur of Montgomery, and Joseph Sheldon and his wife Sally (or Polly) of Southampton sold to George Avery of Montville, Conn., three lots of land in Westfield.

On 14 July 1806 the heirs of Simeon Potter who hold land in common in nine shares divided the estate. One of the shares belonged to Levi Bradford, Mary Chapman, Lucy Sheldon, Elisha Bradford, Margaret Ripley, Lydia Orcutt, and Hannah Bates.

Children of Richard and Hannah (Bradford) Arthur, b. Westfield:

   i   MARY ARTHUR[6] (*Bradford Desc* p. 486 says prob. d.y. No record)
  ii BRADFORD ARTHUR, b. 20 Sept. 1773
 iii HANNAH ARTHUR, b. 25 Jan. 1775
 iv RICHARD ARTHUR, b. 16 Oct. 1776
  v MOLLY ARTHUR, b. 20 June 1778
 vi LEVI ARTHUR, b. 25 March 1780
 vii ELISHA ARTHUR, b. 10 Sept. 1781
viii RUSSELL ARTHUR, b. 15 May 1783
 ix CLARISSA ARTHUR, b. 16 Feb. 1785
  x JOSEPH ARTHUR, b. 18 Dec. 1786
 xi LUCY ARTHUR, b. 13 Aug. 1788
 xii SARAH ARTHUR, b. 2 Oct. 1789

References: *Bradford Desc* pp. 138-9. "An Account or Register of the Deaths of Those Deceased in Westfield 1728-1836 (From the Record of the First Church)," typ. May 1936, p. 14(d. Richard). "Westfield Birth & Death Records, As Obtained From the Files at City Hall, Westfield," 1937 typ. (no pagination) (b. ch. except Mary). Hampden Co. LR 35:677(Hannah Arthur); 45:160(Hannah Arthur *et al.*). Bristol Co. LR 86:439(division). *Lewis Co NY Hist* p. 448.

482. ELISHA[5] BRADFORD (*Abner[4], Israel[3], William[2-1]*), b. Kingston 10 May 1753; d. Cheshire 31 May 1809.

He m. 10 June 1781 **EUNICE BENNETT**, b. poss. Plymouth (not in VR or Ch.) 18 March 1765; d. Cheshire 17 Dec. 1823; poss. dau. of Joseph and Eunice (Ward) Bennett.

On 16 Sept. 1788 Elisha Bradford of Adams, yeoman, sold to John Wells of Adams, yeoman, 90 acres in two pieces.

Elisha Bradford was listed in Adams in 1790 with a household of 2 men, 3 boys, and 4 females.

On 14 July 1806 the heirs of Simeon Potter who hold land in common in nine shares divided the estate. One of the shares belonged to Levi Bradford,

Mary Chapman, Lucy Sheldon, Elisha Bradford, Margaret Ripley, Lydia Orcutt, and Hannah Bates. On 5 Feb. 1807 Elisha Bradford, John Sheldon and his wife Lydia all of Cheshire, Calvin Ripley and his wife Margaret of Kingston, and Lydia Orcutt of Boston widow appointed Levi Bradford their attorney in the matter of the estate of Simeon Potter.

In his will dated 28 March 1809, Elisha Bradford of Cheshire named wife Eunice Bradford; daughters Susannah Brown, Lucy Sayles, and Sally Bradford; and sons William, Joseph, Hopstill, Levi, Simeon, and George.

On 8 Aug. 1817 Eunice Bradford of Cheshire, widow, sold to Levi Bradford and George W. Bradford of Cheshire, yeomen, her right in two pieces of land that had been part of the farm of Elisha Bradford. On the same day Simeon P. Bradford of Cheshire sold to Levi and George W. his right in these properties. And on the same day Levi and George W. sold to Simeon their rights in all land and buildings that Elisha had died seized of. On 10 July 1819 George W. Bradford sold to Zebulon Dean of Cheshire, blacksmith, part of Elisha's farm and on the same day Zebulon sold this land back to George W.

Children of Elisha and Eunice (Bennett) Bradford:

    i SUSANNA[6] BRADFORD, b. Feb. 1782
   ii LUCY BRADFORD, b. 18 March 1784
  iii WILLIAM BRADFORD, b. 3 March 1786
  iv JOSEPH BRADFORD, b. 30 March 1788
   v HOPESTILL BRADFORD, b. 1 March 1790
  vi LEVI BRADFORD, b. 25 Dec. 1791
 vii SIMEON BRADFORD, b. 9 March 1794
viii SARAH BRADFORD, b. 18 March 1796
  ix GEORGE W. BRADFORD, b. 9 May 1798
   x EUNICE BRADFORD (twin), b. 28 Sept. 1800; d. 1800
  xi BENJAMIN BRADFORD (twin), b. 28 Sept. 1800; d. 1800

References: *Bradford Desc* p. 139. Berkshire Co. PR 14:407(Elisha Bradford). Berkshire Co. LR 1:344(Elisha Bradford); 23:512-16(land of Elisha). Bristol Co. LR 86:439(division); 87:163(power of attorney).

482A. LUCY[5] BRADFORD (*Abner[4], Israel[3], William[2-1]*), b. Kingston 10 May 1755.

She m. Cheshire 5 May 1799 **JOHN SHELDON**. He probably m. (1) ABIGAIL PHILLIPS with whom he had John, Nathan, Amasa, Hezekiah, Daniel, Salome, Abigail, Patience, Salome, and Ann.

In the Adams town records John Sheldon had his earmark recorded as a swallow tail in the right ear and a hole through the same ear (no date).

John Sheldon was head of a household of 1 man, 3 boys, and 7 females in Adams in the 1790 census. Cheshire was set off in 1793, but John Sheldon is listed in Adams in 1800, 1810, and 1820.

On 14 July 1806 the heirs of Simeon Potter who hold land in common in nine shares divided the estate. One of the shares belonged to Levi Bradford, Mary Chapman, Lucy Sheldon, Elisha Bradford, Margaret Ripley, Lydia Orcutt, and Hannah Bates. On 5 Feb. 1807 Elisha Bradford, John Sheldon and his wife Lucy all of Cheshire, Calvin Ripley and his wife Margaret of Kingston, and Lydia Orcutt of Boston widow appointed Levi Bradford their attorney in the matter of the estate of Simeon Potter.

Lucy was aged 44 at marriage and she and John probably had no children.

References: Bristol Co. LR 86:439(division); 87:163(power of attorney). IGI(b. of his children in Smithfield RI).

483. PEGGY (or **MARGARET**)[5] **BRADFORD** (*Abner⁴, Israel³, William²⁻¹*), b. Kingston 8 May 1757; d. after 27 May 1810, prob. before 1839 when she was not named in her husband's pension.

She m. Kingston 8 Dec. 1774 **CALVIN RIPLEY**, b. Pembroke 18 May 1748; d. after 11 Jan. 1839; son of Joshua and Alice (Stetson) Ripley.

Calvin Ripley served in the Revolutionary War as a private in Capt. Peleg Wadsworth's company, Col. Theophilus Cotton's regiment; he enlisted 7 May 1775 and served for 3 months and 5 days. He applied for a pension on 7 Sept. 1832 when he was aged 84. On 11 July 1839 he moved to Providence, R.I., to live with a son [not named].

Calvin Ripley was head of a household of 1 man, 4 boys, and 4 females in Kingston in the 1790 census.

At the November 1801 term of the Court of Common Pleas, the inhabitants of the town of Kingston sued Calvin Ripley. The town complained that Joshua Ripley, Calvin's father, "has been a poor and indigent person and unable to support himself and for six months last past has been actually chargeable to the said Town of Kingston." The town prays that Calvin "May be ordered to pay the charges ... and may be further obliged to support the said Joshua Ripley in such way and manner as the court shall direct."

On 14 July 1806 the heirs of Simeon Potter who held land in common in nine shares divided the estate. One of the shares belonged to Levi Bradford, Mary Chapman, Lucy Sheldon, Elisha Bradford, Margaret Ripley, Lydia Orcutt, and Hannah Bates. On 5 Feb. 1807 Elisha Bradford, John Sheldon and his wife Lucy all of Cheshire, Calvin Ripley and his wife Margaret of Kingston, and Lydia Orcutt of Boston widow appointed Levi Bradford their attorney in the matter of the estate of Simeon Potter.

On 27 May 1810 Calvin Ripley of Swanzey, gentleman, sold to Levi Bradford of South Kingstown, R.I., land in Swanzey; wife Peggy gave consent.

Children of Calvin and Peggy (Bradford) Ripley, b. Kingston:

  i   CHARLES RIPLEY[6], b. 14 May 1775
  ii LEVI RIPLEY, b. 16 May 1777
  iii LUCY RIPLEY, b. 16 July 1779
  iv LUTHER RIPLEY, b. 16 June 1781
  v   ZENAS RIPLEY, b. 15 June 1783
  vi BRADFORD RIPLEY, b. 1 Oct. 1785
  vii NANCY RIPLEY, b. 16 Nov. 1787
  viii BETSEY RIPLEY, b. 23 Jan. 1790
  ix SALLY RIPLEY, b. 15 May 1792
  x   POLLY RIPLEY, b. 27 April 1794
  xi SOPHIA RIPLEY, b. 12 Feb. 1797
  xii CALVIN RIPLEY (twin), b. 23 Nov. 1800 [sic]; d. Kingston 25 Feb. 1802
  xiii. PEGGY RIPLEY (twin), b. 24 Nov. 1800 [sic]
  xiv HERVEY RIPLEY, b. 17 Sept. 1802

References: *VR Kingston* pp. 122-4(b. Calvin, b. ch.), 181(m.), 373(d. Calvin Jr.). *Bradford Desc* p. 139. Bristol Co. LR 86:439(division); 87:163(power of attorney); 91:268(Calvin Ripley). *Pensions Abstracts* 2:2894(Calvin Ripley). *Plymouth Co Ct Recs* 11:201(Town of Kingston). *MSSR* 13:343(Calvin Ripley).

484. LEVI[5] BRADFORD (*Abner[4], Israel[3], William[2-1]*), b. Kingston 1 July 1759; d. South Kingstown, R.I., 21 Sept. 1802 in 63rd yr.

He m. Kingston 22 Aug. 1782 **POLLY** (or **MARY**) **RIPLEY**, b. Kingston 29 Oct. 1761; daughter of Joshua and Alice (Stetson) Ripley.

The court records show that Levi Bradford was a constable for the town of Kingston in 1781.

On 19 Jan. 1788 Consider Orcutt of Plymouth, yeoman, sold to Levi Bradford of Kingston, housewright, several tracts of land in Kingston; Lydia made her mark to sign the deed. On 19 Jan. 1791 Levi sold six acres of this land to Nathaniel Goodwin of Plympton, Esqr.

Levi Bradford was head of a household of 1 man, 2 boys, and 2 females in the 1790 census of Kingston.

On 23 Aug. 1799 Levi Bradford of Kingston, housewright, sold to Nathaniel Thomas of Kingston, yeoman, seven and a half acres of cedar swamp in Halifax; his wife Polly signed the deed.

On 14 July 1806 the heirs of Simeon Potter who held land in common in nine shares divided the estate. One of the shares belonged to Levi Bradford, Mary Chapman, Lucy Sheldon, Elisha Bradford, Margaret Ripley, Lydia Orcutt, and Hannah Bates. On 5 Feb. 1807 Elisha Bradford, John Sheldon and his wife Lucy all of Cheshire, Calvin Ripley and his wife Margaret of Kingston, and Lydia Orcutt of Boston widow appointed Levi Bradford their attorney in the matter of the estate of Simeon Potter. Levi Bradford, representing himself and his brothers and sisters, with other heirs of Simeon Potter sold parts of the estate in eight deeds in 1806.

Children of Levi and Polly (Ripley) Bradford, b. Kingston:*

   i   [CHILD] BRADFORD, stillborn 30 Dec. 1783
   ii   POLLY[6] BRADFORD, b. 25 March 1784; bp. 8 Oct. 1786
   iii   PAMELA BRADFORD, bp. 8 Oct. 1786; d. Kingston 7 Dec. 1789
   iv   LEVI BRADFORD, b. 5 April 1789
   v   MARTIN BRADFORD, b. 20 March 1792
   vi   SOPHIA BRADFORD, b. 27 June 1794, bp. 24 Aug. 1794
   vii   LUCY BRADFORD, bp. 14 May 1797
   viii   HOWARD BRADFORD
   ix   WARREN BRADFORD

* Aspinwall lists only Polly, Pamelia, Sophia, and Lucy. The last two children are not in Kingston VR, *MD*, or the old IGI. No Plymouth PR for them to 1850. No So. Kingston RI will, m. or b. for any Bradford. This Levi Bradford not found in the 1800 census.

References: *VR Kingston* pp. 28-31(b. &, bp. ch.), 123(b. Polly), 178(m.), 322(d. stillborn child, Pamela). *Bradford Desc* pp. 139-40. Plymouth Co. LR 67:141(Consider Orcutt); 70:219; 87:21(Levi Bradford). Bristol Co. LR 86:423-4(heirs of Simeon Potter), 439(division); 87:163(power of attorney), 453, 535; 88:293; 90:44; 93:41-3(heirs of Simeon Potter); 106:107(Levi Bradford).

485. CORNELIUS[5] BRADFORD (*Joshua[4], Israel[3], William[2-1]*), b. Kingston 10 Dec. 1737; d. Grand Manan, New Brunswick, 10 Feb. 1790.

He m. ca. 1760 **PATIENCE DAVIS**, d. 9 July 1847; possibly a daughter of Solomon Davis of Falmouth.

On 14 Sept. 1773 Cornelius Bradford appears on a petition to make Meduncook (now Friendship) a town separate from Broad Bay. The next year at a town meeting on 10 March 1774, he was chosen to be on a committee to take care of the ministerial lot and on 16 May an assessor.

Cornelius Bradford was Captain of the Militia in Meduncook 9 Sept. 1775. On 5 Jan. 1776 he was chosen clerk of the committee of safety and the next year their treasurer. He was commissioned a Captain in Col. Mason Wheaton's (4th Lincoln Co.) regiment on 3 July 1776.

On 25 April 1775 the town inhabitants voted to send to the selectmen of Falmouth "for 100 lbs. of Powder, 300 flints, 100 lbs. of Lead & the Loan of 20 fire arms ... Mr. Bradford engaged to make out the chief part of last year's march hire ... into the hands of Ebenezer Davis, who with Bradford undertook to go on the message but did not succeed so the money was returned." At a meeting on 18 May it was reported that "Mr. Bradford is going westward with his Vessel & promises to try again for some ammunition with the marsh hire."

On 19 Sept. 1775 "At a meeting of the Committee of Correspondence Agreed that the Guard be kept at Mr. Bradford's Point so as to have the Benefit of the high land on his lot for a lookout in clear weather, the Centry in the night and in thick weather to be kept down upon the point near the shore."

In 1776 there was some suspicion that Cornelius Bradford had Loyalist leanings. On 6 Feb. 1776 the committee of inspection and correspondence prepared depositions "after Capt. Adams having entered a complaint against Mr. Bradford for inclining to toryism." On the 15th "when Mr. Bradford had his trial, made an acknowledgement & promised Reformation as having considerably offended, but the Committee not finding Sufficient cause to condemn him, gave him an acquitance on condition of his future good behavior."

On 15 Sept. 1790 son Joshua Bradford was appointed administrator of the estate of Cornelius Bradford, late of Meduncook, mariner. Widow Patience Bradford received her dower 8 Dec. 1794.

Patience Bradford was appointed guardian of Cornelius, Bethia, James, Francis, and Winslow.

Children of Cornelius and Patience (Davis) Bradford, all b. Meduncook [now Friendship], Me.:

- i HANNAH[6] BRADFORD, b. 1761
- ii ELSIE BRADFORD, b. 4 Nov. 1763
- iii JOSHUA BRADFORD, b. 4 Sept. 1764
- iv BETSEY BRADFORD, b. 1765
- v JOSEPHUS BRADFORD, b. 10 Feb. 1768

   vi SARAH BRADFORD, b. 1770

  vii SYLVIA BRADFORD, b. 1772

 viii MEHITABLE BRADFORD, b. 1773*

   ix PRUDENCE BRADFORD, b. 5 Oct. 1774

    x WINSLOW BRADFORD, b. 1777

   xi LYDIA BRADFORD, b. 1780

  xii FREDERICK BRADFORD, b. 1782

 xiii JAMES BRADFORD, b. 1784

 xiv CORNELIUS BRADFORD

* Note: *Friendship ME Recs* (p. 9) says a child of Cornelius Bradford d. 21 Oct. 1773 ae 8 or 9 days. This was probably Mehitable.

References: *Bradford Desc* p. 140.   *Lincoln Co ME Probates* p. 199(Cornelius Bradford). GS#63224-Abstract Bradford Fam. Recs.(b. Elsie). *Friendship ME Recs* pp. 8-10, 13-18. *MSSR* 2:401. *Chronicles of Cushing and Friendship* (1892) (b. last 5 ch.)

486. SARAH⁵ BRADFORD (*Joshua⁴, Israel³, William²⁻¹*), b. Kingston 16 Oct. 1739; d. prob. Friendship, Me., 5 Nov. 1797.

She m. ca. 1758 **JOHN DAVIS**, b. Barnstable 1737, bp. East Church 25 April 1742 with siblings; d. 1790, prob. lost at sea; son of John and Anna (Allen) Davis. He resided in Friendship, Me.

John Davis appears on a list of settlers of Meduncook, now Friendship, with William Davis Sr., Zachariah Davis, and William Davis Jr.

John Davis served in the Revolutionary War as a First Lieutenant in Capt. Cornelius Bradford's company, Col. Mason Wheaton's regiment; he was commissioned 3 July 1776 at St. Georges, Me.

Children of John and Sarah (Bradford) Davis:

    i DEBORAH DAVIS⁶, b. 1760

   ii CORNELIUS DAVIS, b. Cushing, Me., 1765; d. 24 Aug. 1845 ae 80y 2m

  iii JOHN DAVIS, b. Friendship, Me., 1764

  iv BRADFORD DAVIS, b. 6 May 1774

   v ROBERT DAVIS

  vi LYDIA DAVIS

References: *Bradford Desc* p. 140. *Barnstable Fams* 1:284. *NEHGR* 46:120(Meduncook settlers). Barnstable Recs on CD. DAR Patriot Index (John lost at sea). GS#61111(g.s. photo Cornelius). *MSSR* 4:507(John Davis).

487. RACHEL⁵ BRADFORD (*Joshua⁴, Israel³, William²⁻¹*), b. Kingston 28 Jan. 1741; d. Friendship, Me., 28 April 1823 aged 81 (g.s.).

She m. Meduncook, Me., 27 May 1765 **EBENEZER MORTON**, b. Kingston 26 June 1746; d. Friendship, Me., 3 Aug. 1831 (g.s.); son of Ebenezer and Sarah (Holmes) Morton.

On 29 Dec. 1769 Ezra King of Pownalborough, Me., housewright, sold to Ebenʳ Morton Junʳ of Meduncook, Me., yeoman, 100 acres in Meduncook. On 5 March 1773 Jacob Graffam of Meduncook, yeoman, and his wife Martha, sold to Ebenezer Morton Jr. of Meduncook, mariner, 30 acres there.

On 14 Sept. 1773 Ebenezer Morton appears on a petition to make Meduncook (now Friendship) a town separate from Broad Bay.

At town meetings on 25 March 1790 and 8 March 1792, Ebenezer was chosen assessor and at a meeting on 17 March 1791, he served as moderator.

Children of Ebenezer and Rachel (Bradford) Morton, b. Meduncook, Me.:*

    i   SUSANNA MORTON⁶, b. 12 Dec. 1765

    ii CORNELIUS MORTON, b. 18 March 1767

    iii ZENAR MORTON, b. 27 Sept. 1768

    iv REBECCA MORTON, b. 24 Sept. 1770

    v   ISAAC MORTON, b. 8 Sept. 1772

    vi HANNAH MORTON, b. 26 Oct. 1774

    vii MARY MORTON, b. 28 Aug. 1776

    viii SALLY MORTON, b. 5 May 1778

    ix JOHN MORTON, b. 15 July 1780

    x   JOSHUA MORTON

*Aspinwall lists also a son Ebenezer 23 Sept. 1778 or 23 Sept. 1780.

References: *Bradford Desc* p. 140. *VR Kingston* p. 111(b. Ebenezer). *Bangor Historical Magazine* p. 2168(m.). *ME Fams 1790* 2:202. Lincoln Co. LR 7:128(Ezra King); 11:67(Jacob Graffam). *Friendship ME Recs* pp. 8, 18, 22.

488. MARY⁵ BRADFORD (*Joshua⁴, Israel³, William²⁻¹*), b. Kingston 16 March 1744; d. Claverack, N.Y., 21 June 1822 aged 77y 2m 16d (g.s.).*

She m. Plympton 1 Dec. 1768 **AUSTIN BEARCE**, b. Halifax 31 Jan. 1747/8, d. Claverack, N.Y., 22 May 1821 aged 73y 3m 26d; son of Austin and Hannah (Stetson) Bearce. Austin and Mary are buried in the cemetery of the Dutch Reformed Church at Claverack, N.Y.

After their parents and brother were killed by Indians at Meduncook in 1758, Mary and her sisters Melatiah and Hannah were sent to live with their aunt Deborah (Bradford) Sampson in Plympton and their brother Elisha was sent to his uncle Benjamin Bradford in Kingston.

On 28 Nov. 1769 Austin Bearce of Halifax, yeoman, sold to Charles Sturtevant of Halifax, yeoman, all his 30-acre homestead farm, it being the farm his father Austin Bearce died seized of; Austin's wife Mary released her dower rights. On 20 April 1770 Austin Bearce of Halifax, cordwainer, sold to Barnabas Briggs and Stephen Bryant Jr. of Halifax ten acres bounded on land owned by Mial Bearce and Obadiah Bearce; Austin's wife Mary signed with her mark. On 1 Oct. 1770 Austin Bearce of Cornwall [Conn.], yeoman, sold to Ignatius Loring of Plimpton land in Halifax "my Father bought of Isaac Sturtevant." And on 2 Nov. 1772 Austin Bearce of Cornwall, yeoman, appointed Nathaniel Bonney Jr. his attorney to dispose of land given him by the will of his father.

On 22 April 1790 Austin Barse of Cornwall was appointed guardian to Bradford and John Sherwood sons of Ebenezer Sherwood late of Cornwall, and on 17 June 1791 he was appointed guardian of Orilla Sherwood daughter of Ebenezer Sherwood late of Cornwall. These were the children of Austin's wife's sister (see #491).

Austin and Mary Bearce were members of the Cornwall Congregational Church on 23 June 1793 and were dismissed to Sheffield, Mass., 5 July 1796.

Austin Bierce and Austin Bierce Jr. bought land on 20 Sept. 1805 from Adam Emerick yeoman and Catherine his wife of Claverack, N.Y. On 10 April 1812 Austin Beirce of Claverack, N.Y., yeoman, sold two parcels of land in Sheffield totaling 200 acres to Salmon Willoughby of Sheffield for $4,083.33; Mary Beirce released her dower right

In his will dated 13 Feb. 1818, proved 6 June 1821, Austin Beirce of Claverack, Columbia Co., N.Y., left half his household furniture and one good cow and half of his books to beloved wife Mary; the other half of the household furniture and books to daughter Hannah; and to "beloved son Austin Beirce Junior the one half of the farm that [he] & myself owns jointly," with farming utensils and livestock, "in consideration of which my son Austin is to support his mother during her natural life and pay unto my son Winslow Beirce fifty dollars."

Children of Austin and Mary (Bradford) Beirce, b. Cornwall, Conn., first 3 bp. together 3 April 1774:

> i   AUSTIN BEIRCE[6], b. 28 Oct. 1769 [fragmentary record; has been misread as "Allen"]

    ii ZEBULON BEIRCE, b. 5 Sept. 1772; d. 20 April 1776

   iii HANNAH BEIRCE, b. 18 Jan. 1774

   iv WINSLOW BIERCE, b. 21 Sept. 1775; bp. 28 Oct. 1775

* Note: It has been supposed that the wife Mary buried with Austin was not Mary Bradford (b. 16 March 1744) because the age on her g.s. calculates to a birth date of 5 April 1745. However, ages on gravestones are often miscalculated, and the 1752 calendar change may or may not have been taken into consideration. The facts are that Austin referred to his wife Mary in his will as mother of his son Austin Jr., and he made none of the bequests typical in cases of second marriages ("goods she brought with her," etc.).

References: *Bradford Desc* p. 140. *VR Plympton* p. 264(m.). *Halifax VR* pp. 45(b. Austin), 64(int). Cornwall CT VR 2:12(b. Hannah, Winslow), 13(b. 1st 2 ch.). Cornwall 1st Ch. records 1:5(bp. 1st 3 ch.), 8(bp. Winslow), 33(members 1793). Plymouth Co. LR 58:117, 178; 59:148; 66:91(Austin Bearce). Litchfield CT PR 5:134, 218 (guard. Sherwood ch.). Columbia Co., N.Y. LR (Emerich to Beirce). Berkshire Co. LR 50:121-2(Beirce to Willoughby). Columbia Co., N.Y., Surrogate's Record, Bk E: 22-23(will of Austin Beirce). Photocopies of will and deeds cited, and additional deeds and tax lists from Richard Batt.

489. MELATIAH⁵ BRADFORD (*Joshua⁴, Israel³, William²⁻¹*), b. Kingston 16 March 1744; d. Chittenden, Vt., 15 Aug. 1826 aged 82y or in 83rd yr., buried Bump or Churchill Cemetery.

    She m. Plympton 1 Aug. 1765 **ISAAC CHURCHILL**, b. Plympton 11 Feb. 1735/6; d. Chittenden, Vt., 25 Feb. 1826 aged 90, buried Bump or Churchill Cemetery; son of Ebenezer and Leah (Keen) Churchill. On 9 Jan. 1762 Rebekah Churchill and Leah Churchill of Plimpton sold to Isaac Churchill Jr. of Plimpton land that had been part of the homestead farm of their father Ebenezer Churchill including half of the barn, right in an old saw mill, and right in a pew in the meeting house.

    After their parents and brother were killed by Indians at Meduncook in 1758, Melatiah and her sisters Mary and Hannah were sent to live with their aunt Deborah (Bradford) Sampson in Plympton.

    At the January 1765 term of the Court of General Sessions, Elijah Mcfarland of Plympton, Laborer, was presented (and judged guilty and punished) for stealing a sheep belonging to Isaac Churchill on 2 Sept. 1764 "being the Lords day."

    The court records show that Isaac Churchill served the town of Plympton as a constable in 1782 and as a selectman in 1784 and 1785. After that he and his family removed to Vermont.

Children of Isaac and Melatiah (Bradford) Churchill, first 5 bp. Plympton:

    i   MICHAEL/MICAL CHURCHILL[6], b. 26 Jan. 1766

   ii   ZERULAH CHURCHILL, b. 16 March 1767

  iii   RACHEL CHURCHILL, b. 4 Jan. 1769; bp. 12 May 1776

  iv   WINSLOW CHURCHILL, b. 30 Dec. 1770; bp. 12 May 1776

   v   SETH CHURCHILL, b. 28 June 1773; bp. 12 May 1776

  vi   ISRAEL CHURCHILL, b. 5 May 1775; d. 16 Dec 1775 ae 7m 11d

 vii   HANNAH CHURCHILL, b. 28 March 1777

viii   ISRAEL CHURCHILL, b. 30 Oct. 1779

  ix   ELISHA CHURCHILL, b. 16 Aug. 1781

   x   DRUSILLA CHURCHILL, b. 16 Aug. 1783

  xi   CHRISTIANA CHURCHILL, b. 14 Sept. 1789

References: *VR Plympton* pp. 58(b. Isaac), 61(b. Mical), 62-3(bp. Rachel, Winslow, Seth), 264(m.), 461(d. Israel). *Bradford Desc* p. 141. *Churchill Fam* pp. 30, 32, 71. Plymouth Co. LR 47:165(Rebekah Churchill). Margaret R. Jenks, *Chittenden, Mendon, Pittsfield and Sherburne Cem. Inscrip., Rutland Co VT* (1991) p.9(d. Isaac, Maltiah). *Plymouth Co Ct Recs* 3:203. Research report from Charles C. Loper.

490. JOSHUA[5] BRADFORD (*Joshua[4], Israel[3], William[2-1]*), b. Kingston 3 April 1746; d. Friendship, Me., 9 May 1827 (or 1837).

He m. Meduncook, Me., 26 April 1773 **MARTHA JAMESON***, b. Friendship, Me., 30 June 1751; d. there 3 Nov. 1837; daughter of Paul and Elizabeth (Pebbles) Jameson.

Joshua Bradford was one of the captives taken when Indians attacked Meduncook on 22 May 1758. From the *Boston Newsletter*: "the Indians falling upon the Inhabitants there this Morning half an Hour after Sunrise; killed and scalped Mr. Bradford, his Wife and Mr. Mill's Wife and kill'd her Children; two of the Bradford's Boys they carried off Prisoners."

Joshua Bradford appears on a list of settlers of Meduncock, now Friendship, Me. On 14 Sept. 1773 Joshua Bradford appears on a petition to make Meduncook a town separate from Broad Bay.

On 21 Aug. 1778 Joshua Bradford of Meduncook, Me., yeoman, sold to James Thompson of Meduncook, Gentleman, 150 acres on Cranberry Island.

At a Meduncook town meeting on 8 March 1779 Joshua Bradford was chosen for a committee to oversee the rate bill.

Children of Joshua and Martha (Jameson) Bradford:

    i   RACHEL[6] BRADFORD, b. 9 Aug. 1774

ii PAUL BRADFORD, b. 17 Aug. 1776; d. 9 Sept. 1798

iii ISAIAH BRADFORD, b. 18 July 1778

iv NANCY BRADFORD, b. 6 Dec. 1780

v ROBERT BRADFORD, b. 14 Dec. 1783

vi ANN BRADFORD, b. 10 Jan. 1785

vii CORNELIUS BRADFORD, b. 19 Dec. 1788

viii JOSHUA BRADFORD, b. 30 (or 8) July 1791

*Note: *Bradford Desc* p. 141 calls her Martha *Johnson.* That is apparently an error. She is called Martha Jameson in the 16 Jan. 1773 int. in *Friendship ME Recs* p. 6 which is apparently correct.

References: *Bradford Desc* p. 141. *Maine Hist Mag* p. 2170(m.). *Jameson Gen* pp. 191-2. *NEHGR* 46:120(Meduncock list). *ME Fams 1790* 2:23, 155. Lincoln Co. LR 13:55(Joshua Bradford). *Friendship ME Recs* pp. 8, 20. *New England Captives* p. 283.

491. HANNAH⁵ BRADFORD (*Joshua⁴, Israel³, William²⁻¹*), b. Kingston 9 March 1748; living Nelson, Ohio, in 1825 (church record); d. probably Nelson, Ohio, after 1830 when she was probably one of the women between 80 and 90 in the household of her son Joshua Sherwood in Portage, Ohio.

After their parents and brother were killed by Indians at Meduncook in 1758, Hannah and her sisters Melatiah and Mary were sent to live with their aunt Deborah (Bradford) Sampson in Plympton.

She m. (1) Cornwall, Conn., 2 Jan. 1772 **EBENEZER SHERWOOD**, b. 10 April 1737; d. Cornwall, Conn., 24 Jan. 1785 aged 39; son of John and Azubah (Grant) (Allen) Sherwood. He m. (1) Cornwall, Conn., 10 April 1769 AZUBA ALLEN with whom he had Azubah.

She m. (2) Cornwell, Conn., 30 Sept. 1788 **FREDERICK CRONER**, b. in Germany as **CHRISTOPH FRIEDRICH GRÜNNER** (Jacobus in *Old Fairfield* calls him Frederick Augustus Crowner). He had come to America as a soldier with the Bayreuth Regiment, whose members were largely from the margravate of Ansbach, in British pay, and deserted to the colonial troops while on a foraging party in the Hudson Valley on 15 Sept. 1782. He left Hannah in March 1789 and they were divorced on 13 Aug. 1792. In her petition for divorce Hannah says that from the time of the marriage she "lived with him … in the Chearful Obedient & Willin performance of all & singular the Duties of her station as a good, Faithful loving & Obedient Wife until the 17ᵗʰ day of March A.D. 1789 at which Time he … did without any Provocation or Fault … Abscond Desert & Leave." He may be the Frederick Croner who appears in the 1790 census of Northumberland Co., Pa.

She m. (3) before 22 Dec. 1803 (deed) **THADDEUS BALDWIN**; d. Brookfield, Conn., 25 July 1815, buried in Gallows Hill Cemetery, New Milford, Conn.

The April 1788 distribution of the estate of Ebenezer Sherwood names widow Hannah; eldest son Bradford; second son John; eldest daughter Azubah; second daughter Mary; third daughter Orilla; fourth daughter Hannah; third son Ebenezer; and youngest daughter Sarah.

On 22 April 1790 Austin Barse of Cornwall was appointed guradian to Bradford and John Sherwood sons of Ebenezer Sherwood late of Cornwall. And on 17 June 1791 Austin Beirce of Cornwall was appointed guardian of Orilla Sherwood daughter of Ebenezer Sherwood late of Cornwall. Austin was the husband of Hannah's sister Mary (see #488).

On 1 Dec. 1795 Hannah Croner alias Hannah Sherwood of Cornwall sold to Seth Pierce part of the homestead of her late husband Ebenezer Sherwood.

On 22 Dec. 1803 Hannah Sherwood of Cornwall sold to Seth Pierce her right in the estate of her father Ebenezer Sherwood. The land is described as "under the Incumbrance of the Widows Right of Dower who is now Hannah Baldwin."

On 15 Aug. 1805 Thaddeus Baldwin and his wife Hannah of Brookfield, Conn., leased to John Bonney of Cornwall land that had been set out to Hannah as her right of dower in the estate of Ebenezer Sherwood, being her right in the land set out to Azubah Millard, John Sherwood, Mary Sherwood, Orilla Bonney, and Hannah Payne the children and heirs of Ebenezer Sherwood.

Hannah was re-admitted to the Cornwall First Congregational Church on 3 Jan. 1819 and was then dismissed by letter to Nelson, Ohio.

On 3 May 1823 Hannah Baldwin of Cornwall sold to Seth Pierce part of the land of her late husband Ebenezer Sherwood.

Children of Ebenezer and Hannah (Bradford) Sherwood, b. Cornwall, Conn.:

    i JOSHUA BRADFORD SHERWOOD[6], b. 19 May 1772

    ii JOHN SHERWOOD, b. 25 Sept. 1773

    iii EBENEZER SHERWOOD, b. 1775; d. 22 April 1790

    iv MARY (MOLLY) SHERWOOD, b. 2 March 1777; d. 22 April 1790. On 20 March 1793 Austin Beirce of Cornwall was appointed administrator on the estate of Mary Sherwood late of Cornwall.

    v EBENEZER SHERWOOD, b. 28 Jan. 1779; d. 24 Jan. 1796

    vi ORILLA SHERWOOD, b. 10 Nov. 1780

    vii HANNAH SHERWOOD, b. 5 Sept. 1782

viii   SARAH SHERWOOD, b. 2 March 1784

Child of Frederick and Hannah (Bradford) (Sherwood) Crowner, b. Cornwall, Conn.:

ix   DIANA CROWNER, b. ca. 1789

References: *Bradford Desc* p. 141.   Cornwall VR LR4:15(1st m.; b. Joshua, John, Mary, Ebenezer); 2:12(b. last 3 ch.).   Litchfield CT PR 5:134(guard. Bradford, John), 135-9(Ebenezer Sherwood), 218(guard. Orilla), 348(admin. Mary Sherwood).   Cornwall CT LR 7:37(Hannah Crowner); 8:170(Hannah Sherwood), 448(Thaddeus & Hannah); 11:509 (Hannah Baldwin).   Cornwall 1st Cong. Ch. Recs. 1:125(m. to Frederick); 2:138(admittance & dismissal of Hannah).   Nelson OH Cong. Ch. list of members 1 April 1825(Hannah Baldwin).   Conn. Superior Court for Litchfield Co. 28:344-5(divorce).   *NGSQ* 60 [1972]:269, 272 (Frederick Crooner, deserter); letter 7 June 1992, Nürnberg Archives to Elinor D. Titus, N. Chatham (Ansbach origins of Frederick)

492.   JOSEPH⁵ BRADFORD (*Joshua⁴, Israel³, William²⁻¹*), b. Meduncook [now Friendship], Me., 19 March 1751; d. Farmington, Me., between 27 Oct. 1812 and 9 March 1813.

He m. Wiscasset, Me., 20 Jan. 1774 **ABIGAIL STARLING**, b. Windham, Me., 13 Nov. 1752; d. Farmington, Me., 16 Jan. 1832; daughter of Joseph and Mary (Wooster) Starling.

On 14 Sept. 1773 Joseph Bradford appears on a petition to make Meduncook (now Friendship) a town separate from Broad Bay.

He moved from Meduncook, Me., to Sandy River Twp., Me., in 1786.

On 15 Aug. 1800 Moses Bradford of Farmington, Me., yeoman, sold to Joseph Bradford of Farmington, 56 acres. On 20 Sept. 1800 Joseph Bradford of Farmington, yeoman, sold to Elisha Bradford of Farmington, yeoman, one-third of 230 acres; Joseph's wife Abigail also signed the deed.

Joseph Bradford of Farmington, Me., yeoman, made his will 27 Oct. 1812, proved 9 March 1813, naming his wife Abigail; youngest son Joseph; son Moses (now living in the northwest Territory of the Ohio); son Elisha; daughters Sally Parker wife of Peter, Huldah Britten wife of Benjamin Jr., Polly Gordon wife of Jonathan, Betsey Pinkham wife of Nathan, Hannah Bradford, and Dorothy Bradford; and grandchildren Lyman Eaton and Martha Eaton children of Jacob Eaton.

Children of Joseph and Abigail (Starling) Bradford, first six b. Meduncook, Me.; last five b. Farmington, Me.:

i   ELISHA⁶ BRADFORD, b. 25 Oct. 1775

    ii MOSES BRADFORD, b. 13 Nov. 1776
   iii SARAH BRADFORD, b. 6 Dec. 1768 [*sic - should be 1778*]
    iv HULDAH BRADFORD, b. 7 Feb 1781
     v POLLY BRADFORD
    vi ABIGAIL BRADFORD
   vii BETSY BRADFORD, b. 12 Dec. 1788
  viii HANNAH BRADFORD, b. 21 May 1791
    ix DOROTHY BRADFORD, b. 8 Dec. 1793
     x JOSEPH BRADFORD, b. 22 Jan. 1797
    xi RICHARD BRADFORD, b. 11 Nov. 1801; d.y.

* Note: *Bradford Desc* says his will was dated 2 Oct. 1812, but this is inconsistent with date of death.

References: *Bradford Desc* p. 142. *Friendship ME Recs* pp. 8, 12(m.; b. 1ˢᵗ 4 ch.). Farmington ME VR p. 15(b. last 5 ch.). *ME Fams 1790* 1:21; 3:46. *Farmington Hist* p. 396. Kennebec Co. ME LR 3:488(Joseph Bradford); 4:291(Moses Bradford). Kennebec Co. ME PR 8:28(Joseph Bradford).

493. BENJAMIN⁵ BRADFORD (*Joshua⁴, Israel³, William²⁻¹*), b. Meduncook [now Friendship], Me., 28 May 1753; d. probably Bayside, N.B., after 11 Sept. 1804.

He m. int. Bristol, Lincoln Co., Me. (date missing; bet. 15 Sept. 1773 and 30 June 1775) **MILIA (or MEETE, MITEA, MARTHA, MILLITY) STUDLEY** of Bristol, b. Bristol, Me., 16 Nov. 1754; daughter of Daniel and Mary (Pittee) Studley.

Benjamin's father, Joshua Bradford, was one of the captives taken when Indians attacked Meduncook on 22 May 1758. From the *Boston Newsletter*: "the Indians falling upon the Inhabitants there this Morning half an Hour after Sunrise; killed and scalped Mr. Bradford, his Wife and Mr. Mill's Wife and kill'd her Children; two of the Bradford's Boys they carried off Prisoners."

Benjamin Bradford is on the 4 July 1783 list of Penobscot Loyalists who removed to Nova Scotia with three persons over 10 and three under 10 in addition to himself and wife Millity. In 1783 he moved to St. Andrews, Charlotte Co., N.B., and was assigned lots #61 and PF4. His son Benjamin in a petition in 1821 says that he "was born in Castine while in possession of the British and removed while an Infant with his parents and other Loyalists to Saint Andrews in 1784 where he has resided and in the Neighborhood, ever since."

Benjamin Bradford was living in St. Andrews, Charlotte Co., N.B., when he sold a yoke of oxen to Robert Pagan 11 Sept. 1804.

On 5 Sept. 1823 Benjamin Bradford of St. Andrews (or perhaps his son) sold to Christopher Scott of St. Andrews a tract of land known as Bradford's Farm at Oak Point.

Children of Benjamin and Milia (Studley) Bradford (only first 3 in Aspinwall):

 i DANIEL[6] BRADFORD, b. ca. 1775 (ae 75 in 1850 census)
 ii BENJAMIN BRADFORD, b. Castine, Me.
 iii JOSHUA BRADFORD, b. Bayside, N.B., 13 May 1789
 iv HULDAH BRADFORD
 v POLLY BRADFORD
 vi MARTHA BRADFORD
 vii RACHEL BRADFORD
 viii ANNIEL BRADFORD (or AMMIEL)

References: *Bradford Desc* p. 142. *Downeast Ancestry* 7:133 (move to Nova Scotia). *Loyalists To Canada* p. 163. Legal documents at the Archives of New Brunswick(1804 sale). *ME Fams 1790* 6:433-4. 1850 Census Calais ME(ae Daniel). Provincial Archives of New Brunswick; Charlotte Co. Land Petitions (Benj.'s petition). *New England Captives* p 283.

494. ELISHA[5] BRADFORD (*Joshua[4], Israel[3], William[2-1]*), b. Kingston 15 Oct. 1755; d. Plattsburg, N.Y., 23 Sept. 1833.

He m. Cornwall, Conn., 10 Aug. 1786 **LUCY ROSSITER**, b. Litchfield, Conn., 7 April 1760; d. Plattsburg 16 Nov. 1849; daughter of Stephen and Ann (____) Rossiter.

After their parents and brother were killed by Indians at Meduncook in 1758, Elisha was sent to his uncle Benjamin Bradford in Kingston and his sisters Melatiah, Mary and Hannah were sent to live with their aunt Deborah (Bradford) Sampson in Plympton.

In 1790 Elisha Bradford was in Pittsford, Vt., with a household of 1 man, 2 boys, and 2 females, and he was still in Pittsford in 1800. He appears in 1810, 1820, and 1830 census in Plattsburg, Clinton Co., N.Y. In 1830 Joshua Bradford is also listed in Plattsburg.

Elisha Bradford applied for a Revolutionary War pension from Plattsburg, Clinton Co., N.Y., on 7 April 1818, stating that he enlisted from Cornwall, Conn., was now aged 62 and his wife Lucy was aged 60. Their children were Joshua, 26, Hannah, 20, and Elisha Jr., 15. His widow Lucy applied for a pension from Clinton Co. 4 Aug. 1838, aged 77. Family records show that they were married 10 Aug. 1786, he was b. 20 Oct. 1755, Lucy was b. 7 April 1761, and their children were Nancy b. 21 Oct. 1790, Cornelius b. 27 Feb.

1793, Joshua b. 24 June 1795, Abigail b. 8 March 1797, Hannah b. 19 Feb. 1799, Rachel b. 8 May 1801, and Elisha Jr. b. 18 Dec. 1805.

Children of Elisha and Lucy (Rossiter) Bradford, all b. Pittsford, Vt.:

    i   NANCY[6] BRADFORD, b. 21 Oct. 1790
   ii CORNELIUS BRADFORD, b. 27 Feb. 1793
  iii JOSHUA BRADFORD, b. 24 June 1795
  iv ABIGAIL BRADFORD, b. 8 March 1797
   v HANNAH BRADFORD, b. 19 Feb. 1799
  vi RACHEL BRADFORD, b. 8 May 1801
 vii ELISHA BRADFORD, b. 18 Dec. 1806

References: *Bradford Desc* p. 142. *Rev War Pensions* 1:356, W24676(Elisha Bradford; b. ch. from Bible). Cornwall CT VR 2:16(m.).

495. ICHABOD[5] BRADFORD (*Ichabod[4], Israel[3], William[2-1]*), b. Kingston 28 Aug. 1744; d. 6 April 1791 aged 77y.

He m. (1) Kingston 2 Nov. 1775 **RACHEL WRIGHT**.

He m. (2) Kingston 19 Oct. 1780 **RUTH FULLER**, b. Kingston 17 Sept. 1764; daughter of Barnabas and Rebecca (Cushman) Fuller, a descendant of Pilgrims **Isaac Allerton, Francis Eaton** and **Samuel Fuller**.

In 1790 Ichabod Bradford was head of a household in Kingston consisting of 1 man and 1 woman.

Ichabod left no known issue.

References: *VR Kingston* pp. 84(b. Ruth), 178(2nd m.), 180(1st m.), 320(d. Ichabod). *Bradford Desc* pp. 142-3. *MF* 10:39-40.

496. ELIZABETH[5] BRADFORD (*Ichabod[4], Israel[3], William[2-1]*), b. Kingston 10 July 1747; d. after 1820.

She m. Kingston 23 Dec. 1765 **MICAJAH DRINKWATER**, b. No. Yarmouth, Me., 25 Jan. 1739; d. Northport, Me., July 1825; son of Joseph and Jane (Latham) Drinkwater, a descendant of Pilgrims **James Chilton** and **George Soule**.

On 18 Nov. 1801 Josiah Drinkwater of Northport, Me., sold land bounded on land of Micajah Bradford. On 16 June 1806 Micajah Bradford of Northport, yeoman, sold to Lemuel Drinkwater of Northport, mariner, 40 acres. On 7 May 1822 Micajah Drinkwater Jr. of Northport, mariner, sold 12 acres to Ammi Drinkwater of Northport, yeoman.

Children of Micajah and Elizabeth (Bradford) Drinkwater, b. most prob. Northport, Me.:

    i   MARY DRINKWATER[6], b. No. Yarmouth, Me., 13 May 1766
    ii ZENAS DRINKWATER, b. York, Me., 9 Nov. 1768
   iii JOSIAH DRINKWATER, b. 18 Nov. 1770
   iv LEMUEL DRINKWATER, b. 29 Jan. 1773
    v WILLIAM DRINKWATER, b. 16 Oct. 1775
   vi RHODA DRINKWATER, b. 24 March 1778
  vii BETSEY DRINKWATER, b. 23 Aug. 1781
 viii MICAJAH DRINKWATER (twin), b. 27 April 1783
   ix JAMES DRINKWATER (twin), b. 27 April 1783
    x JOHN DRINKWATER, b. 5 Oct. 1785
   xi NANCY DRINKWATER, b. 27 Dec. 1788
  xii AMMI DRINKWATER, b. 27 Dec. 1792

References: *MF* 3:358. *Bradford Desc* p. 143. *VR Kingston* p. 179(m.). *No Yarmouth VR* p. 25(b. Micajah). *Penobscot Patriot* of 20 July 1825(obit Micajah). Hancock Co. ME LR 9:316(Josiah Drinkwater); 35:255(Micajah Drinkwater); 43:205(Micajah Drinkwater Jr.).

497. RHODA[5] BRADFORD (*Ichabod[4]*, *Israel[3]*, *William[2-1]*), b. Kingston 20 July 1751.

She m. Cumberland, Me., 22 Jan. 1770 **SAMUEL DRINKWATER**, b. No. Yarmouth, Me., 24 Feb. 1743; d. Northport, Me., July 1825; son of Joseph and Jane (Latham) Drinkwater, a descendant of Pilgrims **James Chilton** and **George Soule**.

In the 1771 Valuation List, Samuel Drinkwater appears in North Yarmouth as 1 poll, with a vessel of 18 tons.

The 1790 census listed Samuel Drinkwater in North Yarmouth as head of a household of 1 man, 2 boys, and 7 females.

Children of Samuel and Rhoda (Bradford) Drinkwater, b. No. Yarmouth, Me.:

    i   SUSANNA DRINKWATER[6], b. 6 Dec. 1770
    ii SEBAH DRINKWATER, b. 1 Dec. 1772
   iii BETSEY DRINKWATER, b. 24 July 1774
   iv RUFUS DRINKWATER, b. 24 April 1778
    v AZUBAH DRINKWATER, b. 24 Dec. 1779
   vi HEBZABAH DRINKWATER, b. 14 Dec. 1781
  vii RHODA DRINKWATER, b. 11 Jan. 1783 ("Arohada" in birth rec.)
 viii BRADFORD DRINKWATER, b. 13 Dec. 1785

ix CYNTHIA DRINKWATER, b. 11 Oct. 1789
x MARY DRINKWATER, b. 20 Dec. 1792
xi SEWELL DRINKWATER, b. 30 Oct. 1795

References: *No Yarmouth VR* pp. 25(b. Samuel), 26(b. ch.). *1771 Valuation* p. 497.

498. ANNE⁵ BRADFORD (*Ichabod⁴, Israel³, William²⁻¹*), b. Kingston 15 April 1758; d. Cumberland, Me., Oct. 1824.

She m. No. Yarmouth, Me., 27 May 1784 **JOSIAH WYMAN**, b. Cumberland, Me., 5 Oct. 1762, bp. No. Yarmouth 4 July 1762; d. there 13 Jan. 1830; son of John and Mercy (Johnson) Wyman.

On 24 March 1785 Josiah Wyman, yeoman, and William Wyman, yeoman of No. Yarmouth, Me., agreed to divide land (lot #47) given to them by the will of their father John Wyman. On 5 April 1797 John Wyman, mariner, and Joseph Shaw, yeoman, and his wife Sarah, all of No. Yarmouth sold to Josiah Wyman of No. Yarmouth, yeoman, 16 acres of lot #47 given to them by the will of their father. On 6 June 1797 Josiah Wyman sold to William Wyman 25 acres part of lot #74 given to him by the will of his father.

Anne is called Nancy (nickname for Anne) in the N. Yarmouth, Me., VRs.

Children of Josiah and Anne (Bradford) Wyman, b. No. Yarmouth, Me., to "Josiah and Nancy":

i LEMUEL WYMAN⁶, b. 6 Sept. 1784
ii ELIZABETH WYMAN, b. 24 March 1786
iii MARY WYMAN, b. 22 July 1801

References: *Bradford Desc* p. 143. *No Yarmouth VR* pp. 113 (b. ch.), 281(m.). Cumberland Co. ME LR 27:517(Josiah Wyman, 2 deeds); 32:327(John Wyman *et al.*). *Old Times* p. 714(bp. Josiah).

499. ISRAEL⁵ BRADFORD (*Ichabod⁴, Israel³, William²⁻¹*), b. Kingston 28 Oct. 1766; d. Plymouth 5 Jan. 1855 aged 88y 4m 10d.

He m. (1) Kingston 15 Dec. 1785 **HANNAH EVERSON**, b. Kingston 2 Nov. 1767; d. there 11 June 1823 aged 56y; daughter of Robert and Hannah (Putnam) Everson. [Robert and Hannah named a son William Putnam Everson]

He m. (2) Kingston 4 Dec 1840 **OLIVE (DELANO) JEFFERS**, b. Duxbury 20 Sept. 1793; daughter of Charles and Hannah (Pierce) Delano. She m. (1) WILLIAM JEFFERS.

Israel Bradford served in the Revolutionary War as a matross with Capt. Amos Lincoln's company in Col. Craft's (artillery) regiment. He enlisted on 23 May 1781 and was discharged on 21 Aug. 1783. He applied for a pension on 14 Aug. 1832 when he was aged 67, a resident of Kingston. His widow Olive applied on 31 March 1855 aged 61. He and Olive were m. on 4 Dec. 1840 and he d. 5 Jan. 1855 aged 88y 2m 8d.

Izrael Bradford's household consisted of 1 man, 1 boy and 2 females in Plymouth in the 1790 census.

On 5 Feb. 1849 Lemuel Bradford of Plymouth sold to Israel Bradford of Plympton a dwelling house and two acres in Plympton, and the following month, on 12 March 1849, Israel sold this house and land to Martin Cobb of Kingston, sailmaker.

Children of Israel and Hannah (Everson) Bradford (a child of Israel Bradford d. Plymouth 30 Oct. 1796):

  i POLLY⁶ BRADFORD, b. 7 Oct. 1786
  ii LEMUEL BRADFORD, b. Feb. 1788
  iii SALLY BRADFORD
  iv HANNY (or HANNAH) BRADFORD
  v LUCY BRADFORD
  vi NANCY BRADFORD, b. 26 April 1801
  vii BETSY BRADFORD, b. 9 Nov. 1803
  viii [DAUGHTER] BRADFORD (twin), d. Kingston 15 Oct. 1806, ae 9w
  ix [DAUGHTER] BRADFORD (twin), d. Kingston 16 Oct. 1806, ae 9w
  x WILLIAM PUTNAM BRADFORD

References: *VR Kingston* pp. 180(both m.), 322(d. Hannah, twins). *Bradford Desc* p. 143. *Rev War Pensions* 1:356(Isreal Bradford). Plymouth Co. LR 231:32(Lemuel Bradford); 232:82(Israel Bradford). *Plymouth Ch Recs* 1:426(d. child). *MSSR* 2:403.

500. LYDIA CHANDLER⁵ (*Anna⁴ Bradford, Ephraim³, William²⁻¹*), b. Duxbury 14 March 1740/1; d. Kingston Jan. 1813.

She m. (1) Duxbury 11 Jan. 1763 **ABRAHAM EVERSON**, b. Kingston 31 Aug. 1736; d. before 27 July 1769 (2ⁿᵈ m.); son of John and Silence (Staples) Everson.

She m. (2) Kingston 27 July 1769 **JOSIAH WATERMAN**, b. Kingston 13 Aug. 1732; d. Plymouth 13 April 1817 aged 84; son of Josiah and Joanna (Bryant) Waterman, a descendant of Pilgrim **Isaac Allerton**. He m. (1) Plymouth 9 Dec. 1756 FEAR TINKHAM with whom he had Joshua, Josiah, Jerusha, Lucy, and Fear.

Josiah Waterman, his wife Lidia and their sons Joshua, Josiah, and Chandler were warned from Kingston 5 Dec. 1770.

In the 1771 Valuation List, Josiah Waterman appears in Kingston with 1 poll and 1 house.

Josiah Waterman was head of a household of 1 man, 1 boy and 4 females in Kingston in the 1790 census.

No Plymouth Co. probate records were found for Josiah Waterman.

Children of Abraham and Lydia (Chandler) Everson, b. Kingston:

> i ABRAHAM EVERSON[6] (twin), b. 1 Sept. 1763; d. 18 March 1765
> ii LYDIA EVERSON (twin), b. 1 Sept. 1763

Children of Josiah and Lydia (Chandler) (Everson) Waterman, 2nd b. Kingston:

> iii CHANDLER WATERMAN (in warning)
> iv EBENEZER WATERMAN, b. 1 July 1782

References: *Waterman Gen* pp. 165-6. *VR Duxbury* p. 231(1st m.). *VR Kingston* pp. 69-70(b. Abraham, b. Everson ch.), 156(b. Josiah, Ebenezer Waterman), 156(2nd m.), 344(d. Abraham). *Bradford Desc* p. 144. *Plymouth Co Ct Recs* 3:304 (warning). *Plymouth VR* p. 348(m.). *MF* 7:110-1. *1771 Valuation* p. 642.

501. SCEVA CHANDLER[5] (*Anna⁴ Bradford, Ephraim³, William²⁻¹*), b. Duxbury 12 June 1757; d. there 14 March 1832 aged 76.

He m. (1) Duxbury 20 June 1782 **EDITH SAMSON**, d. Duxbury 2 June 1796 aged 37y 10m 18d.

He m. (2) Duxbury March 1798 **ELIZABETH (CHANDLER) DARLING**, b. Duxbury 13 June 1758; d. Duxbury 5 June 1836 aged 78 of consumption and palsey; daughter of Perez and Rhoda (Wadsworth) Chandler. She m. (1) Duxbury 21 Dec. 1780 JOSEPH DARLING.

Sceva Chandler was a Private in the Revolutionary War.

On 24 Oct. 1786 Ebenezer Chandler of Duxbury, miller, sold his house and land in Duxbury to Sceva Chandler of Duxbury, blacksmith.

"Aviva" Chandler's household consisted of 1 man and 3 females in Duxbury in the 1790 census.

On 10 March 1803 Nathan Chandler of Kingston, yeoman, and his wife Rebecca sold to Sceva Chandler of Duxbury, blacksmith, their share in the homestead of their father Joseph Darling late of Duxbury. On 18 March 1803 Nathan and Rebecca with Asa King and his wife Betsey, sold to Sceva their share in the widow's thirds.

On 12 May 1803 Perez Chandler, yeoman, Daniel Chandler, blacksmith, Sceva Chandler, yeoman, and wife Betty, Zenos Delano, blacksmith, and wife Welthea, all of Duxbury, Nathaniel Holmes, carpenter, and his wife Aseneth of Kingston, and Seth Chandler, physician, for himself and for Benjamin Chandler, physician, both of Minot, Me., sold to Wadsworth Chandler their rights in the estate of Perez Chandler late of Duxbury; Ruth, the wife of Perez, and Joanna, the wife of Daniel, released their dower rights.

On 10 March 1825 Sceva Chandler of Duxbury, blacksmith, and his wife Betsey, sold to Nathan Chandler of Kingston, yeoman, the easterly half of a lot formerly belonging to our father Perez Chandler that was divided between Asenath wife of Nathaniel Holmes and Betsey wife of Sceva Chandler, and another lot from the estate of Joseph Darling late of Duxbury.

No Plymouth County probate records have been found for Sceva Chandler.

Child of Sceva and Edith (Samson) Chandler:

   i [CHILD] CHANDLER⁶; d. Duxbury 18 Feb. 1804 ae 4

References: *VR Duxbury* p. 48(b. Elizabeth), 233(m.), 240(1ˢᵗ m. Elizabeth), 358(d. Elizabeth), 360(d. child), 364(d. Edith). *Small Desc* 2:1076. Plymouth Co. LR 66:238(Ebenezer Chandler); 96:70(Perez Chandler *et al.*); 104:128(Nathan Chandler); 154:12(Sceva Chandler).

502. PATIENCE WHITING⁵ (*Elizabeth⁴ Bradford, Ephraim³, William²⁻¹*), b. Plympton 21 Jan. 1757; d. Abington 5 June 1844 aged 87.

She m. Plympton 19 Feb. 1778 **JOHN CHAMBERLAIN**, b. Plympton 2 Jan. 1755 (pension, not in VR); d. Abington 14 Sept. 1834 aged 79; son of Phillips and Mehetable (Scott) Chamberlain.

John Chamberlin of Plymouth, retailer, was granted a license to sell liquor from 1791 to 1794. John Chamberlin, of Abington, retailer or innholder, was granted a license to sell liquor in 1794, 1801, and 1802.

John Chamberlin's household consisted of 1 man, 1 boy and 5 females in Plympton in the 1790 census.

John Chamberlin served in the Revolutionary War as a private in Capt. James Harlow's company, Col. Thomas Lothrop's regiment which marched to Bristol, R.I., in March 1777. He applied for a pension on 27 Aug. 1833 aged 78, a resident of Abington. His widow applied for a pension on 2 April 1839 when she was 82.

John Chamberlin of Abington, yeoman, in his will dated 31 Dec. 1817, proved 25 Nov. 1834, named his wife Patience, sons Ezra and John, and daughters Mehitable Dyer, Patience Jenkins, Rebecca Chamberlin, Elizabeth Chamberlin, and Hannah Chamberlin.

On 20 July 1836 Ezra Chamberlain sold to Patience Jenkins of Abington all his right in the homestead farm of Zenas Jenkins deceased.

On 30 March 1837 Ezra Chamberlain of Boston, trader, sold to John Chamberlain of Abington, yeoman, all his claim to the estate of John Chamberlain late of Abington including land bounded on land owned by their sisters, Rebecca, Elizabeth, and Hannah; Ezra's wife Hannah released her dower rights. Also in 1837 (ack. 9 June) John sold to Ezra land and John's wife Mary P. Chamberlain released her dower rights. On 7 May 1837 Ezra and John sold land to their three single sisters. On 9 June 1837 Ezra mortgaged land with buildings to his sisters.

Children of John and Patience (Whiting) Chamberlain, first six b. Plympton:

   i   EZRA CHAMBERLAIN[6], b. 5 Oct. 1778

   ii MEHITABLE CHAMBERLAIN, b. 10 Sept. 1780

  iii REBEKAH CHAMBERLAIN, b. 6 Nov. 1784; d. Abington 20 March 1871 ae 86y 4m 14d of old age.

  iv ELIZABETH CHAMBERLAIN, b. 21 Dec. 1786; d. Abington 8 March 1843 ae 56y. The inventory of Elizabeth Chamberlain's estate was taken 24 Jan. 1845 and the estate was declared insolvent by administrator Jared Whitman on 1 April 1845. On 1 Sept. 1845 the only claimants against the estate were her sisters Rebecca and Hannah.

   v PATIENCE CHAMBERLAIN, b. 2 Nov. 1788

  vi JOHN CHAMBERLAIN, b. 22 June 1792

 vii HANNAH CHAMBERLAIN, b. Abington 4 April 1800; d. Abington 27 May 1895 ae 95y 1m 3d of old age; her death record says her father John was b. in Boston.

References: *VR Abington* 1:46(b. Hannah); 2:261 (d. John, Patience, Elizabeth). *VR Plympton* pp. 53-46(b. 1ˢᵗ 6 ch.), 277(m.). *Bradford Desc* p. 144. Plymouth Co. LR 191:91; 193:52, 193:105, 234(Ezra Chamberlain), 93(John Chamberlain). Plymouth Co. PR 76:508(John Chamberlin); 87:83(Elizabeth Chamberlain). MAVR 239:319(d. Rebecca Chamberlain); 455:570(d. Hannah Chamberlain). *Plymouth Co Ct Recs* Vol. 4. *Rev War Pensions* 1:589. *MSSR* 3:265(John Chamberlin).

503. ELIZABETH WHITING⁵ (*Elizabeth⁴ Bradford, Ephraim³, William²⁻¹*), b. Plympton 6 Oct. 1759; d. Turner, Me., 16 Feb. 1842; buried New Keene Mills cemetery.

She m. Plympton 13 Dec. 1780 **JONATHAN CUSHMAN**, b. Kingston 12 May 1753; d. Turner, Me., 6 April 1814; son of Jonathan and Susanna (Benson) Cushman, a descendant of Pilgrim **Isaac Allerton**.

On 24 Oct. 1788 Jonathan Cushman of Kingston, yeoman, sold to Silvester Holmes of Kingston, laborer, all his land and buildings in Kingston and a piece of meadow in Plympton; his wife Elizabeth released her dower rights and signed the deed. On 13 Sept. 1794 Jonathan Cushman of Green, Lincoln Co. [Maine], yeoman, sold to Silvester Holmes an acre and a half of cedar swamp in Halifax given to him by his father Jonathan Cushman's will.

Jonathan Cushman's daughter Elizabeth Martin, aged 59, applied for a Revolutionary War pension on 3 Aug. 1852 in Oxford Co., Me. She stated that Jonathan d. 6 April 1814 and his widow d. 30 Jan. 1842 leaving children Artemas, Hosea, Benson, Bradford, and Elizabeth Martin.

Children of Jonathan and Elizabeth (Whiting) Cushman, first two b. Kingston, rest from pension application:

    i ARTEMUS CUSHMAN⁶, b. 20 April 1782

    ii SARAH CUSHMAN, b. 2 April 1784

    iii HOSEA CUSHMAN

    iv BENSON CUSHMAN

    v BRADFORD CUSHMAN

    vi ELIZABETH CUSHMAN, b. ca. 1793 (ae 59 in 1852)

References: *VR Kingston* pp. 53-6(b. Jonathan; b. 2 ch.). *VR Plympton* pp. 53(b. Artemus), 56(b. Sarah), 427(m.). *Bradford Desc* p. 144. *MF* 17:83. Plymouth Co. LR 68:232; 75:234(Jonathan Cushman). *Cushman Fam* p. 87. *Rev War Pensions* 1:855.

504. ABIGAIL HOLMES⁵ (*Abigail⁴ Bradford, Ephraim³, William²⁻¹*), b. Kingston 6 July 1746; living 6 Nov. 1829 (see deed below).

She m. Yarmouth, N.S., 16 Dec. 1763 **CORNELIUS ROGERS**, b. Kingston 26 Aug. 1739; d. before 10 April 1816 when administration of his estate was granted to Benjamin Rogers; son of Benjamin and Phebe (Harding) Rogers; a descendant of Pilgrim **Thomas Rogers**.

Cornelius Rogers received 110 acres in lot #23 in the First Division division of land in Yarmouth, 557 acres in lot #107 in the Second Division, and 216 acres in lot #33 in the Third Division.

On 10 July 1779 John Rogers of Yarmouth sold Cornelius Rogers of Yarmouth land that he bought of Ruth Rogers, widow of Thomas.

On 6 July 1791 Elishama Eldredge of Yarmouth, Gentleman, sold Cornelius Rogers of Yarmouth, yeoman, 107 acres; Elishama's wife Mary also signed this deed.

On 6 June 1805 Cornelius Rogers Sr. of Yarmouth, yeoman, sold John Rogers Sr. of Yarmouth, yeoman, land in Yarmouth; Cornelius' wife Abigail made her mark.

On 7 Nov. 1815 Abigail Rogers, one of the heirs of Peleg Holmes, sold Elkanah Clements of Yarmouth, her right in land of Peleg Holmes; Abigail signed by making her mark.

Administration on the estate of Cornelius Rogers late of Yarmouth was granted to Benjamin Rogers on 10 April 1816. The inventory taken on 15 April 1816 included over £870 in land and buildings and one yoke of oxen, 15 cattle, a horse, and 10 sheep. The division of his estate on 1 July 1817 was among the widow Abigail, John Rogers, Cornelius Rogers, Benjamin Rogers, Deborah Clement wife of Elkanah, the heirs of Abigail Durkee, Lydia Sanders wife of Nathaniel, Hannah Hilton wife of Amos, Elizabeth Landers wife of Selea, and Sarah Rogers.

On 22 June 1817 Cornelius Rogers Jr. of Yarmouth, son of Cornelius Rogers late of Yarmouth, paid Benjamin Rogers for 44 acres that their father had given Benjamin on 1 Oct. 1802 and for which Cornelius had never paid.

On 3 April 1827 Abigail Rogers of Yarmouth, spinster, sold to Thomas Eldredge of Yarmouth, yeoman, her eighth share in the estate of Peleg Holmes. On 28 July 1829 Abigail Rogers, widow of Cornelius, sold to David Landers part of Second Division lot #142 which was part of her share in her father's estate.

On 6 Nov. 1829 Samuel Ellis of Yarmouth, yeoman, sold to the heirs of Cornelius Rogers the share of his deceased wife Sarah in the estate of Cornelius Rogers; the heirs were to maintain the widow Abigail Rogers.

On 17 Aug. 1835 Cornelius Rogers, John Rogers and wife Lydia, David Landers and wife Lucy, Elkanah Clements and wife Deborah, Amos Hilton and wife Hannah all of Yarmouth, heirs of Cornelius Rogers, sold to Isaac Miller of Yarmouth their right in the Third Division lot #140.

Children of Cornelius and Abigail (Holmes) Rogers, b. Yarmouth, N.S.; first three bp. 3 Dec. 1764:

i DEBORAH ROGERS[6], b. 1 Oct. 1764

ii ABIGAIL ROGERS, b. 9 March 1766

iii JOHN ROGERS, b. 28 Jan. 1768

iv LYDIA ROGERS, b. 4 May 1771; bp 10 June 1770

v HANNAH ROGERS, b. 21 Oct. 1772; bp. 31 May 1772

vi CORNELIUS ROGERS, b. 26 Feb. 1775; bp. 21 May 1775

vii BENJAMIN ROGERS, b. 22 May 1777; bp. 22 June 1777

viii ELIZABETH ROGERS, b. 23 Jan. 1780

ix SARAH ROGERS, b. 26 Aug. 1788

References: *VR Kingston* p. 125(b. Cornelius). *Yarmouth NS VR* p. 37(m.). *Yarmouth NS Herald Gen* #80(b. ch.). *MF* 19:91. *Jebogue Ch Recs* pp. 120(first 3 bp.), 121(bp. Lydia, Hannah); bp. 123(bp. Cornelius, Benjamin). Yarmouth N.S. LR 1A:263(Cornelius Rogers); B:135(Elishama Eldredge); E:13; L:91(Cornelius Rogers); K:77; O:233; R:422(Abigail Rogers), 456(Samuel Ellis); U:341(Cornelius Rogers *et al.*). *Yarmouth Hist. Sequel* p. 177(division lots). Yarmouth N.S. PR 1:63, 133, file papers(Cornelius Rogers).

505. ELIZABETH HOLMES[5] (*Abigail[4] Bradford, Ephraim[3], William[2-1]*), b. Kingston 18 Feb. 1751; d. 2 July 1809.

She m. Tisbury 5 Aug. 1779 **JAMES WINSLOW**, b. poss. Middleboro 6 Jan. 1733/4; d. Tisbury 26 Aug. 1805 in 73rd year; poss. the son of James and Susanna (Connant) Winslow. He m. (1) Tisbury 3 Nov. 1757 RHODA CHASE with whom he had Susanna, James, Isaac, Peleg, Newell, and Timothy.

James Winslow served in the Revolutionary War as a corporal in Capt. Nathan Smith's company which was stationed at Martha's Vineyard for defense of the coast; enlisted 5 Oct. 1775 with service until 1 Dec. 1775. He served in the same company as a private from 18 Jan. 1776 with service of 7m 14d. And he served in the same company as a sergeant from 1 Sept. 1776 to 21 Nov. 1776.

James Winslow was head of a household of 3 men, 3 boys, and 6 females in Tisbury in the 1790 census.

Children of James and Elizabeth (Holmes) Winslow:

i ABIGAIL BRADFORD WINSLOW[6], b. 17 April 1780

ii JAMES WINSLOW, d. Nov. 1795

iii NEWELL WINSLOW, d. Nov. 1795

iv   POLLY WINSLOW, d. Nov. 1795

v   ZEBULON WINSLOW, d. Nov. 1795

vi   [CHILD] WINSLOW, d. Nov. 1795

vii GEORGE WINSLOW, b. ca. 1797

viii ELIZABETH WINSLOW, b. 21 Oct. 1801

References: *VR Tislbury* pp. 192(1st m.), 193(m.), 243(d. James), 244(d. ch.). *Martha's Vineyard By Banks* 3:513. *MSSR* 17:632(James Winslow). *Middleboro VR* 1:72(b. James).

506. NATHANIEL HOLMES⁵ (*Abigail⁴ Bradford, Ephraim³, William²⁻¹*), b. Kingston 21 Oct. 1755; d. Yarmouth, N.S., before 22 March 1831.

He m. Yarmouth, N.S., 14 June 1784 **ABIGAIL KIMBALL**, b. ca. 1759; d. Yarmouth, N.S., 21 March 1846 aged 87 yrs.

On 24 Nov. 1821 Nathaniel Holmes Sr. of Yarmouth, yeoman, sold to his son Nathaniel Holmes Jr. of Yarmouth, yeoman, part of First Division lot #20 where Nathaniel Jr. had erected a house.

On 19 July 1825 Nathaniel Holmes of Yarmouth, yeoman, and his wife Abigail sold Thomas Eldredge of Yarmouth, yeoman, sold their right in 27 acres from the division of the estate of Peleg Holmes; this land was also in the possession of Lydia Holmes and Samuel Kimball.

Nathaniel Holmes of Yarmouth made his will 24 Nov. 1821, proved 22 March 1831, naming his wife Abigail; sons Peleg, Nathaniel, Elisha, Joseph, and John; daughters Abigail wife of John Trefry and Ruth Holmes; and sister Lydia Holmes. The inventory taken 2 April 1731 included 474 acres of land.

On 5 Oct. 1832 Elisha Holmes of Yarmouth, farmer, and his wife Lydia, sold to Nathaniel Holmes of Yarmouth their right in the estate of Nathaniel Holmes Sr. On 12 Oct. 1832 Joseph Holmes formerly of Yarmouth, yeoman, and his wife Sarah sold to Peleg Holmes of Yarmouth, yeoman, their share in the estate of Nathaniel Holmes. On 23 June 1834 Peleg Holmes formerly of Yarmouth and his wife Mary sold to Nathaniel Holmes their right in the estate of Nathaniel Holmes Sr.

Children of Nathaniel and Abigail (Kimball) Holmes, b. Yarmouth, N.S.:

i   PELEG HOLMES⁶, b. 15 April 1785

ii   NATHANIEL HOLMES, b. 7 Feb. 1787

iii ELISHA HOLMES, b. 11 March 1789

iv   JOHN HOLMES, b. 13 April 1791; an invalid; d. unm.

v   JOSEPH HOLMES, b. 8 June 1793

vi SAMUEL HOLMES, b. 30 Aug. 1795; d. 15 Sept. 1796

vii ABIGAIL HOLMES, b. 25 July 1797 [in VRs as Samuel, but the father's will names a dau. Abigail, but no son Samuel]

viii RUTH HOLMES, b. 15 June 1802

References: *Yarmouth NS VR* pp. 2:10(b. 1st 7 ch.), 1:19(m.). *Yarmouth NS Herald Gen* #86(b. ch.; deaths). *Yarmouth NS Gen* (BROWN) pp. 577, 578(m.; deaths; b. of ch.). Yarmouth N.S. PR 2:49, file papers(Nathaniel Holmes). Yarmouth N.S. LR P:301; S:246(Nathaniel Holmes); T:27(Joseph Holmes), 114(Elisha Holmes), 340(Peleg Holmes).

507. MARY HOLMES⁵ (*Abigail⁴ Bradford, Ephraim³, William²⁻¹*), b. Kingston 20 Feb. 1758; living 6 July 1791.

She m. (1) Yarmouth, N.S., 11 Dec. 1776 **SAMUEL KIMBALL**, bp. Yarmouth 11 Jan. 1756; d. at sea shortly before 5 Oct. 1777; son of Thomas and Mary (Ingalls) Kimball.

She m. (2) Yarmouth, N.S., 27 Jan. 1785 **ELISHAMA ELDREDGE**, b. Mansfield, Conn., 9 Sept. 1752; living 6 July 1791; son of Elisha and Priscilla (Paddock) Eldredge. He m. (1) 17 Jan. 1775 SARAH (WING) CROSBY.

The History of the Kimball Family in America says: Samuel Kimball "was a seaman and was wrecked at Chebogue, Yarmouth, Nova Scotia, remained some time among the people of that section, and married there. Shortly after his marriage he sailed for the West Indies, and was never heard from afterwards, either dying on the voyage or being lost at sea."

On 12 Jan. 1787 Elisha Eldredge of Yarmouth, yeoman, sold to Elishama Eldredge of Yarmouth, Gentleman, 115 acres of upland and 14 acres of salt marsh.

On 6 July 1791 Elishama Eldredge of Yarmouth, Gentleman, sold to Cornelius Rogers of Yarmouth, yeoman, 107 acres; Elishama's wife Mary also signed this deed.

On 19 July 1825 Nathaniel Holmes of Yarmouth, yeoman, and his wife Abigail sold to Thomas Eldredge of Yarmouth, yeoman, their right in 27 acres from the division of the estate of Peleg Holmes; this land was also in the possession of Lydia Holmes and Samuel Kimball. On 3 April 1827 Abigail Rogers of Yarmouth, spinster, sold to Thomas Eldredge of Yarmouth, yeoman, her eighth share in the estate of Peleg Holmes.

Child of Samuel and Mary (Holmes) Kimball, b. Yarmouth, N.S.:

i SAMUEL KIMBALL⁶, b. 11 Oct. 1777

Children of Elishama and Mary (Holmes) (Kimball) Eldridge:

  ii THOMAS ELDRIDGE

  iii MARY ELDRIDGE

  iv SARAH ELDRIDGE

  v   BETHIAH ELDRIDGE

References: *Yarmouth NS VR* p. 18(1ˢᵗ m.; b. son Samuel). *Yarmouth NS Genealogies* pp. 257, 258(Elishama Eldridge; m., b. of 4 ch.; m. of ch.). *Kimball Fam* p. 236. Yarmouth N.S. LR B:135(Elishama Eldredge); P:301(Nathaniel Holmes); R:422(Abigail Holmes).

508. SARAH HOLMES⁵ (*Abigail⁴ Bradford, Ephraim³, William²⁻¹*), b. Kingston 23 April 1760.

  She m. Yarmouth, N.S., 25 March 1788 **JOSEPH SANFORD BAILEY**, bp. Newport, R.I., 4 Nov. 1759; d. Newport, N.S., 4 Nov. 1791; son of Joseph and Hannah (Sanford) Bailey. Joseph Baley of Newport, N.S., made his will 7 April 1787 naming his son Joseph Sanford Baley and giving him "the farm on which I now live."

  On 11 July 1815 Sarah Bailey, one of the heirs of the estate of Peleg Holmes, sold to Elkanah Clements of Yarmouth her right in Peleg's land; she signed by making her mark.

Children of Joseph Sanford and Sarah (Holmes) Bailey, b. Newport, N.S.:

  i   JOSEPH SANFORD BAILEY, b. 25 Dec. 1788

  ii ABIGAIL BAILEY, b. 9 Oct. 1790

  iii poss. WILLIAM BAILEY, b. ca. 1813

References: Yarmouth NS Herald Gen pp. 212, 577(m.). Yarmouth N.S. LR K:44(Sarah Bailey). Newport N.S. PR 1:67(Joseph Baley). *Newport, Nova Scotia – A Rhode Island Township* pp.97-9. *RIVR* 8:401(bp. Joseph).

509. LUCY HOLMES⁵ (*Abigail⁴ Bradford, Ephraim³, William²⁻¹*), b. Yarmouth, N.S., 12 Sept. 1762; d. there 22 March 1799.

  She m. Yarmouth, N.S., 19 March 1782 **ELKANAH CLEMENTS**, b. Marblehead 1 Feb. 1761 (not in VR); d. Yarmouth, N.S., 17 July 1845; son of John and poss. Hannah (Eaton) Clements. He m. (2) DEBORAH ROGERS, Yarmouth 1 Oct. 1764; daughter of Cornelius and Abigail (Holmes) Rogers (see #504) with whom he had Deborah and William.

On 21 March 1787 John Clemens Jr. of Yarmouth, mariner, sold Elkanah Clemens of Yarmouth 34 acres of upland and 15 acres of salt marsh; John's wife Sarah also signed this deed.

Between 1806 and 1815 Elkanah Clements owned 6 schooners. In 1809 he was a shareholder and director of the Marine Insurance Company of Yarmouth.

On 11 July 1815 Sarah Bailey, one of the heirs of the estate of Peleg Holmes, sold to Elkanah Clements of Yarmouth her right in Peleg's land; she signed by making her mark.

On 27 Jan. 1831 Elkanah Clements Sr. and his wife Deborah, Reuben Clements and his wife Elizabeth, Elkanah Clements Jr. and his wife Mary, John Pinkney Jr. and his wife Abigail, Ziba Clements, and Lucy Robbins widow of Benjamin all of Yarmouth and Timothy Labeau/Sabeau and his wife Lydia of Weymouth, N.S., and Joseph Haycock and his wife Elsey of Grand Passage, N.S., sold to Nathaniel Saunders of Yarmouth part of the Second Division lot #20 assigned to Peleg Holmes.

The will of Silas Clements of Yarmouth made 15 June 1832, proved 8 Sept. 1836, names his brother Elkanah Clements, sisters, and heirs of sisters.

On 17 Aug. 1835 Cornelius Rogers, John Rogers and his wife Lydia, David Landers and his wife Lucy, Elkanah Clements and his wife Deborah, Amos Hilton and his wife Hannah all of Yarmouth, heirs of Cornelius Rogers, sold to Isaac Miller of Yarmouth their right in Third Division lot #140.

Children of Elkanah and Lucy (Holmes) Clements, b. Yarmouth, N.S.:

    i   REUBEN CLEMENTS[6], b. 14 Aug. 1783

   ii   LYDIA CLEMENTS, b. 28 Aug. 1785

  iii   ELKANAH CLEMENTS, b. 1 April 1788

  iv   ABIGAIL CLEMENTS, b. 30 June 1790

   v   LUCY CLEMENTS, b. 12 Aug. 1792

  vi   ELSIE CLEMENTS, b. 27 Aug. 1795

 vii   ZIBA CLEMENTS, b. 28 Dec. 1797; d. 25 Jan. 1864; unm.

viii   DEBORAH CLEMENTS, b. 15 July 1801; d. 17 May 1804

References: *Yarmouth NS VR* pp. 1:21(m.; b. ch.); 2:56(b. 2 ch. by Deborah). Yarmouth N.S. LR B:69(John Clemens); K:44(Sarah Bailey); S:305(Elkanah *et al.*). Yarmouth N.S. PR 2:160(Silas Clements); U:341(Cornelius Rogers *et al.*). *Yarmouth Hist Sequel* pp. 210(schooners); 362-3(insurance co.).

510. HANNAH EVERSON[5] (*Lusanna*[4] *Bradford, Ephraim*[3], *William*[2-1]), bp. Kingston 15 April 1753; d. Scituate 24 Nov 1836 aged 84y.

She m. Kingston 13 June 1774 **JAMES LINCOLN**, b. Scituate 20 June 1752; d. Machiasport, Me., 1839 or Scituate 17 July 1839 aged 87; son of Isaac and Mary (Neall) Lincoln.

James Lincoln was head of a household of 1 man, 5 boys, and 3 females in Scituate in the 1790 census.

Children of James and Hannah (Everson) Lincoln, b. Scituate:

    i   JOHN LINCOLN[6], b. 13 Dec. 1774

    ii JAMES LINCOLN, b. 7 Aug. 1776

    iii LUCY LINCOLN, b. 14 May 1778

    iv OLIVER LINCOLN, b. 16 May 1781 [not in Aspinwall]

    v   BARTLETT LINCOLN, b. 2 Aug. 1783

    vi SETH LINCOLN, b. 1 Oct. 1786

    vii MARY LINCOLN, b. 25 March 1789; d. 13 Oct. 1793 ae 3y 6m 18d

    viii LYDIA LINCOLN, b. 2 May 1791

References: *Bradford Desc* pp. 145-6. *VR Kingston* p. 216(m.). *VR Scituate* 1:219-20(b. James, b. ch.); 2:411(d. Hannah, James, Mary).

511. JAMES EVERSON[5] (*Lusanna*[4] *Bradford, Ephraim*[3], *William*[2-1]), bp. 29 Sept. 1754; d. Kingston 17 April 1787 aged 33y 7m 16d.

He m. Kingston 29 June 1780 (int. 8 April 1780) **LYDIA (HOLMES) THOMAS**, b. ca. 1752; d. Kingston 16 May 1836 aged 84y. She m. (1) Plymouth 17 April 1772 MICAH THOMAS with whom she had Sally.

The court records show that James Everson served the town of Kingston as a constable in 1781.

On 10 Dec. 1781 Lydia Everson of Kingston, weaver, sold to [her brother] James Everson Jr. of Kingston her right in the estate of their father Seth Everson deceased.

On 19 Dec. 1787 the widow Lydia Everson was granted her dower rights to the estate of James Everson.

On 18 May 1788 Lydia Everson of Kingston, adminstratrix of the estate of James Everson Jr. late of Kingston, sold to Seth Everson of Kingston, yeoman, part of the homestead farm and the easterly part of a dwelling house; the land was bounded by land of the widow Lusanna Everson and included

"Orchard set off to me for my Dower." This deed was not recorded until 22 Sept. 1817.

Lydia Everson's household consisted of 5 females in Kingston in the 1790 census.

Children of James and Lydia (Holmes) Everson, b. Kingston:

    i   LUCY EVERSON[6], b. 1 Sept. 1781

    ii JOANNA EVERSON, b. 26 June 1784

    iii NANCY EVERSON, b. 20 Aug. 1786

References: *VR Kingston* pp. 70(b. ch.), 216(m. int.), 345(d. James, Lydia). *Thomas Gen* p. 33. Plymouth Co. PR 30:405(James Everson Jr.). *Plymouth VR* p. 352(her 1st m.). Plymouth Co. LR 67:55; 132:151(Lydia Everson).

512.   SETH EVERSON[5] (*Lusanna[4] Bradford, Ephraim[3], William[2-1]*), b. Kingston 11 July 1761; d. there 10 June 1832 aged 71.

He m. Kingston 12 Feb. 1797 **LUCY WATERMAN**, b. Plymouth 5 June 1765; d. Kingston 20 Jan. 1839 aged 73y 7m; daughter of Josiah and Fear (Tinkham) Waterman, a descendant of Pilgrim **Peter Brown**.

Seth Everson's household consisted of 1 man and 2 females in Kingston in the 1790 census.

On 18 May 1788 Lydia Everson of Kingston, adminstratrix of the estate of James Everson Jr. late of Kingston, sold to Seth Everson of Kingston, yeoman, part of the homestead farm and the easterly part of a dwelling house; the land was bounded by land of the widow Lusanna Everson and included "Orchard set off to me for my Dower." This deed was not recorded until 22 Sept. 1817.

On 3 March 1794 Seth Everson of Kingston, yeoman, sold to Amos Cook of Kingston, cordwainer, land in Kingston.

Some sources say that Seth and Lucy had no children, but on 26 March 1823 Seth Everson of Kingston, yeoman, sold to his son Oliver Everson of Kingston the reversion of real estate set off to the widow Simmons and sold to Seth by Josiah [Cook?] Jr., the administrator of Simmons' estate.

At the April 1739 term of the court of Common Pleas, Seth Everson sued Daniel Weston Ring of Kingston, yeoman, Martin Howard of Plympton, Gentleman, Francis Holmes, Sampson Holmes, Bela Sturtevant, and Asa Sherman Jr. all of Plympton, yeomen, for trespass. Seth claimed that, using force and arms at diverse times since 20 Feb. 1828, the defendants did break and enter a close of 18 acres in Kingston and carry away 5 rods of fence and tread down 50 rods of soil. The defendants defaulted.

On 15 Oct. 1833 Lucy Everson, widow of Seth Everson of Kingston, yeoman, deceased, was appointed administratrix of his estate.

On 10 April 1835 Lucy Everson, administratrix of the estate of Seth Everson, sold land in Kingston to pay debts to Oliver Everson of Kingston, yeoman.

Possible child of Seth and Lucy (Waterman) Everson:

    i. OLIVER EVERSON[6]

References: *VR Kingston* p. 217(m.). *Waterman Gen* 1:359. *MF* 7:110. Plymouth Co. PR 68:350; 71:100; 73:430; 74:7, 168(Seth Everson). Plymouth Co. LR 132:151(Lydia Everson); 147:75; 169:155(Seth Everson); 217:62(Lucy Everson). *Plymouth Co Ct Recs* 14:165(Seth Everson).

513. EPHRAIM CHANDLER[5] (*Ruth[4] Bradford, Ephraim[3], William[2-1]*), b. Duxbury 18 May 1750; d. Kingston 28 Jan. 1795 in 44th yr.

He m. Plympton 11 Oct. 1775 **MARY DOTEN**, b. Plympton 28 Jan. 1755; d. Kingston 27 April 1808 "Molly widow of Ephraim"; daughter of Edward and Joanah (Whiting) Doten, a descendant of Pilgrim **Edward Doty.**

On 13 May 1779 Joanna Doten of Kingston, widow of Edward Doten late of Plympton, John Doten, James Doten, Ephraim Chandler and his wife Molly, Ichabod Churchill and his wife Abigail, and Ephraim Doten's children sold to Jacob Doten of Plympton, husbandman, their rights in the widow's thirds.

Eph[m] Chandler was head of a household of 1 man, 3 boys, and 4 females in Kingston in the 1790 census.

On 5 March 1794 John Faunce of Kingston was appointed administrator of the estate of Ephraim Chandler of Kingston. The division of 1 Aug. 1796 went to Molly Chandler, widow; Selah, wife of Melzar Russell; sons Nathan, Isaac, Ephraim, and John Chandler; and daughter Rispa Chandler. Division of the widow's share on 1 July 1808 names the same children.

Children of Ephraim and Mary (Doten) Chandler, b. Kingston:

    i SELAH CHANDLER[6], b. 13 Aug. 1776
    ii RISPAH CHANDLER, b. 23 June 1778; d. 1 Nov. 1779 ae 17m
    iii NATHAN CHANDLER, b. 5 Sept. 1780
    iv ISAAC CHANDLER, b. 3 Sept. 1782

v RISPAH CHANDLER, b. 22 June 1785

vi MOLLY CHANDLER, b. 5 April 1788; d. 23/25 Dec 1793 ae 5y 8m 18d

vii EPHRAIM CHANDLER, b. 22 April 1790

viii JOHN CHANDLER, b. 11 Nov. 1793

References: *VR Kingston* pp. 39(b. ch.), 93(b. Mary), 277(m.), 327(d. Ephraim, Mary, Rispah, Molly). *VR Plympton* p.93(b. Mary). *Bradford Desc* p. 146. Plymouth Co. PR #3759(Ephraim Chandler); 47:53(Mary Chandler). Plymouth Co. LR 66:142(Joanna Doten *et al.*).

514. RUTH CHANDLER[5] (*Ruth[4] Bradford, Ephraim[3], William[2-1]*), bp. Duxbury 24 Oct. 1762; d. there 8 Feb. 1811 aged 48y.

She m. Duxbury 2 Feb. 1787 **JOSHUA BREWSTER**, b. Duxbury 2 May 1761; d. there 20/22 Sept. 1832 aged 71y; son of Nathan and Hannah (Kent) Brewster, a descendant of Pilgrim **William Brewster**. He m. (2) SARAH _____.

Joshua Brewster served in the Revolutionary War as a private from Duxbury raised for service in the Continental Army during 1780; he marched on 3 July 1780 and was discharged 14 Jan. 1781. He applied for a pension on 21 Aug. 1832, aged 71, stating that he had a wife Sarah aged 56 and children Joshua aged 20 and Ruth aged 17, and also the care of a granddaughter, Roxalana Weston.

In Duxbury in the 1790 census there were two Joshua Brewsters; one with a household of 1 man, 1 boy and 1 female, the other with 3 men, 1 boy and 2 females. The second is most likely this Joshua since listed near him was Joshua Brewster Jr. with 1 man and 3 females.

On 10 Oct. 1793 Joshua Brewster of Duxbury, yeoman, sold to Amos Phillips of Duxbury, yeoman, his right in four acres. On 29 Dec. 1796 Joshua Brewster of Duxbury, Gentleman, sold to Abner Dingley Jr. of Duxbury, yeoman, 3+ acres. Joshua's wife Ruth signed both these deeds.

On 1 Oct. 1831 Joshua Brewster 3rd petitioned the probate court saying, "... my father Joshua Brewster has for sometime been afflicted with mental derangement & is incapable of taking proper care of himself & his property" and prayed that Nathan C. Brewster be appointed his guardian. The inventory taken 4 Nov. 1831 included 100 acres in various lots and a pew in the Congregational Church.

On 6 Nov. 1832 Nathan C. Brewster was granted the administration on the estate of Joshua Brewster late of Duxbury.

On 5 Nov. 1833 Nathan C. Brewster, Joshua Brewster, yeomen, Hosea Delano, housewright, and his wife Hannah, and Ruth Brewster, singlewoman, divided the land they held in common from the estate of their father Joshua Brewster; Abigail, the wife of Nathan, and Deborah, the wife of Joshua, released their dower rights. On the same day they sold to Wadsworth Chandler their part of a lot that their father Joshua Brewster and Wadsworth Chandler had bought of the heirs of Oliver Sampson.

Children of Joshua and Ruth (Chandler) Brewster, b. Duxbury (these children are incorrectly listed as children of Joshua and Deborah; it was Joshua Jr. who m. a Deborah):

   i   DEBORAH BREWSTER[6], b. 15 Dec. 1787; d. Duxbury 3 Jan. 1820 ae 32

   ii RACHEL BREWSTER, b. 3 Aug. 1790; d. Duxbury 21 Oct. 1812 in 24th yr.

   iii SELAH BREWSTER, b. 9 June 1792; may be the ____ dau. of Joshua d. Duxbury 1819.

   iv NATHAN CHANDLER BREWSTER, b. 30 April 1796

   v   HANNAH BREWSTER, b. 31 March 1798

   vi JOSHUA BREWSTER, b. 16 May 1801

   vii RUTH BREWSTER, b. 10 April 1803

References: *VR Duxbury* p. 33-5(b. Joshua, b. ch.); 233(m.); 354(d. Deborah), 355(d. Joshua, Ruth, Rachel), 356(d. dau.). *Bradford Desc* p. 146. Plymouth Co. LR 76:28; 82:77(Joshua Brewster); 178:118; 180:2(Nathan C. Brewster *et al.*). Suffolk Co. PR 70:477(guardianship), 546(inv.); #2758, 71:104(Joshua Brewster). *Rev War Pensions* 1:377(Joshua Brewster). *MSSR* 2:471(Joshua Brewster).

515. EPHRAIM[5] BRADFORD (*Ezekiel[4], Ephraim[3], William[2-1]*), b. Kingston 13 Dec. 1750; d. New Gloucester, Me., 1817.

He m. (1) int. No. Yarmouth, Me., 10 Oct. 1778 and New Gloucester, Me., 25 Nov. 1778 **JUDITH MOULTON**, b. No. Yarmouth, Me., 30 June 1754; daughter of Stephen and Elizabeth (Stevens) Moulton.

He m. (2) New Gloucester, Me., 4 Oct. 1790 **ANNA WARREN**, b. ca. 1761; daughter of Walter and Mary (Cotton) Warren.

Ephraim Bradford's household consisted of 1 man, 3 boys, and 4 females in the 1790 census of New Gloucester, Me..

Ephraim Bradford was called a cordwainer in 1780, 1805, and 1809 when he bought land in New Gloucester, Me.

Children of Ephraim and Judith (Moulton) Bradford, b. prob. New Gloucester, Me.:

    i BETSEY[6] BRADFORD, b. Aug. 1779; d. Turner 12 July 1836 ae 59y; unm.

    ii STEPHEN BRADFORD, b. 21 Feb. 1780

    iii REBECCA BRADFORD, b. 1782

    iv ISAAC BRADFORD, b. 15 Oct. 1784

    v REUBEN BRADFORD, b. 1789; d. New Gloucester, Me., 14 April 1805

Children of Ephraim and Anna (Warren) Bradford, b. prob. New Gloucester, Me.:

    vi JUDITH BRADFORD, b. 1804; d. Augusta, Me., 1840

    vii CHARLES BRADFORD, b. 1806

References: *Bradford Desc* pp. 146-7. *No Yarmouth ME VR* pp. 70(b. Judith), 123(int. 1st m.). ME VR cards(d. Betsey). New Gloucester typescript marriages 1:5(1st int.), 7(his 2nd m.). Cumberland Co. LR 27:123; 45:408; 90:10(Ephraim Bradford). *ME Fams 1790* 2:243

516. DEBORAH[5] BRADFORD (*Ezekiel[4], Ephraim[3], William[2-1]*), b. Kingston 18 Aug. 1752; d. 13 March 1833.

She m. New Gloucester, Me., 13 June 1776 (int. 11 May 1776) **BARNABAS WINSLOW**, b. No. Yarmouth, Me., 1 March 1745; d. New Gloucester, Me., 12 (or 1) Dec. 1812; son of Barnabas and Mercy (Glass) Winslow, a descendant of Pilgrim **Richard Warren**.

Barnabas Winslow served in the Revolutionary War as a private in Capt. Isaac Parsons' company, Lieut. Col. Joseph Prime's regiment; he enlisted 1 May 1780 and was discharged 21 Dec. 1780.

On 12 Feb. 1768 a committee representing the Proprietors of New Gloucester sold to Barnabas Winslow of New Gloucester, yeoman, six acres; this deed was not recorded until 20 Feb.1802. On 10 June 1788 the heirs of David Millet late of New Gloucester sold to Barnabas the homestead lot from the estate; again not recorded until 20 Feb.1802.

Children of Barnabas and Deborah (Bradford) Winslow:

    i ZILPAH WINSLOW[6], b. 11 March 1777; d. 5 Aug. 1779

    ii LORANA WINSLOW, b. 17 Feb. 1779

    iii CLARISSA WINSLOW, b. 29 May 1781; d. 7 Oct. 1799

    iv EDWARD PARSONS WINSLOW, b. 2 April 1783; d. 26 March 1805

    v   DEBORAH WINSLOW, b. 25 April 1786
    vi REBECCA WINSLOW, b. 28 April 1788
    vii PHILLIP WINSLOW, b. 7 Oct. 1790

References: *Bradford Desc* p. 147. New Gloucester typescript marriages 1:2(int.); deaths 1:16(d. Deborah, Barnabas). *Winslow Mem* 2:726. Cumberland Co. ME LR 36:161(Proprietors to Barnabas), 162(heirs of David Millet). *MF* 18:3:15. *No. Yarmouth VR* p. 126(b. Barnabas). *MSSR* 17:628(Barnabas Winslow).

517. WILLIAM⁵ BRADFORD (*Ezekiel⁴, Ephraim³, William²⁻¹*), b. Kingston; d. Turner, Me., 26 May 1828 aged 74y.

He m. int. New Gloucester, Me., 8 Nov. 1776 **ASENATH MASON**, b. New Gloucester, Me., 4 Sept. 1758; d. Turner, Me., 25 Dec. 1833 aged 75y; son of Ebenezer and Rebecca (Winslow) Mason, a descendant of Pilgrim **Richard Warren**.

On 3 Nov. 1780 Ebenezer Mason of New Gloucester, Me., yeoman, William Bradford of a place commonly called "Silvester", Me. (now Turner, Me.), yeoman, and his wife Asenath, Ebenezer Mason Jr., blacksmith, and Marcy Mason, spinster, both of New Gloucester, Me., sold 50 acres in No. Yarmouth, Me., to John Lawrence of No. Yarmouth, Me. On the same day William Bradford of a place called "Sylver," Me., and his wife Asenath sold more land with the above Masons.

On 24 May 1790 William Bradford of Turner bought a piece of land for back taxes from Mark Andrews tax collector. On 1 April 1795 Jesse Bradford tax collector for the town of Turner sold to William Bradford of Turner three pieces of land for back taxes. On 30 May 1795 William bought another piece of land for back taxes from Benjamin Chamberlain, constable.

On 3 Aug. 1795 William Bradford of Turner, yeoman, sold to Chandler Bradford and Daniel French, Jr., of Turner, yeomen, 112 acres in lot #102.

On 3 July 1797 William Turner of Boston, Gentleman, and his wife Eunice sold to William Bradford of Turner, Gentleman, the 112ᵗʰ lot in Turner. On 6 June 1798 Caleb Torrey of Scituate, yeoman, Robert Lenthill Eells of Hanover, Gentleman, and James Warren of Plymouth, Esq., a standing committee of the Proprietors of the Town of Turner, granted a proprietor's right for the 56ᵗʰ lot to William Bradford for having "fulfilled the conditions of settlement."

On 24 July 1815 William B. Sever of Kingston, Gentleman, sold to William Bradford, Ezekiel Bradford, Chandler Bradford, and Asa Bradford all of Turner, yeomen, his one undivided 12ᵗʰ part of 19 lots in Turner which were the property of William Sever late of Kingston, Esq. On the same day John Sever sold the above his 12th part. On 9 Dec. 1817 William and Asa Bradford sold to Ezekiel and Chandler Bradford their part of nine of the lots.

On 10 April 1817 William Bradford of Turner, yeoman, sold to Asa Bradford of Turner, yeoman, lots #142 and #192.

On 23 June 1828 Asenath Bradford declined administration on the estate of her husband William Bradford late of Turner and requested that her sons William and Asa Bradford be appointed.

Children of William and Asenath (Mason) Bradford, b. prob. Turner, Me.:

    i   WILLIAM[6] BRADFORD, b. 6 Aug. 1778

    ii ASA BRADFORD, b. 4 Feb. 1780

References: ME VR cards(d. William, Asenath). Turner ME TR 1:60(b. ch.). New Gloucester typescript births 1:27(b. Asenath). Cumberland Co. LR 27:49(Ebenezer Mason *et al.*); 15:69(William Bradford). *Hugh Mason* pp. 122-3. Oxford Co. ME PR 5:554(William Bradford). Cumberland Co. ME LR 24:380-83; 27:358(land bought for back taxes); 29:382(William Turner), 383(Proprietor's right). Oxford Co. ME LR 6:487(William Bradford); 11:244(William Sever), 245(John Sever); 14:238; 15:34(William Bradford).

518. REBECCA[5] BRADFORD (*Ezekiel[4], Ephraim[3], William[2-1]*), b. Kingston 22 Sept. 1756; d. Turner, Me., 22 Sept. 1832. They are both buried in Fern St. Cem., Turner, Me.

She m. Turner, Me., 19 Jan. 1786 **WILLIAM TRUE**, b. 15 June 1760; d. Turner, Me., 10 April 1855; son of William and Sarah (Tuttle) True.

On 15 March 1815 William True of Minot, Me., Gentleman, sold to Philip True of Minot, Me., yeoman, 50 acres.

On 15 April 1822 Chandler Bradford of Turner, yeoman, and Ezekiel Bradford of Turner, yeoman, sold to Phillip True of Minot, Gentleman, the northerly half of lot #42 in Turner; this deed was not recorded until 18 Nov. 1856.

Children of William and Rebecca (Bradford) True, b. Poland, Me.:

    i   ELIZABETH TRUE[6], b. 17 Oct. 1786

    ii PHILIP TRUE, b. 1 Sept. 1791

    iii REBEKAH TRUE, b. 1 Jan. 1796

References: *Bradford Desc* p. 147. *NEHGR* 98:57(b. ch.). Cumberland Co. LR 73:189(William True). *ME Fams 1790* 3:285. *Hist Turner ME* p. 159(m.). "Poland Vital

Records 1780-1850" p. 36(b. ch.).   Androscoggin Co. ME LR 15:568(Chandler Bradford).
MOCA, Series 1, p. 231.

519.   JESSE[5] BRADFORD (*Ezekiel[4], Ephraim[3], William[2-1]*), b. Kingston 7
March 1758; d. Turner, Me., 19 May 1829 aged 71y 2m.

He m. 1781 **JUDITH WESTON**, b. Kingston 17 Aug. 1762; d. Turner,
Me., 6 Nov. 1842 aged 79y; daughter of John and Mercy (Sampson) Weston.

On 3 March 1812 Jesse Bradford of Turner, Gentleman, sold to William
Bradford of Turner, yeoman, 240 acres being lots #218 and 212; Hira and
Dura Bradford were the witnesses. On 30 July 1812 Jesse sold to William an
undivided 1/6th part of lot #115 which he had bought from Isaac Cushman.

On 24 July 1815 William B. Sever of Kingston, Gentleman, sold to
William Bradford, Ezekiel Bradford, Chandler Bradford, and Asa Bradford all
of Turner, yeomen, his one undivided 12th part of 19 lots in Turner which was
the property of William Sever late of Kingston, Esq. On the same day John
Sever sold the above his 12th part. On 9 Dec. 1817 William and Asa Bradford
sold to Ezekiel and Chandler Bradford their part of 9 of the lots.

On 26 March 1822 Jesse Bradford of Turner, Gentleman, sold to Phillip
Bradford of Turner, physician, 21 ½ acres, part of lot #171.

On 16 June 1826 Dura Bradford of Turner, Gentleman, sold to Ethelbert
of Turner, yeoman, the southerly half of lot #173 except 4 acres; this deed was
not recorded until 12 Feb. 1856.

In September 1829 Judith Bradford declined administration on the estate
of her husband Jesse Bradford. On 3 Nov. 1829 Philip Bradford, administrator, made oath to the inventory. On 5 Jan. 1830 Philip declared the estate
insolvent and the court ordered that Judith could have $200 in personal
property from the estate.

On 26 Feb. 1831 Hira Bradford of Turner, Gentleman, mortaged to
Phillip Bradford, physician, Thayer S. Whitman, and William B. Bray, yeoman,
part of lot #163 bounded on land formerly owned by Jesse Bradford. On 10
Aug. 1821 Hira Bradford, Gentleman, Dura Bradford, Gentleman, Ethelburt
Bradford, yeoman, Joel Fairbanks, millwright, and his wife Judith, Isaac Allen,
yeoman, and his wife Jennett, and Amos Shaw, Gentleman, and his wife
Salome all of Turner and heirs of Jesse Bradford, sold to Philip Bradford of
Turner, physician, all their right in the estate of Jesse Bradford. Also signing
the deed were Rebecca the wife of Hira, Sally the wife of Dura, and Rebeckah
the wife of Ethelburt.

Children of Jesse and Judith (Weston) Bradford, first six b. Turner, Me.:

   i   HIRA/HERAH⁶ BRADFORD, b. 5 Dec. 1783

   ii DURA BRADFORD, b. 7 March 1785

  iii CHARLES BRADFORD, b. 1787; d.y. (not in TR or in above deed)

  iv PHILIP BRADFORD, b. 15 July 1789

   v ALFRED BRADFORD (twin), b. 16 July 1791; d. 12 Dec. 1812 ae 21y 4m 23d, unm.

  vi ETHELBERT BRADFORD (twin), b. 16 July 1791

? vii ELIPHALET BRADFORD, b. 1792, probably the same child as Ethelburt, above, but if not, d. y.

viii JUDITH BRADFORD, b. 13 June 1793

  ix MARY BRADFORD, b. 17 Aug. 179- [not in Aspinwall; not in above deed]

   x JEANNETTE (or JENNET) BRADFORD, b. 13 June 1797

  xi SALOME BRADFORD, b. 23 July 1799

  xii CYRUS BRADFORD d.y. [not in Aspinwall]

Note: *Bradford Desc* includes another child Betsey, b. 6 Dec. 1789, but see Philip above.

References: *Bradford Desc* pp. 147-8. *VR Kingston* p. 158(b. Judith). ME VR cards(d. Jesse, Judith, Alfred). Turner ME TR 1:60(b. Herah, Dura, Philip, Alfred, Ethelbert), 359(b. Jennet), 368(b. Salome). Oxford Co. ME PR 5:838, 890-93(Jesse Bradford). Oxford Co. ME LR 10:97, 98(Jesse Bradford); 11:244(William Sever), 245(John Sever); 15:34(William Bradford). 22:49(Jesse Bradford); 36:456(Hira Bradford); 48:163(Hira Bradford *et al.*). Androscoggin Co. ME LR 14:536(Dura Bradford).

520. EZEKIEL⁵ BRADFORD (*Ezekiel⁴, Ephraim³, William²⁻¹*), b. Kingston 15 Dec. 1759; d. Turner, Me., 28 Oct. 1829 aged 70y.

He m. Turner, Me., 14 Dec. 1786 **MARY HOUSE**, b. Abington 26 Feb. 1763; d. Turner, Me., 25 April 1852 aged 86y; daughter of Caleb and Elizabeth (Randall) House.

Ezekiel Bradford served in the Revolutionary War as a private from 28 June to 19 Nov. 1776, 25 Sept. to 30 Oct. 1777, and 5 Nov. 1777 to 3 April 1778. His widow Mary applied for a pension on 18 Aug. 1846 aged 83, a resident of Turner, Me., stating that they were m. 14 Dec. 1786 at Turner and he d. 26 Oct. 1829. She d. 25 April 1852.

On 3 Jan. 1785 Elias Merrill of New Gloucester, Me., yeoman, sold to Ezekiel Bradford Jr.of Sylvester, Me., (now Turner), yeoman, 100 acres in the

First Division of Sylvester. Ezekiel Bradford Jr. of Turner continued to buy land in 1787, 1790, 1791, and 1795.

On 24 July 1815 William B. Sever of Kingston, Gentleman, sold to William Bradford, Ezekiel Bradford, Chandler Bradford, and Asa Bradford all of Turner, yeomen, his one undivided 12th part of 19 lots in Turner which were the property of William Sever late of Kingston, Esq. On the same day John Sever sold the above 12th part. On 9 Dec. 1817 William and Asa Bradford sold to Ezekiel and Chandler Bradford their part of nine of the lots.

On 15 April 1822 Chandler Bradford of Turner, yeoman, and Ezekiel Bradford of Turner, yeoman, sold to Phillip True of Minot, Gentleman, the northerly half of lot #42 in Turner; this deed was not recorded until 18 Nov. 1856.

On 2 July 1825 Chandler sold to Ezekiel one undivided 4th part of lot #162.

On 29 Dec. 1829 Mary Bradford declined administration on the estate of her husband Ezekiel Bradford.

Children of Ezekiel and Mary (House) Bradford, b. Turner, Me.:

  i   BETSEY[6] BRADFORD, b. 6 Dec. 1789
  ii MARY (or POLLY) BRADFORD (twin), b. 17 Aug. 1794; d.y.
  iii SARAH (or SALLY) BRADFORD (twin), b. 17 Aug. 1794
  iv CYRUS BRADFORD, b. 10 Aug. 1798
  v   NANCY BRADFORD, b. 19 Aug. 1804

References: *Bradford Desc* p. 148. *VR Abington* p. 113(b. Mary). *Samuel House Of Scituate MA*, Robert B. and Barbara B. Pierce, 1992. ME VR cards(d. Ezekiel, Mary). Turner ME TR 1:351A(b. Betsey), 362(b. Nancy), 364(b. Poley), 368(b. Sarah). *Rev War Pensions* 1:356(Ezekiel Bradford). Cumberland Co. ME LR 18:434-37; 24:54(Ezekiel Bradford buying). Oxford Co. ME PR 5:894(Ezekiel Bradford). *MSSR* 2:402. *Hist Turner ME* p. 159(m.). Oxford Co. ME LR 11:244(William Sever), 245(John Sever); 15:34(William Bradford); 35:428(Chandler Bradford). Androscoggin Co. ME LR 15:568(Chandler Bradford).

521. CHANDLER[5] BRADFORD (*Ezekiel[4], Ephraim[3], William[2-1]*), b. Kingston 15 Aug. 1761; d. Turner, Me., 22 Feb. 1849 aged 87y.

He m. 1783 **SARAH FRENCH**, b. ca. 1764; d. 31 Oct. 1840 aged 76y; daughter of Daniel and Waitstill (Sumner) French.

Chandler Bradford served as a private in the Revolutionary War in Capt. Ichabod Bonney's company in Col. Nathan Sparhawk's regiment which marched on 19 Oct. 1778 with service of 1 month 26 days.

On 14 May 1794 Ezekiel Bradford of Turner, yeoman, quitclaimed half a lot in Turner "I now live on" to son Chandler Bradford of Turner, yeoman. On the same day Ezekiel and Chandler Bradford of Turner, yeomen, quitclaimed a lot in Turner to Martin Bradford of Turner, yeoman.

On 3 Aug. 1795 William Bradford of Turner, yeoman, sold to Chandler Bradford and Daniel French Jr., of Turner, yeomen, 112 acres in lot #102.

On 6 Nov. 1797 Chandler Bradford of Turner, Me., yeoman, sold to Martin Bradford of Turner, Me., yeoman, lot #43; Chandler's wife Sarah released her dower rights.

On 1 April 1809 Chandler Bradford of Turner, yeoman, sold to Seth Bradford of Turner, yeoman, 125 acres in lot #12; this deed was not recorded until 10 June 1834. On 16 Aug. 1833 Chandler sold to Seth lot #8 and 15 acres in lot #287.

On 15 April 1822 Chandler Bradford of Turner, yeoman, and Ezekiel Bradford of Turner, yeoman, sold to Phillip True of Minot, Gentleman, the northerly half of lot #42 in Turner; this deed was not recorded until 18 Nov. 1856. On 2 July 1825 Chandler sold to Ezekiel one undivided fourth part of lot #162.

On 25 Sept. 1823 Chandler Bradford of Turner, yeoman, sold to Benjamin Bradford of Livermore, 2 acres in Livermore. On 14 June 1837 Chandler sold Benjamin another 31 acres in Livermore.

On 31 May 1841 Chandler Bradford of Turner, yeoman, sold to Chandler Bradford Jr., of Turner, yeoman, the northwest quarter of lot #68; this deed was not recorded until 5 Jan. 1863. On 23 April 1841 Chandler sold to Chandler, Jr., his right in 3 pieces of land.

Chandler Bradford, age 85, was mentioned in the Revolutionary War pension of his brother Ezekiel in 1847.

Children of Chandler and Sarah (French) Bradford, b. Turner, Me.:

- i BENJAMIN[6] BRADFORD, b. 5 March 1784
- ii LAURANA BRADFORD, b. 4 May 1786; d.y.
- iii SETH BRADFORD, b. 16 March 1788
- iv SARAH BRADFORD, b. 15 March 1790
- v BETSY BRADFORD, b. 27 Feb. 1792
- vi CELIA BRADFORD, b. 29 Dec. 1793; d. 29 May 1812
- vii OLIVE BRADFORD, b. 10 May 1796
- viii LAURA BRADFORD, b. 28 Nov. 1798
- ix ROXANA BRADFORD, b. 16 Oct. 1800; d.y.
- x XOA BRADFORD, b. 28 Sept. 1803

    xi CHANDLER BRADFORD, b. 10 March 1806
    xii ROXA BRADFORD, b. 29 Oct. 1807; d.y.
    xiii LAURANA BRADFORD, b. 2 June 1810

References: *Bradford Desc* p. 148. ME VR cards(b. Luranan, Roxa; d. Chandler, Sarah). Turner ME TR 1:351A(b. Benjamin, Betsy), 352(b. Chandler, Celia), 361(b. Laura), 364(b. Olive), 367(b. Roxana), 368(b. Seth, Sarah), 373(b. Xoa). Cumberland Co. ME LR 21:230(Ezekiel Bradford), 231(Ezekiel & Chandler); 39:318(Chandler Bradford). *Rev War Pensions* 1:356(Ezekiel Bradford). *MSSR* 2:401. Androscoggin Co. LR ME 15:568; 32:186(Chandler Bradford). Oxford Co. ME LR 6:487(William Bradford); 35:428; 41:414; 42:270; 56:559-60; 78:312(Chandler Bradford).

522. MARTIN⁵ BRADFORD (*Ezekiel⁴, Ephraim³, William²⁻¹*), b. Kingston 17 Oct. 1763; d. Turner, Me., 7 June 1832.

He m. (1) Turner, Me., 10 Aug. 1790 **PRUDENCE DILLINGHAM**, b. probably Middleboro or Turner, Me., 17 Oct. 1757; d. there 5 Sept. 1822; probably daughter of Paul and Anna (Paull) Dillingham.

He m. (2) int. Minot, Me., 15 Feb. 1823 **SARAH READ**.

On 14 May 1794 Ezekiel and Chandler Bradford of Turner, yeomen, quitclaimed a lot in Turner to Martin Bradford of Turner, yeoman.

On 21 Jan. 1828 Martin Bradford of Turner, yeoman, sold to Martin Bradford Jr., of Turner, yeoman, 139 acres being lot #82 and part of lot #83 where Martin Jr., was living. On the same day Martin sold to Calvin Bradford of Turner, yeoman, 150 acres, it being lot #84 and part of lot #62 where Calvin was living. On 12 Jan. 1833 Martin sold to Calvin half of lot #104.

On 25 June 1832 Sarah Bradford requested that Richmond Bradford, son of her late husband Martin Bradford, be appointed administrator of the estate. The inventory taken on 28 Aug. 1832 included 2 pews and 5 and 2/3 gallery pews in the church of Turner and 1 pew in the E. Meetinghouse in Minot. On 4 March 1834 Sarah Bradford, Martin's second wife, stating that she had married him 9 years ago, petitioned for some of the personal estate claiming that she had brought $150 worth of furniture and $200 in cash to the marriage.

On 15 Jan. 1836 Richmond Bradford of Danville, physician, sold to Charles Briggs of Minot, Gentleman, several pieces of land in Turner formerly owned and occupied by Deacon Martin Bradford.

On 5 July 1849 Charles Briggs of Turner, yeoman, sold to Cyrus Briggs of Auburn 60 acres of the farm formerly owned and occupied by Deacon Martin Bradford, deceased, excluding a graveyard and another lot.

Children of Martin and Prudence (Dillingham) Bradford, b. Turner, Me.:

    i   MARTIN[6] BRADFORD, b. 2 Feb. 1791

   ii   CALVIN BRADFORD, b. 15 Jan. 1793

  iii   ANNA BRADFORD, b. 22 May 1794; d. 9 Oct. 1796 ae 2y 6m 17d

  iv   EZEKIEL BRADFORD, b. 1 Feb. 1796

   v   FREEMAN BRADFORD, b. 11 Sept. 1797

  vi   RICHMOND BRADFORD, b. 30 April 1801

References: *Bradford Desc* p. 149. ME VR cards(d. Prudence). Turner ME TR 1:51(m.), 351A(b.&d. Anna), 352(b. Calvin), 354(b. Ezekiel), 355(b. Freeman), 362(b. Martin). A Genealogy of the Dillingham Family of New England, Winthrop Alexander (typescript at NEHGS) p. 214. Cumberland Co. ME LR 21:231(Ezekiel & Chandler). *Turner ME Hist* pp. 58, 161(m.). Oxford Co. ME PR 6:464, 487; 7:107(Martin Bradford). Oxford Co. ME LR 43:369; 45:270-1(Martin Bradford); 59:126(Richmond Bradford). Androscoggin Co. ME LR 21:86(Charles Briggs).

523. PHILIP[5] BRADFORD (*Ezekiel[4], Ephraim[3], William[2-1]*), b. Kingston 8 June 1765; d. June 1789.

He m. Pembroke 9 April 1789 (also recorded in Turner, Me.) **MARY BONNEY**, b. Pembroke 13 Sept. 1764; daughter of Ichabod and Mary (Turner) Bonney. She m. (2) Turner, 17 May 1792, BENJAMIN CHAMBER-LAIN.

References: *Bradford Desc* p. 149. *VR Pembroke* pp. 44(b. Mary), 246(m.). *Hist Turner ME* pp. 160(m.), 164(her 2nd m.).

524. BETTY[5] BRADFORD (*Ezekiel[4], Ephraim[3], William[2-1]*), b. Kingston 22 Aug. 1767; d. Turner, Me., 2 Nov. 1815.

She m. Turner, Me., 14 Feb. 1788 **DANIEL BRIGGS**, b. Taunton 9 May 1764; d. Minot, Me., 8 Feb. 1839; son of Daniel and Silence (Hart) Briggs. He m. (2) Turner, Me., 5 May 1817 MARY (_____) MILLIKEN.

On 29 Jan. 1800 James Harsey, Aaron Dwinel, and Samuel Pool, yeomen, a committee to make good and sufficient deeds for the Proprietors of Poland, Me., sold to Daniel Briggs of Poland, yeoman, lot #9 containing 200 acres.

On 9 May 1808 James Hill, tax collector of Minot, sold 23½ acres to Daniel Briggs Jr. of Minot, yeoman, for back taxes.

Children of Daniel and Betty (Bradford) Briggs, first four b. Minot, Me.:

    i   CHARLES BRIGGS[6], b. 29 Nov. 1788

    ii LURANA BRIGGS, b. 20 Sept. 1790

   iii TYLIE (or SILENCE) BRIGGS, b. 4 March 1792

   iv BETSY BRIGGS, b. 18 Jan. 1794

    v DANIEL BRIGGS, b. Poland, Me., 28 March 1796

   vi RISPAH BRIGGS, b. 25 Dec. 1797

  vii CYRENE BRIGGS, b. 7 March 1800; d.y.

 viii CHANDLER BRIGGS, b. 16 July 1802; d. 21 July 1804

   ix JANNET MUNROE BRIGGS, b. 24 March 1804

    x ROXANNA BRADFORD BRIGGS, b. 16 Feb. 1806

   xi HIRAM BRIGGS, b. 12 Nov. 1808

  xii ANN HATHAWAY BRIGGS, b. 5 Jan. 1814; d. Lewiston, Me., 8 June 1859; unm.

References: *Bradford Desc* p. 149.   *NEHGR* 126:272.   Cumberland Co. ME LR 32:111(deed to Daniel Briggs); 67:192(James Hill). *Hist Turner ME* p. 160(m.).

525. ASA[5] BRADFORD (*Simeon[4], Ephraim[3], William[2-1]*), b. Kingston 5 July 1758.

He m. **THANKFUL** _____; d. Springfield, Vt., 1 April 1796.

Asa Bradford was head of a household consisting of one man and one female in the 1790 census at Springfield, Vt.

On 10 Dec. 1796 Joel Bradford and Hosea Bradford of Springfield sold to Asa Bradford of Springfield 29 acres and 9½ acres, part of their mother's thirds "being the whole of the Land sett off to us out of our late Father's Estate likewise Two Thirds of the House & Barn."

References: *1790 Census VT* p. 64.   Springfield VT LR 2:316(Joel Bradford *et al.*). Springfield VT VR cards(d. Thankful).

525A. SIMEON[5] BRADFORD (*Simeon[4], Ephraim[3], William[2-1]*), b. Kingston 3 Sept. 1760.

He m. **MARY SMITH**.

Simeon Bradford's household in the 1790 census of Springfield, Vt., consisted of 4 men aged 16 or older, 1 boy, and 4 females. He appears in Crown Point, Essex Co., N.Y., in 1820. He did not have any transactions in the Essex Co. land records but his sons Otis, Alden, and Enos did. No probate records were found in Essex Co. for Simeon.

Children of Simeon and Mary (Smith) Bradford:

    i ORIN[6] BRADFORD, b. 1800 (IGI shows an Orren Bradford, b. Springfield, Vt., 11 May 1800)

    ii OTIS BRADFORD, b. 1801

    iii ALDEN BRADFORD, b. 1804

    iv ENOS BRADFORD

References: *Bradford Desc* pp. 149-50. Children from Bowman Microfiche.

526. LUCY[5] BRADFORD (*Simeon[4], Ephraim[3], William[2-1]*), b. Kingston 2 Oct. 1762; d. Pittsfield Twp., Lorain Co., Ohio, 27 July 1845 aged 83y 9m 25d.

She m. Springfield, Vt., 4 Jan. 1782 **JOHN McROBERTS**; called John W. Roberts in her father's will; d. Orwell, Vt., 4 April 1813, buried. Sudbury, Vt., in 54th y.; son of _____ and Polly (_____) McRoberts.

In 1773 or 1774 John McRoberts and his mother, widow Polly McRoberts, came to America from Scotland and settled in Springfield, Vt.

John McRoberts served as a Sergeant in the Rev. War in Capt. Thomas Lee's company, Col. Warner's regiment.

John McRoberts's household consisted of 1 man, 2 boys, and 2 females in the 1790 census of Springfield, Vt.

On 30 Aug. 1851 James McRoberts made application on behalf of himself and the other surviving children of the soldier, John McRoberts and his wife, Lucy, namely Peter McRoberts, Polly Worcester, Cynthia Sheldon, Lucetta Hall, and Balsora Clark all of Pittsfield Twp., Ohio, for the pension of their mother.

Children of John and Lucy (Bradford) McRoberts, b. Springfield, Vt.:

    i DAVID McROBERTS[6], b. 23 March 1782

    ii PETER McROBERTS, b. 12 Feb. 1784; d. 9 Oct. 1789

    iii JAMES McROBERTS, b. 20 March 1786

    iv MARY McROBERTS, b. 3 Oct. 1788; d. 9 Oct. 1789

    v POLLY McROBERTS, b. 24 July 1790

    vi CYATHA/CYNTHIA McROBERTS, b. 8 March 1793

    vii LUCETTA McROBERTS, b. 26 Oct. 1796

    viii JANE McROBERTS, b. 12 July 1799

References: VTVR (m., b. ch.; cem.). *Rev War Pension* W4023, 2:2309(b. ch.; d. ch.).
DAR Patriot Index p. 459.

527. HOSEA⁵ BRADFORD (*Simeon⁴, Ephraim³, William²⁻¹*), b. Springfield,
Vt., 25 July 1773; d. Olmsted Fields, Ohio, 28 Dec. 1863.

He m. (1) Springfield, Vt., 5 Oct. 1794 **PARTHENIA SMITH**, b. 7
Sept. 1767; d. before 1806; daughter of Isaac and Mary (Briggs) Smith.

He m. (2) 1806 **HANNAH EASTMAN**, b. 7 Jan. 1784; d. Bucksville,
Ohio, 14 June 1869; daughter of Ebenezer and Susannah (Wheeler) Eastman.

On 13 June 1794 a Springfield town committee sold to Joel Bradford and
Hosea Bradford pew #3 in the gallery of the meeting house.

On 10 Dec. 1796 Joel Bradford and Hosea Bradford of Springfield sold to
Asa Bradford of Springfield 29 acres and 9½ acres, part of their mother's
thirds "being the whole of the Land sett off to us out of our late Father's
Estate likewise Two Thirds of the House & Barn."

On 8 Jan. 1806 Hosea Bradford and Joel Bradford of St. Armonds,
Province of lower Canada, sold to Allen Smith of Springfield pew #3 in the
gallery of the meeting house.

In the pension application of Hosea' brother-in-law John McRoberts,
Hosea states that in 1851 he had lived in Lomstead [*sic*], Ohio, for 31 years and
he was a brother of John's wife.

In 31 July 1851 Hosea Bradford in his 79th year, of Olmstead, Cuyahoga
Co., Ohio, where he had lived for 31 years, stated he was born 20 July 1773 in
Springfield, Vt., where he lived until he was 24 years old, and that he was the
brother of Lucy Bradford who m. John McRoberts.

Children of Hosea and Hannah (Eastman) Bradford:

   i   PHILO⁶ BRADFORD, b. 10 Oct. 1807

   ii LESTER BRADFORD, b. 17 July 1809

   iii CYNTHIA BRADFORD, b. 12 April 1811

   iv SALLY BRADFORD, b. 31 Nov. 1812 [sic]

   v   FANNY BRADFORD, b. 31 July 1814; d. 11 June 1816

   vi EASTMAN BRADFORD, b. 8 June 1816

   vii LAURA BRADFORD, b. 21 April 1818

   viii ORIN BRADFORD, b. 5 March 1820; d. 8 Aug. 1851; unm.

   ix HIRAM BRADFORD, b. 31 Aug. 1821; d. 20 March 1851; unm.

   x   MIRIAM BRADFORD, b. 14 Sept. 1824; d. Olmstead, Ohio, 16 Oct.
       1850

References: *Bradford Desc* p. 150. *Rev War Pensions* W4023, 2:2309(John McRoberts). Springfield VT VR cards(1st m.). Springfield VT LR 2:155(buying pew), 316(Joel Bradford *et al.*); 3:253(selling pew).

528. ABIGAIL⁵ BRADFORD (*Simeon⁴, Ephraim³, William²⁻¹*), b. Springfield, Vt., 23 Jan. 1765; d. Hubbardton, Vt., 1 Dec. 1831.

She m. Springfield, Vt., 16 April 1789 **WALTER HOLMES** (see her father's will), bp. Plympton 2 May 1762; d. Hubbardton, Vt., 18 June 1831; son of Simeon and Abiah (Sturtevant) Holmes. He was a fifth-generation descendant of Pilgrim **Henry Samson.**

Wally Holmes served in the Revolutionary War as a private in Capt. Ebenezer Washburn's company, Col. Eleazer Brook's regiment from 19 Nov. 1777 to 3 April 1778. His name appears on a list dated 8 July 1778 of men raised in Plymouth County for a term of 9 months from their arrival at Fishkill. He also served in Capt. Calvin Partridge's company, Lieut. Col. Samuel Pierce's regiment in 1779.

Walter Holmes was head of a household consisting of 1 man and 2 females in Springfield, Vt., in the 1790 census. "Water" Holmes was listed in 1800 in Hubbardton, Vt. Walter Holmes was listed there in 1810 and 1820. In 1830 "Watty" Holmes was listed with Pliny and Harvey Holmes in Hubbardton.

On 13 April 1793 Walter Holmes of Springfield, yeoman, sold to Thomas Marble and Abigail Bel 26 acres in Springfield; Walter's wife Naby also signed this deed. On 6 May 1793 Abner Ashley of "Hobarton" sold to Walter Holmes of Springfield 100 acres in Hubbardton. On 12 Sept. 1802 Abner sold to Walter another 50 acres.

On 8 May 1824 Walter Holmes of Hubbardton sold to Harvey Holmes of Hubbardton 50 acres. On 23 March 1830 Walter gave the land he had bought from Abner Ashley and a house to Harvey provided Harvey supply Walter and his wife yearly with firewood "properly fitted for the stove and put into my woodhouse," two cows (and if either of them died due to Harvey's neglect he was to replace it), provide on demand a suitable horse, 20 pounds of wool "well washed and Dried," 15 pounds of flax, a hog "well fatted killed and Dressed," 100 pounds of beef or mutton, 12 bushels of corn, 8 bushels of rye, 4 bushels of wheat, 20 bushels of potatoes, "needfull and nessary sauce," 6 barrels of cider, 30 bushels of apples, 1 bushel of butter salt, 1 bushel of coarse salt, 3 gallons of molasses, 10 pounds of sugar, 3 pounds of green tea, and 20 pounds of tallow. Finally Harvey was to provide a home for Harriet Holmes while she remained unmarried. Fortunately for Harvey, both his parents died the next year.

Children of Walter and Abigail (Bradford) Holmes:

    i   ESTHER HOLMES[6], b. 15 May 1791

    ii   NANCY HOLMES, b. 1 Sept. 1793

    iii HORACE HOLMES, b. 7 Aug. 1795

    iv PLINY HOLMES, b. 29 Jan. 1798

    iv HARVEY HOLMES, b. 15 April 1800

    vi POLLY HOLMES, b. 20 Sept. 1803

    vii HARRIET HOLMES, b. 17 Aug. 1806; unm. 23 Aug. 1830

References: *Bradford Desc* p. 161. GS#66626(abstract Bible, b. ch.). Springfield VT LR 1:635(Walter Holmes). Hubbardton VT LR 1:220; 3:219(Abner Ashley); 5:7, 416(Walter Holmes). *MSSR* 8:177, 184(Wally Holmes).

529. RUTH[5] BRADFORD (*Simeon⁴, Ephraim³, William²⁻¹*), b. Springfield, Vt., 17 Jan. 1768; d. Abbott's Corner, Missisquoi Co., Quebec, Canada.

She m. **ISAAC SMITH** (11 April 1794 division of father's estate), b. 22 Dec. 1766; d. Abbott's Corner March 1803; son of Isaac and Sarah (Clarke) Smith.

On 28 Jan. 1789 Isaac Smith of Springfield, Vt., Gentleman, sold to Isaac Smith Jr. of Springfield, blacksmith, 52 acres.

Child of Isaac and Ruth (Bradford) Smith:

    i. ISAAC SMITH[6], b. ca. 1803 (d. 3 Dec. 1871 ae 68y 7m 26d)

References: *Bradford Desc* p. 161. Springfield VT LR 1:335(Isaac Smith).

530. JOEL[5] BRADFORD (*Simeon⁴, Ephraim³, William²⁻¹*), b. Springfield, Vt., 25 Jan. 1773; d. Patriot, Ind., 12 July 1837.

He m. Springfield, Vt., 15 Oct. 1794 **TRYPHENA SMITH**, b. Norton 27 Sept. 1767; d. Patriot, Ind., 6 June 1837; daughter of Isaac and Mary (Briggs) Smith.

On 13 June 1794 a Springfield town committee sold to Joel Bradford and Hosea Bradford pew #3 in the gallery.

On 10 Dec. 1796 Joel Bradford and Hosea Bradford of Springfield sold to Asa Bradford of Springfield 29 acres and 9½ acres, part of their mother's thirds "being the whole of the Land sett off to us out of our late Father's Estate likewise Two Thirds of the House & Barn."

On 8 Jan. 1806 Hosea Bradford and Joel Bradford of St. Armonds, Province of Lower Canada sold to Allen Smith of Springfield pew #3 in the gallery of the Springfield meeting house.

Children of Joel and Tryphena (Smith) Bradford, b. Springfield, Vt.:

    i WILLIAM⁶ BRADFORD, b. 7 Sept. 1795

    ii LURINA BRADFORD, b. 22 Dec. 1796

    iii THEDA BRADFORD, b. 25 Nov. 1798

    iv OREN BRADFORD, b. 11 May 1800

    v JESSE BRADFORD, b. 15 April 1802

    vi ELI BRADFORD, b. 30 Dec. 1805

    vii HARLOW BRADFORD, b. 15 Dec. 1806

    viii HAIL BRADFORD, b. 15 July 1808

    ix LOUISANNA BRADFORD, b. 8 June 1810

    x LEWIS BRADFORD, b. 23 July 1812

References: *Bradford Desc* p. 150. Letter from Springfield VT town clerk (m.). *VR Norton* p. 103(b. Tryphena). Bible rec. with GS #57618. Springfield VT LR 2:155(buying pew), 316(Joel Bradford *et al.*); 3:253(selling pew). Springfield VT VR cards(m.).

531. EPHRAIM⁵ BRADFORD (*Simeon⁴, Ephraim³, William²⁻¹*), b. Springfield, Vt., ca. 1785; d. prob. Plainfield, Vt., 10 Nov. 1855.

He m. Barnard, Vt., 24 March 1809 **JANE JACQUES**, b. Plainfield, Vt., ca. 1790; d. there 16 March 1860. The 1860 mortality schedule shows that Jane Bradford, widow, d. Plainfield in March aged 70.

Ephraim Bradford aged 55 [*sic*], Jane Bradford aged 30 [*sic*], and John M. Bradford aged 36 are listed in Plainfield in the 1850 census.

Children of Ephraim and Jane (Jacques) Bradford:*

    i ORENDA⁶ S. BRADFORD, b. 9 Feb. 1810; d. 1817

    ii SHIPLEY M. BRADFORD, b. 19 Dec. 1811

    iii ADALIZA M. BRADFORD, b. 19 Feb. 1814

    iv JOHN BRADFORD, b. 15 Dec. 1815

    v MILTON BRADFORD, b. 31 Aug. 1818

* Springfield VT VR cards list a fourth child as Milton John Bradford, b. 31 Aug. 1818 and no 5th child. The 1850 census seems to support only one child John Milton Bradford, but b. Dec. 1815.

References: *Bradford Desc* p. 151.   Springfield VT VR cards(b. ch.).   *NSDAR* 18:312(mortality schedule).   1850 VT census p. 76 Plainfield. Barnard VT Vital Records 1774-1897, 1:83(m.).

532. SARAH[5] BRADFORD (*Wait[4], Ephraim[3], William[2-1]*), b. Pembroke 8 June 1769; d. 25 Oct. 1857. Both are buried in Bonney Cemetery, Turner, Me.

She m. Turner, Me., 26 Oct. 1794 **SNOW KEENE**, b. Pembroke 27 Jan. 1770; d. Hebron, Me., 23 Feb. 1849; son of Snow and Rebecca (Burbank) Keene.

In the 1850 census for Hebron, Sarah Keen was aged 84 and living with Asa Keen and his family.

Children of Snow and Sarah (Bradford) Keene, b. Hebron, Me.:

 i BETSEY KEENE[6], b. 29 Sept. 1798

 ii SNOW KEENE, b. 26 Feb. 1801

 iii MOSES KEENE, b. 7 Oct. 1803

 iv ALVIN KEENE, b. 13 Oct. 1807

 v ASA KEENE, b. 17 July 1812

 vi DEBORAH KEENE

References: *Bradford Desc* p. 151. *VR Pembroke* p. 132(b. Snow). *Hebron ME VR* p. 38(b. all ch. exc. Alvin; d. Snow). Turner ME TR(m.). GS#71243(g.s. photos-b. & d. Snow and Sarah). *Hist Turner ME* p. 165(m.). 1850 census p. 42 in Hebron. MOCA, Series 1, p. 227.

533. SIMEON[5] BRADFORD (*Wait[4], Ephraim[3], William[2-1]*), b. Kingston ca. 1770.

He m. Turner, Me., 11 May 1800 **MARTHA TRUE**, b. 1777; d. Wayne, Me., 21 May 1831; daughter of Benjamin and Rhoda (Merrill) True.

On 17 May 1791 Oliver Otis of Littleborough, Me., yeoman, sold to Simeon Bradford of Turner, Me., carpenter, 125 acres in Turner.

On 28 April 1806 Simeon Bradford of Turner, carpenter, sold to Ephraim Bradford of Turner, yeoman, 70 acres, half of lot #261. On 20 Feb. 1810 Simeon Bradford of Turner, housewright, sold to Jesse Bradford of Turner,

Gentleman, his right in the southeast quarter of lot #51, the north half of lot #261, and the south quarter of lot #262.

The True Family calls him of Farmersville, N.Y.

Children of Simeon and Martha (True) Bradford:

    i WELTHEA⁶ BRADFORD, b. Turner, Me., 4 Nov. 1803

    ii LYDIA BRADFORD

    iii EPHRAIM BRADFORD

    iv JAMES BRADFORD

    v ALMIRA BRADFORD

    vi CHARLES BRADFORD, b. 30 April 1811

    vii JABEZ BRADFORD, b. 1813 (37 in 1850 census)

    viii LAVERNA BRADFORD

    ix JANE BRADFORD

    x TRUE BRADFORD

References: *Bradford Desc* p. 152. *True Fam* p. 66. Oxford Co. ME LR 5:128; 6:56(Simeon Bradford). (Lydia, Laverna, and Jane are not in Aspinwall.)

534. DEBORAH⁵ BRADFORD (*Wait⁴, Ephraim³, William²⁻¹*), b. Kingston ca. 1777; d. Turner, Me., 10 Nov. 1848, widow.

She m. Turner, Me., 24 March 1808 **WILLIAM PUTMAN** of Topsham, Me.; d. Turner, Me., 12 Aug. 1831.

On 1 Nov. 1807 Nathaniel Robinson of Turner, yeoman, sold to William Putman of Topsham, yeoman, 100 acres, the westerly part of lot #283.

Child of William and Deborah (Bradford) Putman:

    i HANNAH PUTMAN⁶

References: *Bradford Desc* p. 152. Turner ME TR 1:300(m.). ME VR cards(d. Deborah, William). Oxford Co. ME LR 3:233(Nathaniel Robinson).

535. EPHRAIM⁵ BRADFORD (*Wait⁴, Ephraim³, William²⁻¹*), b. Kingston ca. 1783 or 14 Jan. 1784; d. Turner, Me., 11 Feb. 1851 aged 67y 27d.

He m. Turner, Me., 7 June 1807 **LOUISA DELANO**, b. 30 Nov. 1779; d. Turner, Me., 22 Nov. 1860 aged 80y 11m 22d; daughter of Ebenezer and Lydia (Wormall) Delano.

On 26 March 1841 Ephraim Bradford of Turner, yeoman, sold to Philamon A. Bradford of Turner, 35 acres bounded by the farm Ephraim was living on.

In the 1850 census for Turner, Ephraim Bradford aged 66 and Louisa Bradford aged 70 are listed in the household of Philemon Bradford. In the 1860 census for Turner, Alfred Bradford has a Louisa Bradford age 75 in his household.

Children of Ephraim and Louisa (Delano) Bradford:

    i   LUCIA[6] BRADFORD, b. ca. 1808

    ii LOIS BRADFORD, b. 14 June 1808 [not in Aspinwall]

    iii MARIA GREELY BRADFORD, b. 19 July 1811

    iv SETH BRADFORD, b. 13 Jan. 1815

    v PHILEMON BRADFORD, b. 10 Dec. 1816

References: *Bradford Desc* p. 152. ME VR cards(d. Ephraim, Louisa). Turner ME TR 1:300(m.), 366(b. Maria). 1850 census Turner p. 10. 1860 census Turner p. 91. Oxford Co. ME LR 64:389(Ephraim Bradford).

536.   NATHANIEL[5] BRADFORD (*Nathaniel[4], David[3], William[2-1]*), b. Plymouth 26 July 1748, bp. 31 July 1748; d. there 24 Nov. 1837 in 90th yr.

He m. Plymouth 28 May 1775 **REBECCA HOLMES**, b. Plymouth 5 July 1753; d. there 15 June 1838 in 85th yr.; daughter of Ichabod and Rebecca (Gillis) Holmes.

Nathaniel Bradford served in the Revolutionary War as a private in Capt. Jesse Harlow's company with service from 29 Jan. 1776 to 18 Nov. 1776. He applied for a pension on 4 Dec. 1832 at age 84.

Nath[l] Bradford was head of a household consisting of 1 man, 4 boys, and 3 females in Plymouth in the 1790 census.

On 12 April 1792 Nathaniel Bradford of Plymouth, cordwainer, and Lemuel Bradford of Plymouth, housewright, sold meadow land.

On 5 Nov. 1805 Nathaniel Bradford of Plymouth, mariner, sold to Joseph Bradford of Plymouth, Gentleman, a garden spot on Mill Street bounded on land owned by Lemuel Bradford. On 16 July 1806 Nathaniel appointed Joseph Bradford of Plymouth, hatter, his agent to sell a houselot in Plymouth on South Street adjoining the land of brother Lemuel Bradford.

Children of Nathaniel and Rebecca (Holmes) Bradford, b. Plymouth:

    i NATHANIEL[6] BRADFORD, b. 26 Nov. 1775

ii JOSEPH BRADFORD, b. 18 March 1778

iii JOHN BRADFORD, b. 14 July 1780; d. 7 Dec. 1863; unm.

iv SARAH BRADFORD, b. 8 Jan. 1783; d. 19 April 1882; unm.

v EPHRAIM BRADFORD, b. 28 June 1785

vi REBECCA BRADFORD, b. 15 Feb. 1788

vii BENJAMIN WILLIS BRADFORD, b. 15 Jan. 1791

viii ELIZABETH BRADFORD, b. 25 Dec. 1794; d. Oct. 1800 ae 6y (a child of Nathaniel Bradford d. 9 Nov. 1800 in Church recs.)

References: *MD* 12:85(b. Rebecca). *NGSQ* 74:217. *Plymouth Ch Recs* 1:444(bp. Nathaniel); 2:498(m.), 623(d. child); 681(d. Nathaniel), 682(d. Rebecca). *(Plymouth) Burial Hill* p. 191(d. Nathaniel, wife Rebecca, Elizabeth). *Bradford Desc* p. 152. *Plymouth VR* pp. 51(b. Rebecca), 237(b. 1st 7 ch.), 361(m.). Plymouth Co. LR 72:220; 102:233; 106:226(Nathaniel Bradford). *Pension Abstracts* 1:357. *MSSR* 2:405.

537. LEMUEL⁵ BRADFORD (*Nathaniel⁴, David³, William²⁻¹*), b. Plymouth 25 Feb. 1751, bp. 24 Feb. 1751 [*sic*]; d. there 12 May 1828 aged 77 yrs.

He m. (1) Plymouth 23 March 1775 **MARY SAMPSON**, b. Plymouth 4 June 1755; d. there 21 Dec. 1790 in 36th yr.; daughter of Ebenezer and Hannah (Harlow) Sampson, a descendant of Pilgrims **Henry Sampson** and **Richard Warren**.

He m. (2) Plymouth 28 Aug. 1791 **LYDIA HOLMES**, b. ca. 1761; d. Plymouth 6 June 1838 aged 77 yrs.; daughter of Cornelius and Lydia (Drew) Holmes.

Lemuel Bradford served as a private in the Revolutionary War in Capt. Jesse Harlow's company which marched on the alarm of 19 April 1775.

In several terms of the court of General Sessions, Lemuel Bradford was paid for working on the courthouse and jail: July 1786 Lemuel was one of the "persons paid for construction of goal and courthouse"; Nov. 1787 paid for "mending the Court House Doors and Clabbords, making Benches, Raising a Sill, and mending the Floor"; Jan. 1789 paid for "Work done on the Goal and Goal-House, and for Boards and Nails"; April 1789 paid for "work done by him and his apprentice on the court house"; Nov. 1792 paid for "Laying a Floor and sealing one Room in the Goal, and for making Cabbins in said Goal"; April 1797 paid for "fixing a Room in the Goal for an House of Correction"; April 1798 paid for "work done on the Goal, viz, Cutting out a Door, making and casing it, and making Stairs and porch"; and Aug. 1803 paid for "work done on the Court House."

Lemuel Bradford was head of a household of 2 men, 3 boys, and 4 females in Plymouth in the 1790 census.

On 12 April 1792 Nathaniel Bradford of Plymouth, cordwainer, and Lemuel Bradford of Plymouth, housewright, sold meadow land.

On 29 Jan. 1799 the Plymouth church chose a committee to "talk with our Brethren *John Carver & Lemuel Bradford,* respecting their *playing at Cards,* in a public place, before several, who were not of the Chh, (& who express^d their surprize at such Conduct in Members of the Church)." On 12 Feb. it was reported "with respect to our Brother *Lemuel Bradford* ...that having conversed with him, he acknowledged the Fact charged against him – that he did not, at the time of it, reflect so much upon it or think it so great an Evil – that he was drawn in to it – & was ignorant of the explicit Vote of this Chh against playing Cards, (having lived out of town for some years) but, that had he known what he now does, he sho^d not have comply^d – he own'd he did it, thro the Temptation of Satan, & his own wicked heart, & is sorry." The church voted to "forgive & restore to their christian Charity, our brother *Lem^l Bradford.*"

On 24 May 1821 Lemuel Bradford of Plymouth, housewright, mortgaged to his son David Bradford of Plymouth, part of the dwelling house "I now live in" on Summer Street; Lemuel's wife Lydia released her dower rights.

Stephen Lucas and David Holmes made a deposition in front of the Registrar of Deeds that on 10 Feb. 1830 they "were present and within the dwelling house now occupied by David Bradford of said Plymouth, Gentleman, and formerly the residence of his late father Lemeul Bradford deceased, and that ... David Bradford was then and their present holding in his hands a deed of Mortgage of the premises upon which we were then standing from ... Lemuel Bradford deceased to the said David Bradford dated" 24 May 1821. Duly notified William H. Bradford, Lydia Bradford, John Tribbel and Mary Tribbel, Eleanor Faunce, and Andrew Mechic and Mehitable Mechic "being all the persons to us known as interested in the property."

On 11 Feb. 1830 David Bradford of Plymouth, gentleman, sold to William H. Bradford of Wareham, nailor, a undivided half part of land with a dwelling house that Lemuel Bradford (now deceased) had mortgaged to David in 1821; David's wife Betsey released her dower rights.

No Plymouth Co. probate records have been found for Lemuel or Mary Bradford.

Children of Lemuel and Mary (Sampson) Bradford, b. Plymouth:

    i LEMUEL^6 BRADFORD, b. 1 Dec. 1775; killed in battle 17 Sept. 1814

    ii THOMAS BRADFORD, b. 25 Feb. 1778

    iii MARY BRADFORD, b. 19 Dec. 1780

    iv GEORGE BRADFORD, b. 19 Sept. 1783

    v ELEANOR BRADFORD, b. 25 Aug. 1785

Children of Lemual and Lydia (Holmes) Bradford, b. Plymouth:

    vi CORNELIUS [HOLMES, per Aspinwall] BRADFORD, b. 28 March 1793; d. New Orleans 16 Aug. 1824-as

    vii LYDIA BRADFORD, b. 25 Jan. 1795; d. Plymouth 14 April 1863 ae 68y 2m 18d of typhoid fever.

    viii DAVID BRADFORD, b. 20 April 1796

    ix WILLIAM HOLMES BRADFORD, b. 12 Feb. 1798

    x LEWIS BRADFORD, b. 1 April 1801; d. 13 April 1802

    xi LEWIS BRADFORD, b. 6 Dec. 1802

References: *Plymouth Ch Recs* 1:447(bp. Lemuel); 2:498(1st m.); 2:505(2nd m.) 535-7(playing cards), 557, 625(d. Lewis), 682(d. Lydia). *(Plymouth) Burial Hill* pp. 65(d. Mary), 159(d. Lemuel, Lydia). *Bradford Desc* pp. 152-3. *TAG* 51:54-6. *Plymouth VR* pp. 123(b. Mary), 361(1st m.), 368(2nd m.), 390(b. ch.; d. Lemuel). Plymouth Co. LR 72:220(Nathaniel Bradford); 144:212(Lemuel Bradford); 166:32(David Bradford); 167:98(deposition); 168:198(David Bradford). MAVR 166:311(d. dau. Lydia). *Plymouth Co Ct Recs* Vol. 4. *MSSR* 2:405.

538. ELKANAH CUSHMAN⁵ (*Lydia⁴ Bradford, David³, William²⁻¹*), b. Plymouth 13 Nov. 1741.

He m. **MARY LOTHROP**, b. Plymouth 1 Oct. 1739; daughter of Ansel and Mary (Thomas) Lothrop.

On 13 Aug. 1743 Lazarus LeBaron, physician, and his wife Lydia as guardians to Elkanah Cushman, only son and heir of Elkanah Cushman late of Plymouth deceased, and James Hovey, administrator of the estate of James Cushman, divided land in Kingston held in common. On 20 Aug. 1767 Elkanah Cushman of Plymouth, goldsmith and jeweler, sold to Dr. Lazarus LeBaron 3 acres of upland "Said Land ... set off to me as my Father's Right in the Division betwixt him and my Uncle James Cushman."

On 19 June 1764 Elkanah Cushman of New Providence "in the Bahama Islands," goldsmith, represented by Benjamin Goodwin of Boston, merchant, to whom Elkanah gave his power of attorney on 21 Nov. 1763, sold to William Seva of Kingston, Esqr., 1 ½ acres in Kingston.

At a Plymouth town meeting 8 March 1770, Elkanah Cushman was chosen one of the hogreeves and on 8 March 1773 a surveyor of highways.

At the April 1773 term of the Court of Common Pleas, "Elkanah Cushman of Plymouth in the county of Plymouth jeweller was appointed by the justices of this court to be Cryer of our said Inferior Court of Common Pleas."

Elkanah Cushman was a Loyalist and in 1776 embarked for Halifax, N.S., with the British Army.

Child of Elkahah and Mary (Lothrop) Cushman:

    i ELKANAH CUSHMAN[6], b. 1 June 1769

Note:: *Lo-Lathrop Gen* p. 97 says Mary Lothrop d. single about 1792.

References: *Bradford Desc* p. 153. *MD* 15:114(b. Mary). *Plymouth VR* p. 121(b. Mary). Plymouth Co. LR 49:116; 53:229(Elkanah Cushman). *Plymouth Co Ct Recs* 9:3. *Plymouth Town Recs* p. 220, 267.

539. ISAAC LEBARON[5] (*Lydia[4] Bradford, David[3], William[2-1]*), b. Plymouth 25 Jan. 1743/4; d. there 23 Dec. 1819.

He m. Plymouth 1 Dec. 1774 **MARTHA HOWLAND**, b. Plymouth 22 Dec. 1739; d. there [?26] June 1825; daughter of Consider and Ruth (Bryant) Howland, a descendant of Pilgrim **John Howland**.

In December 1773 he was called "late of Boston and now of Plymouth" and was a cordwainer.

At a Plymouth town meeting 23 June 1777, the following complaint was made against Isaac Lebarron:

> When Speaking of the Cruize he (Mr Coye) had been in the armed Sloop America Calld it Pirateing, Mr Thomas Southth Howland says that he has heard Mr Joshua Thomas and many others of their family lament Isaac Lebarrons being a Tory & that they Count not Change his principalls & Prevent his making Such bad Speaches Against America. Mr Abraham Hammet Says that he had Several time heard Isaac Lebarron blame all the measures taken by the Country in the Common Cause. Then Inasmuch as the Committee reported Several things against Isaac Lebarron … After hearing what Each had to say in his defence, The Vote was Seperately Calld to know if their names Should be put upon the list. It Passed in the Negative respecting them all.

On 30 March 1778 Isaac was chosen to be on a committee "for Supplyg the Grammer School with a Suteable Schoolmaster." On 5 March 1781 he was chosen a warden.

Isaac LeBaron's household in Plymouth in 1790 consisted of 1 man, 2 boys under 16, and 4 females.

Children of Isaac and Martha (Howland) Lebaron, b. Plymouth:

    i ISAAC LEBARON[6], b. 11 March 1777; bp. 23 March 1777

    ii MARTHA HOWLAND LEBARON, b. 14 June 1778; bp. 21 June 1778

    iii FRANCIS LEBARON, b. 27 April 1781; bp. 6 May 1781; d. 20 June 1829; unm.

    iv MARY HOWLAND LEBARON, b. 14 May 1786; bp. 21 May 1786

References: *MD* 13:175(b. Martha). *Bradford Desc* p. 153. *(Plymouth) Burial Hill* p. 135(d. Isaac, Martha). *Plymouth VR* pp. 80(b. Martha), 353(m.). *Plymouth Ch Recs* pp. 462-4, 467(bp's ch.). *LeBaron Gen* pp. 30-1. *Plymouth Town Recs* 3:332-3, 341, 417.

540. ELIZABETH LEBARON[5] (*Lydia*[4] *Bradford, David*[3], *William*[2-1]), b. Plymouth 21 Dec. 1745; d. 28 Sept. 1829 in her 84th yr.

She m. Plymouth 13 May 1762 **AMMI RUHAMAH ROBBINS**, b. Branford, Conn., 25 Sept. 1740; d. Norfolk, Conn., 31 Oct. 1813 in his 74th yr.; son of Philemon and Hannah (Foote) Robbins.

Ammi Robbins began his college at Princeton because his father was a good friend of Pres. Burr, but when Burr died he transferred to Yale. He graduated from Yale in 1760. He was settled over the church in Norfolk, Conn., in 1761 and remained pastor until his death. He served as a chaplain in the Revolutionary War; took several missionary trips to northern Vermont and New York between 1783 and 1796; and served as a trustee for Williams College from 1794 to 1810. *Yale Grads* says: "In his special work as a Christian minister he had gratifying success, the church in Norfolk growing under his care to be one of the largest and most prosperous in the State, and during his lifetime no other religious denomination obtained a foothold in the town."

On 29 Jan. 1772, at the ordination of Mr. Lemuel LeBaron at the Rochester church, Rev. Mr. Robbins of Norfolk made the concluding prayer at this service for his wife's sister.

Children of Ammi R. and Elizabeth (LeBaron) Robbins, b. Norfolk, Conn.:

    i PHILEMON ROBBINS[6], b. 13 May 1763; d. 20 March 1763

    ii PHILEMON ROBBINS, b. 28 Feb. 1764; d. 26 Sept. 1766

    iii ELIZABETH ROBBINS, b. 5 Jan. 1766; d. 9 Jan. 1766

    iv MARY [MARA in VRs] ROBBINS, b. 8 Jan. 1767; d. 9 Jan. 1767

    v AMMI RUHAMAH ROBBINS, b. 3 Jan. 1768

vi   ELIZABETH ROBBINS, b. 8 Jan. 1770

vii   NATHANIEL ROBBINS, b. 18 June 1772

viii   FRANCIS LEBARON ROBBINS, b. 9 March 1775; d. 3 Sept. 1777

ix   THOMAS ROBBINS, b. 11 Aug. 1777; d. 13 Sept. 1856; unm.

x   SARAH ROBBINS, b. 22 Aug. 1779

xi   JAMES ROBBINS, b. 19 April 1782

xii   SAMUEL ROBBINS, b. 29 Aug. 1784 [not in Barbour VRs]

xiii   FRANCIS ROBBINS, b. 30 Dec. 1787

References: *Bradford Desc* pp. 153-4. *MD* 26:41(int.). Branford CT VR 3:39(b. Ammi Ruhanah). Norfolk CT VR TM 1(b. & d. 1st Philemon), TM 12(b. & d. 2nd Philemon), TM 13(b. & d. Elizabeth), TM 16(b. Ammi R.), TM 19(b Elizabeth, Nathaniel); 1:1(b. Francis, Thomas), 5(b. Sarah, James; d. Francis). *Plymouth VR* p. 355(m.). *LeBaron Gen* pp. 31-2. *Plymouth Ch Recs* 1:340(ordination Lemuel). *Yale Grads* 2:670.

541.   LEMUEL LeBARON⁵   (*Lydia⁴ Bradford, David³, William²⁻¹*), b. Plymouth 1 Sept. 1747; d. Mattapoisett 26 Nov. 1836 aged 92.

He m. Rochester 24 Nov. 1774 (int. 14 Nov. 1774) **ELIZABETH ALLEN**, b. Chilmark 20 April 1752; d. Rochester 9 Nov. 1830 aged 78; daughter of John and Ann (Mayhew) Allen.

Lemuel LeBaron graduated from Yale in 1768. He settled in Rochester as pastor of the Mattapoisett parish in 1772 and served until his death. He served as a chaplain in the Revolutionary War. *Yale Grads* says "All accounts of him agree that he was a man of eminent piety, marked by habitual cheerfulness and great humility; a ripened saint, and a peacemaker among his people. His preaching, like his religion, was above all practical; and although himself strictly orthodox, he was a man of great liberality of feeling."

On 29 Jan. 1772 Lemuel was ordained in Rochester. The Plymouth church sent the pastor and delegates, including Lemuel's father Lazarus LeBaron, to this service. The concluding prayer at the service was given by Rev. Mr. Robbins of Norfolk, Conn., his brother-in-law.

Lemuel LeBaron served as a Chaplain in Capt. Nathaniel Hammond's company which marched 20 April 1775 to the alarm of 19 April 1775.

Lemuel LeBaron's household in Rochester in 1790 consisted of 2 men over 16, 5 boys, and 3 females.

On 29 Dec. 1837 John A. Lebaron of Rochester, Gentleman, for love and affection gave to his son James Lebaron of Rochester, yeoman, 38 acres which his father Lemuel Lebaron had bought of Amittai Barlow.

Children of Lemuel and Elizabeth (Allen) LeBaron, b. Rochester:

    i   LEMUEL LeBARON[6], b. 1 Aug. 1775 (bp. 7 Sept.); d. 17 Sept. 1775

   ii ANN LeBARON, bp. Dec. 1777

  iii ANN LeBARON, b. 9 Jan. 1778; d. 27 May 1779 ae 16m 3d

   vi LEMUEL LeBARON, b. 10 Jan. 1780

    v JOHN ALLEN LeBARON, b. 27 April 1782

   vi ELIZABETH LeBARON, b. 23 March 1784; d. 2 Jan. 1815 ae 30; unm.

  vii WILLIAM LeBARON, b. 27 April 1786

 viii LAZARUS LeBARON, bp. 1788

   xi LAZARUS LeBARON, b. 27 July 1789

    x SALLY AULDEN LeBARON, b. 11 Sept. 1791

  xii JAMES LeBARON, b. 19 Oct. 1794; d. 12 Dec. 1801 ae 7

References: *VR Chilmark* p. 10(b. Ann). *VR Rochester* 1:200-1(b. ch.); 2:200(int.), 405(d. Lemuel, Elizabeth, d. ch.). *Bradford Desc* p. 154. *LeBaron Gen* p. 32. Plymouth Co. LR 190:99(John A. LeBaron). *Plymouth Ch Recs* 1:340(Lemuel's ordination). *Yale Grads* 3:285. *MSSR* 4:617(Lemuel LeBaron).

542. WILLIAM LeBARON[5] (*Lydia[4] Bradford, David[3], William[2-1]*), b. Plymouth 8 Aug. 1751; d. Fairhaven 23 Oct. 1816 aged 65 yrs; he and his wife are buried in Burial Hill.

He m. Plymouth 15 Dec. 1774 **SARAH CHURCHILL,** b. Plymouth 11 June 1750; d. there 29 Oct. 1796 aged 46 yrs.; daughter of John and Sarah (Cole) Churchill.

On 9 April 1780 Sarah, wife of William LeBaron, joined the Plymouth church.

At the April 1783 term of the Plymouth Court of Common Pleas, Abraham Hammett and William LeBaron of Plymouth, traders, sued James Warren Esq. of Milton and John Deshon Esq. of New London, Conn., for a broken covenant. On 10 June 1778 Abraham and William agreed with James and John, as the Continental Navy Board for the Eastern Department, to:

> ... grant and let to freight the Schooner named the *Dispatch,* furniture and Appurtenances whatsoever to her belonging ... for a voyage to be made in her from the Port of Boston to any Port in the Kingdom of France and back again ... [and] the said Navy Board ... did further Covenant and agree ... that they would pay or cause to be paid to the said Abraham and William for the hire of the said Schooner ... [and] in case the said Schooner should be lost or taken on her return

from said Voyage that then they would pay ... the rate ... to the Time of her being lost or taken ... yet the said James Warren and John Deshon have not kept, but wholly broken their Covenant and Agreements aforesaid.

James and John pleaded that in their capacity as part of the Navy Board they had "never been possessed of any Monies belonging to the said United State since any became due in Consequence of the said Charter." The court ruled that the defendants' plea was good since it had "not been by reason of any neglect of them."

At the April 1784 term of the Court of Common Pleas, William Weston, Lewis Weston, John Cotton III, Joseph Jennings all of Plymouth, traders, sued Samuel Bartlett and Isaiah Doane both of Boston, merchants, and William LeBaron of Plymouth, hatmaker. On 11 Aug. 1779 the plantiffs "who were owners of the schooner *Lively*" agreed with the defendants to "let one half of said schooner ... to them for a voyage from said Plymouth to the West Indies and back again." The defendants agreed to pay a rate per tonnage for the use of the schooner and to insure the schooner "against the seas, Enimey and all danger that may happen to her during said voyage." On 11 Sept. 1779 the schooner was "on the high seas to wit in said Plimouth taken by the enemy and thereby to them lost." The parties agreed to refer the suit to referees who reported that plantiffs should recover.

At a Plymouth town meeting 15 March 1779, William Lebarron was chosen a juror; 19 March 1781 and 4 March 1782 a selectman; and 11 March 1782 a warden.

William Lebaron of Plymouth, retailer, was granted a license to sell liquor in 1784, 1784, and 1786.

Wm. LeBaron was head of a household consisting of 1 man and 6 females in Plymouth in the 1790 census.

The court records show that William was a Justice of the Peace in the 1790s and early 1800s.

On 2 Nov. 1806 William LeBaron joined the Plymouth church. On 16 July 1813 he was dismissed from the Plymouth church to the Fairhaven church.

On 30 Sept. 1819 Thomas Jackson of Plymouth, yeoman, and his wife Sarah, William LeBaron, Eliza LeBaron of Rochester, Wyatt Hammond of Rochester and his wife Mary, Ansell Gibbs of Fairhaven and his wife Lucy, and Francis LeBaron Robbins of Enfield, Conn., and his wife Priscilla, sold to William Davis Esq. of Plymouth England meadow land in Plymouth that had descended to them from their mother Sarah LeBaron.

Children of William and Sarah (Churchill) LeBaron, b. Plymouth; Sarah, Mary, and Lucy, bp. 23 April 1780:

 i WILLIAM LEBARON[6], b. 9 Nov. 1775; d. 17 Nov. 1775

 ii SARAH LEBARON, b. 16 Dec. 1776

 iii MARY LEBARON (twin), b. 27 Aug. 1778

 iv LUCY LEBARON (twin), b. 27 Aug. 1778

 v PRISCILLA LEBARON, b. 7 March 1781, bp. 11 March 1781

 vi ELIZABETH LEBARON, b. -- May 1785, bp. 22 May 1785; d. 21 Oct. 1788

Note: The *LeBaron Gen* adds a son William, b. 6 May 1787, d. 21 Oct. 1788; it also has Elizabeth marrying and dying long after 1788.

References: *(Plymouth) Burial Hill* p. 76(d. Sarah), 127(d. William). *Plymouth VR* pp. 141(b.&d. Sarah), 198(b. & d. ch.), 361(m.). *LeBaron Gen* pp. 32-3. Plymouth Co. LR 138:158(Thomas Jackson *et al.*). *Plymouth Ch Recs* 1:405(d. son William), 416(d. Elizabeth), 426(d. Sarah), 463(bp. Sarah, Mary, Lucy), 464(bp. Priscilla), 467(bp. Elizabeth); 2:473(Sarah joined), 498(m.), 637(William joined), 655(William dis.). *Plymouth Co Ct Recs* 9:150(Abraham Hammett *et al.*). *Plymouth Town Recs* 3:367, 419, 439, 441

543. PRISCILLA LEBARON[5] (*Lydia⁴ Bradford, David³, William²⁻¹*), b. Plymouth 3 Aug. 1753; d. there 14 Aug. 1803 aged 50 yrs.

She m. Plymouth 14 Dec. 1774 **ABRAHAM HAMMATT**, b. Plymouth 13 Feb. 1750; d. there 12 (13 in church recs) Oct. 1797 aged 47; son of Abraham and Lucy (Howland) Hammatt, a descendant of Pilgrim **John Howland**. He is called "Capt." in church records.

At a Plymouth town meeting 23 June 1777, a complaint was made against Isaac Lebarron for "...being a Tory & that they Count not Change his principalls & Prevent his making Such bad Speaches Against America. Mr Abraham Hammet Says that he had Several time heard Isaac Lebarron blame all the measures taken by the Country in the Common Cause."

At a Plymouth town meeting 26 June 1780, Abraham Hammett was chosen as a collector. In 1781 he was on the ballot for election as a state senator. On 11 March 1782 Capt. Abraham Hammit was chosen a warden.

At the April 1783 term of the Plymouth Court of Common Pleas, Abraham Hammett and William LeBaron of Plymouth, traders, sued James Warren Esq. of Milton and John Deshon Esq. of New London, Conn., for a broken covenant. On 10 June 1778 Abraham and William agreed with James and John, as the Continental Navy Board for the Eastern Department, to

... grant and let to freight the Schooner named the *Dispatch,* furniture and Appurtenances whatsoever to her belonging ... for a voyage to be made in her from the Port of Boston to any Port in the Kingdom of France and back again ... [and] the said Navy Board ... did further Covenant and agree ... that they would pay or cause to be paid to the said Abraham and William for the hire of the said Schooner ... [and] in case the said Schooner should be lost or taken on her return from said Voyage that then they would pay ... the rate ... to the Time of her being lost or taken ... yet the said James Warren and John Deshon have not kept, but wholly broken their Covenant and Agreements aforesaid.

James and John pleaded that in their capacity as part of the Navy Board they had "never been possessed of any Monies belonging to the said United State since any became due in Consequence of the said Charter." The court ruled that the defendants' plea was good since it had "not been by reason of any neglect of them."

Ab^m Hammatt's household in 1790 consisted of 2 men over 16, 3 boys, and 8 females in Plymouth.

On 25 Aug. 1800 Priscilla Hammatt of Plymouth, administratrix to the estate of Abraham Hammatt, Gentleman, deceased, being impowered to sell land to pay debts, sold to William Hammatt of Plymouth, ropemaker, a ropewalk with all tools and implements.

On 27 Sept. 1803 "Wid. Priscilla Hammat made a profession & owned the Covenant in her own house considering herself on her death bed as it proved to be." In Nov. 1803 "Priscilla Hammat daughter of the deceased admitted to the Chh. & baptized." On 28 Sept. 1803 Elizabeth, Consider Howland, and George Hammat, children of the widow Priscilla Hammat, were "baptized at her own house on account of the sickness of the mother."

Children of Abraham and Priscilla (LeBaron) Hammatt:

    i   PRISCILLA HAMMATT^6, b. 14 July 1776

   ii WILLIAM HAMMATT, b. 15 May 1778

  iii SAMUEL A. HAMMATT, b. 4 Feb. 1780; d. 6 Feb. 1780 (a child of Abraham Hammatt's d. 18 Feb. 1780 in church recs.)

  iv ABRAHAM HAMMATT, b. 26 March 1781

   v CONSIDER HOWLAND HAMMATT, b. 12 April 1782; d. 14 (7 per Aspinwall) April 1783 (a child of Abraham Hammatt d. 26 Feb. 1783 in church recs)

  vi SOPHIA HAMMATT, b. 4 June 1784; d. 1 Dec. 1797 ae 13

 vii LUCIA HAMMATT, b. 20 Aug. 1786

viii ELIZABETH HAMMATT, b. 10 Jan. 1789

ix CHARLES HOWLAND HAMMATT, b. 7 April 1791; d. 8 Oct. 1837; unm.

x GEORGE HAMMATT, b. 29 Jan. 1793

xi HENRY HAMMATT, b. 3 March 1795; d. 23 March 1795

References: *MD* 17:124(int.); 27:176(m.). *(Plymouth) Burial Hill* pp. 78(d. Abraham, Priscilla), 100(d. Priscilla). *Bradford Desc* p. 155. *Plymouth VR* p. 361(m.). *LeBaron Gen* p. 33. Plymouth Co. LR 89:28(Priscilla Hammatt). *Plymouth Ch Recs* 1:409, 412(d. child) 427(d. Abraham, Sophia); 2:498(m.), 606(bp. Elizabeth, Consider, George), 636(profession Priscilla, dau. admitted). *Plymouth Co Ct Recs* 9:150(Abraham Hammett *et al.*). *Plymouth Town Recs* 3:332, 397, 421, 441.

544. JONATHAN⁵ BRADFORD (*Nathan⁴, David³, William²⁻¹*), b. Kingston 15 May 1752; d. 18 Sept. 1805.

He m. 10 May 1789 **MARY SOUTHWORTH**, b. No. Yarmouth, Me., 13 April 1763; d. 25 Feb. 1822; daughter of John and Joanna (Mitchell) Southworth.

Jonathan Bradford served as a private in the Revolutionary War in Capt. Noah Nichol's company in Col. Jeduthan Baldwin's regiment in Gen. Knox's brigade of Artillery artificers. He served from 15 March 1777 to 15 March 1780.

On 7 Jan. 1797 Jonathan Bradford of Poland, Me., housewright, sold to his brother David Bradford of Kingston one-half of the real estate of his father Nathan Bradford; his wife Mary also signed the deed.

On 3 April 1837 Asenath Bradford of Minot, widow of David Bradford late of Minot, sold to Elisha Hall a "parcel of land situate in said Minot containing about Eighty acres be the same more or less that part of the Estate of Jonathan Bradford of said Minot deceased which was set of[f] to and occupied by Mary Bradford widow of said Jonathan as her dower and which said Mary & the heirs of said Jonathan agreed should be the Estate of the said late David Bradford ... the same Estate devised by said David Bradford to said Asenath and his three children with power for said Asenath to dispose of the same while she remained his widow."

Children of Jonathan and Mary (Southworth) Bradford, first 5 b. Poland, Me., next 3 b. Minot, Me.:

i ELIZABETH⁶ BRADFORD, b. 25 Feb. 1790

ii DAVID BRADFORD, b. 25 Jan. 1792

   iii MARY BRADFORD, b. 12 March 1794

   iv JOANNA BRADFORD, b. 9 Aug. 1796

   v JONATHAN BRADFORD, b. 26 July 1798

   vi LUCY BRADFORD, b. 2 Dec. 1800; d. unm.

   vii WILLIAM BRADFORD, b. 6 Jan. 1803

   viii JOHN BRADFORD, b. 2 April 1805; d. 25 May 1825; unm.

References: *No Yarmouth ME VR* p. 96(b. Mary). *Bradford Desc* p. 155. Plymouth Co. LR 81:182(Jonathan Bradford). *NEHGR* 98:149(b. first 4 ch.). Cumberland Co. ME LR 155:480(Asenath Bradford). *MSSR* 2:404. "Poland, Maine, Vital Records, 1780-1850" p. 110(b. 1st 5 ch.).

545. DAVID⁵ BRADFORD (*Nathan⁴, David³, William²⁻¹*), b. Kingston 27 March 1757; d. there 29 Feb. 1840 aged 83y.

He m. Duxbury 16 Feb. 1779 **BETSY** [a duplicate record says **LUCY**] **(ROBINSON) THOMAS**, b. Duxbury 16 Sept. 1754; d. Kingston 7 June 1825 aged 70y 8m 22d; daughter of John and Elizabeth (_____) (Thomas) Robinson. She m. (1) Kingston 10 Dec. 1772 ROBERT THOMAS.

David Bradford served in the Revolutionary War as a private in Capt. Peleg Wadsworth's company in Col. Theophilus Cotton's regiment in April 1775; as a Corporal from 1 May 1775 to 6 Nov. 1775; and as a private in Capt. Joseph Wadsworth's company in Col. Gamaliel Bradford's regiment in 1778. He applied for a pension on 17 April 1818 as a resident of Plymouth. His wife Elizabeth was age 65.

David Bradford's household in the 1790 census consisted of 1 man, 1 boy under 16, and 3 females in Kingston.

On 7 Jan. 1797 Jonathan Bradford of Poland, Me., housewright, sold to his brother David Bradford of Kingston one-half of the real estate of his father Nathan Bradford; his wife Mary also signed the deed.

David Bradford of Kingston made his will 27 Aug. 1839, proved 3rd Monday of May 1840, naming Francis Drew, Sarah Bailey wife of Ward Bailey, Thomas B. Drew son of Job W. Drew, and Julius G. Glynn grandson of Joseph Bartlett, but no relationships are stated.

Children of David and Betsy (Robinson) Bradford, b. Kingston, neither in David's will:

   i LUCY⁶ BRADFORD, b. 26 Oct. 1778 [*sic* –date from a census taken in Kingston in 1796]

   ii THOMAS BRADFORD

References: *VR Duxbury* pp. 135(b. Betsey), 179(m.). *VR Kingston* pp. 28(b. Lucy), 179(m.), 319(d. David, Betsy). *Bradford Desc* pp. 155-6. Plymouth Co. LR 81:182(Jonathan Bradford). *Rev War Pensions* 1:356(David Bradford). *MSSR* 2:401. Plymouth Co. PR 82:140(David Bradford).

546. MARY McFARLIN[5] (*Laurana⁴ Bradford, Elisha³, Joseph², William¹*), b. Plympton 18 July 1746.

She m. int. Plymouth 11 June 1768 **JAMES MURFEE.**

References: *MD* 26:139(int.). *Plymouth VR* p. 256(int.).

547. ELIJAH McFARLIN[5] (*Laurana⁴ Bradford, Elisha³, Joseph², William¹*), b. Plympton ca. 1751; d. Fairfield, Somerset Co., Me., 7 Nov. 1827.

He m. Plympton 12 May 1774 **SARAH MARSHALL**, b. Plympton 16 Aug. 1751; d. Waterville, Me., 14 Dec. 1840; daughter of Josiah and Sarah (Churchill) Marshall.

Elijah McFarlin served in the Revolutionary War in Capt. Thomas Newcomb's company, Col. Theophilus Cotton's regiment which marched to R.I. on a secret expedition with service of 35 days from 28 Sept. 1777. From 20 Feb. to 31 Dec. 1778, he served with the Continental Army.

On 11 May 1814 Elijah McFarlin of Fairfield, Me., yeoman, sold to Joseph Burgess of Fairfield, yeoman, 60 acres. On 23 May 1814 Elijah and Joseph sold to Job Bates of Fairfield, yeoman, land in Fairfield.

On 27 March 1820 Elijah Mcfarlin had his earmark recorded: a half crop of the underside of each ear and a happeny the far side of the left ear.

An undated deposition of Elijah McFarland states that he was 67 and had been born in Plympton, but was then living at Fairfield, Me., and gives his Revolutionary service which totaled four years. On 2 June 1820 he deposed again, aged 69 of Fairfield. On 18 Aug. 1836 Sarah McFarland, resident of Wasterfield, Me., aged 85, swore that she was the widow of Elijah, gave their marriage date at Plympton, and stated that Elijah died at Fairfield 7 Nov. 1827. Sarah died before 10 Feb. 1844 when her children claimed the balance of her pension.

On 3 March 1829 Joseph Burges of Fairfield, Me., was appointed administrator of the estate of Elijah Mcfarland late of Fairfield who died the 7th of November 1827.

Children of Elijah and Sarah (Marshall) McFarlin, first 3 b. Plympton, last 2 b. Dudley:

    i   JOSIAH McFARLIN⁶, b. 31 Oct. 1774

    ii ELIJAH McFARLIN, b. 29 Dec. 1777

    iii DAVID McFARLIN, b. 26 Oct. 1780

    iv SALOME McFARLIN, b. 2 Nov. 1786

    v   BRADFORD McFARLIN, b. 4 Nov. 1788

References: *VR Dudley* p. 82(b. ch.). *VR Plympton* pp. 138(b. Sarah), 135-6(b. 1ˢᵗ 3 ch.), 348(m.). Rev. War Pension W23949(Elijah McFarlin). *MSSR* 10:486. Somerset Co. ME PR 4:81(Elijah McFarlin). Somerset Co. ME LR 4:459; 5:150(Elijah McFarlin). Fairfield TR & VR p. 75(earmark). *Holland MA Hist* p.595.

548. HANNAH McFARLIN⁵ (*Laurana⁴ Bradford, Elisha³, Joseph², William¹*), b. Plympton.

She m. Plymouth 15 Dec. 1768 **CALEB RIDER**, b. Plymouth 22 Aug. 1746; son of Josiah and Experience (Jenny) Rider.

In the 1771 Valuation List, Caleb Ryder appears in Plymouth with one poll.

No probate records have been found for Caleb Rider in Plymouth Co.

Child of Caleb and Hannah (McFarlin) Rider:

    i   [Child] RIDER⁶ d. 7 March 1771

References: *MD* 13:167(b. Caleb); 26:139(int.). *Plymouth Ch Recs* 1:399(d. child). *Plymouth VR* pp. 71(b. Caleb), 352(m.). *1771 Valuation* p. 656.

549. LAURANA McFARLIN⁵ (*Laurana⁴ Bradford, Elisha³, Joseph², William¹*), b. Plympton 18 Aug. 1755; d. East Bridgewater 5 March 1834 aged 78y 6m 17d.

She m. Dartmouth 7 Nov. 1776 **DAVID CHURCHILL**, b. Plympton 9 Aug. 1729; d. Hingham 23 or 28 Feb. 1812 aged 82y 6m 8d; son of David and Mary (Magoun) Churchill. He m. (1) Plympton 20 Feb. 1751 JANE ELLIS with whom he had Hannah, Molly, Jenne, Levy, Patte, Sylvia, and David.

David Churchill of Plympton, retailer, was granted a license to sell liquor from 1766 to 1773.

On 14 April 1769 David Churchill of Plympton, yeoman, sold to David Churchill Jr. of Plympton the house and land on which David Jr. lived, one-third of his right in the tan yard, meadow and upland, cedar swamp, and one-third of his right in an old furnace and saw mill.

David Churchill's household in Plympton in the 1790 census consisted of 1 man, 5 boys under 16 and 3 females.

In court records he is called of Hingham, laborer, in 1803 and "now a resident of Cambridge, brickmaker," in 1805.

Children of David and Laurana (McFarlin) Churchill, b. Plympton:

    i DAVID CHURCHILL[6], b. 11 June 1778

    ii LEVI CHURCHILL, b. 20 Feb. 1780

    iii THADDEUS CHURCHILL, b. 18 March 1782

    iv JESSE CHURCHILL, b. 28 Aug. 1784

    v ASABA/SABA CHURCHILL, b. 1 Feb. 1787; d. 12 Jan. 1794 ae 7

    vi RUFUS/RUPHAS CHURCHILL, b. 10 Oct. 1789

    vii LYDIA CHURCHILL

    viii OTIS CHURCHILL, b. 1797; d. 1 Jan. 1798 ae 11 mos.

References: *VR Dartmouth* 2:300(m.). *VR Plympton* pp. 58(b. David), 64-69(b. ch.), 374(m.), 457(d. David), 462(d. Laurana), 463(d. Saba). *Churchill Fam* pp. 31, 73. Plymouth Co. LR 58:133(David Churchill). *Plymouth Co Ct Recs* Vol. 3; 11:334.

550. ABIGAIL McFARLIN[5] (*Laurana⁴ Bradford, Elisha³, Joseph², William¹*), b. prob. Plympton; living 7 Feb. 1822 (deed).

She m. Plymouth 1 June 1775 **STEPHEN MARTIN** of Dartmouth; who d. before 4 July 1783, when Abigail Martin of Rochester was appointed administratrix of the estate of her husband Stephen Martin late of Rochester, deceased.

On 22 March 1811 Abigail Martin of Rochester, widow, sold to Jesse Martin of Rochester, mariner, land in Rochester. On 7 Feb. 1822 Abigail Martin of Rochester, widow, Jesse Pratt of Rochester, yeoman, and his wife Anna, and Jesse Martin of Rochester, yeoman, sold to Otis Shearman of Rochester, gentleman, their right in an estate jointly owned; Betsey wife of Jesse Martin released her dower rights.

No probate records were found in Plymouth Co. for Abigail Martin.

Children of Stephen and Abigail (McFarlin) Martin, last 3 b. Rochester:

    i ANNA MARTIN[6], b. prob. Dartmouth 1776; d. Dartmouth 10 Aug. 1777 ae 1y 3d

    ii STEPHEN MARTIN, b. 2 Oct. 1777

    iii JESSE MARTIN, b. 21 July 1780

    iv ANNA MARTIN, b. 17 March 1782

References: *Plymouth Ch Recs* 2:498(m.). *VR Dartmouth* 2:300(m.); 3:47(d. Anna). *VR Rochester* 1:211(b. 3 ch.). *Plymouth VR* p. 361(m.). Plymouth Co. LR 127:134; 147:15(Abigail Martin).

551. JONATHAN SAMPSON[5] (*Deborah*[4] *Bradford, Elisha*[3], *Joseph*[2], *William*[1]), b. Plympton ca. 1753.

He m. before 27 Nov. 1780 **BETHIA (EDSON) BARDEN**, b. Bridgewater 2 March 1754; daughter of Abel and Margaret (Conant) Edson. She m. (1) int. Bridgewater 6 Nov. 1773 CONSIDER BARDEN with whom she had Margaret, Betsey, and Consider.

Jonathan Samson was head of a household consisting of 1 man, 2 boys under 16 and 7 females in Middleboro in the 1790 census.

On 23 May 1807 Jonathan Samson of Middleboro, yeoman, and his wife Bethiah in her right as she "has heretofore been the widow of Consider Barden" of Middleboro and she is heir to Betsey Barden her daughter deceased; Consider Barden of Uxbridge, laborer, as son and heir of Consider and heir to his sister Betsey; and Lewis Finney of Middleboro, laborer, and his wife Margaret as daughter and heir of Consider and heir to her sister Betsey, sold to John Barden Jr. of Middleboro, yeoman, 24 acres with a house.

On 4 May 1808 Jonathan Samson of Plymouth, yeoman, sold to William Davis of Plymouth, Esq., his right in the dwelling house he lives in.

Children of Jonathan and Bethia (Edson) (Barden) Sampson, b. Middleboro:

    i OLIVE SAMPSON[6], b. 13 June 1781

    ii LEVI SAMPSON, b. 26 March 1783

    iii HANNAH SAMPSON, b. 5 July 1785

    iv PARNEL SAMPSON, b. 26 April 1787

    v LUCY SAMPSON, b. 12 March 1789

    vi JONATHAN SAMPSON, b. 20 June 1791

    vii BETHIA SAMPSON, b. 8 July 1798

References: *Middleboro VR* 1:203(b. Margaret), 207(b. Consider); 2:8(b. 1st 7 ch.). *MQ* 48:175-6. *VR Bridgewater* 1:100(b. Bethia); 2:38(int. her 1st m.). Plymouth Co. LR 107:6, 265(Jonathan Samson *et al.*).

552. HANNAH SAMPSON[5] (*Deborah[4] Bradford, Elisha[3], Joseph[2], William[1]*).

She prob. m. Halifax 10 April 1785 **BENJAMIN BOSWORTH** Is he the Benjamin Bosworth, son of John and Sarah, b. Halifax 3 Sept. 1760 (p. 36)?

Note: *Bosworth Gen.* pt. 6 p. 802 says "Elisha[3] who dau. Deborah m. Jonathan Sampson said to be the parents of Hannah, but after diligent search I fail to find that these last had a dau. Hannah who could have m. Benjamin Bosworth, and to date the parents of Hannah cannot be found."

References: *MD* 7:52(m.). *MQ* 48:172-7. *Halifax VR* p. 22(m.).

553. EPHRAIM SAMPSON[5] (*Deborah[4] Bradford, Elisha[3], Joseph[2], William[1]*) d. South Carver 1810.

He m. (1) Middleboro 27 July 1783 **ELIZABETH (EDSON) BARDEN**; d. Middleboro about 1791; daughter of Abel and Margaret (Conant) Edson. She m. (1) Middleboro 20 Aug. 1774 RODOLPHUS BARDEN with whom she had Abel and David.

He m. (2) Middleboro 7 Feb. 1808 **MARY (BESSE) COVILL**; dau. Benjamin Besse of Wareham. She m. (3) SAMUEL GIBBS with whom she had Enos.

Ephr[m] Samson's household in the 1790 census consisted of 1 man, 2 boys under 16 and 4 females, in Middleborough.

Mary applied for a Revolutionary War pension at Sandwich on 9 Aug. 1854 at age 85. She says "shortly after their marriage [to Ephraim Sampson] they moved to Sandwich & later moved to Nantucket & also lived at what became South Carver where sol d in 1810." The pension papers mention 3 children from Ephraim's first m.: "Ephraim, Jr who d at West Bridgewater (no date given) but would have been aged 50 in 1854, Sylvia who was a wid of Jeremiah Thomas in 1854 at which time she was aged 70 & was a res of West Bridgewater & Polly wife of Abraham Thompson & she was b in March 1787 & in 1854 was a res of West Bridgewater."

Children of Ephraim and Elizabeth (Edson) (Barden) Sampson, b. Middleboro:

    i   SYLVIA SAMPSON[6], b. 14 June 1784

   ii   PRISCILLA SAMPSON, b. 23 Nov. 1785

  iii   EPHRAIM SAMPSON, b. 16 Jan. 1793

  iv   THOMAS SAMPSON

   v   POLLY SAMPSON, b. March 1787

Child of Ephraim and Mary (Covill) Sampson, b. Middleboro:

vi   THEODORE SAMPSON, b. ca. 1809 (1 year old when father d.)

References: *MD* 32:21(2nd m.). *MQ* 48:172-7. *Middleboro VR* 1:349(b. Ephraim); 2:77(2nd m. of Eliz.), 181(2nd m.). *Rev War Pensions* 3:3004.

554. DEBORAH SAMPSON[5] (*Deborah[4] Bradford, Elisha[3], Joseph[2], William[1]*), b. Plympton 17 Dec. 1760; d. Sharon 29 April 1827 in 68th yr.

She m. Stoughton 7 April 1785 **BENJAMIN GANNETT**, b. Stoughton 29 June 1757; d. Sharon 9 Jan. 1837 in 80th yr.; son of Benjamin and Mary (Copeland) Gannett.

Deborah Sampson served in the Revolutionary War as a soldier for three years. See the first *MQ* references for an account of this most unusual woman.

In a 1795 deed (acknowledged 23 Jan. 1797), Benjamin Gannett of Sharon, tanner, sold to Benjamin Gannett Jr. of Sharon, yeoman, eight acres with a tanhouse and tanyard and three other pieces of land; Benjamin's [second] wife Anne also signed the deed.

In several deeds Benjamin Gannett of Sharon, tanner, and his wife Anne, sold land to their grandson and grandson-in-law: on 20 April 1811 20 acres to Earl B. Gannett of Sharon, laborer; on 10 Feb. 1812 six acres to Seth Gay of Roxbury, housewright; and on 14 April 1812 the homestead of 100 acres to Earl and Seth. On 20 July 1814 Earl sold his half to Seth.

On 25 Dec. 1821 Seth Gay of Roxbury, tallow chandler, sold to Benjamin Gannett and Earl B. Gannett of Sharon, yeomen, the land he had bought on 10 Feb. 1812; Seth's wife Patience also signed the deed.

On 21 May 1816 Benjamin Gannett of Sharon, yeoman, sold to Earl B. Gannett of Sharon, yeoman, one-half of five pieces of land. One piece included half a house and barn; Earl was to have the other half after the death of Benjamin and his wife.

The will of Benjamin Gannett, yeoman of Sharon, Norfolk Co., dated 3 June 1828, proved 7 Feb. 1837, names daughter Polly, wife of Judson Gilbert; daughter Patience, wife of Seth Gay; and son Earl B. Gannett.

Children of Benjamin and Deborah (Sampson) Gannett, b. Sharon:

i   EARLE BRADFORD GANNETT[6], b. 8 Nov. 1785
ii   MARY GANNETT, b. 19 Dec. 1787
iii PATIENCE GANNETT, b. 25 Nov. 1790

References: *MQ* 39:56-8; 48:172. Norfolk Co. PR #7680(Benjamin Gannett). *Canton-Stoughton VR* pp. 88(b. Benjamin), 149(m.). *VR Sharon* p. 28(b. ch.). Norfolk Co. LR 9:27; 39:127; 41:63, 163(Benjamin Gannett); 48:46(Earl Gannett); 66:53(Seth Gay), 53(Benjamin Gannett).

555. NEHEMIAH SAMPSON[5] (*Deborah[4] Bradford, Elisha[3], Joseph[2], William[1]*), b. Plympton 17 July 1764; d. Rochester, N.H., 26 April 1818.

He m. Stoughton 1 Oct. 1789 **BATHSHEBA BAKER**, bp. Sharon 22 April 1770; d. poss. Strafford, N.H., after 13 Sept. 1824; daughter of Elijah and Hannah (Puffer) Baker.

Nehe Sampson's household in the 1790 census consisted of 1 man, 1 boy, and 1 female, in Stoughton.

Dr. Nehemiah Sampson first appears on the tax lists in Rochester, N.H., in 1813 and is listed through 1817. In 1813 he is listed with 1 poll and 1 horse. In 1814, 1815, and 1816 he is listed with 1 poll, 1 cow, and 1 horse. In 1817 he is listed simply as "Doct^r Neh^h Sampson poor." In 1816 and 1817 his name is followed by a listing for Jonathan Sampson and in 1818 Jonathan Sampson is listed as "gone."

On 21 March 1817 Nehemiah B. Sampson of Rochester, N.H., husband-man, and his wife Bathsheba, appointed Jonathan Sampson of Rochester, N.H., their attorney for any land due them from the estates of John Puffer and Abel Puffer of Canton or Stoughton. On 23 Sept. 1818 Jonathan Sampson of Rochester, carpenter, sold to Phineas Bronsdon of Milton, blacksmith, all Nehemiah and Bathsheba's right in 31 acres in Randolph being one-eleventh part that was set off to them from the estates of John and Abel Puffer, Bathsheba being the daughter of Hannah Baker. On 12 Nov. 1817 Nehemiah and Bathsheba sold to Phineas Bronsdon their right in three acres of meadow in Canton from the estates of John and Abel Puffer as heirs of Hannah Baker eldest sister of John and Abel. On 1 Dec. 1818 Bathsheba Sampson, as an heir of Hannah Baker deceased, participated in a division of land. On 13 Sept. 1824 Bathsheba Samson of Strafford, N.H., widow of Nehemiah, sold to John F. Gerald of Canton, yeoman, her portion from the estate of Joseph Puffer deceased.

Their son Jonathan Sampson is listed in Strafford, N.H., in an 1822 tax list.

Children of Nehemiah and Bathsheba (Baker) Sampson:

   i JOEL SAMPSON[6]

  ii JONATHAN SAMPSON

    iii SUSANNA SAMPSON

    iv SALLY SAMPSON

    v JAMES SAMPSON

    vi LUTHER SAMPSON

References: *Stoughton VR* p. 169(m.). *MQ* 48:172-7. *VR Sharon* p. 9(bp.). Rochester NH TR 2:598, 627, 642, 673, 692, 704; 4:119, 202, 239, 273(tax lists). Norfolk Co. LR 58:63, 81(Nehemiah Sampson), 81(Jonathan Sampson), 106(partition); 95:79 (Bathsheba Samson). Delmar W. Goodwin, *Stafford N.H., U.S. Census & Town Tax Records...1790-1880*, p. 71(tax list).

556. SYLVIA SAMPSON[5] (*Deborah*[4] *Bradford, Elisha*[3], *Joseph*[2], *William*[1]), b. Plympton 1 April 1766; d. Plympton 27 Jan. 1836 aged 69y 9m 26d.

    She m. Plympton 16 April 1799 **JACOB CUSHMAN**, b. Plympton 29 [sic] Feb. 1748/9; d. there 11 July 1842 aged 94y 4m; son of Benjamin and Zerviah (Samson) Cushman, a descendant of Pilgrim **Isaac Allerton.**

    Jacob Cushman served in the Revolutionary War as a private several times: in Capt. John Bradford's company, Col. Theophilus Cotton's regiment on the alarm of 19 April 1775; in the same company and regiment for 3 months 7 days from his enlistment 2 May 1775; in Capt. James Harlow's company, Col. Thomas Lothrop's regiment in March 1777; and in Capt. Ichabod Bonney's company, Col. Nathan Sparhawk's regiment with service of 25 days from 29 Nov. 1778.

    At the November 1803 term of the Plymouth Court of Common Pleas, Zabdiel Bradford of Plympton, husbandman, sued Jacob Cushman of Plympton, yeoman, for refusal to deliver a deed for a pew in Rev. Brigg's meetinghouse. On 24 March Jacob "caused the Pew to be exposed to public Sale" and agreed "that whoever should bid most...should be deemed the buyer." Zabdiel was the highest bidder "Yet the said Cushman ... refused to execute and deliver a deed of said Pew." The jury found for Zabdiel.

    Children of Jacob and Sylvia (Sampson) Cushman, b. Plympton:

    i JACOB CUSHMAN[6], b. 30 April 1800

    ii IRENE CUSHMAN, b. 3 Nov. 1801

    iii WINSLOW BRADFORD CUSHMAN, b. 1 May 1805

References: *VR Plympton* pp. 84(b. Jacob, Irene), 87(b. Winslow), 89(b. Jacob), 381(m.), 470(d. Jacob), 472(d. Sylvia). *MQ* 48:172-7. *Cushman Fam* pp. 106. *Plymouth Co Ct Recs* 11:283(Zabdiel Bradford). *MSSR* 4:310(Jacob Cushman).

557. ASA WATERS[5] (*Alice*[4] *Bradford, Elisha*[3]*, Joseph*[2]*, William*[1]), b. Stoughton 11 Feb. 1760; d. there 8 April 1845 (pension). He is buried in Dry Pond Cemetery, Stoughton, with his three wives.

He m. (1) Stoughton 10 Nov. 1785 **LYDIA SMITH**, b. Stoughton 10 Jan. 1763; d. there 22 June 1809, daughter of Joseph and Experience (Talbot) Smith. On 28 Jan. 1800 the estate of Joseph Smith late of Stoughton was distributed among his heirs including Lydia Waters wife of Asa.

He m. (2) Stoughton 14 June 1810 **MARY (LYON) SMITH**, b. Stoughton 26 March 1763; d. there 25 Feb. 1839 aged 76 yrs, daughter of Elhanan and Rebecca (Belcher) Lyon. She m. (1) Stoughton 14 Dec. 1780 ELIJAH SMITH. The will of Elhanan Lyon made on 1 Feb. 1768, proved 9 July 1770, named children including Mary.

He m. (3) Stoughton 17 Nov. 1839 **SUSAN BAKER SHEPARD**, b. Sharon 25 Sept. 1796; d. Stoughton 3 Nov. 1883; daughter of Oliver and Susanna (Baker) Shepard.

Asa Waters served in the Revolutionary War and his name appears on an 1779 descriptive list of men raised in Suffolk County to reinforce the Continenal Army; he was 19 years old 5 ft. 8 in., light hair, gray eyes, a husbandman. He served in Capt. Talbut's company, Col. Gill's regiment He applied for a pension on 13 April 1818 and d. 8 April 1845. His widow applied 9 July 1853 at Stoughton when she was aged 50.

On 20 March 1787 Zebulon Waters of Stoughton, yeoman, sold to Asa Waters of Stoughton, farmer, 40 acres with a dwelling house and barn.

Asa Waters' household in the 1790 census consisted of 1 man, 2 boys under 16 and 1 female, in Stoughton.

On 11 Sept. 1811 Asa Waters of Stoughton, Gentleman, and his wife Mary, sold to James Smith Jr. of Stoughton, housewright, all their right in the estate of Elijah Smith late husband of Mary.

On 24 April 1819 Asa Waters of Stoughton, Gentleman, sold to Lewis Waters of Stoughton, yeoman, 36 acres; Asa's wife Mary also signed the deed. On 8 March 1820 Asa and Mary sold to Lewis two pieces of land. And on 7 Sept. 1835 Asa and Mary sold to Lewis Waters of Wareham 32 ¾ acres in Stoughton with buildings.

Asa Waters of Stoughton in his will dated 2 March 1842, proved 3 May 1845, named his wife Susan B. Waters; sons Oren and Lewis; only daughter Lydia Weddell wife of Robert; and grandchildren, children of son Asa deceased: Eliza, Mary S., Keziah, Hannah, Asa, and Israel.

On 16 Oct. 1846 Oren Waters of Pittsburgh, Pa., and Robert Waddel of Mercer, Pa., and his wife Lydia sold to Jesse Pierce Esq. of Stoughton their right in 41 acres left to them by the will of their father Asa Waters; Oren's wife Juliet also signed the deed. On 24 April 1847 William A. Gill of Columbus, Ohio, Gentleman, and his wife Hannah H.M. Gill sold to Jesse Pierce their right in the estate of their grandfather Asa Waters. On 30 Oct. 1848 Asa B. Waters and his wife Annette H. Waters and Noah L. Wilson and his wife Keziah B. Wilson all of Marietta, Ohio, sold to Jesse Pierce their right in the estate of their grandfather Asa Waters. And on 2 March 1849 John L. Gill and his wife Mary S. Gill and Eliza P. Sisson all of Columbus, Ohio, sold to Jesse Pierce their right in the estate of their grandfather Capt. Asa Waters.

Children of Asa and Lydia (Smith) Waters:

  i   ASA WATERS⁶, b. Stoughton 14 Dec. 1786
  ii OREN WATERS, b. 26 Nov. 1788
  iii LEWIS WATERS, b. Stoughton 28 March 1791
  iv HENRY WATERS, b. 13 April 1793; d. 7 May 1795
  v   LYDIA WATERS, b. 9 May 1797

References: *Bradford Desc* p. 158. *Stoughton VR* pp. 46(2nd m.), 83(3rd m.), 94(b. Mary), 114(b. Lydia), 121(b. son Asa), 148(Mary's 1st m.), 149(1st m.), 200(b. Susan). Suffolk Co. LR 160:131(Zebulon Waters). Norfolk Co. PR #16938, 6:130(Joseph Smith); #19461, 78:99(Asa Waters). Norfolk Co. LR 40:249; 61:253; 64:18; 107:244(Asa Waters); 169:61(Oren Waters *et al*.); 173:53(William A. Gill *et al*.); 187:233(John L. Gill *et al.* and Asa B. Waters *et al.*). *Rev War Pensions* 3:3695(Asa Waters). *MSSR* 16:693(Asa Waters).

558.   MATILDA WATERS⁵ (*Alice⁴ Bradford, Elisha³, Joseph², William¹*), b. Stoughton 31 May 1761.

She m. Stoughton 15 March 1781 **JAMES NASH,** possibly the James Nash son of Daniel and Rebecca (Wiswall) Nash b. Dorchester 2 Oct 1756.

They removed to Gilson, N.H., after 1784.

Children of James and Matilda (Waters) Nash, first two b. Stoughton:

  i   JAMES NASH⁶, b. 23 Feb. 1782
  ii DANIEL NASH, b. 13 Feb. 1784
  iii ASA NASH
  iv SAMUEL NASH
  v   LEVI NASH
  vi CHARLES NASH
  vii ELISHA NASH

References: *Stoughton VR* pp. 95(b. ch.), 148(m.). *Bradford Desc* p. 158. *Oren Waters Anc.*

559. HANNAH WATERS[5] (*Alice[4] Bradford, Elisha[3], Joseph[2], William[1]*), b. Stoughton 12 Jan. 1767; d. Sharon 13 July 1817.

She m. Stoughton 18 Sept. 1788 **DAVID DRAKE**, b. Stoughton in 1756; d. 20 March 1829 aged 72y; son of David and Hannah (Clark) Drake.

David Drake's household in the 1790 census consisted of 1 man and 2 females, in Sharon.

Children of David and Hannah (Waters) Drake, b. Sharon:

    i ALICE BRADFORD DRAKE[6], b. 2 June 1789

    ii OTIS DRAKE, b. 16 June 1791; d. before 11 Jan. 1812 "on board ship *Dromo*, on his passage from Africa to Havana, aged 21"; unm.

    iii MACE DRAKE, b. 31 May 1793; d. Boston 10 Oct. 1829; unm.

    iv CHARLES BRADFORD DRAKE, b. 22 Jan. 1795; d. Boston 10 Aug. 1814; unm.

    v HANNAH WATERS DRAKE, b. 21 April 1798 (listed as Rhoami in VR)

    vi ELIZA HOWARD DRAKE, b. 21 April 1801 (listed as Live in VR)

    vii ROXANNA DRAKE, b. 26 Sept. 1803

References: Bradford Desc pp. 158-9. Stoughton VR p. 169(m.). VR Sharon pp. 22-3(b. ch.), 161(d. Hannah, David). Lois Stoughton, *The Drake Family in England and America, 1630-1895*, and *The Descendants of Thomas Drake of Weymouth, Mass.* (Boston, 1896) pp. 32, 78. *Columbian Centinel*, issue 11 Jan. 1812(d. Otis). *Oren Waters Anc.*

560. ZEBULON WATERS[5] (*Alice[4] Bradford, Elisha[3], Joseph[2], William[1]*), b. Stoughton 23 Aug. 1768; d. Sharon 6 Jan. 1831.

He m. (1) Sharon 18 March 1794 **ZILPHA (DRAKE) LOVEL**, b. 17 April 1759; d. Sharon 2 April 1800; daughter of John and Mary (Cone) Drake. She m. (1) 5 April 1778 EBENEZER LOVEL with whom she had Ebenezer, Mary, Cyrus, and Zilpha.

He m. (2) Sharon 18 April 1802 (int. Stoughton 27 March 1802) **LUCY BELCHER**, b. Stoughton 16 Oct. 1772; d. Sharon 22 May 1847, daughter of Joseph and Abiel (____) Belcher.

On 21 May 1816 and 10 Feb. 1817 Zebulon Waters and his wife Lucy sold land formerly of Zebulon Waters deceased. On 7 Dec. 1818 Thompson Allen of Charlestown, yeoman, and his wife Nancy ("she residing in Sharon") and William Waters of Dedham, tinplate worker, sold 25 acres formerly belonging to Zebulon Waters.

Children of Zebulon and Zilpha (Lovel) Waters, b. Stoughton:

    i NANCY WATERS[6], b. 25 Nov. 1794

    ii WILLIAM BRADFORD WATERS, b. 3 Aug. 1797

Children of Zebulon and Lucy (Belcher) Waters, b. Stoughton:

    iii CAROLINE DAVIS WATERS, b. 11 Dec. 1802

    iv JOSEPH B. WATERS, b. 22 June 1804

    v MARY ANN WATERS, b. 10 March 1806

    vi DOLLY HODGES WATERS, b. 28 Jan. 1808

    vii JOHN B. WATERS, b. 17 Feb. 1812

    viii CHARLES E. WATERS, b. 28 Oct. 1815

References: *Stoughton VR* pp. 6(int. 2nd m.), 122(b. William B.), 124(b. Nancy), 173(b. John B., Charles E.), 268(m.). *Bradford Desc* p. 159. *VR Sharon* p. 142(m.). *The Drake Fam.* p. 15. Norfolk Co. LR 49:170; 54:202(Zebulon Waters); 58:205(Thompson Allen).

561. MOLEY (or **MARY**) **WATERS**[5] (*Alice[4] Bradford, Elisha[3], Joseph[2], William[1]*), b. Stoughton 6 April 1773; d. 18 May 1823.

She m Stoughton 18 July 1802, **GEORGE RANDALL** of Easton, b. 1779; d. 1841; son of Jonathan and Amity (Morse) Randall. The distribution of the estate of Jonathan Randall of Easton in May 1837 following the death of the widow names eldest son George Randall.

Drake Fam. states that her "husband left her and went to Richmond, Va." where he died.

Child of George and Mary (Waters) Randall, b. Easton:

    i GEORGE RANDALL[6], b. Sept. 1802

References: *Bradford Desc* p. 159. "Easton Families" pp. 236(b. George), 275(m.). Bristol Co. LR 156:492 (John Randall division).

562. CHLOE WATERS[5] (*Alice[4] Bradford, Elisha[3], Joseph[2], William[1]*), b. Stoughton 19 Sept. 1775; d. there 18 Feb. 1816 aged 40y.

She m. Stoughton 4 Aug. 1794 **LEMUEL MONK**, b. Stoughton 7 May 1769; d. there 21 Feb. 1816 aged 47y; son of William and Mary (Wedlock) Monk.

On 8 April 1806 William Monk of Stoughton, yeoman, sold to Lemuel Monk of Stoughton, yeoman, 20 acres in Stoughton with buildings and on the same day, William and Lemuel agree that William will have the use of this land and buildings during the lifetime of William and his wife Mary. On 1 Sept. 1806 Lemuel sold to William 18 acres with buildings; Lemuel's wife Chloe also signed this deed. On 16 May 1817 William sold to Lemuel another 9 ¾ acres.

On 12 May 1818 administration was granted to Benjamin Richards Esq. on the estate of Lemuel Monk late of Stoughton, yeoman. The inventory taken 1 June 1818 included two acres of land with buildings in Stoughton with "the Incumbrances of a life lease of the same to William Monk father of the said deceased." The estate was insolvent and creditors were paid on 6 April 1819.

On 6 April 1819 Benjamin Richards, administrator of the estate of Lemuel Monk, sold land to Lemuel Monk of Stoughton, cordwainer; William Monk had a life interest in this land. On 26 Sept. 1823 Benjamin Richards, administrator of the estate of William Monk, sold to Lemuel Monk more land.

Children of Lemuel and Chloe (Waters) Monk:*

prob. i. LEMUEL MONK, b. Stoughton 26 Jan. 1795

  ii POLLY MONK[6] d. 27 June 1800

  iii STEPHEN MONK, b. 24 March 1803

  iv WILLIAM MONK, b. 10 July 1810

  v ORIN MONK, b. 1 April 1812

  vi OTIS MONK, b. 2 March 1814

* Possible additional children: Luther, Sally, Benjamin Waters, and Mary.

References: *Stoughton VR* pp. 117(b. Lemuel), 168(d. Polly), 170(m.). *Bradford Desc* p. 159. Norfolk Co. PR #12913, 30:530, 607(Lemuel Monk). Norfolk Co. LR 23:279(William Monk); 26:88(Lemuel Monk); 31:195(agreement); 54:287(William Monk); 62:44; 72:213(Benjamin Richards). "Stoughton VRs" (Holbrook Microfilm) no pagination(d. Chloe, Lemuel; b. Stephen, William, Orin, Otis).

563.   BETHIA WATERS[5] (*Alice[4] Bradford, Elisha[3], Joseph[2], William[1]*), b. Stoughton 28 Dec. 1757; d. Camden, Me., 12 Feb. 1837.

She m. Stoughton 15 Dec. 1774 **SAMUEL PACKARD**, b. Easton Sept. 1751; d. after 23 Feb. 1778; son of Joseph and Hannah (Manley) Packard.

On 24 April 1773 Joseph Packard of Easton, yeoman, sold to Samuel Packard of Easton, laborer, 15 acres in Easton; Joseph's wife Hannah made her mark on this deed.

On 19 April 1776 Samuel Packard of Easton, yeoman, sold to Solomon Randall of Easton, yeoman, three or four acres with Samuel's house; Samuel's wife Bethia made her mark on this deed. On 6 Aug. 1777 Samuel sold his orchard. And on 25 Feb. 1778 Samuel sold to James Packard of Easton, yeoman, a "Piece of Land the Northeast part that Samuel Packard owns which was given to him by a deed of his father Joseph Packard"; Bethiah made her mark on this deed.

On 23 Feb. 1778 Samuel Packard of Stoughton, laborer, and his wife Bethiah sold to Joseph Smith of Stoughton, yeoman, their right in land left them from the estate of Daniel Waters excepting the right in their mother's thirds.

Samuel Packard does not appear in the index to N.H. town records.

Children of Samuel and Bethia (Waters) Packard:

     i   HANNAH PACKARD[6], b. Easton 7 June 1775

    ii   JAMES PACKARD, b. Easton 24 Nov. 1776

   iii   NATHANIEL PACKARD

   iv   DANIEL PACKARD, b. Surrey, N.H., 22 Sept. 1782

    v   MARY PACKARD

   vi   BETHIA PACKARD, b. Surrey, N.H., 1786

? vii   SAMUEL PACKARD, b. 1787 (in IGI, no confirmation found)

  viii   JOHN PACKARD, b. 1791

References: *Bradford Desc* p. 159. *Stoughton VR* p. 147(m.). *Camden-Rockport ME VR* (1985) p. 93(d. Bethia). *Desc. Samuel Packard* p. 25. "Easton Families" pp. 63(b. Samuel), 133(b. Hannah, James). Bristol Co. LR 56:458(Joseph Packard); 59:46; 60:49, 225(Samuel Packard). Norfolk Co. LR 11:102(Samuel Packard).

564. JOHN PACKARD[5] (*Azenath*[4] *Bradford, Elisha*[3], *Joseph*[2], *William*[1]), b. Stoughton 19 Dec. 1765.

He m. Easton 10 Sept. 1789 **HANNAH RANDALL**, b. Easton b. 14 Aug. 1767, daughter of Ephraim and Mary (____) Randall.

John Packard's household in the 1790 census consisted of 1 man, 1 boy, and one female, in Stoughton.

Children of John and Hannah (Randall) Packard, b. Stoughton [according to IGI; Eunice only one in VRs]:

    i   SALLY PACKARD[6], b. 29 Oct. 1789

   ii   EUNICE PACKARD, b. 23 Aug. 1791

  iii   RHODA PACKARD, b. 12 April 1794

iv EPHRAIM PACKARD, b. 17 July 1796

v JOHN PACKARD, b. Sept. 1798

References: *Stoughton VR* p. 273(m.). *Bradford Desc* pp. 159-60. "Easton families" p. 132(b. Hannah), 168(m.).

565. JEDEDIAH PACKARD[5] (*Azenath*[4] *Bradford, Elisha*[3], *Joseph*[2], *William*[1]), b. Stoughton 18 Feb. 1771; d. 1816.

He m. Easton 4 Oct. 1792 **ANNE BRETTON**; d. 1816 (was she the "Mrs. Packard" who d. in "Eastham" 19 Feb. 1816; C.C. 28 Feb.?); daughter of Zachariah and Freelove (Drake) Bretton.

Jedediah Packard's household in the 1790 census consisted of 1 man, 1 boy and 1 female, in Easton. [This is probably the Jedediah Packard who married Kezia Williams on 9 Aug. 1789 and had Mason, b. Easton 30 Jan. 1790. On 29 Jan. 1808, Jedediah was made guardian to his children Mason and Abigail (over 14) and Kezia (under 14) for their inheritance from their grandparents Ebenezer and Anna Williams.]

On his marriage to Anne Bretton, Jedediah is called "2d." In the 1800 census for Easton there are two Jedediah Packards. The one called "2d" had only one boy in the 10 to 16 age category in the household; this must be a mistake since a child under 16 would not be living on his own. The other Jedediah had 1 boy under 10, 1 boy 10 – 16, 1 man 26 – 45, 3 girls under 10, and 1 woman 26 – 45. Our Jedediah would have been 29 in 1800, but if the birth years of Bradford and Marcus are correct, both should be listed as under 10 in 1800. In 1810 there are still problems with the two Jedediah Packards in Easton and neither of them is identified as "2d." One has 1 boy under 10, 1 young man 16 – 26, and 1 woman 26 – 45. The other has 1 boy under 10, 1 boy 10 to 16, 1 man over 45, 3 girls under 10, 2 girls 10 to 16, and 1 woman 26 – 45. Our Jedediah would have been 39, but neither of these households have a male in the 26 to 45 age category. To further confuse things there is a marriage in Easton for a Jedediah Packard and Mrs. Mehitable Witterell on 22 Nov. 1795.

On 16 May 1810 Samuel Packard of Easton, yeoman, sold to Barnabas Packard, yeoman, and Jedediah Packard the 2nd, blacksmith, of Easton three acres with buildings. On 12 Feb. 1811 Barnabas sold to Jedediah the 2nd, blacksmith, the three acres. Jedediah then witnessed a deed on the same day in which Barnabas and his wife Sarah sold their right in the thirds of "our late mother Lidia Willis."

On 12 April 1816 Barnabas Packard of Easton, yeoman, sold to Jedediah Packard the 2nd of Easton, yeoman, three acres with a house; Barnabas' wife Sarah signed and Martin Packard was a witness.

Children of Jedediah and Anne (Bretton) Packard:

> i BRADFORD PACKARD[6], b. 1793 (d. Lee 31 Jan. 1869 ae 76)
> ii MARCUS PACKARD, b. Jan. 1796

Note: There were apparently 8 more children.

References: *Bradford Desc* p. 160. "Easton families" p. 171(m.). Bristol Co. LR 92:179(Samuel Packard; Barnabas Packard), 181(witness); 110:515(Barnabas Packard).

566. MELATIAH PACKARD[5] (*Azenath[4] Bradford, Elisha[3], Joseph[2], William[1]*), b. Stoughton 21 July 1773; d. Manorville, N.Y., 20 Jan. 1852.

She m. (1) int. Stoughton 26 Sept. 1794 **ELIJAH BLISS**, b. at "Lebanon Crank," now Columbia, Conn., about 1759-1760; d. before 13 Feb. 1797; son of John Bliss. He m. (1) REBECCA _____. The *Bliss Genealogy* says that Elijah "in a year or two is said to have left his wife and small child, and removed to Stoughton."

She m. (2) Stoughton 13 Feb. 1797 **ELIPHAT/ELIPHALET WORTHINGTON**, b. ca. 1766; d. New Haven, Conn., 11 Aug. 1825; son of William and Sarah (Rogers) Worthington [according to the *Worthington Genealogy*, but in "Springfield Families" no son Eliphalet is listed for them].

Elijah Bliss was in Capt. James Clark's Co. at the Battle of Bunker Hill, served seven years and eight months, and was discharged as a Sergeant Major.

Eliphalet Worthington applied for a Revolutionary pension on 21 Dec. 1818 as a resident of West Springfield. In 1821 he was 54 with a wife Meletiah and children Meletiah aged 12, Henry aged 9, and Benjamin aged 7. He stated that he had married Meletiah or Ameletiah Bliss at Stoughton on 13 Feb. 1797. He had moved to Connecticut by 1823 and d. at New Haven 11 Aug. 1825. His widow applied for a pension 16 July 1849 as a resident of Brookhaven, Suffolk Co., N.Y. She had five children: Linus, b. Stoughton 18 Dec. 1797 living at Riverhead, N.Y., in 1849; Sarah, b. Easton 17 Oct. 1799 and in 1849 living Ulster Co., N.Y., as Sarah Hutton; Amelia or Ameletiah who was d. by 1849; Henry living in 1849; and Benjamin living in 1849. In 1849 Alpheus Bliss of Suffield, Conn., aged 59, stated he was b. at Stoughton and had known the soldier since childhood.

Child of Elijah and Meletiah (Packard) Bliss, b. Stoughton:

  i ALPHEUS BLISS[6], b. 1 May 1795 (listed as "Alpheus Bliss son of Milletiah Packard"

Children of Eliphat and Melatiah (Packard) (Bliss) Worthington:

  ii LINUS[6] WORTHINGTON, b. Stoughton 18 Dec. 1797

  iii SARAH WORTHINGTON, b. Easton 17 Oct. 1799

  iv AMELIA (or AMELETIAH) WORTHINGTON, b. ca. 1809

  v HENRY WORTHINGTON, b. Springfield 20 April 1811

  vi BENJAMIN WORTHINGTON, b. ca. 1814

References: *Stoughton VR* p. 162(int. 1st m.). *Bradford Desc* p. 160. Rev. War Pension W 2310. John Homer Bliss, *Genealogy of the Bliss Family in America* (Boston, 1881) pp. 163-4. George Worthington, *The Genealogy of the Worthington Family* (1894) pp. 112, 161-4. "Stoughton VRs" (Holbrook microfilm) no pagination(b. Elijah).

567. AZUBAH[5] BRADFORD (*Carpenter[4], Elisha[3], Joseph[2], William[1]*), b. Truro, N.S., 21 May 1765; d. Cushing, Me., 11 Nov. 1823 aged 58y.

She m. Friendship, Me., 4 Jan. 1791 **ENOCH WENTWORTH**, b. Stoughton 9 May 1766; d. Cushing, Me., 23 Oct. 1859 aged 91y 6m; son of Sion and Hannah (Pettingill) Wentworth.

On 7 Nov. 1811 Carpenter Bradford of Friendship, Gentleman, sold to William Jameson of Friendship, Gentleman, and Enoch Wentworth of Cushing, blacksmith, 9 acres in Friendship. On 26 June 1815 Carpenter sold to William Jameson, Enoch Wentworth, and Levi Morse of Union, Maine, yeoman, 91 acres in Friendship, the northerly half of the land Carpenter lived on.

In the 1850 census for Cushing, Enoch Wentworth age 84, blacksmith, is listed in the household of Benjamin Wentworth.

Children of Enoch and Azubah (Bradford) Wentworth, b. Cushing, Me.:

  i EMILY WENTWORTH[6], b. 12 Oct. 1792

  ii NANCY WENTWORTH, b. 29 Dec. 1794

  iii MARY WENTWORTH, b. 14 Jan. 1797

  iv LUCY WENTWORTH, b. 4 Dec. 1798; d. 4 Jan. 1799

  v SARAH WENTWORTH, b. 6 Dec. 1799

  vi HANNAH WENTWORTH, b. 6 Dec. 1801; d. 12 Dec. 1801

  vii ENOCH WENTWORTH, b. 14 Nov. 1802; d. 18 Nov. 1809

    viii CHARLOTTE WENTWORTH, b. 6 Nov. 1805; d. 24 Oct. 1810

    ix BENJAMIN WENTWORTH, b. 13 July 1809

References: *Bradford Desc* p. 160. *The Wentworth Genealogy, English And American*, John Wentworth 1878, pp. 616-9. GS#69738(g.s. photo-d. Enoch, Azubah). Lincoln Co. ME LR 91:46; 94:135(Carpenter Bradford). 1850 census Cushing p. 149.

568. HANNAH⁵ BRADFORD (*Carpenter⁴, Elisha³, Joseph², William¹*), b. Onslow, N.S., 28 June 1767; d. Friendship, Me., 31 Aug. 1840 (g.s.).

She m. (1) **ZENAS COOKE**, b. ca. 1753; drowned at East Friendship, Me., 4 Sept. 1789 aged 36; son of James and Abigail (Hodges) Cooke, a descendant of Pilgrim **Francis Cooke**.

She m. (2) Friendship, Me., 19 Nov. 1791 **WILLIAM JAMESON**, b. Friendship, Me., 24 May 1764; d. 21 Sept. 1848 aged 85y 4m (g.s.); son of Paul and Elizabeth (Peebles) Jameson.

On 15 Sept. 1789 widow Hannah Cooke was appointed administratrix of the estate of Zenas Cooke. The account of 16 Jan. 1801 mentions that the widow had married William Jameson.

On 7 Nov. 1811 Carpenter Bradford of Friendship, Gentleman, sold to William Jameson of Friendship, Gentleman, and Enoch Wentworth of Cushing, blacksmith, 9 acres in Friendship. On 26 June 1815 Carpenter sold to William Jameson, Enoch Wentworth, and Levi Morse of Union, Maine, yeoman, 91 acres in Friendship, the northerly half of the land Carpenter lived on.

Children of Zenas and Hannah (Bradford) Cooke, b. Meduncook (now Friendship), Me.:

    i HANNAH COOKE⁶, b. March 1786

    ii ELIJAH COOKE, b. 20 Oct. 1788

Children of William and Hannah (Bradford) (Cooke) Jameson, first two b. Meduncook (now Friendship), Me.:

    iii POLLY JAMESON (twin), b. 31 July 1792

    iv ELIZABETH JAMESON (twin), b. 31 July 1792

    v ISAAC JAMESON, b. 20 Sept. 1798

    vi WILLIAM JAMESON, b. 5 April 1801

    vii CHARLOTTE JAMESON, b. 16 Dec. 1806

  viii – xii 5 JAMESON children who d. in infancy

References: *Bradford Desc* pp. 160-1.   Manuscript of The Cooke Family of Meduncook/Friendship ME by Clifton R. Sargent, Jr. of Yarmouth ME. *Lincoln Co ME Probates* p. 189 (Zenas Cooke). Lincoln Co. ME LR 91:46; 94:135(Carpenter Bradford).

569.   WILLIAM⁵ BRADFORD (*Carpenter⁴, Elisha³, Joseph², William¹*), b. Onslow, N.S., 15 Dec. 1770.

He m. **SARAH SWEETLAND**; daughter of Samson and Ruth (Wade) Sweetland of Waldoboro, Me.

William Bradford's household in the 1790 census, in Winslow, Me., consisted of 1 man, 2 boys, and 3 females.

Children of William and Sarah (Sweetland) Bradford, b. Friendship, Me.:

    i   LYDIA⁶ BRADFORD

    ii   ELISHA BRADFORD, b. 27 March 1794

   iii CHARLES BRADFORD, b. 15 Nov. 1795

   iv MARY BRADFORD, b. 7 March 1797

    v   WILLIAM BRADFORD, b. 17 Nov. 1798

   vi NEHEMIAH BRADFORD, b. 7 June 1801

  vii ENOCH BRADFORD, b. 12 Dec. 1802; d. 1 Oct. 1829; unm.

References: *Bradford Desc* p. 161.

570.   MARY GAY⁵ BRADFORD (*Carpenter⁴, Elisha³, Joseph², William¹*), b. Onslow, N.S., 8 Nov. 1772; d. Union, Me., 25 Oct. 1845.

She m. 8 March 1792 **LEVI MORSE**, b. Sherburne 5 Jan. 1762; d. Union, Me., 3 Feb. 1844; son of Obadiah and Mary (Walker) Morse.

Union ME Hist says:

> Among the settlers who came soon after the incorporation was Levi Morse. He was hired 'for forty shillings a month, and found' by Dr. Johnson, then of Brookfield, to chop for him *three* or *six* months, as Morse should choose…it appears that he returned from Sherburne to Union every spring for several years…
>
> Levi Morse went in a privateer to France. He served six weeks in Rhode Island at the time of Gen. Sullivan's expedition, under the command of Capt. Perry, of Sherburne, in Col. Hawes's regiment. A memorandum found among his papers, dated July 24, 1832, says: 'In 1788, was engaged several days and nights in constructing redoubts, and exposed to cannon shot and shells several days. We were overtaken with a severe storm, whilst on the island, without tents to cover us. In 1779 and '80, I served in Sherburne fifteen months; enlisted under Reuben Partridge, commanding officer, in the State of Massachusetts, for the term of three

months at each engagement. In 1781, I served three months in the State of New York, at West Point, Peekskill, and vicinity.'

Levi Morse served the town of Union on the school committee in 1798, as a fish warden in 1791, and as treasurer from 1801 to 1810.

On 7 Nov. 1811 Carpenter Bradford of Friendship, Gentleman, sold William Jameson of Friendship, Gentleman, and Enoch Wentworth of Cushing, blacksmith, 9 acres in Friendship. On 26 June 1815 Carpenter sold William Jameson, Enoch Wentworth, and Levi Morse of Union, Maine, yeoman, 91 acres in Friendship being the northerly half of the land Carpenter lived on.

Levi Morse of Union made his will 9 June 1842, proved 15 May 1844, naming his wife Mary; sons Barnard (a farm in Belmont, Me., where he now lives), William B., John P., and George W.; daughters Hannah, Sally, Nancy, and Harriet; children of his deceased daughter Mary; children of his deceased daughter Chloe Lunt: Mary Grace Morse Lunt and Chloe Morse Lunt; and grandchildren John P. Morse, Levi Morse, and Mary B. Morse. On 12 May 1847 George W. Morse, administrator of the estate of Levi Morse, paid legacies to William B. Morse, Hannah Bachelder wife of Lewis, Sally Hahn wife of Jacob, Aaron Starrett husband of deceased daughter Nancy, and Hannah Starrett wife of Benjamin.

Children of Levi and Mary Gay (Bradford) Morse, b. Union, Me.:

  i   PERSIS MORSE[6], b. 11 Nov. 1792; d. 4 Oct. 1839; unm.

  ii WALTER MORSE, b. 16 July 1794

  iii HANNAH MORSE, b. 24 April 1796

  iv SALLY MORSE, b. 13 May 1798

  v   BARNARD MORSE, b. 11 June 1800

  vi MARY MORSE, b. 12 Sept. 1802

  vii LEVI MORSE, b. 18 Oct. 1804; d. 11 July 1844

  viii NANCY MORSE, b. 6 Jan. 1807

  ix SAMUEL MORSE, b. 18 March 1809; d. 7 March 1831 of consumption

  x   CHLOE BRADFORD MORSE, b. 6 April 1811

  xi GEORGE WASHINGTON MORSE (twin), b. 24 Aug. 1813

  xii WILLIAM BRADFORD MORSE (twin), b. 24 Aug. 1813

  xiii HARRIET NEWELL MORSE, b. 14 May 1816

References: *Bradford Desc* p. 161.   Union ME VR 1789-1876 pp. 106(b. & d. ch.), 215(d. Polly, Levi).   Bible in ME application GS #1495.   Lincoln Co. ME LR 91:46;

94:135(Carpenter Bradford). *Union ME Hist* pp. 126, 129, 303, 329, 476-80. Lincoln Co. ME PR 57:355; 64:139-40(Levi Morse).

571. CHLOE⁵ BRADFORD (*Carpenter⁴, Elisha³, Joseph², William¹*), b. Truro, N.S., 5 Jan. 1776; d. prob. Cushing, Me., after 1860.

She prob. m. ca. 1802 **WILLIAM BURTON**; who d. March 1842; son of Benjamin and Alice (Davis) Burton.

In the 1850 census for Cushing, Me., Chloe Burton aged 73 is living with William Burton aged 26. In the 1860 census, Chloe aged 82 is living with John R. Burton.

Children of William and Chloe (Bradford) Burton, prob. b. Cushing, Me.:*

    i THOMAS BURTON, b. ca. 1802 (48 in 1850 census)

    ii SARAH BURTON, b. ca. 1803 (47 in 1850 census)

    iii CHLOE BURTON, b. ca. 1807 (43 in 1850 census)

    iv JOHN R. BURTON, b. ca. 1816 (34 in 1850 census)

* Poss. other children. From the Cushing vital records there are marriages for James Burton in 1832, Nancy Burton in 1830, and Church Burton in 1834.

NOTE: *Bradford Desc* says that she m. (1) Thomas Knight and (2) Thomas Palmer, but research for years has not turned up men of either name with a wife Chloe. John R. Burton died Cushing, Me., 28 Aug. 1874 age 77y 9m 24d. His death record lists his parents as William and Chloe (Davis) Burton, but since his grandmother was Alice Davis, this mistake is understandable.

References: *Bradford Desc* p. 161. ME VR cards(d. John R. Burton). 1850 census Cushing p. 150-1. 1860 census Cushing p. 626.

Appendix

ROBERT BRADFORD OF BOSTON

A Non-*Mayflower* Bradford Family

Descendants of Robert Bradford, who immigrated to New England before 1639 and lived his life in Boston, are sometimes confused with those of William Bradford of the *Mayflower*. For the convenience of researchers, Robert's line has been traced for five generations. A much more thorough presentation of Robert's family, by Ann S. Lainhart and Scott Andrew Bartley, is scheduled to appear in the *Mayflower Descendant*, Volume 53 #1, Winter 2004.

1. ROBERT[1] BRADFORD; d. Boston bef. 28 Dec. 1680 (will).

He m. (1) **MARTHA** _____.

He m. (2) bef. 16 Nov. 1677 **MARGARET** _____, b. ca. 1605; d. 1697 aged 92.

Robert Bradford was admitted an inhabitant of Boston 27 Feb. 1639/40. Robert Bradford, a taylor, became a member of the First Church 4 5th mo. 1640.

On 22 Sept. 1673 Robert Bradford of Boston, tailor, gave to his son Moses Bradford a house which Moses had built and now lived in and land next to the house and land of Robert Bradford.

In his will dated 16 Nov. 1677, proved 28 Dec 1780, Robert Bradford of Boston, tailor, named his wife Margaret, son Moses Bradford, and daughter Martha wife of Peter Maverick.

Children of Robert and Martha (_____) Bradford, b. Boston, bp. First Ch.:

2   i   MOSES[2] BRADFORD, b. 2 1st mo. 1644, bp. 10 1st mo. 1644 about 10 d. old

      ii   MARTHA BRADFORD, b. 9 9th mo. 1645, bp. 16 9th mo. 1645 about 3 d. old; d. 13 Aug. 1661

3   iii   MARTHA BRADFORD

References: *BRC* 2:46(inhabitant); 9:17(b. Moses), 18(bp. Moses), 21(b. Martha), 22(bp. Martha), 80(d. Martha). Suffolk Co. LR 9:105(Robert Bradford). *First Ch Recs* 1:29(Robert member), 294(bp. Moses), 300(bp. Martha).

2. MOSES[2] BRADFORD (*Robert[1]*) was bp. at the First Church of Boston 10 1st mo. 1644; drowned in 1692.

He m. bef. 1668 **ELIZABETH** _____; bur. Boston 29 March 1713/4.

Moses Bradford was admitted to the First Church on 4 Nov. 1665; his wife Elizabeth was admitted on 1 3rd mo. 1670. On 27 April 1690 Moses Bradford was "Excommunicated ... for drunkenesse."

On 22 Sept. 1673 Robert Bradford of Boston, tailor, gave to his son Moses Bradford a house which Moses had built and was now living in and land next to the house and land of Robert Bradford.

He became a member of the Ancient and Honorable Artillery Company in 1674.

Children of Moses and Elizabeth (_____) Bradford, b. Boston:

     i JOHN[3] BRADFORD, b. 15 Aug. 1668.

4   ii MOSES BRADFORD, b. 24 Nov. 1670, bp. First Ch. 26 9th mo. 1670

     iii ROBERT BRADFORD , bp. First Ch. 16 12th mo. 1672; d. 1673

     iv ROBERT BRADFORD, b.1674

     v THOMAS BRADFORD, b. 20 Nov. 1678

     vi HANNAH BRADFORD, b. 15 Nov. 1681

References: *BRC* 9:106(b. John), (b. Moses), 117(bp. Moses), 126(bp. Robert), 144(b. Thomas), 154(b. Hannah), 205(d. Moses). Suffolk Co. LR 9:105(Robert Bradford). *Boston Deaths* 1:104(bur. Elizabeth). *First Ch Recs* 1:60(Moses admitted), 63(Elizabeth admitted), 90(excommunicate), 294(bp. Moses); 2:349(bp. son Moses), 353(bp. Robert)

3. MARTHA[2] BRADFORD (*Robert[1]*); d. by 17 Oct. 1681.

She m. **PETER MAVERICK;** son of Elias and Ann (Harris) Maverick. Elias Maverick of Charlestown made his will 19 Oct. 1681, proved 6 Nov. 1684, naming his son Peter among his other children.

Martha Mavericke was admitted to First Ch. Boston 11 2nd mo. 1675.

On 17 Oct. 1681 Moses Bradford, taylor, and Isaac Walker, shopkeeper, both of Boston were granted administration of the estate of Martha Maverick late of Boston deceased. On 4 Sept. Moses Bradford presented an account of the funeral expenses for Martha which included 5 gallons of Madera wine, 6 pairs of gloves, digging the grave, ringing the bell, the "Hearse Cloath," the coffin, posts, and "vayle." On 29 Sept. Moses presented "An Inventory of what goods Robert Bradford dec[d] left to his daughter Martha Maverick that was the wife of Peter Maverick & to her children after her ... the s[d] Martha being dec^d." The inventory included the easternmost end of a house and land and household goods. Moses also presented an inventory of "what goods of Peter Maverick was found in the house Robert Bradford gave to his daughter Martha and after to her children" which included a small amount of household goods.

Children of Peter and Martha (Bradford) Maverick, b. Boston:

i MARTHA³ MAVERICK, b. 8 Feb. 1670, bp. First Ch. 25 2nd mo. 1675

5   ii JAMES MAVERICK, bp. First Ch. 25 2nd mo. 1675

References: *BRC* 9:115(b. Martha). *NEHGR* 96:232(Maverick family). Suffolk Co. PR #1198, 9:54-5; new series 1:171-2(Martha Maverick). *First Ch Recs* 1:72(Martha admitted); 2:256(bp. Martha, James).

4. MOSES³ BRADFORD (*Moses², Robert¹*) was born Boston 24 Nov. 1670, bp. First Ch. 26 9th mo. 1670; d. Boston 22 Jan.1729/30 aged 59y.

He m. Boston 8 Dec. 1692 **ELIZABETH ALLEN**, b. ca. 1672, bp. First Ch. 24 1st mo. 1671/2; d. Boston bef. 20 Sept. 1731; dau. of Edward and Lydia (Ludkin) Allen.

Moses Bradford and his wife Elizabeth were admitted to the First Ch. on 27 Dec. 1696.

On 5 Oct. 1725 Thomas Bradford of Boston, goldsmith, and his wife Abigail; Robert Bradford of Boston, carpenter, and his wife Lydia; Elizabeth Bradford of Boston, spinster; Joseph Bradford of Boston, sadler; and James Bradford of Boston, shipchandler, sold to John Bradford of Boston, sadler, land near the town dock. On 16 Nov. 1730 John Bradford, sadler, and wife Sarah; Thomas Bradford, goldsmith, and wife Abigail; Robert Bradford, carpenter, and wife Lydia; Joseph Bradford, sadler, and wife Ruth; and James Bradford, merchant, and wife Hepzibah all of Boston sold to John Billings and Richard Billings land and buildings on Wing's Lane. On 23 Sept. 1731 Thomas Bradford of Boston and his wife Abigail; Robert Bradford of Boston; Thomas Nowell of Boston and his wife Elizabeth; and James Bradford of Boston and his wife Hepzibah, sold to Joseph Bradford of Boston, sadler, an old house and land about the middle of Wings Lane which was given to their mother Elizabeth Bradford, dec., by their grandmother Allen, deceased.

Children of Moses and Elizabeth (Allen) Bradford, b. Boston, bp. First Ch.:

6   i   JOHN³ BRADFORD, b. 18 Sept. 1693, bp. 24 Sept. 1693

7   ii THOMAS BRADFORD, b. 24 Dec. 1697, bp. 26 Dec. 1697

          iii ROBERT BRADFORD, b. 30 Aug. 1699, bp. 3 Sept. 1699; m.
              Boston 1722 Lydia Rogers, prob. d. by 5 April 1740 when she did not
              release her dower rights (see deed above).

8   iv ELIZABETH BRADFORD, b. 21 Sept. 1701, bp. 28 Sept. 1701

9   v   JOSEPH BRADFORD, b. 14 May 1705, bp. 20 May 1705

10   vi JAMES BRADFORD, b. 22 Sept. 1707, bp. 28 Sept. 1707

References: BRC 9:113(b. Moses), 203(m.), 205(b. John), 213(bp. John), 232(b. Thomas), 239(bp. Thomas), 246(b. Robert), 253(bp. Robert); 24:5(b. Elizabeth), 33(b. Joseph), 47(b. James); 28:113(m.).   Suffolk Co. LR 46:117, 152(Thomas Bradford *et al.*), 200(John Bradford *et al.*). *First Ch Recs* 2:365(bp. John), 368(bp. Thomas), 369(bp. Robert), 371(bp. Elizabeth), 374(bp. Joseph); 377(bp. James). *Boston Deaths* 1:104(d. Moses).

5. JAMES MAVERICK³ (*Martha², Robert¹*) was bp. Boston 1st Ch. 25 2nd mo. 1675; d. about 1695.

He m. Boston **ESTHER/HESTER** _____. She m. (2) Boston 7 Aug. 1705 BENJAMIN WHITNEY of Framingham.

James Maverick received 15 acres of land from the 1681 will of his grandfather Elias Maverick.

On 16 July 1703 Hester Maverick of Lynn, widow of James Maverick late of Boston, petitioned the Governor and Council for permission to sell part of her husband's estate on Wing Lane in Boston. She stated that her "husband did about Eight years Since go out of this Port in a Voyage bound for London, & was then taken by the French, & Since not heard of by and of his Relations, he Left me two Children a boy & a girl, with very Small matters to Support & maintain them."

On 18 June 1718 depositions that the children of Hester Whitney, wife of Benjamin Whitney of Framingham, were James Maverick , born 2 Oct. 1699, and Martha Maverick, born 17 April 1693.

On 6 Sept. 1728 James Maverick, cordwainer, and his wife Mary and Thomas Bellows and his wife Martha sold to Eleazer Rice, trader, part of a house and land bounded on land of Moses Bradford and John Bradford. On 10 Sept. 1728 Benjamin Whitney, yeoman, and his wife Esther sold to Thomas Bellows, carpenter, and James Maverick, cordwainer, a house and land part of the estate of James Maverick dec. the former husband of Esther Whitney and father of James Maverick and Martha Bellows wife of Thomas Bellows. On 28 Sept. 1728 Eleazer Rice and his wife Thankfull sold to John Bradford, sadler, one-half of a wooden house and land bounded on land of Moses Bradford and John Bradford.

Children of James and Esther/Hester (_____) Maverick:

11   i   MARTHA MAVERICK[4], b. 17 April 1693

12   ii   JAMES MAVERICK, b. 2 Oct. 1699 [prob. incorrect since father died about 1695]

References: Suffolk Co. LR 33:15(deposition); 46:149(Eleazer Rice), 151(James Maverick, Benjamin Whiting). *BRC* 28:17(her 2nd m.). *NEHGR* 11:225; 96:239-40, 364-5. *Chelsea Hist*, pp. 43-5.

6. JOHN[4] BRADFORD (*Moses[3-2], Robert[1]*) was born at Boston 18 Sept. 1693, bp. First Ch. 24 Sept. 1693; d. bet. 17 Feb. 1734 and 17 Aug. 1735 when he was called dec. on his son John's bp.

He m. int. Boston 21 March 1716, Topsfield 9 May 1717 **SARAH CAPEN**, b. Topsfield 6 April 1699; d. Boston Feb. 1772 aged 74; dau. of Joseph and Priscilla (Appleton) Capen. She m. (2) int. Boston 22 Dec. 1739 EDWARD JENNINGS.

John Bradford was admitted to the First Ch. Boston 26 Feb. 1715/6 and his wife Sarah was admitted 26 Jan. 1717/8.

On 5 Oct. 1725 Thomas Bradford of Boston, goldsmith, and his wife Abigail; Robert Bradford of Boston, carpenter, and his wife Lydia; Elizabeth Bradford of Boston, spinster; Joseph Bradford of Boston, sadler; and James Bradford of Boston, shipchandler, sold to John Bradford of Boston, sadler, land near the town dock. On 16 Nov. 1730 John Bradford, sadler and wife Sarah; Thomas Bradford, goldsmith and wife Abigail; Robert Bradford, carpenter and wife Lydia; Joseph Bradford, sadler and wife Ruth; and James Bradford, merchant and wife Hepzibah all of Boston sold to John Billings and Richard Billings land and buildings on Wing's Lane. On 16 Sept. 1731 Robert Bradford of Boston, carpenter, sold to John Bradford of Boston, sadler, a house and land near Sudbury St.; Joseph and James Bradford were witnesses. In Nov. 1731 John Bradford of Boston sold his right in this land to Joseph Bradford of Boston, shopkeeper.

He was chosen a constable in 1727.

John Bradford of Boston made his will 17 Feb. 1734, proved 25 March 1735, naming his wife Sarah and his four children Joseph, Sarah, Elizabeth, and Abigail.

On 3 Sept. 1737 Sarah Bradford, widow, and Joseph Bradford, shopkeeper and executor of the estate of John Bradford, sold to Charles Apthrop, merchant, a house and land on Wing's Lane.

On 10 Oct. 1746 Edward Jennings, sadler, and his wife Sarah and Joseph Bradford, shopkeeper and executor to the estate of John Bradford, sadler, dec., sold to Simon Rogers, cooper, a house and land near Sudbury St.

On 5 June 1747 Edward Jennings and his wife Sarah mortgaged to Nathan Peabody, cooper, a house and land near the town dock bounded with land of Robert Bradford. On 2 July 1747 Nathan Peabody of Newbury, cooper, agreed that Edward Jennings of Boston, sadler, and his wife Sarah, would have possession of this house during the natural life of Sarah [Nathan's mother-in-law].

On 1 May 1781 Elisha Dunham, mariner, and his wife Abigail sold to William Dall Jr. one-half of undivided land formerly the property of John Bradford deceased.

Children of John and Sarah (Capen) Bradford, b. Boston, bp. First Ch.:

      i   JOHN[5] BRADFORD, b. 21 March 1717/8, bp. 23 March 1717/8; d. 8 Oct. 1720 ae 2y

13   ii SARAH BRADFORD, b. 10 Aug. 1719, bp. 16 Aug. 1719

     iii JOHN BRADFORD, b. 8 March 1720, bp. 12 March 1720/1; d. 30 April 1728 ae 7y

     iv NATHANIEL BRADFORD, b. 11 Feb. 1722, bp. 17 Feb. 1722/3; d. 16 Dec. 1723 ae 10m

     v PRISCILLA BRADFORD, b. 10 Oct. 1724, bp. 25 Oct. 1724; d. bef. 17 Feb. 1734 (not in father's will)

14   vi ELIZABETH BRADFORD, b. 24 Oct. 1726, bp. 20 [sic]Oct. 1726

     vii MARY BRADFORD, b. 15 Sept. 1728, bp. 15 Sept. 1728; d. 4 Sept. 1730 ae 2y

     viii MARY BRADFORD, bp. 22 Nov. 1730; d. bef. 17 Feb. 1734 (not in father's will)

15   ix JOSEPH BRADFORD, b. 13 March 1731, bp. 19 March 1732

     x JOHN BRADFORD, b. 19 May 1733; d.y.

16   xi ABIGAIL BRADFORD, b. 22 June 1734; bp. 23 June 1734

     xii JOHN BRADFORD, bp. 17 Aug. 1735 (father is deceased)

References: *BRC* 24:127(b. John), 135(b. Sarah), 148(b. John), 154(b. Nathaniel), 163(b. Priscilla), 174(b. Elizabeth), 185 (b. Mary), 201(b. Joseph), 211(b. John), 215(b. Abigail); 28:96(m.), 232(her 2nd m.). *BRC* 8:202(constable). Suffolk Co. LR 46:117(John Bradford);

150(Robert Bradford); 152(Thomas Bradford *et al.*), 200(John Bradford *et al.*); 54:228(Sarah Bradford); 72:193; 74:4(Edward Jennings), (Nathan Peabody); 160:283(Elisha Dunham). *VR Topsfield* pp. 22(b. Sarah), 128(m.). Suffolk Co. PR #6708(John Bradford), #7383, 7384, 7385(guardianships). *First Ch Recs* 1:107(John admitted), 108(Sarah admitted); 2:387(bp. son John), 389(bp. Sarah, John), 391(bp. Nathaniel), 392(bp. Priscilla), 395(bp. Elizabeth), 397(bp. Mary), 399(bp. Joseph), 401(bp. Abigail), 404(bp. John). *Boston Deaths* 1:522(d. Sarah).

7. THOMAS[4] BRADFORD (*Moses[3-2], Robert[1]*) was born at Boston 24 Dec. 1697, bp. First Ch. 26 Dec. 1697.

He m. (1) 11 Dec. 1721 **ABIGAIL DYER,** prob. b. 7 April 1695; prob. dau. of Benjamin and Mary (_____) Dyer.

He m. (2) **DORCAS _____**.

Thomas Bradford was admitted to the First Church Boston 29 May 1715. Abigail Dyer was admitted 28 Sept. 1718.

On 5 Oct. 1725 Thomas Bradford of Boston, goldsmith and his wife Abigail; Robert Bradford of Boston, carpenter and his wife Lydia; Elizabeth Bradford of Boston, spinster; Joseph Bradford of Boston, sadler; and James Bradford of Boston, shipchandler, sold to John Bradford of Boston, sadler, land near the town dock. On 16 Nov. 1730 John Bradford, sadler and wife Sarah; Thomas Bradford, goldsmith and wife Abigail; Robert Bradford, carpenter and wife Lydia; Joseph Bradford, sadler and wife Ruth; and James Bradford, merchant and wife Hepzibah all of Boston sold to John Billings and Richard Billings land and buildings on Wing's Lane. On 23 Sept. 1731 Thomas Bradford of Boston and his wife Abigail; Robert Bradford of Boston; Thomas Nowell of Boston and his wife Elizabeth; and James Bradford of Boston and his wife Hepzibah, sold to Joseph Bradford of Boston, sadler, an old house and land about the middle of Wings Lane which was given to their mother Elizabeth Bradford, dec., by their grandmother Allen, dec.

On 5 April 1740 Thomas Bradford of Boston, goldsmith, and Robert Bradford of Boston, housewright, sold to Joseph Bradford of Boston, shopkeeper, a house and one acre in Brookline; Thomas' wife Abigail released her dower rights.

Children of Thomas and Abigail (Dyer) Bradford, b. Boston, bp. First Ch.:

    i THOMAS[5] BRADFORD, b. 17 June 1723, bp. 23 June 1723; d. 21 April 1724 ae 10m

17   ii JOHN BRADFORD, b. 12 Aug. 1724, bp. 16 Aug. 1724

iii ABIGAIL BRADFORD, b. 26 Dec. 1726, bp. 1 Jan. 1727

18 iv THOMAS BRADFORD, b. 27 Sept. 1728, bp. 29 Sept. 1728

v MARY BRADFORD, b. 18 Oct. 1729, bp. 6 Oct. 1730

vi ELIZABETH BRADFORD, bp. 20 Sept. 1730

vii ABIGAIL BRADFORD, bp. 5 Sept. 1732

References: *BRC* 24:158(b. Thomas), 163(b. John), 174(b. Abigail), 185(b. Thomas), 191(b. Mary); 28:99(m.). Suffolk Co. LR 46:117, 152(Thomas Bradford *et al.*), 200(John Bradford); 65:250(Thomas Bradford). *Boston Deaths* 1:105(d. son Thomas). Harrison Gray Dyar, *A Preliminary Genealogy of the Dyar Family* (Washington D.C., 1903) p. 5. *NH State Papers* 37:347-8(Thomas Bradford). *First Ch Recs* 2:391(bp. Thomas), 393(bp. John), 395(bp. Abigail), 397(bp.Thomas), 398(bp. Elizabeth), 399(bp. Mary), 401(bp. Abigail).

8. ELIZABETH⁴ BRADFORD (*Moses³⁻², Robert¹*) was born at Boston 21 Sept. 1701, bp. First Ch. 28 Sept. 1701.

She m. (1) Boston First Ch. 12 Aug. 1730 **THOMAS NOWELL;** d. bef. 6 Oct. 1741.

She m. (2) Boston 6 Oct. 1741 **BENJAMIN EMMONS;** d. Boston bef. 17 Aug. 1752; son of Benjamin and Mary (Windsor) Emmons. He m. (1) Boston 10 Sept. 1694 MARY AMORY with whom he had Benjamin and Thomas.

Elizabeth Nowell was admitted to the Boston Second Church on 29 July 1733.

Benjamin Emmons of Boston, trader, made his will 29 Dec. 1741, proved 17 Aug. 1752, naming his wife Elizabeth, son Benjamin, and grandchild Benjamin Emmons under 21. To his wife he left "all that Plate she brought to me And all the Goods Household Stuff that was her former Husband Mʳ Thomas Nowell, Glazier of Boston, and Goods she has in my Shop so that she pay all the Debts of her former Husband Mʳ Nowell & what Debts she Contracted in her Widowhood with her brother Mʳ Joseph Bradford."

Children of Thomas and Elizabeth (Bradford) Nowell, b. Boston:

i THOMAS NOWELL⁵, b. 15 May 1731, bp. New Brick Ch. 16 May 1731; d. 30 Dec 1739 in 9ᵗʰ yr, bur. Copp's Hill Burial Ground.

ii EBENEZER NOWELL, b. 6 Feb. 1732

Child of Benjamin and Elizabeth (Bradford) (Nowell) Emmons:

    iii ELIZABETH EMMONS, bp. First Ch. 30 Oct. 1743; d. Boston 23 Jan. 1743 ae 3m., bur. Granary Burial Ground.

References: *BRC* 24:22(b. Thomas), 204(b. son Thomas), 208(b. Ebenezer); 28:156(m.). Suffolk Co. PR 46:500(Benjamin Emmons). *Boston Cemeteries* p. 302(d. son Thomas), 444(d. dau. Elizabeth). *First Ch Recs* 2:412(bp. Elizabeth).

9. JOSEPH⁴ BRADFORD (*Moses³⁻²*, *Robert¹*) was born at Boston 14 May 1705, bp. First Ch. 20 May 1705; d. Boston 3 Aug. 1782 aged 78.

He m. New South Ch., Boston 17 July 1729 **RUTH BAKER**; d. bef. 3 July 1782 (husband's will).

Joseph Bradford was admitted to the First Ch. Boston 26 Jan. 1723/4.

On 5 Oct. 1725 Thomas Bradford of Boston, goldsmith, and his wife Abigail; Robert Bradford of Boston, carpenter, and his wife Lydia; Elizabeth Bradford of Boston, spinster; Joseph Bradford of Boston, sadler; and James Bradford of Boston, shipchandler, sold to John Bradford of Boston, sadler, land near the town dock. On 16 Nov. 1730 John Bradford, sadler, and wife Sarah; Thomas Bradford, goldsmith and wife Abigail; Robert Bradford, carpenter and wife Lydia; Joseph Bradford, sadler and wife Ruth; and James Bradford, merchant and wife Hepzibah all of Boston sold to John Billings and Richard Billings land and buildings on Wing's Lane. On 23 Sept. 1731 Thomas Bradford of Boston and his wife Abigail; Robert Bradford of Boston; Thomas Nowell of Boston and his wife Elizabeth; and James Bradford of Boston and his wife Hepzibah, sold to Joseph Bradford of Boston, sadler, an old house and land about the middle of Wings Lane which was given to their mother Elizabeth Bradford, dec., by their grandmother Allen, dec. On 5 Nov. 1731 Joseph and his wife Ruth sold the Wing's Lane land that had come from his grandmother Lydia Allen to James Dolbeare of Boston, brazier.

On 5 April 1740 Thomas Bradford of Boston, goldsmith, and Robert Bradford of Boston, housewright, sold to Joseph Bradford of Boston, shopkeeper, a house and one acre in Brookline; Thomas' wife Abigail released her dower rights.

On 28 April 1762 Joseph Bradford of Boston, shopkeeper, sold to his son Joseph Bradford of Boston, glazier, land near Cambridge St.

Joseph Bradford of Boston, shopkeeper, made his will on 3 July 1782, proved 13 Aug. 1782, naming his son Joseph; dau. Elizabeth Greenwood; grandson John Bradford, son of his late son John; granddaus. Rebecca and

Elizabeth Bradford, daus. of late son of Richard; grandchildren Caleb Loring, Joseph Loring, Sarah Loring, and Ruth Loring, children of Caleb Loring and his late dau. Sarah.; and son John Bradford.

Children of Joseph and Ruth (Baker) Bradford, b. Boston:

      i JOSEPH[5] BRADFORD, b. 12 Aug. 1730; d.y.

     ii RUTH BRADFORD, b. 28 Aug. 1731, bp. New South Ch. 29 Aug. 1731

19   iii JOSEPH BRADFORD, b. 17 Feb. 1732, bp. New South Ch. 18 Feb. 1731

20   iv ELIZABETH BRADFORD, b. 14 Aug. 1734, bp. New South Ch. 18 Aug. 1734

     v JOHN BRADFORD, b. 29 Nov. 1735, bp. New South Ch. 30 Nov. 1735; living 3 July 1782

21   vi SARAH BRADFORD, b. 7 March 1736, bp. New South Ch. 13 March 1736

22   vii RICHARD BRADFORD, bp. West Ch. 2 July 1738

References: *BRC* 24:196(b. Joseph), 201(b. Ruth), 206(b. Joseph), 215(b. Elizabeth), 220(b. John), 224(b. Sarah); 28:148(m.). Suffolk Co. LR 46:117, 152(Thomas Bradford *et al.*), 200(John Bradford *et al.*); 47:10(Joseph Bradford); 65:250(Thomas Bradford); 97:249(Joseph Bradford). Suffolk Co. PR 81:402.

10. JAMES[4] BRADFORD (*Moses[3-2], Robert[1]*) was born Boston 22 Sept. 1707, bp. First Ch. 28 Sept. 1707; d. by 31 May 1741 when he was called dec. on the bp. of William.

He m. Boston 23 Oct. 1729 **HEPZIBAH WILLIAMS**, b. Boston, 2 Jan. 1707; living 2 July 1762 (deed); dau. James and Abigail (Baxter) Williams. James Williams made his will 9 March 1733, proved 8 May 1734, named his dau. Hepzibah Bradford and grandchildren James and Hepzibah Bradford.

James Bradford was admitted to the First Ch. Boston 28 Sept. 1729 and his wife Hepzibah was admitted 26 Dec. 1731.

On 5 Oct. 1725 Thomas Bradford of Boston, goldsmith, and his wife Abigail; Robert Bradford of Boston, carpenter and his wife Lydia; Elizabeth Bradford of Boston, spinster; Joseph Bradford of Boston, sadler; and James Bradford of Boston, shipchandler, sold to John Bradford of Boston, sadler, land near the town dock. On 16 Nov. 1730 John Bradford, sadler and wife Sarah; Thomas Bradford, goldsmith and wife Abigail; Robert Bradford, carpenter and wife Lydia; Joseph Bradford, sadler and wife Ruth; and James

Bradford, merchant and wife Hepzibah, all of Boston, sold to John Billings and Richard Billings land and buildings on Wing's Lane. On 23 Sept. 1731 Thomas Bradford of Boston and his wife Abigail; Robert Bradford of Boston; Thomas Nowell of Boston and his wife Elizabeth; and James Bradford of Boston and his wife Hepzibah, sold to Joseph Bradford of Boston, sadler, an old house and land about the middle of Wing's Lane which was given to their mother Elizabeth Bradford, dec., by their grandmother Allen, dec.

On 31 Oct. 1740 the administration on the estate of James Bradford of Boston, merchant, was granted to his widow Hepzibah. On 23 Jan. 1741 Robert Williams of Boston, baker, was appointed the guardian of Hepzibah age 11, James age 6, and William age 1, children of James Bradford dec.

On 17 March 1762 John Larrabee of Boston, cabinet maker, sold to Honorable James Bradford Esq. of New Providence, Bahamas, a house and 4 acres in Brookline. On 11 July 1762 James Bradford Esq. late of New Providence and now of Boston sold to his mother Hepsibah Bradford of Boston, widow, this house and land in Brookline; James' wife Sarah released her dower rights. The witnesses were John Churchill and Hephz. Churchill [James' sister and brother-in-law] and the deed was acknowledged in Plymouth.

Children of James and Hepzibah (Williams) Bradford, b. Boston, bp. First Ch.:

23   i   HEPZIBAH[5] BRADFORD, b. 22 Aug. 1730, bp. 23 Aug. 1730

        ii   JAMES BRADFORD, b. 26 Nov. 1732, b́p. 3 Dec. 1732; d. 21 June 1734 ae 19m.

24   iii   JAMES BRADFORD, b. 11 May 1736, bp. 16 May 1736

       iv   ABIGAIL BRADFORD, bp. 15 July 1739

25   v   WILLIAMS BRADFORD, b. 26 May 1741, bp. 31 May 1741 (father is deceased)

References: *BRC* 24:52(b. Hepzibah), 196(b. dau. Hepzibah), 206(b. James), 224(b. James), 242(b. William); 28:148(m.). *Boston Deaths* 1:104(d. son James). Suffolk Co. PR #7510, 35:185(James Bradford); #7699-7701, 35:579-81(guardianships). Suffolk Co. LR 46:117, 152(Thomas Bradford *et al.*), 200(John Bradford *et al.*); 98:153(John Larrabee), 154(James Bradford). *First Ch Recs* 1:113(James & Hepzibah admitted)2:398(bp. Hepzabah), 401(bp. James), 406(bp. 2nd James), 407(bp. Abigail), 410(bp.Williams).

11. MARTHA MAVERICK[4] *(James³, Martha², Robert¹)*, b. 17 April 1693.

She m. Framingham 29 May 1716 **THOMAS BELLOWS**, b. Marlboro 30 Sept. 1693; d. by 2 Feb. 1742/3; son of Eleazer and Esther (Barrett) Bellows.

On 30 Dec. 1723 Thomas Bellows of Marlborough, carpenter, sold to Caleb Bridges of Framingham, bricklayer, 28 acres in Marlborough.

On 29 June 1732 Thomas Bellows of Southborough, carpenter, sold to William Johnson of Southborough, yeoman, land in Southborough. Thomas Bellows of Southborough, housewright, sold to Ezekiel Collins of Lynn, 13 acres in Southborough being all of Thomas' land in town. This deed was acknowledged 2 Feb. 1742/3 by Samuel Lyman one of the witnesses since Thomas was deceased.

Child of Thomas and Martha (Maverick) Bellows:

	i	ELIAS BELLOWS⁵, b. Marlborough 12 May 1717, bp. 22 Aug. 1717
26	ii	MARGARET BELLOWS, b. Marlborough 16 Oct. 1718
	iii	ESTHER BELLOWS, b. Marborough 25 Jan. 1720/1
	iv	ZERUIAH BELLOWS, b. Marlborough 15 Jan. 1722/3
27	v	MARTHA BELLOWS, b. Marlborough 26 Dec. 1724
28	vi	KEZIAH BELLOWS, b. Hopkinton 15 March 1727
29	vii	LYDIA BELLOWS, b. Southborough 30 April 1729
	viii	THOMAS BELLOWS, b. Southborough 28 Feb. 1731/2
	ix	ABIGAIL BELLOWS, b. Southborough 6 March 1734
	x	MAVERICK BELLOWS, b. Hopkinton 9 Feb. 1734/5
30	xi	JAMES BELLOWS, b. Hopkinton 6 March 1738/9, bp. 5 July 1741

References: *VR Framingham* pp. 22(bp. Elias), 332(m.). *NEHGR* 96:365. *VR Hopkinton* pp. 28(b. James, Keziah, Maverick, bp. James). *VR Marlborough* pp. 25 (b. Elias), 26(b. Esther, Margaret, Martha, Zeruiah). *VR Southborough* pp. 14-6(b. Lydia, Thomas, Abigail). Thomas Bellows Peck, *The Bellows Genealogy or John Bellows, The Boy Emigrant of 1635 and his Descendants* (Keene NH, 1898) p. 6-7. Middlesex Co. LR 22:499(Thomas Bellows). Worcester Co. LR 5:275; 16:445(Thomas Bellows).

12. JAMES MAVERICK[4] *(James³, Martha², Robert¹)*, b. 2 Oct. 1699 [year prob. incorrect since father d. ca.1695]; d. Sudbury 17 Dec. 1749 (1750 in VR, but see PR).

He m. (1) **MARY** _____

He m. (2) **MARY WALKER**, b. Sudbury 30 Oct. 1706; d. there 17 Nov. 1740; dau. of William and Sarah (Goodnow) Walker. In his will dated 27 June 1732 William Walker named his dau. Mary Maverick and on 28 Dec. 1732 James Maverick signed a receipt for her share of her father's estate.

He m. (3) Sudbury 28 April 1742 **LYDIA SANDERSON**; d. by 10 Feb. 1756.

On 10 Sept. 1718 James Maverick of Sherborn, cordwainer, sold 5 acres in Sherborn to Isaac Coolidge of Sherborn, cordwainer. On 12 Nov. 1719 James sold 10 acres in Sherborn to Joseph March of Medfield, wheelright.

On 18 March 1735 John Walker, James Maverick and his wife Mary, all of Sudbury sold to their brother Thomas Walker of Sudbury, their right in the estate of their father William Walker.

On 11 Feb. 1750 Lydia Maverick and children requested administration on the estate of James Maverick late of Sudbury and Silas Moore was appointed that day. The division of the estate on 23 April 1752 was among the three youngest children Easter, Silence, and Barsheba; Sarah the wife of John Putnam; Mary the wife of David Molton; and Abigail the wife of Moses Hill. On 25 April 1752 Silas Moore of Sudbury, administrator of the estate of James Maverick, sold to Joseph Berry of Framingham 6 acres bounded on land set off to the widow.

On 20 May 1751 Benjamin Whitney was appointed the guardian of Esther and Silence Maverick above the age of 14 and on 28 Oct. 1751 he was appointed the guardian of Bersheba Maverick under 14 years of age.

On 17 June 1754 John Putnam of Sudbury, husbandman, and his wife Sarah, sold to Daniel Hapgood of Stow, yeoman, 1/6th part of 1/3rd part of land in Sudbury. On 5 Jan. 1756 Daniel Hapgood sold to Joseph Stanhope of Sudbury, 1/6th part of 1/3rd part of the estate of James Maverick which was set off to his widow.

On 10 Feb. 1756, now that James' wife was now deceased, it was decided that the land left to Esther, Silence, and Barsheba could not be further divided, so Jedediah Parmenter, who married James' dau. Silence, agreed to take the land and pay the others.

On 6 Jan. 1756 Jedediah Parmenter of Sudbury, yeoman, and his wife Silence, sold to Joseph Stanhope of Sudbury, yeoman, all their right in 1/6th part of 1/3rd part of the estate set off from the estate of their father James Maverick, late of Sudbury, that was set off to his widow; also their right in James' dwelling house; and also their right in 5 acres given by William Walker to James and Mary Maverick.

On 9 June 1766 Moses Hill of Sherburn, and his wife Abigail; Elijah Moore of Sudbury, yeoman; Ephraim Potter of Marlboro, yeoman, and his wife Esther; Bathsheba Maverick of Marlboro, spinster; and Daniel Ward of Marlborough, yeoman, sold to Elijah Parmenter of Sudbury 6 acres in Sudbury.

Children of James and Mary (____) Maverick:

31   i   SARAH MAVERICK[5], b. Sherborn 13 Aug. 1718.

32   ii MARY MAVERICK, b. Sudbury 4 March 1720/1.

Children of James and Mary (Walker) Maverick:

33   iii ABIGAIL MAVERICK, b. Sudbury 4 June 1725

        iv   JAMES MAVERICK, b. Sudbury 4 Aug. 1729

        v   ESTHER MAVERICK, b. Sudbury 30 April 1732

34   vi   SILENCE MAVERICK, b. Sudbury 16 April 1735

35   vii BEARSHEBA MAVERICK, b. ca. 1737

References: *Boston Deaths* 2:614(d.Mary). *NEHGR* 96:365. *VR Sudbury* pp. 86(b. James, Esther, Silence), 315(d. James, Mary). *VR Sherborn* p. 64(b. Sarah). Middlesex Co. PR #14792(James Maverick); #14793, #14794(guardianships); #236491(William Walker). Middlesex Co. LR 20:496; 24:531(James Maverick); 37:9(John Walker *et al.*); 52:270(Silas Moore); 53:5(John Putnam); 54:242(Daniel Hapgood); 243(Jedediah Parmenter); 70:69(Moses Hill *et al.*).

13.   SARAH[5] BRADFORD (*John[4], Moses[3-2], Robert[1]*) was born Boston 10 Aug. 1719, bp. 1st Ch. 16 Aug. 1719; d. Newbury 17 Sept. 1753 in her 35th yr.

She m. Boston 29 Nov. 1739 **NATHAN PEABODY**, b. Boxford 13 March 1716; son of Nathan and Hannah (Putnam). He m. (2) Newbury 2 June 1754 MARY (____) GREENLEAF with whom he had Bradford.

On 5 June 1747 Edward Jennings and his wife Sarah mortgaged to Nathan Peabody, cooper, a house and land near the town dock bounded with land of Robert Bradford. On 2 July 1747 Nathan Peabody of Newbury, cooper, agreed that Edward Jennings of Boston, sadler, and his wife Sarah, would have possession of this house during the natural life of Sarah [Nathan's mother-in-law].

Poss. child of Nathan and Sarah (Bradford) Peabody, b. Boxford:

        i   SARAH PEABODY[6], b. 26 Sept. 1740

        ii NATHAN PEABODY, b. Feb. 1742; bp. Feb. 1741/2

        iii NATHAN PEABODY, bp. 10 Aug. 1745

iv JOHN PEABODY, b. 3 July 1748

References: *BRC* 24:135(b. Sarah); 28:212(m.). Suffolk Co. LR 74:4(Edward Jennings), 5(Nathan Peabody). *VR Boxford* p. 66(b. Nathan, bp. son Nathan), 67(b. Sarah). *VR Newbury* 1:379(b. John, bp. 2nd Nathan); 2:372(2nd m.), 683(d. Sarah). Selim Hobart Peabody, *Peabody (Paybody, Pabody, Pabodie) Genealogy* (Boston, 1909), pp. 22, 30.

14. ELIZABETH[5] BRADFORD (*John[4], Moses[3-2], Robert[1]*) was born Boston 24 Oct. 1726, bp. 1st Ch. 20 [*sic*] Oct. 1726; d. Boston 14 Dec. 1771, wife of William Dall, sugar baker, suddenly.

She m. Boston 25 April 1750 **WILLIAM DALL,** b. ca. 1716; d. Boston 1 June 1803 aged 87y. His death notice in the *Columbian Centinel* calls him formerly a sugar refiner.

On 20 June 1759 William Dall, sugar baker, and his wife Elizabeth sold to John Scollay, merchant, ¼ of a shop and land on Union St.

On 23 Oct. 1772 William Dall of Boston, sugar baker, was appointed guardian to his children, the grandchildren of John Bradford late of Boston, sadler, James, Joseph, and Sarah over age 14 and John and Elizabeth under 14.

On 1 May 1781 Elisha Dunham, mariner, and his wife Abigail sold to William Dall Jr. one-half of undivided land formerly the property of John Bradford dec.

On 1 July 1789 Sarah Dall and Elizabeth Dall of Boston sold land on Wing's Lane to their brother Joseph Dall of Milton.

Children of William and Elizabeth (Bradford) Dall, b. Boston, bp. Brattle St. Ch.:

    i JOSEPH DALL[6], b. 25 May 1752, bp. 7 June 1752

    ii WILLIAM DALL, b. 22 Dec. 1753, bp. 30 Dec. 1753

    iii JAMES DALL, b. 11 March 1755, bp. 16 March 1755

    iv SARAH DALL, b. 21 April 1758, bp. 23 April 1758

    v JOHN DALL, b. 5 July 1762, bp. 11 July 1762; d. Boston 29 Oct. 1782 ae 21y, bur. Granary Burial Ground

    vi ELIZABETH DALL, b. 10 Dec. 1763, bp. 18 Dec. 1763

References: *BRC* 24:174(b. Elizabeth), 279(b. Joseph), 281(b. William), 286(b. James), 293(b. John), 305(b. Elizabeth). Suffolk Co. LR 93:66(William Dall); 160:283(Elisha Dunham); 176:58(Sarah & Elizabeth Dall). *Boston Deaths* 1:242(d. Elizabeth, John, Mary). *Boston Cemeteries* p. 493(d. John, William). Suffolk Co. PR 72:177(guardianships).

15. JOSEPH⁵ BRADFORD (*John⁴, Moses³⁻², Robert¹*) was born Boston 13 March 1731, bp. First Ch. 19 March 1731.

He m. New North Ch., Boston 20 Jan. 1757 **SUSANNAH EDES**, bp. New North Ch. 15 May 1737; dau. of Edward and Sarah (Mills) Edes.

In Feb. 1758 Joseph Bradford Jr. and Mrs. Susanna Bradford were admitted to the West Ch. in Boston.

On 16 Feb. 1759 Joseph Bradford of Boston, tin plate worker, and his wife Susanna, mortgaged to John Scollay ¼ of a house and land "expectant on the life of Sarah, mother of the Grantor."

On 19 Nov. 1778 Joseph Bradford of Boston, shopkeeper, sold to William Cunningham of Boston, wharfinger, 4 pieces of land one of which was "laid out to Henry Emmes in the Division of his father's estate."

References: *BCR* 24:201(b. Joseph); 39:370(m.). Suffolk Co. LR 92:206; 129:136(Joseph Bradford). *New North Ch.* (m.) (bp. Susanna).

16. ABIGAIL⁵ BRADFORD (*John⁴, Moses³⁻², Robert¹*) was born Boston 22 June 1734, bp. 1st Ch. 23 June 1734.

She m. First Ch. Boston 30 Jan. 1752 **PETER SLATER**.

On 7 June 1759 Peter Slater, mariner, and his wife Abigail sold to John Scollay, merchant, ¼ shop and land on Union St.

Children of Peter and Abigail (Bradford) Slater, bp. Boston 1st Ch.:

    i   SARAH SLATER⁶, bp. 19 Sept. 1756; d.y.

    ii PETER SLATER, bp. 7 May 1758

    iii SARAH SLATER, bp. 17 May 1761

References: *BRC* 24: 215(b. Abigail); 28:299(m.). *First Ch Recs* 2:418(bp. Sarah), 419(bp. Peter), 422(bp. Sarah). Suffolk LR 93:63.

17. JOHN⁵ BRADFORD (*Thomas⁴, Moses³⁻², Robert¹*) was b. Boston 12 Aug. 1724, bp. 1st Ch. 16 Aug. 1724; d. bet. 12 March 1784 and 15 June 1784. 18 May 1784 in Boston Deaths

He m. Boston int. 30 Oct. 1746 **MARGARET BARTON**, bp. New South Ch. Boston 27 Dec. 1724; is she the Margaret Bradford who d. Boston bef. 17 Dec. 1791; dau. of John and Katherine (Burrel) Barton.

On 9 Feb. 1756 John Bradford, mariner, and his wife Margaret, and Katherine Barton, spinster, sold to Thomas Hitchborn, boatbuilder, and Gibbons Sharp, shipwright, land and wharf formerly part of the estate of their grandfather James Barton, set off to their dec. brothers John and Michael Barton in the division of the estate. On 1 Oct. 1761 they sold a house and land.

Margaret Hamilton, widow, made her will 28 Dec. 1775, proved 28 March 1780, naming among others Margaret Bradford wife of Capt. John Bradford and Margaret's sister Catherine Barton.

John Bradford Esq. made his will 12 March 1784, proved 15 June 1784, naming his wife Margaret; sons John, Samuel, and William; his negro servant Dinah who was to receive her freedom at age 21; blind servant Lot to be maintained by his estate; and Mrs. Katherine Barton who was to pay 10 shillings weekly if she remained with the family.

On 10 Nov. 1785 John Bradford of Roxbury, clerk, and wife Mary, sold to Samuel Bradford of Boston, merchant, 1/3 of a house and land on Hanover St. On the same day William Bradford of Billerica and wife Sarah, sold 1/3 of the same house and land to Samuel Bradford.

On 7 June 1789 Margaret Bradford of Boston, widow, released her right in a house on Hanover St. that Thomas Perkins of Boston, merchant, had bought from Samuel Bradford on 7 Nov. 1788.

On 9 Jan. 1791 Samuel Bradford Esq. was admitted administrator in the estate of Margaret Bradford late of Boston, widow; sureties were Jonathan Freeman Jr., merchant, and William Bradford, merchant. On 23 Dec. 1791 Samuel Bradford of Boston, merchant, sold to John Bradford of Roxbury, clerk, his right in a dwelling house on Cole Lane and the warehouses or stores on Mill Creek with land lately the property of John Bradford dec.; Samuel's wife Ann also signed the deed.

Children of John and Margaret (Barton) Bradford, b. Boston:

   i JOHN[6] BRADFORD, b. 18 Aug. 1756

  ii SAMUEL BRADFORD

 iii WILLIAM BRADFORD

References: *BRC* 24:163(b. John), 288(b. son John). Suffolk Co. PR 79:21(Margaret Hamilton); 83:575(John Bradford). Suffolk Co. LR 88:11(John Bradford); 97:7; 162:169(John Bradford), 170(William Bradford); 166:159(Margaret Bradford); 171:181(Samuel Bradford). *Boston Deaths* 1:104(d. Margaret). Suffolk PR #19867, 91:29(Margaret Bradford).

18. THOMAS⁵ BRADFORD (*Thomas⁴, Moses³⁻², Robert¹*) was b. Boston 27 Sept. 1728, bp. 1ˢᵗ Ch. 29 Sept. 1728.

He m. Boston int. 27 July 1749 **MEHITABLE ADAMS**.

Thomas Bradford was admitted to the New South Church on 3 June 1750.

On 5 Oct. 1762 John Bradford of Boston, mariner, was granted the administration of the estate of his brother Thomas Bradford late of Portsmouth, N.H., mariner.

Children of Thomas and Mehitable (Adams) Bradford, bp. New South Ch.:

    i   THOMAS⁶ BRADFORD bp. 22 July 1750

   ii   JOSEPH BRADFORD bp. 1 March 1752

  iii   THOMAS BRADFORD bp. 21 Oct. 1753

  iv   ELIJAH BRADFORD bp. 24 Oct. 1756

References: *BRC* 24:185(b. Thomas); 28:284(m. int.). Suffolk Co. PR 61:125(Thomas Bradford).

19. JOSEPH⁵ BRADFORD (*Joseph⁴, Moses³⁻², Robert¹*) was born Boston 17 Feb. 1732, bp. New South Ch. 18 Feb. 1732; d. Boston 10 Dec. 1787 aged 54 or 55.

He m. Boston 5 Dec. 1762 **ELIZABETH ALLEN**, bp. Hollis St. Ch. 26 May 1745; d. after 10 July 1799 when ack. deed; dau. of John and Susannah (Walker) Allen. She m. (2) Boston 23 Nov. 1789 AARON MAY.

Joseph Bradford Jr. was admitted to the West Ch. in Boston in Feb. 1758.

On 23 May 1760 Joseph Bradford Jr. of Boston, glazier, sold to Joseph Bradford of Boston, shopkeeper, land in the North End.

On 19 May 1787 Joseph Bradford of Boston, glazier, and his wife Elizabeth, sold to Ebenezer Pope of Boston, tailor, land formerly belonging to John Allen.

Joseph Bradford owned the covenant in the Hollis St. Ch. 15 June 1766.

Joseph Bradford of Boston, glazier, made his will 13 Nov. 1787, proved 18 Dec. 1787, naming his wife Elizabeth and sister Elizabeth Greenwood wife of Samuel.

On 14 Aug. 1790 Aaron May of Boston, hatter, and his wife Elizabeth, widow of the late Joseph Bradford, sold to Nathaniel Balch of Boston, hatter, land and buildings part of Joseph Bradford's estate.

Aaron May of Boston made his will, 16 Oct. 1798, proved 27 Nov. 1798, naming his wife Elizabeth, son Samuel C. May, and two orphan grandchildren Thomas and Nancy May.

On 6 July 1799 Elizabeth May of Boston, widow, sold to Thomas Emmons of Boston, cooper, land on Warren St.; Elizabeth ack. this deed on 10 July 1799.

Child of Joseph and Elizabeth (Allen) Bradford, b. Boston:

>   i JOHN ALLEN[6] BRADFORD, bp. Hollis St. Ch. 15 June 1766; d. bef. 13 Nov. 1787

References: *BRC* 24:206(b. Joseph); 30:44(m.), 126(her 2nd m.). *Hollis St. Ch.* (bp. Elizabeth) p. 26(covenant, bp. John Allen). Suffolk Co. LR 94:145; 160:243(Joseph Bradford); 168:109(Aaron May); 192:95(Elizabeth May). Suffolk Co. PR 86:610(Joseph Bradford); 96:572(Aaron May). *Boston Deaths* 1:104(d. Joseph).

20.   ELIZABETH[5] BRADFORD (*Joseph[4], Moses[3-2], Robert[1]*) was born Boston 14 Aug. 1734, bp. New South Ch. 18 Aug. 1734; d. after 13 Nov. 1787 (brother's will).

She m. **SAMUEL GREENWOOD.**

Joseph Bradford of Boston, glazier, made his will 13 Nov. 1787, proved 18 Dec. 1787, naming his wife Elizabeth and sister Elizabeth Greenwood wife of Samuel.

References: *BRC* 24:215(b. Elizabeth). Suffolk Co. PR 86:610(Joseph Bradford).

21.   SARAH[5] BRADFORD (*Joseph[4], Moses[3-2], Robert[1]*) was b. Boston 7 March 1735, bp. New South Ch. 13 March 1735; d. 11 July 1769.

She m. int. Boston 30 April 1760 **CALEB LORING**, b. Hull 29 March 1736; d. Hingham 6 Aug. 1787 aged 52nd y., bur. Granary Burial Ground, Boston; son of Caleb and Rebecca (Lobdell) Loring.   He m. (2) 1770 MARGARET (TIDMARSH) LORING, his brother Joshua's widow, with whom he had William, Edward, and Giles.

Caleb Loring was a distiller with the firm of Loring & Snelling and a shipowner of the vessels *The Rising Sun* and *The Neptune.*

Caleb Loring of Hingham, merchant, made his will 31 March 1778, proved 31 Aug. 1787, naming his wife Margaret; children Caleb, Sarah, Jospeh, and Ruth, children of his former wife Sarah; and children William, Edward, and Giles born to his present wife Margaret.

Margaret Loring of Boston, widow, made her will 29 April 1797, proved 9 June 1801, naming her sons-in-law [step-sons] Caleb Loring and Joseph Loring; sons William and Edward; and daus.-in-law [step-daus.] Sarah Loring and Ruth Loring.

Children of Caleb and Sarah (Bradford) Loring, b. Boston:

    i CALEB LORING[6], b. 20 Aug. 1762; d. in two weeks

    ii CALEB LORING, b. 13 Jan. 1764

    iii SARAH LORING, b. 22 Aug. 1765; d. Aug. 1846; unm. Sarah Loring of Boston, gentlewoman, made her will 3 Aug. 1836, proved 31 Aug. 1846, naming her nephew Francis S. Loring.

    iv JOSEPH LORING, b. 11 Aug. 1767

    v RUTH LORING, b. 26 Aug. 1768; d. 8 Sept. 1768

    vi RUTH LORING, b. 2 July 1769; d. 1830; unm. Ruth Loring of Boston, now a resident of Hingham, singlewoman, made her will 13 Jan. 1830, proved 25 Oct. 1830, naming Mrs. Anne Pierce Loring, wife of Charles Loring, Esq.; Helen Curtis Loring and William J. Loring, ch. of her brother Caleb Loring, Esq.; Mrs. Frances Curtis; her sister Sarah Loring; and Edward Greeley Loring, son of her late brother Edward Loring.

References: *BRC* 24:224(b. Sarah); 30:36(m. int.). *NEHGR* 85:1. *Boston Deaths* 1:579(d. Caleb). *Boston Cemeteries* p. 622(d. Caleb). Charles Henry Pope, *Loring Genealogy* (Cambridge, 1917) pp. 32-3, 56-7. Suffolk Co. PR 86:462(Caleb Loring); 99:333(Margaret Loring); 128[2]:410(Ruth Loring); 144[2]:122(Sarah Loring).

22. RICHARD[5] BRADFORD (*Joseph[4], Moses[3-2], Robert[1]*) was bp. Boston West Ch. 2 July 1738; d. by 3 July 1782 (father's will).
He m. Boston 2 Nov. 1763 **RACHEL LORING.**

Children of Richard and ____ (____) Bradford, in grandfather's will:

    i REBECCA[6] BRADFORD

    ii ELIZABETH BRADFORD

References: Charles Henry Pope, *Loring Genealogy* (Cambridge, 1917), p.33.

23. HEPZIBAH[5] BRADFORD (*James[4], Moses[3-2], Robert[1]*) was born Boston 22 Aug. 1730, bp. First Ch. 23 Aug. 1730; d. Boston 1 Dec. 1814 aged 85y, bur. Central Burial Ground.

She m. (1) First Ch. Boston 22 Oct. 1752 **JAMES PEMBERTON**.

She m. (2) First Ch. Boston 26 Feb. 1761, m. First Ch. 26 Feb.1761(int. Plymouth 7 Feb. 1761) **JOHN CHURCHILL** of Plymouth.

She m. (3) _____ **DANZEL** of Milton.

James Pemberton of Boston made his will 26 Feb. 1755, proved 28 July 1756, naming only his wife Hepzibah.

On 30 Nov. 1756 Hepzibah Pemberton, widow and executor of the estate of her late husband James Pemberton, received of Joseph Greenleaf a house and land as security. On 30 Nov. 1757 she bought ½ of a house and land from Joseph. A receipt dated 21 June 1760 says that Samuel Pemberton was to pay the heirs of his brother James Pemberton dec. £171.13.5 with interest.

On 17 March 1762 John Larrabee of Boston, cabinet maker, sold to Honorable James Bradford Esq. of New Providence, Bahamas, a house and 4 acres in Brookline. On 11 July 1762 James Bradford Esq. late of New Providence and now of Boston sold to his mother Hepsibah Bradford of Boston, widow, this house and land in Brookline; James' wife Sarah released her dower rights. The witnesses were John Churchill and Hephz. Churchill [James' sister and brother-in-law] and the deed was acknowledged in Plymouth.

At a meeting of the Plymouth church on 16 Aug. 1775, several charges against Deacon Thomas Foster were considered. One of them was "his calling John Churchills Wife a cursed, murderous Bitch – The Church, 1. Voted it proved. Upon which Deacon Foster, saying that tho. he had no Remembrance of it, yet that if he did say it, he was sorry for it, & condem^d ye Expression The Chh Voted satisfied."

On 29 Oct. 1787 Hepzibah Dansel of Milton, widow, formerly Hepzibah Pemberton, sold land in Boston to Sarson Belcher of Boston, hatter.

Mrs. Dansell was listed in Milton in the 1790 census with 0-1-1.

Hepzibah Dansel of Boston made her will on 14 Sept. 1809, proved 26 Dec. 1814, in which she left her entire estate to William Bradford of New Providence, one of the Bahama Islands, physician [poss. her nephew]. The inventory taken 2 Jan. 1815 included a house and land on Green St. in Boston.

Poss. child of James and Hepzibah (Bradford) Pemberton:

    i MARY PEMBERTON[6]

References: *BRC* 24:196(b. Hepzibah); 30:4(1st m. int.), 39(2nd m. int.). Suffolk Co.LR 89:169; 92:14(Hepzibah Pemberton); 98:153(James Larrabee), 154(James Bradford); 163:252(Hepzibah Danzel).   Suffolk Co. PR 57:419(James Pemberton); 112:660; 113:3(Hepzibah Dansel). *Boston Cemeteries* p. 66(d. Hepzibah Dansell). *Plymouth VR* p. 250(int. 2nd m.). *Plymouth Ch Rec* 1:350(Deacon Foster).

24. JAMES⁵ BRADFORD (*James⁴, Moses³⁻², Robert¹*) was b. Boston 11 May 1736, bp. First Ch. 16 May 1736.

He m. **SARAH** _____.

On 17 March 1762 John Larrabee of Boston, cabinet maker, sold to Honorable James Bradford Esq. of New Providence, Bahamas, a house and 4 acres in Brookline. On 11 July 1762 James Bradford Esq. late of New Providence and now of Boston sold to his mother Hepsibah Bradford of Boston, widow, this house and land in Brookline; James' wife Sarah released her dower rights. The witnesse were John Churchill and Hephz. Churchill [James' sister and brother-in-law] and the deed was acknowledged in Plymouth.

Hepzibah Dansel of Boston made her will on 14 Sept. 1809, proved 26 Dec. 1814, in which she left her entire estate to William Bradford of New Providence, one of the Bahama Islands, physician [poss. her nephew]. The inventory taken 2 Jan. 1815 included a house and land on Green St. in Boston.

Poss. child of James and Sarah (_____) Bradford:

     i   WILLIAM⁶ BRADFORD

References: Suffolk Co. LR 98:153(James Larrabee), 154(James Bradford). Suffolk Co. PR 112:660; 113:3(Hepzibah Dansel).

25. WILLIAMS⁶ BRADFORD (*James⁴, Moses³⁻², Robert¹*) was b. Boston 26 May 1741, bp. 31 May 1741 (father called deceased); New Providence, Bahamas, d. 1801.

July 1757 "The said Annuity ordered by the Elders and Deacons to be for the Use of Williams Bradford a Student at Harvard College."

Harvard Grads says "Bradford's mother in 1761 married James Churchill of Plymouth, and it was probably in connection with his business that Williams went to New Providence. He was there when his second Commencement approached, so he requested his M.A. *in absentia* ... The early death of his stepfather and the remarriage of his mother severed any ties he may have had with Plymouth, so he spent the rest of his days at New Providence. At the time of his death, in 1801, he was described as 'King's Counsellor.' He has been listed among the American Loyalists under the mistakened assumption that he had gone into exile."

References: *First Ch Recs* 2:465(annuity). *Harvard Grads* 14:567.

26. MARGARET⁵ BELLOWS (*Martha⁴, James³, Martha², Robert¹*) was b. Marlborough 16 Oct. 1718.

She m. int. Hopkinton 27 Nov. 1747, **JAMES FANNING**.

References: *VR Hopkinton* p. 224(m. int.). *VR Marlborough* p. 26(b. Margaret).

27. MARTHA⁵ BELLOWS (*Martha⁴, James³, Martha², Robert¹*) was b. Marlborough 26 Dec. 1724.

She m. Southborough 27 Jan. 1741/2, **ABRAHAM PIKE**, b. Framingham 12 Feb. 1712; d. Jan. 1810 aged near 90; son of Mikel and Mehetabell (Brown) Pike.

On 10 April 1760 Abraham Pike of Framingham, husbandman, sold to John Pike and his wife Sarah, 21 acres; Abraham's wife Martha also signed this deed and William Pike, Jr., and Rachel Pike were witnesses.

Children of Abraham and Martha (Bellows) Pike, b. Framingham:

    i NAOMI⁶ PIKE, b. 1745, bp. 20/26 April 1747

    ii DANIEL PIKE, bp. 9 Aug. 1747

    iii SILAS PIKE, bp. 5 Aug. 1750

    iv MOSES PIKE, b. 12 Feb. 1752, bp. 18 Feb. 1753; "Slane by a Cannon Ball (Shot by the Ministeral Troops), on Plow'd Hill, Aug. 28, 1775 – and buried on the Southwesterly part thereof," ae 22y 6m 16d.

References: Ruth G. Pike, *Some Descendants of James Pike of Charlestown and Reading, Massachusetts*, type. at NEHGS, pp. 90-1. *VR Framingham* pp. 160(b. Abraham, bp. Daniel), 161(bp. Moses, Naomi, Silas), 458(d. Moses). *VR Southborough*, p. 94(m.). Middlesex Co. LR 101:411(Abraham Pike).

28. KEZIAH⁵ BELLOWS (*Martha⁴, James³, Martha², Robert¹*) was b. Hopkinton 15 March 1727.

She m. Framingham 3 April 1747, **MOSES PARKER**.

In 1790 Moses Parker was head of a household consisting of one man and 3 females in Gerry (now Phillipston) Listed next to him were Samuel Parker (1 man, 4 boys, 7 females), and Assa Parker (1 man, 2 boys, 4 females).

Children of Moses and Keziah (Bellows) Parker, b. Framingham:

    i ASA[6] PARKER, b. 15 March 1747

    ii ELIAS PARKER, bp. 21 Feb. 1749/50

References: *VR Hopkinton* p. 28(b. Keziah). *VR Framingham* pp. 154(b. Asa, Elias), 238(m.).

29. LYDIA[5] BELLOWS (*Martha[4], James[3], Martha[2], Robert[1]*) was b. Southborough 30 April 1729.

She m. (1) Southborough 6 Aug. 1753, as his second wife, **EBENEZER DUNTON**. He m. (1) Southborough 5 Feb. 1744/5, REBECCA LYSCOM, with whom he had Ebenezer, Nathaniel, Reuben, and Samuel.

She m. (2) Southborough 28 Oct. 1773, **EBENEZER PHILLIPS**. He m. (1) Southborough HANNAH LYSCOM, with whom he had Hannah, Ruth, and Susannah.

On 18 Sept. 1771 Lydia Dunton, widow of Ebenezer Dunton late of Southborough, declined administration on his estate and requested his son Nathaniel be appointed. On the same day Nathaniel was appointed administrator with William Collins, Gentleman, and Jonathan Champney, yeoman, both of Southborough, as sureties. The inventory taken on 17 Oct. 1771 included a house and land valued at £60.

References: *VR Southborough* p. 94(1st m.), 105(2nd m., Dunton's 1st m.), 135(Phillips' 1st m.). Worcester Co. PR 11:522;177:332; 461:274(Ebenezer Dunton).

30. JAMES[5] BELLOWS (*Martha[4], James[3], Martha[2], Robert[1]*) was b. Hopkinton 6 March 1738/9, bp. 5 July 1741; d. Southborough bet. 25 June 1804 and 3 June 1810.

He m. (1) Southborough 18 Jan. 1754, **ELISABETH CAMPBELL**; d. Southborough, 23 May 1754 "w. James Jr."

He m. (2) Southborough 11 Dec. 1758, **JOANNA LENARD**, b. Southborough 13 Nov. 1735; d. Southborough, 16 Jan. 1812, widow aged 76; dau. Ezekiel and Joannah (Hudson) Lenard.

James Bellows of Southborough, yeoman, made his will 25 June 1804, proved 3 June 1810, naming his wife Joanna; granddaughter Joanna Rice (to whom he gave his cooper shop and tools); and daughter Elizabeth Rice and her other children Austin, Willard, and Betsey.

Children of James and Joanna (Lenard) Bellows, b. Southborough:

 i ELIZABETH[6] BELLOWS, b. 28 Feb. 1763

 ii JOSIAH BELLOWS, b. 20 July 1766

 iii EZEKIEL BELLOWS, b. 16 June 1771

References: *VR Southborough* pp. 15(b. ch.), 50(d. James) 94(m.), 156(d. Elizabeth, James, Joanna). Worcester Co. PR 39:351(James Bellows).

31. SARAH[5] MAVERICK (*James[4-3], Martha[2], Robert[1]*) was b. Sherborn 13 Aug. 1718.

 She m. Sudbury 25 April 1737, **JOHN PUTNAM**, b. Salem 8 Oct. 1715, son of Samuel and Mary (Leach) Putnam; d. Oswego, N.Y., April 1762.

 On 17 June 1754 John Putnam of Sudbury, husbandman, and his wife Sarah, sold to Daniel Hapgood of Stow, yeoman, 1/6th part of 1/3rd part of land in Sudbury. On 5 Jan. 1756 Daniel Hapgood sold to Joseph Stanhope of Sudbury, 1/6th part of 1/3rd part of the estate of James Maverick which was set off to his widow.

Children of John and Sarah (Maverick) Putnam, b. Sudbury:

 i ELIZABETH[6] PUTNAM, b. 18 Jan. 1737/8

 ii JOHN PUTNAM, b. 13 June 1746

 iii NATHAN PUTNAM, bp. 15 July 1749

 iv ENOS PUTNAM, b. 8 June 1752

 v DANIEL PUTNAM, b. 27 Sept. 1755

 vi ASA PUTNAM, b. 5 Sept. 1758

 vii SARAH PUTNAM, b. 25 Sept. 1761

References: Middlesex Co. LR 53:5(John Putnam); 54:242(Daniel Hapgood). *VR Salem* 2:213(b.John). *VR Sudbury* p. 116(b. ch.).

32. MARY[5] MAVERICK (*James[4-3], Martha[2], Robert[1]*) was b. Sudbury 4 March 1720/1.

 She m. Framingham 20 June 1744, **DAVID MELLEN**, b. Framingham 10 March 1721/2, son of Simon and Esther (Towne) Mellen (called Daniel in VR, David in *Hist. Framingham*); d. Oxford 10 Oct. 1801, aged 80.

On 23 May 1765 David Mellen, husbandman, of Oxford, and his wife Mary, sold to Elijah Parmenter of Sudbury, yeoman, sold 1 acre in Sudbury given by William Walker to his dau. Mary (Mary Maverick's mother). David and Mary were heirs of a 1/6th part of the land.

Children of David and Mary (Maverick) Mellen, 1st b. Framingham, rest b. Oxford:

    i   ANN6 MELLEN, b. 8 Feb. 1844

    ii JOHN MELLEN, b. 10 Aug. 1750

    iii MARY MELLEN, b. 19 March 1753

    iv LUCY MELLEN, b. 30 Aug. 1756

    v DAVID MELLEN, b. 14 May 1759

References: Middlesex Co. LR 70:68(David Mellen). *VR Oxford* pp. 76(b. last 4 ch.), 295(d. David). *VR Framingham* pp. 138(b. David), 139(b. Ann). William Barry, *A History of Framingham* (Boston, 1847), p. 326.

33. ABIGAIL5 MAVERICK (*James4-3, Martha2, Robert1*) was b. Sudbury 4 June 1725.

She m. Sudbury 10 Aug. 1749, **MOSES HILL**, b. Sherborn 26 April 1728; son of Nathaniel and Elizabeth (Phipps or Hardy) Hill.

On 9 June 1766 Moses Hill of Sherborn, yeoman, and his wife Abigail; Elijah Moor of Sudbury, yeoman; Ephraim Potter of Marlboro, yeoman, and wife Esther; Bathsheba Maverick of Marlboro, spinster; and Daniel Ward of Marlboro, yeoman, sold to Elijah Parmenter of Sudbury, yeoman, 6 acres of swamp and upland in Sudbury.

Children of Moses and Abigail (Maverick) Hill, b. Sherborn:

    i   MARY6 HILL, b. 15 Sept. 1749

    ii   ELIZABETH HILL, b. 26 March 1751

    iii MERCY HILL, b. 29 Oct. 1753

    iv MOSES HILL, b. 24 Aug. 1755

    v   JESSE HILL, b. 17 Aug. 1757

    vi NATHANIEL HILL, b. 1 July 1760

    vii BEZELEEL HILL, b. 17 Sept. 1763

   viii SILVANUS HILL, b. 10 July 1765

References: *VR Sherborn* pp. 44-6(b. Moses, b. ch.). Middlesex Co. LR 70:69(Moses Hill et.al.).

34. ESTHER⁵ MAVERICK (*James⁴⁻³, Martha², Robert¹*) was b. Sudbury 30 April 1732; d. ca. 1810.

She m. **EPHRAIM POTTER,** born Marlborough, 25 Jan. 1728; died 9 June 1792; son of Ephraim and Sarah (___) Potter.

On 9 June 1766 Moses Hill of Sherborn, yeoman, and his wife Abigail; Elijah Moor of Sudbury, yeoman; Ephraim Potter of Marlboro, yeoman, and wife Esther; Bathsheba Maverick of Marlboro, spinster; and Daniel Ward of Marlboro, yeoman, sold to Elijah Parmenter of Sudbury, yeoman, 6 acres of swamp and upland in Sudbury.

Children of Ephraim and Esther (Maverick) Potter, bp. Marlborough:

    i STEPHEN⁶ POTTER, bp. 27 June 1762

    ii ANNA POTTER, bp. 29 Oct. 1763

    iii EPHRAIM POTTER, bp. 17 Nov. 1765

    iv PERSIS POTTER, bp. 14 Aug. 1768

    v SARAH POTTER, bp. 12 May 1771

    vi JAMES POTTER, bp. 6 June 1773

References: Middlesex Co. LR 70:69(Moses Hill *et al.*). *VR Marlborough* pp. 147-8(b. Ephraim, bp. ch.).

35. SILENCE⁵ MAVERICK (*James⁴⁻³, Martha², Robert¹*) was b. Sudbury 16 April 1735.

She m. Sudbury 5 Feb. 1755, **JEDEDIAH PARMENTER,** b. Sudbury 9 July 1728; son of Solomon and Deborah (Pratt) Parmenter.

Jedediah Parmenter of Sudbury, yeoman, made his will 5 Dec. 1800, proved 12 Jan. 1808, naming his wife Silence, dau. Azubah Dalrymple, grandson Henry Dalrymple, and only son Ezekiel Parmenter.

Children of Jedediah and Silence (Maverick) Parmenter, b. Sudbury:

    i AZUBAH⁶ PARMENTER, b. 25 Jan. 1764

    ii EZEKIEL PARMENTER, b. 2 Nov. 1771

References: Middlesex Co. PR #16928(Jedediah Parmenter). Middlesex Co. LR 54:243(Jedediah Parmenter). *VR Sudbury* pp. 104(b. Azubah), 106(b. Jedediah), 109(b. Ezekiel).

BIBLIOGRAPHY AND KEY TO SOURCES

Abbe-Abbey Gen
Abbe, Cleveland and Josephine Genung Nichols, *Abbe-Abbey Genealogy, in Memory of John Abbe and his Descendants* (New Haven, 1916).

Adams Fam (1861)
Adams, George, *Genealogy of the Adams Family of Kingston, Mass.* (Boston, 1861).

Adams Gen
Adams, Andrew N., *Genealogical History of Henry Adams of Braintree, Massachusetts, and His Descendants; also John Adams of Cambridge, Massachusetts, 1632-1897* (Rutland, Vt., 1898).

Aldrich Gen
Aldrich, Alvin James, *The George Aldrich Genealogy*, Vol. 1 (1971); Vol. 5 (1982).

Anc Of One Atwood Fam 1965
Atwood, C. A., *Ancestry of One Atwood Family* (Antioch, Illinois, 1965).

Bangor Hist Mag
Porter, Joseph W., ed., *The Bangor [Maine] Historical Magazine, later the Maine Historical Magazine* (1885-1894).

Barker Gen
Barker, Elizabeth Frye, *Barker Genealogy* (New York, 1927).

Barnstable Fams
Swift, C. F., *Genealogical Notes of Barnstable Families, Being a Reprint of the Amos Otis Papers* (Barnstable, Mass., 1888-90; reprint Baltimore, Md., 1979).

Barstow-Bestor
Radasch, Arthur Hitchcock, *Barstow-Bestor Genealogy, Descendants of John[1] Barstow and George[1] Barstow* (1964).

Bass Desc
Bass, Clarissa T., *Descendants of Samuel and Ann Bass* (Freeport, Ill., 1940).

Bingham Fam
Bingham, Theodore Alfred, *The Bingham Family in the United States* 3 vols. (Easton, Pa., 1927-1930).

Boston Cems
Dunkle, Robert J. and Ann S. Lainhart, *Inscriptions and Records of the Old Cemeteries of Boston* (Boston, 2000).

Boston Deaths 1700-1799
Dunkle, Robert J. and Lainhart, Ann S., *Deaths in Boston, 1700 to 1799*, 2 vols. (Boston, 1999).

Boston Evening Transcript
Genealogical column of newspaper *Boston Evening Transcript*, Boston, 1906-1941.

Boston News Obits
Index of Obituaries in Boston Newspapers 1704-1800, 3 vols. (Boston, 1968).

BRC or Boston VR
Reports of the Record Commissioners of the City of Boston, Vols. 9 and 24 [Boston births, marriages and deaths, 1630-1699 and births 1700-1800] (Boston, 1883 and 1894). Vols. 28 and 30 [Boston marriages 1700-1751 and 1751-1809] (Boston, 1898 and 1902; reprinted Baltimore, Md., 4 vols. in 2, 1977 and 1978).

Bradford Desc
Hall, Ruth G., *Descendants of Governor William Bradford* (n.p., 1951).

Braintree Recs
Bates, Samuel A., *Records of the Town of Braintree 1640-1793* (Randolph, Mass., 1886).

Brattle St Ch Recs
Brattle Street Church Records, on *Boston Churches* CD (Boston: NEHGS 2001).

Brimfield Hist
Historical Celebration of the Town of Brimfield, Hampden County, Mass. (Springfield, 1879).

Buell Fam
Welles, Albert, *History of the Buell Family in England...and in America* (New York, 1881).

Burnap-Burnett Gen
Belknap, Henry W., *The Burnap-Burnett Genealogy* (Salem, Mass., 1925).

Cambridge Hist
Paige, Lucuis R., *History of Cambridge, Massachusetts, 1630-1877* (Boston,1877).

Canaan Reflections
Reflections, Canaan, New York, Bicentennial (1976).

Canterbury 1st Ch
Records of the Congregational Church in Canterbury, 1711-1844 (Hartford, Conn., 1932).

Canton VR
Endicott, Frederic, *The Record of the Births, Marriages and Deaths, in the Town of Stoughton from 1727 to 1800, and in the Town of Canton from 1797 to 1845* (Canton, Mass. 1896).

Charlestown By Wyman
Wyman, Thomas B., *The Genealogies and Estate of Charlestown*, 2 vols. (Boston, 1879, reprint Somersworth, N.H., 1982).

Charlestown VR
Joslyn, Roger D., comp.and ed., *Vital Records of Charlestown, Massachusetts, to the Year 1850*, 2 vols. (Boston, 1984).

Chipman Gen
Chipman, A. L., *Chipmans of America* (Poland, Me., 1904).

Churchill Fam
Churchill, Gardner Asaph and Nathaniel Wiley Churchill, *The Churchill Family in America* (Boston, 1904; reprint, Baltimore, 1991).

Clapp Fam in Amer
Clapp, E., *The Clapp Memorial* (Boston, 1876).

Cleveland Gen
Cleveland, Edmund J., *The Genealogy of the Cleveland and Cleaveland Families*, 3 vols. (Hartford, Conn., 1899).

Coggeshall Fam
Coggeshall, Charles Pierce and Thellwell Russell Coggeshall, *The Coggeshalls in America* (Boston, 1930).

Cogswell Desc
Cogswell, Donald James, *Descendants of John Cogswell* (Westminster, Md., 1998).

Columbian Centinel
Columbian Centinel, newspaper published in Massachusetts 1740+.

CT Hist Coll
Connecticut Historical Society Collections (Hartford, Conn.).

Conn Marrr
Bailey, Frederick W., *Early Connecticut Marriages as Found on Ancient Church Records Prior to 1800*, 7 vols. (New Haven, Conn., 1896-1906; reprinted in 1 vol., Baltimore, Md., 1968, 1982).

CT Men in Rev War
Johnston, Henry Phelps, *Records of Service of Connecticut Men in the Military and Naval Service during the Revolutionary War, 1773-1783* (Hartford, 1889).

CT Settlers By Goodwin
Goodwin, Nathaniel, *Genealogical Notes or Contributions to the Family History of Some of the First Settlers of Connecticut and Massachusetts* (Hartford, Conn., 1856, reprinted Baltimore, Md., 1969).

Cooke (Thomas)
Fiske, Jane Fletcher, *Thomas Cooke of Rhode Island* (Boxford, Mass., 1987).

Cornish NH Hist
Child, William H., *History of the Town of Cornish, New Hampshire*, 2 vols. (Concord, N.H., 1911).

Cornwall By Starr
Starr, Edward C., *A History of Cornwall Conn., a Typical New England Town* (New Haven, 1926).

Cornwall Documents
Gannett, Michael R., *Cornwall Documents, Town Meeting Minutes, 1740-1875* (1994).

Cowles Fam
Cowles, Col. Calvin Duvall, *The Genealogy of the Cowles Family in America* (New Haven, 1929).

Cushman Fam
Cushman, Joseph Augustine, *The First Seven Generations of the Cushman Family in New England* (1964).

John Damon
Damon, D. Bradford, "John Damon of Scituate, Massachusetts," typescript at NEHGS, Boston.

DAR Patriot Index
DAR Patriot Index, Publ. by the National Society of the Daughters of the American Revolution (Washington, D.C., 1966; Supplements: 1, 1969; 2, 1973; 3, 1976).

Dedham Ch
Hill, Don G., *Record of Baptisms, Marriage and Deaths transcribed from the Church Records in the Town of Dedham, Massachusetts, 1638-1845. Also All Epitaphs in the Ancient Burial Place in Dedham* (Dedham, 1888).

Dewey Gen
Dewey, Louis M., *Life of George Dewey...and Dewey Family History* (Westfield, 1898).

Dexter's Memoranda
Dunkle Robert J., and Ann S. Lainhart, *John Haven Dexter's Memoranda of the Town of Boston in the 18th & 19th Centuries* (Boston, 1997).

Downeast Ancestry
Bachelor, Rosemary E., *Downeast Ancestry,* 1976.

Drake Fam
Stoughton, Lois, *The Drake Family in England and America, 1360-1895 and The Descendants of Thomas Drake of Weymouth, Massachusetts* (Boston, 1896).

Durant Gen
Durant, Rev. William, and Alexander G. Rose III, "The Durant Genealogy: A History of the Descendants of George and Elizabeth (----) Durant of Malden, Mass. and Middletown, Conn.," 1966, typescript at NEHGS, Boston.

Dyar Gen
Dyar, Harrison Gray, *A Preliminary Genealogy of the Dyar Family* (Washington, D.C., 1903).

Early Ohio Census Records
Jackson, Ronald Verne, *Early Ohio Census Records: Cincinnati 1798, 1799–1817;* (Bountiful, Utah, 1981).

"Easton Families"
"Births, Deaths, and Marriages by Families 1697–1847," manuscript, NEHGS, Boston, and on FHL microfilm 1059951.

Enfield CT Hist
Allen, F. O., *History of Enfield Connecticut* (Lancaster, Pa., 1900).

Ensign Desc
Nelson, Martha Eunice Ensign, *Record of the Descendants of James Ensign and his Wife Sarah Elson,* 3 vols. (1939, 1960, 1977).

Fairfield CT Fams
Jacobus, Donald L., *History and Genealogy of the Families of Old Fairfield,* 2 vols. in 3 (1930-34; reprint Cleveland, Ohio, 1967).

Farmington Hist
Butler, Francis G., *A History of Farmington, Franklin County, Maine* (Farmington, Me., 1885).

Finney-Phinney
Finney, Howard, *Finney-Phinney Families in America: Descendants of John Finney of Plymouth and Barnstable, Mass. and Bristol, R.I.; of Samuel Finney of Philadelphia, Penn.; and of Robert Finney of New London, Pa.* (Richmond, Va., 1957).

Fitch Fam
Fitch, Roscoe Conkling, *History of the Fitch Family, A.D. 1400-1930*, 2 vols, (1930).

Fitch Gen
Fitch, John T., *Descendants of the Reverend James Fitch 1622-1702* (Cambridge, Mass., 1997).

Fowler Hist
Fowler, Christine, *Fowler History* (Batavia, N.Y., 1950).

Friendship ME Recs
Cook, Melville B., *Records of Meduncook Plantations and Friendship, Me., 1762-1899* (Rockland, Me., 1985).

Frink Gen
Humphrey, Peggy Frink, *The Frink Family in America* (Ann Arbor, Mich., 1971).

Gager Fam
Gager, Edmund R., *The Gager Family* (Baltimore, Md., 1985).

Gen Advertiser
Greenlaw, Lucy H., ed., *The Genealogical Advertiser, a Quarterly Magazine of Family History*, Vols. 1-4 (1898-1901, reprint Baltimore, 1974).

Gilberts of NE
Gilbert, George Gordon and Geoffrey; Homer W. Brainard, and Clarence A. Torrey, *Gilberts of New England. Part I, Descendants of John Gilbert of Dorchester. Part II, Descendants of Matthew Gilbert of New Haven, Humphrey Gilbert of Ipswich, and William Gilbert of Boston* (Victoria, B.C., 1959).

Giles Mem
Vinton, John A., *The Giles Memorial. Genealogical Memoirs of the Families Bearing the Names of Giles, Gould, Holmes (and others)* (Boston, 1864).

Goodwins of Hartford
Goodwin, James Janius, *The Goodwins of Hartford, Connecticut, Descendants of William and Ozias Goodwin* (Hartford, Conn., 1891).

Granary Bur Gd
Gravestone Inscriptions and Records of the Tomb Burials in the Granary Burying Ground, Boston, Mass. (Salem, Mass., 1918).

Great Migration Begins
Anderson, Robert C., *The Great Migration Begins*, 3 vols. (Boston, 1995).

Greenman Fam
Greenman, Peter Holden, *The Greenman Family in America*, R.I. (Delmar, N.Y.,1998).

Hale Cem Coll
Hale collection of cemetery records copied from the WPA of Connecticut cemeteries about 1932. Bound volumes for each town and a single alphabetical card index; at Connecticut State Library.

Hale House
Jacobus, Donald Lines and Waterman, Edgar Francis, *Hale, House and Related Families* (Hartford, Conn., 1952, reprinted Baltimore, 1978).

Halifax VR
Bowman, George Ernest, *Vital Records of the Town of Halifax, Massachusetts, to the End of the Year 1849* (Boston, 1905).

Hammond Gen
Hammond, Frederick S., *History and Genealogy of the Hammond Families in America*, 2 vols. (Oneida, N.Y., 1902).

Desc Benjamin Hammond
Hammond, Roland, *History and Genealogy of Descendants of William Hammond of London, England, and His Wife Elizabeth Penn, Through Their Son, Benjamin, of Sandwich and Rochester, Massachusetts, 1600-1894* (1894).

Hanover First Ch
Briggs, L. Vernon, *History and Records of the First Congregational Church, Hanover, Massachusetts, 1727-1865 and Inscriptions from the Headstones and Tombs in the Cemetery at Centre Hanover, Mass., 1727-1894* (Boston, 1895).

Hanover VR
A Copy of the Records of Births, Marriages, and Deaths, and of Intentions of Marriage, of the Town of Hanover, Massachusetts, 1727-1757, as Recorded by the Several Town Clerks for the Said Town of Hanover (1898).

Hardwick Hist
Paige, Lucius Robinson, *History of Hardwick, Massachusetts* (Boston, 1883).

Hartford By Barbour
Barbour, Lucius B., *Families of Early Hartford, Connecticut* (Baltimore, 1977) (includes records of the First Church).

Hartford CT Second Ch
Parker, Edwin Pond, *History of the Second Church of Christ in Hartford* (Hartford, Conn., 1892).

Harlow Gen
Williams, Alicia Crane, ed., *Harlow Family, Descendants of Sgt. William Harlow [1624/5-1691] of Plymouth, Massachusetts* (Baltimore, 1997).

Harvard Grads
Sibley, John L., *Biographical sketches of Graduates of Harvard University in Cambridge, Massachusetts*, (Cambridge, vol. 1, 1873).

Hathaway Gen (1970)
Versailles, Elizabeth Starr, *Hathaways of America* (Northampton, Mass., 1965, 1970).

Hazen Fam
Hazen, Tracy Elliot, *The Hazen Family in America* (Thomaston, Conn., 1947).

Hempstead Diary
Diary of Joshua Hempstead of New London, Connecticut, 1711-1758 (New London, Conn., 1901, reprinted 1985).

Hibbard Fam
Hibbard, Augustine George, *The Genealogy of the Hibbard Family* (Hartford, Conn., 1901).

Hingham Hist
History of the Town of Hingham, Mass., 3 vols. (Hingham, Mass., 1893; reprinted Somersworth, N.H., 1982).

Hist A. & H.A.C.
Whitman, Zachariah Gardner, *The History of the Ancient and Honorable Artillery Company* (1842).

Holland Hist
Lovering, Rev. Martin, *History of the Town of Holland, Mass.* (Rutland, Vt., 1915).

Hollis St Ch
Dunkle, Robert J., and Ann S. Lainhart, *Hollis Street Church, Boston, Records of Admissions, Baptisms, Marriages, and Deaths, 1732-1887* (Boston, 1998).

Hopkins Desc 1932
Hopkins, Timothy, *John Hopkins of Cambridge, Massachusetts, 1634, and Some of his Descendants* (Stanford University, Palo Alto, Calif., 1932).

Hosmer Gen
Hosmer, James B., *Genealogy of the Hosmer Family* (Hartford, Conn., 1861).

House of Scituate
Pierce, Robert B. and Barbara B., *Samuel House of Scituate, Mass.* (1992).

Hyde Gen
Walworth, Reuben H., *Hyde Genealogy* (Albany, N.Y., 1864).

IGI
International Genealogical Index, Salt Lake City, Utah (Microfiche).

Jameson Gen
Jameson, Ephraim Orcutt, *The Jamesons in America, 1674-1900. Genealogical Records and Memoranda* (Concord, N.H., 1901).

Jewett Gen
Jewett, Fredric Clarke, *History and Genealogy of the Jewetts of America*, 4 vols. (reprint, Bowie, Md., 1992).

Jebogue Ch Recs
The Records of the Church at Jebogue in Yarmouth, Nova Scotia, 1766-1851 (Yarmouth, N.S.: Stonycroft Press, 1992).

The Kelloggs
Hopkins, Timothy, *The Kelloggs in the Old World and the New World* (San Francisco, Calif., 1903).

Kimball Fam
Morrison, Leonard, and Stephen Sharples, *The History of the Kimball Family in America* (Boston, 1897).

Killingly Ch Rec
Larned, E. D., *Church Records Of Killingly, Conn.* (Lambertville, N.J., 1984).

Kinne Gen
Robertson, Florance Keeney, *The Genealogy of Henry and Ann Kinne, Pioneers of Salem, Massachusetts* (Los Angeles, Calif., 1947).

Kingsley Fam
Kingsley, William Arthur, *Kingsley Family in America* (Baltimore, 1980).

Knowles Desc
Hufbauer, Virginia Knowles, *Descendants of Richard Knowles, 1637-1973* (San Diego, Calif., 1974).

Lanesboro Hist
Palmer, Charles J., *History of the Town of Lanesborough* (Lanesboro, Mass., 1905).

Lawrence Co Cem
"Illinois Cemeteries: Cemeteries of Lawrence Co." typescript FHL, Salt Lake City, Utah.

LeBaron Gen
Stockwell, Mary LeBaron, *Descendants of Francis LeBaron of Plymouth, Mass.* (Boston, 1904).

John Lee and Desc
Lee, L. and S. F., *John Lee and His Descendants* (1897).

Lewis Co Hist
Hough, Franklin B., *1805 History of Lewis County, New York* (Syracuse, N.Y., 1883).

Lincoln Co ME Probates
Patterson, William D., ed., *The Probate Records of Lincoln County, Maine, 1760 to 1800* (Portland, Me., 1895; reprint, Camden, Me., 1991).

Litchfield Co Rev Soldiers
Richards, Josephine Ellis, ed., *Honor Roll of Litchfield County Revolutionary Soldiers* (Litchfield: Mary Floyd Tallmadge Chapter, D.A.R., 1912).

Little Compton Fams
Wilbour, Benjamin F., *Little Compton Families* (Providence, R.I., 1967).

Lo-Lathrop Fam
Huntington, E. B., *A Genealogical Memoir of the Lo-Lathrop Family* (Ridgefield, Conn., 1884; reprinted 1971).

Lord Gen
Lord, Kenneth, *Genealogy of the Descendants of Thomas Lord* (New York, 1946).

Loring Gen
Pope, Charles H., *Loring Genealogy compiled from "The Chronicles or Ancestral Records" of James Spear Loring; from the Manuscripts of John Arthur Loring; and from Many Other Sources* (Cambridge, 1917).

Loyalists to Canada
Holmes, Theodore C., *Loyalists to Canada: The 1783 Settlement of Quakers and others at Passamaquoddy* (Camden, Me., 1992).

Loyalists of Mass
Jones, E. Alfred, *Loyalists of Massachusetts* (London, 1930).

Luddington-Saltus
Ludington, Ethel Saltus, *Luddington-Saltus Records* (New Haven, 1925).

Lunenburg Hist
Des Brisay, Mather Byles, *History of the County of Lunenburg*, 3rd ed. (Nova Scotia, 1967).

Lyme CT VR
Hall, Verne M. and Elizabeth B. Plimpton, *Vital Records of Lyme, Connecticut to the End of the Year 1850* (Lyme, Conn., 1976).

ME Fams 1790
Maine Families in 1790, 8 vols. to date, ongoing (Camden and Rockport, Me., 1988 – 2003)

Manning Fam
Manning, Charles W., *The Manning Families of New England* (Salem, 1902).

Mansfield CT VR
Dimock, Susan W., *Births, Baptisms, and Marriages and Deaths from the Records of the Churches in Mansfield, Connecticut. Births, Marriages and Deaths of Mansfield* (New York, 1898).

Manwaring
Manwaring, Charles W., *A Digest of the Early Connecticut Probate Records*, 3 vols. (Hartford, Conn., 1902-6).

Marcy Gen
Marcy, Charles Edney, *History and Genealogy of John Marcy, 1662-1724, Woodstock, Conn., and Many of his Descendants, Eleven Generations* (privately pub., 1980).

Marshfield by Richards
Richards, Lysander Salmon, *History of Marshfield*, 2 vols. (1901, 1905).

Marshfield VR
Sherman, Robert M. and Ruth Wilder, *Vital Records of the Town of Marshfield, Massachusetts, to the Year 1850* (Warwick, R.I., 1970).

Martha's Vineyard By Banks
Banks, Charles E., *History of Martha's Vineyard, with Genealogy*, 3 vols. (Boston, 1911-25; reprint Edgartown, Mass., 1966).

Hugh Mason
Mason, Edna Warren, *Descendants of Capt. Hugh Mason in America* (New Haven, Conn., 1937).

Mass Officers French & Indian War
Voye, Nancy S., *Massachusetts Officers in the French and Indian Wars, 1748-1763* (Boston, 1975).

MD
The Mayflower Descendant: a Quarterly Magazine of Pilgrim History and Genealogy, Vol. 1, 1899.

Mayflower Source Recs
Mayflower Source Records (From the New England Historical and Genealogical Register) (Baltimore, 1986).

MF
Mayflower Families Through Five Generations, published by the General Society of Mayflower Descendants, 21 vols.

MQ
The Mayflower Quarterly, Vol. 1, 1935; a publication of the General Society of Mayflower Descendants.

Middleboro Deaths
Wood, Alfred, *Records of Deaths, Middleboro, Massachusetts* (Boston, 1947).

Middleboro VR
Merrick, Barbara Lambert, and Alicia Crane Williams, *Middleborough, Massachusetts, Vital Records*, 2 vols. (Boston, 1986, 1990).

Montville CT His
Baker, Henry A., *History of Montville, formerly the north parish of New London, from 1648-1896* (Hartford, Conn., 1895).

MSSR
Massachusetts Soldiers and Sailors of the Revolutionary War, a Compilation from the Archives, 17 vols. (Boston, 1896-1908).

Nash Fam
Benson, Richard H., *The Nash Family of Weymouth, Massachusetts* (Boston, 1998).

NGSQ
National Genealogical Society Quarterly, Vol. 1., 1912; quarterly journal of the National Genealogical Society, Arlington, Va.
    60 [1972]:267 Clifford Neal Smith, "Some British and German Deserters During the American Revolution."
    71 [1983]:87   Robert S. Wakefield and Robert M. Sherman, "Arthur Howland of Plymouth, Mass., 1640, his Wife Margaret (____) Walker, and Their Children."
    74 [1986]:214 Eugene A. Stratton, "Descendants of Mr. John Holmes, Messenger of the Plymouth Court."

Newcomb Gen
Newcomb, Bethuel M., *Andrew Newcomb 1618-1686 and his Descendants*, a revised edition of *Genealogical Memoir*, of the Newcomb Family published 1874 by John Bearse Newcomb (New Haven, Conn., 1923).

New England Captives
Coleman, Emma, *New England Captives Carried to Canada Between 1677 and 1760, During the French and Indian Wars* (Portland, Me., 1925).

NEHGR
New England Historical and Genealogical Register, quarterly journal of the New England Historic Genealogical Society, Boston, Mass., 1847 – ongoing.
    2:404, "Inscriptions from the Burying Ground in Norwich, Conn."
    9:127, Rev. William Allen, "Descendants of Alice Bradford."
    13:122, J. Gardner White, "Tileston."
    25:192, "Notes & Queries."
    46:120, A List of the Settlers in St. George's River, Meduncook and Broadbay."
    51:316, Harvey Hebard and Ralph D. Smith, "Descendants of Robert Hebert of Salem and Beverly, Mass."
    58:128, William R. Cutter and Arthur G. Loring, "The Brooks Family of Woburn, Mass."
    61:281, Ralph D. Smith, "Edward and John Collins and Their Descendants."

81:292, Grace Williamson Edes, "Timothy Williamson of Marshfield, Mass., and his Descendants."

82:140, Alfred Gooding, "Records of the South Church of Portsmouth, N.H."

107:260, Bradford Adams Whittemore and Edgar Whittemore, "The Whittemore Family in America."

117:298, Lydia B. (Phinney) Brownson and Maclean W. McLean, "Michael Blackwell of Sandwich, Mass. (c. 1620-1710)."

119:260, Lydia B. (Phinney) Brownson and Maclean W. McLean, "Lt. John[1] and Elizabeth (Freeman) Ellis of Sandwich, Mass."

126:95, "Vital Records of Liverpool N.S."

126:272, Edna Anne Hunnibal and Claude W. Barlow, "Richard, William, and Hugh, Sons of John Briggs of Taunton, Massachusetts."

150:157, Helen S. Ullmann, "Hubbell Steevens of Killingworth, Connecticut."

New Haven Fams
Jacobus, Donald L., *Families of Ancient New Haven*, 3 vols. (Rome, N.Y., 1923, 1927, New Haven, Conn., 1931; reprint Baltimore, Md., 1974).

New Haven 1ˢᵗ Ch
Dexter, Franklin Bowditch, *Historical Catalogue of the Members of the First Church of Christ in New Haven, Connecticut* (New Haven, Conn., 1914).

New North Ch Recs
Wyman, Thomas Bellows, *The New North Church, Boston, 1714-1799* (Baltimore, 1995).

New South Ch Recs
Records of the New South Church, on *Boston Churches* CD (Boston: NEHGS, 2001).

Newton Bio Dir
Ritter, Priscilla R., and Thelma Fleishman, *Newton, Massachusetts, 1679-1779, A Biographical Directory* (Boston, 1982).

Newton Hist
Jackson, Francis, *A History of the Early Settlement of Newton, County of Middlesex, Massachusetts, From 1639 to 1800* (Boston, 1854).

NYGBR
The New York Genealogical and Biographical Record, quarterly journal of the New York Genealogical and Biographical Society, New York, N.Y., 1870 – ongoing.
>	64:34, Howard S. F. Randolph, "Abial[5] (Metcalf) Fitch of Greenbush, Rensselaer Co., N.Y., Her Mayflower Ancestry and Her Descendants."

Nickerson Fam
The Nickerson Family; The Descendants of William Nickerson, 1604-1689, 4 vols. (1973).

No Yarmouth ME VR
Sherman, Ruth Wilder, *Vital Records of North Yarmouth Maine to the Year 1850* (Society of Mayflower Descendants in the State of Rhode Island, 1980, 2nd ed. Camden, Me., 1993).

Norwich CT VR
Society of Colonial Wars in the State of Connecticut, *Vital Records of Norwich, 1659-1848* (Hartford, Conn., 1913).

Norwich Hist
Caulkins, Frances Manwaring, *History of Norwich, Connecticut, From its Possession by the Indians to the Year 1866* (Hartford, 1866, 1874).

Old Times
Corliss, Augustus W., *Old Times: A magazine devoted to the Preservation and Publication of Documents Relating to the Early History of North Yarmouth, Maine. Including...the towns of Harpswell, Freeport, Pownal, Cumberland and Yarmouth...Also, Genealogical Records of the Principal Families and Biographical Sketches of the Most Distinguished Residents of the Town*, 8 vols. (Yarmouth, Me., 1877-1884; reprinted 8 vols. in 1, Somersworth, N.H., 1977).

Ontario Loyalists
Reid, William D., *The Loyalists in Ontario ...* (Baltimore, 1973).

Oxford CT by Sharpe
Sharpe, W.C., *History of Oxford* (Seymour, Conn., 1885).

Desc Samuel Packard
Wight, Charles Packard, "Descendants of Samuel Packard," typescript at NEHGS, Boston.

Pawlet VT Cem Recs
Jenks, Margaret R., *Pawlet Cemetery Inscriptions, Rutland County, Vermont* (1984).

Pensions Abstracts
White, Virgil D., *Genealogical Abstracts of Revolutionary War Pension Files*, 4 vols. (Waynesboro, Tenn., 1992).

(Plymouth) Burial Hill
Kingham, Bradford, *Epitaphs from Burial Hill, Plymouth, Massachusetts, from 1657 to 1892. With biographical and historical notes* (Brookline, Mass., 1892; reprint Baltimore, 1977).

Plymouth Ch Recs
Plymouth Church Records, 1620-1859, 2 vols. (New York, 1920-23; reprint Baltimore, 1975).

Plymouth Co Ct Recs
Konig, David T., *Plymouth Court Records 1686-1859*, 16 vols. (Wilmington, Del., 1978).

Plymouth Colony Recs
Shurtleff, Nathaniel B. & Pulsifer, David, *Records of the Colony of New Plymouth in New England*, 12 vols. (Boston, 1855-61; reprint 12 vols. in 6; New York, 1968).

Plymouth Town Recs
Records of the Town of Plymouth, 3 Vols. (1889-1903).

Plymouth VR
Van Antwerp, Lee D., and Ruth Wilder Sherman, *Vital Records of Plymouth, Massachusetts, to the Year 1850* (Camden, Me., 1993).

PN&Q
Bowman, George E., *Pilgrim Notes and Queries*, 5 vols. (Boston, 1913-17).

Raymond Gen
Raymond, Samuel E., *Raymond Genealogy, Descendants of Richard Raymond,*
Seattle, 1969.

Hist Redding CT
Todd, Charles Burr, *The History of Redding, Connecticut* ... (New York, 1880).

Redding CT Ch
Manual of the Congregational Church in Redding, Conn. (1896).

Richford Settlers
Gibson, Leon, *"Genealogy of Early Settlers of Richford,"* from the *Richford
Gazette* from 1935 and 1936.

Richford VT Cem
Simmons, Marlene, *Index to Grave Stones Inscriptions, Richford, Vermont* (1994).

Richmond NH Hist
Bassett, William, *History of the Town of Richmond, Cheshire County, New Hampshire,
From its First Settlement, to 1882* (Boston, 1884).

Ripley Gen
Ripley, H. W., *Genealogy of The Ripley Family* (Newark, N.J., 1867).

RIVR
Arnold, James N., *Vital Records of Rhode Island, 1636-1850*, 21 vols.
(Providence, R.I., 1891-1912).

Rockingham VT Hist
Hayes, Lyman Simpson, *History of the Town of Rockingham, Vermont* (Bellows
Falls, Vt., 1907).

Root Gen
Root, James Pierce, *Root Genealogical Records 1600-1870. Comprising the general
history of the Root and Roots families in America* (New York, 1870).

Ruggles Gen
Ruggles, Henry Stoddard, *Ruggles Genealogy* (Boston, 1892).

Rutland Co VT Cem
Jenks, Margaret R., *Chittenden, Mendon, Pittsfield, and Sherburne Cemetery Inscriptions, Rutland Co., Vermont* (1991).

St. John Gen
Alexander, Orline St. John, *The St. John Genealogy* (New York, 1907).

Salem First Ch
Pierce, Richard D., *The Records of the First Church in Salem, Massachusetts, 1629-1736* (Salem, 1974).

Sandwich VR
Kardell, Caroline Lewis, and Russell A. Lovell, Jr., *Vital Records of Sandwich, Massachusetts, to 1884*, 3 vols. (Boston, 1996).

Savage
Savage, James., *A Genealogical Dictionary of the First Sett-lers of New England showing three generations of those who came before May 1692 …*, 4 vols. (Boston, 1860-62; reprints Baltimore, 1965, 1981).

Swansea VR
Rounds, H.L. Peter, *Vital Records of Swansea, Massachusetts to 1850* (Boston, 1992).

Saybrook Colony VR
Plimpton, Elizabeth B., *The Vital Records of Saybrook Colony, 1635-1860; including the towns of Chester, Deep River, Essex, Old Saybrook, and Westbrook, Connecticut* (1985).

Seymour Gen
Seymour, George Dudley and Donald Lines Jacobus, *A History of The Seymour Family, Descendants of Richard Seymour of Hartford, Connecticut, for Six Generations* (New Haven, 1939).

1771 Valuation List
Pruitt, Bettye Hobbs, *The Massachusetts Tax Valuation List of 1771* (2nd printing, Camden, Me., 1998).

Sharon Bury Gr
Van Alstyne, L., *Burying Grounds of Sharon, Connecticut, Amenia and North East, New York* (1983).

Shepard Fam
Shepard, Gerald F., *The Shepard Families of New England*, 3 vols. (New Haven, Conn., 1971-1973).

Sherman Gen
Holman, Mary Lovering, *Descendants of William Sherman of Marshfield, Massachusetts* (Brookline, Mass., 1936).

Skinner Kinsmen
Fernald, Natalie R., *The Skinner Kinsmen, The Descendants of John Skinner of Hartford, Connecticut* (Washington, D.C., 1926).

Small Desc
Underhill, Lora A. W., *Descendants of Edward Small of New England and the Allied families, with tracings of English Ancestry*, 3 vols. (Cambridge, Mass., 1910).

Southington Cem
Barbour, Lucius B., *Genealogical Data from Connecticut Cemeteries, Southington.*

Southington CT by Timlow
Timlow, Heman R., *Ecclesiastical and other Sketches of Southington, Conn.*, (Hartford, 1875).

Spooner Desc
Spooner, Thomas, *Records of William Spooner of Plymouth, Mass., and his Descendants*, Vol. 1 (Cincinnati, Ohio, 1883).

Stearns Gen
Van Wagenen, Avis S., *Genealogy of Charles and Nathaniel Stearns* (Syracuse, N.Y., 1901).

Steele Fam
Durrie, Daniel Steele, *Steele Family. A Genealogical History of John and George Steele, (Settlers of Hartford, Conn.,) 1635-6, and Their Descendants* (Albany, N.Y., 1859).

Steevens Desc
Barlow, Claude W., *John Steevens of Guilford, Connecticut; Five Generations of 17th and 18th Century Descendants with Surnames* (Rochester, N.Y., 1976).

Stonington CT Hist
Wheeler, R. A., *History of Stonington, Conn. with a genealogical register* (New London, Conn., 1900; reprint Baltimore, Md., 1977).

Stoughton VR see Canton VR

Stratford CT Hist
Orcutt, Rev. Samuel, *A History of the Old Town of Stratford and the City of Bridgeport, Connecticut*, 2 vols. (New Haven, 1886).

Strong Desc
Dwight, Benjamin W., *The History of the Descendants of Elder John Strong, of Northampton, Mass.* (Albany, N.Y., 1871).

Suffolk Deeds
Suffolk (MA) Deeds, 14 vols. (Boston, 1850-1906).

TAG
The American Genealogist, private quarterly journal, 1922 – ongoing; published in 2004 at Demorest, Georgia.

Terry Fam
Terry, Stephen, *Notes of Terry Familes in the United States of America* (Hartford, 1887).

Thomas Gen
Raymond, John M., *Thomas Families of Plymouth County, Massachusetts, Genealogies of the Families of David Thomas of Middleboro (1620-1689), John Thomas of Marshfield (1621-1691), and William Thomas of Marshfield (1573-1651)* (Menlo Park, Calif., 1980).

Torrey's Marriages
Torrey, Clarence Almon, *New England Marriages Prior to 1700* (Baltimore, Md., 1985), based on manuscript at NEHGS, on CD (2001).

Tracy Gen
Tracy, Evert E., *Tracy Genealogy: Ancestors and Descendants of Lieutenant Thomas Tracy of Norwich, Conn., 1660* (Albany, N.Y., 1898).

True Fam
True, Charles Wesley, Jr., *The True Family* (revised 1991).

Turner ME Hist
French, Rev. W. R., *A History of Turner, Maine, From its Settlement to 1886* (Portland, Me., 1887).

Union CT Hist
Lawson, Harvey M., *The History of Union, Connecticut* (New Haven, 1893).

Union ME Hist
Sibley, John Langdon, *A History of the Town of Union, in the County of Lincoln, Maine* (Boston, 1851).

VR of Eastern NY
Bowman, Fred Q., *10,000 Vital Records of Eastern New York* (Baltimore, 1987).

Wadsworth Fam
Wadsworth, Horace A., *250 Years of the Wadsworth Family in America* (Lawrence, Mass., 1883).

Waldo Fam
Lincoln, Waldo, *Genealogy of the Waldo Family* (Worcester, Mass., 1902).

Warner Desc
Warner, Lucien C., and Josephine Genung Nichols, *The Descendants of Andrew Warner* (New Haven, 1919).

Warren Desc
Foster, Warren Woden, *Some Descendants of Arthur Warren of Weymouth, Massachusetts Bay Colony* (Washington, D.C., 1911).

Waterman Gen
Jacobus, Donald L., *Descendants of Robert Waterman of Marshfield, Mass.*, Vols. 1 & 2 (New Haven, Conn., 1939-42). *Descendants of Richard Waterman of Providence, R.I*, Vol. 3 (New Haven, Conn., 1954).

Oren Waters Anc.
Harrell, Elizabeth J., *The New England Ancestry of Oren Waters (1778-1873) of Stoughton, Massachusetts, and Pittsburgh, Pennsylvania* (Los Altos, Calif., 1988).

Watertown by Bond
Bond, Henry, *Genealogies of the Families and Descendants of the Early Settlers of Watertown, Massachusetts, including Waltham and Weston* (Boston, 1860).

Watertown Recs
Watertown Records, Comprising the First and Second Book of Town Proceedings, with Land Grants and Possessions. Also, the Proprietors' Book, and the First Book and Supplement of Births, Deaths, and Marriages, 5 vols. (1894).

Webster Fam
Webster, William Holcomb, *History and Genealogy of the Gov. John Webster Family of Connecticut* (Rochester, N.Y., 1915).

Wentworth Gen
Wentworth, John, *The Wentworth Genealogy, English and American* (Boston, 1878).

W Hartford Fams
This source, referenced by earlier researchers on the project, has not been identified by the present compiler.

Westbrook CT Ch Recs
Rumsey, Jean, *First Congregational Church of Westbrook, Conn.* (1979).

Wethersfield CT by Stiles
Adams, Sherman W., and Henry R. Stiles, *The History of Ancient Wethersfield, Connecticut*, 2 vols. (1904, reprint Rockport, Me., 1996).

Weymouth By Chamberlain
Chamberlain, G. W., *History of Weymouth with Genealogies*, 4 vols. (Boston, 1923).

Wheat Gen
Wheat, Silas Carmi, and Helen Love Scranton, *Wheat Genealogy* (Guilford, Conn., 1960).

Whiton Fam
Whiton, Augustus Sherrill, *The Whiton Family In America* (Whiton, N.Y., 1932).

Windham Ch Rec
Records of the Congregational Church in Windham, Conn. 1700 – 1851 (Hartford: Conn. Historical Society and Society of Mayflower Descendants in Conn., 1943).

Windsor CT by Stiles
Stiles, Henry R., *The History of Ancient Windsor*, 2 vols. (Hartford, 1891, 1892; reprinted Somersworth, N.H., 1976).

Winslow Mem
Holton, David Parsons, and Frances K. Holton, *Winslow Memorial, Family Records of Winslows and Their Descendants in America*, 2 vols. (New York, 1877, 1888).

Woodstock CT by Bowen
Bowen, Clarence W., *The History of Woodstock, Connecticut*, 8 vols. (Norwood, 1926-1943).

Woodward Gen
Woodward, Norma Slater and Thomas R. Steadman, *Descendants of Richard, Nathaniel, Robert and Henry Woodward of New England, 1589-1996* (1982, 1996).

Woodworth Gen
Pierce, James R., *Woodworth Family of America* (1975).

Worcester Co Warnings
Worcester County, Massachusetts, Warnings, 1737-1788 (Camden, Me., 1992).

Worcester Inscrip
Barton, William Sumner, *Inscriptions from the old burial grounds in Worcester, Massachusetts, from 1727 to 1859: with biographical and historical notes* (Worcester, Mass., 1878).

Worthington Fam
Worthington, George, *The Genealogy of the Worthington Family* (1894).

Yale Grads
Dexter, Franklin Bowditch, *Biographical Sketches of the Graduates of Yale College*, series 1, 2, and 3 (New York, 1885).

Yarmouth NS Herald Gen
Brown, George F., *Yarmouth, Nova Scotia, Genealogies from Genealogical Columns in the* Yarmouth, Nova Scotia Herald, *November 1896 to May 1902* (1993). Columns also on microfilm at NEHGS, Boston.

Yarmouth NS VR
Early Vital Records of the Township of Yarmouth, Nova Scotia, 1762-1811 (Yarmouth County Historical Society, 1982).

Yarmouth VR
Sherman, Robert M., *Vital Records of Yarmouth, Massachusetts, to the Year 1850,* 2 vols. (Warwick, R.I., 1975).

INDEX OF NAMES

Surnames have been grouped under the most common variant, unless a particular spelling was so unique that it left room for doubt. Almost all given names have been standardized.

Readers should be aware of nicknames commonly used as alternative names for women, particularly *Betsey* or *Betty* for Elizabeth, *Polly* or *Molly* for Mary, *Patty* for Martha, *Nabby* for Abigail, and *Nancy* for Ann. The same woman may be indexed on different pages under both names. Women are indexed under both maiden and married names.

CHURCHILL *cont'd*
John 541, 579, 588-590
Laurana (McFarlin) 548
Leah 491
Leah (Keen) 491
Levi 548, 549
Lydia 549
Mary (Bradford) 156
Mary (Magoun) 548
Melatiah (Bradford)
 491, 492
Mercy 184
Michael 492
Molly 548
Otis 549
Patte 548
Peleg 184
Rachel 492
Rebecca 125, 491
Rufus 549
Saba 549
Sarah 184, 541, 547
Sarah (Cole) 541
Seth 492
Stephen 43, 51, 181-184
Sylvia 548
Thaddeus 549
Winslow 492
Zadock 183, 184
Zerulah 492
CLAPP / CLAP
Ann (Benton) 278
Anne 210
Bethiah (Winslow) 403
Earl 407
Ebenezer 106, 421
Elijah 277, 278
Eunice 277, 278
Increase 403
Keziah 421
Lucy (Sprague) 106, 421
Mary 210, 278, 279
Mary (Benton) 277
Mary (Haynes) (Lord)
 (Saltonstall) 210

CLAPP *cont'd*
Mary (Whiting) 210
Mary (Winslow) 421
Nathaniel 105, 106, 421,
 424
Sarah (Tileston) 388
Stephen 210
Temperance 210
Temperance (Gorham)
 210
Thomas 56, 210-212
CLARK / CLARKE
Abigail 329, 330, 409,
 437
Abigail (Wicom) 437
Ann (Dimmick) 110,
 437
Anna 437
Balsora (McRoberts)
 527
Daniel 237, 437
Ebenezer 437
Elizabeth 379
Eunice 437
Hannah 356, 557
James 562
Jane (___) 329
Joanna 175
Joannah 437
John 329
Jonathan 437
Margaret 457
Mary 437
Mary (Phinney) 356
Mary (Tracy) 208
Priscilla (Bradford) 445
Richard 437
Salomon 437
Samuel 50, 356
Sarah 532
Simon 437
Temperance 437
Timothy 272, 437
Wycom 437

**CLEMENTS /
 CLEMENS**
Abigail 511
Deborah 510, 511
Deborah (Rogers) 506,
 510, 511
Elizabeth (___) 511
Elkanah 126, 506, 510,
 511
Elsie 511
Hannah (Eaton) 510
John 510, 511
Lucy 511
Lucy (Holmes) 126,
 510, 511
Lydia 511
Mary (___) 511
Reuben 511
Sarah (___) 511
Silas 511
William 510
Ziba 511
**CLEVELAND /
 CLEAVELAND**
Abby 246
Abigail (Paine) 188
Abijah 246
Alice 192, 246
Alice (Dyer) 227
Amasa 247
Ann (Bradford) 192
Anna 192
Anna (Bradford) 52
Arunah 200
Azariah 247
Bradford 192
Charlotte 249
Deliverance 247
Dinah (Brown) 246, 247
Dorothy 200
Eleazer 52, 192
Elizabeth 251
Ezra 199
Frederick 200, 249

LITTLE *cont'd*
Constant 416
Constant (Fobes) 414, 416
Doty 417
Ephraim 7, 103, 414-416
George 415, 416
Hannah Briggs (___) 417
John 414-417
Josiah 165
Luce 416
Lucy (Dingley) (Bourn) 416, 417
Luther 416
Mary 416
Nathaniel 392, 414
Otis 417
Pamela (Bradford) 392
Parthena (Alden) 301
Patience 416
Peabody 415, 416
Ruth 417
Ruth (___) 415
Sarah 417
Sarah (Baker) 103, 416, 417
Sarah (Hall) (Porter) 414
Selah 415
Thomas 103, 416, 417
William Henry 417
Woodbridge 301
Zintha/ Zinthia 415, 416

LOBDELL / LOBDEL
Isaac 156, 161-163
Molly (Bradford) 156, 161-163
Rebecca 587

LOCKWOOD
Abigail (Hawley) 258
Hannah 258, 259
Peter 258

LOOMIS
Abigail 116
Ann (Allyn) 242
David 243
Elisha 243
Elizabeth 243, 244
Elizabeth (Norman) 243
Fitch 242, 243
George 243
Joseph 234
Margaret (Bissell) 63, 241-245
Mary 234, 235
Mary (Cooley) 234
Molly 243
Nathan 153
Nathaniel 242, 243
Phebe (Freeman) 153
Prudence 243
Prudence (___) 243
Rhoda (___) 243
Ruth 361
Selina Matilda (Holmes) 475
Triphena 243
Watson 242, 243

LORD
Alathea (Ripley) 81, 323
Alletheiah 323
Elisha 82, 323
Elizabeth 397
Experience 323
Hezekiah 323
Jerusha (Webster) 281
Mary 323
Mary (Haynes) 210
Pamlia 323
Sarah 323
Sarah (Fish) 323
Tamasine (Kimball) (Coit) 323

LORING
Abigail 395
Anne (Pierce) 588
Asa 150

LORING *cont'd*
Caleb 577, 587, 588
Charles 588
Christiana 150, 151
Edward 587, 588
Edward Greeley 588
Francis S. 588
Giles 587
Helen Curtis 588
Ignatius 490
Jane 151
Jane (Baker) 150
John 150
Joseph 577, 587, 588
Joshua 587
Jotham 150
Leah 148
Margaret (Tidmarsh) 587
Nathaniel 395
Nicholas 390
Perez 118
Polycarpus 41
Priscilla (Gray) 395
Rachel 150, 151
Rachel (___) 588
Rebecca (Lobdell) 587
Richmond 390
Ruth 577, 587, 588
Sarah 151, 577, 587, 588
Sarah (Bradford) 577, 587, 588
Sarah (Hearsey) 38, 150
Thomas 150, 151
Welthean 5
William 587, 588
William J. 588
Zilpha (Bradford) 144
Lothrop *see* Lathrop
LOVEL
Cyrus 557
Ebenezer 557
Mary 557
Zilpha 557
Zilpha (Drake) 557